LABOR RELATIONS LAW
IN THE PUBLIC SECTOR

CASES AND MATERIALS

CONTEMPORARY LEGAL EDUCATION SERIES

CONTEMPORARY LEGAL EDUCATION SERIES

ADVISORY COMMITTEE

Alfred F. Conard, *Chairman*

Ralph S. Brown, Jr.

A. Kenneth Pye

Maurice Rosenberg

Murray L. Schwartz

Jerre S. Williams

Labor Relations Law in the Public Sector

CASES AND MATERIALS

RUSSELL A. SMITH
Professor Emeritus of Law
University of Michigan

HARRY T. EDWARDS
Professor of Law
University of Michigan

R. THEODORE CLARK, JR.
Partner
Seyfarth, Shaw, Fairweather &
Geraldson

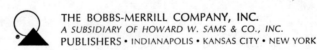
THE BOBBS-MERRILL COMPANY, INC.
A SUBSIDIARY OF HOWARD W. SAMS & CO., INC.
PUBLISHERS • INDIANAPOLIS • KANSAS CITY • NEW YORK

ISBN 0-672-81788-8

Copyright © 1974
by THE BOBBS-MERRILL COMPANY, INC.
Library of Congress Catalog Card Number: 73-20863
Printed in the United States of America
All Rights Reserved

To

Berta, Becky and Sandy
David, Brent and Steven
Sarah and Michelle

Preface

Several premises underlie the preparation and offering of the materials contained in this volume. The first is that public sector "unionization" and collective bargaining represent the most important development in "labor relations" since the post-Wagner Act period of the 1930s and 1940s. This significance derives both from the sheer magnitude and success of organizing efforts in the public sector and from its major impacts on the management of governmental affairs and public employees at all levels of government—federal, state and local.

During the past decade, dramatic changes have occurred in the body of relevant public sector law, as was true in the private sector in the earlier era. These changes have both contributed to and resulted from public sector unionization. While labor relations law in the public sector has naturally drawn heavily on private sector precepts and models, it has also involved major departures, in response to numerous problems peculiar to the public sector. These are not only substantive. In contrast with the preemptive "federalization" in the private sector, the most important body of public sector labor relations law is state and local. Thus, there are wide variations, resting on differing judgmental evaluations and determinations of public policy. Indeed, the states have proven to be "laboratories" for socio-political experimentation in the development of the law in this area.

In our judgment, a law school curriculum is incomplete which does not afford students the opportunity to examine in some depth the parameters, important variations and problems of public policy embodied in this area of the law. The traditional law school Labor Law curriculum has given primary attention to the private sector, and the typical Labor Law "casebook" reflects this fact. It is quite apparent now, however, that adequate treatment of both private and public sectors is not feasible in a single volume. Hence a basic objective has been to provide a separate set of teaching materials for use in law schools and in other educational contexts. We have also sought to achieve a kind of approach and treatment of the relevant materials which will be of interest and value to those directly concerned on a working basis with public sector labor relations (lawyers, administrators, officials of labor organizations and public employees).

We have not sought to treat many of the obviously important problems relating to collective bargaining techniques, substantive collective bargaining provisions or the numerous practical aspects of labor relations, except to the extent these matters are affected or influenced by the applicable legal structure or rule. In many of these areas, the law does have significant relevance. But it has not seemed to us to be feasible to attempt to deal fully, in a single volume, with the process of collective bargaining or with the more practical aspects of administering labor agreements. In dealing with collective bargaining, therefore, we concentrate on the legal framework and not on specific techniques of collective negotiations or contract administration.

Although the body of "law" in the public sector is now substantial, it is still in the formative stage. As a consequence, we have sought to supplement the judicial decisions reported herein with numerous excerpts from other publications and with substantial text and note material written by the editors. It is our hope that this textual material, much of which has been written by some of the outstanding scholars and practitioners in the field, will raise significant policy questions for consideration in connection with the proper course of the development of labor relations law in the public sector.

The original footnote numbers from judicial opinions have been retained and bracketed. The editors' footnotes are numbered consecutively within each chapter. For the future, we plan to provide annual softbound supplements so that the work will be up-to-date at the start of each school year.

Our thanks to the following students who served as research assistants during the preparation of this volume: Donald Anderson, Zachary Fasman, Dianne Fraser, and Richard Moon. We are also especially indebted to Miss Patt Alfs and Miss Ruth Iverson, who toiled tirelessly to type the final manuscript.

Mr. Clark wishes to thank his wife, Sandy and children, David, Sarah and Steven; Professor Edwards wishes to thank his wife, Becky and children, Brent and Michelle; and Professor Smith wishes to thank his wife, Berta—their patience, faith and encouragement helped to make possible the contribution of each of us.

Chicago, Illinois   *R. Theodore Clark, Jr.*
Ann Arbor, Michigan   *Harry T. Edwards*
Ann Arbor, Michigan   *Russell A. Smith*
June, 1973

Summary Table of Contents

Summary Table of Contents

Table of Contents

Table of Cases

Principal cases are those with page references in italics

Chapter 1

PUBLIC SECTOR UNIONISM— ORIGINS AND PERSPECTIVES

A. An Historical Survey

1. Generally

PROJECT: COLLECTIVE BARGAINING AND POLITICS IN PUBLIC EMPLOYMENT, 19 U.C.L.A.L. Rev. 887, 893-96 (1972)†

Unionism among government employees began in the 1830's, when mechanics, carpenters and other craftsmen employed by the federal government joined craft unions which already existed to serve those employed by private industry. The natural affinity among skilled craftsmen overcame the differences between public and private employ, and encouraged public employees to join the unions.[1] Within ten years, the embryonic public employee movement began to assert itself, presenting employers across the country with demands for a shorter work day.[2] Private trade unions had already adopted this demand, encouraging their public sector brethren to follow suit.[3] Private sector employers had agreed to a ten hour work day in 1835, and ultimately public employers also acquiesced, not necessarily because they sanctioned union-type activity on the part of their employees, but rather because they competed with private industry for the same workers, and thus had to ensure the availability of their labor supply. Undoubtedly, however, union activities by public employees had some effect in gaining concessions by the government. Moreover, private sector employees, having won their own battle, assisted public employees in applying pressure on local governmental

---

† Copyright © 1972 by The Regents of the University of California. Reprinted by permission.

[1] *See* M. Moskow, Collective Bargaining in Public Employment 29-30 (1969). . . . According to Moskow, the reasons for the affinity among craftsmen were that they "received the same training, associated socially and moved interchangeably between public and private sector jobs." *Id.*

[2] S. Spero, Government as Employer 77 (1948) [hereinafter cited as Spero].

[3] *Id.*

units,[4] and in most cases these combined efforts contributed to the change in policy by the public employers.[5]

While state and local government employees found relative success in union activity, workers in federal employ had less favorable results. Their employers were department heads who were divorced from popular pressure. Moreover, most of the federal artisans and craftsmen were employed by the War and Navy Departments, which were run by military officers whose jobs were unaffected by public opinion. In the face of unalterable resistance by their employers, the federal workers resorted to the strike; in 1836, workers at the Washington, D.C. Naval Shipyard walked off the job. The strike continued for several weeks without any sign of ending, until finally, as had occurred many times at the local level the previous year, a mass demonstration involving strikers and their comrades from private sector organizations confronted President Jackson. The President yielded, establishing the shorter work day for federal employees.

In succeeding years, public employees maintained their status as secondary characters in the struggles of the labor movement. Any benefits secured by these employees generally resulted from the fact that the private sector labor union in their particular industry had already secured such benefits. Public employees benefitted from the fact that public employers adopted the policy of making pay rates and labor standards conform to those prevailing in private employment in the surrounding area.[6]

Until the 1880's, there were few organizations primarily for public employees; indeed, the trade union movement as a whole

---

[4] In Philadelphia, for example, the ten-hour work day was adopted by the city council after a large demonstration involving privately employed artisans who were joined by a great number of public workers. *See* 6 J.R. COMMONS, DOCUMENTARY HISTORY OF AMERICAN INDUSTRIAL SOCIETY 41-42 (1918).

[5] SPERO, *supra* note 2, at 77. Most strike and pressure activity engaged in during this period was by private sector unions acting on behalf of their government-employed members. Public employees did not have their own union, nor was the right of public employees to organize officially recognized by public officials. Thus, where the ten-hour work day movement was unsuccessful in private industry, the public officials of the same area were able to maintain their own resistance. *Id.*

[6] *See, e.g.,* Act of July 16, 1862, ch. 184, 12 Stat. 587, *amending* Act of December 21, 1861, ch. 1, § 8, 12 Stat. 330:

[T]he hours of labor and the rates of wages of the employees in the navy yards shall conform as nearly as is consistent with the public interest with those of private establishments in the immediate vicinity of the respective yards . . . .

This policy of making government employment standards conform with those in private industry was reversed by President Van Buren. Under his direction the foundation was laid for a government employment policy which later became the leader in setting labor standards that were followed by private employers; rather than vice versa. SPERO, *supra* note 2, at 83-84.

was just recovering from the Great Panic of 1873. However, with the return of prosperity, a substantial number of public employee organizations were formed. These organizations, which were called associations, were formed primarily for benevolent purposes, and thus they did not join in the renewed militancy of the labor movement which occurred in the late 1800's.[7] One result of the relatively docile attitude of these associations was that the great labor activities of the two decades preceding the twentieth century, which brought labor in the United States to a position of great importance, occurred virtually without the participation of government workers. Perhaps the alienation of government workers from the mainstream of the labor movement resulted from the fact that militant activity in government employment was not essential, since public employers usually followed private industry job standards; if improvements secured by private sector unions would be granted to public employees without any effort on the part of their own unions, there was virtually no need for a strong, independent bargaining organization.

This situation remained static until well into the twentieth century. However, with the inflationary trend that preceded World War I, state and local government employees began to show an interest in affiliating with the private sector union movement. Significant progress in organizing public employees was stopped, however, in 1919, when the Boston police strike occurred. The great public opposition which resulted from that incident wiped out the progress of public employee unionization for several years; only in the great labor upsurge of the 1930's did public employees begin to take renewed interest in labor organizations.

In 1936, the American Federation of Labor (AFL) founded the first national union for state and local government employees —the American Federation of State, County and Municipal Employees (AFSCME).[8] At the same time, all types of govern-

----

7 . . . "Benevolent" purposes included such goals as the upkeep of morale through association-sponsored social functions. Sometimes associations were formed primarily to take advantage of group insurance benefits. . . . In any event, activity was generally restrained and little, if any, pressure was exerted on public employers by the associations on their members' behalf.

8 . . . By this time, the federal service was already well-organized—particularly the Post Office Department. The first national union composed solely of government employees to receive an AFL charter was the National Federation of Post Office Clerks, founded in 1906. Unionism outside the Post Office was also well established with the foundation of the National Federation of Federal Employees in 1917 and, later, the American Federation of Government Employees, chartered by the AFL when the NFFE withdrew from the parent organization in 1935.

ment employees began joining organizations comprised principally of workers of their own occupation; teachers, firemen and policemen being among the first to organize. But despite these developments unionization in the public sector progressed slowly, and not until the 1960s did organized public employees become a prominent national labor force. . . .

NOTES

1. Although widescale organization of public employees is a relatively recent phenomenon, some groups of public employees have been organized for decades. For example, the Illinois Supreme Court in Fursman v. Chicago, 278 Ill. 318, 116 N.E. 158 (1917), noted that of the

> . . . more than 7,000 teachers employed by the board of education of the city of Chicago . . . more than 3,500 of these teachers have been and are members of the Chicago Teachers' Federation, which is affiliated with a federation of trade unions; that the Chicago Teachers' Federation is a corporation not for profit organized on April 9, 1898 . . . ; that in November, 1902, the Chicago Teachers' Federation became and has since continued to be affiliated with the Chicago Federation of Labor; . . . that in 1914 members of the Chicago Teachers' Federation affiliated with the American Federation of Labor . . . .

2. Among the many useful books and articles examining the history of public sector unionism are S. SPERO, GOVERNMENT AS EMPLOYER (1948) ; Rosenblum & Steinbach, *Federal Employee Labor Relations: From the "Gag Rule" to Executive Order 11491*, 59 Ky. L.J. 833 (1971) ; Wagner, *TVA Looks at Three Decades of Collective Bargaining*, 22 IND. & LAB. REL. REV. 20 (1968) ; Klaus, The Right of Public Employees to Organize—In Theory and in Practice (New York City Dep't of Labor Serial No. L.R. 1, March 1955) .

The history of collective bargaining in New York City has been the subject of several books and articles. *See generally* Cook, *Public Employee Bargaining in New York City*, 9 IND. REL. 246 (1970); Russo, *Management's View of the New York City Experience*, in ACAD. POL. SCI. PROC., Vol. 30, at 81 (1970); R. HORTON, MUNICIPAL LABOR RELATIONS IN NEW YORK CITY: LESSONS OF THE LINDSAY-WAGNER YEARS (1973) . For a critical review of the latter book by the Executive Director of District Council 37 of the American Federation of the State, County, and Municipal Employees, see Gotbaum, Book Review, THE NEW LEADER, May 14, 1973, at 21.

REHMUS, LABOR RELATIONS IN THE PUBLIC SECTOR,
Paper prepared for the 3rd World Congress, International
Industrial Relations Association, London, England (Sept. 3-7, 1973)†

Scope of Public Employment

Public service is the most rapidly growing major sector of employment in the United States. In the last 30 years, public employment has tripled, growing from 4.2 million to 13.1 million employees. Today nearly one out of five workers in the United States is on a government payroll.

Part of this dramatic increase in public employment can be attributed simply to population growth, necessitating a proportional increase in publicly provided services. More fundamental to growth than simple demographic change, however, have been increases in demand for new services, shifts from private to public provision of certain kinds of service, and advances in technology which have intensified the need for new levels of existing public services. Ever since the Great Depression of the 1930's, United States citizens have expected government to provide more and more service for more and more people. As an example, provision for social welfare services to the poor and those too young and too old to work has created many new public jobs. At state and local levels of government, education, health care, the public highway system and police and fire protection are the largest sources of employment. At the federal level, the government's role in the international arena has steadily increased as the United States has become more and more involved in military assistance and economic aid throughout the world.

This growth of government service has not been steady or equal at all levels of government in the United States federal system. Any consideration of public employment, and public employee labor relations within each, must distinguish between three primary levels of government—federal, state, and local— as well as the large postal and educational subsections of federal and local government. Each level of government has specific areas of administrative authority and service responsibility which are in turn affected by specific constituency demands. Each of these levels of government has its own laws regulating public employer-employee labor relations.

Federal Government. Federal government employment has increased the least of the three primary levels of government, expanding by only 40 percent between 1950 and 1970. Hence the federal proportion of all public employment has declined

---

† Reprinted by permission of the Institute of Labor and Industrial Relations.

from 33 to 23 percent during the same period. It should be
noted, however, that the federal government's share of total
government expenditures has not declined proportionately.
Nearly half of all federal expenditures go into national defense.
If this component of federal expenditures were eliminated, the
federal expenditure share would be approximately the same as
the federal employment share, about 23 percent. In the United
States the federal government's income is derived primarily from
individual and corporate income taxes and, in addition to defense and military expenditures, is spent for social welfare insurance and trust programs, veterans' benefits, agricultural and
natural resources programs, international gifts and loans, space
research, and a multitude of general welfare programs.

State Government. State employment represents 27 percent of
total government employment in the United States. State governments derive their income primarily from sales and excise taxes,
and increasingly from individual and corporate income taxes as
well. Primary state expenditures go for public education, for
maintenance of highways and waterways, and for administration
of public welfare and health programs.

Local Government. Local government represents 50 percent of
all public employment in the United States. Local governments
derive their incomes primarily from taxes on real property and
from subventions out of state and federal revenue-sharing funds.
Local governments carry out the police, public safety, and sanitation functions and, more recently, expend a large share of the
monies that are devoted to urban renewal programs.

Education. Education ranks second only to national defense
in terms of public economic expenditures in the United States.
Twenty-nine percent of all government expenditures go for
national defense and related purposes, and approximately 16
percent goes to education. Education accounts for 32 percent of
all public employment and represents slightly over half of all
state and local employment. Although state governments bear
the responsibility for establishing and maintaining the system of
public schools, the actual operation of the schools is ordinarily
delegated to local school districts. Over 90 percent of all local
school districts are administratively independent of any other
local governmental unit. Moreover, most school districts are
atypical in the United States governmental structures in that
their local governing bodies—school boards or the equivalent—
have both executive and legislative authority. School boards
both make and administer educational policy, and most school

boards have been given the authority to levy property taxes, subject to voter approval.

Postal Service. The fifth substantial sector of public employment in the United States is unusual: The United States Postal Service is by far the largest and only major public corporation in the United States. Until 1970, the Post Office Department had been one of the component agencies of the federal government. Its employees were federal civil servants whose conditions of employment were legislated by the U.S. Congress. Its work force was also unusual in having been overwhelmingly union-organized since the 19th Century, and was restless and militant. An unprecedented major strike by postal workers, beginning on the Eastern Seaboard and extending to many other parts of the nation, created pressure for the immediate realization of a long-discussed idea; the transformation of the Post Office Department into a public corporation. Postal service employees are now in general subject to the labor relations rules and regulations that pertain in the private sector. The main remnant of postal employees' former civil servant status is the retention of the ban on their right to strike in the event of bargaining impasses and the substitution for it of compulsory binding arbitration.

This striking modification in the status of postal employment is only one of many fundamental changes that came to public service in the United States in the 1960's—a period that has been called by some "the decade of the public employee revolution."

Background of Public Employee Labor Relations

Workers in the industrial private sector in the United States were given the statutory right to organize and bargain collectively in the 1930's. By 1960, approximately 30 percent of all non-agricultural private sector employees were represented by unions. Yet by this same date there was practically no unionization in the public sector other than in the traditionally-organized postal service and in a few other isolated situations.

The reasons for the delay in union organization of employees in the public sector in the United States are complex. In part they stem from certain philosophical ideas long prevalent in the nation. Traditional concepts of sovereignty asserted that government is and should be supreme, hence immune from contravening forces and pressures such as that of collective bargaining. Related to this concept was that of the illegality of delegation of sovereign power. This assertion was that public decision-making could only be done by elected or appointed public officials, whose unilateral and complete discretion was therefore unchallengeable.

More practical considerations also delayed the advent of public employee unionism in the United States. The private sector unions and their international federations were fully occupied in trying to increase the extent of organization in the private sector. They had neither the money nor energy to turn to the public sector until the 1960's. Equally or more importantly, public employees were not generally dissatisfied with their terms and conditions of employment and therefore, except in isolated cases, did not press for collective bargaining rights. Though the wages and salaries of public employees in the United States had traditionally lagged slightly behind comparable private sector salaries, the greater fringe benefits and job security associated with public employment were traditionally thought to be adequate compensation.

By the late 1950's and early 1960's several of these practical considerations which had delayed public employee unionism had disappeared. Moreover, new factors came into play that are difficult to assess as to sequence or relative importance, but in total added to a new militancy. Change increasingly became endemic in American society as more and more groups, including public employees, found it commonplace to challenge the established order. Some public employees were made less secure by organizational and technological changes as government came under pressure to reduce tax increases and therefore turned to devices to increase efficiency and lower unit labor costs. Public employee wages and salaries began to lag further behind those in the unionized private sector as the post-war inflationary spiral continued. The private sector international unions saw the large and growing employment in the non-union public sector as a fertile alternative which might substitute for their failure after 1956 to increase membership steadily in the private sector. Finally, many observers of public employment both in and out of government began strongly and publicly to question the logic behind governmentally-protected collective bargaining in the private sector and government's complete failure to grant similar privileges and protections in the public sector.

By the 1960's these practical challenges to the traditional arguments of sovereignty and illegal delegation of powers came to be seen as overriding in a number of government jurisdictions. The City of New York, the school board of that same city, and the State of Wisconsin gave modification collective bargaining rights to their public employees. Most importantly, in 1962 President Kennedy by executive order gave federal employees a

limited version of the rights that private employees had received
30 years before. These seminal breakthroughs in granting some
form of bargaining right to public employees led increasingly
to similar kinds of state legislation, particularly in the more industrialized states. Today over 30 American states have granted
some form of collective bargaining rights to some or all of their
public employees. President Nixon in two subsequent executive
orders has expanded and clarified the bargaining rights of federal
employees. . . .

NOTE

In recommending that federal employees be affirmatively
granted the right to join and participate in employee organizations and to bargain collectively, President Kennedy's Task Force
referred to the following statement in ABA Section of Labor
Relations Law, REPORT OF COMMITTEE ON LABOR RELATIONS OF
GOVERNMENTAL EMPLOYEES 89, 90 (1955) :

> A government which imposes upon other employers cer-
> tain obligations in dealing with their employees may not
> in good faith refuse to deal with its own public servants
> on a reasonably similar favorable basis, modified, of course,
> to meet the exigencies of the public service. It should set
> the example for industry by being perhaps more considerate
> than the law requires of private enterprise. THE TASK
> FORCE, A POLICY FOR EMPLOYEE-MANAGEMENT COOPERATION
> IN THE FEDERAL SERVICE 4 (1961).

2. The Rise and Fall of the Sovereignty Doctrine

K. HANSLOWE, THE EMERGING LAW OF LABOR RELATIONS IN PUBLIC EMPLOYMENT 11-20 (1967)†

[V]arying policies have grown up at the state and federal levels
with respect to the organizing and bargaining rights of public
employees and . . . a discernible trend toward enhanced recognition and protection of these rights is now evident. At one time
and place or another, however, virtually all aspects of collective
bargaining have been deemed incompatible with government employment. Thus, courts have ruled that public employees can be
prohibited from joining unions. To the assertion that this interferes with the constitutional right of freedom of association, government has responded that, there being no constitutional right to
government employment, it may insist on non-membership as a
condition of such employment because of the governmental right
and need to maintain operations without interference and interruption. Consequently, it has been ruled that state governments
may condition employment on relinquishment of the right to or-

---

† Reprinted by permission of the New York State School of Industrial and
Labor Relations, Cornell University.

ganize, and that no one has a constitutional right to work for the government on his own terms.

Even where public employees are allowed to join unions, this right has often been restricted to organizations not affiliated with the general labor movement. Where not so restricted, affiliation, in any event, must not be with an organization that asserts the right to strike against the government. The reason for the latter restriction is fairly obvious. Strikes of government employees are almost universally deemed to be unlawful. The reasons for the former restriction are thought to be as follows:

(1) Affiliation increases the possibility that conflicting loyalties will arise. For example, it is argued that policemen who are members of a labor federation such as AFL-CIO, or who are members of an international union also representing employees in private industry, cannot be expected to perform in disinterested fashion and with no reservations when called out to eliminate violence on a picket line maintained by their fellow union members.

(2) Affiliation increases the funds available to public employee organizations and thereby increases their capacity to strike.

(3) Affiliation increases the likelihood of sympathetic strikes by private or public employees to help their fellow union members.

(4) Affiliation with the general labor movement may result in placing too much power in the hands of organized labor. Employees in both sectors might use their respective political and economic power each to enhance the position of the other group at the expense of the rest of society.

The government trend in recent years has been to relax previous restrictions on affiliation. Most jurisdictions which now allow their public employees to organize, also allow them to affiliate with the general labor movement, at least so long as the affiliations are not with organizations asserting the right to strike against the government. More stringent restrictions can still be found in some instances, however, especially with respect to bans on the affiliation of policemen's organizations with other unions.

Other facets of collective bargaining, familiar in the private sector, have been similarly deemed inappropriate in government employment. This is true not only of the strike, but of exclusive recognition of an organization representing a majority of the employees involved, the closed or union shop, the checkoff by the employer of union dues from the employees' wages, and the arbitration of disputes as well. Indeed, the very possibility of *bargaining* with the government has been questioned, and agreements reached between public officials and labor unions have been held invalid as constituting unauthorized abdications of governmental power with respect to conditions of public employment.

These views are reflected in legal opinion. For instance, the attorney general of Florida advised the city manager of Miami that:

. . . no organization, regardless of who it is affiliated with, union or non-union, can tell a political sub-division possessing the attributes of sovereignty, who it can employ, how much it shall pay them, or any other matter or thing relating to its employees. To even countenance such a proposition would be to surrender a portion of the sovereignty that is possessed by every municipal corporation and such a municipality would cease to exist as an organization controlled by its citizens, for after all, government is no more than the individuals that go to make up the same and no one can tell the people how to say, through their duly constituted and elected officials, how the government should be run under such authority and powers as the people themselves give to a public corporation such as a city.[9]

A judicial decision, in 1946, asserted:

There is an abundance of authority, too numerous for citation, which condemns labor union contracts in the public service. The theory of these decisions is that the giving of a preference [to unions and their members] is against public policy. It is declared that such preferences, in whatever form, involve an illegal delegation of disciplinary authority, or of legislative power, or of the discretion of public officers; that such a contract disables them from performing their duty; that it involves a divided allegiance; that it encourages monopoly; that is defeats competition; that it is detrimental to the public welfare; that it is subversive of the public service; and that it impairs the freedom of the individual to contract for his own services. . . .[10]

At the core of this position is the concept of sovereignty.

. . . In our polity, sovereignty, of course, ultimately reposes in the people but is, out of the practical necessities of circumstance, exercised for them by the constituted state governments and the federal government. It is these governments and their delegates (such as local governments, municipalities, and exec-

---

[9] Florida Attorney General's Opinion, March 21, 1944, reproduced in Rhyne, *Labor Unions and Municipal Employee Law* (Washington: National Institute of Municipal Law Offices, 1946), pp. 252-54.

[10] Mugford v. Mayor and City Council of Baltimore, opinion Nov. 6, 1944, *aff'd*, 185 Md. 266, 44 A.2d 745 (1946).

utive and administrative agencies) which exercise, within constitutional and statutory limitations, the sovereign power to make and enforce law. To the extent that collective bargaining entails joint determination of conditions of employment, such bargaining with the government is seen as unavoidably creating an interference in the sovereign's affairs. Unionization is similarly thought to involve intolerable splitting of the civil servant's loyalty between the government of which he is a part and his union. Furthermore, such practices as exclusive recognition, the closed or union shop, and the checkoff of union dues are thought not only to invite organized interference with the conduct of public business but to involve improper preference for one group at the expense of others in society. The use of arbitrators to resolve disputes is seen to entail an improper abandonment by the sovereign of a portion of his authority. And the strike, needless to say, involving, as it does, concerted coercion of the employer, falls little short of insurrection when the employer is the government.

What this position comes down to is that governmental power includes the power, through law, to fix the terms and conditions of government employment, that this power reposes in the sovereign's hand, that this is a unique power which cannot be given or taken away or shared, and that any organized effort to interfere with this power through a process such as collective bargaining is irreconcilable with the idea of sovereignty and is hence unlawful.

> The [police] commission . . . not only had the power but it
> was the manifest duty to adopt and enforce the resolution
> [prohibiting policemen from joining a labor union]. . . .
> The failure to do so in effect would have amounted to a
> surrender of power, a dereliction of duty, and a relinquish-
> ment of supervision and control over public servants it was
> their sworn duty to supervise and direct.[11]

This is the orthodox position. We shall see below that in practice it has been widely modified, although not wholly abandoned.

Still another line of analysis must be indicated. What has been said thus far flows from political or legal theory. It can also be argued that the theory is grounded in functional necessity. The sovereign, whether absolute or representative, acts for the entire political entity involved. The functions which the sovereign performs are governmental tasks which need to be discharged on behalf of the whole society. These tasks, whether they be national

---

11 Perez v. Board of Police Commissioners, 78 Cal. App. 2d 638, 651, 178 P.2d 537, 545 (1947).

defense, local security, running an educational system, or whatever, are carried on to further the public weal. Any conduct which interferes with the performance of these tasks is inimical to that weal and is therefore intolerable. Strikes of civil servants clearly constitute such interference. So, likewise, to the extent that unionization and collective bargaining may have a tendency to lead to strikes, they can and, indeed, must be outlawed as running counter to the public interest. Thus the functional necessity of governmental tasks is asserted to combine with the theoretical nature of sovereign power to render collective bargaining on the part of public employees undesirable and unlawful.

Sovereignty Delimited

So goes the traditional argument. Its difficulty lies in the circumstance that life has a way of running ahead of logic and that history tends to be more complex than political theory. Implicit in the argument is the idea that the sovereign is absolute, allpowerful, and always right. The idea is open to question.

We derive our notions of sovereignty from the English common law which reposed sovereign authority in the king as the fountainhead of law, justice, and government. "The king can do no wrong," wrote Blackstone in his *Commentaries.* This maxim assumed concrete meaning in the context of law suits by citizens against the Crown. If the king can indeed do no wrong, the Crown is necessarily immune from suit. Applied to government employment, the Blackstone maxim means that, when the sovereign has fixed the terms of public employment, these are inescapably fair and just, and hence any employee effort to alter them is wrong and runs counter to law.

One difficulty with this is that, insofar as sovereign immunity from suit is concerned, the Blackstone maxim has been misunderstood, and the English kings did not enjoy the absolute immunity commonly thought to be conveyed by the notion that they could "do no wrong." Professor Louis Jaffe writes:

It is the prevailing view among students of this period that the requirement of consent [to be sued] was not based on a view that the King was above the law "[T]he king, as the fountain of justice and equity, could not refuse to redress wrongs when petitioned to do so by his subjects." Indeed, it is argued by scholars on what seems adequate evidence that the expression "the King can do no wrong" originally meant precisely the contrary to what it later came to mean. "[I]t meant that the king must not, was not allowed, not entitled to do wrong. . . ." It was on this basis that the King,

though not suable in his court . . ., nevertheless endorsed on
petitions "let justice be done," thus empowering his courts
to proceed.[12]

The petitions referred to were "petitions of right." They
were granted when other remedies against the government were
unavailable. Thus legal procedure combined with political
theory to delimit sovereign immunity even at its source—the
kings of England. By what Professor Jaffe calls a "magnificent
irony," these limitations upon sovereign immunity were substantially destroyed in North America when the Colonies, by
revoking their allegiance to the Crown, eliminated the king
who could "let justice be done."

So it seems that the king was not always absolutely right, and
he has, of course, for a long time not been absolute. Absence of
absolute power has, in any case, been a dominant characteristic
of American government from the start. Yet the doctrine of
sovereign immunity has had a sturdy history in American law
which, perhaps, helps to explain the reluctance with which American governments have moved in the direction of accepting collective bargaining with their employees.

. . . .

Mr. Justice Holmes spoke in favor of the immunity of the
sovereign:

A sovereign is exempt from suit, not because of any formal
conception or obsolete theory, but on the logical and practical ground that there can be no legal right as against the
authority that makes the law on which the right depends.[13]

Nevertheless, the doctrine of sovereignty, in areas other than
the labor relations context, as well as in the labor relations field
itself, has come to be limited. Indeed, Professor Kenneth Culp
Davis has recently written: "Sovereign immunity in state courts
is on the run."

The traditional position, for one thing, has been substantially
modified by legislative enactments, the effect of which is to
"waive" sovereign immunity for certain purposes. A court of
claims was established in 1855 to entertain citizens' claims that
their private property has been unconstitutionally taken by the
federal government for public use without just compensation.
Tort claims against the federal government may be asserted under the Federal Tort Claims Act of 1946. Contract claims may

---

12 Louis Leventhal Jaffe, Judicial Control of Administrative Action
(Boston: Little, Brown & Company, 1965), p. 199. Professor Jaffe's footnotes
have been omitted.

13 Kawananakoa v. Polyblank, 205 U.S. 349, 353 (1907).

be similarly asserted under the Tucker Act of 1948. Several states have legislated in similar vein. . . .

More recently the courts, often without legislative aid, have, in Professor Davis' words, "abolish[ed] large chunks of immunity." According to Professor Davis, thirteen jurisdictions have so acted between 1957 and 1965. Some of the decisions collected by Professor Davis speak in such terms as:

"[S]overeign immunity" may be a proper subject for discussion by students of mythology but finds no haven or refuge in this Court.[14]

With respect to municipal tort liability, the Supreme Court of Florida made this observation:

The modern city is in substantial measure a large business institution. . . . To continue to endow this type of organization with sovereign divinity appears to us to predicate the law of the Twentieth Century upon an Eighteenth Century anachronism.[15]

. . . .

One may well ask, therefore, whether conceptions of sovereignty should remain as a barrier to collective bargaining in governmental labor relations. If the "sovereign" government is increasingly assuming ordinary legal responsibility in its relations with its citizens, why should not the same hold true for governmental relations with civil servants?

One point emerges. Whatever immunities the sovereign may possess, there is no barrier to such immunities being delimited. The sovereign power does, indeed, include the power within constitutional limitations to make policy. But does this not include the power to establish, as a matter of public personnel policy, a system of collective bargaining with respect to civil servants. This is, in fact, the position which seems to be emerging. One leading writer has concluded that, while *the* [sovereignty] *doctrine is a clear and effective bar to any action on the part of government employees to compel the government to enter involuntarily into any type of collective bargaining relationship, . . . the doctrine does not preclude the enactment of legislation specifically authorizing the government to enter into collective bargaining relationships with its employees."* . . .[16]

---

[14] Colorado Racing Commission v. Brush Racing Ass'n, 136 Colo. 279, 284 (1957).

[15] Hargrove v. Town of Cocoa Beach, 96 So. 2d 130, 133 (Fla. 1957).

[16] WILSON R. HART, COLLECTIVE BARGAINING IN THE FEDERAL CIVIL SERVICE, (New York: Harper & Row, 1961), p. 44.

NOTES

1. While the judge in the *Mugford* case quoted by Hanslowe condemned an agreement that gave the union a preferential position which was specifically denied to any other organization, the judge nevertheless stated:

> With the pattern of collective dealing so firmly established in the industrial field, is it reasonable to expect to maintain the fiction of personal relationship between employer and employe in the municipal field among a large number of workers engaged in performing the same tasks as are performed in the industrial field? I think not. To maintain even a semblance of individual contact with a large force of workers would require an increase of supervisory workers, who would still fail to detect and deal grievances and complaints as effectively as an organization of workers would do. The right to organize, and bargain collectively, can be exercised without interference with the exercise of the discretion committed to public officers, without preferment of organization members, without discrimination against others, and without detriment to the public service. Mugford v. Mayor and City Council of Baltimore (Cir. Ct. No. 2, Baltimore City, 1944), *reproduced in* C. RHYNE, LABOR UNIONS AND MUNICIPAL EMPLOYE LAW 166, 168 (1946).

2. In denying public employees many of the rights which their counterparts in the private sector possessed, the courts also relied on the theory that public employees owed extra-loyalty to their governmental employers. The following critique of this "extra-loyalty" theory is contained in Edwards, *The Developing Labor Relations Law in the Public Sector*, 10 DUQUESNE L. REV. 357, 360-61 (1972):

> A close relative of the sovereignty doctrine is the theory that public employees have a commitment to further the programs of government even at a sacrifice of their own interests. . . .
> It would seem the extra-loyalty theory is open to the same criticism as the sovereignty theory: it too is vague, conclusory, and not adequately founded in the realities of the modern situation. Based upon an assumed concensus as to the proper role of government in society, it offers no guidance as to what the employee must give up. Further, it puts forth no reason for this sacrifice, save the equation government equals sovereign equals absolute fealty. Such an equation is hardly a viable alternative in our modern

society. Indeed, with so many "urgent" demands on the government's admittedly inadequate resources—coupled with the great gains of private sector unions (creating a considerable controversy as to just what the public employee's fair share really is)—it outrages modern notions of industrial democracy to relegate a large segment of the work force to dependence upon the conscience of the government. A degree of self-determinism has become a way of life for the American worker, and nowhere is it more necessary than in the public sector.

NORWALK TEACHERS' ASSOCIATION v. BOARD OF EDUCATION OF THE CITY OF NORWALK
Connecticut Supreme Court of Errors
138 Conn. 269, 83 A.2d 482 (1951)

JENNINGS, J. This is a suit between the Norwalk Teachers' Association as plaintiff and the Norwalk board of education as defendant for a declaratory judgment, reserved on the admitted allegations of the complaint for the advice of this court.

The complaint may be summarized as follows: The plaintiff is a voluntary association and an independent labor union to which all but two of the teaching personnel of approximately 300 in the Norwalk school system belong. In April, 1946, there was a dispute between the parties over salary rates. The board of estimate and taxation was also involved. After long negotiations, 230 members of the association rejected the individual contracts of employment tendered them and refused to return to their teaching duties. After further negotiations, in which the governor and the state board of education took part, a contract was entered into between the plaintiff and the defendant, and the teachers returned to their duties. The contract, subject to conditions precedent therein set forth, recognized the plaintiff as the bargaining agent for all of its members, defined working conditions and set up a grievance procedure and salary schedule. Similar contracts were entered into for the succeeding school years, including 1950-51. From September, 1946, to the present, and particularly with reference to the contract for 1950-1951, much doubt and uncertainty have arisen concerning the rights and duties of the respective parties, the interpretation of the contract and the construction of the state statutes relating to schools, education and boards of education. "In addition," the complaint states, "there has been the possibility of strikes, work stoppage or collective refusals to return to work by the teachers through their organization and the possibility of discharges or suspensions by the defendant by reason of difficult personnel relations, all of which tends to disharmony in the operation of the school system and to the ever present possibility that either, or both, the parties may be unwittingly violating statutes by reason of mistaken or erroneous interpretation thereon." The parties agreed that the contract for the school year 1949-1950 would govern their relations for the school year 1950-1951, that they would join in the action, and "that whatever contractual obligations exist will be forthwith modified so soon as they shall have received from the Court judgments and orders declaring their respective rights, privileges, duties and immunities." The specific points of dispute are stated in the questions reserved, printed in the footnote.[1] . . .

. . . Question (e) will be considered first.

Under our system, the government is established by and run for all of the people, not for the benefit of any person or group. The profit motive, inherent in the principle of free enterprise, is absent. It should be the aim of every employee of the government to do his or her part to make it function as efficiently and economically as possible. The drastic remedy of the organized strike to enforce the demands of unions of government employees is in direct contravention of this principle. It has been so regarded by the heads of the executive departments of the states and the nation. Most of the text writers refer to one or more of the following statements by three of our recent presidents. They are quoted, for example, in 1 Labor Law Journal 612 (May, 1950):

---

[1] The plaintiff claimed a declaratory judgment answering and adjudicating the following questions:

" (a) Is it permitted to the plaintiff under our laws to organize itself as a labor union for the purpose of demanding and receiving recognition and collective bargaining?

" (b) Is it permitted to the plaintiff organized as a labor union to demand recognition as such and collective bargaining?

" (c) Is it permissible under Connecticut law for the defendant to recognize the plaintiff for the purpose of collective bargaining?

" (d) Is collective bargaining to establish salaries and working conditions permissible between the plaintiff and the defendant?

" (e) May the plaintiff engage in concerted action such as strike, work stoppage, or collective refusal to enter upon duties?

" (f) Is arbitration a permissible method under Connecticut law to settle or adjust disputes between the plaintiff and the defendant?

" (g) Is mediation a permissible method under Connecticut law to settle or adjust disputes between the plaintiff and the defendant?

" (h) If the answer to the previous questions is yes, are the State's established administrative facilities, such as the State Board of Mediation and Arbitration and the State Labor Relations Board, available, as they are available in industrial disputes, to the plaintiff and the defendant?

" (i) Does the continuing contract law, so-called, create a status of employment within which the plaintiff may claim employment subject to the right to bargain salaries and working conditions?

" (j) Has the plaintiff the right to establish rules, working conditions and grievance resolution procedures by collective bargaining?"

"There is no right to strike against public safety by anybody anywhere at any time" (Calvin Coolidge on the Boston police strike). This same strike was characterized by President Wilson as "an intolerable crime against civilization." President Franklin D. Roosevelt said in a letter to the president of the National Federation of Federal Employees on August 16, 1937: "Particularly, I want to emphasize my conviction that militant tactics have no place in the functions of any organization of Government employees. . . . [A] strike of public employees manifests nothing less than an intent on their part to prevent or obstruct the operations of Government until their demands are satisfied. Such action, looking toward the paralysis of Government by those who have sworn to support it, is unthinkable and intolerable." As the author of the article cited says, "The above statement by President Roosevelt, who certainly was no enemy of labor unions, epitomizes the answer to the problem. It seems to be axiomatic."

The commentators, generally, subscribe to this proposition. National Institute of Municipal Law Officers Reports No. 76, 116, 129; 1 Teller, Labor Disputes & Collective Bargaining (1947 Sup.) § 171; 18 N.Y.U.L.Q. Rev. 247; 94 U. of Pa. L. Rev. 427. Notwithstanding this fact, Ziskind was able to publish a well-documented book entitled "One Thousand Strikes of Government Employees," which contains an elaborate bibliography. See also Spero, Government as Employer. This would indicate that the law on the subject is still in the process of development.

Few cases involving the right of unions of government employees to strike to enforce their demands have reached courts of last resort. That right has usually been tested by an application for an injunction forbidding the strike. The right of the governmental body to this relief has been uniformly upheld. It has been put on various grounds: public policy; interference with governmental function; illegal discrimination against the right of any citizen to apply for government employment (where the union sought a closed shop). The following cases do not necessarily turn on the specific right to strike, but the reasoning indicates that, if faced with that question, the court would be compelled to deny that right to public employees. For example, Perez v. Board of Police Commissioners, 78 Cal. App. 2d 638, 178 P.2d 537, held that the board could, by rule, prevent police officers from joining a labor union. If it could do this, it would certainly be upheld in an attempt to enjoin a strike called by the union. . . . [Citations omitted] The court puts the matter succinctly in the *Miami* case [Miami Water Works Local 654 v. Miami, 157 Fla. 445, 26 S.2d 194 (1946)]: "While strikes are recognized by the statute to be lawful under some circumstances, it would seem that a strike against the city would amount, in effect, to a strike against government itself—a situation difficult to reconcile with all notions of government."

The plaintiff, recognizing the unreasonableness of its claims in the case of such employees as the militia and the judiciary, seeks to place teachers in a class with employees employed by the municipality in its proprietary capacity. No authority is cited in support of this proposition. "A town board of education is an agency of the state in charge of education in the town. . . ." Board of Education of Stamford v. Board of Finance, 127 Conn. 345, 349, 16 A.2d 601. In fulfilling its duties as such an agency, it is acting in a governmental, not a proprietary, capacity. . . .

In the American system, sovereignty is inherent in the people. They can delegate it to a government which they create and operate by law. They can give to that government the power and authority to perform certain duties and furnish certain services. The government so created and empowered must employ people to carry on its task. Those people are agents of the government. They exercise some part of the sovereignty entrusted to it. They occupy a status entirely different from those who carry on a private enterprise. They serve the public welfare and not a private purpose. To say that they can strike is the equivalent of saying that they can deny the authority of government and contravene the public welfare. The answer to question (e) is "No."

Questions (a) and (b) relate to the right of the plaintiff to organize itself as a labor union and to demand recognition and collective bargaining. The right to organize is sometimes accorded by statute or ordinance. See, for example, the Bridgeport ordinance adopted June 17, 1946 (Bridgeport Munic. Reg. [1947] p. 15), discussed in National Institute of Municipal Law Officers Report No. 129, p. 51. The right to organize has also been forbidden by statute or regulation. Perez v. Board of Police Commissioners, 78 Cal. App. 2d 638, 178 P.2d 537. In Connecticut the statutes are silent on the subject. Union organization in industry is now the rule rather than the exception. In the absence of prohibitory statute or regulation, no good reason appears why public employees should not organize as a labor union. Springfield v. Clouse, 356 Mo. 1239, 1246, 206 S.W.2d 539. It is the second part of question (a) that causes difficulty. The question reads: "Is it permitted to the plaintiff under our laws to organize itself as a labor union for the purpose of demanding and receiving recognition and collective bargaining?" The question is phrased in a very peremptory form. The common method of enforcing recognition and collective bargaining is the strike. It appears that this method has already been used by the plaintiff and that the threat of its use again is one of the reasons for the present suit. As has been said, the strike is not a permissible method of enforcing the plaintiff's demands. The answer to questions (a) and (b) is a qualified "Yes." There is no objection to the organization of the plaintiff as a labor union, but if its organization is for the purpose of "demanding" recognition and collective bargaining the demands must be kept within legal bounds. What we have said does not mean that the plaintiff has the right to organize for all of the purposes for which employees in private enterprise may unite, as those are defined in § 7391 of the General Statutes. Nor does it mean that, having organized, it is necessarily protected against unfair labor practices as specified in § 7392 or that it shall be the exclusive bargaining agent for all employees of the unit, as provided in § 7393. It means nothing more than that the plaintiff may organize and bargain collectively for the pay and working conditions which it may be in the power of the board of education to grant.

Questions (c) and (d) in effect ask whether collective bargaining between the plaintiff and the defendant is permissible. The statutes and private acts give broad powers to the defendant with reference to educational matters and school management in Norwalk. If it chooses to negotiate with the plaintiff with regard to the employment, salaries, grievance procedure and working conditions of its members, there is no statute, public or private, which forbids such negotiations. It is a matter of common knowledge that this is the method pursued in most school systems large enough to support a teachers' association in some form. It would seem to make no difference theoretically whether the negotiations are with a committee of the whole association or with individuals or small related groups, so long as any agreement made with the committee is confined to members of the association. If the strike threat is absent and the defendant prefers to handle the matter through negotiation with the plaintiff, no reason exists why it should not do so. The claim of the defendant that this would be an illegal delegation of authority is without merit. The authority is and remains in the board. This statement is not to be construed as approval of the existing contracts attached to the complaint. Their validity is not in issue.

As in the case of questions (a) and (b), (c) and (d) are in too general a form to permit a categorical answer. The qualified "Yes" which we give to them should not be construed as authority to negotiate a contract which involves the surrender of the board's legal discretion, is contrary to law or is otherwise ultra vires. For example, an agreement by the board to hire only union members would clearly be an illegal discrimination. Mugford v.

Baltimore, 185 Md. 266, 270, 44 A.2d 745; Rhyne, Labor Unions & Municipal Employe Law, pp. 34, 137, 157. Any salary schedule must be subject to the powers of the board of estimate and taxation. "The salaries of all persons appointed by the board of education . . . shall be as fixed by said board, but the aggregate amount of such salaries . . . shall not exceed the amount determined by the board of estimate and taxation. . . ." 21 Spec. Laws 285, No. 315, § 3; Board of Education of Stamford v. Board of Finance, 127 Conn. 345, 349, 16 A.2d 601. One of the allegations of the complaint is that the solution of the parties' difficulties by the posing of specific issues is not satisfactory. Whether or not this is so, that course will be necessary if this discussion of general principles is an insufficient guide.

Question (f) reads, "Is arbitration a permissible method under Connecticut law to settle or adjust disputes between the plaintiff and the defendant?" The power of a town to enter into an agreement of arbitration was originally denied on the ground that it was an unlawful delegation of authority. Griswold v. North Stonington, 5 Conn. 367, 371. It was later held that not only the amount of damages but liability could be submitted to arbitration. Hine v. Stephens, 33 Conn. 497, 504; Mallory v. Huntington, 64 Conn. 88, 96, 29 A. 245. The principle applies to the parties to the case at bar. If it is borne in mind that arbitration is the result of mutual agreement, there is no reason to deny the power of the defendant to enter voluntarily into a contract to arbitrate a specific dispute. On a proposal for a submission, the defendant would have the opportunity of deciding whether it would arbitrate as to any question within its power. Its power to submit to arbitration would not extend to questions of policy but might extend to questions of liability. Arbitration as a method of settling disputes is growing in importance and, in a proper case, "deserves the enthusiastic support of the courts." International Brotherhood of Teamsters v. Shapiro, 138 Conn. 57, 69, 82 A.2d 345. Agreements to submit all disputes to arbitration, commonly found in ordinary union contracts, are in a different category. If the defendant entered into a general agreement of that kind, it might find itself committed to surrender the broad discretion and responsibility reposed in it by law. For example, it could not commit to an arbitrator the decision of a proceeding to discharge a teacher for cause. So, the matter of certification of teachers is committed to the state board of education. General Statutes §§ 1432, 1433, 1435. The best answer we can give to question (f) is, "Yes, arbitration may be a permissible method as to certain specific, arbitrable disputes."

From what has been said, it is obvious that, within the same limitations, mediation to settle or adjust disputes is not only permissible but desirable. The answer to question (g) is "Yes." The state board of mediation and arbitration and the state labor relations board, however, are set up to handle disputes in private industry and are not available to the plaintiff and defendant for reasons given in the opinion of the attorney general dated July 6, 1948. 25 Conn. Atty. Gen. Rep. 270. This was confirmed as to Norwalk teachers by an opinion dated June 12, 1950, not yet published. See also United States v. United Mine Workers, 330 U.S. 258, 269, 67 S. Ct. 677, 91 L. Ed. 884. The answer to question (h) is "No."

General Statutes, Sup. 1949, § 160a, provides in part: "The contract of employment of a teacher shall be renewed for the following school year unless such teacher has been notified in writing prior to March first of that year that such contract will not be renewed." Question (i) asks whether this law creates "a status of employment within which the plaintiff may claim employment subject to the right to bargain salaries and working conditions?" The meaning of this is not clear and the briefs do not clarify it. It is the type of question that should be related to a specific state of facts. It cannot be answered in vacuo.

As to question (j), the plaintiff has no right to establish rules. As stated above, the right is and remains in the board. . . .

NOTES

1. For a good review of the case law prior to 1953, see Annot., 31 A.L.R.2d 1142 (1953).

2. The *Norwalk* case at the time of its issuance in 1951 was hailed by public sector unions since the court recognized that collective bargaining was permissible in the public sector. Although the sovereignty doctrine was not utilized to prevent collective bargaining, the court clearly felt that it was pertinent to the various issues presented for decision.

3. The issues which were raised in the *Norwalk* case mirror many of the issues which are explored in subsequent chapters, *e.g.*, the right of public employees to join and form unions, the authority of a public employer to recognize and negotiate with a union, the right to strike, the legality of an agreement to arbitrate disputes, and so forth.

4. The changing judicial attitude concerning the applicability of the sovereignty theory is graphically illustrated by two New York court decisions issued thirteen years apart. In Railway Mail Ass'n v. Murphy, 180 Misc. 868, 44 N.Y.S.2d 601, 607-08 (1943), *rev'd on other grounds*, 326 U.S. 88 (1945), the court stated:

To tolerate or recognize any combination of Civil Service employees of the Government as a labor organization or union is not only incompatible with the spirit of democracy, but inconsistent with every principle upon which our Government is founded. Nothing is more dangerous to public welfare than to admit that hired servants of the state can dictate to the Government the hours, the wages and conditions under which they will carry on essential services vital to the welfare, safety and security of the citizen. To admit as true that Government employees have power to halt or check the functions of Government, unless their demands are satisfied, is to transfer to them all legislative, executive and judicial power. Nothing would be more ridiculous. . . .

Collective bargaining has no place in government service. The employer is the whole people. It is impossible for administrative officials to bind the Government of the United States or the State of New York by any agreement made between them and representatives of any union. Government officials and employees are governed and guided by laws which must be obeyed and which cannot be abrogated or set aside by an agreement of employees and officials.

Thirteen years later the court in Civil Serv. Forum v. New York City Transit Auth., 3 Misc. 2d 346, 151 N.Y.S.2d 402, 408 (Sup. Ct. 1956), rev'd on other grounds, 4 App. Div. 2d 117, 163 N.Y.S.2d 476 (1957), stated:

The agreement . . . executed with these unions was negotiated for the purpose of protecting the health, safety and vital interests of the people of the City and State of New York and to establish and maintain harmonious and stable labor relations with the unions. In the circumstances it seems clear that these compelling reasons were sufficient to warrant the defendant authority in fostering a peaceful settlement of its prospective labor disputes by entering into the challenged agreement.

5. The full text of President Roosevelt's frequently quoted letter to the President of the National Federation of Federal Employees is reproduced in C. RHYNE, LABOR UNIONS AND MUNICIPAL EMPLOYE LAW 436-37 (1946). This book, by the General Counsel of the National Institute of Municipal Law Officers, contains an invaluable collection of decisions, attorney general's opinions, and other documentation concerning public sector labor relations prior to 1946. For the period from 1946 to 1949, see C. Rhyne, Labor Unions and Municipal Employee Law—A Supplementary Report, NAT'L INSTITUTE MUN. L. OFFICER REP. No. 129 (1949).

B. Public Employee Organizations

1. Generally

ADVISORY COMMISSION ON INTERGOVERNMENTAL RELATIONS,
LABOR-MANAGEMENT POLICIES FOR STATE AND
LOCAL GOVERNMENT 5-10 (1969)

. . . .

Public Employee Organizations

While the growth of public employee organizations at local, State, and national levels has not been commensurate with the growth of government itself, the organizations affiliated with national unions nevertheless comprise the most rapidly expanding sector of unionized labor. In 1956, the 915,000 organized government employees constituted approximately 5 percent of the total AFL-CIO membership; by 1964, 1.45 million such employees represented 8 percent of the total. The unionized public sector reached the 1.7 million mark in 1966 (the latest year for reliable figures) or 9 percent of all union members. In addition, while the proportion of unionized workers in relation to the entire labor force had dropped in recent years, the proportion of government employees—unionized and nonunionized—in the country's labor force rose from 12 percent in 1956 to 16 percent in 1964, but dipped to 15.4 percent in 1966 and 15.0 percent in 1968.

Unionization efforts, however, have scored differing records at the various levels of government, with the greatest success occurring at the Federal level. Fifty two percent, or 1.4 million members, of all Federal executive branch employees in 1968 belonged to unions recognized for discussion purposes. Only 8 percent, or 644,000 members, of all State and local government workers belonged to affiliates of national unions in 1966. Two years later the figure edged up to 9.6 percent or approximately 890,000 members. These figures, of course, do not include professional associations such as those affiliated with the National Educational Association (NEA) or independent unions. Of the 1,026 organized cities over 10,000 population responding to a 1969 Advisory Commission survey made in cooperation with the International City Management Association (ICMA) and the National Association of Counties (NACO), 38 percent of the reporting jurisdictions with organized employees indicated that some of their employees were members of national unions, while 48 percent reported that organized employees belonged only to nationally affiliated local unions. Of the 117 organized metropolitan counties participating in the survey, 48 percent stated that some of their employees were members of national unions and 38 percent replied that their organized personnel were wholly in the unionized sector.

Yet unions constitute only one portion of the organized sector. Independent State and local employee associations loom large in the overall organized personnel picture with more than one-fifth of the total. For the municipalities participating in the ACIR-ICMA survey, 38 percent reported that some of their personnel were members of such associations and 14 percent indicated that their organized employees were exclusively associational members. Of the organized counties participating in the ACIR-NACO poll, 48 percent had some of their organized employees belonging to local associations and 14 percent had all such personnel in these organizations. Finally, professional associations with or without national organizations account for over 45 percent of the total organized State and local public sector.

Most public employee organizations at the State, county, and municipal levels may be divided into three major categories. The professional associations include — among others — employee groups for teachers and school administrators, nurses, and social and welfare workers. The craft unions primarily consist of single occupational groups of employees—while the industrial type of union or association cuts across broad occupational categories in various departments and sometimes in whole governmental jurisdictions.

Professional Associations. Professional associations represent a great variety of professional and semi-professional public employees at the State and local levels. All of them, however, are concerned with certification, training, codes of ethics, the right to exclude nonprofessionals from their organization, and the economic and social welfare of their members. Some of them are hardly distinguishable from unions with respect to employer relations and other related activities.

Among the largest is the National Education Association (NEA) with approximately one million members. Public school teachers constitute approximately 85 percent of the total membership of NEA with supervisors, principals, administrators and other school specialists accounting for the remaining 15 percent. This policy underscores a major difference between the NEA and the American Federation of Teachers, which limits its membership only to classroom teachers. Members of each of the 50 NEA State affiliates and most of the 8,000 local associations include teachers, supervisors, and administrators. At the same time, the State affiliates enjoy a relatively high degree of autonomy in membership policies as well as in other matters.

The NEA in its early history emphasized activities centering on better schools and improved professional status of teachers. It frowned upon any overt activity of State and local affiliates lobbying for higher teachers' salaries and displayed a singular lack of interest in affiliating with the labor movement. Salary discussions and other "bread and butter" concerns were deemed unprofessional and labor unions were considered special interest groups.

In the 1960's the NEA affiliates in large cities across the country began what has since amounted to a complete about-face. Prompted in part by classroom teacher gains of the AFL-CIO American

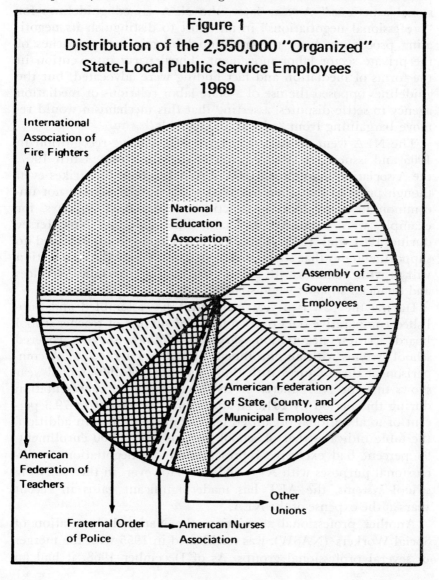

Figure 1
Distribution of the 2,550,000 "Organized"
State-Local Public Service Employees
1969

Federation of Teachers in the large urban systems, NEA's doctrine of passive professionalism came under mounting criticism. At its 1961 convention, the Association for the first time called for discussions between local boards of education and the teaching profession for the purpose of achieving common consent on matters of interest to its members. While the word negotiation was not used, the resolution declared that a board of review should be established to resolve differences arising between local affiliates and boards of education. By 1962, however, the NEA began to use the term "professional negotiations" and in that year passed a landmark resolution establishing a system of "professional sanctions." A year later, the NEA issued guidelines for "professional negotiations" in an effort to distinguish its negotiating procedures from the traditional bargaining approaches of the private sector labor movement. Third party intervention in the forms of mediation and fact finding were advocated, but the guidelines opposed the use of a State labor relations or mediation agency to settle disputes, asserting that this mechanism would remove bargaining from "education channels."

The NEA went on record in favor of exclusive recognition in 1965 and issued a revised edition of the guidelines. Until 1967, the Association maintained its traditional disdain for strikes even though prior to that time forms of work stoppages were not uncommon in many local jurisdictions. Professional holidays, for example, were organized in Utah, Oklahoma, and New Jersey during 1964 and 1965. The 1967 NEA convention resolved to support affiliates that strike school systems. Today the Association will provide affiliates with substantial legal and technical services and financial support when strikes occur.

During the past two years, the NEA has assembled and published comparative data on two national surveys of teacher-school board written negotiation agreements. Both surveys covered school systems with an enrollment of 1,000 or more. . . . A comparison of these figures with those for the 1966-1967 school year shows that the NEA increased its share of teacher representation during this period by 201,844, up from 77.7 percent to 79.3 percent of total national organized teacher membership. In addition, the table indicates that of school districts over 1,000 enrollment, 93 percent had exclusive representation for negotiation or discussional purposes with NEA affiliates. However, in the really big school systems, the AFT has made significant gains in recent years at the expense of the NEA.

Another professional association, the National Association of Social Workers (NASW), was established in 1955 with the merger of several professional groups. As of December 1968, it had an overall membership of slightly over 50,000 including student and private sector worker members. "Bread-and-butter" economic activities are carried on only in a limited way by NASW, but they are a focal point of concern of separate, local social worker unions. The Association, however, has never viewed the latter as a threat to its existence, probably because less than 15 percent of all social welfare workers are unionized. The American Nurses Association is another such professional group with 204,000 members (1967) or 31 percent of all nurses working in public and private institutions. The ANA is concerned with more than just professional standards. It actively engages in employer discussions and collective bargaining, seeks exclusive recognition, negotiates contracts and agreements, and has, on a few occasions, engaged in walkouts. In the summer of 1968, the ANA removed the clause from its constitution prohibiting strikes.

Another national organization, the Fraternal Order of Police, is independent of labor movement organizations and is the principal professional organization for policemen. FOP does not consider itself a union, although local lodges in some communities engage in collective bargaining, handle grievances and represent the interests of their members to their employer. In general, however, the FOP concentrates on police pension matters and improvement in police working conditions. The Grand Lodge of FOP was organized in 1915 and today claims to have over 620 lodges in 18 States, with a total of 62,600 members.

Craft-Type Unions. One of the largest among the craft-type unions is the International Association of Firefighters (IAFF), an affiliate of the AFL-CIO. The organization had its origins in the fraternal and social clubs of the 1880's and today claims that better than 90 percent of the nation's uniformed firemen are enrolled within its membership. In 1935, Association members numbered approximately 26,000. Nearly three decades later, the union claimed 115,000 members. Last year (1968), the total came to 131,356. The Association has operated traditionally without written contracts or agreements and adhered loyally to its constitutional ban on strikes. At its 1968 convention, however, the membership removed the fifty-year-old no-strike pledge from its constitution. The union's international president, William Buck, stated:

> . . . certain arbitrary public officials, knowing that we cannot and will not strike—because we voluntarily gave up this right when we were founded—have certainly taken advantage of the professional firefighters across the negotiating table.

Another major public employee "craft" union is the American
Federation of Teachers, which affiliated with the old American
Federation of Labor in 1919. Their greatest success has been in
the large cities . . . with about 80 percent of the Federation's members employed in school systems with an enrollment
of 100,000 or more. In terms of size, the AFT has a membership
of 175,000 or about 20 percent of the country's organized teachers. For collective negotiation and discussion purposes, the AFT
claims that their locals, in effect, serve as the representatives of
approximately a quarter of a million school teachers.

Blue collar craft unions also are found frequently at national,
State, county and municipal levels. Organization of some of these
governmental employees has kept pace with the unionization
of the counterpart trades in private industry. International unions
active at the State, county, and municipal levels include the International Association of Machinists and Aerospace Workers; International Brotherhood of Teamsters, Chauffeurs, Warehousemen;
Service Employees' International Union; United Brotherhood of
Carpenters and Joiners of America; United Association of Journeymen and Apprentices of the Plumbing and Pipefitting Industry of the United States and Canada; International Union of
Operating Engineers; International Brotherhood of Electrical
Workers; International Hod Carriers, Building and Common Laborers' Union; and United Mine Workers. No accurate count,
however, is available concerning the number of State and local
employees belonging to these craft unions.

Finally, establishment of a national police union has been announced with the goal of enrolling 325,000 law enforcement
officers.

Industrial-Type Unions. The dominant "industrial-type" union
at these levels is the American Federation of State, County, and
Municipal Employees (AFSCME), an affiliate of the AFL-CIO.
AFSCME traces its ancestry back to 1932 when a small group of
Wisconsin State employees formed the Wisconsin State Employees
Association and received an AFL charter. A month later, the local
had 53 members. Within a year, the organization was exploring
the possibility of establishing a national union, but this effort
soon generated jurisdictional problems with the American Federation of Government Employees, another AFL affiliate. AFGE's
charter from the AFL gave it ill-defined jurisdiction over all government employees, but its organizational activity had been confined almost exclusively to the Federal service. With the emerging
threat of a rival national organization, the union's leadership decided to clarify AFGE's position and in 1935 amended its consti-

tution to claim jurisdiction over State and local employees as well as those in the Federal sector.

At that time, the AFL leadership generally was indifferent to the unionization of public employees. Some heads of the older craft unions wanted no part of the public employee field. Yet, the AFL faced another far more difficult problem in 1935: the withdrawal of industrial unions to form the Congress of Industrial Organizations under the leadership of the Mineworker's President, John L. Lewis. The AFL leadership realized that unless the jurisdictional disputes between AFGE and the new organization of State and local employees were resolved, the newly organized CIO might issue a national charter to the ambitious newcomers.

Consequently, the AFL Executive Council promoted an agreement whereby the State and local group would become a semi-autonomous affiliate of AFGE, with its own convention and leadership. In effect, the AFGE would be merely the channel of communication with the parent AFL. The new group then held its first national convention in December 1935 and ratified the agreement. The organization thus formally became the American Federation of State, County, and Municipal Employees, adopted a constitution and elected its own officers.

But the AFGE-AFSCME relationhsip continued to be competitive. AFGE sought to limit AFSCME organizing to white-collar workers in State and local agencies—a restriction AFSCME would not accept. When AFGE voted in new leadership in 1936, the matter again was placed before the AFL Executive Council, and it finally decided to grant AFSCME independent status.

While the early growth of AFSCME was not impressive, its membership, as of July 1969, had soared to 425,000. It claims—with good reason—to be the fastest growing union in the country. Although two-thirds of its members hold blue collar jobs, its occupational categories range from garbage collectors to zoo keepers, from architects to psychologists, from laborers to lawyers. The Federation's chief aim is to achieve establishment of a system of collective bargaining which produces written agreements. Its basic procedural concerns then center on recognition, bargaining, union security, checkoff, and the use of signed contracts. In recent years, the union's members have not hesitated to strike even in jurisdictions where walk-outs are not permitted. In December 1968, the Federation reported that of its 700 local agreements 16 percent provided for a union shop, 12 percent for a modified union shop, and 10 percent contained a maintenance of membership provision. Five percent of the total stipulated an "agency shop" arrangement and half of the 700 agreements, concluded with jurisdictions in at least 24 States, call for binding arbitration of grievance disputes.

AFSCME reports that to date more than 1,850 local affiliates have been organized. Locals may represent an entire city or county, or alternatively a particular department, **part of a department**, or a group of employers in a particular occupational classification which cuts across many departments.

In addition to AFSCME, independent unaffiliated associations of public employees exist in at least 37 State governments and an indeterminate number of local governments. Their membership is drawn from all departments and agencies of these jurisdictions. Nearly all have non-selective enrollment policies and may count as members elected and appointive officials, department heads, supervisors, as well as rank and file workers. At least 14 States have two or more statewide public employee organizations and several associations have local unit affiliates organized on a sub-state regional basis.

These associations in the past generally have been satisfied with informal recognition by employers, and membership has never been required as a condition of employment. They usually have relied on lobbying to achieve better working conditions and have depended upon civil service procedures rather than on collective negotiations to settle disputes. Their affiliated competitors have frequently referred to them as "company unions."

With the recent passage of public labor-management legislation, however, a good deal of competition has been generated between these independent associations and the affiliated unions, both for membership and exclusive recognition rights. In California, Connecticut, Michigan, New Jersey, New York, Ohio, Oregon, and Rhode Island, State employee associations are now considered strong competitors with AFSCME affiliates. A number of associations at both the State and local levels now are beginning to scrap their traditional passive practices and are adopting a fairly militant stance. For example, the New York State Civil Service Employees Association—representing over 170,000 public workers—by a unanimous vote of its convention delegates dropped its 19-year-old no-strike pledge in March 1967 claiming that, ". . . while strikes may be abhorrent to the public and damage the image of public employees generally, they have proven a benefit to the employees and organizations involved." Similarly, in October 1969 the 111,000-member California State Employees' Association abandoned the no-strike pledge it had adopted in 1959. The attitude of the Oregon State Employees' Association toward collective bargaining also shows signs of change. The Association now asserts that collective bargaining is another tool to represent their membership better, and written and enforceable agreements on employment matters presently are among its goals.

Published material on these unaffiliated organizations is limited and detailed anaylsis of the scope and nature of their membership and activities is virtually nonexistent. What evidence there is, however, suggests that some of them are more than holding their own against unions in representation elections, partly because of their own increased militance and concern with establishing viable discussion and negotiation procedures. In the most recent instance, for example, the 1969 representation election for New York State employees was won overwhelmingly by the independent employees' association. In 1969, the 32 State affiliates of the Assembly of Governmental Employees (AGE)—a loose confederation of State and local public employees associations—reported a total paid membership of approximately 500,000 State employees, a 41 percent increase since 1964.

NOTES

1. The most recent report of union and association membership issued by the Bureau of Labor Statistics in August 1973 shows that 4,514,000 public employees are members of unions or associations. Of this total, 1,381,000 are at the Federal level and 3,133,000 are at the State and local level. Whereas approximately 33 percent of all public employees presently belong to unions or associations, only 24.3 percent of the total U.S. labor force are members of unions or associations. U.S. BUREAU OF LABOR STATISTICS, DEP'T OF LABOR, LABOR UNION AND EMPLOYEE ASSOCIATION MEMBERSHIP, 1972, RELEASE No. 73-390 (Aug. 22, 1973).

The continuing surge in the unionization of public employees is revealed by the rapid growth which many public sector unions and employee organizations have experienced. The membership of six of the major public sector unions and associations as of mid-1973 is as follows:

American Federation of Government Employees (AFGE)	293,000
American Federation of State, County and Municipal Employees (AFSCME)	615,000
American Federation of Teachers (AFT)	385,000
Assembly of Government Employees (AGE)	600,000
International Association of Fire Fighters (IAFF)	165,000
National Education Association (NEA)	1,400,000

Of all the unions in both private and public sectors that gained 100,000 members or more between 1962 and 1972, the three that showed the greatest percentage increases were the AFT, AFGE, and AFSCME, which registered increases of 250 percent, 176 percent, and 140 percent, respectively. U.S. BUREAU OF LABOR STATISTICS, DEP'T OF LABOR, RELEASE NO. 73-390, at 6 (Aug. 22, 1973).

2. A survey of union recognition in the federal government released by the United States Civil Service Commission showed that as of November 1972, 55 percent of all executive branch employees (1,082,587) were represented by unions holding exclusive recognition rights. U.S. CIVIL SERV. COMM'N BULL. NO. 711-27 (1973), GERR Ref. File 71:201. This is up sharply from the 21 percent of all executive branch employees (excluding postal employees) that were in exclusive bargaining units in 1966, four years after President Kennedy promulgated Executive Order 10988. GERR No. 186, C-1 to C-29 (1967).

At the municipal level, a 1972 Bureau of Labor Statistics study concluded:

> Representation of Municipal employees is no longer confined solely to major American cities. In fact, it encompasses a majority of the 2,064 municipalities studied, even towns of 10,000. In total, more than three-fifths of the cities surveyed reported unions and associations within their jurisdictions. (See table 1.) These occurred in direct relation to city size. That is, all cities of 1 million or more reported employee organizations, more than 90 percent of cities having populations of one-quarter to 1 million, and over 80 percent of cities of 50,000 to one-quarter million. There was a significant drop in coverage among smaller cities but more than 50 percent noted the presence of organizations. . . .
>
> In the past, efforts to organize were directed toward large cities because of the concentration of workers. In recent years, the focus of organizing drives has shifted toward smaller towns. Aware of successes by unions and associations in large cities, employee associations in smaller towns have pressed for collective bargaining, in addition to their normal fraternal, social, and legislative activities, and have often been successful.
>
> Most cities reporting unions and associations were in the East North Central and Middle Atlantic regions. In both regions, the proportion of cities reporting unions and associations exceeded the national average. This was not unexpected, because these States have strong traditions of union-

ism in the private sector. However, the highest proportions of cities reporting employee organizations were in New England and the Pacific States, where unions are also common in private industry. California also has a long history of dealing with public employee associations, many of which have now converted to collective bargaining representation. Nelson & Doster, *City Employee Representation and Bargaining Policies,* MONTHLY LAB. REV., November 1972, at 43.

3. For a particularly comprehensive study of public sector unions and associations, see J. STIEBER, VARIETIES OF PUBLIC EMPLOYEE ORGANIZATION: UNIONS AND ASSOCIATIONS IN STATE AND LOCAL GOVERNMENT (1973). *See generally* U.S. BUREAU OF LABOR STATISTICS, DEP'T OF LABOR, BULL. No. 1702, MUNICIPAL PUBLIC EMPLOYEE ASSOCIATIONS (1971); Donoian, *The AFGE and the AFSCME: Labor's Hope for the Future?,* 18 LAB. L.J. 727 (1967); Gitlow, *Public Employee Unionism in the United States: Growth and Outlook,* 21 LAB. L.J. 766 (1970).

4. For an excellent account of the founding and growth of AFSCME, see L. KRAMER, LABOR'S PARADOX—THE AMERICAN FEDERATION OF STATE, COUNTY, AND MUNICIPAL EMPLOYEES, AFL-CIO (1962).

5. For many years there was a fierce and frequently bitter rivalry between the National Education Association (NEA) and the American Federation of Teachers (AFT). For example, as recently as 1966, the President of the NEA categorized the AFT in the following manner:

> The American Federation of Teachers merely serves as a front for organized labor in general, and the Industrial Union Department [of the AFL-CIO] in particular in their drive to unionize white collar workers and professionals in American society. . . .
>
> It is also important that you are aware also of another motivation in this unionizing drive for teachers in particular. This second motivation represents to us one of the most dangerous threats that American education will ever face. . . . [This second motivation] is indoctrination of the pupils and teachers to the labor movement philosophy in order to advance the interests of unionism in this country. White Collar Report No. 464, A-4 to A-5 (1966).

Increasingly, however, there are signs that these two teacher organizations will eventually merge. At its 1973 convention, the NEA voted in favor of merger talks with the AFT. GERR No.

512, B-10 (1973). Subsequently, David Selden, President of the AFT, stated that the AFT Executive Council was ready to begin merger discussions between the two organizations immediately. Mergers of the two organizations have already occurred at the state level in New York and at the local level in such cities as New Orleans, Los Angeles, and Flint. GERR No. 512, B-11 (1973).

Among the many studies of the American Federation of Teachers (AFT) and the National Education Association (NEA) are R. DOHERTY & W. OBERER, TEACHERS, SCHOOL BOARDS, AND COLLECTIVE BARGAINING: A CHANGING OF THE GUARD (1967); M. LIEBERMAN & M. MOSKOW, COLLECTIVE NEGOTIATIONS FOR TEACHERS (1966); E. SHILS & T. WHITTIER, TEACHERS, ADMINISTRATORS, AND COLLECTIVE BARGAINING (1968); C. PERRY & W. WILDMAN, THE IMPACT OF NEGOTIATIONS IN PUBLIC EDUCATION: THE EVIDENCE FROM THE SCHOOLS (1970); M. MOSKOW & R. DOHERTY, United States, in TEACHER UNIONS AND ASSOCIATIONS 295 (A. Blum ed. 1969). For a critical examination of the AFT, see R. BRAUN, TEACHERS AND POWER (1972). For an excellent article on the development of collective bargaining between the New York City Board of Education and the United Federation of Teachers, see Klaus, The Evolution of a Collective Bargaining Relationship in Public Education: New York City's Changing Seven-year History, 67 MICH. L. REV. 1033 (1969).

6. The development of collective bargaining among faculty members at colleges and universities is explored in FACULTY POWER: COLLECTIVE BARGAINING ON CAMPUS (T. Tice ed. 1972); EMPLOYMENT RELATIONS IN HIGHER EDUCATION (S. Elam & M. Moskow eds. 1969); Collective Negotiations in Higher Education: A Symposium, 1971 WIS. L. REV. 1; R.S. Brown, Collective Bargaining in Higher Education, 67 MICH. L. REV. 1067 (1969); Ferguson, Collective Bargaining in Universities and Colleges, 19 LAB. L.J. 778 (1968); R.C. Brown, Professors and Unions: The Faculty Senate: An Effective Alternative to Collective Bargaining in Higher Education, 12 WM. & MARY L. REV. 252 (1970); Coe, A Study of the Procedures Used in Collective Bargaining with Faculty Unions in Public Universities, J. COLLEGE & UNIV. PERSONNEL ASS'N, Vol. 24, No. 2, pp. 1-22 (March 1973).

7. In addition to the AFT and the NEA, the American Association of University Professors (AAUP) also seeks to represent college and university faculty members for the purpose of collective bargaining. The AAUP's Statement on Collective Bargaining, GERR No. 478, B-6 to B-7 (1972), states, in relevant part:

Collective bargaining, in offering a rational and equitable means of distributing resources and of providing recourse for an aggrieved individual, can buttress and complement the sound principles and practices of higher education which the American Association of University Professors has long supported. Where appropriate, therefore, the Association will pursue collective bargaining as a major additional way of realizing its goals in higher education, and it will provide assistance on a selective basis to interested local chapters. . . .

The longstanding programs of the Association are means to achieve a number of basic ends at colleges and universities: the enhancement of academic freedom and tenure; of due process; of sound academic government. Collective bargaining, properly used, is essentially another means to achieve these ends, and at the same time to strengthen the influence of the faculty in the distribution of an institution's economic resources. The implementation of Association-supported principles, reliant upon professional traditions and upon moral suasion, can be effectively supplemented by a collective bargaining agreement and given the force of law.

Commenting on this 1972 statement, the General Secretary of the AAUP, Bertram H. Davis, stated:

The action of the 1972 Annual Meeting did not . . . constitute a total break with the Association's past; it would be inaccurate, however, to state that it was merely another step in an evolution which had begun some seven years earlier. It represented, most particularly, a change in emphasis and attitude, for it was the Association's first decisive affirmation of the view that collective bargaining provides a suitable means to achieve the Association's objectives for higher education. Although there was full recognition that collective bargaining was not the only means to that end and that chapters ought to have complete discretion in deciding whether or not to employ it, there was a clear determination to devote more of the Association's resources to collective bargaining and to give greater assistance, on a selective basis, to chapters seeking exclusive bargaining status. Report of General Secretary Bertram H. Davis to 59th Annual Meeting of AAUP, GERR No. 503, F-1 (1973).

2. The Union vs. the Association Model

GOVERNOR'S COMMITTEE ON PUBLIC EMPLOYEE RELATIONS, FINAL REPORT 55-62 (State of New York, March 31, 1966)†

There are at least 8600 governmental employing entities in the State of New York the employees of which might conceivably desire to exercise the right of association for the purpose of negotiating collectively the terms of their employment and the handling of their grievances. These include 20 State Departments, the State University, 62 cities, 62 counties, 932 towns, 553 villages, 1199 school districts, 53 public authorities, 84 housing authorities, 5540 special districts, an unknown but large number of city departments, and 21 urban renewal agencies. Moreover, many of these entities run special installations (such as hospitals, prisons, etc.) the employees of which have a plausible community of interest in collective representation.

To assume that a single mode of collective participation for the employees of all of these entities can or should be established by state law would exceed the limits of common sense. As a matter of fact, an extensive range of arrangements for that collective participation has developed out of experience in satisfying the interests of not only employees, but also employee organizations, government agency executives, and legislative bodies.

It is widely considered, however, that there are basically two models characterizing those arrangements, sometimes referred to as the *Union* model and the *Association* model. . . .

The differences between those two models can be painted with a broad brush. Leaders of particular employee organizations do identify themselves with one or the other model. And when their organizations are competitors with each other for members among the same group of employees, their recruiting appeal frequently stresses the advantages of the type which they represent. Yet, the problem to which they must adapt their activity in representing public employees is, in many essentials, the same for all employee organizations. It is not surprising, therefore, that over time it becomes harder to distinguish between unions and associations and that each tends to adopt successful practices of the other.

The differences between the two models are normally considered to be related to the following six dimensions:

---

† The members of the Committee were George W. Taylor, Chairman, E. Wright Bakke, David L. Cole, John T. Dunlop, and Frederick H. Harbison.

A. The character of the claimed employee-employer unit.

In the Union model the unit desired is subject to pragmatic determination at the moment, not only in accordance with a community of interests of employees in regard to their sharing of the same conditions of work, the same grievances, the same "boss," the same locality, or the same craft skills, but with regard to a favorable opportunity for organizing them and thus for extending the membership of the organizing union. There is thus a tendency for fragmentized units to appear originally in a number of cases. It is pragmatic opportunity rather than a policy of occupational oriented organizing, however, which predominantly governs their practice.

The unit claimed by those organized on the Association model is also subject to pragmatic organizing strategy considerations, but there is a traditional policy of seeking to represent the employees of more comprehensive units defined by reference to employment in a common-employer unit. . . .

Another dimension of the unit problem has to do with the status level of the members eligible to join the organization. In the Union model supervisors and professional and confidential employees are normally excluded. In the Association model they are normally included.

B. Formality of recognition and for what, and for whom.

The recognition sought ultimately by organizations identified with the Union model is for exclusive representation of all employees of a bargaining unit where the union has been chosen as representative by a majority of the employees. Representation for members only is considered an undesirable second best to be accepted only until the union has sufficient strength to demand exclusive representation. . . .

The Associations do not differ from the Unions in their predisposition to desire exclusive representation.

The terms of employment about which the two models of organizations negotiate are determined not so much by the policies of the organizations as by the willingness of the executives of the government agencies to negotiate on certain issues. Different executives have different ideas about the scope of issues concerning which they have the discretion to negotiate to a conclusion.

In the case of both Union and Association, however, the kind of representative action for which recognition is sought includes the process of grievance settlement. The expectations of both Associations and Unions concerning what they can negotiate

about are limited by the fact that certain terms of employment
are mandated by legislative enactment. . . .

Moreover, both the Union and the Association model organizations are subject to the restriction that "nothing in
conflict with law and Civil Service rules or benefits" shall be
negotiated or made part of a grievance settlement. The tendency
of both models, however, is to take the mandated terms as
minima, and to negotiate from there. Also, one gets the impression that the Union model organizations stress the amplification
of those minima through direct negotiation, and that the Association model organizations have a greater tendency to seek direct
legislative modification of the minima.

As experience grows, it is possible that the differences in the
two models in regard to the type of recognition sought, for whom,
and for what, will be even less significant than in the present.
Such predispositions are, after all, not so much a function of what
organization leaders want, as a function of what they can expect
in view of the possibilities they experience. Those possibilities
are constrained by many of the same factors for both of them.

C. *The check off.*

Both the Unions and the Associations are interested in and
strive to obtain the check off.

D. *Character of participating activity.*

The phrase "collective bargaining with management" is frequently used to describe the kind of collective participating
activity in which organizations oriented toward the Union model
engage. The Association model organization is popularly supposed to accept a more informal type of participation in relations
with "management" and to emphasize achievement of results
through influencing legislative action. Let us set down several
concepts of participating activity in order to see what the reality
is at the moment.

1. Discussion of and consultation between the parties followed by ultimately unilateral decision by the executives
   or the legislative body of the governmental entity involved.
2. Joint study of and negotiation of terms with both parties
   assuming the desirability of a consensus and mutual
   agreement.
3. Negotiation of terms on the assumption of the necessity
   for a joint commitment of the negotiating parties to the
   terms, but with the necessity to seek approval and the

appropriations to implement any agreement from a legislative body.

4. Direct political action before a legislative body in order to acquire statutory confirmation of desired terms.

5. Efforts to obtain a "prevailing rate" arrangement by which legislative authority (and private agreement) is sought to gear wages and benefits to the wages and benefits enjoyed by comparative and relevant groups of employees in private industry.

6. Bargaining with government executives to a mutually acceptable agreement, binding on both parties, both of whom have authoritative discretion to come to such a final and binding agreement, and both of whom have economic power to sustain their veto of any terms to which they do not agree.

A widely-held concept of the two models places the emphasis in the Union model on a demand for the last type of collective participation on the assumption that, in the minds of union leaders, this is the only *real* kind of collective bargaining, as indeed it is considered to be in private industry where the Unions have their longest tradition. The concept of the Association model places the emphasis on the fourth type of collective participation.

These concepts do not correspond with the emphasis which employee organizations actually find it practicable to make in New York State at the present time. Neither is really satisfied with the first type of participation, that is, discussion and consultation before unilateral employer decision. Partly because this is the only kind of collective participation with their "employers" envisioned in public policy proclaimed for State employees and for most local public employees outside of New York City, and partly because of the resistance of public employers to anything but this discussion-and-consultation type participation, many locals both of the Union and the Association type find themselves able to go no further than this. That they go no further arises not from their character or fixed policies, but from the constraints of necessity.

Organizations of both types prefer the second type of negotiations to the first. The second type is distinguished from the first primarily because it involves the assumption that both parties desire to come to a mutually satisfactory consensus.

Practically speaking, the closest approach to "collective bargaining" in the traditional sense that either model of organization can come to in the case of political entities is the third type of collective participation. This, of course, is due to the fact that legislative or Civil Service Commission approval must be obtained for negotiated terms related to those legislatively mandated and in which legislative appropriations must be obtained to implement money terms. Both types of organizations in the public sector can be expected to perfect their strategies and tactics along these lines as long as they are negotiating with the agents of legislatively-governed and tax-supported governmental entities or their subagencies.

The first stage in the "prevailing rate" type of bargaining (type 5) is normally essentially a political process. It involves convincing a legislature to authorize the setting of certain terms of employment for public employees which shall be equitable in relation to terms prevailing for other comparable groups of employees. Once such authorization is given, the succeeding stage consists of convincing whoever is charged with the responsibility for determining what, in fact, the prevailing rate is that certain comparisons are more relevant than others. There is a sense in which this approach to the determination of terms places in the hands of negotiators beyond the organization representing the employees involved the power to determine what the terms for public employees shall be.

This method can be used only by employee organizations representing employees (usually in the "labor" occupations) whose terms are not mandated by Civil Service regulations. In fact, Section 220 of the Labor Law uses this approach. Such employees are usually, but not universally, represented by a union-type organization. The method is thought of, therefore, as characteristic of the union model.

The nearest possibility for the exercise of the kind of collective bargaining envisaged in point 6 is in negotiating with certain Public Authorities (thruway, bridges, transit and publicly-owned utilities), whose governing boards are not only responsible for operating the services but have the authority to meet their needs by revenues from prices charged, from taxes, or from the sale of bonds. The Public Authorities, it should be noted, are the closest approximation to private enterprise which exists in the public sector. Even in these cases, however, such revenues are frequently supplemented by appropriations from the public treasury or are constrained by public policy with respect to the level of prices or taxes which legislatures permit (the New York City Transit Authority is a case in point). The negotiating process must, therefore, be modified to deal with others than the agency in question. Both Unions and Associations have recognized this and have sought political access to those "others."

Neither Unions nor Associations can move, however, to the

sixth type of allegedly *real* collective bargaining with the executives of political entities only if the public, through the action of its legislatures is ready to delegate to a bargaining "team" composed of the executives of government agencies and the negotiators for employee organizations the virtual determination of its budget, the allocation of public revenues to alternative uses, and the setting of the tax rate necessary to balance that budget. The delegation of those powers is not likely in the foreseeable future. The public, the leaders of employee organizations, and prospective recruits for these organizations would be wise to recognize this and modify their expectations accordingly as to what "collective bargaining" in the public sector can be expected to accomplish unless recognition is given to the practical limitations on public employers to commit themselves unconditionally to a bargain.

The Associations have a long experience in the use of the fourth method, that involving direct political action for terms of employment beneficial to the employees they represent. This mode of collective activity is certainly characteristic of the Association model. Yet, some of the most successful of the employee organizations which, by virtue of their affiliation with the AFL-CIO, are considered to be "unions,". . . . The Firefighters and Postal Clerks, are well known for their traditional *primary* utilization of this method.

E. Type of pressure used.

The concept of "collective bargaining" used to describe the mode of collective participation characterizing the Union model employee organization involves at least two other elements in addition to the kind of activity involved. The first of these elements has to do with the kind of pressure employed to achieve the objective of a joint decision. The Union model pressure is frequently described as economic, and the ultimate actualization of that pressure is the threat of or the actual slowdown or the strike. There is little question that the history and tradition of unions supports this description. The present public insistence by many labor leaders that public as well as private sector employees should not be denied the right to strike gives evidence that their position, at least their strategic public position, is that collective bargaining without the right to apply realistically the strike threat pressure is a contradiction in terms.

The position of Association model organizations on the other hand is widely assumed to have been that economic pressure, including the threat of or an actual strike, is not only illegitimate but irrelevant for organizations of public employees. They are assumed to place greater reliance on political pressure brought upon elected political executives and legislators either in support before a legislative body of proposals mutually agreed to by agency executives and employee representatives or in direct pursuit of legislative action, or in appeals directly to the public.

This differentiation, as indicating traditional emphasis in the two models respectively, is accurate, although association types of organization have employed economic pressure and tactics, and locals of union types of organization have renounced the right to employ the kind of economic power actualized in the strike weapon.

Decision making by executives of government agencies and their calculations of the cost to them of agreement or disagreement on terms desired by employees is often influenced by public or political considerations. Any organization representing public employees knows that from experience. They are also fully aware of the fact that there are normally strata of "employers," including ultimately a legislature, to whom any agreements made with negotiating executives must be referred for approval and financial implementation. They are also aware that sometimes the most dependable process is to work directly for legislation favorable to their members, which legislation will be binding on the government agencies whose employees they represent. It is to be expected that any successful employee organization, whether of the Union or Association type, will understand and utilize the strategy and tactics associated with political activity as a major re-enforcement of, and, on occasion, as a substitute for, the strategy and tactics associated with skill in negotiating with government agency executives.

As both the Union and the Association model organizations adapt their strategies of action and power to the realities of public employment relationships, they may be expected to gear that adaptation to the peculiarities of that type of relationship. . . .

NOTES

1. The differences between independent employee organizations and employee organizations affiliated with the AFL-CIO are indicated in the following excerpt from the Statement of John R. Doyle, President of the Assembly of Governmental Employees (AGE), in ADVISORY COMMISSION ON INTERGOVERNMENTAL RELATIONS, LABOR-MANAGEMENT POLICIES FOR STATE AND LOCAL GOVERNMENT 123, 124-25 (1969):

AGE, the Assembly of Governmental Employees, is a nationwide federation of independent public employee asso-

ciations which represents public employees at the federal,
state and local jurisdiction levels. AGE works cooperatively
with independent public employee organizations in Canada
and Puerto Rico.

Founded in 1952, AGE has been growing steadily and
currently has a membership of over 500,000 public employees, mostly at the state level. However, recent applications under board consideration are from organizations
representing federal, county and city groups. . . .

[T]he question usually comes to mind as to what degree
this public employee group differs from others—say those
affiliated with the American Federation of Labor-Congress
of Industrial Organization.

[T]here are distinct differences and these differences stem
from basic philosophies and historical practices. The more
obvious differences are these:

1. *Merit System*—The independent associations are extremely strong advocates of the merit system principle. They
believe that the selection and promotion of public employees
should be based upon demonstrated merit as determined
by competitive examination. In this way, the public through
the merit system furnishes the manpower to government.
In most jurisdictions, the merit system or civil service has
been established and is being maintained through the efforts
of the independent associations.

Employee organizations affiliated with international unions
tend to give "lip service" to civil service. On the one hand,
they call for the preservation of the merit principle while
on the other they espouse the philosophy of the unions'
furnishing the labor force to government through the hiring
hall. Their philosophy is diametrically opposed to the essence of the merit system.

2. *Control of Policy*—The internal policies which guide
the independent public employee organizations are conceived
and executed at the local jurisdictional level. They brook
little or no interference from authorities outside their jurisdiction. On the contrary, the union groups' policies are
strongly influenced and even dictated by the international
councils located outside of the jurisdiction. . . .

6. *Tactics*—In representing public employees the inde-
pendents rely heavily upon possession of the facts and persistent yet dignified persuasion. They believe that impasses
can be resolved through mediation and arbitration and
contend that adult sophisticated public management and

employees should be able to resolve impasses without the
pressure of work stoppage through strikes. Those affiliated
with international unions tend to use pressure tactics in the
presentation of their requests and generally advocate the
threat of strikes at the outset of their presentations or negotiations.

2. *See generally* Krislov, *The Independent Public Employee
Association: Characteristics and Functions,* 15 IND. & LAB. REL.
REV. 510 (1962); K. WARNER & M. HENNESSY, PUBLIC MANAGE-
MENT AT THE BARGAINING TABLE 28-31, 220-24 (1967); *American
Federation of State, County, and Municipal Employees Policy
Statements,* in K. WARNER & M. HENNESSY, PUBLIC MANAGEMENT
AT THE BARGAINING TABLE 401 (1967).

C. The Role of the Federal Government

MARYLAND v. WIRTZ
Supreme Court of the United States
392 U.S. 183, 88 S. Ct. 2017, 20 L. Ed. 2d 1020 (1968)

MR. JUSTICE HARLAN delivered the opinion of the Court.

As originally enacted, the Fair Labor Standards Act of 1938
required every employer to pay each of his employees "engaged
in commerce or in the production of goods for commerce" a
certain minimum hourly wage, and to pay at a higher rate for
work in excess of a certain maximum number of hours per week.
The Act defined the term "employer" so as to exclude "the
United States or any State or political subdivision of a State . . . ."
This case involves the constitutionality of two sets of amendments
to the original enactment.

In 1961, Congress changed the basis of employee coverage:
instead of extending protection to employees individually connected to interstate commerce, the Act now covers all employees
of any "enterprise" engaged in commerce or production for
commerce, provided the enterprise also falls within certain listed
categories.[1] In 1966, Congress added to the list of categories
the following:

---

[1] The minimum wage requirement, 29 U.S.C. § 206 (1964 ed., Supp. II),
now reads as follows: " (a) Every employer shall pay to each of his employees
who in any workweek is engaged in commerce or in the production of goods
for commerce, or is employed in an enterprise engaged in commerce or in
the production of goods for commerce, wages at the following rates. . . ."
The maximum hours requirement, 29 U.S.C. § 207 (1964 ed., Supp. II), now
contains a similar definition of covered employees. The term "enterprise
engaged in commerce or in the production of goods for commerce" is defined
by 29 U.S.C. § 203 (s) (1964 ed., Supp. II) to mean "an enterprise which has
employees engaged in commerce or in the production of goods for commerce,

"(4) is engaged in the operation of a hospital, an institution primarily engaged in the care of the sick, the aged, the mentally ill or defective who reside on the premises of such institution, a school for the mentally or physically handicapped or gifted children, an elementary or secondary school, or an institution of higher education (regardless of whether or not such hospital, institution, or school is public or private or operated for profit or not for profit."[5]

At the same time, Congress modified the definition of "employer" so as to remove the exemption of the States and their political subdivisions with respect to employees of hospitals, institutions, and schools.

The State of Maryland, since joined by 27 other States and one school district, brought this action against the Secretary of Labor to enjoin enforcement of the Act insofar as it now applies to schools and hospitals operated by the States or their subdivisions. The plaintiffs made four contentions. They argued that the expansion of coverage through the "enterprise concept" was beyond the power of Congress under the Commerce Clause. They contended that coverage of state-operated hospitals and schools was also beyond the commerce power. They asserted that the remedial provisions of the Act, if applied to the States, would conflict with the Eleventh Amendment. Finally, they urged that even if their constitutional arguments were rejected, the court should declare that schools and hospitals, as enterprises, do not have the statutorily required relationship to interstate commerce.

A three-judge district court, convened pursuant to 28 U.S.C. § 2282, declined to issue a declaratory judgment or an injunction. Three opinions were written. Judges Winter and Thomsen, constituting the majority, concluded for different reasons that the adoption of the "enterprise concept" of coverage and the extension of coverage to state institutions could not be said, on the face of the Act, to exceed Congress' power under the Commerce Clause. Both declined to consider the Eleventh Amendment and statutory contentions. Judge Northrop dissented, concluding that the amendments exceeded the commerce power because they transgressed the sovereignty of the States.

We noted probable jurisdiction of the plaintiffs' appeal, 389 U.S. 1031. For reasons to follow, we affirm the judgment of the District Court.

---

including employees handling, selling, or otherwise working on goods that have been moved in or produced for commerce by any person, and which— [falls in any one of four listed categories] . . . ."

[5] 80 Stat. 832, 29 U.S.C. § 203 (s) (4) (1964 ed., Supp. II).

I.

We turn first to the adoption in 1961 of the "enterprise concept." Whereas the Act originally extended to every employee "who is engaged in commerce or in the production of goods for commerce," it now protects every employee who "is employed in an enterprise engaged in commerce or in the production of goods for commerce." Such an enterprise is defined as one which, along with other qualifications, "has employees engaged in commerce or in the production of goods for commerce. . . ." Thus the effect of the 1961 change was to extend protection to the fellow employees of any employee who would have been protected by the original Act, but not to enlarge the class of *employers* subject to the Act.

In United States v. Darby, 312 U.S. 100, this Court found the original Act a legitimate exercise of congressional power to regulate commerce among the States. Appellants accept the *Darby* decision, but contend that the extension of protection to fellow employees of those originally covered exceeds the commerce power. We conclude, to the contrary, that the constitutionality of the "enterprise concept" is settled by the reasoning of *Darby* itself and is independently established by principles stated in other cases.

Darby involved employees who were engaged in producing goods for commerce. Their employer contended that since manufacturing is itself an intrastate activity, Congress had no power to regulate the wages and hours of manufacturing employees. The first step in the Court's answer was clear: "[Congress may] by appropriate legislation regulate intrastate activities where they have a substantial effect on interstate commerce."

The next step was to discover whether such a "substantial effect" existed. Congress had found that substandard wages and excessive hours, when imposed on employees of a company shipping goods into other States, gave the exporting company an advantage over companies in the importing States. Having so found, Congress decided as a matter of policy that such an advantage in interstate competition was an "unfair" one, and one that had the additional undesirable effect of driving down labor conditions in the importing States. This Court was of course concerned only with the finding of a substantial effect on interstate competition, and not with the consequent policy decisions. In accepting the congressional finding, the Court followed principles of judicial review only recently rearticulated in Katzenbach v. McClung, 379 U.S. 294, 303-304:

"Of course, the mere fact that Congress has said when particular activity shall be deemed to affect commerce does not preclude further examination by this Court. But where we find that the legislators . . . have a rational basis for finding a chosen regulatory scheme necessary to the protection of commerce, our investigation is at an end."

There was obviously a "rational basis" for the logical inference that the pay and hours of production employees affect a company's competitive position.

The logical inference does not stop with production employees. When a company does an interstate business, its competition with companies elsewhere is affected by all its significant labor costs, not merely by the wages and hours of those employees who have physical contact with the goods in question. Consequently, it is not surprising that this Court has already explicitly recognized that Congress' original choice to extend the Act only to certain employees of interstate enterprises was not constitutionally compelled; rather, Congress decided, at that time, "not to enter areas which it might have occupied [under the commerce power]." Kirschbaum Co. v. Walling, 316 U.S. 517, 522.

The "enterprise concept" is also supported by a wholly different line of analysis. In the original Act, Congress stated its finding that substandard labor conditions tended to lead to labor disputes and strikes, and that when such strife disrupted businesses involved in interstate commerce, the flow of goods in commerce was itself affected.[14] Congress therefore chose to promote labor peace by regulation of subject matter, wages, and hours, out of which disputes frequently arise. This objective is particularly relevant where, as here, the enterprises in question are significant importers of goods from other States.

Although the Court did not examine this second objective in *Darby,* other cases have found a "rational basis" for statutes regulating labor conditions in order to protect interstate commerce from labor strife. The National Labor Relations Act had been passed because

"[t]he denial by employers of the right of employees to organize and the refusal by employers to accept the procedure of collective bargaining lead to strikes and other forms of industrial strife or unrest, which have the intent or the necessary effect of burdening or obstructing commerce. . . ."

In Labor Board v. Jones & Laughlin, 301 U.S. 1, this Court held that the National Labor Relations Act (NLRA) was within the commerce power. The essence of the decision was contained in

---

[14] Section 2, 29 U.S.C. § 202, declares in part that the existence of substandard labor conditions "leads to labor disputes burdening and obstructing commerce and the free flow of goods in commerce."

two propositions: "the stoppage of those [respondent's] operations by industrial strife would have a most serious effect upon
interstate commerce," *id.*, at 41; and "[e]xperience has abundantly
demonstrated that the recognition of the right of employees
to self-organization and to have representatives of their own
choosing for the purpose of collective bargaining is often an
essential condition of industrial peace." *Id.*, at 42.

The Fair Labor Standards Act, including the present "enterprise" definition of coverage, may also be supported by two
propositions. One is identical with the first proposition supporting the NLRA: strife disrupting an enterprise involved in commerce may disrupt commerce. The other is parallel to the
second proposition supporting the NLRA: there is a basis in
logic and experience for the conclusion that substandard labor
conditions among any group of employees, whether or not they
are personally engaged in commerce or production, may lead to
strife disrupting an entire enterprise.

Whether the "enterprise concept" is defended on the "competition" theory or on the "labor dispute" theory, it is true
that labor conditions in businesses having only a few employees
engaged in commerce or production may not affect commerce
very much or very often. Appellants therefore contend that
defining covered enterprises in terms of their employees is sometimes to permit "the tail to wag the dog." However, while Congress has in some instances left to the courts or to administrative
agencies the task of determining whether commerce is affected
in a particular instance, *Darby* itself recognized the power of
Congress instead to declare that an entire class of activities affects
commerce. The only question for the courts is then whether the
class is "within the reach of the federal power." The contention
that in Commerce Clause cases the courts have power to excise,
as trivial, individual instances falling within a rationally defined
class of activities has been put entirely to rest. Wickard v. Filburn, 317 U.S. 111, 127-128; Polish Alliance v. Labor Board,
322 U.S. 643, 648; Katzenbach v. McClung, *supra,* at 301. The
class of employers subject to the Act was not enlarged by the
addition of the enterprise concept. The definition of that class
is as rational now as it was when *Darby* was decided.

II.

Appellants' second contention is that the commerce power
does not afford a constitutional basis for extension of the Act
to schools and hospitals operated by the States or their subdivisions. Since the argument is made in terms of interference with
"sovereign state functions," it is important to note exactly what

the Act does. Although it applies to "employees," the Act specifically exempts any "employee employed in a bona fide executive, administrative, or professional capacity (including any employee employed in the capacity of academic administrative personnel or teacher in elementary or secondary schools). . . ."[20] We assume, as did the District Court, that medical personnel are likewise excluded from coverage under the general language. The Act establishes only a minimum wage and a maximum limit of hours unless overtime wages are paid, and does not otherwise affect the way in which school and hospital duties are performed. Thus appellants' characterization of the question in this case as whether Congress may, under the guise of the commerce power, tell the States how to perform medical and educational functions is not factually accurate. Congress has "interfered with" these state functions only to the extent of providing that when a State employs people in performing such functions it is subject to the same restrictions as a wide range of other employers whose activities affect commerce, including privately operated schools and hospitals.

It is clear that labor conditions in schools and hospitals can affect commerce. The facts stipulated in this case indicate that such institutions are major users of goods imported from other States. For example:

> "In the current fiscal year an estimated $38.3 billion will be spent by State and local public educational institutions in the United States. In the fiscal year 1965, these same authorities spent $3.9 billion operating public hospitals. . . .
>
> "For Maryland, which was stipulated to be typical of the plaintiff States, 87% of the $8 million spent for supplies and equipment by its public school system during the fiscal year 1965 represented direct interstate purchases. Over 55% of the $576,000 spent for drugs, x-ray supplies and equipment and hospital beds by the University of Maryland Hospital and seven other state hospitals were out-of-state purchases."[23]

Similar figures were supplied for other States. Strikes and work stoppages involving employees of schools and hospitals, events which unfortunately are not infrequent, obviously interrupt and burden this flow of goods across state lines. It is therefore clear that a "rational basis" exists for congressional action prescribing minimum labor standards for schools and hospitals, as for other importing enterprises.

---

[20] U.S.C. § 213 (1) (1964 ed. Supp. II).
[23] 269 F. Supp., at 833 (opinion of Judge Winter).

Indeed, appellants do not contend that labor conditions in all schools and hospitals are without the reach of the commerce power, but only that the Act may not be constitutionally applied to state-operated institutions because that power must yield to state sovereignty in the performance of governmental functions. This argument simply is not tenable. There is no general

"doctrine implied in the Federal Constitution that 'the two governments, national and state, are each to exercise its powers so as not to interfere with the free and full exercise of the powers of the other.'" Case v. Bowles, 327 U.S. 92, 101.

In the first place, it is clear that the Federal Government, when acting within a delegated power, may override counter-vailing state interests whether these be described as "governmental" or "proprietary" in character. As long ago as Sanitary District v. United States, 266 U.S. 405, the Court put to rest the contention that state concerns might constitutionally "outweigh" the importance of an otherwise valid federal statute regulating commerce. Congress had imposed statutory limits on the diversion of water from Lake Michigan. A unanimous Court, speaking through Mr. Justice Holmes, declared that the sanitary district's alleged need for more water than federal law allowed was "irrelevant" because federal power over commerce is "superior to that of the States to provide for the welfare or necessities of their inhabitants." Id., at 426. See Oklahoma v. Atkinson Co., 313 U.S. 508.

There remains, of course, the question whether any particular statute is an "otherwise valid regulation of commerce." This Court has always recognized that the power to regulate commerce, though broad indeed, has limits. Mr. Chief Justice Marshall paused to recognize those limits in the course of the opinion that first staked out the vast expanse of federal authority over the economic life of the new Nation. Gibbons v. Ogden, 9 Wheat. 1, 194-195. Mr. Chief Justice Hughes, speaking only one Term after he delivered the opinion for the Court in Jones & Laughlin, supra, put the matter thus:

"The subject of federal power is still 'commerce,' and not all commerce but commerce with foreign nations and among the several States. The expansion of enterprise has vastly increased the interests of interstate commerce but the constitutional differentiation still obtains." Santa Cruz Co. v. Labor Board, 303 U.S. 453, 466.

The Court has ample power to prevent what the appellants purport to fear, "the utter destruction of the State as a sovereign political entity."[27]

But while the commerce power has limits, valid general regulations of commerce do not cease to be regulations of commerce because a State is involved. If a State is engaging in economic activities that are validly regulated by the Federal Government when engaged in by private persons, the State too may be forced to conform its activities to federal regulation. This was settled by the unanimous decision in United States v. California, 297 U.S. 175. The question was whether a railroad, operated by the State, and entirely within the State, as a nonprofit venture for the purpose of facilitating transportation at a port, was nevertheless subject, like other railroads, to the Safety Appliance Act. The Court first held that although the railroad operated only between points in California, it was within the reach of federal regulation of interstate rail transportation. 297 U.S., at 181-183. The Court then proceeded to consider the claim that the State "is not subject to the federal Safety Appliance Act," and reasoned as follows:

"[W]e think it unimportant to say whether the state conducts its railroad in its 'sovereign' or in its 'private' capacity. That in operating its railroad it is acting within a power reserved to the states cannot be doubted. The only question we need consider is whether the exercise of that power, in whatever capacity, must be in subordination to the power to regulate interstate commerce, which has been granted specifically to the national government. The sovereign power of the states is necessarily diminished to the extent of the

---

[27] The dissent suggests that by use of an "enterprise concept" such as that we have upheld here, Congress could under today's decision declare a whole State an "enterprise" affecting commerce and take over its budgeting activities. This reflects, we think, a misreading of the Act, of Wickard v. Filburn, *supra,* and of our decision. The Act's definition of "enterprise" reads in part as follows:

" 'Enterprise' means the related activities performed (either through unified operation or common control) by any person or persons for a common business purpose . . . but shall not include the related activities performed for such enterprise by an independent contractor . . . ." 29 U.S.C. § 203 (r). We uphold the enterprise concept on the explicit premise that an "enterprise" is a set of operations whose activities in commerce would all be expected to be affected by the wages and hours of any group of employees, which is what Congress obviously intended. So defined, the term is quite cognizant of limitations on the commerce power. Neither here nor in *Wickard* has the Court declared that Congress may use a relatively trivial impact on commerce as an excuse for broad general regulation of state or private activities. The Court has said only that where a general regulatory statute bears a substantial relation to commerce, the *de minimis* character of individual instances arising under that statute is of no consequence.

grants of power to the federal government in the Constitution.
. . . .

"[W]e look to the activities in which the states have traditionally engaged as marking the boundary of the restriction
upon the federal taxing power. But there is no such limitation upon the plenary power to regulate commerce. The
state can no more deny the power if its exercise has been
authorized by Congress than can an individual." 297 U.S.,
at 183-185 (citations omitted).

See also Board of Trustees v. United States, 289 U.S. 48, where
the Court rejected a claim of "state sovereignty" and held that
a state university that imported scientific apparatus from abroad
could be made to pay import duties imposed pursuant to the
power over foreign commerce.

The principle of United States v. California is controlling
here. Appellants' argument that the statute involved there was
somewhat more directly and obviously a regulation of "commerce," and that the state activity involved there was less central
to state sovereignty, misses the mark. This Court has examined
and will continue to examine federal statutes to determine
whether there is a rational basis for regarding them as regulations of commerce among the States. But it will not carve up
the commerce power to protect enterprises indistinguishable in
their effect on commerce from private businesses, simply because those enterprises happen to be run by the States for the
benefit of their citizens.[28]

III.

Appellants raise two further issues, both of which the District
Court found it inappropriate to explore fully in a declaratory
judgment proceeding. We agree. In each case we conclude that
no showing has been made that warrants declaratory or injunctive relief. In neither instance, however, do we mean to preclude
future consideration on the facts of individual cases.

The first question is whether the Act violates the States' sovereign immunity from suit guaranteed by the Eleventh Amendment.[29] The Act provides as follows:

---

[28] Nor is it relevant that Congress originally chose to exempt all state
enterprises and later partially removed that exemption. Congress was as free
to include state activities within the general regulation at a later date as it
would have been to omit the exemption in the first place.

[29] "The Judicial power of the United States shall not be construed to
extend to any suit in law or equity, commenced or prosecuted against one
of the United States by Citizens of another State, or by Citizens or Subjects
of any Foreign State."

"Any employer who violates the provisions of section 206 [wages] or section 207 [hours] of this title shall be liable to the employee or employees affected in the amount of their unpaid minimum wages, or their unpaid overtime compensation as the case may be, and in an additional equal amount as liquidated damages. Action to recover such liability may be maintained in any court of competent jurisdiction . . . ." 29 U.S.C. § 216(b).

The Act also provides for suits by the Secretary of Labor to recover unpaid minimum wages or overtime compensation, 29 U.S.C. § 216(c) and for injunctive relief against violations, 29 U.S.C. § 217.

Percolating through each of these provisions for relief are interests of the United States and problems of immunity, agency, and consent to suit. Cf. Parden v. Terminal R. Co., 377 U.S. 184. The constitutionality of applying the substantive requirements of the Act to the States is not, in our view, affected by the possibility that one or more of the remedies the Act provides might not be available when a State is the employer-defendant. Particularly in light of the Act's "separability" provision, 29 U.S.C. § 219, we see no reason to strike down otherwise valid portions of the Act simply because other portions might not be constitutional as applied to hypothetical future cases. At the same time, we decline to be drawn into an abstract discussion of the numerous complex issues that might arise in connection with the Act's various remedial provisions. They are almost impossible and most unnecessary to resolve in advance of particular facts, stated claims, and identified plaintiffs and defendants. Questions of state immunity are therefore reserved for appropriate future cases.

Appellants' remaining contention presents similar problems. In order to be covered by the Act, an employer hospital or school must in fact have

"employees engaged in commerce or in the production of goods for commerce, including employees handling, selling, or otherwise working on goods that have been moved in or produced for commerce by any person . . . ." 29 U.S.C. § 203(s) (1964 ed., Supp. II).

Appellants ask us to declare that hospitals and schools simply have no such employees. The word "goods" is elsewhere defined to exclude "goods after their delivery into the actual physical possession of the ultimate consumer thereof other than a producer, manufacturer, or processor thereof." 29 U.S.C. § 203(i). Appellants contend that hospitals and schools are the ultimate consumers of the out-of-state products they buy, and hence none of their employees handles "goods" in the statutory sense.

We think the District Court was correct in declining to decide, in the abstract and in general, whether schools and hospitals have employees engaged in commerce or production. Such institutions, as a whole, obviously purchase a vast range of out-of-state commodities. These are put to a wide variety of uses, presumably ranging from physical incorporation of building materials into hospital and school structures, to over-the-counter sale for cash to patients, visitors, students, and teachers. Whether particular institutions have employees handling goods in commerce, cf. Walling v. Jacksonville Paper Co., 317 U.S. 564, may be considered as occasion requires.

The judgment of the District Court is

Affirmed.

Mr. Justice Douglas, with whom Mr. Justice Stewart concurs, dissenting.

The Court's opinion skillfully brings employees of state-owned enterprises within the reach of the Commerce Clause; and as an exercise in semantics it is unexceptionable if congressional federalism is the standard. But what is done here is nonetheless such a serious invasion of state sovereignty protected by the Tenth Amendment that it is in my view not consistent with our constitutional federalism.

The case has some of the echoes of New York v. United States, 326 U.S. 572, where a divided Court held that the Federal Government could tax the sale of mineral waters owned and marketed by New York. My dissent was in essence that the decision made the States pay the Federal Government "for the privilege of exercising the powers of sovereignty guaranteed them by the Constitution." 326 U.S., at 596.

The present federal law takes a much more serious bite. The 1966 amendments to the Fair Labor Standards Act require the States to pay school and hospital employees a minimum wage escalating to $1.60 per hour in 1971. As a general rule, the amendments make the States pay their employees who work over 40 hours a week overtime compensation of $1\frac{1}{2}$ times their regular wage. There are civil sanctions against the State and its political subdivisions, and state officials may, apparently, be subjected to criminal penalties. The impact is pervasive, striking at all levels of state government. As Judge Northrop said in his dissent below, 269 F. Supp. 826, 853:

"By this Act Congress is forcing, under threat of civil liability and criminal penalties, the state legislature or the responsible political subdivision of the state

"1. to increase taxes (an impossibility in some of the political subdivisions without a state constitutional amendment) ; or

"2. to curtail the extent and calibre of services in the public hospitals and educational and related institutions of the state; or

"3. to reduce indispensable services in other governmental activities to meet the budgets of those activities favored by the United States Congress; or

"4. to refrain from entering new fields of governmental activity necessitated by changing social conditions."

There can be no doubt but that the 1966 amendments to the Fair Labor Standards Act disrupt the fiscal policy of the States and threaten their autonomy in the regulation of health and education. Yet, the Court considers it irrelevant that these federal regulations are to be enforced against sovereign States and limits its consideration to "whether there is a rational basis for regarding them as regulations of commerce among the States."

The States are not totally immune from federal regulation under the commerce power of Congress. Parden v. Terminal R. Co., 377 U.S. 184, and United States v. California, 297 U.S. 175, subjected state-owned railroads to the Federal Employers' Liability Act, 45 U.S.C. § 51 et seq., and the Safety Appliance Act, 45 U.S.C. § 1 et seq.; Board of Trustees v. United States, 289 U.S. 48, required a state university to pay federal customs duties on educational equipment it imported. In Oklahoma v. Atkinson Co., 313 U.S. 508, the Federal Government was permitted to condemn 100,000 acres of state land for a reservoir to control commerce-paralyzing floods. In Sanitary District v. United States, 266 U.S. 405, a State was prohibited from diverting water from the Great Lakes necessary to ensure navigability, a phase of commerce.

In none of these cases, however, did the federal regulation overwhelm state fiscal policy. It is one thing to force a State to purchase safety equipment for its railroad and another to force it either to spend several million more dollars on hospitals and schools or substantially reduce services in these areas. The commerce power cases the Court relies on are simply not apropos.

In the area of taxation, on the other hand, the Court has recognized that the constitutional scheme of federalism imposes limits on the power of the National Government to tax the States. E.g., New York v. United States, 326 U.S. 572. The Court will not permit the Federal Government to utilize the taxing power to snuff out state sovereignty, Metcalf & Eddy v. Mitchell, 269 U.S. 514, recognizing that the power to tax is the power to destroy. M'Culloch v. Maryland, 4 Wheat. 316, 431. The exercise of the commerce power may also destroy state sovereignty. All activities affecting commerce, even in the minutest degree, Wickard v. Filburn, 317 U.S. 111, may be regulated and controlled by Congress. Commercial activity of every stripe may in some way interfere "with the [interstate] flow of merchandise" or interstate travel. Katzenbach v. McClung, 379 U.S. 294, 299-300. The immense scope of this constitutional power is demonstrated by the Court's approval in this case of regulation on the basis of the "enterprise concept"—which is entirely proper when the regulated "businesses" are not essential functions being carried on by the States.

Yet state government itself is an "enterprise" with a very substantial effect on interstate commerce, for the States spend billions of dollars each year on programs that purchase goods from interstate commerce, hire employees whose labor strife could disrupt interstate commerce, and act on such commerce in countless subtle ways. If constitutional principles of federalism raise no limits to the commerce power where regulation of state activities are concerned, could Congress compel the States to build superhighways crisscrossing their territory in order to accommodate interstate vehicles, to provide inns and eating places for interstate travelers, to quadruple their police forces in order to prevent commerce-crippling riots, etc? Could the Congress virtually draw up each State's budget to avoid "disruptive effect[s] . . . on commercial intercourse."? Atlanta Motel v. United States, 379 U.S. 241, 257.

If all this can be done, then the National Government could devour the essentials of state sovereignty, though that sovereignty is attested by the Tenth Amendment. The principles which should guide us in this case are set forth in the several opinions in New York v. United States, supra. As Mr. Chief Justice Stone said there, the National Government may not "interfere unduly with the State's performance of its sovereign functions of government." 326 U.S., at 587. It may not "impair the State's functions of government," id., at 594 (dissenting opinion of MR. JUSTICE DOUGLAS, joined by MR. JUSTICE BLACK). As Mr. Justice Frankfurter observed, "[t]here are, of course, State activities . . . that partake of uniqueness from the point of view of intergovernmental relations." Id., at 582.

Whether, in a given case, a particular commerce power regulation by Congress of state activity is permissible depends on the facts. The Court must draw the "constitutional line between the State as government and the State as trader . . . ." New York v. United States, *supra,* at 579 (opinion of MR. JUSTICE FRANK-FURTER). In this case the State as a sovereign power is being seriously tampered with, potentially crippled.

I would reverse the judgment below.

NOTES

1. In Municipal Government, City of Newark and State, County, and Municipal Workers of America, Local 277, CIO, Case Nos. 47 and 726 (December 23, 1942), reprinted in C. RHYNE, LABOR UNIONS AND MUNICIPAL EMPLOYE LAW 226 (1946), the National War Labor Board unanimously held that it did not have jurisdiction over labor disputes between state governments, including political subdivisions thereof, and their public employees. In so ruling, the National War Labor Board, in an opinion written by Wayne Morse, stated

> It has never been suggested that the Federal Government has the power to regulate with respect to the wages, working hours, or conditions of employment of those who are engaged in performing services for the states or their political subdivisions. Any action of the National War Labor Board in attempting to regulate such matter by directive order would be beyond its powers and jurisdiction. The employees involved in the instant cases are performing services for political subdivisions of state governments. Any directive order of the National War Labor Board would purport it to regulate the wages, the working hours, or the conditions of employment of state or municipal employees would constitute a clear invasion of the sovereign rights of the political subdivisions of local state government.

Among the labor members who concurred in the foregoing opinion was George Meany, the current president of the AFL-CIO. George W. Taylor, the principal author of the New York Public Sector Collective Bargaining Law, was a public member who likewise concurred in the opinion.

The wage-price freeze imposed by President Nixon on August 15, 1971, was applicable to both the private and public sectors. In State of Ohio *ex rel.* Fry v. Ferguson, 34 Ohio St. 2d 252, 298 N.E.2d 129 (1973), the Ohio Supreme Court held that the Pay Board established under the Economic Stabilization Act of 1970 "lacks jurisdiction to prevent enforcement of otherwise valid state statutes establishing the compensation for classified state employees in the absence of clear authorization from Congress acting under specific power granted by the Constitution." [Subsequently the United States Temporary Emergency Court of Appeals upheld the constitutionality of the Economic Stabilization Act in United States v. Ohio, 21 WH Cases 322 (1973).]

2. In addition to extending coverage under the FLSA to certain employees of states and their political subdivisions, Congress has enacted other legislation which affects the terms and conditions of public sector employment. Thus, the 1972 amendments to the Civil Rights Act extended coverage under Title VII to employees of any state or any political subdivision of any state. 42 U.S.C. § 2000e (a), (b), and (f) (1973). *See* Chapter IX, *infra.* The Urban Mass Transportation Act provides for grants to states and local public agencies to be used for the acquisition of transit facilities of private mass transportation companies. In order to be eligible to receive such a grant, the following requirement, *inter alia,* must be met:

> It shall be a condition of any assistance under this chapter that fair and equitable arrangements are made, as determined by the Secretary of Labor, to protect the interests of employees affected by such assistance. Such protective arrangements shall include, without being limited to, such provisions as may be necessary for (1) the preservation of rights, privileges, and benefits (including continuation of pension rights and benefits) under existing collective bargaining agreements or otherwise; (2) the continuation of collective bargaining rights; (3) the protection of individual employees against a worsening of their positions with respect to their employment; (4) assurances of employment to employees of acquired mass transportation systems and priority of reemployment of employees terminated or laid off; and (5) paid training or retraining programs.
> . . .

Urban Mass Transportation Act § 13 (c) , 49 U.S.C. § 1609 (c) (1972) . *See generally* Barnum, *From Private to Public: Labor Relations in Urban Transit,* 25 IND. & LAB. REL. REV. 95 (1971) .

3. In Employees of Dep't of Public Health & Welfare v. Missouri, — U.S. —, 93 S. Ct. 1614 (1973) , employees of a state operated hospital and training school brought an action against the State of Missouri for overtime compensation under the Fair Labor Standards Act. In holding that Congress did not intend to deprive Missouri of her constitutional immunity by virtue of the Eleventh Amendment, the Court stated in relevant part:

> Where employees in state institutions, not conducted for profit, have such a relation to interstate commerce that

national policy, of which Congress is the keeper, indicates that their status should be raised, Congress can act. And when Congress does act, it may place new or even enormous fiscal burdens on the States. Congress acting responsibly would not be presumed to take such action silently. . . . We deal here with problems that may well implicate elevator operators, janitors, charwomen, security guards, secretaries and the like in every office building in a State's governmental hierarchy. . . .

. . . It is not easy to infer that Congress in legislating pursuant to the Commerce Clause, which has grown to vast proportions in its applications, desired silently to deprive the States of an immunity they have long enjoyed under another part of the Constitution. Thus, we cannot conclude that Congress conditioned the operation of these facilities on the forfeiture of immunity from suit in a federal forum.

Although the Court held that state employees could not institute suit in federal court, it observed that the extension of coverage to state employees under the Fair Labor Standards Act was not meaningless since the Act "gives the Secretary of Labor authority to bring suit for unpaid minimum wages or unpaid overtime compensation under FLSA." The Court further noted that the Act allows an employee to bring suit in "any court of competent jurisdiction" and "[a]rguably that permits suit in the Missouri courts but that is a question we need not reach."

STATEMENT OF JERRY WURF, INTERNATIONAL PRESIDENT, AMERICAN FEDERATION OF STATE, COUNTY, AND MUNICIPAL EMPLOYEES, AFL-CIO
Hearings on H.R. 12532, H.R. 7684, & H.R. 9324
Before the Special Subcomm. on Labor of the House Comm. on Education and Labor, 92d Cong., 2d Sess., 25, 28, 31-32 (1972)

. . . We appear before you this morning in behalf of the over 525,000 public employees who are members of our Union to urge the enactment of Federal legislation dealing with labor relations in state and local government. We are convinced that only through national legislation can public employees be guaranteed full rights to organize and bargain collectively and thereby end unnecessary labor strife in the public sector.

Our views also reflect the concerns and interests of the Coalition of Public Employee Organizations, representing more than two million public employees throughout the nation. This Coalition, formed last March, includes our Union, the National Education Association and the International Association of Fire Fighters, AFL-CIO. The Coalition was established to bring the collective power of public employees to bear on matters of mutual concern.

Over the past several months, our organizations have been working toward a common position on Federal legislation to establish a uniform national labor relations policy in the public sector. We have reached agreement on the substantive provisions of such a bill and the specific legislative recommendations made in behalf of the American Federation of State, County, and Municipal Employees this morning are shared by the other organizations associated with this Coalition. . . .

In the absence of a national uniform labor-management relations policy, labor law in the public sector has developed on a piecemeal, state-by-state, city-by-city basis. State laws are a shameful hodgepodge designed largely to frustrate unionization and collective bargaining.

Inconsistency and confusion best describe the legal setting of labor relations for state and local government employees. Each of the 50 states and the 80,000 units of local government does its own thing. There is no set pattern. The labor programs are regulated by state laws, city ordinances, court decisions, attorneys general opinions, county charters, civil service rules, executive orders, school board policies, and other regulations. . . .

There is clear need for change in public sector labor relations. The choice, in our view, is between continued chaos or Federal legislation.

New state laws are proliferating. Each is different. Most merely add to the confusion and chaos that already exists. Hawaii and Pennsylvania are outstanding exceptions. Although both have provisions with which we disagree, or lack provisions we believe necessary.

The frustrations deriving from the astonishing jungle of state laws, have led our Union to the call for a single, comprehensive Federal law addressing itself to labor relations in the public sector.

There have been enough confrontations. There have been enough studies and experiments. It is time for responsible change.

The problem is national in scope and it requires a national solution.

We need uniformity of law in the public sector, so that a body of law and tradition and practice can be developed. This will only occur under Federal legislation, much like that which governs labor relations in business and industry. We are convinced that the majority of the states are either unwilling or unable to move toward the establishment of rational and reasonable mechanisms.

The needs of public employees do not differ across state lines. They are one and the same throughout the nation. There should be no more difference between the job rights of a public employee in Wisconsin and Virginia than there is between an aerospace worker in California and New York. The labor relations situation of public employees today is different in every city, county, and state—not just between states, but between cities and counties within the same state. There is more reason to justify fragmentation of labor relations between states and their cities and counties than there is to fragment any other system of dealing with problems on a national level.

We believe it is outrageous to conduct labor relations without a set of uniform rules. We are advocating uniformity of law of this matter for the same reason we advocate government by law rather than by force.

You can say what you want about labor relations in business and industry, but a free society could not get along without the mechanisms that exist there. The mechanisms are firmly established and clearly understood. They have a history of legal precedents applicable to almost every work place in America. Contrast that with the public sector where you can go from one city to the next and find a different mechanism and a different set of precedents and procedures.

Finally, we know what state legislatures have to offer us in the way of labor legislation. We know what the needs are. The two just don't fit and probably never will. We are not turning our backs on the new laws in Hawaii and Pennsylvania. They are good laws, although we have serious points of difference with them. If we continue to rely on state legislation, we will continue to face a crazy quilt-work pattern of law. A national approach is the only answer to meeting them uniformly and fairly. . . .

STATEMENT OF JAMES F. MARSHALL, PRESIDENT, ASSEMBLY OF GOVERNMENTAL EMPLOYEES

Hearings on H.R. 12532, H.R. 7684 & H.R. 9324 Before the Special Subcomm. on Labor of the House Comm. on Education and Labor, 92d Cong., 2d Sess., 259-60, 261, 263, 264 (1972)

. . . Although we oppose the legislation pending before this Subcommittee, we welcome the opportunity to discuss the issues facing labor relations of non-federal public employees. We were encouraged to note that your Subcommittee Chairman, in announcing these hearings on January 20th, correctly observed that one of the recognized alternatives of your Subcommittee action would be no action. In other words, leave the requirements affecting the working conditions of non-federal employees to state and local governments as is presently the case. We would sincerely hope that at the conclusion of the Subcommittee's deliberations such a recommendation will be made. . . .

AGE differs from other public employee groups on basic philosophy. One of the largest public employee groups in this country is the American Federation of State, County and Municipal Employees, AFL-CIO (AFSCME), which testified before this Subcommittee on March 8th. Both AGE and AFSCME are obviously dedicated to improving public employee labor conditions. The techniques used in such representation are only similar in that they include, where appropriate, action by administrative means, action through boards and commissions, court review, collective negotiation, legislative enactments, and action through initiative or referendum. The major differences stem from basic philosophic and historical practices and underscore our opposition to the legislation presently pending before this committee. . . .

The internal policies which guide the independent public employee organizations are conceived and executed at the local jurisdictional level. They brook little or no interference from authorities outside their jurisdiction. The union group policies are strongly influenced and even dictated by the international councils located outside of the local jurisdiction. Consequently, it is understandable that they would support legislation that would eliminate any local control of policy. Conversely, this point is one of the main reasons AGE does not support the pending legislation.

Certainly we support the achievement of equality for public employees, but we seriously question whether or not this goal can be better regulated on a national level rather than at the State and local level. This is particularly true when the industrial union concept of collective bargaining would be essentially recognized by the passage of this legislation. . . .

The real issue is whether or not federally controlled collective bargaining will deter the strike concept or, if in fact, it can be successfully employed absent this tool. The position has been advocated before this committee that there is no difference between the public employee and the employee in private industry, and the right to strike is the sine qua non of the public employment bargaining process.

AGE is not convinced. . . .

Another byproduct of the national institution of the industrial collective bargaining concept would be the demise of the merit system. Supported by independent public employee associations, the merit system advocates the selection and promotion to positions in government service on the basis of merit as demonstrated by competitive examination; the removal or suspension of an employee only for cause after a fair hearing; the right of every citizen to compete for a public position without regard to race, creed, color, religion or political affiliation; and the exemption from the merit system of those who are elected and those involved in policy making functions. It is the belief of AGE that the legislation pending before this Subcommittee does not encourage or promote the merit system concept but would, in fact, be the most devastating blow to the merit system ever proposed. . . .

There is no room for debate that for those States which have yet to develop successful State policies in public employee labor relations, time is running out. There is room for doubt, however, as whether or not the answer to the problem is to impose legislation which even its original author admits is silent on the strike issue and overrules all State and local laws governing public employee relations. Through the political processes, it has been demonstrated that procedures can be developed to meet the peculiar problems of the jurisdiction, short of the industrial concept of collective bargaining mandated by the Federal Government.

It is therefore suggested that if state and local governments are to truly serve the increasing needs of the citizens they represent, the interests of public employees must be met through appropriate merit system and bargaining techniques on the State and local level. . . .

STATEMENT OF ARVID ANDERSON, CHAIRMAN, NEW YORK CITY OFFICE OF COLLECTIVE BARGAINING

Hearings on H.R. 12532, H.R. 7684, & H.R. 9324 Before the Special Subcomm. on Labor of the House Comm. on Education and Labor, 92d Cong., 2d Sess., 404-07 (1972)

[W]hat is really needed, as I see it, is the enactment of State and local legislation. But where the States are unwilling to act, I favor the enactment of a nonpreemptive Federal law regulating the structure of employment relations at the State and local level under the following conditions:

1. The statute should establish the right to organize and bargain collectively.

2. The rights and duties established by the statute for both employer and employees should be protected from improper practices, including the duty to bargain and the duty of fair representation.

3. The statute should establish a Federal agency to administer the statutes including questions of representation, improper practices, and impasse resolution.

4. The statute should be nonpreemptive in that State and local procedures should be allowed to stand or to come into being unless the Federal agency was able to prove in Federal court that the State and local statute and procedures were not substantially similar to Federal procedures.

5. The means of impasse resolution, whether by the protected right to strike, by arbitration, voluntary or binding, or by factfinding, would be determined by State law.

6. In the absence of State procedures, Federal impasse and factfinding procedures would apply.

7. The statute should provide procedures for the resolution of grievances, including questions over the arbitrability of grievances and disputes over the scope of bargaining.

8. The issue of union security would be handled in the same manner as the private sector. In other words, union security agreements will be allowed except where barred by State law.

I have made these recommendations for the following reasons:

During the 1960's, as I view it, a debate existed as to whether there was to be collective bargaining for public employees. While the process is far from fully accepted or implemented, which is part of why we are here today, the question of whether or not there will be collective bargaining for public employees is really over. The process is here to stay. The question to be answered in the 1970's is what form it will take and whether or not public sector labor relations will be regulated at the State or Federal level.

A growing number of States and localities, as you know, have demonstrated their creative responsibility by developing and administering comprehensive labor relations procedures regulating the conditions of employment of their public employees. The response of some States to enact laws dealing with public sector employee relations has been much more positive than was true in the period following the enactment of the Wagner Act and the Taft-Hartley law. I believe that the enactment or even the serious possibility of the enactment of a comprehensive but non-preemptive Federal law will further stimulate and encourage those States and localities which have not done so to enact public sector bargaining laws.

Moreover, I believe that sound labor relations and effective administration of the public service at the State and local levels will be advanced by the enactment of a comprehensive but non-preemptive Federal law.

Again, although I believe that State and local legislation is to be preferred, I also believe that Federal legislation is far preferable to the no man's land which now exists in many jurisdictions. Then, of course, you have a whole very large area and I don't know whether it has been brought to your attention, bi-state agencies and authorities, port authorities, airport authorities, harbor commissions employing large numbers of public servants who have no formal structure for resolving employment relations. . . .

I stress that Federal law should not be preemptive because the experience of the administration of the Labor Management Relations Act by the National Labor Relations Board throughout its entire history demonstrates conclusively that a Federal administrative agency will, if left to its own discretion, refuse to cede to any competent State authority administration over any phase of its statute. The administrators of the National Labor Relations Board consistently took the position that those sections of the national act which provided the authority to cede affirmative administrative authority to States if such State laws or administration were not inconsistent with Federal law, that the State statute must be identical with Federal law, and, thus, in effect refused to cede any authority to the States. . . .

I don't think that the problem was with the language of the statute. It was in the lack of willingness of the Federal authorities to cede any jurisdiction to State agencies. Thus, States with competent professional administrative agencies in the private sector, such as Wisconsin, New York, Connecticut, and Michigan, although they repeatedly tried to obtain the consent of the Federal Government to assume some responsibility over the administration of private sector labor relations, were unable to complete such agreements.

I believe that State agencies and local agencies are generally competent and, thus, as well or better equipped than a Federal agency because of their thorough knowledge of the local scene to administer a public sector labor relations statute. Therefore, I believe the right of the States to do so should be protected. I suggest this can be done by providing in any Federal statute which may regulate public employees relations that any State or local statute, which is similar in its basic provisions and administration to the provisions and administration of the Federal act shall remain intact and free from preemption. . . .

The Federal statute could provide that in the event the administrators of the Federal statute believe that State or local procedures were not similar to the Federal procedures nor administered in a similar fashion, then it would be the Federal administrators who would have the burden of proof of such fact in an action in Federal court. Absent such Federal judicial restraint, State and local procedures would continue. Such limitation on Federal preemption would permit the freedom of State experimentation which now exists to continue and would encourage additional States to enact bargaining procedures for their State and local employees.

I make this suggestion because a limitation similar to what is proposed here has worked effectively under the New York State Taylor law with respect to its relationship to the New York City collective bargaining law. The New York City law is not identical to the Taylor law; but it is our belief that its purposes and administration are substantially equivalent to the Taylor law. Such procedures have worked for the past 4 years even though both laws have been amended during that period.

Both the New York City law and the Taylor law contain procedures for the determination of questions of representation, the resolution of improper practices and for the resolution of impasses. Under the New York City law, a recent amendment provides for finality in bargaining impasses, which is the equivalent to binding arbitration. Under the Taylor law, factfinding with recommendations is the procedure provided for finality. However, this significant difference in impasse resolution is permissible under New York laws and I believe similar differences in impasse resolutions should be allowed under any Federal statute. . . .

STATEMENT OF JAMES D. HODGSON, SECRETARY OF LABOR

Hearings on H.R. 12532, H.R. 7684, & H.R. 9324 Before the Special
Subcomm. on Labor of the House Comm. on Education and Labor,
92d Cong., 2d Sess., 281-83, 285 (1972)

Mr. Chairman and members of the Sub-Committee on Labor, I appreciate the opportunity to present the views of the Department of Labor on the advisability of enacting Federal legislation at the present time to regulate labor relations in the public sector at the State and local level. The Department of Labor has been giving careful consideration to the question of the proper role for the Federal Government to play in the developing area of labor relations in State and local govern-

ment units. Under the present circumstances, we have concluded that the body of knowledge and experience in State and
local government labor relations is inadequate to justify Federal
legislation in this area. We believe that it is important for State
and local governments to develop their own mechanisms for
peaceful settlement of labor disputes among public employees,
because it is the States and localities that can best assess their
local needs and create frameworks for public sector bargaining
that are responsive to those needs. As the States develop new
and innovative laws regulating labor relations in the public sector, the proper role for the Federal Government will become
clearer. The following four reasons have led us to conclude that
Federal legislation under the current circumstances would be
inappropriate:

1. The relative lack of experience at all levels of government in public sector labor relations,

2. The differences in economic, social and political considerations bearing on collective bargaining in the public sector, as
distinguished from those in private sector,

3. The diversity of approach in dealing with this subject that
we find in current state laws, and

4. The inability of acknowledged experts to agree as to the
wisest course of action in this area, especially with respect to
the extent if any, that the Federal Government should intrude
upon State and local public sector labor relations.

I will elaborate on these factors and then suggest what I consider to be the proper role for the Federal Government to play
in this formative stage of public sector labor relations at the
State and local levels.

Lack of Experience in Public Employee-Management Relations

The first reason that I consider it important not to enact
Federal legislation at the present time is the relative lack of
experience in public sector labor relations. Although the first
State statute dealing with public employee bargaining appeared
in the late 1950's, the bulk of State legislation did not come
until after 1965. As I will point out later, this State legislation
has been extremely diverse in its provisions and coverage.

The important point, however, is the very short period of
time that both the Federal Government and State governments
have had to build experience in public sector labor relations.
This lack of experience makes it impossible to adequately evaluate the efficiency and effect of various statutory provisions upon
the governmental unit, public employees, and the public interest. Without additional experience and an evaluation of that

experience it would be short-sighted and ill-advised to try to draft a comprehensive Federal statute covering labor management relations at the State and local level. Even at the Federal level the first Executive Order establishing bargaining in the Federal Service was not signed until 1962. Since 1962 clarification of federal employee bargaining rights has been in the developing stages. During these 10 years, four study groups and three Executive Orders have focused on Federal labor-management relations and there is a continuing need for further delineation of the rights and responsibilities of Federal employees. The Federal Labor Relations Council, established by Executive Order 11491, is attempting to build a body of case precedent and experience in Federal public sector bargaining, but the area is clearly still in the formative stages. This Federal experience emphasizes the importance of allowing State and local governments to more fully develop their own public sector labor relations policies.

The need for Federal legislation would be more compelling if such legislation were as urgently needed today in the public sector as the Wagner Act was needed in the private sector in 1935. But, there is clearly no such urgency at the present time. Federal labor legislation in the private sector was passed at a time when it was clear that a balancing mechanism was necessary to protect labor from the power and anti-union bias of private employers.

State legislation could not adequately deal with this issue because of the interstate nature of the market in which businesses compete in the sale of their products. Varying State practices would have disrupted competition and limited the effectiveness of laws encouraging collective bargaining. There is no such pressure in the public sector. Public employers do not compete in an interstate product market that would require immediate uniformity in State labor-management relations policies.

The States are taking advantage of this opportunity to adapt various public sector labor relations models to their local needs. The past six years has been a period of great activity in public sector labor relations at the State level. Not only have States developed various initial approaches to public sector labor relations, but they are refining and perfecting these approaches on the basis of their experience. For example, Wisconsin and New York have both amended their comprehensive statutes. Minnesota has replaced two "meet and confer" laws with one collective bargaining statute. Connecticut is involved in a major legislative study of possible revision of its law. Thus, the States are not neglecting the problems of labor and management in the public sector. Rather than being detrimental as in the private sector, experimentation on a State-by-State basis in the public sector takes into account important State differences and contributes substantially to our understanding of the issues in public sector labor relations. This process of development should not be interrupted when there is no urgency for Federal legislation. Under these circumstances, variation rather than uniformity among the States is the more valuable pattern for policy development.

Transfer of Experience from Private Sector to Public Sector

Sufficient information is not available about public sector bargaining to demonstrate what concepts and mechanisms of private sector bargaining can be adapted to the public sector. Labor and management in the private sector have been developing experience in labor relations since 1935. Beginning at that time with the Wagner Act, a sophisticated set of mechanisms has evolved for handling labor negotiations and disputes in the private sector. Case precedent, legislation, and structural evolutions have refined the efficiency of labor-management relations in the private sector.

It would be convenient if this wealth of experience in the private sector could be transferred to the public sector, but given the unique problems encountered in public sector labor relations, it is not at all clear to what extent such a transfer is possible or desirable. Various mechanisms and concepts including those that are applied in the private sector should be experimented with in the public sector at the State level before any determination is made regarding the feasibility or provisions of Federal legislation. Certainly there are some obvious and important differences between private and public sector bargaining. Bargaining in the private sector is based on an interplay between capital and labor. In the public sector "capital" as such and the quantitatively measurable profits derived therefrom are absent. There is certainly management in the public sector, but there is not the entrepreneurial thrust associated with capital and the corresponding competitive pressures with their own unique force of influence and discipline.

An even more important difference is that private sector bargaining does not deal with such broad issues as public budget priorities and public policy decisions that often cannot be best framed by the adversary process of collective bargaining. Other differences include the often overriding political influences in the public sector, the importance of many public services to the public welfare, the controlling and limiting effect of statutory or constitutional law, and the division of managerial power between legislative and executive branches. Adaptation of experience in the private sector to public sector bargaining would require some adaptation of mechanisms to meet the special needs of public employment.

Before any proposals for Federal legislation are considered, the individual states should have an opportunity to develop their own variations and adaptations of private sector techniques in labor relations. For example, the important right to strike question might be better dealt with several years from now after the experience of Hawaii and Pennsylvania in granting a limited right to strike to public employees can be evaluated. After some experience is accumulated on the extent to which State and local governments are able to transfer private sector experience to the public sector, the question of Federal legislation can be examined on the basis of systematic analysis of state experience. Any Federal attempt to transfer the principles and mechanisms of the National Labor Relations Act to the Public Sector would be premature at this time.

Another question for which an adequate response cannot be developed because of the lack of experience in State and local government labor relations is whether a Federal law could be drafted that would be sufficiently flexible to adequately handle peculiarly local labor problems or whether the States should be left to regulate public sector bargaining at the local level. Federal legislation would impose uniform law and rules on diverse State and local governments. Professor Harry Wellington, one of the foremost experts in the field of public sector bargaining, objects to Federal legislation on this ground. Any Federal legislation would require an enforcement tribunal which would involve at least some minimal intrusions into sensitive matters of local government. Complex fiscal structures, local budgetary practices, charter limits on taxes, statutes concerning the type and mode of provision of services, and other uniquely local matters could be involved in the bargaining process without regard to whether this is appropriate in each situation. Federal legislation governing this process could lead to the establishment of uniform rules for the structure of local government. Even Federal legislation which allows local administration of the system would be an intrusion into local government to some extent. The Federally-imposed structure is inherently an intrusion. In labor relations policy the structure of bargaining relationships and the definition of terms are often determinative of substantive issues regardless of Federal or local administration of the system. The need for diversity and local regulation requires that the question of state or Federal regulation of public employee labor relations be determined only after the sufficient State experience in uniquely local needs has been developed.

Wide Variation in State Approaches

The third reason that Federal legislation should not be enacted is the lack of any common pattern in current State legislation dealing with public employee bargaining. No model system has emerged. A haphazard mixture of statutes, local executive orders, resolutions, ordinances, court decisions, and civil service statutes and procedures has developed in the States. By the end of 1970, approximately 40 States had legislation authorizing some form of formalized employee relations for public employees, eight had no legislation, and two prohibited such activity. Mandatory negotiations, in either the "meet and confer" or traditional collective bargaining form, were required in 25 States. The remainder of the States divided between statutes permitting bargaining or conferring and statutes merely permitting the presentation of proposals. Including the statutes enacted by Pennsylvania and Hawaii in 1970, and by Minnesota in 1971, 17 States now have mandatory collective bargaining laws. . . .

Thus, the States are clearly involved in developing a wide variety of models for public sector labor relations. As was previously pointed out, to impose Federal uniformity would prematurely halt this healthy process and would deprive us of the experience that is being derived through an infinite number of variations in approaches. The Federal Government should take advantage of the unique opportunity to study and evaluate the impact of these variations at the state level.

Divergent Expert Opinion

The question of Federal legislation dealing with State and local government labor relations has sparked heated controversy among scholars and experts in the field of public sector labor relations. This controversy focuses both on the issue of whether Federal legislation should be enacted at all, and, if so, what features it should include. Several groups have considered these questions. In April 1970, the Twentieth Century Fund Task Force on Labor Disputes in Public Employment issued its report Pickets at City Hall in which it recommended collective bargaining and execution of written agreements, provision for final settlement of grievances including binding arbitration, and establishment of an impartial administrative agency responsible for public employee-management relations policies. On the other hand, the Advisory Commission on Intergovernmental Relations in its March 1970 report Labor Management Policies for State and Local Governments endorsed enactment of "meet and confer" statutes by States rather than the collective bargaining approach of Twentieth Century Fund. On the right to strike question, the Twentieth Century Task Force opposed a complete ban on the right for all public employees under all circumstances but would ban strikes during the course of impasse procedures and strikes by policemen and fire fighters. ACIR endorsed an absolute prohibition on strikes by public employees. The American Assembly on Collective Bargaining in American Government in 1971 endorsed a limited right to strike by public employees after procedures have been exhausted. The ACIR specifically opposed Federal legislation regulating State and local government labor relations.

Several individual scholars of labor relations disagree on the appropriate framework for State and local government labor relations. Most notably, Theodore Kheel, well-known mediator and arbitrator, and Dr. George W. Taylor, a foremost expert in public sector labor relations, in a continuing dialogue on this subject, have taken opposing views on such key issues as the right to strike and appropriate impasse procedures.

Thus, even the experts do not agree on how to deal with the burgeoning area of public employment labor relations. In light of this divergent expert opinion, and the lack of experience, substantial variations in State practices, and philosophical and practical differences between private and public sector labor relations noted above, we believe that the firm foundation upon which Federal legislation must be based does not exist.

Proper Role for the Federal Government at the Present Time

Because of the need for further State experience and careful analysis of that experience, the Federal Government can serve most usefully as a source of information and technical assistance. By working in close cooperation with State and local governments in the effort to develop some sound principles and mechanisms for handling public sector labor relations, the agencies of the Federal Government can be instrumental in continuing to build the base of information necessary to adequately determine whether Federal legislation should be enacted at some time in the future or, if so, what features that legislation should include. The Department of Labor and the Civil Service Commission have recently become increasingly involved in providing assistance in labor-management relations to state and local governments. . . .

NOTE

See generally Baird, *National Legislation for Public Employees: "End Run" on the Wagner Act,* 61 ILL. B.J. 410 (1973); ADVISORY COMMISSION ON INTERGOVERNMENTAL RELATIONS, LABOR-MANAGEMENT POLICIES FOR STATE AND LOCAL GOVERNMENT 111-13 (1969).

D. The Impact of Public Sector Unions

TAX FOUNDATION, INC., UNIONS AND GOVERNMENT EMPLOYMENT 37-41 (1972)

FINANCIAL CONSEQUENCES OF UNIONIZATION OF PUBLIC EMPLOYEES

The increasing activity of public employee unions raises two interesting, and related, questions. Have the unions made any real gains for their members? and, if so, what have these gains cost the taxpayer?

Neither question can be answered unequivocally, because data directly to the point are very difficult to find. Indirect evidence, however, does yield some interesting hints.

Government Expense

Payroll expenditures represent a substantial proportion of total government outlays, particularly at the local level (Table 13). Total payroll for all three levels of government had climbed to $110 billion by 1970, of which about $48 billion was attributable to Federal payrolls, $18 billion to the states, and $45 billion to local governments. Put another way: expenditures for payroll in 1970 exceeded all of the receipts from the biggest revenue-raiser of all, personal income taxes.

The wage bill at each of the three levels has shot up dramatically in the period shown in the table, approximately doubling between 1960 and 1970. Even when outlays are adjusted for changes in price levels, the increases are spectacular for so brief a period: 88 percent for all levels combined, 79 for Federal, 123 for state, and 87 for local.

Outlays devoted to payroll compared with all other expenditures differ markedly between the local level and the other two, but have been increasing at all levels. Between 1960 and 1970, payroll as a percentage of all other expenditures rose from 42 to 50 percent for all levels combined; from 26 to 30 percent at the

Federal level; from 24 to 36 percent at the state level, and from 89 to 96 percent at the local level.

Two major factors operating at the Federal level probably will continue to exert upward pressures on payroll costs. The "comparability" principle, introduced in 1960 with the goal of keeping Federal pay more or less equivalent with that for similar work in private industry, has resulted in annual increases for virtually all Federal employees. At the same time, these increases set a model for state and local pay scales. Overlaid on the "comparability" approach, there has developed a tendency to what some observers consider excessive upgrading. Recent studies show organizational fragmentation has sharply increased the number of employees at higher grade levels.

The examination of government costs cannot stop with payroll expenditures, however, since fringe benefits occupy quite an important place in negotiations. The cost of many of these elude quantification. For instance, a union might win shorter hours for its members, or teachers might bargain for assistants to do chores ordinarily performed by the teachers themselves. In such cases, the original employees continue to receive the same pay but do less work or different kinds of work; the additional payroll resulting from supplementary workers really must be considered as costs of the settlement, but never could be isolated for computational purposes.

Peripheral information can be found, however, on the costs of one type of employee benefits, retirement plans. These outlays have shot up very rapidly over the last decade. State and local government contributions to employee retirement plans have risen from $1.7 billion in 1960 up to $4.6 billion in 1970, or nearly a threefold increase. Federal agency contributions to civil service retirement plans more than doubled over the same period, from .7 to 1.7 billon. But such figures only scratch the surface of what actually may be happening. The full impact of increases in pension arrangements may not be felt for years, depending on the funding practices of the governmental unit involved. All that can be said with certainty is that government outlays for pension plans have been increasing rapidly, in general more rapidly than outlays for direct compensation for wages—suggesting but of course not proving that an emphasis on fringe benefits may characterize many settlements.

Advantage to Employees

As a corollary of government costs, are public employees making gains? A look at trends in civil service income, shown in Table 14, would be the first step in finding an answer. Certainly average earnings have gone up, from whatever point they are measured. Taken from 1961 to 1970, earnings for government employees as a whole have risen 64 percent, compared with 53 percent for the private sector. Moreover, average earnings, particularly in the Federal jobs, are markedly higher than in private industry: for example, Table 14 shows an industry average of $7,462 compared with a Federal civilian average of $10,597 in 1970.

Table 13

Expenditures for Compensation of Employees, by Level of Government

Fiscal 1960-1970

Level of government	Expenditures for compensation of employees						
	1970	1969	1968	1966	1964	1962	1960
Amount (billions)							
All	$110.5	$99.1	$89.4	$73.0	$61.4	$54.1	$44.8
Federal	47.5	43.4	40.4	32.9	28.1	25.4	20.3
State	17.8	15.6	13.8	10.6	8.4	7.1	6.1
Local	45.2	40.1	35.2	29.5	24.9	21.6	18.4
Amount (billions of 1970 dollars)							
All	110.5	105.0	99.7	87.3	76.8	69.5	58.8
Federal	47.5	46.0	45.1	39.4	35.2	32.6	26.6
State	17.8	16.5	15.4	12.7	10.5	9.1	8.0
Local	45.2	42.5	36.3	35.3	31.2	27.7	24.2
Compensation as percentage of all other expenditures							
All	50	47	46	48	45	44	42
Federal	30	28	28	30	29	29	26
State	26	27	26	26	25	24	24
Local	96	94	95	94	95	91	89

Source: Based on Department of Commerce data.

Table 14

Average Annual Earnings, Industry and Government

1929-1970

Year	All industries	Private industry	All government	Federal		State and local	
				All employees	Civilian only	All employees	Public education
1929	$1405	$1391	$1551	$1684	$1933	$1504	$1445
1939	1264	1250	1337	1215	1843	1476	1403
1949	2844	2841	2862	3024	3348	2700	2671
1959	4594	4615	4499	4667	5682	4345	4522
1961	4884	4889	4859	4942	6274	4787	5097
1963	5243	5252	5205	5234	6792	5180	5448
1965	5705	5706	5701	5844	7605	5592	5846
1967	6230	6231	6222	6100	7985	6324	6605
1969	7087	7071	7188	7131	9442	7232	7529
1970	7564	7462	7965	8175	10597	7818	8141
Percent increase, 1961-1970	55	53	64	65	69	63	60

Source: Office of Business Economics.

Table 15

Municipal Government Salaries Compared to Private Industry for Selected Occupational Groups[a]
(Private industry average salaries = 100) 1970

Occupation	Atlanta	Boston	Buffalo	Chicago	Houston	Kansas City, Mo.	Los Angeles	New Orleans	New York	Newark	Philadelphia
Office clerical group[b]	108	109	122	108	121	97	118	92	101	106	133
Bookkeeping-machine operators, class B	96	—	135	118	104	112	—	79	96	106	141
Clerks, accounting, class A	115	106	101	94	114	87	—	92	—	96	123
Clerks, accounting, class B	128	113	113	101	149	94	—	86	96	98	—
Messengers (office boys or girls)	—	107	115	98	123	—	107	99	114	125	136
Stenographers, general	93	102	126	106	97	93	110	98	94	95	126
Stenographers, senior	95	107	135	121	102	98	115	98	100	106	130
Switchboard operators, class B	119	—	127	112	142	—	134	105	105	107	—
Typists, class A	—	100	122	107	—	98	—	92	107	107	142
Typists, class B	102	108	104	105	96	101	123	89	102	119	122
Data processing group[b]	—	117	119	105	96	94	—	85	96	—	125
Computer operators, class A	—	103	—	110	98	94	124	95	111	123	—
Computer operators, class B	—	—	94	112	106	90	120	97	106	144	—
Computer operators, class C	—	—	96	113	111	97	118	76	90	87	—
Computer programers, class A	85	95	—	106	—	95	123	77	93	—	109
Computer programers, class B	93	95	98	101	87	96	113	74	82	—	119
Computer programers, class C	—	—	—	104	92	88	117	—	—	—	106
Computer systems analysts, class A	86	118	—	99	—	—	—	88	—	122	144
Computer systems analysts, class B	74	107	98	106	84	—	—	88	—	120	131
Keypunch operators, class A	104	103	—	101	—	—	120	91	102	—	—
Keypunch operators, class B	112	114	115	103	111	—	—	83	—	—	—
Tabulating-machine operators, class B	—	—	—	—	—	—	—	—	—	—	—
Maintenance and custodial group[b]	98	101	91	126	105	86	118	81	142	142	113
Carpenters, maintenance	98	91	88	125	91	80	118	76	162	141	106
Electricians, maintenance	91	—	82	148	113	87	121	87	162	141	107
Helpers, maintenance trades	—	—	83	—	—	—	119	—	—	171	113
Janitors, porters, and cleaners	100	99	111	137	124	95	122	88	98	109	131
Mechanics, automotive	101	127	92	—	100	88	107	78	135	152	110
Painters, maintenance	100	87	93	108	95	81	121	75	136	139	114
Plumbers, maintenance	—	101	—	111	—	—	—	—	160	144	113

a. Each of the intracity comparisons, except for Chicago and New York, was based on private industry data for the entire standard metropolitan statistical area scope of the respective area wage surveys. For Chicago and New York, however, it was possible to isolate data limited to each of the two cities, instead of using data for the entire metropolitan area. In those cities where the municipal government and area wage survey payroll reference periods were different, the area wage survey data were adjusted to reflect the same month of reference as the municipal government data. The adjustments were made by prorating the private industry salary increases for occupational groups between the two area wage surveys which occurred earlier and later than the reference period of the particular municipal government survey. No adjustments were made to compensate for differences in standard workweeks.

b. Relative salaries of municipal government groups were obtained by averaging the percent differences of the individual jobs.

c. Dashes indicate no municipal government employees matching the categories were reported or lack of comparable private industry data.

Source: Bureau of Labor Statistics.

But the real question is, have civil servants improved their earnings relative to employees in other industries? Table 15 helps to answer that question, showing the difference between government and private industry salaries in 11 large municipalities, for a number of typical occupational categories. These figures come from a Bureau of Labor Statistics survey conducted during 1970 and 1971. Generally, municipal employees fared better than individuals performing equivalent work in private industry. In only two municipalities, Kansas City and New Orleans, the private sector worker usually earned a higher salary. In two other cities, Los Angeles and Philadelphia, the municipal worker without exception received higher pay than his private counterpart. In the remaining seven cities studied, the great majority of civil service positions offered a pay advantage over the equivalent private job.

Some of the differences can only be called astonishing. For instance, in New York City maintenance plumbers, carpenters, and electricians receive approximately 60 percent more pay than men doing similar work for a private employer. In Newark, a helper in the maintenance trades earns 71 percent more working for government than for private industry. In Philadelphia, clerical workers—clerks, stenographers, typists, etc.—are paid 30 to 40 percent higher wages by the city than by private employers.

A differential between government and industry salaries does not, in itself, demonstrate whether unionization has exerted an impact on pay scales. A study by Paul T. Hartman provides some indication, however, that unions exert a substantial effect. His analysis of the results of a survey of 400 representative school districts throughout the United States showed that both beginning and experienced teacher salaries were higher in unionized districts. More than one-third of the districts were unionized, and in these districts, the average salary at the entry level (after adjustments for the general level of wages in a district, teacher shortages, size and urban characteristics of a district) proved to be a little more than 4 percent higher than in the non-union districts. Moreover, the top salary for teachers with a bachelor's degree averaged 12 percent higher in the unionized districts and the top for master's degrees, 15 percent higher.

NOTE

The effect of unionization on the wages of various categories of public employees has been the subject of considerable discussion. In Kasper, *The Effects of Collective Bargaining on Public School Teachers' Salaries*, 24 IND. & LAB. REL. REV. 57, 71

(1970), the author concluded that "collective representation does not seem to have had much, if any, effect on teachers' salaries. . . ." On the other hand, in Hall & Carroll, *The Effect of Teachers' Organizations on Salaries and Class Size*, 26 IND. & LAB. REL. REV. 834, 841 (1973), the authors observed that their "findings strongly indicate that teachers' organizations do indeed increase salaries." *See also* Ashenfelter, *The Effect of Unionization on Wages in the Public Sector: The Case of Fire Fighters*, 24 IND. & LAB. REL. REV. 191 (1971).

REHMUS, LABOR RELATIONS IN THE PUBLIC SECTOR,
Paper prepared for the 3rd World Congress, International
Industrial Relations Association, London, England (Sept. 3-7, 1973)†

. . . A basic underlying reason for the extension of collective bargaining rights to public sector employees in the United States is the argument that collective bargaining rights which have been mandated by law in the private sector should in equity be given to the government's own employees. This is not to suggest that there are not important differences between private and public employment, however, and that these differences have not created some difficult problems as the private sector bargaining model increasingly pervades the public sector.

Probably the most fundamental of these problems lies in the different purposes of public and private undertakings. The public employer is an artificial creature of the electorate established to minister to the needs and desires of the public and to provide the mechanical and administrative structure to carry on these functions. In a democratic system of government it is elected officials who are normally charged with the control and determination of budget and tax rates, which is the primary way of setting goals and priorities. While extra-parliamentary influences are both inevitable and necessary elements of the democratic process, they should not be allowed to overcome the fact that elected legislative bodies are supposed to be essentially deliberative bodies. If democratic governments are to distinguish between public passions and public interests, legislatures have to be at least partially insulated from group pressures. In a number of major American cities the crisis pressures that result from actual or threatened withdrawal of public employment services has at times usurped the legislature's deliberative process in this most fundamental governmental function of setting goals and priorities.

---

† Reprinted by permission of the Institute of Labor and Industrial Relations.

A second problem lies in the existence of the merit system and civil service in the public sector in the United States. These systems, basically designed to ensure that the selection, retention, and promotion of public employees is based on qualifications and meritorious performance alone, are often considered to be the warp and woof of public employment. To employees, however, merit is sometimes considered a euphemism for favoritism. Public employee organizations therefore attempt to weave into this tight fabric somewhat coarser threads such as strict seniority, across-the-board wage adjustments, and the like. It is a yet-unsettled question whether civil service and the merit system can survive the assault of traditional collective bargaining practices. It is clear that the protection of public employees' right to continued employment, assuming meritorious service, is increasingly being enforced through bargained grievance procedures culminating in binding neutral arbitration rather than through statutory devices such as the tenure system.

A third general problem is that of supervisory unionism. In private industry in the United States the lines of authority and supervision are ordinarily clearly drawn, even in areas of white collar employment. In the public sector, however, the lines between supervisor and employee are far more indistinct. There are several reasons for this. The appellation of supervisor tends to be pushed further down in the organizational hierarchy in public than in private bureaucracies. Where all are dedicated to serving the public, there is a greater community of interest among all employees. In the public service both supervisors and non-supervisors alike are often compensated within an identical and fairly rigid salary payment structure. As a reflection of these facts many existing state collective bargaining laws have not drawn traditional distinctions between supervisors and employees. Hence labor relations boards that implement the state laws have permitted supervisory unionism. In some cases they have required the recognition of supervisory units as components of the same union that organized those who are supervised. Whether conflict of interest is inevitable between the supervisory goals of the organization and the fraternal goals of the union is as yet uncertain. It is clearly a danger, however.

A fourth serious problem in public employee bargaining arises because of the diffusion of decision-making authority which frequently exists in the public sector. Parliamentary systems of government permit a greater unity of legislative and executive authority than is common in United States governmental systems which are more often characterized by division of authority with checks and balances operating between the executive and legislative powers. In federal, state and local governments an agency head may have authority to negotiate only on a portion of the issues which are normally subjects of collective bargaining—other bargainable subjects may be retained within the control of the legislative body or an independent civil service board. Often a chief executive may not have final authority on distribution of funds and can only submit recommendations to the appropriate legislature. May the legislative body repudiate his decisions? Does it have the responsibility to provide the funds to pay for the salary structure which the chief executive has negotiated? Finally, where voter approval of increased millage is necessary to pay for the negotiated increases, local taxpayer revolts and disapproval are increasingly common. What is to be done in these situations? Questions of this kind are extremely difficult within many, though not all, governments in the United States. But the inherent logic of public employee bargaining is leading to considerable centralization of power and to increased executive power vis-a-vis both legislatures and civil service boards.

Related to but distinguishable from the previous problem is one characterized as "end-run" or "double-deck" bargaining. Some public employee unions attempt by lobbying to secure from the state legislature those items which they had failed to obtain or which were traded away at the municipal bargaining table. In many states, civil service organizations have been one of the strongest lobbies in the state legislature. These powers can hardly be taken away from such organizations. But from the municipal government's point of view, freedom to trade cost reductions in one area for contractually bargained new expenditures in another is an essential element of bargaining flexibility and bargaining equality. Where state legislatures mandate wage and fringe bargaining at the municipal level and yet continue to legislate on municipal employee benefits they place local units of government in a Procrustean bed. Public employee bargaining may be desirable and inevitable, but public employees hardly seem entitled to the benefits both of collective bargaining and of traditional protective state laws.

A final problem of collective bargaining in the public sector, one which perhaps receives more attention than it deserves, is that of public employee strikes. Most contemporary discussions of this subject in the United States concern the issue of whether public employees have or should be given the legal right to strike. The fact is, of course, that despite the fact that *de jure* in almost all United States governmental jurisdictions they do not have the right to strike, *de facto* they can and do, often with impunity. Moreover, though it is not commonly recognized, the public employee strike problem exists both in jurisdictions which permit collective bargaining and in those which have not yet granted public employees these rights.

The public employee strike problem is not overwhelming on a national basis. In the last decade such strikes have grown in frequency from approximately one per month to one per day in the whole nation. But strike activity in the public sector is still far below that in the private sector. Public employees involved in work stoppages in recent years represent about 1½ percent of total employment, compared to nearly 4 percent in the private sector. In the most recent year for which data are available, 1970, strike idleness represented 0.08 percent of mandays worked by government employees; for the economy as a whole this figure was 0.28 percent. The average duration of public employee strikes is less that five days for what might be termed "essential" employees; for those in less crucial occupations the average duration is over twice as great. Among teachers, and unlike municipal employees, the absolute number of strikes has declined substantially in the last two years.

Mediation and non-binding neutral recommendations are the most common governmental devices used to help to resolve collective bargaining impasses. While they are effective in the large majority of disputes, they are obviously not a panacea. Where it is deemed that no strike can be permitted, as is almost invariably the decision with police and firemen, compulsory binding arbitration is the most frequently used alternative. Eight states are now experimenting with variants of this device. The newest, though largely untested, idea in compulsory arbitration is "final offer selection," in which the neutral is given no power to compromise issues in dispute, but must select one or the other of the parties' final offers.

Conclusion

The coming of collective bargaining to the public sector is the most significant development in the industrial relations field in the United States in the last thirty years. Its growth has been both rapid and extensive and appears to be continuing. Even now, however, bargaining does not occur in more than half of all governmental jurisdictions in the United States. In many areas where bargaining has begun it is less than ten years old. Hence one must be cautious in making generalizations about the future of public employee labor relations. A few may be put forward tentatively, however.

The coming of unionism to the public sector has provided enough new recruits to the labor movement to reverse the decline in trade union membership which took place during the latter 1950's and early 1960's. Moreover, it is at least possible that as government employees join unions, or convert their traditional professional associations to union-like behavior, that this will change the general blue-collar image of the labor movement in the United States. Private sector trade unionism has never exceeded 30 percent of the non-agricultural workforce and has never had any strong appeal to white collar workers. Organizing successes among white collar and professional employees in the public sector may make unionism acceptable and normal to private sector white collar workers who in the near future, if not already, will represent a majority of employment in private industry. In summary, public employee unionism has halted the decline in trade union size in the United States and may in fact contribute to substantial new growth in the private sector in the next decade or two.

Public employee unionism appears to have contributed to the centralization of governmental decision-making power in the United States, though it is by no means the sole cause of such developments. At the municipal level it is clear that the exigencies of collective bargaining have forced decision-making power toward the chief executive at the expense of municipal legislatures and civil service boards. In the educational field organized teacher pressures along with a number of constitutional decisions are forcing a shift away from the local property tax toward the state-imposed income tax as the primary means of financing public education. Almost inevitably this will mean that many financial decisions will be removed from local school boards and centralized to intermediate or statewide decision-making bodies. At the federal level the movement toward nation-wide bargaining units of federal civil servants may slow or halt efforts toward federal decentralization that were undertaken in the 1960's. In short, public employee unionism appears in many areas to be leading to more centralized decision-making in the United States, similar to the way it has in many other industrialized democracies.

The economic results of public employee bargaining are as yet unclear and controversial. Some authorities believe that public employees have driven their salary and benefit levels far higher than would have been the case in the absence of collective bargaining, and higher than can be justified on the basis of economic equity. Others challenge this assumption. They state that recent increases in public employee compensation are largely reflective of inflationary pressures in the society and the temporary need for public employees to "catch up" with others to whom their wages and salaries should be compared. Quantitative data that would support either argument are still scanty. Public employees in some occupations clearly have fared more favorably in recent years than has the average employee in the private sector. The differences are not large, however, and during 1971 and 1972 increases in both sectors were held down by government wage policies.

As yet, at least, the impact of public employee unionism on governmental decision-making has not been as great as the numerical increase in public union membership and bargaining unit growth might suggest. In the federal sector it is estimated that employees as yet have the right to bargain on perhaps only 25 percent of the subjects that are bargainable in the private sector. Though the scope of bargaining is increasing at the federal level, and is already more extensive at the local and educational levels, it cannot be said with any certainty that the large majority of governmental and public policy decisions are fundamentally different than they would have been in the absence of collective bargaining.

Finally, and most speculatively, it is possible that public employee unionism will bring changes to the whole of the labor relations environment in the United States. As previously noted, white collar and professional organization in the public sector may bring a greater acceptability of white collar unionization in the private sector. If devices such as compulsory arbitration become common and effective for resolving collective bargaining impasses in the public sector, such devices may increasingly be urged for use in the private sector. In general, and with many obvious exceptions, public sector labor relations practices and laws in the United States have thus far been strongly modeled on the private sector structures which had evolved earlier. Over time, experience in the public sector may prove certain procedures and practices, now uncommon or unknown in the private sector, to be useful or effective. It is not at all unlikely that such practices might then become acceptable in the private sector. In sum, the future may well be one of simultaneous changes in both sectors, each tending generally to become more like the other.

NOTES

1. For other prognostications on the future of public sector collective bargaining, see Bakke, *Reflections on the Future of Bargaining in the Public Sector,* MONTHLY LAB. REV., Vol. 93, pp. 21-25 (July 1970); Couturier, *Crisis, Conflict and Change:*

The Future of Collective Bargaining in Public Service, GOOD GOVERNMENT, Vol. 86, pp. 7-11 (Spring 1969); Oberer, *The Future of Collective Bargaining in Public Employment,* 20 LAB. L.J. 777 (1969); Zagoria, *The Future of Collective Bargaining in Government,* in PUBLIC WORKERS AND PUBLIC UNIONS 160 (S. Zagoria ed. 1971); M. MOSKOW, J. LOEWENBERG & E. KOZIARA, COLLECTIVE BARGAINING IN PUBLIC EMPLOYMENT 286-92 (1970).

2. Collective bargaining in the public sector has been the subject of numerous books and symposia. The following are particularly useful in gaining a broad overview of the issues and problems: M. MOSKOW, J. LOEWENBERG, E. KOZIARA, COLLECTIVE BARGAINING IN PUBLIC EMPLOYMENT (1970); SORRY . . . NO GOVERNMENT TODAY: UNIONS VS. CITY HALL (R. Walsh ed. 1969); *Symposium: Labor Relations in the Public Sector,* 67 MICH. L. REV. 891 (1969); *A Symposium: Collective Negotiations in the Public Service,* PUBLIC ADMIN. REV., Vol. 27, pp. 11-147 (March-April 1968); H. WELLINGTON & R. WINTER, THE UNIONS AND THE CITIES (1971); PUBLIC WORKERS AND PUBLIC UNIONS (S. Zagoria ed. 1972); COLLECTIVE BARGAINING IN THE PUBLIC SERVICE (D. Kruger & C. Schmidt eds. 1969); K. WARNER & M. HENNESSY, PUBLIC MANAGEMENT AT THE BARGAINING TABLE (1967). One of the most concise yet most perceptive discussions of the principal policy issues raised by public sector unionism is D. Bok & J. Dunlop, *Collective Bargaining and the Public Sector,* in LABOR AND THE AMERICAN COMMUNITY 312 (1970). Among the many useful bibliographies on public sector labor relations are: PEZDEK, PUBLIC EMPLOYMENT BIBLIOGRAPHY (N.Y. State School of Ind. & Lab. Rel., Bibliography Series No. 11, 1973); PEGNETTER, PUBLIC EMPLOYMENT BIBLIOGRAPHY (N.Y. State School of Ind. & Lab. Rel. 1971); SHIMAOKA, SELECTED REFERENCES ON PUBLIC EMPLOYEE COLLECTIVE BARGAINING WITH EMPHASIS ON STATE AND LOCAL LEVELS (Univ. of Hawaii Ind. Rel. Center, Occasional Publication No. 87, 2d ed. 1972); U.S. CIVIL SERVICE COMM'N, EMPLOYEE-MANAGEMENT RELATIONS IN THE PUBLIC SERVICE (Personnel Bibliography Series No. 44, 1972); U.S. DEP'T OF LABOR, DIV. OF PUBLIC EMPLOYEE LABOR RELATIONS, CURRENT REFERENCES AND INFORMATION SERVICES FOR POLICY DECISION-MAKING IN STATE AND LOCAL GOVERNMENT LABOR RELATIONS: A SELECTED BIBLIOGRAPHY (1971).

Another invaluable source of information on public sector collective bargaining are the reports and recommendations of various advisory commissions. *See generally* ADVISORY COMMISSION ON INTERGOVERNMENTAL RELATIONS, LABOR-MANAGEMENT

POLICIES FOR STATE AND LOCAL GOVERNMENT (1969); 1967 EXECUTIVE COMMITTEE, NATIONAL GOVERNORS' CONFERENCE, REPORT OF TASK FORCE ON STATE AND LOCAL GOVERNMENT LABOR RELATIONS (1967), and 1968, 1969 and 1970 Supplements to REPORT OF TASK FORCE ON STATE AND LOCAL GOVERNMENT LABOR RELATIONS; THE COUNCIL OF STATE GOVERNMENTS, STATE-LOCAL EMPLOYEE LABOR RELATIONS (1970); TWENTIETH CENTURY FUND TASK FORCE ON LABOR DISPUTES IN PUBLIC EMPLOYMENT, PICKETS AT CITY HALL (1970); TAX FOUNDATION, INC., UNIONS AND GOVERNMENT EMPLOYMENT (1972); AFL-CIO MARITIME TRADES DEPARTMENT, COLLECTIVE BARGAINING IN THE PUBLIC SECTOR (1969). Many of the reports issued by state and local advisory commissions are also useful. For one of the most comprehensive as well as the most recent report, see FINAL REPORT OF THE ASSEMBLY ADVISORY COUNCIL ON PUBLIC EMPLOYEE RELATIONS, STATE OF CALIFORNIA (March 15, 1973). *See generally* Smith, *State and Local Advisory Reports on Public Employment Labor Legislation: A Comparative Analysis,* 67 MICH. L. REV. 891 (1969).

Chapter 2

THE RIGHT TO JOIN AND FORM UNIONS

A. Constitutional Protection

LOCAL 201 v. CITY OF MUSKEGON

Supreme Court of Michigan
369 Mich. 384, 120 N.W.2d 197
Cert. denied, 375 U.S. 833 (1963)

CARR, C.J. The question at issue in this litigation concerns the validity of a rule adopted by the chief of police of the city of Muskegon on March 16, 1961. . . .

The rule in question was duly approved by the city manager and was filed as required by the code provisions. It reads as follows:

"Sec. 101: No police officer of the city of Muskegon police department shall hereafter be, or become a member of any organization in any manner identified with any federation or labor union which admits to membership persons who are not members of the Muskegon police department, or which would in any way exact prior consideration and prevent such officer from performing full and complete police duty at any time. Any police officer now a member of such unions shall disassociate himself within 30 days from this date. Failure to comply will constitute reason for immediate dismissal."

The situation to which the rule was intended to apply obviously had been under consideration by municipal officers prior to the adoption of the rule. Under date of March 14, 1961, the Muskegon city commission took the action indicated by the following statement and resolution:

"61-165. *Resolution on banning of union affiliation by police officers adopted.*

"Certain of the police officers of the city of Muskegon police department are dues paying members of Local No. 201, Muskegon County and Municipal Employees Union affiliated with the American Federation of State, County and Municipal Employees, AFL-CIO.

89

"This commission, as well as past commissions, have seriously questioned whether a police officer can be a member of such a union and still enforce, impartially and without prejudice the laws of our city, county and State of Michigan.

"Every police officer who joins the Muskegon police department must take an oath of office to support the Constitution and bear allegiance to his city and State and its Constitution and laws and to the best of ability, skill and judgment, diligently and faithfully, without partiality or prejudice, execute his office. Police officers are invested with broad powers, few of which are given to any other government employee. They have the legal right to carry a weapon, their powers of restraint, arrest, and control of moral and physical behaviour of others are grave and serious. A police officer is required by law and invariably becomes a neutralizer in controversies involving the right of public assemblage, neighborhood disputes, domestic difficulties and strikes, between labor and management. Again, his actions in these instances must be governed by his oath of office. He must recognize certain rights of people among which is the right of collective bargaining on the part of labor. Yet, at the same time, he must protect the rights and the property of management. In this instance, again, his neutrality must be the watchword of his every activity in the effort to protect the life and property of all those involved and to preserve peace and order during periods of such difficulty.

"This commission subscribes to this statement of responsibility and, as such, cannot further condone police officers of the city of Muskegon to continue to be members of a union.

"In the belief that we are acting in the best interest of all of the citizens of the city of Muskegon, the following resolution is presented.

"Commissioner Carlson offered the following resolution and moved its adoption:

"No police officer of the city of Muskegon police department shall hereafter be, or become, a member of any organization in any manner identified with any federation or labor union which admits to membership persons who are not members of the Muskegon police department, or which would in any way exact prior consideration and prevent such officer from performing full and complete police duty at any time. Any police officer now a member of such unions shall disassociate himself within 30 days from this date. Failure to comply will constitute reason for immediate dismissal." . . .

The basic question at issue is whether the defendant city may through its duly constituted authorities prescribe a regulation of the character here involved for the members of its police department. It may be assumed that in taking the action in question due consideration was given to local conditions and to the protection of the public interest generally. That a municipality maintaining a police department may adopt reasonable rules in connection therewith is not open to question. Opinions may perhaps differ as to what may be regarded as reasonable, or as the converse thereof. In the instant case the presumption of validity attaches to the regulation adopted by the chief of police pursuant to the code of ordinances of the city, and the burden rests on those assailing it to establish that there is an unwarranted, and therefore arbitrary, interference with rights protected by constitutional guaranties. If the municipality has acted within the scope of its powers, the regulation must be sustained.

Basically the question at issue is whether the city may exercise over the members of its police department the right of control asserted by the rule in question, rather than the effect of such rule on those employees who are within its scope. The restriction imposed is not directed at a class as such but, rather, solely at those who have sought and obtained employment in the police department of the defendant city. . . .

In Fraternal Order of Police v. Lansing Board of Police & Fire Com'rs, 306 Mich. 68, this Court had before it a suit brought by the plaintiff to restrain the defendant board from enforcing a resolution designed to prevent members of the police department from becoming members of the plaintiff organization. Plaintiff accepted as associate members private citizens who paid small fees for joining and were given identification tags that might be attached to their automobiles. It was held that defendant had acted within the scope of its authority and that neither plaintiff organization nor any of its members had been deprived of constitutional rights. . . .

The above decision was followed in State Lodge of Michigan, Fraternal Order of Police v. City of Detroit, 318 Mich. 182, which involved a regulation of the police commissioner of defendant city forbidding members of the police force from being members of a fraternal order allowing other citizens to become associate members. The Court quoted (p. 189) with approval from the opinion in Carter v. Thompson, 164 Va. 312, 317 (180 S.E. 410), as follows:

" 'Police and fire departments are in a class apart. Both are at times charged with the preservation of public order, and for manifold reasons they owe to the public their undivided allegiance. The power in the city of complete control is imperatively necessary if discipline is to be maintained.' "

In accord with prior holdings of this Court is the decision in Perez v. Board of Police Commissioners of the City of Los Angeles, 78 Cal. App. 2d 638 (178 P.2d 537). At issue there was a resolution of the board of police commissioners of Los Angeles forbidding police officers of the city to become members of any organization identified with "any trade association, federation or labor union which admits to membership persons who are not members of the Los Angeles police department, or whose membership is not exclusively made up of employees of the city of Los Angeles." The action of the trial court in sustaining the resolution was upheld. It was specifically held that there was no violation of the 14th amendment to the Federal Constitution, and that the order of the defendant board was not arbitrary or unreasonable. . . .

The regulation involved in the instant case is limited in its application to members of the police department of the city of Muskegon and it applies to them solely in their capacity as such members. As this Court pointed out in City of Detroit v. Division 26 of the Amalgamated Association of Street, Electric Railway & Motor Coach Employees of America, 332 Mich. 237, there is no provision of either State or Federal Constitution which gives to individuals the right to be employed in government service or the right to continue therein. . . .

Plaintiffs herein have not borne the burden of proof of showing that members of the police department of Muskegon are deprived by the enforcement of the regulation in question of any constitutional rights to which they are entitled. As before suggested, they cannot claim a constitutional right to be appointed as members of said department, or to continue therein. They are subject to the authority of the municipality, granted by the Constitution and laws of the State, to manage its local affairs and to regulate the departments of municipal government. The duly constituted authorities of the city have concluded that the regulation here under attack is reasonably required in the interests of a fair and impartial administration of the law by those entrusted with its enforcement, without discrimination or partiality. The basic principles recognized in the prior decisions of this Court and by courts in other States as well are applicable here. On the record before us it may not be said that the rule is unreasonable or arbitrary in its application. . . .

MC LAUGHLIN v. TILENDIS
United States Court of Appeals, Seventh Circuit
398 F.2d 287 (1968)

CUMMINGS, Circuit Judge. This action was brought under Section 1 of the Civil Rights Act of 1871 (42 U.S.C. § 1983) [1] by John Steele and James McLaughlin who had been employed as probationary teachers by Cook County, Illinois, School District No. 149. Each sought damages of $100,000 from the Superintendent of School District No. 149 and the elected members of the Board of Education of that District.

Steele was not offered a second-year teaching contract and McLaughlin was dismissed before the end of his second year of teaching. Steele alleged that he was not rehired and McLaughlin alleged that he was dismissed because of their association with Local 1663 of the American Federation of Teachers, AFL-CIO. Neither teacher had yet achieved tenure.

In two additional Counts, Local 1663 and the parent union, through their officers and on behalf of all their members, sought an injunction requiring the defendants to cease and desist from discriminating against teachers who distribute union materials and solicit union membership.

The District Court granted the defendants' motion to dismiss the complaint, holding that plaintiffs had no First Amendment rights to join or form a labor union, so that there was no jurisdiction under the Civil Rights Act. The District Court's memorandum opinion did not consider the alternative defense presented in the motion that defendants were immune from suit under the Illinois Tort Immunity Act (Ill. Rev. Stats. 1967, Ch. 85, Sec. 2-201). Concluding that the First Amendment confers the right to form and join a labor union, we reverse on the ground that the complaint does state a claim under Section 1983.

It is settled that teachers have the right of free association, and unjustified interference with teachers' associational freedom violates the Due Process clause of the Fourteenth Amendment. Shelton v. Tucker, 364 U.S. 479, 485-487. Public employment may not be subjected to unreasonable conditions, and the assertion of First Amendment rights by teachers will usually not warrant

---

[1] Section 1983 of Title 42 of the U.S. Code provides:

"Every person who, under color of any statute, ordinance, regulation, custom, or usage, of any State or Territory, subjects, or causes to be subjected, any citizen of the United States or other person within the jurisdiction thereof to the deprivation of any rights, privileges, or immunities secured by the Constitution and laws, shall be liable to the party injured in an action at law, suit in equity, or other proper proceeding for redress."

their dismissal. Keyishian v. Board of Regents, 385 U.S. 589, 605-606; Garrity v. New Jersey, 385 U.S. 493, 500; Pickering v. Board of Education, 36 U.S. Law Week 4495. Unless there is some illegal intent, an individual's right to form and join a union is protected by the First Amendment. Thomas v. Collins, 323 U.S. 516, 534; see also Hague v. C.I.O., 307 U.S. 496, 512, 519, 523-524; Griswold v. Connecticut, 381 U.S. 479, 483; Stapleton v. Mitchell, 60 F. Supp. 51, 59-60, 61 (D. Kan. 1945; opinion of Circuit Judge Murrah), appeal dismissed, 326 U.S. 690. As stated in N.A.A.C.P. v. Alabama, 357 U.S. 449, 460:

"It is beyond debate that freedom to engage in association for the advancement of beliefs and ideas is an inseparable aspect of the 'liberty' assured by the Due Process Clause of the Fourteenth Amendment, which embraces freedom of speech."

Even though the individual plaintiffs did not yet have tenure, the Civil Rights Act of 1871 gives them a remedy if their contracts were not renewed because of their exercise of constitional rights. . . .

Just this month the Supreme Court held that an Illinois teacher was protected by the First Amendment from discharge even though he wrote a partially false letter to a local newspaper in which he criticized the school board's financial policy. Pickering v. Board of Education, 36 U.S. Law Week 4495. There is no showing on this record that plaintiffs' activities impeded "the proper performance of [their] daily duties in the classroom." *Idem* at p. 4498. If teachers can engage in scathing and partially inaccurate public criticism of their school board, surely they can form and take part in associations to further what they consider to be their well-being.

The trial judge was motivated by his conclusion that more than free speech was involved here, stating:

"The union may decide to engage in strikes, to set up machinery to bargain with the governmental employer, to provide machinery for arbitration, or may seek to establish working conditions. Overriding community interests are involved. The very ability of the governmental entity to function may be affected. The judiciary, and particularly this Court, cannot interfere with the power or discretion of the state in handling these matters."

It is possible of course that at some future time plaintiffs may engage in union-related conduct justifying their dismissal. But the Supreme Court has stated that

"Those who join an organization but do not share its unlawful purposes and who do not participate in its unlawful
activities surely pose no threat, either as citizens or as public
employees." Elfbrandt v. Russell, 384 U.S. 11, 17.

Even if this record disclosed that the union was connected with
unlawful activity, the bare fact of membership does not justify
charging members with their organization's misdeeds. *Idem.*
A contrary rule would bite more deeply into associational freedom than is necessary to achieve legitimate state interests, thereby violating the First Amendment.

Illinois has not prohibited membership in a teachers' union,
and defendants do not claim that the individual plaintiffs engaged in any illegal strikes or picketing.[3] Moreover, collective
bargaining contracts between teachers' unions and school districts are not against the public policy of Illinois. Chicago Education Association v. Chicago Board of Education, 76 Ill. App.
2d 456, 222 N.E.2d 243 (1966). Illinois even permits the automatic deduction of union dues from the salaries of employees
of local governmental agencies. Ill. Rev. Stats. 1967, Ch. 85,
Sec. 472. These very defendants have not adopted any rule,
regulation or resolution forbidding union membership. Accordingly, no paramount public interest of Illinois warranted the
limiting of Steele's and McLaughlin's right of association. Of
course, at trial defendants may show that these individuals were
engaging in unlawful activities or were dismissed for other
proper reasons, but on this record we hold that the complaint
sufficiently states a justiciable claim under Section 1983. There is
nothing anomalous in protecting teachers' rights to join unions.
Other employees have long been similarly protected by the
National Labor Relations Act. See National Labor Relations
Board v. Jones & Laughlin, 301 U.S. 1, 33.

The second ground of defendants' motion to dismiss was that
they are protected against suit by the Illinois Tort Immunity
Act (Ill. Rev. Stats. 1967, Ch. 85, Sec. 2-201).[4] Under the
Supremacy Clause, that statute cannot protect defendants against
a cause of action grounded, as here, on a federal statute. Legislators and judges have broad immunity under Section 1983

---

[3] In Illinois, strikes and certain picketing by public employees are enjoinable. Redding v. Board of Education, 32 Ill. 2d 567, 207 N.E.2d 427 (1965).

[4] Sec. 2-201 provides:

"Except as otherwise provided by Statute, a public employee serving
in a position involving the determination of policy or the exercise of
discretion is not liable for an injury resulting from his act or omission
in determining policy when acting in the exercise of such discretion
even though abused."

because in enacting that statute Congress did not intend to overturn their pre-existing defense. Tenney v. Brandhove, 341 U.S. 367, 376; Pierson v. Ray, 386 U.S. 547, 554-555. However, other officials, such as present defendants, retain only a qualified immunity, dependent on good faith action. . . . Even under the Illinois Act, immunity is conditioned upon a showing of good faith (Baum, *Tort Liability of Local Governments and Their Employees: An Introduction to the Illinois Immunity Act,* Ill. Law Forum (1966) 981, 1003-1004), and there has been no hearing on that question. In this Court and in their brief below the defendants also rely on common law immunity, but we rejected a similar contention in Progress Development Corp. v. Mitchell, 286 F.2d 221, 231 (7th Cir. 1961), where it was held that common law immunity did not extend to members of the Deerfield, Illinois, Park Board charged with discriminating against Negroes. Unless they can show good faith action, the reach of that decision extends to the present defendants who are alleged to have discriminatorily discharged Steele and McLaughlin for their union membership. To hold defendants absolutely immune from this type of suit would frustrate the very purpose of Section 1983. Jobson v. Henne, 355 F.2d 129, 133 (2nd Cir. 1966). At best, defendants' qualified immunity in this case means that they can prevail only if they show that plaintiffs were discharged on justifiable grounds. Thus here a successful defense on the merits merges with a successful defense under the qualified immunity doctrine.

Finally in this connection, it should be noted that immunity was *sub silentio* denied to the school officials involved in the *Johnson, Bomar, Smith, Rackley* and *Williams* cases, *supra;* see also Board of Education v. Barnette, 319 U.S. 624, 637-638.

The judgment of the District Court is reversed and the cause is remanded for trial.

NOTES

1. *See generally* Leahy, *From McAuliffe to McLaughlin: A Revolution in the Law of Constitutional Rights of Public Employees,* 57 ILL. B.J. 910 (1969) ; Eisner, *First Amendment Right of Association for Public Employee Union Members,* 20 LAB. L.J. 438 (1969).

2. Does the constitutional right of public employees to join and form unions extend to supervisory personnel? In Shelofsky v. Helsby, 39 App. Div. 2d 168, 332 N.Y.S.2d 723 (1972), *aff'd,* 32 N.Y.2d 54, 295 N.E.2d 774, — N.Y.S.2d —, *appeal dismissed,* 84 L.R.R.M. 2421 (U.S. Oct. 9, 1973), the court held that an amendment to the New York Taylor Law which excludes man-

agerial and confidential personnel from coverage under the law does not violate the employees' rights of due process, freedom of association, or equal protection. *See also* AFSCME Local 2183 v. New Mexico Personnel Bd., 81 L.R.R.M. 2397 (N.M. Dist. Ct. 1972), where the court held "that it is not arbitrary, capricious, unreasonable or unlawful to prohibit supervisors from being in a bargaining unit." On the other hand, in Orr v. Thorp, 308 F. Supp. 1369 (S.D. Fla. 1969), the court held that a state act that prohibited membership by supervisory and administrative personnel in unions that represented teachers violated the equal protection and freedom of association provisions of the Constitution.

Under the National Labor Relations Act the NLRB has uniformly held that since supervisors are excluded from the definition of the term "employee," they do not have the right to join or form unions and that it is not an unfair labor practice for employers to discharge supervisors who engage in union activity as long as such discharge is not intended to inhibit the right of rank and file employees to join or form unions. *See* NLRB v. Inter-City Advertising Co., 190 F.2d 420 (4th Cir. 1951).

3. Must a public employee first exhaust whatever state *judicial* remedies may exist before maintaining a suit in federal court under the Civil Rights Act of 1871? The courts have held that "exhaustion of state *judicial* remedies is not a prerequisite to the invocation of federal relief under section 1983 since the cause of action established by that statute is fully supplementary to any remedy, adequate or inadequate, that might exist under state law." Hobbs v. Thompson, 448 F.2d 456 (5th Cir. 1971). *But see* Askew v. Hargrave, 401 U.S. 476 (1971); Egner v. Texas City Independent School District, 338 F. Supp. 931 (S.D. Tex. 1972).

4. Most of the comprehensive state public employee labor relations statutes specifically provide that it is an unfair labor practice for a public employer to discriminate against a public employee because of his union activities. Most of these statutes further establish a public employee relations agency to hear complaints of alleged unfair labor practices and authorize the agency to issue orders remedying any unfair labor practices that are found to exist. Where such a state *administrative* remedy exists, should the employee be required to exhaust this remedy before seeking relief in the federal courts under the Civil Rights Act of 1871? In McNeese v. Board of Education, 373 U.S. 668, 83 S. Ct. 1433, 10 L. Ed. 2d 622 (1963), the Supreme Court held that federal plaintiff need not exhaust state administrative

remedies, noting that one of the purposes of the Civil Rights Act
was "to provide a remedy in the federal courts supplementary
to any remedy any State may have." *Accord,* Houghton v. Shafer,
392 U.S. 639, 88 S. Ct. 2119, 20 L. Ed. 2d 1319 (1968) ; Damico
v. California, 389 U.S. 416, 88 S. Ct. 526, 19 L. Ed. 2d 647
(1967) . *But see* Gibson v. Berryhill, — U.S. —, 93 S. Ct. 1689,
36 L. Ed. 2d — (1973) ; Askew v. Hargrave, 401 U.S. 476, 91
S. Ct. 856, 28 L. Ed. 2d 196 (1971) . The broad negation of the
exhaustion doctrine has been critically examined in Note, *Exhaustion of State Remedies Under the Civil Rights Act,* 68
COLUM. L. REV. 1201 (1968) ; Note, *Limiting the Section 1983
Action in the Wake of Monroe v. Pape,* 82 HARV. L. REV. 1486
(1969) . For a rebuttal to the latter note, see Comment, *Section
1983 Jurisdiction: A Reply,* 83 HARV. L. REV. 1352 (1970) . Does
the result in *McNeese* make sense in the labor relations context where the public employee's right to join and form unions
is affirmatively protected and where the state provides an administrative remedy to protect such right? Should exhaustion
be required where such an administrative remedy exists and
the inquiry is essentially factual in nature, *i.e.,* did the public
employer unlawfully discriminate against the public employee
because of his union activities? In Teamsters Local 594 v. City of
West Point, 338 F. Supp. 927 (D. Neb. 1972) , the court, noting
that the Nebraska Court of Industrial Relations had recently
been granted authority to hear public sector labor disputes, including charges of discrimination against public employees because of their union activities, stated that it "would be prone
toward application of the exhaustion of remedies doctrine . . . ."
"[I]n view of the time and cost already expended," however, the
court held that "it would be manifestly unjust to apply the
doctrine in the instant matter."

5.   If a public employee, whether required to or not, exhausts
his state administrative remedy and a decision is issued finding
that his right to engage in union activity was not unlawfully
interfered with, may the employee subsequently relitigate the
same matter in a suit in federal court? Is the determination by
the state agency *res judicata?* In Nigosian v. Weiss, 343 F. Supp.
757 (E.D. Mich. 1971) , the court held that "[i]t would be
improper to accord a determination of the State Labor Mediation Board binding effect where the examiner specifically limited
his decision to examination of state, not federal, law."

6.   What remedies are available in a section 1983 suit? If,
for example, it is found that a public official is interfering with
a public employee's right to engage in union activities, can the

federal court issue injunctive relief? Does the Norris-LaGuardia Act's broad prohibition against federal courts issuing injunctions in cases arising out of labor disputes apply to suits brought under section 1983? In Lontine v. VanCleave, 80 L.R.R.M. 3240 (D. Colo. 1972), *aff'd,* 483 F.2d 966 (10th Cir. 1973), the court granted an injunction and ordered reinstatement of an employee who was discharged because of union membership.

7. Suppose it is found in a section 1983 suit that a public official has unlawfully discharged a public employee and an order requiring reinstatement and back pay is issued. Can the public employer be held liable for the back pay or is this the responsibility of the public official or officials directly involved? In Monroe v. Pape, 365 U.S. 167, 81 S. Ct. 473, 5 L. Ed. 2d 492 (1961), the Supreme Court held that a municipal corporation was not a "person" within the meaning of section 1983. *Accord,* Moor v. County of Alameda, — U.S. —, 93 S. Ct. 1785, 36 L. Ed. 2d — (1973). Subsequent to the decision in *Monroe,* the lower federal courts were divided with respect to whether it precluded suit against a public employer for equitable relief as well as for damages. *Compare* Harkless v. Sweeny, Independent School Dist., 427 F.2d 319 (5th Cir. 1970), *cert. denied,* 400 U.S. 991 (1971) (equitable relief permissible), *with* Deane Hill Country Club, Inc. v. City of Knoxville, 379 F.2d 321 (6th Cir.), *cert. denied,* 389 U.S. 975 (1967) (equitable relief not permissible). In City of Kenosha, Wisconsin v. Bruno, — U.S. —, 93 S. Ct. 2222, — L. Ed. 2d — (1973), the Court resolved this question in holding that municipal corporations were outside the ambit of section 1983 "for purposes of equitable relief as well as for damages." *See generally* Comment, *Injunctive Relief Against Municipalities Under Section 1983,* 119 U. PA. L. REV. 389 (1970).

8. What is the statute of limitations for suits under section 1983? Suppose a state statute provides, as most do, that unfair labor practice charges must be filed within six months from the occurrence of the event giving rise to the allegation. Would this be binding on a federal court in a suit under section 1983?

9. Does a union have standing to bring an action under section 1983 alleging that a public employer interfered with the constitutional right of employees to join or become members of the union? *Compare* Lontine v. VanCleave, 80 L.R.R.M. 3240 (D. Colo. 1972), *aff'd,* 483 F.2d 966 (10th Cir. 1973) (union does not have standing), *with* Service Employees Int'l Union v. County of Butler, 306 F. Supp. 1080 (W.D. Pa. 1969) (union "has standing to complain on behalf of its members").

10.   Is a successful plaintiff in a suit under section 1983 entitled to attorneys' fees? *Compare* NAACP v. Allen, 340 F. Supp. 703 (M.D. Ala. 1972) (attorneys' fees allowed), *with* Webb v. Lake Mills Community School Dist., 344 F. Supp. 791 (N.D. Iowa 1972) (". . . attorneys' fees are only to be awarded as a punitive measure where a defendant has acted with obdurant recalcitrance").

ATKINS v. CITY OF CHARLOTTE

United States District Court, Western District of North Carolina
296 F. Supp. 1068 (1969)

CRAVEN, Circuit Judge:

This is a civil action brought to obtain a declaratory judgment and injunctive relief declaring unconstitutional and preventing enforcement of Sections 95-97, 95-98 and 95-99 of the General Statutes of North Carolina. We hold G.S. 95-97 unconstitutional on its face. We hold G.S. § 95-98 a valid and constitutional exercise of the legislative authority of the General Assembly of North Carolina. As for G.S. § 95-99, we hold it to be so related to G.S. § 95-97 that it cannot survive the invalidation of that section. . . .

[T]he court finds the facts to be as follows:

FACTS

The statutes sought to be invalidated are these:

N.C.G.S. § 95-97: . . . [Prohibits any employee employed by any governmental unit engaged full-time in law enforcement or fire protection activity from being or becoming a member of any labor organization or aiding or assisting any labor organization] which is, or may become, a part of or affiliated in any way with any national or international labor union, federation, or organization, and which has as its purpose or one of its purposes, collective bargaining. . . .

N.C.G.S. § 95-98: . . . [Any agreement or contract between any unit of government and any labor organization] is hereby declared to be against the public policy of the State, illegal, unlawful, void and of no effect.

N.C.G.S. § 95-99: . . . [Violations of §§ 95-97 and 95-98 are misdemeanors] punishable in the discretion of the court.

All of the plaintiffs are members of the Charlotte Fire Department, and the gist of the complaint is that the statutes are overbroad and prohibit constitutionally guaranteed rights of the plaintiffs in violation of the First Amendment and the Due

Process and Equal Protection Clauses of the Fourteenth Amendment to the Constitution of the United States. Specifically, plaintiffs want to become dues paying members of a Local which would become affiliated with International Association of Fire Fighters, the intervenor. Affidavits of some 400 fire fighters of the Charlotte Fire Department have been put into evidence to the effect that, if allowed to do so by law, affiants would join the Union.

The City of Charlotte is a municipal corporation which operates and maintains the Charlotte Fire Department pursuant to the City Charter. The Chief of the Department is appointed by the City Council and is accountable to the Council for the faithful performance of his duties. He is responsible for the discipline and efficiency of the Department and for carrying out all orders, rules and regulations approved by the Council. He is also responsible for approving all promotions of members in the Department subject to the approval of the Civil Service Board.

The Department has approximately 438 employees, consisting of the Chief, two assistant chiefs, 14 deputy chiefs, 60 fire captains, and 56 fire lieutenants, with the remainder being fire fighters, inspectors, fire alarm personnel and office personnel. The plaintiffs consist of deputy chiefs, captains, lieutenants and fire fighters and range in service with the department from two to 40 years.

For many years prior to the enactment in 1959 of the North Carolina General Statutes complained of, the International Association of Fire Fighters operated or maintained a union made up of Charlotte Fire Department members and designated as Local 660, an affiliate of the International Association of Fire Fighters. A number of Fire Department members paid dues to that organization which was engaged in collective bargaining activity. Further, the City checked off dues for union membership.

During 1959, the North Carolina Legislature enacted General Statutes §§ 95-97 through 95-99. Following the enactment of these statutes, Local 660 terminated its affiliation with the International Association of Fire Fighters and became, or took the name, Charlotte Fire Fighters Association. This organization continued the activities and representations very much as had been the practice with Local 660. The Fire Fighters Association continued to negotiate with the City and to represent the Charlotte firemen with respect to wages, grievances, and other conditions of employment, and the City continued its recognition of the association and permitted dues check-off. This practice continued from 1959 until 1962. On January 29, 1962, the City Council received and ap-

proved a report compiled by the City Manager. One of the recommendations of this report as it was approved established as a
condition of continued employment in the Fire Department
non-membership in the Fire Fighters Association or in any successor thereto. The City Council approved this report after having been advised by the City Attorney that the Fire Fighters Association was not illegal per se under the statutes complained of,
but that the association and its recognition by the City was in
violation of public policies of the State. Sometime after this action
on the part of the City Council, the Fire Fighters Association
terminated its activities and the City discontinued its recognition and dues checkoff. A grievance procedure was established to
allow individual employees to process grievances, but no provisions were made for group grievance procedure or for collective
bargaining with respect to grievances, wages, and conditions of
employment.

During March of 1967, members of the Charlotte Fire Department, the plaintiffs herein, organized the Charlotte Firemen's Assembly. This organization has as its purpose collective
bargaining with the City of Charlotte with respect to wages, grievances, hours of employment and other conditions of employment.
It would like to become a local affiliate of intervenor but is prevented by the statutes. The Firemen's Assembly has not been
recognized by the City as a representative of firemen. . . .

THE CONSTITUTIONAL QUESTION AND THE REMEDY

We think N.C.G.S. § 95-97 is void on its face as an abridgment of
freedom of association protected by the First and Fourteenth
Amendments of the Constitution of the United States. The flaw
in it is an intolerable "overbreadth" unnecessary to the protection
of valid state interests. Cf. United States v. Robel, 389 U.S. 258,
88 S. Ct. 419, 19 L. Ed. 2d 508 (1967). The Supreme Court of
the United States has accorded "freedom of association" full
status as an aspect of liberty protected by the Due Process Clause
of the Fourteenth Amendment and by the rights of free speech and
peaceful assembly explicitly set out in the First Amendment. In
NAACP v. Alabama ex rel. Patterson, the Court said:

"It is beyond debate that freedom to engage in association
for the advancement of beliefs and ideas is an inseparable
aspect of the 'liberty' assured by the Due Process Clause of
the Fourteenth Amendment, which embraces freedom of
speech. [Citations omitted.] Of course, it is immaterial whether the beliefs sought to be advanced by association pertain
to political, *economic,* religious or cultural matters, and state
action which may have the effect of curtailing the free-

dom to associate is subject to the closest scrutiny." 357 U.S. 449, 460-461, 78 S. Ct. 1163, 1171, 2 L. Ed. 2d 1488, 1498- 1499 (1958) . (Emphasis ours.)

The Court had previously noted the close connection between the freedoms of speech and assembly. In De Jonge v. Oregon, 299 U.S. 353, 364, 57 S. Ct. 255, 81 L. Ed. 278, 283-284 (1937), the Court held that the right of peaceable assembly is a right cognate to those of free speech and free press and equally fundamental. It was said that the right is one that cannot be denied without violating fundamental principles of liberty and justice which lie at the base of all civil and political institutions. The Court made a careful distinction between the proper exercise of legislative power to protect against abuse of the right of assembly and legislative infringement per se of that right, holding that the latter is not permissible. Especially pertinent to the problem confronting us is the following:

"[C]onsistently with the Federal Constitution, peaceable assembly for lawful discussion cannot be made a crime. The holding of meetings for peaceable political action cannot be proscribed. Those who assist in the conduct of such meetings cannot be branded as criminals on that score. The question, if the rights of free speech and peaceable assembly are to be preserved, is not *as to the auspices under which the meeting is held* but as to its purpose. . . ." DeJonge v. Oregon, 299 U.S. 353, 365, 57 S. Ct. 255, 260, 81 L. Ed. 278, 284 (1937) . (Emphasis ours.)

We would make the same distinction here. It matters not, we think, whether the firemen of the City of Charlotte meet under the auspices of the intervenor, a national labor union, but whether their proposed concerted action, if any, endangers valid state interests. We think there is no valid state interest in denying firemen the right to organize a labor union—whether local or national in scope. It is beyond argument that a single individual cannot negotiate on an equal basis with an employer who hires hundreds of people. Recognition of this fact of life is the basis of labor-management relations in this country. Charlotte concedes in its brief that the right of public employees to join labor unions is becoming increasingly recognized (with the exception of firemen and policemen) and even admits that collective bargaining might be beneficial in many situations in the case of municipal firemen. But Charlotte insists that the State has a valid interest in forbidding membership in a labor union to firemen. It is said that fire departments are quasi-military in structure, and that such a structure is necessary because individual firemen must be ready to respond instantly and without question to orders of a superior, and that such military discipline may well mean the difference between saving human life and property, and failure. The extension of this argument is, of course, that affiliation with a national labor union might eventuate in a strike against the public interest which could not be tolerated, and the very existence of which would imperil lives and property in the City of Charlotte. This is the only state interest that can be validly asserted for N.C.G.S. § 95-97. The thought of fires raging out of control in Charlotte while firemen, out on strike, Neroically watch the flames, is frightening. We do not question the power of the State to deal with such a contingency. We do question the overbreadth of G.S. § 95-97, which quite unnecessarily, in our opinion, goes far beyond the valid state interest that is suggested to us, and strikes down indiscriminately the right of association in a labor union—even one whose policy is opposed to strikes.

Since the only valid state interest suggested by defendants in support of the constitutionality of G.S. § 95-97 is the quite legitimate fear that fire protection for the people of Charlotte might be disrupted by violence or by strike, it seems quite clear that the statute must be invalidated for "overbreadth."

The Supreme Court "has repeatedly held that a governmental purpose to control or prevent activities constitutionally subject to state regulation may not be achieved by means which sweep unnecessarily broadly and thereby invade the area of protected freedoms." NAACP v. Alabama ex rel. Flowers, 377 U.S. 288, at 307, 84 S. Ct. 1302, at 1314, 12 L. Ed. 2d 325, at 338 (1964).

Again, "even though the governmental purpose be legitimate and substantial, that purpose cannot be pursued by means that broadly stifle fundamental personal liberties when the end can be more narrowly achieved." Shelton v. Tucker, 364 U.S. 479, 488, 81 S. Ct. 247, 256, 5 L. Ed. 2d 231, 237 (1960). As previously indicated, the plaintiffs and intervenor do not question the power of the State to prohibit strikes against the public interest.

What we have said thus far supports our ultimate conclusion: that the firemen of the City of Charlotte are granted the right of free association by the First and Fourteenth Amendments of the United States Constitution; that that right of association includes the right to form and join a labor union—whether local or national; that membership in such a labor organization will confer upon the firemen no immunity from proper state regulation to protect valid state interests which are, in this case, the protection of property and life from destruction by fire. We think such a conclusion flows inevitably from the enunciations of the United States Supreme Court set out above. Our decision is consistent with that of the Seventh Circuit according the same right to teachers. McLaughlin v. Tilendis, 398 F.2d 287 (7th Cir. 1968). We do not think the *McLaughlin* decision is distinguishable on the asserted ground that the State in that case had not undertaken to prohibit membership in a teachers' labor union. The court's recitation that there was no such state legislation went to the question of whether there was a valid state interest. It held that there was no such state interest, and that the right of a teacher to join a labor union rested upon the First Amendment to the United States Constitution. In our case, we hold that the valid state interest may be served by more narrowly drawn legislation so as not to infringe the First Amendment.

We find nothing unconstitutional in G.S. § 95-98. It simply voids contracts between units of government within North Carolina and labor unions and expresses the public policy of North Carolina to be against such collective bargaining contracts. There is nothing in the United States Constitution which entitles one to have a contract with another who does not want it. It is but a step further to hold that the state may lawfully forbid such contracts with its instrumentalities. The solution, if there be one, from the viewpoint of the firemen, is that labor unions may someday persuade state government of the asserted value of collective bargaining agreements, but this is a political matter and does not yield to judicial solution. The right to a collective bargaining agreement, so firmly entrenched in American labor-management relations, rests upon national legislation and not upon the federal Constitution. The State is within the powers reserved to it to refuse to enter into such agreements and so to declare by statute. . . .

Finally, we are asked to enjoin the defendants from enforcing these statutes now adjudged to be unconstitutional, *viz.*, N.C.G.S. § 95-97 and § 95-99. We decline to do so. There has not been the slightest intimation that our decision adjudging these statutes invalid will be ignored by the City of Charlotte or by any of the other defendants. If our decision should be thought wrong, we may properly assume it will be appealed—not ignored. There is no evidence that the solicitor of the district has sought indictments against any firemen or that he intends doing so. We adhere to the philosophy of federalism and think it unseemly that a federal court should issue its injunctive process against state or local officers except in situations of the most compelling necessity. Entry of a declaratory judgment decreeing G.S. § 95-97 and § 95-99 invalid because in violation of the First and Fourteenth Amendments of the United States Constitution seems to us, on the facts of this case, a fully sufficient remedy.

Declaratory judgment granted. Injunction denied.

Addendum:

The Eighth Circuit has decided that public employees have a right, grounded in the Constitution, to join a labor union, in the absence of a "paramount public interest of the State of Nebraska or the City of North Platte [which] warranted limiting the plaintiffs' right to freedom of association." *See* American Federation of State, County, and Municipal Employees v. Woodward, 406 F.2d 137 (8th Cir. Jan. 17, 1969) (Jan. 28, 1969).

NOTES

1. The *Atkins* case is noted in 55 VA. L. REV. 1151 (1969).

2. In Alabama Labor Council v. Frazier, 81 L.R.R.M. 2155 (Ala. Cir. Ct., Madison County, 1972), the court held unconstitutional a state act that provided any public employee who joined or participated in the activities of a labor union lost all rights "afforded him under the state merit system, employment rights, re-employment rights, and other rights, benefits or privileges which he enjoys as a result of his public employment." ALA. CODE tit. 55, § 317 (2) (1958).

3. A three-judge federal district court in Melton v. City of Atlanta, 324 F. Supp. 315 (N.D. Ga. 1971), held unconstitutional a Georgia statute that made it a misdemeanor for a policeman to join or belong to a labor union. The court stated:

> . . . we are faced with the problem of weighing the plaintiffs' interests in the First Amendment rights and the defendants' interest in securing and having an impartial police force. While the statutes here undoubtedly tend toward securing the desired impartiality, their practical effect in that direction would not appear so efficacious or certain as to offset or outweigh the obvious impairment in plaintiffs' First Amendment rights. This is particularly true where, as we are informed by plaintiffs, the FOP [Fraternal Order of Police] has no members outside the Atlanta Police Department, and no affiliation with any organizations other than the national FOP. We accept these assurances in ruling as we do.

In Lontine v. VanCleave, 80 L.R.R.M. 3240 (D. Colo. 1972), *aff'd,* 483 F.2d 966 (10th Cir. 1973), the court in an action under the Civil Rights Act of 1871 ordered the reinstatement of a deputy sheriff who had been suspended because he "refused to indicate whether he would disaffiliate with the union." The court observed that the plaintiff has "a constitutional right to join a union and may not be discharged from employment for joining or continuing membership in a union, absent a showing of compelling state interest." *See generally* Juris & Hutchison, *The Legal Status of Municipal Police Employee Organizations,* 23 IND. & LAB. REL. REV. 352 (1970); Hilligan, *Police Employee Organizations: Past Developments and Present Problems,* 24 LAB. L.J. 288 (1973).

The New Jersey Act states that unless "established practice, prior agreement, or special circumstances dictate the contrary, no policeman shall have the right to join an employee organization that admits employees other than policemen to membership." N.J. STAT. ANN. § 34:13A-5.3 (Supp. 1968). Is this provision constitutional? Are there any legitimate reasons for restricting the kind of labor organization that policemen can join? In ABA PROJECT ON STANDARDS FOR CRIMINAL JUSTICE, THE URBAN POLICE FUNCTION 171 (Tentative Draft, March 1972), the Advisory Committee on the Police Function made the following recommendations:

> The need to preserve local control over law enforcement and over the resolution of law enforcement policy issues requires that law enforcement policy not be influenced by a national police union.
>
> The maintenance of police in a position of objectivity in engaging in conflict resolution requires that police not belong to a union which also has non-police members who may become party to a labor dispute.

See also Illinois Governor's Advisory Commission on Labor-Management Policy For Public Employees 14 (March 1967).

Executive Order 11491, adopting the NLRA approach, provides that no unit shall "be established if it includes . . . any guard together with any other employees." Section 10 (b) (3). Is this provision constitutional? In terms of a constitutional challenge, is there any difference between this provision and the provision contained in the New Jersey Act?

B. Statutory Protection

Virtually all of the public sector collective bargaining statutes set forth the rights of public employees. This statutory statement frequently parallels the statement of the rights of employees in section 7 of the National Labor Relations Act, as amended. For example, the Pennsylvania statute, PA. STAT. ANN. tit. 43, § 1101.-401 (1970), provides that:

> It shall be lawful for public employes to organize, form, join or assist in employe organizations or to engage in law-

ful concerted activities for the purpose of collective bargaining or other mutual aid and protection or to bargain collectively through representatives of their own free choice and
such employes shall also have the right to refrain from any
or all such activities, except as may be required pursuant
to a maintenance of membership provision in a collective
bargaining agreement.

Most of the comprehensive statutes, again adopting the NLRA
model, specify unfair labor practices by both public employers and
employee organizations. Thus, these comprehensive statutes generally provide that it is an unfair labor practice (sometimes referred to as an "improper practice" or "prohibited practice") for
a public employer to

(1) interfere with, restrain or coerce public employees in
     the exercise of their enumerated rights;
(2) dominate or interfere with the formation or admin-
     istration of an employee organization;
(3) discriminate in regard to hire or tenure of employment
     or any term or condition of employment to encourage
     or discourage membership in any employee organiza-
     tion;
(4) discharge or otherwise discriminate against an employee
     because he has filed charges or given testimony under
     the act; and
(5) refuse to bargain in good faith with the duly designated
     bargaining agent.

Similarly, these statutes also provide, with some exceptions, that
it is an unfair labor practice for an employee organization to

(1) restrain or coerce employees in the exercise of their
     enumerated rights;
(2) cause or attempt to cause an employer to interfere with,
     restrain or coerce employees in the exercise of their
     enumerated rights;
(3) restrain or coerce employers in the selection of their
     representatives for the purposes of collective bargaining
     or the adjustment of grievances; and
(4) refuse to bargain in good faith.

Some of the comprehensive state statutes, however, contain broader
proscriptions than those set forth in the NLRA. For example,
the Pennsylvania Act provides that it is an unfair labor practice
for both employers and employee organizations to violate "any
of the rules and regulations established by the board regulating the conduct of representation elections." PA. STAT. ANN.

tit. 43, §§ 1101.1201 (a) (7) and (b) (4) (1970). Under the Hawaii Act, it is an unfair labor practice for either employers or employee organizations to "[v]iolate the terms of a collective bargaining agreement." HAWAII REV. STAT. §§ 89-13 (a) (8) and (b) (5) (Supp. 1971). The unfair labor practice provisions in the Pennsylvania, Michigan, Hawaii, New York, and Wisconsin (municipal employees) statutes are set forth in the Statutory Appendix.

The determination of whether an unfair labor practice has occurred is generally left to a public employment relations agency. If the agency finds that the person named in the complaint has engaged in or is engaging in an unfair labor practice, the agency is generally empowered, as the Pennsylvania Act provides, to "cause to be served on such person an order requiring such person to cease and desist from such unfair practice, and to take such reasonable affirmative action, including reinstatement of employes, discharged in violation of Article XII of this act, with or without back pay, as will effectuate the policies of this act." PA. STAT. ANN. tit. 43, § 1101.1303 (1970).

NOTES

1. Should the complaining party have the burden of prosecuting an unfair labor practice charge before a public employment relations agency? The contrasting approaches under the NLRA and under several of the comprehensive public sector statutes is discussed in 1967 EXECUTIVE COMMITTEE, NATIONAL GOVERNOR'S CONFERENCE, REPORT OF TASK FORCE ON STATE AND LOCAL GOVERNMENT LABOR RELATIONS 15 (1967):

In the administration of the unfair labor practice provisions of their statutes, the states have tended *not* to follow the National Labor Management Relations Act. The federal act originally conferred responsibility for investigating, prosecuting, and determining the merits of charges of unfair practices to the National Labor Relations Board. This led to the accusation that the board was both prosecutor and judge. Later the judicial functions were administratively separated from the investigatory and prosecuting functions. This softened the accusation but did not totally eliminate it. To avoid this functional conflict, the state laws in Wisconsin and Michigan have restricted the board's function to hearing and deciding a charge, and leaving to the complaining party the responsibility of raising the issue at the outset and also of making a valid case in support of the charge. The Illinois Commission reviewed these procedural

questions and concluded that it was basically sound to limit
the board's function to deciding charges even though this
practice might in some instances place a burden on an
individual employee. At the same time, it also warned the
board against holding formal hearings on trivial charges.

2. The handling of unfair labor practices in the public
sector is explored in Smith, *Unfair Labor Practices in Public
Employment,* GERR No. 268, E-1 (1968); Kahn, *Unfair Labor
Practices Under the Taylor Law,* IND. & LAB. REL. FORUM, VOL.
6, pp. 57-76 (March 1969).

3. As noted above, most of the comprehensive statutes protect the right of public employees to bargain collectively and
specifically provide that it is an unfair labor practice for an
employer to refuse to bargain collectively. This area is discussed in detail in Chapter IV.

4. Section 14 (b) of the NLRA permits the states to enact
right-to-work legislation, 29 U.S.C. § 164 (b) (1970), and at present nineteen states have enacted right-to-work laws.[1] The
general purpose of most of these laws is to make it illegal to
condition employment on membership *or* non-membership in a
labor organization. Although right-to-work laws have been
vehemently attacked by organized labor, public sector unions
have occasionally relied on such laws to support their contention
that public employees have the right to join labor organizations
of their own choosing. For example, in Levasseur v. Wheeldon,
79 S.D. 442, 112 N.W.2d 894 (1964), a resolution adopted by
a municipality which prohibited fire, police, and health department employees from becoming members of any labor
organization whose membership was not exclusively confined
to employees of the municipality was held to contravene the
"right-to-work" provision in the state's constitution. The court
held that the "constitutional amendment does not exclude public
employment and that membership among city employees cannot
be banned by municipal legislation or rule." *Accord,* Potts v.
Hay, 229 Ark. 830, 318 S.W.2d 826 (1958); Beverly v. City of
Dallas, 292 S.W.2d 172 (Tex. Civ. App. 1956). *Contra,* Keeble
v. City of Alcoa, 204 Tenn. 286, 319 S.W. 2d 249 (1958).

---

[1] Alabama, Arizona, Arkansas, Florida, Georgia, Iowa, Kansas, Mississippi,
Nebraska, Nevada, North Carolina, North Dakota, South Carolina, South
Dakota, Tennessee, Texas, Utah, Virginia, and Wyoming. In addition,
Louisiana has a right-to-work law applicable only to agricultural employees.

1. Employer Interference, Restraint and Coercion

CHARLESTON NAVAL SHIPYARD

Assistant Secretary for Labor-Management Relations
A/SLMR No. 1 (1970), GERR Ref. File 21:4003

. . . The complaints in the instant cases filed by the Charleston Metal Trades Council (herein called the Union) against the Charleston Naval Shipyard (herein called the Shipyard) alleged violations of Sections 19 (a) (1) and 20 of Executive Order 11491 based on the Shipyard's notice of February 18 and its subsequent memoranda of March 16 and 27, 1970. The Union contends that the notice and memoranda effectively coerced, restrained, and intimidated employees in the exercise of their rights assured under Executive Order 11491. The Shipyard, on the other hand, defends its conduct in issuing the above-mentioned directives on the basis that it was merely acting in accordance with outstanding instructions of the Civil Service Commission which provide, in part, that during the period subsequent to the filing of a valid challenge requiring a redetermination of exclusive status, an "agency should not authorize the use of agency facilities to either the incumbent exclusive or the challenging organization (s) to conduct membership or election campaigns."[4] In this respect, the Shipyard contends that the Assistant Secretary of Labor is without authority to find that a directive, regulation, order or policy issued by the Civil Service Commission, Department of Defense, or any other "higher authority" over the Shipyard is invalid because such a determination would violate Sections 4 (b) and 25 (a) of the Order.

The Hearing Examiner concluded that the directives governing union electioneering activities promulgated by the Shipyard[5] interfered with, restrained, or coerced employees in the

---

[4] Federal Personnel Manual Letter 711-6 also provides in part, that "There shall be no restriction at any time on the right of employees to freedom of normal person-to-person communication at the workplace provided there is no interference with the work of the agency. Employees may engage in oral solicitation of employee organization membership during nonwork periods on agency premises."

[5] The Shipyard's notice of February 18, 1970, provided, in pertinent part, that:

a. Neither the currently recognized Charleston Metal Trades Council nor the challenging National Association of Governmental Employees shall conduct any type of electioneering on Naval Base premises until campaign procedures are established. Prohibited actions include:

(1) Posting or distribution on Naval Base premises of any poster, bulletin or other material which relates to the challenge;
(2) Meetings on Naval Base premises for the purpose of electioneering or campaigning;

rights assured by Executive Order 11491 since such rules infringed on the employees' right under Section 1 of the Order to "assist a labor organization."

In reaching his recommendation, the Hearing Examiner relied on precedent developed under the National Labor Relations Act. He reasoned that in view of the similarity of language between Sections 7 and 8 (a) (1) of the Act and Sections 1 and 19 (a) (1) of the Order, that "the decisions under the statute dealing with employee rights in solicitation and in distribution of literature are applicable under the Order (footnote omitted)." The Hearing Examiner also rejected the Shipyard's contention that in issuing the disputed regulations it was acting under a legal obligation to follow the directives of the Civil Service Commission and the Department of Defense. In this regard he stated that rights of employees established under the Executive Order "are not diminished by erroneous rulings of the Civil Service Commission or the Department of Defense."

There is no indication in the reports and recommendations which preceded Executive Orders 10988 and 11491 that the experience gained in the private sector under the National Labor Relations Act would necessarily be the controlling precedent in the administration of labor-management relations in the Federal sector. Thus, many of the provisions of Executive Order 10988 constituted clear attempts to take into account situations peculiar to Federal sector labor-management relations. Moreover, in 1969, when it was determined that improvements in the Federal labor-management relations program were warranted, it was made clear by the Study Committee that the proposed changes dealt only with deficiencies found to exist under Executive Order 10988, and there was no intention to adopt some other model for Federal labor-management relations.

Based on the foregoing, it is my belief that decisions issued under the Labor-Management Relations Act, as amended, are not controlling under Executive Order 11491. I will, however, take into account the experience gained in the private sector

---

(3) Solicitation of authorization revocations by the challenged union on Naval Base premises;

(4) Solicitation of further authorizations by the challenging union on Naval Base premises.

b. The prohibitions stated in paragraph 3a above, apply equally to employees and non-employee representatives of the organizations involved. . . .

The Shipyard's memorandum of March 16, 1970, as amplified on March 27, 1970, placed certain restrictions on the Union's stewards with respect to the time allowed for their conducting of union business. The March 16 memorandum also stated, in part, that "Electioneering or campaigning at this time is prohibited."

under the Labor-Management Relations Act, as amended, policies and practices in other jurisdictions, and those rules developed in the Federal sector under the prior Executive Order. Accordingly, I reject the reasoning of the Hearing Examiner in the instant case insofar as he implies that all of the rules and decisions under the Labor-Management Relations Act, as amended, would constitute binding precedent on the Assistant Secretary with respect to the implementation of his responsibilities under Executive Order 11491.

Also, I reject the Shipyard's assertion that I am without authority to determine whether directives or policy guidance issued by the Civil Service Commission, Department of Defense or any other agency are violative of the Order when those directives or policies are asserted by the activity as a defense to allegedly violative conduct. Both the Study Committee's Report and Recommendations and the Order itself clearly indicate the role which the Assistant Secretary was intended to play in the processing of unfair labor practice complaints under the Order. Thus, the Study Committee's Report and Recommendations stated that the lack of a third party process in resolving unfair labor practice charges was a serious deficiency under the prior Federal Labor-Management program. To rectify this deficiency, it was recommended that the Assistant Secretary of Labor-Management Relations be authorized to issue decisions to agencies and labor organizations subject to a limited right of appeal to the Federal Labor Relations Council. The Study Committee stated that as the Assistant Secretary issues decisions a body of precedent would be developed from which interested parties could draw guidance. The recommendations of the Study Committee culminated in Section 6 (a) (4) of the Order which provides, in part, that the Assistant Secretary of Labor for Labor-Management Relations shall ". . . decide complaints of alleged unfair labor practices and alleged violations of the standards of conduct for labor organizations." Hence, neither the Study Committee's Report and Recommendations nor the Order itself require that in processing unfair labor practices complaints I am bound to accept as determinative those directives or policies of the Civil Service Commission, the Department of Defense or any other agency which in my view contravene the purposes of the Order.

Accordingly, I reject the Shipyard's contention that I am without authority to find a violation in the instant case because its conduct was based on directives issued by the Civil Service Commission and the Department of Defense.

As did Executive Order 10988, Executive Order 11491 guarantees to employees of the Federal Government the right "to form, join and assist" a labor organization "without fear of penalty or reprisal." Section 19 (a) (1) of Executive Order 11491 states that "Agency management shall not interfere with, restrain or coerce employees in the exercise of the rights assured by this Order." That provision raises the basic issue to be resolved herein, i.e.—were the Shipyard's attempts to control employee electioneering on its premises, as evidenced by its February 18 notice to employees and its subsequent memoranda of March 16 and 27, in derogation of expressly guaranteed employee rights under Executive Order 11491?[11]

In attempting to resolve this issue, I have carefully reviewed the policy and practice developed in the Federal sector under Executive Order 10988 pursuant to the Civil Service Commission's Personnel Manual Letter 711-6. As noted above, such policy and practice was adopted to cover a particular period prior to the execution of an election agreement when a valid and timely challenge had been filed with respect to an incumbent labor organization's exclusive representative status. During this period, agencies were counseled not to authorize the use of their facilities to either the incumbent exclusive representative or the challenging organization for the purpose of conducting membership or election campaigns.[12]

The Civil Service Commission contended that this procedure represents "the most reasonable approach we have discovered to achieving among the contending unions the requisite fairness or equality of opportunity which alone can guarantee a genuinely free and representative election."

The Shipyard and the Department of Defense offered further justification for the Civil Service Commission policy on the grounds that the Government, as an employer, is "more neutral" in these matters than private employers and that there exists a substantial past practice under this policy which, if changed, would result in instability in Federal labor-management relations.[14]

---

[11] As noted in footnote 2 of the Hearing Examiner's Report and Recommendations, the subject cases involve only the rights of employees and not the rights of non-employee union representatives.

[12] As noted above in footnote 4 and as distinguished from the Shipyard's directives herein, normal employee "person-to-person communication at the workplace" was permitted under Federal Personnel Manual Letter 711-6 and employees were allowed to "engage in oral solicitation of employee organization membership during non-work periods on agency premises."

[14] In its exceptions to the Hearing Examiner's Report and Recommendations, the Department of Defense contended, among other things, that to

The basic rules governing employee solicitation and distribution were established by the Supreme Court in Le Tourneau Co. of Georgia v. NLRB, 324 U.S. 793 (1945) and Republic Aviation Corp. v. NLRB, 324 U.S. 793 (1945). The Court held that the enforcement of no-distribution and no-solicitation rules against employees during their non-working time was unlawful except where there were unusual circumstances present.

In the instant cases there is no evidence to establish that employee solicitation activity with respect to the forthcoming election or their distribution of campaign literature had the effect or would have had the effect of creating a safety hazard or interfering with work production or the maintenance of discipline in the Shipyard. Moreover, the argument that a moratorium on electioneering prevents the incumbent from exercising its natural advantage over the challenger is likewise unpersuasive since equality also can be maintained by granting full communication rights to both unions. A prohibition on any reasonable form of solicitation or election campaigning, works not only to the detriment of unit employees who may seek to become informed, but also to the detriment of the challenging union, which, unlike the incumbent, has not enjoyed the advantage of a prior relationship among the unit employees. I conclude, therefore, that the purposes sought to be achieved by the operation of the Shipyard's rules are neither attained, nor do they justify limiting the employees' right established under Executive Order 11491 "to assist a labor organization."

Accordingly, in the absence of any evidence of special circumstances which would have warranted the Shipyard's limiting or banning employee solitation during nonwork time and the distribution of campaign materials on its premises during employee nonwork time and in nonwork areas, I find that the Shipyard's notice of February 18, 1970, and its subsequent memoranda of March 16 and 27, 1970, [15] interfered with em-

---

the extent the Shipyard's notice of February 18, 1970, attempted to restrict the solicitation rights of individual employees it was too broad since Section 11 of Federal Personnel Manual Letter 711-6 made it clear that nothing therein was intended to interfere with freedom of normal person-to-person communication at the work place which does not disrupt work operations. The Department of Defense further asserted that a valid and meaningful distinction should be made between such constitutionally protected communication on the one hand, and, on the other, participation in organized electioneering activities on behalf of a union on activity premises during a period before mutually agreed upon rules for such electioneering have been adopted.

[15] As noted above, the Shipyard's memoranda of March 16 and 27, 1970, placed certain restrictions on the Union's stewards with respect to their handling of union business at the facility. Under these restrictions, before

ployee rights assured under Executive Order 11491 and were therefore violative of Section 19 (a) (1) of the Order.[17]

Conclusion

The promulgating and maintaining a rule which prohibits employees from engaging in solicitation on behalf of the Union or any other labor organization during nonwork time and from distributing literature for the Union of any other labor organization on Activity premises in nonwork areas during nonwork time, the Shipyard has violated Section 19 (a) (1) of the Executive Order. . . .

NOTES

1. Can an employer prohibit solicitation and distribution of union materials on his premises by *nonemployees?* Under the NLRA, the courts and the NLRB have made a distinction between the rights of employees and the rights of nonemployees. The leading NLRB decision concerning the legality of an employer's no-solicitation and no-distribution rules is Stoddard-Quirk Mfg. Co., 138 N.L.R.B. 615 (1962). In NLRB v. Babcock & Wilcox Co., 351 U.S. 105, 76 S. Ct. 679, 100 L. Ed. 975 (1956), the Court stated:

> . . . an employer may validly post his property against nonemployee distribution of union literature if reasonable efforts by the union through other available channels of communication will enable it to reach the employees with its message and if the employer's notice or order does not discriminate against the union by allowing other distribution.

Should the same distinction be made in the public sector where public property rather than private property is involved?

---

being granted time off to carry out their responsibilities to the unit employees, stewards were required to specify to management representatives the type of union business to be conducted and, unless such business was included on a list of 18 permissible activities, excused time would be denied. The Shipyard admitted that the desire to limit electioneering activities was one of the reasons for issuance of these memoranda. Although, under Article VI, Section 5 of the parties' agreement, stewards must first obtain oral permission from their supervisor when they desire to leave their work area to transact appropriate union business during work hours, insofar as the Shipyard's March 16 and 27 memoranda constituted a broad restriction against electioneering by stewards during their nonwork time, they violated Section 19 (a) (1) of the Order.

[17] The fact that the Government, as an employer, must remain neutral during an election campaign was not considered to require a contrary result. Thus, standing alone, this factor would not warrant a curtailment of *employee* rights under the Order.

2. Even though an employee's right to join and form a union is affirmatively protected by statute or executive order, are there any legitimate restrictions which an employer can place on such activity? In Department of Transportation, Federal Aviation Admin., FLRC No. 72A-1 (1973), GERR Ref. File 21:7035, the Federal Labor Relations Council held that the teacher-student relationship between instructors and new employees justified greater restrictions on union activity than those which may be placed on other employees. The FLRC stated:

It is a generally-felt belief that instructors have suasion over their students, even if they do not "supervise" the students. Students inherently feel pressure to "please" instructors and to be deferential to their desires. This is particularly significant in the circumstances of this case where students are often in attendance at the academy and away from their normal workplaces for extended periods of time. If the student is "solicited" by the instructor — for example, is asked to sign a union authorization card or membership application or to tender an initiation fee, this places undue pressure upon the student to respond affirmatively, notwithstanding the sophisticated judgment that the instructor is neither a management official nor a supervisor. Further, such action on the part of an instructor places agency management in an equally untenable position. The agency must insure the efficiency of its employees and the administration of a total labor relations program. It is required to insure that undue pressures do not distort true employee choices or the viability of the representation process or impair the efficiency of agency operations.

The FLRC held, however, that it was an unfair labor practice for the agency to ban instructors from wearing union buttons:

There is a great difference between actively soliciting in behalf of a labor organization and merely wearing a union membership button, particularly in the facts of the instant case where the buttons at issue are described as "unobtrusive membership pins bearing no campaign propaganda." We see no reasonable potential for employee coercion or adverse impact on the operation of the facility resulting from instructors wearing union membership buttons. While a balancing of competing rights and obligations justifies permitting the agency to restrict the right of instructors to solicit students in behalf of a labor organization, the same kinds of considerations do not exist—certainly, at least, not to a comparable degree—when the restriction goes to the very personal act of wearing a union membership button.

3. The statutory proscription against interfering with, restraining, or coercing an employee in the exercise of his rights to join or form a union and to engage in collective bargaining has been held to cover numerous matters:

(a) *Surveillance.* An employer's surveillance of union activities constitutes illegal interference, restraint and coercion. For example, in Green Lake County, WERC Decision No. 6061 (1962), the Wisconsin Employment Relations Commission held that it was illegal for an employer to spy on a union meeting for the purpose of determining who attended. In City of Midland, 1971 MERC Lab. Op. 1129, the Michigan Employment Relations Commission held that "[t]he representation of a city government in the bargaining process does not include infiltration and subversion of the union's strategy meetings."

(b) *Interrogation.* An employer's action in interrogating or questioning employees about their union activities, about whether they have signed union cards, about how they intend to vote in a representation election, etc., constitutes illegal interference. *See* Baraga County Memorial Hospital, 1969 MERC Lab. Op. 6.

(c) *Promise of benefit or threat of reprisal.* The granting or withholding of benefits for the purpose of influencing employees with respect to union activity constitutes illegal interference, restraint, and coercion. As the Supreme Court stated in NLRB v. Exchange Parts Co., 375 U.S. 405, 84 S. Ct. 457, 11 L. Ed. 2d 435 (1964):

We think the Court of Appeals was mistaken in concluding that the conferral of employee benefits while a representation election is pending, for the purpose of inducing employees to vote against the union, does not "interfere with" the protected right to organize.

. . . The danger inherent in well-timed increases in benefits is the suggestion of a fist inside the velvet glove. Employees are not likely to miss the inference that the source of benefits now conferred is also the source from which future benefits must flow and which may dry up if it is not obliged. The danger may be diminished if, as in this case, the benefits are conferred permanently and unconditionally. But the absence of conditions or threats pertaining to the particular benefits conferred would be of controlling significance only if it could be presumed that no question of additional benefits or renegotiation of existing benefits would arise in the future; and, of course, no such presumption is tenable.

. . . Other unlawful conduct may often be an indication of the motive behind a grant of benefits while an election is pending, and to that extent it is relevant to the legality of the grant; but when as here the motive is otherwise established, an employer is not free to violate § 8 (a) (1) by conferring benefits simply because it refrains from other, more obvious violations. We cannot agree with the Court of Appeals that enforcement of the Board's order will have the "ironic" result of "discouraging benefits for labor." 304 F.2d, at 376. The beneficence of an employer is likely to be ephemeral if prompted by a threat of unionization which is subsequently removed. Insulating the right of collective organization from calculated good will of this sort deprives employees of little that has lasting value.

In addition to the actual conferral or withdrawal of benefits, employer statements which contain promises of benefit or threats of reprisal constitute unlawful interference, restraint, and coercion. *See, e.g.,* City of Marysville, 1970 MERC Lab. Op. 458.

2. Employer Domination or Assistance of Employee Organizations

MICHIGAN NURSES ASSOCIATION
Michigan Employment Relations Commission
1972 MERC Lab. Op. 564

[The Charging Party, approximately 40 members of the Michigan Nurses Economic Security Organization (MNESO), alleged that the Michigan Nurses Association (MNA) was an illegally dominated labor organization under both the Michigan Labor Mediation Act (LMA) and the Michigan Public Employment Relations Act (PERA), primarily on the basis that most of its officers were supervisory employees of various employers. The Charging Party further alleged that the MNA, as an agent for various employers, illegally dominated MNESO. To remedy these alleged violations, the Charging Party requested, *inter alia,* that MNA be disestablished and enjoined from dominating MNESO and that MNA's labor negotiating staff be ordered to cease and desist from representing MNESO.]

. . . As the Charging Party presents the facts, the Michigan Nurses Association membership was divided in 1968 into those who were eligible to participate in a labor organization and those who were not. The rank and file members then formed MNESO and began to engage in collective bargaining, although allowing MNA to collect all dues. During the period within six months of the filing of the charge, the president of MNA was the director of nursing at a hospital. A vice president and executive board member was an assistant administrator of a health center. Another vice president was "in charge" of nursing education at a hospital. The treasurer of MNA was director of nursing at a nursing home. Another MNA board member was director of nursing at a hospital, and another was head nurse at a health center.

During the statutory period of limitations, the Charging Party alleges various acts of domination. These include the fact that the executive director of MNA exercised "administrative leadership over MNESO"; the executive director of MNESO reported to the MNA board of directors; the MNA director appointed professional labor negotiators who functioned for MNESO. The by-laws of MNA and MNESO provided that MNA would appoint three members to the executive board of MNESO and MNA would approve MNESO's budget. The MNA director terminated the employment of the MNESO director.

Based on the foregoing recited facts, the Charging Party argues that MNESO is a separate organization in its own right. The Charging Party argues that it is irrelevant that MNA acted illegally and assisted in the original separation or division of its membership so as to comply with Michigan labor law in the creation of MNESO. The Charging Party regards this as irrelevant because it occurred before the April 1, 1970 statute of limitations date. Charging Party argues, however, that the relationship described above constituted complete domination of MNESO by MNA. It is argued that although employers did not participate in MNESO, by the acts of the supervisors as agents, the employers effectively controlled and inhibited MNESO's operation as a labor organization. Charging Party contends that if MNESO had been allowed to elect its own officers, hire its own negotiators, and handle its own grievances with its own "philosophy," it could have been an appropriate non-dominated labor organization. The Charging Party urges that since Respondents have illegally dominated MNESO, an unfair labor practice has occurred, and the "fraternal relationship" which had existed for a period of time between MNA and MNESO has been irreparably damaged. Where MNA has secured collective bargaining agreements, Charging Party's brief holds then to have been "fraudulently" secured. . . .

In addition to those facts relied upon by the Charging Party in support of its theory, the facts are not substantially in dispute. . . .

The Michigan Nurses Association, an affiliate of the American Nurses Association, was founded in 1904 and incorporated in 1924. It admits to membership all graduate nurses licensed to practice nursing in the State of Michigan. It is essentially a professional organization including approximately 6,000 active members. It is open to all levels of the nursing profession. The members annually elect delegates who constitute the "house of delegates" at an annual convention. The house of delegates selects the officers and certain of the board of directors. The board of directors consists of the officers, six directors, and seven section chairmen. . . .

The officers are not full-time employees of MNA. MNA employs an executive director who is not an employee of any hospital employer. The organization was and is financed primarily from members' dues.

As early as 1946, MNA turned its attention to the economic interests of its members. The American Nurses Association instituted a program to deal with these needs and the state organizations followed suit. In approximately 1960, MNA formalized its program under the title of Economic Security Program (ESP) and began collective bargaining. In approximately 1967, MNA began to separate ESP from other activities. Appropriate steps were taken to draft by-laws and create a structure for an independently operating economic security program. MNA engaged a labor relations consulting firm to conduct collective bargaining and to assist in this program. An executive director was appointed for the program which was established by resolution of MNA as a separate division known as Michigan Nurses Employment Security Organization (MNESO) .

This division was to include all MNA members except nursing directors or administrators. The members elected their own officers and board of directors, although one-third of the directors were to be appointed by the MNA board.

The organizational meeting of the new division took place during the MNA annual convention in 1968. Only members of MNA could belong to MNESO and membership was automatic for all eligible members. Participation in the organizational and subsequent meetings and conventions was limited to eligible MNESO members. . . .

The record establishes that collective bargaining for members of the Michigan Nurses Association or those involved in MNESO takes place at the level of the local employing unit or the so-called "staff council." The staff council is the equivalent of the local bargaining unit. It is limited in its membership to the employees of a single employer. The general pattern followed is that within a given employer's establishment, hospital or other institutional setting, a staff council "Unit I" is made up of non-supervisory nurses. A staff council "Unit II" is made up of supervisory employees of the employer. In some situations, a third "Unit III" is set up to include teaching faculty in schools of nursing located within a hospital or other employing situation. The supervisory unit, of course, is found only in institutions within the sphere of public employment under the policy of the Commission permitting collective bargaining by public employee supervisors. These units do not include executive employees.

Where a supervisory and non-supervisory unit is found within the same employer institution, the two units do not bargain together. Only members of Unit I and Unit II may participate in negotiations for their respective units. The negotiating teams are selected by the members of the unit and unit officers elected from within the unit. Each unit or staff council may adopt by-laws. Only the members of the unit vote on ratification of a proposed contract. Some of them have their own dues structure.

The only part played by MNA in collective bargaining is the providing of professional labor relations staff. The unit may conduct its own bargaining without calling upon this staff. The record indicates that there were never more than one or two persons provided for this service, although it is not clear how many persons were involved when the MNA contracted for this service from an outside firm.

The officers of MNA do not play any part in the ordinary collective bargaining process or in any negotiating. There is no evidence that collective bargaining goals, technique, or content are the subject of any binding resolution or discussions at the general conventions of MNA. It should also be noted that, as to conventions, there is no evidence in the record of the ratio of voting delegates who are supervisory and non-supervisory or how the voting is handled.

It appears from the record that MNA is a certified bargaining agent in at least forty or more certifications issued by the Commission between the years 1967 and 1970. Most of these certifications run to the "Michigan Nurses Association." Some show the certified representative as "Michigan Nurses Economic Security Organization, a division of Michigan Nurses Association."

Discussion and Conclusions of Law

Nature of the Parties:

In approaching the analysis of the Charging Party's position, an anomaly in its theory immediately becomes obvious. Briefly stated, the theory of the Charging Party appears to be that MNA is a dominated labor organization and that MNA, as a dominated labor organization and an employer agent, has in turn dominated MNESO. The wrong complained of is the domination of MNESO by MNA. The remedies sought go to alleviate this alleged wrong.

The essence of the violations alleged is the domination of MNESO by MNA. Put another way, MNESO is portrayed as the dominated union. Nevertheless, the remedies sought by the Charging Party call for ending the domination of MNESO by MNA with no other remedy being mentioned. Merely to state this is to demonstrate the serious problem which Charging Party must face. If MNA has dominated MNESO, and MNESO is a dominated union, why should the remedy be limited to lifting this domination of MNESO. If indeed MNESO was dominated, it, too, may need to be disestablished as part of the remedy.

Following the logic of the Charging Party's theory, it would be possible for a union which was directly dominated and created by an employer to salvage itself and avoid the corrective actions of the law. Such a union might file a charge against the employer involved and argue that once the employer's domination is lifted, it, the charging union, is free of taint. But that is not the law. The dominated union may be deemed to be an unacceptable vehicle for future employee representation in collective bargaining.

If a charge had been filed by another party, an individual or another labor organization, naming MNESO as well as MNA as dominated unions, then clearly the remedy would extend to MNESO, as well as MNA.

By anticipating this action, and arguing as if it had itself filed the charge, MNESO may believe it has insulated itself against the remedial action which might otherwise be warranted. By casting itself in the role of the injured party, MNESO seeks to avoid the impact of a remedial order. However, as LMA and PERA are drawn, it is the protected activities of employees which are protected, not the interests of labor organizations as such. The evil in the existence of the dominated or assisted union is not that the union is harmed or hindered in some way. It is rather that a dominated union cannot be a proper means to properly express the collective bargaining needs of the employees.

Since this is the case, a remedy substituting the "secondarily" dominated union for the "primarily" dominated union would be a dubious means of protecting employee rights. Charging Party cannot achieve this dubious goal by pointing to MNA and shouting "unclean, unclean," while it, too, bears the scars of the same disease. . . .

There are situations in which a "cease and desist" order is appropriate without disestablishment of the labor organization. Livonia Schools, 1968 MERC Lab. Op. 202. This is generally found in the assistance-type violation. Here the employer can be ordered to cease assisting the labor organization when the labor organization is found to be subject to less than employer domination. The labor organization may be allowed to continue as an employer representative once the assistance has been ended. In the instant case, Charging Party has not alleged an assistance theory. None of the evidence would show assistance as the term is usually used. This is a domination situation. The Charging Party argues that it is irrelevant that MNESO was originally created by the actions of employer agents because this took place prior to the six-month statutory period of limitations. However, if that is the case, and Charging Party is saying, implicitly, that no domination can be shown during the statutory period, then no violation at all can be shown. If, on the other hand, domination of MNESO by MNA can be shown, then the remedy must apply to MNESO as well as to MNA. . . .

In applying case law to the matter at hand, it becomes clear that this is a multi-faceted situation. The presence of supervisors and non-supervisors in the same labor organization requires attention to possible domination, the status of the organization, and to policy regarding the protected activities of both non-supervisors and supervisors.

Decisions of the Commission as well as the federal board and courts have considered the nature of the dominated union. We do not deal here with the blatant "company union" cases in which employers deliberately created puppet "Blue Card Union" organizations to defeat the efforts of legitimate bargaining agents. See Ford Motor Co., 31 NLRB 994, 8 LRRM 173 (1941); Weirton Steel Co., 32 NLRB 1145, 8 LRRM 247 (1941). In the administration of the federal and our state acts the problem has arisen of the labor organization in which employees and supervisors jointly hold membership. These were organizations which employees voluntarily joined, although supervisory personnel also held membership or even constituted the majority of the members. These usually resulted from situations in which professional trade or craft interests led persons in the occupation to feel a mutuality of interest despite the existence of the division between the employer and the employed.

It is not necessary to extensively discuss the federal cases in the area, beyond a brief statement of representative decisions. In Nassau & Suffolk Contractors Ass'n, Inc., 118 NLRB 174, 40 LRRM 1146 (1957), the NLRB delineated the permissible participation of minor supervisors as union members.

In Anchorage Businessmen's Ass'n, 124 NLRB 662, 44 LRRM 1453 (1959), union members who were managerial level supervisors were found to have participated in union affairs in areas which could affect the administration of the union. This was held to be illegal assistance. The NLRB has distinguished between intraunion activity as opposed to participation in negotiations or adjustments of grievances by union member supervisors. See E. E. E. Co., Inc., 171 NLRB 982, 68 LRRM 1267 (1968).

As will be discussed below, the Commission followed certain leading federal cases. These are Local 636, Plumbers v. NLRB, 287 F. 2d 354, 47 LRRM 2457, (D.C. Cir. 1961) and Machinists v. NLRB, 311 US 72, 7 LRRM 282 (1940). The doctrine of the federal cases is well summarized in the following statement in NLRB v. Typographical Union, 452 F.2d 976, 78 LRRM 3063 (10th Cir. 1971):

"Our conclusions are: (1) there is no statutory right of a supervisor to participate actively in a journeymen's union; (2) whether the activities of supervisors are an impermissible interference must be determined on a case by case basis; (3) the Board is best able to judge if there is an interference, subtle or otherwise; (4) . . . there was interference with the free exercise of the employees' rights because of the nature of the supervisory positions and the participation by the supervisors in actions connected with the collective bargaining process; . . ."

Because of the nature of certain public employment situations, the Commisison has faced a number of such cases in public as well as private employment. Grand Rapids Schools, 1966 MERC Lab. Op. 282; Benton Harbor Bd. of Ed., 1966 MERC Lab. Op. 334; Livonia Schools, 1967 MERC Lab. Op. 780 and 1968 MERC Lab. Op. 202. . . .

The basic conclusions of these cases are that supervisors may be members of a labor organization but may not actively participate in the collective bargaining function.

An examination of these cases will show that the determining factor is the finding of circumstances that hinder the exercise of free collective bargaining by employees. One of the obvious examples of such circumstances is the holding of responsible union office by supervisors. Grand Rapids Schools, *supra;* Livonia Schools, *supra.* Their participation in the collective bargaining function of the union or membership in the unit has been found to conflict with the statutory purpose of affording untrammeled freedom to employees in the exercise of their statutory rights. The Commission has held that a labor organization in which an employer was president could not seek the benefits of this Commission's services. . . .

At the same time, the Commission has faced another facet of this larger issue. The Commission has found, with court approval, that public employee supervisory personnel are entitled to the protection of PERA. . . . The Commission has further held that such supervisory personnel may select bargaining agents who also represent rank and file employees, even of the same employer. . . . In such situations, it must be assumed that such supervisory personnel would exercise their rights as members of the labor organization even though not included in the same bargaining units with non-supervisory personnel.

The Commission has said that it would deal with such situations on a case by case basis as they are presented. . . .

Under LMA, of course, supervisors have no organizing rights so the context is comparable to the federal act. Examination of these lines of cases reveals that the prohibited contact between an employer and a union, relevant herein, involves membership of supervisors in the bargaining unit or their participation in the bargaining process.

By these criteria, our record takes on a different hue. From the time of the adoption of the collective bargaining process within the framework of MNA, separate bargaining units were created for rank and file employees and supervisory employees. It is not contended by Charging Party that any of the bargaining units were or are tainted by the admixture of supervisors to non-supervisory units. It was also uncontradicted that negotiating committees are chosen only from the membership of the unit, ratification of contracts is solely within the discretion of the voting membership of the unit. There is little if anything in the record showing any part played by supervisory personnel in the collective bargaining process in a non-supervisory unit. There is no evidence that any collective bargaining issues or policies were set by the board of directors of MNA or, for that matter, of MNESO. There is no evidence that the members of the MNESO board appointed by MNA were supervisors. It appears, further, that this particular practice was changed.

Although none of the parties discuss this question, it would seem entirely within the law for a supervisory unit in the organization to seek the help of professional negotiators hired by the organization. Implicit in the [Commission's decisions allowing supervisory personnel to select a bargaining agent that also represents non-supervisory employees] is the assumption that there would be some sharing of facilities within the labor organization although supervisory employees and non-supervisory would be segregated in separate bargaining units. There is no evidence in the record as to whether the professional staff engaged by MNA ever took part in actual bargaining on behalf of the non-supervisory units, and if so, what part they did take. One may assume that some part of their time must have been involved in collective bargaining involving non-supervisors, but no actual evidence is presented. Query: If both types of units will use the services of the staff, shouldn't all have a voice in selecting the staff?

What we find, then, is that MNA, originally including in its membership supervisory and non-supervisory personnel, when faced with the phenomenon of collective bargaining attempted to restructure itself so as to permit collective bargaining to be carried out on behalf of its members in a manner constant with the applicable statutes without, at the same time, rupturing the organization as originally formed for the overall professional benefit of its members. Other jurisdictions have dealt with this problem. . . . [I]n International Paper Co., 172 NLRB 933, 68 LRRM 1360 (1968), the NLRB certified the Alabama Nurses Association as collective bargaining agent for a unit of nurses after disposing of contentions that it could not be certified because supervisors were members and officers in the organization.

The board noted that, "Although petitioner does have supervisors as members and supervisors serve on the board of directors, the record indicates substantial participation by the employee members in the affairs of petitioner, and that no employer supervisors or employees are presently serving on the board of directors. Further . . . goals in negotiations involving the unit herein would be determined and pursued solely by members of the unit." The Board went on to find that the petitioner was a labor organization under Section 2 (5) of the Act. This case, it must be noted, is a representation case in which the NLRB would not consider unfair labor practice allegations. Nevertheless, the criteria cited serve to emphasize that domination must be proven in each case and is not to be assumed.

In a detailed decision, the New Jersey Superior Court has also considered the relationship between a state affiliate of the nurses association. In Bowman v. Hackensack Hospital Ass'n, 78 LRRM 3103 (1971), the New Jersey Superior Court, Chancery Division, considered both the labor organization status and alleged domination of an economic security program created by a state nurses association, comparable, if not identical with, the instant fact situation. The court there found that the organization was a labor organization and that the economic security program or organization was sufficiently insulated from the overall organization to avoid domination. The court found facts quite similar to the instant record as to the internal relationship and control over the economic security program exercised by the overall state organization. The determinative factor was that the collective bargaining units of non-supervisory employees acted completely independent in terms of setting collective bargaining goals and engaging in collective bargaining.

Although the undersigned concludes that no violation has been shown as a matter of law, it appears appropriate to examine whether any policy considerations are implicit in the Commission's decisions which would conflict with or support this conclusion.

. . . The fact that supervisors under PERA belong to the same organization as supervisors under LMA may raise a question. Will rights of public employee supervisors be curtailed if they join an organization which includes non-supervisors or supervisors under LMA? No such limitation is expressed, nor is it even implied, in the Commission's decisions granting the right to supervisors to belong to the same organizations as non-supervisory employees. Therefore, it may be concluded that the overall organization will be subject to standards applicable under PERA, if, in fact, they may differ from those applying under LMA. Upon closer analysis, however, it does not appear that there is any difference in regards to finding domination. The language of the unfair labor practice sections of the two statutes are identical, although LMA includes the additional "company union" provision. Thus, although supervisory employees under PERA may belong to the same organization, it should not be understood that the Commission intended to grant them any further latitude than would be accorded private sector supervisors who might belong to a labor organization. It was not the intention of *Hillsdale* [See chapter III, p. 266], and its progeny, to vitiate the prohibition against domination or assistance.

However, in evaluating practices of the organization, there are policy implications. The supervisory employees have a right to participate fully in the overall labor organization which they have chosen to belong to.

To hold otherwise would mean that they have something less than fully protected rights under the Act. No limitation was placed upon them as, for example, on guards, under Section 9 (b) of the NLRA, who may not belong to a labor organization which is affiliated directly or indirectly with an organization which admits to membership employees other than guards.

If supervisors can participate as members in the "umbrella" labor organization which has separate supervisory and non-supervisory units, there appears to be no impediment to such an employee eventually finding a place in the leadership of the umbrella organization. This eventuality is not limited to the nursing profession. Cf. Battle Creek Police Dept., Case No. C70 K-201, Trial Examiner's Decision, April 8, 1971. The Commission has issued certifications in supervisory units to labor organizations which include and primarily represent non-supervisory employees. It appears that in any such case the relationship between the umbrella organization and the non-supervisory units must be recognized as requiring careful self-policing. The Commission may face situations as extreme as that which the federal court described in the Mates & Masters v. NLRB, 321 F.2d 376, 53 LRRM 2585 (D.C. Cir. 1963), in which the ordinary seamen chose to belong to a labor organization which was almost entirely composed of supervisory personnel. The Michigan Supreme Court has recognized that suitable internal structuring can be devised to meet this contingency. See Sweet v. Local 552, Barbers, 365 Mich. 79, 112 N.W.2d 218 (1961)....

Shortly after the passage of PERA, the Commission dealt with cases in which it had to apply the law under PERA to pre-existing fact situations which clearly raised questions of unfair labor practices. Grand Rapids Schools, *supra;* Benton Harbor Bd. of Ed., *supra.* In several of those cases, the Commission found it appropriate to defer application of the statute to organizations which were in the process of reorganizing and restructuring themselves to meet the demand of the law. There may be provisions of the MNA-MNESO by-laws and the internal relationship which could lead to assistance or domination even though the total relationship, as found herein, is not an impermissible one. The record shows that MNA and MNESO have been engaged since the creation of MNESO in further defining the identity of each by amendments to the respective by-laws and other internal procedures. The most recent amendments to the by-laws, shown on this record, reflect an attempt to avoid ambiguities and clarify provisions which raised questions of domination or assistance. Even as amended, certain of the provisions may be subject to questioning. As applied in practice, according to the evidence in this record, none of those provisions have been shown to create an actual violation. Nevertheless, careful attention to them is warranted to avoid leading to practices that would violate the integrity of the bargaining effort.

It is to be expected that there will be variations depending on the nature of the trade or occupation involved and even the size of the organization involved. Where the organization is very small, the number of persons available to hold the various offices and act on the various committees may be so few as to necessarily lead to supervisors playing too great a role in the functioning of the individual bargaining units. In the instant case, individual bargaining units function in collective bargaining with very little contact with the overall governing body of the statewide organization.

We may conclude that organizations with a mixed membership complement will need to constantly police their internal practices and organizational principles to avoid violations of the law.

At the same time such organizations may seek means to accord full membership to members of supervisory and nonsupervisory units, as long as these means do not impinge on the collective bargaining rights of the members. . . .

NOTE

Where it is found that an employer has illegally assisted or dominated a labor organization, what is the appropriate remedy? Because of the wide range of acts that might be found to constitute illegal assistance or domination, the NLRB under the National Labor Relations Act determines the remedy on a case by case basis. Where it is found that the employer's conduct constitutes illegal domination of the union, the NLRB orders disestablishment of the union and permanently prohibits the employer from recognizing the union. This remedy is considered necessary by the Board "in order effectively to remove the consequences of an employer's unfair labor practices and to make possible a free choice of representatives. . . ." Carpenter Steel

Co., 76 N.L.R.B. 670 (1948). On the other hand, ". . . when the Board finds that an employer's unfair labor practices were limited to interference and support and never reached the point of domination, . . . [it] order[s] that recognition be withheld until certification. . . ." *Ibid.*

3. Employer Discrimination

MUSKEGO-NORWAY CONSOLIDATED SCHOOLS v. WERB

Wisconsin Supreme Court
35 Wis. 2d 540, 151 N.W.2d 617 (1967)

. . . In 1960 the Muskego-Norway Education Association (MNEA), an organization composed of practically 100 percent of all teaching and administrative personnel in the employ of the school district, was organized. The MNEA is affiliated with the Wisconsin Education Association (WEA), which renders assistance to local affiliates in regard to their representation of teachers in conferences and negotiations concerning salaries and other conditions of employment.

This controversy concerns certain activities in the school district during the period from 1960 through early 1964. On the one hand is a group of teachers employed by the district who in May, 1964, complained of violations of sec. 111.70, Stats., on the part of the school board and certain of its supervisory personnel. These teachers alleged that the school district coerced the teachers into joining the WEA, MNEA, or the Wisconsin Federation of Teachers Union by threatening to enforce a rule providing that wages would be deducted from the salary of any teacher taking off the two days of the annual teachers' convention who was not a member of any convening labor organization, and discouraged labor activity on the part of the teachers by its failure to renew the teaching contract of Carston C. Koeller because of his labor activities on behalf of the MNEA.

On the other hand are the school district; Robert J. Kreuser, superintendent of schools; Jack C. Refling, high school principal; Paul J. Ussel, assistant principal; and Charles A. Ladd, coordinator of instruction.

Certain facts in this involved dispute are uncontroverted and best be set forth here. Other pertinent facts, some controverted, are detailed in the opinion. . . .

Carston Koeller, a first-year teacher in the district, was elected chairman of a reorganized and enlarged MNEA welfare committee for the 1963-1964 year. (He remained chairman at all times pertinent herein.) In September of 1963 the committee began operations by requesting salary information from Superintendent Kreuser. When this information was not forthcoming, the committee obtained it by circulating questionnaires to the teachers. The MNEA also began sending representatives to board meetings. Largely through Koeller's efforts, this information was tabulated prior to mid-January, 1964, and proposals for the year 1964-1965 were formulated. The committee worked hard and held as many as 26 meetings. Its proposals, which were very comprehensive and were approved by the MNEA membership, were presented to the personnel committee of the school board. The proposals dealt with matters of teacher salaries, insurance, personal and sabbatical leaves, class size and load, job security, teacher qualifications, and other matters supporting said proposals including various tables and graphs.

The personnel committee took these proposals under advisement. The personnel committee met again with MNEA representatives and questioned the accuracy of these proposals and whether they represented the wishes of a majority of the teachers. Further questionnaires were circulated and modified proposals were submitted (as approved by the MNEA membership). The report and proposals were submitted to the board meeting on March 2, 1964. What transpired at that meeting and subsequently will be described later in the statement of facts.

Paralleling in importance the development of the MNEA as an effective representative of the teachers are the activities of the chairman of its welfare committee, Carston Koeller, both educational and as a leader in the MNEA. Mr. Koeller was hired by the school district in 1962 following three years of teaching experience in the air force and one year at Belleville, Wisconsin. Mr. Koeller taught five classes of general mathematics, a subject taken by students deficient in mathematics and incapable of comprehending algebra. These students were also slower learners in other subjects as well. In 1963, at the end of Koeller's first year of teaching, a report was filed by the then principal, Donald Helstad, listing him in the bottom quarter of the faculty in teaching ability, although this did not necessarily mean he was a poor teacher. Helstad advised that Koeller had shown as much progress as any other high school teacher at the time and Helstad unqualifiedly recommended that Koeller be rehired for the year 1963-1964. Koeller was retained. Subsequently, Koeller engaged in a number of activities related to his duties as a teacher rather than to his extracurricular duties with the MNEA.

1. On October 2, 1963, Koeller mailed to six parents a statement asking them to sign a request to give Mr. Koeller permis-

sion to use whatever physical means was necessary in order to enforce discipline. On October 7th the new principal, Refling, held a conference with Koeller informing him he was not to determine a course of discipline contrary to established school procedures. At this conference, Koeller's difficulty in handling students in study hall was also discussed. (Koeller had placed a female student in a large unlighted closet as a disciplinary procedure.)

2. On October 14th Koeller suggested in writing to a committee of teachers established to create procedures for disciplining study halls that enforcement of discipline could be implemented by "tweak or pull an ear, rap on head, pull hunk of hair or sit in front closet with door shut."

3. In the fall of 1963, football players were excused from their seventh-hour classes on the day of the game. On October 22d Koeller sent a note to Principal Refling, objecting to this practice. Koeller was then called into a conference with Ussel and Refling, in which conference Koeller's disagreement with school policies and his lack of judgment in handling student situations were discussed. Koeller then appealed by letter directly to Mr. Guhr (school board president) but was told to go through the normal grievance procedures. No further action was taken on this matter except that on October 28th Refling sent Koeller a letter warning him about insubordination.

4. On December 2, 1963, following a visit to Koeller's classroom, coordinator of instruction Ladd made the following comments and suggestions for improving inadequacies in Koeller's teaching techniques: (a) More student "involvement," (b) "less teacher talk," (c) the elicitation of "clear, confident responses" from students, (d) personal supervision of assignments, (e) various approaches to various students, and (f) permitting students to make their own evaluations. Koeller visited an experienced mathematics teacher from a Racine school and his class, and thereafter Ladd noticed that Koeller's teaching techniques improved.

5. On December 10, 1963, as a layman, Koeller wrote the state department of public instruction, concerning state aids formulas and the financial condition of the Muskego-Norway district. In this letter Koeller complained of inadequate facilities in the district.

6. On January 28, 1964, Koeller scheduled a meeting of the National Honor Society which conflicted with the meeting of the high school P. T. A. Koeller was given oral confirmation from Ussel but school policy required a written approval. A

memo from the principal chastized Koeller for failing to obtain the approval of the principal, and Koeller circulated the memo.

7. On February 5, 1964, Koeller sent a student to the office with a note indicating he had suspended the student for three days. Koeller was told that the administration decided whether suspensions were in order. Koeller then publicly challenged the position of the administration in the MNEA newsletter, quoting from the private memo he had received from the administration. In the newsletter, Koeller maintained he had the right to suspend students for disciplinary reasons. Koeller was called into conference with the principal, where he was advised he was skating on "thin ice" in utilizing the MNEA newsletter to vent a private grievance.

8. On February 18th Koeller read the memo received in regard to the scheduling problem to the National Honor Society students and announced that this was the reason for resigning as adviser from the group. Koeller then sent Kreuser a note explaining his reasons for resigning and charging that Kreuser had exhibited vindictiveness toward him. Koeller subsequently withdrew this statement.

9. Koeller's record as a teacher includes having 43 disciplinary referrals to Principal Refling, while the 49 other teachers on the faculty had a total of 150 disciplinary referrals.

There is a dispute about what transpired at the March 2, 1964, meeting of the board. In addition to the salary-and-working-conditions proposals of the MNEA during executive session the board also considered whether to rehire Koeller. Kreuser denied that he made any recommendations at that session against renewing Koeller's contract. He denied that the subject was even discussed. Yet board member Vogel recalled that Kreuser had advised him on March 3d that Kreuser had made this recommendation at the meeting the previous night. Between March 2 and March 9, 1964, a summary of Koeller's activities was prepared and, upon the recommendation of Kreuser, at another executive session on March 9, 1964, the school board formally determined not to offer Koeller a teacher's contract for 1964-1965. On March 11, 1964, conditions of employment were again announced at a general teachers' meeting. No prior notice of action taken on its proposals was received by the MNEA.

On March 12, 1964, Koeller was called to Kreuser's office and given a notice that his contract would not be renewed. Kreuser read from a sheet of paper a number of reasons for the dismissal, but he did not give Koeller a copy of the list of the reasons even though Koeller requested one. Kreuser also advised Koeller that a successful contest of the discharge was unlikely, because all statutory requirements had been met. Further, Kreuser advised Koeller that such an appeal would be professional suicide because Koeller needed Kreuser's signature to obtain a life-time teaching certificate.

A dispute exists as to whether or not Kreuser first offered to give Koeller a recommendation for another job if Koeller would resign. Koeller's testimony indicates this is true while the testimony of Kreuser and Refling is that Koeller was only offered the opportunity to resign. Nonetheless, Koeller refused to resign and was then handed a prepared notice of termination, the letter stating that the action was "deemed advisable in view of actions and conduct on your part which have previously been discussed with you."

After a full hearing on the complaints, the WERB found:

"29. That the primary motivation of Kreuser's recommendation to the School Board not to renew Koeller's teaching contract for the 1964-1965 school year was not based on any shortcomings Koeller may have had as a teacher, nor upon his differences with certain policies with the School Board, but rather upon Koeller's activity and efforts on behalf of the MNEA Welfare Committee as the collective bargaining representative of the majority of the professional teaching personnel in the employ of the School District; that the discriminatory refusal of the School Board to renew Koeller's teaching contract and the recommendations with respect thereto made by Superintendent Kreuser and other supervisory employes of the School District, interfered, restrained and coerced not only Koeller, but also the remaining teachers in the employ of the School District in the exercise of their right to engage in lawful concerted activities."

And it reached the following conclusion of law:

"2. That Muskego-Norway Consolidated Schools Joint School District No. 9, Town of Muskego, Waukesha County, and Town of Norway, Racine County, by its School Board, by refusing and failing to renew Carston C. Koeller's teaching contract for the year 1964-1965 upon the recommendation of Kreuser, Refling, Ussel and Ladd, discriminated against him in regard to the conditions of his employment, for the purpose of discouraging membership in and activities on behalf of the Muskego-Norway Education Association and, thereby, has committed, and is committing, prohibited practices, within the meaning of Section 111.70 (3) (a) 1 and 2 of the Wisconsin Statutes."

As to the allegation that the school board and supervisory personnel had interfered with the freedom of the teachers to join or not join employee organizations, the following appeared in a statement of school policy in a manual for teachers:

"It is expected that when school is closed for the purpose of attending professional meetings, teachers shall be in attendance at such meetings."

The WEA convention was planned for November 7 and 8, 1963. The Wisconsin Federation of Teachers also met on this date. In a November, 1963, memorandum from Kreuser to the administrators of the district it was stated:

"That as a matter of professional ethics no teacher that is not a member of the groups holding convention at this time can really expect time off with pay during these days."

This policy was implemented on the faculty of Muskego-Norway by Refling, who issued a memo (also on November 1, 1963) stating:

"We are making plans for everyone to attend next week's teachers convention. This brings up a matter of professional ethics that might be called to your attention at this time. That anyone *not* a member of either of the convening groups can hardly expect time off with pay."

Refling told one teacher that this meant he would have to join a teachers' organization in order to get paid.

As a conclusion of law on this matter, the WERB declared:

"1. That the Muskego-Norway Consolidated Schools Joint School District No. 9, Town of Muskego, Waukesha County and Town of Norway, Racine County, by its agents Robert J. Kreuser and Jack G. Refling, by threatening its teachers with the forfeiture of two days pay, if they failed to attend teachers' conventions and failed to retain membership in the sponsoring organization, interfered with, coerced, and restrained teachers in its employ in the exercise of their right to freely affiliate with, or decline to affiliate with, any employee organization, and, thereby, has committed, and is committing, prohibited practices within the meaning of Section 111.70 (3) (a) 1 of the Wisconsin Statutes."

The WERB ordered the school district and individual supervisory personnel to cease and desist from similar activities, to offer Koeller his former position without prejudice, to pay Koeller any damages he may have suffered and to post a notice to all teachers notifying them of the actions taken and future policy to be followed by the district.

A petition for review of the WERB's order was filed under ch. 227, Stats. Thereafter, judgment was entered setting aside the order of the WERB. On the merits the trial court found that the finding of the WERB that the school board's primary motivation for firing Koeller was his labor activities was based on speculation and conjecture. As to the teachers' convention issue, the trial court also set aside the WERB order, declaring that state law requires schools to be closed and authorizes teachers' time off with pay only if they attend the conventions. Further, the trial court ruled that there had been no proof of any relationship between the school board and the administrators. The WERB has appealed.

WILKIE, J. Four issues are raised on this appeal:

First, is the authority of school boards under secs. 40.40 and 40.41, Stats., subject to the limitations of sec. 111.70?

Second, is the WERB finding that respondents interfered with, coerced and restrained teachers in its employ in the exercise of their right to freely decline to affiliate with employee organizations supported by substantial evidence?

Third, is the WERB finding that the refusal of respondents to renew Koeller's contract was prompted by his labor activities supported by substantial evidence?

Fourth, must the WERB make an express finding that Kreuser, Refling, Ladd and Ussel were agents of the Muskego-Norway school board in order to impute their actions to the board in deciding whether unfair labor practices were committed?

Relation of Secs. 40.40, 40.41 and 40.45 and Sec. 111.70, Stats.

One of the principal premises for the trial court's decision was that secs. 40.40 and 40.41, Stats., require the school board to contract individually with each teacher each year. The trial court also approved the school board's policy of offering its teachers the choice of attending conventions or losing two days' pay. This policy, according to the trial court, merely complied with sec. 40.40 (3), which provides:

> "The board *may* give to any teacher, without deduction from her wages, the whole or part of any time spent by her in attending a teacher's institute held in the county, or a school board convention or the meeting of any teach-

ers' association, upon such teacher's filing with the school clerk a certificate of regular attendance at such institute, convention or association, signed by the person conducting the institute or convention, or by the secretary of the association." (Emphasis added.)

The WERB found that by threatening its teachers with the forfeiture of two days' pay if they failed to attend teachers' conventions, the school district interfered with the teacher's rights guaranteed by sec. 111.70 (2), Stats., to freely affiliate with or decline to affiliate with any employee organization.[3]

The provisions of sec. 111.70, Stats., apply to the authority of school districts to the same extent as the authority of other municipal governing bodies. Sec. 111.70 was enacted after secs. 40.40 and 40.41 and is presumed to have been enacted with a full knowledge of preexisting statutes. Construction of statutes should be done in a way which harmonizes the whole system of law of which they are a part, and any conflict should be reconciled if possible.

Sec. 40.40 (3), Stats., provides that a school board may give to a teacher without deducting from her wages the whole or any part of time spent in attending a teachers' convention upon filing with the clerk a certificate showing such attendance. Sec. 40.45 provides that days on which state and county teachers' conventions are held are considered to be school days. Under sec. 111.70 (2) teachers have the right to refrain from affiliating with labor organizations and forcing teachers to join employee organizations is expressly forbidden by sec. 111.70 (3) (a) 1. These statutes are not necessarily in conflict. They can all be given effect by construing them together and ruling that teachers cannot be required to attend such conventions under threat of loss of pay, but that teachers who do not attend such conventions can be required to work for the school. In this way teachers can avoid deductions from their salaries while the right to refuse to join a labor organization guaranteed by sec. 111.70 (2) is preserved. If the teacher refuses to work, deductions from his salary could be made, but if the school does not offer work to teachers not attending conventions, the school cannot deny pay to such teachers.

---

[3] "111.70 (2) RIGHTS OF MUNICIPAL EMPLOYES. Municipal employes shall have the right of self-organization, to affiliate with labor organizations of their own choosing and the right to be represented by labor organizations of their own choice in conferences and negotiations with their municipal employers or their representatives on questions of wages, hours and conditions of employment, and such employes shall have the right to refrain from any and all such activities."

Respondents also contend that secs. 40.40 and 40.41, Stats., permit the school board to refuse to rehire on any ground or for no reason at all. Assuming this to be true, secs. 40.40 and 40.41 can be modified by subsequent statutes which forbid refusing to rehire a teacher for a particular reason. For example, a school board may not refuse to rehire a teacher because of his race, nationality or political or religious affiliations. Modification of statutes is a question of legislative policy. In 1959 the legislature enacted sec. 111.70 (3) (a), which prohibits municipal employers, including school districts, from:

"1. Interfering with, restraining or coercing any municipal employe in the exercise of the rights provided in sub. (2).
"2. Encouraging or discouraging membership in any labor organization, employe agency, committee, association or representation plan by discrimination in regard to hiring, tenure or other terms or conditions of employment."

This also restricts the reasons a teacher can be refused reemployment. A school board may not terminate a teacher's contract because the teacher has been engaging in labor activities.

Scope of Judicial Review

The second and third issues concern whether crucial findings of the WERB are supported by credible evidence. This makes it necessary to state the standard of judicial review of the findings of the WERB. It is well established that under sec. 227.20 (1) (d), Stats., judicial review of the WERB findings is to determine whether or not the questioned finding is supported "by substantial evidence in view of the entire record." This court has held that the key to the application of this standard is to determine what is meant by "substantial evidence."[10]

In *Copland* this court quoted from an article by E. Blythe Stason[11] as follows:

" '[T]he term "substantial evidence" should be construed to confer finality upon an administrative decision on the facts when, upon an examination of the entire record, the evidence, including the inferences therefrom, is found to be such that a reasonable man, acting reasonably, *might* have reached the decision; but, on the other hand, if a reasonable man, acting reasonably, *could not* have reached the

[10] Copland v. Department of Taxation (1962), 16 Wis. (2d) 543, 554, 114 N.W. (2d) 858.

[11] "Substantial Evidence" in Administrative Law, 89 University of Pennsylvania Law Review (1941), 1026, 1038.

decision from the evidence and its inferences then the decision is not supported by substantial evidence and it should be set aside.' "

Moreover, in *Copland* we reiterated that " 'substantial evidence' is 'such relevant evidence as a *reasonable mind* might accept as adequate to support a conclusion.' (Emphasis supplied.) "[13] In *Copland* we declared that the test of reasonableness "is implicit in the statutory words 'substantial evidence.',", and that the "[u]se of the statutory words 'in view of the entire record as submitted' strongly suggests that the test of reasonableness is to be applied to the evidence as a whole, not merely to that part which tends to support the agency's findings."

Interference with Right to Affiliate with Employee Organizations

In the instant case the evidence supports the WERB's finding and related conclusion that the respondents interfered with, coerced, and restrained teachers in the exercise of their right to freely affiliate with or decline to affiliate with any employee organization. The school district's policy expressed in the teacher's manual strongly implied that teachers were required to join the WEA. Memos circulated by Superintendent Kreuser and Principal Refling indicated that time off with pay would be granted only to teachers who were members of the convening groups (the WEA or the Federation of Teachers). The minutes of an executive committee contain the following statement:

"It was brought to the attention of the executive committee by the membership committee that some of our professional staff are not joining the WEA. Mr. Ussel stated that he had talked to the district office and said that wages will be deducted for anyone not attending the WEA Convention."

One of the complainants stated to Principal Refling, "It appears I have the choice of paying the seven bucks or losing two days pay," to which Refling replied, "That's about the size of it."

All these statements and actions indicate a policy of coercing teachers into joining the WEA (or its competitor organization) by threatening them with the loss of pay for failing to join. The

---

[13] Copland v. Department of Taxation, *supra*, footnote 10, at page 554, quoting from Gateway City Transfer Co. v. Public Service Comm. (1948), 253 Wis. 397, 405, 406, 34 N.W. (2d) 238; and Consolidated Edison Co. v. National Labor Relations Board (1938), 305 U.S. 197, 59 Sup. Ct. 206, 83 L. Ed. 126.

WERB found that the WEA was an employee organization and, although this finding was not challenged, it is supported by the evidence. Coercing teachers to join an employee organization is a prohibited practice of sec. 111.70 (3) (a) 1, Stats. The WERB's order to the respondents to cease and desist from this action is valid.

Termination of Employment for Labor Activities

The WERB found that the primary motivation for the refusal of the school board to renew Koeller's contract was because of his activities and efforts on behalf of the MNEA welfare committee. The WERB concluded that the school board discriminated against Koeller in regard to the conditions of his employment for the purpose of discouraging membership in and activities on behalf of the MNEA and was thereby committing a prohibited practice under sec. 111.70 (3) (a) , Stats.

A major premise in the trial court's argument for reversing the WERB's determination in this respect is that if a valid reason for discharging an employee exists, this is a sufficient basis for holding that the employee was not dismissed for union activities. The trial court quotes *Wisconsin Labor Relations Board v. Fred Rueping Leather Co.* as follows:

". . . When a valid reason as heretofore defined is found to be present, it is relatively difficult and may be impossible to more than guess which reason motivated the discharge. The board could find discrimination here only by finding that the assigned reason for the discharge of Assaf was false because if it was not the evidence is in such state that a finding of discrimination would be pure conjecture. Furthermore, we have some misgivings whether, if a valid and sufficient reason for discharge exists, the real or motivating reason has any materiality whatever, unless it can be shown that in other cases where similar grounds for discharge of nonunion men existed, no such action was taken."[16]

In other words, if there was good reason for terminating Koeller's employment because of teaching deficiencies and his differences of teaching philosophy with the school board and the supervisory personnel, it would not matter whether the contract was not renewed for his labor activities. But this is not the law. In *Rueping* there was no speculation as to what the real reason for the discharge was. Moreover, the law concerning discharge for labor activities has changed since 1938. In N.L.R.B.

---

[16] (1938), 228 Wis. 473, 499, 279 N.W. 673, 684.

v. Great Eastern Color Lithographic Corp.[17] the federal courts
[sic] stated:

> "The issue before us is not, of course, whether or not
> there existed grounds for discharge of these employees apart
> from their union activities. *The fact that the employer had
> ample reason for discharging them is of no moment. It was
> free to discharge them for any reason good or bad, so long
> as it did not discharge them for their union activity.* And
> even though the discharges may have been based upon
> other reasons as well, if the employer were partly motivated
> by union activity, the discharges were violative of the Act."
> (Emphasis added.)

Several other federal cases are in accord. Although these cases
all involve a construction of unfair labor practices under the
Wagner Act, the case of *St. Joseph's Hospital v. Wisconsin Employment Relations Board* adopts their legal conclusion that an
employee may not be fired when one of the motivating factors
is his union activities, no matter how many other valid reasons exist for firing him.

The trial court opined that the WERB reached finding of
fact No. 29 "purely upon conjecture." It concluded that there
was ample reason for the school board's actions for Koeller's
deficiencies as a teacher and his philosophical differences with
the individual respondents on school matters.

But in this court's judicial review we are not required to
agree in every detail with the WERB as to its findings, conclusions and order. We must affirm its findings if they are supported
by substantial evidence in view of the entire record. Sec. 227.20
(2), Stats., requires that upon such review due weight shall be
accorded the experience, technical competence, and specialized
knowledge of the agency involved. In short, this means the court
must make some deference to the expertise of the agency.

In *St. Joseph's Hospital v. Wisconsin Employment Relations
Board* the WERB found that the discharge of an employee was
primarily because of her union activities. The court discussed
the scope of review of this finding as follows:

> "Finding 20 is a finding of ultimate fact and is of necessity
> based upon inferences from other testimony before the
> board. Such inferences may not be based upon conjecture
> but must be drawn from established facts which logically
> support them. The drawing of inferences from other facts
> in the record is a function of the board and the weight to be

---

[17] (2d Cir. 1962), 309 F.2d 352, 355.

given to those facts is for the board to determine. International Union v. Wisconsin E.R. Board, 258 Wis. 481, 46 N.W. (2d) 185. Such findings, when made, cannot be disturbed by a court unless they are unsupported by substantial evidence in view of the entire record submitted."

The board is the judge of the credibility of the witnesses and the reviewing court is not to substitute its judgment for the judgment of the board.

In essence, in the instant case we must decide whether the WERB's crucial findings, conclusions and order are based on inferences reasonably drawn on the entire record or whether they are the result of conjecture on the part of the WERB.

On the whole record we conclude that WERB's finding No. 29 is supported by substantial evidence and reasonable inferences drawn therefrom in view of the entire record, that the failure to renew Koeller's teaching contract was motivated by his activities as chairman of the welfare committee of MNEA and not on any shortcomings Koeller may have had as a teacher nor upon his differences with certain policies of the school board and the respondent supervisory personnel.

The WERB's finding No. 29 is the logical final determination as to the motivation behind the failure to renew Koeller's contract following the stepped-up labor activities of the welfare committee in which Koeller had such a major part and the difficulties [he] had in assembling and presenting proposals on salaries and working conditions to Kreuser and the school board.

The WERB placed heavy emphasis on the timing and manner of the dismissal. Although there was dispute about it the WERB could reasonably find that the first recommendation of Koeller's nonrenewal was made at the executive session of the school board on March 2, 1964, immediately following the very meeting when the MNEA proposals for 1964-1965 were submitted to the school board for the first time and were discussed; that at that time no written reasons were given for the dismissal; that on March 9, 1964, a summary of reasons having been prepared since March 2d, the school board acted formally to terminate Koeller's services; that Koeller was not notified of this action until March 12, 1964, the day after the school teachers were called together and told of the school board's determinations about salaries and working conditions for the year 1964-1965 (there having been no negotiations about the MNEA proposals).

In a memorandum accompanying its findings of fact, conclusions of law and order the WERB discussed its reasons for con-

cluding that the respondents were motivated by Koeller's labor
activities in ending his employment. The WERB also thoroughly discussed and rejected the other reasons that were alleged to
have motivated the respondents relating to the shortcomings of
Koeller as a teacher and his disagreement with certain policies
established by the school board.

The WERB carefully considered each one of the reasons compiled in the summary prepared by supervisory personnel prior
to the school board's final action on March 9th as to why
Koeller's contract should not be renewed. The WERB's analysis
is summed up as follows:

"It seems incredible to us that the Superintendent could
be sincere in the gravity of complaints made against Koeller
and at the same time offer to recommend him to another
position. We believe this to be a gross act of intimidation."

The WERB concluded:

". . . in light of the entire record, we do not find that
Koeller's competence as a teacher or disciplinarian motivated the determination not to extend his teaching contract.

"We have therefore concluded that the Respondent School
District refused Koeller a contract in order to discourage
membership and collective bargaining activities on behalf
of the Welfare Committee of the MNEA."

In any event, it may be assumed arguendo that the school
board would have been warranted in terminating Koeller's services on these grounds if the motivation for the action were not
connected with his labor activities. Yet the WERB could reasonably find, as it did, that the motivation for failing to renew
Koeller's contract was his activities in the MNEA and on
behalf of his fellow teachers' welfare.

Agency

The WERB specifically found that Kreuser, Refling, Ussel,
and Ladd were supervisory personnel in the employ of the
Muskego-Norway school district. The WERB considered the
actions of these supervisory personnel in determining whether
unfair labor practices had been committed by the school board
and the school district. The trial court ruled that there was
nothing in the findings of the WERB or in the evidence to
establish that these supervisory personnel were agents of the
Muskego-Norway school board. Therefore, ruled the trial court,
actions of the supervisory personnel could not be attributed
to the board in determining whether unfair labor practices had

been committed, and only actions by school board members could be considered.

The trial court's ruling places form over substance. Where the WERB expressly found that Kreuser, Refling, Ussel, and Ladd were "supervisory personnel in the employ of said School District," such employment is sufficient to constitute an agency relationship. The employment policies of the school district are implemented through the actions of the supervisory personnel. Under the trial court's ruling, the school board could tacitly engage in unfair labor practices through actions by the supervisory personnel, and the employees discriminated against would have no effective recourse. Such a technical interpretation—as made by the trial court—of the findings of the WERB deprives sec. 111.70 (3) , Stats., of any real substance.

By the Court.—Judgment reversed.

HANSEN, J., took no part.

[The dissenting opinion of BEILFUSS, J., is omitted.]

NOTES

1. In City of New Berlin, WERC Decision No. 7293 (1966) , the Wisconsin Employment Relations Commission in holding that an employee's termination was not motivated because of union activities, stated:

> The most that Complainant can assert under the circumstances is that his selection for termination was arbitrary; but if the reason for discharge is not for an unlawful purpose prescribed [sic] by Section 111.70 (3) (a) , this Board has no jurisdiction to remedy mere arbitrary action. . . .

2. The precedents established in the private sector under the National Labor Relations Act have been repeatedly referred to by the various state boards and state courts, especially where there is a parallel or analogous statutory provision involved. As the Connecticut Supreme Court of Errors noted in Town of Windsor v. Windsor Police Dep't Employees Ass'n, Inc. 154 Conn. 530, 227 A.2d 65 (1967) , ". . . the judicial interpretation frequently accorded the federal act is of great assistance and persuasive force in the interpretation of our own act."

3. Normally a labor relations agency conducts an investigation to determine whether an unfair labor practice charge has any merit. If the agency dismisses the charge, to what extent can the individual seek judicial review of such a determination? Under the National Labor Relations Act, the courts have uniformly held that the exercise of discretion by the NLRB General

Counsel in dismissing an unfair labor practice charge is not subject to judicial review. *See, e.g.,* United Electric Contractors Ass'n v. Ordman, 366 F.2d 766 (2d Cir. 1966) (per curiam), *cert. denied,* 385 U.S. 1026 (1967); Hourihan v. NLRB, 201 F. 2d 187 (D.C. Cir. 1952), *cert. denied,* 345 U.S. 930 (1953).

In re FAITH GAGNIER
New York Public Employment Relations Board
1 PERB ¶ 399.90 (1968)
Sub-nom enforcement denied, Helsby v. Board of Education, Central School District No. 2, 34 App. Div. 2d 361 (1970)

Upon a charge filed by Faith Gagnier, employed as a teacher by the Board of Education of the Ockawamick Central School District, Counsel to the Public Employment Relations Board issued a complaint alleging that she was denied reappointment and tenure by her employer because of her activities on behalf of an employee organization, the Ockawamick Teachers Association.

The answer interposed by respondent employer denied that Gagnier was denied tenure because of her activities on behalf of the employee organization. Further, respondent asserted the following defenses: (a) that the Public Employment Relations Board, herein referred to as the Board, lacks jurisdiction to hear or determine this claim; (b) that the denial of tenure was made pursuant to the provisions of § 3013 of the Education Law and is not subject to review by this Board; (c) that if Gagnier feels aggrieved by respondent's action, her sole remedy is that provided by subdivision 4 of § 3013 of the Education Law.

A hearing was held on this complaint before a hearing officer appointed by this Board. At the hearing, attorneys for respondent declined to participate on the ground that this Board lacked jurisdiction. The hearing officer proceeded with the hearing and found that Gagnier was denied tenure "to punish Complainant for her association activities." He recommended that the respondent be directed to employ Gagnier as of September 1, 1968.

The report and recommendation of the hearing officer are now before this Board. The attorneys for respondent have not seen fit to file briefs with this Board on the issues of law raised in respondent's answer. However, as this is the first time that this Board has had to consider these issues, we shall proceed to rule on the merits of said defenses.

Respondent asserts in its answer that Article 14 of the Civil Service Law (Public Employees' Fair Employment Act, hereinafter referred to as the Act), does not confer or grant jurisdiction to this Board to hear or determine claims that a public employer is guilty of reprisal against an employee.

Admittedly, the Act does not *in haec verba* grant power to this Board to hear and determine claims of reprisal against public employees. However, § 205.5 (k) provides that this Board shall have the power "To make . . . such rules and regulations . . . and to exercise such other powers as may be appropriate to effectuate the purposes and provisions of this article."

The purpose of this Act is in part "to promote harmonious and cooperative relationships between government and its employees."[1] This purpose and policy was in the judgment of the Legislature to be best effectuated by granting to public employees the right of organization and representation.[2] Thus, the Legislature, in § 202 of the Act, granted to public employees the right to form, join and participate in any employee organization of their own choosing.

If this grant of rights is to be meaningful and to effectuate the purpose of the Act, then these rights must be exercised in an atmosphere of free choice and not in an area of intimidation or fear of reprisal. If a public employer could with impunity threaten a public employee or transfer, suspend, lay off or discharge him for exercising these rights, then the legislative enactment would be so meaningless as to constitute an act of supreme futility. Clearly this was not the intent of the Legislature.

This Board is charged with the administration and implementation of all of the provisions of the Act, which includes the grant of rights in § 202. The Legislature has mandated this Board to exercise such powers as may be appropriate to effectuate the purposes and provisions of this Act. Clearly for the reasons stated above, the power to deal with acts of reprisals against public employees for exercising their rights is necessary to effectuate the purposes of this Act.

Public employees are prohibited from engaging in a strike; the public expects such employees to obey the law. Certainly when the same employees are granted rights, the public expects the public employers to recognize these rights, to act in accord with them, and not to act in derogation of them.

Respondent further asserts in its answer that the granting or denial of tenure is within the absolute discretion of the board of education and is, therefore, not reviewable by this Board.[3] This Board does not dispute that respondent has broad discretion in granting or denying tenure. However, in this proceeding the Board is simply determining whether the employee was penal-

---

[1] § 200, Civil Service Law.
[2] *Ibid.*
[3] § 3013, Education Law.

ized for exercising the rights granted to her by the Legislature. The agency mandated to effectuate this Act is this Board, and not the public employer, be it a board of education or otherwise.

Thus, we conclude that this Board does have jurisdiction to hear and determine this claim.

On the merits of the claim, we agree with and adopt the conclusion of the hearing officer.

Gagnier has been employed as a teacher for nine years. She was first employed by respondent for the academic year 1965-66. Prior to this, she had been employed for three years by the school district in Dover Plains, New York. Her supervising principal at Dover Plains described her as an "excellent teacher" and she was recommended by him to respondent "without reservation."

At the conclusion of each of her first two years with respondent, she was commended for her work by her supervisors. During her third year she was recommended for reappointment and tenure by grade supervising principal Calvin and supervising principal Benson. On March 8, 1968, the district superintendent Mapes recommended Gagnier along with six other teachers for tenure, stating he found these seven teachers to be "competent, efficient and satisfactory."

Respondent board of education, at a meeting held on March 11, 1968, accepted the recommendation as to the other six and granted them tenure but voted against tenure as to Gagnier. Two members of respondent board testified that this was the first time in their experience where tenure was denied countermanding the recommendation of the professional administrators.

Gagnier was president of the Ockawamick Faculty Organization, which organization was recognized by respondent as the negotiating representative of the teaching faculty employed by respondent. In the summer of 1967, Gagnier called Mr. Giannattasio, president of respondent, concerning the mechanics of recognition. During the conversation, Giannattasio asked her her year of employment and she replied that it was to be her third year. He cautioned her that it was her most important year, obviously alluding to tenure.

In January of 1968, Gagnier was invited to speak to a faculty group in New Lebanon concerning negotiations under the Taylor Law. After this talk, she was called in by her supervisor, who told her that with reference to her talk at New Lebanon she was getting "quite a reputation as a rabblerouser."

On March 5, 1968, a letter was delivered to members of respondent board complaining that the negotiator for respondent,

Giannattasio, did not have the power to reach an agreement. This letter was signed by Gagnier. Giannattasio was described as angry at receiving this letter.

Shortly thereafter, respondent board voted to deny Gagnier tenure. Giannattasio testified at the hearing herein. When questioned as to reasons for denying tenure over the recommendation of the professional administrators, he stated he relied upon what he had heard from other Board members and people on the outside. It was to the effect that Gagnier did not relate well to parents. However, Giannattasio was unable to identify the Board member or the source of the complaint. Similarly, he mentioned a report that complainant spent two [sic] much time away from her classroom but could not identify who made the complaint. Giannattasio did not observe Gagnier in the classroom; rather, the only opportunity he had to observe her was at the negotiating table.

On the record, we find the conclusion of the hearing officer to be well supported by the record. Considering all of the facts herein, particularly Giannattasio's vagueness as to the basis for denial of tenure, coupled with the fact that her immediate supervisors found Gagnier to be competent and efficient, and that it was the first time respondent rejected the recommendations of the professional administrator, warrants a finding that Gagnier was denied tenure because of her activities on behalf of an employee organization.

IT IS THEREFORE ORDERED that respondent offer to reinstate Gagnier to her former employment as of September 1, 1968 and to compensate her for wages lost as a result of respondent's act.

NOTES

1. As indicated in *Gagnier,* the Taylor Law as originally enacted did not contain any specific enumeration of improper practices by either public employers or employee organizations. When the act was amended in 1969, however, a new section was added setting forth improper employer practices and improper employee organization practices. N.Y. CIVIL SERV. LAW § 209-a (McKinney Supp. 1972), as added by A. 6704, L. 1969. The authority of the New York PERB to issue remedial orders such as that involved in *Gagnier* following the 1969 amendment was upheld in City of Albany v. Helsby, 29 N.Y.2d 433, 278 N.E. 2d 898, 328 N.Y.S.2d 658 (1972).

2. In Burlington County Evergreen Park Mental Hosp. v. Cooper, 56 N.J. 579, 267 A.2d 533 (1970), the New Jersey Supreme Court held that the Public Employment Relations

Commission lacked the authority under the New Jersey Act to issue a cease and desist order against a public employer for illegally discharging an employee because of his union activities. In holding that the New Jersey Act did not confer on the commission the authority to hear and decide unfair labor practice charges, the court noted:

> Whether PERC should be invested with authority to hear and decide unfair labor practice charges and to issue various types of affirmative remedial orders respecting them is an important policy question. In our judgment, a policy question of that significance lies in the legislative domain and should be solved there. A court should not find such authority in an agency unless the statute under consideration confers it expressly or by unavoidable implication. In this case, obviously the statute does not expressly confer the power sought to be exercised by PERC. And, in our judgment, the statutory language does not justify a judicial determination that power of such magnitude resides there by implication. 56 N.J. at 598-99.

The *Cooper* case is critically examined in Koch, *Decision in Perspective*, 23 LAB. L.J. 295 (1972).

Chapter 3

ESTABLISHMENT OF THE COLLECTIVE BARGAINING RELATIONSHIP

A. Employers Covered by Public Employee Collective Bargaining Legislation

In our complex society a seemingly endless variety of legal entities have been established for a wide variety of purposes. Entities such as states, cities and counties are clearly public employers; others such as corporations that are privately owned, financed and operated are clearly private employers. While it is an easy task at the extremes to distinguish a public employer from a private employer, there is a gray area in which the entity has the attributes of both a public employer and a private employer. Courts and the various agencies administering labor relations legislation have been faced with the threshold question of distinguishing public and private employers. This determination is important in order to ascertain which statutory provisions, if any, are applicable to a given employer and thus to determine the rights and obligations of the employees and employer. This is particularly significant in those states where public employees are prohibited from striking.

Another problem is the treatment of bi-state or multi-state agencies and authorities established by states and some of the Canadian provinces. Such agencies or authorities exist by virtue of compacts which must be approved by Congress. While employees of these agencies and authorities are undoubtedly public employees, there may be considerable question whether existing public sector collective bargaining legislation is applicable. For example, if a port authority is established pursuant to a compact approved by Congress between two states, or between a state and one of the Canadian provinces, and both jurisdictions have public sector collective bargaining statutes, which statute, if either, governs? Do both statutes apply depending upon where the employees reside and/or work? If only one jurisdiction has such a statute, does it apply?

NLRB v. NATURAL GAS UTILITY DISTRICT OF HAWKINS COUNTY, TENNESSEE

Supreme Court of the United States
402 U.S. 600, 91 S. Ct. 1746, 29 L. Ed. 2d 206 (1971)

Mr. Justice Brennan delivered the opinion of the Court.

Upon the petition of Plumbers and Steamfitters Local 102, the National Labor Relations Board ordered that a representation election be held among the pipefitters employed by respondent, Natural Gas Utility District of Hawkins County, Tennessee, 167 N.L.R.B. 691 (1967). In the representation proceeding, respondent objected to the Board's jurisdiction on the sole ground that as a "political subdivision" of Tennessee, it was not an "employer" subject to Board jurisdiction under § 2 (2) of the National Labor Relations Act, as amended by the Labor Management Relations Act, 1947, 61 Stat. 137, 29 U.S.C. § 152 (2).[1] When the Union won the election and was certified by the Board as bargaining representative of the pipefitters, respondent refused to comply with the Board's certification and recognize and bargain with the Union. An unfair labor practice proceeding resulted and the Board entered a cease-and-desist order against respondent on findings that respondent was in violation of §§ 8 (a) (1) and 8 (a) (5) of the Act, 29 U.S.C. §§ 158 (a) (1) and 158 (a) (5). 170 N.L.R.B. 1409 (1968). Respondent continued its noncompliance and the Board sought enforcement of the order in the Court of Appeals for the Sixth Circuit. Enforcement was refused, the court holding that respondent was a "political subdivision," as contended. 427 F.2d 312 (1970). We granted certiorari, 400 U.S. 990 (1971). We affirm.

The respondent was organized under Tennessee's Utility District Law of 1937, Tenn. Code Ann. §§ 6-2601 to 6-2627 (1955). In First Suburban Water Utility District v. McCanless, 177 Tenn. 128, 146 S.W.2d 948 (1941), the Tennessee Supreme Court held that a utility district organized under this Act was an operation for a state governmental or public purpose. The Court of Appeals held that this decision "was of controlling importance on the question whether the District was a political

---

[1] Section 2 (2), 29 U.S.C. § 152 (2), provides:

"The term 'employer' includes any person acting as an agent of an employer, directly or indirectly, but shall not include the United States or any wholly owned Government corporation, or any Federal Reserve Bank, or any State or political subdivision thereof, or any corporation or association operating a hospital, if no part of the net earnings inures to the benefit of any private shareholder or individual, or any person subject to the Railway Labor Act, as amended from time to time, or any labor organization (other than when acting as an employer), or anyone acting in the capacity of officer or agent of such labor organization."

subdivision of the state" within § 2 (2) and "was binding on the Board." 427 F.2d, at 315. The Board, on the other hand, had held that "while such State law declarations and interpretations are given careful consideration . . . , they are not necessarily controlling." 167 N.L.R.B., at 691. We disagree with the Court of Appeals and agree with the Board. Federal, rather than state, law governs the determination, under § 2 (2) , whether an entity created under state law is a "political subdivision" of the State and therefore not an "employer" subject to the Act.

The Court of Appeals for the Fourth Circuit dealt with this question in NLRB v. Randolph Electric Membership Corp., 343 F.2d 60 (1965) , where the Board had determined that Randolph Electric was not a "political subdivision" within § 2 (2) . We adopt as correct law what was said at 62-63 of the opinion in that case:

"There are, of course, instances in which the application of certain federal statutes may depend on state law. . . .

"But this is controlled by the will of Congress. In the absence of a plain indication to the contrary, however, it is to be assumed when Congress enacts a statute that it does not intend to make its application dependent on state law. Jerome v. United States, 318 U.S. 101, 104 . . . (1943) .

"The argument of the electric corporations fails to persuade us that Congress intended the result for which they contend. Furthermore, it ignores the teachings of the Supreme Court as to the congressional purpose in enacting the national labor laws. In National Labor Relations Board v. Hearst Publications, 322 U.S. 111, 123 . . . (1944) , the Court dealt with the meaning of the term 'employee' as used in the Wagner Act, saying:

" 'Both the terms and the purposes of the statute, as well as the legislative history, show that Congress had in mind no . . . patchwork plan for securing freedom of employees' organization and of collective bargaining. The Wagner Act is federal legislation, administered by a national agency, intended to solve a national problem on a national scale. . . . Nothing in the statute's background, history, terms or purposes indicates its scope is to be limited by . . . varying local conceptions, either statutory or judicial, or that it is to be administered in accordance with whatever different standards the respective states may see fit to adopt for the disposition of unrelated, local problems.'

"Thus, it is clear that state law is not controlling and that it is to the actual operations and characteristics of [respondents] that we must look in deciding whether there is sufficient support for the Board's conclusion that they are not 'political subdivisions' within the meaning of the National Labor Relations Act."

We turn then to identification of the governing federal law. The term "political subdivision" is not defined in the Act and the Act's legislative history does not disclose that Congress explicitly considered its meaning. The legislative history does reveal, however, that Congress enacted the § 2 (2) exemption to except from Board cognizance the labor relations of federal, state, and municipal governments, since governmental employees did not usually enjoy the right to strike.[3] In the light of that purpose, the Board, according to its Brief, p. 11, "has limited the exemption for political subdivisions to entities that are either (1) created directly by the state, so as to constitute departments or administrative arms of the government, or (2) administered by individuals who are responsible to public officials or to the general electorate."

The Board's construction of the broad statutory term is, of course, entitled to great respect. Randolph Electric, *supra*, at 62. This case does not however require that we decide whether "the actual operations and characteristics" of an entity must necessarily feature one or the other of the Board's limitations to qualify an entity for the exemption, for we think that it is plain on the face of the Tennessee statute that the Board erred in its reading of it in light of the Board's own test. The Board found that "the Employer in this case is neither created directly by the State, nor administered by State-appointed or elected officials." 167 N.L.R.B., at 691-692 (footnotes omitted). But the Board test is not whether the entity is administered by "State-appointed or elected officials." Rather, alternative (2) of the test is whether the entity is "administered *by individuals who are responsible to public officials* or to the general electorate" (emphasis added), and the Tennessee statute makes crystal clear that respondent is administered by a Board of Commissioners appointed by an elected county judge, and subject to removal proceedings at the instance of the Governor, the county prosecutor, or private citizens. Therefore, in the light of other "actual operations and characteristics" under that administration, the Board's holding that respondent "exists as an essentially private venture, with insufficient identity with or relationship to the

---

[3] See 78 Cong. Rec. 10351 *et seq.;* Hearings on Labor Disputes Act before the House Committee on Labor, 74th Cong., 1st Sess., 179; 93 Cong. Rec. 6441 (Sen. Taft). See also C. Rhyne, Labor Unions and Municipal Employee Law 436–437 (1946). Vogel, What About the Rights of the Public Employee?, 1 Lab. L.J. 604, 612-615 (1950).

State of Tennessee," 167 N.L.R.B., at 691, has no "warrant in the record" and no "reasonable basis in law." NLRB v. Hearst Publications, 322 U.S. 111, 131 (1944).

Respondent is one of nearly 270 utility districts established under the Utility District Law of 1937. Under that statute, Tennessee residents may create districts to provide a wide range of public services such as the furnishing of water, sewers, sewage disposal, police protection, fire protection, garbage collection, street lighting, parks, and recreational facilities as well as the distribution of natural gas. Tenn. Code Ann. § 6-2608 (Supp. 1970). Acting under the statute, 38 owners of real property submitted in 1957 a petition to the county court of Hawkins County requesting the incorporation of a utility district to distribute natural gas within a specified portion of the county. The county judge, after holding a required public hearing and making required findings that the "public convenience and necessity requires the creation of the district," and that "the creation of the district is economically sound and desirable," Tenn. Code Ann. § 6-2604 (Supp. 1970), entered an order establishing the District. The judge's order and findings were appealable to Tennessee's appellate courts by any party "having an interest in the subject-matter." Tenn. Code Ann. § 6-2606 (1955).

To carry out its functions, the District is granted not only all the powers of a private corporation, Tenn. Code Ann. § 6-2610 (1955), but also "all the powers necessary and requisite for the accomplishment of the purpose for which such district is created, capable of being delegated by the legislature." Tenn. Code Ann. § 6-2612 (1955). This delegation includes the power of eminent domain, which the District may exercise even against other governmental entities. Tenn. Code Ann. § 6-2611 (1955). The District is operated on a nonprofit basis, and is declared by the statute to be "a 'municipality' or public corporation in perpetuity under its corporate name and the same shall in that name be a body politic and corporate with power of perpetual succession, but without any power to levy or collect taxes." Tenn. Code Ann. § 6-2607 (Supp. 1970). The property and revenue of the District are exempted from all state, county, and municipal taxes, and the District bonds are similarly exempt from such taxation, except for inheritance, transfer, and estate taxes. Tenn. Code Ann. § 6-2626 (1955).

The District's records are "public records" and as such open for inspection. Tenn. Code Ann. § 6-2615 (Supp. 1970). The District is required to publish its annual statement in a newspaper of general circulation, showing its financial condition, its earnings, and its method of setting rates. Tenn. Code Ann. § 6-

2617 (Supp. 1970). The statute requires the District's commissioners to hear any protest to its rates filed within 30 days of publication of the annual statement at a public hearing, and to make and to publish written findings as to the reasonableness of the rates. Tenn. Code Ann. § 6-2618 (1955). The commissioners' determination may be challenged in the county court, under procedures prescribed by the statute. *Ibid.*

The District's commissioners are initially appointed, from among persons nominated in the petition, by the county judge, who is an elected public official. Tenn. Code Ann. § 6-2604 (Supp. 1970). The commissioners serve four-year terms and, contrary to the Board's finding that the State reserves no "power to remove or otherwise discipline those responsible for the Employer's operations," 167 N.L.R.B., at 692, are subject to removal under Tennessee's General Ouster Law, which provides procedures for removing public officials from office for misfeasance or nonfeasance. Tenn. Code Ann. § 8-2701 *et seq.* (1955); First Suburban Water Utility District v. McCanless, 177 Tenn., at 138, 146 S.W.2d, at 952. Proceedings under the law may be initiated by the Governor, the state attorney general, the county prosecutor, or ten citizens. Tenn. Code Ann. §§ 8-2708, 8-2709, 8-2710 (1955). When a vacancy occurs, the county judge appoints a new commissioner if the remaining two commissioners cannot agree upon a replacement. Tenn. Code Ann. § 6-2614 (Supp. 1970). In large counties, all vacancies are filled by popular election. *Ibid.* The commissioners are generally empowered to conduct the District's business. They have the power to subpoena witnesses and to administer oaths in investigating District affairs, Tenn. Code Ann. § 6-2616 (5) (1955), and they serve for only nominal compensation. Tenn. Code Ann. § 6-2615 (Supp. 1970). Plainly, commissioners who are beholden to an elected public official for their appointment, and are subject to removal procedures applicable to all public officials, qualify as "individuals who are responsible to public officials or to the general electorate" within the Board's test.

In such circumstances, the Board itself has recognized that authority to exercise the power of eminent domain weighs in favor of finding an entity to be a political subdivision. New Jersey Turnpike Authority, 33 L.R.R.M. 1528 (1954). We have noted that respondent's power of eminent domain may be exercised even against other governmental units. And the District is further given an extremely broad grant of "all the powers necessary and requisite for the accomplishment of the purpose for which such district is created, capable of being delegated by the legislature." Tenn. Code Ann. § 6-2612 (1955). The District's "public records" requirement and the automatic right to a public hearing and written "decision" by the commissioners accorded to all users betoken a state, rather than a private, instrumentality. The commissioners' power of subpoena and their nominal compensation further suggest the public character of the District.

Moreover, a conclusion that the District is a political subdivision finds support in the treatment of the District under other federal laws. Income from its bonds is exempt from federal income tax, as income from an obligation of a "political subdivision" under 26 U.S.C. § 103. Social Security benefits for the District's employees are provided through voluntary rather than mandatory coverage since the District is considered a political subdivision under the Social Security Act. 42 U.S.C. § 418.

Respondent is therefore an entity "administered by individuals [the commissioners] who are responsible to public officials [an elected county judge]" and this together with the other factors mentioned satisfies us that its relationship to the State is such that respondent is a "political subdivision" within the meaning of § 2 (2) of the Act. Accordingly, the Court of Appeals' judgment denying enforcement of the Board's order is

Affirmed.

[The dissenting opinion of MR. JUSTICE STEWART is omitted.]

NOTES

1. In Roza Irrigation Dist. v. State of Washington, 80 Wash. 2d 633, 497 P.2d 166 (1972), the Washington Supreme Court was faced with a question of whether an irrigation district was a "municipal corporation" and thus covered by the Washington public sector collective bargaining statute. In giving the term "municipal corporation" a broad construction, the court stated:

> . . . We find no such restrictive intent expressed in the statute. The service which irrigation district employees render is a vital one in the areas which they serve. It is in the public interest to avoid interruption of irrigation services, just as it is to avoid interruption of services rendered by a city's fire or police department. We are given no plausible reason why the legislature should have chosen to deny such employees the protection of the act or to regard them as private employees, having the right to strike. 497 P.2d at 170.

2. In Nassau Library System, 1 PERB ¶ 399.47 (1968), the New York Public Employment Relations Board held that the library in question was not a "government" or a "public employer" within the meaning of the Taylor Law and that, there-

fore, it did not have jurisdiction over the employer. The PERB noted that

> It would clearly be improper to apply the term "instrumentality or unit of government" to *any* corporate entity solely on the basis of the state or county aid it receives, the fact that it was established pursuant to a charter by permission of the legislature, or the fact that it performs a public service which is performed by other organs in the public sector as well.

Subsequently, the NLRB ruled that it likewise did not have jurisdiction. Nassau Library System, 196 N.L.R.B. No. 125, 80 L.R.R.M. 1112 (1972). In declining to assert jurisdiction over the Nassau Library System, the Board pointed to the "unique relationship" between the System and the state and county, stating:

> [V]irtually all of the System's operating income is derived either directly or indirectly from the State of New York and Nassau County. In addition, the System's board of trustees is appointed by, and the System itself services, various public libraries. . . .
>
> Moreover, the State of New York has intervened in the past over the System's day-to-day operations. The State of New York also places stringent requirements on the System to see that its plan of service is adequate, that its funds are invested in preapproved securities, and that it complies with state regulations regarding the purchase of books.
>
> For these reasons, we conclude, without deciding the System's status under Section 2 (2) of the Act, that it would not effectuate the policies of the Act to assert jurisdiction over the System. Accordingly, we shall dismiss the petition.

In view of these holdings by the New York PERB and the NLRB, where else could a union seeking to represent the System's employees turn? By virtue of these decisions, has a no-man's land been created?

MILWAUKEE AUDITORIUM BOARD
Wisconsin Employment Relations Commission
Decision No. 6543 (1963)

The Union petitioned the Board to conduct an election to determine what, if any, representation the operating engineers employed by the Employer desired, pursuant to Section 111.05 of the Wisconsin Employment Peace Act. At the hearing the Employer, by its Counsel, contended that the Employer was a political subdivision of the state within the meaning of Section 111.70 and that therefore any election by the one operating engineer in its employ should be held pursuant to that subsection.

The Employer operates an auditorium and arena for the purpose of providing facilities for public meetings, conventions, expositions, and other purposes of a public nature for which its buildings are suitable. The Employer is in the nature of a joint Employer having two distinct and separate parts. The first is a private corporation and the second is the City of Milwaukee. This form of organization permitted the Employer to acquire some of the necessary capital for the construction of the auditorium. However, the arena was constructed entirely from public funds. The city owns the land and buildings of the Employer and controls the operation of the Employer by virtue of the fact that a majority of the board of trustees of the Employer are city officials. In recent years, the city has acquired portions of the stock of the corporation. However, not all of the corporation stock of the Employer has been transferred to the city since in such event the corporation would be dissolved and the board of trustees would consist of the city officials exclusively.

The Board has held that the fact that a corporation is authorized to disburse public moneys in performing a public purpose and furthermore that it is, by virtue of its organization and statutory limitations, substantially controlled by the State, is not determinative of the question whether such corporation is a state agency or political subdivision of the state.[1] In this same case, the Board looked to the particular language used in the Statute creating the Employer in determining whether such Employer should be deemed a political subdivision of the state. Section 43.44 Wisconsin Statutes provides in part:

" (1)   Any city of the first class may establish and maintain public auditoriums and music halls; and may establish, maintain and operate the same jointly, share and share alike, by agreement between the common council of such city and private corporation duly organized for that purpose.

" (2)   Such private corporation shall execute to the city a bond, in a sum determined and with sureties approved by said common council, conditioned that the said corporation will furnish its share of money as the same shall be required for the purposes specified in subsection (1) .

---

[1] Milwaukee County War Memorial, Inc., Decision No. 6325, 4/63.

. . . .

"(5)   Whenever the city shall have acquired all the stock of such corporation, the said corporation shall ipso facto be dissolved and the title to all its property of whatsoever nature, shall vest in said city; thereupon the auditorium board provided for in section 43.45 shall consist of only the ex officio members specified in said section.

. . . .

"(7)   Any such city may build additions to such auditoriums and for the purposes of any such addition, by action of the common council, issue revenue bonds under the provisions of section 66.51 payable exclusively from income and revenues of any such addition and of any auditorium to which it is added which said auditoriums and additions thereto for such purpose are declared a public utility. Said private corporation shall not be required to contribute to any such addition. Any such addition shall be subject in all other respects to the provisions of sections 43.44 to 43.48."

The statutory language recognizes that a portion of the Employer's operation will be carried on by a private corporation operating jointly with the city. Part of the funds necessary to build the auditorium were furnished by the corporation. The corporation elects five members to the eleven member board of trustees which is charged by statute with full and complete control of the Employer. The statute further recognizes that stock in the corporation may be transferred to the city and that the corporation may assume a secondary role in furnishing capital for new buildings for the Employer. Nevertheless, the corporation retains its corporate entity, elects the members of the board of trustees that it is entitled to elect, and shares in the operation of the Employer, share and share alike, until such time as all of the stock of the corporation is transferred to the city. Such being the case, the Employer must be deemed a joint operation between a private corporation and a municipality.

The Petitioner herein petitioned the Board to conduct a representation election in a bargaining unit consisting of one operating engineer employed by the Milwaukee Auditorium Board pursuant to 111.05 of the Wisconsin Statutes. The Employer contends that the election should be conducted pursuant to 111.70 (4) (d) of the Wisconsin Statutes since it is a municipal employer and not a private employer subject to the provisions of the Wisconsin Employment Peace Act.

Employes of private employers have greater rights than employes of municipal employers. Section 111.04 grants employes in private industry the right to "engage in collective bargaining through representatives of their own choosing, and to engage in lawful concerted activities, such as strikes, picketing, and bargaining, or other mutual aid or protection," which refers to lawful concerted activities, such as strikes, picketing and boycotts, labor unions traditionally use to induce employers to accede to their demands. Section 111.70 (a), while granting the right to representation in collective bargaining, omits the right to engage in concerted activities. Section 111.70 (1) prohibits strikes by municipal employes and, in its stead, in Section 111.70 (e) through (g) establishes fact finding procedures for the resolution of disputes. The question here before the Board is not merely an administration matter as to which section of the statutes shall be cited when the Board directs its election, but is determinative of the right of the employe involved to engage in certain concerted activity. The representative of the Petitioning Union indicated his awareness of the basic issue when he stated on the record he sought in this proceeding the right to strike. The Milwaukee Auditorium Board operates the Milwaukee Arena and Auditorium. The operation is controlled by a private corporation established by the Wisconsin Statutes and by representatives of the City of Milwaukee. The private corporation was formed to acquire some of the necessary capital, for the construction of the auditorium. However the latter building, the Arena is constructed entirely from municipal funds. The City of Milwaukee has title to the land and buildings and controls the operation by virtue of the fact that a majority of the board of trustees are city officials. Furthermore in recent years the City of Milwaukee has been acquiring portions of the stock of the corporation and eventually all the corporate stock will be transferred to the City of Milwaukee. It appears to the Board that the City of Milwaukee is the senior partner in this organization having the greater control and having made the greater financial contribution and therefore any employes employed by the Milwaukee Auditorium Board are to be deemed municipal employes. Therefore the election shall be conducted pursuant to 111.70 (4) (d) of the Wisconsin Statutes.

NOTE

In Milwaukee County War Memorial Center, Inc., WERC Decision No. 6325 (1963), the Wisconsin Employment Relations Commission held that the war memorial was not a public employer even though (1) eight of the 15 members of the Board

of Directors were elected by the Milwaukee County Board, (2)
the County retained legal title to the building, and (3) the
County made "an annual appropriation to defray the cost of
operating the building and auxiliary facilities, less any revenues
the Employer receives. . . ."

DELAWARE RIVER & BAY AUTHORITY v. NEW JERSEY PERC

Superior Court of New Jersey, Appellate Division
112 N.J. Super. 160, 270 A.2d 704 (1970)
Aff'd, 58 N.J. 388, 277 A.2d 880 (1971)

Halpern, J.A.D.: . . . The narrow issue for determination is
whether the New Jersey Public Employment Relations Commission (PERC) has jurisdiction over plaintiff Delaware River
& Bay Authority (Authority), a bi-state agency created by compact between the States of New Jersey and Delaware.

The Authority was established by interstate compact in 1962,
approved by Congress. In general terms, the Authority was authorized to construct and operate crossings between New Jersey
and Delaware over the Delaware River and Bay. A full recital
of its creation, purposes, powers and functions is set forth in
Delaware River and Bay Authority v. International Org., etc.,
45 N.J. 138 (1965), and need not be repeated here. The principle established by that decision is that plaintiff is a public
agency whose employees have no right to strike.

The New Jersey Employer-Employee Relations Act (act)
was enacted in 1968 (N.J.S.A. 34:13A—1 *et seq.*). In general
terms, the act was designed to permit public employees to organize, join unions and to appoint bargaining representatives to
engage in collective negotiations with public employers. . . .

All the defendants filed petitions with PERC seeking to be
certified as the exclusive bargaining representative for various
designated units of the Authority. Jurisdiction was accepted by
PERC, which directed that notices of election be posted. Judge
Wick enjoined PERC from proceeding with the elections until
the issue of PERC's jurisdiction is judicially determined. Similar
relief was sought by Local No. 326 in the Delaware courts, but
those proceedings have been voluntarily stayed by the parties
pending the disposition of this appeal.

In determining PERC's authority and jurisdiction over public
employers and employees we are, of necessity, relegated to the
statute which created it and the intent of the Legislature as
expressed in the act. The act, N.J.S.A. 34:13A-3 (c), defines "employer" as including

. . . public employers and shall mean the State of New
Jersey, or the several counties and municipalities thereof,

or any other political subdivision of the State, or a school district, or any special district, or any authority, commission, or board, or any branch or agency of the public service.

Defendants lay great stress upon the term "any authority" appearing in the statute, and argue it was intended to include plaintiff. We disagree. If such were the legislative intent it would have specifically provided for bi-state authorities. Its failure to do so evidences an intent not to include them because it realized that bi-state agencies are controlled by the compacts entered into, and it could not act unilaterally.

The meaning and intent of a statute must be gathered from its objective, the nature of the subject matter and its contextual setting. We must not be guided by a single sentence or member of a sentence, but we should look to the provisions of the whole law, and to its object and policy, as well as statutes *in pari materia*. . . .

In using the term "any authority" the Legislature had in mind the myriad authorities created by a municipality, county or state functioning within the State, and over which it has exclusive control. Any other construction would be violative of the interstate compact which gave birth to plaintiff. By the terms of the compact plaintiff became "an agency of government of the State of Delaware and State of New Jersey. . . ." N.J.S.A. 32:11E-1, Art. IV. Plaintiff's powers are derived "not from any single government but from the authority conferred by all parent governments. . . ." Application of Waterfront Comm'n of New York Harbor, 39 N.J. Super. 33, 42 (Law Div. 1956).

It is also clear that the compact gave plaintiff designated powers which were to be jointly controlled by both states. The relevant portion of Article VIII of the compact provides, "but no additional duties or obligations shall be undertaken by the authority under the law of either State or of Congress without authorization by the law of both States."

If PERC is to have jurisdiction over plaintiff and its employees, such power must be expressly given to it by the Legislatures of New Jersey and Delaware, and not inferred by the courts. In short, were we to hold that PERC had jurisdiction over plaintiff, it would authorize New Jersey to impose its will and policies over Delaware contrary to Delaware's wishes and the terms of the compact. In discussing PERC's jurisdiction and power, we must be careful not to intrude on the legislative function in this vitally important field. . . .

Bi-state agencies exist by virtue of compacts between the states involved, entered into by their respective legislatures with the approval of Congress. When formed, they become a single agency of government of both states. Their primary purpose is to cooperate in advancing the mutual interests of the citizens of both states by joint action to overcome common problems. We fail to see how either state could enact laws involving and regulating the bi-state agency unless both states agree thereto. To sanction such practice would lead to discord and a destruction of the purposes for which such bi-state agencies are formed. As previously indicated, the New Jersey Employer-Employee Relations Act, of which PERC is an integral part, was enacted to enable public employees to organize and to engage in collective negotiations with their public employers. However, New Jersey's policy in this regard cannot be foisted upon Delaware and its citizens who are employed by plaintiff. As we see it, to accomplish the result argued for by defendants, the States of New Jersey and Delaware must first amend the compact and agree upon the issue whether plaintiff's employees may organize and engage in collective negotiations, what procedure should be utilized to implement this result, and where and how it should be accomplished. Unless such is done, Delaware and New Jersey could each claim jurisdiction since both states have legislation permitting public employees to organize and negotiate. The confusion and conflicts which would follow if one state assumed jurisdiction, makes it clear that such was never intended by the compact. . . .

To summarize our conclusions, we hold that plaintiff is not a public employer within the definition of N.J.S.A. 34:13A-3 (c) , and need not recognize and collectively negotiate with the exclusive bargaining representative selected through PERC. Since PERC has no jurisdiction over plaintiff its order to hold elections is reversed. No costs.

NOTE

In Palisades Interstate Park Comm'n, PERC Decision No. 60 (1971), the New Jersey PERC held that the decision in the principal case was not applicable where the compact legislation permitted unilateral action by either state that was a party to the compact to amend the responsibilities and powers of the bi-state commission, provided it was accomplished by a law specifically applicable to the commission. The New Jersey PERC held that it did not have jurisdiction to entertain a representation petition, however, since there was no legislation specifically making the commission subject to its jurisdiction.

BUFFALO AND FORT ERIE PUBLIC BRIDGE AUTHORITY
New York Public Employment Relations Board
1 PERB ¶ 399.03 (1968)

Statement

Pursuant to Laws of 1933, Chapter 824, the Buffalo and Fort Erie Public Bridge Authority (hereinafter referred to as the Authority) was established as a public benefit corporation (§ 1) constituting a municipal corporate instrumentality of the State of New York and empowered to act for and become the agency or instrumentality of Canada, with such additional powers and duties as might be conferred by that government (§ 2). The purpose of the Authority is to operate and maintain the international bridge (known as the Peace Bridge) between Buffalo, New York, and Fort Erie, Ontario.

The Authority was created by the State of New York without concurrent legislation by Canada. In the following year, 1934, the Canadian Parliament invested the Authority with basic powers similar to those contained in the New York statute (24-25 George V, Chapter 63). The Authority, however, was conceived and came into existence by virtue of an agreement or compact between Canada and the State of New York (People ex rel., Buffalo and Fort Erie Public Bridge Authority v. Davis et al., 277 N.Y. 292, 299). Congressional consent to the compact was granted by 48 Statutes 662, Chapter 196, 1934.

In 1957, the New York statute was amended to provide, among other things, equal representation for Canada on the board of directors of the Authority and annual rotation of the chairmanship between New York and Canadian residents (Laws of 1957, Chapter 259). Canada concurred by amending its original statute in 6 Elizabeth II, Chapter 10. Congressional consent to the revised compact was granted pursuant to 71 Statutes 367, P.L. 85-145. The Industrial Relations and Disputes Investigation Act, 1948, Chapter 54, Revised Statutes of Canada, 1952, Chapter 152, is applicable to Canadian corporations established to perform governmental duties or functions and to their employees (§ 54). The Canada Labour Relations Board, acting pursuant to such Act, has determined that the Authority is subject to its jurisdiction. By order dated December 15, 1967, the Canadian Board certified General Truck Drivers' Union Local 879 of the International Brotherhood of Teamsters, Chauffeurs, Warehousemen and Helpers of America as the bargaining agent for a unit of Authority employees of various trades who reside in Canada and work in Canada or in Canada and the United States.

On November 24, 1967, Local 375, International Brotherhood of Teamsters, Chauffeurs, Warehousemen and Helpers of America filed a petition for certification as the bargaining representative of a unit of Authority employees comprised of all janitors and toll collectors employed in Buffalo. Counsel for the Authority, on December 13, 1967, moved to dismiss the petition on the ground that the Public Employment Relations Board lacked jurisdiction over the respondent Authority. On the same day, a petition for certification as the bargaining representative of a unit comprised of all painters and sand blasters employed by the Authority in Buffalo was filed by District Council No. 4, Brotherhood of Painters, Decorators and Paperhangers of America. . . .

Opinion

As a public benefit corporation (Laws of 1933, Chapter 824, § 1) and an agency of the State (People ex rel. Buffalo and Fort Erie Public Bridge Authority v. Davis et al., *supra*), the Authority is a government or public employer as defined in Civil Service Law § 201 (7) (e) and (f). The fact that the respondent is not a "state public authority" as that term is defined in Section 201 (9) of the Civil Service Law does not alter its status as a public employer. A "state public employer" is defined only for the purpose of excluding such entities from those which are empowered to enact local procedures pursuant to Sections 206 and 212 of the Civil Service Law; the term has no other relevancy.

The Authority is also an agency of the Canadian government by virtue of the complementary legislation contained in 24-25 George V, Chapter 63, as amended, and by compact assented to by Congress as aforementioned.

The Canada Labour Relations Board on January 23, 1968, issued its reasons for judgment with respect to its aforementioned order. These reasons for judgment reveal that such Board based its determination upon the grounds that "[t]he employees in this unit are within Canadian territorial jurisdiction and are employed upon or in connection with a work or undertaking extending beyond the limits of a province to which Part I of the Industrial Relations and Disputes Investigation Act applies (see paragraph (b) of Sect. 53 thereof)." The Canada Labour Relations Board considered and rejected the arguments raised by the Authority's Canadian counsel:

> Counsel for the Respondent submits that the Board should decline to exercise jurisdiction to give effect to the application on the basis of broad public and international policy and comity in view of, to use his own description, the hybrid

nature of the Bridge Authority which is designated as a public benefit corporation by the aforesaid Act of the New York State Legislature, 1933, c. 824. While the Respondent has been established as a public corporate body in the complementary Acts of Parliament of Canada and the New York State Legislature we do not consider that this constitutes or provides valid grounds for the denial of bargaining rights to the employees of the Respondent affected by the present application. These employees are subject to the penalty provisions for breach of the I.R.D.I. Act and have a right to the benefits and services given thereunder. The respondent in its capacity as employer of these employees is not exempted from the application of the Act and is as such employer likewise subject to the penalty provisions for breach of the Act and has a right to the benefits and services given thereunder. (Reasons for Judgment, paragraph 7)

We concur with the basic reasoning of the Canada Labour Relations Board.

With respect to whether the consent of Congress may be necessary for Article 14 of the Civil Service Law to be applicable to the Authority, we note that only those acts tending to increase state political power which may encroach upon the supremacy of the United States are within the prohibition of Article I, Section 10, Clause 3 of the U.S. Constitution (Virginia v. Tennessee, 148 U.S. 503, 13 S. Ct. 728, 37 L. Ed. 976). We do not believe that Article 14 constitutes an encroachment.

Conclusion

The Authority is subject to the jurisdiction of the New York State Public Employment Relations Board. Accordingly, the Authority's motion to dismiss the petition is denied.

B. Qualification of the Proposed Bargaining Representative

Most of the state labor relations acts provide that labor organizations can file representation petitions seeking to represent employees in an appropriate unit. A preliminary question is occasionally raised as to whether a given organization or group constitutes a "labor organization" or "employee organization" within the meaning of the act. Many of the acts contain the definition of labor organization that is set forth in section 2 (5) of the National Labor Relations Act:

The term "labor organization" means any organization of any kind, or any agency or employee representation committee or plan, in which employees participate and which exists for the purpose, *in whole or in part,* of dealing with employers concerning grievances, labor disputes, wages, rates of pay, hours of employment, or conditions of work. 29 U.S.C. § 152 (5) (1970) (emphasis added).

This definition has been given an expansive interpretation. Thus, an organization that has as one of its purposes negotiations with an employer is a labor organization even though it has no written constitution or by-laws, its officers do not serve for a specified period of time, and it is funded by voluntary contributions. Yale University, 184 N.L.R.B. No. 101, 74 L.R.R.M. 1637 (1970). Moreover, the Supreme Court has held that an organization that deals with an employer concerning grievances is a labor organization within the meaning of the act, even though it does not negotiate collective agreements with the employer in the usual sense. NLRB v. Cabot Carbon Co., 360 U.S. 203 (1959). Social clubs and "flower" committees have also been held to be labor organizations if they serve as the medium for the presentation of employee recommendations and grievances to the employer. NLRB v. Precision Castings Co., 130 F.2d 639 (6th Cir. 1942).

Where the state act's definition of the term "labor organization" parallels the definition found in the National Labor Relations Act, the term has likewise been interpreted liberally. For example, in Wayne County Board of Supervisors, 1965-1966 MERC Lab. Op. 320, the Michigan Employment Relations Commission held that a bar association was a labor organization even though its by-laws did not list collective bargaining as one of the purposes of the organization.

In contrast to the NLRA definition, some state statutes define the term "labor organization" or "employee organization" to mean an organization whose *primary* purpose is to represent employees with respect to wages, hours and other conditions of employment. Does such a definition encompass professional organizations established primarily to advance professional interests rather than to represent employees in negotiations with an employer such as the American Association of University Professors (AAUP) or the American Physical Therapists Association?

CONNECTICUT STATE BOARD OF LABOR RELATIONS, TWENTY-FIRST ANNUAL REPORT 8-9 (1967)

The Act defines this term ["employee organization"] as meaning "any lawful association, labor organization, federation or council having as a primary purpose the improvement of wages, hours and other conditions of employment among employees of municipal employers." Section 7-467 (3). The Commission [to Study Collective Bargaining by Municipalities] explained that this definition "was given a wide sweep but it was the intention of the Commission to require that an employee organization have as a genuinely primary purpose the improvement of working conditions among municipal employees in order to qualify under the Act." *Report*, pages 12, 13. It also cautioned that pre-existing organizations which had not theretofore been concerned with collective bargaining might now become concerned, and concluded: "In such an event it will be incumbent on the organization to demonstrate by its constitution and bylaws the legitimacy of that concern." *Report*, page 13. In heeding that caution and that injunction, the Board found that the Bridgeport Police Officers Association had failed to make the requisite showing. City of Bridgeport (Police Department), [Decision No. 677, 1966]. Other pre-existing employee associations with a history of negotiation about, and concern with, employee working conditions have been found to meet the statutory definition. City of Bridgeport, *supra;* Town of Greenwich [Decision No. 692, 1966].

In two cases where employee associations met this primary purpose requirement, they were challenged on the ground that supervisors, excluded from the unit by the Act, were active members and officers of the association. The Board, following decisions by the federal courts, the National Labor Relations Board, and the New York State Labor Relations Board, ruled that such membership rendered the organization ineligible to be a bargaining representative of municipal employees under the Act. Such membership "inevitably conflicts with the policy of the Act 'to insulate employees' jobs from their organizational rights.'" Local 636, United Association of Journeymen, etc. v. NLRB, 287 F.2d 354, 362 (D.C. Cir. 1961). Therefore the Board concluded:

"These decisions did not, of course, involve the Connecticut statute which we must construe and administer. They were, however, made under statutes which were similar to ours in forbidding domination or interference by the employer in the associations which are to represent the employees. And we find the federal and New York decisions persuasive that the policies underlying this prohibition are violated when supervisory personnel excluded from the bargaining unit are allowed to become active voting members of the association; and more clearly violated when such supervisors became officers of the association.

"The next question is whether an association which permits such supervisors to be active members or officers is a 'lawful association' within Section 1 (3) of our Act. The giving of such permission is not made a prohibited practice on the part of an employee organization under Section 4 (b) of the Act, nor is it unlawful in the sense that it will subject the association to criminal penalties, but this is not, we feel, dispositive of the question. We believe that the legislature used the words 'lawful association' in this connection to mean broadly an association which is so constituted and organized that it is fully capable of serving the law's policy to have a disinterested and independent bargaining representative for employee units which want representation. And we find that an association which acquiesces in or permits voting membership or office-holding by supervisors excluded from the bargaining unit is thereby acquiescing in a practice which is prohibited because it tends to subvert the policies of the Act and render the association incapable of fulfilling the law's policies. This prevents it from being a 'lawful association' within the meaning and purposes of this provision." City of Stamford (Public Works Department), Dec. No. 682, April 1, 1966; City of Hartford, Dec. No. 681, April 6, 1966.

NOTE

The New York Taylor Law defines the term "employee organization" as "an organization of any kind having as its primary purpose the improvement of terms and conditions of public employees. . . ." N.Y. CIV. SERV. LAW § 201 (5) (McKinney Supp. 1971). In view of this definition, it was contended that an organization whose membership included both public employees and private employees was not an "employee organization." The New York PERB refused to accept this interpretation. City of Ogdensburg, 1 PERB ¶ 414 (1968). Joseph Crowley, a member of the New York PERB, explained the Board's position as follows:

> In those situations where the employee organization does admit to membership both public and private employees, it has been held that if the public employee members of the organization select their own negotiating committee and, without participation by private sector members, ratify negotiation agreements, the organization is an employee organization within the meaning of section 201(5). The reasoning of the Board is that the public employees who are responsible for the conduct of the negotiations would, therefore, not be submerged in an organizational structure dominated by private sector employees. Hence, where the independence of action of public employee members in-

volved is protected, such organizations have been found to be within the purview of section 201(5) of the Law.

Crowley, *The Resolution of Representation Status Disputes Under the Taylor Law,* 37 FORDHAM L. REV. 517, 529-30 (1969).

CITY OF MILWAUKEE
Wisconsin Employment Relations Commission
Decision No. 6960 (1964)

Effect of Supervisory Employes as Members of Employe Organization

The Board is confronted herein with a problem as to whether it should permit an employe organization to be on a ballot in an election proceeding which organization has a substantial number of supervisors among its membership. In *Joint School District No. 1 of the City of West Allis, etc.,*[5] the Board stated:

"The fact that supervisory personnel are members of, or any hold office in, any labor organization subject to the provision of Section 111.70 may raise a suspicion, but does not in itself establish domination or interference with the organization by the Municipal Employer employing such supervisory personnel. The number of supervisors among the members of the organization and the ratio of supervisors to other members are factors to be evaluated in each case. Likewise, the office held by supervisors and the extent to which they formulate the bargaining policy and programs of their labor organizations will also be scrutinized in each case."

In said case the issue of participation by supervisors, as members, in a labor organization was raised in a prohibitive practice proceeding before the Board and not in a representation case. The function of the Board in a representation proceeding is to determine whether or not a question of representation exists, to take evidence with respect to the appropriate collective bargaining unit and with respect to the employes eligible to participate in the election if one is ordered by the Board. It is now our opinion that the Board should not, in a representation proceeding, question the internal affairs of an organization, which the Board is satisfied exists for the purpose of representing municipal employes in conferences and negotiations with municipal employers on matters pertaining to wages, hours and conditions of employment. Therefore, in a representation proceeding, we do not believe that we should impose conditions on any organiza-

---

[5] Decision No. 6544.

tion seeking to represent municipal employes, which conditions would limit the right of such organizations to establish rules for the acquisition, retention and rejection of membership. To do so in a representation proceeding would impinge on the voluntary nature of such organizations. If the rules of such an organization permit supervisors to membership and/or excludes classes of employes from membership, the employes involved have a right to refuse to become members thereof, and if said organization is seeking to represent the employes in an election proceeding before this Board, the employes can vote to reject such organization as their collective bargaining representative. If it can be established, in a prohibitive practice proceeding, that any labor organization which has been selected as the collective bargaining representative of municipal employes in an election conducted by the Board, that the rules and regulations of such an organization interfere with the rights of employes under Section 111.70 or that supervisory employes have dominated that organization and thus interfered with the rights granted to the employes, we will, among other remedies, set aside the certification.

We have held that supervisory employes should be barred from the collective bargaining unit since we do not consider them to be employes within the meaning of Section 111.70. Since supervisors are not employes within the meaning of the Statute then they should not participate in the activities of an employe organization concerned with wages, hours and conditions of employment.

As noted previously herein, the inclusion of supervisors in the same bargaining unit with employes would create a conflict of interest since supervisors are agents of the municipal employer. Where supervisory employes are members of the rank and file employe organization, the fact that they are not included in the appropriate collective bargaining unit would not eliminate the possible conflict of interest above noted. Supervisors who are members of an employe organization, with rights and privileges extended to employe members, could exercise a voice and vote in the administration and in the deliberations of the affairs of that employe organization. Their membership in the employe organization would permit them to run for office, to nominate candidates for office, to vote on candidates for office, to act on committees meeting in conferences and negotiations with the municipal employer on questions concerning hours, wages and conditions of employment and to vote and participate in such matters. By such membership they could actively exercise an interest in conflict with that of the employes and thereby dominate or interfere with the internal affairs of the employe organization. The active participation by supervisory employes in the affairs of an employe organization could result in impeding and defeating the primary purpose of the employe organization—that of representing municipal employes in conferences and negotiations concerning their wages, hours and conditions of employment. Since supervisors are the agents of the municipal employer, a municipal employer, by permitting supervisory employes to participate actively, in any manner similar to that described above, in the affairs of an organization representing employes for the purposes set forth in Section 111.70, could, in the proper proceedings, be found to have committed prohibitive practices by interfering, restraining and coercing its employes in the exercise of their rights granted to them under the law. As previously noted in this case, the president of the Association and two members of its Board of Directors have been found to be supervisors by the Board. Whether the activities of supervisors as members of a labor organization constitute prohibitive practices under Section 111.70 will be determined by the Board in formal complaint proceedings before the Board and by the facts established in each case.

Effect of Limiting Membership to Certain Employes

As noted above, during the hearings in the matter, a question arose as to whether or not the Board would consider the Association as a qualified labor organization under Section 111.70 since it admitted to membership only registered engineers and architects, or those who had obtained a degree in their respective fields. The Board has found the unit appropriate here not only to include certain classifications of engineers and architects, but also the Engineering Technician IV, V and VI classifications, the incumbents of which, although not degreed or registered, are performing duties identical to various degreed or registered employes employed in the engineering and architectural classifications.

Section 111.70 (2) confers upon municipal employes the right to affiliate with employe organizations of their own choosing. In our view this provision does not limit employe organizations from adopting reasonable rules for the acquisition, retention or rejection of membership. As noted above, we have indicated that we will not, in a representation proceeding, prescribe or review the rules governing the internal affairs of labor organizations representing municipal employes and, therefore, the fact that the Association's constitution and by-laws do not provide membership for non-degreed or non-registered employes does not affect the right of the Association to appear on the ballot in this election proceeding. Any labor organization selected by a majority of employes in an appropriate collective bargaining unit has the duty and obligation to represent all of the employes in the bargaining unit with equal vigor, whether members of the organization or not. If any labor organization certified by the Board as the exclusive bargaining representative for employes in an appropriate unit fails in that duty and obligation, the Board can, in a proper proceeding, vacate its certification and eliminate the right of such organization to continue as the exclusive collective bargaining representative of said employes. . . .

NOTES

1. *See generally* Michigan Nurses Ass'n, *supra,* pp. 119-30; Comment, *The Role of Supervisors in Employee Unions,* 40 U. CHI. L. REV. 185 (1972) .

2. The Assistant Secretary of Labor has held that an organization composed solely of supervisors is not a "labor organization" within the meaning of section 2 (e) (1) of Executive Order 11491. Social Security Admin., Bureau of Hearings and Appeals, A/SLMR No. 142 (1972) , GERR Ref. File 21:4097.

3. In Wayne State University, 1969 MERC Lab. Op. 670, the Michigan Employment Relations Commission held that an organization composed entirely of students is a "labor organization." The MERC rejected the contention that such an organization "would not have the permanence, experience, or strength necessary to constitute" a labor organization within the meaning of the Michigan Act.

TOWN OF HUNTINGTON
New York Public Employment Relations Board
1 PERB ¶ 399.96 (1968)

This is an appeal from part of a decision by the Director of Representation in this proceeding dated October 11, 1968.

The Director in his decision determined the units he deemed to be appropriate; however, he stayed further proceedings to certification on the ground that one of the intervenors, Local 342, Long Island Public Service Employees, United Marine Division, National Maritime Union, AFL-CIO (NMU), the appellant herein, has a charge pending against it, alleging a violation of § 210.1 of the Public Employees' Fair Employment Act (Act) .[1]

_____

[1] § 210.1, Civil Service Law.

Appellant appeals from this portion of the Director's decision staying the representation proceedings.

This representation proceeding was commenced by the filing of a petition on May 24, 1968. Appellant intervened in this proceeding.

While this proceeding was pending, the Counsel to this Board filed a charge alleging that appellant violated § 210.1 of the Act[2] in that "it caused, instigated, encouraged, condoned and engaged in a strike by certain employes of the Town of Huntington."

The Director reasoned that if this were sustained it ". . . may cause the Board to look behind the NMU's no strike affirmation and conclude that it was a sham." The Director concluded that, "In that event, the NMU would not be permitted to participate in any further proceedings leading to certification." The Director therefore stayed this representation proceeding pending a decision on the charge of violation of § 210.1.

The thrust of appellant's contention on this appeal is that this Board and *a fortiori* the Director of Representation lack the power to deny an employee organization participation in representation proceedings on this ground, or even to inquire into the good faith of an employee organization in making the "no strike" affirmation required by § 207.3 (b) of the Act.

We modify the decision of the Director insofar as he stayed the proceedings herein and direct him to proceed with the certification process in accordance with § 201.6 of the Rules of Procedure of this Board. However, we do, for the reasons set forth below, reserve the right to inquire, upon reasonable grounds, into the good faith of the "no strike" affirmation made by any employee organization prior to its being certified.

The Legislature, in enacting the Act, granted to public employees in this state rights which are unparalleled in this nation— the right to form, join and participate in any employee organization; the right to be represented by employee organizations to negotiate terms and conditions of employment. The Legislature provided procedures for the resolution of disputes concerning representation status. The obvious purpose of these procedures was not only to provide a reasonable and peaceful means of resolving disputes between competing employee organizations but also to assure public employees that they may select employee organizations of their own choosing.

However, the Legislature, not unmindful that strikes by public employees are prohibited, provided that this Board may

---

[2] § 210.1. "No public employee or employee organization shall engage in a strike, and no employee organization shall cause, instigate, encourage, or condone a strike."

not certify an employee organization until such organization has provided an affirmation that it does not assert the right to strike against any government.

What was the purpose of this legislative mandate? The appellant in its brief sets forth a most adequate answer. Appellant states, "The affirmation is simply a formal renunciation of the right to strike or to assist or participate in a strike against a public employer." If this be the purpose of this legislative requirement, and we would concur, then a formal renunciation of the right to strike would seem to require that the entity making such a renunciation has a sense of purpose to act in accord with such a renunciation and to strive to observe the affirmation. Clearly the Legislature did not intend that such affirmation be simply a meaningless recitation or an affirmation without substance or obligation. Simply put, no one would attribute to the Legislature that its enactment in whole or in part was designed to be an exercise in futility. Rather, logic requires us to assume that the Legislature intended this affirmation to be precisely as characterized by appellant, a "formal renunciation of the right to strike."

Consider a situation where an employee organization would make such an affirmation at a time when the same organization was engaged in a strike. To say in such circumstances that this Board should accept such affirmation without question would be such an adherence to form in disregard of substance as to constitute a classic absurdity. Similarly, it would appear to be incumbent upon this Board to make an inquiry in a situation where such affirmation or "formal renunciation" is repudiated soon after it is made and before certification.

Appellant argues in support of its contention that this Board lacks power to so inquire, and to deny certification as a result of such inquiry would constitute a penalty beyond that provided in § 210.3 (f) of the Act, i.e., forfeiture of dues deduction privileges.

In advancing this contention, appellant fails to give effect to the statutory scheme. The statute requires that recognition or certification of an employee organization be conditioned upon an affirmation made in good faith that the organization does not assert the right to strike against any government. A determination by this Board that an employee organization is not qualified for certification by reason of its failure to make such an affirmation in good faith is therefore administrative and not penal.

Appellant is an employee organization which is neither recognized nor certified. Rather, appellant is an employee organization seeking to be certified and a requisite to certification is the making of the affirmation referred to above. For the reasons stated, such an affirmation must be made in good faith, and if there are present facts and circumstances which place the good faith of the affirmation in question, this Board has not only the power but the obligation to make an inquiry and to take such affirmative action as is necessary, including the withholding of certification in order to effectuate the purposes and provisions of the Act.

Accordingly, the stay granted by the Director is vacated and the certification proceedings shall proceed subject to the right of inquiry asserted herein.

NOTES

1. The constitutionality of the Taylor Law's requirement that an employee organization must affirm that it does not assert the right to strike before it can be certified as a collective bargaining representative was upheld by the New York Appellate Division in Rogoff v. Anderson, 34 App. Div. 2d 154, 310 N.Y.S.2d 174 (1970), aff'd, 28 N.Y.2d 880, 271 N.E.2d 553, 322 N.Y.S.2d 718, appeal dismissed for want of a substantial federal question, 404 U.S. 805 (1971). The union argued "that the requirement for an affirmation that Respondent does not assert the right to strike is a violation of Respondent's right of free speech under the Federal and State Constitutions," relying on the decision in National Association of Letter Carriers v. Blount, 305 F. Supp. 546 (D.D.C. 1969), appeal dismissed, 400 U.S. 801 (1970), in which the court struck down as unconstitutional a statutory provision that made it illegal for federal employees to belong to employee organizations that asserted the right to strike. In distinguishing this case, the court held the problem "was not job acquisition for retention, but certification with its attendant benefits." As a result, the court held that "the condition imposed is reasonable for the benefits conferred, and is reasonably calculated to achieve the ultimate desired end." The court further observed that it did not construe the statutory requirement as an infringement "upon the exercise of rights protected by the First Amendment."

2. The Georgia Fire Fighters Bargaining Law provides that a municipal employer shall recognize the organization selected by a majority of the fire fighters in a given fire department if "said organization does not advocate striking and has a 'no-strike' clause in its Constitution and By-laws. . . ." GA. CODE ANN., ch. 54-13, § 54-1305 (Supp. 1972). The Nevada statute provides that a local government employer may only recognize an employee

organization that has affirmatively pledged "in writing not to strike against the local government employer under any circumstances." NEV. REV. STAT. § 288.160 (1971). Are either or both of these requirements constitutionally permissible? In determining the constitutionality of prohibiting the granting of recognition to an employee organization that advocates striking, would it make any difference if the jobs of the employees in question are essential to the safety and health of the public?

3.   The Connecticut statute provides that an employee organization is not "eligible to petition for or participate in a recognition election until it has been in existence for at least six months." CONN. GEN. STAT. ANN. § 7-467a (1972). What reasons can be advanced for including this type of qualification? In its Twenty-Third Annual Report, the Connecticut State Board of Labor Relations stated:

> . . . Its purpose was to prevent mushroom organizations from forestalling organizing efforts by established organizations. The requirement was to add some measure of assurance that the organization has the will and the ability to survive. When an established national or regional organization forms a local or chapter, there is adequate assurance of endurance and effectiveness. Thus, while a petition by the local could not stand alone, when filed in the names of the parent and the newly formed local, Section 7-467a is met and a certification will issue in joint names. CONNECTICUT STATE BOARD OF LABOR RELATIONS, TWENTY-THIRD ANNUAL REPORT 5 (1969).

C. Existence of Question Concerning Representation

1. Showing of Interest

A condition precedent to invoking the representation procedures under most of the public sector collective bargaining statutes is a showing by the union or employee organization that it has substantial support among the employees in the bargaining unit petitioned for. The purpose of such a requirement is "to avoid needless dissipation of P.E.R.B.'s resources on frivolous representation claims." Civil Service Employees Ass'n v. Helsby, 63 Misc. 2d 403, 312 N.Y.2d 386 (Sup. Ct. 1970), aff'd, 35 App. Div. 2d 655, 314 N.Y.S.2d 159 (1971). Most of the statutes incorporate the long standing NLRB rule that the union or employee organization must affirmatively demonstrate that it has the support of at least 30 percent of the employees in the unit claimed to be appropriate. Although there are some statutory variations, this showing of interest is usually made by submitting membership cards or dues checkoff authorizations to the labor relations agency. These cards or authorizations are then checked against a list of employees submitted by the employer. Following the private sector precedent,[1] the determination of whether the employee organization has submitted the requisite showing of interest has been held to be an administrative matter that is within the discretion of the agency to determine and is not a matter that can be litigated. Civil Service Employees Ass'n v. Helsby, *supra;* Union Free School Dist. No. 21, 1 PERB ¶ 405 (1968) ; Defense Supply Agency, Boston, Mass., A/SLMR No. 34 (1971), GERR Ref. File 21:4043; South Redford School Dist., 1965-1966 MERC Lab. Op. 160.

WAUWATOSA BOARD OF EDUCATION
Wisconsin Employment Relations Commission
Decision No. 8300-A (1968)

. . . Under the pertinent statutory provisions a question of representation must exist as a condition precedent to the processing of a petition for an election among employes. The Commission has not required any showing of interest to be demonstrated by any petitioner with respect to the processing of election petitions filed pursuant to the Wisconsin Employment Peace Act or the Municipal Employer-Employe Labor Relations Act. The Commission has considered the filing of the petition, whether it be to certify or decertify a representative, as a good-faith claim that the employes desire to be represented or not to be represented. This policy has been applied in initial and subsequent elections[6] on the basis of our experience that the overwhelming number of petitions have been filed in good faith with the expectation of obtaining the results prompting the petition. . . .

The establishment of a policy which would now require labor organizations seeking representation to present a showing of interest or to require that an employer establish a good faith doubt that the employes desire to continue their representation by an incumbent union, requires a consideration of the rights of employes to select or change their bargaining representative, with the interest of preserving stability in existing collective bargaining relationships. We have considered the above-discussed factors

---

1 "It is well settled that showing of interest is a matter for administrative determination, and is not subject to collateral attack by the parties." Standard Cigar Co., 117 N.L.R.B. 852, 853 (1957).

[6] Kenosha Board of Education, Dec. No. 8301, 5/67.

in order to balance and achieve these objectives when confronted with issues involving the timely filing of petitions for elections.

Although the Commission has not in the past processed a substantial number of petitions which have not been filed in good faith, the results of recent elections seeking a change in the present representative status indicate that an increasing number of petitions have been filed where there was little likelihood of success by the petitioner. The processing of such election petitions has resulted in no change in the bargaining relationship and has had an adverse impact upon such existing relationship, in that such processing has interrupted and delayed negotiations, thus affecting the stability of the collective bargaining relationship. Such unwarranted delays create problems especially in municipal employment with respect to the effect of budgetary deadlines and other special deadlines which may be imposed by statute, and in both the private and public employment where such delays create additional issues for bargaining, such as effective dates of agreements, as well as their retroactive application.

The Commission concludes that there is now sufficient reason requiring parties requesting elections seeking a change in representation or the rejection of the present representative to furnish the Commission with objective data raising the question concerning representation before it will conduct such an election, which if otherwise held, might delay and frustrate the relationship between the recognized or certified labor organization and the employer. . . .

Accordingly, where there is an existing collective bargaining relationship resulting from a good faith voluntary recognition of the labor organization, or where the labor organization has been certified in an election conducted by this agency, an organization filing a petition for an election among the employes involved at the time of filing must administratively demonstrate that at least 30 percent of the employes in the claimed appropriate collective bargaining unit desire the petitioning organization to represent them for the purposes of collective bargaining. Where the petition is filed by an employe or employes seeking to terminate the representative status of the incumbent labor organization, the petitioning employe or employes must administratively demonstrate to this agency at the time of filing that at least 30 percent of the employes in the requested bargaining unit desire to terminate the representative status of the union. An employer petitioning for an election in an existing unit must demonstrate to this agency at the hearing, by objective considerations, that it has reasonable cause to believe that the incumbent organization has lost its majority status since its certification or the date of voluntary recognition. This objective evidence must not have been obtained by the employer through prohibited means. . . .

NOTES

1. Is there a valid question concerning representation if the employee organization does not request the public employer to grant recognition prior to filing a representation petition? Following the long established policy of the NLRB, the Wisconsin Employment Relations Commission has held that the filing of a representation petition is sufficient to raise a question concerning representation. Thus, in Village of Brown Deer, WERC Decision No. 6650 (1964), the Wisconsin Commission stated:

> Our experience in administering Section 111.70 indicates that the Municipal Employer has a different mode of operation which makes it exceedingly difficult, at best, for it to respond with any dispatch to a demand for recognition by a Union. The private employer can recognize or decline to recognize a Union after a decision by the individual owner of the business or after conferences among members of the management. On the other hand, the Municipal Employer must decide upon its action through legislative process, which is often slow and drawn out and which lends itself more to inaction than action. During this same period, disputes concerning the terms and conditions of employment and the representative status of the Union would be aggravated by the Union's and the employes' suspicion that the Municipal Employer might be using the time to undermine its organization. Such delays are eliminated through the unhampered use of the Board's election machinery. . . .
>
> [W]e have encouraged Municipal Employers to extend voluntary recognition to a Union where they are satisfied that the Union is the representative of the majority of the employes in the unit. Indeed, where the Union believes the Municipal Employer will recognize its claim of representation and enters into conferences and negotiations with the employe representative, such action is entirely in keeping with the voluntary nature of the collective bargaining process. However, the fact that the Union may choose to seek voluntary recognition does not mean that it must make known its claim to the Municipal Employer before filing an election petition with the Board.

2. Many of the public sector statutes specifically provide that a decertification petition must be supported by a 30 percent showing of interest.

3. Where a given statute specifically authorizes employees to file a decertification petition but makes no provision for an employer to do so, may an employer nevertheless file a petition challenging the continued majority status of the collective bargaining representative? May an employer test the union's majority status by refusing to bargain with the union and assert as its defense that the union no longer represents a majority of the employees in the appropriate bargaining unit?

4. The NLRB, like the WERC, has held that an employer may file a petition challenging a union's majority status if it can establish that it has a good faith doubt based on objective considerations that the union has lost its majority status. United States Gypsum Co., 157 N.L.R.B. 652 (1966). In Lloyd McKee Motors, Inc., 170 N.L.R.B. 1278, 1278-79 (1968), the Board stated:

> . . . Respondent had engaged in protracted bargaining for a 5-month period over the single issue of the apprentice program followed by absolutely no communication from the Union or the mediator during the final 6 weeks. There had been several changes in the makeup of the union negotiating committee and what appeared to Respondent to be a loss of majority on the part of the Union. The Union failed to fill the post of steward, and there had been a considerable turnover of employees within the unit. In addition, McKee had asked the supervisors to make an "assessment" of the Union's strength, and, thereafter, McKee received various "opinion" reports from the supervisors which were to the effect that the Union had lost its majority status. Finally, on May 21, McKee asked Cook, the Union's vice president and chief employee negotiator, if he had heard from Jones, and Cook replied that he had not seen Jones since the meeting of April 14.
>
> While these factors may not, in and of themselves, establish as a fact a loss of majority, we are of the opinion that taken in their totality they present an objective basis which could furnish reasonable grounds for Respondent to believe in good faith that the Union had lost its majority status. . . .

The NLRB has further held that the determination as to whether the employer has presented sufficient objective considerations is an administrative matter and cannot be litigated. United States Gypsum Co., 161 N.L.R.B. 601 (1966).

5. The Nevada statute is unique in that it expressly provides that a public employer may withdraw recognition if the employee organization "ceases to be supported by a majority of the local government employees in the negotiating unit for which it is recognized." NEV. REV. STAT. § 288.160 (3) (c) (1971). The employee organization may appeal, however, to the Local Government Employee-Management Relations Board. The Board is given the authority to direct an election if it "in good faith doubts whether any employee organization is supported by a majority of the local government employees in a particular negotiating unit." NEV. REV. STAT. § 288.160 (4) (1971).

2. Effect of an Existing Agreement (Contract Bar Doctrine)

TOWN OF MANCHESTER
Connecticut State Board of Labor Relations
Decision No. 813 (1968)

The Municipal Employees' Group, Inc., on March 7, 1968, petitioned for an election in a unit consisting of salaried employees. The employees in this unit are presently represented by the Intervenor, Local 991, of Council #4, American Federation of State, County and Municipal Employees, AFL-CIO, and are covered by a collective agreement between the Intervenor and the Municipal Employer. That Agreement is due to expire January 1, 1969.

The Intervenor objects to the petition on the ground that an election is barred by the present contract and that a petition filed ten months prior to the termination of the contract is premature. We agree and order the petition dismissed. However, because our past decisions have raised some questions as to the operation of the contract bar principle in the field of municipal employment and when a petition will be considered to be timely filed, we feel it appropriate to provide as much clarification as our evolving experience presently permits.

We start with the basic statutory premise that employees have a right to bargain through representatives of their own choosing. That freedom of choice includes the freedom to change their mind as to which, if any, employee organization they want to represent them. At the same time, the purpose of choosing a representative is for collective bargaining, and that purpose cannot be realized unless there is some stability of representation. The employees must be permitted periodically to reconsider their choice, but this ought to be done at a time when it will not disrupt the bargaining process any more than necessary. To that end, the National Labor Relations Board developed the contract bar rule which this Board has generally followed. The least disruptive time for a change of representative is at the end of the contract term. Therefore, the appropriate time for a petition for an election is in that period prior to the end of the contract when a change in the bargaining representative can be most smoothly effectuated with the least disruption of the bargaining process.

The National Labor Relations Board evolved a set of subsidiary rules governing the timeliness of a petition prior to the end of the contract. See Leedom, *Industrial Stability and Freedom of Choice*, in COLLECTIVE BARGAINING AND THE LAW (1959), p. 63; Reed Roller Bit Co., 72 N.L.R.B. 927 (1947). Petitions filed more than 150 days prior to the end of the contract would not be accepted because the holding of an election would leave the incumbent union as a lame duck in administering the old contract. Also, petitions filed less than 60 days prior to the end of the contract would not be accepted so that the parties would have the last 60 days of bargaining undisrupted by any doubts as to the union's status in election proceedings. To these rules governing the timeliness of a petition, the NLRB added a third rule that a petition would not be barred by the negotiation of a new contract prior to the end of the time for filing a petition. Deluxe Metal Furniture Co., 121 N.L.R.B. 995 (1958). For example, if the contract were to expire on December 31, a petition filed on October 30 would not be barred by a new contract made prior to that date. The challenging union could not be blocked by the incumbent union's premature renewal of the contract. Later the NLRB modified these time limits to require filing not more than 90 days or less than 60 days prior to the end of the contract. Leonard Wholesale Meats, Inc., 136 N.L.R.B. 1000 (1962).

These rules were developed by the National Labor Relations Board for collective bargaining in the private sector. Although we have never adopted the rigid time limits set down by the NLRB, we believe that the principles they are built upon are sound and that the time spans indicated are generally appropriate in the sphere for which they were designed. That is, for collective bargaining in the private sector.

Collective bargaining in the public sector raises different considerations. Experience during the last two years has suggested that the bargaining process in public employment is often more protracted than in private employment. This means that bargaining for a new contract may begin longer in advance of the end of the contract term. If there is to be a change of the bargaining representative, that change can be most smoothly made at the time when contract negotiations would normally begin.

Therefore, a petition filed somewhat more than 90 days prior to the end of the contract would be at an appropriate time. Our experience is too limited to now fix limits with certainty, but we are presently persuaded that a petition filed as much as four months prior to the end of that contract should not be considered premature.

Collective bargaining in the public sector often requires quite different time limits for filing petitions for another reason. Collective agreements are often timed to expire at the end of the fiscal year. In that case, the parties usually contemplate that negotiations for a new contract will be held while the budget is being prepared so that when the budget is presented and adopted, it will reflect the costs of the new collective agreement.

Where the collective bargaining process is thus coordinated with the budget-making processes, the normal time for beginning negotiations may be as much as five or six months before the end of the contract term. This time is considered necessary to complete negotiations, get the results of the negotiations reflected in the budget and have the budget adopted before the end of the fiscal year. A petition filed for a change of representatives at the time when negotiations for a new contract normally begin cannot be considered to be premature. On the contrary, it might well be considered to be at the most appropriate time. It would avoid having negotiations disrupted in mid-course by a change of bargaining representatives. For this reason, we ordered an election in the *Greenwich* case (Case No. ME-1631, April 17, 1968), even though the collective agreement still had several months to run.

We are not prepared at this time to establish any rigid time limit in such cases, for our experience is yet too limited to say with any assurance how long a time may be required. Nor do we know in practical terms what difficulties the incumbent union may have in administering the remainder of the existing contract. For the present, we will follow the general guide that a petition filed within a month prior to the time when negotiations will normally begin will be considered timely. We consider it preferable that when negotiations normally begin, everyone will know who are the proper negotiators.

In this case, the contract is not scheduled to coordinate with the fiscal year, but is to expire on January 1, 1969. The parties have testified that, as in private employment, negotiations would normally begin about three months prior to the end of the contract. To hold an election in May could mean that the incumbent union could continue to administer the contract for seven or eight months in a lame duck status. Such problems should and can be avoided. The appropriate time for a petition to be filed in this case is after the first of September. This will permit the question of representation to be resolved in time for negotiations to take their regular course. A petition filed any earlier than the first of September will, in this case, be considered premature.

The petitioner here need have no fear that it will be barred by a new contract made before it files a new petition. If a petition is filed at any time between September 1, and November 1, then a new agreement made prior to the filing of the petition will not constitute a bar to an election.

The petition is hereby dismissed.

CITY OF MILWAUKEE
Wisconsin Employment Relations Commission
Decision No. 8622 (1968)

[On April 17 and 24, 1968, the Teamsters Union filed a representation petition and an amended petition, respectively, seeking to represent all of the truck drivers, including the tractor operators and equipment operators, employed in the Bureau of Municipal Equipment of the City of Milwaukee.]

Both AFSCME [American Federation of State, County and Municipal Employees] and the City contend that the petition was not timely filed and therefore the Commission should dismiss same. In *Wauwatosa Board of Education* the Commission adopted the following policy with respect to the timely filing of representation petitions.

"Where there presently exists a collective bargaining agreement covering the wages, hours and conditions of employment of employes in an appropriate collective bargaining unit, the petition must be filed within the sixty (60) day period prior to the date reflected in the resolution or ordinance for the commencement of negotiations for changes in wages, hours and working conditions of the employes in the unit covered by said resolution or ordinance."

AFSCME is the certified bargaining representative of the employes involved herein. Such employes are presently in an overall unit consisting of employes of the Department of Public Works of the City. AFSCME and the City are parties to an existing collective bargaining agreement which by its terms became effective January 1, 1966, and is to continue until December 31, 1968. Said agreement contains among its provisions the following material herein:

"PART I.

. . . .

B. Conditions and duration of agreement. (1) This Agreement shall remain in full force and effect commencing on the 1st day of January, 1966, and terminating on the 31st day of December, 1966, except as provided below. In accordance with this provision and the intent of the parties and as provided for in paragraphs (2), (3) and (4) of Part I, Section B, the Labor Policy Committee of the Common Council prior to July 31, 1966 agrees to recommend the financial terms of this Agreement for 1967 to the Finance Committee of the Common Council, and prior to July 31, 1967 agrees to recommend the financial terms of this Agreement for 1968 to the Finance Committee of the Common Council.

(2) If the Labor Policy Committee makes the aforementioned recommendation or if the Union fails to exercise the right to terminate this Agreement, which right as provided below results from the Labor Policy Committee's failing to make the aforesaid recommendation, and if the Common Council in its budget for 1967 adopts the financial terms of this Agreement for 1967, the parties agree that this shall constitute a readoption of all the terms of this Agreement from the 1st day of January, 1967 and terminating on the 31st day of December, 1967.

(3) If the Labor Policy Committee makes the aforementioned recommendation or if the Union fails to exercise the right to terminate this Agreement, which right as provided below results from the Labor Policy Committee's failing to make the aforesaid recommendation, and if the Common Council in its budget for 1968 adopts the financial terms of this Agreement for 1968, the parties agree that this shall constitute a readoption of all the terms of this Agreement from the 1st day of January, 1968 and terminating on the 31st day of December, 1968.

(4) If and in the event the Labor Policy Committee of the Common Council fails to act as set forth above prior to July 31, 1966, or July 31, 1967, as the case may be, the Union may within ten (10) days terminate this Agreement.

(5) If and in the event the Common Council in its annual budget in November, 1966, and/or November, 1967, does not adopt the financial terms of this Agreement, the Union may within ten (10) days after passage of the budget terminate this Agreement.

. . . .

C. Negotiations. Either party to this Agreement may select for itself such negotiator or negotiators for purposes of carrying on conferences and negotiations under the provisions of Section 111.70, Wisconsin Statutes, as such party may determine. No consent from either party shall be required in order to name such negotiator or negotiators.

D. Timetable. Conferences and negotiations shall be carried on by the parties hereto in 1968 as follows:

Step 1. Submission of Union demands to the City by Feb. 1

Step 2. Submission of City's answer (within 6 weeks) by Mar. 15

Step 3. Negotiations to begin (within 4 weeks) by Apr. 15

Step 4. Conclusion of negotiations (within 3 months) by July 15

Step 5. Mediation, if any, begins by July 15

Step 6. Fact Finding, if any, begins by Aug. 1

Step 7. Recommendations issued by Oct. 15

Adherence to such timetable shall be effectuated as to its chronological order, as closely as may be practical under the circumstances which attend at the time such conferences and negotiations are undertaken."

AFSCME and the City contend that under the policy adopted by the Commission in *Wauwatosa Board of Education* the petition herein was not timely filed since it was filed more than two months after the date on which AFSCME and the City, in accordance with their collective bargaining agreement, had commenced negotiations toward a succeeding agreement and that in order to be timely, said petition would have had to be filed during the 60-day period prior to February 1, 1968.

The record indicates that AFSCME and the City have proceeded in their negotiations in accordance with the negotiating timetable set forth in their collective bargaining agreement and up to the date of the hearing had met on five occasions with respect to AFSCME's demands for a 1969 agreement and the City's counter proposals thereto. The timetable reflected in the collective bargaining agreement was adopted as a result of a fact finding panel's recommendations issued in 1964. Both AFSCME and the City, because of the number of employes involved, the number of units represented by various labor organizations with which the City must bargain, the number of public hearings that must be held with respect to budgetary problems, and the budgetary deadline, contend that the negotiation timetable set forth in the collective bargaining agreement is not unreasonable but on the contrary necessary to maintain collective bargaining stability.

Teamsters contend that the collective bargaining agreement which contains the negotiating timetable is illegal since it constitutes a three-year agreement contrary to Section 111.70 (4) (i). Further, that the timetable set forth in the agreement, if the agreement is found valid, is excessive and thus deprives employes of their right to freely select a bargaining representative, in that it provides for the commencement of bargaining eleven months prior to the expiration of the agreement, and over eight months prior to the budgetary deadline of the City. Further, Teamsters argue that although the petition was filed approximately 75 days after the negotiations commenced and that five negotiation meetings were held, that said meetings were not substantial and that the first public hearing on AFSCME's proposals was not convened by the City until May 10, after the petition was filed.

A careful reading of the pertinent language in the agreement persuades the Commission that the labor agreement is not in fact a three-year agreement but a one-year agreement providing for the readoption thereof at the end of the year, at least through December 31, 1968, and therefore we conclude that it is not invalid within the meaning of Section 111.70 (4) (i).

In this regard it is to be noted that the pertinent language contemplates the possibility that agreements could not have been reached for the readoption of the agreement for the years 1967 and 1968 and that AFSCME could have terminated same on ten-days' notice prior to July 31, 1966, or July 31, 1967, in the event the Labor Policy Committee of the City failed to act as set forth therein, or within ten days following the failure of the Common Council to adopt the annual budget in November 1966 and 1967. This conditional right to prevent the readoption of the collective bargaining agreement if no agreement was reached on the financial terms thereof for 1967 and 1968, implied that the parties would return to the negotiating table and continue their negotiations, and thus depart from the bargaining schedule reflected in the agreement. We are aware that the negotiation timetable set forth in the agreement was recommended by the eminent fact finding panel in order to promote stability of collective bargaining between employe representatives and the City. However, when making such a recommendation, it is doubtful that the fact finding panel contemplated the effect of such an extended period of negotiation upon the rights of employes to change or reject their collective bargaining representative. We must weigh the rights of the employes to select or reject a bargaining representative and the matter of stability of an existing collective bargaining relationship. The record indicates that the proposal submitted by AFSCME with respect to conditions of employment for employes, including those covered by the petition, for the year 1969 includes a proposal that the agreement be limited to one year. If AFSCME and the City were to enter into a one-year agreement containing the same negotiating time-table, in February 1969, AFSCME normally would submit proposals for the year 1970. If we were to dismiss the petition as being untimely filed, it is probable that the Teamsters would refile a new petition in December 1968 or January 1969, and if the City and AFSCME had reached an agreement on the terms of the 1969 contract and if in an election conducted as a result of the petition filed by the Teamsters in December 1968 or January 1969 the Teamsters were successful in being selected as the bargaining representative, the Teamsters would, in accordance with our policy expressed in *City of Green Bay*,[4] administer the collective bargaining agreement, for at least 11 months of its duration, which had not been negotiated by it. The administration of a collective bargaining agreement for such a substantial period of its term by an organization which did not negotiate same does not create or maintain the type of stability desirable in the collective bargaining relationship.

Although the eleven-month timetable for negotiations may be reasonable as it generally applies to the collective bargaining relationship presently existing involving the City and the Unions which represent its employes, we are of the opinion that where a good faith question of representation exists, initiated by a sufficient showing of interest, this extended period of negotiations should not bar the present petitions. The petition herein was filed more than eight months prior to the expiration date of the current agreement, and following the determination of the question of representation raised thereby, in our opinion, after the employes select their bargaining representative, sufficient time remains for meaningful bargaining prior to the budgetary deadline.

In retrospect, the policy as expressed by the Commission in *Wauwatosa Board of Education* with respect to the time for filing petitions, is too general and we, therefore, modify it as follows: Where there presently exists a collective bargaining agreement, resolution or ordinance covering the wages, hours and conditions of employment of employes in an appropriate collective bargaining unit, a petition requesting an election among

---

[4] Dec. No. 6558, 11/63.

said employes must be filed within the 60-day period prior to the date reflected in said agreement, resolution or ordinance for the commencement of negotiations for changes in wages, hours and working conditions of the employes in the unit covered thereby unless the period of negotiations as set forth therein extends beyond six months prior to the budgetary deadline date of the municipal employer involved. In the latter event, petitions for elections will be entertained by the Commission if they are filed in good faith within sixty days prior to such six-month period. . . .

Commissioner Rice, dissenting in part:

I dissent with the determination of my colleagues to direct an election at this time. I would apply, without exception, the policy expressed by the Commission in *Wauwatosa Board of Education* and would conclude that the Teamsters did not timely file its petition.

In the Wauwatosa case the Commission stated that the reason for the adoption of time limitations ". . . is to promote stability in the collective bargaining relationship, and in municipal employment to insure the parties a reasonable period of time to engage in bargaining and to negotiate an agreement prior to the established budgetary deadlines. . . ." In the 1964 fact finding recommendations involving the City of Milwaukee the fact finders considered the length of time necessary to insure the parties a reasonable period of time to engage in bargaining and to negotiate an agreement and it recommended that those negotiations begin on February 1. They considered such a period of bargaining to be reasonable and necessary and AFSCME and the Employer apparently agreed because they incorporated the timetable into their agreement. I am not prepared to say that the fact finders, who are recognized experts in the field of labor relations, did not contemplate the effect of such a period of negotiation upon the rights of employes to change or reject their collective bargaining representative. Regardless of their considerations, when I weigh the rights of the employes to select or reject a bargaining representative after one has been certified against the goals of (a) stability in an existing collective bargaining unit, and (b) a bargaining period sufficient to negotiate an agreement, I feel that greater consideration should be given to the stability of the bargaining relationship and a sufficient period of time for bargaining. I am not disturbed by the fact pointed out by my colleagues that strict adherence to the Wauwatosa rule might result in the Teamsters administering a collective bargaining agreement which had not been negotiated by it for at least 11 months. . . .

NOTES

1. The Wisconsin Employment Relations Commission in the principal case reiterated its policy that if a rival union unseats an incumbent union prior to the expiration of the agreement between the employer and the incumbent union, the rival union administers the agreement for the balance of its term. In State of New York, 5 PERB ¶ 3060 (1972), GERR No. 489, B-10 (1973), *aff'd sub nom.*, Police Benevolent Ass'n v. Osterman, 73 Misc. 2d 184, 340 N.Y.S.2d 291 (Sup. Ct. 1973), the New York PERB held that the successor organization administers the agreement "until a new agreement can be negotiated effective upon the start of a new fiscal year of the employer or the expiration of the old agreement, whichever is sooner." That not all state agencies have adopted a similar policy is indicated by the following excerpt from the Connecticut State Board of Labor Relations in City of Norwich, Decision No. 804 (1968):

> [E]ven though an election is held prior to the termina-
> tion date of the contract, it is for determining the status of
> the bargaining agent after the termination of the contract.
> During the remainder of the contract term, the Union re-
> tains its right to recognition and its authority to represent
> the employees, regardless of the outcome of the election.

Under the NLRA if an incumbent union is decertified, it loses its status as the bargaining agent and it has no right to administer the agreement for the balance of its term. *See* Modine Mfg. Co. v. Grand Lodge Int'l Ass'n of Machinists, 216 F.2d 326 (6th Cir. 1954); Farmbest, Inc., 154 N.L.R.B. 1421 (1965), *enforced as modified*, 370 F.2d 1015 (8th Cir. 1967). The Supreme Court in NLRB v. Burns Int'l Security Services, Inc., 406 U.S. 272, 92 S. Ct. 1571, 1580 n.8 (1972), held that "[w]hen the union which has signed a collective-bargaining contract is decertified, the succeeding union certified by the Board is not bound by the prior contract, need not administer it, and may demand negotiations for a new contract, even if the terms of the old contract has not yet expired." What are the advantages and disadvantages of each approach? Which approach is more likely to promote labor relations stability?

2. Not infrequently the period of time within which a representation petition may be filed where there is an existing collective bargaining agreement is specifically set forth in the applicable statute. For example, section 967 (2) of the Maine Municipal Public Employees Labor Relations Act provides that "[w]here there is a valid collective bargaining agreement in

effect, no question concerning unit or representation may be raised except during the period not more than 90 nor less than 60 days prior to the expiration date of the agreement." ME. REV. STAT. ANN. tit. 26, § 967 (2) (Supp. 1972). The Hawaii statute contains a similar provision. HAWAII REV. STAT. § 89-7 (Supp. 1971). In other instances the contract bar rules are set forth in rules and regulations promulgated by the agency administering the act. For the applicable contract bar rules under Executive Order 11491, see section 202.3 of the rules promulgated by the Assistant Secretary of Labor.

3. Normally, a representation petition is timely if it is filed after the expiration date of a collective bargaining agreement. Suppose, however, that prior to the expiration date the parties had reached agreement on all but one issue and had agreed to submit that issue to binding arbitration. Would a representation petition filed by a rival union be timely if it was filed after the termination date of the agreement but prior to the receipt of the arbitrator's award that would resolve the one remaining issue in negotiations between the employer and the incumbent union? In City of Norwich, Decision No. 804 (1968), the Connecticut State Board of Labor Relations stated:

[T]he agreement to submit the principal issue in dispute to binding arbitration creates a contractual relationship between the Union and the employer which bars an election, and if that arbitration leads directly to the concluding of a collective agreement, an election is barred until the termination of that collective agreement. The purpose of the contract bar is to promote stability in collective bargaining relations. The arbitration agreement substantially settles the parties' relation and removes the uncertainty and instability of unsettled negotiations. To open the question of representation during the time required for arbitration to crystalize into a completed contract would be to disrupt this peaceful method of resolving disputes. Uncertainty as to the union's status would undermine or distort the arbitration and open the award to a kind of collateral attack. . . .

Would the same considerations be applicable if the parties had agreed to submit the unresolved issues to non-binding fact finding as opposed to binding arbitration? Would it make any difference if non-binding fact finding was legislatively mandated? *See* City of Appleton, WERC Decision No. 7423 (1966).

CITY OF GRAND RAPIDS (HEALTH DEPARTMENT)
Michigan Employment Relations Commission
1968 MERC Lab. Op. 194

. . . On July 11, 1967, MNA [Michigan Nurses Association] petitioned the Board for a representation election in a unit defined as:

"All registered nurses employed by the Health Department of the City of Grand Rapids."

AFSCME and the City oppose this petition on the grounds that (1) there existed as of July 11, 1967, a collective bargaining agreement sufficient under section 14 of PERA to bar the Board from conducting any election. . . .

The 1966 contract contained an expiration date of June 30, 1967. In March, 1967, AFSCME and the City commenced negotiations for a new agreement. Since no new agreement had yet been reached as of June 28, 1967, the parties extended the 1966 agreement to July 7, 1967. On July 5, 1967, the City Commission adopted Ordinance No. 67-43, a general salary ordinance which set pay ranges for the various classifications of work. On July 7, the City Manager completed negotiations with AFSCME and reached an oral agreement on salaries and all other working conditions. This oral agreement called for certain salary increases beyond those just provided in Ordinance No. 67-43 of July 5, 1967. The City Commission followed through by adopting Ordinance No. 67-44, on July 11, 1967, upping salaries to the level orally agreed to on July 7, 1967 by the City Manager and AFSCME. Also on July 11, a two page "letter of agreement" was signed by the City Manager and AFSCME officials, agreeing that the old 1966 Contract would remain in effect until May 31, 1968, with several specific modifications, including the substance of Salary Ordinance 67-43 as amended by 67-44. Other modifications affected the grievance procedure, compensatory time off, pay for work out of classification, vacation pay, number of holidays, hospitalizations, life insurance, safety committee, uniforms, tool allowance, and a parking facilities study committee. The MNA's election petition, as noted earlier, was filed with the Board on July 11, 1967, the same date as the "letter of agreement" and Ordinance No. 67-44. The election petition was not served upon the City and AFSCME until several days later. Section 14 of PERA provides in pertinent part:

"*No election shall be directed* in any bargaining unit or subdivision thereof *where there is in force and effect a valid collective bargaining agreement* which was not prematurely extended and which is of fixed duration. . . ." (emphasis added)

The ultimate issue is whether there was in force and effect as of July 11, 1967, a valid collective bargaining agreement between the City and AFSCME. What existed as of that date was a written agreement between the City Manager and AFSCME, covering all areas of wages and working conditions, coupled with City Commission ordinances confirming the salary portion of the City Manager's agreement. The ordinances were silent as to the several other contract modifications agreed to in the "letter of agreement," except for the following relevant provision of Ordinance No. 67-43:

"Section 21. The City Manager shall make rules not in conflict with Civil Service provisions, *and subject to the approval of the City Commission*, on the subjects of sick leave, annual leave (vacation), military leave, leave without pay, holidays, working hours, and other personnel matters. *Until such rules are approved existing resolutions and rules on such subjects shall remain in full force and effect.*" (emphasis added)

It is clear from the above that the several non-salary modifications agreed to by the City Manager were to be of no effect until the City Commission approved them. There is no evidence that the City Commission ever formally approved these modifications to which the City Manager had agreed. Accordingly, it is concluded that the only collective bargaining agreement "in force and effect" (Section 14 of PERA) as of the date the election petition was filed was the agreement on a salary schedule.[1] The City Manager patently lacked power to bind the City or its City Commission to terms for a new contract. While he was authorized by a 1965 Commission action to "represent" the City in union matters, the Commission never pretended to delegate to him the power to legislate wages and working conditions without the Commission's ratification of any agreement reached by him at the bargaining table. Inasmuch as the "letter of agreement" was legally unenforceable without Commission approval taken at a Commission meeting, it is found that no "collective bargaining agreement" was "in force and effect" as

[1] The Charter of the City of Grand Rapids, Title V, vests all City legislative and administrative powers in the City Commission (sec. 1(a)); provides that no monies shall be paid out except in pursuance of appropriations approved by the City Commission (sec. 20); and provides that the City Commission shall fix by ordinance the salary or rate of compensation of all officers and employees of the City (sec. 35).

of July 11, 1967, except for the salary agreement which was adopted by Commission Ordinances Nos. 67-43 and 67-44.

As a general rule the Board will follow a policy of treating as a section 14 bar only such agreements of public employers as have been rendered legally enforceable by virtue of having been duly enacted, adopted or approved by the competent governing body, e.g., city council or commission, board of education, or county board of supervisors. However, it is apparent that the unavoidable delay[3] between tentative agreement by negotiators at the bargaining table and the convening of an official meeting of the legislative body encourages disruptive rival union activity and consequent raids if the tentative agreement does not serve to bar an election. This is so because it encourages dissident groups of employees to make capital out of their asserted ability to negotiate an even better contract. Such a situation discourages reasonable settlements and responsible representation. Accordingly, in the interest of striking a balance between employee freedom of choice and stability of existing bargaining relationships, the Board announces the following policy which will be applied in implementing PERA section 14 for all petitions filed after the date of this order:

A complete written collective bargaining agreement made between and executed by, authorized representatives of a public employer and the exclusive bargaining agent of its employees will, for a period of up to thirty days thereafter, bar a rival union election petition or a decertification petition pending subsesequent action on the agreement by the legislative body. A petition filed within the thirty day period will not be dismissed if the legislative body meets and votes to reject the proposed agreement or takes no action within the thirty day period. If the legislative body approves the collective bargaining agreement negotiated by its representative within the thirty day period, the petition will be dismissed.

The determinative issue in this case is whether the salary agreement (the only agreement approved by the governing City Commission *at any time*) was sufficient *in scope* to constitute the type of agreement contemplated by section 14 as barring an election.[4] This question must be answered in the negative, con-

---

[3] Administrative notice is taken of the fact that the majority of such local legislative bodies, are composed of citizens who have other occupations, serve on a voluntary basis, and are unable to meet on a continuous basis because of other commitments.

[4] It is unnecessary to apply the 30 day rule, announced above, in reaching a decision in the instant case, since the record contains no evidence that the City Commission *ever* met and approved a complete collective bargaining agreement.

sistent with the holding in School District No. 61, Berrien County-Buchanan Public Schools, 1967 Labor Opinions, 518, 520 wherein we stated:

"The National Labor Relations Board consistently refuses to treat an agreement as a bar to an election petition unless it contains substantial terms and conditions of employment deemed sufficient to stabilize the bargaining relationship. A contract limited to wages only or to one or several insubstantial provisions is not recognized as a bar. Appalachian Shale Products Co., 121 NLRB 1160. We have adopted the NLRB rule. South Redford School District MLMB R65 J-184, 1966 Labor Opinions 160; Sterling Township, MLMB R65 H-20, 1966 Labor Opinions 9. Accordingly, the agreement of June 20, 1966, being limited to a wage schedule, is not a bar, under section 14 of PERA, to the conduct of an election at this time."

Accordingly, it is concluded that no section 14 bar exists to the direction of an election. . . .

NOTES

1. The NLRB has held that "[w]here ratification is a condition precedent to contractual validity by express contractual provision, the contract will be ineffectual as a bar unless it is ratified prior to the filing of the petition. . . ." Appalachian Shale Products Co., 121 N.L.R.B. 1160 (1958). The New Jersey Public Employment Relations Commission adopted a similar policy in Camden County Welfare Board, PERC Decision No. 65 (1972).

2. The Michigan Employment Relations Commission, following the uniform practice of the NLRB, has ruled that "a contract to act as a bar to an election must embrace a unit that is appropriate to the extent that the unit is one neither prohibited by PERA nor contrary to Board policy." Kent County Road Commission, 1969 MERC Lab. Op. 34.

3. Does a contract that does not include any wage or fringe benefit provisions constitute a bar to a representation proceeding? The New York City Office of Collective Bargaining has held that a contract that "contains substantial non-economic provisions" was sufficient to be a bar since the wages and fringe benefits were mandated by the state's "prevailing rate" law and bargaining was prohibited on subjects covered by the law. Teamsters Local Union 237, Decision No. 11-71, GERR No. 396, B-7 (1971).

4. In West India Mfg. & Serv. Co., 195 N.L.R.B. No. 203, 79 L.R.R.M. 1619 (1972), the NLRB held that an employer and a union caught in mid-negotiations by the wage-price freeze ordered by President Nixon in August 1971 were entitled to an additional 60-day period during which they were insulated from an election petition filed by a rival union.

5. A survey published by the Michigan Municipal League in 1970 indicated that over 25 percent of the 158 contracts analyzed contained either union shop or maintenance of membership provisions, both of which were illegal under Michigan law. MICHIGAN MUNICIPAL LEAGUE, LABOR CONTRACT ANALYSIS FOR MICHIGAN MUNICIPALITIES 1970 (Information Bull. No. 117, April 1970); *see* Oakland County Sheriff's Dep't, 1968 MERC Lab. Op. 1, GERR No. 227, F-1 (1968). Does the inclusion of an illegal union security clause remove the contract as a bar to an election? In the private sector, the NLRB has uniformly held that a contract which contains a union-security clause or a check-off clause which is illegal on its face or has been determined to be illegal in an unfair labor practice proceeding does not bar a representation election. Paragon Products Corp., 134 N.L.R.B. 662 (1961); Gary Steel Supply Co., 144 N.L.R.B. 470 (1963). What are the advantages and disadvantages of adopting this policy in the public sector?

6. Does an agreement that is conditioned upon the appropriation of funds by another public body operate as a bar prior to the time the condition is met? In Camden County Welfare Board, PERC Decision No. 65 (1972), the New Jersey PERC stated:

> . . . The incorporation of two conditions regarding funds for salary increases in no way detracts from the substance of the agreement. It simply represents the most that a public employer could do under the circumstances at that time. A collective negotiations agreement in public employment frequently requires a later appropriation of funds after execution of the agreement in order to implement it. Even if that subsequent appropriation is not made an express condition in the contract, it is nevertheless a fundamental condition which is incorporated by necessary implication. Many, probably most, public employers are not self-appropriators; they are dependent for funds upon a political mechanism outside of their direct control. The conditions involved here are of that kind; the contract does not contain a condition, the fulfillment of which is reserved to one of the parties. The parties struck a bargain, the funding of which was necessarily

conditioned by the Board's limitations. The expression of these conditions in their agreement merely recognizes a fact of political life. Under the circumstances, we conclude that the execution date of their written agreement, January 13, 1971, should control for purposes of applying the contract bar rule. . . .

3. Election, Certification and Recognition Bars

Election Bars. In order to balance the right of employees freely to decide whether they wish to be represented with the desirability of providing some degree of finality to the results of an election, most public sector collective bargaining statutes provide for a one-year election bar. Section 23.40.100 (c) of the Alaska statute, which parallels section 9 (c) (3) of the NLRA, is typical: "An election may not be held in a bargaining unit or in a subdivision of a bargaining unit if a valid election has been held within the preceding 12 months." ALAS. STAT. tit. 23, ch. 40, § 23.40.100 (c) (1972). There are some variations, however. The Los Angeles ordinance states that "At least six months shall lapse following an election without a majority representative being chosen before a petition for certification may be filed covering the same group of employees." Los Angeles, Cal., Admin. Code, div. 4, ch. 8, § 4.822 (c) (6) (1971). On the other hand, the Baltimore ordinance provides that a valid election bars another election for a two year period. Baltimore, Md., City Code, art. I, § 117 (d) (1972). An election bar, however, does not prohibit the holding of a runoff election or a second election if the first election has been set aside on the basis of objections filed by a party to the election or has otherwise been ruled invalid.

Under the NLRA the period of time within which another election is barred is computed from the date of the election, not the date on which the results of the election are certified. Bendix Corp., Automation & Measurement Div., 179 N.L.R.B. 140 (1969). *Accord,* Holland Bd. of Public Works, 1968 MERC Lab. Op. 853. While an election in a broad bargaining unit bars an election in a smaller bargaining unit for the specified period of time, an election in a smaller unit does not bar an election in a broader unit. For example, if a group of craft employees were included in a broad overall unit, a subsequent election limited to the craft employees would be barred for the specified period. *See* Vickers, Inc., 124 N.L.R.B. 1051 (1959). On the other hand, if an election were held in a unit limited to craft employees, it would not bar an election in a larger bargaining unit that included the craft employees, even though the specified period of time had not elapsed. *See* Thiokol Chemical Co., 123 N.L.R.B.

888 (1959). Would the same results be required under the Los Angeles ordinance quoted above?

Suppose a valid election is held on June 1 in which Union A fails to poll a majority of the votes cast. Suppose further that within three months thereafter Union B obtains authorization cards from a substantial majority of the same employees that voted in the June 1 election. Does the employer, knowing Union B represents a majority of its employees, commit an unfair labor practice if it refuses to recognize Union B where the act bars the holding of an election if a valid election has been held within the twelve preceding months? Would it be necessary to show that the employer has engaged in unfair labor practices aimed at dissipating the union's majority support? *See* Conren, Inc. v. NLRB, 368 F.2d 173 (7th Cir. 1966), *cert. denied,* 386 U.S. 974 (1967), *noted* 80 HARV. L. REV. 1805 (1967).

Certification Bars. Several public sector collective bargaining statutes expressly provide that no question concerning representation can be raised during a designated period of time from the date of the employee organization's certification as the collective bargaining representative. A one-year period is typically specified. The Maryland Teachers' Statute is an exception; it provides that "the designation of an exclusive representative shall be for a minimum period of two years." MD. ANN. CODE, art. 77, § 160(f) (1969). Under the NLRA there is a conclusive presumption that a union, in the absence of unusual circumstances, continues to represent a majority of the employees during the year following certification and no question concerning representation can be raised during the certification year. Brooks v. NLRB, 348 U.S. 96 (1954). The Michigan Employment Relations Commission has adopted a similar policy. Sunshine Hospital, 1968 MERC Lab. Op. 440; City of Bay City, 1967 MERC Lab. Op. 155. One of the underlying premises is that "a union should be given ample time for carrying out its mandate on behalf of its members, and should not be under exigent pressure to produce hothouse results or be turned out." Brooks v. NLRB, *supra.*

In Kenosha Board of Education, WERC Decision No. 8031 (1967), a local affiliate of the American Federation of Teachers filed a representation petition seeking to represent the District's teachers. In opposing the petition, the Kenosha Education Association, the incumbent bargaining representative, urged, *inter alia,* "that the Board adopt a rule to the effect that where the Board has previously certified an organization as the exclusive bargaining representative of employes in an appropriate unit, the second election should not be conducted within two years of the date of the certification of the results of the first election, and further, that said two-year certification bar rule be extended at two-year intervals." With respect to this contention, the WERC stated:

The Board has seriously considered whether it should adopt a two-year certification bar rule. That is to say, whether the Board should not conduct a second election in a period earlier than two years from the certification of the results of a previous election. In such consideration we must weigh the right of the employes to select or change their bargaining representative with the interest of preserving the stability of the established collective bargaining relationship. The problem is aggravated as a result of the fact that collective bargaining agreements in public employment, and especially those involving teachers, are not coextensive in time with budgetary considerations. Because of its statutory budgetary deadline and because of the nature of teacher employment, the School Board herein normally commences bargaining in May of each year for terms and conditions of employment for the following school year. It therefore becomes a necessity that if the employes are to select a new collective bargaining representative, said representative should be given a reasonable time to negotiate the collective bargaining agreement. If the ordinary contract bar rules were to apply, the election would not be held during the term of an existing agreement, and the selected collective bargaining representative, therefore, normally would not have a reasonable period of time to negotiate a collective bargaining agreement to succeed the existing agreement.

No rule with respect to certification bar is being established because the history of employment relations in municipal employment has not been such as to require such a rule at the present time, and because that history is not sufficiently developed to indicate a pattern of similar conditions. The conditions to be regulated are still too vaguely defined, and the Board prefers to wait until it is sufficiently certain that its rule, once adopted, will not be eroded by exceptions. Each case will be reviewed and determined on its own facts in order to balance the objective of employe choice with the objective of a stable bargaining relationship.

In determining how the two objectives will best be balanced and achieved, the Board will be influenced by various factors such as (1) the presence or absence of a current agreement; (2) the presence or absence of current and active negotiations for an agreement and how long such

negotiations have been in progress; (3) the budgetary deadlines imposed upon the parties; (4) the special deadlines
imposed by statute, such as the case with respect to teachers'
personal contracts; (5) whether the current bargaining agent
was certified or recognized; (6) the period of time since the
current bargaining agent was certified or recognized; and
(7) the employment relations history involved.

What effect would a finding that an employer had not bargained in good faith have on the computation of the certification
year? In City of Norwich, Decision No. 804 (1968), the Connecticut State Board of Labor Relations stated:

> There remains the question whether the petition in this
> case should be barred by the Municipal Employer's past pro-
> hibited labor practices in refusing to fulfill its statutory
> obligation to bargain collectively. In a number of cases
> under the National Labor Relations Act it has been held
> that where a union's majority was dissipated after an
> employer has engaged in unfair labor practices, particu-
> larly the refusal to bargain collectively, the Union is entitled
> to recognition for a reasonable period even though it has
> lost its majority support. For example, in Franks Bros. v.
> NLRB, 321 U.S. 702 (1944) the Supreme Court held that
> even though the union had lost its majority the employer
> should be compelled to continue bargaining with it for a
> reasonable period. The underlying principle expressed by
> the Court was that the union was entitled to a period of
> recognition and stability in order to demonstrate to the
> employees its capacity to represent them and to obtain
> benefits on their behalf. See also NLRB v. Warren Co.
> Inc., 350 U.S. 107 (1955); NLRB v. John S. Swift Co., 302
> F.2d 342 (7th Cir. 1962); Irving Air Chute Co. v. NLRB,
> 350 F.2d 176 (2nd Cir. 1965).
>
> We subscribe to this general principle. The employees
> can have no freedom of choice between whether they will
> engage in collective bargaining or not if the employer's
> refusal to bargain has prevented them from experiencing
> collective bargaining. We will not entertain a petition for
> an election where the employer's unfair labor practices
> have undermined the union's majority before it has had
> an opportunity to demonstrate its capabilities of represent-
> ing the employees in collective bargaining.

Recognition Bars. Under many public sector bargaining statutes an employer may voluntarily grant recognition to an employee organization if it represents a majority of the employees

in an appropriate unit. Should such a voluntary grant of recognition likewise constitute a bar to a representation petition filed by a rival organization? The NLRB has held that voluntary recognition bars a representation election "for a reasonable period." Keller Plastics Eastern, Inc., 157 N.L.R.B. 583 (1969). The so-called "reasonable period" is determined on a case-by-case basis and is frequently much less than one year from the date recognition was granted. See Ruffalo's Trucking Service, Inc., 114 N.L.R.B. 1549 (1955). What reasons, if any, are there for establishing different periods of unchallenged representation depending on whether the union was certified or was voluntarily recognized by the employer? Should the same policy be adopted in the public sector?

4. Effect of AFL-CIO Internal Disputes Plan

The purpose of the AFL-CIO Internal Disputes Plan as set forth in Article XX of the AFL-CIO Constitution is to prevent member unions from raiding the jurisdiction of other member unions. Article XX provides that if a member union feels that another member union is invading its jurisdiction, it can file a complaint and have the complaint heard by the Internal Disputes Tribunal. Article XX provides that the decision of the impartial tribunal is binding on member unions. The NLRB, however, has uniformly refused to dismiss a representation petition on the basis that an appeal to the AFL-CIO Internal Disputes Plan is being made or the petitioner has been found to be in violation of Article XX. In S.G. Adams Co., 115 N.L.R.B. 1012, 1013n.1 (1956), the Board stated:

[T]he pendency of proceedings before an intra-union tribunal for adjudication of representation questions does not affect the duty of the Board to resolve such questions. . . . Nor is the fact that the filing of a representation petition violates a union constitutional provision sufficient ground under Board policy for dismissing the petition. The Board has frequently held that it will not concern itself with the internal regulations of a labor organization.

That the same approach may be adopted in the public sector is indicated by the decision of the New York City Office of Collective Bargaining in Local Union No. 3, IBEW and the City of New York, Decision No. 36-69, GERR No. 305, B-4 (1969), wherein the New York City OCB stated:

Although Article XX may constitute a binding contract between affiliates of the AFL-CIO, it is not binding on third parties. In the State of New York, public employees have the statutory right to bargain collectively through representatives of their own choosing. . . . That statutory right manifestly is paramount to the contract between AFL-CIO affiliates, and must be recognized and effectuated by this Board.

The New York City OCB further noted that "the paramount right of the employees to select a bargaining representative cannot and should not be stultified by the fact that a rival union had represented employees in the past."

D. Determination of the Appropriate Bargaining Unit

1. Introduction

PRASOW, PRINCIPLES OF UNIT DETERMINATION—CONCEPT AND PROBLEMS, in PERSPECTIVE IN PUBLIC EMPLOYEE NEGOTIATION 61-62 (Public Employee Relations Library Special Issue, 1969)†

Unit determination has a considerable impact on the interested parties, which consist of four groups: employees, the employee organization, the public employer, and the public.

Employees prefer the unit which provides the maximum pressure to achieve their economic objectives. Where special skills are involved, they desire tight, compact, small units which preserve their bargaining power in terms of numbers and skill. Also, the smaller unit gives more weight to each vote.

Employee organizations are quite pragmatic in their approach to the unit question. Their first interest is in organization. They seek that unit which strengthens or ratifies the extent of employee organization. A major problem in unit determination arises when there are two or more rival organizations, each seeking recognition for some or all employees. The older and more established organization generally has more members and prefers a broader unit to offset the strength of the rival organization. The newer organization will insist on a narrow unit because its strength is concentrated in that area.

Rival employee organizations occasionally take opposing sides on two different unit questions. One will argue for a narrow unit in the first situation and a wide unit in the second. Exactly the opposite position is taken by the rival organization. There are internal, political, economic, and technological reasons for such apparent contradictions.

In state and local government, management's interest in unit formation is influenced by several factors. Public managers are

---

† Reprinted by permission of the International Personnel Management Association.

subject to inevitable political pressures, from below as well as from above. They must be sensitive and responsive to the views of higher officials, legislative or administrative, who have the ultimate decision-making power. Public managers in state and local government are often reluctant to take a firm stand on the boundaries of the bargaining unit. They may have mixed feelings on whether to include or exclude such categories as supervisors or professional personnel.

Public executives are properly concerned with efficiency in operations, stability of the work force, and administrative convenience. Accordingly they may prefer the all-inclusive unit to avoid the rivalry resulting from fragmentation of employees into competing units. Public management may sometimes press for a wider unit in order to prevent a particular organization from winning an election. In other situations, a unit is sought which favors a more cooperative employee organization.

Public management has a major stake in unit determination because it can significantly affect administrative functioning. For example, the larger the number of units, the greater the tendency, usually, of organizations to multiply. Certain kinds of unit determinations may preclude equitable treatment for *all* employees. The formation of units can be reflected in the quality of work performed. Administrators and public officials are expected to insure that service is rendered promptly, efficiently, and economically.

The Public Interest

We come now to "the public," the fourth and last, but not the least interested party in unit determination. It is altogether impossible to define this term precisely because the public is so diffuse, so heterogeneous and such a conglomerate assortment of individual and group interests.

We are never quite sure what the public interest really is. It is certainly not in the public interest for teachers to strike. Neither is it in the public interest for local officials to maintain an intransigent attitude in the face of reasonable teacher demands.

However, there are some aspects of the public interest which can be stated affirmatively: First, the public does not want any deterioration in the quality of the service rendered. There is an interest in maintaining harmonious relations in public employment. But the greatest concern is over the possibility of a disruption or stoppage of the service. The public has a right to expect uninterrupted service, but public employees also have the right to obtain effective representation. Both rights are legitimate. The difficulty arises when they conflict and are headed on a collision course. . . .

SHAW AND CLARK, DETERMINATION OF APPROPRIATE BARGAINING UNITS IN THE PUBLIC SECTOR: LEGAL AND PRACTICAL PROBLEMS, 51 Ore. L. Rev. 152, 152-54, 157-58 (1971)†

Determination of the appropriate bargaining unit in the public sector is of fundamental importance. It is both a prerequisite to negotiations and a vital factor in their structure and outcome. The more bargaining units public management deals with, the greater the chance that competing unions will be able to whipsaw the employer. Moreover, a multiplicity of bargaining units makes it difficult, if not impossible, to maintain some semblance of uniformity in benefits and working conditions. Unfortunately, in many states and localities bargaining units have been established without consideration of the effect such units will have on negotiations or on the subsequent administration of an agreement. The resulting crazy-quilt pattern of representation has unduly complicated the collective bargaining process in the public sector. . . .

The Legal Framework

State Legislation. In states which do not have applicable legislation, the determination of the appropriate bargaining unit is made by the parties. With increasing frequency, however, the determination of whether a unit is appropriate, in the absence of voluntary agreement by the parties, is made by a public employee relations board. Wisconsin, in 1959, was the first state to enact a comprehensive statute concerning collective bargaining by public employees. Since then there has been a virtual onslaught of legislation. More than thirty states have enacted legislation covering some or all categories of public employees. Various criteria have been suggested for determining the appropriate bargaining unit;[2] the following considerations are most frequently mentioned: (1) whether the employees concerned have a clear and identifiable community of interest; (2) whether the proposed unit will result in effective dealings and efficiency of operations; and (3) whether the employees have a history of representation. Generally the extent of organization may not be a controlling consideration.

Recently, there has been a distinct trend toward prescribing criteria explicitly designed to avoid fragmented bargaining

---

† Reprinted by permission. Copyright © 1971 by University of Oregon.

[2] Most of the statutes covering specific occupational groups such as firefighters, policemen or teachers specifically set forth the boundaries of the collective bargaining unit. . . .

units. The Pennsylvania Act, for example, provides that the board, in determining the appropriate bargaining unit, must take into consideration the effects of over-fragmentation and the existence of an identifiable community of interest. It further requires the board to consider "that when the Commonwealth is the employer, it will be bargaining on a statewide basis unless the issues involve working conditions peculiar to a given governmental locale." Similarly, the Kansas Act directs the public employee relations board to consider "the effects of overfragmentation and the splintering of a work organization."

Hawaii has gone one step further; it has legislatively established statewide bargaining units. Thus there are separate units for supervisory and nonsupervisory employees in blue-collar positions. The same is true for white-collar groups. There are separate units for teachers, for faculty of the University of Hawaii and the community college system, and for employees of the university and community college system other than faculty. Optional appropriate bargaining units are designated for registered nurses, nonprofessional hospital and institutional workers, firemen, policemen, and professional and scientific employees other than nurses.

On both the state and national level, statutory criteria necessarily determine the framework within which decisions of the various public employee relations boards can be made. The Wisconsin and New York statutes illustrate how the statutory framework affects bargaining unit determinations. . . .

Occupational Group Statutes. The Wisconsin and New York statutes are comprehensive in that they (1) cover all categories of employees, (2) provide a method for resolving questions concerning representation, and (3) establish a public employee relations board to administer the act. It should be noted, however, that there are numerous statutes that apply to only one occupational group, such as firefighters, policemen, or teachers. In contrast to the general criteria for determining the appropriate unit set forth in the comprehensive statutes, the occupational group statutes prescribe the boundaries of the bargaining unit. Furthermore, these statutorily prescribed bargaining units usually include supervisory and managerial personnel.[3]

---

[3] The Statutes covering firefighters are a prime example. Occasionally, individual units are prescribed within a comprehensive act. The Michigan Act, for example, provides that ". . . in any fire department, or any department in whole or part engaged in, or having the responsibilities of, fire fighting, no person subordinate to a fire commission, safety director, or other similar administrative agency shall be deemed to be a supervisor." MICH. COMP. LAWS ANN. § 423.213 (1967).

The Florida statute provides, as do the Georgia, Idaho, Rhode Island, and Wyoming statutes, that the organization selected by the majority of the firefighters shall be the sole and exclusive bargaining agent for *all* the classified members of the fire department. The units which have resulted from the application of this statute in Florida include everyone but the fire chief. In a city like Jacksonville, this means that out of a department of 711 members, only one person, the fire chief, is excluded.

NOTES

1. Section 23.40.090 of the Alaska Public Employment Act specifically provides that "bargaining units shall be as large as is reasonable and unnecessary fragmenting shall be avoided." ALAS. STAT. tit. 23, ch. 40, § 20.40.090 (1972).

2. The Nevada statute provides that where a local government employer has recognized one or more employee organizations, the employer is to determine the appropriate bargaining unit, after consultation with the employee organization or organizations, pursuant to the criteria set forth in the statute. If an employee organization disagrees with the unit determination, it may appeal to the PERB which is directed to apply "the same criterion" as the government employer. NEV. REV. STAT. § 288.170 (2) (1971).

Section 160 (d) of the Maryland Teachers' Bargaining Law makes the following provision with respect to the establishment of the appropriate bargaining unit:

> The determination of the composition of the unit shall be made by the public school employer in negotiation with those employee organizations which request negotiation thereon; provided, however, that in no event shall there be more than two units in any county or Baltimore City; and provided further that all public school employees shall be included in one of said units and shall be permitted all the rights granted herein. MD. ANN. CODE, art. 77, § 160 (d) (Supp. 1972).

3. In those states that do not have public sector collective bargaining legislation, the task of determining the appropriate bargaining unit is left to the parties themselves. In some instances where the parties have been unable to reach agreement on the appropriate bargaining unit, they have submitted the question to a mutually selected arbitrator. *See, e.g.,* Rochester Board of Education, 52 Lab. Arb. 1062 (Arb. Jean McKelvey, 1969). *See generally* Rehmus, *Arbitration of Representation and Bargaining Unit Questions in Public Employment Disputes,* in NATIONAL

ACADEMY OF ARBITRATORS, THE ARBITRATOR, THE NLRB, AND THE COURTS, PROCEEDINGS OF THE TWENTIETH ANNUAL MEETING 251 (1967).

4. For other useful discussions, see UNIT DETERMINATION, RECOGNITION, AND REPRESENTATION ELECTIONS IN PUBLIC AGENCIES, PROCEEDINGS OF A CONFERENCE ON PUBLIC SECTOR LABOR MANAGEMENT RELATIONS, 1971 (Univ. of Calif. Institute of Ind. Rel. 1972); H. WELLINGTON & R. WINTER, THE UNIONS AND THE CITIES 97-114 (1971); Anderson, *Selection and Certification of Representatives in Public Employment,* in N.Y.U. TWENTIETH ANNUAL CONFERENCE ON LABOR 277 (1967); Thompson, *Unit Determination in Public Employment,* PUBLIC EMPLOYEE RELATIONS REPORTS, No. 1 (N.Y. State School of Industrial and Labor Relations, 1968); Sullivan, *Appropriate Unit Determinations in Public Employee Collective Bargaining,* 19 MERCER L. REV. 402 (1968); Lahne, *Unit Determinations in the Federal Service,* in N.Y.U. TWENTY-FIRST ANNUAL CONFERENCE ON LABOR 469 (1969); Newman, *Major Problems in Public Sector Bargaining Units,* in N.Y.U. TWENTY-THIRD ANNUAL CONFERENCE ON LABOR 373 (1971). The NLRB's unit policies in the private sector are thoroughly explored in J. ABODEELY, THE NLRB AND THE APPROPRIATE BARGAINING UNIT (1971).

2. Criteria Considered

CONNECTICUT STATE BOARD OF LABOR RELATIONS, TWENTY-FIRST ANNUAL REPORT 1-3 (1967)

Questions concerning the unit and the related questions concerning the supervisory level at which membership in a unit is to be cut off obviously involve competing legitimate interests. The municipal employer, for example, often wants the broadest possible unit for reasons of administrative simplicity and convenience. Some employee organizations also want wide units because of their own traditions and institutional patterns. Other employee organizations have different and narrower traditions and practices, sometimes stemming from those of the old-line trade or craft unions. And some groups, heretofore unorganized or loosely organized, have their own traditions and special communities of interest. The Legislature itself has resolved these conflicts by providing specific guides in the case of uniformed and investigatory members of the police and fire departments, and in the case of professional employees. Even these guides have presented some problems of interpretation. Beyond them the Legislature has charged the Board with the difficult and often delicate task of balancing these competing interests under the broad injunction to insure to employees "the fullest freedom in exercising their rights" under the Act, and "to insure a clear and identifiable community of interest among employees" included in a unit. The Commission which drafted the Act stated that it did "subscribe to the view that the units should be the broadest possible which will reflect a community of interest and at the same time will respect the special interests of certain groups of employees." REPORT OF THE INTERIM COMMISSION TO STUDY COLLECTIVE BARGAINING BY MUNICIPALITIES (1965), p. 15 (hereinafter *Report*).

In attempting to implement this broad legislative mandate, the Board has given attention to the following factors in cases where one or more of them were made to appear:

1. *Agreements by the parties.* The Commission's Report indicates that the framers of the Act believed that questions of this nature should be governed by agreement of the parties where agreement can be had. *Report,* page 15. There has been such agreement in a majority of cases processed by the Agent during the reporting period, upon at least some aspects of the case. The Board has adopted the policy of approving such agreements unless the resulting unit clearly contravenes the policy of the Act, and this has not occurred in practice.

2. *The similarity (or dissimilarity) of work and working conditions.* This includes any aspects of the work which would tend to create a community of interest, or the reverse, and covers a great variety of matters. Whether the work is clerical or manual (white collar or blue collar); whether there is common supervision; whether the work is performed in a single location, are examples of the sort of things the Board will look for and try to weigh. Obviously these considerations may sometimes pull in opposite directions. Employees in the same department may, for instance, perform different kinds of work, and work classifications often cut across department lines. This was the case in Greenwich, Dec. No. 692, June 7, **1966.**

3. *The convenience of the municipal employer* in the light of its personnel and other relevant policies and practices. Thus in the Town of Greenwich the Board declined to carve a unit out of blue collar workers in the Public Works Department alone, when the Town showed that this would disrupt its policy of uniform treatment for all employees in the work classifications involved, many of whom were in other departments, and where there

appeared to be no countervailing consideration. See also City of Bridgeport, Dec. No. 677, February 21, 1966.

4. *Past bargaining history, if any.* The Board has given weight to the municipal employer's past practices and patterns of negotiation and recognition where there have been any. It is true that these would have antedated the Act, and are not legally binding on the parties. Nevertheless they have some tendency to show what the parties themselves have considered appropriate and feasible and what they are used to. And the patterns are likely to reflect any traditions that have evolved in the municipal service. Patterns worked out in other cities and towns, where they have attained a measure of consistency, seem entitled to some consideration in determining what is appropriate (though less than the municipal employer's own practices). They may be compared roughly to the customs of an industry which have often been given similar consideration. Even the employee organization's over-all pattern (in this country), where there is one, seems entitled to some weight, since it has at least a slight tendency on pragmatic grounds to show something about feasibility and about the kind of unit which the organization can effectively represent.

5. *The desires of the members of a group* to be associated together for bargaining purposes. . . .

6. *The Commission's admonition to keep the unit as broad as possible,* where that is consistent with the need for community of interest, and respect for legitimate special interests. . . .

The above discussion should indicate something of the complexity and difficulty of the Board's task. It should be quite apparent that many of the above considerations overlap, and many work at cross-purposes with each other. The problems and practices of the 169 cities and towns of the State vary infinitely, and the extent to which each of the factors listed above appears is not the same in any two of them. . . . For this reason there is great variety among the size and the kinds of units found appropriate in the cases decided by the Board during the reporting period. Just as the Commission "concluded that it would be impossible to lay down any hard and fast rules for the determination by the Board of appropriate units," . . . so the Board has refrained from applying rules which would put a strait-jacket on the types of units it would find appropriate. Rather it has sought to determine the problems in each municipality by applying to them the broad principles which the Act lays down, and by weighing the factors which the Board believes to be relevant to those principles in each individual case.

CITY OF APPLETON
Wisconsin Employment Relations Commission
Decision No. 7423 (1966)

Local 73, AFSCME, hereinafter referred to as the Petitioner, petitioned the Board to conduct an election among employes of the City of Appleton, employed in the Sewerage Division of the Department of Public Works, to determine what representation, if any, the employes therein desired for the purposes of collective bargaining, pursuant to Section 111.70 of the Wisconsin Statutes. At the hearing, Teamsters Local 563, hereinafter referred to as the Intervenor, was permitted to intervene on the basis of its claim to be the recognized representative for all hourly-paid employes employed in the Department of Public Works.

The Intervenor would have the Board dismiss the petition on two grounds, (1) that the unit sought by the Petitioner is inappropriate, and (2) that the petition was untimely filed.

Appropriateness of Unit

The Department of Public Works consists of five separate divisions, Street, Sanitation, Sewerage, Maintenance and Engineering. There are approximately 120 employes in the Department of Public Works, and 18 are employed in the Sewerage Division. The Intervenor, up until at least the date of the filing of the petition, September 27, 1965, has been recognized as the collective bargaining representative of all hourly-paid employes in the first four divisions. The Engineering Division consists of professional engineers and clericals.

While the Intervenor claims that it has been recognized as the representative of the employes in the Department of Public Works and that such a Department is an appropriate unit, it should be noted that the clerical employes in the Engineering Department have not been included as part of that departmental-wide unit.

The Sewerage Division is physically and functionally located separate and distinct from the remainder of the functions and divisions of the Municipal Employer. Its employes primarily carry out their functions at the Sewage Disposal Plant. It has its own Superintendent, who is in charge of the entire Division, and the employes in said Division are not subject to the supervision of any other agent or officer of the Municipal Employer. The employes perform duties which, except for the Laborer I and II classifications, of which there are four positions, are distinct from the duties performed by employes of the Municipal Employer employed in other divisions or departments. There are very few temporary transfers either to or from the Sewerage Division.

The Board's function with respect to the establishment of an appropriate collective bargaining unit of municipal employes is governed by the following statutory provisions:

"Section 111.70 (4) (d). *Collective Bargaining Units.* Whenever a question arises between a municipal employer and a labor union as to whether the union represents the employes of the employer, either the union or the municipality may petition the board to conduct an election among said employes to determine whether they desire to be represented by a labor organization. Proceedings in representation cases shall be in accordance with ss. 111.02 (6) and 111.05 insofar as applicable, except that where the board finds that a proposed unit includes a craft the board shall exclude such craft from the unit. The board shall not order an election among employes in a craft unit except on separate petition initiating representation proceedings in such craft unit."

"Section 111.02 (6). The term 'collective bargaining unit' shall mean all of the employes of one employer . . . , except that where a majority of such employes engaged in a single craft, division, department or plant shall have voted by secret ballot as provided in Section 111.05 (2) to constitute such group a separate bargaining unit they shall be so considered, . . ."

"Section 111.05 (2). Whenever a question arises concerning the determination of a collective bargaining unit as defined in Section 111.02 (6), it shall be determined by secret ballot, and the board, upon request, shall cause the ballot to be taken in such manner as to show separately the wishes of the employes in any craft, division, department or plant as to the determination of the collective bargaining unit."

Whenever a petition for an election is filed with the Board, and wherein the petitioner requests an election among certain employes not constituting all of the employes of the employer, the Board has no power, except if the employes constitute a single craft, to determine what constitutes an appropriate collective bargaining unit. It does determine whether the group of employes set out as being an appropriate bargaining unit does in fact constitute a separate craft, division, department or plant.

The employes involved, if they do constitute a separate division, department, or plant, are given the opportunity to determine for themselves whether they desire to constitute a separate collective bargaining unit.

The Intervenor contends that the statutes should be interpreted to give weight to past bargaining history to determine whether a non-craft group should be permitted to establish itself as a separate unit, whether for the purpose of decertification or for substituting another union for its current bargaining agent. It emphasizes the bargaining history between the Intervenor and the Municipal Employer, and argues that the unit established through bargaining history should not be disturbed.

The bargaining and negotiations in the past have been conducted by the City's Personnel Committee for all of the employes in the Department of Public Works, with the City Personnel Committee consulting with and receiving the advice of the Director of Public Works. The wage increases, fringe benefits and work rules negotiated for the Department of Public Works have been applied to all the employes in the Department and, in some instances, on a City-wide basis. The recommendations made by the Sewerage Division Superintendent with respect to promotions, transfers, discipline and individual wage adjustments, are subject to the approval of the Director of Public Works, and are not made independently by the Superintendent of the Sewage Disposal Plant.

The Intervenor would have the Board establish an appropriate collective bargaining unit on criteria considered by the National Labor Relations Board in establishing appropriate units under the federal labor law. The National Labor Relations Board considers the following factors:

(1)   Duties, skills and working conditions of the employes.
(2)   History of collective bargaining.
(3)   Extent of union organization among the employes.
(4)   Desires of the employes where one or two units may be equally appropriate.

Similarly, in recently adopted labor laws applying to public employes, the Connecticut State Board of Labor Relations and the Michigan Labor Mediation Board determine appropriate collective bargaining units with due consideration to ". . . a clear and identifiable community of interest to employes concerned. . . ."

However, the criteria established in the Wisconsin Employment Peace Act, as quoted above, do not permit the Board to rely on the bargaining history as grounds for denying elections among employes in a separate division to determine for themselves whether they desire to constitute a unit separate and apart from the other employes of the municipal employer.

The Board has also today issued a Direction of Elections in a case involving the City of Kenosha. Another local of the Teamsters filed a petition with the Board requesting the Board to conduct an election among employes in the Waste Division of the Department of Public Works. In that proceeding, another local of the AFSCME has been historically recognized as the representative of all civil service employes of that community, with the exception of uniformed employes. In the instant proceeding, the intervening Teamster's local objects to the fragmentation of an existing unit. In the City of Kenosha case, the petitioning Teamster's local would fragmentize the existing unit. The Intervenor AFSCME Local in the City of Kenosha case would retain the overall unit and opposes fragmentation of an existing unit, while in the instant proceeding, the petitioning AFSCME Local would fragmentize the existing unit. The position of the parties in said two proceedings are inconsistent and demonstrate the problems faced by the Board in establishing units as required by the Statute. Fragmentizing of larger units of employes may result in requiring a municipal employer to engage in conferences and negotiations with more than one labor organization representing the same general category of employes on wages, hours and working conditions of its employes, may encourage needless rivalry among labor organizations, and may disturb an existing legitimate relationship and tend to delay the collective bargaining process. However, these factors must be weighed against the rights of the employes, where they constitute a separate department or division, to determine for themselves whether they desire to constitute a separate appropriate collective bargaining unit and, further, what representation, if any, they desire for the purposes of conferences and negotiations with their municipal employer. It is interesting to note that there has been an insignificant number of cases where the Board has observed fragmentation of bargaining units, in accordance with the statutory requirements, among employes of private employers. Apparently, the employes, labor organizations and employers alike, at least in private employment, have recognized that an effective collective bargaining relationship is best maintained in the absence of fragmentizing an over-all collective bargaining unit. This observation is not intended to apply to those smaller units consisting of craft employes or employes with specialized skills. . . .

The Board, therefore, is today issuing a Direction of Elections wherein the employes in the Sewerage Division will be given an opportunity to determine for themselves whether they desire to constitute a collective bargaining unit separate and apart from other employes of the Municipal Employer, and what, if any, representation they desire for the purposes of conferences and negotiations with the Municipal Employer on questions of wages, hours and conditions of employment.

The results of the unit vote will be tabulated first, and if there is no question that the required number of employes vote in favor of the separate unit, then the ballots with respect to the selection of the bargaining representative will be tallied. However, if the result of the vote on the unit determination does not establish a separate unit, the Board agent conducting the elections will immediately impound the ballots on the question of representation and the results thereof will not be determined. . . .

NOTES

1. Chairman Morris Slavney of the Wisconsin Employment Relations Commission made the following comments with respect to the statutory provisions referred to in the principal case:

[S]uch requirements with regard to the establishment of bargaining units have resulted in an overfragmentation of bargaining units in municipal employment in Wisconsin. For example, the City of Milwaukee has over 20 separate bargaining units. In the City of Appleton, somewhere in the neighborhood of 60,000 population, both AFSCME and Teamsters were engaged in organizational efforts among clerical employees in some six departments of the city hall. As a result of the statutory provision granting employees in each department an opportunity to establish separate units, the City of Appleton ended up with six units of stenographers and clericals in six departments. The Teamsters represented three of the departmental units while AFSCME was certified as the representative in the remaining three departments. You can imagine the frustration of management in having to bargain with two unions, who are forever competing with each other, for the same classification of employees under the same civil service system. Slavney, *Representation and Bargaining Unit Issues,* in DISPUTE SETTLEMENT IN THE PUBLIC SECTOR 35, 49-50 (T. Gilroy ed. 1972).

The Wisconsin Municipal Employment Law was recently revised to broaden the discretion of the WERC in determining appropriate bargaining units, while at the same time mandating it to avoid excessive fragmentation. Wis. Stat. Ann. § 111.70 (4) (d) (Supp. 1972) now provides, in relevant part, that:

The commission shall determine the appropriate bargaining unit for the purpose of collective bargaining and shall whenever possible avoid fragmentation by maintaining as few units as practicable in keeping with the size of the total municipal work force. In making such a determination, the commission may decide whether, in a particular case, the employees in the same or several departments, divisions, institutions, crafts, professions or other occupational groupings constitute a unit. Before making its determination, the commission may provide an opportunity for the employees concerned to determine, by secret ballot, whether or not they desire to be established as a separate collective bargaining unit. . . .

2. Community of interest among the employees in the unit petitioned for is one of the most important determinants of whether the unit is appropriate. The Michigan Employment Relations Commission in City of Warren, 1966 MERC Lab. Op. 25, 28, noted that

Community of interest is determined by a number of factors and criteria, some of which are as follows: similarity of duties, skills and working conditions, job classifications, employee benefits, the amount of interchange or transfer of employees, the integration of the employer's physical operations, the centralization of administrative and managerial functions, the degree of central control of operations, including labor relations, promotional ladders used by employees, supervisory hierarchy, and common supervision.

Even if the employees in the unit petitioned for have an established community of interest, the unit may not necessarily constitute an appropriate bargaining unit. In Kelly Air Force Base, GERR No. 228, at Unit Arbitrations 1 (1968), the arbitrator conceded that there was a community of interest in the proposed unit; nevertheless, he held that "where that homogeneous group is only part of a larger essentially homogeneous group, sharing essentially the same common employment interests, a smaller group may not be found to be an appropriate unit."

3. What is the unit status under state law of employees who are paid from funds provided by the federal government? At least three labor relations agencies have held that employees hired under the Emergency Employment Act (EEA) of 1971

may be properly included in municipal bargaining units even though the federal government provides 90 percent of the funding. City of Chetek, WERC Decision No. 10757-A, GERR No. 457, B-11 (1972); AFSCME District Council 37 and City of New York, New York City Office of Collective Bargaining Decision No. 9-72, GERR No. 457, B-11 (1972); City of Selah, Wash. St. Dep't of Labor & Industries Memorandum Decision No. SK-1216, GERR No. 469, B-6 (1972). In Northumberland County, Case Nos. PERA-R-1996-C *et al.* (1972), GERR No. 485, B-4 (1973), the Pennsylvania Labor Relations Board refused to accept a stipulation excluding employees hired with Emergency Employment Act funds from a bargaining unit. In Clare Public Schools, 1972 MERC Lab. Op. 1002, the MERC held that whether EEA employees were eligible to vote in representation elections depended on whether they share a sufficient community of interest with other employees performing similar work, the nature of their employment, and the manner in which they are paid. *Cf.* Social Service Employees Union and City of New York, New York City Bd. of Certification Decision No. 51-68 (1968) (case-aide trainees paid entirely by federal government and in program terminable at discretion of federal government not employees). The Connecticut State Board of Labor Relations, however, held that EEA employees could not be included in a bargaining unit since the requirements under which the federal funds were provided precluded the employer from having the "sole and exclusive control over the . . . wages, hours and conditions of employment" as required by the Municipal Employment Relations Act. The Connecticut Board noted that the various federal requirements left "no room for the kind of collective bargaining contemplated by the State Act implemented by procedures and sanctions which are exclusively within the control of the state." Housing Authority of the City of Bristol, Decision No. 1067, GERR No. 457, B-11 (1972).

4. Are prisoners in state correctional institutions entitled to representation for the purposes of collective bargaining? In State of New York (Department of Correctional Services), 1 PERB ¶ 3033 (1973), the New York PERB held that prisoners were not public employees, noting that "their employment relationships . . . is too peripheral to be covered by the Taylor Law."

ROCK, THE APPROPRIATE UNIT QUESTION IN THE PUBLIC SERVICE: THE
PROBLEM OF PROLIFERATION, 67 Mich. L. Rev. 1001, 1001-08 (1969)†

I. Introduction

It is becoming increasingly clear that of the numerous problems
which complicate the practice of collective bargaining in the
public sector, none is more important than the appropriate unit
question. In the public sector as well as in private industry, determination of the size and composition of the bargaining unit at
the initial stages of organization and recognition can be decisive
of the question of which employee organization will achieve
majority recognition, or whether any organization will win recognition. Save for the employee organization which limits its
jurisdiction along narrow lines such as the craft practiced by its
members, the normal tendency may be to request initially a
unit whose boundaries coincide with the spread of the organization's membership or estimated strength. The public employer,
on the other hand, may seek to recognize a unit in which the
no-union votes will be in the majority, or a favored employee
organization will have predominant strength; or the employer
may simply seek to avoid undue proliferation of bargaining
units.

The problem in the public sector, however, is of far greater
depth than the initial victory-or-defeat aspect of recognition.
In the private sector, it is clear that the scope and nature of the
unit found to be appropriate for bargaining has acted as an
important determinant of the union's basic economic strength—
that is, its bargaining over bread-and-butter economic issues. In
the public sector, it seems clear that the scope and nature of the
unit found to be appropriate will also affect the range of subjects
which can be negotiated meaningfully, the role played in the
process by the separate branches of government, the likelihood
of peaceful resolution of disputes, order versus chaos in bargaining, and ultimately, perhaps, the success of the whole idea of
collective bargaining for public employees.

Although the appropriate unit question has received much
attention in the private sector during the past thirty years, it has
not received the same attention for public sector employees until
recently. The purpose of this Article is to focus on certain distinguishing aspects of both the problem and the experience in the
public sector, and to discuss a possible approach or philosophy
for the future. The primary concern here is undue proliferation
of units among the large pool of blue-collar and white-collar
employees in the public service.

---

† Reprinted by permission of The Michigan Law Review Association.

II. *Past Tendencies and Patterns*

Traditionally, the public employer and union have given little thought to the appropriateness of a unit that requested recognition. More often than not, in the years prior to the enactment of definitive rules for recognition of public employees, a union requesting and receiving some form of recognition was considered the spokesman for its members—in whatever job classifications, functional departments, or physical locations they happened to be. This lenient approach was facilitated by (and perhaps had its start in) the fact that "recognition" frequently carried no legal consequences beyond the ability to appear before legislative or executive bodies hearing budgetary requests or the power to lobby with key political figures. Even when recognition was followed by a procedure similar to bargaining—including in some instances an embodiment of the bargain in a written agreement or memorandum—little if any consideration was given to the appropriateness of the unit being dealt with. Apart from the obvious problems stemming from the failure to grant "exclusive bargaining rights" to these early public employee units and from the inattention to the matter of excluding supervisors from the units representing those whom they supervise, a groundwork was laid for the creation of illogical unit lines. All too frequently the result was a proliferation of bargaining units. The task of changing this ill-conceived basis has often proved troublesome in the current period of rule-oriented bargaining.

Nor has the enactment of rules in the past ten years invariably led to a different pattern. For example, under New York City's Executive Order 49, issued by Mayor Wagner in the late fifties, certificates of recognition were granted for over 200 separate units, some containing as few as two employees. The proportion of units to number of member-employees found in New York City is perhaps exceeded only in Detroit, where some seventy-eight separate units have come into existence. At the federal level, marked proliferation of units has also characterized the pattern of recognition under Executive Order No. 10,988; a similar tendency seems inherent in a number of recently enacted state legislative standards for unit determination.

Notwithstanding this rather pessimistic summary, the past ten years have clearly been the decisive decade for all aspects of public sector bargaining, and this is particularly true for the specific rules regarding unit determination. A major example of this development occurred in 1962 with President Kennedy's promulgation of Executive Order No. 10,988. In this document, which was originally regarded as the federal employee's Magna Carta of labor relations, the following general standards are specified for appropriate unit determination when "exclusive" recognition is sought by a majority organization:

> Units may be established on any plant or installation, craft, functional or other basis which will ensure a clear and identifiable community of interest among the employees concerned, but no unit shall be established solely on the basis of the extent to which employees in the proposed unit have organized.

Another section of the Order also provides for "formal" recognition in a "unit as defined by the agency" when an employee organization has ten percent of the employees as members, and no other organization holds exclusive representation rights. Finally, another section provides for "informal" recognition when the employee organization does not qualify for exclusive or formal recognition, without regard to whether other employee organizations hold one of the other forms of recognition in the same unit.

Regardless of whether this three-sided format was justified under the state of recognition and bargaining then prevalent in the federal service, there can be little question that the system was calculated to encourage representational footholds on a mass scale within small units. And, it did result in proliferation of units, albeit on a reduced scale, as informal or formal recognition often led to exclusive recognition. Emphasis on the "community of interest" standard in the administration of Executive Order No. 10,988, and the use in some instances of the National Labor Relations Board's technique of the *"Globe* election"—a procedure in which the members of a homogeneous occupational group are allowed to vote on separate recognition for their own unit, as opposed to a rival organization's request that they be included in a larger unit—have undoubtedly contributed further to widespread fragmentation of units in federal employment.

At the state and local levels, virtually all of the significant legislation passed since 1960 has spelled out standards of some type for unit determination. In many instances these state enactments made possible further proliferation by adding to the existing illogical patterns of recognition new units made possible through espousal of the federal "community of interest" standard and its converse, separate units for groups having "conflicting interests"; by providing for *Globe*-type elections or similar approaches designed to facilitate small unit separation; and, in the states of Delaware and Minnesota, by permitting the government agency to rely on the extent of employee organization. Notwithstanding the fact that some of the state laws embody specific standards used by the National Labor Relations Board for the private sector, observers familiar with bargaining conditions in both sectors have contended that the degree of fragmentation in some of the states exceeds that of the private sector.

Clearly, at both state and federal levels the standards place a high premium on the subjective judgment of the decision-making body or individual, and results are also shaped to a high degree by the happenstance of the petitioning organization's requested unit at the time of the petition. Particularly when there is no rival organizational claim for a larger unit—which is often the case—the over-all effect has been to encourage recognition of the smaller unit. Even if a union succeeds in winning recognition in a large unit, employees in that unit are generally not required to become members of the union. The relative lack of union security clauses in the collective bargaining agreements of the public service assures that, to a degree unparalleled in the private sector, dissident small-unit groups are able to maintain their separate identities and to prolong the battle for break-off from the larger group's exclusive bargaining agent.

III. The Case for and Against the Small Unit

It cannot be assumed automatically that the pattern of many small units is wrong. A single craft, classification, department, or installation which would otherwise constitute a small minority if included in a larger unit can argue with some justification that its specialized interests and needs may be subordinated to the wishes of the larger unit's majority. Moreover, the smaller unit which performs a particularly essential function may also be capable of striking a better bargain for itself when left to do its own negotiating.

"Community of interest" is more than a catch phrase. It not only points up that like-situated employees will better understand their own problems and press their unique needs, but it also recognizes the instinct of exclusiveness which causes employees to *want* to form their own organization rather than become a part of a larger organization in which they may feel themselves strangers. The desire to possess such "freedom of choice" or "self-determination" should, it can be argued, receive greater weight for public employees, because they are "public," than for those in the private sector.

There is nothing inherently wrong in permitting an employee organization to gain a foothold in a smaller unit, if the employees in that unit select it; and, if the union is effective in the small unit, it may grow and achieve recognition in other separate units or in a single large unit. This consideration may be particularly significant in the early period after the promulgation of legislation or executive orders encompassing a vast group of employees whose right to representation had not previously been formally legitimized. It is frequently easier for unions to secure employees' allegiance in smaller, distinctive groups than in larger, heterogeneous ones.

At the same time, there are important considerations which, it seems, point toward a unique long-range need for larger units in the public sector. The special problems of unit determination in the public sector were most clearly recognized legislatively in 1967 in New York's Taylor Law, which included, in addition to the common standards of community of interest and necessity to promote the public welfare, the further requirement that in defining an appropriate unit the following standard should be taken into consideration: "the officials of government at the level of the unit shall have the power to agree, or to make effective recommendations to other administrative authority or the legislative body with respect to, the terms and conditions of employment upon which the employees desire to negotiate. . . ." The latter clause clearly reflects awareness of the fact that the employer-negotiator in the public service frequently has only limited authority, and that this condition will affect the scope of bargaining. As pointed out by the New York Governor's Committee on Public Employee Relations, the picture in the public sector is fundamentally different from that in the private sector. In private business, the authority to bargain on all of the normally bargainable matters is present or can be delegated, no matter what the size or make-up of the bargaining unit. By contrast, in the public service the necessary authority may not be delegable to lower-level functional units; legal requirements and tradition often call for uniformity of certain working conditions for like categories of employees throughout the governmental entity, regardless of bargaining unit categorization; and, even at the top of the particular level of government involved, authority is normally divided at least three ways—among the executive branch, the legislative branch, and a civil service commission.

Inherent in the previously quoted section of the Taylor Law, therefore, is the necessity that some consideration be given to the nature of the subject matter sought to be bargained upon in seeking to arrive at the appropriateness of a unit. This provision of the Taylor Law also recognizes that the subject matter of bargaining must normally be limited by the scope of the "employer's" authority to make agreements or effective recommendations, and a likely consequence is that the smaller the unit decided upon, the more restricted the scope of the bargaining by that unit will be.

Apart from this inhibiting effect on the bargaining experience, an approach which permits or favors small units makes it very difficult to resolve other institutional complications which arise in bargaining in the public service. The New York Governor's Committee, in both its 1966 Report and its 1968 Report, pointed out the unique importance of completing a negotiation with public employees in time to incorporate the agreement's financial essence in the budget of the governmental unit—which, by law, generally must be submitted to the legislature by a specified date. However, many of the annual bargaining sessions in the public sector today are extraordinarily prolonged, starting with direct negotiation, followed by resort to mediation and the frequently used machinery of fact-finding or impasse panels. After all of this there may be further extensive dealings with upper-echelon individuals or groups in the executive and legislative branches. Thus, the sheer weight of the process[4] may lead to its breakdown if the trend toward proliferation of bargaining units in numerous jurisdictions continues unabated. It is noteworthy that in the City of Philadelphia[5]—which is frequently cited as an example of well-established, peaceful, and effective bargaining at the municipal level—all employees except policemen and firemen have been represented by a single unit for most of the last two decades. Even with only a single unit and without use of impasse resolution machinery, however, the experience in Philadelphia has been marked by many instances of abnormally prolonged annual negotiations. The Philadelphia experience also demonstrates the need to establish detailed liaison between the executive branch, the legislative branch, and the civil service commission during the course of an annual bargaining program in order to minimize the chaotic effects of overlapping authority on the government side.

While it is possible that a city the size of Philadelphia might also have had a history of successful labor relations in the public sector under a pattern which broke down the public employee bargaining group into a small number of separate units, there is little question that the success could not have been achieved

---

4 For example, a February 27, 1968, report by an impasse panel for the unit of Detroit police officers recommended a procedure for future bargaining. The essential steps which the panel proposed were to extend over a period of nine months in a particular year. *Excerpts from Detroit Police Panel Report*, GOV'T EMPLOYEE REL. REP. [*hereinafter* GERR] No. 235, at D-1, D-10 (March 11, 1968).

5 The author was the labor relations adviser to the City of Philadelphia between 1952 and 1962.

under the patterns of excessive fragmentation found elsewhere. In any event, the existence of the single large unit clearly contributed significantly to that city's ability to surmount effectively the institutional obstacles complicating public sector bargaining. Moreover, proliferation can and does breed excessive competition among rival organizations. One consequence of this may be a high incidence of breakdowns in peaceful bargaining. To be sure, competition in bargaining is to some extent unavoidable; this condition is not necessarily undesirable socially, and will continue to characterize the experience in private and public sector alike, regardless of the size of units involved. Nevertheless, there is hardly a permanent justification for permitting what appears to be a greater proliferation of bargaining units in the public sector than that now prevailing in the private sector. The institutional factors discussed above add a unique dimension to the task of achieving peaceful and successful bargaining in the public sector. Because of this, and because of the likelihood that proliferation will result in an increased number of breakdowns in the bargaining process, larger units must become the accepted norm in the public sector. . . .

STATE OF NEW YORK

New York Public Employment Relations Board
1 PERB ¶ 399.85 (1968), *aff'd per curiam sub nom.* Civil Service Employees Ass'n v. Helsby, 32 App. Div. 2d 131, 300 N.Y.S.2d 424, *aff'd per curiam,* 25 N.Y.2d 842, 250 N.E.2d 731, 303 N.Y.S.2d 690 (1969)

On November 15, 1967, the State of New York, herein referred to as the employer, recognized the Civil Service Employees Association, Inc., herein referred to as CSEA, as negotiating representative of employees in a general unit made up of all State employees other than professional members of the State University of New York and members of the State Police. Timely petitions contesting the designation of the general unit and the recognition of CSEA were filed by many organizations, all of which proposed one or more negotiating units alternative to the unit designated by the employer.

The Petitioners and the Units They Claim

New York State Employees Council 50, American Federation of State, County and Municipal Employees, AFL-CIO, herein referred to as Council 50, directly and through several of its affiliated locals, seeks the following units:

1. All correction officers, correction youth camp officers and correction hospital officers in the Department of Correction, excluding all supervisors and all other persons.

This identical unit is claimed by another of the petitioners, Local 456 of the International Brotherhood of Teamsters, Chauffeurs, Warehousemen and Helpers of America, herein referred to as IBT.

2. All employees in the Psychiatric Attendant Series, including psychiatric attendant, psychiatric senior attendant, psychiatric staff attendant, psychiatric supervising attendant, psychiatric head attendant, psychiatric chief supervising attendant and all (T.B.) titles in this series.

3. All nonsupervisory employees in the Rehabilitation Counselor Series in the Department of Education, including counselors and senior counselors. There are a few rehabilitation counselors in the Department of Social Services and Mental Hygiene and in the State University. Council 50 takes no position on whether these rehabilitation counselors should also be included in the proposed unit.

4. All clerical employees of the Department of Labor, proper.

5. All professional and technical employees of the Department of Labor proper, excluding managerial and confidential employees, nurses, attorneys and safety inspectors.

6. All professional and technical employees of the Division of Employment, excluding managerial and confidential employees, nurses and attorneys.

7. All clerical employees of the Division of Employment.

8. All nonsupervisory office and clerical employees of the State Insurance Fund.

9. All nonsupervisory professional and technical employees of the State Insurance Fund, excluding field service, confidential and managerial employees, nurses and attorneys.

10. All supervising professional and technical employees of the State Insurance Fund, excluding field service, confidential and managerial employees, nurses and attorneys.

11. All investigators of the Workmen's Compensation Board, Grade 12 through Grade 20.

12. All hearing officers of the Workmen's Compensation Board, Grade 14, and all those calendar clerks who are assigned to the Workmen's Compensation Board Referees' Bureau.

13. All assistant workmen's compensation examiners, Grade 8.

Local 30D, International Union of Operating Engineers, AFL-CIO, herein referred to as Operating Engineers, seeks a unit of:

14. Nonsupervisory employees in the power plants and related skilled trade shops.

The Safety Officers Benevolent Association, herein referred to as SOBA, seeks to represent:

15. All nonsupervisory safety officers. SOBA leaves to the discretion of this Board whether all nonsupervisory safety officers should be included in a single unit or whether there should be separate units for those employees in the Department of Mental Hygiene, Department of Correction, and the State University, respectively. It takes no position with respect to the inclusion or exclusion from the proposed unit or units of safety officers, if any, in the Department of Health.

Local 381 of the Building Service Employees International Union, AFL-CIO, herein referred to as BSEIU, seeks two units consisting, respectively, of:

16. Lifeguards employed by Long Island State Park Commission.
17. Seasonal patrolmen employed by Long Island State Park Commission.

District 15, International Association of Machinists and Aerospace Workers, AFL-CIO, herein referred to as IAM, seeks a unit of:

18. Long Island State Park Police, Grade 14 and Grade 16.

The Police Conference of New York, Inc., through two of its affiliates, seeks units of:

19. Niagara State Park Police, excluding the captain and lieutenants.
20. All Capital Buildings Police.

The Correction Officers Association claims a unit of:

21. All correction officers and their supervisors, excluding the deputy warden and correction deputy superintendent.

Local 223 of the Building Service Employees International Union, AFL-CIO, seeks a unit of:

22. Inspectors in the Division of Industrial Safety Service of the Department of Labor, excluding chief inspectors.

The Association of New York State Civil Service Attorneys, Inc., seeks a unit of:

23. Lawyers holding competitive class positions in the attorney series of titles for which permission to practice law

in the State of New York is a mandatory requirement, and persons holding training-level positions whether or not admitted to practice law in New York State. It would exclude lawyers who hold competitive class positions as counsel to a department or agency.

The New York State Nurses Association seeks a unit consisting of:

24. All registered professional nurses and every person lawfully authorized by permit to practice as a registered professional nurse in nursing service or in nursing education. The proposed unit would include persons on the faculty of the State University and, therefore, not within the general unit designated by the employer.

The American Physical Therapy Association claims a unit of:

25. All physical therapists. This unit would include physical therapists employed on the faculty of the State University and, therefore, not within the general unit designated by the employer.

Petitions were also filed by SOBA for a unit of nonsupervisory narcotics security assistants in the Department of Mental Hygiene, by the New York State Council of Carpenters, AFL-CIO, for a unit comprising all carpenters; and by Local 200 of the Building Service Employees International Union, AFL-CIO, for a unit consisting of all nonsupervisory employees of the Syracuse State School. Each of these petitions was withdrawn, as was a petition of the Police Conference, Inc., on behalf of a unit of police officers of the Palisades Interstate Park Commission.

Council 50 and BSEIU both filed timely petitions to decertify CSEA as the negotiating representative of employees in the general unit, on the ground that the general unit is inappropriate for the purpose of collective negotiations.

. . . .

[The Board denied a motion to disqualify the CSEA on the ground that it was not a labor organization within the meaning of the act. The Board granted motions disqualifying the American Physical Therapy Association and the Association of New York State Civil Service Attorneys, Inc., on this basis.]

Unit Determination of Director of Representation

With respect to the unit claims of the petitioners, the Director of Representation gave full consideration to the evidence produced and to the arguments made. He found that the employees within the general unit did not share a community of interest in that the range of their work assignments and of the training required for the performance of such assignments was inordinately broad. On the other hand, he found that, in the language of the employer:

> none [of the petitioners] has related its unit to a meaningful pattern of collective negotiation. Each would leave the State with a jumble of mixed vertical and horizontal units. They would leave it to the State to bring order out of the chaos they had created.

We agree with this analysis of the Director of Representation.

The employees concerned in this representation dispute are employed in over 3,700 job classifications, categorized in some 90 occupational groupings. These job classifications far surpass in diversity and number those usually found in public or private employment. These classifications run the gamut from Aircraft Pilot to Wild Life Trapper.

The enormity of this diversity of occupations and the great range in the qualifications requisite for employment in these occupations would preclude effective and meaningful representation in collective negotiations if all such employees were included in a single unit. The occupational differences found here give rise to different interests and concerns in terms and conditions of employment. This, in turn, would give rise to such conflicts of interest as to outweigh those factors indicating a community of interest.

Thus, the implementation of the rights granted by the Act to all public employees mandates a finding that a single unit would be inappropriate.

On the other hand, to grant the type of narrow occupational fragmentation requested by the petitioners would lead to unwarranted and unnecessary administrative difficulties. Indeed, as the State contends, it might well lead to the disintegration of the State's current labor relations structure.

Having rejected the unit designated by the employer and those proposed by petitioners, the Director of Representation decided that there should be six negotiating units, as follows:

> Operational Services Unit, Inspection and Security Services Unit, Health Services and Support Unit, Administrative Services Unit, Professional, Scientific and Technical Services Unit, and a unit of seasonal employees of the Long Island State Park Commission.

Excluded from all units are all other seasonal and part-time employees inasmuch as there is not sufficient evidence in the record to determine their proper unit placement, and persons claimed to be managerial or confidential employees by the employer. With respect to the latter group, the Director stated that further proceedings would be necessary to develop criteria to be utilized in categorizing an employee as managerial or confidential and to determine the desirability and practicality of their inclusion in the negotiating structure of State employees.

Both the employer and CSEA have contended on this appeal that the decision of the Director constitutes error, in that the units found in his decision do not coincide with any of the units petitioned for in this proceeding. Thus, a most basic question presented on this appeal is whether this Board, in a representation proceeding, may devise a unit that it deems to be most appropriate although such a unit is not sought by any of the parties.

We are convinced that this question must be answered in the affirmative. The statutory grant of authority to this Board to resolve disputes concerning representation status mandates this Board to define appropriate units[3] and does not restrict its power simply to the approval or disapproval of units sought by a party or parties to the proceeding. Even apart from such clear statutory intent, the logic of the situation compels the same conclusion. If the Board's power herein were so restricted, a representation dispute might be interminable, in that it would continue until a party to the proceeding petitioned for a unit which the Board found to be appropriate in the light of statutory criteria. Such a restrictive interpretation of the Act would delay unduly participation by public employees in the determination of their terms and conditions of employment. It is for this reason that the Director of Representation has, in many proceedings, devised negotiating units which were not sought by any of the parties.

We believe that the statutory criteria that "the unit shall be compatible with the joint responsibilities of the public employer and public employees to serve the public" (Civil Service Law, § 207 (c)) requires us to designate negotiating units which provide the employer with a comprehensive and coherent pattern for collective negotiations. Moreover, we believe that this statutory standard requires the designation of as small a number of units as possible consistent with the overriding requirement that the employees be permitted to form organizations of their own choosing to represent them in a meaningful and effective manner. It is our conviction that the approach of the Director of Representation in designating a limited number of negotiating

---

[3] Civil Service Law, § 207.1.

units, each consisting of families of occupations, is reasonably designed to achieve this goal.

In evaluating the specific units determined to be appropriate by the Director of Representation, we defer consideration of the unit for the seasonal employees of the Long Island State Park Commission. The unit itself and the questions it raises regarding seasonal employees in parks and elsewhere throughout the State are separable from problems involving the other State employees. Further, these problems are not ripe for resolution as the seasonal employees of the Long Island State Park Commission are not presently on the State payroll and will not be until the advent of summer.

We find the following five units to be appropriate:

1. Operational Services Unit:

This unit is similar to that determined to be appropriate by the Director of Representation except that we delete those occupations associated with institutions and related to the preparation and distribution of food, and to personal and domestic services. For the reasons discussed below, these occupations are placed in Unit 3.

2. Security Services Unit:

This unit is a contraction of the Inspection and Security Services Unit determined to be appropriate by the Director of Representation in that we delete all inspectors, investigators and examiners from that unit. The unit now comprises all occupations involving the protection of persons and property; the enforcement of laws, codes, rules and regulations concerned with vehicle and highway safety; and the security aspects of correctional institutions. Inspectional services cover a broad range of occupations which are distinct from security services and cannot be properly allocated to the same unit. The inspectors, investigators and examiners who have been deleted from this unit have been placed in Units 4 and 5.

3. Institutional Services Unit:

This unit is an expansion of the Health Services and Support Unit determined to be appropriate by the Director of Representation in that the unit now includes those occupations associated with institutions and related to the preparation and distribution of food and to personal and domestic services. We find that working conditions in institutions are significantly different from working conditions elsewhere. Accordingly, we conclude that employees engaged in these occupations—which are unique to institutions

—have a greater community of interest with their fellow institutional employees than with operational services employees.

4. Administrative Services Unit:

This unit is similar to the unit determined to be appropriate by the Director of Representation except that it also includes certain inspectors, investigators and examiners who were deleted from Unit 2. All inspectors, investigators and examiners are placed in this unit unless their responsibilities are of a professional, scientific or technical nature.

5. Professional, Scientific and Technical Services Unit:

This unit is similar to that determined to be appropriate by the Director of Representation except that it includes inspectors, investigators and examiners, the nature of whose responsibilities are of a technical, professional or scientific nature.

The implementation of these units in this representation proceeding requires a determination as to those eligible for inclusion in each unit. In making this determination, we must consider these as yet unanswered questions—

First—A determination as to which job titles shall be included in each unit. We feel that the delineation of the units heretofore made provides sufficient specificity to allocate the majority of job titles to their respective units. However, there may be a question with respect to some job titles as to which unit they belong.

Second—In his decision, the Director included in each unit those responsible for the supervision of the activities of that unit. It is our policy not to exclude all supervisors arbitrarily from a rank-and-file unit.[5] Rather, supervisors have been excluded when there was a showing that their supervisory duties and obligations were of such a nature to give rise to such a conflict of interest as to preclude their inclusion in the same unit with rank-and-file. Thus, a determination must be made as to what supervisors will be excluded from any unit and the disposition of those excluded.

Third—The dimensions of the exclusion of managerial and confidential employees.

We believe that these specific questions of eligibility and exclusion can be resolved most expeditiously in the following manner: This Board shall prepare a list of job titles to be

---

[5] *See, e.g.,* In the Matter of **New York State Division of State Police, Case Nos.** C-0062, C-0130, C-0133 (1968).

placed in each unit. This list shall include the Board's disposition of the supervision question. A second list prepared by the Board will indicate those excluded as managerial or confidential. Within seven days after these lists have been submitted to the parties, a conference will be scheduled by the Board, at which time the Board will consider and rule on any objections of the parties to such lists. . . .

NOTES

1. In establishing appropriate bargaining units, is it necessary that the agency establish the *most* appropriate unit as distinguished from *an* appropriate unit? In the private sector the NLRB has uniformly held that the unit petitioned for does not have to be the most appropriate unit. In Morand Brothers Beverage Co., 91 N.L.R.B. 409, 418 (1950), the Board stated that "there is nothing in the statute which requires that the unit of bargaining be the *only* appropriate unit, or the *ultimate* unit or the *most* appropriate unit; the Act requires only that the unit be appropriate. It must be appropriate to insure to employees, *in every case,* 'the fullest freedom in exercising the rights guaranteed by this Act.' " Although similar rulings have been made by several state labor relations boards, there are at least two noteworthy exceptions. In the principal case the New York PERB held that the statutory criteria mandated the establishment of the most appropriate bargaining unit. The Michigan Employment Relations Commission (MERC) has adopted a position somewhere between the NLRB approach and the New York PERB approach. Thus, the MERC has stated that in making unit determinations it is guided by the following standard set forth by the Michigan Supreme Court in Hotel Olds v. State Labor Mediation Board, 333 Mich. 382, 387, 53 N.W.2d 302, 304 (1952): "In designating bargaining units as appropriate, a primary objective of the Commission is to constitute the largest unit which in the circumstances of the particular case is most compatible with the effectuation of the purposes of the law and to include in a single unit all common interests." Relying on the *Hotel Olds* decision, the MERC held in City of Charlevoix, 1970 MERC Lab. Op. 404, that a city-wide bargaining unit that included fire and police personnel was appropriate since "the larger overall unit is more in keeping with the policy of the State than separate departmental units, especially in a municipality where only a small number of employees are employed." On the other hand, in Regents of the University of Michigan, 1971 MERC Lab. Op. 337, the MERC stated that "[t]he statute does not require that only the 'ultimate unit' can

be certified. There may be smaller groupings within the employment of a single employer which are appropriate for collective bargaining. . . ."

2.   The Kansas Public Employee Relations Board in Ft. Hays Kansas State College, Case No. 1 (1972), GERR No. 487, B-3 (1973), stated that it "would allow public employees at each unit of higher education to organize on individual institutional units." The Kansas Board stated:

> Each institution, the Board feels is a separate distinct operating entity with a complex relationship already existing between the public employees and the administration therein. The principles of efficient administration will be maintained inasmuch as the evidence before this Board indicates that most problems concerning conditions of employment with university employees have been handled on a local basis; i.e. between the local university administration and the employee. Evidence before this Board also indicates that a distinct "community of interest" is enjoyed by employees at the individual institutions. Particularly, it was expressed that the workers with similar occupations at KU Medical Center and at Kansas University were working under different environments with different benefits in some cases. Contrasted with this, the employees at each institution had a common base in their working conditions and the evidence indicated a similarity of problems at each institution that is not evident between employees of separate institutions.
>
> . . . The difficulties of employees organizing over a great distance (i.e., the distance between Wichita and Ft. Hays) when considered in light of the fact that each institution has operated as a separate identity, made the unit determinations on an individual institutional basis seem most logical. The Board did not view the problems of overfragmentation and splintering of a work force as automatically requiring a statewide unit in every case, but that each case must be reviewed on its own merit, thus our decision of the individual institutional units.

3.   Professional Employees

Section 9 (b) (3) of the NLRA provides that

. . . the Board shall not (1) decide that any unit is appropriate [for the purposes of collective bargaining] if such unit includes both professional employees and employees who are not professional employees unless a majority of such

professional employees vote for inclusion in such unit. . . .
29 U.S.C. § 159 (b) (3) (1970).

A premise underlying this provision is that professional employees should not be automatically included in bargaining units with non-professional employees against their wishes since they usually have distinct professional standards, different working conditions, and are frequently paid on a different basis than non-professional employees. In order to differentiate professional employees from non-professional employees, Congress defined the term "professional employee" as follows:

(a)   any employee engaged in work (i) predominantly intellectual and varied in character as opposed to routine mental, manual, mechanical, or physical work; (ii) involving the consistent exercise of discretion and judgment in its performance; (iii) of such a character that the output produced or the result accomplished cannot be standardized in relation to a given period of time; and (iv) requiring knowledge of an advanced type in a field of science or learning customarily acquired by a prolonged course of specialized intellectual instruction and study in an institution of higher learning or a hospital, as distinguished from a general academic education or from an apprenticeship or from training in the performance of routine mental, manual or physical processes; or

(b)   any employee, who (i) has completed the courses of specialized intellectual instruction and study described in clause (iv) of paragraph (a), and (ii) is performing related work under the supervision of a professional person to qualify himself to become a professional employee as defined in paragraph (a). 29 U.S.C. § 152 (12) (1970).

STATE OF NEW JERSEY

New Jersey Public Employment Relations Commission
Decision No. 68, GERR No. 457, E-1 (1972)

The above-captioned cases raise questions concerning the representation of various groups of professional employees[2] employed by the State of New Jersey. Hearings were conducted on each of the petitions and thereafter Hearing Officers made the following recommendations. In Case No. R-111 *ad hoc* Hearing Officer Joseph McCabe recommended that separate state-wide

---

[2] In most instances the parties do not contest the use of the term "professional" in describing the employees involved. For purposes of this decision, there is an assumption, but no determination, that such description is appropriate.

units of supervisory and non-supervisory Registered Nurses be found appropriate. No exceptions were timely filed to that recommendation. In Case No. RO-196, wherein Petitioner sought certification in a unit of all Social Workers and Social Worker trainees employed by the Bureau of Childrens Services, Hearing Officer Martin Pachman recommended dismissal of that petition on two grounds.

First, since not all social workers in state classified service were included, the unit sought, being less than state-wide in scope, failed to meet the minimum standards set forth by the Commission in its earlier disposition of other state cases.[3] Second, even if that state-wide standard were not a requirement, the exclusion of other social workers located in hospitals, training schools, etc., who share the same characteristics of employment is not consistent with any reasonable definition of community of interest. In Case No. RO-230, wherein Petitioner sought certification in a unit of all Rehabilitation Counselors, their supervisors, aides and trainees employed by the Department of Labor and Industry, the same Hearing Officer recommended dismissal of that petition essentially because the unit, even though state-wide as to the titles sought, would exclude employees with similar duties, skills, functions, goals and job qualifications and thus there was a community of interest which extended beyond those titles which that Petitioner sought to represent. Neither of the two Petitioners involved in these recommendations filed exceptions to the proposed dismissals of their petitions. The Employer took exception to certain observations made by the Hearing Officer which were not material to his recommendations above, but which were relied on to support his suggested resolution of the larger question of appropriate unit or units for professional employees of the State. Finally, in Cases Nos. RO-164 and RO-208, which, by virtue of certain amendments, amount to a single petition for a unit of all professional, non-supervisory, educational employees in the Departments of Education and Institutions and Agencies, Hearing Officer Jeffrey B. Tener recommended that a unit of all professional, educational employees be found appropriate. This is a modification of Petitioner's unit, principally in that it also includes a small number of employees in the Department of Higher Education.[4] The Employer filed exceptions to a variety of the Hearing Officer's

[3] State of New Jersey (Neuro-Psychiatric Institute, et al), P. E. R. C. No. 50.

[4] The unit does not contemplate inclusion of the teaching faculties found within the Department of Higher Education, most of whom are already represented.

findings and conclusions as well as to his ultimate recommendation on unit.

Following submission of all Hearing Officers' Reports and exceptions thereto, a three member panel of the Commission heard oral argument on the positions of the parties in these consolidated cases. The Commission has considered the record, briefs, Hearing Officer's Report and Recommendations, exceptions and oral argument in each of these cases and makes the following dispositions.

The cases will be discussed as one since the bases for disposition are the same in each. The Commission is not persuaded that the above units where recommended as appropriate for collective negotiations be found so. There are two interrelated reasons for this conclusion, the statute's policy and the community of interest of the employees concerned.

It was the Legislature's express determination that Ch. 303 be enacted to promote permanent employer-employee peace and the health, welfare, comfort and safety of the people of the State. N.J.S.A. 34:13A-2. As the Supreme Court later observed, "The nature of the appropriate negotiating unit is a most significant factor in the production and maintenance of harmony and peace in public employment relations."[5]

Against this background the statute provides that the negotiating unit ". . . shall be defined with due regard for the community of interest among the employees concerned . . ." N.J.S.A. 34: 13A-5.3. Community of interest is an accepted term of art and the statute does not attempt to define it. There are several guidelines, however, only one of which is relevant here, namely, that in deciding which unit is appropriate for collective negotiations, the Commission may not include professional employees in the same unit with non-professional employees unless a majority of the former vote for inclusion. N.J.S.A. 34:13A-6 (d) .

When the Commission last examined the question of unit involving State employees, it concluded, with respect to the employees in question there, that to be appropriate the scope of the unit must be state-wide. Expressed and implied in that conclusion was an assessment that the strength and significance of the factors cited—in brief, a high degree of centralization of authority in the top echelon of State government and a general uniformity of major terms and conditions of employment for State employees—required a finding that the first distinctive level of common interest among employees extended state-wide and that this was the minimum level for meaningful negotiation

[5] Board of Education of the Town of West Orange v. Wilton, 57 N.J. 404, 424 (1971).

of terms and conditions of employment. The Commission recognized but refused to give controlling weight to the variety of lesser but more particularized points of common employee interest known to exist in a specific institution or department. Admittedly, a reasonably persuasive case was made for establishing units at the institution or department level by highlighting local differences in conditions and duties, but on balance the factors demonstrating a broader community of interest were considered more compelling. Conceivably, the Commission could have stopped at that point and relied on the factors cited to conclude, as one organization urged, that not only was this the first level of common interest, but that this was the only set of interests to be recognized in determining the unit question, meaning that there would be only one unit for all State employees. Instead, the Commission relied on that set of facts only to establish the base or scope of the unit. It then found, in agreement with the principal parties, that it was appropriate to fashion a unit, statewide in scope, to encompass all employees sharing a broad occupational objective or description. That is, it found an additional mutuality of employee interest arising from the kind of work performed, not expressed in terms of specific job titles or functions, but in terms of the nature of the service provided. As a result of that proceeding, the following three units of non-professional, nonsupervisory employees were established: Health, Care and Rehabilitation Services; Operations, Maintenance and Services; and Craft.

The Commission is now asked to find appropriate several units whose composition would conform to certain individual professions. To do so would require the Commission to recognize as controlling the common attributes and bonds which distinguish a particular profession, be it teaching, nursing, counseling, etc., and find therein the necessary regard for community of interest. The Commission views that concept in much broader perspective in these cases. Community of interest is, as the writers have said, an elusive concept. While it is purposely vague and undefined, a considerable number of factors has been identified as useful indicators. But in given cases some factors are emphasized over others, with still others regarded as insignificant; in other fact settings the weight given the same indicators may be substantially altered. It is essentially a question of weighing the facts in each case and deciding what will best serve the statutory policy.

For example, no one would dispute that registered nurses share an identity simply by virtue of their common background and qualifications required for licensure and by virtue of their common goal to provide care of various kinds to those in medical need. Yet, it is obvious that these professional characteristics do not necessarily create an exclusive community of interest. The statute, which generally provides little insight, does contemplate that there may, in fact, be an identity of interest between professionals and nonprofessionals. In that event it requires a majority vote by professionals for inclusion with nonprofessionals, thereby recognizing the professional interest. But material to this discussion is the recognition that such interest is not so unique that it must be insulated.[6] *A fortiori*, the lines between professional disciplines are not necessarily natural barriers. The goal of providing medical care is common to nurses but it is equally common to medical doctors, clinical psychiatrists and psychologists. True, the particular skills, functions and qualifications of these groups differ, but the same observation may be made of the shop teacher at Bordentown Youth Correction Institution, the teacher of the deaf at Marie Katzenbach and the curriculum consultant for elementary education, all of whom are sought to be included in the educational unit. Given the policy considerations of this statute, the Commission believes that the characteristics of a particular profession should not be the determinant in establishing units for negotiations. If community of interest is equated with and limited to such characteristics, the stability and harmony which this Act was designed to promote are in jeopardy. Potentially, every recognized professional group would be segregated, presenting the Employer with multiplicity of units and the likelihood of attendant problems of competing demands, whipsawing, and continuous negotiations which, disregarding the Employer's inconvenience, are not judged to be in the public interest. Fragmentation to that degree cannot be justified on the ground that individual professional interests are so unique that they cannot be adequately represented in concert with others, especially in the absence of a determination that matters of a professional concern are in every instance negotiable as terms and conditions of employment. At this point in the statute's development the Commission is inclined to believe that the purposes of the Act will be better served if, when dealing with professional employees, the individual distinctions among the professions not be regarded as controlling, but rather the more elementary fact that they are simply professionals and

[6] A graphic example from recent private sector experience is found in Barnes-Hind Pharmaceuticals, 183 N.L.R.B. No. 38 where the Board found it would be appropriate to group professional scientists in the same unit with non-professional technicians and employees such as glassware washer and animal caretaker.

on that basis alone to be distinguished from other groups of employees. This approach would parallel that taken in the case of craft employees where individual craft lines were not observed and the unit was established simply on the basis of a general craft distinction.

The Commission is not unmindful of the fact that several organizations were interested in representing all craft employees in one unit, whereas here the organizations concerned seek representation along the lines of separate professions. We consider the right to organize and be represented, not as an absolute right, but as one that is qualified by the statute's policy and purpose and by the requirement that the exercise of the right be channeled through units appropriate for negotiations. Moreover the Commission takes note of the fact that units already exist at state level containing substantial diversity of function and ranging in size up to 7,500 employees.

The Commission concludes for the reasons above that each of the petitions be and are hereby dismissed.

NOTES

1. The Assistant Secretary of Labor was faced with a somewhat similar problem in a case involving a request by a group of pharmacists for a bargaining unit separate from the other professional employees at a veterans hospital. Veterans Administration, Veterans Administration Hospital, Buffalo, N.Y., A/SLMR No. 60 (1971), GERR Ref. File 21:4059. In finding that such a unit was not appropriate, the Assistant Secretary stated:

[T]he evidence fails to establish that the pharmacists are a distinct and homogeneous unit, but rather, it appears that they share a community of interest with other professional groups of the paramedical service. Moreover, in my view, a unit limited to pharmacists would not promote effective dealings and efficiency of agency operations as required by Section 10 (b) of the Order. Thus, the contrary finding could result ultimately in a myriad of separate units at the Activity, each involving a different professional group in the paramedical service. Clearly, such fragmentation would not promote effective dealings and efficiency of agency operations as required under the Executive Order.

2. Although the New York Taylor Law does not specifically provide that professional employees are entitled to separate units, the New York PERB has allowed professional employees to form their own units, primarily on the basis of their substantially different community of interest from that of non-

professional employees. Chemung County, 1 PERB ¶ 415 (1968); New York State Thruway, 1 PERB ¶ 423 (1968). In New York State, 1 PERB ¶ 424 (1968), the New York PERB placed all of the state's professional employees, *e.g.*, doctors, lawyers, accountants, and economists, in one unit. A member of the New York PERB, Joseph Crowley, commented as follows concerning this decision:

Though the disciplines differed, the interest in the maintenance of professional standards and status would provide a common bond. Further experience is necessary to determine whether this grouping of professions may preclude effective and meaningful negotiations. The desire to avoid unwarranted fragmentation appears to dictate this approach. Fragmentation should be granted only where the evidence to support it is clear and convincing. . . . Crowley, *The Resolution of Representation Status Disputes Under the Taylor Law*, 37 FORDHAM L. REV. 517, 526 (1969).

3. One of the reasons advanced for allowing professional employees to establish separate bargaining units in the private sector is that they would constitute in many instances only a small minority of the bargaining unit if they were included with non-professionals. This consideration may not be as valid in the public sector. The Illinois Study Commission, for example, noted that "there are public agencies in which the non-professionals are a small portion of the total, and they should not automatically be blanketed in with a larger professional group that did not reflect their interests." Based on this finding, the Illinois Study Commission recommended that *both* "[p]rofessional and non-professional employees should be given the opportunity to decide whether they want to be included in the same unit if that issue is raised by either group." ILLINOIS GOVERNOR'S ADVISORY COMMISSION ON LABOR-MANAGEMENT FOR PUBLIC EMPLOYEES, REPORT AND RECOMMENDATIONS 20 (Mar. 1967). The Connecticut State Board of Labor Relations adopted this approach in Clifford W. Beers Guidance Clinic, Decision No. 1104, GERR No. 493, B-11 (1973).

4. One of the current policies of government employers is to encourage job advancement of racial minorities. The Report of the Fortieth American Assembly on Collective Bargaining in American Government included the following recommendation:

As an increasing number of Americans obtain access to the rights inherent in a free society, there is a particular responsibility placed on public employers and public unions. Both unions and public employers have an affirmative obligation to effectuate a change in the racial composition of government's work forces so that the number of minority employees on all levels more adequately reflects the racial balance of residents in the governmental unit. Unions have an affirmative obligation to the full extent of their bargaining capabilities to press employers to hire or promote minorities and to eliminate artificial, non-job related barriers which impede minority employment. Employers have the same obligation to remove such barriers and to withdraw or deny recognition from a union which impedes affirmative action. . . .

None of this will be easy, but public employers and public unions as the beneficiaries of tax revenues derived from the population have a particular responsibility to act on these matters. They may have to revise or overcome collective bargaining agreements if exclusive rights for unions block necessary changes in the work force. . . .

REPORT OF THE FORTIETH AMERICAN ASSEMBLY, COLLECTIVE BARGAINING IN AMERICAN GOVERNMENT 7 (1971). What effect does the establishment of separate bargaining units for professional and non-professional employees have on job mobility? Consider, for example, the various categories of jobs related to nursing, *i.e.*, registered nurses, licensed practical nurses, and nurses aides. If each of these three groups is allowed to form its own separate bargaining unit, it is quite possible that artificial barriers would be created in terms of advancement from a nurses aide to a licensed practical nurse and finally to a registered nurse. This suggests that it might be necessary to review the usual statutory provision, borrowed from the private sector, which provides that professional employees may not be included in the same bargaining unit with non-professional employees unless they affirmatively vote to be included in such a unit. Perhaps some discretion should be given to the agency on a case-by-case basis to determine whether the appropriate unit should include both professional and non-professional employees. *See* State of Alaska, Alaska State Labor Relations Agency Decision No. 1, GERR No. 492, G-1 (1973) (combined unit of technical, professional and clerical employees held appropriate since "the interests of these groups are intertwined and the distinctions between them are often blurred"); Detroit Bd. of Educ. and Michigan Nurses Association, 1969 MERC Lab. Op. 229 (professional employees have no statutory right to separation from non-professional employees and may be included in same bargaining unit).

MICHIGAN STATE UNIVERSITY
Michigan Employment Relations Commission
1971 MERC Lab. Op. 82

[The University College Chapter—MSU District of the Michigan Association for Higher Education filed a petition seeking an election among certain employees of Michigan State University. The American Association of University Professors—MSU Chapter was allowed to intervene on the basis of a sufficient showing of interest.]

The Employer herein is a public employer within the meaning of PERA, and both the Petitioner and the Intervenor are labor organizations within the meaning of PERA.

Michigan State University, an institution of higher learning established under Article VIII, Section 5, of the Michigan Constitution of 1963, is composed of approximately fifteen colleges. The . . . University employs approximately two thousand persons in its teaching faculty from the rank of instructor and up. The unit sought in the petition is composed of approximately two hundred and twenty teaching personnel including all academic rankings from instructor, associate professor, through full professor. While the Petitioner contends that this unit is appropriate, the Employer and the Intervenor take the position that only a university-wide unit of teaching personnel would be appropriate for collective bargaining.

The nature of this case is such that there is minimal dispute over the factual situation. The relationship of University College to the University in terms of administrative structure is comparable to that of the other colleges or schools making up the University. The petitioned for unit includes teaching personnel in all of the academic ranks as does every other college. The range of teaching duties and other obligations, counseling, research and related activities, required and expected of the faculty of University College is comparable, if not identical, with those of faculty members of all the other colleges and schools. The employment relationships of the individual faculty member with the University is uniform throughout all the colleges. The general salary scale and the enjoyment of various employment benefits are uniform throughout the University.

The Petitioner introduced evidence by which it proposed to delineate University College and its faculty as a separate entity within the University with sufficient separate identity to warrant the finding of a unit limited to its faculty. The University catalog and other publications identify the College within the structure of Michigan State University as a separate college. As is the case with each of the other fifteen colleges, it has its own dean. It has two major responsibilities. It offers four courses which are required as a condition of graduation of substantially all students. It also enrolls and is responsible for the academic progress of substantially all freshmen and sophomores in the University. In addition to the four basic courses, which are embodied in four departments, the College maintains a non-instructional department which provides testing services within the college and for other colleges of the University. Virtually all of the students in the University College courses, therefore, are freshmen or sophomores and, it is not unfair to say, that their unique problems and needs form the primary concern of the college. It is one of the few colleges in the University which does not grant a degree.

The Petitioner presented evidence of the separate activities of the University College faculty. The University College faculty has promulgated a set of bylaws which govern its internal procedures. However, it should be noted that these bylaws refer primarily to intra-college matters and are authorized and controlled by the bylaws of the University. Its faculty periodically conducts meetings. It publishes a newsletter written by and distributed to its own faculty. It also publishes the "University College Quarterly," a journal related to the scholarly concerns of the faculty.

The University College faculty participate in a variety of university-wide committees and councils made up of elected or appointed representatives of the various colleges and schools. These committees and councils govern the broad spectrum of academic and internal activities of the University. The broadest based of these is the Academic Senate. All members of the University faculty are members of the Academic Senate of Michigan State University which is made up of all tenured faculty. University College elects representatives to the Academic Council of the University and its faculty are among the appointed Council members. Its faculty participates fully in all faculty standing committees. These standing committees relate in their activities to aspects of the University's functioning in which University College stands on equal footing with the other colleges and schools. Among these committees are the University Curriculum Committee, University Educational Policies Committee, University Faculty Affairs Committee, University Faculty Tenure Committee, and other committees reflecting the multiple concerns and activities of a large university.

With reference to faculty appointments, University College personnel are employed primarily within the College. Dual appointments, that is, an appointment of an individual to different colleges simultaneously, constitute a small percentage of the total appointments within the entire University and a slightly larger percentage of the faculty of this College. More common, although not involving University College, is the joint administration of a department by two or more colleges. This also involves a relatively small percentage of the total faculty.

Testimony of an administrative officer of the University emphasized the centralized control of vital aspects of University academic and personnel activities. As is implicit in the titles of several of the standing committees listed above, significant areas are within the purview of university-wide committees. The University Tenure Committee has jurisdiction over all faculty. Major curriculum decisions must be approved by a university-wide committee. Non-academic administrative control is uniform throughout the University. In matters such as appointments, promotions or tenure, recommendations originate with the department head or dean of the college involved but are then channeled through the office of the Provost and ultimately to the President and Board of Trustees. Recruiting is conducted by the individual department although ultimate approval must come from the central office of the University. Higher ranking appointments involve a personal interview by the office of the Provost, the highest academic officer of the University.

The budget of the University is prepared centrally and allocated by the Legislature to the University rather than to individual schools. The dean prepares the budget request for his school. After the final budget is returned to him, he has certain freedom, with approval of the Provost, to make adjustments. Some members of the University College faculty are involved in the Office of Evaluation Services of the College. These sixteen persons provide technical advice and assistance to other professors and departments in a variety of testing and evaluation procedures. They teach part-time either in University College or in other colleges in the University.

Analysis and Conclusions of Law

The picture painted by this record is one of dual levels of administrative authority within a large university. It reflects significant departmental freedom in many areas, although centralized authority and control is retained. Thus, there is substantial recognition of the competence of each department to find and recommend persons for hire based on their status as scholars and competence as teachers. Generally, recommendations of departmental faculty, approved by the individual dean, are followed by the University. Similarly, in granting tenure, the collegial decisions of each department are generally respected by the central administration. Within each school and within individual departments the chairman or dean is the direct and effective supervisor in terms of immediate day-to-day employment relations. However, policy decisions and administrative control are allocated, as appropriate, between various committees and the central administration.

The Petitioner would now have us find a separate bargaining unit made up of one school composed of five departments. Our prior decisions have expressed the essential elements of evidence of an appropriate bargaining unit. The record must show that the sought-for unit has inherent cohesiveness, that is, an internal community of interest among the employees in the proposed unit, and a cleavage between the community of interest of those employees and all other employees of the employer. City of Warren, 1966 MERC Lab. Op. 225; 61 LRRM 1206; Wayne State University Board of Governors, 1969 MERC Lab. Op. 670. It is clear from this record that the employees in the proposed unit share a community of interest among themselves. They perform basically the same duties under the same conditions and under separate supervision. They are employed in a subdivision of the Employer which is nominally distinguished and, to a limited extent, administratively separate, from the balance of the employing institution.

We must search the record with substantial diligence, however, to discover factors that will create a cognizable line of demarcation between the employees in the proposed unit and the balance of the faculty. They perform the same function. The separate supervision of the College, to the extent that is shown by the record, is not sufficient to support a separate unit finding. City of Warren, supra. The intra-college activities, such as the journal and bylaws, do not significantly affect the community of interest question. No geographical or physical separation of this faculty school is reflected in the record. It is not contended that the professional or academic character of the petitioned for group is sufficiently distinguishable from the overall faculty as to constitute a basis for a separate finding. Although the College is primarily concerned with teaching freshmen and sophomores, there are at least three other colleges in the University which admit and conduct courses for lower classmen.

Accordingly, on the facts on this record, we find that the unit sought does not constitute an appropriate unit for collective bargaining and we will order the petition dismissed. Wayne State University, Board of Governors, 1969 MERC Lab. Op. 670; Grand Rapids Board of Education, 1966 MERC Lab. Op. 241.

NOTES

1. At the university level, the various labor relations agencies have differed on whether a single department or college within a university constitutes an appropriate unit and whether the appropriate unit may be limited to one campus of a multi-campus university. In the private sector, the NLRB has ruled that one college within a university may, in appropriate circumstances, constitute a separate appropriate bargaining unit. For example, in Fordham University, 193 N.L.R.B. No. 23, 78 L.R.R.M. 1177 (1971), the Board held that the faculty of the Fordham Law School constituted a separate appropriate unit, based on a finding that they possessed a community of interest separate and apart from the balance of the university. In Temple University, Case Nos. PERA-R-1123-E and 1137-E, GERR No. 472, B-1 (1972), the Pennsylvania Labor Relations Board held that the law school, medical and dental school faculties constituted separate, identifiable units entitled to representation apart from other university faculty members.

In State of New York (State University of New York), 2 PERB ¶ 3070 (1969), aff'd sub nom., Wakshull v. Helsby, 35 App. Div. 2d 183, 315 N.Y.S.2d 371 (1970), the New York PERB held that a university-wide faculty bargaining unit was appropriate. In so ruling, the PERB affirmed its Director of Representation who held that "the concomitant differences among the campuses do not establish such conflicts of interest between their respective professions as to warrant geographic fragmentation." Similarly, the New Jersey Public Employment Relations Commission, reversing a prior decision holding that each of the six state colleges constituted a separate appropriate unit (New Jersey State Colleges, PERC Decision No. 1 (1969), GERR No. 293, E-1 (1969)), ruled that a statewide faculty unit was appropriate. State of New Jersey, Docket Nos. RO-210 and RO-221 (1972), GERR No. 484, F-1 (1973). See generally McHugh, Collective Bargaining with Professionals in Higher Education: Problems in Unit Determinations, 1971 WIS. L. REV. 55.

2. In Grand Rapids Bd. of Educ., 1966 MERC Lab. Op. 241, an affiliate of the AFT argued that elementary and secondary teachers should not be included in the same bargaining unit in view of the alleged substantial difference in interest. The Michigan Employment Relations Commission disagreed:

[A]ll of the K through 12 teachers of the Grand Rapids school system have a similarity of conditions of employment, qualifications, skills, pay, places of employment, modes of compensation and of duties. There is a difference in the

teaching methods between elementary and secondary areas.
. . . However, this difference in methods does not mean that
the teaching process is basically different in the one than in
the other. . . .

[I]t is the determination of the Mediation Board that the
bargaining unit among the teaching personnel of the Grand
Rapids Board of Education which will best secure to them
their rights of collective bargaining is one consisting of all
teachers, K through 12.

3.   With respect to elementary or secondary school districts,
the various state boards have uniformly denied requests for
bargaining units on less than a system-wide basis. For example,
in Joint School Dist. No. 8 (City of Madison), WERC Decision No. 6746 (1964), the Wisconsin Employment Relations
Commission stated:

The employes involved in this proceeding are engaged in a
single profession—that of teaching. . . . The Wisconsin Federation of Teachers desires to split the statutorily established
unit into various departments or plants. The fact that
teachers perform their duties in separate schools under
separate immediate supervision does not establish that each
school is a separate department or plant. The function of
each school is identical, that is the education of the youth
of Madison. While the facilities may be separately located,
methods and techniques used in such function are for the
most part identical in each school. Generally the curriculum
for all schools is planned, directed and supervised by the
School Board, the Superintendent and other high level administrators, as is the employment of all teachers and the
conditions thereof. The immediate separate supervision of
the principals at the various schools is subject to the scrutiny
and control of the School Board, the Superintendent and
high level administrators. To fragmentize the teachers in
the employ of one school system on a school by school basis
for the purpose of conferences and negotiations with their
municipal employer would not only interfere with the proper
and efficient administration of a school system, but would in
the end result frustrate the intent and purpose of Section
111.70.

THE BOARD OF HIGHER EDUCATION OF THE CITY OF NEW YORK
New York Public Employment Relations Board
1 PERB ¶ 407
Aff'd, 2 PERB ¶ 3056 (1968)

Director of Representation Paul Klein: On November 22, 1967, the Legislative Conference of the City of New York (herein referred to as the petitioner) filed, in accordance with the Rules of Procedure (herein referred to as the Rules) of the New York State Public Employment Relations Board (herein referred to as the Board), a timely petition for certification as the exclusive negotiating representative for all members of the instructional staff of the Board of Higher Education of the City of New York (herein referred to as the employer).

A formal hearing in this matter was conducted on February 27, 28 and 29, and March 15, 18 and 22, 1968. All parties, including the United Federation of College Teachers, AFL-CIO (herein referred to as the intervenor), were present and represented by counsel.

Petitioner contends that the employer's instructional staff should be divided to form two separate negotiating units as follows:

(1)   All members of the permanent instructional staff with tenure and all those members of the temporary instructional staff serving in jobs which automatically lead to tenure upon completion of the applicable period of continuous employment specified in the employer's bylaws (these personnel will be herein referred to as the permanent staff), and all other members of the temporary instructional staff (herein referred to as the temporary staff) paid on an annual basis.

(2)   All other temporary staff except those who work less than six hours.[3]

The employer contends that only one unit, consisting of all instructional personnel, is appropriate for purposes of collective negotiations. However, the employer further contends that lecturers working less than six hours should either be excluded from any unit or, if included in a unit, deemed ineligible to vote in any election that might be held.

The intervenor contends that an overall unit of instructional personnel is appropriate, except that college science technicians and assistants, and college engineering technicians should be in a separate unit.

---

[3] The term "hours," as used throughout this Decision, refers to contact hours of classroom teaching per week and not to the number of courses taught.

The parties stipulated that supervisors, visiting professors and adjunct professors should be excluded from any unit deemed appropriate for purposes of collective negotiations.

The employer is a municipal corporation created by Section 6201 of the Education Law to "govern and administer that part of the public school system within the city which is of collegiate grade and which leads to academic, technical and professional degrees." There are presently 13 institutions subject to the jurisdiction of the employer, including seven senior colleges and six community colleges. As of July 1, 1968, two senior colleges will be added. There is also a graduate division, a teachers education division, and the Mount Sinai School of Medicine.

Under the employer's bylaws, its employees have always been divided throughout its constituent institutions into three categories: the instructional staff, the administrative staff and the custodial staff. The instant case involves only the instructional staff.

. . . .

The employer's bylaws provide that all members of the permanent staff shall have tenure, and all members of the temporary staff shall not. A tenured employee has the right to hold his position during good behavior and efficient and competent service, and thus cannot be removed from his position except for cause and by presentation and investigation of formal charges. Tenure also bestows rights of transfer, retention and preference if a position is discontinued.

All members of the instructional staff may teach the same subjects to the same students. All teachers grade, evaluate and are authorized to discipline students. They instruct in the same buildings, use the same classrooms and laboratories, and have the same privileges with regard to use of dining rooms and other facilities.

As [indicated], the instructional staff has a very definite series of status stratifications by rank and tenure, with certain definite rights, privileges and benefits going with each higher step in the ranking order. This situation creates both major and minor areas of difference in terms and conditions of employment. The ultimate question in this case is whether these differences are sufficiently important or significant to justify division of the instructional staff into separate units for purposes of collective negotiations.

I will deal first with petitioner's basic position that the permanent staff and the nonannual lecturers should not be placed in the same negotiating unit.

The nonannual lecturers, unlike the permanent staff, are appointed (and reappointed) for only one semester at a time, can never achieve tenure as a lecturer, and thus may be "dropped" for any reason whatsoever.[7] Thus, they never achieve the basic right of continued employment which, as has been aptly stated, "lies at the heart of the entire concept of academic freedom." Most nonannual lecturers have full-time employment elsewhere although some, such as a graduate student working to complete his doctoral thesis, may have a long-term career interest in the City University of New York. This highlights a significant difference in interest: the permanent staff has committed itself to the career service of the employer, whereas the nonannual lecturers may well find their chief livelihood elsewhere. In short, the role of the nonannual lecturer is generally that of a second job holder whose primary allegiance is to some other employer or career.

Thus, only the permanent staff is expected, in addition to their regular teaching duties, to engage in all types of committee work, conferences, research and writing, to develop and administer teaching policies, and to have regular hours for consultation with students. The nonannual lecturers cannot serve on personnel, appointments or budget committees. Further, all lecturers are ineligible to vote for the election of department chairmen, who supervise all teachers.

The permanent staff are paid on an annual basis. Their salary schedules and increment steps are fixed by the Board of Higher Education, negotiated on a budget line basis with the budget director of New York City and, after approval by the mayor, have the force of law. The salary rates of the permanent staff alone are, by operation of long existing practice, increased in proportion to any salary increase granted to teachers in the New York City public school system.

There is no established relationship between salaries paid to the permanent staff and those paid to nonannual lecturers. All lecturers (with one minor exception) are paid out of lump-sum funds, which, together with a schedule of maximum rates, also are negotiated as part of the employer's personnel service budget with the budget director of New York City and approved by the mayor. Thus, for the lecturers, only the schedule of maximum rates has the force of law; the employer has an internal policy for minimum rates. The nonannual lecturers are paid on an

---

[7] Although they may eventually be appointed to the tenured positions of instructor, assistant professor, associate professor and professor, this occurs infrequently.

hourly or monthly salary basis which is individually negotiated for one semester at a time.

Similarly, there is a great distinction between the fringe benefits available to the permanent staff and the nonannual lecturers. The permanent staff are entitled to vacation pay, sick leave, sabbatical leave, terminal leave and disability retirement benefits, and may participate in the New York City health program, a faculty welfare plan and a retirement pension and annuity system. The total value of these benefits has been estimated to be worth as much as one-third of the annual salary. The nonannual lecturers are ineligible for all these benefits except sick leave. Sick leave is different in that it may be accumulated from year to year only by the permanent staff. The nonannual lecturers' desire to initiate fringe benefits creates a clear conflict with the desire of the permanent staff to improve them, in terms of competition for available funds.

It is recognized that the permanent staff and nonannual lecturers have some common interests. Their mission is the same (the instruction of students), there is a single grievance procedure, they are still subject to supervision by the chairman of their department,[9] there is a free interchange amongst them in the performance of their duties,[10] and there is a past history of "negotiations" on a single-unit basis.[11]

Despite these common interests, the major differences between the permanent staff and the nonannual lecturers in important terms and conditions of employment such as tenure, fringe benefits and the method of determining salaries, create a sharp conflict of interest which mandates separate representation. The employer has, in effect, recognized that there exists a division between these two groups by creating these differences, and it cannot be said that the history of "negotiations" is so permanent that it establishes an inviolate practice that negates them.[12]

Therefore, I find that the permanent staff should be separated

---

[9] However, the members of the permanent staff who are on the appointments committee observe and report on the nonannual lecturers with regard to possible re-appointment.

[10] However, it should be noted that no employees are ever transferred from the permanent staff to a nonannual lecturer's position.

[11] However, no formal recognition was ever extended by the employer to petitioner or intervenor, nor was any written agreement ever executed.

[12] See *In the Matter of the Petition of Milwaukee Vocational Teachers Union Local 212*, Wisconsin Employment Relations Board Decision No. 6343 (1963), cited in Lieberman and Moskow, "Collective Negotiations for Teachers," Appendix D-6 (1966).

from the nonannual lecturers for purposes of collective negotiations.[13]

I further find that the college science technicians and assistants, and college engineering technicians, who are defined in the bylaws as being permanent employees, belong in a unit which includes all other members of the permanent staff. Although these "satellite personnel" are not primarily concerned with the instruction of students, they share with the rest of the permanent staff a community of professional interest inasmuch as they are engaged in directly supportive activities that are clearly and closely associated with the function of teaching.[14] They do not have any significant conflicting interests with the other permanent staff, which were the basis for excluding the nonannual lecturers, and they do have many common interests. All are professionals, and their functions dovetail. They advise professors and graduate students on the feasibility of projects, and they have contact with students in laboratories and elsewhere. As members of the permanent staff, they have or will have tenure, are paid in accordance with salary schedules set by law as described above, and are eligible for all fringe benefits except that they receive only six weeks paid vacation. Although there is some evidence that their jobs require specialized training and that they wear uniforms or shop aprons, these occupational differences alone do not justify placing them in a separate negotiating unit. Therefore, they shall be included in the same unit as the rest of the permanent staff. A contrary result would, in this case, result in undue and unnecessary fragmentization and would be administratively unwieldy.

I next find that all lecturers, including annual lecturers and both classes of nonannual lecturers, i.e., those who work six hours or more and those who work less than six hours, belong in one negotiating unit. It appears that the reason for employment of these personnel for different time periods is at least partially related to budgetary considerations and the desire to make available money go as far as possible.

The distinctions between the permanent staff and nonannual lecturers have already been discussed. The annual lecturers are distinguishable from the permanent staff in that, among other

[13] Petitioner contends, none of the other parties disagree, and I find, that higher education officers, associates, and assistants, fellows (part-time), college physicians, college dentists, research associates, and research assistants belong in the same unit as the permanent staff.

[14] See the discussion of "satellite personnel" in Doherty and Oberer; "Teachers, School Boards, and Collective Bargaining: A Changing of the Guard," pp. 68-70 (1967).

things, they are not entitled to tenure. Their wages are determined in a different manner than the wages of the permanent staff, and there is no relationship between them. Further, although the annual lecturers are entitled to some of the fringe benefits made available to the permanent staff, they are not entitled to sabbatical, personal or terminal leave, and have waiting periods for the insurance and welfare programs. Whereas the permanent staff automatically move up through the ranks, most annual lecturers do not get promoted to the permanent staff. The annual lecturers do not participate in the leadership role of the tenured permanent staff with regard to policy making, curriculum planning, appointments, personnel or budget matters. Nor are they required to participate in the numerous "extracurricular" activities taken on by the permanent staff.

On the other hand, the annual lecturers have no serious conflict, and much in common, with the nonannual lecturers. Basically, all lecturers are hired to fill openings in the permanent staff for which the employer is unable to otherwise recruit a satisfactory candidate, or to balance uneven teaching schedules, or to secure skilled personnel who are only available on a temporary basis. All lecturers lack tenure and have equal expectations of reappointment, share the same mission, are subject to common supervision, and freely substitute for one another. In terms of job security, salary determination, and interdependence and interchange of employees, the annual lecturers stand in the same shoes as the nonannual lecturers. As the employer has stated in its brief (page 40) :

> "[t]he supreme unworkability of the . . . proposed dividing line [between annual lecturers and nonannual lecturers] is made clearest by considering the example of a lecturer paid one year on an annual line basis, but hired the next year (because of insufficient annual lines or for other reason beyond his control) on a non-annual basis. The example may apply in scores, hundreds, perhaps thousands of cases. To the extent that it occurs it will involve a constant and unnatural shifting of personnel from one unit to another, thereby contributing in a bizarre manner to instability of labor relations at City University."

Thus, there is insufficient justification for separating the annual lecturers from the nonannual lecturers. Similarly, there is nothing in the record to warrant the exclusion from the lecturers' unit of the nonannual lecturers who work less than six hours. None of the parties have been able to ascertain just how many hours an average employee of this type, or an average nonannual lecturer, works and, apparently, this is not a matter of record.

It is, therefore, not possible to determine whether these employees are engaged in the type of assignment that can be deemed casual, sporadic or irregular. Thus, I need not reach the question, raised by petitioner, of whether one who does engage in that type of work is a "public employee" as that term is defined in § 201.8 of the Public Employees' Fair Employment Act (the Taylor Law).

No persuasive reason is apparent for placing the nonannual lecturers who work less than six hours in a separate unit from all other lecturers. Such evidence as there is concerning their terms and conditions of employment applies equally to all the nonannual lecturers whether they work more or less than six hours per week, and to the annual lecturers (except that the annual lecturers are eligible for some fringe benefits).

There being no conflict of interest between the nonannual lecturers who teach less than six hours and all other lecturers, I find that they should be included in the lecturers' unit.[17]

In finding the two units described above to be appropriate, I have seriously considered the employer's concern that the establishment of more than one unit could cause difficult administrative problems. However, while the employer's preference is entitled to consideration, it may not predominate where the other criteria for unit determination set forth in § 207.1 of the Taylor Law indicate the need for a different result by establishing that there are real conflicts of interest among the employees the employer seeks to join together.

The employer need not be unduly dismayed at the possibility of dealing with different employee organizations for the two units I have determined are appropriate. There is nothing in the Taylor Law or the Rules of this Board to prevent the employer from requesting the employee organization or organizations, if any, representing the employees in the two units to make a joint presentation to it and to conduct joint negotiations with regard to matters of concern to all employees. Such a procedure would afford the employer the convenience of unified negotiations on University-wide issues, while assuring to the employees in each unit particularized representation on issues of special concern to them.

NOTES

1. In the subsequent elections that were held, the United Federation of College Teachers was certified as the exclusive

---

[17] Therefore, they will be allowed to vote in any election that might be held.

bargaining agent for the temporary staff members and the Legislative Conference was certified as the exclusive bargaining representative for the tenured staff members. The college's subsequent negotiations with the two bargaining units are explored in detail in Mintz, *The CUNY Experience*, 1971 WIS. L. REV. 112. In describing some of the problems faced by the college, Mintz stated:

> It is important to point out again that these were competing organizations with whom CUNY was required to negotiate. This competition created the additional and rather unique problem of riding the negotiations in tandem. In most instances a specific proposal agreed to by one organization had to be sold pretty much verbatim to the other. 1971 WIS. L. REV. at 117-118.

2. Contrary to the decision in the principal case, the Michigan Employment Relations Commission has held that part-time faculty members who perform the same functions as full-time members should be included in the same bargaining unit since they "share a community of interest with the full-time faculty members. . . ." Lansing Community College, 1971 MERC Lab. Op. 1062.

After assuming jurisdiction over private colleges and universities with revenues in excess of $1,000,000 per year, the NLRB initially determined that "absent a stipulation of the parties to the contrary, only a unit of the full-time and regular part-time professional employees is appropriate." University of New Haven, Inc., 190 N.L.R.B. No. 102, 77 L.R.R.M. 1273 (1971). Subsequently, the Board in a 3-2 decision overruled this decision and held "that part-time faculty do not share a community of interest with full-time faculty and, therefore, should not be included in the same bargaining unit." New York University, 205 N.L.R.B. No. 16, 83 L.R.R.M. 1549 (1973). The Board noted that it was "convinced that the differences between the full-time and part-time faculty are so substantial in most colleges and universities that we should not adhere to the principle announced in the *New Haven* case."

3. In establishing teacher bargaining units the question of whether "fringe" personnel such as counsellors, nurses, psychologists, social workers, and the like, should be included in or excluded from the bargaining unit is frequently raised. In Janesville Board of Education, WERC Decision No. 6678 (1964), the WERC set forth the following standard:

> Where there are issues with respect to the eligibles in an appropriate collective bargaining unit, the Board will

usually include as eligible in a unit consisting of regular full-time certificated teaching personnel those certificated teachers who are regularly employed on a part-time basis and those who, although not directly engaged in normal classroom teaching, work directly with students or with teachers, other than in a supervisory capacity, in support of the educational program.

Applying this standard, the WERC has included the following categories of personnel in teacher bargaining units: social workers and psychometrists, La Crosse City Public School Dist. Joint No. 5, WERC Decision No. 7347 (1965); psychologists, counselors and guidance personnel, reading teachers, and physical and occupational therapists, Joint City School Dist. No. 1, WERC Decision No. 6677 (1964). *See generally* E. SHILS & T. WHITTIER, TEACHERS, ADMINISTRATORS, AND COLLECTIVE BARGAINING 242-305 (1968).

4. Should ROTC instructors, paid by the U.S. Government, be included in a faculty collective bargaining unit? In the private sector, the NLRB has held that they should be excluded since they do not "share sufficient interest in common with the other faculty members" in view of "their responsibilities as officers in the U.S. Army." Florida Southern College, 196 N.L.R.B. No. 133, 80 L.R.R.M. 1160 (1972). *Accord,* Manhattan College, 195 N.L.R.B. No. 23, 79 L.R.R.M. 1253 (1972). In Detroit Bd. of Educ. and Detroit Fed'n of Teachers, 1969 MERC Lab. Op. 360, the MERC held that retired military personnel hired by the Board as ROTC instructors were properly part of a faculty bargaining unit even though the U.S. Army controlled the subject matter taught and provided some of the funds for the maintenance of the program. In the same case, however, the MERC excluded several other ROTC instructors who were still in active military status and were assigned to the program by the Army.

4. Severance Petitions

SHAW AND CLARK, DETERMINATION OF APPROPRIATE BARGAINING UNITS IN THE PUBLIC SECTOR: LEGAL AND PRACTICAL PROBLEMS, 51 Ore. L. Rev. 152, 167-68 (1971)†

Standards for Processing Severance Petitions

Where broad units are established there are occasionally requests to sever certain employees. Typically, a severance petition is limited to a subgroup of employees who claim to have special

---

† Reprinted by permission. Copyright © 1971 by University of Oregon.

interests which entitle them to be separately represented. Under the NLRA, a severance petition will be denied unless it is established that the employees petitioned for constitute "a functionally distinct group with special interests sufficiently distinguishable from those of the Employer's other employees to warrant severing them from the overall unit."[6]

The Assistant Secretary of Labor has adopted a similar approach to severance petitions under Executive Order 11,491. Where an established, effective and fair bargaining relationship exists, severance will not be found appropriate except in "unusual circumstances."[7] Applying this formula, the Assistant Secretary has denied virtually every severance request. The same approach was followed by the New Jersey Public Employee Relations Commission in denying a request by a group of nurses to be severed from a larger school unit, and by the Michigan Commission in denying a petition by a group of community college instructors to be severed from an established unit composed of both elementary and secondary teachers and community college instructors.

Recently, the former chairman of the National Labor Relations Board, Frank W. McCulloch, denied a request to sever a group of licensed practical nurses (LPNs) from an overall unit of nonprofessional employees at the Baltimore City Hospital. After stating that an "established structure for bargaining . . . should be altered or upset only for clear and compelling reasons," McCulloch cogently set forth the reasons why severance petitions should not ordinarily be granted in the public sector:

> To split off the LPNs . . . would result in three separate bargaining representatives for employees who make up the patient care teams. The possibilities for confusion and conflict in developing uniform and efficient working conditions on the job would be considerably enhanced. It is common experience that "whip-sawing" and service interruptions tend to occur more frequently where public agency employees are represented in a multiplicty of bargaining units.

---

[6] Kalamazoo Paper Box Corp., 136 N.L.R.B. 134, 139 (1962). The Board set forth the following considerations for determining whether a substantial difference in interests and working conditions exists: ". . . a difference in method of wages or compensation; different hours of work; different employment benefits; separate supervision; the degree of dissimilar qualifications, training, and skills; differences in job functions . . . the infrequency or lack of integration with the work functions of other employees or interchange with them; and the history of bargaining."

[7] United States Naval Construction Battalion, Davisville, R.I., A/SLMR No. 8 (1971), GERR Ref. File 21:4011. [Eds.]

Of course tensions can arise within as well as between bargaining units. But the bargaining representative in seeking to achieve a harmony or working balance among the interests of various groups within the inclusive unit is one more buffer against dislocations of public service.[8]

NOTE

The Federal Labor Relations Council has upheld the Assistant Secretary's so-called *Davisville* rule in which he held that "where the evidence showed that an established, effective and fair collective bargaining relationship is in existence, a separate unit carved out of the existing unit will not be found to be appropriate except in unusual circumstances."[9] Department of the Navy, Naval Air Station, Corpus Christi, Texas, FLRC No. 72A-24 (1973), GERR Ref. File 21:7079.

E. Unit Status of Certain Categories of Employees

1. Supervisors

ADVISORY COMMISSION ON INTERGOVERNMENTAL RELATIONS, LABOR-MANAGEMENT POLICIES FOR STATE AND LOCAL GOVERNMENT 95-96 (1970)

Supervisors have traditionally been eligible for membership in public employee associations, even though union membership has been denied to them. The issue of inclusion or exclusion of supervisory personnel is particularly controversial in education, the largest field of local government employment, where the National Education Association and the American Federation of Teachers have taken differing positions. NEA favors supervisory employee membership while the AFT, with but few exceptions, is for exclusion. This problem also involves middle-level supervisors in fields other than teaching, where common professional goals and program objectives closely link management and employees.

Whether to accord supervisory and other management personnel the rights granted regular public employees is a basic issue that must be decided by policymakers grappling with proposed public labor-management relations legislation. This subject usually is more complicated in the public than in the private sector, due to the probability that the latter's traditional definitions of "management" and "employee" may not be applicable to the

---

8 Baltimore City Hosp., 56 L.A. 197, 202-03 (McCulloch, 1971).

9 United States Naval Construction Battalion, Davisville, R.I., A/SLMR No. 8 (1971), GERR Ref. File 21:4011.

more complex personnel systems of many States and localities. Yet, whether to exclude or to include such personnel is a question on which State statutes cannot be silent or vague.

Many supervisors and key professionals—such as teachers, policemen, firemen, and social workers—have a strong community of interest with the rank-and-file workers they supervise. Hence, frequently no conventional distinctions are apparent between management and employee functions.

The sensitive question of the status of supervisory and other key personnel in public employee organizations must be dealt with forthrightly in State public labor-management relations legislation. The Commission believes that while such statutes should not prohibit supervisors and managerial personnel from membership in a union or association, they should not be allowed to hold office in or to be represented by an employee organization to which rank-and-file employees belong. Elected officials, key appointive people, and certain "confidential" employees also should not be accorded these employee rights. Participation of any of these personnel in union or associational activities would sharply limit management's effectiveness at the discussion table.

A persistent and perplexing problem is the failure of many key middle-management and supervisory officials to act like "management," even when their role and public responsibilities clearly put them on that side of the discussion table. A clear legislative denial of employee rights to such personnel will prompt a clarification of this attitudinal confusion.

From the viewpoint of a union or association, certain objections also can be raised concerning participation by supervisors and other middle-managers in their activities. Supervisory personnel cannot remove themselves entirely from an identification with certain management responsibilities, and this can generate intraunion strife. Their involvement in union or associational affairs in effect places management on both sides of the discussion table. State legislation dealing with public labor-management relations, then, should clearly define the types of supervisory and managerial personnel which should not be accorded employee rights.

Some observers contend that States should statutorily accord to supervisory employees the rights to organize and to present proposals to the employer's representative. It is generally conceded, however, that this approach is sound only if supervisors, when exercising such rights, act through an organization entirely independent of any which represents non-supervisory employees. Michigan's Public Employment Relations Act for city, county, and district employees, for example, permits supervisors to form their own bargaining units. Establishment of separate units presumably ensures that supervisors will continue to uphold their responsibilities as representatives of management when dealing with rank-and-file employees.

Another body of opinion holds that no State law can deal comprehensively with the status of all supervisors, given the diversity of public employers and their varying supervisory structures. It is difficult if not impossible, so the argument runs, to deal equitably with this problem by statutory definition. This position is taken in New York State's "Taylor Law," which does not attempt to define "supervisory employee" precisely, but empowers the State public employee relations unit to promulgate this definition by rule or decide it on a case-by-case basis and then apply it to such occupational categories as the agency deems appropriate.

The Commission finds both of these approaches defective. Allowing supervisors to organize and to present proposals perpetuates the vocational ambivalence that this group has long exhibited. The need at the present time is for management to identify its members and to develop a healthy community of interest. This, in the long run, will benefit employees more than any short-term gains which might come from supervisors continuing to act as part-time advocates for the rank-and-file.

. . . .

The Commission believes, however, that supervisory and managerial personnel should enjoy certain basic organizational rights. They should be permitted to join and to be represented by an organization that does not include rank-and-file employees on its membership roster. They or their representatives should be authorized to meet on an informal basis with their employer's agent for the purpose of consultation in connection with the terms and conditions of employment or on such other matters as may be determined by the agency head. Yet, regardless of their top or middle echelon status, because they are still members of the management team, supervisors or their representatives should not participate in formal discussions, nor should they be parties to memoranda of understanding with the employer.

NOTES

1. President Nixon's Federal Labor Relations Study Committee similarly concluded that supervisors "should be and are part of agency management and should be integrated fully into that management." Accordingly, the Committee recommended "that recognition should not be granted for any unit which includes supervisors, or managerial executives, and that super-

visors should not participate in the management or representation of labor organizations granted recognition under the Order." *Report and Recommendations on Labor-Management Relations in the Federal Service,* GERR Ref. File 21:1018 (1970). The recommendations of the Study Committee with respect to the treatment of supervisors were incorporated in Executive Order 11491. *See* sections 2 (c), 10 (b) (1), 21 (b), and 24 (2) of Executive Order 11491.

2. Among the many articles examining the status of supervisory personnel in the public sector are Rains, *Collective Bargaining in the Public Sector and the Need for Exclusion of Supervisory Personnel,* 23 LAB. L.J. 275 (1972); Bers, *The Status of Managerial, Supervisory and Confidential Employees in Government Employment Relations,* A Report sponsored by the New York State Public Employment Relations Board (January 1970).

CITY OF WAUSAU
Wisconsin Employment Relations Commission
Decision No. 6276 (1963)

At the hearing the parties stipulated to the description of the collective bargaining unit as being all the employes of the Municipal Employer employed in the Board of Public Works, which consists of the Engineering, Sanitation, Electrical, Public Works and Inspection departments. However an issue exists with respect to whether individuals employed as supervisors should be included as eligibles in the unit.

The Municipal Employer contends that only those employes excluded from the term "municipal employe" as defined in Section 111.70 can be excluded from the unit. It argues that supervisory employes have a right to engage in concerted activity and to be represented for the purposes of collective bargaining since that right is given to "employes," and that therefore no basis exists for their exclusion from the eligibles in the bargaining unit.

The Union, on the other hand, takes the position that the Board should apply the same principles and rules that it applies in determining eligibles in elections conducted by the Board among employes of non-public employers pursuant to Section 111.05 of the Wisconsin Employment Peace Act.

Section 111.70 (1) (b) defines the term "municipal employe" as follows:

". . . any employe of a municipal employer except city and village policemen, sheriff's deputies and county traffic officers."

A municipal employer performs its functions and services through elected and appointed officials and by employes hired by the municipal employer through its administrative and managerial officials and employes. Broadly, any individual receiving compensation for services performed by him on behalf of the municipal employer, with the exception of those services performed under contract, can be said to be an employe of the municipal employer. Such application could encompass the mayor, city manager, alderman and department heads. A municipal employer as such is a corporate being. Governmental units, including municipal employers, are managed by persons who, among their duties, may represent the municipal employer in its relationship to employes thereof who are performing services and who have no connection with any managerial function. As in private industry, the managerial function of the municipal employer is not normally performed by any single individual. The usual chain of command originates with the mayor or city manager, and is channeled to various committees, boards, department heads, and through various supervisory personnel in the various departments. Managerial and supervisory functions are performed in the interest of the municipality as an employer. The representative of the municipal employer has the responsibility and authority connected with the municipal employer's operation and presumably perform their duties in what is the best interest of the municipality as the employer. Their inclusion in a collective bargaining unit consisting of employes whom they supervise is inconsistent with their obligation to the performance of their supervisory function on behalf of the municipal employer. Should supervisors be included in the same bargaining unit with employes they supervise said individuals would be in a position either to prefer the interest of employes over that of the municipal employer or to prefer the interest of the municipal employer as the agents thereof over that of the employes.

Supervisors are generally responsible for the direction of the work force, the maintenance of discipline and the processing of routine grievances. We do not believe that supervisors can properly carry out such responsibilities if they were included in the bargaining unit.

The rights conferred upon municipal employes under Section 111.70 (2) to form and join labor organizations of their own choosing and the right to engage in conferences and negotiations with their municipal employer on the questions of wages, hours, and conditions of employment could be seriously impaired, if not nullified, if the agents of the municipal employer, with whom the representatives of the employes could be expected to negotiate, were included in the employes bargaining unit. To permit supervisory personnel to participate in the election of the representative of the employes he supervises would constitute an interference with their rights as provided in Section 111.70, for it may very well be possible that the ballots of supervisors, if permitted to vote, would affect the results of the representation election. If supervisors were not excluded from bargaining units, then presumably chief executive officers of a municipal employer could be included in the same bargaining unit as other employes. We believe such an interpretation would be clearly at variance with the statutory intent, for who would then be the statutory representative of the municipal employer with whom the municipal employes have a right to confer and negotiate?

Section 111.70 (4) (d) provides:

"(d) *Collective bargaining units.* Whenever a question arises between a municipal employer and a labor union as to whether the union represents the employes of the employer, either the union or the municipality may petition the board to conduct an election among said employes to determine whether they desire to be represented by a labor organization. Proceedings in representation cases shall be in accordance with ss. 111.02 (6) and 111.05 insofar as applicable, except that where the board finds that a proposed unit includes a craft the board shall exclude such craft from the unit. The board shall not order an election among employes in a craft unit except on separate petition initiating representation proceedings in such craft unit."

The legislature by making reference to the election provision in the Wisconsin Employment Peace Act has granted the Board the power to utilize procedures there provided which are not inconsistent with the substantive provisions of Section 111.70. The Board's determination to exclude supervisory personnel from collective bargaining units of public employes is consistent with the policy applied by the Board in elections conducted under Section 111.05 of the Wisconsin Employment Peace Act.

The Board therefore has and will continue to exclude managerial and supervisory personnel from collective bargaining units on the basis that they are agents of the municipal employer in the performance of the "employer" function. . . .

NOTES

1. Unlike the employer in the principal case, employers generally argue for the exclusion of individuals whom they consider to be supervisors. Why do you think the city in the instant case

sought to include supervisors in the bargaining unit? Sometimes the reason is the employer's belief that the individuals in question are likely to vote against union representation and therefore tip the vote in the employer's favor. Is such a short-range consideration valid from an employer's standpoint? Consider the following comments of Wellington and Winter:

Municipalities are frequently not well organized for collective bargaining and never will be if they cannot create positions with effective responsibility for the administration of collective agreements. Such positions must necessarily be filled by persons who identify with, and are part of, management, not by those who are unionized, whether or not the union is exclusively supervisory. Nor can such responsibilities be carried out by persons who are members, much less officers, of the other party to the contract, as might occur when supervisors are in a unit with regular employees. Indeed, the creation of such positions and the delegation of supervisory power are likely to constitute a principal change in municipal structure as a consequence of collective bargaining. The law should not discourage this trend by permitting the holders of these positions to organize or be in units with nonsupervisory employees. H. WELLINGTON & R. WINTER, THE UNIONS AND THE CITIES 114 (1971).

2. Under the National Labor Relations Act as initially enacted in 1935, there was no specific exclusion of supervisors from the definition of the term "employee." In interpreting the Act the National Labor Relations Board vacillated with respect to whether supervisory employees were entitled to organize and have representation petitions processed. *Compare* Godchaux Sugars, Inc., 44 N.L.R.B. 874 (1942) (supervisory employees may organize in an affiliated union), *with* Maryland Drydock Co., 49 N.L.R.B. 733 (1943) (unit of supervisory employees was not appropriate). In Packard Motor Car Co. v. NLRB, 330 U.S. 485, 67 S. Ct. 789, 91 L. Ed. 1040 (1947), the Supreme Court upheld the authority of the Board to establish bargaining units for supervisory employees. In rejecting the various policy arguments that were proffered as to why supervisory employees should not be allowed to organize, the Court noted that "[t]hey concern the wisdom of the legislation; they cannot alter the meaning of otherwise plain provisions."

When Congress amended the National Labor Relations Act in 1947, it specifically excluded supervisors from the definition of the term "employee" and defined the term "supervisor" to mean

. . . any individual having authority, in the interest of the employer, to hire, transfer, suspend, lay off, recall, promote, discharge, assign, reward, or discipline other employees, or responsibly to direct them, or to adjust their grievances, or effectively to recommend such action, if in connection with the foregoing the exercise of such authority is not of a merely routine or clerical nature, but requires the use of independent judgment. 29 U.S.C. § 152 (11) (1970).

The reasons why Congress excluded supervisors from coverage under the NLRA are indicated in the following excerpt from the relevant House Report:

Management, like labor, must have faithful agents.—If we are to produce goods competitively and in such large quantities that many can buy them at low cost, then, just as there are people on labor's side to say what workers want and have a right to expect, there must be in management and loyal to it persons not subject to influence or control of unions. . . .

. . . What the bill does is to say what the law always has said until the Labor Board, in the exercise of what it modestly calls its "expertness," changed the law: That no one, whether employer or employee, need have as his agent one who is obligated to those on the other side, or one whom, for *any* reason, he does not trust. 1 Legislative History of the Labor-Management Relations Act 307, 308 (1948).

See generally Daykin, *Legal Meaning of "Supervisor" Under the Taft-Hartley Act,* 13 LAB. L.J. 130 (1963).

HILLSDALE COMMUNITY SCHOOLS
Michigan Employment Relations Commission
1968 MERC Lab. Op. 859
Aff'd, 24 Mich. App. 36, 179 N.W.2d 661 (1970)

The instant case arose when the Hillsdale Community Schools Principals and Supervisory Association (PSA), a labor organization under the Act, sought an election in a proposed bargaining unit:

"High School, junior high, and elementary school principals, curriculum coordinator, reading coordinator, ESEA coordinator, cooperative education coordinator, head librarian, and physical education director; excluding: teachers, superintendent, assistant superintendent, business manager and all non-certificated employees."

The Hillsdale Education Association (HEA) is a labor organization which is recognized by the School District as exclusive bargaining agent for the District's non-supervisory certificated teachers.

The School District opposes the petition on the grounds that: (1) supervisors and executives have no rights to collective bargaining under PERA; (2) assuming, arguendo, that PERA allows such rights to principals and other supervisors, this Board should deny such rights as a matter of public policy; (3) the proposed unit is inappropriate because it contains six staff specialists who are supervised by seven principals, also included in the unit; and (4) PSA may not be certified as exclusive representative of principals and teachers' supervisors, since it is affiliated with the state organization (MEA) which is the parent organization of many teacher organizations, including the organization of teachers in the petitioner's District.

We now turn to the discussion of the issues individually.

1. The unit of supervisors.

The Trial Examiner, in his Report, rejected the School District's position on this issue, consistent with our decision in Saginaw County Road Commission, 1967 Labor Opinions 196. During oral argument, the School District and certain amici curiae prayed that we reverse Saginaw and hold that supervisory employees are excluded from statutory coverage.

We have studied the briefs and arguments urging reversal of our position, but we are not persuaded that the *Saginaw* decision is contrary to proper construction of PERA.

Our duty as described in Section 13 of PERA is to:

". . . decide in each case, in order to insure *public employees* the full benefit of their right to self organization, to collective bargaining and otherwise to effectuate the policies of this act, *the unit appropriate for the purposes of collective bargaining as provided in Section 9e of Act No. 176* (Labor Mediation Act) . . . ." (Emphasis supplied)

From this section, the argument is made that "employees," as used in 9e, specifically excludes executives and supervisors; that is, "employees" as used in Section 9e is defined in Section 2 (e) of LMA.[3] However, this argument ignores the use of "public employee" in Section 13 of PERA. "Public employee" is defined in Section 2 of PERA and not in Section 2 (e) of LMA. PERA,

---

[3] The customary basis for prohibition of supervisory units is found in the definition of employee, which excludes supervisors. If supervisors are not employees, they cannot avail themselves of the provisions of the Act.

Section 2, does not exclude supervisors or executives from the provisions of PERA as does its counterpart in LMA.

Section 9e is incorporated into PERA only for standards of unit determination and to provide a prohibition against supervisors and executives being included in the same unit with employees they supervise. There is no prohibition against supervisory units except by virtue of LMA's Section 2 (e), which is not included by specific mention in PERA.

The School District maintains that our interpretation of the statutes ignores the canon of construction that statutes which have the same general purpose should be read *in para materia* as constituting one law, especially where there is specific reference from one statute to the other. The purpose of this canon of statutory construction is to avoid a strict construction of one statute which defeats the main purpose of another statute or statutes relating to the same subject.

However, this construction of two statutes dealing with the general subject of labor relations is subject to being made more specific by other canons of construction. *Expressio unius est exclusio alterius* restricts the effect of a statute to the area specifically mentioned, *i.e.*, public employment relations. *E pressum facit cessare tacitum* means that "when the law designates the actors none others can come upon the stage." PERA is restricted to public employees, which term is defined in the Act.

We affirm our *Saginaw* decision and adopt the Trial Examiner's Findings of Fact and Conclusions of Law on this issue.[7]

2. *Public Policy.*

The School District devotes a substantial portion of its brief to urging the adoption of a policy that supervisors should not be allowed rights under PERA. Our *Saginaw* decision was based on

---

[7] We find no merit to the contention that the principals in the instant case are distinguishable from the traffic director supervisor in *Saginaw* because principals have a policy function. This argument is a *non sequitur* if supervisors are not excluded from the definition of employee. We note that the New York State Public Employment Relations Board has included principals and assistant principals in bargaining units, stating that: "Principals act merely as conduits rather than as decision makers." Board of Education, Union Free School District and Depew Teachers Organization, Inc., 255 GERR C-2 (1968). Similarly, see Metropolitan Transit Authority, 48 L.R.R.M. 1296 (Mass. Labor Relations Board, 1961). We also dismiss the argument concerning Governor Romney's veto of HB 3388, which bill would have amended PERA to allow the inclusion of police supervisors in the bargaining unit with patrolmen. The issue raised by the bill was solely the inclusion, or exclusion, of police supervisors in the same unit with the rank and file. Police supervisors had, on the enactment of PERA, the privilege to engage in concerted activities, including the choice of an exclusive bargaining representative in a designated unit.

statutory construction, not policy. The School District's argument is that " (t) he policy as well as the letter of the law is a guide to decision."

We recognize this Board's responsibility as guardian of public policy discussed in National Labor Relations Board v. Atkins & Company, 331 U.S. 398 (1947). While there are certain areas of policy to be considered in every matter, this policy should not be used to frustrate the intent of the Legislature as we interpret it. Thus, it would be inconsistent for us to find supervisory status encompassed within the definition of "public employees," and then deny that status because we believed that the policy should be to the contrary.

We do note that competent authorities have expressed the opinion that supervisory personnel in the public sector have characteristics which differ from supervisors in private employment.[9] These differences, far from disqualifying public employment supervisors from representation, make a stronger case for allowing supervisors separate bargaining units, particularly when they are not excluded from the definition of "employee."[10]

There is a common interest among school boards, superintendents, principals and teachers to provide "a superior education for the nation's youth." All of those parties work professionally toward the same goal. . . .

3. Appropriate Unit.

The Trial Examiner found that the petitioned for unit was appropriate although it contained purported principal supervision of the staff specialists. We affirm the Trial Examiner's Findings that the nature of the supervision was not sufficient to invoke

---

[9] See, for example, Slavney, "The Public Employee—How Shall He Be Represented in Collective Negotiations?" Governor Rockefeller's Conference on Public Employment Relations, 269 GERR E-1 (1968). Mr. Slavney observes at p. E-4: "I think most of us here would admit that supervisors in public employment are for the most part different than supervisors in the private sector, not only in the concept of employer loyalty but also in the performance of identifiable supervisory functions. Under a civil service system, the authority supervisors might have with regard to the hire, transfer, suspension, layoff, recall and promotion is subject to more stringent review than in private employment. Further, in civil service, employees performing normal supervisory duties have the same rights and protections as do rank and file employees with respect to tenure, job security and civil service grievance procedures, and normally their salary increments and increases have a distinct relationship to increments and increases granted to nonsupervisory personnel. These factors tend to create a community of interest with employees supervised rather than with management." See also, New York Public Library, 69-1 ARB § 8067 (Yagoda, 1968).

[10] Metropolitan New York Nursing Home Association, 60 L.R.R.M. 1281 (N.Y. State Labor Relations Board, 1965).

the prohibition against supervisors being included in units with those employees they supervise.

The evidence reveals that the supervision is mere routine direction not requiring the exercise of independent judgment. . . .

Regarding the unit in question, we find a community of interest between the staff specialists and the principals. There are similarities in administrative duties, professional skills and working conditions. Additionally, we agree with the Trial Examiner's conclusion that the staff specialists' distinct community of interest is insufficient to separate them from the principals.

Thus, we find the petitioned for unit appropriate for collective bargaining purposes under PERA.

4. MEA domination of PSA.

The School District argues here that the parent organization (MEA), exercises an overwhelming degree of control over its affiliates, particularly respecting collective bargaining policy. Also, it is alleged that it is impossible for PSA to be truly independent within the MEA organizational framework. Where both the principals' and teachers' organizations are MEA affiliates, the School District maintains that there is a conflict of interest where principals are the first step in the grievance procedure. Hence, if the MEA exercises such a degree of control over its affiliates, it will control the initial stage of the grievance procedure. The Trial Examiner agreed with the School District's contentions.

Perhaps this situation may arise, but it is speculative. We are charged with the duty to protect the organizational rights of *all* public employees. Where, as here, principals are public employees, we should not restrict their free exercise of Sec. 9 rights, which includes the selection of a collective bargaining representative. City of Escanaba, 1966 Labor Opinions 451. The petitioning organization must, however, proceed with the normal proof establishing itself as a labor organization within the terms of the Act.

Similarly, there is no more basis for restricting the choice of bargaining agent to one not representing the rank and file employees here, than there is in restricting that choice respecting craft, technical, or professional employee units. Just as professional, craft, and technical employees are not restricted in their choice of bargaining representative, supervisory employees should also not be so restricted.

We agree with the principals [sic] enunciated by the New York State Labor Relations Board:[14]

---

[14] Yonkers Raceway, Inc., 63 L.R.R.M. 1098, 1100 (N.Y. State Labor Relations Bd., 1966).

"We also have noted that the 'conflict of loyalties,' allegedly resulting from the selection of the same representative by supervisory or protection employees and by rank and file employees, is a misnomer; that it arises, if at all, from the employees' fundamental right of association which exists independent of statute; that the denial of all rights under the Act to one of the two groups of employees provides no solution; and that any problems which arise can and should be adjusted and resolved in the collective bargaining process, when, and if, that eventuality occurs."

. . . .

Before this position is interpreted as allowing the organization of "vice presidents" mentioned in the Packard[15] case, we note that there is a level at which organization must end. That level consists of "executive" employees, and is limited to those employees who formulate, determine and effectuate management policies.[17]

The application of this exclusion is not necessary in this case because there is no evidence that the employees in the proposed unit act in any other manner than as resource people in collective bargaining or as conduits for labor relations policy established without their participation. We do not consider that employees who serve the employer at the first step of the grievance procedure are within the executive category by reason of that responsibility. Thus, we do not feel that our determination impinges upon management's right to have trusted personnel act in its behalf in formulating, determining and effectuating policies and in collective bargaining. . . .

NOTES

1.   A number of commentators have supported the view that supervisory employees should have the right to be represented for the purposes of collective baragining. *See, e.g.,* White, *Rights and Responsibilities in Municipal Collective Bargaining,* 22 ARB. J. (n.s.) 31, 32 (1967) ; Schmidt, *The Question of the Recognition of Principal and Other Supervisory Units in Public Education Collective Bargaining,* 19 LAB. L.J. 283 (1968) .

2.   In City of Detroit, Dep't of Parks and Recreation, 1969 MERC Lab. Op. 661, the MERC noted that it "does not intend

---

[15] Packard Motor Car Company v. NLRB, 330 U.S. 485 (1947). The briefs of some amici curiae noted the comment by Mr. Justice Jackson.

[17] The executive designation is basically synonymous with managerial employees as defined in Ford Motor Co., 66 N.L.R.B. 1317, 17 L.R.R.M. 394 (1946), and as applied in Quincy City Hospital, 60 L.R.R.M. 1244 (Mass. Labor Relations Comm., 1965).

to mechanically apply private employment supervisory concepts to public employment situations," observing:

> Frequently, under governmental employment, by its very nature and history, numerous promotional steps exist in a department or agency in order to provide upward mobility and increased compensation, and each upward step means that the lower classification is in a sense subservient to the higher. Therefore, a series of leader-type steps are instituted, each of which exercises a certain degree of authority over lower classifications without necessarily possessing actual supervisory authority in a labor relations context and as such authority normally exists in private industrial employment where the lines of demarcation between employee and supervisor are often much clearer. Thus, the "responsibility to direct" guideline of Section 2 (11) of the Federal Labor Management Relations Act is not necessarily a viable criteria in determining supervisory status under PERA.

3. Where a civil service commission has the authority to hire and fire employees and to determine which employee is to be promoted, what effect, if any, does this have on the determination of supervisory status? In Wauwatosa Board of Education, WERC Decision No. 6219-D (1967), the Wisconsin Employment Relations Commission made the following observation:

> Because certain conditions of employment are governed by civil service rules and regulations, the employees in the positions in question have limited authority with respect to hiring and promotion and discharge of employees. However, they can make recommendations with respect thereto. The lack of such authority, however, will not preclude the Commission from making a supervisory determination.

4. The various labor relations agencies have had considerable difficulty in deciding whether department chairmen or division chairmen should be considered "supervisors" and therefore excluded from faculty bargaining units or considered "employees" and included in such units. *Compare* Southwestern Michigan College, 1969 MERC Lab. Op. 89 (department chairmen held not supervisors), *with* Henry Ford Community College, 1969 MERC Lab. Op. 64 (division heads and department chairmen held supervisors). The NLRB has likewise struggled with the question of whether department chairmen are "supervisors." *Compare* Fordham Univ., 193 N.L.R.B. No. 23, 78 L.R.R.M. 1177 (1971) (held not supervisors), *with* Syracuse Univ., 204 N.L.R.B. No. 85, 83 L.R.R.M. 1373 (1973) (held supervisors).

See generally Comment, *The Bargaining Unit Status of Academic Department Chairmen,* 40 U. CHI. L. REV. 442 (1973).

2. Managerial Employees

Many of the public sector statutes exclude managerial employees from the definition of the term "employee." The definition of the term "managerial employee" varies, but it usually refers to persons who are involved in formulating, determining or effectuating policies on behalf of the public employer. A number of labor relations agencies have excluded managerial employees even though the applicable statute in question does not contain such a specific exclusion. The Michigan Employment Relations Commission, for example, in City of Detroit and Governmental Accountants and Analysts Ass'n, 1969 MERC Lab. Op. 187, excluded them on the ground that they are creators of policy and thus should not be included in bargaining units. The NLRB has likewise determined, as a matter of policy, that managerial employees should be excluded. *See* J. ABODEELY, THE NLRB AND THE APPROPRIATE BARGAINING UNIT 209-10 (1971).

STATE OF NEW YORK
New York Public Employment Relations Board
5 PERB ¶ 3001 (1972)

On September 21, 1971 the State of New York filed a timely application pursuant to CSL § 201.7, as amended,[1] seeking to have this Board designate as managerial or confidential certain employees of the State of New York in specified job titles. . . .

Discussion

I. *Authority of PERB*

One of the points made by the State is that,

"The initial and primary fact in the determination of whether a position or person should be designated as managerial or confidential is the opinion of the public employer. Only the employer can accurately judge its needs. Accordingly, when the over-all position of the employer appears to

---

[1] CSL § 201.7 provides: "The term 'public employee' . . . shall not include . . . persons who may reasonably be designated from time to time as managerial or confidential upon application of the public employer to the appropriate board in accordance with procedures established pursuant to section two hundred five or two hundred twelve of this article, which procedures shall provide that any such designations made during a period of unchallenged representation pursuant to subdivision two of section two hundred eight of this chapter shall only become effective upon the termination of such period of unchallenged representation. Employees may be

be reasonable, the employer's judgment should be supported by this Board unless for particular positions the employer's judgment is not supported by substantial evidence."

In support of this proposition, the State argues that a managerial employee is defined as one who formulates policy or "may reasonably be required on behalf of the public employer" to exercise certain specified labor relations functions. According to the State, the words, "may reasonably be required on behalf of the public employer," express a legislative intent that this Board should adopt the employer's analysis of what it may reasonably require unless the employer has been arbitrary.

We do not read the quoted language of the statute as creating a presumption in favor of an employer's judgment concerning the employees whom it may reasonably require to conduct its labor relations responsibilities; we understand it as providing a criterion which PERB must observe in making its determination. While an employer's opinion as to the designation of employees as management or confidential is entitled to serious consideration, nevertheless, this Board's determination is not limited simply to a review of the opinion of the employer and of the reasons supporting such opinion. Rather, the determination is based upon the application of the statutory criteria to all the evidence offered by the parties.

The respective responsibilities of PERB and the public employer are set forth in the Taylor Law (CSL § 201.7), which provides for the exclusion of "persons who may reasonably be designated from time to time as managerial or confidential upon application of the public employer to the appropriate board. . . ." It is the function of the public employer to apply; it is the responsibility of the Board to determine. . . .

II. *Managerial and Confidential Employees Before the 1971 Amendment of the Taylor Law*

Even before the enactment of Chapters 503 and 504 of the Laws of 1971, there was a concept of managerial and confidential employment under the Taylor Law. This concept derived from the Report of the Taylor Committee. Although the Taylor Law

---

designated as managerial only if they are persons (a) who formulate policy or (b) who may reasonably be required on behalf of the public employer to assist directly in the preparation for and conduct of collective negotiations or to have a major role in the administration of agreements or in personnel administration provided that such role is not of a routine or clerical nature and requires the exercise of independent judgment. Employees may be designated as confidential only if they are persons who assist and act in a confidential capacity to managerial employees described in clause (b)."

did not expressly exclude persons who were managerial or confidential, the Office of Collective Bargaining of the City of New York interpreted the Taylor Law to require such an exclusion. This Board did not have occasion to rule on whether managerial and confidential employees were covered by the Taylor Law, but it did find that they could not be in the same units as rank-and-file employees because of the conflict of interest between them, and no separate unit of managerial and confidential employees had ever been designated by PERB.

IV. Comparison of Statutory Definition with Prior PERB Definition

The definition used by this Board to exclude persons from the five units established in 1968 was that a person is managerial or confidential if he:

"Formulates or determines State or agency policy (e.g., department and agency heads and their deputies) ; or

"Directs the work of an agency or a major subdivision thereof with considerable discretion in determining the methods, means and personnel by which State or agency policy is to be carried out (e.g., institution heads, administrative directors) ; or

"Is so closely related to or involved with the activities noted above as to present a potential conflict of interest or clash of loyalties in matters concerning employer-employee relationships (e.g., staff agents, confidential assistants) , or in a geographically separated location is responsible for representing the State's position in dealing with a significant number of employees."

The first two paragraphs of the above-quoted PERB definition were intended by this Board to delineate persons who might be deemed "managerial." The two criteria set forth in those paragraphs were clearly not limited to labor relations functions or responsibilities, but were intended to cover all activities that might be deemed "managerial," such as the formulation and determination of State, agency or institutional policy. The Legislature, however, in defining "managerial" in the same broad sense simply said "persons . . . who formulate policy."

A. Criterion One—Formulation of policy.

This criterion is but one of four criteria established by the Legislature for designating persons as managerial. The other three criteria are limited to labor relations functions or responsibilities of the public employer. Thus, it would appear to have been the intent of the Legislature that persons who formulate policy may be designated managerial even though they do not exercise a labor relations function.

We will first discuss the "policy" criterion and later the other three criteria. It would appear desirable to first consider the term "policy." Policy is defined in a general sense as "a definite course or method of action selected from among alternatives and in the light of given conditions to guide and determine present and future decisions."[10] In government, policy would thus be the development of the particular objectives of a government or agency thereof in the fulfillment of its mission and the methods, means and extent of achieving such objectives.

The term "formulate" as used in the frame of reference of "managerial" would appear to include not only a person who has the authority or responsibility to select among options and to put a proposed policy into effect, but also a person who participates with regularity in the essential process which results in a policy proposal and the decision to put such a proposal into effect. It would not appear to include a person who simply drafts language for the statement of policy without meaningful participation in the decisional process, nor would it include one who simply engaged in research or the collection of data necessary for the development of a policy proposal.

We conclude that this legislative criterion is similar in scope and meaning to the earlier one stated by this Board, namely, one who "formulates or determines State or agency policy."

B. *Criterion Two—Involvement in collective negotiations.*

The remaining three criteria for designating an employee as managerial all specifically relate to the labor relations functions of the employee. The first of these is that the employee "may reasonably be required on behalf of the public employer to assist directly in the preparation for and conduct of collective negotiations." This part of the definition is an addition to the criteria set forth in our decision In the Matter of the State of New York, 1 PERB ¶ 399.85 (1968), although many of the persons to whom it is applicable were designated as managerial under other criteria then used and now restated. We interpret this criterion to include those who may reasonably be required to be directly involved in the preparation and formulation of the employer's proposals or positions in collective negotiations. We do not think that the Legislature intended, however, that if an employer consulted with supervisory personnel on the impli-

---

[10] Webster's Seventh New Collegiate Dictionary.

cation or feasibility of negotiation proposals that such supervisory personnel should be deemed managerial. Admittedly, such supervisory personnel would be assisting in the preparation for collective negotiations, but such assistance without participation in the actual conduct of negotiations would not satisfy the statutory criterion. Moreover, we take the phrase "to assist directly" to mean direct involvement or participation in the preparation for collective negotiations so as to be part of the decision-making process therein. Similarly, with respect to "conduct of collective negotiations," there must be direct involvement or participation in the negotiating process, and simply being present at the negotiations as an observer or other non-participatory role would not suffice. The largest group of persons not previously designated as managerial, but encompassed by this part of the definition, are persons holding positions in newly created titles specifically related to the preparation for and conduct of collective negotiations. Examples of these are Labor-Management Relations Officers and Employee Relations Representatives.

C. *Criterion Three—Administration of agreements.*

The third criterion is that a person is managerial if he has "a major role in the administration of agreements . . . provided that such role is not of a routine or clerical nature and requires the exercise of independent judgment." The administration of an agreement involves basically two functions: (1) observance of the terms of the agreement and (2) interpretation of the agreement both within and without the grievance procedures of the contract. The observance of the terms of the agreement is largely a routine and ministerial function. Undoubtedly many supervisory employees have a responsibility to insure that terms and conditions of an agreement are adhered to, but this responsibility does not usually require "the exercise of independent judgment." There will be occasions where the implementation of an agreement will necessitate a change in a government's procedures or methods of operation. The person or persons who effect such implementation and change do exercise independent judgment and would have a "major role" in the administration of an agreement. Such a person is one the Legislature sought to exclude by this criterion.

Many supervisors are involved in grievance procedures. It does not appear, however, that supervisors who participate in first step grievances exercise independent judgment. Rather, such participation generally conforms to policy established at a higher level.

The interpretation of an agreement involving State agency or institution policy involving employee relations would constitute a "major role" in the administration of an agreement, and would require the exercise of independent judgment.

D. Criterion Four—Personnel administration.

The final criterion for defining managerial employees is that they "have a major role . . . in personnel administration, provided that such role is not of a routine or clerical nature and requires the exercise of independent judgment." Many of the persons so defined were previously excluded under the old definition because they were "so closely related to or involved with the activities [of those who formulate policy or direct the work of major subdivisions] as to present a potential conflict of interest or clash of loyalties in matters concerning employer-employee relationships." To some extent, this final criterion is a compression of our prior definition. Some persons were previously excluded from the five units because their relationship to personnel administration was very close, even though it was of a routine or clerical nature. In any event, they are not managerial employees under the new statutory definition. Examples of these are the staff of the health services unit of the Department of Civil Service. . . .

NOTE

The amendment of the Taylor Act which allowed public employers to designate certain employees as either managerial or confidential was held constitutional in Shelofsky v. Helsby, 39 App. Div. 2d 168, 332 N.Y.S.2d 723 (1972), aff'd, 32 N.Y.2d 54, 295 N.E.2d 774, — N.Y.S.2d — (1973), appeal dismissed, 84 L.R.R.M. 2421 (W.S. Oct. 9, 1973). After noting that "similar criteria appear in the definition of 'supervisor' in the National Labor Relations Act," and that "the standards are both familiar and sufficient under established administrative law," the court ruled that the amendment does not violate employees' rights of due process, freedom of association, or equal protection. The court, in relevant part, stated:

There is nothing very novel about the concept of employment units consisting of management employees as distinct from other employees. The State should have a loyal management cadre of employees handling its labor relations. This practice has been accepted in private industry and also in the public sector for State employees . . . and for New York City employees through the City's Office of Collective Bargaining. . . . The statute in this case provides reasonable means for limiting the number of employees designated by the employer.

It is common knowledge that the interests of employees and management are frequently adverse. The government may rightfully require that those charged with the responsibility of implementing and administering collective bargaining agreements be free from any possible conflict of interest either because they are implementing or because they are unsympathetic to management's interest due to associational bias. The State's police power may properly be exercised to this end for the purpose of achieving stability in labor relations, even though the result is to interfere with some employees' personal rights to due process and freedom of association. Furthermore, the classification here involved is reasonable and avoids equal protection criticisms. 332 N.Y.S.2d at 727.

3. Confidential Employees

SHAW AND CLARK, DETERMINATION OF APPROPRIATE BARGAINING UNITS IN THE PUBLIC SECTOR: LEGAL AND PRACTICAL PROBLEMS, 51 Ore. L. Rev. 152, 171 (1971)†

Another common exclusion from bargaining units is confidential employees. Although the breadth of this exclusion varies from state to state, the term "confidential employees" usually refers to "employees who assist and act in a confidence capacity to persons who formulate, determine, and evaluate management policies in the field of labor relations." The rationale for excluding confidential employees from larger bargaining units in the private sector was to separate those employees "who, in the normal performance of their duties may obtain advance information of the Company's position with regard to contract negotiations, the disposition of grievances, or other labor relations matters."

In some states, including Oregon, confidential employees are specifically excluded from bargaining units. In other states, such as Connecticut and Michigan, confidential employees have been excluded from bargaining units on a case-by-case basis by the public employee labor relations board. For example, the Michigan Employment Relations Commission has adopted the following rule:

[W]e are of the opinion that the "confidential" employees rule should be applied cautiously. Only those employees whose work is closely related to that of supervisory employees and

---

† Reprinted by permission. Copyright © 1971 by University of Oregon.

involves matters which should be held in confidence should be excluded from a bargaining unit with nonsupervisory employees. . . .[10]

Applying this rule, the MERC has held that the secretary to a public employer's negotiator, and the secretary to a director of budget, finance, and accounting were confidential employees. On the other hand, persons who from time to time may have access to confidential information are not necessarily confidential employees. Similar decisions have been issued by other public employee relations boards.

NOTES

1.   Are city attorneys who furnish legal opinions to various municipal agencies and in such capacity participate in negotiations between such agencies and the unions that represent their employees confidential employees? In City of Milwaukee, WERC Decision No. 8100 (1967), *aff'd*, 43 Wis. 2d 596, 168 N.W.2d 809 (1969), the WERC stated:

> Although the Assistant City Attorneys do act in a confidential capacity with respect to the determination and implementation of management policies in the field of labor relations, the information available to these attorneys is not directly related to the relationship between the City and their representative. Employees who have access to confidential labor relations information of other employers, unrelated to the relationship between the employer and the employees included in the unit in question, does not mean that such employees should be excluded from one unit because they are "confidential employees."

The WERC did find, however, that the assistant city attorney who represented the city in negotiations and was regularly assigned to furnish legal assistance to the office of the city's labor negotiator should be excluded from the unit. The WERC noted that the individual in question "cannot possibly serve both parties" and that "his relationship with the office of the Labor Negotiator is too intimate to permit him to be included in the unit."

2.   The NLRB's exclusion of confidential employees from bargaining units is thoroughly explored in Note, *Confidential Employees and the National Labor Relations Act*, 29 WASH. & LEE L. REV. 350 (1972).

---

[10] Benton Harbor Bd. of Educ., 1967 MERC Lab. Op. 743, 746.

3. Section 10 (b) (2) of Executive Order 11491 prohibits the establishment of a bargaining unit if it includes "an employee engaged in Federal personnel work in other than a purely clerical capacity."

4. Teaching Assistants and Students

REGENTS OF THE UNIVERSITY OF MICHIGAN v. MERC
Michigan Supreme Court
— Mich. —, 204 N.W.2d 218 (1973)

SWAINSON, J. In 1966, a group of interns, residents and post-doctoral fellows connected with the University of Michigan Hospital and its affiliates organized the University of Michigan Interns-Residents Association (hereinafter referred to as the Association). The Association attempted to bargain with the University Hospital Administrators concerning the compensation of interns and residents. The University asserted its right to unilaterally determine such compensation. On March 19, 1970 the Association filed a written request that the Regents of the University of Michigan recognize it as the bargaining representative of the interns, residents and post-doctoral fellows serving at the University Hospital and its affiliates. The Regents denied this request on or about March 31, 1970.

The Association then filed a petition for representation with the Michigan Employment Relations Commission (hereinafter referred to as MERC) on April 19, 1970. . . .

On March 16, 1971 a majorty of the members of the commission issued a decision holding:

1. That the Association is a labor organization within the meaning of the Michigan Public Employees Relations Act (hereinafter referred to as PERA).

2. That the University of Michigan is a public employer subject to the provisions of PERA and thus the commission has jurisdiction of the matter.

3. That the members of the Association are public employees under the provisions of PERA.

4. The employment relationship between the parties is not a casual one as that term is used to designate exclusions from a bargaining unit.

The majority of the commission further ordered that an election be held and defined the appropriate bargaining unit. One member of the commission held in a dissent that interns and residents are post-graduate students whose activities are primarily educational and are not employees in the traditional sense.

The Regents applied for leave to appeal in the Court of Appeals and such was granted on June 9, 1971. The Court of Appeals denied the Regent's motion to stay the representation election and MERC conducted such an election. Of the 419 individuals who cast votes, 296 voted for representation, 115 voted against, and four ballots were challenged. The Association soon after the election requested that negotiations be instituted, but the Regents refused on the theory that the matter was still pending in court. The Court of Appeals on June 24, 1971 issued an order staying all proceedings until a final decision of that Court.

On January 21, 1972 the majority of the Court of Appeals reversed the findings of the MERC and held as a matter of law that interns, residents, and post-doctoral fellows cannot be characterized as employees. 38 Mich. App. 55. Judge McGregor in dissent held that the members of the Association could be both students and public employees. 38 Mich. App. 66. We granted leave to appeal. 387 Mich. 773. . . .

The key contention of the respondent, concurred in by a majority of the Court of Appeals, that to hold the members of the Association are employees would contravene Article VIII, section 5 of the 1963 Constitution.* This constitutional provision has its roots in Article XIII, section 6-8 of the 1850 Constitution. The desires of the framers of the 1850 and subsequent constitutions to provide autonomy to the Board of Regents in the educational sphere have been protected by our Court for over a century.

This concern for the educational process to be controlled by the Regents does not and cannot mean that they are exempt from all the laws of the state. When the University of Michigan was founded in the 19th Century it was comparatively easy to

---

* "The regents of the University of Michigan and their successors in office shall constitute a body corporate known as the Regents of the University of Michigan; the trustees of Michigan State University and their successors in office shall constitute a body corporate known as the Board of Trustees of Michigan State University; the governors of Wayne State University and their successors in office shall constitute a body corporate known as the Board of Governors of Wayne State University. Each board shall have general supervision of its institution and the control and direction of all expenditures from the institution's funds. Each board shall, as often as necessary, elect a president of the institution under its supervision. He shall be principal executive officer of the institution, be ex-officio a member of the board without the right to vote and preside at meetings of the board. The board of each institution shall consist of eight members who shall hold office for terms of eight years and who shall be elected as provided by law. The governor shall fill board vacancies by appointment. Each appointee shall hold office until a successor has been nominated and elected as provided by law." [Eds.]

isolate the University and keep it free from outside interference. The complexities of modern times makes this impossible. Problems concerning the disputes between employees and public employers were not given full constitutional recognition until the 1963 Constitution. The people, through the passage of Article IV, section 48 of the 1963 Constitution have deemed the resolution of public employee disputes a matter of public policy. This Court must attempt to harmonize the various constitutional provisions and give meaning to all of them. . . .

We agree with the reasoning of the Court of Appeals in Branum v. Board of Regents of University of Michigan, 5 Mich. App. 134 (1966). The issue in that case was whether the Legislature could waive governmental immunity for the University of Michigan because it was a constitutional corporation. The Court of Appeals stated (pp. 138-139):

"In spite of its independence, the board of regents remains a part of the government of the State of Michigan.
. . . .

"It is the opinion of this Court that the legislature can validly exercise its police power for the welfare of the people of this State, and a constitutional corporation such as the board of regents of the University of Michigan can lawfully be affected thereby. The University of Michigan is an independent branch of the government of the State of Michigan, but it is not an island. Within the confines of the operation and the allocation of funds of the University, it is supreme. Without these confines, however, there is no reason to allow the regents to use their independence to thwart the clearly established public policy of the people of Michigan."

Thus, we believe that the two sections of the 1963 Constitution can be harmonized. We hold that interns, residents and post-doctoral fellows may be employees and have rights to organize under the provisions of PERA without infringing on the constitutional autonomy of the Board of Regents. However, as the Court of Appeals pointed out in Regents of the University of Michigan v. Labor Mediation Board, 18 Mich. App. 485 (1969), pp. 490-491:

"While recognizing that the plaintiff is a public employer and the employees in question are public employees, we also recognize that this plaintiff, because of the provisions of Const. 1963, art. 8, § 5, is a unique public employer. Its powers, duties and responsibilities are derived from the constitution as distinguished from other public employers whose authority is derivative from enactments of the legislature."

Because of the unique nature of the University of Michigan, above referred to, the scope of bargaining by the Association may be limited if the subject matter falls clearly within the educational sphere. Some conditions of employment may not be subject to collective bargaining because those particular facets of employment would interfere with the autonomy of the Regents.

For example, the Association clearly can bargain with the Regents on the salary that their members receive since it is not within the educational sphere. While normally employees can bargain to discontinue a certain aspect of a particular job, the Association does not have the same latitude as other public employees. For example, interns could not negotiate working in the pathology department because they found such work distasteful. If the administrators of medical schools felt that a certain number of hours devoted to pathology was necessary to the education of the intern, our Court would not interfere since this does fall within the autonomy of the Regents under Article VIII, section 5. Numerous other issues may arise which fall between these two extremes and they will have to be decided on a case by case basis. Our Court will not, as it has not in the past, shirk its duty to protect the autonomy of the Regents in the educational sphere. Thus, we hold that it does not violate Article VIII, section 5 of the 1963 Constitution if the members of the Association are held to be public employees.

The Regents further contend that interns and residents are not employees as that term is used in the PERA. However, as we stated in the *Eastern Michigan* case, *supra,* (p. 566) concerning the scope of the PERA:

" 'Public employment' is clearly intended to apply to employment or service in all governmental activity, whether carried on by the state or by townships, cities, counties, commissions, boards or other governmental instrumentalities. *It is the entire public sector of employment as distinguished from private employment.* The public policy of this state as to labor relations in public employment is for legislative determination." [Emphasis added.]

The only exception is for the classified civil service. No exception is made for people who have a dual status of students and employees. If the Legislature had intended to exclude students/employees from the operation of PERA, they could have written such an exception into the law. However, as noted above, the only exception is for the classified civil service. We thus hold that members of the Association are employees within the meaning of the PERA.

Finally, we must determine whether the findings by the Michigan Employment Relations Commission that members of the Association are employees is supported by competent, material and substantial evidence on the record. We hold that it is.

There is ample evidence to support the findings of the Commission that the members of the Association are employees. For example, they have a portion of their compensation withheld for the purposes of federal income tax, state income tax, and social security coverage (75a, 149a, 513a, 524a). As Judge McGregor pointed out in his dissent in the Court below, 38 Mich. App. 55 (p. 67):

> Doctors are not eligible for the Internal Revenue Code § 117 exclusion of income for fellowships and education stipend. See Woddail v. Commissioner of Internal Revenue. 321 F.2d 721, (CA 10, 1963).

The interns, residents and post-doctoral fellows receive fringe benefits available only to regular University of Michigan employees through use of the identification cards which are issued to them by the University. (517-518a). This includes partial payment of Blue Cross-Blue Shield coverage, identical to coverage offered to other regular University employees. (91a, 143a, 508-509a). The University furnishes the W-2 forms required by the Internal Revenue Service for all employees. (510-512a). The compensation is paid by University checks drawn from a University account. (65a, 103a, 138a).

All interns and residents are required as a condition of employment to sign a loyalty oath required by Michigan law to be signed by all public employees. (422a, 601a). The interns and residents spend over three-quarters of their time providing patient care services (72-3a, 106a, 120-1a) for which the University is compensated. (333a-4a). In particular, they are entrusted with many responsibilities that medical students are not. These include:

1. Writing of prescriptions without the required approval of a senior person. (46a, 60a, 74a, 200a, 399a).

2. Taking full charge and responsibility for the running of an outpatient clinic. (100-101a, 397a).

3. Admitting and discharging patients. (121-2a, 130a, 375-6a, 397a, 461a).

4. Performing operations and surgical techniques on actual patients under minimal or no supervision. (201a, 376a, 398a).

Moreover, Dr. John A. Gronvall testified that the principal duty and responsibility of interns and residents is to diagnose and prescribe a patient care program and put it into effect. (203-4a). We agree with counsel for the Association that this is far more indicative of an employee (i.e.—in this case a doctor) than a student.

The Regents point out other evidence from the record that would indicate that interns, residents and post-doctoral fellows are students. All internship and residency programs at the University of Michigan are fully approved by the Council of Medical Education of the AMA. The stipend that interns and residents receive is unlike a salary because it has no relation to the number of hours an individual works or the duties they perform. All interns are not licensed to practice medicine. The Regents also relied on the testimony given at the hearing by several doctors which demonstrates that the medical education is different from other professions and graduate school educations. Medical education begins to include patient care responsibilities in the third year of medical school. The type of patient care responsibility given to an intern and resident is part of a continuing medical education and not evidence that an intern or resident is primarily an employee.

We do not regard these categories as mutually exclusive. Interns, residents and post-doctoral fellows are both students and employees. The fact that they are continually acquiring new skills does not detract from the findings of the MERC that they may organize as employees under the provisions of PERA. Members of all professions continue their learning throughout their careers. For example, fledgling lawyers employed by a law firm spend a great deal of time acquiring new skills, yet no one would contend that they are not employees of the law firm. The Regents contend vigorously that the MERC was incorrect in its findings that interns, residents and post-doctoral fellows are employees and contend that they are primarily students. However, since at this point we are dealing with a question of fact, under section 106d of the Administrative Procedures Act, we cannot, pursuant to said section, overturn the findings of the MERC unless they are not supported by competent, material, and substantial evidence on the record. We hold that the findings of the MERC that interns, residents and post-doctoral fellows are employees are supported by competent, material, and substantial evidence on the whole record.

The judgment of the Court of Appeals is reversed and the decision of the MERC is affirmed. No costs, a public question being involved.

NOTES

1. In Iron Mountain Area Public Schools, 1972 MERC Lab. Op. 35, the MERC held that high school students working in office clerical or custodial jobs under a federally financed work-study program did not have a sufficient community of interest with the regular full-time employees to be included in the unit since there was no expectation that they would continue their employment beyond graduation.

2. The NLRB has held that graduate students who serve as teaching assistants "are primarily students and do not share a sufficient community of interest with faculty members to warrant their inclusion in . . . [a faculty bargaining] unit." College of Pharmaceutical Sciences, 197 N.L.R.B. No. 142, 80 L.R. R.M. 1456 (1972) ; Adelphi University, 195 N.L.R.B. No. 107, 79 L.R.R.M. 1545 (1972). In Cornell Univ., 202 N.L.R.B. No. 41, 82 L.R.R.M. 1614 (1973) , the NLRB excluded students from a unit of full-time employees, noting that "for the great majority of student employees, since they have no expectation of remaining permanently in their present jobs, their employment is incidental to their academic objectives."

F. Selection of the Collective Bargaining Representative

1. Secret Ballot Election

Most of the comprehensive public sector collective bargaining statutes provide, as the Alaska statute does, that "[i]f the labor relations agency finds that there is a question of representation, it shall direct an election by secret ballot to determine whether or by which organization the employees desire to be represented and shall certify the results of the election." ALAS. STAT. tit. 23, ch. 40, § 23.40.100 (b) (1972). Adopting the practice under the NLRA, Executive Order 11491 and most of the state acts further provide that an employee organization is to be certified if it receives a majority of the votes *cast* in the election. In other words, if there are 100 employees in the unit and 80 employees vote in the election, only 41 votes favoring representation would be needed for certification, even though this would not constitute a majority of the employees in the unit. There are some exceptions, however. Section 941 (e) of the Vermont State Employees Labor Relations Act, for example, provides that "[i]n order for a collective bargaining unit to be recognized and certified by the board, there must be at least a fifty-one percent affirmative vote of all employees within [the] proposed bargaining unit." VT. STAT. ANN. tit. 3, § 941 (e) (Supp. 1973).

In addition to conducting secret ballot elections, the various labor relations agencies are frequently called upon to decide who is eligible to vote in such elections. Employees who are not on the active payroll because of illness, vacation, leave of absence and those who are on layoff but have a reasonable expectation of being recalled are generally considered eligible to vote in representation elections. Occasionally this is specifically spelled out in the applicable statute or ordinance. For instance, the Los Angeles ordinance provides that employees who did not work in the period immediately prior to the election "because of illness, vacation or authorized leaves of absence" are entitled to vote. Probationary employees are considered eligible voters since they share a community of interest with other employees in the unit and have a reasonable expectation of becoming permanent employees. *See* Taylor County, Highway Dep't, WERC Decision No. 8178 (1967); Department of Navy, Navy Exchange, Mayport, Florida, A/SLMR No. 24 (1971), GERR Ref. File 21:4031.

2. Card Check or Other Means

Several of the comprehensive public sector collective bargaining statutes provide that the labor relations agency has the authority to ascertain whether the employees desire to be represented by methods other than conducting a secret ballot election. For example, section 207 of the New York Taylor Law gives the PERB the authority to resolve questions concerning representation "on the basis of dues deduction authorization and other evidences or, if necessary, by conducting an election." N.Y. CIV. SERV. LAW § 207 (McKinney Supp. 1971). The Connecticut statute provides that the State Board of Labor Relations has the authority to either direct a secret ballot election, or "use any other suitable method to determine whether and by which employee organization the employees desire to be represented . . . ." CONN. GEN. STAT. ANN. § 7-471 (1) (B) (1972). This latter provision is very similar to the language in the National Labor Relations Act as originally enacted in 1935. When Congress amended the NLRA in 1947, the phrase "any other suitable method" was deleted.

UNION FREE SCHOOL DISTRICT NO. 6
New York Public Employment Relations Board
1 PERB ¶ 399.01 (1968)

[The Amityville Federation of Teachers filed a petition seeking to decertify the Amityville Teachers Association. At a conference the parties entered into a consent agreement which set forth the appropriate bargaining unit.]

The consent agreement further provides that an election will be held unless the employee organizations who are parties thereto submit to the Director of Representation (hereinafter called the Director) of the Board within seven days from the execution date of the agreement "dues deduction authorizations and other evidences" sufficient to satisfy the requirements of Section 201.6 (h) (1) of the Rules for certification without an election. The significance and meaning of this Section was carefully explained to all parties by the trial examiner prior to their entering into the consent agreement.

On December 13, 1967, the petitioner submitted to the Board 83 "authorization and designation" cards. These cards contained the following information: the name of the employee, the date of signing, the school involved, the position of the employee, the school district, and the home address and telephone number of the employee. The following statement is also included above the signature of the employee:

I hereby designate and authorize the American Federation of Teachers as my exclusive agent and representative for the purpose of collective negotiations with respect to the terms and conditions of employment, the negotiation of collective agreements, and the administration of grievances arising thereunder.

On December 18, 1967, the Director approved the aforesaid consent agreement.

By letter dated December 20, 1967, the intervenor, pursuant to the consent agreement, submitted to the Director 155 "cards" containing the following information: the name of the individual employee and his position, the school involved, the date of execution, and the following statement:

This is to certify that as a paid member of the Amityville Teachers Association, I hereby designate and authorize the ATA as my exclusive representative for collective negotiations under the New York Public Employees' Fair Employment Act.

The Rules elaborately detail the circumstances under which an employee organization may be certified without an election. If an employee organization can demonstrate by "dues deduction authorizations and other evidences" that a sufficient proportion of the employees in the appropriate unit have designated it as the negotiating agent, it will be certified as long as a sub-

stantial proportion of the employees in the unit have not authorized a competing employee organization to represent them by
executing dues deduction authorizations and other evidences.
The Rules specifically define "dues deduction authorizations and
other evidences" as membership in an employee organization in
addition to proof that such membership is for purposes of
representation in collective negotiations. Further, the Rules
specify (a) the minimum proportion of employees in the negotiating unit which must support an employee organization by
dues deduction authorizations and other evidences for that organization to be certified without an election, and (b) the minimum proportion of employees in the negotiating unit which
must support a competing organization by dues deduction authorizations and other evidences to prevent certification without
an election. The following illustration, taken from Section 201.6
(h) (1) of the Rules, is pertinent:

Column I (Percentage neces- sary to be certified without an election)	Column II (Percentage neces- sary to prevent certification with- out an election)
55	10
60	15
65	20
70	25

In the instant case, while petitioner's submission of cards is
sufficient to constitute a showing of interest, and did indeed
satisfy the applicable 10% showing of interest requirement, it
is clear from the above that they do not satisfy the requirements
of certification without an election, nor do they block the certification of the intervenor without an election, since evidence
of membership is lacking.

On the other hand, the cards submitted by the intervenor
satisfy the requirements for certification without an election in
that they specify the two necessary ingredients: (1) membership,
and (2) proof that such membership is for purposes of representation in collective negotiations.[7] Since these cards were
executed by 55% of the employees in the unit agreed to in the
consent agreement (this percentage has been computed without
taking into consideration the twenty employees who signed cards
on behalf of both competing employee organizations) and since

_____

[7] These ingredients might conveniently be referred to as "membership
plus."

the petitioner has not submitted any "dues deduction authorizations and other evidences," the Board finds that the Amityville Teachers Association is entitled to be certified as the
exclusive negotiating agent for the employees in the unit specified in the consent agreement.

NOTES

1. The Idaho Fire Fighters Bargaining Law provides that

The organization selected by the majority of the Fire
Fighters in any city, county, fire district or political subdivision shall be recognized as the sole and exclusive bargaining agent for all of the members of the Fire Department,
unless and until recognition of said bargaining agent is
withdrawn by a vote of the majority of the Fire Fighters
of such department. IDAHO CODE § 44-1803 (Supp. 1971).

The Florida, Georgia, and Wyoming Fire Fighter bargaining
laws contain substantially similar provisions. Under such a
provision, may an employer require that the petitioning organization demonstrate that it, in fact, has been selected by a majority of the members of a given fire department? May an employer, for example, condition the grant of recognition upon
the holding of a secret ballot election? Under a similar provision
in the Oklahoma law prior to its amendment, the Oklahoma
Attorney General ruled that a city had no right to establish the
standards and procedures for the selection of a bargaining agent.
Okla. Op. Att'y Gen. No. 71-420 (Dec. 29, 1971), GERR Ref.
File 51:4513 (1972).

2. In Bowman v. Hackensack Hospital Association, 116 N.J.
Super. 260, 282 A.2d 48 (1971), the New Jersey Superior Court
rejected an employer's contention that a bargaining order should
not be entered until an election was held to determine the
union's majority status. The court noted that there were relatively few employees in the bargaining unit and that the union's
majority status had been established by the pro-union trial testimony of a substantial majority of the unit members.

3. Post-Election Objections to Representation Election

BRANCH COUNTY ROAD COMMISSION
Michigan Employment Relations Commission
1969 MERC Lab. Op. 247

[At an employee meeting three days before a scheduled representation election employees were informed that the Branch
County Road Commission had previously decided to give the

employees a 25 cents per hour wage increase but that it could not do so because the Teamsters had filed a petition for an election. The employees were also told that if the Teamsters did not win the election the Commission would bargain with the Employees Association (which did not participate in the election) and agree to a three-year contract with a cost-of-living provision, a benefit which the employees had not previously enjoyed. When the Teamsters lost the election, it filed objections to the election based on the foregoing conduct.]

These circumstances establish that the intent and purpose of the Road Commission and its agents in holding the meeting, was to discourage the employees from voting for representation by the Teamsters union, and in addition was showing favoritism towards another organization that was not participating in the election.

We agree with the statement of the National Labor Relations Board, in the Baltimore Catering Company, 148 N.L.R.B. 970, wherein that Board stated:

> "Although the granting of benefits during the relevant period preceding an election is not necessarily cause for setting aside an election, the Board has set aside elections where it appears that the granting of the benefits at that particular time was calculated to influence the employees in their choice of a bargaining representative. In the absence of evidence demonstrating that the timing of the announcement of changes and benefits was governed by factors other than the pendency of the election, the Board will regard interference with employee freedom of choice as the motivating factor. The burden of establishing a justifiable motive remains with the employer. The fact that the employees may have known about or otherwise anticipated the increase in wages is not necessarily controlling. The crucial determination is whether the benefits were conferred for the purpose of influencing the employees in their choice of bargaining representatives and were of a type reasonably calculated to have that effect."

Accordingly, we hereby sustain the Objections to Elections discussed above, and direct an Election Officer of the Board to conduct a new election according to the attached Direction of Second Election, to determine whether the employees in the unit desire to be represented by Teamsters, State, County and Municipal Workers, Local 214, or no labor organization.

NOTE

There is a continuing debate concerning the extent to which a public employer should be allowed to state its views on unionization to employees prior to a representation election. The MERC has adopted the NLRA private sector standard, i.e., an employer is permitted to state its views as long as such expressions of opinion do not contain any threat of reprisal or promise of benefit. The Report of the Fortieth American Assembly on Collective Bargaining in American Government recommended a similar approach, stating:

> Public employers at all levels of government should have the right to be active or passive in the face of a union organizing campaign. This right to free speech should not permit coercive conduct or dismissals of union adherents.

REPORT OF THE FORTIETH AMERICAN ASSEMBLY, COLLECTIVE BARGAINING IN AMERICAN GOVERNMENT 5 (1971). At the other extreme is the approach adopted by the federal government under Executive Order 11491, whereby the federal government, as an employer, maintains "a position of neutrality as far as union representation of its employees is concerned, and Government officials do not mount 'vote no' campaigns." Hampton, *Federal Labor-Management Relations: A Program in Evolution*, 21 CATHOLIC U.L. REV. 493, 502 (1972). A position somewhere between these two approaches was recommended by the Federal Reserve System Labor Relations Panel. Thus, in Federal Reserve Bank of San Francisco, Panel Report and Decision (July 19, 1971), GERR No. 413, A-6 (1971), the Panel, chaired by William E. Simkin, recommended that there be "greater restraint" by the various federal reserve banks in asserting their views on unionization than the NLRB would require of employers in the private sector.

KENT COUNTY ROAD COMMISSION
Michigan Employment Relations Commission
1969 MERC Lab. Op. 314

[Following an election in which the Teamsters defeated the Kent County Road Commission Employees Association by a vote of 127 to 117, the Kent County Road Commission and the Kent County Road Commission Employees Association filed objections to conduct affecting the results of the election.]

The Kent County Road Commission Employees Association made the following objections:

"A.   That contrary to Rule 423.445 (3) an important notice
of election and sample ballot was either insufficient as
posted by the Employer or defaced subsequent to its
posting at the No. 1 garage at Scribner Avenue, Grand
Rapids, Michigan, whereby said notice and said sample
ballot had deleted from its face that this Petitioner was
one of the parties to said election. . . .

"C.   That Teamsters Local 214, did engage in material representation, involving substantial departure from the
truth, just prior to the election ordered herein in the
form of hand-bills and oral representations at a time
which prevented this Petitioner from making an effective reply, said misrepresentations were designed and
could be reasonably expected to have a significant impact on said election."

There is no material dispute as to the facts underlying the
objections contained in Paragraph A above. On the morning of
February 10, 1969, two days prior to the election, the sample
ballot that had been posted prior to the election, was found
to have the name of the Kent County Road Commission Employees Association cut out from the ballot. As far as the record
discloses, this was the only sample ballot that was defaced.
Sample ballots were posted at other places in the same building
where the defaced ballot was found, as well as on various other
properties of the Road Commission. There is no evidence as
to who defaced the one election notice, or that the defacement
of the sample ballot had been brought to the attention of the
Road Commission or the Labor Mediation Board.

Under the circumstances, in absence of evidence as to who is
responsible for the defacement of the face ballot, and the fact
that the sample ballot had been defaced had been posted in
complete form for at least three days, and other notices un-
defaced and containing the names of the Kent County Road
Commission were posted we find that this act by an unidentified
person is not sufficient grounds for setting aside the election.
Eaton County Road Commission, 1967 Lab. Op. 501, Frye Roofing Co., 108 N.L.R.B. 1297, Murray Chair Co., Inc., 117 N.L.R.B.
1385, Snow Canning Co., 119 N.L.R.B. 714.

The main thrust of Objection C by the Kent County Road
Commission Employees Association is that the Teamsters engaged in material misrepresentation. The alleged misrepresentations are that in a handbill distributed by the Teamsters by mail
on or about February 6, 1969, and again on February 9, 1969,
stated that if the Teamsters were the bargaining agent there

would be: "no more staggering hours—to avoid paying over-time," and that there would be "no more reprimands that the Commission is the final judge (we want a grievance procedure with arbitration)" and "no more kangaroo courts—full steward representation and grievance procedure."

An additional matter objected to was a statement contained in a letter mailed to the employees' homes by the Teamsters on or about February 6th or 7th wherein it was stated:

"Another fact must be carefully considered—if the Association commits by accident or voluntarily any unlawful act, the employer will sue the Association and all its employees. Under the Teamsters' contract, the Teamsters Union will stand completely liable and you and your family cannot be sued."

The last statement objected to in the Teamster literature was the statement that the Teamsters' Pension Plan would be available to the employees of the Road Commission.

The National Labor Relations Board has considered various types of campaign misrepresentations for years. We are in agreement with the view taken by the National Labor Relations Board in Hollywood Ceramics Co. Inc., 140 N.L.R.B. 221. In that case the National Labor Relations Board stated:

"We believe that an election should be set aside only where there has been a misrepresentation or other similar campaign trickery, which involves a substantial departure from the truth, at a time which prevents the other party or parties from making an effective reply, so that the misrepresentation, whether deliberate or not, may not reasonably be expected to have a significant impact on the election. However, the mere fact that a message is inartistically or vaguely worded and subject to different interpretations will not suffice to establish such misrepresentation as would lead us to set the election aside. Such ambiguities, like extravagant promises, derogatory statements about the other party, and minor distortions of some facts, frequently occur in communication between persons. But even where a misrepresentation is shown to have been substantial, the Board may still refuse to set aside the election if it finds upon consideration of all the circumstances that the statement would not be likely to have had a real impact on the election. For example, the misrepresentation might have occurred in connection with an unimportant matter so that it could only have had a de minimis effect. Or, it could have been so extreme as to put the employees on notice of its lack of truth under the particular circumstances so that they could not reasonably have relied on the assertion. Or, the Board may find that the employees possess independent knowledge with which to evaluate the statements."

We are, however, of the opinion, that the Teamsters, in their campaign literature which was specifically directed to the wives of the employees of the Road Commission in the unit, exceeded the permissible bounds of election propaganda, allowed by the *Hollywood Ceramics* case. The statements that the Employer will sue the Association and all its employees because of any accidental or voluntarily unlawful act, is an outright falsehood. The untruth of the statement, when accompanied with the taint of threat inherently contained therein, can [sic] have prevented a fair election. The National Labor Relations Board stated in United Aircraft Corporation, 31 L.R.R.M. 1437:

> "Although the Board has traditionally declared its intention not to censor or police pre-election propaganda by parties to elections, it has imposed some limits on free campaigning which, when transgressed, require corrective action. Thus, exaggerations, inaccuracies, partial truths, name-calling, and falsehoods, while not condoned, may be excused as legitimate propaganda, provided they are not 'so misleading' as to prevent the exercise of a free choice by the employees in the selection of their bargaining representative. Propaganda of this sort, the Board has said, will not be censored or policed if it remains within 'bounds,' and in this connection the question to be decided is 'one of degree.' In sum, the ultimate consideration is whether the challenged propaganda has lowered the standards of campaigning to the point where it may be said that the uninhibited desires of the employees cannot be determined in an election."

As indicated above, we are of the opinion that what has occurred here, has prevented the employees from exercising their uninhibited desires in selection of a bargaining agent. . . .

Order and Direction of Election

It is ordered that an Election Officer of the Board, shall conduct a new election. . . .

NOTES

1. The Assistant Secretary of Labor has ruled that under Executive Order 11491 an employee organization which has been eliminated from the ballot in a run-off election because it was not one of the two top vote getters in the first election

has no standing to object to the conduct of the run-off election. Report No. 17, GERR No. 376, A-5 (1970).

2. The NLRB in Excelsior Underwear Inc., 156 N.L.R.B. 1236 (1966), held that an employer is required to furnish a petitioning union, as well as any other employee organizations on the ballot, with the names and addresses of all eligible voters within a specified time period prior to the election and that an employer's failure to provide the names and addresses of its employees constitutes a valid ground for setting aside an election. The so-called *Excelsior* rule was upheld by the Supreme Court in NLRB v. Wyman-Gordon Co., 394 U.S. 759, 89 S. Ct. 1426, 22 L. Ed. 2d 709 (1969). The Michigan Employment Relations Commission has incorporated similar policies in its rules and regulations. Is it an unfair labor practice for a public employer to refuse to provide an employee organization which is attempting to organize the employer's employees with their names and addresses? *See* Eastern Michigan University, 1971 MERC Lab. Op. 346.

WISCONSIN EMPLOYMENT RELATIONS COMMISSION v. CITY OF EVANSVILLE

Wisconsin Circuit Court, Rock County
80 L.R.R.M. 3201 (1972)

LUEBKE, J.: The facts are involved and lengthy and are set forth in great detail in both the record and briefs of counsel and for the most part need not be repeated in this decision.

Briefly, Local 579 filed a complaint of prohibited practices wherein it alleged that the City violated Section 111.70 (3) (a) (1), Wis. Stats., by engaging in acts of intimidation and coercion of its employees, thereby restraining and interfering with their rights to affiliate with and be represented by a labor organization of their own choosing.

This is a proceeding for the review of related decisions and orders of the WERC upholding certain findings of its Examiner that the City had in fact committed certain prohibited practices, that possibilities of holding a fair election were at best marginal, and that the Union should therefore be certified without a new election.

In opposing the petition of the WERC in this Court to enforce its decision, the City asks for a review of the Commission's findings and orders. The City maintains that (1) the record fails to establish that the City committed any prohibited practices; (2) the remedy ordered by the WERC is in excess of its authority and jurisdiction; and (3) the conduct complained of, even if unlawful, does not justify the Commission's drastic remedy.

The Circuit Court's scope of review in proceedings of this kind is set forth in Sections 110.07 and 227.20, Wis. Stats. In addition, two cases clarify the role of the reviewing court and set up guidelines between the two extremes of judicial rubber-stamping on one hand and judicial meddling on the other.

Muskego-Norway v. WERC, 35 Wis. 2d 540, for instance, emphasizes that the Court should show some deference to the expertise of the Commission and give due weight to its experience, technical competence, and specialized knowledge in determining whether the Commission's findings are supported by substantial evidence in view of the entire record. If so, then the Court must not substitute its wisdom for that of the Commission merely because the Court doesn't agree in every detail with the Commission's findings.

Kenosha Teachers Union v. WERC, 39 Wis. 2d 196, however, makes it clear that the Court must not abdicate its judicial power to the Commission. The Commission exercises administrative and not judicial authority. Therefore, substantial evidence must be further defined as such relevant evidence as a reasonable mind might accept as adequate to support a conclusion in view of the record as a whole, rather than of just that portion of the record which tends to support the Commission's decision.

1. Is the Commission's finding that the City engaged in prohibited practices, within the meaning of Section 111.70 (3) (a) (1), Wis. Stats., supported by substantial evidence in view of the entire record?

Section 111.70 (2), Wis. Stats., provides that municipal employees shall have the right of self-organization and to affiliate with and be represented by a labor organization of their own choosing.

Section 111.70 (3), on Prohibited Practices, provides, in part, that municipal employers, their officers and agents are prohibited from

" (1)   Interfering with, restraining or coercing any municipal employee in the exercise of the rights provided in sub. (2) ."

Determinations of unfair labor practices normally involve a consideration of the totality of the conduct undertaken by the employer and its agents. Isolated facts taken out of context must be treated cautiously. Conduct and acts may be harmless in one situation and prejudicial in another. Here the Examiner has an advantage over both the Commission and the Court in evaluating the nuances of credibility in the testimony of the witnesses.

A study of the transcript of testimony and the documents submitted at the Examiner's hearing clearly supports the finding
by the Commission that the employer's conduct had an actual
tendency to coerce or intimidate its employees. Acts that under
other circumstances might individually create merely an aroma
of coercion, or a strong suspicion of intimidation, when examined
together in the entire context of their dealings amply support the
Commission finding that the employer engaged in a low-key but
no less persistent campaign of public and private threats and
coercive conduct designed to undermine the Union's majority
status before the election. Among others, the following Commission findings of prohibited practices are affirmed by the Court
or are otherwise established to the satisfaction of the Court.

1. The contents of the newspaper article published on November 27, 1969 threatened the employees with loss of fringe
benefits if the Union won the election. Even assuming that the
writers of the article were operating under an innocent misunderstanding of law that fringe benefits would have to be
negotiated, such misunderstanding is not a defense to an unlawful threat. This statement, taken in consideration of the
entire context of the letter and the other conduct of the employer, could be reasonably determined to be chillingly coercive in its consequences.

2. From another statement of the employer in the same letter,
notwithstanding its disclaimers that no threats were intended, it
appears that the employees were threatened with the loss of certain specific benefits, such as the future installation of time
clocks, regulated coffee breaks, and possible loss of presently enjoyed freedoms. Here, again in the entire context of the letter
and all of the employers conduct, this statement could be found
to be much more than a mere pointing out of the disadvantages
of Union membership and what the Union could negotiate. Instead, there was ample basis for the Commission to find that it
was a threat designed to intimidate.

3. The employer's statement dealing with possible sub-con-
tracting, made during the pendency of an election proceeding,
could be found to be under the circumstances then existing to
amount to a threat coercive in its consequences. While the employer may have had a legal right to subcontract certain municipal
functions, the threat to do so under these circumstances was
unlawful and interfered with the right of the employees to engage in concerted activity.

4. While this Court questions the inferential conclusion of
the Examiner that the employer would improve its offer if the
Union were defeated in the election, the record does support a

finding that there was a promise of benefit to the employees if they would reconsider their position and by talking with an aldermanic committee completely resolve this situation, without Union interference.

2. Did the WERC have statutory authority to issue a bargaining order without an election?

In order to remedy the violations which it found, the Commission ordered the City to recognize the Union, without an election, as the bargaining representative of all the employees for whom an election had been directed.

To this extreme remedy, the City strenuously objects, emphasizing that the order not only deprives the employees of their statutory right to vote by secret ballot on whether they want to be represented by the Union, but also deprives them of their ability to determine the description of the bargaining unit. The statute provides that the majority status of labor organizations seeking to become bargaining representatives is to be established by a government conducted secret ballot election.

The WERC, in turn, relies on its general remedial authority to go beyond the mere granting of a cease and desist order. The Commission's statutory authority to issue remedial orders stems from Section 111.07 (4), Wis. Stats., wherein it is provided that if the Commission finds that prohibited practices have been committed it can then require the City

". . . to take such affirmative action, . . . as the Board may deem proper. . . ."

Section 111.70 (4) (h) (2), Wis. Stats., states in part:
"only labor unions which have been certified . . . or which the employer has recognized . . . shall be proper parties in initiating fact finding proceedings. . . ."

Thus, it seems clear from the above statute that the City could have chosen voluntarily to recognize the Union as being the representative of its employees. What the City can do voluntarily, the Commission obviously can direct it to do.

The Commission has held that if the Union loses an election it may nevertheless secure bargaining rights through an unfair labor practice proceeding wherein it proves (1) its majority status in an appropriate bargaining unit at the time of the demand for recognition, (2) Employer conduct aimed at dissipating the majority, and (3) the futility of conducting a new election in view of the Employer's effective misconduct. Hotel, Motel, Restaurant Employees and Bartenders Union, Local 122 v. Colonial Restaurants, Inc., Decision No. 7604-C.

The City contends that the Commission should order a municipal employer to recognize an employee organization without an election only when the employer has "destroyed all possibility of a free secret-ballot election." Such a theory, however, would appear to be an open invitation to the employer to engage in as much minor misbehavior as he could get away with (knowing that some acts would go undetected or unreported anyway), and only to be careful not to be caught doing anything so flagrant as would destroy all possibility of a free secret-ballot election. Such an interpretation would condone, not discourage, minor abuses and irregularities by the employer.

For instance, what would an employer have to lose? If the Union wins the election, the employer's misconduct would be moot. If the Union loses the election, it is obliged to appeal to the Commission and the Courts at great loss of time and expense, where time is on the side of the employer, and with loss of interest or discouragement on the part of employees.

In the last analysis, we must also recognize that a municipal employer, with its elected and appointed public officials who do not own the business, should be able to behave more like Caesar's wife than the private owner (or his agents) who feels this is *his* business and that he has a personal concern in its future that outweighs at times his prudence and respect for the letter of the law. At least his excesses are more understandable than those of public officials who are presumed to be more responsive to the necessity of respecting and obeying the Employment Relations law as established by the Legislature, whether they agree with its wisdom or not.

Admittedly, the function of the Commission is to assist in the creation and maintenance of peaceful employer-employee collective bargaining relationships, and that the Commission is required to balance the interests of the public, the employees, and the employer in doing so. The instant case is an eloquent example of the sad consequences to the public interest resulting from a municipal employer's failure to recognize the sensitivity of its role in informing but not manipulating its employees and public opinion around them.

Under all the circumstances, the Commission was entitled to find that the timing of the acts engaged in by the City was motivated to discourage the employees from engaging in lawful concerted activities and from selecting the Union as their bargaining representative. The Court agrees with the Commission that to require the employees to cast a ballot to determine their bargaining representative, after such unlawful acts had occurred, would permit the City to take advantage of its own misconduct.

Prior to the City's having engaged in prohibited practices the great majority of employees had selected and designated the Union to be their bargaining representative. The Commission was entitled to believe from the entire record that after these prohibited practices had taken place the consequences flowing from such misconduct could not reasonably be expected to be expunged from the minds of the employees by a new election, simply upon subsequent reassurances of the municipal employer made in response to an order of the Commission.

NOTE

The Supreme Court has upheld the authority of the NLRB to issue a bargaining order if it finds that the employer has engaged in unfair labor practices which tend to dissipate the union's majority status and make a fair election unlikely. NLRB v. Gissel Packing Co., Inc., 395 U.S. 575, 89 S. Ct. 1918, 23 L. Ed. 2d 547 (1969). In so ruling, the Court stated:

> If the Board finds that the possibility of erasing the effects of past practices and of insuring a fair election (or a fair rerun) by the use of traditional remedies, though present, is slight and that employee sentiment once expressed through cards would, on balance, be better protected by a bargaining order, then such an order should issue . . . . *Id.* at 614-15.

G.   Judicial Review of Representation Proceedings

CITY MANAGER OF MEDFORD v. STATE LABOR RELATIONS COMMISSION

Supreme Judicial Court of Massachusetts
353 Mass. 519, 233 N.E.2d 310 (1968)

CUTTER, Justice. On April 4, 1966, the president of International Association of Firefighters, Local 1032 . . . , filed with the commission a petition for certification of the union as collective bargaining agent for Medford's firefighters. See G.L. c. 149, §§ 178G-178N (inserted by St. 1965, c. 763, § 2; see amendment of § 178G by St. 1966, c. 156), regulating collective bargaining by municipal employees. The commission on June 9, 1966, filed a decision. After meager findings of subsidiary facts it stated (1) that a question of representation had arisen; (2) that the appropriate unit consisted "of all fire fighters employed by the . . . [city] including lieutenants, captains, district chiefs, [and] deputy chiefs, but excluding the [c]hief . . . and . . . all other [city] employees," and (3) that an election should be held on July 7, 1966, to determine whether a majority of the employees had selected the union as collective bargaining agent.

The city manager, on June 28, 1966, filed this petition for judicial review. He contends that the commission's decision improperly "lumps together all uniformed employees of the Medford [f]ire [d]epartment as an appropriate [bargaining] unit with the . . . exception of the [c]hief . . . and orders an unnecessary election." A Superior Court judge overruled a plea to the jurisdiction filed by the interveners. This plea was based primarily on the ground that the commission's decision was not a final order. By final decree, the commission's decision was affirmed. The city manager appealed.

We first consider whether this petition is premature. The commission ordered an election by secret ballot "as part of the investigation authorized by" it.

The statutes permitting collective bargaining by municipal employees . . . contain no express provision for judicial review. General Laws c. 30A, § 14 (as amended through St. 1957, c. 193, § 1), however, provides for judicial review of "a final decision of any agency in an adjudicatory proceeding." The commission and the interveners contend that there has been no "final decision" by the commission.

Precedents under G.L. c. 150A, § 6 (f), as amended through St. 1954, c. 681, § 11, are not directly controlling. Nevertheless, there are numerous similarities between c. 150A, the State Labor Relations Law (see c. 150A, § 12) which is applicable to private industry, and the 1965 statute . . . concerning municipal employment. Accordingly, precedents under c. 150A are likely to furnish helpful guidance if differences between the two statutes and between public and private employment are appropriately taken into account.

In Jordan Marsh Co. v. Labor Relations Comm., 312 Mass. 597, 602, 45 N.E.2d 925, 927, this court held that "in ordinary cases" judicial review of certification issues within the commission's jurisdiction could take place only after there had been a commission decision based upon an unfair labor practice.[4] At that stage, "the whole proceeding, including any errors in the certifying of the representatives . . . [becomes] open to court review." The court in the Jordan Marsh Co. case (p. 602, 45 N.E.2d p. 928) left open the possibility that cases might exist "where the effect of a mere certification might be so immedi-

---

[4] Such postponement of court review, however, is not necessary in cases where the commission acts outside its jurisdiction. In such instances judicial proceedings have been permitted in advance of any final order on an unfair labor practice. See e.g. Saint Luke's Hosp. v. Labor Relations Comm., 320 Mass. 467, 469-474, 70 N.E.2d 10; Wheaton College v. Labor Relations Comm., Mass. (Mass. Adv. Sh. [1967] 1071, 1074-1077, 227 N.E.2d 735).

ately and completely disastrous to the legally protected interests of the employer that the Legislature must be presumed to have intended" to permit other avenues of review.

In cases reviewing action of the National Labor Relations Board, similar principles have been applied. See American Fedn. of Labor v. National Labor Relations Bd., 308 U.S. 401, 412, 60 S. Ct. 300, 84 L. Ed. 347. An order for an election has not been regarded as a final order. Inland Empire Dist. Council v. Millis, 325 U.S. 697, 707, 65 S. Ct. 1316, 89 L. Ed. 1877, reh. den. 326 U.S. 803, 66 S. Ct. 11, 90 L. Ed. 489. See Boire v. Greyhound Corp., 376 U.S. 473, 476-481, 84 S. Ct. 894, 11 L. Ed. 2d 849. The Supreme Court of Connecticut has recently reached a similar conclusion under its statute (Conn. Gen. Sts. Ann. [1965] §§ 7-467 to 7-477; see Pub. Act No. 159, 1965) regulating collective bargaining by municipal employees.[5] See Windsor v. Windsor Police Dept. Employees Assn. Inc., 154 Conn. 530, 536-539, 227 A.2d 65.

We conclude that the principles stated in the *Jordan Marsh Co.* case, 312 Mass. 597, 602, 45 N.E.2d 925 (at least in the absence of extraordinary circumstances making certification questions of vital significance, or of questions relating to the commission's jurisdiction), should be applied to postpone judicial review of certification questions until, upon complaint, the commission has issued or denied an order (see c. 149, § 178L) to the municipal employer or to employees to desist from a practice prohibited by the statute. When such an order is issued, the propriety of the commission's decision on certification issues will be open for appropriate judicial scrutiny.

The city manager contends that the commission had no authority to order an election and that, in any event, an election is unnecessary (see White, Rights and Responsibilities in Municipal Collective Bargaining, 22 Arbit. J. 31, 32), because the city in fact recognizes the union as the firefighters' exclusive bargaining agent. Certainly, there appears to be no real objection by the city to recognizing the union as representing all the fire-

---

[5] The Connecticut statute was adopted a few months earlier than the Massachusetts statute, which in many respects appears to follow the Connecticut language. The Connecticut court, however, rested its decision (p. 535, 227 A.2d 65) in part upon § 7-471 (4) (D), a provision not included in the comparable Massachusetts section. See G.L. c. 149, § 178L. On general principles, however, we reach essentially the same result. Precedents under other somewhat different State statutes afford little guidance. See Mich. Comp. L. Ann. §§ 423.201 to 423.216; Wis. St. 1965 subd.-c. IV, § 111.70 (see also Milwaukee County Dist. Council 48 v. Wisconsin Employment Relations Bd., 23 Wis. 2d 303, 306-307, 127 N.W.2d 59, 11 A.L.R.3d 810; note, 1965 Wis. L. Rev. 652); 7 Wyo. St. (1965 supp.) c. 14, §§ 27-265 to 27-273; note, 8 B.C. Ind. and Com. L. Rev. 273. Cf. annotation, 31 A.L.R.2d 1142.

fighters except the deputy chiefs and officers (for convenience here called the officer group). The only real dispute appears to be whether the officer group should be included in the bargaining unit. Nevertheless, we cannot say that under c. 149, § 178H (3), the commission was not justified in ordering an election as part of its investigation, to obtain assurance, through an uncoerced, free, secret ballot, that the firefighters really wished to be represented by the union. See, however, the provisions for waiving an election by stipulation in St. 1967, c. 746, amending § 178H.

The petition does not set forth any facts showing (a) that the commission has exceeded its jurisdiction, (b) that there is any extraordinary occasion for varying the usual procedure for review, or (c) that special injury to the public interest or inconvenience to the city or its firefighters will occur if the commission's investigation takes the usual course. Accordingly, it was premature for the Superior Court to exercise jurisdiction to review the commission's action. The petition should have been dismissed.

Because the petition was brought prematurely, the case is remanded to the Superior Court, where a new final decree is to be entered dismissing the petition.

So ordered.

NOTES

1. Under the NLRA, decisions of the NLRB establishing appropriate bargaining units, determining the eligibility of voters, ruling on objections to an election, and other issues raised in representation proceedings are not generally subject to direct judicial review. In Boire v. Greyhound Corp., 376 U.S. 473, 476-80, 84 S. Ct. 894, 11 L. Ed. 2d 849 (1964), the Supreme Court discussed the underlying rationale, as well as the two major exceptions to the general rule:

In the normal course of events Board orders in certification proceedings under § 9 (c) are not directly reviewable in the courts. This Court held as long ago as American Federation of Labor v. Labor Board, 308 U.S. 401, that the "final order[s]" made reviewable by §§ 10 (e) and (f) in the Courts of Appeals do not include Board decisions in certification proceedings. Such decisions, rather, are normally reviewable only where the dispute concerning the correctness of the certification eventuates in a finding by the Board that an unfair labor practice has been committed as, for example, where an employer refuses to bargain with a certified representative on the ground that the election was held in an inappropriate bargaining unit. In such a case, § 9 (d) of the Act makes full provision for judicial review of the underlying certification order by providing that "such certification and the record of such investigation shall be included in the transcript of the entire record required to be filed" in the Court of Appeals.

That this indirect method of obtaining judicial review imposes significant delays upon attempts to challenge the validity of Board orders in certification proceedings is obvious. But it is equally obvious that Congress explicitly intended to impose precisely such delays. At the time of the original passage of the National Labor Relations Act in 1935, the House Report clearly delineated the congressional policy judgment which underlay the restriction of judicial review to that provided for in § 9 (d) :

> "When an employee organization has built up its membership to a point where it is entitled to be recognized as the representative of the employees for collective bargaining, and the employer refuses to accord such recognition, the union, unless an election can promptly be held to determine the choice of representation, runs the risk of impairment of strength by attrition and delay while the case is dragging on through the courts, or else is forced to call a strike to achieve recognition by its own economic power. Such strikes have been called when election orders of the National Labor Relations Board have been held up by court review."

And both the House and the Senate Reports spelled out the thesis, repeated on the floor, that the purpose of § 9 (d) was to provide "for review in the courts only after the election has been held and the Board has ordered the employer to do something predicated upon the results of the election." Congressional determination to restrict judicial review in such situations was reaffirmed in 1947, at the time that the Taft-Hartley amendments were under consideration, when a conference committee rejected a House amendment which would have permitted any interested person to obtain review immediately after a certification because, as Senator Taft noted, "such provision would permit dilatory tactics in representation proceedings."

In light of the clear import of this history, this Court has consistently refused to allow direct review of such orders in the Court of Appeals. American Federation of Labor v. Labor Board, *supra*. In two cases, however, each characterized by extraordinary circumstances, our decisions have permitted district court review of orders entered in certification proceedings. In Leedom v. Kyne, 358 U.S. 184, despite the injunction of § 9 (b) (1) of the Act that "the Board shall not (1) decide that any unit is appropriate . . . if such unit includes both professional employees and employees who are not professional employees unless a majority of such professional employees vote for inclusion in such unit," the Board—without polling the professional employees— approved as appropriate a unit containing both types of employees. The Board conceded in the Court of Appeals that it "had acted in excess of its powers and had thereby worked injury to the statutory rights of the professional employees." 358 U.S., at 187. We pointed out there that the District Court suit was "not one to 'review,' in the sense of that term as used in the Act, a decision of the Board made within its jurisdiction. Rather it is one to strike down an order of the Board made in excess of its delegated powers and contrary to a specific prohibition in the Act." 358 U.S., at 188. Upon these grounds we affirmed the District Court's judgment setting aside the Board's "attempted exercise of [a] power that had been specifically withheld." 358 U.S., at 189. And in McCulloch v. Sociedad Nacional, 372 U.S. 10, in which District Court jurisdiction was upheld in a situation involving the question of application of the laws of the United States to foreign-flag ships and their crews, the Court was careful to note that "the presence of public questions particularly high in the scale of our national interest because of their international complexion is a uniquely compelling justification for prompt judicial resolution of the controversy over the Board's power. No question of remotely comparable urgency was involved in Kyne, which was a purely domestic adversary situation. The exception recognized today is therefore not to be taken as an enlargement of the exception in Kyne." 372 U.S., at 17. . . .

2. Assume that Union A and Union B are vying for the right to represent the employees of a public employer and that Union A loses the election and subsequently files timely objections to the election alleging that Union B engaged in illegal pre-election conduct that affected the outcome of the election. Assume further that the PERB overrules the objections and certifies Union B as the exclusive bargaining representative of the employees. On the basis of the decision of the Massachusetts Supreme Judicial Court in the principal case, could Union A obtain judicial review of the PERB decision overruling its objections?

3. Decisions of the Assistant Secretary of Labor directing elections under Executive Order 11491 are not subject to judicial review. In holding that it did not have jurisdiction to entertain such an action, the court in National Alliance of Postal & Federal Employees v. United States, 339 F. Supp. 1343 (W.D. Pa. 1971), stated, *inter alia,*

> . . . that no judicial review can be had of an order directing [an] election under this Executive Order for the reason that these Executive Orders have no basis in Statute, are promulgated fully by the President and he can revoke or modify them at any time. They are purely a matter of grace with the Executive. . . . There may be exceptions to this where acting under the Executive Order, the Assistant Secretary has violated constitutional rights of government workers or has acted in an arbitrary or discriminatory manner as was claimed in National Association of Government Employees v. White, 135 U.S. App. D.C. 290, 418 F.2d 1126. . . . 339 F. Supp. at 1344-45.

The court further observed in dictum "that a mere order of the Assistant Secretary ordering an election is not a final agency order under any circumstances but only an interlocutory decision. There is no final order at least until such time as the election has been held and one bargaining unit or the other or neither has been certified."

CIVIL SERVICE EMPLOYEES ASSOCIATION v. HELSBY
New York Supreme Court, Appellate Division
31 App. Div. 2d 325, 297 N.Y.S.2d 813
Aff'd per curiam, 24 N.Y.2d 993, 250 N.E.2d 230, 302 N.Y.S.2d 822 (1969)

STALEY, JR., J. This is an appeal from a judgment of the Supreme Court at Special Term, entered in Albany County on January 9, 1969, which dismissed a petition in a proceeding under article 78 of the CPLR to review a determination of the Public Employment Relations Board in a representation status dispute, and denied an application to vacate an order issued by such board temporarily restraining the State Negotiating Committee from continuing negotiations with the Civil Service Employees Association pending final certification of representation status.

Following the enactment of the Public Employees' Fair Employment Act (Civil Service Law, art. 14; L. 1967, ch. 392, also known as the Taylor Law), the State Negotiating Committee determined that it would negotiate collectively with three units of State employees and recognized the Civil Service Employees

Association to negotiate on behalf of employees of one such unit commonly called the general unit. Employee organizations opposed to the association filed petitions with the Public Employment Relations Board contesting both the establishment of the general unit and the recognition of the association. The board issued an order on November 30, 1967 restraining exclusive negotiations between the State Negotiating Committee and the association until the representation status dispute initiated by the filing of such petitions was resolved, which order was vacated in a prior proceeding in which the statute was construed as "conferring of power on the public employer to recognize and negotiate with employee organizations, untrammeled by representation dispute proceedings until they have been resolved by the Board through certifications of appropriate bargaining units and employee organizations." (Matter of Civil Serv. Employees Assn. v. Helsby, 21 N.Y.2d 541, 548.)

Following extensive hearings upon the petitions filed by the employee organizations opposed to the association, the board, on November 27, 1968, handed down its decision which rejected the general unit designated by the State Negotiating Committee and found five separate units to be appropriate. The question of which job titles should be included in each unit and the ascertainment of the employees' choice of employee organizations as their representatives were reserved pending further proceedings before the board. The association promptly commenced the present proceeding to review such determination by petition and order to show cause issued November 27, 1968. Before service of the petition and order to show cause was effected, the board issued an order, also dated November 27, 1968, in which it ordered the State Negotiating Committee and the association to refrain from conducting further negotiations until the representation status dispute was resolved through certifications of employee organizations for employees in each of the five units.

Respondents moved to dismiss the petition upon the ground that the determination sought to be reviewed is not final within the meaning of subdivision 1 of CPLR 7801, which motion was granted. Special Term also denied the association's application, apparently made upon the argument of the motion to dismiss its petition, for judgment vacating the order restraining negotiations between the State Negotiating Committee and the association.

The first issue raised on this appeal is whether the board's determination is subject to judicial review under article 78 of the CPLR. CPLR 7801 provides that article 78 "shall not be used to challenge a determination which is not final or can be adequately reviewed by appeal to a court or some other body or officer." It is this exception upon which the board relies to defer judicial review.

The board in its decision concluded that in a representative proceeding it was empowered to devise a unit that it deemed most appropriate, although such a unit was not specifically sought by any of the parties. It further held that the general unit designated by the employer was not appropriate and approved five separate units as appropriate. The board contends that its determination is not final and, therefore, the association is not, at this time, free to question the appropriateness of the units it has devised.

The pertinent provisions of the Taylor Law to the issues involved on this appeal read as follows:

"§ 205. Public employment relations board. . . . 5. In addition to the powers and functions provided in other sections of this article, the board shall have the following powers and functions . . . (f) To conduct studies of problems involved in representation and negotiation, including, but not limited to . . . (ii) the problems of unit determination. . . .

"§ 207. Determination of representation status. For purposes of resolving disputes concerning representation status, pursuant to section two hundred five or two hundred six of this article, the board or government, as the case may be, shall

"1. define the appropriate employer-employee negotiating units taking into account the following standards:

" (a)   the definition of the unit shall correspond to a community of interest among the employees to be included in the unit;

" (b)   the officials of government at the level of the unit shall have the power to agree, or to make effective recommendations to other administrative authority or the legislative body with respect to, the terms and conditions of employment upon which the employees desire to negotiate; and

" (c)   the unit shall be compatible with the joint responsibilities of the public employer and public employees to serve the public."

It should be noted that subdivision 1 of section 207 of the Civil Service Law provides for the determination of the negotiating unit, while subdivisions 2 and 3 provide for the implementation of the unit for the purpose of certification.

Nothing in the Taylor Law or the CPLR makes the certification of an employee organization a prerequisite to judicial review of the determination establishing separate negotiating units. If that determination is final as to the rights of the parties, with respect to the matter involved, it should be reviewable.

The units deemed to be appropriate by the board are as final now as they will be upon certification. The matter involved in this proceeding is the propriety of the recognition of the association as a negotiating representative for the employees of the general unit, as contrasted with the board's determination that the general unit should be divided into five separate negotiating units. The determination mandated by subdivision 1 of section 207 of the Civil Service Law having been accomplished, the procedure provided by statute to implement that determination cannot alter the original determination. Whatever organization may ultimately be certified to represent the employees involved cannot affect the determination with respect to the structure of the five units.

The argument that the determination of the board establishing the five negotiating units should be reviewed only after certification as provided by subdivision 3 of section 207 of the Civil Service Law is contrary to prompt disposition of a dispute where a party is aggrieved as of the moment of the determination.

Judicial review at this time may avoid costly and time-consuming intermediate procedures. There would be no economy in deferring the question of the correctness of the board's determination until after all the proceedings required to ascertain and establish the employee representative for the five proposed units, should the courts ultimately decide that the five units established were not appropriate. Resolution of the issues in this proceeding at the earliest possible moment is in the best interest of the State and its employees. Unless there is some statutory prohibition, there is no reason to defer judicial review. As the Court of Appeals said of a comparable situation in Long Is. Coll. Hosp. v. Catherwood (23 N.Y.2d 20, 36) : "A decision that the validity of the board's certification cannot be tested in the court until time-consuming mediation, fact-finding and compulsory arbitration proceedings have been exhausted can only serve to delay a prompt determination of the representation issue—a delay which is not in the interest of the public, the nonprofitmaking hospitals or the unions, since unresolved representation issues may cause the very strife which the 1963 amendments were enacted to prevent."

We are here required to construe a unique statutory scheme, one that has as its main purpose the promotion of harmonious and co-operative relationships between government and its employees to protect the public by assuring at all times the orderly and uninterrupted operations and functions of government. Certainly such a statute should be construed with the liberality needed to carry out its public benefit purposes and, therefore,

the determination involved should be afforded prompt and
effective judicial review.

The board's decision finally and irrevocably rejected the bargaining unit designated by the State Negotiating Committee and
determined appropriate alternate units. Such determination is
in no sense interlocutory or merely an intermediate procedural
ruling incident to the administrative process (cf. Matter of Car-
ville v. Allen, 13 A.D.2d 866), but instead as to such matters it is
final and thus reviewable under article 78. . . .

NOTES

1. The decision in the principal case was relied on by the
New Jersey Superior Court, Appellate Division, in holding that
a decision of the New Jersey PERC denying a request for review
of an order directing an election was subject to judicial review.
County of Gloucester v. PERC, 107 N.J. Super. 150, 257 A.2d
712 (1969). The court rejected the proffered arguments based on
decisions under the NLRA that representation proceedings are
only subject to judicial review following a finding that an unfair
labor practice has been committed, observing that it found these
"arguments and their supportive rationale unpersuasive." On
appeal, the New Jersey Supreme Court affirmed the decision,
with the following modification: "We deem the final order
under the statute to be an order certifying the results of an
election. An order certifying the appropriate unit or directing
an election is merely interlocutory and is reviewable only upon
motion for leave to appeal." County of Gloucester v. PERC,
55 N.J. 333, 262 A.2d 1 (1970).

2. The Michigan Supreme Court in Board of Trustees of
Michigan State University v. State Labor Mediation Board, 381
Mich. 44, 158 N.W.2d 873 (1968), held that a decision of the
MERC establishing an appropriate bargaining unit and directing
an election was subject to judicial review. Without elaboration
or further explanation, the court relied on a provision in the
Michigan Constitution which provides that "[a]ll final decisions,
findings, rulings and orders of any administrative officer or agency
existing under the constitution or by law, which are judicial
or quasi-judicial and affect private rights or licenses, shall be
subject to direct review by the courts as provided by law" [Mich.
Const. art. 6, § 27]. Is the establishment of an appropriate bargaining unit and the direction of an election a "final decision"?
Does the court's decision beg the question?

Chapter 4

THE OBLIGATION AND DUTY TO BARGAIN

A. The Obligation to Bargain Collectively

1. Constitutional Considerations

ALANIZ v. CITY OF SAN ANTONIO

United States District Court, Western District of Texas
80 L.R.R.M. 2983 (1971)

Before THORNBERRY, Circuit Judge, and SUTTLE and WOOD, District Judges.

The essential facts in this case have been stipulated. The named plaintiffs are members of the Associacion de Obreros Mexico-Americanos (Associacion), an unincorporated labor and social organization formed in part to engage in collective bargaining, negotiation and arbitration of grievances with respect to wages, hours, and conditions of employment of its members. Plaintiffs are employed as utility workers in the General Construction Department of the City Public Service Board of San Antonio, Texas (Board), created by Trust Indenture to manage and operate electric and gas utilities owned by the City. The Associacion sought recognition by the Board as the bargaining agent for the unit in which plaintiffs worked, claiming to represent a majority of such employees. The Board refused to recognize the Associacion or to participate in collective bargaining because prohibited by a State statute, art. 5154c, Tex. Rev. Civ. Stat. Ann. Plaintiffs filed the instant suit against the City, its Mayor and Clerk, the Board, and its Manager, seeking a judgment declaring sections 1 and 2 of art. 5154c unconstitutional and an injunction against their enforcement. Locals 500, 831 and 1019, International Brotherhood of Electrical Workers, AFL-CIO, have intervened, claiming majority representation of various units of Board employees and adopting the position of plaintiffs.

Art. 5154c, enacted in 1947, deals generally with State policy regarding labor relations with public employees. Section 1 declares collective bargaining contracts between an official of the State or any subdivision thereof, including a City, and any labor organization, as broadly defined in section 5, to be against the public policy of the State and void. Section 2 declares recognition

313

by any such official of a labor organization as the bargaining agent for any group of employees against public policy. Section 3 likewise classifies strikes and organized work stoppages, and provides for full forfeiture of rights of any public employee involved in such concerted activity. Sections 4 and 6 protect public employees' right to membership (or nonmembership) in a labor organization and to "present grievances concerning their wages, hours of work, or conditions of work individually or through a representative that does not claim the right to strike," and other statutes provide for dues check-offs in favor of labor organizations representing public employees. Finally, section 7 provides for severability of sections.

This Court has jurisdiction under 42 U.S.C. § 1983 and 28 U.S.C. § 1343 (3) and 28 U.S.C. § 1331. It has been suggested that this case does not require the convening of and consideration by a three-judge District Court under 28 U.S.C. §§ 2281 et seq. We find that it does. First, we cannot say that the constitutional questions raised are either "obviously without merit" or foreclosed by decisions of the Supreme Court, and hence "insubstantial." Second, plaintiffs attack as unconstitutional the effect of a State statute embodying statewide policy declarations and seek to enjoin the officials who, though localized in geographic activities and mode of selection, execute and enforce the statute by their adherence thereto, and hence perform a state function within the meaning of § 2281. The case is therefore properly before this tribunal.[6]

The issue presented in this case is narrow. The Associacion does not claim the right to strike and plaintiffs do not attack section 3 of art. 5154c prohibiting such concerted activity. Nor is there any question about the individual public employee's right to join or not join a labor organization or be individually represented by any organization not claiming the right to strike. Sections 4 and 6 of art. 5154c protect these rights and it has been stipulated that the Board meets with the Associacion or its representative regarding grievances relating to wages, hours and other conditions of employment of its members. The only issue is the validity of the prohibitions in sections 1 and 2 of art. 5154c against recognition of a labor organization as bargaining agent for a *group* of public employees and *collective* bargaining contracts.

---

[6] While we need not here deal with defendants' suggestion that we lack power to afford the affirmative relief requested, we point out that, in addition to declaratory judgment under 28 U.S.C. § 2201 . . . , "[o]nce a right and a violation have been shown, the scope of a district court's equitable powers to remedy past wrongs is broad, for breadth and flexibility are inherent in equitable remedies." Swann v. Board of Education, 402 U.S. 1, 15 (1971).

Plaintiffs first contend that bargaining-agent recognition and collective bargaining are constitutionally protected rights, either as part of their First Amendment right to assemble, partially guarded here by section 4 of art. 5154c, or as part of those "retained by the people" through the Ninth Amendment, protected from unreasonable governmental interference by the Fourteenth Amendment to the United States Constitution. The "freedom" of individuals to organize into labor unions recognized at common law, however, was a narrow one. National legislation has added to the private employee's right of self-organization the right to engage in certain concerted activities for the purpose of collective bargaining, including selection and recognition of a bargaining representative. While it is now clear that public employees have a constitutionally protected right to self-organization, this right has never been extended to include collective bargaining through a recognized group representative. The private employee's right to such concerted activity, now "fundamental" under national legislative policy in the private arena, is not guaranteed to public employees such as plaintiffs, either by national legislation or the constitution. The State, in declaring its policy against bargaining-agent recognition and collective bargaining contracts in its dealing with public employees, is not interfering with any constitutionally protective [sic] rights of plaintiffs.

Plaintiffs further contend that the public policies embodied in sections 1 and 2 of art. 5154c with regard to public employees are arbitrary, irrational, and without reasonable justification, and hence in violation of the Equal Protection Clause of the Fourteenth Amendment. But, in addition to the many differences inherent in the nature of public as opposed to private employment justifying no-strike statutes, the nature and purpose of collective bargaining itself gives rise to reasons justifying different public and private treatment. To the extent the function of collective bargaining is to limit and restrict the control and direction of the working force by the employer, there is doubt as to a public employer's power to contract away these "management prerogatives." Any contract negotiated runs the risk of being "legislated away" by the ultimate governmental authority. Where the private employee relies on concerted action through collective bargaining to protect himself from arbitrary and discriminatory action by the employer, the State and its officials are always prohibited such conduct when dealing with its citizen-employees by the Constitution. Finally, while private employees must rely upon collective bargaining and other concerted activities to change management policies, the public employee always has the guaranteed political avenues, either individually through the ballot box or together through "petition,"[16] to effect a change in management personnel and/or policies. In short, there are facts and considerations which reasonably justify the policies embodied in sections 1 and 2 of art. 5154c sufficient to withstand equal protection scrutiny under the Fourteenth Amendment.

Whatever the wisest course for the State of Texas to follow in its labor relations with its employees, its choice of a public policy against recognition of a labor organization as bargaining representative for any group of employees and against collective bargaining contracts is not barred by the United States Constitution. Plaintiffs' constitutional rights under the First Amendment are adequately protected by sections 4 and 6 of art. 5154c, and sections 1 and 2 thereof are constitutional. . . .

NOTE

In Indianapolis Educ. Ass'n v. Lewallen, 72 L.R.R.M. 2071 (7th Cir. 1969), a school board entered into an agreement with a teachers' association in which the board agreed that it would recognize the association as the exclusive bargaining representative for a unit of teachers and would bargain in good faith with the association if the association received a majority of the votes cast in a representation election. Although the association received approximately 95 percent of the votes, it alleged that the school board thereafter refused to bargain in good faith and that this refusal violated the First and Fourteenth Amendments. The court rejected this contention, stating:

> The gravamen of the complaint goes to the failure on the part of the defendants-appellants to bargain collectively in good faith. But there is no constitutional duty to bargain collectively with an exclusive bargaining agent. Such duty, when imposed, is imposed by statute. The refusal of the defendants-appellants to bargain in good faith does not equal a constitutional violation of plaintiffs-appellees' positive rights of association, free speech, petition, equal protection, or due process. Nor does the fact that the agreement to collectively bargain may be enforceable against a state elevate a contractual right to a constitutional right.

Accord, Hanover Township Fed'n of Teachers v. Hanover Community School Corp., 457 F.2d 456 (7th Cir. 1972); Beauboeuf v. Delgado College, 428 F.2d 470 (5th Cir. 1970); Newport News Fire Fighters Ass'n, Local 794 v. City of Newport News, 339 F.

---

[16] See U.S. Const. amend. I. It is perhaps here where an organization like the Associacion may be most effective.

Supp. 13 (E.D. Va. 1972); Atkins v. City of Charlotte, 296 F. Supp. 1068 (W.D.N.C. 1969); Gary Teachers Union, Local 4 v. School City of Gary, 427 Ind. App. 211, 284 N.E.2d 108 (1972). *But see* School Comm. of the Town of Westerly v. Westerly Teachers Ass'n, — R.I. —, 299 A.2d 441 (1973) (dissenting opinion).

RICHMOND EDUCATION ASSOCIATION v. CROCKFORD
United States District Court, Eastern District of Virginia
55 F.R.D. 362 (1972)

MERHIGE, District Judge:—This is a class action brought pursuant to 28 U.S.C. §§ 1343 (3) and (4) and 42 U.S.C. § 1983, seeking declaratory and injunctive relief against the School Board of the City of Richmond and its individual members in their representative capacities. . . .

The complaint and exhibits filed therewith reflect that plaintiff, Richmond Education Association ("REA"), is an unincorporated association organized under the laws of the Commonwealth of Virginia, whose sole purpose is to represent certified professional employees of the defendant school board, in their employment relationships. REA membership currently lists 2,085 members of an eligible 3,350. This action is based upon an alleged refusal of the defendants to meet and discuss with the REA concerning conditions of employment, to recognize REA as a representative of the aforementioned employees for purposes of discussion, and to recognize REA as the exclusive representative of the class which it purports to represent. The defendants have allegedly refused all recognition of and discussions with REA.

Through the motions filed, defendants have attacked the complaint on several grounds:

1. Motion to Dismiss For Lack of Jurisdiction and/or Failure To State A Claim Upon Which Relief Can Be Granted

The plaintiffs herein premise their complaint in the First and Fourteenth Amendments to the Constitution of the United States. The Court is satisfied that jurisdiction exists pursuant to 42 U.S.C. § 1983 and 28 U.S.C. §§ 1343 (3) and (4).

The complaint herein clearly and succinctly alleges that the plaintiffs have a constitutional right as public sector employees to organize and associate for the purpose of collectively representing their employment interests. It is contended that by their actions, the defendants have effectively blunted the exercise of these rights. The plaintiffs allege, in essence, that:

Nothing could have a greater chilling effect upon plaintiffs' fundamental rights to associate and bargain collectively, than the stoppage of all communication and dealings between the School Board and REA as a representative association. See, Plaintiffs' Memorandum in Opposition, at page 11.

The grant of approval to organize and associate without the corresponding grant of recognition may well be an empty and meaningless gesture on the part of the defendant School Board. See, Williams v. Rhodes, 393 U.S. 23, 41 (1968); NAACP v. Button, 371 U.S. 415 (1963); Lamont v. Postmaster General, 381 U.S. 301 (1965).

Without embarking into a discussion of a remedy herein, the Court finds that plaintiffs' allegation that the defendants' wrongful actions have a chilling effect upon the exercise of plaintiffs' First Amendment rights does indeed state a claim upon which relief, if due, can be granted. The plaintiffs have stated a constitutional claim, which on the present status of the pleadings is sufficient under the Constitution and laws of the United States. . . .

2. Authority of Public Employers to Bargain in the Absence of Legislation

INTERNATIONAL UNION OF OPERATING ENGINEERS, LOCAL 321 v. WATER WORKS BOARD OF THE CITY OF BIRMINGHAM

Alabama Supreme Court
276 Ala. 462, 163 So. 2d 619 (1964)

SIMPSON, Justice. The question presented by this appeal is res integra in this jurisdiction, viz.: Can a public agency in Alabama bargain with and enter into an enforceable collective agreement with a labor organization concerning the wages, hours, and conditions of employment of its employees in the absence of express constitutional or statutory authorization to do so? Appellant has represented the employees of appellee for some thirty years, during which period a series of twelve collective contracts were executed between the parties. (There is no question of union membership, per se, involved on this appeal.)

The lower court, in a declaratory judgment action, ruled, inter alia, that such a contract was ultra vires and unenforceable and therefore the relief sought by appellant (union) was denied.

This Court has been favored with excellent and exhaustive briefs from both appellant and appellee and also from amicus curiae which present every conceivable facet of arguments, citing numerous cases from other jurisdictions where the question has arisen.

Concededly, appellee, as the Water Works Board of the City of Birmingham, is a public agency and its employees are public employees. . . .

It appears from the cases cited to us in brief, and our research also reveals, that the strongest current of opinion from the highest courts of states where the question has been presented has ruled that a public agency has no legal authority to bargain or contract with a labor union in the absence of express statutory authority. Appellant argues to the contrary and asks us to adopt a rule that would permit such contracts or agreements where there is no statutory prohibition against collective bargaining.

The Supreme Court of Florida in Miami Water Works Local No. 654 v. City of Miami, 157 Fla. 445, 26 So. 2d 194, 165 A.L.R. 967 (where the Union sought a declaratory judgment that the city might bargain with it) held, and we think correctly so, that the City was under no obligation to bargain with the Union and stated:

> "The City of Miami is a governmental entity created by the state. It derives its powers and jurisdiction from the sovereign authority. It is limited to the exercise of such powers as are expressly granted to it by the state, or as are necessarily and fairly implied in or incident to the powers expressly granted. . . . It is a public institution designed to promote the common interests of the inhabitants in their organized capacity as a local government. Its objects are governmental, not commercial. . . . It has no authority to enter into negotiations with the labor union, or any other organized group, concerning hours, wages, or conditions of employment. . . ."

The Florida Court of Appeals (1963) in the case of Dade County v. Amalgamated Association of Street Electric Railway and Motor Coach Employees of America, 157 So. 2d 176, held in part:

> " 'Unless clearly authorized to do so by the enactment of legislation, the plaintiffs would not be authorized and are not now authorized to enter into collective bargaining agreements, within the labor relations meaning of the term, with the defendants. . . .
>
> " 'The courts have said that as a general rule collective bargaining has no place in government service. The employer is the whole people. This is a government of law, not men. For the courts to hold otherwise than as I have just explained would be to sanction control of governmental functions not by laws but by men. Such policy, if followed to its logical conclusion, would inevitably lead to chaos.' "

The Supreme Court of Colorado in Fellows v. LaTronica, Colo., 377 P.2d 547, held that an action to compel the city to arbitrate a claim for vacation pay for city firemen under a collective agreement should be dismissed because the City had no authority to enter into such a contract with the union in the first instance.

The Maryland Court of Appeals, in Mugford v. Mayor and City Council of Baltimore, 185 Md. 266, 44 A.2d 745, 162 A.L.R. 1101 (affirming the lower court) in an action by a taxpayer to enjoin enforcement of and to have declared invalid a collective agreement between the City and Union, held that the City did not have the power to "delegate its governing power to any agency" and that such a contract was void.

See also Nutter v. City of Santa Monica, 74 Cal. App. 2d 292, 168 P.2d 741; City of Los Angeles v. Los Angeles Building and Construction Trades Council, 94 Cal. App. 2d 36, 210 P.2d 305; City of Springfield v. Clouse, 356 Mo. 1239, 206 S.W.2d 539; City of Alcoa v. International Brotherhood of Electrical Workers, 203 Tenn. 12, 308 S.W.2d 476; Weakley County Municipal Electric System v. Vick, 43 Tenn. App. 524, 309 S.W.2d 792; International Longshoremen's Assn., etc. v. Georgia Ports Authority, 217 Ga. 712, 124 S.E.2d 733, cert. den., 370 U.S. 922, 82 S. Ct. 1561, 8 L. Ed. 2d 503, all of which are in accord.

The rule stated by the annotator in 31 A.L.R.2d 1142 at page 1170 seems to be the rule of the majority, and supported by well reasoned cases:

> "Public employers cannot abdicate or bargain away their continuing legislative discretion and are therefore not authorized to enter into collective bargaining agreements with public employee labor unions. Constitutional and statutory provisions granting the right to private industry to bargain collectively do not confer such right on public employers and employees."

The opinions of the Alabama Attorneys General are likewise without conflict to the effect that state, county, and municipal agencies of this State are without legal authority to negotiate or to enter into collective bargaining agreements with labor unions. . . . In the April 10, 1941 opinion of the Attorney General of Alabama, . . . it appears that the President of the County Board of Revenue of Gadsden, Alabama presented an inquiry to the Attorney General as to whether or not said Board of Revenue "may legally enter into a contract or agreement with a labor organization . . . as a bargaining agent for county employees with respect to hours of employment, wages, etc." The opinion of the Attorney General was as follows:

"It is my opinion that your inquiry must be answered negatively.

"In reaching this conclusion, I have not failed to recognize the fact that the county employees have a legitimate interest in collective action for the purpose of improving their economic and social situation wherever change is needed. I think it cannot be seriously questioned by anyone that beneficial results to society, as well as to employees individually and as a class, have come from an assertion of the collective economic force of employees. The beneficial results of cooperative action on the part of labor generally is apparent. But the question raised by your inquiry does not involve the power or authority of the employee class. Solely presented is the right of a county, a mere political subdivision of the State (First National Bank v. Jackson County, 227 Ala. 448, 150 So. 690; Pickens County v. Williams, 229 Ala. 250, 156 So. 548; Moore v. Walker County, 236 Ala. 688, 185 So. 175)—an agency of limited jurisdiction having only those powers expressly authorized by statute or necessarily implied therefrom (Corning v. Patton, 236 Ala. 354, 182 So. 39)—to enter into a contract, the ultimate effect of which might be to remove the control of the government from the people as a whole, acting through their duly constituted officials.

"I have found no specific authorization for such a contract, nor has there come to my attention a provision of law from which the right to enter such an agreement might be necessarily implied. . . .

> "Thomas S. Lawson,
> "Attorney General"

Thus the public agencies of Alabama have long been advised, without conflict, that matters of wages, hours, and conditions of employment never have been, and cannot become, a matter of collective bargaining and contract in the absence of constitutional or statutory authority and of course such administrative rulings having been in force and effect for many years, are highly persuasive authority of the correctness of the rule. State v. Southern Electric Generating Co., 274 Ala. 668, 151 So. 2d 216; Haden v. McCarty, 275 Ala. 76, 152 So. 2d 141. Such administrative construction is neither binding on the State nor its agencies nor on the court. Therefore, the use of the word "bound" in the last paragraph of the opinion in State v. Southern Electric Generating

Co., supra, was not intended to impinge upon the longstanding rule hereinabove adverted to. A clearer statement of what was there intended is that where an administrative construction by proper officials is fair and reasonable and has been followed for the prescriptive period of twenty years or longer, the courts are not disposed to alter that construction merely because the highest officials may have changed their minds about the matter under consideration.

On a thorough canvass of the pertinent authorities and a careful study of the entire case, despite the cogent arguments of learned counsel for appellants and amicus curiae, we are constrained to hold that the trial court ruled correctly.

Affirmed.

LIVINGSTON, C.J., and MERRILL and HARWOOD, JJ., concur.

NOTES

1. *Accord,* Wichita Public Schools Employees Union, Local No. 513 v. Smith, 194 Kan. 2, 397 P.2d 357 (1964); State of Delaware v. AFSCME, Local 1726, 81 L.R.R.M. 2836 (Del. Ch., New Castle County, 1972) (dictum) ("The prevailing rule at common law is that, absent such a statute, public employees are not entitled to collective bargaining and public employers are without power to enter into such agreements"). *Cf.* Local 283, IBEW v. Robison, 91 Idaho 445, 423 P.2d 999 (1967). *See* Comment, *Municipal Collective Bargaining Agreements: Are They Ultra Vires?,* 20 CASE W. RES. L. REV. 637 (1969).

2. The court in the principal case discussed both a public employer's authority to bargain *and* to enter into an enforceable collective bargaining agreement. Is there any legal distinction between an employer's authority to bargain and its authority to execute a binding contract?

3. Should the *capacity* in which the government employer acts, rather than the *fact* of government employment, be determinative of a public employee's collective bargaining rights? In several cases courts have held that employees of a government agency performing a proprietary function are entitled to collective bargaining rights similar to private sector employees. Civil Service Forum v. New York City Transit Authority, 4 App. Div. 2d 117, 163 N.Y.S.2d 476 (1957); Local 266, IBEW v. Salt River Project Agricultural Improvement & Power Dist., 78 Ariz. 30, 275 P.2d 393 (1954); Christie v. Port of Olympia, 27 Wash. 2d 534, 179 P.2d 294 (1947). Most courts, however, have rejected the proprietary/governmental dichotomy, citing one or more of the following reasons: (a) it is unfair to discriminate

among employees in this fashion; (b) the proprietary/governmental distinction is too hard to apply in practice; (c) state law makes no such distinction, indicating the legislative intent that all public employees are subject to the same rules; and (d) even when a government agency is performing a proprietary function, this function becomes no less public than the agency's governmental functions. *See* Nutter v. City of Santa Monica, 74 Cal. App. 2d 292, 168 P.2d 741 (1946) ; City of Alcoa v. IBEW Local 760, 203 Tenn. 12, 308 S.W.2d 476 (1957) ; Weakley County Municipal Elec. Sys. v. Vick, 43 Tenn. App. 524, 309 S.W.2d 792 (1957) ; Miami Waterworks Local 654 v. City of Miami, 157 Fla. 445, 26 So. 2d 194 (1946) .

4. Over the years there have been numerous opinions issued by state attorneys general with respect to the obligation and legal right of public employers to bargain collectively, or to enter into collective bargaining agreements, as well as their obligations and duties under public sector collective bargaining statutes. In most states, it is one of the duties of a state attorney general to issue opinions to the Governor and the heads of the various executive agencies. For example, the Illinois statute provides that the attorney general is "to consult with and advise the Governor and other state officials, and give, when requested, written opinions upon all legal or constitutional questions relating to the duties of such officers respectively." ILL. ANN. STAT. ch. 14, § 14 (1963) . The Illinois courts, in accord with the overwhelming weight of authority, have held that opinions rendered by the Attorney General are persuasive, but are not binding upon the court. In City of Champaign v. Hill, 29 Ill. App. 2d 429, 173 N.E.2d 839, 846 (1961), the Illinois Appellate Court stated that opinions of the State Attorney General ". . . are the legal opinions of the chief law officer of the State of Illinois on the precise question before this Court, and will be accorded considerable weight." *See* Scott, *The Role of Attorney General's Opinions in Illinois,* 67 Nw. U.L. Rev. 643 (1972) ; Larson, *The Importance and Value of Attorney General Opinions,* 41 Iowa L. Rev. 351 (1956) .

BOARD OF REGENTS v. PACKING HOUSE, FOOD & ALLIED WORKERS, LOCAL 1258

Iowa Supreme Court
— Iowa —, 175 N.W.2d 110 (1970)

STUART, Justice. Sometime prior to February 20, 1968, the non-academic personnel who operate the physical plant of the University of Northern Iowa (UNI) organized themselves into a union and received a charter as Local No. 1258 United Packing

House Food and Allied Workers of America AFL-CIO (UPWA).
On February 20, 1968 the union and its members struck against
plaintiff, who has the administrative authority over U.N.I., and
established picket lines. Plaintiff brought this action which ultimately resulted in a permanent injunction:

> ". . . enjoining and restraining the defendants and each of
> them individually and collectively from engaging in a strike
> or concerted work stoppage against the University of North-
> ern Iowa and from picketing on or near the campus or in the
> vicinity of the campus . . . in furtherance of any strike or
> concerted work stoppage or for the purpose of coercing plain-
> tiff to bargain collectively with the defendant union Local
> No. 1258 . . . except that nothing contained herein shall be
> deemed to prevent informational picketing which in no
> way interferes with or impedes the operation of the Univer-
> sity of Northern Iowa."

Plaintiff appealed from that part of the Ruling and Order and
Decree which holds the Board of Regents has the power to enter
into collective bargaining and collective bargaining agreements.

Defendants appealed from that portion of the injunctive order
which prohibits them from picketing the campus for the purpose
of coercing plaintiff to bargain collectively with defendant union.

Because of the narrow questions presented by this appeal, it
might be helpful to point out that the following propositions are
accepted as the law of the case. (1) Public employees have the
right to organize and join labor organizations. (2) Public employees do not have the right to strike. (3) Defendants have the
right to picket for informational purposes if the picketing does
not interfere with or impede the operation of the university.

I.   Does the Board of Regents, as the administrative agency of
the state charged with the duty of operating the state institutions
of higher learning, have the power and authority to bargain collectively with defendant union?

The employer-employee relationship in public employment "is
governed by statutory law and administrative regulation, it is
not fixed, either in whole or in part, by contract, as in the field
of private industry." City of Los Angeles v. Los Angeles Bldg. &
C. Tr. Council, 94 Cal. App. 2d 36, 210 P.2d 305, 310. Defendants
concede there is no specific legislation giving the board such
authority. They rely on the rule of statutory construction that
whenever a power is conferred by statute, everything necessary
to carry out the power and make it effectual and complete will
be implied. . . . They claim the authority is necessarily implied
in section 262.9 (2) (4) (7) (11), Code of Iowa which gives the

Regents the general power to hire employees, fix their salaries and wages, direct the expenditure of money and to perform all other acts necessary and proper for the execution of the powers and duties conferred by law upon it.

The answer to the question depends upon the definition of the term "collective bargaining." Neither party nor the trial court defines the term. There is a vast difference between implying authority in the Regents to meet with selected representatives of a group of employees to discuss wages, working conditions and grievances on behalf of those who have agreed to such representation and implying authority in the Regents to recognize the union as the exclusive employee representative for collective bargaining on behalf of all employees.

It is not clear for which concept of collective bargaining the parties are contending. Plaintiff seems to take the position that all sort of representative bargaining and discussion is improper without specific authority. In oral argument counsel for defendant stated that if one person spoke for himself and another this was "collective bargaining." However, their brief contains extensive quotes from Richard F. Dole, Jr., State and Local Public Employee Collective Bargaining in the Absence of Explicit Legislative Authorization, 54 Iowa L. Rev. 539, 542-543, which is focused "on the legality of negotiating and contracting with an exclusive employee representative, and that is the sense in which collective bargaining is hereafter used. As a practical matter, execution of a collective bargaining contract almost never occurs without some form of exclusive recognition."

The power to hire employees, fix their salaries and wages, direct expenditures of money and to perform all other acts necessary and proper for the execution of the powers and duties conferred upon the Regents carries with it the power and authority to confer and consult with representatives of the employees in order to make its judgment as to wages and working conditions. We hold the Regents have authority to engage in collective bargaining in this context.

"A public employer's general power to carry out its assigned functions is sufficiently inclusive to permit consultation with all persons affected by those functions. . . . This consultation serves the public interest by permitting informed governmental action without abridging governmental freedom of action." Dole, ibid., 54 Iowa L. Rev. at 542. . . .

The Board of Regents has the power and authority to meet with representatives of an employee's union to discuss wages, working conditions and grievances if it so desires. It can do so without becoming obligated to meet with the representatives of any other group of employees. The agreed terms could be adopted by the Regents in a proper legislative manner. Such action does not involve an improper delegation of legislative powers to private persons as there is no compulsion to sign an agreement and the final decision remains in the Board of Regents.

On the other hand, if the legislature desires to give public employees the advantages of collective bargaining in the full sense as it is used in private industry, it should do so by specific legislation to that effect. We cannot imply authority under these general powers to agree to exclusive representation, depriving other employees of the right to be represented by a group of their choosing or an individual the right to represent himself. Dole, in 54 Iowa L. Rev. 539, presents many sound reasons why collective bargaining, with limitations, should be authorized for public employees. But the limitations, provisos and exceptions which the author suggests should be imposed by the court in implying the power to bargain collectively are persuasive arguments for holding it is a matter for the legislature, not the courts. The power to fix the terms and conditions of public employment is a legislative function which, with proper guidelines from the legislature, can be delegated to its administrative agencies. . . .

The following cases from other jurisdictions support our position.

In City of Springfield v. Clouse (1947) 356 Mo. 1239, 206 S.W.2d 539, 543, Mr. Wood testified for the union: "Now, collective bargaining means a good many things. There are many types of collective bargaining. When you sit down at a table, representative of the employees of the city sits down at a table and discusses the matter concerning employees relations between an employee and the city, that is collective bargaining."

The Missouri Supreme Court said: "This is confusing collective bargaining with the rights of petition, peaceable assembly and free speech. Certainly public employees have these rights for which Mr. Wood was contending; and can properly exercise them individually, collectively or through chosen representatives, subject, of course, to reasonable legislative regulation as to time, place and manner in the interest of efficient public service for the general welfare of all the people."

The court refused to apply the industrial concept of collective bargaining to public employees. . . .

Norwalk Teachers' Ass'n v. Board of Education (1951) 138 Conn. 269, 83 A.2d 482, 486, 31 A.L.R.2d 1133, which is cited as approving of collective bargaining, does not use the term in the full industrial sense. . . .

See also: Nutter v. City of Santa Monica (1946) 74 Cal. App. 2d 292, 168 P.2d 741, 747-748; Fellows v. LaTronica (1962) 151 Colo. 300, 377 P.2d 547, 550-551; Delaware River and Bay Auth. v. International Organization etc. (1965) 45 N.J. 138, 211 A.2d 789, 792-793; Philadelphia Teacher's Association v. LaBrum (1964) 415 Pa. 212, 203 A.2d 34, 36; City of Pawtucket v. Pawtucket Teachers' Alliance (1958), 87 R.I. 364, 141 A.2d 624, 629; Opinion of the Attorney General, State of Iowa, August 16, 1961; Anno. 31 A.L.R.2d 1142.

The following cases hold the public employer has no authority to engage in collective bargaining or enter into collective bargaining contracts without specific legislation to that effect. They contain no reference to the power to meet and consult with representatives of groups of employees. International Union of Operating Engineers Local 321 v. Water Works Board (1964, Ala.), 163 So. 2d 619, 620-621; Miami Water Works Local No. 654 v. City of Miami (1946) 157 Fla. 445, 26 So. 2d 194, 165 A.L.R. 967; Dade County v. Amalgamated Association of S.E.R. & M.C. Emp. (1963, Fla. App.) 157 So. 2d 176, 183; International Longshoremen's Ass'n v. Georgia Ports Authority (1962) 217 Ga. 712, 124 S.E.2d 733, 737; Wichita Public School Employees Union, Local No. 513 v. Smith (1964), 194 Kan. 2, 397 P.2d 357, 359-360; Mugford v. Mayor and City Council (1945) 185 Md. 266, 44 A.2d 745, 162 A.L.R. 1101; Weakley County Mun. Elec. Sys. v. Vick (1957) 43 Tenn. App. 524, 309 S.W.2d 792, 804; City of Alcoa v. International Brotherhood of Elec. Workers (1957) 203 Tenn. 12, 308 S.W.2d 476.

Most of the cases cited by defendants for the proposition that power to engage in collective bargaining in the industrial sense may be implied involve employees working for the government in its corporate or proprietary capacity. Local 266, etc. v. Salt River Project Agr. Imp. & P. District (1954) 78 Ariz. 30, 275 P.2d 393; International Brotherhood of Electrical Workers v. Town of Farmington (1965) 75 N.M. 393, 405 P.2d 233; Civil Service Forum v. New York City Transit Authority (1957) 4 A.D.2d 117, 163 N.Y.S.2d 476; Christie v. Port of Olympia (1947) 27 Wash. 2d 534, 549-550, 179 P.2d 294.

We are not, by pointing out this distinction in the instant case indicating we would follow this line of authority if a proprietary function were involved. There is a strong line of authority to the contrary. International Operating Engineers Local No. 321 v. Water Works Board, supra; Nutter v. City of Santa Monica, supra; Miami Water Works Local No. 654 v. City of Miami, supra; Dade County v. Amalgamated Association of S.E.R. & M.C. Emp., supra; International Longshoremen's Ass'n v. Georgia Ports Authority, supra; City of Springfield v. Clouse, supra; Weakley Co. Mun. Elec. Sys. v. Vick, supra; City of Alcoa v. Int. Brotherhood of Electrical Workers, supra.

Chicago Div. of Ill. Ed. Ass'n v. Board of Education (1966), 76 Ill. App. 2d 456, 222 N.E.2d 243, is the only case cited which implies authority to enter into a collective bargaining agreement with a sole collective bargaining agency selected by employees working in a governmental capacity. We prefer the logic and reasoning behind those cases which hold this is a matter for specific legislation.

II.   There is also confusion about the meaning of collective bargaining agreements. In the industrial sense they are not contracts of employment but trade agreements entered into between the employer and representatives of the employees resulting in an accord as to wages, working conditions, grievances and such other matters as may be agreed upon. J.I. Case Co. v. Nat. Lab. Rel. Board (1944), 321 U.S. 332, 64 S. Ct. 576, 88 L. Ed. 762, 766. Almost without exception they include a provision making the union the exclusive bargaining agent. Dole, ibid. at 543. Under our holding in Division I, it is obvious that the Regents would have no authority to enter into a collective bargaining agreement in the sense recognized in private industry.

However, we can see no reason why the Regents, if they so desire, could not enter into one written contract with the union binding all members of the union agreeing to such representation as long as the terms of the contract are within the statutory authority of the board and contains no terms of employment which could not be included in a standardized contract for individual employees. . . .

We have heretofore held that the Board of Regents has no authority to enter into collective bargaining or collective bargaining agreements in the industrial context. We have also held the Board of Regents may voluntarily meet and consult with representatives of groups of employees to discuss wages, working conditions and grievances. The decision whether to do so or not remains that of the Board of Regents. Therefore, any picketing to coerce the Board of Regents to bargain collectively against its better judgment would either be illegal, against public policy or both. . . .

Modified and affirmed.

BECKER, Justice (concurring specially).

I concur in the announced result; i.e., the trial court's order is affirmed. I cannot concur in certain limitations which are imposed by way of dicta in connection with acknowledgment of the Board of Regents' power to bargain collectively.

I. One must first determine just what the majority holds. As I read the opinion the court holds the Board has power to:

1. Meet with, confer and consult with representatives of labor employees in order to make its judgment as to wages, grievances and working conditions. (Opinion, pp. 112 and 113).

2. They may implement their decision by: (a) appropriate legislation (Opinion, page 113), (b) by a proper contract with the union binding all members of the union. (Opinion, page 117).

3. The Board is not compelled to exercise the power noted but may do so if it pleases.

This is all the case calls for us to decide and I agree with these decisions. But the court goes on to mandate certain affirmative actions and prohibit other actions, to wit:

1. The Board cannot agree to exclusive representation by a designated union. (Opinion, page 113).

2. It may deal with as many groups (presumably within the same classification) as decide to associate themselves together for the purpose of collective bargaining, but may also refuse to deal with any one or more groups if it so desires. Thus making the group of its choice the exclusive bargaining agent in fact if not in theory. (Opinion, page 113).

These two pronouncements are not within the issues presented to us and they should not be decided at this time. They have not been adequately briefed and argued. Nor do we have a reasonably complete record on the subject. If the questions are to be decided without adequate argument or briefing, then I must disagree with the majority conclusion on the basis of what has been submitted. . . .

IV. There cannot be much doubt that the issues of exclusive bargaining and mandatory recognition of multiple bargaining agencies are not in this case. But if the court elects to ignore this fact and proceeds with an advisory opinion we all have to vote on the advice.

I cannot agree that public collective bargaining must be interpreted to prohibit exclusive bargaining with one recognized agency. Within limits, this court can tell an administrative agency what it can and cannot do under the law. But we cannot, and normally do not, attempt to tell the agency *how* to do what it can do.

This is what we are doing here. We say they may bargain collectively but they may not bargain exclusively. In the same breath we say the agency has the right to refrain from bargaining with any groups of employees it chooses. The positions are inconsistent. If the agency can recognize one group and refuse to bargain with all others isn't it bargaining exclusively? We are not here talking about closed shops, or union shops, or any of the other restrictive types of contracts in the broad spectrum of the labor law. We are speaking only of the agency's right to limit its discussion to one representative.

As a practical matter we are placing public agencies in an impossible position. While Professor Dole's article should be treated as an additional brief, the majority opinion makes it germane. The article poses the underlying difficulty of non-exclusive bargaining rather well: "Power to confer exclusive recognition is a corollary of power to execute a master contract. Where there are actual or potential rival employee representatives, it is difficult for a public employer to obtain a master contract without resort to exclusive recognition. Competitive pressures make each representative reluctant to reach agreement until every representative is willing to accept the same terms. Exclusive recognition also simplifies the administration of a master contract. In the absence of exclusive recognition, employees claiming infringement of their rights under a master contract can shop around for a representative who is willing to press their claims. This, of course, introduces competitive considerations into contract administration and can require a public employer to deal with an inordinately large number of employee representatives. Exclusive recognition both relaxes competitive pressure on the recognized representative and permits a public employer to channel all employee claims through a single representative. . . .

"Some courts seem to have been as perturbed by exclusive recognition as by the negotiation of collective bargaining contracts. There are several older decisions indicating that it is an abuse of discretion for a public employer to grant exclusive recognition to an employee representative if all employees concerned are not already supporters of the exclusive representative. However, the more recent cases conclude that exclusive representation of both members and nonmembers is permissible where there is satisfactory evidence of at least majority employee support for the exclusive representative, the exclusive representative is required to represent all employees regardless of union membership, and employees are given assurances that exclusive representation will not preclude individual presentation of complaints to the public employer." 54 Iowa Law Rev. 546, 547, 548. With the above limitations, exclusive bargaining should not pose the problems envisioned by the majority. But again, at this time, we should not attempt to explore the subject.

V. One of the phrases most often used in the majority opinion is "collective bargaining in the industrial sense." There is an implication that if the employee's bargaining unit is recognized as an exclusive agent there is collective bargaining "in an industrial sense." This is not true. The legal right to strike has been eliminated. The *legal necessity* to bargain has been eliminated. The *right* to deal with non-union individuals is preserved. The open shop—as it is commonly known—is preserved. So that even if the public agency finds it more efficient—or even necessary—to bargain exclusively, there are many factors which remove the process from bargaining "in the industrial sense." If this phrase is a shorthanded way of making a point it is an oversimplification that commands a poor result.

RAWLINGS, J., joins in this special concurrence.

NOTE

In Chicago Div. of Ill. Educ. Ass'n v. Board of Educ., 76 Ill. App. 2d 456, 222 N.E.2d 243 (1966), the court held "that the Board of Education of the City of Chicago does not require legislative authority to enter into a collective bargaining agreement with a sole collective bargaining agency selected by its teachers, and we hold that such an agreement is not against public policy." *Accord,* Cook County Police Ass'n v. City of Harvey, 8 Ill. App. 3d 147, 289 N.E.2d 226 (1972). However, the court held that a public employer "has no enforceable duty to recognize a representative of its employees or to bargain collectively." In Mayor and City Council of Cumberland v. Municipal Employees Local 812, 70 L.R.R.M. 2650 (Md. Cir. Ct., Allegheny County 1969), the court upheld the legality and constitutionality of an ordinance which authorized the holding of an election to determine the exclusive representative of certain of the city's employees for the purposes of collective bargaining. The court concluded "that the City has the power to enter into a collective bargaining agreement with a representative union, so long as the agreement does not discriminate against non-union employees." By implication, the Indiana Court of Appeals in Gary Teachers Union, Local 4 v. School City of Gary, 427 Ind. App. 211, 284 N.E.2d 108 (1972), held that a school board had the discretionary authority to grant exclusive recognition to a teachers union for the purposes of negotiating a collective bargaining agreement.

3. Legal Authorization

Increasingly the right of public employees to bargain collectively is established and protected by legislation, executive orders, or municipal ordinances. The right of federal employees to bargain collectively was initially authorized in 1962 by Executive Order 10988. In 1969 Executive Order 10988 was reissued and modified by Executive Order 11491.* The approximately 750,000 United States Postal employees who were formerly covered by Executive Orders 10988 and 11491 now come under the labor relations provisions of the Postal Reorganization Act* which incorporates most of the provisions of the Labor-Management Relations Act.

Wisconsin in 1959 was the first state to enact legislation authorizing collective bargaining for public employees. Since then, well over half the states have enacted legislation permitting collective bargaining by some or all categories of public employees. The following is a summary of the legislation enacted to date:

Twenty-five states have enacted reasonably comprehensive statutes of general applicability: Alaska (all public employees), California (all municipal and state employees; two statutes),* Connecticut (all municipal employees), Delaware (all public employees), Hawaii (all public employees),* Kansas (all public employees; local option as to coverage), Maine (all municipal employees), Massachusetts (all public employees; two statutes), Michigan (all public employees except classified state employees),* Minnesota (all public employees),* Missouri (all public employees except policemen and teachers), Montana (all state and local government employees), Nebraska (all public employees), Nevada (all local government employees including teachers), New Hampshire (classified state employees and non-academic university employees), New Jersey (all public employees), New York (all public employees),* North Dakota (all public employees), Oklahoma (all municipal employees), Oregon (all state and local government employees including teachers), Pennsylvania (all public employees),* Rhode Island (all public employees; five statutes), South Dakota (all public employees), Vermont (all state and municipal employees; two statutes), Washington (all local government employees), Wis-

---

* Included in Statutory Appendix.

consin (all state and municipal employees including teachers; two statutes).*

Fifteen states have enacted separate statutes granting teachers the right to bargain collectively: Alaska, California,* Connecticut,* Delaware, Idaho, Indiana, Kansas, Maryland, Montana, Nebraska, North Dakota, Oklahoma, Rhode Island, Vermont, Washington.

Twelve states have enacted collective bargaining laws covering firemen and/or policemen: Alabama (firemen), Florida (firemen),* Georgia (firemen), Idaho (firemen), Kentucky (both, but only covers Louisville and Jefferson County), New Hampshire (policemen), Oklahoma (both), Pennsylvania (both), Rhode Island (both; two statutes), South Dakota (both), Texas (both), Wyoming (firemen).

Several states have also enacted collective bargaining legislation that is limited to transit authorities, port authorities, or other special districts.

In addition to the numerous states laws referred to above, a number of municipalities in states that do not have collective bargaining legislation have passed charter provisions or enacted ordinances granting their employees the right to bargain collectively. Jacksonville, Florida, and Baltimore, Maryland are two prominent examples.

NOTES

1. Whereas some states such as New York and Hawaii have one law which covers all public employees, other states such as California have numerous statutory enactments covering various categories of public employees.[1] In Vail, *The Scope of Bargaining Controversy: Substantive Issues vs. Procedural Hangups,* CALIFORNIA PUBLIC EMPLOYEE RELATIONS No. 15, at 4 (1972), the author made the following commentary on the California situation:

> This complex of state laws creates a coverage maze for public employees. The Meyers-Milias-Brown Act (Government Code Sections 3500-3510) provides the legal framework for employees of cities, counties, and local public agencies other than school districts. State employees are covered by a separate statute—the original Brown Act (Government Code Sections 3525-36), augmented by an Executive Order. Fire Fighters have a separate statute (Labor Code Sections

---

* Included in Statutory Appendix.

[1] The California statutes covering local employees, state employees, and teachers are included in the Statutory Appendix.

1960-3), but they are also covered under the MMB and Brown Acts. School district employees fall under still another public employee relations law—the Winton Act (Ed. Code Sections 13080-90) —but its provisions, including those affecting the subject areas of meeting and conferring, differ for certified employees (teachers) and classified employees. Among public institutions of higher learning, employees of community colleges, as district colleges, are placed under the Winton Act; employees of the state colleges and university system fall under the legal framework governing other state employees; and the University of California, which until recently asserted its "constitutional" independence regarding labor relations policies, appears to have finally decided that its employees are also covered by the state employees statute. Finally, each of the nine state statutes providing for transit districts in various parts of the state carries its own, separate labor relations provisions. Only the latter fully embrace the concept of bilateral decision-making through collective negotiations.

A number of advisory commissions, however, have recommended the enactment of one comprehensive statute rather than separate statutes for different categories of public employees. The Advisory Commission on Intergovernmental Relations in its Report "endorse[d] the single law approach," noting that "the State statute should deal with all occupational categories of public employees" since "separate statutory treatment of certain types of public employees is incompatible with the need for a smoothly-functioning labor-management relations process in the public sector." ADVISORY COMM'N ON INTERGOVERNMENTAL RELATIONS, LABOR-MANAGEMENT POLICIES FOR STATE AND LOCAL GOVERNMENT 103-04 (1969). More recently a Rhode Island Study Commission recommended that the state's five public sector collective bargaining laws be encompassed in one comprehensive law. In Discussion and Recommendations for Changing Public Employee Legislation in Rhode Island, GERR No. 498, E-1, E-2 (1973), the following critique was made of the state's existing patchwork of laws:

> There is little question that the evolution of public sector legislation within the state was accomplished without any real consideration as to the totality of the impact of all of the legislation. We have in the state five collective bargaining laws each relating to a specific type of public employee, i.e., teachers, police, firefighters, municipal employees and state employees. Each of these laws was framed only with

reference to that particular class of employee. The major deficiency in this individual approach is that the impact of the bargains ultimately made draws upon common tax revenues and crosses administrative lines and if the laws are not considered together the administration of the acts as well as the requirements for dispute resolution are also inevitably handled independently. It is only incidental that the total economic and organizational impact is ever effectively understood. *In a word, we have over-legislated* and this "over legislation" in itself (since it has not taken into consideration the total system of impacts) has and will continue to have a serious, detrimental effect upon the collective bargaining process and the decisions made thereby.

2.   If a municipality, in the absence of applicable state legislation, enacts an ordinance establishing bargaining rights for its employees, can the ordinance be challenged on preemption grounds, i.e., that collective bargaining legislation is a matter of statewide concern and can only be enacted by the state legislature? Would it make any difference if the municipality had home rule powers? In Louisville Fire Fighters v. Burke, 75 L.R.R.M. 2001 (Ky. Cir. Ct., Jefferson County, 1970), the court upheld the power of the City of Louisville to enact a collective bargaining ordinance. The court noted, *inter alia,* "that the Legislature meant to and did confer home rule upon the City of Louisville except where specifically denied by statute." *But see* Midwest Employers Council v. City of Omaha, 131 N.W.2d 609 (Neb. 1964), where the court held that the City of Omaha did not have authority to enact a fair employment practices ordinance since "the power relating to labor relations and practices, and civil rights lies in the state, and such matters are of statewide concern and not of local concern nor municipal government concern."

3.   Several of the state public sector bargaining laws permit local governmental jurisdictions to adopt their own procedures. The New York Law, for example, provides that provisions and procedures enacted by a local government, with certain exceptions, are applicable if the New York PERB has determined "that such provisions and procedures and the continuing implementation thereof are substantially equivalent to the provisions and procedures set forth . . . with respect to the state. . . ." N.Y. CIVIL SERV. LAW § 212 (McKinney, 1972). With respect to New York City, however, the Act provides that the PERB is not required to make such a determination, but rather may file suit for declaratory judgment alleging that the provisions

and procedures are not substantially equivalent. The Kansas Act requires that local provisions and procedures be "reasonably equivalent" rather than "substantially equivalent." KAN. STAT. ANN. § 75-4334 (Supp. 1972). What is the difference between "reasonably equivalent" and "substantially equivalent"? *See* Statement of Arvid Anderson, pp. 65-68, *supra*.

ADVISORY COMMISSION ON INTERGOVERNMENTAL RELATIONS, LABOR-MANAGEMENT POLICIES FOR STATE AND LOCAL GOVERNMENT 100-02 (1969)

Existing legislation which deals comprehensively with public employer-employee relations takes one of two basic forms: collective negotiation or meet and confer. Great interstate differences, of course, exist in the treatment accorded public employees under either approach. Both types of statute may deal extensively, or sketchily, with the rights of employees, the strike question, and coverage by level of government or occupation. But meet and confer laws generally are less comprehensive than those governing collective negotiations. In particular, they usually treat more superficially the questions of representation, administrative machinery, dispute settlement, and unfair practices. Moreover, they usually accord a different status—a superior one —to the public employer vis-a-vis employee organizations.

While both systems involve continuing communication between the employer and employee representatives, under collective negotiations both parties meet more as equals. The employee organization's position is protected by statutory provisions relating to organization rights, unfair practices, third party intervention in disputes, and binding agreements. The labor and management negotiators hopefully will arrive at a mutually binding agreement which is a byproduct of bilateral decisions. If they reach an impasse, the law generally sets forth a range of procedures to be followed, including such third-party assistance as mediation, fact-finding, and arbitration. The strike ban and the practical difficulties in making agreements binding, however, sometimes produces a system that is much less than bilateral.

Under a meet and confer system, the outcome of public employer-employee discussions depends more on management's determinations than on bilateral decisions by "equals." In some jurisdictions, the public employer may be under statutory obligation to "endeavor" to reach agreement or to "meet and confer in good faith" with an employee organization. If an agreement is reached, it is put into writing, but it normally does not become binding on the employer until such time as the legislative body takes appropriate action with executive concurrence. In other jurisdictions, the meet and confer system does not go this far, since management retains the exclusive right to act when and how it chooses concerning procedures for entering into discussions with employee organizations. Most meet and confer laws also give the employer the final "say" in the adoption and application of rules for employee organization recognition and of methods for settling disputes and handling grievances. Legislative criteria relating to these matters usually are lacking.

Fourteen States have enacted mandatory collective negotiations laws, while two have passed legislation permitting management to negotiate with unions and associations. Five States have meet and confer statutes under which the public employer is required to discuss the terms and conditions of employment with employee organizations and authorized to enter into non-binding memoranda of understanding with such representatives. In the absence of an express statutory authorization or laws to the contrary, other jurisdictions have conferred or negotiated with their employees on a *de facto* basis. Finally, a few States and some local governments have flatly refused to engage in either negotiations or discussions with employee organizations.

A major reason for these wide differences in practice is lack of consensus on the relationship between governmental sovereignty and the public labor-management dialogue. While some jurisdictions continue to cling to traditional interpretations of this doctrine, others are seeking to adapt it to, or as some would argue, move it ahead of contemporary conditions. A related issue is the belief of some public employers that they, as well as their employees, have certain "rights" which should not be surrendered or abridged through entering into a negotiating relationship with unions and associations. Some phrase this argument in terms of the multiple responsibilities falling upon anyone assuming the tough assignment of political executive at this point in time, and the corresponding duty of the public employer to balance the conflicting demands and pressures swirling around him.

The existence of certain basic differences between the private and public sectors also affects the extent to which public employers are willing and able to deal with their employees and with employee organizations. The major and perhaps controlling distinction between labor-management relations in the private sector and those in State and local governments is that neither the employer nor the employee in the latter case are really at liberty to bargain freely. Both parties must operate within the limits of applicable laws and regulations, the full view of public opinion, and the very real world of politics. Both parties must recognize that essential public services, especially in the fields of health and safety, have to be maintained and cannot be allowed to be disrupted by slowdowns or work stoppages. Public employers, in contrast to their counterparts in the private sector, do not have the option of shutting down services and facilities if they feel employee demands are unreasonable. Correspondingly, employee organizations do not have the option of striking legally. Another unique dimension of the problem is the political overtones inherent in confrontations between public management and employee unions and associations. Many services of government are monopolistic, mandated by law, and supported by revenue derived from taxation. Consumers cannot refuse to "buy" them, nor can they lawfully refuse to pay taxes. Any constraints on the availability of these services as a result of public employee activities inevitably will generate hostile public attitudes and possibly political retaliation. Finally, the fact that government is directly responsible to a general electorate, not to any specific segment thereof, is a paramount factor differentiating the public and private sectors.

Those supporting the meet and confer approach to public employer-employee relations stress the differences between public and private employment, and consequently seek to maximize managerial discretion. Those favoring collective negotiations recognize these differences, but find them no major or insuperable barrier to meaningful bilateral relations among "equals."

The Commission is aware that a strong case can be made in support of the collective negotiations approach. It has heard the argument that equitable and workable public labor-management relations can only result from reciprocal and bilateral dealings. It fully recognizes that 16 States have enacted legislation either requiring or permitting public employers to engage in collective negotiations with employee organizations. It understands that this procedure generally imposes a mutual obligation on the public manager and the exclusive bargaining representative to meet at reasonable times and to negotiate in good faith, and that the results of negotiations over grievance procedures and other personnel matters—including wages, hours, and working conditions—must be reduced to a binding, written agreement.

The Commission has heard the argument that the sovereignty of government tenet should not preclude collective negotiations in the public service. It accepts the fact that the traditional doctrine of sovereignty has been modified already through practice; obviously, if government allows itself to be sued and if it signs contracts with private contractors which contain provisions for the binding arbitration of disputes, then acceptance of certain restrictions on its discretion in dealing with public employees does not undermine its sovereign status. It has considered the related contention that rather than delegating or abdicating sovereign authority a public employer only agrees to limit its powers in a certain area for a given period of time when it enters into a contract with its employees. But it is also cognizant of the fact that, if necessary, agreements which the public employer made on a voluntary basis can be repudiated, and affected employees would lack any legal recourse. This, of course, makes a mockery of one of the distinguishing features of collective bargaining systems. The Commission fully understands the implications of the broad claim that willingness of a government to engage in collective negotiations with its employees should be viewed mainly as a matter of enlightened personnel policy designed to improve labor-management relations through bilateral—rather than unilateral—determination of the terms and conditions of public employment.

On balance, however, the Commission believes another approach is more appropriate, given contemporary and evolving conditions in State and local employment. Twenty-nine States have taken no general legislative action in this controversial field, and it is these States as well as those having unworkable public labor-management laws to which the Commission's recommendation is addressed. What kind of system can be established which will bring about real progress in ensuring employee and employer rights; in promoting the position, pay, and prestige of public employees; and in preventing work disruptions?

At this point in time, the crying need in a majority of situations is for a general statute that balances management rights against employee needs, recognizes the crucial and undeniable differences between public and private employment, and establishes labor-management relationships in which the public-at-large and their elected representatives have confidence.

The Commission believes that legislation embodying the essentials of a meet and confer in good faith system constitutes this kind of statute. "Meet and confer in good faith," as we view it, means the obligation of both the public employer and an employee organization to meet at reasonable times, to exchange openly and without fear information, views, and proposals, and to strive to reach agreement on matters relating to wages, hours, and such other terms and conditions of employment as fall within the statutorily defined scope of the discussion. The resulting memorandum of understanding is submitted to a jurisdiction's governing body, and it becomes effective when the necessary implementary actions have been agreed to and acted on by pertinent executive and legislative officials.

To a greater degree than collective negotiations, the meet and confer approach is protective of public management's discretion. To a greater extent, it seeks a reconciliation with the merit system since agreements reached through the discussional process and actions taken as an implementary follow-up cannot contravene any existing civil service statute. To a far greater degree than collective negotiations, it is candid and squarely confronts the reality that a governmental representative cannot commit his jurisdiction to a binding agreement or contract, and that only through ratifying and implementing legislation and executive orders can such an agreement be effected. To a greater extent, it avoids detailed, statutorily prescribed procedures applicable to all situations, and this lack of specificity in some degree and in some areas permits greater flexibility and adaptability in actual implementation. To a much greater degree, it recognizes—indeed, is rooted in—the vital differences existing between private and public employment, and does not make the mistake of relying heavily on the National Labor Relations Act as a blueprint for action in the public service.

"In good faith" has a number of important connotations as it applies to the meet and confer process. It obligates the governmental employer and a recognized employee organization to approach the discussion table with an open mind. It underscores the fact that such meetings should be held at mutually agreeable and convenient times. It recognizes that a sincere effort should be made by both parties to reach agreement on all matters falling properly within the discussion's purview. It signifies that both sides will be represented by duly authorized spokesmen prepared to confer on all such matters. It means that reasonable time off will be granted to appropriate agents of a recognized employee organization. It calls for a free exchange to the other party, on request, of non-confidential data pertinent to any issues under discussion. It implies a joint effort in drafting a non-binding memorandum of understanding setting forth all agreed upon recommendations for submission to the jurisdiction's appropriate governing officials. It charges the governmental agent to strive to achieve acceptance and implementation of these recommendations by such officials. It affirms that failure to reach agreement or to make concessions does not constitute bad faith when real differences of opinion exist. It requires both parties to be receptive to mediation if *bona fide* differences of opinion produce an impasse. Finally, it means that the State public labor-management relations law should list as an unfair practice failure to meet and confer in good faith, thereby providing a basis for legal recourse.

These special obligations convert the system into something broader and more balanced than the usual "meet and confer" setup, but still something less than the glittering and often unfulfilled promises of a collective bargaining statute.

HAYES v. ASSOCIATION OF CLASSROOM TEACHERS
California Superior Court, County of Los Angeles
66 LC ¶ 52,622 (1970)

STRATTON, J.: . . . .

Neither in the Winton Act* nor in the Education Code is authority given the Los Angeles Teachers, or the School Board, the right to collectively bargain or strike.

But the teachers did strike—and they and the Board did collectively bargain. And the Court has concluded and has found as a fact that the subject Contract and Rule 3700 were the product of such bargaining, and except for the strike, the Board would not have considered execution of the contract nor adoption of Rule 3700.

On April 13, 1970, after demands made by the teachers upon the Board relative to the subjects of the disputed Contract, (Exhibit 19 and Rule 3700) were refused, 8,000 to 10,000 of the certificated employees of the Los Angeles School District walked out of the classrooms, remaining away until May 13, 1970, when, by vote of 6,702 to 2,007, the strike terminated.

During the strike there were intensive negotiations between the School Board and the negotiating council, and the representatives of United Teachers of Los Angeles (UTLA); a labor negotiator with a staff was engaged; a mediator was engaged, and thereafter the efforts of the negotiator and his staff became insignificant, resulting in the resignation of the negotiator in protest. Numerous meetings, some of which extended far into the night, were held by the Board with the representatives of the teachers; drafts of contracts were submitted by both sides in an attempt to reach agreement. On May 11, 1970, at a meeting of the Board, the atmosphere of which appears to have been quite acrimonious, it decided by a 4 to 3 vote to finalize and execute an agreement submitted by the mediator.

On May 20, 1970, the Board by the same majority decided to execute the subject Contract, Exhibit 19.

On the same date, in proceedings preliminary to this trial, the defendants in *Grasko, et al. v. Board of Education, et al.* and

---

* Editors' Note: The Winton Act is set forth in the Statutory Appendix.

Miles, et al. v. United Teachers—Los Angeles, et al., two of the four cases consolidated for the present trial, were enjoined and restrained as set forth in the files of those cases.

On June 4, 1970, the Board, by formal Resolution indicated its intention to "sign the recently negotiated agreement when legal restrictions confronting the Board were removed," namely the above injunctions.

Faced with the restraints of the Court's injunctions, the Board prepared to mold the subject agreement into a rule, which is Rule 3700 in evidence and the subject of *Citizens Legal Defense Alliance, Inc. v. Los Angeles City Board of Education,* another of the four cases consolidated for this trial.

On May 28, 1970, the Board Rule 3700 was drafted in its final form, but action on the adoption thereof was postponed until June 4, 1970.

The Court has concluded that unless enjoined the Board will adopt and implement said Rule.

Preliminary to the trial in the aforesaid *Citizens Alliance* matter, the Court in proceedings preliminary to this trial enjoined the Board from adopting and implementing the Rule.

Rule 3700 is substantially the same document as the subject Contract except that it is in the form of a unilateral statement of policies, employment relation procedures and goals, instead of a bilateral binding agreement. . . .

We proceed on the assumption that the defendant School Board has those powers expressly granted to it by Statute and those *necessarily* implied, and the Statutes granting such powers are strictly construed.

The powers of the Board in respect to employer-employee relations are determined by the Winton Act. One of the specific issues to be determined is whether or not the Board has the power and authority to enter into the subject Contract with UTLA, ACTLA, or the negotiating council.

The Court has concluded that it does not, and that the defendants in *Grasko* and *Miles* should be permanently restrained, as they were heretofore restrained by this Court by a temporary restraining order and preliminary injunction.

We have looked to California Federation of Teachers v. Oxnard Elementary School, 272 Cal. App. 2d, 514, for guidance. While the Court therein indicates, "The issue of central significance in this appeal is the validity and constitutionality of the Winton Act," the case does provide a thorough analysis of the intention of the Legislature in the enactment of the Winton Act, and in doing so reviews the historical background of the Act, including legislation proposed since its enactment.

The situation in Los Angeles School District rather dramatically demonstrates one of the mischiefs aimed at by the Winton Act in its provision for a negotiating council. This council comes into being when there is more than one organization of certificated employees in a School District. In the Los Angeles School District there are more than 80 officially recognized Board employee organizations, 50 of which appear to be organizations of certificated employees. (See Exh. 34) And it is through the negotiating council that the Board meets and confers with the representative of certificated employee organizations regarding "the definition of educational objectives, the determination of the content of courses and curricula, the selection of textbooks, and other aspects of the instructional program to the extent matters are within the discretion of public school employer or the governing board under the law."

One can readily see the confusion if the Board should be burdened with the necessity of meeting and conferring in respect to the above-mentioned items with every certificated employee organization in the District. Thus, under the facts of the case, the Board was required to *meet and confer* with the negotiating council. However, the meeting and conferring is confined to the subjects above indicated, and does not, in the opinion of this Court, permit the hardcore bargaining and labor negotiations which took place, nor contracting as contemplated by the execution of the subject contract.

The contract, Exh. 24, both in form and in substance, undertakes to recognize the Negotiating Council as the sole bargaining agent for certificated teachers. The Agreement also recognizes UTLA as the agent of the Negotiating Council.

This Court has concluded that the Negotiating Council is not an entity legally qualified to enter into a contract.

The Court has further concluded that the Board is without express statutory authority, or necessarily implied authority, to enter into a binding bilateral agreement

> ". . . with regard to all matters relating to the definition of educational objectives, the determination of the content of courses and curricula, the selection of textbooks, and other aspects of the instructional program to the extent such matters are within the discretion of the public school, employer or governing board under the law." (Section 13085, Ed. Code.)

The law with which we deal has attempted to give the certificated teacher a voice in the above-enumerated matters, and on matters dealt with in the subject Contract via the Negotiating

Council, but it has not yet given them an arm which permits the procedures and conduct contemplated by the Board and defendants in the *Grasko* and *Miles* cases.

The results of meeting and conferring sessions under the present state of the law cannot result in more than a unilateral determination of policy in the form of rules or resolutions in regard to the subjects above enumerated. The rules and policies of the Board must be subject to change and modification at its pleasure, with the possible exception of those rules which by implication are a part of an employers [sic] contract of employment.

The Court is not unmindful in arriving at its conclusions of the difficult problems confronting the Board regarding employee relations. It is also well aware that many demands of the teachers reflected in the contract are sincere and may be justified. And we can well understand the wishes of the witness Gordon, a member of the Board, when he succinctly stated in his testimony the hope of the Board that they might develop "a package deal" in respect to employment relations that would set the die for a definite period, thus avoiding the necessity of continuous and piecemeal approaches to the solution of employee relations and other matters of concern to teachers.

This Court believes that school teachers are dedicated professional persons, just as concerned with the effecting [sic] of educational policies for the benefit of pupils, as they are with their own working conditions. But the sympathies of this Court are not permitted as an item of consideration in arriving at its conclusion.

Should this Court's decision withstand the rigors of an appellate procedure, then the remedy of the teachers is clear, namely legislation via the legislative process. It has been said:

> "Teachers are earnest and devoted people, with a high degree of training and experience. They know children and what goes on in the classroom and in the learning process. A lay board should make full use of their willingness and their knowledge and experience in matters of vital concern to both. Their voices should be heard and their recommendations thoughtfully considered. This should be rudimentary in good procedure. If boards and superintendents aren't doing this, they should. The critical question now is this: Is the superimposing of the already outgrown and inadequate industrial bargaining theory and techniques upon this quite different set of conditions the best way to achieve our purpose? Is this the desired spirit and procedure? Is in-

dustrial type 'bargaining' the way to select a reader for the third grade, or decide whether to introduce the new math for the eleventh, or whether the class size shall be 22 or 27, or which teacher shall teach in which school? Can't we find a better way, in a different context, to solve difficult professional questions that must be reasoned and analyzed and decided, but not 'bargained' in this ritualistic sense?" (Hatcher, Alexander F. Morrison Lecturer, 42 State Bar. J., pp. 50-51, cited in California Federation of Teachers v. Oxnard Elementary School, 272 Cal. App. 2d, pp. 515, 539.)

We are not allowed to opine in answer to the above questions but we do believe the philosophy urged by the quotation parallels the philosophy in the Winton Act in its creation of a Negotiating Council to "meet and confer." . . .

NOTE

The court's determination that a school board has no authority to enter into a binding agreement under the Winton Act was affirmed on appeal. Grasko v. Los Angeles City Bd. of Educ., 31 Cal. App. 3d 290, 82 L.R.R.M. 3098 (1973). The appellate court noted, however, that "the legality of the proposed Board Rule 3700 is not presented in the instant appeal."

EDWARDS, AN OVERVIEW OF THE "MEET AND CONFER" STATES—WHERE ARE WE GOING?,
Law Quadrangle Notes, Vol. 16, Winter 1972, at 10-15†

. . . .

As a theme for my speech, my first inclination was to share with you my strong opposition to the "meet and confer" bargaining model in the public sector and to suggest to you that "meet and confer" should be conceived as nothing more than an interim measure to bridge the gap between no collective bargaining and full collective bargaining rights for public employees. Most critics of the "meet and confer" model argue that it forces a union to engage in "collective begging" in place of collective bargaining in the public sector. While this criticism is not wholly without justification, it surely is too simplistic to afford a realistic appraisal of the "meet and confer" bargaining model. So while I am still inclined to reject the "meet and confer" approach as obsolete, I nevertheless feel that public sector labor questions are too complex to be disposed of by reference to one's subjective inclinations.

---

† Reprinted by permission of the University of Michigan Law School.

Before I launch into an appraisal of "meet and confer" legislation, it may be helpful to attempt to define what is meant by the "meet and confer" approach, particularly in contrast to the "collective negotiations" approach presently recognized in the private sector. The glossary in the *Government Employee Relations Report* defines "meet and confer negotiations" as a—

"Term for process of negotiating terms and conditions of employment intended to emphasize the differences between public and private employment conditions. Negotiations under 'meet and confer' laws usually imply discussions leading to unilateral adoption of policy by legislative body rather than written contract, and take place with multiple employee representatives rather than an exclusive bargaining agent."

I think this definition fairly describes what was originally intended by the "meet and confer" standard of bargaining. Implicit in this *pure* meet and confer approach is the assumption that the private sector bargaining model is overly permissive and therefore not applicable in the public sector. In other words, it is argued that public employers—who are by definition political souls—should retain broad managerial discretion in the operation of a governmental agency, subject only to the recall of the electorate pursuant to the lawfully designed political process. Thus, under the pure "meet and confer" bargaining model, the outcome of any public employer-employee discussions will depend more on management's determinations than on bilateral decisions by "equals" at the bargaining table.

On the other hand, in the private sector the parties meet as equals at the bargaining table and are free to discuss all matters concerning wages, hours, and conditions of employment. Except for "illegal" terms, there really is no statutorily created class of subjects which are not deemed to be bargainable. The only distinction of consequence in the private sector is between those "mandatory" items which may be negotiated to a point of impasse and those merely "permissible" subjects which may not be insisted upon. Since the NLRB has tended to construe "mandatory" subjects liberally, the result has been that when the parties face each other across a private sector bargaining table, they are in effect free to discuss virtually all matters which touch on the employment relationship.

It is generally assumed that most states which have passed statutes dealing with public sector labor relations problems have opted for the private sector "collective negotiations" model over the "meet and confer" approach. Upon close study of the applicable state legislation, however, it can be seen that this statement is somewhat of an overstatement and at best misleading. Actually it is true that most states have rejected the pure "meet and confer" bargaining model as it has been here defined, but by the same token, most states also rejected the traditional private sector "collective negotiations" approach. So, in practice, what we have really seen is the adoption by most states of either a *"modified* meet and confer" statute (which is more liberal than the traditional model) or a *"modified* collective negotiations" statute (which is more restrictive than its private sector counterpart). For this reason alone, it is often difficult to distinguish between "meet and confer" and "collective negotiations" as viable working concepts in the public sector. . . .

Most critics of "meet and confer" have argued that any bargaining structure which presumes to relegate the employees' representative to the status of a "conferee" or "discussant," rather than a negotiator, is patently deficient. But this criticism rests on the assumption that the bargaining process is *in fact* different under a "meet and confer" as opposed to a "collective negotiations" model. I would suggest, however, that, based upon the recent history of collective bargaining experiences which we have witnessed in the public sector in the United States, there is little to support the notion that there is any wide-spread difference in tactic or technique in the bargaining processes under these two models. Notwithstanding the statutory terminology used, unions in the public sector have pressed for the same type of demands and with the same vigor under both statutory bargaining models.

Furthermore, and with all due respect to the recent Supreme Court pronouncement that public employees do not have a constitutional right to strike, there has developed a *de facto* right to strike among public employees in this country—the threat or exercise of which appears to be no less effective than the legalized right enjoyed by employees in the private sector.

I would maintain, then, that in practice there has been no measurable difference in the *bargaining process* as seen in those states which have opted for "meet and confer" versus those states which have enacted statutes following the more traditional "collective negotiations" approach in the public sector. Indeed, many of the states which have passed "meet and confer" statutes have so distorted the pure "meet and confer" bargaining model that it is no longer accurate to say that the parties governed by some of these statutes do not meet as "equals" at the bargaining table.

At last count, I was able to identify ten states which have enacted some form of "meet and confer" legislation covering various groups of government employees: California, Idaho, Kansas, Minnesota, Missouri, Montana, Oregon, South Dakota, Maine, and Alabama.

With the exception of the Missouri and Alabama laws, and the recently enacted law in California covering state employees, none of these so-called "meet and confer" states has passed a statute which embodies what I have labelled the *pure* "meet and confer" bargaining approach. The two noticeable exceptions to this observation are California and Missouri. The Supreme Court of Missouri, in Missey v. City of Cabool, 441 S.W.2d 35, 41 (1969), ruled that the Missouri Statute did

> ". . . not purport to give to public employees the right of collective bargaining guaranteed to employees in private industry. . . . The act does not constitute a delegation . . . to the union of the legislative power of the public body, and therefore . . . the prior discretion in the legislative body to adopt, modify or reject outright the results of the discussions is untouched. . . . The act provides only a procedure for communication between the organization selected by public employees and their employer without requiring adoption of any agreement reached."

The recently enacted statute covering state employees in California seems to follow the principles espoused in *Missey,* for it simply requires the state representatives to "meet and confer" with employee representatives upon request, and to "consider" as fully as is deemed reasonable by the government representative, presentations made by the employee representative. However, the statute seems to make it clear that after the state has reasonably "considered" union proposals it may then act unilaterally with respect to wages, hours, and conditions of employment.

Thus, it is plain that at least in California (at the state level) and in Missouri, the parties do not meet as equals at the bargaining table. But the matter surely has not been so clearly resolved in other "meet and confer" states.

The other jurisdictions mentioned almost uniformly define the "meet and confer" obligation as

> ". . . the process whereby the representatives of a public agency and representatives of recognized employee organizations have the mutual obligation to meet and confer in order to exchange freely information, opinions and proposals to endeavor to reach agreement on conditions of employment."

The last-quoted definition is found in the Kansas statute and it is noteworthy that the law requires bargaining with an eye toward reaching an agreement. This clearly is at variance with the pure "meet and confer" model, which in theory does not require the employer to agree.

Other "meet and confer" statutes are even more explicit on this point. For example, the Montana statute makes it an unfair labor practice for a government employer to refuse to "meet, confer, or negotiate in good faith." The duty to "meet and confer in good faith" was proposed by the report of the Advisory Commission on Intergovernmental Relations published in March 1970. In its report, the Commission opted for a "modified meet and confer" approach; that is, one requiring meeting and conferring in "good faith." . . .

It is noteworthy that the ACIR recommendations, which have been followed by many of the states adopting "meet and confer" statutes, include the suggestion that the parties may be required to bargain in "good faith" to a point of impasse. Surely, if this is a part of the definition of "meet and confer" then the *bargaining process* is arguably not much different from what is seen in states which have followed the "collective negotiations" approach in dealing with public sector labor problems.

The marked distinction between the ACIR "modified meet and confer" approach, and the traditional "collective negotiations" approach, is the ACIR suggestion that the result of bargaining should be "a non-binding memorandum of understanding setting forth all agreed upon recommendations for submission to the jurisdiction's appropriate governing officials." This is essentially the approach taken by the California Meyers-Milias-Brown Act, which sets forth a modest scheme for local government collective bargaining.

But the required adoption of a *conditional agreement* at the conclusion of bargaining does not really distinguish the "modified meet and confer" states from some of the states which have followed the "collective negotiations" model. For example, under the New York Taylor Act it is provided that any labor agreement between a public employer and a union must include, "in type not smaller than the largest type used elsewhere in the agreement," the following clause:

"It is agreed . . . that any provision of this agreement requiring legislative action to permit its implementation by amendment of law or by providing the additional funds therefore, shall not become effective until the appropriate legislative body has given approval."

Thus, even in New York, which has enacted one of the most comprehensive "collective negotiations" statutes governing public sector labor relations, the end product of bargaining may be nothing more than a *conditional* agreement. . . .

. . . I am persuaded that there is no compelling evidence to demonstrate that the parties do not meet as "equals" under existing "meet and confer" bargaining statutes. It is true that, under the *pure* "meet and confer" model, adopted by California (for state employees), Missouri, and Alabama, the employee representative may be reduced to a role of "collective begger" rather than a collective bargainer. But most "meet and confer" states have adopted the *modified* ACIR design which substantially enhances the role of the employees' agent at the bargaining table. On this score then, it can be concluded that, excluding those few states which rely on outmoded notions of "sovereign authority," the *bargaining process*—as distinguished from the problem of the scope of permissible bargaining—is very similar under existing "meet and confer" and "collective negotiations" statutes. . . .

In conclusion, and in partial answer to the question posed by my speech topic, I would suggest to you that the term "meet and confer" is a misnomer in public sector labor relations. Excluding the two or three statutes, such as the one covering state employees in California and the one in Missouri, I would argue that the actual differences between the "meet and confer" and "collective negotiations" approaches have been grossly overstated. This is so because less than a handful of states have adopted what I have called the *pure* "meet and confer" bargaining model. As a consequence, the bargaining process and the techniques used to seek to reach an agreement are very similar in both those states which have followed and rejected "meet and confer." I think that we sometimes see a greater sophistication at the bargaining table in the states where a comprehensive and comprehensible state statutory scheme has been enacted, but this sophistication is not a necessary by-product of having public sector bargaining governed by a "collective negotiations" versus a modified "meet and confer" statute. Indeed, in Illinois, which has *no* state statutory scheme to regulate public sector bargaining, many highly sophisticated bargaining relationships have nevertheless developed.

My prognostications:

(1) Notwithstanding the recent enactment in California, I am inclined to think that the *pure* "meet and confer" approach to bargaining is obsolete and will pass with time. Labor leaders probably will not tolerate, for too much longer, any bargaining system which is founded on the worn-weary notion of sovereign-authority.

(2) "Meet and confer" will soon pass from the lexicon of labor relations terminology. To the extent that "meet and confer" suggests that the parties do not meet as "equals" at the bargaining table, it is a bad term; and to the extent that it suggests that there is a meaningful distinction between "meet and confer" and "collective negotiations," it is a misleading term. (I personally think that the *failure* by some states to embody the principles of "majority rule" and "exclusive representation" in their public sector labor laws has had a more profound effect on public sector bargaining relationships than has the modified "meet and confer" bargaining model.)

I think we can excuse the present chaotic state of affairs of labor relations in the public sector by reference to the statement once made by Justice Holmes that: "The life of the law has not been logic; it has been experience."

For those states which have yet to deal with the problem of public sector labor relations, and for those states still wallowing in obsolete notions of sovereign authority under the guise of "meet and confer," I would quote Justice Stewart's admonition in the recent *Boys Markets* case, to the effect that—

"Wisdom too often never comes, and so one ought not to reject it merely because it comes late."

NOTE

The interpretation and application of the Meyers-Milias-Brown Act is exhaustively explored in Grodin, *Public Employee Bargaining in California: The Meyers-Milias-Brown Act in the Courts,* 23 HASTINGS L.J. 719 (1972).

4. The Principle of Exclusive Representation

LULLO v. FIRE FIGHTERS, LOCAL 1066

Supreme Court of New Jersey
55 N.J. 409, 262 A.2d 681 (1970)

FRANCIS, J. In this action plaintiffs Lullo and Wood, individually and as officers of the plaintiff Firemen's Mutual Benevolent Association of New Jersey, Branch No. 1, attacked the constitutionality of L. 1968, c. 303, known as "New Jersey Employer-Employee Relations Act." N.J.S.A. 34:13A-1 *et seq.* The challenge was two pronged. One was directed at section 7 (N.J. S.A. 34:13A-5.3) of the Act which provides that the representative duly elected by a majority of the public employees in an appropriate unit shall be *the exclusive representative* of all employees in the unit. The other challenged the portion of section

7 which authorizes such representative and the employer in the appropriate unit involved to engage in *collective negotiations* concerning the terms and conditions of their employment. It was alleged that in these two respects section 7 is repugnant to Article I, paragraph 19 of the *New Jersey Constitution* of 1947. The trial court sustained the Act, and this Court certified the ensuing appeal while it was awaiting hearing in the Appellate Division.

Since 1895 the Firemen's Mutual Benevolent Association (FMBA), Branch No. 1, has been an incorporated association of this State. Its membership has always been made up of Jersey City firemen who desired to join. It is not a labor organization in the usual sense and has never held itself out as a negotiating agent for all the firemen of the City. However, on a purely voluntary basis it has interceded for and spoken on behalf of its members with the proper City representatives in matters affecting salaries, working conditions and grievances.

After L. 1968, c. 303, became effective, the New Jersey Public Employment Relations Commission (PERC) which was created by the Act, acceded to a request of defendant International Association of Fire Fighters, Local 1066 (IAF), a labor organization, and ordered an election to determine if those firemen eligible to vote wished to be represented by IAF for purposes of collective negotiation with Jersey City. N.J.S.A. 34:13A-5.2, 5.3, 6. Notice of the time and place of the election and a sample ballot were given to the firemen. As stated in the ballot the question to be voted upon was:

> Do you desire to be represented for purposes of collective bargaining by International Association of Fire Fighters, Local 1066? . . .

Plaintiffs were notified of the election but declined to participate because of their view that L. 1968, c. 303 is unconstitutional. Instead they instituted this action in the Superior Court, Chancery Division, seeking a declaration of the statute's invalidity and a temporary and permanent injunction against holding the election. The trial judge declined a temporary restraint and directed that the election be held, the result not to be certified until disposition of the court proceeding. See N.J.S.A. 34:13A-11; PERC Rule 19:11-19 (g) . The election was held and 417 of the 430 eligible firemen voted; 399 voted for representation by IAF, 17 voted against such representation, and one vote was not counted. Thereafter the trial court heard the attack on the statute, and as already indicated sustained its constitutionality.

I

The Exclusive Representation Issue

The right of employees in private and public employment to organize and to deal with their employers was dealt with in general terms in Article I, paragraph 19 of the 1947 *Constitution*. It provides:

> Persons in private employment shall have the right to organize and bargain collectively. Persons in public employment shall have the right to organize, present to and make known to the State, or any of its political subdivisions or agencies, their grievances and proposals through representatives of their own choosing.

. . . In general language it grants and secures to employees in the private and public sectors certain basic rights. At the same time, it recognizes and clearly projects a difference as between private and public employees in the quality and substance of the rights thus elevated to constitutional stature. Obviously, as Delaware River & Bay Auth. v. International Org., etc., 45 N.J. 138, 145 (1965) suggests, employees in private employment were endowed in broad terms with the right to organize and bargain collectively. However, public employees were invested inviolably in significantly narrower terms with the right to organize, present and make known to their public employers their grievances and proposals through representatives of their own choosing. But it is important to note that the delegates made no effort to detail or to prescribe the nature or scope of the representation or the authority of the representative to act for the employees whether their employment was in the public or private sector. The decision as to whether there should be a single representative to speak exclusively for all the employees, or multiple representatives to speak for different groups of employees or whether an individual employee should have the right to represent himself in all dealings with his employer, or whether all three forms of representation should be authorized, was left to the Legislature.

This Court declared in Board of Ed., Borough of Union Beach v. N.J.E.A., 53 N.J. 29, 44-45 (1968) that the purpose of Article I, paragraph 19 was to secure the specified rights of employees in private and public employment against legislative erosion or denial. It reveals no intention to deprive the Legislature of the power to grant to public employees a further right designed to implement or effectuate those rights secured by Article I, paragraph 19, or to grant more expansive relevant rights which do not conflict with that article. *Id.*, at 45. . . .

In 1966 the Legislature, noting that Article I, paragraph 19 of the *Constitution* "explicitly distinguishes between persons in private employment and persons in public employment with respect to the constitutional right to bargain collectively," created a commission to study the need for establishing an effective procedure for considering the grievances of public employees. L. 1966, c. 170. A number of other states have created similar study groups. See Smith, "State and Local Advisory Reports on Public Employment Labor Legislation: A Comparative Analysis," 67 Mich. L. Rev. 891 (1969). The New Jersey Commission Report[1] which was filed on January 9, 1968 asserted broadly that "the public interest requires that public employers and public employees be provided with an effective procedure for the mutual resolution of disputes involving terms and conditions of employment." It recommended "legislation setting forth a procedure that is fully compatible with and complementary to existing Civil Service systems and present laws and regulations governing personnel matters in public employment at all governmental levels in New Jersey." . . .

Under the heading "Administrative Procedures," the Report contains a strong recommendation respecting a primary problem in the present case. It says:

> a. When a majority of employees in a given negotiating group or unit indicate by secret election a preference for a specific representative organization, no other organization should be designated, certified, or recognized for the purpose of collective negotiations. (Report, p. 2).

In a later portion of the Report setting forth the recommendations in greater detail, the following appears at the end of the above paragraph and as a continuation thereof:

> . . . but this should not preclude an employee's right to process grievances individually. (Report, p. 22, par. c).

On the subject of exclusive representation by a representative duly elected by public employees in an appropriate unit, the Commission observed:

> Multiplicity of organizations claiming or possessing representation rights for the same group or unit of employees has long been regarded as undesirable. Multiple representation of employees encourages rivalries among employee groups and severely handicaps private and public employers

---

[1] Final Report to the Governor and the Legislature of the Public and School Employees' Grievance Procedure Study Commission, 1.

in the development of effective negotiations and stable relationships.

Expert witnesses and representatives of interested employer and employee groups appearing before the Commission were almost unanimous in their opposition to multiple representation within any employee negotiating unit. . . . The New Jersey Department of Civil Service, in its presentation to the Commission, accepted this viewpoint and advocated restriction of multiple bargaining following the pattern of the federal executive order. . . . (Report, p. 15).

In preparing the article in 67 Michigan Law Review, supra, Professor Smith surveyed similar reports of special advisory groups of other states. In discussing them he said:

It was generally agreed that public sector labor legislation should embrace the principle of exclusive recognition of the union or organization selected by the majority of employees in a defined bargaining unit. 67 Mich. L. Rev. at 897.

Chapter 303, L. 1968, was adopted in response to the New Jersey Commission Report and incorporated most of its recommendations. The controversy now before us centers around section 7 of Chapter 303. N.J.S.A. 34:13A-5.3. It provides among other things:

Representatives designated or selected by public employees for the purposes of collective negotiation by the majority of the employees in a unit appropriate for such purposes or by the majority of the employees voting in an election conducted by the commission as authorized by this act *shall be the exclusive representatives for collective negotiation concerning the terms and conditions of employment of the employees in such unit.* Nothing herein shall be construed to prevent any official from meeting with an employee organization for the purpose of hearing the views and requests of its members in such unit so long as (a) the majority representative is informed of the meeting; (b) any changes or modifications in terms and conditions of employment are made only through negotiation with the majority representative; and (c) a minority organization shall not present or process grievances. Nothing herein shall be construed to deny to any individual employee his rights under Civil Service laws or regulations. When no majority representative has been selected as the bargaining agent for the unit of which an individual employee is a part, he may present his own grievance either personally or through an appropriate representative or an organization of which he is a member and have such grievance adjusted.

A majority representative of public employees in an appropriate unit shall be entitled to act for and to negotiate agreements covering all employees in the unit and shall be responsible for representing the interests of all such employees without discrimination and without regard to employee organization membership. Proposed new rules or modifications of existing rules governing working conditions shall be negotiated with the majority representative before they are established. In addition, the majority representative and designated representatives of the public employer shall meet at reasonable times and negotiate in good faith with respect to grievances and terms and conditions of employment.

When an agreement is reached on the terms and conditions of employment, it shall be embodied in writing and signed by the authorized representatives of the public employer and the majority representative.

Public employers shall negotiate written policies setting forth grievance procedures by means of which their employees or representatives of employees may appeal the interpretation, application or violation of policies, agreements, and administrative decisions affecting them, provided that such grievance procedures shall be included in any agreement entered into between the public employer and the representative organization. Such grievance procedures may provide for binding arbitration as a means for resolving disputes. (Emphasis added.)

Plaintiffs allege that this section which constitutes IAF the exclusive representative of all the employees in the unit for collective bargaining negotiation concerning their terms and conditions of employment violates Article I, paragraph 19 of the *Constitution*. In support of the contention they point to the language of paragraph 19 which gives "persons" in public employment the right to organize, present to and make known to their public employers their grievances and proposals "through representatives of their own choosing." Then they seize upon the pluralistic significance of "persons" and urge that the language authorizes any "person" in public employment to present *his* grievances and proposals through a representative of his own choosing. Thus they say that each public employee has been vested with the basic right to present his proposals and grievances to the employer through his individually chosen representative, and that this right, being entrenched in the organic charter, is beyond the power of the Legislature to qualify or dilute. Consequently they claim that section 7 of the statute is invalid because it undertakes to place effectuation of this right exclusively in the hands of a representative elected by a majority of an individual's fellow employees in the designated unit, even though the individual did not vote with the majority or does not belong to the organization selected as the representative.

We cannot accept such a narrow view of the constitutional purpose. It seems obvious to us that the very general language of Article I, paragraph 19 was oriented toward collectivity. The purpose was to secure to employees collectively in the various employer divisions and agencies of government the right to get together—to organize—and to select representatives to present their (*i.e.*, all employees in all divisions and agencies) proposals and grievances. The use of the plural form—"representatives"— signifies an awareness that there would be many different organizations involved and that they would represent many different groups or units of employees in many separate divisions or agencies of government. It is not reasonable to say that the delegates to the Constitutional Convention, many of whom were described as well informed in the field of labor relations, intended the broad language they employed in paragraph 19 to prevent the Legislature from establishing a commonly known means of giving potency and practical effect to the guaranteed right to organize. Delaware River & Bay Auth. v. International Org., etc., supra, 45 N.J., at 144. Surely it could not have been the purpose of such knowledgeable men to give constitutional sanction to the scene of each employee or group of employees in a public agency presenting proposals and grievances through a substantial number of different representatives. Such delegates would have known that "multiplicity of organizations claiming or possessing representation rights for the same group or unit of employees has long been regarded as undesirable. Multiple representation of employees encourages rivalries among employee groups and severely handicaps private and public employers in the development of effective negotiations and stable relationships." Report, supra, at 15.

It cannot be overlooked that the delegates to the Convention realized that the particular aspect of labor relations in the public employment sector was being drawn into a New Jersey Constitution for the first time. They were in virgin territory and although they wished to ensconce certain basic guarantees in the charter, obviously they felt the need to phrase them in most general terms and leave to legislative judgment their implementation and augmentation, and particularly the decision as to whether there should be a single representative for all employees, or multiple representation or individual self-representation.

When Chapter 303, L. 1968, was under consideration by the Legislature, experience on a vast scale in the private employment sector on the national scene had demonstrated that just and harmonious labor relations for both employer and employee are best achieved when the employees' cause is in the hands of an exclusive representative freely and fairly chosen by a majority of the employees in an appropriate unit.

It seems hardly necessary to explain this principle of majority representation in light of the common acceptance of that principle as an integral part of our democratic form of government. Moreover, that principle of representation was adopted by the National War Labor Board during World War II and likewise was embodied in the Railway Labor Act. See 2 *Teller, Labor Disputes and Collective Bargaining,* § 243, p. 688 (1940). As far back as 1903 the pertinency of the principle in industrial relations was spoken of as beyond dispute. In Wabash Railroad v. Hannahan, 121 F. 563, 571 (E.D. Mo. 1903) the court said:

> The will of the individual must consent to yield to the will of the majority, or no organization either of society into government, capital into combination, or labor into coalition can ever be effected. The individual must yield in order that the many may receive a greater benefit. The right of labor to organize for lawful purposes and by organic agreement to subject the individual members to rules, regulations, and conduct prescribed by the majority is no longer an open question in the jurisprudence of this country.

In 1935 when the National Labor Relations Act was adopted to regulate employer-employee relations in the private employment sector, section 7 thereof, 29 U.S.C.A. § 157, provided:

> Employees shall have the right to self-organization, to form, join, or assist labor organizations, to bargain collectively through representatives of their own choosing. . . .

In the 35-year history of the Act the phrase "representatives of their own choosing" has become a phrase of art, designed to convey the intention that the employees' selection of a bargaining representative should be an uncoerced and free choice. . . . It has never been deemed to be inconsistent with the grant of exclusive representation in section 9 (a), 29 U.S.C.A. § 159 (a), which says:

> Representatives designated or selected for the purpose of collective bargaining by the majority of the employees in a

unit appropriate for such purposes, shall be the exclusive representatives of all the employees in such unit. . . . (Emphasis added.)

This meaning of the phrase and the absence of any indication or ruling by the courts that it was inconsistent with the existence of the exclusive representation concept in section 9 (a) obviously did not escape the attention of the framers of the 1947 *New Jersey Constitution*. Thus in using the phrase in paragraph 19 of Article I, it is reasonable to assume that their intention was to assure that the choice of a representative in the public sector would be uncoerced and free. Knowing, as they must have, that the language "representatives of their own choosing" had always been considered consistent with exclusive representation in the federal statutory scheme, they could not have intended, as plaintiffs argue here, to exclude such representation in the future simply by using the words "representatives of their own choosing" in the *Constitution*.

When we pass on to an examination of L. 1968, c. 303, attention is drawn immediately to the almost identical language of its section 7 and that of section 9 (a) supra, of the Labor Management Relations Act. Since, as we have noted above, there is no conflict between section 7 and 9 (a) (29 U.S.C.A. § 157, 159 (a)) of the federal statute it would seem to follow logically that Article I, paragraph 19 of the *Constitution* and section 7 of our 1968 Act are likewise harmonious and may stand together.

A wide-ranging consideration of the problem makes it particularly noteworthy that both section 9 (a) of the federal act and our section 7 speak of "representatives designated or selected . . . by the majority of the employees in a unit appropriate for such purposes"; also that both say that representatives "shall be the exclusive representatives" of all the employees in the appropriate unit. The parallelism is not merely coincidental. It is obvious from the Report that the New Jersey Study Commission was conscious of the federal legislation, its mandate for exclusive recognition of the bargaining representative chosen by a majority of the employees involved, the need for such a mandate, the accepted consistency between its sections 7 and 9 (a) , 29 U.S.C.A. §§ 157, 159 (a) , and the satisfactory experience resulting from its application on the national scene in the private employment sector. Manifestly such knowledge was responsible for the Commission's disparagement of multiple representation of employees in the appropriate unit and its recommendations of exclusivity for the representative freely and fairly chosen by the majority of such employees. See Smith, supra, 67 Mich. L. Rev., at 897-98, 901. Adoption by the Legislature of the federal act's language establishing the exclusive representation of the elected representative demonstrates acceptance of the Commission's recommendation in that regard. Further, for purposes of judicial interpretation in a context such as is presented to us here, such legislative approval brings to the fore the well known tenet of statutory construction that the experience and the adjudications under the copied act were probably accepted as an intended guide for the administration of the later act. See 2 *Sutherland, Statutory Construction* (3d ed. 1943) § 5209, p. 551. . . .

The labor union movement was born of the realization that a single employee had no substantial economic strength. He had little leverage beyond the sale of his own efforts to aid him in obtaining fair wages, hours of work and working conditions. . . . Realization by individual employees that their reasonable expectations were common to their fellow workers turned them toward organization to strengthen and further that community of interest. The concept that in union there is strength and a means of achieving an equitable balance of bargaining power with employers flourished in this country. Ultimately it found legislative acceptance of monumental proportions in the 1935 National Labor Relations Act and its subsequent revisions. It is undisputed the major purpose of Congress in enacting that legislation was to bring about such a balance in private employment.

However, the major aim could not be accomplished if numerous individual employees wished to represent themselves or groups of employees chose different unions or organizations for the purpose. Such absence of solidarity and diffusion of collective strength would promote rivalries, would serve disparate rather than uniform overall objectives, and in many situations would frustrate the employees' community interests. See *Chamberlain, Labor* 179 (1958). Obviously parity of bargaining power between employers and employees could not be reached in such a framework. So the democratic principle of majority control was introduced on the national scene, and the representative freely chosen by a majority of the employees in an appropriate unit to represent their collective interests in bargaining with the employer was given the exclusive right to do so. 29 U.S.C.A. § 159(a). Thus this policy was built on the premise that by pooling their economic strength and acting through a single representative freely chosen by the majority, the employees in such a unit achieve the most effective means of bargaining with an employer respecting conditions of employment. N.L.R.B. v. Allis-Chalmers Mfg. Co., 388 U.S. 175, 87 S. Ct. 2001, 18 L. Ed. 2d 1123 (1967); Medo Photo Supply Corp. v. N.L.R.B., 321 U.S. 678, 684, 64 S. Ct. 830, 88 L. Ed. 1007, 1011 (1944);

J.I. Case Co. v. N.L.R.B., 321 U.S. 332, 338, 64 S. Ct. 576, 88 L. Ed. 762, 768 (1944). Experience in the private employment sector has established that investment of the bargaining representative of the majority with the exclusive right to represent all the employees in the unit is a sound and salutary prerequisite to effective bargaining. Beyond doubt such exclusivity—the majority rule concept—is now at the core of our national labor policy. N.L.R.B. v. Allis-Chalmers Mfg. Co., supra, 388 U.S. at 180, 87 S. Ct. 2001.

Application of the majority rule concept strengthens the right of the individual employee to obtain fair and equitable terms of employment. It brings the collective strength of all the employees in the unit to the negotiating table and thus enhances the chances of effectuating their community purposes and serving the welfare of the group. The employee who votes against the representative chosen by the majority or who exercises his privilege not to join the organization of the representative suffers no constitutional infringement of his basic freedom of contract right because of the exclusivity principle. Freedom of contract is a qualified, and not an absolute right. There is no absolute freedom to do as one wills or to contract as one chooses.

It follows from what has been said that in the private employment sector the individual employee's right to organize and to bargain collectively has been implemented and made truly meaningful by the legislative mandate for exclusive representation. The exclusivity concept carries with it an equally heavy responsibility toward dissident employees in the unit as for employee-members of the representative organization. Although the representative has the sole right to negotiate and consummate a contract respecting the terms and conditions of employment and the processing of grievances for all employees in the unit, the right to do so must always be exercised with complete good faith, with honesty of purpose and without unfair discrimination against a dissident employee or group of employees. This is true not only in the negotiating of the employer-employee agreement but in its administration as well. N.L.R.B. v. Allis-Chalmers Mfg. Co., supra, 388 U.S. at 180-181, 87 S. Ct. 2001; Vaca v. Sipes, 386 U.S. 171, 177, 87 S. Ct. 903, 17 L. Ed. 2d 842 (1967). When the collective bargaining agreement has been made, it becomes the code of the plant and in policing it the union cannot trample upon the rights of a non-member minority. All must be treated fairly and evenly, particularly with respect to employment of procedures established therein to adjust and settle individual grievances. Vaca v. Sipes, supra; Donnelly v. United Fruit Co., 40 N.J. 61, 76, 80 (1963) · Wellington, "Union Democracy and Fair Representation: Federal Responsibility in a Federal System," 67 Yale L.J. 1327 (1958) . . . .

Undoubtedly the delegates to the 1947 Constitutional Convention were aware of the exclusivity doctrine which was at the heart of the national employer-employee labor relations policy in the private employment sector. The broad general language they used in drafting Article I, paragraph 19, particularly the portion referring to public employment reveals no express or implied intention to control or regulate, approve or disapprove the rule of majority representation. The Commission plainly was familiar with it and its successful operation as a means of stabilizing industrial relations in the private sector. For that reason the Report opposed multiple representation of public employees for purposes of negotiating with their employer. It is significant that the Legislature agreed and in adopting section 7 of L. 1968, c. 303, used almost the identical language of the federal act, 29 U.S.C.A. § 159 (a) in mandating that the representative selected by the majority of the employees in an appropriate unit for purposes of collective negotiation shall be the exclusive representative of all the employees for that purpose.

The legislative aim in writing section 7 was to aid, not to hinder, public employees in their relationship with their employers. The purpose was to discourage rivalries among individual employees and employee groups and to avoid the diffusion of negotiating strength which results from multiple representation. On the positive side the Legislature was seeking through the medium of the collective agreement to supersede separate agreements with employees and to substitute a single compact with terms which reflect the strength, negotiating power and welfare of the group. The benefits and advantages of the collective agreement are then open to every employee in the unit whether or not he is a member of the representative organization chosen by the majority of his fellow workers. He can be certain also that in negotiating with the employer the representative is obliged to be conscious of the statutory obligation to serve and protect the interests of all the employees, majority and minority, equally and without hostility or discrimination. And he can rest secure in the knowledge that so long as the union or other organization assumes to act as the statutory representative, it cannot lawfully refuse to perform or neglect to perform fully and in complete good faith the duty, which is inseparable from the power of exclusive representation, to represent the entire membership of the employees in the unit. The obligations of the exclusive representative as they have been described herein evolved largely from experience in administering section 9 (a)

of the National Labor Relations Act, 29 U.S.C.A. § 159 (a).
The absence of any express specifications of the obligations by
Congress made it necessary for the courts to define them. The
New Jersey Legislature accepted the judicial exposition of the
exclusive representative's duty to all employees in the appropriate unit, and made it part of L. 1968, c. 303, N.J.S.A. 34:13A-
5.3. . . .

The above considerations lead us to the conviction that the
creation in section 7 of an exclusive representative under the
conditions stated therein is not repugnant to Article I, paragraph 19 of the *Constitution*. Fairly construed in light of the
history of employer-employee relations, the section enhances,
implements and effectuates the right secured public employees
to organize, present and to make known to their public employers
their grievances and proposals through representatives of their
own choosing. . . .

NOTES

1. In Dade County Classroom Teachers Ass'n Inc. v. Ryan,
225 So. 2d 903 (Fla. 1969), the Florida Supreme Court held
that a Florida constitutional provision which provides that
"[t]he right of employees, by and through a labor organization,
to bargain collectively shall not be denied or abridged" and a
statute which substantially restated the constitutional provision
were applicable to public employees. The court held that the
statute precludes a labor organization from acting as the sole
bargaining agent for all the employees in a given unit, noting
that "a labor organization can represent all those [employees]
who are members of the organization or who freely and expressly
give their consent for that organization to act as their collective
bargaining agent." Accordingly, a collective bargaining agreement, as well as the grievance procedure set forth therein, was
held to apply only to those teachers who specifically consented to
be bound by it.

2. In California the Winton Act, CAL. EDUC. CODE §§ 13080-
13088 (West 1969), which applies to teachers in elementary and
secondary schools, establishes a system of proportional rather
than exclusive representation. The Act provides that where
there is more than one certificated employee organization in a
unit, a negotiating council is to be formed to represent all
employees. Seats on the council are apportioned according to a
ratio formula. The courts have ruled, however, that once a
council is formed, minority unions not participating on the
council do not have the right to make individual presentations
to a school board, except through the council. An individual

employee, however, has the right to appear directly before the school board. California Fed'n of Teachers v. Oxnard Elementary Schools, 272 Cal. App. 2d 514, 77 Cal. Rptr. 497 (1969); West Valley Fed'n of Teachers, Local 1953 v. Campbell Union High School Dist., 24 Cal. App. 3d 297, 101 Cal. Rptr. 83 (1972). Why should an employee have the right to appear before his employer's decision-making body in an individual capacity, yet not in his capacity as the representative of an employee organization? The Winton Act is discussed in Hayes v. Association of Classroom Teachers, *supra* p. 341.

3. Obviously, an exclusive bargaining representative is entitled to certain rights and privileges not granted to minority organizations. Yet, it may be claimed that the grant of some privileges to a majority union results in an unfair discrimination against minority unions and an effective denial of freedom of association to employees. Should this be a matter of concern for a state legislature? Since the principles of majority rule and exclusive representation are well-established in the private sector, are there any legitimate reasons for rejecting these principles in the public sector? *See generally* Comment, *The Privilege of Exclusive Recognition and Minority Union Rights in Public Employment,* 55 CORNELL L. REV. 1004 (1970).

B. Scope of Bargaining

1. Public Policy Considerations

H. WELLINGTON AND R. WINTER, THE UNIONS AND THE CITIES 21-30 (1971)†

The Public Sector Model: Nonmonetary Issues

In the private sector, unions have pushed to expand the scope of bargaining in response to the desires of their members for a variety of new benefits (pension rights, supplementary unemployment payments, merit increases). These benefits generally impose a monetary cost on the employer. And because employers are restrained by the market, an expanded bargaining agenda means that, if a union negotiates an agreement over more subjects, it generally trades off more of less for less of more.

From the consumer's point of view this in turn means that the price of the product he purchases is not significantly related to the scope of bargaining. And since unions rarely bargain about the nature of the product produced, the consumer can be rela-

---

† Reprinted by permission. Copyright © 1971 by The Brookings Institution, Washington, D.C.

tively indifferent as to how many or how few subjects are covered in any collective agreement. Nor need the consumer be concerned about union demands that would not impose a financial cost on the employer, for example, the design of a grievance procedure. While such demands are not subject to the same kind of trade-off as are financial demands, they are unlikely, if granted, to have any impact on the consumer. Their effect is on the quality of life of the parties to the agreement.

In the public sector the cluster of problems that surround the scope of bargaining are much more troublesome than they are in the private sector. The problems have several dimensions.

First, the trade-off between subjects of bargaining in the public sector is less of a protection to the consumer (public) than it is in the private. Where political leaders view the costs of union demands as essentially budgetary, a trade-off can occur. Thus, a demand for higher teacher salaries and a demand for reduced class size may be treated as part of one package. But where a demand, although it has a budgetary effect, is viewed as involving essentially political costs, trade-offs are more difficult. Our paradigmatic mayor, for example, may be under great pressure to make a large monetary settlement with a teachers' union whether or not it is joined to demands for special training programs for disadvantaged children. Interest groups tend to exert pressure against union demands only when they are directly affected. Otherwise, they are apt to join that large constituency (the general public) that wants to avoid labor trouble. Trade-offs can occur only when several demands are resisted by roughly the same groups. Thus, pure budgetary demands can be traded off when they are opposed by taxpayers. But when the identity of the resisting group changes with each demand, political leaders may find it expedient to strike a balance on each issue individually, rather than as part of a total package, by measuring the political power of each interest group involved against the political power of the constituency pressing for labor peace. To put it another way, as important as financial factors are to a mayor, political factors may be even more important. The market allows the businessman no such discretionary choice.

Where a union demand—such as increasing the disciplinary power of teachers—does not have budgetary consequences, some trade-offs may occur. Granting the demand will impose a political cost on the mayor because it may anger another interest group. But because the resisting group may change with each issue, each issue is apt to be treated individually and not as a part of a total package. And this may not protect the public. Differing from the private sector, nonmonetary demands of public sector unions do have effects that go beyond the parties to the agreement. All of us have a stake in how school children are disciplined. Expansion of the subjects of bargaining in the public sector, therefore, may increase the total quantum of union power in the political process.

Second, public employees do not generally produce a product. They perform a service. The way in which a service is performed may become a subject of bargaining. As a result, the nature of that service may be changed. Some of these services—police protection, teaching, health care—involve questions that are politically, socially, or ideologically sensitive. In part this is because government is involved and alternatives to governmentally provided services are relatively dear. In part, government is involved because of society's perception about the nature of the service and society's need for it. This suggests that decisions affecting the nature of a governmentally provided service are much more likely to be challenged and are more urgent than generally is the case with services that are offered privately.

Third, some of the services government provides are performed by professionals—teachers, social workers, and so forth—who are keenly interested in the underlying philosophy that informs their work. To them, theirs is not merely a job to be done for a salary. They may be educators or other "change agents" of society. And this may mean that these employees are concerned with more than incrementally altering a governmental service or its method of delivery. They may be advocates of bold departures that will radically transform the service itself.

The issue is not a threshold one of whether professional public employees should participate in decisions about the nature of the services they provide. Any properly run governmental agency should be interested in, and heavily reliant upon, the judgment of its professional staff. The issue rather is the method of that participation.

Conclusions about this issue as well as the larger issue of a full transplant of collective bargaining to the public sector may be facilitated by addressing some aspects of the governmental decision-making process—particularly at the municipal level—and the impact of collective bargaining on that process.

Public Employee Unions and the Political Process

Although the market does not discipline the union in the public sector to the extent that it does in the private, the municipal employment paradigm, nevertheless, would seem to be consistent with what Robert A. Dahl has called the " 'normal' American political process," which is "one in which there is a high probability that an active and legitimate group in the population can make itself heard effectively at some crucial stage in the process of decision," for the union may be seen as little more than an "active and legitimate group in the population." With elections in the background to perform, as Mr. Dahl notes, "the critical role . . . in maximizing political equality and popular sovereignty," all seems well, at least theoretically, with collective bargaining and public employment.

But there is trouble even in the house of theory if collective bargaining in the public sector means what it does in the private. The trouble is that if unions are able to withhold labor—to strike —as well as to employ the usual methods of political pressure, they may possess a disproportionate share of effective power in the process of decision. Collective bargaining would then be so effective a pressure as to skew the results of the " 'normal' American political process."

One should straightway make plain that the strike issue is not simply the importance of public services as contrasted with services or products produced in the private sector. This is only part of the issue, and in the past the partial truth has beclouded analysis. The services performed by a private transit authority are neither less nor more important to the public than those that would be performed if the transit authority were owned by a municipality. A railroad or a dock strike may be more damaging to a community than "job action" by police. This is not to say that governmental services are not important. They are, both because the demand for them is inelastic and because their disruption may seriously injure a city's economy and occasionally impair the physical welfare of its citizens. Nevertheless, the importance of governmental services is only a necessary part of, rather than a complete answer to, the question: Why be more concerned about strikes in public employment than in private?

The answer to the question is simply that, because strikes in public employment disrupt important services, a large part of a mayor's political constituency will, in many cases, press for a quick end to the strike with little concern for the cost of settlement. This is particularly so where the cost of settlement is borne by a different and larger political constituency, the citizens of the state or nation. Since interest groups other than public employees, with conflicting claims on municipal government, do not, as a general proposition, have anything approaching the effectiveness of the strike—or at least cannot maintain that relative degree of power over the long run—they may be put at a significant competitive disadvantage in the political process.

The private sector strike is designed to exert economic pressure on the employer by depriving him of revenues. The public employee strike is fundamentally different: its sole purpose is to exert political pressure on municipal officials. They are deprived, not of revenues but of the political support of those who are inconvenienced by a disruption of municipal services. But precisely because the private strike is an economic weapon, it is disciplined by the market and the benefit/unemployment trade-off that imposes. And because the public employee strike is a political weapon, it is subject only to the restraints imposed by the political process and they are on the whole less limiting and less disciplinary than those of the market. If this is the case, it must be said that the political process will be radically altered by wholesale importation of the strike weapon. And because of the deceptive simplicity of the analogy to collective bargaining in the private sector, the alteration may take place without anyone realizing what has happened.

Nor is it an answer that, in some municipalities, interest groups other than unions now have a disproportionate share of political power. This is inescapably true, and we do not condone that situation. Indeed, we would be among the first to advocate reform. However, reform cannot be accomplished by giving another interest group disproportionate power, for the losers would be the weakest groups in the community. In most municipalities, the weakest groups are composed of citizens who many believe are most in need of more power.

Therefore, while the purpose and effect of strikes by public employees may seem in the beginning designed merely to establish collective bargaining or to "catch up" with wages and fringe benefits in the private sector, in the long run strikes may become too effective a means for redistributing income; so effective, indeed, that one might see them as an institutionalized means of obtaining and maintaining a subsidy for union members.

As is often the case when one generalizes, this picture may be considered overdrawn. In order to refine analysis, it will be helpful to distinguish between strikes that occur over monetary issues and strikes involving nonmonetary issues. The generalized picture sketched above is mainly concerned with the former. Because there is usually no substitute for governmental services, the citizen-consumer faced with a strike of teachers, or garbage men, or social workers is likely to be seriously inconvenienced. This in turn places enormous pressure on the mayor, who is apt to find it difficult to look to the long-run balance sheet of the municipality. Most citizens are directly affected by a strike of sanitation workers. Few, however, can decipher a municipal budget or trace the relationship between today's labor settlement and next year's increase in the mill rate. Thus, in the typical case the impact of a settlement is less visible—or can more often be concealed—than the impact of a disruption of services. Moreover, the cost of settlement may fall upon a constituency much larger—the whole state or nation—than that represented by the mayor. And revenue sharing schemes that involve unrestricted funds may further lessen public resistance to generous settlements. It follows that the mayor usually will look to the electorate that is clamoring for a settlement, and in these circumstances the union's fear of a long strike, a major check on its power in the private sector, is not a consideration.[2] In the face of all of these factors other interest groups with priorities different from the union's are apt to be much less successful in their pursuit of scarce tax dollars than is the union with power to withhold services.[3]

With respect to strikes over some nonmonetary issues—decentralization of the governance of schools might be an example—the intensity of concern on the part of well-organized interest groups opposed to the union's position would support the mayor in his resistance to union demands. But even here, if the union rank and file back their leadership, pressures for settlement from the general public, which may be largely indifferent as to the underlying issue, might in time become irresistible.[4]

The strike and its threat, moreover, exacerbate the problems associated with the scope of bargaining in public employment. This seems clear if one attends in slightly more detail to techniques of municipal decision making.

Few students of our cities would object to Herbert Kaufman's observation that:

---

[2] Contrast the situation in the private sector: ". . . management cannot normally win the short strike. Management can only win the long strike. Also management frequently tends, in fact, to win the long strike. As a strike lengthens, it commonly bears more heavily on the union and the employees than on management. Strike relief is no substitute for a job. Even regular strike benefits, which few unions can afford, and which usually exhaust the union treasury quite rapidly (with some exceptions), are no substitute for a job." E. Livernash, "*The Relation of Power to the Structure and Process of Collective Bargaining,*" 6 JOURNAL OF LAW & ECONOMICS 10, 15 (October 1963).

[3] A vivid example was provided by an experience in New Jersey. After a twelve-hour strike by Newark firefighters on July 11, 1969, state urban aid funds, originally authorized for helping the poor, were diverted to salary increases for firemen and police. See *New York Times*, Aug. 7, 1969, p. 25. Moreover, government decision makers other than the mayor (for example, the governor) may have interests different from those of the mayor, interests that manifest themselves in pressures for settlement.

[4] Consider also the effect of such strikes on the fabric of society. See, for example, M. MAYER, THE TEACHER STRIKE: NEW YORK, 1968 (Harper and Row, 1969).

Decisions of the municipal government emanate from no single source, but from many centers; conflicts and clashes are referred to no single authority, but are settled at many levels and at many points in the system: no single group can guarantee the success of any proposal it supports, the defeat of every idea it objects to. Not even the central governmental organs of the city—the Mayor, the Board of Estimate, the Council—individually or in combination, even approach mastery in this sense.

Each separate decision center consists of a cluster of interested contestants, with a "core group" in the middle, invested by the rules with the formal authority to legitimize decisions (that is to promulgate them in binding form) and a constellation of related "satellite groups" seeking to influence the authoritative issuances of the core group.

Nor would many disagree with Nelson W. Polsby when, in discussing community decision making that is concerned with an alternative to a "current state of affairs," he argues that the alternative "must be politically palatable and relatively easy to accomplish; otherwise great amounts of influence have to be brought to bear with great skill and efficiency in order to secure its adoption."

It seems probable that such potential subjects of bargaining as school decentralization and a civilian police review board are, where they do not exist, alternatives to the "current state of affairs," which are not "politically palatable and relatively easy to accomplish." If a teachers' union or a police union were to bargain with the municipal employer over these questions, and were able to use the strike to insist that the proposals not be adopted, how much "skill and efficiency" on the part of the proposals' advocates would be necessary to effect a change? And, to put the shoe on the other foot, if a teachers' union were to insist through collective bargaining (with the strike or its threat) upon major changes in school curriculum, would not that union have to be considerably less skillful and efficient in the normal political process than other advocates of community change? The point is that with respect to some subjects, collective bargaining may be too powerful a lever on municipal decision making, too effective a technique for changing or preventing the change of one small but important part of the "current state of affairs."

Unfortunately, in this area the problem is not merely the strike threat and the strike. In a system where impasse procedures involving third parties are established in order to reduce work stoppages—and this is common in those states that have passed public employment bargaining statutes—third party intervention must be partly responsive to union demands. If the scope of bargaining is open-ended, the neutral party, to be effective, will have to work out accommodations that inevitably advance some of the union's claims some of the time. And the neutral, with his eyes fixed on achieving a settlement, can hardly be concerned with balancing all the items on the community agenda or reflecting the interests of all relevant groups.

The Theory Summarized

Collective bargaining in public employment, then, seems distinguishable from that in the private sector. To begin with, it imposes on society more than a potential misallocation of resources through restrictions on economic output, the principal cost imposed by private sector unions. Collective bargaining by public employees and the political process cannot be separated. The costs of such bargaining, therefore, cannot be fully measured without taking into account the impact on the allocation of political power in the typical municipality. If one assumes, as here, that municipal political processes should be structured to ensure "a high probability that an active and legitimate group in the population can make itself heard effectively at some crucial stage in the process of decision," then the issue is how powerful unions will be in the typical municipal political process if a full transplant of collective bargaining is carried out.

The conclusion is that such a transplant would, in many cases, institutionalize the power of public employee unions in a way that would leave competing groups in the political process at a permanent and substantial disadvantage.

NOTES

1. The Advisory Commission on Intergovernmental Relations recommended that certain "management rights" be removed from the scope of bargaining. The Commission stated:

> The Commission believes statutory description of management rights is necessary if well defined parameters to discussions are to be established. In a democratic political system, dealings between public employers and public employee organizations—whether they are called negotiations or discussions—must necessarily be limited by legislatively determined policies and goals. This may involve merely a restatement of basic management prerogatives and civil service precepts. Listing such rights in law eliminates many of the headaches of administrative elaboration and some of the cross pressures generated by ambiguities. Wages, hours, and other terms and conditions of employment, however,

are left for the conference table. Hence, the framework for a meaningful dialogue remains intact. ADVISORY COMMISSION ON INTERGOVERNMENTAL RELATIONS, LABOR-MANAGEMENT POLICIES FOR STATE AND LOCAL GOVERNMENT 102-03 (1969).

2. Should the determination of whether public employees are allowed to strike have any bearing on the scope of bargaining? Bok and Dunlop answered affirmatively:

[T]he scope of bargaining will be influenced by the procedures adopted to resolve impasses in negotiations. If public employees are permitted to strike, the range of bargainable topics presumably should be closely confined. The exercise of economic pressure through disruption of public services is too haphazard a way of deciding significant issues affecting the public, such as institution of a police review board, decentralization of administrative services, and initiation or discontinuation of a specific government facility. This is especially true in the public sector, where decisions are much less restricted by competition and related market pressures. If disputes are settled by the more reasoned process of fact finding or arbitration, on the other hand, the scope of negotiation may be somewhat broader, although there will still be many important matters excluded from bargaining on the ground either that they should be within the province of management or that they seem more suited to resolution through the political process. Finally, a system that does not provide for strikes or arbitration, but reserves final power in a legislative body to settle bargaining disputes, can appropriately entrust a broad range of subjects to the bargaining process. D. BOK & J. DUNLOP, LABOR AND THE AMERICAN COMMUNITY 327 (1970).

WOLLETT, THE BARGAINING PROCESS IN THE PUBLIC SECTOR: WHAT IS BARGAINABLE?, 51 Ore. L. Rev. 177, 177-82 (1971)†

Bargainability is a subject which seems to have a peculiar fascination for the National Labor Relations Board, and for lawyers, law professors, law students, directors of industrial relations, union representatives, and other persons in the labor relations business. A vast body of jurisprudence dealing with what the parties *must* bargain about, what they *may* bargain about, and what they *cannot* bargain about has developed in the last 30 years.

Predictably, as collective bargaining has come to public em-

---

ployment, the same concern has been demonstrated. For example, Professors Wellington and Winter have recently argued that collective bargaining is too powerful a lever on governmental decision-making and too effective a technique for changing or maintaining public policies to allow it to run unchecked. Therefore, the subject matter which is negotiable should be more sharply circumscribed in the public sector than in the private sector.

My thesis is that the vast literature concerning the scope of bargaining is much ado about nothing and that the preoccupation with this subject is mischievous as well as mistaken. Many practitioners will regard this as a glossing over of a fundamental issue, as an oversimplification, and as a blithe ignoring of vital matters.

The case for my thesis lies in the attitude which one brings to the bargaining table. If the negotiator conceives his function to be one of establishing immutable principles, winning points and outscoring the adversary, massaging his client's ego, or building a reputation as a protagonist of ordered government and managerial sovereignty, the issue of what is bargainable is fertile ground. If, on the other hand, he approaches the table in a spirit of meeting problems rather than avoiding them, and of trying to find ways to reach agreement rather than identifying obstacles which make a negotiated settlement impossible, I submit that the question of scope of bargaining becomes of little significance.

During my eight years of law practice in New York City, exclusively on the management side in the private sector, I cannot recall a single instance when my colleagues and I refused, on behalf of our client, to bargain about *anything* in the sense of refusing to discuss it on its merits. If we perceived that the proposal reflected a problem of genuine concern to the employees, we were willing to talk about it. In focusing on the facts, it often turned out that the problem was more fanciful than real, or that it could be more appropriately handled outside the context of periodic crisis bargaining, that it made no sense from either party's point of view to deal with it as a fixed provision of a collective agreement, that it could be dealt with without invading interests in respect to which management felt it must retain the power to act unilaterally, or that it could be traded off. In my experience, this approach to scope of bargaining questions is both realistic and constructive. If one is willing to be imaginative in dealing with a proposal and is motivated by a desire to reach a negotiated settlement, an acceptable accommodation can generally be reached. If one is unwilling to consider new proposals, conflict is a certainty and exacerbation of the dispute a likelihood.

Although some union proposals represent institutional impera-
tives, most of them (in the public sector as well as in the private
sector) are manifestations of the ambitions, fears, and frustrations of the employees represented. For purposes of this discussion, union proposals may be categorized into three groups.
The first group contains those proposals which are psychological
and political. These wash out in the bargaining process not
because they are nonnegotiable but because they are frivolous,
and for management to react to them by asserting that they invade
prerogatives or sovereignty would be gratuitous and counterproductive. The second group includes those proposals which
arguably intrude into policy matters usually thought to be within
the sole control of management, which, while seriously made,
are subject to trade-offs for improvements in wages, hours, and
working conditions.[5] The third group consists of proposals which
arguably intrude into managerial prerogatives or governmental
sovereignty, which are seriously made and which are not readily
tradable. The proposals in the last category do present problems,
but they are not usually insoluble if they are dealt with on their
merits rather than avoided on conceptualistic grounds.

The fourth set of negotiations between the New York City
School Board and the United Federation of Teachers provides an
excellent example of how problems encompassed in the third
category above can be resolved. The fourth set of negotiations
involved in part a proposal by the union that the collective bargaining agreement provide for the removal of disruptive children
from regular classrooms. The parties had great difficulty with this
issue because it involved educational policy as well as conditions
of work, but the result of their negotiations was an acceptable
compromise which preserved management's basic concern by
agreeing that the procedures would be embodied in a "Special
Circular" of the School Board which would be *appended to,* but
would not be *a part of,* the collective bargaining agreement.

The Wellington-Winter thesis is based on two assumptions:
(1) that public employee unions aspire to take over the responsibility for the management of governmental enterprises,
and (2) that they have the power to do so. Both assumptions
are, in my judgment, unsound. The scope of bargaining is partly
a function of relative bargaining power, and most employee
organizations in the public sector lack the power to force bargaining (or to force agreement) over such matters as opera-

---

[5] This subject is, of course, academic unless the aggressive party, usually the
union, has enough bargaining power to compel trade-offs.

tional efficiency, educational policy, and other matters which relate to the so-called "mission" of the enterprise.

Most public employee unions, even those which are professional in nature, do not think of collective bargaining primarily as a vehicle for social change. They do not have ambitions to take over the responsibility for running the agency. Specific aspirations will vary, of course, according to the skills and traditions of the occupational group involved. For example, teachers as a group tend to be interested in social change; and some agreements resulting from teacher-school board bargaining have worked changes in educational programming. But it is not true, at least in my experience, that teachers use collective bargaining primarily as an instrumentality for promoting social change. Public employees, including those whose responsibilities and skills are professional or quasi-professional, think of collective bargaining primarily as a vehicle for protecting and advancing their interests as an employed occupational group.

The key word is "interests." If classes are large, teachers will express their concern at the bargaining table because the size of the class creates problems affecting their working conditions. The same is true of disruptive children and student disciplinary problems. If school facilities are inadequate or poorly designed, teachers will manifest their concerns at the bargaining table, not because they want to take over the schools, but because they are frustrated by their working milieu.

It is fashionable to argue that teachers must be held "accountable" for what students can or cannot do, what they learn or do not learn. The criteria for accountability and how these criteria apply are not clear, but student performance on achievement tests appears to be a major factor. Presumably, the teacher will be rewarded with merit salary increases or penalized with decreases or perhaps dismissal once the system of academic due process (i.e., tenure) has been "decimated." Given this threatening circumstance, one can expect teachers to have an expansive view of their occupational interests. At the bargaining table, they can be expected to demand authority over those areas for which they are held accountable. If they are to be held accountable for the behavior of their colleagues, they will want a voice in recruiting; if their accountability is to be determined by tests, they will want a voice in determining what those tests are and who applies them. Clearly they will want a voice over what is taught and how it is taught. Class size and procedures for handling the disruptive child will be more important than ever.

An argument frequently made in support of a limited scope of bargaining is that third-party intervenors (i.e., mediators, fact-finders, arbitrators) will, absent such constraints, invade the business of government itself. The contention is that even though an organization lacks the power to make a credible strike threat, it may be able to gain its ends by enlisting the support of an outsider.

This argument is unpersuasive. First, mediators or fact-finders who make recommendations in respect to matters regarded by management as being in the area of prerogatives or sovereignty will not be taken very seriously by the public employer unless the employee organization has sufficient bargaining power to enforce those recommendations. Thus a mediator or a fact-finder will not be able to force incursions into the prerogatives of management or government which the organization could not achieve on its own.

The situation is different when the arbitrator has the authority to bind the parties. However, the concern still seems more fanciful than real. To illustrate, what is an arbitrator likely to do in a typical situation where the parties have bargained on a package basis and a multiplicity of issues remain unresolved (for example, wages, holidays, shift premiums, overtime, transfer procedures, work rules, or seniority in general employee units; class size, student discipline, or curricular reform in education; or civilian review boards for police)? He will be inclined to deal solely with those issues with which he feels comfortable because these are acceptable criteria, ducking other issues in respect to which he feels uncomfortable, if not incompetent. It would be a rare arbitrator presumptuous enough to make a binding determination on class size, student discipline, curriculum reform, or the existence of a civilian police review board.

Law professors and management negotiators are not the only persons who are "uptight" about the scope of collective bargaining in public employment. Many legislative bodies suffer from the same syndrome.

The Nevada statute governing public employee bargaining specifies that a local government employer need not negotiate over its right to direct its employees, to hire, to promote, to classify, transfer, assign, retain, suspend, demote, discharge, or take disciplinary action against an employee, to relieve any employee from duty because of lack of work or for any other legitimate reason, to maintain the efficiency of its governmental operations, to determine the methods, means, and personnel by which its operations are to be conducted, and to take whatever actions may be necessary to carry out its responsibilities in emergency situations. . . .

The Hawaiian statute goes even further. It makes it *illegal* for an employer and a labor organization to agree to any proposal which interferes with the right of a public employer to direct its employees, to determine qualifications, standards for work, the nature and content of examinations, to hire, to promote, transfer, assign, and retain employees in positions; to suspend, demote, discharge, or take other disciplinary action against its employees for proper cause; to relieve an employee from duty because of lack of work or other legitimate reasons; to maintain the efficiency of government operations; and to determine methods, means and personnel by which the employer's operations are to be conducted.

Even the most imaginative negotiators will have their work cut out for them under this language. Can they agree to a standard job security clause, to a provision requiring posting and bidding on promotions, to an article which makes seniority a controlling factor in lay-off and recall?

Such laws, which encourage or require public employers to avoid problems rather than deal with them, are mischievous because they produce strife and frustration rather than understanding and peaceful accommodation of conflicts between government and its employees. In the public sector, as well as the private, what is bargained about, as well as what the terms of the bargain are, should be a function of the bargaining process, not of abstract concerns over sovereignty or responsiveness to misconceived legislative constraints.

C. PERRY AND W. WILDMAN, THE IMPACT OF NEGOTIATIONS IN PUBLIC EDUCATION: THE EVIDENCE FROM THE SCHOOLS 165-71 (1970)†

The effect of collective bargaining is to grant to employees a greater measure of control over the decisions of management. A question does exist, however, as to the range of such decisions over which this control can or should be extended. On what kinds of issues have teachers sought to exercise influence through collective bargaining?

At a pragmatic level, this question centers on the scope of bargaining and the definition of the appropriate subject matter for collective bargaining. The issue, at this level, is whether collective bargaining shall be limited to "wages, hours, and conditions of employment" or shall extend to "anything that affects the

---

† Reprinted by permission of Charles A. Jones Publishing Company, Worthington, Ohio.

working life of the teacher" and "all matters which affect the quality of the educational program."

On a more basic level, the question involves the extent to which collective bargaining will alter the distribution of lay and professional control over basic educational policy. This has been raised by one union leader in the following terms:

The coming of age of the teaching profession, through collective bargaining, forces us to meet, head-on, the critical problem of the respective roles of teachers and civic and parent groups in the system of public education. . . . It is inconceivable that laymen will insist on keeping the educational process out of the control of educators, any more than they would think of depriving doctors, lawyers and theologians of the ultimate control of their respective professions. Lay groups will have to recognize and accept the realities of the new world of collective bargaining by teachers in the educational system. By definition, bargaining means co-determination, together with Boards of Education, and not unilateral decisions.

Boards of education have generally taken quite the opposite position. In the words of one board member:

It is the belief of our scheme of public education that the objectives of the school system, the basic emphasis on the teaching effort, the goals to be achieved, shall be determined by the community itself, and not by the professionals. . . . I do not believe that this philosophy is altered, or modified by the fact that a Board of Education has entered into a collective bargaining agreement with an organization which represents the teachers in that system.

Collective bargaining in the private sector has not raised a comparable issue. Despite perennial concern over management prerogatives in the face of an expanding scope of bargaining, unions have generally been more than willing to leave the basic direction of the enterprise to management. To do otherwise would require the organization to compromise its adversary role and assume responsibility for management decisions. Except in crisis situations, unions have not been willing or able to make this change in role.

It is not yet wholly clear what the experience will be in public education. The extension of collective bargaining beyond its traditional scope—salaries, benefits, a narrow range of employment conditions, and protection of individual rights in the day-to-day application of the agreement—requires two things. First, teachers must enjoy the expertise required to set policy and be able to achieve a consensus on policy issues. Second, the teacher organization must be willing to accept responsibility as well as authority in policy areas. It remains to be seen whether these conditions can be met within the adversary framework of collective bargaining, or whether they will require some other decision-making structure.

The Definition Problem

First, it should be noted that it is exceedingly difficult to distinguish between "educational policy" and "salaries and working conditions" where teacher bargaining is concerned. For instance, it is generally accepted that salary schedule and teacher benefits are "bargainable" if anything is. However, if raising teacher salaries in a district as a result of bargaining forces a budget reallocation of sums set aside for textbooks, hiring of additional professional personnel, building maintenance, or even new school construction, a decision on school district "policy" is clearly involved and may, indeed, be discussed as such, although all that is ostensibly under consideration is the salary schedule.

Or, take for example the problem of teacher transfers. Transfer rules and procedures have long been considered, in both private and public employment, as falling clearly within any reasonable definition of "working conditions." Yet, in our major cities, where schools in lower socio-economic areas have a grossly disproportionate share of the system's inexperienced teachers who are minimally qualified in terms of training and advanced degrees, the problem of fairly and equitably balancing teaching staffs, and thus curtailing the right of transfer by seniority, has become, for large city boards, a "policy" issue of great significance.

Examples of this kind pointing up the difficulty of distinguishing between "policy" and "working conditions" can be cited endlessly. Similarly, no really satisfying distinction can be made between "policy" matters and many so-called "professional" issues. For instance, basic decisions concerning many aspects of curriculum, methodology, or textbook selection are clearly at one and the same time both "policy" questions for the board or the administration and "professional" concerns of the teaching staff. However, despite overlap and untidiness, it is necessary and possible for purposes of analysis and discussion to establish a rough, somewhat arbitrary category of "policy" and "professional" issues.

It is, of course, true that in many school systems in this country, teachers, through one medium or another, have exercised significant influence over numerous policy and professional questions long before the advent of formal collective negotiation relationships. However, our focus here is the extent to which collective negotiations in the schools has been used as a vehicle for gaining a greater measure of teacher control over or participation in decisions in these areas.

Overall Impact

Investigations indicate that, as yet, the direct impact of collective negotiations on the board's freedom to set basic policy and on administrative discretion to implement that policy and decide questions involving school or system-wide "professional" judgment is not as great as might be assumed.

The evidence from the districts studied by the authors—a survey of substantive collective negotiation agreements from around the country, and awareness of the reality behind many seemingly significant contract clauses—has led to the conclusion that there are few cases where negotiations have actually forced a significant shift in basic school district policy on a reluctant, unwilling board, and few examples of a board being blocked from initiating action or change on a basic policy matter solely as a result of teacher power exercised through the negotiation process.[6] Also, administrative discretion in areas calling for significant exercise of professional judgment, while curbed or modified in certain instances, has rarely been radically altered.

It should be remembered, though, that collective negotiations in education is a quite recent and immature phenomenon, and it must be recognized that there is evidence that the potential clearly exists for the power generated by negotiations to bring about significant changes in the distribution of authority among boards, administrators, and teacher organizations with respect to "policy" and "professional" matters.

As yet, there are relatively few instances where specific, substantive issues which might be considered in the policy or "professional" realm have become the focus of pointed conflict at the bargaining table.[7] However, while bargaining over specific,

---

[6] As has been pointed out previously in this book, teacher power exercised in negotiations on salary and other cost items has resulted in significant reassessment of budget priorities and forced boards to make reallocations with definite policy consequences, at least in the short run. The present focus here, however, is on the impact of negotiations in policy areas not directly budget related.

[7] There are exceptions, of course, and dramatic ones at that. The most recent significant instance of a "policy" question providing bargaining table conflict occurred in the fall of 1967 between the New York City Board of Education and the United Federation of Teachers. A key teacher demand in New York was for the extension to more inner city schools of the expen-

tangible issues of policy or professional judgment may be rare
as yet, bargaining is being used as a vehicle for establishing procedures and structures for interaction assuring teachers a voice
in so-called policy and "professional" matters outside and independent of the process of negotiations over the collective
agreement.[8] For instance, a number of contracts have provided
for committees to be established for a wide variety of research—
deliberative and decision-making purposes embracing subjects
such as curriculum, methodology, textbook selection, promotion
to the principalship, screening and recommendations of candidates for openings at any level in the system (including the
superintendency), methods of achieving pupil and teacher integration in the system, pupil discipline, and many more. In
some instances the establishment of committees for such purposes has constituted a dramatic departure from past practice. In
other cases, the functioning reality behind the exciting contract
clause may be anything but impressive. Also, in some cases,
clauses which seem to represent significant inroads on a board's

---

sive "saturation services" More Effective Schools program. The board, which
had judged that the additional outlay for the MES program had not been
justified by the results and that extra sums might better be spent on
alternative compensatory educational activities, argued that the issue was
clearly an educational policy matter, not appropriate for resolution through
collective bargaining. Ultimately, the issue was compromised by establishment of a committee which included parent and community representatives.
This important confrontation took place well after the authors' work in the
New York system was completed; thus, a thorough investigation of this issue
is not a part of this research.

It should be noted here, too, that in several cities besides New York, the
AFT has induced boards in negotiations to allot funds for compensatory
experiments similar in nature to the New York More Effective Schools
program. Also, of course, the fall and early winter of 1968 saw the teachers
in New York City striking the system three separate times in the struggle
over decentralization and community control. The community control
dispute in New York is most complex and of a magnitude which seems to
threaten destruction or wholesale restructuring of the system; in the authors'
judgment, an escalation of basic conflict is involved which far transcends
the "normal" negotiating process. In the final chapter of this book, there
will be a brief discussion concerning the anticipated impact of teacher power
on attempts to effectively decentralize large city systems.

[8] A distinction should be recognized at this point between "teacher" in a
system and the organization representing teachers in the system. Particularly
in systems where the exclusive representative organization has far from all of
the teachers enrolled, the board and the administration may evidence much
desire to assure a continuing voice for teachers who are not in the majority
organization, especially with regard to issues involving subject matter expertise and professional judgment generally. On the other hand the right
to appoint teachers to any and all committees or councils in a school (particularly those which have been established by contract) regardless of the
subject to be considered has important organizational security and prestige
implications for the exclusive representative. Thus, the stage may be set in
bargaining for significant conflict over an important issue.

traditional, unilateral discretion over "policy" are actually not a source of conflict in negotiations; indeed, in some instances what may appear to be "revolutionary" commitments are actually encouraged by the administration and the board.

Some boards of education have agreed to clauses in collective agreements calling for mutual agreement between board and teacher organization before adoption and installation of innovative programs which might force modification of fixed class size, programming, or assignment provisions in the agreement. In one district studied, the administration rationale for accepting such a clause was to the effect that "we haven't given anything up, because if the teachers aren't in favor of a new program, it wouldn't succeed and there wouldn't be any sense in trying it out anyway." Reflecting on the need or desirability in some circumstances for administration to exercise innovative leadership, and given what is known of frequent resistance to change in large organizations (especially, perhaps, schools) one might find this justification less than satisfying. However, in none of the systems studied had new programs or innovations been proposed which might have made such a clause the focal point of conflict or dispute between a school administration and teacher organization.

In a somewhat related vein, boards have agreed to general clauses committing them to negotiate any new "policies" and/or "policy changes" which might "affect" professional personnel before adoption or implementation of same. Here again, while one can note from the board and administration point of view the loss of flexibility potentially inherent in such a clause, no issues had yet arisen in any of the districts studied which became the subject of dispute under such an agreement.

REHMUS, CONSTRAINTS ON LOCAL GOVERNMENTS IN PUBLIC EMPLOYEE BARGAINING, 67 Mich. L. Rev. 919, 921-28 (1969)†

II. Financial Limitations on Local Governmental Units

Three major sources of revenue are available for financing government: taxes on sales, on income, and on property. Of these, the property tax is the workhorse of local government; it accounts for ninety per cent of local tax revenues in the United States. Local governments in Michigan—municipalities, counties, and school districts—have no authority to levy sales taxes, and the development of city income taxes is just begin-

---

† Reprinted by permission of The Michigan Law Review Association.

ning.[9] Thus, Michiganders have traditionally relied heavily on the property tax not only to finance city and village governments, but also to support townships, counties, and school districts. In many areas, three or four local governing units, not to mention special district authorities, all depend upon the same overburdened property tax base. Nevertheless, the state legislature, jealous of its own tax sources and protective of its citizens, has not permitted much change in local taxing structure. The new Michigan Constitution adopted in 1963 theoretically delegated broad taxing powers to home rule charter cities. Despite this, the state legislature has reserved most nonproperty taxes to itself and has prohibited municipalities from levying such taxes without specific legislative authorization. Moreover, Michigan, like most states, limits the total amount of millage that can be levied upon property without specific authorization from the voters.[10] The specific constitutional limit in Michigan upon a city council's unrestricted taxing power is eighteen mills, and another fifteen mills must be divided among township boards, county supervisors, and school boards.

Even those cities that desire to tax themselves more heavily often find that the legislature forces them to beg for the privilege. States that permit cities to levy income taxes frequently place limitations upon the amounts that can be obtained through this resource. It is common to find statutes which restrict municipalities to a flat rate rather than a progressive income tax, limit the percentage of residents' income which they can tax, and place even more severe limitations upon the percentage of commuters' incomes which they can reach. Michigan, for example, limits city income taxes to a flat rate of one per cent and the tax on commuters' incomes to half that amount. Moreover, state legislatures commonly allow voters a veto over new city income taxes, a privilege seldom if ever accorded for similar state levies. Under the uniform Michigan city income tax law, the imposition of city income taxes is subject to a protest referendum. In order for city councils to obtain an affirmative vote in these referendum elections, they must often promise the voters major property tax reductions. Thus, the amount of new money generated is limited, and much of the purpose of the new taxes is defeated. Related to this, the Michigan Consti-

---

[9] At the present time, fewer than 200 cities in the United States levy an income tax, but growth of this form of taxation will undoubtedly expand rapidly.

[10] MICH. CONST. art. 9, § 6. Pennsylvania is an important exception. It is alone among the states whose public employees are strongly organized and which permit local governing bodies to levy unlimited property taxes without specific voter authorization.

tution prohibits cities from issuing general obligation bonds without an affirmative vote of property owners. Consequently, many cities, rather than attempting to get the voters to approve capital bonds, squeeze capital improvements out of their operating millage and further limit the resources available for short-run operational flexibility.

These constitutional and legislative constraints upon the taxing powers of home rule charter cities are sometimes aggravated by the cities themselves. Some cities have in their original charters limited the total operating millage which they can levy administratively to an amount lower than the state-imposed twenty-mill maximum. This handicaps them further in generating the funds necessary to meet employee demands.

In summary, a state-imposed obligation upon local governments to negotiate wages and fringe benefits inevitably entails increased budget expenditures for employee compensation. If the state simultaneously maintains existing limitations upon the unilateral taxing power of local governments, the situation often becomes intolerable. Local government administrators are helplessly caught between employee compensation demands, public unwillingness to vote for increased operating millage levied on property, and the state legislature's reluctance to allow local governments the freedom to impose income, sales, or excise taxes.

An example which highlights the problem recently occurred in Detroit. Following both a "ticket-writing strike" and a "blue flu" epidemic among police officers, the disputants finally referred the issue of police salaries to a neutral three-member panel for recommendations. The panel found that police officers' salaries should be substantially increased. Money to pay the recommended increases could be found on an emergency basis within Detroit's current operating budget, but beyond the first year, the panel concluded:

> the City of Detroit urgently needs new taxing authority which can be granted only by the State Legislature. . . . Detroit is in serious financial trouble, and we join others who have suggested that the State Legislature raise the authorized level of the municipal income tax, to restore the authority to levy local excise taxes, and to revise the 2 percent restriction on property tax levies.[11]

The problem of financial straight-jacketing in the face of collective bargaining pressure is equally serious for school dis-

---

[11] Detroit Police Dispute Panel, Findings and Recommendations on Unresolved "Economic" and Other Issues 32-33 (Feb. 27, 1968, unpublished mimeo).

tricts. Collective bargaining for Michigan public school teachers appears to have produced annual pay increases averaging ten to twenty per cent higher than those which the teachers would otherwise have received. Over all, the salaries of Michigan teachers have increased by about one third in the last three years. Most, if not all, of these increases were long overdue, but they resulted in severe pressure on school district budgets. In the 1966-1967 academic year, the first full year of teacher bargaining under the 1965 Act, these increases in teacher compensation were paid for largely from minor economies and from new revenues. Among the new revenue sources were increases in state aid, imposition of previously authorized millage, and growth in assessed valuation. In the second full year of collective bargaining, however, school districts began to use less desirable sources of funds to pay the wage increases demanded by organized teachers. Administrators generated new sources of funds through liquidation of operating reserves and contingency funds, transfer of millage from building and site reserves to operating accounts, and substantial program cutbacks. Most important— and despite the fact that Michigan law is generally construed to forbid school districts from deficit financing—a quarter of the school districts studied in one survey showed a deficit by the end of fiscal 1968.

The financial constraints on local governments constitute the most serious problem they face in coping with public employee collective bargaining. However, public officials must contend with at least three other problems which, although related to financing, are not as severe as the shortage of funds per se. The first problem is that of coordinating the budget-making process with collective bargaining. An acute aspect of this problem is the difficulty which local governmental units face in meeting budget deadlines, particularly when the state legislature itself imposes the deadline. The collective bargaining process often entails months of negotiations, mediation, and fact-finding or arbitration; it does not respect time limits. Yet budgets must be filed under the law, and this requires local officials to make preliminary estimates. As a result, municipalities may often feel constrained to take rigid positions based upon estimates which were submitted to the legislature before bargaining is completed. A second aspect of the coordination problem arises after budget submission deadlines have been passed: the issue then is whether negotiated pay increases should apply prospectively from the date of the agreement or retroactively from the beginning of the budget period. Finally, it may be difficult to synchronize legislative decisions concerning the amount of funds to be allocated to local governmental units with local governmental responsibilities in the bargaining process. For instance, teacher bargaining for the 1967-1968 school year in Michigan proved exceptionally difficult because the state legislature failed to act on the school aid formula until August 1967. Consequently, spring and summer bargaining in many school districts dragged on beyond budget submission deadlines because school administrators were unable to predict how much state funding would be available to help them meet teacher demands. The state legislature avoided this problem the following year by acting on the school aid formula in April, well before budget deadlines. Perhaps as a result, a smaller number of bargaining impasses occurred during teacher negotiations for the 1968-1969 school year. This problem of coordinating the budget-making process with collective bargaining is more an irritating than an insurmountable obstacle. The difficulties can be minimized by using open-ended budgets, resorting to short-term internal and external borrowing, allowing more time for bargaining before budget deadlines, and negotiating collective bargaining contracts for longer terms than are currently settled upon.

A second complication of collective bargaining in the public sector results from the tradition that public budgets and accounts are not secret documents. In the private sector the employer may under most circumstances refuse to disclose his profit and loss figures, but the public employer is forced to open his books to all interested persons. As a result, any operating reserves or contingency funds that may be available simply become targets for the employees to shoot at. Prudent management —whether in business or in public administration—ordinarily requires the retention of some operating reserves. It is not reprehensible for a public administrator to maintain a reserve account to pay operating costs in periods before tax money becomes available or to provide for unforeseen contingencies. In practice, however, even if cities and school districts have not had to resort to deficit financing in order to meet collective bargaining demands, the retention of operating reserves has proved almost impossible. Many cities and most school districts in Michigan, their reserves depleted to satisfy the bargaining demands of employees, are now operating on little better than a year-to-year cash basis. In jurisdictions where reserves remain, this result has often been accomplished by padding various budget items—a recurrent practice but hardly one to be encouraged.

A third anomaly of collective bargaining in the public sector is that the union can often invade the management decision-making structure. Particularly in public school and junior college districts, organized teacher groups have succeeded in electing their members, relatives, or sympathizers to school and governing boards. Under these circumstances it is often impossible for the management decision-making group to hide its bargaining strategy and tactics from employees. Democratic government does allow almost anyone to run for office, but this tactic may make collective bargaining a farce.

III. Other State-Imposed Constraints on Collective Bargaining

State legislatures have imposed many limitations upon the authority of local governmental units to manage their own personnel systems. One of the most common limitations is the statutory or de facto requirement that home rule cities establish a civil service and merit system for recruitment and promotion of personnel. This requirement, although beneficial in its thrust and general impact upon city government, operates to reduce substantially the flexibility of local governmental units at the collective bargaining table. State legislatures have seldom given enough thought to the problems that may be encountered when they impose a collective bargaining requirement covering "terms and conditions of employment" upon an existing merit structure.

The civil service concept ordinarily contemplates the establishment of a nonpartisan board or commission at the local or state level with rulemaking authority to assure adherence to the merit principle. In practice, merit systems have over the years grown to encompass many aspects of employee relations and personnel management other than recruitment, classification, and promotion. These new areas of concern include the handling of grievances, employee training, salary administration, safety, morale, and attendance control programs—the very subjects that most employee organizations regard as appropriate for bargaining. If an independent civil service commission has authority over bargainable matters, then perhaps bargaining responsibilities should lie with the commission. But as it is, authority to bargain is usually vested in the chief executive officer of the local government unit. If he has the duty to bargain over the terms and conditions of employment while authority over many personnel matters remains with an independent commission, the scope of negotiations will be unduly restricted.

This problem is not insoluble. If the principle of collective bargaining by local governments is to be effectuated, all non-merit functions should be transferred from the civil service commission to a personnel department under the chief executive officer of each local unit. In practice, however, such a transfer of authority has seldom been made. In Massachusetts, for example, the state collective bargaining law for public employees specifically states that it shall not "diminish the authority and power of the civil service commission, or any retirement or personnel board established by law. . . ." The Wisconsin public employment relations statute excludes from the mandatory scope of bargaining a large range of matters established by law or governed by civil service. In practice, in localities where public employee collective bargaining is fully developed, informal bargaining arrangements to deal with these problems are already appearing.[12] At the very least, any state considering collective bargaining legislation for public employees should carefully analyze its personnel system in order to minimize the potential conflict between bargaining relationships, existing merit systems, and the rules promulgated by civil service boards and commissions.

State legislatures contemplating collective bargaining in the public sector should also ensure that they have not imposed undue restrictions upon the permissible scope of bargaining. Some years ago the Michigan legislature imposed upon its municipalities a fifty-six-hour maximum duty week for firemen. This law not only raised municipal fire protection costs substantially, but also eliminated from the scope of bargaining one of the major subjects which should have been left there. In Pennsylvania, the state legislature prohibited combined police-fire departments, another potentially bargainable subject. Laws of this kind place many local governments, particularly smaller communities, in a Procrustean bed. These municipalities are obligated to bargain over wages and hours, yet uniform state laws fundamentally weaken their negotiating position by creating mandatory high-cost requirements without the freedom to trade cost reductions in one area for new expenditures in another.

State legislatures have also limited the negotiating flexibility of school boards. For example, the Attorney General of Michigan has recently ruled that under existing law boards of education lack statutory authority to award severance pay, to pay for any unused portion of sick leave at the end of a school year or upon termination of employment, or to reimburse teachers' tuition

---

12 For example, Michigan's Wayne County has created special labor boards with the power to negotiate collective agreements with employees. The labor board for a negotiation is composed of a representative of the county Civil Service Board, a representative of the county Board of Supervisors, and a representative from the particular administrative unit involved (such as the county Highway Department).

for college credit courses beyond the baccalaureate degree. Under the Michigan collective bargaining statute, school boards had assumed prior to the Attorney General's ruling that they were obligated to bargain on all of these subjects, and concessions had in fact been made on many. Probably a majority of existing teacher collective bargaining agreements in Michigan call for one or more of these payments that have now been declared to be unlawful. The attempt of school boards to negotiate such benefits back out of existing contracts is likely to engender bitter conflict. A new grant of authority to make the disputed payments would seem to be a preferable alternative. . . .

NOTES

1. Increasing attention is being paid to the structure of bargaining in the public sector. As indicated in the following comments of Irving Sabghir, there are a number of alternative approaches:

Although definitive data are not available, it is assumed that within a particular labor market, there is a high degree of clustering on wages, benefits, and other central bargaining items. It may also be hypothesized that such clustering has probably increased as a consequence of the Taylor Act as both employee organizations and public employers, at least informally or more purposefully, improve their respective channels of communication. If this is so, one may seriously question whether balkanization of bargaining, especially in schools, is sensible. A number of alternative bargaining structures may be considered.

First, with respect to schools, the Act might establish regions for purposes of bargaining. These might be on the basis of labor markets, or 100,000 pupil groupings. New units and bargaining agents would have to be determined. There could be one region-wide agreement for each bargaining unit, i.e., teachers, administrators, service personnel, etc.[13] The "employer" could be a duly constituted body established especially for this purpose representing the school boards in the area. Although this is the most radical possibility it may well be the most rational in that it gives full recognition to the current impact of key settlements within a labor market or region.

---

[13] This would be quite analogous to the bargaining structure for New York state employees. Indeed, a statewide approach could ultimately flow from a regional structure. It might be noted that in Hawaii teachers bargain statewide and are certified on the basis of a single statewide unit.

This approach would, admittedly, enlarge the geographical area of bargaining and thus intensify the impact of a possible dispute. However, the increased "monopoly" power this could give to teachers might be matched by a higher order of responsibility on the part of both parties arising out of their recognizing the expanded scope of a possible conflict and thus lead to more realistic and good faith bargaining over mutual problems. It should also be noted that adoption of this approach may have far-reaching consequences on the financing of schools because of the differences in fiscal abilities among districts that may be placed in a common region. Indeed, this could hasten the advent of full State assumption of school costs, at least for certain major items, and even statewide bargaining.

This regional structure of bargaining may also be applicable to other public employees where pattern settlements are significant. For example, the police and firemen in Albany-Schenectady-Troy (Tri-City area) are attempting to forge a body that would present a single front to the public employers. It is possible that such developments in bargaining structure might, of necessity, rekindle interest in the metropolitanization of certain public services.

A second possibility would be to permit individual bargaining agents for each school district as at present, but for the Act to mandate certain issues as regionwide, e.g., wages, benefits, school year calendar, and other matters such as local district issues, e.g., school day, teacher aides, use of school facilities. Employee organizations and school boards would have to establish bargaining structures appropriate to this two-tiered system.[14] This structure, too, could be applicable to other public employers.

A third approach would be for the Act explicitly to permit and encourage such structural groupings indicated above but not to mandate them. This would legalize co-ordinated or coalition bargaining, which might otherwise be challenged under the present representation structure.

---

[14] This structure might be more acceptable to the parties since it does retain, at least initially, some local control. Significantly, this approach is being developed at the state level where "national" issues will be bargained at the state level, while "local" issues will be bargained at the departmental or even work-site level. It will, evidently, also be applied at the State University where a single statewide unit has been established for faculty and other professional employees. Thus, university-wide salaries, benefits, etc., will be negotiated centrally, while certain purely local matters could be bargained at each campus.

Sabghir, *The Taylor Act: A Brief Look After Three Years,* in 1970 SUPPLEMENT TO REPORT OF TASK FORCE ON STATE AND LOCAL GOVERNMENT LABOR RELATIONS 30, 34 (1971). *See generally* Simon, *The School Finance Decisions: Collective Bargaining and Future Finance Systems,* 82 YALE L.J. 409 (1973).

2. New York City's bargaining law expressly provides for multi-level bargaining. The New York City Office of Collective Bargaining explained it as follows:

The bargaining structure provided by the New York City Collective Bargaining Law divides the subjects of bargaining into five distinct levels that do not overlap. The first four relate to employees other than those in the uniformed forces and include the general area of bargaining on salaries, hours, and working conditions applicable to particular citywide job titles. There are three special areas "in which efficiency of operation mandate uniformity." These include matters which must be uniform for:

—all employees in a department
—all employees in the Career and Salary Plan
—all employees in a pension system.

The fifth area of bargaining relates solely to all employees in the uniformed forces: police, fire, sanitation, and correction services.

"Designation" to bargain on matters which must be uniform is obtained from the Board of Certification upon verification that the union is the certified representative of bargaining units which include more than 50% of all employees of the department, career and salary plan or pension system involved.

It should be noted that such designation of a bargaining representative does not impair the right of the unions holding citywide job title certifications to continue to negotiate salaries, hours, and working conditions for employees in these titles. Also, the check-off right extends only to the unions which hold citywide job title certifications and not to the union which may be designated to represent employees in the three special areas. NEW YORK CITY OFFICE OF COLLECTIVE BARGAINING, 1970-1971 ANNUAL REPORTS 11 (1972).

SMITH, STATE AND LOCAL ADVISORY REPORTS ON PUBLIC
EMPLOYMENT LABOR LEGISLATION: A COMPARATIVE ANALYSIS,
67 Mich. L. Rev. 891, 904-08 (1969)†

C. *The Scope of Collective Bargaining*

The advisory reports generally recognize that the determination of appropriate subjects for collective bargaining in the
public sector involves problems of the first magnitude. One
critical problem is that public agencies, without some accommo-
dating change in applicable law, may lack the authority to
make binding contractual commitments relating to certain subjects. For instance, limitations on discretionary authority are
found in civil service legislation, municipal charter provisions,
school codes, and other special legislation. A second question,
more of policy than of law, is whether some subject matters
should be entirely excluded from the scope of collective bargaining because of the special responsibility of public agencies
to carry out public service functions. If there is to be a mandate for collective bargaining in the public sector, to what extent
can or should the legislation take cognizance of these factors?
Alternatively, should the state legislation merely include a broad
duty to bargain, modeled on the NLRA, which would leave
legal questions to be decided by the courts and policy questions
to be decided by the processes of collective bargaining?

The Michigan Act of 1965 followed the NLRA pattern by
prescribing a general obligation to bargain collectively on wages,
hours, and other terms and conditions of employment. The Act
also contained a proviso similar to those in the NLRA guaranteeing the right of an individual employee to have his grievance
adjusted at any time.

The Taylor Committee recognized that, as in the private
sector, labor organizations in the public sector have broad bargaining aspirations. However, it noted that "the expectations
. . . concerning what they can negotiate about are limited by
the fact that certain terms of employment are mandated by
legislative enactment." As an example, the Committee referred
to employees whose terms of employment are fixed by civil
service legislation. The Committee ultimately concluded that, as
a practical matter, the closest that political entities can come to
traditional collective bargaining is "negotiation of terms on
the assumption of the necessity for a joint commitment of the
negotiating parties to the terms, but with the necessity to seek
approval and the appropriations to implement any agreement
from a legislative body." The Committee noted that there can

---

† Reprinted by permission of The Michigan Law Review Association.

be traditional collective bargaining only "if the public through the action of its legislatures is ready to delegate to a bargaining 'team' composed of the executives of government agencies and the negotiators for employee organizations the virtual determination of its budget, the allocation of public revenues to alternative uses, and the setting of the tax rate necessary to balance that budget"—a "delegation scarcely likely to occur in the foreseeable future."

The New Jersey Commission tersely recommended "that the scope of negotiations should be limited by the discretionary or recommending power of the appointing authority in public employment. . . ." The reference to "recommending power," if written into law, could leave the range of negotiations very broad indeed. Of course, if the "discretionary power" of the employing authority is limited, the results of the bargaining process might not be conclusive. One possible solution to this problem is to specify that the results reached in collective bargaining shall prevail over any pre-existing statutory limitation on the authority of the employing agency. For example, the draft statute proposed by the Connecticut Commission included the following provision:

> Where there is a conflict between any agreement reached by a municipal employer and an employee organization and approved in accordance with the provisions of this Act and any charter, special act, ordinance, or rules and regulations adopted by the municipal employer or its agents . . . or any general statute regulating the hours of work of policemen or firemen, the terms of such agreement shall prevail.

The Connecticut body recognized only two qualifications to this principle: first, collective bargaining should not interfere with civil service control of merit-rating systems; second, every collective bargaining agreement must be approved by the legislative body with authority over the employing agency. Under these qualifications, the legislative body would retain ultimate authority to reject demands which it considered inconsistent with sound fiscal or other policies. Despite these limitations, the Connecticut recommendations on the scope of bargaining represent a position strikingly different from the far more cautious approach taken by the Taylor Committee.

Most of the advisory groups considered whether the legislature should pass an explicit statutory requirement wholly reserving certain managerial "prerogatives" as outside the scope of collective bargaining. Following the pattern set by the Goldberg Task Force Report at the federal level, most of the groups favored such provisions. Exceptions are found in the Connecticut and Michigan reports. Public employers represented to the Michigan Advisory Committee that the 1965 Michigan Act should be amended in order to preserve certain managerial prerogatives. The Michigan Committee, while cognizant of the potentially serious problems underlying these suggestions, did not consider them of such immediate importance as to warrant legislative changes without further study.

The Taylor Committee did not deal as explicitly with this matter as did some of the groups, but its perceptive analysis of the problems, discussed under the caption "Character of Participating Activity," assumed that collective bargaining should not interfere with subject areas now delegated to various governmental authorities. The Report also noted that "the issue of 'retained rights' of the employer (related in public service to the proper performance of both the legislative and executive functions) is more difficult to deal with in the public sector than in the private sector." The Illinois Report stated:

> It should be the exclusive function of each public employing agency to determine the mission of the agency, set standards of services to be offered to the public, and exercise control and discretion over its organization and operations.
>
> It should be the right of each public employing agency to direct its employees, take disciplinary action, relieve its employees from duties because of lack of work or for other legitimate reasons, and determine the methods, means, and personnel by which the agency's operations are to be conducted. But this should not preclude employees from negotiating or raising grievances about the practical consequences that decisions on these matters may have on wages, hours, and working conditions.

The Pennsylvania Report simply stated that collective bargaining should be "appropriately qualified by a recognition of existing laws dealing with aspects of the same subject matter and by a carefully defined reservation of managerial rights."

The Los Angeles Report followed a more conservative (or some would say, more sophisticated) view of the scope of public employee collective bargaining. It also presented perhaps the most complete supporting rationale. Employee organizations, of course, had argued before the Committee that the "duty to bargain" should be stated in general terms such as those employed in the NLRA in order to leave the broadest scope for collective bargaining. County officials maintained that failure clearly to enumerate certain functions and duties as reserved to various agencies of county government would invite meaningless and unlawful attempts on the part of employee organizations to widen the legally permissible scope of negotiation. The Committee stated its position as follows:

> On this issue we believe that attempts to draw an exact analogy with the private sector are misguided and dangerous. The extent to which private employers have agreed to share traditional managerial decisions with labor organizations has varied widely between industries and sometimes between enterprises in the same industry. Concessions on this subject are often merely pragmatic adjustments to special situations. In the event of bargaining impasses over this question, private employers and unions can usually resort to the economic weapons of lockout and strike.
>
> In the public sector, however, the situation is quite different. Managers of governmental agencies must insure that the functions intrusted to them are carried out promptly and without interruption. We think they should have the right initially to determine the manner in which these functions are to be performed. Accordingly, the provision we recommend explicitly sets forth those rights that County management may exercise unilaterally and without prior negotiation with employees or their organizations.
>
> At the same time, we recognize that actions taken by management, purportedly "in the public interest," sometimes are unnecessary or arbitrary. We have therefore provided that nothing in the section on employer rights shall preclude employees from raising grievances about the practical consequences that decisions on matters reserved for management may have on wages, hours, and other terms and conditions of employment.

The Los Angeles Committee then distinguished between the "scope of consultation" and the scope of "negotiation": those matters explicitly made nonnegotiable by ordinance, but which affect employee relations, should be subject to "consultation" between employees and the employing agency. Thus under the proposed ordinance "every reasonable effort shall be made by management to consult with employees or their representatives prior to initiating basic changes in any rule or procedure affecting employee relations." Since the distinction between negotiation and consultation will "not always [be] clearly discernible," the Committee felt that it would be unwise "to try to draw [such a line] once and for all and for all subjects. . . ." Rather, the Committee suggested that "in close and doubtful cases the [proposed] enforcement commission be empowered to draw the line on an *ad hoc* basis." It will be interesting to follow the experience in Los Angeles County to see whether the somewhat ambiguous distinction between negotiation and consultation produces results markedly different than those that would be expected under the NLRA's general definition of the scope of collective bargaining.

Some proposals for an explicit reservation of managerial prerogatives in public employers would constitute, if adopted, a mandate that collective bargaining agreements in the public sector should include something approaching—perhaps even more comprehensive than—the "management rights" provisions frequently negotiated into private sector contracts. I have some doubt about the feasibility, or even the desirability, of this kind of attempted restriction on the scope of public employee collective bargaining. Private sector unions generally do not quarrel with the position that the ability of a private firm to determine such matters as the kind and quality of its products or services is and should remain a managerial prerogative. However, there are some categories of employees in the public sector who, by virtue of the nature of their occupations and professional interests, might claim to have a negotiable concern with the "mission" or goals of particular public agencies. For example, public school teachers may reasonably assert that they have a legitimate interest not only in compensation and "conditions" of employment, but also in the fundamental educational policies to be followed in a school system. Perhaps the same could be said of police and fire fighters. Obviously, a public agency cannot abdicate all of its public responsibility to teachers, policemen, or fire fighters, but an obligation to negotiate—to share in decision-making—does not necessarily involve abdication. Indeed, it can be argued that the quality of many public services would be substantially improved if those most directly involved in, and dedicated to, the "mission" of the agency had a more direct hand in the policy-making process.

NOTE

Among the many useful articles examining the scope of bargaining in the public sector are Sabghir, *The Scope of Bargaining in Public Sector Collective Bargaining*, A Report sponsored by the New York State Employment Relations Board (October 1970) ; U.S. Dep't of Labor, Scope of Bargaining in the Public Sector—Concepts and Problems (1972) ; Edwards, *The Emerging Duty to Bargain in the Public Sector*, 71 Mich. L. Rev. 885 (1973) ; Kilberg, *Appropriate Subjects for Bargain-*

ing in Local Government Labor Relations, 30 MD. L. REV. 179 (1970) ; Gerhart, *The Scope of Bargaining in Local Government Negotiations,* 20 LAB. L.J. 545 (1969) ; Blair, *State Legislative Control Over the Conditions of Public Employment: Defining the Scope of Collective Bargaining for State and Municipal Employees,* 26 VAND. L. REV. 1 (1973) ; Vial, *The Scope of Bargaining Controversy: Substantive Issues vs. Procedural Hang-ups,* CALIFORNIA PUBLIC EMPLOYEE RELATIONS No. 15, at 4 (Nov. 1972).

2. Wages, Hours and Working Conditions—What is Negotiable?

WESTWOOD COMMUNITY SCHOOLS
Michigan Employment Relations Commission
1972 MERC Lab. Op. 313

[The Westwood Education Association (Association) filed an unfair labor practice charge against the Westwood Community Schools (Employer) alleging, *inter alia,* that the Employer vio-lated Section 10 (a) and (e) of the Michigan Public Employment Relations Act (PERA) by refusing to negotiate with the Asso-ciation over the beginning and ending dates of the school term and by unilaterally establishing said dates. The Trial Examiner ruled "that there is no obligation on the Employer to bargain in regard to the opening of school and that subject is a voluntary subject of bargaining." The Association filed a timely exception to the Trial Examiner's recommendation that this portion of the Association's unfair labor practice charge be dismissed.]

The issue of whether the opening date of the school term is a mandatory subject of bargaining is one of first impression for this Commission. We have never definitively established a list of subjects which lie within the scope of bargaining, nor does PERA define such subjects. Section 15 of the statute provides that the collective bargaining duty of the Employer is ". . . to meet at reasonable times and confer in good faith with respect to wages, hours and other terms and conditions of employ-ment. . . ." Disputes involving bargainable subjects have been resolved on a case by case basis. City of Detroit, Police Depart-ment, 1971 MERC Lab. Op. 237, 241.

This ad hoc method of determination has, however, embraced the traditional private sector distinctions between mandatory, non-mandatory and illegal subjects of bargaining. Bullock Creek School District, 1969 MERC Lab. Op. 497, 504; City of Detroit, Police Department, *supra;* Coleman Community Schools, 1970 MERC Lab. Op. 813. While we have made no extensive analysis of these categories of bargaining proposals, we have held that the words ". . . other terms and conditions of employment . . ." from Section 15 of PERA mean "those items which *affect* employees after they have become employees." City of Detroit, Police Department, *supra* at 249 (emphasis added).

The traditional classification of bargaining proposals was enunciated in the leading United States Supreme Court case, National Labor Relations Board v. Wooster Division of Borg-Warner, 356 U.S. 342, 42 L.R.R.M. 2034 (1958). Here, the employer insisted that its collective bargaining contract with some of its employees contain a ballot clause calling for a pre-strike secret vote of the employees as to the employer's last offer, and a recognition clause which excluded as a party to the contract the International Union which had been certified by the NLRB as the employees' exclusive bargaining agent and substituted for it the agent's uncertified local affiliate. The NLRB found that the employer's insistence upon either of such clauses amounted to an unlawful refusal to bargain. Borg-Warner Corporation, 113 N.L.R.B. 1288, 36 L.R.R.M. 1439 (1955). The Sixth Circuit of the United States Court of Appeals upheld the Labor Board's finding as to the recognition clause, but reversed on the ballot clause issue. NLRB v. Wooster Division of Borg-Warner, 236 F.2d 898, 38 L.R.R.M. 2660 (6th Cir., 1956). In reversing the Court of Appeals' decision as to the latter issue, the Supreme Court sustained the Labor Board's opinion.

The Court held that both the ballot clause and the recognition clause are not mandatory subjects of bargaining; thus, the employer could not insist upon contractual inclusion of these subjects. It reached this result by reading together Sections 8 (a) (5) and 8 (d) of the National Labor Relations Act. The former makes it an unfair labor practice for an employer to "refuse to bargain collectively with the representatives of his employees." National Labor Relations Act, 29 U.S.C. § 158 (a) (5). The latter defines collective bargaining as the

". . . performance of the mutual obligation of the employer and the representative of the employees to meet at reasonable times and confer in good faith with respect to wages, hours and other terms and conditions of employment . . . but such obligation does not compel either party to agree to a proposal or require the making of a concession." *Id.,* 29 U.S.C. § 158 (d) .[3]

The court found that the duty to bargain is limited to the subjects (mandatory) "wages, hours and other terms and conditions of

_____

[3] The PERA analogues to these provisions can be found at Sections 10 (e) and 15 of the Act.

employment," and that neither party is legally obligated to yield. "As to other matters (non-mandatory), however, each party is free to bargain or not to bargain, and to agree or not to agree." 356 U.S. at 349, 42 L.R.R.M. at 2036. The Court explicitly held that ". . . (I) t is lawful to insist upon matters within the scope of mandatory bargaining and unlawful to insist upon matters without. . . ." *Id.*, 42 L.R.R.M. at 2037.

Thus, the teaching of *Borg-Warner*, is that the employer cannot take unilateral action with regard to a mandatory subject of bargaining where there has been no bargaining. But the parties do not have to agree. In the absence of agreement, the employer may act unilaterally. NLRB v. American National Insurance Co., 343 U.S. 395, 30 L.R.R.M. 2147 (1952). Under *Borg-Warner*, the employer may act without bargaining as to non-mandatory subjects of bargaining.

The elusive question that continually plagues courts, administrative tribunals and practitioners focuses on the phrase "other terms and conditions of employment." No satisfactory answer has been formulated to resolve this problem; *Borg-Warner* provides little help.

The Supreme Court again dealt with this issue in Fibreboard Paper Products Corp. v. NLRB, 379 U.S. 203, 57 L.R.R.M. 2609 (1964). The Court held that an employer is required to bargain over the contracting out of bargaining unit work, within the limits of the evidence in that case. This decision has not been universally acclaimed; indeed, it has generated substantial criticism. M. Bernstein, "The NLRB's Adjudication—Rule Making Dilemma under the Administrative Procedure Act," 79 Yale L.J. 571, 580 (1970). However, the tests established in *Fibreboard* for the determination of a mandatory subject of bargaining are helpful. Summers, "Labor Law in the Supreme Court," 1964 Term, 75 Yale L.J. 59, 60 (1965). The Court noted that industrial practices in this country are a factor in determining a statutory subject of bargaining. The majority in *Fibreboard* held that bargaining is compelled to promote one of the primary purposes of the National Labor Relations Act, viz., ". . . the peaceful settlement of industrial disputes by subjecting labor-management controversies to the mediatory influence of negotiation. . . ." 379 U.S. at 211, 57 L.R.R.M. at 2612. From this premise flow two tests: (1) Is the subject of such vital concern to both labor and management that it is likely to lead to controversy and industrial conflict? And (2) is collective bargaining appropriate for resolving such issues?

The most recent decision by the Court dealing with this issue reaffirmed the *Fibreboard* test. Chemical Workers v. Pittsburgh

Plate Glass Co., 40 U.S.L.W. 4043, 78 L.R.R.M. 2974 (U.S., Dec. 7, 1971). In holding that benefits of retired employees are not within the mandatory rule the Court said, ". . . in each case the question is . . . whether it (the subject) vitally affects the terms and conditions of their (bargaining unit employees) employment." *Id.*, at 4050, 78 L.R.R.M. at 2982. However, the Court carefully pointed out in footnote No. 19 that the effect on the employer's freedom to conduct business must also be considered. *Id.*

This caveat specifically refers to Mr. Justice Stewart's concurring opinion in *Fibreboard,* wherein he argued that the majority's interpretation of the equivocal phrase "conditions of employment" ". . . seems to imply that any issue which may reasonably divide an employer and his employees must be the subject of compulsory collective bargaining." 379 U.S. at 221, 57 L.R.R.M. at 2616. After concluding that the term "conditions of employment" offers no workable guide, the opinion intuitively distinguished between ". . . managerial decisions which lie at the core of entrepreneurial control . . . and (those) not in themselves primarily about conditions of employment." *Id.* at 223, 57 L.R.R.M. at 2617. Those decisions which are fundamental to the basic direction of a corporate enterprise should not be subject to compulsory bargaining. *Id.*

The instant case presents the challenge the Court faced in *Fibreboard*. The Employer argues that establishment of the opening day of school is a management function not subject to mandatory bargaining. The Education Association responds that the Employer's unilateral act affected a vital employee interest. We agree with the Association that the careful planning of summer interlude activities, e.g., advanced study, supplementary employment, travel and vacation, causes the teachers to have a substantial interest in the opening date of school. Thus, the classic confrontation between management rights and employee interests is created. This conflict can be appropriately reconciled by balancing the interests involved.

In this process, we are confined by the doctrine of illegal delegation of power which commands that certain discretionary decisions be made solely by a designated official rather than through the collective bargaining process. Wellington and Winter, "The Limits of Collective Bargaining in Public Employment," 78 Yale L.J. 1107, 1109 (1969). In the instant case, neither the Michigan Statutes nor the regulations of the State Department of Education interfere with a holding that the school calendar is a subject which must be bargained. With respect to the opening of school, the Michigan law provides only that the school year of all school districts shall commence on the first day of July. MCLA 340.353. State law also requires that every school district shall determine the length of the school term, but that the length of the term shall be a minimum of 180 days. MCLA 340.575, as amended. Since these rules are silent as to establishing the opening day of school, we find that there are no delegation problems created by submitting the school calendar to bargaining.

The rather substantial interest which the school teachers have in planning their summer activities outweigh any claim of interference with the right to manage the school district.

We agree with the holding of the Wisconsin Supreme Court, which has said, in affirming a Wisconsin Employment Relations Commission decision, that the school calendar (including the opening day of school) has a direct and intimate relationship to the salaries and working conditions of the teachers. City of Madison v. Wisconsin Employment Relations Board, 37 Wis. 2d 43, 155 N.W.2d 78, 65 L.R.R.M. 2488 (1967). In accord with that decision is Norfolk Education Association v. South District of Norfolk, Nebraska Court of Industrial Relations, Case No. 40, October 6, 1971, 430 GERR B-7 (December 6, 1971).

Since a Michigan school district has already been required to bargain collectively with respect to certain aspects of the school calendar, e.g., holiday and vacation dates (Reese Public School District, 1967 MERC Lab. Op. 489), requiring the employer to bargain about the beginning and terminating dates of the school term does not impair significantly its right to manage. Nor are we impressed by the argument that bargaining with the teachers over the school calendar would foreclose bargaining on this subject with other school district employees. Other subjects of bargaining affect more than one bargaining unit. Bargaining over such subjects as fringe benefits, holidays, hours and the work day, vacations and wages, as well as the school calendar, would be facilitated by joint or coalition bargaining. Furthermore, the order to bargain does not command that there be agreement; we only order that the parties bargain in good faith about this subject.

A balancing approach to bargaining may be more suited to the realities of the public sector than the dichotomized scheme— mandatory and non-mandatory—used in the private sector. The Supreme Court in *Fibreboard* argued that this private sector concept was necessary to preserve a primary purpose of the National Labor Relations Act—industrial peace. The Court argued that labor disputes should be peacefully settled by subjecting the controversies to the "mediatory influence of negotiation." This scheme prohibits the use of economic weapons to compel agreement to discuss non-mandatory subjects of bargaining but strikes are permissible once the point of impasse concerning mandatory subjects of bargaining is reached. Economic force is illegal in the public sector in Michigan as PERA prohibits strikes by public employees. In Michigan, in the public sector, economic battle is to be replaced by invocation of the impasse resolution procedures of mediation and fact finding.

An expansion of the subjects about which the public employer ought to bargain, unlike the private sector, should not result in a corresponding increase in the use of economic force to resolve impasses. In the absence of legal public sector strikes, our only proper concern in the area of subjects of bargaining is whether the employer's management functions are being unduly restrained. All bargaining has some limiting effect on an employer.

Therefore, we will not order bargaining in those cases where the subjects are demonstrably within the core of entrepreneurial control. Although such subjects may affect interests of employees, we do not believe that such interests outweigh the right to manage.

In reversing the Trial Examiner on this issue, we hold that the opening and terminating days of the school term are subjects about which the employer must bargain. However, we apply this decision prospectively, and we hold that the Employer did not commit an unfair labor practice in its unilateral setting of the opening day of school. . . .

Chairman Howlett, dissenting: . . .

The opening (and, indeed, the closing) date for the school year is a function which should be within the province of the school board. It is a power which should not be delegated, even to the extent of bargaining.

While Michigan statutes do not specifically vest this power in boards of education, it flows logically from MCLA 340.353 (Mich. Stat. Ann. 15.3353) which specifies that the school year of all school districts commences on the 1st day of July, and the requirement of MCLA 340.575 (Mich. Stat. Ann. 15.3375) that the length of the term shall be a minimum of 180 days. Within these two specifications, the school board should determine when the schools open and the period within which the 180 days (or more, at the option of the school board) shall be held.

It is urged that the opening day of school (as well as the calendar) has a direct and intimate relationship to the salaries and working conditions of the teachers. The majority opinion notes the contention of the Association "that the careful planning of summer activities, e.g., advance study, supplementary employment, travel and vacation causes the teachers to have a substantial interest in the opening date of school." And, the parents of children have summer interlude activities which cause them to have a substantial interest in the opening day of school. The parents are not—and should not be—part of the bargaining process. Under the school law, the members of the school board are elected to represent the citizens of the district, including the parents. The parents' interest in the opening date of school is equal, if not paramount, to that of the teachers. This interest of the citizens of the district, including the parents, is not, however, within the sphere of collective bargaining. Their rights are in the political (using the word in its broad sense) arena. The legislative body—the school board—should make the decision of the period that school will be in session for all citizens of the district.

The majority notes that the United States Supreme Court, in Allied Chemical and Alkali Workers v. Pittsburgh Plate Glass Co., — U.S. —, 92 S. Ct. 383, 78 L.R.R.M. 2974 (1971), said that ". . . in each case the question is . . . whether it (the subject) vitally affects the terms and conditions of their (bargaining unit employees) *employment.*" (Emphasis supplied.)

Here I depart from the rationale of the majority. Is the opening date of school a term or condition of *employment?* While teachers may be considered employees for some purposes from the date they are required by law to notify the school board that they will return for the next school year (MCLA 38.83, Mich. Stat. Ann. 15.1983), or, in the case of non-tenured teachers, have signed a contract, teachers' active employment does not start until the day they are required to report at the beginning of the school year.

We have held, as the majority opinion notes, that bargaining is required with respect to holiday and vacation dates (Reese Public School District, 1967 MERC Lab. Op. 489). These are working conditions within the period of employment. Actual employment does not start until teachers report to work. There is no term or condition of employment prior to the *start* of employment. This is consistent with our decision in City of Detroit, Police Department, 1971 MERC Lab. Op. 237, that recruitment standards (before employment begins) are not included with "other terms and conditions of employment," as that phrase is used in Section 15 of PERA.[1]

---

[1] Teachers are often paid over the 12 months of the year. This is, in most instances, at the choice of the teacher. However, the teacher is paid for services *performed* from the day school opens until the day school closes.

Perhaps the nearest parallel in the private sector is the right of management to determine when an establishment shall be opened for the manufacture of the product produced or performing of the service offered, by the employer.

NOTES

1. In North Dearborn Heights School Dist., 1966 MERC Lab. Op. 434, 445, Trial Examiner Robert Pisarski held that a teacher union's proposals concerning, *inter alia,* class size, selection of text book materials, planning of facilities and special education, and procedures for rating the effectiveness of teachers were "proper subjects of bargaining." The MERC granted the union's request that the proceedings be dismissed and, therefore, never ruled on the Trial Examiner's decision. Are any of the subjects which the Trial Examiner held negotiable "demonstrably within the care of entrepreneurial control"?

2. In Burlington County College Faculty Ass'n v. Board of Trustees, Burlington County College, 119 N.J. Super. 276, 291 A.2d 150 (1972), the court held that a college was obligated to negotiate but not reach agreement with the faculty association on the format of the academic calendar. Although the court held that the calendar constituted a term or condition of employment within the meaning of the state's public employee bargaining law, it noted:

> The Board of Trustees need not surrender its discretion in determining calendar policy nor come to an agreement in the collective bargaining sense. The Board must, however, confer and negotiate, and this included a consideration of the suggestions and reasons of the faculty representatives. There is no duty upon the Board to agree against its judgment with the suggestions and it is not a forbidden practice for the School Board to determine in its own judgment what the school calendar should be even though such course of action rejects the faculty's wishes. The refusal may place the Board in a position where, under the rule of the New Jersey Public Employment Relations Commission, it will result in the appointment of a mediator and upon his failure to resolve the impasse, a fact-finding board. However, the fact finders, if adverse to the Board, are not binding upon it. The force of the fact-finding procedure is public opinion and the legislative process thrives on such enlightenment in a democracy. . . . 119 N.J. Super. at 285.

The court noted, however, that "[a] curriculum . . . would appear to rest entirely with the Board of Trustees [and] should not be confused with a calendar."

3. The *Borg-Warner* distinction between mandatory, permissive, and illegal subjects of bargaining has been utilized by several state labor relations agencies. *See, e.g.,* Mayor Samuel E. Zoll and the City of Salem, Mass. Labor Rel. Comm'n Case No. MUP-309 (1972); Town of Stratford, Conn. St. Bd. Labor Rel. Decision No. 1069 (1972). The scope of bargaining in the private sector and the role of the NLRB has been the subject of extended discussion. Among the many excellent articles are Cox & Dunlop, *Regulation of Collective Bargaining by the National Labor Relations Board,* 63 HARV. L. REV. 389 (1950); Cox, *The Duty to Bargain in Good Faith,* 71 HARV. L. REV. 1401 (1958).

4. In Allied Chemical & Alkali Workers Local 1 v. Pittsburgh Plate Glass Co., 404 U.S. 157, 92 S. Ct. 383, 30 L. Ed. 2d 341 (1971), the Supreme Court held that retirees were not "employees" within the meaning of the National Labor Relations Act and that therefore an employer was not mandatorily required to negotiate over a union's proposal that the pension benefits for retirees be increased. The New York City Office of Collective Bargaining in District Council 37, AFSCME and City of New York, NYC OCB Decision No. B-21-72 (1972), held that the City's collective bargaining law should be construed similarly. Accordingly, it held that retired city employees could not appropriately be included in a unit with active employees for the purposes of collective bargaining and that a union could not bargain on behalf of retired city employees for contributions to the health and welfare fund.

5. In a number of instances state attorneys general have issued opinions concerning the scope of bargaining under a public sector collective bargaining law, even though a labor relations agency has been established under such legislation. *See, e.g.,* Pa. Op. Att'y Gen. No. 133 (1972) (whether full wages or reduced wages must be paid if schools close before end of school year concerns wages, hours and other conditions of employment and therefore negotiable). Should an attorney general abstain from issuing an opinion where the same question is within the jurisdiction of a state public employment relations board? If the state public employment relations board and the attorney general issue conflicting decisions on the same question, which decision prevails in the absence of applicable court precedent? *See generally* Note 4, p. 323, *supra.*

WEST HARTFORD EDUCATION ASSOCIATION v. DECOURCY
Connecticut Supreme Court
162 Conn. 566, 295 A.2d 526 (1972)

[The plaintiff, West Hartford Education Association, was selected as the bargaining representative of the professional employees of the defendant, West Hartford Board of Education.]

. . . Although the representatives of the parties met frequently, they were unable to agree on the following topics: class size, teacher load, length of school day, school calendar, extracurricular activities, and binding arbitration of grievances. The defendant maintained throughout the negotiations that those items were not negotiable under § 10-153d of the General Statutes and should be determined unilaterally by the board or its agents. . . .

The questions which have been reserved for our advice are: (a) Are the following items conditions of employment with respect to which the defendant board of education has a duty to negotiate with the plaintiff under the provisions of § 10-153d of the General Statutes as amended: class size, teacher load, length of school day, school calendar, extracurricular activities, and binding arbitration of grievances? (b) If the answer to (a) is "Yes," does the defendant board of education violate its duty to negotiate with the plaintiff association by doing any of the following: (i) not making counterproposals on these topics, or (ii) taking the position that such matters be reserved for unilateral action by the board, or (iii) taking the position that such matters be included in the "board prerogatives" clause of the contract? (c) Did the actions of the defendant Richter in communicating directly with teachers and members of the association about the new work year, vacation schedule and salary schedule proposed by the board for department chairmen, coordinating teachers and subject area specialists and about the "extended plan" or "resource teacher program" violate § 10-153b of the General Statutes? (d) Did the actions of the defendant board of education in unilaterally implementing the above-mentioned proposals after the parties had failed to reach an agreement on them violate the provisions of § 10-153d?

In order to determine the questions presented it is necessary to examine the powers and duties of boards of education in the light of the statutory provisions of the Teacher Negotiation Act, §§ 10-153a—10-153h of the General Statutes. The chief function of local boards of education is to serve as policy maker on behalf of the state and for the local community on educational matters. The state has had a vital interest in the public schools from the earliest colonial times. . . . Article VIII, § 1, of the Connecticut constitution provides that "[t]here shall always be free public elementary and secondary schools in the state. The general assembly shall implement this principle by appropriate legislation." Obviously, the furnishing of education for the general public is a state function and duty. . . . By statutory enactment the legislature has delegated this responsibility to the local boards who serve as agents of the state in their communities. . . . Our statutes have conferred on the local board broad power and discretion over educational policy. . . . Section 10-220 of the General Statutes sets forth the duties of boards of education.[2] Section 10-221 of the General Statutes provides that boards of education shall "prescribe rules for the management, studies, classification and discipline of the public schools and, subject to the control of the state board of education, the textbooks to be used; shall make rules for the arrangement, use and safekeeping, within their respective jurisdictions, of the school libraries and approve the books selected therefor, and shall approve plans for schoolhouses and superintend any high or graded school in the manner specified in this title."

In 1951, this court, in Norwalk Teachers' Assn. v. Board of Education, 138 Conn. 269, 83 A.2d 482, 31 A.L.R.2d 1133 [*supra*, p. 17], held that although, teachers' strikes were unlawful, in the absence of statute or regulation there was no good reason why public employees should not organize as a labor union. "The stat-

---

[2] "[General Statutes] Sec. 10-220. DUTIES OF BOARD OF EDUCATION. Boards of education shall maintain in their several towns good public elementary and secondary schools and such other educational activities as in their judgment will best serve the interests of the town; provided any board of education may secure such opportunities in another town in accordance with provisions of the general statutes and shall give all the children of the town as nearly equal advantages as may be practicable; shall have charge of the schools of their respective towns; shall make a continuing study of the need for school facilities and of a long-term school building program and from time to time make recommendations based on such study to the town; shall have the care, maintenance and operation of buildings, lands, apparatus and other property used for school purposes; shall determine the number, age and qualifications of the pupils to be admitted into each school; shall employ and dismiss the teachers of the schools of such towns subject to the provisions of sections 10-151 and 10-158a; shall designate the schools which shall be attended by the various children within their several towns; shall make such provisions as will enable each child of school age, residing in the town, who is of suitable mental and physical condition, to attend some public day school for the period required by law and provide for the transportation of children wherever transportation is reasonable and desirable, and for such purpose may make contracts covering periods of not more than five years; may arrange with the board of education of an adjacent town for the instruction therein of such children as can attend school in such adjacent town more conveniently; shall cause each child between the ages of seven and sixteen living in the town to attend school in accordance with the provisions of section 10-184, and shall perform all acts required of them by the town or necessary to carry into effect the powers and duties imposed upon them by law."

utes and private acts give broad powers to the defendant with reference to educational matters and school management in Norwalk. If it chooses to negotiate with regard to the employment, salaries, grievance procedure and working conditions of its members, there is no statute, public or private, which forbids such negotiations. It is a matter of common knowledge that this is the method pursued in most school systems large enough to support a teachers' association in some form. It would seem to make no difference theoretically whether the negotiations are with a committee of the whole association or with individuals or small related groups, so long as any agreement made with the committee is confined to members of the association. If the strike threat is absent and the defendant prefers to handle the matter through negotiation with the plaintiff, no reason exists why it should not do so. The claim of the defendant that this would be an illegal delegation of authority is without merit. The authority is and remains in the board." Id., 277.

In 1965, the legislature adopted the Teacher Negotiation Act which, through sundry amendments, is now §§ 10-153a to 10-153h of the General Statutes. Section 10-153a provides that teachers shall have the right to join or refrain from joining an organization for professional improvement through which teachers can establish a bargaining unit and elect an organization to represent them in negotiations with the board of education. Section 10-153d provides in pertinent part as follows: "The town or regional board of education and the organization designated or elected as the exclusive representative for the appropriate unit, through designated officials or their representatives, shall have the duty to negotiate with respect to salaries and other conditions of employment about which either party wishes to negotiate, and such duty shall include the obligation of such board of education to meet at reasonable times, including meetings appropriately related to the budget-making process, and confer in good faith with respect to salaries and other conditions of employment, or the negotiation of an agreement, or any question arising thereunder and the execution of a written contract incorporating any agreement reached if requested by either party, but such obligation shall not compel either party to agree to a proposal or require the making of a concession." Section 10-153e prohibits strikes and § 10-153f provides for mediation and nonbinding arbitration of disputes concerning the making of a contract as to the terms and conditions of employment.

Question (a)

The defendants contend that the items involved in question (a) are all matters of educational policy which the legislature has reserved exclusively to boards of education for their determination. The plaintiff, on the other hand, asserts that the items are conditions of a teacher's employment and are, therefore, within the statutorily defined scope of negotiations. The significance of calling something a "condition of employment" is that it then becomes a mandatory subject of collective bargaining, under the reasoning of N.L.R.B. v. Wooster Division, Borg-Warner Corporation, 356 U.S. 342, 78 S. Ct. 718, 2 L. Ed. 2d 823. The duty to negotiate is limited to mandatory subjects of bargaining. As to other matters, however, each party is free to bargain or not to bargain. Id., 349; N.L.R.B. v. American National Ins. Co., 343 U.S. 395, 72 S. Ct. 824, 96 L. Ed. 1027. To the extent that such permissive bargaining results in an accord between the parties, their agreement may be incorporated into a binding contract, provided, however, that the board, in so contracting, may not abdicate any duty which the law has charged that the board and the board alone shall perform.

At the outset, however, the defendants take issue with the proposition that the scope of negotiations under the statute is defined by the phrase "salaries and other conditions of employment." They maintain that the area of negotiability is circumscribed by the narrower phrase "salary schedules and personnel policies relative to employment." They point to § 10-153b (d) which establishes the election procedure, and wherein it is stated that the representative designated or elected in accordance with the section "shall be the exclusive representative of all the employees in the unit for the purposes of negotiating with respect to salary schedules and personnel policies relative to employment of certified, professional employees." We take note, however, of the language of subsection (c) of this same statute, wherein it is provided that the employees may designate an organization "to represent them in negotiations concerning salaries and all other conditions of employment." The broader phrase "conditions of employment" appears in three additional places in the act and most significantly in § 10-153d wherein the legal duty of the parties to negotiate is defined. It also appears in § 10-153f concerning mediation of disputes, and in § 10-153g which provides: "Notwithstanding the provisions of any special act, municipal charter or local ordinance, the provisions of sections 10-153a to 10-153f shall apply to negotiations concerning salaries and conditions of employment conducted by boards of education and certified personnel." There can be no doubt that it was the intention of the legislature to require negotiations between the representatives of teachers and boards of education as to "salaries and other conditions of employment."

The meaning of "salaries" is clear and requires no interpretation, but the determination of the matters embraced within the phrase "other conditions of employment" does require interpretation. . . . We look, therefore, to the legislative history of the Teacher Negotiation Act.

Historically, Connecticut statutes dealing with labor relations have been closely patterned after the National Labor Relations Act. This is particularly evidenced by the phraseology our legislature has adopted to define the scope of negotiations in the various Connecticut acts. The National Labor Relations Act provides that it shall be an unfair labor practice for an employer to refuse to bargain collectively with the representatives of his employees "in respect to rates of pay, wages, hours of employment or other conditions of employment." 29 U.S.C. §§ 158(a) (5) ; 159 (a) ; The Connecticut Labor Relations Act requires collective bargaining in respect to "rates of pay, wages, hours of employment or other conditions of employment." §§ 31-105 (6) , 31-106 (a) . The Municipal Employee Relations Act imposes on the parties the duty to confer in good faith "with respect to wages, hours and other conditions of employment." §§ 7-469, 7-470 (c) . The language of these three acts is essentially the same and for this reason the judicial interpretation frequently accorded the federal act is of great assistance and persuasive force in the interpretation of our own acts. . . .

The Connecticut Teacher Negotiation Act, on the other hand, states that the board of education shall have the duty to negotiate with respect to "salaries and other conditions of employment." The phrase "hours of employment" is omitted. This is highly significant in view of the labor acts previously adopted by the legislature of this state.[3] Its importance may be better understood on an examination of decisions under the National Labor Relations Act.

"Hours of employment have caused little difficulty in the area of mandatory subjects of bargaining in light of the express terms of § 8 (d) of the act. Thus, over the years there have been few cases involving this particular topic." Morris, The Developing Labor Law, 403. The cases that have discussed the subject, however, show that such topics as working hours and work days (Gallenkamp Stores Co. v. N.L.R.B., 402 F.2d 525 [9th Cir.]) ;

---

[3] It is noteworthy that certified teachers were specifically excluded from the provisions of the Municipal Employee Relations Act. General Statutes § 7-467.

overtime, Sunday and holiday work (N.L.R.B. v. Boss Mfg. Co., 118 F.2d 187 [7th Cir.]) ; and shift work (N.L.R.B. v. Laney & Duke Storage Warehouse Co., 369 F.2d 859 [5th Cir.]) , are all included within the phrase "hours of employment."

It is apparent that these topics from the private sector are not easily superimposed on the field of education. The omission of the words "hours of employment" in the Teacher Negotiation Act evidences a legislative judgment that teachers' "hours of employment" determine students' hours of education and that this is an important matter of educational policy which should be reserved to the board of education.

Accordingly, we may dispose of two of the items in question (a), length of school day and school calendar, before we begin our consideration of what is covered by the term "conditions of employment." The length of the school day is defined as the number of hours during which a teacher is required to be in attendance at a school each day. School calendar means the number of days and distribution of days during which schools are in session or teachers may be assigned to duties. Under any definition, these items would be "conditions of employment," however, since they are directly related to "hours of employment," it is our conclusion that these matters were specifically excepted from the act with great deliberation. Thus, the length of the school day and school calendar are not mandatory subjects of negotiation.

To decide whether the rest of the items in question (a) are mandatory subjects of negotiation, we must direct our attention to the phrase "conditions of employment." This problem would be simplified greatly if the phrase "conditions of employment" and its purported antithesis, educational policy, denoted two definite and distinct areas. Unfortunately, this is not the case. Many educational policy decisions make an impact on a teacher's conditions of employment and the converse is equally true. There is no unwavering line separating the two categories. It is clear, nevertheless, that the legislature denoted an area which was appropriate for teacher-school board bargaining and an area in which such a process would be undesirable.

The particular phrase the legislature designated to represent the area suitable for negotiations permits us to draw certain inferences about the types of subjects which are negotiable. The legislature was not required to use the phrase "conditions of employment." Apparently, it intended to encompass a larger range of topics than did the Oregon legislature, which restricted the area of negotiability to "salaries and related economic policies affecting professional services." Ore. Rev. Stat. §§ 342.450-342.470 (1969). But the legislative body was not prepared to venture as far as the Washington legislature, which enumerated a long and detailed list of negotiable items in a statute, e.g., curriculum, textbook selection, in-service training, student teaching programs, personnel, hiring and assignment practices, salaries, and noninstructional duties, to name but a few. Wash. Rev. Code Ann. §§ 28A.72.010-28A.72.090 (1969). The use of the phrase "conditions of employment" reflects a judgment that the scope of negotiations should be relatively broad, but sufficiently flexible to accommodate the changing needs of the parties.

The intended breadth of the area of negotiability is evidenced by the experience under the National Labor Relations Act. 49 Stat. 449, as amended, 29 U.S.C. § 151 et seq. These cases indicate that the National Labor Relations Board and the courts have consistently expanded the number of items which fall within the penumbra of the phrase "other conditions of employment." . . .

Nevertheless, the phrase "conditions of employment" limits the area of negotiability. In Fibreboard Paper Products Corporation v. N.L.R.B., *supra,* 222, 223, Mr. Justice Stewart, concurring with the majority, attempted to articulate those limits. "In common parlance, the conditions of a person's employment are most obviously the various physical dimensions of his working environment. . . . [p. 223] In many of these areas the impact of a particular management decision upon job security may be extremely indirect and uncertain and this alone may be sufficient reason to conclude that such decisions are not 'with respect to . . . conditions of employment.' . . . Nothing the court holds today should be understood as imposing a duty to bargain collectively regarding such managerial decisions which lie at the core of entrepreneurial control."

The notion that decisions concerning the "core of entrepreneurial control" are solely the business of the employer appears to have a special kind of vitality in the public sector. For instance, under Presidential Executive Order 10988, pursuant to which federal agencies dealt with organizational representatives of their employees, the obligation to negotiate does not extend to "such areas of discretion and policy as the mission of the agency, its budget, its organization and the assignment of its personnel, or the technology of performing its work." 27 F.R. 551, 554 § 6 (b) ; Wollett & Chanin, Law and Practice of Teacher Negotiations, 6:34-6:45.

Educational policy is the parallel concept limiting the scope of negotiations in teacher-school board relations. It is the sum total of the powers conferred by §§ 10-220 and 10-221. But like its counterpart "conditions of employment," it requires interpretation. Suffice it to say that, at the very least, matters of educational policy are those which are fundamental to the existence, direction and operation of the enterprise.

There are two other factors which we must consider in order to determine if an item falls within the scope of negotiability. The National Labor Relations Board and the courts in interpreting the federal labor act have frequently turned to the history and custom of the industry in collective bargaining. In holding that the contracting-out of work is a mandatory subject of collective bargaining, the Supreme Court of the United States stated that "[w]hile not determinative, it is appropriate to look to industrial practices in appraising the propriety of including a particular subject within the scope of mandatory bargaining. . . . Industrial experience is not only reflective of the interests of labor and management in the subject matter but it is also indicative of the amenability of such subjects to the collective bargaining process." Fibreboard Paper Products Corporation v. N.L.R.B., *supra*, 211. The United States Supreme Court, in the *Fibreboard* case, observed that provisions concerning the contracting-out of work exist in many contracts and that the subject is the basis of many grievances.

We must consider also the policies underlying the Teacher Negotiation Act. The act divests boards of education of some of the discretion which they otherwise could exercise under the provisions of §§ 10-220 and 10-221, since it imposes on the board the duty to negotiate certain matters with the representatives of teachers. The legislature by this enactment expressed the view that the state's best interest will be served by according teachers the right to negotiate in accordance with the terms and conditions of the act. It eliminates any need for resort to illegal and disruptive tactics. The statute does not compel the parties to agree nor does it require them to make concessions. The board, if it negotiates in good faith, retains the ultimate power to say "No." But, by submitting matters to the mediating influence of negotiations, it is more likely that disputes will be resolved and that agreement will be reached. This is also the basis of federal labor policy. "The National Labor Relations Act is designed to promote industrial peace by encouraging the making of voluntary agreements governing relations between unions and employers. The Act does not compel any agreement whatsoever between employees and employers. Nor does the Act regulate the substantive terms governing wages, hours and working conditions which are incorporated in an agreement. The theory of the Act is that the making of voluntary labor agreements is encouraged by protecting the employees' rights to organize for collective bargaining and by imposing on labor and management the mutual obligation to bargain collectively." N.L.R.B. v. American National Ins. Co., 343 U.S. 395, 401-2, 72 S. Ct. 824, 96 L. Ed. 1027.

Turning, then, to the remaining items in question (a), the stipulation defines class size as the number of pupils assigned to a class. Teacher load means the number of teaching classes per day or per week and the number of different preparations per day or per week. The defendant board urges that both of these subjects are questions of policy within the exclusive province of the board of education. There can be no doubt that policy questions are involved in these matters but that cannot be decisive in the present case. The basic question for this court to determine is whether these matters are mandatory subjects of negotiation in accordance with the legislative mandate by its adoption of the Teacher Negotiation Act. Class size and teacher load chiefly define the amount of work expected of a teacher, a traditional indicator of whether an item is a "condition of employment." Further, we see from the stipulation that of the ninety-six group teacher contracts negotiated in Connecticut, sixty-one have class size provisions and forty-one have provisions dealing with teacher load. The legislative intent is clear that class size and teacher load are mandatory subjects of negotiation.

Extracurricular activities are activities generally outside of regular hours of pupil attendance at which a teacher's attendance is either required or voluntary and which may or may not involve additional pay. As the defendants point out in their brief, this topic involves three separate issues. First, is the defendant board free to decide unilaterally what extracurricular activities shall be conducted in the West Hartford schools, or must the existence of such programs be negotiated with the plaintiff? Second, may the defendant assign teachers to participate in such activities, without first negotiating assignments with the plaintiff? Third, must compensation for extracurricular duties be negotiated with the plaintiff? "Boards of education shall maintain in their several towns good public elementary and secondary schools, implement the educational interests of the state . . . and provide *such other educational activities as in their judgment* will best serve the interests of the town." (Emphasis supplied.) Section 10-220. There can be no doubt that the defendant board of education alone is empowered to determine whether there shall be extracurricular activities and what such activities shall be. The second and third issues involving assignment of teachers to such activities and the question of compensation for such extracurricular activities affect salaries and other conditions of employment and are, to that extent only, mandatory subjects of negotiation.

The final item listed under question (a) is whether binding arbitration of grievances is a mandatory subject of negotiation. Binding arbitration of grievances is defined as submission to an impartial arbitrator or arbitrators with the advance stipulation that both parties shall be bound by the decision of the arbitrator or arbitrators. The arbitration procedure provided for in § 10-153f applies only "[i]f any town or regional board of education cannot agree with the exclusive representatives of a teachers' or administrators' unit after negotiation concerning the terms and conditions of employment applicable to the employees in such unit." This concerns the making of a contract between the board of education and the teachers' organization and is advisory only. It could not be otherwise, since it would involve an unlawful delegation of the board's statutory authority to the arbitrators. The question reserved for our advice involves binding arbitration of a grievance which is a quite different thing.

Traditionally, the establishment of a grievance procedure concerning alleged violations and misinterpretations of the existing collective bargaining agreement is a negotiable item under most labor relations acts. Hughes Tool Co. v. N.L.R.B., 147 F.2d 69 (5th Cir.). If it is unlawful, however, for the board of education to submit these disputes to binding arbitration the topic would be beyond the scope of negotiability no matter how great an effect it might have on teachers. Cf. Penello v. United Mine Workers, 88 F. Supp. 935 (D.D.C.). The defendant contends that such a procedure would be illegal in that it would involve an abdication by the school board of its statutory power.

In Norwalk Teachers' Assn. v. Board of Education, 138 Conn. 269, 83 A.2d 482, we held that "[a]rbitration may be a permissible method for a school board to use to settle certain specific, arbitrable disputes" it has with a teacher. This power of the school board would not extend to questions of liability. The court also stated that if the defendant entered into a general agreement to submit all disputes to arbitration it might find that it had surrendered the broad discretion and responsibility reposed in it by law. "For example, it could not commit to an arbitrator the decision of a proceeding to discharge a teacher for cause." Id., 280.

It is clear that under the general legal concepts recited in the *Norwalk Teachers'* case and pursuant to the Teacher Negotiation Act, the board of education could not relinquish its authority to decide what the terms and conditions of a collective bargaining agreement are to be. In other words, it could not abdicate its responsibility for making the contract.

The question presented in the present case is not whether the defendant board must agree to arbitrate all disputes but only whether it is under a duty to negotiate with the plaintiff as to what, if any, grievance matters can be submitted to arbitration. A grievance procedure involves the interpretation and enforcement of an existing group teacher contract. Insofar as the board has the power to make such a contract it follows that it has the power to agree on a method and forum for the purpose of settling disputes arising under the terms of the contract. It is an amicable and efficient means of resolving any differences within a contract previously acceptable to and executed by the parties. Obviously, the board cannot delegate to an arbitrator its statutory authority as to matters of policy nor can it agree to binding arbitration of matters concerning which a statutory duty rests on the board alone. If the board sees fit to agree to binding arbitration it obviously must confine the subjects involved to those matters which are not ultra vires. Within these limitations binding arbitration of grievances within the terms and conditions of an existing group teacher contract is a permissible method for settling disputes and is a mandatory subject of negotiation between the parties. . . . [The court's decision as to the other question appears later in chapter 4.]

NOTES

1. In National Educ. Ass'n of Shawnee Mission, Inc. v. Board of Educ. of Shawnee Mission Unified School Dist. No. 512, — Kan. —, 512 P.2d 426, 84 L.R.R.M. 2223 (1973), the Kansas Supreme Court was faced with the task of defining what was negotiable under the Kansas Teachers Statute which requires the parties to negotiate in good faith "with respect to terms and conditions of professional service." In addition to wages and other economic matters, the court held that negotiations were required over "such things as probationary period, transfers, teacher appraisal procedure, disciplinary procedure, and resignations and termination of contracts." On the other hand, the court held that the negotiations were not required over "curriculum and materials, payroll mechanics, certification, class size and the use of paraprofessionals, the use and duties of substitute teachers, and teachers' ethics and academic freedom." The court stated that "the key . . . is how direct the impact of an issue is on the well-being of the individual teacher, as opposed to its effect on the operation of the school system as a whole."

2. Both the National Education Association and the American Federation of Teachers have asserted that the scope of

negotiations in education should be virtually unlimited. The National Education Association in 1965 stated:

A professional group has responsibilities beyond self-interest, including a responsibility for the general welfare of the school system. Teachers and other members of the professional staff have an interest in the conditions which attract and retain a superior teaching force, in the in-service training programs, in class size, in the selection of textbooks and in other matters which go far beyond those which would be included in a narrow definition of working conditions. Negotiations should include all matters which affect the quality of the educational system. NATIONAL EDUCATION ASSOCIATION, GUIDELINES FOR PROFESSIONAL NEGOTIATIONS 21-22 (1965).

The past president of the American Federation of Teachers, Charles Cogen, stated that "class size, number of classes taught, curriculum, hiring standards, textbooks and supplies, extra curricular activities—in fact anything having to do with the operation of the school—is a matter for professional concern and should thus be subject to collective bargaining." Cogen, *Collective Negotiations in Public Education*, in SORRY . . . NO GOVERNMENT TODAY 141, 148 (R. Walsh ed. 1969).

3.   What has been the impact of negotiations, either *de jure* or *de facto*, over class size? In Hall and Carroll, *The Effect of Teachers' Organizations on Salaries and Class Size*, 26 IND. & LAB. REL. REV. 834, 840 (1973), the authors concluded:

[I]t appears that teachers' organizations are associated with a larger student-teacher ratio. This lends support to the common allegation that school boards are offering teachers higher salaries in exchange for larger classes and that these offers are being accepted. Certainly, there is nothing to suggest that teachers' organizations have had any success in reducing the number of pupils per classroom. . . .

See generally C. PERRY & W. WILDMAN, THE IMPACT OF NEGOTIATIONS IN PUBLIC EDUCATION: THE EVIDENCE FROM THE SCHOOLS (1970).

4.   In Oakland County Sheriff's Dep't, 1968 MERC Lab. Op. 1, the Michigan Employment Relations Commission held "that binding arbitration of grievances concerning the interpretation and enforcement of a collective bargaining agreement was a mandatory subject of bargaining. . . ." *Accord,* Local 1226, AFSCME v. City of Rhinelander, 35 Wis. 2d 209, 151 N.W.2d 30 (1967); City of Auburn v. Nash, 34 App. Div. 2d 345, 312

N.Y.S.2d 700 (1970); Rockland Professional Fire Fighters Ass'n v. City of Rockland, 261 A.2d 418 (Me. 1970); Central City Educ. Ass'n v. School Dist. of Central City, Neb. Ct. of Ind. Rel. Case No. 35 (1971). *But see* Allegheny County Firefighters Local 1038 v. County of Allegheny, 299 A.2d 60, 82 L.R.R.M. 2425 (Pa. Commonwealth Ct. 1973).

5. Several statutes expressly provide that the parties may negotiate over a grievance procedure with binding arbitration as the terminal step. The Hawaii Act, for example, provides that the parties may include in their labor agreement a provision "setting forth a grievance procedure culminating in a final and binding decision, to be invoked in the event of any dispute concerning the interpretation or application of a written agreement." HAWAII REV. STAT. § 89-11 (a) (Supp. 1972). The New Hampshire, Washington, and Wisconsin statutes covering state employees and the Kansas, Oregon, and Vermont statutes covering teachers contain similar provisions. Executive Order 11491 is somewhat broader in that it provides that "[n]egotiated procedures may provide for the arbitration of employee grievances *and* of disputes over the interpretation or application of existing agreements." E.O. 11491, § 14(a). In United States Kirk Army Hospital, Aberdeen, Md., FLRC No. 70A-11 (1971), GERR Ref. File 21:7005, however, the Federal Labor Relations Council held "that the arbitration of union disputes over the 'interpretation or application' of 'any policy, regulation, or practice' within the employer's discretion . . . is violative of sections 13 and 14 of the Order and is not negotiable."

A number of states mandate the inclusion of a provision providing for the binding arbitration of disputes concerning the interpretation and application of the agreement. The Minnesota statute is illustrative: "All contracts shall include a grievance procedure which shall provide compulsory arbitration of grievances." MINN. STAT. ANN. ch. 179, § 179.70 (1) (Supp. 1973). The Minnesota Act provides that if the agreement does not contain such a procedure the parties are subject to the grievance procedure promulgated by the Director of the Bureau of Mediation Services. Both the Kansas and South Dakota acts contain similar provisions.

6. Would a proposal by one party that any unresolved issues in the negotiations for a successor agreement be submitted to binding arbitration be a mandatory subject of bargaining? A permissive subject of bargaining? An illegal subject of bargaining? Would it make any difference if the applicable statute provides, as the New York Taylor Law does, that the parties may

agree to an impasse procedure which includes "the undertaking by each party to submit unresolved [negotiation] issues to impartial arbitration." N.Y. Civ. Serv. Law § 209 (2) (McKinney Supp. 1973). *Cf.* Mechanical Contractor's Ass'n of Newburgh, 202 N.L.R.B. No. 1, 82 L.R.R.M. 1438 (1973).

WEST IRONDEQUOIT BOARD OF EDUCATION
New York Public Employment Relations Board
4 PERB ¶ 3070
Aff'd on rehearing, 4 PERB ¶ 3089 (1971)
Aff'd, 346 N.Y.S.2d 418 (N.Y. Sup. Ct., App. Div. 1973)

The West Irondequoit Teachers Association (charging party) filed an improper practice charge against the West Irondequoit Board of Education (employer) alleging that the employer violated Section 209-a.1 (d) of the Public Employees' Fair Employment Act by refusing to negotiate on two issues.

The parties submitted the case to the hearing officer on stipulated facts. In summary, the charging party is the recognized negotiating representative for all of the full-time and part-time certificated personnel excluding some job titles which are immaterial herein.

During negotiations for the 1970-71 academic year, the charging party submitted a proposal entitled "Class Size and Teaching Load."[1]

In response to the charging party's proposal, the employer submitted its own proposal.[2]

---

[1] "Class Size and Teaching Load."
The pertinent provisions are: "B. Maximum Class Size:
  (Definition: The number of pupils for whom a teacher is responsible during a single period in a single day.)
  1. The class size of the kindergarten shall be 20 pupils.
  2. The class size of the first grade in the elementary schools shall be 20 pupils.
  3. The class size of the second-fourth grades in the elementary schools shall be 25 pupils.
  4. The class size of the fifth-sixth grades and vocal music classes in the middle schools shall be 25 pupils. . . . [The proposal also specified class sizes for other grades.]
Classes that increase beyond the *maximum* must be agreed upon by the teacher and the building principal involved. Any disagreement over such an exception shall be subject to the procedure set forth in the Grievance Procedure." (emphasis in original)

[2] The pertinent provisions of respondent's proposal on "Class Size" are as follows:
D.1. Basic Understandings.
  a. One key to effective learning is the quantity and quality of interrelations between and among pupils and teachers.
  b. Excessive class size or teacher load may affect the emotional or mental well-being of the teachers.

The charging party also submitted to the employer a proposal entitled "Promotional Policy."

The respondent in May 1970 informed the charging party that it would not negotiate with respect to numerical limitations of class size (hereinafter referred to as class size) or on promotional policy in that both subject matters involved nondelegable duties and responsibilities of the employer.

The charging party has contended that class size is a term and condition of employment and inasmuch as the negotiations on class size do not contravene any law, it is a mandatory subject of negotiations. Further, the charging party argued that since the employer in its counter-proposal stated that excessive class size may affect the emotional or mental well-being of a teacher, the employer had conceded that class size is a term and condition of employment.

The hearing officer stated that, in resolving this matter, we must weigh the duty of government officials to make decisions affecting the entire electorate against the statutory obligation of public employers to negotiate on subjects directly affecting the terms and conditions of employment.

The hearing officer further found that class size does have a major impact on a teacher's working conditions and that class size is not an expression of a primary policy goal of the basic direction of government. The hearing officer concluded that class size is a term and condition of employment and, as such, is a mandatory subject of negotiation.[4]

The issue before this Board raised in this proceeding is a most serious one because of the effect such decisions will have upon school negotiations throughout the State.

---

c.   A number of factors, such as available space, degrees of difficulty of the subject or grade level, the methodology utilized, the particular strengths of the teachers, and the individual characteristics of pupils must be considered by administrators when arranging classes and teacher assignments.
2. Agreements.
The Board and the Association agree that:
a.   The relationships between effective learning and class size and teacher load shall be subject to continued examination by the parties, in order to determine optimal classroom conditions for pupils.
b.   Administrative flexibility in arranging class sizes and teacher loads shall be maintained in order to allow for program diversity and innovation, and to allow for arrangements among teachers which are equitable. The district's administrators shall consider the guidelines established by the NYSTA Special Committee on the Duties of Teachers as optimal conditions in their planning for the 1971-72 school year.

[4] This conclusion of the hearing officer was reached prior to this Board's decision in City School District of the City of New Rochelle v. New Rochelle Federation of Teachers, 4 PERB ¶ 4-3060, 3704.

In the *New Rochelle* case[5] this Board stated that the determination as to the manner and means by which education service is rendered and the extent of such service is the duty and obligation of the public employer. A public employer should not be required to delegate this responsibility. The decisions of a public employer as to the carrying out of its mission—a decision to eliminate or curtail a service—are not decisions that a public employer should be compelled to negotiate with its employees.

Specifically in the *New Rochelle* case we held that budgetary cuts with concomitant job eliminations were not mandatory subjects of negotiations. Underlying this determination was the concept that basic decisions as to public policy should not be made in the isolation of a negotiation table, but rather should be made by those having the direct and sole responsibility therefor, and whose actions in this regard are subject to review in the electoral process. It would appear that class size is also a basic element of education policy. This follows our decision in the *New Rochelle* case. In that case, the budgetary decisions involved the elimination of a substantial number of teacher positions. These eliminations affected class size.

While we state that such decisions may be determined unilaterally by a public employer, nevertheless the employer is obligated to negotiate with the representative of its public employees on the impact of such decisions on terms and conditions of employment. Clearly such negotiations on the impact of decisions will have an effect on the allocation of resources. Nevertheless, impact is a matter for negotiations. Thus, it is not the thrust of this decision that an employer is not required to negotiate on subjects which affect the allocation of resources because salaries clearly have such an effect; rather, the thrust of this decision and the decision in the *New Rochelle* case is that basic policy decisions as to the implementation of a mission of an agency of government are not mandatory subjects of negotiations.[6]

It should be noted that the line of demarcation between a basic policy decision and the impact on terms and conditions of employment may not always be clear. For example, a policy decision as to class size may have an impact on teaching load. At first look, class size and teaching load may seem the same, but as we see them, they are not. The first represents a determination by the public employer as to an educational policy made in the light

---

[5] See Footnote 4, *supra*.

[6] However, the impact which such decisions have on the terms and conditions of employment is a mandatory subject of negotiation.

of its resources and other needs of its constituency. This decision may have an impact on hours of work and the number of teaching periods which are clearly mandatory subjects of negotiations.

Further, we would make clear that this decision does not prohibit negotiations on class size. *A fortiori,* neither does it preclude a public employer, such as a school board, from consulting with teacher organizations in making basic decisions as to educational policies; rather this should be encouraged so as to take advantage of the teachers' professional expertise.

WE, THEREFORE, modify the decision of the hearing officer and hold that class size is a policy decision of government and thus is not a mandatory subject of negotiations. As to that portion of the charge dealing with negotiation on promotional policy, we agree with the distinction and decision of the hearing officer and affirm and adopt the recommendations of the hearing officer.

Thus, we find that promotional policy for job titles outside the negotiating units, as well as the determination of qualifications for promotion into positions within the negotiating unit, are not terms and conditions of employment and, therefore, are not mandatory subjects of negotiations.

The employer is therefore

ORDERED to negotiate upon the request of the charging party with respect to promotional policy relating to job titles within the negotiating unit; in all other respects, the charge herein is dismissed.

NOTES

1. Is manning on fire trucks and engines a mandatory subject of bargaining under the Taylor Law? In City of White Plains, 5 PERB ¶ 3008, *enf'd* 5 PERB ¶ 7019 (N.Y. Sup. Ct. 1972), the New York PERB stated:

> Unlike the circumstance in the *West Irondequoit* case in which the teachers' interest was limited to workload, the interests of the Fire Fighters in this case also involve safety. We do not mean to imply that the Fire Fighters' demands are proper in order to protect them; that determination is for the negotiators. But it is clear that there is a relationship between the numbers of Fire Fighters who man a piece of equipment and their safety. We believe that the demand that a minimum number of Fire Fighters be on duty at all times with each engine and each truck constitutes a mandatory subject of negotiations.

In the same case the PERB held that while the number of firemen on duty at any given time is not a mandatory subject of negotiations, the scheduling of tours of duty is negotiable.

2. Did the New York PERB hold that the decisions with respect to class size or promotional policy are not conditions of employment? In *New Rochelle,* a decision referred to in the principal case, the New York Board noted that a proposed budgetary cut that would have resulted in the termination of 140 positions "[o]bviously . . . does effect 'conditions of employment'. . . . However, it does not follow that every decision of a public employer which may affect job security is a mandatory subject of negotiations." City School Dist. of the City of New Rochelle, 4 PERB ¶ 3060 (1971).

3. In Board of Educ. of Union Free School Dist. No. 3 v. Associated Teachers of Huntington, Inc., 30 N.Y.2d 122, 282 N.E.2d 109, 331 N.Y.S.2d 17 (1972), the New York Court of Appeals held that "[u]nder the Taylor Law, the obligation to bargain as to all terms and conditions of employment is a broad and unqualified one, and there is no reason why a mandatory provision of that Act should be limited, in any way, except in cases where some other applicable statutory provision explicitly and definitively prohibits the public employer from making an agreement as to a particular term or condition of employment." Is the holding of the New York PERB in the principal case consistent with this statement? The New York Supreme Court, Appellate Division, in confirming the decision of the New York PERB in West Irondequoit Teachers Ass'n v. Helsby, 346 N.Y.S. 2d 418 (N.Y. Sup. Ct., App. Div. 1973), noted that *Huntington* was distinguishable on its facts, stating:

> In that case the parties had agreed that five subject items were terms and conditions of employment and sought a determination whether specific statutory authority was required before a board of education could act, whereas in the instant matter we are asked to determine whether or not numerical class size is a term and condition of employment.

4. The MERC in City of Detroit, 1968 MERC Lab. Op. 492, held that the procedural requirements and the substantive criteria for promotions to positions within the bargaining unit are mandatory subjects of bargaining.

5. Contrast the decision in the principal case with the decision of the Los Angeles County Employee Relations Commission in Los Angeles County Department of Public Social Services and Department of Personnel, *infra.*

6. Would a union's demand that a negotiated wage increase be made retroactive be a mandatory subject of negotiation? The Wisconsin Employment Relations Commission in Racine County, WERC Decision No. 10917-B (1972) held that "[t]he retroactive application of matters relating to wages, hours and conditions of employment . . . are proper subjects of collective bargaining under the Act." In so ruling, the WERC rejected the employer's contention that it was prohibited from making retroactive payments by a County ordinance, noting that "what the County enacted with respect to retroactivity, it can repeal if it so desires." *Accord,* Town of Groton, Conn. St. Lab. Rel. Bd. Decision No. 806 (1968); Allegheny County, Pa. Lab. Rel. Bd. Case No. PERA-C-2443-W, GERR No. 517, B-13 (1973).

Many state constitutions include prohibitions against the payment of extra compensation after the services or work have been performed. For example, Article XI, Section 10 of the California Constitution reads as follows:

> A local government body may not grant extra compensation or extra allowance to a public officer, public employee, or contractor after service has been rendered or a contract has been entered into and performed in whole or in part, or pay a claim under an agreement without authority of law.

In San Joaquin County Employees Ass'n v. County of San Joaquin, 69 LC ¶ 52,964 (Cal. Super. Ct. 1972), the court held that the foregoing constitutional prohibition does not "prohibit the Board [of County Supervisors] from providing in the salary ordinance or by appropriate agreement for retroactive pay increases." *But see* Biennial Report of the Fla. Att'y Gen. 402 (1952).

7. It is not unusual in public sector negotiations for a union to propose that there be parity between the wages of the employees it represents and the wages of employees in another bargaining unit. Frequently unions representing fire fighters propose that there be parity between fire fighters and policemen. Is such a proposal requiring parity between the wages of two separate units of employees a mandatory subject of bargaining? In City of New London, Decision No. 1128, GERR No. 505, F-1 (1973), the Connecticut State Board of Labor Relations declared illegal a provision requiring a parity between policemen and fire fighters with respect to wages and other monetary benefits. In so ruling the Board stated:

> The question whether two separate bargaining units should receive *equal* treatment is necessarily one of vital concern to *both* of the concerned groups. Equality is a term

of relationship; by its very nature it cannot characterize a single entity. Where one of two groups has already made its terms with the city, the other may then of course seek to attain equal treatment without impinging on the former group's freedom to bargain. But that is not this case. Where *equality in future treatment* is in question, then each of the groups sought to be equated has a statutory right to bargain about the point. It is this right which the parity clause in the firemen's contract actually interferes with and restrains. If this clause is given effect, the policemen will be bound to a rule of equality in negotiating their own terms and conditions, without ever having had a chance to negotiate the rule itself. This we conclude constitutes a violation of the Act. Only by joint bargaining can a rule of parity properly be imposed by contract. . . .

What we find to be forbidden is an agreement between *one* group (*e.g.,* firemen) and the employer that will impose equality for the future *upon another group* (*e.g.,* policemen) that has had no part in making the agreement. We find that the *inevitable* tendency of such an agreement is to interfere with, restrain and coerce the right of the later group to have untrammeled bargaining. And this affects *all* the later negotiations (within the scope of the parity clause) even though it may be hard or impossible to trace by proof the effect of the parity clause upon any specific terms of the later contract (just as in the case before us). The parity clause will seldom surface in the later negotiations but it will surely be present in the minds of the negotiators and have a restraining or coercive effect not always consciously realized. . . .

But see City of Detroit v. Killingsworth, 80 L.R.R.M. 2752 (Mich. Cir. Ct. Wayne County, 1972). *See generally* Lewin, *Wage Parity and the Supply of Police and Firemen,* 12 IND. REL. 77 (1973).

3. Effect of Statutory Statement of Management Prerogatives

Following the lead of the federal government in Executive Orders 10988 and 11491, several states have also limited the scope of bargaining by enumerating certain management rights or prerogatives. New Hampshire, for example, provides that

The State retains the exclusive right through its department heads and appointing authorities, subject to the provisions of law and the personnel regulations (a) to direct and supervise employees, (b) to appoint, promote, dis-

charge, transfer or demote employees, (c) to lay off unnecessary employees, (d) to maintain the efficiency of government operations, (e) to determine the means, methods
and personnel by which operations are to be conducted, and
(f) to take whatever actions are necessary to carry out the
mission of the agency or department in situations of emergency. N.H. REV. STAT. ANN. ch. 98-C, § 98-C:7.

Hawaii, Kansas, and Nevada have similar provisions. The Minnesota Act provides that

A public employer is not required to meet and negotiate
on matters of inherent managerial policy, which include,
but are not limited to, such areas of discretion or policy
as the functions and programs of the employer, its overall
budget, utilization of technology, the organizational structure and selection and direction and number of personnel.
MINN. STAT. ANN. ch. 179, § 179.66 (1) (Supp. 1972).

The Pennsylvania Act contains a nearly identical provision.
Vermont (for state employees) and California (for local government employees) have also exempted to a lesser extent certain
management prerogatives from the scope of negotiations. Thus,
the California Act provides "that the scope of representation
shall not include consideration of the merits, necessities, or organization of any service or activity provided by law or executive order." CAL. GOV'T CODE § 3504 (West Supp. 1971).

Numerous questions have arisen concerning the scope of bargaining under state statutes that include a statement of management prerogatives since most of these statutes also provide that
the parties are required to negotiate in good faith over wages,
hours and other terms and conditions of employment. The basic
problem is to what extent items which would otherwise be considered "wages, hours and other terms and conditions of employment" are removed from the mandatory area of bargaining
by a statutory statement of management rights.

DEPARTMENT OF THE ARMY CORPS OF ENGINEERS
Federal Labor Relations Council
FLRC No. 71A-46 (1972), GERR Ref. File 21:7023

Background of the Case

The activity (Little Rock District, Corps of Engineers) is
headquartered at Little Rock, Arkansas. Among its responsibilities, the activity operates five hydroelectric power plants, located
in Arkansas and Missouri, called Bull Shoals, Dardanelle, Greers
Ferry, Norfolk and Table Rock.

In October 1966, the union was granted exclusive recognition for a bargaining unit consisting of approximately 90 operating and maintenance personnel employed by the activity. Negotiations for an agreement ensued. All issues were ultimately resolved except one concerning the rotating shift work schedules of power plant operators or, more specifically, the activity's practice of assigning "swing" operators in such a way as to avoid overtime and holiday pay. That issue is the subject of the instant proceeding and the pertinent circumstances surrounding the dispute are as follows:

1. *Method of work scheduling at activity*. The five power plants operate on a continuous, 24-hour day, 7-day week basis, and each is manned by at least one full-time operator at all times. In order to cover the 21 8-hour shifts per week, and accommodate normal absences for annual leave, sick leave, holidays and usual days off, each plant has a complement of five operators, working on rotating shifts. In any one week four employees occupy the classification of regular operator and one employee that of "swing" operator (the nature of "swing" assignments is described below). All five employees take turns working in each classification and the change is made weekly. Thus, a given employee will be a regular operator on each of the four regular operator shifts for four weeks and swing operator in the fifth week, and then the cycle repeats. In this manner the week's twenty-one shifts are covered.

At the beginning of each calendar year, the activity draws up and posts at each power plant a tentative work schedule which lists each operator's scheduled workdays, off days and, insofar as known at that time, annual leave hours for the coming year. From this annual schedule, 35-day (5-week) final work schedules are posted two weeks prior to their effective dates showing any changes from the tentative schedule for the coming 5-week period. The administrative workweek is Sunday through Saturday.

In practice, when none of the operators at a plant is to be absent during an entire week it is necessary for two operators to work on a single shift, as four employees working forty hours each week cover twenty shifts. In such circumstances, "doubling up" is necessary on four shifts during that week and is scheduled on the first shift (8:00 am to 4:00 pm) on Monday through Thursday. The second man on the doubled-up shifts is the so-called "swing" operator. The swing operator returns as the sole operator on the day shift on Friday and is then scheduled for non-work days on the Saturday and Sunday immediately following. (This is the only time an operator is scheduled for consecutive Saturday and Sunday days off during the 5-week cycle.)

However, in the case of absence of a regular operator during the Monday-Thursday period the swing operator is subject to assignment to the second (4:00 pm to midnight) or third (midnight to 8:00 am) shift.

In addition, where leave is taken by a regular operator on a Saturday or Sunday which has not been accounted for in the posted 5-week schedule, it has been the practice of the activity, in order to avoid paying overtime to one of the other regular operators, to relieve that week's swing operator of work on a scheduled workday and require that he work instead on the uncovered Saturday or Sunday which was scheduled as his off day.

Likewise, it appears that when a holiday occurs on a day on which the regular operator and swing operator are scheduled to work the day shift together, the activity, in order to avoid the payment of holiday pay to both operators, often cancels the scheduled day off of the swing operator (i.e., Saturday or Sunday) and relieves him of his scheduled workday which falls on the holidays.

2. *Disputed proposals.* The union has not objected to the activity's practice of changing the shifts for which the swing operator is scheduled within his regular workdays, i.e., moving a swing operator from the first to the second or third shifts on his scheduled workdays. It has objected to the changing of the swing operator's off days as specified in the annual schedule, to avoid the payment of overtime and holiday pay, on the ground that this creates a situation where the swing employees can neither make advance personal plans for the use of his off time nor be compensated for his inconvenience by receiving premium pay. To remedy this situation, the union submitted the following proposals during the course of negotiations:

[Article 4, Section D (2) (d)] No operator's nonwork days shall be changed unless he receives overtime pay for said change.

[Article 6, Section D] Schedules will provide for tours which will allow holidays off to all operators to the maximum extent possible; and which will use the swing operator to avoid the unnecessary payment of holiday pay, except that the swing operator will not be scheduled to return to duty with less than sixteen (16) hours off, when the purpose of the return is to avoid payment of unnecessary holiday pay to another operator. The swing operator's nonwork

day(s) will not be changed for the sole purpose of avoiding
the payment of holiday pay.

The activity refused to accept the union's proposals and an
impasse resulted.

The dispute was thereafter submitted by the union to the
Federal Service Impasses Panel; however, in the course of the
Panel's proceedings the agency claimed that the proposals were
in fact violative of applicable law and regulations, and the negotiability issue was referred to the procedures of section 11 (c)
of the Order. . . .

The union then appealed to the Council, which accepted the
union's petition for review. Both the union and the agency have
filed briefs in this proceeding.

3. *Positions of the parties.* The agency in effect determined
and asserts before the Council that both of the union's proposals
violate management's right under section 12 (b) (4) of the
Order ". . . to maintain the efficiency of Government operations
entrusted to them," and management's responsibilities under
5 U.S.C. sections 301, 302 and 305 to maintain and improve "efficiency and economy in the operation of the agency's activities,
functions, or organization units." . . .

The union argues that its proposals concern matters affecting
working conditions upon which an agency has an obligation to
bargain under section 11 (a) of the Order. Also, the union
denies that its proposals are violative of any statutory requirements.

Opinion

The questions presented for Council decision are whether the
union's proposals are negotiable under section 11 (a) of the
Order as matters affecting working conditions, or non-negotiable,
as contended by the agency, because: (1) they interfere with
management's right under 5 U.S.C. sections 301, 302 and 305
and under section 12 (b) (4) of the Order, to run its operations
efficiently and economically. . . .

Section 11 (a) of the Order, which relates to the negotiation
of agreements, provides that the parties shall meet and confer in
good faith regarding "personnel policies and practices and matters affecting working conditions, so far as may be appropriate
under applicable laws and regulations, including . . . this Order."

Plainly, management policies and procedures concerning the
assignment of employees to particular shifts or the assignment
of overtime or holiday work directly affect the jobs of employees
and are "matters affecting working conditions." They have traditionally been so recognized. Without more, the union's pro-

posals, which are directed to such management actions, would be negotiable under section 11 (a).

1. *5 U.S.C. sections 301, 302 and 305, and section 12 (b) (4) of Order.* As already mentioned, the agency contends that the union's proposals are nevertheless excepted from the obligation to negotiate, on the grounds that they would violate applicable law (5 U.S.C. sections 301, 302 and 305) and section 12 (b) (4) of the Order.

Section 12 (b) of the Order establishes rights expressly reserved to management officials under any bargaining agreement, including "the right, in accordance with applicable laws and regulations . . . (4) to maintain the efficiency of the Government operations entrusted to them." Section 305 of Title 5, along with the general agency authority in sections 301 and 302, indirectly requires management to maintain "efficiency and economy in the operation of the agency's activities, functions, or organization units."

(Although the statute refers to both efficiency and economy, the term "efficiency" in section 12 (b) (4) likewise embraces the concept of "economy" and will be so regarded in the discussion which follows.)

The agency argues principally that "the *raison d' etre* for the swing shift is the minimizing of overtime and other premium costs to the employer"; and that the proposals would thwart "management's efforts to use the 'swing' operator effectively and [attack] the very purpose for establishing a 'swing' shift, by imposing prohibitions and limitations on the use of the fifth operator to reduce premium pay costs." In essence, therefore, it is the agency's position that, since the union's proposals would constrain the agency in reducing premium pay costs, the proposals of necessity would impair the agency's ability to maintain efficiency and economy in its operations.

In our opinion, the agency position equating reduced premium pay costs with efficient and economical operations improperly ignores the total complex of factors encompassed within the concept of "efficiency and economy." It fails to take into account, for example, the adverse effects of employee dissatisfaction with existing assignment practices, and the very real possibility that revised practices along the lines proposed, by reason of their actual impact on the employees, might well increase rather than reduce overall efficiency and economy of operations.

In general, agency determinations as to negotiability made in relation to the concept of efficiency and economy in section 12 (b) (4) of the Order and similar language in the statutes require consideration and balancing of all the factors involved, including the well-being of employees, rather than an arbitrary determination based only on the anticipation of increased costs. Other factors such as the potential for improved performance, increased productivity, responsiveness to direction, reduced turnover, fewer grievances, contribution of money-saving ideas, improved health and safety, and the like, are valid considerations. We believe that where otherwise negotiable proposals are involved the management right in section 12 (b) (4) may not properly be invoked to deny negotiations unless there is a substantial demonstration by the agency that increased costs or reduced effectiveness in operations are inescapable and significant and are not offset by compensating benefits.

Applied to the instant case, the agency has asserted that increased premium pay costs would derive from the union's proposals. However, it has not established in the record before us that such costs would be significant in nature, nor that offsetting factors such as adverted to above would fail to overcome those increased costs. On the other hand, the union has shown that its proposals are limited in scope to certain aspects of swing operator scheduling and assignment, and that its proposals seek to reduce what the employees feel are unusual hardships in the working conditions of the unit.

In these circumstances, we find that the agency's determination of nonnegotiability under section 12 (b) (4) of the Order and similar language in related statutes is insufficiently supported and must be set aside. . . .

NOTES

1. In Plum Island Animal Disease Laboratory, FLRC No. 71A-11 (1971), GERR Ref. File 21:7013, the Federal Labor Relations Council held that the establishment or change of tours of duty was not negotiable since the Executive Order reserved to management the right to determine "the numbers, types, and grades of positions for employees assigned to an organizational unit, work project, or tour of duty." The Council stated:

. . . Clearly, the number of its work shifts or tours of duty, and the duration of the shifts, comprise an essential and integral part of the "staffing patterns" necessary to perform the work of the agency. Further, the specific right of an agency to determine the "numbers, types, and grades of positions or employees" assigned to a shift or tour of duty, as provided in section 11 (b), obviously subsumes the agen-

cy's right to fix or change the number and duration of those
shifts or tours. To hold otherwise, *i.e.*, to interpret section
11 (b) as sanctioning the right of the agency to determine
the composition of the shift or tour and not the framework
upon which that composition depends, would render the provisions of section 11(b) virtually meaningless.

While the obligation to bargain does not therefore extend
to the establishment or change of tours of duty under section 11 (b), negotiations may be required on the *impact* of
such actions on the employees involved. For example, as indicated in the Report, bargaining may be required on the
criteria for the assignment of individual employees to particular shifts; on appropriate arrangements for employees
who are adversely affected by the realignment of the work
force; and the like. . . .

In Immigration and Naturalization Service, U.S. Border Patrol,
FLRC No. 70A-10 (1970), GERR Ref. File 21:7007, the Council ruled that a proposal that surveillance roads used by the
Border Patrol be maintained relatively smooth and free from
excessive dust was negotiable since it related more to employee
safety and health than to technology of work.

2.   The restricted scope of bargaining under Executive Order
11491 has been the subject of considerable criticism. *See, e.g.,*
Matthews, *Federal Labor Relations: A Program in Transition,*
21 CATHOLIC U.L. REV. 512 (1972). On the other hand, Robert
Hampton, the Chairman of the Civil Service System, has defended
the limited scope of bargaining, noting that labor-management
relations in the federal government differs significantly from the
private sector since "union negotiations with management in the
executive departments and agencies are only subsidiary and
supplemental to the major employee benefits and protections
which have been granted and are periodically improved through
the legislative process." Hampton, *Federal Labor-Management
Relations: A Program in Evolution,* 21 CATHOLIC U.L. REV.
493, 503 (1972).

STATE COLLEGE EDUCATION ASSOCIATION v. PENNSYLVANIA LABOR RELATIONS BOARD

Commonwealth Court of Pennsylvania
306 A.2d 404 (1973)

JUDGE MENCER: The State College Education Association
(Teachers) and the Pennsylvania Labor Relations Board (Labor
Board) filed separate appeals from a final order of the Court of
Common Pleas of Centre County, under date of November 7,

1972, affirming in part and reversing in part a final order of the Labor Board.

The Teachers, on February 26, 1971, filed a charge of unfair labor practices with the Labor Board and against the State College Area School District (School Board). It was alleged by the Teachers that the School Board had engaged in unfair labor practices contrary to the provisions of Section 1201, subsection (a), clause (5) of Article XII of the Act of July 23, 1970, P.L. 563, 43 P.S. § 1101.1201 (a) (5) (Act 195). These provisions prohibit public employers, their agents or representatives from refusing to bargain collectively in good faith with an employe representative which is the exclusive representative of employes in an appropriate unit, including but not limited to the discussing of grievances with the exclusive representative.

The refusal alleged here centers around 21 items about which the Teachers sought to bargain with the School Board. The School Board admits its refusal to bargain on these items[1] and asserts that they were items of inherent managerial policy and, therefore, were not subject to collective bargaining because of the provisions of Section 702 of Act 195, 43 P.S. § 1101.702. Following hearings before a hearing examiner, during which all parties were afforded the opportunity to present testimony, introduce evidence and cross-examine witnesses, the Labor Board issued a nisi decision and order on October 14, 1971, dismissing the charge of unfair labor practice against the School Board. Exceptions were filed to this order by the Teachers and after oral argument and the presentation of briefs, the Labor Board, on June 26, 1972, issued its final order in which it ruled that the School Board had failed to bargain in good faith with the Teachers on five of the 21 items. The Labor Board affirmed its rulings as to the other 16 items and held that these were not bargainable and, therefore, the School Board had not violated the provisions of Act 195 as to those 16 items.

Both the School Board and the Teachers petitioned the Court of Common Pleas of Centre County for review of the final order of the Labor Board in accord with the provisions of Section 1502, as amended, of Act 195, 43 P.S. § 1101.1502. The Court of Common Pleas of Centre County affirmed the final order of the Labor Board as to the 16 items which were held to be nonbargainable and reversed the final order of the Labor Board as to the five items which the Labor Board had ruled to be proper

---

[1] The School Board had offered to "meet and discuss" with the Teachers in respect to the 21 items, in accord with the provisions of Section 702 of the Act, 43 P.S. § 1101.702.

subjects for mandatory collective bargaining. These appeals followed.

In Pennsylvania Labor Relations Board v. Kaufmann Department Stores, Inc., 345 Pa. 398, 29 A.2d 90 (1942), the Supreme Court held that the scope of appellate review is limited to a determination of whether the findings of the Labor Board are supported by substantial and legally credible evidence and whether the conclusions deduced therefrom are reasonable and not capricious, arbitrary or illegal. *Kaufmann* was interpreting in this regard identical language as we have here.

Section 1501 of Act 195, 43 P.S. § 1101.1501, provides, *inter alia,* that "[t]he findings of the board as to the facts, if supported by substantial and legally credible evidence shall be conclusive."

The difficult question posed by these appeals can be stated thus: Do any of the 21 items about which the Teachers sought to bargain come within the scope of collective bargaining required under Act 195, known as the Public Employe Relations Act? The answer to this question must encompass a careful consideration of the meshing and intertwining provisions of Sections 701, 702 and 703 of Act 195, 43 P.S. §§ 1101.701, 1101.702 and 1101.703. These three sections read as follows:

"Section 701 [§ 1101.701. Matters subject to bargaining]. Collective bargaining is the performance of the mutual obligation of the public employer and the representative of the public employes to meet at reasonable times and confer in good faith with respect to wages, hours and other terms and conditions of employment, or the negotiation of an agreement or any question arising thereunder and the execution of a written contract incorporating any agreement reached but such obligation does not compel either party to agree to a proposal or require the making of a concession.

"Section 702 [§ 1101.702. Matters not subject to bargaining]. Public employers shall not be required to bargain over matters of inherent managerial policy, which shall include but shall not be limited to such areas of discretion or policy as the functions and programs of the public employer, standards of services, its overall budget, utilization of technology, the organizational structure and selection and direction of personnel. Public employers, however, shall be required to meet and discuss on policy matters affecting wages, hours and terms and conditions of employment as well as the impact thereon upon request by public employe representatives.

"Section 703 [§ 1101.703. Implementation of provisions in violation of, or inconsistent with statutes or home rule charters].

"The parties to the collective bargaining process shall not effect or implement a provision in a collective bargaining agreement if the implementation of that provision would be in violation of, or inconsistent with, or in conflict with any statute or statutes enacted by the General Assembly of the Commonwealth of Pennsylvania or the provisions of municipal home rule charters."

Perhaps our point of departure should be to recall the legal posture of public labor relations prior to Act 195. The Act of June 30, 1947, P.L. 1183, 43 P.S. § 215.1 et seq., known as The Public Employe Act of 1947, and which Act 195 specifically repealed as to public employes, prohibited all strikes by public employes and did not require public employers to bargain collectively with their employes. Although strikes by public employes were particularly forbidden, numerous illegal strikes did occur and labor unrest in the public sector became widespread. This situation led to the creation of a Commission for the Revision of Pennsylvania Public Employe Laws which became known as the Hickman Commission.

Subsequent to the issuance of the report of the Hickman Commission various pertinent bills were introduced in the General Assembly of Pennsylvania. The final result was the enactment into law of Act 195. Article I, Section 101 of Act 195 is captioned "Public Policy" and reads as follows:

"The General Assembly of the Commonwealth of Pennsylvania declares that it is the public policy of this Commonwealth and the purpose of this act to promote orderly and constructive relationships between all public employers and their employes subject, however, to the paramount right of the citizens of this Commonwealth to keep inviolate the guarantees for their health, safety and welfare. Unresolved disputes between the public employer and its employes are injurious to the public and the General Assembly is therefore aware that adequate means must be established for minimizing them and providing for their resolution. Within the limitations imposed upon the governmental processes by these rights of the public at large and recognizing that harmonious relationships are required between the public employer and its employes, the General Assembly has determined that the overall policy may best be accomplished by (1) granting to public employes the right to organize and choose freely their representatives; (2) requiring public employers to negotiate and bargain with employe organizations representing public employes and to enter into written agreements evidencing the result of such bargaining; and (3) establishing procedures to provide for the protection of the rights of the public employe, the public employer and the public at large."

This declaration underscores two important factors. Act 195 is dealing in the public sector of labor relations and, secondly, it is intended to afford public employes a limited right of collective bargaining with public employers, subject, however, to the paramount rights of the public at large.

Since Act 195 deals with the public sector of labor relations and has as an integral part of its plan the limiting provisions to collective bargaining of Sections 702 and 703, it is unique and lends itself more to interpretation than to comparisons. Consequently, the myriad of National Labor Relations Board cases and Federal decisions dealing with statutes that do not contain such limitations to collective bargaining and generally dealing in the private sector of labor relations are of little precedent or real assistance, at least in the interpretation of Section 701.

Although in this case we have public employes who also come within the definition of professional employes as set forth at Section 301 (7) of Act 195, 43 P.S. § 1101.301 (7), it would appear that this fact has no relevance to interpreting Sections 701, 702 and 703. The definition of "professional employes" would seem to be solely for the purpose of separating them from nonprofessional employes in making the determination of the appropriate public employer unit in accord with the provisions of Section 604 of Act 195, 43 P.S. § 1101.604. The definition of "public employe" as set forth at Section 301 (2) of Act 195, 43 P.S. § 1101.301 (2), covers and does not exclude professional employes. Therefore, in considering Section 701, we are confined to public employes, and this section has the same application to school teachers as it does to all other public employes.

These preliminary observations then provide us with general concepts which serve as a basis upon which to launch our analysis of Sections 701, 702 and 703 and to thereafter make application to the specific 21 items here in question.

Applicable General Concepts

1. Prior to Act 195, public employes in Pennsylvania had no legal right to strike and public employers were not required to bargain collectively with their employes.

2. Act 195 was enacted to govern labor relations between public employes and public employers and cannot be solely interpreted by reference to rulings, decisions, or case law inter-

preting statutes enacted to govern the private sector of labor relations.

3. Act 195 affords to public employes a limited and qualified right to strike and to bargain collectively.

4. Act 195 places an overriding limitation on collective bargaining by public employes as to matters of inherent managerial policy and those that would be inconsistent with or in conflict with any statute of the Commonwealth of Pennsylvania or provision of a municipal home rule charter.

5. Professional employes, including school teachers, arrive at the bargaining table under Section 701 in the same posture as any other public employes.

6. Act 195 must be construed as intending to favor the public interest.

Analysis of Sections 701, 702 and 703

A careful reading of these sections discloses that the Legislature designated whether items were (a) bargainable items or (b) not bargainable items but subject to a "meet and discuss" requirement.

Section 701 expressly requires the public employer to participate in good faith in collective bargaining with respect to wages, hours and other terms and conditions of employment. However, we are unable to stop here as it is just not a question of whether the item involves wages, hours and other terms and conditions of employment. Assuming that a proposed item for collective bargaining does involve such matters, the further and controlling question must be asked and answered as to whether the item *also* involves matters of inherent managerial policy and, if the answer to this question is in the affirmative, the item is not bargainable under the provisions of Section 702.

Section 702 provides that public employers shall not be required to bargain as to any matter of inherent managerial policy[4] *but,* if the policy matter affects wages, hours and terms and conditions of employment as well as the impact thereon, upon request, the public employers must meet and discuss such policy matter. However, *the controlling provision,* not to be overlooked, is that under Section 702 a public employer is not required to bargain on any policy matter *notwithstanding the effect or impact that it may have on wages, hours, and terms and conditions of employment.*

Likewise, the duties and prerogatives imposed upon and granted to school boards under the Public School Code of 1949 cannot

---

[4] Public employers are of course free to so bargain but are not required to do so by Act 195.

be the subject of collective bargaining because of the restriction and prohibition contained *in Section 703.*

The definition of "public employer" as set forth at Section 301 (1) of Act 195, 43 P.S. § 1101.301 (1), includes school districts and the boards thereof. Since Section 702 provides that public employers shall not be required to bargain over matters of inherent managerial policy, we ought to consider what responsibilities for the operation of the public schools have been placed on school boards by the Legislature. In Slippery Rock Area Joint School System v. Franklin Township School District, 389 Pa. 435, 442, 133 A.2d 848, 852 (1957), it was stated that " '. . . a school district is an agency of the State, created by law for the purpose of promoting education, deriving all of its powers from the statute, and discharging only such duties as are imposed upon it by statute. The school district is an agency of the State charged with the sovereign duty of building and maintaining the schools within its particular territory and with the further duty of securing, managing, and spending the necessary funds in the interest of public education . . .' " Article 10, Section 1 of the Pennsylvania Constitution of 1874 directed the Legislature to maintain a "thorough and efficient system of public schools." Article 3, Section 14 of our present Pennsylvania Constitution provides that "[t]he General Assembly shall provide for the maintenance and support of a thorough and efficient system of public education to serve the needs of the Commonwealth." The school districts are agencies of the Legislature to administer this constitutional duty. Wilson v. Philadelphia School District, 328 Pa. 225, 195 A. 90 (1937). The Public School Code of 1949, Act of March 10, 1949, P.L. 30, as amended, 24 P.S. § 1-101 et seq., contains Section 211, 24 P.S. § 2-211, which provides that "[t]he several school districts in this Commonwealth shall be, and hereby are vested as, bodies corporate, with all necessary powers to enable them to carry out the provisions of this act [Public School Code of 1949]." Thus we must conclude that school boards have traditionally been given by the Legislature, under constitutional mandates, broad inherent managerial powers to operate the public schools and to determine policy relative thereto. If Act 195 represents a departure from the traditional principle of our public schools being operated and managed by school boards, it would be a sharp departure not to be presumed but the result of clear legislative declaration. A statute is never presumed to deprive the state of any prerogative or right unless the intention to do so is clearly manifest, either by express terms or necessary implications. Hoffman v. Pittsburgh, 365 Pa. 386, 75 A.2d 649 (1950).

What then is encompassed by the phrase "matters of inherent managerial policy"? Section 702 itself provides the initial interpretive guides when it states that this phrase "shall include but shall not be limited to such areas of discretion or policy as the functions and programs of the public employer, standards of services, its overall budget, utilization of technology, the organizational structure and selection and direction of personnel."

We know there are other areas of discretion or policy since the illustrative list provided in Section 702 is specifically stated as not being all inclusive. As to school boards, we note that in Smith v. Darby School District, 388 Pa. 301, 130 A.2d 661 (1957), Mr. Justice (now Chief Justice) JONES wrote the following apropos observations:

> "This court has said: 'By the School Code, the school directors are given power to administer the public school system; they are commanded to employ the necessary qualified teachers to conduct school affairs and keep the schools open': Ehret v. Kulpmont Borough School District, *supra,* p. 523; Walker et al. v. Scranton School District, 338 Pa. 104, 108, 12 A.2d 46; Houtz Appeal, *supra,* p. 541. 'It is the administrative function of the school directors and superintendents to meet changing educational conditions through the creation of new courses, reassignment of teachers, and rearrangement of curriculum.': Jones v. Holes et al., 334 Pa. 538, 542, 6 A.2d 102; Mazzei v. Scranton School District, 341 Pa. 255, 260, 19 A.2d 155; Wesenberg Case, *supra,* p. 444; Welsko v. Foster Township School District, *supra,* p. 394.
>
> "The right of a school board to make reasonable rules and regulations, reassign teachers and take other steps necessary for a proper administration of the school system has been recognized on many occasions." 388 Pa. at 312-13, 130 A.2d at 668.
>
> "School authorities must be given broad discretionary powers to ensure a better education for the children of this Commonwealth and any restrictions on the exercise of these powers must be strictly construed on the basis that the public interest predominates and private interests are subordinate thereto. . . ." 388 Pa. at 314, 130 A.2d at 668-69.

In Commonwealth v. Sunbury School District, 335 Pa. 6, 6 A.2d 279 (1939), Mr. Justice (later Chief Justice) DREW wrote as follows:

> "The fundamental policy of our public school system is to obtain the best educational facilities for the children of

the Commonwealth. To this end must be subordinated all personal and partisan considerations: Walker's Appeal, 332 Pa. 488. The duty of devising methods by which this important obligation can be discharged devolves upon the school boards." 335 Pa. at 11, 6 A.2d at 281.

"All legislation must be construed as intending to favor the public interest; and when it conflicts with private interests, the public interest to be primarily served is the dominating one, not that of the individual: Walker's Appeal, *supra*." 335 Pa. at 12, 6 A.2d at 282.

We believe the Labor Board was correct when it stated in its nisi decision the following:

"Broad discretionary powers have been given school authorities to enable them in exercising their policymaking function to ensure a thorough, efficient, effective and better education for the children of this Commonwealth and any erosion of these powers should be strictly constructed on the basis that the public interest is paramount. It has been long recognized that school officials are trustees of the powers vested in them and cannot divest themselves of the powers which have been conferred upon them for a public purpose. . . .

"Policy matters are thought of as rules of conduct and to the extent they *affect* (influence, impinge, encroach, bear upon, or concern) wages, hours and terms and conditions of employment as well as their *impact* (used metaphorically to mean the result, effect or consequence) thereon become mandatory meet and discuss items by the public employer upon request of the public employe representative."

Matters of "inherent managerial policy" over which public employers are not obligated to bargain are such matters that belong to the public employer as a natural prerogative or essential element of the right (1) to manage the affairs of its business, operation or activity and (2) to make decisions that determine the policy and direction that the business, operation or activity shall pursue.

What then is encompassed by the phrase "wages, hours and other items and conditions of employment" as used in Section 701? First, it is important to note that they are words of limitation and do not require collective bargaining upon other subjects. The enumeration of wages, hours and other items and conditions of employment defines a limited category of issues on which the public employer is required to bargain. The word "wages" would seem the least troublesome to understand and obviously represents the remuneration one will receive for his services or labor. This is *not* a managerial policy matter but rather is inherent in the establishment and continuation of the threshold relationship of employer and employe. How many hours one is going to work; what periods of time will be covered; the starting time; the ending time; and the rest or time out from work periods are all included in the commonly understood word "hours." These items are the subject of collective bargaining under Section 701, but the question of whether a teacher shall be present at a parent-teacher meeting held in the evening would be an example of school board policy affecting hours and would be subject to the meet and discuss requirements of Section 702.

The words "other items and conditions of employment" are no doubt susceptible to varying interpretations. At one extreme they could be considered to apply to any subject which is insisted upon as a prerequisite for continued employment. At the other extreme they could be so narrowly interpreted as to have little or no consequence. We believe they refer to such things as the various physical conditions of one's working surroundings; what quantity and quality of work is required during one's work period; what safety practices prevail at and near the job site; what sick and hospital benefits are available and what vacation benefits are available; what retirement benefits will be provided and how eligibility will be determined. More examples could undoubtedly be mentioned but always we must recall the provisions of Section 702 that none of these things are subject to collective bargaining on a required basis if they are affected by policy matters.

Our analysis of Sections 701, 702 and 703 of Act 195 produces these applicable criteria:

1. The required bargainable items of Section 701 are of a limited nature.

2. Any item involving matters of inherent managerial policy is a nonbargainable item by virtue of Section 702.

3. Any item of wages, hours, and other items and conditions of employment, if affected by a policy determination, is not a bargainable item.

4. Duties and responsibilities imposed upon and granted to public employers by statutes or the provisions of municipal home rule charters are not subject to collective bargaining by virtue of Section 703.

5. The Legislature has vested broad powers in school boards

to administer the public school system[5] and to determine policy pertaining thereto.

6.   Any statutory departure from the school board's traditional role of operating and managing our public school must be the result of clear legislative declaration.

7.   Inherent managerial policy is a broad term and includes the right to manage and to make decisions that determine policy.

The 21 Items

We apply these concepts, criteria, and the provisions of Sections 701, 702 and 703 of Act 195 to the 21 specific items about which the Teachers contend the School Board is required to engage in collective bargaining. In doing so, we keep ever before us our limited scope of review.

The 21 items, retaining for clarity the same item numbers used before the Labor Board, are:

1.   The availability of proper and adequate classroom instructional printed material;

2.   The provision for time during the school day for team planning of required innovative programs;

3.   The timely notice of teaching assignment for the coming year;

4.   Providing separate desks and lockable drawer space for each teacher in the district;

5.   Providing cafeteria for teachers in the senior high school;

6.   Eliminating the requirement that teachers perform non-teaching duties such as but not limited to hall duty, bus duty, lunch duty, study hall, and parking lot duties;

7.   Eliminating the requirement that teachers teach or supervise two consecutive periods in two different buildings;

8.   Eliminating the requirement that teachers substitute for other teachers during planning periods and teaching in noncertificated subject areas;

9.   Eliminating the requirement that teachers chaperone athletic activities;

10.   Eliminating the requirement that teachers unpack, store, check or otherwise handle supplies;

11.   Providing that there shall be one night each week free for Association meetings;

12.   Providing that a teacher will, without prior notice, have free access to his personnel file;

---

[5] Few other public employers have such broad power to manage or control as is inherent in school boards as a result of the power traditionally given them by the Legislature.

13.   Permitting a teacher to leave the building any time during the school day unless he has a teaching assignment;

14.   Providing special teachers with preparation time equal to that provided for other staff members;

15.   Provision for maximum class sizes;

16.   Provision that the Association will be consulted in determining the school calendar;

17.   Provision that school will officially close at noon of the last day of classes for Thanksgiving, Christmas, Spring and Summer vacation;

18.   Provision that at least one-half of the time requested for staff meetings be held during the school day;

. . . .

20.   A provision that the present Tuesday afternoon conference with parents be abolished and teachers hold conferences with parents by appointment at a mutually convenient time;

21.   Provision that secondary teachers not be required to teach more than 25 periods per week and have at least one planning period per day; and

22.   A provision that elementary teachers shall have one period or fifteen minutes per day for planning purposes.

Although there is some overlapping, we conclude that the 21 items are not bargainable for the following reasons:

Items 2, 3, 6, 7, 8, 10, 11, 13, 14, 15, 16, 17, 18, 20, 21, and 22, because they are within the scope of matters of inherent managerial policy specifically in the area of functions and programs of the public employer;

Items 1, 7, 8, 13, 14, 15, 20, and 22, because they are within the scope of matters of inherent managerial policy specifically in the area of standards of services of the public employer;

Items 1, 4, 5, 6, 10, 15, and 21, because they are within the scope of matters of inherent managerial policy specifically in the area of the overall budget of the public employer;

Items 3, 6, 14, 18, 21, and 22, because they are within the scope of matters of inherent managerial policy specifically in the area of organizational structure;

Items 2, 3, 6, 7, 8, 9, 10, 13, 14, 18, 20, 21, and 22, because they are within the scope of matters of inherent managerial policy specifically in the area of direction of personnel; and

Items 1, 3, 4, 5, 6, 9, 10, 12, 16, and 17, because they are within the scope of inherent managerial policy in areas other than those enumerated in Section 702.

Perhaps in the future the Legislature may decide to grant public employes the right to collective bargaining in areas which until now have been within the prerogatives of employer management. Such a legislative decision would be a further departure from the tenet that public employes should not have the right to strike or bargain collectively. Act 195 was a limited step in the direction of equating public employes with private employes in the field of labor relations but whether we should go further in this direction is for the Legislature to determine. However, the Legislature did not go beyond the first step when it enacted Act 195.

Order of the Court of Common Pleas of Centre County is affirmed.

Concurring and Dissenting Opinion of KRAMER, J.: First, I would like to state that I concur in the legal analysis and rationale as stated by my brother, Judge Mencer, in his excellent majority opinion; however, in utilizing his analysis, I must dissent as to the majority's application of the law to two of the 22 items over which the teachers sought collective bargaining or a "meet and discuss" conference.

My reading of the statute (Act 195) leads me to find a legislative intent to provide for good faith collective bargaining whenever the teachers' employment rights are directly affected by "wages, hours and other terms and conditions of employment." I draw a distinction between the school authority's "inherent managerial policy" as it relates to the mandated constitutional and statutory duty to provide a thorough and efficient system of public education, and those matters, which while touching on policy, directly affect the public employe teacher. In other words, following the reasoning of the majority, I believe it would be relatively easy for me to argue that almost everything touching upon teachers' employment could be argued to be a matter of "inherent managerial policy." If that is the result of the tack taken by the majority in analyzing what is meant by "inherent managerial policy," then I believe the legislative intent of Act 195 will have been thwarted.

In reading over the 22 items set forth in the majority opinion, I must agree that, as they are worded, it is difficult to fit most of the items into any one category. For instance, in item No. 4, "Providing separate desks and lockable drawer space for each teacher in the district; . . . ," I agree with the majority that whether or not each teacher shall be provided with a desk appears to come within the intent of "inherent managerial policy." If, however, the teachers had intended to raise an item for collective bargaining concerning the security of the teachers' personal property while on school premises, then I would find that such an item must be considered personal to the teachers in their employment rights, and would hold that such an item would be subject to good faith in collective bargaining. However, inasmuch as item No. 4, as submitted, is ambiguous, I must agree with the majority's disposition of that item.

Item No. 9 states, "Eliminating the requirement that teachers chaperone athletic activities; . . . ." Once again the item, as submitted, is lacking in specificity. If the teachers are attempting to collectively bargain on whether or not they shall be paid for chaperoning athletic events, or whether the number of hours they work shall include such activities, then I would find and hold that item No. 9 is one which must be collectively bargained. As stated, however, it is ambiguous, and I must agree with the majority.

Item No. 3 states, "The timely notice of teaching assignment for the coming year; . . . ." It seems to me that this item is direct and personal to the teacher, when compared with the "inherent managerial policy" of the school district. The timely notice of teaching assignments will permit a teacher to so arrange his or her personal life, and preparation for work as to become an item personal to the teacher and outside the "inherent managerial policy" of the school district. I would hold item No. 3 to be subject to collective bargaining.

Item No. 22 reads, "A provision that elementary teachers shall have one period or fifteen minutes per day for planning purposes." This item also appears to me to be direct and personal to the teacher and comes within the purview of a "condition of employment," and therefore, subject to collective bargaining.

What I am trying to say in this short dissent is that while I agree with the majority's analysis of Act 195, I am concerned that the majority's opinion will be interpreted to mean that teachers have no right to collectively bargain items which may be directly related to their employment. I believe that general interpretations of a complex statute, such as Act 195, could lead to a dissipation of the employment rights intended by the Legislature. It seems to me that the Board and the courts will have to evaluate each item as it is presented and strike a balance. If the item directly affects the "inherent managerial policy" of the school district as it applies to its mandate to provide an education system, then it is not subject to collective bargaining. If the item directly affects a teacher's personal rights, as it relates to wages, hours and conditions of employment, then it is subject to collective bargaining. In between these two ends of the spectrum are varying shades, which are not subject to any prospective rule making.

I would reverse the court below on items Nos. 3 and 22.

NOTES

1. The Pennsylvania Labor Relations Board in Nazareth Area Educ. Ass'n, Case No. PERA-C-1884-C (1972), held that preparation time for teachers is an "inherent managerial policy" and therefore not a bargainable subject. *Contra,* Clark County Teachers Ass'n, Nev. Local Gov't Employee-Management Rel. Bd. Item #5 (1972).

2. In Bristol Educ. Ass'n v. Bristol Township Bd. of School Directors, 55 Pa. D. & C.2d 605, 81 L.R.R.M. 2282 (Pa. C.P., Bucks County, 1972), the court stated:

The question of the quality of the programs in a school district has always been a matter of policy determination for the board. Whether or not the money should be spent to purchase new and better laboratory equipment; or to institute a new modern language course, or to hire more experienced and better qualified teachers; or to enlarge the school library; and an infinite number of similar examples of improving the quality of the education provided in a school district have always been policy decisions reserved to the board. Similarly, whether or not the board, should, hire nonprofessional personnel to supervise recess and free the teachers to better fulfill their professional teaching duties falls squarely within the board's policy making duties. If the board chooses not to spend the extra money to hire the non-professional personnel to supervise recess periods, that policy decision is equivalent to a similar policy decision not to purchase new laboratory equipment, no matter how essential the science department may deem the equipment to be. Here, the teachers may believe, as the science teachers in the example, that the quality of the educational program is completely emasculated by the board's policy. Nevertheless, such policy making is exclusively the board's prerogative.

3. In Aberdeen Educ. Ass'n v. Aberdeen Bd. of Educ., 82 L.R.R.M. 2287 (S.D. Cir. Ct., Brown County, 1972), the court held, *inter alia,* that class size and planning periods were "within the scope of the board of education's policy and management responsibilities" and therefore are not "conditions of employment."

DEPARTMENT OF EDUCATION (HAWAII)
Hawaii Public Employment Relations Board
Decision No. 26 (1973)

The HSTA [Hawaii State Teachers Association] is certified by this Board as the exclusive bargaining representative of Unit 5 (teachers and other personnel of the DOE [Department of Education] under the same salary schedule) for the purpose of collective bargaining on "wages, hours and other terms and conditions of employment." The DOE and the HSTA, after protracted and trying negotiations which reached an impasse, and after having exhausted the mandatory statutory steps which must be utilized in an attempt to settle disputes including a 60-day cooling-off period, agreed on a contract on the morning a teachers' strike was scheduled to begin, February 17, 1972. The contract, covering the period from February 29, 1972, through August 31, 1974, provides for the reopening of negotiations on salaries, fringe benefits, preparation periods and work load levels under Article XXIII A 1, which states:

> "Between August 1st and August 15th in 1972, either party may give written notice of its desire to amend or modify this Agreement with respect to salaries, fringe benefits, preparation periods and work load levels, to be effective for the school year 1973-74.
> "Upon such written notice, negotiations shall commence on said topics no later than September 15, 1972."

On August 11th the HSTA gave notice to the DOE of its desire to reopen negotiations with respect to salaries, fringe benefits, preparation periods and work loads for the 1973-74 school year. The *Reopening Proposal* of the HSTA, dated September 13, 1972, includes, in part, proposals on work load and the scheduling of preparation periods within the students' instructional day.

Article VI CC entitled WORK LOAD, proposes that beginning with the 1973-74 school year the daily work loads of various bargaining unit personnel shall not exceed responsibility for the following number of students:

Elementary
   self-contained classes
      Grade K (20 students)
      Grades 1-2 (23 students)
      Grades 3-6 (25 students)
      "3 on 2" (50 students)

   departmentalized programs (not more than the number of students in a self-contained classroom times the number of teaching periods)

   specialists (125 students) . . .

[The proposal in similar fashion spelled out the daily work loads for secondary education, special education, special services, and team teaching.]

Article VI X, entitled PREPARATION PERIODS, proposes, in part, that:

"Beginning with the 1973-74 school year each teacher shall be provided with at least one daily duty-free preparation period within the students' instructional day. . . ."

Negotiations on the *Reopening Proposal* commenced on September 13, 1972. At the outset, the DOE claimed that the work load proposal and that portion of the proposal on preparation periods, which requires that preparation periods be scheduled within the students' instructional day, are non-negotiable because they interfere with the rights and responsibilities vested in the Board of Education by the State Constitution at Article IX, Section 3, and by Section 89-9 (d) of the Hawaii Revised Statutes. Consequently, the DOE petitioned this Board for a declaratory ruling on the negotiability of said issues.

The HSTA, on the other hand, during the hearing submitted that the proposal on work load did not interfere with management rights under Section 89-9 (d) and was, therefore, negotiable. The HSTA pointed out that work load is directly related to class size and that this Board had already ruled that average class size ratio is negotiable in an earlier case. (In the Matter of Hawaii State Teachers Association, Petitioner, and Department of Education, Respondent, HPERB Case No. CE-05-4, Dec. No. 22, October 24, 1972) [GERR No. 480, E-1] With respect to the proposals requiring that preparation periods be scheduled within the students' instructional day, the HSTA's position was that such a proposal is negotiable since the DOE has scheduled preparation periods within the students' instructional day in the past and preparation periods definitely affect working hours and the ability of the teacher to perform teaching tasks.

In determining the negotiability of these proposals, we are guided by Chapter 89, Hawaii Revised Statutes. Therein, public employers are required to negotiate with and enter into written agreements with exclusive representatives on matters of "wages, hours and other terms and conditions of employment." Such duty to bargain is not unrestricted, however. Section 89-9 (d) sets forth, in pertinent part, the following:

". . . The employer and the exclusive representative shall not agree to any proposal . . . which would interfere with the rights of a public employer to (1) direct employees; (2) determine qualifications, standards for work, the nature and contents of examinations, hire, promote, transfer, assign, and retain employees in positions and suspend, demote, discharge, or take other disciplinary action against employees

for proper cause; (3) relieve an employee from duties because
of lack of work or other legitimate reason; (4) maintain
efficiency of government operations; (5) determine methods,
means and personnel by which the employer's operations are
to be conducted; and take such actions as may be necessary
to carry out the missions of the employer in cases of emer-
gencies."

Therefore, the question with which we are faced herein is
whether the evidence in the record supports the DOE's claim
that the work load proposal and that portion of the proposal
requiring that preparation periods be scheduled within the students' instructional day so interfere with its rights as a public
employer as enumerated in Section 89-9 (d) above as to render
the proposals non-negotiable. . . .

Conclusions of Law

Inasmuch as the HSTA contends that the work load proposal
is negotiable since it is directly related to class size, which this
Board, it declares, has determined to be negotiable in an earlier
case . . . we find a review of that prior case necessary.

In that case, we held that "wages, hours and other terms and
conditions of employment" which are negotiable, and the rights
of the employer reserved in Section 89-9 (d) were not mutually
exclusive categories. We found that class size was a hybrid issue;
it involved both policy making and had a significant impact on
working conditions.

We determined therein that the provision calling for a reduction in the average class size ratio throughout the statewide educational system by approximately one student was negotiable. In
reaching our decision, this Board balanced the employer's broad
right to establish educational policy, unfettered by a collective
bargaining agreement on the one hand, against the direct impact
the average class size ratio had on the teachers' working conditions. Notwithstanding its admitted relation to educational policy, we found in that instance that the element of impact on
teachers' working conditions was great, while the imposition of
an average, statewide class size ratio had minimum impact on
the DOE's right to establish educational policy.

While we held that Section 89-9 (d) should not be narrowly
construed so as to negate the purposes of bargaining, we con-
comitantly expressed the view that said section should not be too
liberally construed so as to divest the employer of its managerial
rights and prevent it from fulfilling its duty to determine policy
for the effective operation of the public school system. Therefore, we further found that other issues raised in that case, which

dictated the number of teachers the employer was to hire in order to implement the reduction and which dictated the assignment of teachers to specific roles, were in violation of Section 89-9 (d) .

Unlike our earlier determination on class size, which concerned a reduction in the average class size ratio throughout the state-wide educational system, the instant work load issue is distinguishable. The work load proposal, in effect, would rigidly fix the maximum number of students for which a teacher, team of teachers, or specialist has daily responsibility.

Here, again, we are faced with a hybrid proposal, which involves both educational policy making and has a significant impact on working conditions. Therefore, while the work load proposal is admittedly a significant term and condition of employment, we must determine, nevertheless, whether the proposal so interferes with management's right to establish educational policy and operate the school system efficiently as to render it non-negotiable under Section 89-9 (d).

The DOE has the right and duty as an employer to maintain efficiency of its operations pursuant to Section 89-9 (d) (5) .

The *Random House Dictionary of the English Language (College Edition)* defines "efficiency" as:

". . . accomplishment or ability to accomplish a job with a minimum expenditure of time and effort. . . ."

The effect of the work load proposal, in the instant case, would be to force the DOE to hire personnel and expand facilities regardless of its rights and duty to maintain efficiency of operations. Some of the alternatives which might be forced upon the DOE would constitute inefficient, wasteful use of personnel and equipment. Other consequences that may ensue if the DOE is required to implement the work load proposal would run counter to the mission of the DOE, *i.e.*, to provide the best educational system possible for the children of Hawaii. In providing educational service, the DOE must be responsive to the needs of the students, to the extent possible, given available resources. Hence, when the DOE is required to utilize methods which would cause deterioration of the learning environment of the students, such as, placing two teachers in the same classroom or increasing team teaching regardless of a teacher's ability to team teach, it becomes obvious that the DOE's right and duty to provide the best educational system possible is being interfered with. Furthermore, when the DOE is relegated to such alternatives as busing students or decreasing course offerings solely for the purpose of implementing the work load proposal, it loses its ability to remain responsive to the needs of the students.

Additionally, the work load proposal does not give any consideration to the fact that the DOE is dealing with humans, not machines, where input and output cannot be standardized. Teachers' talents vary; some are more experienced than others, some do better in large group instruction, others may be particularly suited for team teaching. Students' needs vary; some have problems in a particularly [sic] instructional area, some students are able to learn more readily. An experienced teacher may be effectively able to handle more students than an inexperienced teacher. An experienced teacher may be effectively able to handle more students than another teacher with comparable experience and ability if he had a group of above-average students.

The DOE must have enough flexibility to determine matters such as work load and curriculum based on the admixture of all the factors which affect the educational process at a given time and in a given situation. Furthermore, as developments occur in the field of education, the DOE should not be hampered in its efforts to experiment with innovative strategies and new technology in striving toward its objective of providing an excellent educational system.

Therefore, it is our opinion that the specific proposal on work load which is here at issue, while admittedly concerned with a condition of employment because it may affect the amount of work expected of a teacher, nevertheless, in far greater measure, interferes with the DOE's responsibility to establish policy for the operation of the school system, which cannot be relinquished if the DOE is to fulfill its mission of providing a sound educational system and remaining responsive to the needs of the students while striving to maintain efficient operations. Hence, the DOE and the HSTA may not agree to the subject work load proposal because such agreement would interfere substantially with the DOE's right to determine the methods, means, and personnel by which it conducts its operations and would interfere with its responsibility to the public to maintain efficient operations.

Moreover, the Legislature declared when it enacted Chapter 89, Hawaii Revised Statutes, that its policy was to "promote harmonious and cooperative relations between government and its employees and to protect the public by assuring effective and orderly operations of government." We are convinced that the proposal on work load would not protect the public by assuring effective and orderly operations of government as the Legislature intended.

While we find that preparation periods constitute a condition of employment, the specific issue herein concerns the *scheduling* of preparation periods. It is our opinion that the scheduling of preparation periods is, in effect, the scheduling of work, which has been, and should remain, the right of the DOE as an employer. Inasmuch as preparation periods are periods of work like any other for which teachers are being compensated, the DOE should continue to have the freedom to schedule preparation periods in the same manner as any other period of work, at any time during the teachers' work day (whether within or outside of the students' instructional day) as it deems feasible.

We are aware that it would be more advantageous to teachers if preparation periods are scheduled within the students' instructional day because of the likelihood of interruptions by students and the performance of non-professional, routine chores done prior to, or after, the students' instructional day. However, this should not affect the right of the DOE, as an employer, to schedule and assign the work of its employees. Nearly every employee in any enterprise must also perform routine, non-professional chores daily, at the beginning and end of the work day. Many employees similarly have less time to spend on their work due to questions arising from the people to whom they provide services. These are happenings during the normal course of a work day which all employees experience and do not, in any way, affect the employer's right to assign and schedule employees' work as it deems feasible.

Therefore, we find that the portion of the reopening proposal on preparation periods, which calls for the scheduling of such periods within the students' instructional day, would interfere with the employer's rights to assign employees and to determine the methods, means, and personnel by which it operates the public school system in a manner necessary to maintain efficient operations. Hence, that particular portion of the proposal on preparation periods may not be agreed to by the parties. . . .

NOTES

1. Contrast the Hawaii Act which specifically provides that "[t]he employer and the exclusive representative shall not agree to any proposal which would be inconsistent with merit principles . . . or which would interfere with the rights of a public employer to . . .," HAWAII REV. STAT. § 89-9 (d) (Supp. 1971), with the Pennsylvania Act which provides that "[p]ublic employers shall not be required to bargain over matters of inherent managerial policy, which shall include but shall not be limited to such areas of discretion or policy as . . ." PA. STAT. ANN. tit. 43, § 1101.702 (Supp. 1972). Whereas the parties are prohibited from bargaining over certain subjects by virtue of the Hawaii Act, the

Pennsylvania Act only provides that the employer is not required to negotiate over certain matters. In other words, while the Pennsylvania Act specifically provides that certain matters are not *mandatory* subjects of bargaining, such matters may nevertheless be *permissible* subjects of negotiations, *i.e.,* the employer could voluntarily negotiate over such matters and include any agreements reached in a written labor contract.

2. The Nevada Local Government Employee Relations Act provides that employers are required to negotiate in good faith with employee organizations on matters "concerning wages, hours, and conditions of employment." NEV. REV. STAT. § 288.150(1). The Act, however, further provides:

> Each local government employer is entitled, without negotiation or reference to any agreement resulting from negotiation:
>
> (a) To direct its employees;
>
> (b) To hire, promote, classify, transfer, assign, retain, suspend, demote, discharge or take disciplinary action against any employee;
>
> (c) To relieve any employee from duty because of lack of work or for any other legitimate reason;
>
> (d) To maintain the efficiency of its governmental operations;
>
> (e) To determine the methods, means and personnel by which its operations are to be conducted; and
>
> (f) To take whatever actions may be necessary to carry out its responsibilities in situations of emergency.
>
> NEV. REV. STAT. § 288.150 (2).

In Washoe County School Dist., Item #3 (1971), the Nevada Local Government Employee-Management Relations Board held, *inter alia,* that proposals concerning class size, student discipline, school calendar, and teacher load were negotiable. In so ruling, the Board stated:

> Although it has been urged upon this Board by the counsel for the Washoe County School District that the provisions of Subsection 2 limit the areas of negotiability on matters relating to wages, hours, and conditions of employment if said matters also involve any items in Subsection 2, the Board rejects this view as untenable.
>
> It is presumed the Legislature in enacting Chapter 288 did not enact a nullity. Under the school district's interpretation of the relationship between NRS 288.150, Subsection 1, and NRS 288.150, Subsection 2, any matter, including the

very question of wage scale, involves management prerogative; and consequently, under said view would not be negotiable.

The Board does not believe that the Legislature so intended such an interpretation. Public employees by this Act have been denied perhaps their most valuable right— the right to strike. On the other hand, the local government employer has retained the right to define and recognize particular bargaining units, the right to exercise its management prerogatives without reference to negotiation or any prior negotiated agreement.

It is the opinion of the Board, therefore, that any matter significantly related to wages, hours, and working conditions is negotiable, whether or not said matters also relate to questions of management prerogative; and it is the duty of the local government employer to proceed and negotiate said items.

LOS ANGELES COUNTY DEPARTMENT OF PUBLIC SOCIAL SERVICES AND DEPARTMENT OF PERSONNEL

Los Angeles County Employee Relations Commission
Case No. UFC 55.3 (1971)
Aff'd 83 L.R.R.M. 2916 (Cal. Ct. App. 1973)

Commissioner Alleyne: In this case the Commission has been asked to decide whether the Los Angeles County Employee Relations Ordinance obligates a department of the County to negotiate with a union on the subject of caseloads for Eligibility Workers employed by the Los Angeles County Department of Public Social Services. The charge in this case was filed against the County on December 3, 1970, by the Joint Council of Los Angeles County Employees Association and Service Employees International Union, Local 535. The charge alleges that since May 14, 1970 the County has consistently refused to bargain on the negotiable matter of workload for Eligibility Workers. Sections 12 (a) (1) and 12 (a) (3) of the Los Angeles County Employee Relations Ordinance are alleged to have been violated by the County's conduct. . . .

An answer to the charge was filed on February 17, 1971. The answer admits that the County refused to negotiate with the Union "concerning the specific number of cases assigned to individual eligibility workers." A hearing was held before the Commission on March 11, April 27 and May 14, 1971. The County's admission that it refused to negotiate with the Union on the question of caseloads for Eligibility Workers removes essential factual issues from this case, but leaves open for consideration the legal question of whether the subject of caseloads for Eligibility Workers is a negotiable subject as the Union con tends, or a non-negotiable subject as the County contends.

Section 12 (a) (3) of the Ordinance requires that the County negotiate with a certified employee organization only with respect to "negotiable matters." Therefore, if the subject of an Eligibility Worker's caseload is a negotiable matter within the meaning of Section 12 (a) (3) of the Ordinance, the County violated that provision by refusing to negotiate with the Union on that subject. If, on the other hand, that subject is not a negotiable matter within the meaning of Section 12 (a) (3) of the Ordinance, the County had every right not to negotiate with the Union on that subject.

The County's Position

While admitting that the County refused to negotiate with the Union concerning the number of cases assigned to Eligibility Workers, . . . the County contends that the specific level or quantity of work to be assigned to County employees "is a matter within the exclusive jurisdiction of the [County] to determine, and is therefore not a subject within the scope of required negotiations." . . .

DECISION

After carefully considering the positions of the parties and paying particular attention to the detailed defenses raised in the County's answer to the charge, we have decided that the charge has merit; that the subject of an Eligibility Worker's caseload is a negotiable matter within the meaning of Section 12 (a) (3) of the Ordinance; and that the County was therefore obligated to negotiate with the Union on that subject. It follows that the County's failure to do so constitutes a violation of Sections 12 (a) (1) and (3) of the Ordinance.

The text of Section 12 (a) (3) of the Ordinance provides in pertinent part:

(a) It shall be an unfair employee relations practice for the County

. . . .

(3) To refuse to negotiate with representatives of certified employee organizations *on negotiable matters*. [Emphasis added.]

The Ordinance does not expressly list what subjects are and what subjects are not "negotiable" within the meaning of Section 12 (a) (3) . In resolving that issue in the factual context of this case, we have looked to other general language in the Ordinance and the reported views of the Consultants' Committee which drafted the Ordinance. This being the first case of its nature presented to this Commission, we of course have no precedents under the Ordinance which we might look to for guidance.

The Intent of the Ordinance's Draftsmen

When the Ordinance was in the proposal stage, the Consultants' Committee which drafted it did not recommend—though the County urged that it do so—that the Ordinance specifically enumerate those matters which are non-negotiable within the meaning of Section 12 (a) (3). The Consultants' Committee recognize that "The line between nonnegotiable management rights and subjects over which certified employee organizations would have the right to negotiate under the recommended Ordinance is not always clearly discernible." They accordingly recommended "that in close and doubtful cases the [Employee Relations] Commission be empowered to draw the line on an *ad hoc basis*." In these respects the Ordinance was adopted by the Board of Supervisors as recommended by the Consultants' Committee. Thus, we view this case as one of those *ad hoc* cases envisioned by the drafters of the Ordinance and the County Board of Supervisors as a step in the administrative process of defining what constitutes a Section 12 (a) (3) negotiable matter.

After rejecting the urgings of County officials that the Ordinance specifically define the kinds of subjects concerning which negotiations would not be mandatory, the Consultants' Committee adopted the view that this approach would be unworkable inasmuch as the definition of "negotiation" as used in the Ordinance would have to "take on color and meaning from [its] surrounding context." The Consultants' Committee then gave one hypothetical example of what might be regarded as a negotiable as distinguished from a non-negotiable matter. Fortuitously, the example given bears almost directly on the issue involved in this case. Concerning the subject of a maximum caseload for social workers, the Consultants' Committee report contains the following statement:

Viewed in the abstract, the demand to negotiate over "the level of service to be provided" for example, would seem to be . . . not negotiable except at the discretion of the County. . . . In the context of a specific situation, however, a demand for a lower maximum caseload for social workers, for example, although theoretically related to the level of service to be provided, might be much more directly related to terms and conditions of employment.

This statement by the Consultants' Committee may be regarded as dispositive of the issue at hand. At very least, we think it militates strongly in favor of the Union's position and against the position maintained by the County. The Consultants' Committee report is more than a mere statement of the consultants' personal views concerning the Ordinance's intent. The Ordinance was adopted by the Board of Supervisors on September 3, 1968 by a unanimous vote of the Board. In addition to adopting the Ordinance, the Board of Supervisors at the same time adopted the following resolution:

> That the document entitled "an Employee Relations Ordinance for Los Angeles County—Report and Recommendations of the Consultants' Committee" filed with this Board on July 25, 1968 by Benjamin Aaron, Lloyd H. Bailer, and Howard Block, the three employee relations Consultants previously retained by this Board to prepare and submit a proposed Employee Relations Ordinance . . . and accompanying report . . . *are hereby found to be accurate statements of this Board's intent and purpose in adopting [the] Ordinance. . . .* [Emphasis added.]

It thus appears that the Board of Supervisors in adopting the Consultants' report as an expression of the Ordinance's intent clearly intended to make the subject of caseloads for Social Workers a negotiable matter. Concerning the caseload issue immediately before us, we see no discernible difference between Social Workers and Eligibility Workers. But our decision does not rest on this statement alone. We think there is more to sustain the charge.

The Meaning of "Negotiation" under the Ordinance

Although the Ordinance does not explicitly define what is and what is not a negotiable matter within the meaning of Section 12 (a) (3), the Ordinance's definition of "negotiation," as found in Section 3 (o), and the meaning of "scope of negotiation," as found in Section 6 (b), are of some assistance. Section 3 (o) provides as follows:

> "Negotiation" means performance by duly authorized management representatives and duly authorized representatives of a certified employee organization of their mutual obligation to meet at reasonable times and to confer in good faith with respect to *wages, hours, and other terms and conditions* of employment, and includes the mutual obligation to execute a written document incorporating any agreement reached. [Emphasis added.]

Section 6 (b) of the Ordinance describes the "scope of negotiation" under the Ordinance as including "wages, hours, and other terms and conditions of employment. . . ." Thus, the issue involved here might be narrowed to the following: Is the subject of an Eligibility Worker's caseload among the "terms and conditions of employment" contemplated by Sections 3 (o) and 6 (b) of the Ordinance?

Framing the issue in this fashion does not provide a complete answer to the question before us. The question of what constitutes "terms and conditions of employment," as defined by the National Labor Relations Act, has been a difficult question for courts to decide in borderline cases. As Mr. Justice Stewart noted in a concurring Supreme Court opinion, "The phrase 'conditions of employment' is no doubt susceptible of diverse interpretations."[6]

An appropriate criterion here is one which a United States Court of Appeals has applied, namely, "that since practically every managerial decision has some impact on wages, hours, or other conditions of employment, the determination of which decisions are mandatory bargaining subjects must depend upon whether a given subject has a significant or material relationship to wages, hours, or other conditions of employment."[7] We think that a County Eligibility Worker's caseload falls within this standard.

An Eligibility Worker interviews public assistance applicants or recipients, and determines initial or continuing eligibility. Eligibility Workers I perform these duties under supervision. Eligibility Workers II independently make initial and continuing eligibility and grant determinations for public assistance applicants or recipients; they refer problems requiring social services to the social service staff.

A witness for the Union, an Eligibility Worker employed by the Department of Public Social Services, testified that an Eligibility Worker is responsible for an assigned number of cases. It was the Union's attempt to negotiate with the County for a ceiling on that number and the County's refusal to do so which led to the charge in this case. Although the record in some respects is unclear on the matter of whether the Union was seeking an agreement on an average number of cases or a maximum number of cases, it appears to be undisputed that the Union was

---

[6] Fibreboard Paper Products Corp. v. NLRB, 379 U.S. 203, 221, 57 L.R.R.M. 2609, 2616 (1964).

[7] Westinghouse Electric Corp. v. NLRB, 387 F.2d 542, 548, 66 L.R.R.M. 2634, 2638 (4th Cir. 1966).

initially seeking an agreement on a maximum number of case assignments to an Eligibility Worker. . . .

Following this unsuccessful attempt to negotiate an agreement concerning a ceiling on an Eligibility Worker's caseload, the Union discussed with the County a concept relating to an average caseload. It is, however, the initial refusal of the County to discuss a maximum caseload for Eligibility Workers which is the essence of the unfair employee relations practice charge. While the record contains evidence that the County was willing to discuss this matter with the Union, the County, in those instances, was not negotiating with the Union; on the contrary, the County, as its answer to the charge states, was consulting with the Union. The difference is that "negotiating" may possibly lead to a binding contract while "consulting" places no legal obligation on the parties to attempt to reach an agreement.[10] It was of course a binding agreement which the Union sought in this case, and which the County admittedly refused to attempt to negotiate.

We think that the subject of a maximum caseload has a clear and direct relationship to an Eligibility Worker's conditions of employment. The rate at which their work is performed as well as the amount of work they perform within a given unit of time depend upon the number of cases assigned to them. Whether and to what extent that number might be beyond the capacity of the average Eligibility Worker to perform, whether that number is generally equitable or inequitable, excessive or moderate, are matters which are inseparable from the concept of working conditions. These are but examples of the kinds of questions concerning which the Ordinance binds the parties in this dispute to attempt to resolve through negotiations. The subject of workloads for Eligibility Workers may not be equated with routine job directions or detailed decisions relating to the manner in which work is to be performed. In those areas and of course other areas, there is no duty to negotiate.

While private sector cases decided under the National Labor Relations Act have no binding effect on questions arising under our Ordinance, we do note that the subject of workloads is a mandatory subject of bargaining under the National Labor Relations Act.[11] We also note that the National Labor Relations

---

[10] Section 6 (a) of the Ordinance provides in part: "All matters affecting employee relations, including those that are not subject to negotiations, are subject to consultation between management representatives and the duly authorized representatives of affected employee organizations."

[11] See, for example, Bonham Cotton Mills, Inc., 121 N.L.R.B. No. 159, 42 L.R.R.M. 1542; Little Rock Downtowner, Inc., 145 N.L.R.B. 1286, 55

Act and our Ordinance have the same objective—to protect the public from the effects of work stoppages, strikes and other forms of employee unrest.

The "County Rights" Provision in the Ordinance

Section 5 of the Ordinance is entitled "County Rights." It broadly sets out those general areas within which the County has the exclusive right to make unilateral decisions. Section 5 provides:

> It is the exclusive right of the County to determine the mission of each of its constituent departments, board, and commissions, set standards of services to be offered to the public, and exercise control and discretion over its organization and operations. It is also the exclusive right of the County to direct its employees, take disciplinary action for proper cause, relieve its employees from duty because of lack of work or for other legitimate reasons, and determine the methods, means and personnel by which the County's operations are to be conducted; provided, however, that the exercise of such rights does not preclude employees or their representatives from conferring or raising grievances about the practical consequences that decisions on these matters may have on wages, hours, and other terms and conditions of employment.

The County relies heavily upon this language to sustain its position that caseloads for Eligibility Workers is not a negotiable matter. We do not so read Section 5. We have determined on the basis of the expressed intent of the Board of Supervisors in adopting the Ordinance, that Eligibility Workers' caseloads are negotiable "conditions of employment" as defined in Sections 3 (o) and 6 (b) of the Ordinance. We find nothing in the general language of Section 5 which detracts from that determination. The Section 3 (o) definition of "negotiation," the Section 6 (b) definition of "scope of negotiation" and Section 12 (a) (3) 's refusal to negotiate language are more specific in content than the general provisions of Section 5. We believe that the generalities of Section 5 must be read in the light of, and are in fact limited by, the more specific provisions of Sections 3 (o) , 6 (b) and 12 (a) (3) . For example, Section 5 provides in part that the County has the exclusive right to "exercise control and discretion over its organization and operations. . . ." When read alone, this

---

L.R.R.M. 1156 (1964); Irvington Motors, Inc., 147 N.L.R.B. 565, 56 L.R.R.M. 1257, *enforced*, 343 F.2d 759, 58 L.R.R.M. 2816 (3rd Cir. 1965); Tex-Tan Welhausen Company, 172 N.L.R.B. No. 93 (1968).

might be interpreted to mean that the County may unilaterally determine wages for County employees. Yet, it is clear from a reading of Sections 3 (o), 6 (b) and 12 (a) (3) that the County must—as it does—negotiate with certified employee organizations on the subject of wages. Only by reading those sections as limitations on the broad language found in Section 5 may the County's unquestionable obligation to negotiate on the subject of wages be supported. Specifically, we conclude that the validity of the charge in this case is not affected by the "County Rights" provision of the Ordinance. . . .

CONCLUSION

On the basis of the foregoing, we conclude that the County violated Sections 12 (a) (1) and (3) of the Ordinance by refusing to negotiate with the Union on the subject of a maximum caseload for Eligibility Workers. This does not mean that the County is obligated to reach an agreement with the Union on that issue. Section 3 (o) of the Ordinance precludes this by providing that the obligation to negotiate "does not compel either party to agree to a proposal or to make a concession." Our conclusion does mean that the County has an obligation to make a good faith attempt to reach an agreement with the Union concerning caseloads for Eligibility Workers. We express no opinion on the matter of what appropriate agreement the parties should attempt to conclude on this subject. This is a matter for the parties to negotiate. . . .

Commissioner Nathanson, concurring:

I concur with Commissioner Reginald H. Alleyne, Jr. in his findings, with these additional comments:

My concurrence is based upon the "ad hoc" circumstances pertinent to this case. Whether the undersigned would come to the same conclusions under different circumstances involving a different class of employees should by no means be considered certain.

The instant case, however, involves a category of workers on whose behalf a maximum workload was once established by the employer as peculiar to the work requirements. Subsequently, due to budgetary problems, the numerical maximum was abolished in favor of a more flexible yard-stick. But the employer acknowledged that the workload had progressively increased to an extent that it expressed its intent to avoid adding to the burden. Its reluctance, however, to negotiate on and include such a commitment in a Memorandum of Understanding caused this proceeding.

A Decision by the Board of Collective Bargaining with regard to Workload and Manning in the Fire Department in the City of New York almost parallels the question before the County of Los Angeles Employee Relations Commission (Decision No. B-9-68: Docket No. BCB-16-68) in which the Board said in part ". . . the City will be required expeditiously to take whatever action is necessary to relieve the 'impact'. Relieving the impact can be done by the City on its own initiative if it chooses to act through the exercise of rights reserved to it in Section 5c." (Note: Section 5c of the applicable legislation in the City of New York is essentially similar to Section 5 of the County of Los Angeles Employee Relations Ordinance.) "If it cannot relieve the 'impact' in that manner, or it chooses to take action by offering changes in wages, hours and working conditions— means which are not reserved to the City specifically under Section 5c—then, of course, the City cannot act unilaterally but *must bargain out these matters with the Union.*" (Emphasis supplied.)

The Board went on to say: "We believe that the conclusions reached here are also supported by logic and sound labor relations as well as the provisions of the statute and Executive Order. It is unrealistic to believe that the City and its municipal unions would have agreed . . . that an unreasonable workload or manning problem could be found to exist, but that no appropriate remedy ultimately could be recommended for the alleviation of the problem. To deny this avenue of relief negates the purpose of the statute and opens the door for the very labor strife which the statute was expressly designed to prevent."

The only distinction in the case cited above and that before this Commission is that the Board in the City of New York had to determine first that an impact existed and if it did so, then the remedies quoted must be applied.

Agreement to limit the impact in the employer's offered letter of intent acknowledges the impact. Relief, therefore, is the issue before us.

Peter Seitz, arbitrator, in an award dated October 9, 1966, involving the Patrolmen's Benevolent Association of the City of New York, Inc., and the Uniformed Firemen's Association, Local 94, and the City of New York, said there is an obligation to bargain on matters related to unsatisfactory working conditions, though how the government agency accomplishes the relief is the latter's prerogative. Which is to say, as does Commissioner Alleyne, that it is the County's obligation to bargain on eligibility workers' working conditions, including caseloads, though it need not mandatorily agree with the certified labor organization on the requested method of relief. That's this Commissioner's belief, also.

NOTES

1. After the issuance of the decision in the principal case, the Consultants' Committee, in reviewing the experience with the ordinance, agreed with the Commission's decision that the issue of workload was negotiable. *Proposed Revision of the Los Angeles County Ordinance,* submitted by Consultant Benjamin Aaron, as printed in CALIFORNIA PUBLIC EMPLOYEE RELATIONS No. 14, pp. 12-13 (August 1972).

2. The San Diego County Employee Relations Panel held that the workload of supervisory probationary officers, *i.e.,* the number of employees supervised, was a negotiable item under the San Diego ordinance. As noted in CALIFORNIA PUBLIC EMPLOYEE RELATIONS No. 11, at 37 (November 1971), "The majority of the Panel held that the main impact of the supervisory ratio is on working conditions, rather than on the merits, necessity or organization of the service or on exclusive management rights. The impact on working conditions is direct, whereas the impact on service is indirect."

3. The Vallejo City Charter mandates negotiations, and binding arbitration if negotiations are unsuccessful, between the city and its firefighters on wages, hours, and working conditions, but not on "the merits, necessity or organization of any service or activity provided by law." GERR No. 372, B-5 to B-6 (1970). In Fire Fighters Union, Local 1186 v. City of Vallejo, 69 LC ¶ 52,914 (Calif. Super. Ct., Solano County, 1972), the court held that proposals submitted by the union concerning personnel reduction, promotion, schedule of hours, and manning were negotiable and therefore could be submitted to binding arbitration if the parties were at impasse on any of these issues.

4. The New York City Collective Bargaining Law, which is included in the Statutory Appendix, contains a fairly lengthy enumeration of management rights and provides that "[d]ecisions of the city or any other public employer on those matters are not within the scope of bargaining." The New York law further provides, however, that "questions concerning the practical impact that decisions on [management prerogatives] have on employees, such as questions of workload or manning, are within the scope of collective bargaining." N.Y. CITY ADMIN. CODE, ch. 54, § 1173-4.3 (b). The New York City Office of Collective Bargaining has held that the following items are embraced within the City's management prerogatives and therefore not

negotiable: determination of whether to grant merit increases, City of New York and Civil Service Ass'n, Decision No. B-9-69 (7/18/69); job content and shift hours, City of New York and District Council 37, AFSCME, Decision No. B-4-69 (6/12/69); creation of new positions, District Council 37, AFSCME and City of New York, Decision No. B-3-69 (6/2/69). On the other hand, the OCB has held that the following matters are mandatory subjects of negotiations: procedures and criteria used to determine eligibility for merit increases, City of New York and Civil Service Ass'n, Decision No. B-9-69 (7/18/69); seniority and examination eligibility, City of New York and District Council 37, AFSCME, Decision No. B-4-69 (6/12/69); free parking facilities, availability of office supplies, educational leave, legal counsel for employees in court on official business, and theft and damage funds, City of New York and Social Service Employees Union, Decision No. B-11-68 (1/8/69).

4. Effect of Civil Service Laws

The origins of civil service systems can be traced to passage of the Pendleton Act of 1883. This Act was viewed as the *modus operandi* for protecting federal employees from the spoils system. The core concept underlying the Act and other civil service legislation is that public employees should be selected and retained solely on merit. But over the years these systems have expanded to cover many matters not essential to implementation of the merit principle.

In many respects the development of civil service systems paralleled the growth of collective bargaining in the private sector. George Shultz observed: "Civil service regulations set forth the law of the public workplace. The governing charter in the private sphere is normally the collective bargaining agreement." GERR No. 319, F-2 (1969). In fact, for many years unions representing public employees staunchly supported the strengthening of civil service systems. The American Federation of State, County and Municipal Employees (AFSCME) was founded in 1934 in Wisconsin in order to lobby against proposed legislation that would have gutted that state's civil service system. *See generally* L. KRAMER, LABOR'S PARADOX 27-38 (1962). As late as its 1960 convention AFSCME's official position was to "stimulate the growth and extension of civil service and to improve existing merit systems." Proceedings, AFSCME, 12th Int'l Convention, Philadelphia, April 25-29, 1960, p. 341. Increasingly over the past 15 years, however, AFSCME and other unions representing public employees have come to view civil service as an arm of management. More and more they are demanding that matters covered by civil service be made negotiable. The obvious conflict between civil service and collective bargaining has resulted in numerous problems concerning the scope of negotiations.

1967 EXECUTIVE COMMITTEE, NATIONAL GOVERNORS' CONFERENCE, REPORT OF TASK FORCE ON STATE AND LOCAL GOVERNMENT LABOR RELATIONS 18-19 (1967)†

A critical issue for many governments is how the merit principle can be preserved and how collective bargaining can be accommodated within the merit system.

Because the two terms, "merit principle" and "merit system" are frequently confused, they should be defined. The merit principle is the concept that public employees should be selected and retained solely on the basis of merit. Political, religious, or racial considerations should play no part in such employment practices as selection, promotion, wages, career progression, assignment, and discharge. The merit principle was originally conceived to minimize the effect of patronage on the efficiency of government operations.

The merit system (or civil service system) is a public employment procedure designed to implement the merit principle. The procedure varies from place to place, but it commonly involves the establishment of a board (civil service commission) with rule-making authority to insure adherence to the merit principle. The essential elements of a merit system are: an impartial recruiting, examining and selecting program; position classification plans based on duties and responsibilities; promotion on merit; protection against arbitrary disciplinary action.

In practice, many merit systems over the years have come to encompass other aspects of employee relations and personnel management not essentially related to the merit principle. These aspects include the handling of grievances, labor-management relations, employee training, salary administration, safety, morale, and attendance control programs.

In discussing the implications of collective bargaining for the merit system, consideration should be given to the determination of those procedures necessary to the merit principle as compared to procedural aspects of personnel management. Most public administration experts agree that merit system rules on examination, placement and promotion are indispensable to the merit

---

† Reprinted by permission of the International Personnel Management Association.

principle and should therefore not be subject to collective bargaining. Many would like to extend the list of exemptions.

Most employee organizations regard every aspect of work as subject to bargaining. They want a voice in all areas that may affect the lives of their members. These areas include position classification, compensation, grievance procedures, discipline, discharge, layoff, and other subjects.

Care should be exercised not to restrict collective bargaining so unreasonably as to nullify the values of the process. Experience has shown that employee organizations denied reasonable scope in bargaining—particularly over the matter of wages—resort to lobbying and political pressure. They attempt a quasi-negotiation of sorts with the group that sets salaries, whether it is a civil service commission or a legislative body.

To the extent that a civil service commission has authority over personnel administration beyond the merit principle, the introduction of collective bargaining raises other problems. One problem is that if an independent civil service commission has authority over bargainable matters, then bargaining responsibility must lie with the commission rather than with the executive department. Conversely, if full authority over personnel matters is vested in an independent commission which is not the bargaining agent, then the scope of negotiation is unduly restricted. In Michigan, for example, a constitutional provision gives the independent commission full authority over salaries, wages, and other conditions of work for state employees.

A possible solution to these problems would be to transfer non-merit functions from a civil service commission to a personnel department under the chief executive. Negotiators would thus have full authority to conclude an agreement. In Canada, a new law gives the Treasury Board, as management's bargaining representative, responsibility for pay, classification, and conditions of employment. The Public Service Commission (formerly the Civil Service Commission) retains authority over examinations, promotions, staffings, and career development of Canadian federal employees.

Attitudes Toward the Civil Service Commission

In this connection it is pertinent to examine how the role of the civil service commission is perceived by different groups. Some public administrators look upon the civil service commission as an arm of management. Others view it as an impartial third party that protects employees from patronage or from excessively arbitrary management.

Unions generally regard the commissioners, who in their eyes represent management, as adversaries. They do not believe that a commission is an impartial third party. Rather, they feel that the duties of the commission should be confined to recruitment, hiring, and the prevention of patronage. Union leaders have asserted that if their unions are to achieve a full, mature relationship with public employers through collective bargaining, they must be free to negotiate on all matters.

Independent associations tend to take a less hostile position. They speak of "working with" civil service commissions, but they also want a share in decision-making and a change in the traditionally paternalistic method of administration.

Employee organizations often contend that bargaining will have an influence on agencies that are not covered by a merit system or those whose system is weak and does not preserve the merit principle. It is argued that strong employee groups can act as an effective counter to patronage and bring pressure to bear for efficient, impartial administration. Others argue that strong employee organizations may actually reinforce a patronage system.

Legislation in the United States for public employee collective bargaining has attempted in different ways to protect the merit principle and fit collective bargaining into the existing merit system structure. . . .

NOTES

1. In recommending that federal employees be given the right to organize and bargain collectively, President Kennedy's Task Force, headed by then Secretary of Labor Arthur Goldberg, stated:

> The principle of entrance into the career service on the basis of open competition, selection on merit and fitness, and advancement on the same basis, together with the full range of principles and practices that make up the Civil Service system govern the essential character of each individual's employment. Collective dealing cannot vary these principles. It must operate within their framework.

1961 Task Force Report on Employee-Management Cooperation in the Federal Service, in LABOR-MANAGEMENT RELATIONS IN THE PUBLIC SERVICE, Pt. 1, at 14 (H. Roberts ed. 1968). Executive Order 11491 provides, as did Executive Order 10988, that an agreement between an agency and a labor organization is subject to the "existing or future laws and the regulations of appropriate authorities, including policies set forth in the Federal

Personnel Manual." E.O. 11491, Section 12 (a). *See* Statutory Appendix.

2. The extent of potential conflict between the civil service laws and collective bargaining agreements is illustrated by the growing popularity of civil service systems. In 1955, only 23 states had civil service laws covering approximately 65 percent of full-time state employees. H. KAPLAN, THE LAW OF CIVIL SERVICE 24, 25 (1958). In 1970, 84 percent of the cities, 83 percent of the counties, and 96 percent of the states in a National Civil Service League survey reported adoption of some form of merit system. Approximately 80 percent of all public employees are now covered by merit systems. National Civil Service League, *Survey of Current Personnel Systems in State and Local Governments,* GOOD GOVERNMENT 1-28 (Spring 1970).

3. Among the many articles examining the relationship between collective bargaining and civil service are Comment, *The Civil Service—Collective Bargaining Conflict in the Public Sector: Attempts at Reconciliation,* 38 U. CHI. L. REV. 826 (1971); Stanley, *What are Unions Doing to Merit Systems?,* 31 PUBLIC PERSONNEL REV. 109 (1970); Camp & Lomax, *Bilateralism and the Merit Principle,* PUBLIC ADMINISTRATION REV., Vol. 28, at 132-34 (March/April 1968); Morse, *Shall We Bargain Away the Merit System,* 24 PUBLIC PERSONNEL REV. 239 (1963); U.S. DEP'T OF LABOR, COLLECTIVE BARGAINING IN PUBLIC EMPLOYMENT AND THE MERIT SYSTEM (1972).

HELBURN AND BENNETT, PUBLIC EMPLOYEE BARGAINING AND THE MERIT PRINCIPLE, 23 Lab. L.J. 618, 623-26 (1972)†

Discussion below includes the laws of 20 states which afford general coverage to at least one major category of public employees, state, county, and/or municipal.[15] In general, the laws may be classified into two broad categories with respect to the accommodation of polar views of merit systems: (1).—11 states

---

† This material appeared originally in the October 1972 issue of *Labor Law Journal,* published and copyrighted 1972 by Commerce Clearing House, Inc., Chicago and is reproduced with permission.

[15] The states include California, Connecticut, Delaware, Hawaii, Maine, Massachusetts, Michigan, Minnesota, Missouri, Nevada, New Hampshire, New Jersey, New York, Oregon, Pennsylvania, Rhode Island, South Dakota, Vermont, Washington, and Wisconsin. Joel Seidman has made a general analysis of the public employee labor relations laws of the 16 states which he considers to have the most advanced and comprehensive statutes. Included were all the above except California, Missouri, Nevada, and New Hampshire. See "State Legislation on Collective Bargaining by Public Employees," LABOR LAW JOURNAL, XXII (January, 1971), pp. 13-22.

with legal provisions related to the problem; and (2).—10 states with no related provisions.[16]

Accommodation Provisions

The 11 state laws which have provisions bearing on the accommodation problem basically attempt to resolve the conflict by excluding certain matters from the scope of negotiations. This exclusion takes three general forms: (1).—blanket exclusion of all matters covered by law; (2).—specific exclusion of matters covered by merit system laws and regulations; and (3). —selective exclusion only of certain merit-related items.

The statutes of New Hampshire, Vermont, and Pennsylvania exemplify the blanket exclusion approach. The New Hampshire and Pennsylvania laws do not specifically mention the merit system, but appear to limit bargaining to matters not covered by merit system laws. Vermont law includes the blanket exclusion plus the stipulation that bargaining law should not be construed to contravene the spirit and intent of the merit principle. However, since these laws fail to adequately clarify the relationship between merit systems and collective bargaining, they provide little guidance for a viable approach to the problem of accommodation.

The laws of California, Massachusetts, Rhode Island, and Washington, and the Wisconsin law covering state employees only are of the specific exclusion type. The California statute provides that:

> Nothing contained herein shall be deemed to supersede the provisions of existing state law and the charters, ordinances and rules of local public agencies which establish and regulate a merit or civil service system or which provide for other methods of administering employer-employee relations.

The Wisconsin law for state employees is even more specific:

> Nothing herein shall require the employer to bargain in relation to statutory and rule provided prerogatives of promotion, layoff, position classification, compensation and fringe benefits, examinations, discipline, merit salary determination policy, and other actions provided for by law and rules governing civil service.

Rhode Island law exempts from bargaining only those matters exclusively reserved for merit systems by law or regulation. The Massachusetts and Washington statutes are least specific of this

---

[16] Because two sets of Wisconsin laws were considered, the states appear to add to 21. One Wisconsin law was placed in each of the two major groups.

group, merely exempting matters delegated to civil service and personnel boards. Wellington and Winter note that the Washington statute appears "to subordinate collective bargaining provisions to civil service rules and regulations. However, there is some uncertainty among local officials . . . as to which statute takes precedence."

Problems in Definition

While all of these specific exclusion laws provide to some extent a basic framework for accommodation, there still exist problems in defining the merit system-bargaining relationship and in establishing a reasonable scope of bargaining. Merely excluding merit system matters from the scope of bargaining does not necessarily bring about the proper relationship between the merit principle and bargaining, especially if the merit systems involved have authority over personnel matters not essentially related to the merit principle.

Generally, the selective exclusion laws manage to avoid this pitfall. By extending bargaining to all matters not deemed essential to the merit principle, they provide a reasonably broad scope of bargaining and at the same time apparently maintain a viable merit system. The statutes of Hawaii, Connecticut, and Maine are in this category.

All three laws remove the appointment and promotion functions from the scope of bargaining, with the Connecticut law providing that:

Nothing herein shall diminish the authority and power of any municipal civil service commission, personnel board, personnel agency or its agents established by statute, charter or special act to conduct and grade merit examinations and to rate candidates in order of their relative excellence from which the appointments or promotions may be made to positions in the competitive division of the classified service of the municipal employer served by such civil service commission or personnel board. The conduct and grading of merit examinations, the rating of candidates and the establishment of lists from such examinations and the appointments from such lists and any provisions of any municipal charter concerning political activity of municipal employees shall not be subject to collective bargaining.

The above law is affected, however, by a previous subsection:

Where there is a conflict between any agreement reached by a municipal employer and an employee organization and approved in accordance with the provisions of [this act] on matters appropriate to collective bargaining, as defined in this act, and any charter, special act, ordinance, rules or regulations adopted by the municipal employer or its agents such as a personnel board or civil service commission . . . the terms of such agreement shall prevail.

The Connecticut, as well as the Maine, law permits bargaining over personnel movements other than appointment and promotion, indicating that at least in these states the protection of all personnel movements is not deemed essential to the merit principle. While the Hawaii law does not specifically exclude all personnel movements from bargaining, it does stipulate that agreements cannot contain provisions inconsistent with [the] merit principle. However, "merit principles" are not defined.

Despite problems in specifying the items essential to the merit principle, the above laws confront the problem of accommodation. Unfortunately this is not true of those state laws which have no provisions pertaining to the accommodation of collective bargaining and the merit principle.

The public employee labor relations statutes of Delaware, Michigan, Minnesota,* Missouri, Nevada,** . . . New York, Oregon, and South Dakota, and the municipal employee law of Wisconsin contain no provisions dealing with accommodation. Although the Oregon bargaining statute does not deal with the problem, the state's civil service law attempts to achieve accommodation by redesignating the state Civil Service Board as the Public Employee Relations Board with the authority to interpret and administer the bargaining statutes. The Board is to make rulings which will preserve the merit principle.

In Michigan, the lack of provisions has resulted in legal conflict between collective bargaining and local merit systems. Since

---

* Editors' Note: The Minnesota Act, however, does contain the following provision:

Any provision of any contract . . . which of itself or in its implementation would be in violation of or in conflict with any statute of the State of Minnesota or rule or regulation promulgated thereunder or provision of a municipal home rule charter or ordinance or resolution adopted pursuant thereto, or rule of any state board or agency governing licensure or registration of an employee, shall be void and of no effect. MINN. STAT. ANN. ch. 179, § 179.66 (5) (Supp. 1972).

** Editors' Note: While the Nevada Act does not have a specific provision with respect to civil service, NEV. REV. STAT. § 288.150 (2) provides that "[e]ach local governmental employer is entitled, without negotiation or reference to any agreement resulting from negotiation . . . [t]o hire, promote, classify, transfer, assign, retain, suspend, demote, discharge or take disciplinary action against any employee. . . ." What effect would a provision such as this have on resolving whether the terms of a collective bargaining agreement superseded inconsistent civil service rules and regulations?

the Michigan Public Employee Relations Act does not specifically exempt the various aspects of merit systems from the scope of bargaining, both the Wayne County and Macomb County Circuit Courts have held that agreements reached through collective bargaining guaranteed by the bargaining statute supersede the provisions of the state civil service law when the two conflict. The Michigan experience suggests a great need for legislation clarifying the relationship between merit systems and public employee bargaining if the merit principle is to be preserved.

NOTE

The New Jersey Public Employment Relations Act provides that "Nothing herein shall be construed to deny to any individual employee his rights under Civil Service Laws or regulations." N.J. STAT. ANN. tit. 13, § 13A-5.3 (Supp. 1972). In Lullo v. Firefighters Local 1066, 55 N.J. 409, 440, 262 A.2d 681, 697 (1970), the New Jersey Supreme Court indicated that this provision, in conjunction with the balance of the law, precluded negotiations which resulted in any changes or modifications of civil service regulations. Does the court's conclusion necessarily follow from the quoted statutory provision?

CIVIL SERVICE COMMISSION v. WAYNE COUNTY BOARD OF SUPERVISORS
Michigan Supreme Court
384 Mich. 363, 184 N.W.2d 201 (1971)

PER CURIAM:—Two admittedly conflicting statutes compete in litigious depth for jurisdiction over the process of collective bargaining by Wayne county employees with their employer (or employers). As two courts already have come to know in painful and dissentient succession (see Wayne County Civil Service Comm. v. Wayne County Bd. of Supervisors, 22 Mich. App. 287), the competition presents that most difficult of all appellate problems; the ascertainment of legislative intent when there is no evidentiary or other reasonably authoritative guide to pertinent meaning or purpose of the legislators. For such difficulty Cardozo has provided our first and most dependable range light (The Nature of the Judicial Process, pp. 14, 15, published 1921):

"Interpretation is often spoken of as if it were nothing but the search and the discovery of a meaning which, however obscure and latent, had nonetheless a real and ascertainable pre-existence in the legislator's mind. The process is, indeed, that at times, but it is often something more. The ascertainment of intention may be the least of a judge's troubles in ascribing meaning to a statute. 'The fact is,' says Gray in his lectures on the 'Nature and Sources of the Law,' 'that the difficulties of so-called interpretation arise when the legislature has had no meaning at all; when the question which is raised on the statute never occurred to it; when what the judges have to do is, not to determine what the legislature did mean on a point which was present to its mind, *but to guess what it would have intended on a point not present to its mind, if the point had been present.*" (emphasis presently supplied).

The first of these competing statutes (1941 PA 370; MCLA 38.401 et seq; 1948 CL 38.401 et seq; MSA 5.1191[1]), stated and now states expressly its purpose. Section 1 thereof reads, in full:

"Section 1. Civil service act; purpose. The purpose of this act is to guarantee to all citizens a fair and equal opportunity for public service; to establish conditions of service which will attract officers and employees of character and capacity, and to increase the efficiency of the county governmental departments, commissions, boards and agencies, by the improvement of methods of personnel administration."

The second of these statutes (1965 PA 379; MCLA 423.201 et seq; MSA 17.455[1]), correspondingly stated and now states the legislative purpose; this time by a redesigned title of that which previously was known as the Hutchinson Act of 1947 (No. 336). The new title:

"An act to prohibit strikes by certain public employees; to provide review from disciplinary action with respect thereto; to provide for the mediation of grievances and the holding of elections; to declare and protect the rights and privileges of public employees; and to prescribe means of enforcement and penalties for the violation of the provisions of this act."

(We insert here a significant farse. It is that there is no hint in this new title or, for that matter, in any of the sections of the act of 1965, of legislative thought that the prohibition of strikes by public employees, effected by legislatively authorized collective bargaining and administratively enforced mediation, might conflict in whole or in part with the authority vested, by the act of 1941, in an established county civil service commission. Thus the issue of 1965 legislative intent, vis-a-vis the act of 1941, was deposited in Wayne county as a first class vexer.)

A majority of 3 judges of the circuit court concluded that "the employer of all county employees is the county of Wayne and that the board of supervisors is the legally constituted body authorized to act for and on behalf of the county as the public employer."

. . . .

On application for rehearing the majority stood by its first ruling after having noted that, as against the "complex and apparently contradictory statutes that have been adopted," it would be better to hurry on its way the inevitable appeal "in the public interest." The opinion on rehearing concluded, appropriately by this bullet pass of the male deer:

"The slightest modification at this time would unduly prolong and delay conclusive and complete decision by the High Court. This would hopefully put to rest once and forever the turbulence so clearly existent within the county and between county agencies. Should such a decision fail in this respect, it is for the legislature to act promptly and with dispatch."

On appeal a majority of the assigned panel of the Court of Appeals ruled that plaintiff Wayne County Civil Service Commission is possessed of statutory power to classify positions in the county employment service and to submit uniform pay plans for the standardization of salaries; but does not have exclusive control over such classification and standardization, since all such must be approved by the county board of supervisors. To its reasoning the panel, having finally made a judgment, added this declaration of heartfelt relief (p. 299):

"While this is not the simplest solution to the difficult problem with which we are faced, and though it may even tend to confuse and complicate the area of collective bargaining within Wayne county, it is the only plausible solution under the confines of the present statutory law."

This Court granted leave (383 Mich. 782) to settle if possible what was regularly termed below a "chaos of legislation."

The plaintiff Civil Service Commission contends that act 370 has made it the exclusive bargaining agent for all employees of the county of Wayne, subject only "to concurrence of the board of supervisors on salaries and wages," and that it is entitled to a judicial declaration that "collective bargaining shall be conducted by the Civil Service Commission for all County employees and in accordance with the requirements of act 370."

The defendant County Board of Supervisors, searching the involved statutes in somewhat greater depth, contends that:

"3. Act 379, to the extent that it places rates of pay, hours of work and other conditions of employment of public employees, including employees of Wayne county, into the area of collective bargaining supersedes *pro tanto* those provisions or parts of Act 370 dealing with the same subject matters."

. . . .

Having arrayed these contentions for scrutiny, our ensuing views doubtless will be understood better by an outset declaration of specific decision. We disagree with the stated position of the plaintiff Civil Service Commission. We agree with what in our view is the generally dispositive contention of the defendant Wayne County Board of Supervisors.

First: To read the act of 1941, carefully in conjunction with the act of 1965, is to understand the judicial difficulty. The earlier act was conceived and enacted immediately after the people had adopted the civil service amendment of 1940, effective January 1, 1941 for State employment (Const. 1908, art. 6, § 22). Designed as that act was for adoption by counties having a *population of 300,000 or more,* the measure strove in applicable terms to provide the same rights for employees of such counties, and the same betterment of public service in such counties, as the people had just approved hopefully with respect to the State service. In neither instance could collective bargaining by public employees have been in the minds of the people, or of the legislators. The thought of strikes by public employees was unheard of. The right of collective bargaining, applicable at the time to private employment, was then in comparative infancy and portended no suggestion that it ever might enter the realm of *public* employment.

However, the act of 1941 brought within its purposefully inclusive as well as exclusive purview "all positions not specifically included by this act in the unclassified service." (§ 10[b]). Then, by section 27, headed "Scope," it provided that *all* of its declared aims should apply to the employees of *all* boards, commissions and departments of each statute-adopting county. So, upon adoption of the act by Wayne county, there came into being a Wayne county civil service commission, the authority of which in important if not exclusive part extended to control of the relation of public employer and public employee within the county.

The view taken here of these separate statutes is that they cannot be harmonized, as in *pari materia* or otherwise. The attempts and counter-attempts made below do not prove that premise. In the course of our review of the act of 1965, the conviction grows that it did not occur to the legislators that the manifestly well thought out provisions of the act would both encroach upon and impair, to some extent, the previously assigned authority and duty of a civil service commission operating under the act of 1941, and that serious trouble might arise on account of that fact.

The drafting and enacting legislature of 1965, as with this equally mortal Court on occasion when it endorses an opinion of public moment, did not foresee what since has come to pass. It did not include that needed exclusory clause or proviso, as Judge Fitzgerald noted (22 Mich. App. 287, 294), and therefore left no specific evidence of intent either way. In the words of Cardozo, we are left to *guess* what the 1965 legislature would have done had the point come to its attention, and our *guess* is that it would have advised all established county civil service commissions as we now do by today's judgment.

This is not to say that the act of 1965 repeals outright the act of 1941. Respecting as always our long since declared and regularly maintained rule that repeals by implication are not favored, and that it is only when the two measures in view are so incompatible that both or all cannot fully stand, we can only find that this is a striking instance for application of that rule which, back in 1877, was written into the Court's opinion of Breitung v. Lindauer, 37 Mich. 217, 233 (1887):

> "The rule is that the latter act operates *to the extent of the repugnancy,* as a repeal of the first, or, if the two acts are not in express terms repugnant, yet if the latter *covers the whole subject of the first,* and contains new provisions showing that it was intended as a substitute, it will operate as a repeal."

Note the emphasis supplied by the writer of Breitung; Justice Marston for himself and Justices Cooley, Campbell and Graves. We stress it anew and hold that the act of 1965 operates, *"to the extent of the repugnancy,"* as a partial repeal of the act of 1941; but no more than that. In short shrift this means that the purposed thrust of the act of 1965, that of prohibiting strikes by public employees and providing collective bargaining, negotiation and enforced mediation of labor disputes arising out of public employment coming within the scope of the act, must be implemented and administered exclusively as provided therein. Hence, the original authority and duty of the plaintiff civil service commission was diminished *pro tanto* by the act of 1965, to the extent of free administration of the latter according to its tenor. . . .

To summarize and restrict:

1. Our instant rulings are limited to

(a) Determination that the plaintiff Civil Service Commission has no lawful part in the administration, directly or indirectly, of the act of 1965. . . .

NOTES

1. Subsequent to the principal case, the Michigan Supreme Court affirmed the general terms of its holding in Sloan v. Warren Civil Service Comm'n, 386 Mich. 437, 192 N.W.2d 499 (1971). At least one major arbitration award in Michigan has also upheld the precedence of the collective bargaining agreement. In AFSCME Local 1390 and City of Lansing, GERR No. 411, B-2 (1971), Arbitrator Alan Walt sustained the grievances of three employees who contended that pay increases were withheld in violation of the collective bargaining agreement. The arbitrator held that the city's past practice of granting or withholding pay raises according to merit was superseded by the contract which called for automatic wage progressions based on seniority. The city's personnel rules, embodying the merit increase concept, were held not to have been negotiated or incorporated by reference in agreement.

The rule in the principal case, however, does not apply to employees in the state classified civil service. The 1963 Michigan Constitution states that "[t]he legislature may enact laws providing for the resolution of disputes concerning public employees, except in the state classified civil service." Mich. Const. art. 4, § 48. The Constitution grants to the State Civil Service Commission the power to "regulate all conditions of employment in the classified service." Mich. Const. art. 11, § 5. In Welfare Employees Union v. Michigan Civil Service Comm'n, 28 Mich. App. 343, 184 N.W.2d 247 (1970), the Michigan Court of Appeals held that these Constitutional provisions exempted the petitioning employees from the coverage of the Public Employment Relations Act and that the Civil Service Commission was not required to bargain about the effect on working conditions of a reorganization plan in the State Department of Social Services. The union, the court held, would have to pursue its grievances according to rules established by the Civil Service Commission.

2. One of the primary features of the conflict between collective bargaining and the civil service is the philosophical difference between the seniority principle, characteristic of labor contracts, and the merit principle embodied in civil service legislation. Consider the distinction between the merit *principle* and

the merit *system*. Should public employers and unions be allowed to substitute seniority provisions for competitive examinations and merit pay raises? In New York, the Supreme Court for Erie County held, in Kenmore Club, Police Benevolent Ass'n v. Civil Service Commission, 61 Misc. 2d 685, 307 N.Y.S.2d 63 (Sup. Ct. 1969) and in Selover v. Civil Service Comm'n, 61 Misc. 2d 688, 307 N.Y.S.2d 66 (Sup. Ct. 1969), that the petitioning unions, notwithstanding contract provisions, had no right to orders cancelling or regulating the preparation, conduct or rating of competitive examinations. The court said:

> The authority of municipal civil service commissions to prescribe certain minimum qualifications in a promotional examination as here is authority granted by the Civil Service Law. The above agreement although arising from the Taylor Act can take no precedence under the above-mentioned provisions of the Civil Service Law. The Civil Service Law gives to the municipal commission the right to prescribe minimum training and experience qualifications for promotional examinations. No agreement between a municipal corporation and its employees although basically sanctioned by the Taylor Act has any precedence and makes no claim to any precedence over the Civil Service Law.

Compare the two New York cases cited above with the principal case. Can the cases be distinguished?

UNIVERSITY OF OREGON MEDICAL SCHOOL AND THE STATE PERSONNEL DIVISION
Oregon Public Employe Relations Board
Decision No. C-70 (1972)

Findings of Fact

1. Local 1723, AFSCME, is the certified bargaining representative of the employes of the physical plant at the University of Oregon Medical School.

2. There are approximately 1,400 employes in other state agencies and institutions who are working in the same classes of work as found in the Medical School physical plant. These 1,400 employes make up about 90 percent of the state's work force in these classifications and, for the most part, they are represented by the Oregon State Employes Association.

3. Maintaining that ORS 240.235 requires that wage or salary rates for a class of work must be uniform throughout the state service, the Personnel Division proposed that negotiations on economic matters be conducted simultaneously with the inter-

ested employe organizations. Local 1723, AFSCME, rejected this proposal for coalition bargaining.

4. The Personnel Division refused to bargain separately with Local 1723 on salaries and wages.

5. An agreement was negotiated between the State Personnel Division and the Oregon State Employes Association fixing salaries to be effective July 1, 1972, subject to funding by the State Emergency Board.

Conclusions of Law

As stated in its letter of February 10, 1972, "The Executive Department further contends that the Merit System Law (ORS 240.235 (3)) intends that the rate of pay applied to any single classification in the classified state service will be uniform regardless of certified representation for incumbent personnel in that class being split between one or more employe organizations." The Department admits that it has refused to bargain further with the employe organization involved but defends that refusal on the ground that it is legally prohibited from paying a different scale to the physical plant employes involved in this dispute and those employed elsewhere throughout the state. The Department would contend that this legal conclusion excuses it from the responsibility to bargain with the employe organization as to wages on the ground that the appropriate wage scale is already established by force of law.

We conclude that the Department misreads the obligation of good faith bargaining. Good faith bargaining is not satisfied by a unilateral determination of what is right or even of what is lawful. It still requires an honest attempt to reach agreement within the confines of legal requirements. As long as there is any avenue of potential agreement unexplored and as long as either party wishes to explore that avenue, the process of good faith bargaining has not been exhausted. As stated by the Fourth Circuit in National Labor Relations Board v. Highland Park Mfg. Co., 110 F.2d 632 (C.A. 4 1940),

"... (T)he act, it is true, does not require that the parties agree; but it does require that they negotiate in good faith *with the view of reaching an agreement if possible;* ...."
(110 F.2d at 637; emphasis supplied.)

While the concept of good faith bargaining is a difficult one to define, it has been generally agreed that it includes an approach and an attitude towards negotiations indicative of a willingness to discuss the claims of both parties fully and freely and, when one party is opposed to the claims of the other, that he be willing to justify that opposition on the basis of reasoning.

It may be that the Department is correct in its interpretation of the Merit System Law. On the other hand, it may be possible for the employes organization to present persuasive countervailing arguments. In any event, good faith bargaining requires that they be given that opportunity.

We would further note that even if it be true that the statute requires a single rate, this does not foreclose the obligation to bargain with the smaller unit nor does it force the smaller unit to sit by submissively while the larger group has determined its fate. We cannot catalog all of the possible results of bargaining with the smaller unit but, as examples of possible results, it might be that the smaller unit would be persuaded to accept the pre-set rates or that the Department would agree to some different and higher rates which might then become the standard for all employes. It is also possible that the parties would reach an impasse. It is also conceivable that ORS 240.235 (3), while requiring a uniform rate, does not require that that rate be uniform throughout the state but only in geographical areas.

The State complains that if it must bargain with each unit, there is a possibility of fragmentization. Fragmentization is always possible where employes are in different bargaining units. This is an inherent possibility in collective bargaining. It results from the conclusion reached when the employer's interest in a single bargaining unit is balanced against the employe's right to speak through his chosen representative. While fragmentization is undesirable from an employer's standpoint and perhaps from the employe's standpoint, nevertheless it is a possibility which cannot be used as a basis for refusing to bargain. The results of collective bargaining will not always meet the desires or the needs of either party.

In his letter to the Board dated May 18, 1972, the Attorney General alleges "that Local 1723 has refused to bargain collectively with the employer by refusing to take part in coalition bargaining together with the Oregon State Employes Association, OSEA representing approximately 90 percent of the classified employes in the classification involved in this dispute." The employes in the unit involved are represented by Local 1723. They are therefore entitled to have Local 1723 speak for them. They are entitled to refuse to let any other organization or group of organizations speak for them. Coalition or, as it is referred to in the private sector, multi-unit bargaining is an acceptable and often desirable method of collective bargaining but it requires the mutual consent of all parties involved. Failure to give such consent, whether by employer or labor organization, does not constitute a refusal to bargain in good faith.

Accordingly, we conclude that the respondent's position constitutes a violation of the obligation to bargain collectively in good faith. . . .

5. Effect of Other Statutory Provisions

HANSLOWE & OBERER, DETERMINING THE SCOPE OF NEGOTIATIONS UNDER PUBLIC EMPLOYMENT RELATIONS STATUTES (1971), A special Report Prepared for the New York Public Employment Relations Board

1. General Problem

The general problem examined herein is the relationship of the Taylor Law and of PERB to other laws of the State of New York and to the agencies which administer them, with regard to the determination of the scope of negotiations under the Taylor Law—i.e., the subjects as to which there is a duty to negotiate.

A question within the foregoing question is: What impact, if any, does the Taylor Law have on the pre-existing authority of public employers to determine "terms and conditions of employment" of their employees? In other words is the scope of negotiations under the Taylor Law coterminous with or greater than the scope of the unilateral power held by the particular public employer under pre-existing law, as declared by the Constitution, Legislature, courts, State Comptroller, Attorney General, etc.?

2. A Hypothetical Case: PERB vs. the Comptroller as to Local Government Conditions of Employment

Employee Organization, duly certified representative of certain professional employees, presents to School Board, the public employer, a list of negotiating demands which includes the following item: "Payment of accrued sick leave to the estate of a deceased employee."

School Board refuses to discuss the above item on the ground that inclusion of such a provision in the collective agreement would be illegal, citing 23 Op. State Compt. 649 (1967, #67-735) and Article VIII, § 1 of the State Constitution, prohibiting government entities, including school districts, from giving gifts.

Employee Organization files a charge with PERB under Section 209-a.1 (d), alleging that the above-described action of the School Board constitutes a refusal to negotiate concerning "terms and conditions of employment."

What should PERB do?

Under the 1969 amendments it is clearly PERB's responsibility to determine whether or not the alleged improper practice occurred. Section 205.5, as amended, provides:

In addition to its powers and functions provided in other sections of this article, the board shall have the following powers and functions: . . . (d) To establish procedures for the prevention of improper employer and employee organization practices as provided in section two hundred nine-a of this article. . . . The board shall exercise exclusive nondelegable jurisdiction of the powers granted to it by this paragraph. . . .

PERB must, therefore, determine whether the unused sick leave demand falls within the scope of "terms and conditions of employment," within the meaning of the Taylor Law.

Concerning the relationship of the above-cited opinion of the State Comptroller to this determination, PERB has three courses of action available: PERB might accept the opinion of the Comptroller as conclusive of the matter and dismiss the charge; PERB might ignore the opinion of the Comptroller as irrelevant; PERB might take into account the opinion of the Comptroller, giving it, however, only such weight as, in the judgment of PERB, its persuasive force merits.

The third course of action is patently the proper one. The decision as to the scope of negotiability is PERB's in the first instance. The first two options—abandonment of decision to the Comptroller and ignoring the opinion of the Comptroller—have little to commend them. As to the first, the Comptroller has no mandate under the law to resolve such questions; his opinions with respect to such local government expenditures are admitted by himself to be "informal and advisory" only. . . . As to the second, the Comptroller has, by arrogation or otherwise, been in the business of advising local governments as to their powers under a broad body of law for a substantial period of time; in the process he has accumulated considerable experience concerning the legal framework within which local governments of the State of New York operate. For PERB to ignore completely this source of potential guidance would seem unwise.

The burden of demarcating those subjects which are within the scope of the statutory criterion "terms and conditions of employment" is initially PERB's, not merely because PERB has been designated by the State Legislature to make such determinations in the first instance, but because the vitality of the administrative process lies in the development and application of expertise in specially difficult areas of government regulation. The definition of the scope of negotiations under the Taylor Law is such an area.

One way of validating the foregoing position is to consider the matter of judicial review. However the decision as to the scope of negotiability under the Taylor Law is made in the first instance, it is subject to review in the courts. Such review is dependent upon the quality of the record made below and the sophistication of the trial tribunal with regard to the questions before it. Employment relations, as several decades of experience in the private sector demonstrate, is a complex and delicate area in which the adequacy of judicial review is particularly dependent upon the quality of the proceedings, record, and judgment below.

It is instructive to note, in the foregoing regard, that Comptroller opinions are typically rendered on the basis of a mere exchange of letters, without the sharpening of issues through pleadings, the presentation of evidence, confrontation and cross examination of witnesses, oral or written argument. Proceedings before PERB, on the contrary, under sections 209-a and 205.5 (d), entail all of these aids to administrative adjudication and judicial review.

Turning now to the merits of the hypothetical case posed, namely, whether the issue of "payment of accrued sick leave to the estate of a deceased employee" is within the statutory mandate of "terms and conditions of employment," the problems presented to PERB are the following: (1) whether the demand concerning the treatment of accrued sick leave is a term or condition of employment, and (2) whether Article VIII, § 1 of the State Constitution and/or some other state constitutional or legislative provision takes the matter out of the scope of negotiability. The answer to the first question would seem quite clearly to be yes. The real question for the purposes of this memorandum is the second. As to this, PERB must determine, within the limiting context of all relevant constitutional and statutory provisions (i.e., all relevant "law"), whether, as a matter of sound employment relations in the public sector, including such a subject within the scope of negotiability makes sense.

Stated more clearly perhaps, in cases such as the hypothetical one posed, PERB has two questions potentially before it: (1) whether the particular subject should be deemed, as a matter of sound public employment relations, to be within "terms and conditions of employment," (2) whether, even if it should be so deemed, the particular subject has been withheld or withdrawn from negotiability by the operation of some competing provision of law. Where the answer to the second question is unclear by reason of ambiguity in the competing law, the question of negotiability should be decided by PERB on the basis of sound public employment relations.

Whatever the determination of PERB, that determination is of course reviewable in the courts pursuant to Section 210.4 of the Taylor Law. . . .

4. The Relationship of PERB to Other Competing Agencies

What has been said of the Comptroller is dispositive of PERB's relationship with other potentially competing agencies of state government. Whatever the competing agency, the question of negotiability is to be answered by PERB in the first instance. In the process of answering the question, PERB should take into account all pertinent constitutional and statutory provisions; its consideration should not be confined to the Taylor Law alone. Neither the Taylor Law nor PERB exists in a void. (Cf., e.g., Southern Steamship Co. v. NLRB, 316 U.S. 31, 47 (1942) (". . . the Board has not been commissioned to effectuate the policies of the Labor Relations Act so single-mindedly that it may wholly ignore other and equally important Congressional objectives. Frequently the entire scope of Congressional purpose calls for careful accommodation of one statutory scheme to another, and it is not too much to demand of an administrative body that it undertake this accommodation without excessive emphasis upon its immediate task."); American News Co., 55 NLRB 1302 (1944).)

In addition to taking into account other constitutional and statutory provisions, PERB should consider the decisions of tribunals competent to interpret those constitutional and statutory provisions. The weight which PERB gives to any aspect of the foregoing array of law (constitutional, statutory, decisional) should depend on PERB's own interpretation of such of that law as it deems relevant. PERB's interpretation would, of course, be oriented to sound public employment relations as perceived through its own expertise. While PERB cannot and should not ignore clear mandates from the Constitution, the Legislature, or the Court of Appeals, it should deem itself free in the absence of such mandates to exercise its own best judgment, understanding of course that its decisions are themselves subject to judicial review. It would be obviously wasteful for PERB to determine questions of negotiability in the context of the Taylor Law alone, leaving to the reviewing courts in the first instance the questions of the relevance and force of competing law. Such an approach would deny to the reviewing courts the benefit of PERB's developing expertise with respect to the implications of such competing law for sound public employment relations (which is to say, sound public policy in a public employment context) in the State of New York.

Applying the foregoing principles to a concrete case, the decision of the Supreme Court of Nassau County in the *Central High School District No. 3* case (72 LRRM 2858, 305 N.Y.S.2d 724, November, 1969)—to the effect that an arbitration award, granting a sum of money to a deceased employee's estate in lieu of unused sick leave, was unenforceable by reason of the unconstitutional gift provision—should be accorded no more weight by PERB than the persuasive force of the court's reasoning merits. Without repeating again all of the considerations leading to this conclusion, it would seem quite incongruous for important questions of public employment relations to be resolved without any participation in the decisional process by the agency specially constituted by the Legislature to superintend such matters.

5. The Relationship of Scope of Negotiations to the Unit Problem

A somewhat different variety of scope of negotiations question confronts PERB in the following type of situation: where the subject sought to be negotiated is quite clearly within the statutory scope, "terms and conditions of employment," but is not within the authority of management at the unit level. An example of this type of subject is annuities and pensions under the State Employees' Retirement System. (Retirement and Social Security Law, Article 2.) This system applies not only to state employees but also to the employees of "participating" municipalities and other local government entities. The State Comptroller is declared by § 11 of the Retirement and Social Security Law to be the "administrative head" of the Retirement System, with the express power, among others, to adopt and amend "rules and regulations for the administration and transaction of the business of the retirement system. . . ."

Without delving more deeply into the Retirement and Social Security Law, it may be seen that two sets of potential questions for PERB as to scope of negotiations are presented thereunder. The first set of questions has to do with negotiations in *state* employment; the second set has to do with negotiations in *local* employment.

As to the *state* negotiations, a tug-of-war seems possible between the Office of Employee Relations, on the one hand, and the State Comptroller, on the other. With whom, it may be asked, do state employees have the right to negotiate concerning those aspects of the pension program which the Legislature has expressly placed in the discretionary control of the Comptroller. Those aspects may be said to be (1) not negotiable except with the Comptroller himself (is the Comptroller a "public employer" with regard to employees not employed in the Department of Audit and Control?), (2) negotiable only if the Comptroller *chooses* to negotiate concerning the exercise of his discretionary authority, (3) negotiable only to the extent that the state employer (Office of Employee Relations?) and the employee organization involved may agree upon joint recommendations to be made to the Comptroller and/or to the Legislature.

A possible legislative resolution of the foregoing type of problem may be foreshadowed by a very recent amendment to § 8 of the State Finance Law. The duties of the Comptroller with regard to a related matter have been modified as follows in subdivision 16 thereof:

> Notwithstanding any inconsistent provision of law, no change shall be made in the rate or eligibility standards for state employees' travel, meals, lodging, and other expenses for which the state makes payment (either in advance or by reimbursement), without the approval of the director of employee relations.

As to negotiations over pensions involving *local* governments participating in the State Retirement System, the only practical effect of such would be to produce joint proposals to be presented in the form of requests to the Comptroller and/or the State Legislature. This is an instance of a larger question which will confront PERB in several different contexts. The question is whether PERB should require a particular public employer to negotiate with regard to a subject as to which the employer has no control *except* the power to make recommendations. This question is dealt with in the ensuing section.

6. Subjects of Negotiation: Mandatory, Permissible, Illegal?

The subjects of bargaining in the private sector have been trichotomized into mandatory, permissible, and illegal. Mandatory subjects are those which fall within the meaning of "wages, hours, and other terms and conditions of employment" (National Labor Relations Act, Section 8 (d)); as to these, the proposing party may bargain to impasse, and the other party has a duty to bargain in response. Permissible subjects are those not within "wages, hours, and other terms and conditions of employment," but not illegal; as to these, the proponent may propose, but not insist upon, and the other party need not, but may, bargain; if agreement is reached on a permissible subject, that agreement is an enforceable part of the contract. Illegal subjects are those which, even if agreed upon, are unenforceable; of course there is no duty to bargain over such a subject. (See generally, sections

8 (a) (5), 8 (b) (3), 9 (a), and 8 (d) of the National Labor Relations Act, and NLRB v. Wooster Division of Borg-Warner Corporation, 356 U.S. 342 (1958).)

The situation in public employment is sufficiently different as to impugn the relevance of the trichotomy. The *terminology* may, however, be helpful for purposes of analysis. Assuming a subject to be clearly within "terms and conditions of employment" and at the same time not within the authority of management at the level of the unit, should PERB enforce a duty to negotiate at that level? To put it otherwise, should such a subject be treated as mandatory, permissible, or illegal—i.e., should negotiation be required, permitted, prohibited?

The real choice would seem to lie between the mandatory and permissible approaches; little purpose would be served in *prohibiting* negotiations on such a subject. Even where public management at the level of the unit is without authority to control subject X, it would ordinarily have authority to agree with the employee organization involved to make a joint recommendation to the appropriate higher echelon of authority as to the desired disposition of subject X. Accordingly, subjects found to be within the statutory language "terms and conditions of employment" but not within the authority of management at the unit level might, nonetheless, be treated as mandatory subjects and negotiations over them therefore required. A difficulty with this approach is that it might tend to clutter up negotiations with a laundry list of demands for joint importuning of distant and perhaps intractable holders of pertinent powers. On the other hand, a good deal of negotiations in the public sector concerning the most central of subjects is conducted by "public employers" who lack authority to resolve finally those issues. Examples of this are (1) a dependent school board negotiating teacher salaries and (2) the State Office of Employee Relations negotiating state employee salaries; in the case of the first, the pertinent authority resides in the city council; in the second, it resides in the State Legislature.

Perhaps guidance toward a middle course between the mandatory and permissible approaches is offered by Section 207.1 (b) of the Taylor Law when it speaks of *"effective* recommendations." Subjects which the particular employer does not control but as to which he has the power to make *effective* recommendations might be treated as mandatory subjects. On the other hand, subjects as to which the employer could make only *ineffective* recommendations might be treated as permissible subjects only.

7. The Impact of the Taylor Law on the Pre-Existing Authority of Public Employers

The array of positions with regard to the effect of the enactment of the Taylor Law on the pre-existing authority of public employers to confer benefits on their employees ranges from the response of the Comptroller at the right extreme, "nil," to a hypothetical position at the left extreme to the effect that the Taylor Law impliedly repeals all prior inconsistent legislation and judicial and administrative rulings. . . .

The Comptroller's position, "a fundamental premise which underlies every Opinion of the State Comptroller, concerning situations involving Article 14, of the Civil Service Law (known as the Taylor Law) " (see Comptroller's Memorandum of Law in the *Town of Huntington* case, page 4), was stated in 23 Op. State Compt. 316, 318-19 (1967, #67-378) :

> The new statutory provisions [the Taylor Law] do not in any way enlarge the legal benefits which public employers may confer on their employees nor has there been any expansion of the authority of such public employers in regard to these benefits. Therefore, it will be necessary for us to consider in order each of the employee demands herein to determine whether, irrespective of collective bargaining, this school district may legally comply with the same.

We disagree with the position thus taken by the Comptroller (and also with the position at the opposite extreme of the spectrum). At least two pertinent changes, both, in our judgment, rather basic, have been produced by the Taylor Law. The effect of these two changes is potentially to expand the scope of negotiations beyond the scope of pre-Taylor *exercise* of employer power. The first change is that a new public agency, PERB, has been created and empowered by the Legislature to deal with and decide issues of public employment relations in the State of New York—issues previously presided over (to the extent they were presided over at all) by other agencies. To the extent that those other agencies lacked authority or occasion to render final decisions on questions of employer power presently falling within the purview of PERB, such questions are still open. This means that the only questions of employer power definitively answered at the time of this writing are those questions which have heretofore been unambiguously resolved by the Constitution of the State of New York, the State Legislature, or the Court of Appeals. Opinions of the State Comptroller, and even decisions of lower state courts never challenged in the ultimate through appellate review to the Court of Appeals, establish no controlling precedents.

A second basic change in the public policy of the State of New York occasioned by the enactment of the Taylor Law is the introduction into public employment relations of the whole new concept of resolving employer-employee disagreements through the institution of collective negotiations. We concede that matters unambiguously resolved by the State Constitution, by statutory enactment, or by Court of Appeals interpretation of either of the foregoing are not affected by the passage of the Taylor Law. Where ambiguity exists, however, or where the source of the competing "law" is of a lower order than Constitution, Legislature, Court of Appeals—i.e., in the gray area of public employer authority over "terms and conditions of employment"—strong reason exists for concluding that the legislative intent was to have such gray-area problems resolved through the process of collective negotiations. Indeed, the Taylor Law declares it to be the public policy of the State of New York to resolve disputes between public employees and public employers by that process. (Section 200) . . . .

NOTE

Oberer and Hanslowe suggested that a PERB should (1) determine whether a given subject is within the "terms and conditions of employment," and, if it is, (2) determine whether such subject should nevertheless be "withheld or withdrawn from negotiability by the operation of some competing provision of law." Is there or should there be any difference in the scope of judicial review with respect to these two determinations? Should the scope of judicial review be greater with respect to the second determination?

BOARD OF EDUCATION OF UNION FREE SCHOOL DISTRICT NO. 3 v. ASSOCIATED TEACHERS OF HUNTINGTON, INC.

New York Court of Appeals
30 N.Y.2d 122, 282 N.E.2d 109, 331 N.Y.S.2d 17 (1972)

FULD, CH. J.: We are called upon to decide (1) whether a school board has the authority to enter into a collective bargaining agreement granting economic benefits to schoolteachers, absent specific statutory authorization to do so and (2) whether such a board lacks the power to enter into a collective bargaining agreement containing a clause which provides for the arbitration of disputes concerning disciplinary action taken against tenure teachers.

The facts are undisputed. The plaintiff (hereafter called the "Board"), as a public employer under the Taylor Law (Civil Service Law, art. 14), recognized the defendant (hereafter referred to as the "Association") as the employee organization representing the school district teachers. The parties—following recommendations by a fact finding panel appointed by the New York State Public Employment Relations Board—entered into a collective bargaining agreement for the 1969-70 school year. Included in this agreement are five provisions which gave rise to this litigation. Four of them relate to the payment of economic benefits in the form of either salary increases or reimbursement for certain expenses incurred, and the fifth provides for arbitration in cases in which tenure teachers have been disciplined.

The first two challenged provisions deal with the reimbursement of teachers for job related personal property damage (the damage reimbursement provision).[1] The next provides partial reimbursement to teachers for graduate courses taken with the approval of the school administration (the tuition reimbursement provision).[2] The fourth questioned clause (Article XXI) provides for a salary increment for teachers during their last year of service before retirement (the retirement award provision) and reads as follows:

"Each member who hereafter indicates his intention to retire one year prior to such retirement under the New York State Teachers Retirement System or whose retirement is mandatory under such system shall receive at the start of the last school year of service a salary increase for that year equal to 5/10 of 1% (0.5%) of his current salary multiplied by the number of years of service in this school district, such salary increase not to exceed $1500."

---

[1] These clauses—contained in Article VIII—read as follows:

"E.   The Board will provide protection of teachers by reimbursement for cost of replacing or repairing dentures, eyeglasses, etc., not covered by Workmen's Compensation, destroyed or lost as the result of an injury sustained in the course of his or her employment.

"F.   The Board will provide reimbursement for repair or value, whichever is less, of clothing and personal effects damaged or destroyed during the course of and incident to employment, provided loss is not caused by negligence of the claimant. Personal effects do not include automobiles and/or other vehicles."

[2] The provision (Section A of Article XI) reads in this way:

"Any member of the professional staff shall, upon presentation of his transcript and a bursar's receipt, be reimbursed in a lump sum in an amount equal to 50% of the cost per credit hour of such work up to a maximum of ten hours per year; provided the courses are of a content related to the curriculum or course of study taught by the teacher and are approved in advance by the Principal and Superintendent. The benefits provided above may be extended to other courses with the approval of the Superintendent."

The remaining disputed provision (Section C of Article XVIII) relates to the arbitration of disputes regarding disciplinary action taken against tenure teachers (the grievance provision):

> "No tenure teacher shall be disciplined, reprimanded, reduced in rank or compensation, suspended, demoted, transferred, terminated or otherwise deprived of any professional advantage without just cause. . . . Any such action, including adverse evaluation of teacher performance or a violation of professional ethics asserted by the Board or any agent thereof, shall be subject to the grievance procedure set forth in this Agreement."

The Board, questioning its own power to agree and bind itself to the provisions set out above, raised the issue of their legality, in September 1969, during the negotiations leading up to the execution of the collective bargaining agreement, and shortly thereafter it brought this action for a judgment (1) declaring those provisions illegal and of no effect and (2) staying arbitration proceedings which had been commenced by the Association under the grievance provision. The court at Special Term held the provisions relating to tuition reimbursement and to the grievance procedure were illegal but sustained the validity of the remaining provisions; it rendered judgment to that effect and enjoined the arbitration proceedings. On appeal, the Appellate Division agreed with Special Term in all respects except one; it concluded that the tuition reimbursement provision was also valid (36 AD2d 753). Two of the justices, dissenting in part, believed that the retirement award provision was illegal.

In our view, all of the challenged provisions are valid.

The basic question posed by this appeal is whether there is any fundamental conflict between the provisions of the Taylor Law and the provisions of any other statute dealing with the powers and duties of school boards. Under the Taylor Law, a public employer, in order "to promote harmonious and cooperative relationships between government and its employees" (§ 200), is empowered to recognize an employee organization for the purpose of collective bargaining negotiations (§ 204, subd. 1). When such an organization is recognized, the public employer "is required"—in the words of section 204, subdivision 2—"to negotiate collectively with such employee organization in the determination of, and administration of grievances arising under, *the terms and conditions of employment of the public employees as provided in this article,* and to negotiate and enter into written agreements with such employee organizations in determining such terms and conditions of employment." (Emphasis supplied.)

In other words, the validity of a provision found in a collective agreement negotiated by a public employer turns upon whether it constitutes a term or condition of employment. If it does, then, the public employer must negotiate as to such term or condition and, upon reaching an understanding, must incorporate it into the collective agreement unless some statutory provision circumscribes its power to do so.

It is manifest that each of the provisions here challenged constitutes a term or condition of employment. It is certainly not uncommon for collective agreements in the public sector—as well as in the private sector—to contain "damage reimbursement" provisions similar to the one before us. If, during the course of performing his duties, an employee has his clothing, eyeglasses or other personal effects damaged or destroyed, it is certainly reasonable to reimburse him for the cost of repairing or replacing them.

The tuition reimbursement provision as well clearly relates to a term and condition of employment. School boards throughout the State pay teachers a salary differential for completing a specified number of credit hours above the baccalaureate degree. Since graduate work tends to increase teacher skills and is beneficial to the school district, there is no reason why the Board should not encourage such work by absorbing one-half of the tuition expense.

The so-called retirement award provision also involves a term and condition of employment. Employers, both in the public and private sectors, have traditionally paid higher salaries based upon length of service and training. In addition to the fact that the payment was to be for services actually rendered during their last year of employment, the benefit provided for served the legitimate purpose of inducing experienced teachers to remain in the employ of the school district. It is not, therefore, a constitutionally prohibited "gift" of public monies. (N. Y. Const., art. VIII, § 1) , since the retiring teachers who benefit from this provision have furnished a "corresponding benefit or consideration to the State." (Mtr. of Teachers Assn. [Bd. of Educ.], 34 AD2d 351, 353.) Nor may the provision be regarded as creating a retirement plan since the additional compensation was made payable only upon completion of the required services during the year prior to retirement. If this were to be deemed a retirement benefit, then, it would be equally logical to argue that increases in compensation in the years immediately prior to retirement were part and parcel of the retirement plan.

This brings us to the grievance provision. It assures teachers with tenure that no disciplinary action will be taken against them without just cause and that any dispute as to the existence of such cause may be submitted to arbitration. It is a provision commonly found in collective bargaining agreements in the private and public sectors and carries out Federal and State policy favoring arbitration as a means of resolving labor disputes. . . .

In sum, each of the provisions under attack clearly relates to a term or condition of employment and, accordingly, the Board was, in light of the Taylor Law, required to negotiate—unless its contentions, to which we turn, compel a different conclusion.

Although the Board raises specific objections that are peculiar to each of the challenged items, its basic premise is the same—that, absent a statutory provision expressly authorizing a school board to provide for a particular term or condition of employment, it is legally prohibited from doing so. Proceeding from that premise, the Board would have us hold that school boards possess only those powers granted by a single provision, section 1709, of the Education Law. Quite apart from the fact that that section contains a broad grant of powers, the Board's premise is fallacious. Under the Taylor Law, the obligation to bargain as to all terms and conditions of employment is a broad and unqualified one, and there is no reason why the mandatory provision of that act should be limited, in any way, except in cases where some other applicable statutory provision explicitly and definitively prohibits the public employer from making an agreement as to a particular term or condition of employment.

Were it otherwise, a school board would have a hard time bargaining effectively with its teachers concerning terms of employment, since it would frequently be difficult, if not impossible, to find an express grant of power with respect to any particular subject. To adhere to the restrictive view advanced by the Board "would," the Appellate Division recently wrote in Mtr. of Teachers Assn. (34 AD2d, at p. 356), "virtually destroy the bargaining powers which public policy has installed in the field of public employment and throttle the ability of a Board of Education to meet the changing needs of employer-employee relations within its district."

Public employers must be presumed to possess the broad powers needed to negotiate with employees as to all terms and conditions of employment. The presumption may, of course, be rebutted by showing statutory provisions which expressly prohibit collective bargaining as to a particular term or condition but, "[i]n the absence of an express legislative restriction against bargaining for that term of an employment contract between a public employer and its employees, the authority to provide for such [term] resides in the [school board] under the broad powers and duties delegated by the statutes." (Mtr. of Teachers Assn. [Bd. of Educ.], 34 AD2d 351, 355, *supra;* see, also, Rayburn v. Board of Education, 71 LRRM 2177, 2178 [Mich. Cir. Ct.].) It is hardly necessary to say that, if the Board asserts a lack of power to agree to any particular term or condition of employment, it has the burden of demonstrating the existence of a specific statutory provision which circumscribes the exercise of such power. It has failed to meet this burden in the present case.

The Board cites no legislation which expressly or even impliedly prevented it from including the tuition and damage reimbursement provisions. Nor does section 113a of the Retirement and Social Security Law—to which the Board points—prohibit inclusion of the retirement award provision; that provision merely provided for the payment of a salary increment based upon length of service. We also find without substance the Board's claim that the grievance provision violates section 3020-a of the Education Law, generally known as the Tenure Law. That statute provides that, prior to any disciplinary action being taken against a teacher, the latter must be afforded a hearing before an impartial panel, which then submits recommendations to the school board (Education Law, § 3020-a, subds. 2, 3, 4). The Board is not bound by these recommendations and may disregard them in making its decision. Since a decision by the Board itself to impose discipline is a prerequisite to arbitration, the grievance provision in no way supplants this aspect of the Tenure Law. In addition, section 3020-a, subdivision 5, declares that any employee "feeling himself aggrieved" may either appeal to the Commissioner of Education or commence an article 78 proceeding. The procedure thus set up is not mandatory, its implementation resting entirely in the teacher's discretion. In other words, the Legislature has given a tenure teacher a choice of two methods of statutory appeal if he desires to challenge an adverse decision of the school board. But it does not follow from this that the Board is inhibited from agreeing that the teacher may choose arbitration as a third method of reviewing its determination.

It is of more than passing significance that the Taylor Law explicitly vests employee organizations with the right to represent public employees not only in connection with negotiations as to the terms and conditions of employment but also as to *"the administration of grievances arising thereunder"* (Civil Service Law, § 203). Indeed, it is the declared policy of this State to encourage "public employers and . . . employee organizations to agree upon procedures for resolving disputes" (§ 200, subd.

[c]) . And arbitration is, of course, part and parcel of the administration of grievances. . . . There is, therefore, no reason to infer that the Legislature intended that the provisions of the Tenure Law should, by implication, deprive employee organizations of a right to represent employees in the administration of disciplinary grievances.

Nor can we agree that a board of education is better qualified to decide whether a teacher in its employ should be dismissed for incompetency or misconduct than an arbitrator. It may not be gainsaid that arbitrators, selected because of their impartiality and their intimate knowledge of school board matters are fully qualified to decide issues such as those under consideration. Moreover, if the school board's contentions were sustained, it would be the Supreme Court, not the board of education, which would pass upon the correctness of the determination in an article 78 proceeding. In any event, though, we cannot subscribe to the view that the legality of an arbitration provision turns on the relative competency of arbitrator and judge.

We would but add that there is no basis for the fear expressed that to permit the grievance to go to arbitration will enable the employee to appeal—pursuant to section 3020-a of the Education Law—to the arbitrator *after* he has lost before the commissioner or the court, or, conversely, to the Commissioner of Education or the Supreme Court *after* he has submitted to arbitration and lost before the arbitrator. Once the controversy is heard and a decision arrived at *either* by the arbitrator *or* by the commissioner *or* by the judge, that is the end of the matter. As already indicated, the collective bargaining agreement does no more than give the employee a possible third means of reviewing a Board determination.

The order appealed from should be modified, without costs, by reversing so much thereof as holds illegal the provision permitting arbitration with respect to the disciplining of tenure teachers and, except as so modified, affirmed.

BREITEL, J. (dissenting in part) :

I quite agree with all but one feature of the majority determination, that dealing with the retirement award. While that feature may seem a small part of the collective bargaining agreement negotiated and executed, it has, as a precedent, marked significance in the relations between public employers and employees and critical impact on public retirement systems. Moreover, the retirement feature is one that falls in an area where government has been especially concerned because of accumulating economic burdens on retirement systems and the public fisc out of which some or all retirement reserves come. Indeed, the condition has become so critical that the Legislature in recent sessions has, as is publicly known, invoked a "freeze" on the general increase of retirement benefits.

As did two dissenting justices at the Appellate Division, I conclude that the collective bargaining provision granting to retiring teachers a salary increase for their terminal year is invalid. Unlike the dissenting justices, however, I do not find that the provision violates constitutional limitations on making gifts (Art. VII, § 8, subd. 1) ; but do find in agreement with the dissenters that it is invalid because it violates applicable statute law.

Article XXI of the collective agreement reads:

"Retirement Award

"Each teacher who hereafter indicates his intention to retire one year prior to such retirement under the New York State Teachers Retirement System or whose retirement is mandatory under such system shall receive at the start of the last school year of service a salary increase for that year equal to 5/10 of 1% (0.5%) of his current salary multiplied by the number of years of service in this school district, such salary increase not to exceed $1,500."

Preliminarily, the provision is entitled as a "retirement award," and therefore the parties so regarded it. Moreover, it reads as a retirement formula would with a fraction determined by years of service as a numerator and the current salary as a base.

Section 113 of the Retirement and Social Security Law forbids any municipality from creating any retirement system for its officers or employees (subd. a) . Section 526 of the Education Law provided since the merger of school retirement systems into the state system in 1923 for the abolition and discontinuance of local school retirement systems.

The "retirement award" provided by the collective agreement violates both statutes. Nor may the provision be regarded simply as a salary increase payable out of funds available to the school district. Its pivotal effect, by increasing final average salary in determining retirement allowances, is to increase the allowances payable by the state teachers' retirement system out of its reserves contributed by employers and employees (see, e.g., Education Law, §§ 510, 511, 511-a) .

There may be a further consequential effect. Because the agreement, if valid, affects retirement system benefits it may be prospectively binding under the constitutional provision prohibiting the diminishment or impairment of retirement benefits (Art. V, § 7; Kranker v. Levitt, — NY2d —, decided Feb. 18, 1972). All this under a locally-negotiated agreement and, of course, subject to arbitration in the event of disputes.

If there were any doubt, and there should be none, that the provision, or its like, has direct bearing on retirement systems, and that "increases" in benefits of precisely this kind have been a matter of deep current concern, the recent enactment of chapter 503 of the Laws of 1971 resolves the doubt. Chapter 503 enacts, among others, a new section 431 to the Retirement and Social Security Law, which reads:

> "In any retirement or pension plan to which the state or municipality thereof contributes, the salary base for the computation of retirement benefits shall in no event include any of the following earned or received, on or after April first, nineteen hundred seventy-two:
>
> . . . .
>
> "2.   any form of termination pay,
>
> "3.   any additional compensation paid in anticipation of retirement, or
>
> "4.   That portion of compensation earned during any twelve months included in such salary base period which exceeds that of the preceding twelve months by more than twenty per centum."

It is difficult to avoid the conclusion that everyone, including the Legislature, and even the parties to the collective agreement, regard a final year's salary in anticipation of retirement, as a retirement benefit under a retirement system. That tinkering locally or administratively with such benefits may invoke constitutional limitations on impairment, see Kranker v. Levitt, *supra*.

To further point the analysis, the State Comptroller in opinions rendered in 1967 and 1968 held invalid, because beyond the statutory power of local boards of education, salary increases for final years in anticipation of retirement (op. #67-355, dated June 5, 1967; op. #68-232, dated March 26, 1968).

Obviously, the Taylor Law (Civil Service Law, art. 14) was not intended, and should not have the effect, of overriding the statutes discussed, simply because it authorizes collective bargaining between public employers and employees over the terms and conditions of employment (Civil Service Law, § 204). Otherwise, the whole body of statute and decisional law affecting public employment, penal and civil, would be subject to repeal or revision in public collective agreements so long as there is any effect on "the terms and conditions of employment."

Nor do the strictures apply to any increases in compensation which happen to occur in the final years of employment. The strictures do apply to increases in anticipation of and conditioned on retirement. Which also suggests that the provision is hardly an inducement to continued employment. On the contrary, it is an inducement to retire. To say that the purpose is "to induce experienced teachers to remain in the employ of the school district" is to state the contrary of the provision's effect. Of course, it is irrelevant whether the retirement award promotes or deters earlier retirement, so long as there is no power by local agreement to vary the retirement system's balanced incentives for encouraging continued employment and at certain points to encourage retirement.

Accordingly, I dissent in part and vote to modify except as to the provision for a retirement award which should be held invalid for the reasons indicated.

NOTES

1. In light of the decision in the principal case, could the school district and the teachers' union agree that the arbitration procedure was the sole and exclusive avenue of relief open to a tenured teacher who was terminated or otherwise disciplined by the school board?

2. In Pennsylvania Labor Relations Bd. v. Richland School Dist., Case No. PERA-C-2169-C (November 20, 1972), the Pennsylvania Labor Relations Board observed that the School Code did not set concrete limits or ceilings on the powers and duties of school districts, but rather defined the minimums in various areas that must be given to teachers. The Board noted that the upper limits of what teachers may receive is subject to negotiations between the parties.

UNITED STATES MERCHANT MARINE ACADEMY
Federal Labor Relations Council
FLRC No. 71A-15 (1972), GERR Ref. File 21:7019

Background of Case

The U.S. Merchant Marine Academy, Kings Point, N.Y. (herein referred to as the Academy), is an installation operated by the Maritime Administration, Department of Commerce, to train civilian officers for the merchant fleet.

In 1971, the Merchant Marine Act was amended to clarify the status of the Academy, its faculty, and other personnel (75 Stat. 212). Among other changes, section 216 (e) was added and provides as follows:

> To effectuate the purposes of this section, the Secretary of Commerce is authorized to employ professors, lecturers, and instructors and to compensate them without regard to the Classification Act of 1949, as amended.

In 1965, the United Federation of College Teachers (UFCT) was granted recognition as the exclusive bargaining representative of the Academy faculty and an agreement was executed in 1968. That agreement did not include a negotiated article on faculty salary.

During subsequent negotiations, UFCT submitted two proposals relating to faculty compensation: (1) reduction in the number of steps from entry to top of grade in the current Faculty Salary Schedule; and (2) change in the salary ratio from 120 to 133 1/3 percent for adjusting the related U.S. Naval Academy pay schedule to compensate for the 12-month year at the Academy.

The agency determined that these proposals by the union were non-negotiable. UFCT appealed to the Council from this determination, and the Council accepted the petition for review under section 11 (c) (4) of the Order.

Opinion

The agency based its determination of non-negotiability principally on the grounds that the union's proposals are: (1) contrary to the Merchant Marine Act; (2) beyond the scope of negotiation by reason of Office of Management and Budget constraints; (3) contrary to published policy as specified in various pay acts; and (4) contrary to agency regulations, as interpreted by the agency head. Each of these grounds is disputed by UFCT.

The questions raised will be separately considered below.

1. Do the union's proposals violate the Merchant Marine Act?

The agency asserts in substance, contrary to the union, that: (a) section 216 (e) of the Merchant Marine Act grants sole jurisdiction to the Secretary of Commerce to establish faculty salary scales; and (b) the act, according to its legislative history, requires salary scales to be "similar" to those of the U.S. Naval Academy, and the union's proposals are inconsistent with that requirement. We find that the agency's contentions are without merit.

As to (a), nothing in either the act or its legislative history expressly or impliedly precludes negotiations on faculty compensation with the exclusive representative of such personnel.

As to (b), the legislative history of section 216 (e) indicates that Congress intended for Academy faculty salaries to be "comparable" or "similar" to those of the faculty of the U.S. Naval Academy. Identity of compensation was not required. Here, the union's proposals would reduce the number of steps within grades and would increase by approximately 10 percent the bonus factor already established by the agency for the longer teaching year at the Academy as compared to the Naval institution. Obviously, these proposals fall within the range of "comparability" or "similarity." And without in any manner passing upon the desirability of such proposals, we are of the opinion that they are not violative of section 216 (e) of the Merchant Marine Act.

2. *Do the union's proposals violate OMB directives to the agency?*

A letter from the Chief of the Commerce and Finance Division of the Bureau of the Budget (now Office of Management and Budget), dated April 7, 1965, and addressed to the Assistant Secretary for Administration of Commerce, criticized the Academy's then current practice of basing its faculty pay schedule upon a survey of three academic institutions in the New York area. The letter pointed to the above-mentioned legislative history of section 216 (e) of the Merchant Marine Act and advised the agency to reexamine the Academy faculty personnel system to conform it "more closely to congressional intent by patterning it after that of the Naval Academy." To this end, the letter counseled the Department to make certain comparative analyses of the Kings Point and U.S. Naval Academy programs and suggested that it work with the Navy Department and consult with Civil Service Commission and Budget Bureau experts in the study.

Contrary to the agency's determination, the Budget Bureau letter plainly is not regulatory in form or content, but, instead, reflects policy guidance by the Bureau. Moreover, such guidance does not extend beyond the need for the agency to conform more closely to the legislative intent, under the Merchant Marine Act, of "similarity" between the faculty salary structures of the Academy and the Naval institution. As already indicated, nothing in the union's proposals is violative of that legislative intent.

Accordingly, we find that the union's proposals are not inconsistent with OMB directives.

3. *Are the union's proposals violative of policies specified in various pay acts?*

The agency determined that the union's proposals are contrary to the policies of the Federal Salary Reform Act of 1962 (76 Stat. 841) and the Federal Pay Comparability Act of 1970 (84 Stat. 1946).

However, these statutes apply, with exceptions not here relevant, to employees paid under the Classification Act. As previously indicated, section 216 (e) of the Merchant Marine Act specifically excepts faculty compensation at the Academy from the Classification Act. Thus, there is no necessary linkage between

Academy faculty salary practices and the policies of the above-cited statutes.

We find, therefore, that the union's proposals are not in violation of the pay acts relied upon by the agency.

4. Do agency regulations, as interpreted by the agency head, render the union's proposals non-negotiable?

The agency determined that the union's proposals are non-negotiable because: (a) they are governed by Maritime Administrator's Order No. 181, the agency's personnel policy issuance for the Academy faculty; and (b) they are outside the delegated bargaining authority of the Superintendent of the Academy by virtue of Department of Commerce Administrative Orders 202-250 and 202-711.

The union does not contest the agency's interpretation of its own regulations. However, it contends, in effect, that these regulations, as so interpreted, violate the bargaining obligation imposed by section 11 (a) of the Order.

The essential question presented is whether the agency head's determination that his regulations bar negotiations on the union's proposals is proper and should be sustained, or whether the determination improperly interprets the bargaining obligation of the Order and should be set aside.

The circumstances in the present case are quite unique. To recapitulate, the proposals for negotiation relate to a salary plan and schedule which applies only to a single, relatively small unit of professional employees (81), in a single activity of the agency and at a single location, who have a recognized union representative. The agency established the salary plan and schedule for these employees by detailed regulation (M.A.O. 181) and reserved authority to alter the plan or schedule to its Director of Personnel at departmental headquarters (or a member of his staff at grade GS-14 or above). Some other personnel policies applicable only to the unit are prescribed by the same agency regulation; other special policies for the group, such as those relating to faculty promotions, teaching loads, sabbatical leave, academic freedom, etc., have been established through negotiated agreement between representatives of the local activity and the recognized union.

In these particular circumstances, if the Council were to sustain the agency head's determination of non-negotiability as to the faculty salary plan and schedule, based on M.A.O. 181, it would be holding, in effect, that an agency may unilaterally limit the scope of its bargaining obligation on otherwise negotiable matters peculiar to an individual unit, in a single field activity, merely by issuing regulations from a higher level. We believe the bargaining obligation in section 11 (a) of the Order may not be diluted by unilateral action of this kind.

We do not, of course, question the statutory authority of the agency head to issue regulations for the operation of his department and the conduct of his employees. Moreover, we are fully aware of, and endorse, the policy of the Order to support such regulatory authority, in order to protect the public interest and maintain efficiency of government operations. This policy is incorporated in section 11 (a) by express reference to "published agency policies and regulations" as an appropriate limitation on the scope of negotiations.

However, the policies and regulations referred to in section 11 (a) as an appropriate limitation on the scope of negotiations are ones issued to achieve a desirable degree of uniformity and equality *in the administration of matters common to all employees of the agency, or, at least, to employees of more than one subordinate activity.* Any other interpretation of the phrase "published agency policies and regulations," in the context of the Order, which would permit *ad hoc* limitations on the scope of negotiations in a particular bargaining unit, would make a mockery of the bargaining obligation. For it would mean that superior official could unilaterally dictate any limit on the scope of negotiations in a particular agency activity merely by publishing instructions to the activity head with respect to personnel policies and working conditions unique to that activity.

In other words, with particular reference to the present case, while higher level published policies and regulations that are applicable uniformly to more than one activity may properly limit the scope of negotiations in the faculty unit at the Academy, higher level "published policies and regulations" which deal only with terms and conditions of employment in that individual unit, such as the faculty salary plan and schedule in M.A.O. 181, do *not* properly limit the scope of negotiations on this subject matter—since unilateral prescription of these terms and conditions conflicts with the bargaining obligation of section 11 (a). This is not to say that the Maritime Administrator's Order 181 is invalid. Rather, its publication does not, within the meaning of section 11 (a), limit the agency's obligation to negotiate with the recognized union on the union's proposed changes in matters covered by that directive, subject of course to the Merchant Marine Act and legislative intent.

There remains for consideration the agency's determination that the union's proposals are non-negotiable by virtue of Department of Commerce Administrative Orders 202-250 and 202-

711. According to the agency, Commerce's A.O. 202-711 assigns to the Superintendent of the Academy, as the official who accorded recognition to the union, the responsibility for fulfilling the bargaining obligation of the Order in the Academy unit. However, authority to alter the faculty salary plan or schedule is reserved by Commerce's A.O. 202-250 to the Director of Personnel (or appropriate member of his staff). The agency reasons that the effect of these two regulations is to bar negotiations on the salary plan or schedule for Academy faculty since these matters are not within the Superintendent's delegated authority.

We do not agree. The obligation in section 11(a) of the Order reads:

> An agency and a labor organization . . . through *appropriate* representatives, shall meet . . . and confer. . . . [Emphasis added.]

Clearly, the Order requires the parties to provide representatives who are empowered to negotiate and enter into agreements on all matters within the scope of negotiations in the bargaining unit. Since we have held that the union's proposals in this case are within the scope of negotiations, then to the extent Commerce's A.O. 202-711 bars such negotiations in the Academy unit, it is inconsistent with the Order and may not stand as a bar. Agency regulations, such as A.O. 202-711, which are issued to implement the Order must be consistent *therewith,* as required by section 23 of the Order.[10] Further, since the authority to take action on the matters covered by the union's proposals is reserved by Commerce's A.O. 202-250 to the Director of Personnel, it is apparent that he becomes the "appropriate" official responsible for fulfilling the agency's section 11(a) obligation on those matters.

In summary, we find that the agency's regulations, as interpreted by the agency head, do not render the union's proposals non-negotiable.

Conclusion

For the foregoing reasons, we are of the opinion that the union's proposals are negotiable as "personnel policies and practices and matters affecting working conditions" under section 11(a) of the Order. We do not hold that such proposals are desirable or must be accepted by the agency. We decide only that the proposals are matters subject to the obligation to negotiate by the parties involved.

---

[10] Section 23 of the Order requires that each agency "issue appropriate policies and regulations consistent with this Order for its implementation."

Therefore, pursuant to section 2411.27 of the Council's rules of procedure, we find that the determination by the Department of Commerce that the union's proposals are non-negotiable is improper, and the determination must be set aside. . . .

DETROIT POLICE OFFICERS ASSOCIATION v. CITY OF DETROIT
Michigan Court of Appeals, Division 1
41 Mich. App. 723, 200 N.W.2d 722 (1972)

Before BRONSON, P.J., and V.J. BRENNAN and O'HARA, J.J.

O'HARA, Judge.

Once again we become arbiter in the continuing tug of war between the municipalities asserting their rights under the "Home Rule Act" and the rights of municipal employees who are denied the legal right to strike, but who are also granted the right to collective bargaining representation.

Because of the length of the names of the parties and the concerned agencies and a statute, namely the Detroit Police Officers Association, the City of Detroit, the Michigan Employment Relations Commission and the Public Employment Relations Act, we will use throughout the opinion the acronyms DPOA, MERC, PERA and refer to the City of Detroit simply as the "City."

With the adoption in 1965 of section 15 of the P.E.R.A., municipalities became bound to bargain collectively with the representatives of their employees. Accordingly, the City recognized the DPOA as the bargaining representative of all patrolmen and policewomen of the Detroit Police Department on January 18, 1966. Negotiations for a collective bargaining agreement began in March, 1966 between the City and the DPOA and continued with interruptions through the Spring of 1968. This case grows out of the complexities of those negotiations.

It would appear from the record that both parties approached the bargaining table with certain preconceived objectives. In addition to the traditional wage demands, the representatives for the DPOA sought to remove a thirty-year-old residency requirement as a condition of employment. The DPOA also opposed the lowering of several recruitment qualifications initiated by the police commissioner apart from negotiations. The City, for its part, sought to initiate certain changes in the Policemen and Firemen Retirement Systems, (Detroit Charter, Title 9, Ch. 7) recommended by the Mayor's Task Force Committee on City Finances. The proposed changes were to provide: (1) a retirement pay of 2% of average final compensation for each year of service without a ceiling of 50%; (2) a minimum retirement age of 55,[6] (3) an escalation clause of 2% per year, identical to that of general city employees; and (4) a guaranteed pension after 25 years of service. The pension changes were to be prospective in application with respect to future members while present members would have the option to come under the new program; an option exercisable within a limited deadline period.

In the course of negotiations the City took certain actions to which the DPOA took exception. While the Detroit Labor Relations Bureau, with the support of the mayor, neared agreement with the DPOA in bargaining on the elimination of residency requirements, the Common Council, in separate action, conducted hearings and adopted a new ordinance which required all city employees to reside within the city limits, to which the DPOA expressed strong opposition. The association also opposed modification of police recruitment qualifications mentioned earlier.

Finally, the DPOA took issue with the Common Council's unilateral submission of the mayor's proposed amendments to the Policemen and Firemen Retirement System charter provision to popular referendum[8] absent meaningful bargaining on pension matters. Moreover, the association objected to the City's insistence on discussing pension matters apart from other items subject to agreement such as promotion, seniority and job classification.

On July 10, 1968 the DPOA filed a formal unfair labor practice complaint under M.C.L.A. § 423.210 (a) and (e); M.S.A. § 17.455 (10) (a) and (e) with the State Labor Mediation Board. The DPOA amended its complaint following passage of the retirement system referendum amendment charging the foregoing actions on the part of the City constituted a failure to bargain under PERA. Issue was joined on the following stipulated questions:

"1. Did the City of Detroit have the duty to bargain with the DPOA regarding residency requirements for policemen? If so, did the City of Detroit violate this duty to bargain by enactment of a residency ordinance?

"2. Did the City of Detroit have the duty to bargain with the DPOA regarding recruiting requirements for patrolmen? If so, did the City of Detroit violate this duty by making changes in the existing recruiting requirements?

---

[6] Prior to the proposed changes, the existing system provided that police officers could retire after twenty-five years of service, regardless of age.

[8] The referendum passed November 5, 1968.

"3. When an economic item which is the subject of bargaining, has been agreed to by the respective bargaining agents of the City of Detroit and the Union, which has been approved by the Mayor, does the Common Council's action in deleting said item from the budget constitute a refusal to bargain in good faith?

"4. Under all the facts and circumstances, did the City of Detroit have a duty to bargain at one time on all mandatory subjects of bargaining at the time of the conferences concerning the proposed retirement provisions changes?

"5. Did the City of Detroit bargain in good faith with the DPOA on the subject matter of retirement provision changes?"

Successive hearings were conducted by the MERC trial examiner who decided that the DPOA charges were without merit. Exceptions were filed by the DPOA to the examiner's decision and upon review by the commission a decision and order issued March 18, 1971.

While MERC, in its opinion and order, passed upon all of the five issues set forth herein, only three of them were appealed to this Court—numbers 1, 4 and 5. We treat them *seriatim*.

As to issue 1, MERC ruled there had been no violation of the applicable section of PERA. Subsequent to the time this case was submitted to us, our Supreme Court spoke with finality thereto. See Detroit Police Officers Association v. City of Detroit, 385 Mich. 519, 190 N.W.2d 97 (1971). We read this opinion to mean that the City is entitled to impose such residency requirement. It did so. Hence, we hold that issue no longer mandatorily negotiable.

Issues 4 and 5 both relate to the pension and retirement system. On issue 4 MERC determined that pension and retirement terms are an essential part of an employee's terms and conditions of employment and thus a mandatory subject for collective bargaining. It further held that the City's insistence "on isolating one mandatory subject of collective bargaining from other unresolved issues constitutes a refusal to bargain under Section 10 (e) of PERA." This position has been taken by MERC in earlier employment decisions. We do not disagree therewith, except, of course, as to the constitutional guarantee of the contractual nature of pensions already vested and the absolute inviolability thereof. Const. 1963, art. 9, § 24. To this extent then we affirm the holding of MERC as to issue 4.

Issue 5 as stated, in our view, does not delineate with precision the important legal question we are called upon to decide. In irreducible simplicity it is whether "Home Rule" city charter provisions which are in conflict with municipal obligations under PERA will prevail over the statute.

For the guidance of other municipalities and public collective bargaining units, we will try to strip that issue to its bare bones. What really happened in this case was that the mayor as the chief executive officer enlisted the aid of a "Task Force Committee on City Finances." He also had an executive staff member functioning as a bargaining representative. Under the charter, however, each or both for that matter, had limited powers because that document reposes final authority to approve "all contracts to which the city or any board or commission thereof" is a party in the Common Council. But even though the mayor, his committee and his executive assistant had advocated changes in the policemen's retirement system and the Council by resolution had unanimously approved the recommended changes, there remained a barrier to effective municipal action. In 1941, the policemen's and firemen's retirement system had been made part of the city charter, amendable solely by popular vote. M.C. L.A. § 117.21, M.S.A. § 5.2100. Hence, the mayor, the council and all the king's horses and all the king's men could not change the involved charter provision without approval of the electorate. So the plan advocated by the City was referred by referendum to the electorate. It was approved.

But meanwhile back at the bargaining table, the DPOA was clamorously contending that the referendum was of no legal force. Prospective changes in a pension and retirement system, said DPOA, are mandatory subjects of bargaining under PERA, and this requirement of the statute obtains over the charter provision.

We agree with DPOA. If the course followed by the City in this case were to receive judicial approval, the rights legislatively granted to public employees in return for divesting them of their legal right to strike would become meaningless.

It takes little insight to appreciate what a municipal employer and its electorate could do to the collective bargaining process if this procedure were allowed to stand. Any "Home Rule" city could merely write its pension and retirement system into its charter, and insulate any change therein from negotiations and settlement save with electoral approval. This to us is the exact converse of what the Legislature intended when it inserted bargaining rights for public employees into the statute.

We hold that the City did fail to bargain in good faith as to prospective changes in its retirement and pension system as here involved. We further hold to so do was an unfair labor practice remediable by an order of MERC. If necessary, we will issue an enforcement order compelling the City to bargain in good faith on this issue as required by MERC's decision. PERA prevails over the city charter for, among other reasons, the reason that it is a "general" law of the state. The Home Rule Act itself writes into its grant of powers the exception which pertains here. M.C.L.A. § 117.36; M.S.A. § 5.2116.

"Sec. 36. No provision of any city charter shall conflict with or contravene the provisions of any general law of the state."

To the extent then that the city charter conflicts with PERA, the charter must yield.

Affirmed as delineated herein. No costs—a public question.

NOTE

Are the various public sector labor relations acts applicable to both the executive and legislative branches of government? This question was recently raised in a case before the Pennsylvania Labor Relations Board in which the City of Pittsburgh was alleged to have committed an unfair labor practice by subcontracting the work of five meter collectors. PLRB v. City of Pittsburgh, PLRB Case No. PERA-C-1488-W, GERR No. 521, at B-5 (1973). Although the Board held that the subcontracting of work which affects bargaining unit employees is a mandatory subject of bargaining, the Board nevertheless held that the unilateral action of the City Council did not violate Act 195. The Board stated:

The Act consistently indicates and the legislature, it would appear, intended a separation between the executive and legislative branches of the public employer in the operation and application of the act. Unstated, but existing by the very nature of state government, the act exists and remains in existence at the sufferance of the legislature. Certainly an act which is a creature of the legislature cannot restrict or limit legislative discretion in matters of budget, services offered, or services withheld. The act can and does regulate the relationship between the executive branch of government and the states' employees. . . .
The foregoing can only lead to the conclusion that where the executive and legislative branches of the government (whether state or any subdivision thereof) are separate entities, the legislative branch in its considerations and application of its legislative duties cannot be bound by the application of Act 195 which regulates the conduct of the public employer acting in its executive capacity. Thus, the

charge of a violation under Section 1201 (a) (5), refusing to bargain cannot be sustained against the employer, the City of Pittsburgh.

Can the decision of the PLRB be squared with the decision of the Michigan Court of Appeals in the principal case?

6. Effect of Federal Mandating

HOUSING AUTHORITY OF THE CITY OF NEW HAVEN
Connecticut State Board of Labor Relations
Decision No. 715 (1966)

[Local 713, Council 4, AFSCME (Union) filed a charge alleging that the Housing Authority of the City of New Haven (Authority) had and was engaging in a prohibited practice when it put into effect a new wage schedule without any discussion or negotiation with the Union. As an affirmative defense, the Authority asserted that it had negotiated in good faith with the Union "to the fullest extent permitted under the terms of the Consolidated Annual Contributions Act and relevant federal statutes and regulations."]

The principal legal issue presented here is whether the Connecticut Municipal Employee Relations Act and, in particular, its collective bargaining provisions, apply to the Authority.

The Authority claimed that, as a matter of statutory construction, the provisions of the Act, and especially the Act's collective bargaining provisions, are inapplicable to it. The Authority further claimed that, by virtue of applicable federal housing statutes and federal action taken thereunder, the constitutional doctrine of federal supremacy requires that the collective bargaining provisions of the Act, even if construed to be applicable to the Authority, must yield to the contrary methods of fixing wages and conditions of employment of employees of local housing authorities pursuant to the federal housing laws. The Authority also contends that, if construed as applicable to it, the Act would be unconstitutional as impairing the contractual obligations of the Authority to the Federal Public Housing Administration (hereinafter referred to as PHA), which obligations were assumed pursuant to federal and Connecticut statutes.

There was little factual disagreement between the parties. The record showed that, at least since January 20, 1959, the date upon which one of the working agreements between the Union and the Housing Authority (Exhibit 1) was executed, the Authority has recognized the Union as "representing employees who are members of a certain Local among the regular full-time employees of the Housing Authority." This language appears in the current working agreement dated July 7, 1965 (Exhibit 8). The principal allegations of the complaint are those in Paragraphs 8 and 9. These allege that the Housing Authority has engaged in and is continuing to engage in activities prohibited to municipal employers by Sec. 4 (a) (1) and (4) of the Act.

The Housing Authority, in Paragraph 5 of its answer, has denied these allegations. In addition, in its affirmative statement the Authority recites that it has "for many years entered into a Consolidated Annual Contributions Contract with the Federal Public Housing Administration pursuant to federal law," which contract still remains in effect, and that the current working agreement of July 7, 1965, provides that "compensation rates for custodian and maintenance employees of the Authority who are members of the Union shall be established by the Public Relations Branch of the PHA."

It appears to us that the Union was aware that the Authority had and has a Consolidated Annual Contributions Act with the Federal Public Housing Administration under the applicable federal law, and that the Authority was, and still is, subject to the terms of such contract and of the federal law.

The Connecticut Municipal Employee Relations Act is a modified "Little Wagner Act" applicable to municipal employers and their employees. The provisions of the Act require both parties to do certain things and to refrain from doing certain things, as contained in the Act. The key provision for purposes of this proceeding is the requirement of Section 3 that the municipal employer and the appropriate employee organization shall have the duty to bargain collectively. The reverse of this affirmative duty is the prohibition of Sec. 4 (a) and Sec. 4 (b) which prohibits an employer and an employee organization, respectively, from refusing to bargain collectively.

The Housing Authority is included in the definition of "Municipal Employer" under Sec. 1 (l). However, Sec. 8 (d) of the Act provides:

> (d) If the municipal employer is a district school board, housing authority or other authority established by law which by statute, charter, special act, or ordinance has sole and exclusive control over the appointment of and the wages, hours and conditions of employment of its employees, such district, school board, housing authority or other authority, or its designated representatives, shall represent such municipal employer in collective bargaining and shall have the authority to enter into collective bargaining agree-

ments with the employee organization which is the exclusive representative of such employees.

It appears to us that Sec. 8 (d) of the Act recognizes the fact that local housing authorities, operating low-rent housing projects, are subject to federal law and that by virtue of the analysis of the federal law are exempt from the provisions of our Act.

Any conflict between federal authority operating within its constitutional sphere and state authority must be resolved in favor of the federal authority under the supremacy clause of the Constitution (U.S. Const. Art. VI, Clause 2). The Connecticut Legislature cannot compel the Public Housing Administration, a federal agency, to do anything inconsistent with federal policy as embodied in a federal statute or an administrative regulation or policy adopted within the authority conferred by such statute. Commissioner of Labor & Industries v. Boston Housing Authority, 345 Mass. 406, 188 N.E.2d 150 (1963). And Connecticut has not in fact sought to govern or regulate the conduct of the Public Housing Administration by the Municipal Employee Relations Act. Section 7-467 of the General Statutes defines an employer subject to the Act as a "political subdivision of the state," thus clearly excluding the Public Housing Administration, a federal agency.

The New Haven Housing Authority, on the other hand, is clearly an employer under the Act since it is a creature of the Legislature and is specifically included under the express words "housing authority." This local authority is created to perform state as well as federal functions. Conn. Gen. Stat. Sec. 8-69 et seq.; Austin v. Housing Authority of Hartford, 143 Conn. 338 (1956). And when it is performing state functions this authority is within the Act and must conform to the requirements of the Act with respect to employees on any projects not financed by federal funds. Commissioner of Labor & Industries v. Boston H.A., *supra,* 188 N.E.2d at 158.

When the Authority is engaged in a federally financed project, however, the considerations mentioned in the first paragraph come into play. The Act contemplates bargaining by a municipal employer over whom the Legislature has control. Thus it makes specific provisions for resolving problems posed when an agreement reached by negotiators (a) necessitates a request for funds, or (b) conflicts with any statute, ordinance or administrative rule or regulation, Sec. 7-474 (b). And Sec. 7-474 (c) provides assurance that needed funds will be forthcoming if a problem is resolved in favor of the negotiated agreement. See also Clause 7-474 (f). None of these provisions can be made effective so as to bind the PHA. Yet, clearly, the federal and state statutes dealing with federally financed housing projects contemplate that the local authority "administer its affairs in accordance with the regulations promulgated by the Public Housing Authority." See *Austin v. Housing Authority, supra,* 143 Conn. at 342. See also the *Boston Housing Authority* case, *supra.* As the Boston case points out, the ultimate control over the budget and over expenditures rests with the PHA and is beyond state power.

Since neither the federal statutes (42 U.S.C., Clause 1401 et seq.) nor the state statutes (Conn. Gen. Stat., Clause 8-44 et seq.) seem to forbid it, Connecticut may well have the constitutional power to require a kind of bargaining between the local authority and its employees on federally financed projects, viz., the negotiation of proposals to be submitted to a federal agency for its acceptance, modification or rejection by the application of purely federal standards over which Connecticut does not and cannot have any control. Compare the *Boston Housing Authority* case, *supra.* This does not, however, appear to be the kind of bargaining contemplated by the Act. Moreover, it would involve a procedure not provided for by the Act, and the Act expressly declares that the procedure it provides for the making of a contract "shall be the exclusive method for making a valid agreement for municipal employees represented by an employee organization." Sec. 7-474 (e) .

We conclude, therefore, that the Act does not compel the Housing Authority when administering a project financed by federal funds pursuant to 42 U.S.C., Clause 1401 et seq., to bargain collectively with its employees *on that project.* In this aspect the authority is not one "which by statute . . . has the sole and exclusive control over the . . . wages, hours and conditions of employment of its employees. . . ." Sec. 7-474 (d) .

We therefore conclude that the Housing Authority is not subject to the provisions of the Act.

Order

For the foregoing reasons the complaint in this matter is DISMISSED for lack of jurisdiction.

NOTES

1. In providing financial assistance to state and local governments Congress frequently specifies certain conditions which must be met as a condition precedent to receiving such assistance. For example, in authorizing the Surgeon General to "make grants to State, health or mental health authorities to assist the States in establishing and maintaining adequate public health

services . . . ," Congress stipulated that a state must submit a plan which must, *inter alia,*

> Provide such methods of administration (including methods relating to the establishment and maintenance of personnel standards on a merit basis, except that the Surgeon General shall exercise no authority with respect to the selection, tenure of office, and compensation of any individual employed in accordance with such methods) as are found by the Surgeon General to be necessary for the proper and efficient operation of the plan.

42 U.S.C. § 246 (d) (2) (F) (1970). To what extent does such a statutory provision affect the scope of bargaining?

The Urban Mass Transportation Act of 1964 provides for grants to states and local agencies for the purpose, among others, of acquiring privately-operated transit facilities. As a condition precedent to receiving such a grant, however, the Act requires that there be "fair and equitable arrangements . . . , as determined by the Secretary of Labor, to protect the interest of employees affected by such assistance." Among the protective arrangements which must be provided for is "the continuation of collective bargaining rights." Urban Mass Transportation Act § 13 (c), 49 U.S.C. § 1609 (c) (1972). What effect, if any, does this statutory provision have on the interpretation or application of a public sector bargaining statute which provides for a narrower scope of bargaining than that allowed under the National Labor Relations Act? Would the state act apply? *See* Regional Transp. Dist., Inc. v. Local Div. 282 of Amalgamated Transit Union, 316 N.Y.S.2d 325, 64 Misc. 2d 865 (Sup. Ct. 1970).

2. In ADVISORY COMMISSION ON INTERGOVERNMENTAL RELATIONS, LABOR-MANAGEMENT POLICIES FOR STATE AND LOCAL GOVERNMENT 111 (1969), the following recommendation is made:

> Having assessed [the] various facets of present and potential federal mandating and recognizing that further intervention is quite possible, the Commission adopts the general position that Congress should refrain from any additional mandating of requirements related to the working conditions of State and local employees or the authority of these governments to deal with their personnel in whatever fashion they see fit.

See generally pp. 59-60, *supra.*

7. Effect of Budgetary Process

D. STANLEY, MANAGING LOCAL GOVERNMENT UNDER UNION PRESSURE 112, 115-19 (1972)†

Local government employee unions have added new stresses to the already difficult financial situation of these governments but have not basically altered the budget and finance processes. Department heads still prepare preliminary estimates of expenditures. Budget and finance officers organize and adjust the requests of department heads and estimate available revenues. Chief executives make "final" decisions on the budget to be submitted to the legislative body, and the latter holds hearings, approves the budget, and sets tax rates. All this is familiar. What the unions have done is to assume a greatly strengthened and highly visible role in decisions that ultimately have a major impact on the size of the budget. Their political and emotional effect is heightened by the fact that the larger local governments are generally either in or approaching a condition of financial crisis. . . .

In [the] nineteen localities [studied], as in most fair-sized local governments, budget preparation begins about six months before the start of the new fiscal year when the budget office sends to the various department heads instructions on the format and schedule to be followed in preparing estimates. Departments may or may not be told how rigorously to economize or what programs to emphasize as they look ahead. Generally using the current budget figures as a base, department heads make their estimates, often in consultation with a member of the budget staff. Where it is feasible they use workload figures, past and estimated, to back up their calculations—numbers of fires, miles of streets, cubic yards of rubbish. The department heads do not consult unions at this time and are influenced by union pressures only to the extent that previous union-sponsored changes in work rules or pay provisions have changed the expense outlook. Meanwhile the budget office (or the finance staff if it is a separate organization) is estimating expected revenues. Then both revenue and expenditure sheets go to the chief executive, who, aided by the budget and finance staff, must trim the expense estimates, or plan to seek extra revenues, or both, in order to balance his budget before it goes to the legislative body.[17]

---

† Reprinted by permission. Copyright © 1972 by The Brookings Institution, Washington, D.C.

[17] For a concise, sophisticated summary of local government budgeting, see John P. Crecine, *A Computer Simulation Model of Municipal Budgeting,* MANAGEMENT SCIENCE, Vol. 13 (July 1967), pp. 786-815.

In the days before unions acquired collective bargaining rights, this budget process readily accommodated changes in pay and benefits. Modifications were proposed by the personnel office or civil service commission, approved by the budget office and chief executive, and ultimately enacted by the legislative body. They were kept within anticipated financial resources and were usually timed to begin at the start of the next fiscal year. In the present era of collective bargaining, even though most of the budget process is unrelated to union activities, the schedule has become less controllable for three reasons. First, the bargaining process is time-consuming. Second, unions may adopt a strategy that calls for bargaining to reach a climax at the time the legislative body is considering the budget. Third, the results of bargaining may require new financing measures involving further legislation locally, or a referendum, or action by the state legislature. However, in situations where there is a multi-year union agreement, without pay reopener provisions, such problems are spaced out and therefore less troublesome.

Cities in New York State (including, among those studied, Binghamton and Buffalo but not New York City) are expected to be kept on schedule by the Taylor Law, which provides that negotiations, including mediation and fact finding, must be concluded sixteen [sic] days before the budget is submitted to the local legislative body.[18] Despite the law, Buffalo ran late in 1968. That city's charter requires the mayor to submit the budget to the council by May 1 for adoption by June 1. However, when the 1968 union negotiations (the first under the law) had not been completed by June 1, the city had to include a lump-sum "salary adjustment fund" in the budget to cover the estimated costs of the union settlements.

Several of the cities and counties in other states try to complete bargaining before the legislative body starts work on the budget. Hartford has been successful thus far in concluding negotiations well before the budget is closed, even though state law permits bargaining to run on beyond that time. The city aims to finish bargaining by January 1 and to pass the budget in February; the fiscal year begins April 1. Still another method was found in Detroit, where pay discussions are part of the budget process and separate from union negotiations on other matters. Pay settlements there are not included in agreements, but are recommended by the mayor to the common council along with the budget.

---

[18] New York, Public Employees' Fair Employment Act of 1967, sec. 209, as amended, March 4, 1969. Section 212 of the law exempts New York City from this requirement.

Two governments, Dade County and Philadelphia, bargain while the legislative body has the budget under review but before it completes action.

In a still later category are cities and counties where bargaining continues even after the budget is adopted. This means that if the budget does not contain enough funds to finance the agreement, additional revenues must be obtained. Boston, Dayton, New Castle County, and New York have all been in the position of concluding agreements after the budget has been decided. Boston lacks a fixed schedule for both budget submissions and bargaining. Although the fiscal year there begins in January, departmental estimates trickle in until April, when a supplementary budget request based on bargaining settlements is submitted to the city council. The tax rate is set the following July. New York City's scores of agreements are concluded at different times of the year (usually January or July) and vary in their duration; hence it is virtually impossible to budget realistically for bargaining settlements. Budgeting and bargaining have become two very separate operations.

Turning to the four governments that do not have general collective bargaining, in Los Angeles County, New Orleans, and San Francisco the personnel authorities recommend salaries and benefits for consideration by the legislative bodies before budgets are adopted. St. Louis has found it necessary in the past to consider the salary demands of the unions after the budget is adopted. However, tentative agreement has now been reached between the city and four unions to conduct annual negotiating sessions *before* the budget is drafted.

Reconciling the budget schedule with the bargaining schedule is an annual problem where the agreements are for one year only. Elsewhere these coordination problems have to be faced only in the years when agreements are up for renewal.

What Timing Is Best?

Financial management is obviously more efficient when negotiations are finished before the budget goes to the legislature. Under such circumstances the executive branch has considered the unions' demands along with other spending needs and with estimated revenues, reconciled any problems, and prepared a budget package that is fully ready for legislative action. This is hard to achieve for reasons already stated: slow bargaining, union strategies, and authorization of supplementary financing. The experience of the governments studied here suggests that bargaining results can feasibly go to the legislative body *after* it has begun work on the budget. It is even possible for bargaining to be completed after the budget has been approved by the legislature. In either event the budget process becomes more protracted, less businesslike, and less controllable from a management standpoint. The city council may have to enact supplementary appropriations and new revenue measures after the start of the new fiscal period.

Several of the governments studied have adapted themselves to these difficulties. The problems perhaps would be lessened if elected officials, citizens' groups, and the news media brought pressure for timely conclusion of bargaining. The union members too would like to have their uncertainties ended sooner— but not at the cost of lower settlements. It seems inevitable on the whole that rigid bargaining schedules to meet budget deadlines will be viewed with more nostalgia than respect. Delayed and revised budgets are inconvenient and stressful for executives and staffs and are more difficult for citizens to understand, but they can be expected to continue, and local governments will make the necessary adaptations.

Reserves For Settlements

Representatives of all the cities and counties, regardless of their budget schedules, were asked if they budgeted any "cushions" (contingency funds) or if they "hid" any money to pay for union settlements that were higher than they had anticipated. A majority of the governments studied answered in the negative. Buffalo, Hartford, Milwaukee, and New Castle County all reported that they use contingency funds for this purpose. One other county and three cities, whose identity will not be disclosed, candidly said that they "hid" money in the estimates for various departments. The former method (use of an earmarked fund) is risky. It may become a "sitting duck" for legislators who want to eliminate it or use it for another purpose; or it may become a target for bargaining demands—unions may ask for the total amount and more too. Cincinnati operates under another method, financing settlements out of an "income tax permanent improvement fund," which receives income tax revenues that exceed estimates. The city manager commits part of the fund to capital improvement projects, but it is difficult for the unions to find out how much is uncommitted, thus giving the city some bargaining leeway.

NOTES

1. The impact of bargaining on the budgetary process and on public finance is explored in Hayes, *Collective Bargaining*

and the Budget Director, in PUBLIC WORKERS AND PUBLIC UNIONS 89 (S. Zagoria ed. 1972).

2.   Concerning the impact of bargaining on municipal pay plans, Kenneth O. Warner, then Executive Director of the Public Personnel Association, stated:

> The traditional approach to pay plans may have to be tossed out the window. With bargaining there is a good chance that the tidy, systematic, integrated pay plan—designed to give equitable treatment to all employees in a given jurisdiction—will undergo considerable change. The 64-dollar question is how do you maintain fairness and equity when many unions bargain for wages in several different units of an organization. It should be noted that union representatives argue that anything would be an improvement over what now exists. The reason: Pay administration is not really scientific.

Warner, *Financial Implications of Employee Bargaining in the Public Service,* in SORRY . . . NO GOVERNMENT TODAY 189, 197 (R. Walsh ed. 1969).

CITY OF SAGINAW
Michigan Employment Relations Commission
1967 Lab. Op. 465

Trial Examiner James McCormick: *Refusal to Bargain After Budget Adopted.* That leaves for consideration the charge that the City . . . adopted a budget for the 1966-67 fiscal year, thereby putting into effect its final offer and foreclosing further bargaining, despite the fact no final agreement had been reached. . . . I find merit in [this charge].

Act 279, P.A. of 1909, CL 1948 sec. 117.1 et seq., M.S.A. sec. 5.2071 et seq. (Home Rule Act), pursuant to which the City of Saginaw is incorporated, provides in Section 3 as follows:

"Each city charter shall provide:

(g)   for annually laying and collecting taxes. . .
(h)   for an annual appropriation of money for municipal purposes."

City charter provisions implementing the Home Rule Act generally are much more specific as to the detail required in the schedule of appropriations, or budget. Chapter VII of the Saginaw City Charter, for example, requires each department to submit an itemized estimate of expenditures for the next fiscal year. A budget is then prepared "in such detail and with such supporting schedules as the (city) manager shall require." The manager must submit the budget to the City Council "on or before the last Monday in April." A public hearing must be held before the Council adopts the final budget by resolution, makes appropriations for the new year, and sets the tax levy. The Council thereafter "may transfer any unencumbered appropriation balance or any portion thereof from one department, fund, or agency, to another." The Council may also reduce or increase overall appropriations thereafter, if revenues are less or greater than anticipated when the budget was adopted. (Charter, Section 46, 47).

It appears clear that adoption of the budget on June 20, 1966, did not, under the terms of the Charter, make it impossible for the Council to negotiate further concerning economic items for the ensuing fiscal year. While setting a tax levy put a ceiling on *overall* City expenditures, absent greater revenue than expected, it did not prevent the City from reallocating funds from one purpose or department to another. The Council could still, for example, transfer funds from proposed material purchases or capital outlays to wages, and could transfer funds allocated to the public works department to the fire department, or vice versa. (This might necessitate a further public budget hearing. Storolow v. City of Pontiac, 339 Mich. 199, 63 N.W.2d 611 (1954)). Even if the transfer of funds, once budgeted and appropriated, would violate a city charter or ordinance, the undersigned concludes that the goal of meaningful negotiations leading to a collective bargaining agreement requires that such charter provisions give way to the policy of the Legislature as reflected in the PERA. It is noted that the Home Rule Act itself is not in conflict with the PERA. Under the Home Rule Act, estimated expenditures need not be itemized in detail. Worden v. City of Detroit, 241 Mich. 139, 216 N.W. 461 (1927). In any event, the charter of a home rule city is subject to the general laws of the state, and charter provisions contravening state law are void. City of Highland Park v. F.E.P.C., 364 Mich. 508, 111 N.W.2d 797 (1962); People v. Pickett, 339 Mich. 294 (1954).

Here, it is not clear whether a true impasse had been reached in June, at which time the Council granted its last offer by adopting a budget and setting the tax rate. Since the tax levy must be in effect by the beginning of the new fiscal year, the Council cannot be criticized for the action it took on June 20, regardless of whether an impasse had been reached. On the other hand, its unwillingness to meet further relative to any issue involving the expenditure of funds improperly foreclosed bargaining and, in my opinion, constituted a violation of the bargaining duty. Any other conclusion would put a premium on the public employer's use of tactics designed to stall until the budget deadline, and then avoid bargaining altogether by adopting a budget.

This is not to say that negotiations must be continued *ad infinitum*. Once a true impasse has been reached the public employer may, like his private counterpart, end negotiations and put into effect its last offer, subject to returning to the bargaining table when either side is prepared to make a significant further concession in the interests of reaching agreement.

While the conclusion arrived at here undoubtedly poses problems, it is an interpretation of the statute which at least avoids the absolute frustration of bargaining in the public sector which would result from a holding that a budget deadline tolls the obligation of the employer to seek agreement. The super-imposition of a comprehensive collective bargaining law onto the labyrinth of statutes, charters, ordinances and other forms of regulation of local government operations presents many real or apparent conflicts of laws not encountered in the traditional application of collective bargaining laws to private industry. This case involves such conflicts in the areas of delegation of power to negotiators, insistence upon an ordinance in lieu of a contract, and refusal to negotiate after adopting the annual budget. Here, the City's reliance on the finality of a budget as grounds for refusing to bargain was, in the estimation of the undersigned, misplaced, even though the City may be assumed to have acted in good faith, consistent with its own interpretation of the City Charter.

It should be noted that a more difficult problem of harmonizing seemingly conflicting statutory provisions would be presented if Saginaw were incorporated under the Fourth Class Cities Act (Act 215, P.A. of 1895 as amended, CL 1948 sec. 81.1 et seq., M.S.A. sec. 5.1591 et seq.) which requires a detailed budget and appropriations ordinance and restricts further appropriations after passage of the annual appropriations bill. (M.S.A. secs. 5.1939, 5.1941, 5.1943, 5.1944).

[The Trial Examiner's decision was affirmed by the MERC.]

NOTE

Several of the comprehensive public sector collective bargaining statutes contain impasse procedures which are specifically geared to the budget submission date and contemplate that collective bargaining will be concluded prior to said date. Suppose a union is recognized or certified as a bargaining representative subsequent to the budget submission date and the union requests that the public employer negotiate over wages and fringe benefits for the year covered by the budget. If the public employer refused to negotiate on the grounds that the budget submission date had already passed, would it be committing an unfair labor practice? In Ligonier Valley School Dist., Case No. PERA-C-1542-W (September 29, 1972), the Pennsylvania Labor Relations Board held that an employer had a duty to bargain even though the budget submission date had passed. *Cf.* Town of New Canaan, Decision No. 828 (Conn. SLRB 1968).

C. Elements of Good Faith Bargaining

1. Generally

WEST HARTFORD EDUCATION ASSOCIATION v. DECOURCY
Connecticut Supreme Court
162 Conn. 566, 295 A.2d 526 (1972)

RYAN, Associate Justice: . . . Since [the court has ruled that class size, teacher load, the assignment to and compensation for extracurricular activities, and the submission of grievances to binding arbitration were mandatory subjects of bargaining], the parties ask us to decide whether or not the board violated its duty to negotiate with the plaintiff by: (i) Not making counter-proposals on those topics, or (ii) taking the position that such matters be reserved for unilateral decision by the board, or (iii) taking the position that such matters be included in the "board prerogatives" clause of the contract.

Section 10-153d requires the board to "confer in good faith with respect to salaries and other conditions of employment, or the negotiation of an agreement, or any question arising thereunder and the execution of a written contract incorporating any agreement reached if requested by either party, but such obligation shall not compel either party to agree to a proposal or require the making of a concession." This language is almost identical to the corresponding portion of the National Labor Relations Act.

The duty to negotiate in good faith generally has been defined as an obligation to participate actively in deliberations so as to indicate a present intention to find a basis for agreement. N.L.R.B. v. Montgomery Ward & Co., 133 F.2d 676, 686 (9th Cir.). Not only must the employer have an open mind and a sincere desire to reach an agreement but a sincere effort must be made to reach a common ground. Ibid.

This duty does not require an employer to agree to a proposal or require the making of a concession. The National Labor Relations Board has interpreted this provision as freeing an employer from any duty to make counterproposals in the form of concessions, so that the failure to make counterproposals is not a per se violation of the act, but must be tested against the usual standard of good faith. N.L.R.B. v. Arkansas Rice Growers Assn., 400 F.2d 565, 571 (8th Cir.). The answer to question (b) (i) is "No." The board of education does not violate its duty to negotiate by refusing to make counterproposals on the mandatory subjects listed in question (a) as long as it is negotiating in good faith.

Questions (b) (ii) and (b) (iii) should be discussed together. Question (b) (ii) is somewhat vague because there are insufficient facts contained in the stipulation to indicate what is meant by reserving matters for the "unilateral action of the board." If the conduct of the board amounted to a complete refusal to negotiate with the teachers' representatives on mandatory subjects of bargaining, such conduct would, of course, constitute a violation of its statutory duty to negotiate. On the other hand, the board's insistence on a broad "board prerogatives clause," or as it is referred to in nonpublic labor relations cases, a "management rights clause," would not constitute a per se violation of § 10-153d. In N.L.R.B. v. American National Ins. Co., 343 U.S. 395, 72 S. Ct. 824, 96 L. Ed. 1027, the Supreme Court of the United States held that employer-bargaining for a clause under which management retains the exclusive right to control what certain conditions of employment will be does not amount to conduct which constitutes refusal to bargain per se, nor does it alone demonstrate a lack of good faith. In effect, the court was saying that this type of provision is itself a condition of employment, and a mandatory subject of collective bargaining. Long Lake Lumber Co., 185 N.L.R.B., No. 65, 74 L.R.R.M. 1116.

"While it is well established that an employer's insistence upon a management rights clause does not itself violate . . . [the act], the nature of the employer's proposals on management's rights . . . are material factors in assessing its motivations in approaching negotiations." Stuart Radiator Core Mfg. Co., 173 N.L.R.B., No. 27, 69 L.R.R.M. 1243. Thus, if the employer insisted on retaining for himself absolute unilateral control over wages, hours and other conditions of employment in effect requiring the union to waive practically all of its statutory rights his good faith is suspect. Stuart Radiator Core Mfg. Co., supra; I.T.T. Corporation, Henze Valve Service Division, 166 N.L.R.B. No. 65, 65 L.R.R.M. 1654; East Texas Steel Castings, 154 N.L.R.B., No. 94, 60 L.R.R.M. 1097; "M" System, Inc., 129 N.L.R.B., No. 64, 47 L.R.R.M. 1017; Dixie Corporation, 105 N.L.R.B., No. 49, 32 L.R.R.M. 1259. Where the subject of a dispute is a mandatory bargaining point adamant insistence on a bargaining position is not necessarily a refusal to bargain in good faith. N.L.R.B. v. Wooster Division, Borg-Warner Corporation, 356 U.S. 342, 349, 78 S. Ct. 718, 2 L. Ed. 2d 823. To determine the question of good faith the totality of the parties' conduct throughout the negotiations must be considered. N.L.R.B. v. Alva Allen Industries, Inc., 369 F.2d 310, 321 (8th Cir.) ; New Canaan v. Connecticut State Board of Labor Relations, 160 Conn. 285, 293, 278 A.2d 761.

Questions (b) (ii) and (b) (iii) cannot be answered categorically.

Question (c)

The issue in this question is the extent to which the school board may communicate with its teachers about salaries and other conditions of employment while collective bargaining negotiations are being conducted. Section 10-153d makes it unlawful for the board to interfere with, restrain or coerce employees in the exercise of their rights under the Teacher Negotiation Act. A similar prohibition appears in the National Labor Relations Act, 29 U.S.C. §158 (a) (1) which makes it an unfair labor practice to interfere with, restrain or coerce employees who seek to pursue their rights under that act. Thus, we can again turn to cases arising under the federal act for guidance.

The National Labor Relations Act makes it an employer's duty to bargain collectively with the chosen representatives of his employees, and since this obligation is exclusive, it exacts the negative duty to treat with no other. Medo Photo Supply Corporation v. N.L.R.B., 321 U.S. 678, 64 S. Ct. 830, 88 L. Ed. 1007; International Ladies' Garment Workers' Union v. N.L.R.B., 108 U.S. App. D.C. 68, 280 F.2d 616, aff'd, 366 U.S. 731, 81 S. Ct. 1603, 6 L. Ed. 2d 762. After a duly authorized collective bargaining representative has been selected, the employer cannot negotiate wages or other terms of employment with individual workers. Medo Photo Supply Corporation v. N.L.R.B., supra, 321 U.S. 684, 64 S. Ct. 830; N.L.R.B. v. United States Sonics Corporation, 312 F.2d 610 (1st Cir.) . Thus, an employer interferes with his employees' right to bargain collectively in violation of 29 U.S.C. § 158(a)(1) when he treats directly with employees and grants them a wage increase in return for their promise to repudiate the union which they have designated as their representative. N.L.R.B. v. Katz, 369 U.S. 736, 92 S. Ct. 1107, 8 L. Ed. 2d 230. The statutory obligation thus imposed is to deal with the employees through the union rather than dealing with the union through the employees. Attempts to bypass the representative may be considered evidence of bad faith in the duty to bargain. The conduct proscribed in the *Medo* case was direct negotiation with the employees and bypassing the union. The act does not prohibit an employer from communicating in noncoercive terms with his employees while collective negotiations are in progress. Proctor & Gamble Mfg. Co., 160 N.L.R.B., No. 36, 62 L.R.R.M. 1617. The element of negotiation is critical. Another crucial factor in these cases is whether or not the communication is designed to undermine and denigrate the union. Flambeau Plastics Corporation v. N.L.R.B., 401 F.2d 128 (7th Cir.), cert. denied, 393 U.S. 1019, 89 S. Ct. 625, 21 L. Ed. 2d 563.

The question in the present case is whether the defendant Richter was engaging in direct negotiation with teachers offering something in return for a consideration, dealing with them in a manner calculated to subvert the union, or merely communicating with them without interfering, restraining or coercing them.

The first situation occurred in March, 1969, while negotiations between the parties were continuing. During that month the defendant board proposed a new work year, vacation schedule and salary schedule for department chairmen, coordinating teachers and subject area specialists. The program involved a substantially different length of work day, length of work year and a salary schedule for the personnel involved, and was to take effect July 1, 1969. Before this program was presented to the plaintiff association the defendant Richter called special meetings on March 5 and 6, 1969, and discussed the plan directly with the staff members who would be affected.

It is proper for an employer to discuss his proposals with his employees and to defend his position. Tobasco Prestressed Concrete Co., 177 N.L.R.B., No. 101, 71 L.R.R.M. 1565. Moreover, it is permissible for an employer to discuss certain items with his employees before he presents them to the union. In Little Rock Downtowner, Inc., 168 N.L.R.B., No. 107, 66 L.R.R.M. 1267, an employer had discussed with two employees the possibility of giving them additional duties and additional compensation before any proposal had been made at the bargaining table. The board found that the communication was for the purpose of exchanging ideas and did not constitute negotiation or a violation of the act where the employees understood that the matter would be determined between the employer and the union at the bargaining table.

The law as to attempts to negotiate with employees for the purpose of bypassing or denigrating the union is clear. On this very limited stipulation of facts, however, we cannot conclude that communicating to these special employees some of the details of a new program was unlawful. There is nothing to indicate that the defendant Richter was engaged in negotiations with the teachers nor that this was an attempt to bypass or subvert the union. The proposed new program was discussed later at the bargaining table with the union.

The plaintiff next alleges that the defendant board violated § 10-153d by communicating directly with the teachers concerning the "resource teacher program." On February 13, 1970, during negotiations, the board proposed that the teaching staff be differentiated into two groups, one working more days and more hours per day than heretofore and the other group continuing to work the same days and hours as in the past. This became known as the "extended plan" or "resource teacher program." Despite failure to reach accord on the working conditions of this plan, the board adopted a resolution resolving to implement the program and directing the superintendent to solicit the advice of the plaintiff association and of individual teachers in order to develop a tentative guide for this position. On April 6, 1970, the defendant Richter, acting as superintendent and with the knowledge and assent of the defendant board, informed the entire teaching staff of the West Hartford school system of the adoption of said resolution by distributing copies of it in the Staff Bulletin.

The defendants contend that this conduct on the part of the board and the defendant Richter did not violate the law because the board was merely implementing a policy decision to employ certain personnel as resource teachers. The decision to create a new type of position is a matter which goes to the heart of educational policy. It is true that the salary and working conditions of the resource teachers were mandatory subjects of negotiation, and these matters were actually being negotiated between the plaintiff and the defendants. The adoption of the resolution in question and the communication of this to the teachers and to the plaintiff association did not involve direct negotiations with employees on mandatory subjects of negotiation nor can it be construed as an attempt to bypass the union.

The answer to question (c) is "No."

Question (d)

The final question presented in this case involves the legality of the board of education's unilateral implementation of their contract proposals after the parties had failed to reach agreement on them. The particular proposals which the board put into effect were those dealing with the salary and working conditions of department chairmen, coordinating teachers and subject area specialists for the school year 1969-70. Contrary to the claims of the plaintiff the stipulated facts do not indicate that the proposals involving the extended program or resource teacher program, first made on February 13, 1970, were "implemented." We have no occasion, therefore, to discuss the subject under question (d).

The duty to bargain under the National Labor Relations Act is similar to the duty to negotiate that is created by our Teacher Negotiation Act. A breach of this duty in the federal area is deemed a refusal to bargain and an unfair labor practice under § 158 (a) (5). It is a fundamental tenet of the federal labor law that an employer who unilaterally changes wages and other working conditions which are under negotiation commits a § 158 (a) (5) unfair labor practice. N.L.R.B. v. Katz, 369 U.S. 736, 743, 82 S. Ct. 1107, 8 L. Ed. 2d 230. The employer who engages in such conduct circumvents his duty to deal exclusively with the union and is refusing to bargain in fact with the employee organization. Id., 743, 82 S. Ct. 1107.

The defendants contend that there was a legally cognizable impasse in negotiations over these topics such that it had the right to put its plans into operation. There is no acid test for determining whether or not an impasse exists. N.L.R.B. v. Tex-Tan, Inc., 318 F.2d 472 (5th Cir.), describes it as a state of facts in which the parties, despite the best of faith, are simply deadlocked. In most cases, the National Labor Relations Board and the courts have looked at the fact pattern for certain indicia of impasse. Have the parties stopped talking? How many bargaining sessions were held? Have the positions become solidified and the parties intransigent? Was a mediator called in? See American Ship Building Co. v. N.L.R.B., 380 U.S. 300, 85 S. Ct. 955, 13 L. Ed. 2d 855; 44 Tex. L. Rev. 769. Here, although the stipulated facts reveal that the parties had negotiated but were unable to agree on the topics in question, we note that both sides remained at the bargaining table and continued to negotiate on a wide range of topics. Neither party expressed a desire to terminate these discussions. Moreover, the record indicates that mediation was not requested until after the board had suggested implementation of its proposals. It would appear that at this point the parties believed that a continuation of discussions might be fruitful. On this limited statement of facts, we cannot conclude that the parties were "simply deadlocked." Newspaper Drivers & Handlers', Local No. 372 v. N.L.R.B., 404 F.2d 1159 (6th Cir.).

The defendants, however, claim that impasse may exist with reference to a particular issue, and, even though the parties are still negotiating about other topics, the deadlock on the individual issue permits the board to implement its last proposal thereon.

This claim is inaccurate. The relevant federal cases deal with the situation where the inability to resolve one or two key issues creates a general impasse, and, despite agreement or willingness to talk about other subjects, it is apparent that further negotiations would not produce a broad meeting of the minds. American Federation of Television & Radio Artists v. N.L.R.B., 129 U.S. App. D.C. 399, 395 F.2d 622; Dallas General Drivers, Local No. 745 v. N.L.R.B., 122 U.S. App. D.C. 417, 355 F.2d 842; N.L.R.B. v. Intercoastal Terminal, Inc., 286 F.2d 954 (5th Cir.). "It cannot be doubted that a deadlock on one critical issue can create as impassable a situation as an inability to agree on several or all issues." American Federation of Television & Radio Artists v. N.L.R.B., supra, 395 F.2d 627 n.13. Some bargaining may go on even though the parties are unable to agree on many topics. But, only if the deadlock on the critical issue demonstrates that there is no realistic possibility that further discussions would be fruitful in bringing the parties together generally on salaries and other conditions of employment, can we conclude that there is an impasse.

Even though an impasse had not been reached, however, it does not follow on the facts in the present case that the defendants were in violation of the statute. While N.L.R.B. v. Katz, supra, holds "that an employer's unilateral change in conditions of employment under negotiation is . . . a violation of § 8 (a) (5)," because it is circumvention of the duty to negotiate, the court did, however, note that circumstances might justify unilateral employer action. The language of the court, 369 U.S. on page 745, 82 S. Ct. on page 1113, is significant: "Of course there is no resemblance between the situation wherein an employer, after notice and consultation, 'unilaterally' institutes a wage increase identical with one which the union has rejected as too low. See National Labor Relations Board v. Bradley Washfountain Co., 192 F.2d 144, 150-152 [7th Cir.]; National Labor Relations Board v. Landis Tool Co., 193 F.2d 279 [3d Cir.]." In the *Bradley Washfountain* case, the employer, before an impasse had been reached, after notice and consultation with the union, unilaterally instituted a wage increase identical to the one which the union had rejected as too low, it was held that the employer did not violate the statute.

In the case at bar the defendant board, in March, 1969, proposed a new work year, vacation schedule and salary schedule for department chairmen, coordinating teachers and subject area specialists involving changes in work day, work year and salary schedules. During April, 1969, the parties negotiated but were unable to agree as to the salary and conditions of employment

for these positions and neither party offered further proposals
on these subjects. In May and June, 1969, the defendant Richter
with the approval of the board hired teachers to fill these positions on the basis of the salary schedule and conditions of employment originally proposed by the board but rejected by the plaintiff. During the 1969-70 school year the persons hired to fill these
positions performed duties on the basis of the conditions of
employment originally proposed, and received salaries based on
the salary schedule originally proposed but on which the parties
had been unable to agree in their negotiations. A letter appointing the department head of the high school informed the appointee as follows: "Your salary rate cannot be determined
precisely until the salary schedule is finally negotiated with the
W.H.E.A. I suspect, however, that you may already know the
approximate range in which it will fall and that you are informed as to how you will be placed within that range. For your
information, this formula is enclosed." A letter from this department head to the superintendent acknowledged receipt of a check
for initial services as a department head and informed the superintendent that the employee was cashing the check "with the
express understanding and stipulation that it is received on
account as part payment and that it does not necessarily constitute my total compensation for my services in the West Hartford
schools for the initial pay period of the 1969-70 school year." On
these facts it is clear that the defendants did not "interfere,
restrain or coerce employees in derogation" of their rights under
the statute. There was no attempt to bypass or denigrate the
union. We recognize the fact that the terms of the board's proposal embraced not only subjects which are clearly matters of
board policy but mandatory subjects of negotiation as well. Our
statutes have given the boards of education a clear mandate to
"maintain . . . good public elementary and secondary schools."
§ 10-220. It was not the intention of the legislature to permit
progress in education to be halted until agreement is reached
with the union. . . .

NOTES

1.　To what extent, if any, may an employer communicate with
his employees concerning the negotiations while negotiations are
in progress? In General Electric Co., 150 N.L.R.B. 192 (1964),
enf'd, 418 F.2d 736 (2d Cir. 1969), cert. denied, 397 U.S. 965
(1970), the NLRB held that an employer's communications program, in conjunction with its take it or leave it approach to bargaining, constituted bad faith bargaining. In so ruling, the NLRB
stated:

It is not consistent with . . . [the obligation to bargain in good faith] for an employer to mount a campaign, as Respondent did, both before and during negotiations, for the purposes of disparaging and discrediting the statutory representative in the eyes of its employee constituents, to seek to persuade the employees to exert pressure on the representative to submit to the will of the employer, and to create the impression that the employer rather than the union is the true protector of the employees' interest. As the Trial Examiner phrased it, the employer's statutory obligation is to deal with the employees through the union, and not with the union through the employees.

The NLRB, however, has held that it is permissible for an employer to communicate its position on the various issues in negotiations as long as the purpose of such communications does not undermine the union's role as the collective bargaining representative of the employees. Proctor & Gamble Mfg. Co., 160 N.L.R.B. 334, 339-41 (1966). In Grand Haven Bd. of Educ., 1973 MERC Lab. Op. 1, the MERC held that an employer did not commit an unfair labor practice when it communicated to bargaining unit employees the offer it had previously presented to the union where such communication was not coercive and did not contain threats or offers of benefit. *Accord,* Town of Sharon, Mass. Labor Relations Comm'n Case No. MUP-275 (1972).

2. Does a board of education violate its duty to bargain in good faith if it allows a representative of a minority employee organization to address the board at a regularly scheduled board meeting and to present its views in opposition to an agency shop agreement which the exclusive bargaining representative is seeking to negotiate? The Wisconsin Employment Relations Commission held that such conduct "constituted an erosion of its duty to bargain exclusively with the MTI [Madison Teachers, Inc.] and with no other organization, group of employees, or a single employee." Joint School District No. 8, City of Madison, WERC Decision No. 11271 (1972). In denying the board's assertion that if it had denied the minority representative the right to speak it would have abridged his right to free speech, the WERC noted that the Wisconsin Supreme Court in Milwaukee Bd. of School Directors v. WERC, 42 Wis. 2d 637, 168 N.W.2d 92 (1969), ". . . rejected the contention that prohibiting a representative of a minority union to speak before the school board, while the latter had not completed its negotiations with the majority organization, violated the constitutional rights of said minority organization."

3. For a helpful discussion of the determination of when an impasse exists under the National Labor Relations Act, see Stewart & Engeman, 39 U. Cin. L. Rev. 233 (1970).

INTERNATIONAL ASSOCIATION OF FIREFIGHTERS
v. CITY OF HOMESTEAD

Florida Circuit Court, Eleventh Judicial Circuit
Case No. 72-9285 (1973)

JUDGE GROSSMAN: . . .

I. *Factual Background of This Litigation*

Plaintiff, Local No. 2010 of the International Association of Firefighters, is a labor organization representing a majority of the persons employed as firefighters by the Defendant, City of Homestead. In January, 1971, Plaintiff sent to the City Manager and the City Councilmen of the City of Homestead a letter seeking recognition as collective bargaining agent for the firefighter employees of the City of Homestead. Subsequently, recognition was granted by the City Council and thereafter the council designated Homestead City Manager, Olaf R. Pearson, as the City's bargaining representative. Negotiations between Pearson and Plaintiff commenced with the mutual understanding that any agreement reached between the parties would be subject to the approval of the City Council.

In November, 1971, after more than 50 hours of negotiations, the City Manager and the Plaintiff reached accord on a collective bargaining agreement. This agreement with the recommendations of the City Manager attached was submitted to the Homestead City Council for its approval. The council met with representatives of Plaintiff on January 10th, 1972 for that purpose. At this meeting, however, the City Council proceeded to renegotiate the contract from the beginning and, in fact, changed every provision of the contract brought up before the meeting terminated. Among the changes made, the Council altered the "bargaining unit" clause (which had been agreed to by City Manager Pearson and Plaintiff) by excluding certain members of the Union from the contract's coverage, and proposed that the entire negotiated wage provisions be stricken from the contract and in substitution therefor these wages unilaterally established by the City Council in their budget hearings of the year before be inserted in the contract. In addition, notwithstanding the fact that the City had recognized the Plaintiff and had bargained with their representatives, the Council directed the City Attorney to write an opinion concerning the City's duty to further recognize and bargain with the Plaintiff.

In response to these actions of the City Council, Plaintiff's representatives walked out of the meeting, and on January 27th, 1972, sent a letter to the City Manager invoking the arbitration provisions of the Firefighters Collective Bargaining Act. However, Defendant City failed to respond to said letter except by passing an Ordinance (No. 72-01-4) designed to supersede the Firefighters Collective Bargaining Law.

During the proceedings herein described, Defendant Councilman Fred Rhodes, Jr. made statements indicating his dislike of the Union, his unwillingness to bargain with or continue to recognize the Union, and his hope that the City's firemen would abandon their support of the Union. Testimony establishes that Defendant Rhodes made promises of benefits to Union members if they would abandon their Union support, including a promise that the Union's long-sought pay parity with policemen would be granted if the firemen would just "forget about the Union." Councilman Rhodes admitted before this Court that he was hostile to the Union and that he would like to have the City relieved of the duty to bargain with Plaintiff if it could be done.

During this period, the Union suffered a loss of membership. In November, 1971, one member and in February, 1972, an additional two members resigned their Union membership, expressing displeasure with the Union's inability to sign a collective bargaining agreement.

This action was brought by Plaintiffs to enforce their constitutional right to bargain collectively and to bring the City once again to the bargaining table.

II. *Issues Before This Court*

This litigation presents several issues to the Court for decision. First, the Court must determine whether the City has performed its obligation of negotiating in good faith with its employees under Article I, Section 6 of the Florida Constitution. Second, the Court must determine if the Firefighters Collective Bargaining Law establishes collective bargaining guidelines in support of the Constitutional obligation and, if so, the respective duties of the parties thereunder. Third, the Court must determine whether the activities of Councilman Fred Rhodes, Jr., as an individual, served to deny Plaintiff and its members their constitutional right to bargain collectively and whether damages may be awarded for such denial.

III. *The City Did Not Meet Its Duty to Bargain in Good Faith*

Article I, Section 6 of the Constitution of the State of Florida grants public employees the right of collective bargaining. The

Florida Supreme Court and the Circuit Courts of this State have on several occasions held that this Section imposes a duty upon the public employer to negotiate in good faith with their employees through an organization such as Plaintiff Union.

This Court finds that the practices followed by the Defendant City in this case did not constitute good faith collective bargaining. The defendant's conduct in attempting to renegotiate the entire contract after the lengthy negotiations between the Union and the City Manager, indicates that the bargaining between the City Manager and the Union was only surface bargaining and not a good faith effort by the City to reach agreement with Plaintiff Union. This change in the ground rules after the lengthy contract negotiations were completed demonstrates that the City Manager's function was not to negotiate with the Union on behalf of the City, but rather *to induce the Union to compromise some of its demands in the belief that they were reaching an agreement and then present these compromises to the City Council where further concessions from the Union were to be demanded.* The refusal of the City to show any confidence in the preliminary agreement reached by its City Manager (its appointed negotiator) and its attempt to renegotiate the entire agreement and gain further concessions from the Union on almost every provision of the preliminary agreement, is not good faith bargaining and does not fulfill the duty imposed by the Florida Constitution. . . .

IV. *The Activities of Defendant Councilman Fred Rhodes, Jr.*
Injured the Plaintiffs Insofar as They Denied Plaintiffs
Members of Their Constitutional Rights to
Bargain Collectively

The activities of Councilman Rhodes have been intended and designed to discourage the employees of the Homestead Fire Department from exercising their right to bargain collectively and to defeat the Union as an effective representative of the employees in the exercise of that right. Mr. Rhodes' testimony in deposition and before this Court shows him to have a complete disregard for the constitutional rights of the Homestead Fire Department employees and his intent to do all in his power as a public official to avoid the City's obligation to bargain collectively with its employees. Mr. Rhodes has engaged in practices which are commonly regarded in the private sector as unfair labor practices, such as promises of benefits to employees if they abandon their support for the Union and statements made to undermine the Union's effectiveness. (As a City Councilman of the City of Homestead, the recognition of the right of the City's employees to collectively bargain was one of Councilman Rhodes' duties. His campaign, personally and as a City councilman to defeat the Union, was directly contrary to this official duty imposed upon him as a Councilman.)

The responsibility of a public officer to persons damaged by acts performed in his personal or official capacity was recognized by the Florida Supreme Court in First National Bank of Key West v. Filer, 145 So. 204 (1933). Holding that: "Whenever there is a wrong, there is a remedy," the Court said:

"That public officers should be held to a faithful performance of their official duty and made to answer in damages to all persons who may have been injured through their malfeasance, omission or neglect, to which the persons injured have in no respect contributed, cannot be denied, and it well settled where the law imposes upon a public officer the performance of ministerial duties in which a private individual has a special and direct interest, the officer would become liable to such individual for any injury which he may proximately sustain in consequence of the failure and neglect of the officer either to perform the duty at all or to perform it properly." 145 So. 207.

Councilman Rhodes was held to a faithful performance of his official duty to recognize the right of the City's employees to bargain collectively and he must answer in damages to those persons who may have been injured through his malfeasance, omission, neglect, or intentional course of conduct designed to defeat and deny their constitutional rights. *See also* Fidelity and Deposit Company of Maryland v. Cone, 190 So. 268 (Fla., 1939).

V. *Compensatory and Punitive Damages Are Properly Awardable Against Councilman Rhodes as an Individual*

It is difficult to establish the amount of damages properly awardable to Plaintiff for the denial of its right to represent its members in collective bargaining, as the Court does not have before it testimony of all benefits denied the Plaintiff had good faith collective bargaining been engaged in. However, testimony has established that the conduct of the City and of Defendant Rhodes induced resignations from the Union. The amount of lost dues is not less than one month's dues ($6.00) for each of the three members who resigned from the Union, and this Court hereby finds that the Union suffered damages of not less than $18.00.

Councilman Rhodes has acted deliberately, willfully and intentionally, not only in disregard of Plaintiff's constitutional rights, but for the admitted purpose of defeating those rights. This is a proper case for the award of punitive damages; this is especially so since the compensatory damages awarded for actual losses to the persons deprived by his conduct are small and difficult to ascertain. The denial of a constitutional right, however, even without any accompanying financial loss, is reprehensible. It is the duty of the Court to protect the constitutional rights of our citizens and to punish those who deliberately subvert these rights. To that end, the Court hereby declares that Councilman Rhodes is a violator of the constitutional rights of the citizens of this State and reprimand him for his unlawful activities which are unbecoming to any American citizen and are even more unworthy in one who purports to be a public servant. There is no higher duty in one who serves in government than obedience to the law. When an elected official acts as Councilman Rhodes has acted, in deliberate violation of his oath of office (that is, to support the Constitutions of this State and of the nation), he sets a shameful and humiliating example of lawlessness.

Since this is the first instance of judicial action upon one of the many recalcitrant public employers who wish to purposely ignore the new collective bargaining mandates of Article I, Section 6 of our State's Constitution, this Court will, in addition to the foregoing reprimand, only impose $1.00 as punitive damages upon Councilman Rhodes. Such judgment should, however, be a warning and an indication of the intent of this Court to compel obedience to our laws and to the Constitution of this State in the future, by whatever means may be required. . . .

NOTES

1. Does a PERB have the authority to issue a "make-whole" order where it finds that an employer has failed to bargain in good faith? In IUE v. NLRB (Tiidee Products), 426 F.2d 1243 (D.C. Cir.), *cert. denied,* 400 U.S. 950 (1970), the Court of Appeals for the District of Columbia held that where an employer's refusal to bargain constituted "a clear and flagrant violation" of the NLRA, a cease-and-desist order was not sufficient. The court noted "that damages can be awarded on an assessment of the contract terms that would have been in effect if the law had been complied with even though the law-violating employer has not yet entered into the contract." On remand, however, the Board declined to issue a "make-whole" remedy, reasoning as follows:

We have carefully considered the Union's request for a make-whole remedy in light of the record herein and have decided that it is not practicable. The Union suggests that we determine what the parties *"would* have agreed to" in 1967 and thereafter on the basis of a record which contains only a proposed collective-bargaining agreement submitted by the Union to Respondent on December 18, 1967; a chart comparing the wages then paid by Respondent for certain job classifications with those paid by other employers in comparable industries in the Dayton area who were then under contract with the Union; testimonial evidence of employee wage rates as of the date of the hearing herein and a list thereof as of May 25, 1970; certain testimony about the time required to negotiate a first contract; and several charts and tables depicting nationwide changes in wages and benefits since 1967. We know of no way by which the Board could ascertain with even approximate accuracy from the above what the parties *"would* have agreed to" if they had bargained in good faith. Inevitably, the Board would have to decide from the above what the parties *"should* have agreed to." And this, the court stated, the Board must not do.

Tiidee Products, Inc., 194 N.L.R.B. 1234 (1972). Nevertheless, the Board devised certain "alternative remedies . . . [to] undo some of the baneful effects pointed out by the court as having resulted from Respondent's 'clear and flagrant violation of the law.'" The Board thus ordered the employer to (1) mail copies of the notice to employees to all employees in the unit, (2) give the union reasonable access to the employer's bulletin boards during the period of contract negotiations, and (3) reimburse the union and the NLRB for litigation costs and expenses.

2. Does an employer have an obligation to bargain in good faith following the issuance of a fact finder's recommendations? The MERC in City of Dearborn, 1972 MERC Lab. Op. 749, responded affirmatively, stating:

Statutory fact finding may be invoked only after the parties have bargained and a genuine impasse has occurred. Although the duty to bargain does not mean that parties must engage in futile bargaining in the face of a genuine impasse, changed circumstances may develop, and therefore require compliance with the bargaining requirement. . . . Even though there may be a strike, the duty to bargain may not necessarily be suspended. . . . Just as a strike may create conditions in which the parties would be more willing to make concessions to compromise the matters in difference, the fact finder's recommendations may enlighten or persuade them of the reasonableness or unreasonableness of their bargaining position. The fact finder's report, thus, is the functional equivalent of a strike and may change the factual situation regarding "the negotiation of an agreement, or any question arising thereunder." MCLA 423, 215; MSA 17.455 (15). It must be given the same serious consideration as the initial bargaining proposals. Therefore, there is an affirmative obligation to bargain in good faith about the substantive recommendations of the report of a statutory fact finder. *Accord,* East Hartford Educ. Ass'n v. East Hartford Bd. of Educ., 30 Conn. Supp. 63, 299 A.2d 554 (Conn. Super. Ct. 1972).

The MERC further held that "the duty to bargain requires that the employer make a reasonable effort in some direction to close the differences with the union." Does this mean that the employer in order to meet its obligation to bargain in good faith must modify its position on some of the issues? If so, would this be consistent with the statutory provision that the duty to bargain "does not compel either party to agree to a proposal or require the making of a concession"? Would an employer meet its obligation to bargain in good faith if it stated in detail its reasons for rejecting the fact finder's recommendations?

3. Prior to an amendment in 1971, the Wisconsin statute covering municipal employment did not specifically provide that the refusal to bargain was a prohibited practice and the WERC held that it could not be so interpreted. *See* City of New Berlin, WERC Decision No. 7293 (1966). In this context, the WERC in City of Portage, Decision No. 8378 (1968), noted that "fact-finding recommendations are not binding upon the parties, and failing to adopt them is not a prohibited practice."

4. In Sanilac County Road Comm'n, 1969 MERC Lab. Op. 461, the MERC held that an employer's sincere, but mistaken, belief that a given proposal was illegal does not constitute a valid defense to an unfair labor practice charge.

2. Selection and Authority of the Parties' Representatives

CITY OF SAGINAW

Michigan Employment Relations Commission
1969 MERC Lab. Op. 293

Trial Examiner Joseph Bixler: The charge in this matter was filed by the Charging Party on November 19, 1968. The charge alleges a violation of Section 10 (e) of PERA, and reads as follows:

"At meetings between parties hereto, conducted January 9, 15, February 15, and October 30, 1968, the City agreed to a 'modified agency shop' in return for several concessions made by the Union. The City representative later repudiated his agreement and contended that he did not have authority to bind the City and refuse[d] to submit Union proposal to City Council. The City is, therefore, guilty of refusing to bargain in good faith in that they:

1. Did not provide a Negotiator that had authority to negotiate.
2. Repudiated a previously agreed provision.
3. Refused and failed to submit Union proposals to City Commission."

The Facts

The parties in 1966, began negotiating on a collective bargaining contract. During the years of 1967 and 1968, various economic matters were agreed upon and put into effect. The non-economic portions of the contract, however, were not completed during either of these years.

In January, 1968, the parties were at a standstill, and a Mediator of the State Labor Mediation Board was called in, and tentative agreement was finally reached on all of the non-economic matters of the contract in May, of 1968. Among the various matters tentatively agreed upon between the parties was a "modified agency shop." The parties then went to economic matters and an agreement was reached which was rejected by the membership of the Charging Party. Final economic agreement was reached in July, of 1968.

On September 10, 1968, the following agency shop provision was agreed upon:

"Requirements of Union membership.

All employees *covered by this agreement who are members of the Union at the time this agreement is ratified or who hereafter become members thereof during the term of this agreement must as a condition of continued employment retain their membership in the Union for the duration of this agreement.* New employees covered by this agreement who fail to acquire or maintain membership in the Union shall be required, as a condition of employment beginning on the 91st day following the beginning of such employment or the date of the signing of this agreement, whichever is later, to pay to the Union each month a service charge as a contribution towards the administration of this agreement and the representative of such employee. The service charge for the first month shall be an amount equal to the Union's regular and usual initiation fee and monthly dues and for each month thereafter, an amount equal to the regular and usual monthly dues." (Emphasis added)

Apparently, after the last bargaining meeting, by agreement of the parties, the City of Saginaw undertook to type up the final agreement. The Charging Party received its copy of the final draft of the agreement in September, 1968. The City negotiators explained that the reason that it took so long to type up the agreement was because they were engaged in negotiations with other Unions.

After the final draft of the agreement had been checked through by the Charging Party, it was then ready for submission to the City Council. In mid-October, 1968 Jack Houk, the head of the City's Personnel Department and the chief negotiator for the City, informed the Charging Party that they had presented another contract to the Council for approval involving the Registered Nurses in the City hospital, and that the Council had rejected the union security provisions of the nurses contract which were similar to the one contained in the contract involving the unit represented by the Charging Party. Houk informed the Charging Party that he did not think there was any sense in submitting the contract reached by the Charging Party and the City's negotiators to the Council as long as it contained the union security provisions. Houk further informed the representatives of the Charging Party that as the City Council in all likelihood would not accept the union security provision, the Charging Party could take back those concessions that had been given by the Charging Party in exchange for the union security clause, and that he, Houk, was prepared to negotiate something else in exchange for the Charging Party relinquishing the union security clause.

This proposition by Houk was rejected by the Charging Party. Sometime during the month of November or December, 1968, the agreement that had been reached between the City's negotiators and the Charging Party was submitted to the Council, and the union security clause was rejected by the Council by a five to two vote.

On January 2, 1969, Houk met again with the Charging Party's representatives. Houk again offered to give back the management rights clause and the no strike clause of the proposed agreement that had been given to the City in return for agreement on agency shop. This was again rejected by the Charging Party.

Conclusion and Recommendation

The main thrust of the charge as filed by the Charging Party is that the bargaining representative of the City did not have sufficient authority to commit the City to matters agreed upon at the bargaining table. It is urged that because the bargaining representative of the City agreed to the union security clause as set forth above, that the City was thereby committed and the Council had no right to refuse to agree to this clause. A similar argument was made to the Board by the Charging Party in City of Saginaw, 1967 Labor Opinions, 465. In that case, the Trial Examiner stated:

> Obviously, the negotiating team must receive instructions from the governing body and submit oral or written reports to it, if its concessions and tentative commitments are to be meaningful, that it need not, and probably cannot, be vested with final authority to bind the public employer, since that would seem to involve an illegal delegation of the lawmaking power of the City Council. People vs. Sell, 310 Michigan, 305, 17 NW2d 193 (1945); C. F. Millard vs. Guy, 334 Michigan, 649.

I agree that as indicated by the Trial Examiner in the earlier *Saginaw* case cited above, the requirement that the governing body be present at the bargaining table would be far too burdensome in public employment. I am also of the opinion that if a governmental body gave its negotiator absolute right to make a labor agreement it would be improperly delegating the legislative function as indicated in the *Saginaw* case. The undersigned however, does find that, as stated in the *City of Saginaw* decision by the Trial Examiner, the bargaining representative of a governmental body is under an obligation to keep that governmental body advised as to the progress of negotiations. Further, in those cases where, as here, the governmental body has taken the position that it will not agree on principle to some contractual provision within the range of mandatory bargaining, that the bargaining agent be informed of this fact, and that at the request of the bargaining agent, the governmental body itself will meet at the negotiating table to discuss the rejected subject matter.

In the case at hand, the undersigned is of the opinion that the Charging Party had no opportunity to bargain in regard to union security in the form of agency shop, a mandatory subject of bargaining. Oakland County Sheriff's Department & Oakland County Board of Supervisors, 1968 Labor Opinions 1. This deprivation of the bargaining right of the Charging Party does not arise from the rejection of union security, but from the City negotiators removal of the subject from the bargaining table without affording the bargaining agent the opportunity to bargain or discuss the subject matter with those making the rejection.

The Charging Party should have requested bargaining on union security with the City Council, and that body would under these circumstances, have been obligated to bargain on the subject.

Under the circumstances evidenced by this record I do not believe, however, that a bargaining order should be granted. My reasons for so concluding are that: (1) The union did not request bargaining on the matter of "agency shop" with the city Council after they were notified of the rejection of such a contract provision. (2) The clause contained in the proposed agreement negotiated by the Charging Party and the City negotiators and presented to the City Council, is one not permitted by PERA.

[The Trial Examiner's decision was adopted by the MERC in the absence of exceptions.]

NOTES

1. Does the principal case stand for the proposition that a public employer (city council, board of education, etc.) has to negotiate with the union on each and every proposal within the mandatory area of negotiations which its designated representative has rejected at the bargaining table? If so, does the ruling in the instant case undermine the right of the employer to designate its representative for the purposes of collective bargaining? Suppose a union agrees to a proposal but later seeks to withdraw it on the basis that the membership would never accept it. Would the employer then have the right, upon making a request, "to bargain or discuss the subject with those making the rejection," *i.e.*, the rank-and-file?

2. A year after the decision in *City of Saginaw*, the MERC in City of Detroit, Bd. of Fire Comm'rs, 1970 MERC Lab. Op. 953, 957, stated:

It is not required that Municipal Councils, Commissions and Boards bargain directly with the representatives of their employees. This may be done by administrative employees or other agents who are clothed with authority to participate in effective collective bargaining but reserving final approval to the governing body. Such is common practice in the private sector, and it is effective and workable.

Does this statement conflict with the holding in *City of Saginaw?*

3. The Wyoming Fire Fighter Bargaining Law provides that a city, town, or county is required to negotiate in good faith

through its corporate authorities with the bargaining agent chosen by a majority of the firefighters. The law defines the term "corporate authorities" to "mean the council, commission or other proper officials of any city, town, or county, whose duty or duties it is to establish wages, salaries, rates of pay, working conditions, and other conditions of employment of firefighters." WYO. STAT. § 27-265 (b). In Fire Fighters Local 279 v. Holland, 77 L.R.R.M. 2732 (Wyo. Dist. Ct. 1971), the court held that the corporate authorities of the City of Cheyenne, including the Mayor and Council, were required to negotiate in person with representatives of the fire fighters union "and not through agents of said corporate authorities."

4. Most commentators have recommended that the ultimate policy-making body, whether it be a school board, city council or board of county commissioners, should not directly participate in collective bargaining. As one commentator observed,

> The problems arising from the delegation of bargaining to staff personnel are far outweighed by greater proficiency, objectivity and continuity. Elected officials are rarely trained in personnel matters. . . . Further, elected officials offer no guarantee of continuity for future bargaining sessions.

Mulcahy, *A Municipality's Rights and Responsibilities Under the Wisconsin Municipal Labor Law,* 49 MARQ. L. REV. 512, 515 (1966). Herbert Haber, the Director of Labor Relations for New York City, made the following comments concerning the need for establishing a separate labor relations function in the public sector:

> [D]ealing with the unions is a full-time job requiring professional help. Anyone who has authority over a given agency is well-advised to secure full-time professional help or regular professional consultations, whatever he can manage. In running a large scale public operation, he has innumerable responsibilities of which only one small part is dealing with the union. The union, on the other hand, devotes its full time to representing its members and can therefore concentrate on the specifics of each individual matter. Professional assistance from people who can work exclusively on collective bargaining problems is a must for dealing effectively with the unions.

Haber, *The Relevance of Private Sector Experience to Public Sector Collective Bargaining,* in Proceedings of a Conference held by the Institute of Management and Labor Relations, The State University of New Jersey, May 23, 1968, p. 7.

5. May either party refuse to negotiate with the other party because it objects to the presence of one or more members of the other party's negotiating team? In City of Superior, WERC Decision No. 8325 (1967), the Wisconsin Employment Relations Commission stated:

> Personal differences arising between the representatives of the parties engaged in negotiations with respect to wages, hours and working conditions of municipal employes do not constitute a valid reason for refusing to bargain in good faith. Both municipal employers and representatives of their employes have the right to designate whomever they choose to represent them at the bargaining table. To allow either or both parties to refuse to bargain with each other because of alleged or actual conflicts between their representatives would be contrary to the intent and purpose of Section 111.70. . . .

In Fort Jackson Laundry Facility, A/SLMR Decision No. 242 (1972), the Assistant Secretary of Labor held that with respect to formal discussions under Section 10 (e) of Executive Order 11491, "The right to choose its representatives at such discussions must be left to the discretion of the exclusive bargaining representative and not to the whim of management." Accord, United States Postal Service (Tampa, Florida), 202 N.L.R.B. No. 119, 82 L.R.R.M. 1641 (1973).

6. The NLRB has held that a union can include on its bargaining team "observers" from other unions representing an employer's employees. General Electric Co., 173 N.L.R.B. 253 (1968), enf'd as modified, 412 F.2d 512 (2d Cir. 1969). This tactic, commonly referred to as coordinated bargaining, is discussed in Comment, Coordinated—Coalition Bargaining: Theory, Legality, Practice and Economic Effects, 55 MINN. L. REV. 599 (1971). What are the advantages and disadvantages of coordinated bargaining in the public sector? See University of Oregon Medical School and the State Personnel Division, supra p. 478. Would the same legal principles be applicable to a public employer if it sought to include a taxpayer's representative or a representative of another public employer of its bargaining team?

3. Duty to Supply Information

SAGINAW TOWNSHIP BOARD OF EDUCATION
Michigan Employment Relations Commission
1970 MERC Lab. Op. 127

. . . The Charging Party [Saginaw Township Education Association] takes exceptions to the Trial Examiner's decision that the Respondent [Saginaw Township Board of Education] did not violate the Act by its refusal to submit to the union certain information requested. The information is set forth as:

1. Audited financial statements for the fiscal year ending June 30, 1967, including the general fund balance sheet;
2. The proposed budget for the ensuing fiscal year;
3. A list of the teachers who had left the school system; and
4. A list of the new teachers who had been hired for the 1967-68 school year.

The Trial Examiner held that all requests by the Charging Party for information must be set forth in writing.

The Employer in its cross-exceptions contends that it had a right to insist that demands for information by the Charging Party be specific written requests for information so that the Respondent could properly evaluate each request and therefore be able to give an answer to the Charging Party.

The National Labor Relations Board and federal courts have, over a period of many years, wrestled with the subject of the employer's duty to submit information to the bargaining agent. It is clear that there is a duty on the employer to furnish relevant data and information to the bargaining agents of its employees. Whitin Machinery Works, 108 N.L.R.B. 1537, 34 L.R.R.M. 1251 (1954), enf'd 217 F.2d 593; General Controls, 88 N.L.R.B. 1341, 25 L.R.R.M. 1475 (1950); International Telephone & Telegraph Corporation v. N.L.R.B., 62 L.R.R.M. 1339, enf'd in part, 65 L.R.R.M. 3002 (1967); National Labor Relations Board v. Item Company, 108 N.L.R.B. 1634, 34 L.R.R.M. 1255, enf'd, 220 F.2d 956 (5th Cir., 1955); Aluminum Ore Co., 39 N.L.R.B. 1286, 10 L.R.R.M. 49, enf'd 131 F.2d 485, 11 L.R.R.M. 693 (7th Cir., 1942).

In the above cases, the National Labor Relations Board and the courts have laid down the general rule that an employer is required on request to furnish a union with sufficient data with respect to wage rates, job classifications and other allied matters to permit the union to:

1. Bargain understandingly;
2. Police the administration of the contract; and
3. Prepare for coming negotiations.

A union is not required to show the purpose of their requested data unless the data appears to be clearly irrelevant. The data should also be reasonably available from the employer's records. General Controls, *supra;* Oliver Corporation, 162 N.L.R.B. No. 68, 64 L.R.R.M. 1092 (1967); KCMO Broadcasting, 145 N.L.R.B. 550, 55 L.R.R.M. 1001 (1963).

The federal courts and the NLRB have held that unions need not place their request for relevant information in writing. In the International Telephone & Telegraph Corporation, *supra,* decision, the employer had suggested that the union incorporate its request for information in a letter to the company so that the employer could give it to its counsel for review. The letter was submitted by the union after unfair labor practice charges had been filed. The NLRB held that the company had unlawfully refused to give the union the requested information. The NLRB's order was eventually enforced by the U.S. Court of Appeals for the Third Circuit, which held as follows:

> "We have considered the petitioner's argument that the union's failure to put its request for information in writing until after the unfair labor practice charges had been filed shows that the earlier oral requests for such data were not made in good faith and were merely 'to set the company up' for an unfair labor practice charge. This argument is without merit. *No rule requires that requests for information be in writing."* (Emphasis added)

While the above cases deal with private employees, it is clear that in the field of public employment much of the information is in the public domain. Records of public employers such as school boards, in the absence of specific statutes, do not enjoy immunity from public scrutiny. Any citizen or taxpayer may review the public records of a school board. The statutes involving the Board of Education deal specifically with this matter.

Section 562 of the School Code of 1955, M.S.A. Section 15.5362, provides, among other things, as follows:

> "All records of the board shall be public records subject to inspection under Section 750.492 of the Compiled Laws of 1948 (CL 48, Section 350.562)."

Section 750.492, as referred to above, reads as follows:

> "Any officer having the custody of any county, city or township records of this state who shall when requested fail or

neglect to furnish proper and reasonable facilities for the inspection and examination of records and files in his office and for making memoranda of transcripts therefrom during the usual business hours which shall not be less than four (4) hours per day, to any person having occasion to make examination of them for any lawful purpose, shall be guilty of a misdemeanor, punishable by imprisonment in a county jail of not more than one (1) year or by a fine of not more than five hundred ($500) dollars."

It is accordingly clear that the Charging Party was entitled to receive the information requested above. We reject Respondent's cross-exceptions that the Employer is entitled to evaluate each request for information. The duty to request and supply information is part and parcel of the fundamental duty to bargain. This duty is not an additional negotiable subject matter of the bargaining process. The employer cannot make the subject of bargaining the submission of relevant data needed by a labor organization. Washtenaw Community College and Washtenaw College Education Association, 1968 MERC L. Op. 956.

The employer would also impose the condition that the Union must have no reasonable way to obtain the information except from the employer's records. We reject this contention for the reasons set forth above. Whitin Machinery Works, *supra;* Aluminum Ore Co., *supra;* Curtiss-Wright Corporation v. National Labor Relations Board, 59 L.R.R.M. 2433, 347 F.2d 61 (3rd Cir., 1965) ; J. I. Case Company v. National Labor Relations Board, 253 F.2d 149 (7th Cir., 1958) .

We also reject the Employer's proposed criteria for the additional reasons that the information requested is in the public domain, and there should be an obligation on the part of a labor organization to seek alternative methods of obtaining the information prior to the request made to the employer. Alternative sources of information could require the Charging Party to use secondhand data which would impede rather than expedite intelligent bargaining.

There was no showing in this case that any of the information was available for public inspection in a public location. When information is accessible to the public, we have held that a public employer is not required to furnish it. Washtenaw Community College and Washtenaw College Education Association, *supra....*

NOTES

1. The failure to provide relevant information in *timely* fashion is also considered to be an unfair labor practice. West-

wood Community Schools, 1972 MERC Lab. Op. 313; Kohler Co., 128 N.L.R.B. 1062, 1074 (1960), *aff'd in relevant part,* 300 F.2d 699, *cert. denied,* 370 U.S. 911 (1962).

2. The Supreme Court in NLRB v. Truitt Mfg. Co., 351 U.S. 149 (1956), held that the employer committed an unfair labor practice under the NLRA when it failed, upon request, to supply financial data in support of its claim that it could not afford to pay higher wages. In so ruling, the Court stated:

> We think that in determining whether the obligation of good faith bargaining has been met, the Board has a right to consider an employer's refusal to give information about its financial status. While Congress did not compel agreement between employer and bargaining representatives, it did require collective bargaining in the hope that agreements would result. Section 204(a)(1) of the Act admonishes both employers and employees to "exert every reasonable effort to make and maintain agreements concerning rates of pay, hours, and working conditions. . . ." In their effort to reach an agreement here, both the union and the company treated the company's ability to pay increased wages as highly relevant. The ability of an employer to increase wages without injury to his business is a commonly considered factor in wage negotiations. Claims for increased wages have sometimes been abandoned because of an employer's unsatisfactory business condition; employees have even voted to accept wage decreases because of such conditions.
>
> Good-faith bargaining necessarily requires that claims made by either bargainer should be honest claims. This is true about an asserted inability to pay an increase in wages. If such an argument is important enough to present in the give and take of bargaining, it is important enough to require some sort of proof of its accuracy. And it would certainly not be farfetched for a trier of fact to reach the conclusion that bargaining lacks good faith when an employer mechanically rejects a claim of inability to pay without making the slightest effort to substantiate the claim. Such has been the holding of the Labor Board since shortly after the passage of the Wagner Act. In *Pioneer Pearl Button Co.,* decided in 1936, where the employer's representative relied on the company's asserted "poor financial condition," the Board said: "He did no more than take refuge in the assertion that the respondent's financial condition was poor; he refused either to prove his statement, or to permit

independent verification. This is not collective bargaining."
1 N.L.R.B. 837, 842-843. This was the position of the Board
when the Taft-Hartley Act was passed in 1947 and has been
its position ever since. We agree with the Board that a refusal to attempt to substantiate a claim of inability to pay
increased wages may support the finding of a failure to
bargain in good faith.

3. Does an employer's obligation to provide relevant information to a union extend to a request for information concerning a grievance which is being processed in accordance with
the contractual grievance procedure? In NLRB v. Acme Indus.
Co., 385 U.S. 432, 87 S. Ct. 565, 17 L. Ed. 2d 495 (1967), the
Court answered this question affirmatively, stating that the
"duty to bargain unquestionably extends beyond the period of
contract negotiations and applies to labor-management relations
during the term of an agreement." *Accord*, Commonwealth of
Mass., Dep't of Public Works, Mass. Lab. Rel. Comm'n Case No.
SUP-20 (1972).

4. An employer is not required to supply the information
in the same form requested as long as it is submitted in a
manner which is not unreasonably burdensome to interpret.
Westinghouse Electric Corp., 129 N.L.R.B. 850 (1960); Mc-
Lean-Arkansas Lumber Co., 109 N.L.R.B. 1022 (1954).

5. Articles examining an employer's duty to furnish information under the NLRA include Cox, *The Duty to Bargain in
Good Faith*, 71 HARV. L. REV. 1401 (1958); Huston, *Furnishing
Information as an Element of Employer's Good Faith Bargaining*, 35 U. DET. L.J. 471 (1958); Miller, *Employer's Duty to
Furnish Economic Data to Unions—Revisited*, 17 LAB. L.J. 272
(1966).

4. Unilateral Action

Once a union has been duly designated as the collective bargaining representative for a given group of employees, the employer is thereafter obligated to negotiate and bargain in good
faith with the union with respect to matters that are negotiable.
Concomitant with this obligation is the requirement that an
employer refrain from taking unilateral action with respect to
matters that are subject to negotiation without first offering to
negotiate with the union. Thus, in NLRB v. Katz, 369 U.S. 736,
82 S. Ct. 1107, 8 L. Ed. 2d 230 (1962), the Court stated:

> The duty "to bargain collectively" enjoined by § 8 (a) (5)
> is defined by § 8 (d) as the duty to "meet . . . and confer
> in good faith with respect to wages, hours, and other terms

and conditions of employment." Clearly, the duty thus defined may be violated without a general failure of subjective
good faith; for there is no occasion to consider the issue of
good faith if a party has refused even to negotiate *in fact*—
"to meet . . . and confer"—about any of the mandatory subjects. A refusal to negotiate *in fact* as to any subject which
is within § 8 (d), and about which the union seeks to
negotiate, violates § 8 (a) (5) though the employer has every
desire to reach agreement with the union upon an overall collective agreement and earnestly and in all good faith
bargains to that end. We hold that an employer's unilateral
change in conditions of employment under negotiation is
similarly a violation under § 8 (a) (5), for it is a circumvention of the duty to negotiate which frustrates the objectives of § 8 (a) (5) much as does a flat refusal.

    . . . Unilateral action by an employer without prior dis-
cussion with the union does amount to a refusal to negotiate
about the affected conditions of employment under negotiation, and must of necessity obstruct bargaining, contrary to
the congressional policy. It will often disclose an unwillingness to agree with the union. It will rarely be justified by
any reason of substance. It follows that the board may
hold such unilateral action to be an unfair labor practice
in violation of § 8 (a) (5), without also finding the employer
guilty of over-all subjective bad faith. While we do not foreclose the possibility that there may be circumstances under
which the Board could or should accept as excusing or
justifying unilateral action, no such case is presented here.

Citing *Katz*, the Connecticut State Board of Labor Relations in
Town of Stratford, Decision No. 1069 (1972), observed that "[i]t
is well recognized that unilateral employer action upon a matter
which is the subject of current collective bargaining between
the parties constitutes a failure and refusal to bargain in good
faith upon the issue in question." *Accord,* Borough of Nauga-
tuck, Conn. State Bd. of Lab. Rel. Decision No. 769 (1967)
(unilateral adoption of a new classification plan while negotiations were in progress). *See generally* West Hartford Educ. Ass'n
v. DeCourcy, *supra* pp. 521, 525-28.

5. Effect of Illegal Strike

SAGINAW TOWNSHIP BOARD OF EDUCATION

Michigan Employment Relations Commission
1970 MERC Lab. Op. 127

Commissioner Milmet:

. . . The Trial Examiner, found that on August 30, 1967, there was a "withholding of services" by the teachers in the bargaining unit. The Charging Party disputes the finding that there existed a strike and alleges that the school term had started on time.

The Trial Examiner relied on Section 15, which reads as follows:

"A public employer shall bargain collectively with the representatives of its employees as defined in Section 11 and is authorized to make and enter into collective bargaining agreements with such representatives. For the purposes of this section, to bargain collectively is the performance of the mutual obligation of the employer and the representative of the employees to meet at reasonable times and confer in good faith with respect to wages, hours and other terms and conditions of employment, or the negotiation of an agreement, or any question arising thereunder, and the execution of a written contract, ordinance or resolution incorporating any agreement reached if requested by either party, but such obligation does not compel either party to agree to a proposal or require the making of a concession."

He found that there exists a mutual obligation between the employer and the bargaining organization to bargain in good faith and that when a representative of public employees uses the pressure of an unlawful strike to gain its demands, it cannot be said to be conferring in good faith within the meaning of Section 15.

He further concluded that such unlawfulness relieves the employer, during the duration of the strike, from any obligation to confer.

Relevant to the decision of this issue is Section 6 of the Act, which reads as follows:

"Notwithstanding the provisions of any other law, any person holding such a position who, by concerted action with others, and without the lawful approval of his superior, wilfully absents himself from his position, or abstains in whole or in part from the full, faithful and proper performance of his duties for the purpose of inducing, influencing or coercing a change in the conditions or compensation, or the rights, privileges or obligations of employment shall be deemed to be on strike but the person, upon request, shall be entitled to a determination as to whether he did violate the provisions of this act. The request shall be filed in writing, with the officer or body having power to remove or discipline such employee, within 10 days after regular compensation of such employee has ceased or other discipline has been imposed. In the event of such request the officer or body shall within 10 days commence a proceeding for the determination of whether the provisions of this act have been violated by the public employee, in accordance with the law and regulations appropriate to a proceeding to remove the public employee. The proceedings shall be undertaken without unnecessary delay. The decision of the proceeding shall be made within 10 days. If the employee involved is held to have violated this law and his employment terminated or other discipline imposed, he shall have the right to review to the circuit court having jurisdiction of the parties, within 30 days from such decision, for determination whether such decision is supported by competent, material and substantial evidence on the whole record."

The legislature having set forth statutory penalties with respect to an alleged illegal strike, it is not within the purview of this Commission to add to the statute. The Employment Relations Commission cannot add language to the Act. This is a legislative function. Saginaw County Road Commission, 1967 MERC L. Op. 196; City of Detroit, 1966 MERC L. Op. 254.

The proper forum for the enforcement of the prohibitions contained in Sections 2, 3 and 6 of the Public Employment Relations Act is relegated to the public employer, which has the power to discipline and discharge, and in the courts, which may exercise their traditional equity powers. We leave to the legislature the decision of determining whether or not additional legislation is needed or desired. City of Detroit, supra.

In this matter, we are not only dealing with the rights of an employer and labor organization, but the rights of all employees. The issue raised by the Trial Examiner has been litigated in the federal courts and the National Labor Relations Board. The courts and the NLRB have held that violation by a Charging Party of a state criminal statute does not under all circumstances preclude the filing of unfair labor practice charges under the National Labor Relations Act and the finding that the employer violated that Act.

The U.S. Supreme Court, in the matter of National Labor Relations Board v. Indiana & Michigan Electric Company, 318 U.S. 9, 29, 30 (1943) found that dynamiting the company's premises by some union members during the course of a strike did not justify a refusal to bargain by the employer. It found that freedom to bargain collectively is a public right, and criminal or unlawful activity by some employees cannot justify destroying the freedom and rights of all employees.

Likewise, the U.S. Supreme Court, in the Matter of National Labor Relations Board v. Insurance Agents International Union, 361 U.S. 477, 494-496 (1960), held that certain unprotected activities by union members during collective bargaining negotiations with the employer did not breach the union's duty to bargain in good faith. The U.S. Supreme Court, in this case, answered this issue when it was stated, as follows:

"But surely that a union activity is not protected against disciplinary action does not mean that it constitutes a refusal to bargain in good faith. The reason why the ordinary economic strike is not evidence of a failure to bargain in good faith is not that it constitutes a protected activity but that, as we have developed, there is simply no inconsistency between the application of economic pressure and good faith collective bargaining. The Board suggests that since (on the assumption we make) the union members activities here were unprotected, and they could have been discharged, the activities should also be deemed unfair labor practices, since thus the remedy of a cease-and-desist order, milder than mass discharges of personnel and less disruptive of commerce, would be available. The argument is not persuasive. There is little logic in assuming that because Congress was willing to allow employers to use self-help against union tactics, if they were willing to face the economic consequences of its use, it also impliedly declared these tactics unlawful as a matter of federal law. Our problem remains that of construing Sec. 8 (b)(3)'s terms, and we do not see how the availability of self-help to the employer has anything to do with the matter. . . . Further, the Board cites what it conceives to be the public's moral condemnation of the sort of employee tactics involved here. But again we cannot see how these distinctions can be made under a statute which simply enjoins a duty to bargain in good faith. Again, these are relevant arguments when the question is the scope of the concerted activities given affirmative protection by the Act. But as we have developed, the use of economic pressure by the parties to a labor dispute is not a grudging exception to some policy of completely academic discussion enjoined by the Act; it is part and parcel of the process of collective bargaining. On this basis, we fail to see the relevance of whether the practice in question is time-honored or whether its exercise is generally supported by public opinion. *It may be that the tactics here deserve condemnation, but this would not justify attempting to pour that condemnation into a vessel not designed to hold it."* (Emphasis added)

While we may personally condemn work stoppages of public employees, our problem is even greater than that posed before the U.S. Supreme Court in the *Insurance Agents* case, *supra*. We are faced with not only the problem of being unable to pour our condemnation in a vessel not designed to hold it, but, additionally, we lack the vessel. Such vessel should be supplied by the Legislature if it wishes the Commission to have power to determine the legality or illegality of strikes by public employees and the impact thereof on the bargaining process. City of Detroit, *supra*. This the Legislature has done in the private sector. . . .

The National Labor Relations Board and the federal courts have held that a breach of the statute by one party to a collective bargaining relationship does not justify a violation of the duties under the National Labor Relations Act by the other party. Unions cannot justify their unlawful restraint and coercion on the grounds that the employer refused to bargain. . . .

Labor laws do not deal with purely private rights, but also with public rights. Legislation is enacted in the public interest. If a violation of the Act occurs, there is no justification for reciprocal violation of the law nor a license to violate the Act.

While union bargaining techniques may violate good faith bargaining requirements of the National Labor Relations Act, they are no defense for an employer's refusal to bargain in good faith. . . .

We reject the Trial Examiner's rationale that a violation of the Act by one party to a collective bargaining relationship justifies violation of the Act by the other party. The employer's remedy under our statute is limited to Section 6 and the equity powers of the courts.

In the Holland School District, 380 Mich. 314 (1968), a majority of the Michigan Supreme Court recognized that the remedy by a court of equity in matters of strikes by public school teachers is not available to all boards of education for the sole reason that the employees went on strike. It held that in determining whether an injunction should be issued, inquiry was to be made into the obligation of the employer to bargain in good faith. The proper forum for enforcing the no-strike provisions of the Public Employment Relations Act, with the exception of the remedy provided in Section 6, is confined to the equity powers of the court. Holland School District, *supra*.

[Commissioner Walsh's concurring opinion is omitted.]

Chairman Howlett, dissenting:

I would . . . affirm the Trial Examiner's dismissal of the charges and complaint. I believe it advisable to discuss the Trial Examiner's conclusion

". . . that the duty to 'confer in good faith' does not require a public employer to continue to bargain while the public employees and their representative are engaged in a strike prohibited by Section 2 of PERA."

The Commission should not, as a matter of policy, encourage the use of the strike weapon as the majority opinion will do.

The majority rely on decisions of the courts and the National Labor Relations Board (NLRB) interpreting the National Labor Relations Act, as amended (NLRA). My reading of the decisions by both the courts and the NLRB leads me to conclude that they sustain the principle enunciated by the Trial Examiner that a strike by a union suspends the requirement of an employer to bargain during the period of the strike. This is the principle which should be applied under PERA. Public officials are representatives of the public, concerned with the public interest. They have a responsibility to uphold public policy greater than that of private employers. Prohibited acts under NLRA and under PERA are public policy, which *public* officials are sworn to uphold. To the extent the public employers in Michigan refuse to bargain with a union which is violating PERA they encourage statutory compliance by the unions. As the courts and NLRB have held (see discussion below) the principle does not *relieve* the employer of its statutory duty to bargain, but does *suspend* the obligation during the period of the union's illegal activity.

PERA not only prohibits strikes by all public employees, but interdicts any person exercising authority, supervision or direction over a public employee from authorizing, approving or consenting to a strike. The prohibition is absolute.

While the Michigan Supreme Court, in School District for the City of Holland v. Holland Education Association, 380 Mich. 314 (1968), has held (and in my opinion correctly) that an injunction will not issue per se because public employees have breached the statute, the refusal of an injunction does not render the act of striking legal. Indeed, the *Holland School District* case, by its reference to public employers who have refused or failed to comply with their obligations under the statute, implies that labor organizations should be required to exercise similar responsibility.

As the duty to bargain in good faith is mutual, a circuit court mandatory injunction should be a remedy to require a labor organization to bargain in good faith. The processes of the circuit courts were used under the Labor Mediation Act (LMA), before the 1965 amendments, to require employers to comply with their obligations. . . .

There have been 165 strikes by public employees since the enactment of PERA. Perhaps the magnitude of the strikes has brought into play the law of diminishing returns. We may view strikes with lessened concern than we did in 1965 and 1966, simply because they have occurred—and have been effective. But because public employees have disregarded the statute should not persuade that the use of the strike is right, or other than illegal.

The obligation of Section 15 of PERA is *"the mutual obligation of the employer and the representative of the employees."* As in the case of substantial non-performance or breach of contract where an innocent party to a contract may rescind, the innocent public employer should be freed from its obligation to perform its part of the mutual obligation when a labor organization breaches its obligation by striking. (17 Am. Jur. Contracts, Para. 504; Rosenthal v. Triangle Development Co., 261 Mich. 462 (1933)).

NLRB and the courts hold that a private sector employer is not obligated to bargain during strikes which are in breach of a collective bargaining agreement which includes a "no-strike" clause. This is parallel to a strike by public employees in breach of PERA. Indeed, it may be urged that there is a greater basis for a public employer's release from its obligation, as public employees violate a statute rather than a contract.

The court cases enunciating this principle are well illustrated by United Electrical, Radio & Machine Workers of America v. National Labor Relations Board, 223 F.2d 338 (D.C. Cir.,

1955) ; cert. denied, 350 U.S. 981, 76 S. Ct. 466 (1956). The Court of Appeals held that an employer did not violate Section 8(a)(5) and 8 (d) of NLRA by terminating a collective bargaining contract when the UE staged a walkout in breach of a no-strike clause of the contract. The strike, the court held, was a material breach of the contract. In its opinion, the court said:

"The next point concerns the refusal of the Company to bargain with UE after the strike had been called. As to such a refusal on February 28th, the Board reasoned that, even if UE was still the bargaining representative of the employees, the Company was under no obligation to bargain in the absence of notification that the illegal strike had been terminated. This has been the policy of the board. . . . As we have indicated, when UE, seeking a modification of an existing contract by proposing wage adjustments into the agreed scale, called a strike in flat violation of the contract and of the explicit terms of Section 8 (d) of the Act, it was guilty of failure to bargain in good faith as that term is defined in Section 8 (d). The statute has in it many provisions valuable to labor organizations, and protects them in the exercise of their rights, but it does not give them authority to violate the Act wantonly and at the same time to insist upon full measure of the privileges afforded them when proceeding properly." (p. 344)

The Court of Appeals of the Sixth Circuit, in a per curiam opinion, enforced Valley City Furniture Company, 110 N.L.R.B. 1589, 35 L.R.R.M. 1265 (1954), in National Labor Relations Board v. Valley City Furniture Company, 230 F.2d 947 (1956). A union directed employees to refuse to work overtime after an employer unlawfully increased the hours of work without consulting or notifying the union. The union action, the NLRB held, was not a protected activity; hence the employer had a right to refuse to bargain with the union, even though the employer had violated NLRA Section 8 (a) (5). In its opinion, NLRB said:

"In view of the well settled rule that an employer's duty to bargain is suspended while a union is engaged in unprotected activity, we are constrained to find the (employer) was under no obligation to speak with the union while it was engaging in such threats." (p. 1269)

. . . .

Analysis of the cases, both court and Board, cited in the majority opinion, discloses that they are not applicable to PERA, which renders a strike illegal; and in several instances, the rationale supports my thesis that an employer is freed from its duty to bargain while its employees engage in an illegal strike.

[The portion of Chairman Howlett's opinion in which he distinguishes the cases cited by the majority is omitted.]

There should, in my opinion, be no requirement that public officials be required to bargain with employees while the employees are in violation of the no-strike policy declared by the Michigan Legislature. I agree with my colleagues that "it is not within the purview of this Commission to add to the statute" and that "we leave to the Legislature the decision of determining whether or not additional legislation is needed or desired." The decision which should be made by the Legislature is whether to relax the prohibition against strikes in those areas where the public health, safety and welfare is not endangered by a public employees' strike.

The refusal by public officials to bargain with a striking union, while its members are on strike, is not only consistent with the private sector policy applicable to wildcat strikes, but as official action by public employers, upholds state policy.

NOTES

1. The Los Angeles County Employee Relations Commission in County of Los Angeles and Los Angeles County Employees Association, SEIU, Local 660 AFL-CIO (August 25, 1972), held that a sick-out was not a refusal to bargain in violation of the Los Angeles County Collective Bargaining Ordinance. The Commission stated that it was unprepared to hold that the union had unlawfully refused to bargain when its conduct stemmed directly from the County's unlawful refusal to negotiate over a matter which the Commission had earlier held to be negotiable.

2. The WERC in City of Portage, Decision No. 8378 (1968), in response to the city's assertion that a work stoppage constituted a defense to a prohibited practice charge, noted that it did "not apply the unclean hands' doctrine as a defense to prohibited practices . . . ." However, in City of Milwaukee (Department of Public Works), Dec. No. 6575B (Dec. 12, 1963), the WERC held:

> The fact finding procedure set forth in the statute is designed to give representatives of municipal employes an opportunity to persuade the municipal employer and the public of the merits of their particular requests with reference to the wages, hours and working conditions of municipal employes. As administrators of this statute we do not believe

that labor organizations, who ignore these considerations by engaging in a strike, should at the same time be entitled to the benefits of fact finding or other rights granted to them by statute. The Board as a general policy and in the absence of good cause shown will decline to process any fact finding petition filed by a labor organization which is engaged in a strike.

3. The National Labor Relations Board has held "that it is a defense to a charge of employer bad faith [bargaining], that the union was not itself in good faith." Roadhome Constr. Corp., 170 N.L.R.B. 91 (1968). In Times Publishing Co., 72 N.L.R.B. 676, 682-83 (1947), the NLRB reasoned as follows:

> . . . The test of good faith in bargaining that the Act requires of an employer is not a rigid but a fluctuating one, and is dependent in part upon how a reasonable man might be expected to react to the bargaining attitude displayed by those across the table. It follows that . . . a union's refusal to bargain in good faith may remove the possibility of negotiation and thus preclude the existence of a situation in which the employer's own good faith can be tested. If it cannot be tested, its absence can hardly be found.

Is this statement consistent with the holding of the majority in the principal case?

6. Duty to Execute an Agreement

CITY OF SAGINAW
Michigan Employment Relations Commission
1967 MERC Lab. Op. 465

Trial Examiner James McCormick: I . . . am unable to conclude that the City's announced unwillingness to enter into a signed bilateral labor contract is a breach of the bargaining duty as spelled out in Section 15 of PERA. It is true that, under federal law, the refusal of either party to labor negotiations to enter into a signed contract covering agreements reached constitutes an unlawful failure to bargain in good faith. H.J. Heinz Company v. N.L.R.B. 311 U.S. 514, 7 L.R.R.M. 291 (1941); National Labor Relations Act, as amended, sec. 8(d). As stated by National Labor Relations Board Solicitor William Feldesman in a speech reported in the October 31, 1966, Labor Relations Reporter, 63 L.R.R. 186:

> "Of course the labor contract has always been regarded as the hoped-for product of collective bargaining, as it brings to the industrial community concerned a charter of volun-

tarily made law and palpably evidences labor relations stability."

Professor Archibald Cox (Cases on Labor Law, p. 2) refers to the basic labor relations statutes as the "constitution" of industrial self-government and views the written collective bargaining agreements as the "statutory law" of the employer-employee relationship. It can be seen from such an analogy how important the written contract is to effective collective bargaining in private enterprise. Local governmental bodies, however, must conduct business in a way appropriate to the making of a proper official record. They may act by ordinance, resolution, motion or order. Fordham, *Local Government Law*, p. 403. (In Michigan practice an ordinance ordinarily prescribes a permanent rule for the conduct of government, while a resolution is of a special or temporary character.) Kalamazoo Municipal Utilities Assn. v. City of Kalamazoo, 345 Mich. 318, 76 N.W.2d 1 (1956). Modifications in wages, hours and working conditions have generally been effected by adoption of a resolution approving changes in the governmental body's personnel "plan" or "policy." Even where such action has followed upon, and represented the fruit of, consultation with a union, the resolution of the City Council or other legislative body has not reflected that fact, but has appeared to be a unilateral act.

One of the problems created by incorporating collective bargaining agreements into ordinances or resolutions is the fact that these are subject to being modified or repealed by the body that enacted or adopted them. City of Saginaw v. Consumers Power Co., 213 Mich. 460, 182 N.W. 146 (1921). Imagine the situation which would exist if a private employer could modify or repeal its contracts at will. Enforcement of an ordinance or resolution against the public employer also presents legal difficulties.

In any event, the Michigan legislature has specified in Section 15 of the PERA that the "execution of a written contract, ordinance or resolution incorporating any agreement reached if requested by either party" satisfies the bargaining duty. While the language is ambiguous, the more reasonable interpretation is that any of these three ways of evidencing or memorializing the verbal understanding is sufficient, and that either party may lawfully hold out for its preferred way, not being obliged to sign a bilateral written contract if it prefers an ordinance or resolution.

It may be, however, that an ordinance or resolution which represents and incorporates a final meeting of minds on a collective bargaining agreement results in contractual rights in both employees and public employer, and is, in fact, a contract, even though it is, in another sense, the free and unilateral decree of a duly-empowered governing body. In Dodge v. Board of Education of Chicago, 302 U.S. 74, 58 S. Ct. 98 (1937) the issue was whether a statute providing for pensions for retired teachers created a contract with the teachers, the obligations of which could not be impaired by a later statute decreasing the annuities. The Court recognized that a state may enter into contracts with citizens, the obligation of which the legislature cannot impair by subsequent enactment, but said "On the other hand, an act merely fixing salaries of officers creates no contract in their favor, and the compensation named may be altered at the will of the legislature. . . . The presumption is that such a law is not intended to create private contractual or vested rights, but merely declares a policy to be pursued until the legislature shall ordain otherwise. He who asserts the creation of a contract with the state in such a case has the burden of overcoming the presumption." It would appear that where an ordinance or resolution "incorporates" a collective bargaining "agreement," following extensive "negotiations," any presumption against the creation of contractual rights could be rebutted. In either event, the peculiar language used in Section 15 of the PERA precludes the finding of a violation in the City's anticipatory refusal to enter into a written contract.

[The Trial Examiner's decision was adopted by the MERC.]

NOTES

1. If the parties reach agreement on a substantial number of issues in negotiations but are nevertheless at impasse on a number of other issues, is the employer obligated to reduce to writing and execute an agreement on those issues on which the parties have reached agreement? In Local 1363, International Association of Fire Fighters v. DiPrete, 103 R.I. 592, 239 A.2d 716 (1968), the union, relying on a statutory provision which imposed on employers "the duty to cause any agreement resulting from negotiations to be reduced to a written contract," alleged that the statute required "that whatever matters may have been agreed upon, even though less than all in issue, shall be embodied in a formal writing which, upon execution, will become the collective bargaining agreement governing the working conditions of the Cranston firefighters." The Rhode Island Supreme Court, noting that the word "agreement" "presumes that the parties have arrived at a mutual understanding on all of the matters in negotiation," held that there was no obligation

on the city to execute an incomplete collective bargaining agreement.

2. Where a union is certified as the exclusive bargaining agent for a unit of public employees, can the union limit a ratification vote on a proposed collective bargaining agreement to only its members and exclude nonmembers from participating? *Compare* Wald v. Civil Serv. Employees Ass'n, 72 Misc. 2d 723, 340 N.Y.S.2d 451 (Sup. Ct., Nassau County, 1973) (union may limit ratification in vote to its own members unless the parties agree otherwise), *with* National Educ. Ass'n of Shawnee Mission, Inc. v. Board of Educ. of Shawnee Mission Unified School Dist. No. 512, — Kan. —, 512 P.2d 426, 84 L.R.R.M. 2223 (1973) (". . . ratification is required by a majority of the entire negotiating unit, not just of the negotiating organization").

3. Is a collective bargaining agreement which extends beyond the contracting officials' term of office binding on their successors? In AFSCME Dist. Council No. 33 v. Philadelphia, 83 Pa. D. & C. 537 (C.P. 1952), the court held that a collective bargaining agreement was binding on a successive administration. *But see* City of Springfield v. Clouse, 356 Mo. 1239, 206 S.W.2d 539 (1947) (". . . of course, no legislature could bind itself or its successor to make or continue any legislative act").

D. The Duty to Bargain During the Term of a Collective Bargaining Agreement

1. Generally

CITY OF MILWAUKEE
Wisconsin Employment Relations Commission
WERC Decision No. 8505 (1968)

[A union alleged that an employer violated the Wisconsin Municipal Employment Act when it unilaterally made certain revisions in the duties of several employees during the term of the parties' agreement. The employer asserted that it was under no obligation to bargain with the union before taking the action on the ground that the management rights clause in the agreement gave it the right to revise the duties in question.]

In private employment labor relations an employer is under a continual duty to bargain with the representative of the majority of its employes despite the existence of a collective bargaining agreement, except where such collective bargaining representative, in the agreement, surrenders its right to insist upon bargaining on certain conditions of employment by agreeing to permit the employer to make unilateral determinations in that regard. There is no provision in Section 111.70 of the Wisconsin Statutes which prevents the representative of municipal employes from making such an agreement with the municipal employer involved.

We recognize and agree with the rule that a waiver of the right to bargain on a mandatory subject of bargaining will not be readily inferred, and that a waiver of such a statutory right, in order to be recognized, must be "clear and unmistakable." We conclude that the "management rights" clause in question here specifically provides, "thoroughly and unmistakably," that the Municipal Employer has the authority, during the term of the agreement, to unilaterally make revisions in duties of employes in order to increase the efficiency of the particular operation involved. . . .

NOTE

The NLRB has ruled "that an employer's duty to give a union prior notice and an opportunity to bargain normally arises where the employer proposes to take action which will effect some change in existing employment terms or conditions within the range of mandatory bargaining." Westinghouse Electric Corp., 150 N.L.R.B. 1574 (1955). If the applicable collective bargaining agreement, however, gives the employer the right to take the action in question, then the employer can act unilaterally without bargaining with the union. See, e.g., Ador Corp., 155 N.L.R.B. 1658 (1965). Finally, the NLRB has consistently held that an employer, in the absence of mutual agreement, cannot modify a condition of employment which is set forth in an agreement during the term of the agreement even though it has given the union advance notice and an opportunity to bargain over the proposed modification. In this regard, the NLRB relies on Section 8 (d) of the NLRA which provides "[t]hat where there is in effect a collective-bargaining contract . . . , the duty to bargain collectively shall also mean that no party to such contract shall terminate or modify such contract. . . ." For example, in Standard Oil Co., 174 N.L.R.B. 177 (1969), the NLRB held that an employer violated Section 8 (d) when it unilaterally increased certain wage rates during the term of the parties' agreement without obtaining the union's consent. The Board observed that the employer "was not free . . . to modify the unexpired agreement over the Union's objections, but was obligated to maintain in effect all preexisting contractual commitments for the contract term."

2.   Effect of Negotiated Grievance Procedure

BOARD OF COUNTY ROAD COMMISSIONERS OF THE COUNTY OF WAYNE

Michigan Employment Relations Commission
1972 MERC Lab. Op. 1035

[The employer, the Board of County Road Commissioners of the County of Wayne, filed exceptions to a Trial Examiner's Decision and Recommended Order finding that the employer refused to bargain in violation of Section 10 (e) of the Michigan Public Employment Relations Act.]

On March 21, 1972, the Union [Wayne County Road Commission Supervisory Employees] filed an unfair labor practice charge against the Employer because the Employer filled a vacancy in the Accountant V job classification by hiring Datis Norton from outside while none of the five members of the Union who were employed by the Employer as accountants in the Accountant IV job classification who were qualified to fill the vacancy were promoted.

Datis Norton is black. Early in 1971, the Federal Aviation Administration (FAA), which furnishes substantial federal funds to provide facilities at the Wayne County Metropolitan Airport operated by Employer, investigated the practices of the Employer, its contractors and tenants at the airport in providing equal employment and contracting for service opportunities for minorities.

FAA determined that the Employer did not comply with requirements of the Civil Rights Act and the Executive Order. It recommended that the Employer develop an Affirmative Action Program to accomplish such compliance. The Employer, motivated both by a desire to afford equal opportunity and business opportunities to minorities and by a fear of loss of federal airport funds, did, with the assistance of FAA, develop an Affirmative Action Program approved by FAA and adopted on February 24, 1972.

By this program, so far as is relevant to this proceeding, the Employer committed itself to a policy of increasing its minority work force from 12.6% to 27% over a five-year period.

Wayne County has elected to be subject to the County Civil Service Act (MSA 5.1191 (1) — (28.1)). Pursuant to the Act, the Wayne County Civil Service Commission adopted Rules and Regulations on December 31, 1943. These regulations, as revised and amended, have continued in force and effect.

The Rules and Regulations, among other things, established a job classification, a salary plan, procedures for applying for county employment, procedures for examinations to qualify for employment, a rating system for examinations, eligibility lists for employment, provisions for re-employment, provisions for promotions and types of job appointments.

Article 11 of the collective bargaining agreement in effect at the time Norton was hired incorporated by reference the current Rules and Regulations of the Civil Service Commission as the Employer's Manual of Personnel Procedures.

Norton was hired by the Respondent shortly before the adoption of the Affirmative Action Program as a provisional employee. The Employer considered five accountants working in job classification Accountant IV for the job, but they were not interviewed by any responsible supervisory employees. Other applicants from outside were interviewed. Upon the recommendation of the responsible supervisory employees, Norton was hired.

The reasons offered by the Employer for hiring Norton over the Accountant IV employees were his superior experience and qualifications, the need to bring qualified outside personnel into the finance division and implementation of the Affirmative Action Program by placement of a black in the vacancy. There was no Civil Service Eligibility List for the Accountant V job classification. The Civil Service Commission approved the hiring of Norton as a provisional employee under Section 10 of the Civil Service Rules and Regulations.

The Union contends that the sole basis for Norton's selection was to further the implementation of the Affirmative Action Program and avers that this constitutes discrimination against the five Accountant IV employees. It also urges that as all of the Accountant IV employees were qualified, one of them should have been promoted to Accountant V; that the Employer's failure to do so was contrary to established practice. The Union also asserts that to fill the vacancy without consultation with it was a refusal to bargain, therefore, an unfair labor practice in violation of Section 10 (c) of PERA.

The Union also contends that the action of the Employer constitutes a violation of the Equal Protection clause of the Fourteenth Amendment to the United States Constitution and Section 1981 of the Civil Rights Act.

The Employer contends that it had the right to hire Norton rather than promoting one of the Accountant IV employees, because the Civil Service Rules and Regulations, which are made part of the collective bargaining agreement, do not require that vacancies be filled by promotion. The Employer also avers that it may hire from outside to fill a vacancy under those Rules and

Regulations when there is no Civil Service Eligibility list for the vacant position provided the person hired is given a provisional appointment under Section 10 (a) of Rule 8.

The Trial Examiner found that the failure of the Employer to consult with the Union regarding the filling of the vacancy and the adoption of the Affirmative Action Program without the consent of the Union regarding promotions constituted an unfair labor practice under Section 10 (e) of PERA.

Article VII of the collective bargaining agreement contains provisions of the settlement of grievances arising under it. It provides for a grievance procedure of six steps. The final or sixth step provides for binding arbitration in the event that the grievance has not been previously solved. Step six clearly provides for arbitration to settle disputes over the interpretation of the agreement such as is involved here.

The transcript as well as the exceptions to the Trial Examiner's Decision and the briefs of the parties on review make no reference to Article VII, nor is it discussed by the Trial Examiner in his Decision and Recommended Order.

In two instances, we have had occasion to consider similar situations where parties have reviewed Trial Examiners' decisions in unfair labor practice cases where contractual arbitration provisions have not been followed.

In City of Flint and Flint Fire Fighters Union No. 352, I.A.F.F. (AFL-CIO), 1970 MERC Lab. Op. 367, we returned a dispute to the parties for processing under the contract grievance procedure. We thus not only concurred in the philosophy of Spielberg Mfg. Co., 112 N.L.R.B. 1080, 36 L.R.R.M. 1152 (1955), but antedated Collyer Insulated Wire, 192 N.L.R.B. No. 150, 77 L.R.R.M. 1931 (1971). These cases enunciate the policy of the NLRB that it will, with exceptions not relevant here, require the parties to resolve their differences through arbitration where they have agreed to this method in those cases where the controversy involves both an alleged unfair labor practice and failure to comply with the terms of the collective bargaining agreement. We said, in City of Flint:

> "There will be situations in which we should and will take jurisdiction of controversies which may involve contract construction as well as an alleged unfair labor practice. But employers and unions should make every effort to resolve issues primarily contractual under the contract dispute settling procedure." (1970 MERC Lab. Op. 371)

In Detroit Income Tax Investigators Association, et al. and Detroit Firefighters Association, Local 334, I.A.F.F., 1971 MERC

Lab. Op. 212, we upheld the Trial Examiner's Decision on the merits where the parties did not use the arbitration provisions of the collective bargaining agreement to resolve a contract interpretation dispute. We concluded that it would have been advisable for the parties to arbitrate the dispute, but upheld the Trial Examiner on the merits because: (1) several labor organizations were involved in the dispute, (2) there was need for an expeditious decision, and (3) there were no arbitration provisions in some of the collective agreements involving certain of the employees affected by the dispute.

In dismissing the charge in *Collyer,* the NLRB made several observations pertinent in the disposition of the instant case. It said:

> "We find merit in Respondent's exceptions that because this dispute in its entirety arises from the contract between the parties, and from the parties' relationship under the contract, it ought to be resolved in the manner which that contract describes. . . ." (77 L.R.R.M. at 1934)

We concur in this conclusion and conclude that this dispute arises under the contract and should be resolved in the manner prescribed therein.

The Board also said in *Collyer:*

> "In our view, disputes such as these can better be resolved by arbitrators with special skill and experience in deciding matters arising under established bargaining relationships than by the application by this Board of a particular provision of our statute. . . ." (77 L.R.R.M. at 1934)

We also concur in this statement of the NLRB.

In *Collyer,* the Board also said, quoting from International Harvester Co., 138 N.L.R.B. 923, 51 L.R.R.M. 1155 (1962):

> "There is no question that the Board is not precluded from adjudicating unfair labor practice charges even though they might have been the subject of an arbitration proceeding and award. Section 10 (a) of the Act expressly makes this plain, and the courts have uniformly so held. However, it is equally well established that the Board has considerable discretion (in) respect (to) an arbitration award and (may) decline to exercise its authority over alleged unfair labor practices if to do so will serve the fundamental aims of the Act.
>
> "The Act, as has repeatedly been stated, is primarily designed to promote industrial peace and stability by encouraging the practice and procedure of collective bargaining. Ex-

perience has demonstrated that collective bargaining agreements that provide for final and binding arbitration of grievance and disputes arising thereunder, 'as a substitute for industrial strife,' contribute significantly to the attainment of this statutory objective."

The State of Michigan declared its public policy with respect to the disposition of labor disputes in Section 1 of the Michigan Labor Relations and Mediation Act, MSA 17.454 (1) :

"It is hereby declared as the public policy of this state that the best interests of the people of the state are served by the prevention or prompt settlement of labor disputes; that strikes and lockouts and other forms of industrial strife, regardless of where the merits of the controversy lie, are forces productive ultimately of economic waste; that the interests and rights of the consumers and the people of the state, while not direct parties thereto, should always be considered, respected and protected; and that the voluntary mediation of such disputes under the guidance and supervision of a governmental agency will tend to promote permanent industrial peace and the health, welfare, comfort and safety of the people of the state."

It is clear from reading this Section that it is the policy of the State of Michigan, as well as the policy of the Federal Government as declared in the National Labor Relations Act to promote the prevention or prompt settlement of labor disputes and other forms of industrial strife.

Under this policy, the Commission has the authority to decline to accept jurisdiction in a proceeding such as this one, and to defer to arbitration as a means which the parties themselves have agreed to for the prompt and efficient resolution of disputes arising over contract terms.

Such disposition works no hardship on either the Union or the Accountant IV's. There is no deprivation of remedy. Article VII of the collective contract provides no time limitation for the initiation of this grievance procedure. Moreover, the delay in the disposition of this grievance will not cause irreparable loss for the employee who is finally promoted, should the Union prevail, because the arbitrator can make him whole for any loss of increased earnings occasioned by the delay.

For the foregoing reasons, unlike the Trial Examiner, we decline to assert jurisdiction in this proceeding. In doing so, we call attention to the fact that the issue we raised and upon which this Decision is based was not raised by the parties or considered by the Trial Examiner. . . .

NOTES

1. Did the MERC hold that it did not have jurisdiction of the dispute or only that it was deferring resolution of the dispute to the arbitration procedure set forth in the parties' agreement? Is there a difference between these two concepts? Consider the following holding of the Hawaii Public Employment Relations Board in Department of Educ., Decision No. 22 (1972), GERR No. 480, E-1:

> [I]t would appear that the Legislature intended the Board to take the responsibility for settling prohibited practice cases. However, the language which confers this duty upon the Board is broad enough to permit the Board considerable leeway in determining whether, when faced with prohibited practice charges involving situations for which arbitration has been provided, to commit the parties to their contractual remedy. This procedure would best seem to foster legislative intent and the Board would not be an impotent bystander.
>
> The practice in Wisconsin is also informative. Under Wisconsin law it is an unfair labor practice to breach a collective bargaining agreement and the Wisconsin Board, keeping in step with the NLRB, defers to arbitration unless arbitration would be fruitless or the parties jointly waive arbitration. *Laborers' International Union of North America, Local No. 1440, Complainant, vs. D. L. Bordley Company, Inc., Respondent,* Case I, No. 13524, CE-1285, Decision No. 9526-A, Case II, No. 13525, CE-1286, Decision No. 9527-A.
>
> . . . [I]t is clear that the Board has jurisdiction over prohibited practice charges, including those involving alleged breaches of contract, regardless of the presence of a grievance arbitration provision in a collective bargaining agreement. It appears further that in the exercise of this jurisdiction, the Board may require parties to utilize negotiated grievance arbitration procedures when and to the extent appropriate.

2. Should a policy of deferral to arbitration of disputes concerning the interpretation or application of the terms of the parties' agreement be followed if the terminal step in the contractual procedure provides for advisory rather than binding arbitration? The MERC in City of Flint, 1970 MERC Lab. Op. 367, held that it should, noting that "[t]he contract procedure should be exhausted before the parties seek to have their contract disagreement settled by government." On the other hand, the NLRB has held that "[u]nfair labor practice charges will not be deferred for arbitration under *Collyer* policy if the arbitration provisions of the contract do not make the results reached in

such proceedings 'binding' or 'final and binding' on the parties."
Revised Memorandum of NLRB General Counsel Nash on
Processing of Deferral to Arbitration Cases, BNA Daily Labor
Report No. 90, F-1, F-10 (1973).

3. In Southeastern Pennsylvania Transportation Authority,
Case No. PERA-C-1044-E, GERR No. 450, C-9 (1972), the
Pennsylvania Labor Relations Board held that a union may not
appeal to the Board when it "has not complied with the grievance
procedure specified by a collective bargaining agreement, where
the practice charge is properly subject to such procedure." Under
Executive Order 11491, the Assistant Secretary of Labor has
ruled that where a complaint involves essentially a disagreement
over the interpretation of an existing collective-bargaining agreement which sets forth a procedure for resolving the disagreement,
the parties should pursue their contractual remedies rather than
unfair labor practice remedies. NASA, Kennedy Space Center,
A/SLMR No. 223 (1972), GERR Ref. File 21:4158. *Accord,*
Cohasset School Comm., Mass. Lab. Rel. Comm'n Case No.
MUP-419, GERR No. 510, B-8 (1973).

4. If a labor relations agency defers a dispute to the contractual arbitration procedure but retains jurisdiction to review
the resulting award, what criteria should the agency use in
reviewing the award? The NLRB in Collyer Insulated Wire,
192 N.L.R.B. No. 150, 77 L.R.R.M. 1931 (1971), held that it
would not contravene an arbitrator's award unless there was "a
proper showing that . . . the grievance or arbitration procedures
have not been fair and regular or have reached a result which is
repugnant to the Act."

The NLRB's policies with respect to deferral of contractual
disputes are thoroughly reviewed in Revised Memorandum of
NLRB General Counsel Nash on Processing of Deferral to Arbi-
tration Cases, BNA Daily Labor Report No. 90, F-1 (1973).
See generally Comment, *Deference of Jurisdiction by the NLRB
and the Arbitration Clause,* 25 VAND. L. REV. 1057 (1972); Com-
ment, *Some Post-Deferral Considerations Prompted by the NLRB
New Collyer Doctrine,* 12 WM. & MARY L. REV. 824 (1972). The
NLRB's *Collyer* doctrine received judicial approval in Nabisco,
Inc. v. NLRB, 479 F.2d 770 (2d Cir. 1973).

5. Section 111.70 (3) (a) (5) of the Wisconsin Statute covering municipal employees provides that it is a prohibited practice
for a municipal employer to refuse to comply with an ". . .
arbitration award, where previously the parties have agreed to
accept such award as final and binding upon them." The Wisconsin Act contains a similar prohibition on labor organizations.

In City of Franklin, WERC Decision No. 11296 (1972), the Wisconsin Commission held that an employer violated this section of the Act when it refused and failed to comply with an arbitration award.

E. Public Sector Collective Bargaining and the Public Interest

1. Politics and the "End Run"

BAKKE, REFLECTIONS ON THE FUTURE OF BARGAINING IN
THE PUBLIC SECTOR, Monthly Labor Review, Vol.
93, No. 7, pp. 21, 24-25 (July 1970)

. . . [T]he combination of political and economic bargaining strategies by unions in the public sector will produce a confusing pattern of collective bargaining interactions. It will be similar to a situation in private industry in which the union could go around management and make deals with the board of directors representing the stockholders, and union members had an important voice in electing the board of directors.

There will be an uneasy relationship between the administrative managers of public agencies and the elected legislative and executive officials to whom they are responsible and upon whom they depend for support in the pursuit of their professional interests. The labor movement, particularly in local and State situations, can and often does play a very important part in the electoral process. The working class vote can make the difference in elections. When the union, which is ostensibly bargaining with the management administrators, bypasses them in the hope of getting a better deal directly with city hall or the state house, a serious modification of collective bargaining as developed in the private sector occurs. The management administrators can find their efforts at reaching a settlement shortcircuited.

Collective bargaining as it is defined by practice in the private sector does not involve back-door deals with the board of directors, and directors are not elected either by the union members and their allies in the labor movement or by the ultimate consumers of their services or goods. Collective bargaining in the private sector assumes the existence of two relatively independent parties, the management and workers represented by their union, trying to accommodate their differences and satisfy their respective interests through negotiation and administration of a contract.

NOTE

In its 1968 Interim Report the Taylor Committee stated:

One feature of the relations between collective negotiations and traditional civil service regulations and legislation deserves particular attention. It is possible for labor organizations to seek the maximum benefits available through negotiations and then to seek further benefits through changes in civil service regulations or other legislation in the locality or at the state level. This procedure—whether related to state or local employees—is likely to be detrimental to constructive negotiations. It is not always easy, however, to draw the boundary between negotiations and the rights of members to petition a legislative body for benefits nor to enforce a division between the two. These issues deserve continuing attention. GOVERNOR'S COMMITTEE ON PUBLIC EMPLOYEE RELATIONS, INTERIM REPORT 18-19 (N.Y. 1968).

2.   Open vs. Closed Bargaining Sessions

NEW YORK PUBLIC EMPLOYMENT RELATIONS BOARD, SURVEY ON DISCLOSURE DURING PUBLIC SECTOR NEGOTIATIONS, GERR No. 463, D-2 to D-6 (1972)

Introduction

On January 3, 1972, Governor Rockefeller requested that the Public Employment Relations Board give top priority to the problem of public disclosure following negotiations with public employee groups.

For some time the problem of disclosure at various stages of the negotiating process had been discussed by PERB with the parties, the media, and knowledgeable people in the labor relations field. To completely encompass this field, PERB's analysis of the question was broadened beyond the Governor's request to include all stages of the negotiating process. Opinions on disclosure throughout the process were solicited from the media, mediators and fact-finders, and recognized industrial and labor relations experts. In addition, a questionnaire soliciting information on what actually occurred with respect to disclosure during the course of negotiations and their opinions was sent to the parties in impasse situations in which the fact-finding report and recommendations had not been acted upon within 10 days.

For purposes of structuring the analysis, the negotiating process was broken into the following stages:

1.   Negotiations prior to thrid-party assistance.
2.   During the course of mediation.

3. During the course of fact-finding.

4. After the fact-finder has rendered his report and recommendations but before agreement.

5. After agreement has been reached but prior to employee ratification.

6. After agreement has been reached but prior to enactment of legislation required to implement the agreement.

In addition to the above points, the respondents also were requested to recommend whether disclosure should be mandated by statute.

A full discussion of the issue follows PERB's Recommendations.

Recommendations

On the basis of the inquiry and responses from the affected parties and others, PERB recommends that:

No amendments to the Taylor Law are required with respect to disclosure of agreements negotiated between public employers and employee groups.

1. Legislation regarding disclosure is unnecessary because:

(a) Inquiry indicates that the basic details of most such agreements are made public either when agreement is reached or after ratification by the employee groups.

(b) If the negotiations reach the fact-finding stages, the fact-finding report and recommendations are made public by PERB five days after receipt by the parties as required by law. Often the parties themselves release the substance of the report within the five-day period. Subsequent negotiations, if any, take place within the framework of the fact-finder's report.

(c) If a legislative hearing is required, the law mandates a *public* hearing.

(d) In almost all instances the agreement is made available to the public by the employer, and sometimes by the employee organization. Normally, the contract is also available from PERB on request.

(e) A substantial part of all memoranda of agreement, including the fiscal aspects, requires legislative implementation. Public sector labor agreements appear to receive essentially the same amount of disclosure as do other government matters.

2. Legislation regarding disclosure is *undesirable* because:

(a) It would deny governments necessary flexibility. Given the diversity of negotiating situations among the

1,100 public employers and 2,500 negotiating units (varying from three-man police departments to units with 30,000 or more employees), it would be difficult to devise legislation which would fit this wide variety of situations.

(b)   It subverts the authority of elected officials.

Negotiations under the Taylor Law are, in theory at least, between the Chief Executive and the employee organization on behalf of the public and as the public's agent. The Chief Executive is authorized to pursue his policies, and by entering into the contracts to obligate the government to carry out those policies. If disclosure of an agreement of the Chief Executive is not designed to induce renunciation or modification of that agreement, it is meaningless, adding nothing but costs and delay to ordinary disclosure requirements. If disclosure contemplates renunciation or modification of the agreement, it subverts the authority of the Chief Executive and imperils the negotiation process.

This analysis suggests one caveat. Most employee organizations require disclosure of their agreements to—and ratification by—their members. The possibility of the agreement of labor officials being renounced by their constituency is no less troublesome than the possibility of the agreement of a Chief Executive being renounced under pressure from his constituency. A case could be made for giving to the constituency of the Chief Executive an opportunity to be informed of an agreement before it is executed by the Chief Executive if the employee organization reserves to its members the right of ratification. We would not mandate such disclosure by law but recognize that under such circumstances, the government might choose to disclose the terms of the proposed agreement before executing it.

Discussion

The Study

In making his request of PERB to study the question of disclosure, the Governor said:

"The public has a right to know the full details of agreements reached with public employee groups. More often than not, these agreements involve large sums of public funds. At the same time every effort should be made to avoid interference with the collective negotiating process.

"I have, therefore, called upon the State Public Employment Relations Board to make specific recommendations on this subject, including any necessary amendments to the Taylor Law."

As noted earlier in this report, PERB expanded the inquiry to include disclosure at various stages of negotiations. Among those queried were the parties to actual impasses, media representatives and recognized labor relations experts. A discussion of the responses received from each group follows:

Media Responses

In discussions with representatives of the Public Employment Relations Board from time to time throughout the years, representatives of the media have generally taken a strong position that much, if not all, of the negotiating process should be "public." However, responses from media representatives were generally somewhat more conservative.

The following is a representative response:

"While there is one element of even public sector bargaining which concededly should be private—that is, the bargaining session itself (to assure the maximum opportunity for fruitful discussion and expeditious reaching of agreement), it is in the public interest that full and prompt public disclosure be made, presumably by a PERB spokesman, on the following points as they develop:

"1.   The issues.
"2.   The points of difference, including the sums of public money involved.
"3.   Progress or lack of progress in the negotiations.
"4.   The basis of agreement, including the amount of public money involved."

Another respondent stated:

"We agree wholeheartedly with the Governor's position that the public has a right to know the full details of agreements reached with public employee groups.

"We also feel that since public money is involved, there should be disclosure from the start of negotiations of what the employees are asking and what the employer is offering. . . ."

Another respondent, a distinguished long-time observer of the labor relations scene, said in part:

"The notion that disclosure interferes with the bargaining process has little validity in my experience. There might be something to be said for it if unions in the public sector clothe their bargainers with full power to conclude an agreement. Then, it could be argued that both sides ought to go

in prepared to put their best offers on the table, confident
that a final deal can be made.

"But, desirable as such a procedure would be in narrow
terms of the efficacy of bargaining, it has distinct flaws in a
period of institutional upheaval when union leaders are
hard pressed to hold their members in line even when the
contracts are superb in every respect. Rank and file ratification is a fact of life and must be reckoned with in unions
that were once the acme of conservatism.

"By the same token, taxpayers will have every right to
rebel if they keep finding themselves stuck with a *fait ac-
compli* that pushes up cost while necessitating reductions in
service. Such rebellion is even more likely where the basic
issues of public policy affecting schools, hospitals or other
vital agencies are determined by union and public management with no direct voice for the neighborhood or other
affected groups. Whatever embarrassments disclosing may
create, they are vastly preferable in a democracy to shutting
the public away from knowledge of things that the community has committed itself to until after the commitment
is irrevocable."

The essence of the media response would appear to be that
there should be disclosure with respect to the opening position
of the parties, limited disclosure during the course of negotiations
with periodic progress reports dealing with how far apart the
parties are or how near they are, but not necessarily with substance, and full disclosure once agreement has been reached.

Clientele Responses

Public Employers

The responses summarized below are those received from representatives of organizations representing public employers, e.g.,
Conference of Mayors, N.Y.S. School Boards Association, etc.
Answers received from public employers as such are summarized
in a later section dealing with questionnaire responses as previously indicated.

There appears to be substantial consensus among public employer representatives that there should be no disclosure until
the fact-finder has rendered his report and recommendations. If
no third-party assistance is required or if third-party assistance is
confined to mediation, there appears to be agreement that disclosure should not take place until the parties have ratified the
contract. Response to the specific questions are summarized
below:

1. During the course of negotiations without third-party assistance.

Employer representatives felt that the least possible disclosure should be made during the normal course of negotiations. The situation should be kept flexible. When either side makes public pronouncements of its position, it must then answer to its constituents for any deviation from the stated position. This has the effect of prolonging the negotiations and defeats the normal give-and-take which should be available to the negotiating teams.

2. During the course of mediation.

Mediation is an extension of the negotiating process with a third party present in an informal procedure. The considerations discussed under Question 1 were held to apply to Question 2.

3. During the course of fact-finding.

Fact-finding is a more formalized procedure for impasse resolution. However, none of the public employer representatives advocated making the fact-finding proceeding public or for disclosure of the positions of the parties during fact-finding.

4. After the fact-finder has rendered his report and recommendations but before agreement.

Section 209.3 (c) provides that a fact-finding report and recommendations shall be made public within five days of its transmission to the parties. Thus, at this point, some disclosure is mandated in that the fact-finding report in some manner is reported to the public. (See section on questionnaire responses below.) Representatives of public employers generally felt that public pressures have little effect upon employee groups. All the respondents agreed that the public does have a right to know prior to the legislative hearing. The opinion was expressed that if agreement had not been reached at this point, it would be difficult to predict when agreement would be reached. Therefore, the public employer, at least, should be free to make such disclosure as he sees fit at the time the fact-finder's report becomes public.

Section 209.3 (e) provides that if either party does not accept the fact-finder's recommendations in whole or in part, the chief executive officer shall, within ten days after receipt of the recommendations, submit to the legislative body both the fact-finding report and recommendations and his own recommendations for settling the dispute. The employee organization also is authorized to submit its recommendations.

The legislative body is then directed to "forthwith conduct a public hearing at which the parties shall be required to explain their positions with respect to the report of the fact-finding board." These provisions led to the following comments by one respondent:

> "These considerations lead me to conclude that the public's right to know about contracts with public employee groups arises at either of two points: when the contract has been negotiated *and executed*, or when agreement has not been possible and a public hearing is to be held on the fact-finder's report, and public opinion is to play its part in the legislative decision." The respondent added: "This conclusion is consistent with the rights and responsibilities that are a part of our representative system of government."

5. After agreement has been reached, but prior to employee ratification.

This question brought forth a two-part response. Assuming that negotiations have proceeded with no third-party assistance, there was agreement that public disclosure should await ratification by the parties. Full public disclosure should take place, employer associations felt, when ratification is accomplished so that the public may know what its elected representatives are doing and how public funds are being used.

If there has been fact-finding assistance, then the answers to Question 4 pertain—there should be disclosure simultaneously or shortly after the publication of the fact-finder's report and recommendations.

6. After agreement has been reached, but prior to the enactment of legislation required to implement the agreement.

At this point there was some disagreement. All agreed that there would be disclosure, but one respondent had a reservation:

> "To reveal all of the details of an agreement and heed public reaction is tantamount to allowing the public to veto the agreement, or, in fact, to be a party to the negotiations. In a representative form of government . . . the responsibility rests with the elected official to perform his duty . . . and a remedy for the voter who does not approve of his representative's actions is in the ballot box."

This particular respondent felt that the above quote pertained in a situation where the parties had arrived at an agreement without third-party assistance and where the legislature, of course, has not been required to make a determination but to implement an agreement bilaterally negotiated.

The final, but unnumbered question, was:

Should such disclosure as you consider to be appropriate be mandated by statute?

Significantly, none of the respondents felt that disclosure, in the sense of full publication of the text of the contract, should be mandated prior to legislative implementation. Some felt that this was not necessary at all. Others felt that the full text of the agreement should be published in an official newspaper after ratification and after implementation but within a specified period. An alternative would be to print the agreement and to make it available to all interested parties including employees, residents, etc. It was pointed out that to require publication of the full text of an agreement in an official newspaper would be to impose a substantial financial burden upon an employer, particularly if there were several units.

Public Employee Organizations. The views of parent labor organizations representing public employees also were solicited. The views of locals were solicited by questionnaire and are discussed in a later section of this report.

The views of the leadership of parent organizations representing public employees can best be summarized by the following comment:

"I have no quarrel with full disclosure after the contract has been agreed upon or certainly disclosure to the legislative body as legislation is needed. . . . Only after a contract is consummated and ratified would I give it full public disclosure. Labor relations, like international relations, is much too sensitive and difficult a process without putting it in the glare of public emotion. The public has a right to know— after it's negotiated. The . . . legislature should be kept fully informed in terms of the process of negotiations, the goals of negotiations. . . ."

Public employee union leadership was in general agreement that there should be no disclosure until:

1. Agreement has been reached and ratified; or
2. The matter is before the legislative body.

Panel Member Responses

Because of a wide variation in a number of impasses coming to the Public Employment Relations Board at various times of the year—half of the total impasses brought to the Board come in the second calendar quarter—and because PERB staff members do not engage in fact-finding the Board makes extensive use of panel mediators and fact-finders. These panel members are drawn from a variety of sources and have varying backgrounds and experience. The reactions of a sample of the members of the panel were sought to the same questions submitted to representatives of employer and employee organizations.

One panel respondent summarized the comments of most panel members who were queried.

"1.   No disclosure should be required or even encouraged during the stages of negotiations, mediation or fact-finding. Such disclosure would not only inhibit the making of offers and counterproposals *between* the parties, but might also cause serious problems of internal communications within the ranks of the bargainers. Just as one example, when I entered the XYZ school district negotiations last May, the parties had wasted ten entire bargaining sessions engaging in mutual recriminations about releases of information to the press. The minutes of these sessions reflect the progressive animosities which developed over the winter—feelings which had hardened to such an extent that absolutely no discussion had taken place on substantive issues. I was able to get the dispute settled by mediation only after both parties had agreed that no one (including the mediator) would talk to the press until settlement had been achieved, or until the mediator released the parties from their pledge of silence both to the press *and* to their constituents.

"2.   After a fact-finding report has been issued and following the expiration of the five-day negotiating period the Law already mandates the release of the report. I see nothing harmful in disclosure of the report at this point.

"3.   Once agreement has been reached, the parties themselves should agree on the ground rules for disclosure of the terms to their constituents. Otherwise, the agreement may blow up or be rejected because of mistrust, misunderstandings, or mutual recriminations.

"4.   After an agreement has been ratified and signed, I have no objection to its terms being disclosed before implementing legislation is enacted. In fact, such disclosure would seem to be in the public interest.

"5.   I am opposed to any form of disclosure being mandated by law. [It] could more appropriately be handled by administrative rule making."

Disagreement with the positions articulated above centered on two factors:

1.   The nature of the fact-finding process; and
2.   The problem of disclosure itself.

Those panelists who had different views were, nevertheless, in agreement that there should be no disclosure at least until the beginning of fact-finding.

Some of the panelists felt that certain advantages might flow from public fact-finding proceedings, and perhaps more formalized ones. One advocate of public fact-finding hearings, operating on the assumption that only organized public groups would participate, summarized his position this way:

"1. The immediate advantage, it seems to me, would result from allowing parent groups in teacher disputes and general taxpayer groups involving other classes of public employees to get at first hand all the facts relating to the dispute. . . .

"2. Participation by the public in the fact-finding proceeding may alert the disputants to adopt a reasonable and rational approach to the ultimate solution of the dispute.

"3. Since participation should assume a real recognition of the opinions and judgments of the participants, the third parties (taxpayer groups, et al.) will bring to the proceedings evidence of the public interest and thus may affect the positions of the disputants. . . .

"4. Psychologically, public participation may result in public acceptance of the findings and recommendations even when they may be at variance of the opinions of the public participants. The right to participate in itself is a form of due process which in time makes adverse decisions palatable and acceptable. . . .

"5. Exposure of the fact-finding proceedings to the glare of interested public groups may result in a reduction of the many peripheral issues commonly raised by the disputants under existing procedures. . . ."

The problem of *how* to disclose bothered some panelists. One put it this way:

"As you well know, there are at least two ways to multiplying and adding the same set of figures—employer's way and union's way—and at least one more way of doing it objectively . . . it may seem possible to avoid all this by merely listing tersely the items in the memorandum of agreement or list of demands without costing or explanation. But what will it mean to the public? Very little. . . .

"I see one possible avenue in the direction of involving the taxpayers. That is, in enlarging the concept of the 'legislative body' as responsive to the community as a whole. Provide that no settlement may be finalized until there is a public hearing on it by the legislative body—similar to the 'show cause' hearing on the fact-finder's report, but for both instances with mandated advance notice to the public—at least 25 days. That is, no settlement may be final until it has been 'shown' to the public and an opportunity given to them to react to it."

Another panelist, accepting the concept that there should be no disclosure until the fact-finder has reported, commented as follows:

"After the fact-finder has issued his report and recommendations, the rules of the game change. The fact-finder is the voice of the public and his document, once issued, becomes public property. At the same time, however, I am fully aware that a fact-finder's report is subject to modifications and exchanges by the parties and they should be given the opportunity to make these changes within a reasonable time after the report is issued, and a period of five days appears reasonable.

"The activities of the parties starting with the sixth day after the issuance of a fact-finder's report should be given the full public exposure and the element of distortion by the media is substantially reduced because the fact-finder's document contains in written form . . . all the ingredients of the dispute and thus it is relatively easier for the media to give accurate, objective information when this document is available as a foundation.

"As a statutory provision for disclosure, I would advise amendment of the existing language on legislative hearing which would require same to be held within a precise and exact time insofar as the public employer is concerned. In order to put an end point to delay by design, I would further recommend that the results of the legislative hearing must be publicly communicated by a time certain after the issuance of the fact-finder's report and failure to so communicate would constitute acceptance of the report as final and binding, that this is also true as to the public employee organization where the employee organization does assert a definitive position within a time certain, and I think 20 days would be ample for the parties. The public employee organization would be deemed to have accepted the report as a final and binding document in the case of failure to declare within the specified time. . . ."

Thus the position of the panelists can be summed up by saying that they were unanimous in holding that there should be no disclosure until the beginning of fact-finding. A few thought that public participation in the fact-finding process might be helpful, but the vast majority did not. All of the panelists appeared to be in agreement with the present provision of the Taylor Law which requires disclosure of the fact-finding report and recommendations five days after receipt by the parties.

There was disagreement, and fairly wide disagreement, among the panelists as to whether some form of disclosure should be mandated by law. Many felt that if such action was required it could be done by administrative rule. They felt that this procedure would allow for some experimentation and less rigidity if whatever was proposed did not work.

Those panelists who felt that some form of disclosure should be mandated after issuance of the fact-finding report coupled such proposals with proposed modifications of the impasse procedure.

"Expert" Respondents

A variety of labor relations "experts" also were canvassed. These included members of the Taylor Committee, heads of public sector labor relations agencies in other states, academic experts, and distinguished practitioners.

In those states which have "anti-secrecy" statutes, the mediation process is either exempt from such laws or the process has escaped being affected by such laws. In Michigan, a school board which insisted that the press be present during negotiations was held to be guilty of bad faith bargaining. In Wisconsin the Supreme Court held, contrary to the ruling of the Labor Relations agency, that a school board did not interfere with the rights of an employee who was a member of a minority organization by denying that individual the opportunity to speak at a public hearing conducted by the school board with reference to the negotiated agreement. All of the heads of the state labor relations agencies with public sector responsibilities canvassed were essentially in agreement. Their position can best be summarized by the following response:

> "It has been our opinion that once the collective bargaining agreement has been tentatively approved by the negotiators for the public employer [and the] union, the details of the agreement should be made known. All three of the Commissioners—as well as our two staff men who do quite a bit of public speaking—have taken this position. We do so on the basis you state in your letter: that the agreements most often involve large sums of public funds and that the public is entitled to know."

There only disagreement among administrators of state agencies is *when* there should be disclosure. Some feel that disclosure should occur at the tentative agreement stage while others contend that disclosure should not occur until after ratification.

Other experts and practitioners canvassed were similarly divided on this point. One stated:

". . . when agreement is reached by negotiators, there are often very delicate situations involved in achieving ratification, sometimes on both sides—by the union's general membership or by the legislative body involved. For this reason it is probably advisable to guard against premature release of the terms of the contract because of possible interference with the ratification. While I recognize the strength of the argument that the people who pay the bills should be entitled to know the cost of the agreement before it is finalized, I am experienced enough in the bargaining process to realize that such disclosure would make agreement more difficult to achieve. We must rely on the good faith of the municipal negotiators and the power of the public to change them by the process of recall or election, to assure the community that the agreement is a sound one.

"On the other hand, I do believe that a great deal more can be done to inform the public of the actual cost of finalized agreements—after ratification—so that they may be in a better position to judge the correctness of the agreement which has been acted upon. I refer to effective costing out of fringe benefits in general and pensions in particular. . . ."

Other groups of respondents were as concerned with the "how" of disclosure as with the "when" of disclosure. Among the academic-practitioner respondents concerned with this question, the following is a typical comment:

"The 'how' question is even more difficult. Even in the public sector, I have grave reservations about the ability of the general public to digest and appraise complicated issues. Simple publication of the terms usually is somewhat a waste of paper since few people will read a complete agreement. Moreover, even if they do, most people outside of the immediate scene cannot intelligently appraise the terms. Consequently well-written summaries that are interpretive are almost required. Who is to do this job? Good labor reporters are increasingly hard to find. Moreover, whoever prepares a summary can always be accused, sometimes rightly, of 'slanting the story.' I suspect that there is no perfect way of meeting these problems. The mediator, or the fact-finder, or

P.R. personnel in the agency can be most helpful in the preparation of an accurate and understandable summary but some risks are involved. Probably the potential values are worth the risk."

Responses of Parties

The comments from the parties generally opposed disclosure citing reasons as inhibiting the negotiations process, creating a fish bowl effect and polarizing the parties.

One employer replied:

"If agreements are made public before ratification, political pressures to turn down negotiated agreements will be brought against the legislative body with the only possible results being the rejection of negotiated agreements in greater numbers than have existed in the past and even greater distrust of the negotiating procedure on the part of employee organizations than at present."

The replies as to the actual amount of disclosure indicate that there was very little public disclosure. . . .

Most of the clients responding did not favor additional disclosure. Majorities ranging from 90 to 60 per cent were opposed to more disclosure. The highest vote for more disclosure was for releasing the fact-finding report to the public and the press at the same time it is released to the parties. Slightly under 40 per cent of the respondents favored this step.

There was slightly less support for public fact-finding hearings. The support for this viewpoint was strongest by employers. More than 44 per cent of them supported this idea. However, it seemed apparent that many of the replies favoring more disclosure were not advocating public policy but were advancing ideas that they thought would have aided their cause in recent negotiations.

In the instances in which there was public disclosure, the side making it often claimed that the "public" supported their side. It seems apparent that public disclosure is not being used as a means of informing the citizens but rather as a means of marshalling support for their respective position. There also were several comments that indicated that disclosure inhibited flexibility and compromise.

In terms of public impact, the comments varied from no impact to support of position by community (on both sides). There were several comments that positions as reported by media were distorted. However, in most cases the impact of the community toward reaching an agreement even after the fact-finder's report was published appeared to be slight. Those who commented on attendance at legislative hearings indicated that the public did not attend.

BASSETT v. BRADDOCK
Florida Supreme Court
262 So. 2d 425 (Fla. 1972)

DEKLE, Justice. We affirm on this direct appeal the findings and judgments of the learned chancellor. An injunction was sought by certain Dade County citizens as plaintiffs (appellants) against Appellees-Dade County School Board for alleged failure to comply with the so-called "Government in the Sunshine" law.[1] Dade County Classroom Teachers' Assoc., Inc., was intervenor upon counterclaim for declaratory decree as to teachers' "collective bargaining" rights. The injunction was properly denied; the declaratory decree was correct as to "bargaining rights."

The principal issues are framed as follows:

1.   Whether labor negotiators employed by the Board in preliminary or tentative teacher contract negotiations with the teachers' representatives may negotiate outside of public meetings without being in violation of the "Sunshine Law"?

2.   Whether the Board may instruct and consult with its labor negotiators in private without such violation?

The appeal is from the chancellor's affirmative answers to these queries. We affirm.

The constitutional question vesting jurisdiction in this Court (Fla. Const. art. V, § 4(2)), F.S.A. relates to Fla. Const. art. I, § 6, which guarantees collective bargaining for employees.[2] See also this Court's expression thereon in Dade County Classroom Teachers' Assoc., Inc. v. Ryan, 225 So. 2d 903 (Fla. 1969).

Implementing legislation unfortunately has not yet been passed to give guidance and meaning to this vital constitutional protec-

---

[1] Fla. Stat. § 286.011 F.S.A.: *"Public meetings and records; public inspection; penalties.*— (1) All meetings of any board or commission of any state agency or authority or of any agency or authority of any county, municipal corporation or any political subdivision, *except as otherwise provided in the constitution, at which official acts are to be taken* are declared to be public meetings open to the public at all times, and no resolution, rule, regulation or *formal action* shall be considered binding except as taken or made at such meeting. (2) The minutes of a meeting of any such board or commission of any such state agency or authority shall be promptly recorded and such records shall be open to public inspection. The circuit courts of this state shall have jurisdiction to issue injunctions to enforce the purposes of this section upon application by any citizens of this state." (emphasis ours)

[2] *"Section 6. Right to Work.*—The right of persons to work shall not be denied or abridged on account of membership or nonmembership in any labor union or labor organization. The right of employees, by and through a labor organization, to bargain collectively shall not be denied or abridged. **Public employees shall not have the right to strike."**

tion. Public employees are also entitled to their place in the "sunshine." At the 1972 regular legislative session, which is the third since passage of this 1968 provision, proposals in this regard have again been considered without passage. It is to be hoped that this will in time reach fruition. Meanwhile, however, this Court remains hesitant to allow itself to be propelled into "judicial implementation." For purposes of this appeal, therefore, we merely affirm the lower court's action in these respects. To do otherwise could well deny the public employees' rights to "bargain collectively" as guaranteed by Fla. Const. art. I, § 6. Such "intensity" of the "sunrays" under the statute, as urged by this appeal, could cause a damaging case of "sunburn" to these employees or to the public which elected the Board. It quite possibly would conflict with the protective umbrella of the constitutional guarantee of § 6.

Here we have a literal *constitutional* exception expressly provided within the Sunshine Law which states: ". . . except as otherwise provided in the *constitution*. . . ." (emphasis ours) The "sunshine" of the statute is still afforded in the debate and adoption of the ultimate employment contract at a public meeting but with the constitutional polaroid filter from the damaging "ultra violet rays" of preliminary skirmishing.

The able chancellor's finding as to bargaining negotiations was based on impressive, uncontroverted testimony by respectable national authorities in the field, that meaningful collective bargaining in the circumstances here would be destroyed if full publicity were accorded at each step of the negotiations. It would pit the public body as a virtual "David" without benefit of "sling" against the Goliath champion (negotiators) for 7,500 employees in this immediate case and over 200,000 employees who could be ultimately involved.

The public's representatives must be afforded at least an equal position with that enjoyed by those with whom they deal. The public should not suffer a handicap at the expense of a purist view of open public meetings, so long as the ultimate debate and decisions are public and the "official acts" and "formal action" specified by the statute are taken in open "public meetings." This affords the adequate and effective protection to the public on the side of the "right to know" which was intended.

The Board's employed attorney for the negotiations ("negotiator") was employed in public; he had no authority to bind the Board (and in fact his recommendations were later modified by the Board in open meetings) ; he made his report to the Board in public where the discussions were spirited and the ultimate vote was 4 to 3! Full consideration of the *recommendations* of the Board's negotiator was accordingly had in a public meeting and aired and voted upon in public. Those recommendations were in a sense simply the acorn from which the final contract grew—in the sunshine. There is no violation.

Appellants urge that the Act and our prior decisions compel public meetings for "not only formal acts, but also acts of deliberation, discussion and deciding, occurring, prior to and leading up to affirmative formal action." While conceding that our opinions have been as broad as possible to let in the sunshine under the Legislature's enactment, nevertheless a careful rereading of our opinions and the Act fail to support the foregoing contention. It was not specifically involved in our prior decisions which have dealt principally with "meetings" (some informal) of a board. We have in earlier opinions referred to "matters on which foreseeable action will be taken by the Board" and "any discussions on matters pertaining to the duties and responsibilities of the Board of Public Instruction of Broward County." These are broad considerations but they still do not invade the areas of deliberation here involved, for it will be noted that in all of these observations by the Court, they are predicated upon a "meeting." Here the required action under the statutes *was* taken in a public meeting; changes were made and voting had, all in public. The *discussions* and *deliberations,* however, in an executive process often take place beyond the veil of actual "meetings" of the body involved. It is only in those "meetings" that official action is taken. Preliminary "discussions" may never result in any action taken. There may be numerous informal exchanges of ideas and possibilities, either among members or with others (at the coke machine, in a foyer, etc.) when there is no relationship at all to any meeting at which any foreseeable action is contemplated.[9] Such things germinate gradually and often without really knowing whether any action or meeting will grow out of the exchanges or thinking.

---

[9] Massachusetts has a "right-to-know" law. Massachusetts General Laws, Annot. Ch. 39, § 23A (Supp. 1969). An Attorney General opinion has held this law to be inapplicable to collective bargaining sessions conducted between negotiators.

"After careful considerations, I have concluded that this statute does not apply to collective bargaining sessions with school employees. The decisive point is that such sessions are not 'meetings' within the meaning of that term in the statute. The meetings to which the statute refers are rather those in which the internal discussions, deliberations and voting of an agency are of public concern. A collective bargaining session, on the other hand, is a meeting at which the employer and employees are engaged in a process of an interchange and analysis of each other's proposals and counterproposals. This is a different kind of process from that involved in the conduct of an agency's internal deliberations or the making of its official decisions." Letter from State Attorney General to Commissioner of Education, Owen B. Kiernan, Sept. 12, 1967,

Every action emanates from thoughts and creations of the mind and exchanges with others. These are perhaps "deliberations" in a sense but hardly demanded to be brought forward in the spoken word at a public meeting. To carry matters to such an extreme approaches the ridiculous; it would defeat any meaningful and productive process of government. One must maintain perspective on a broad provision such as this legislative enactment, in its application to the actual workings of an active Board fraught with many and varied problems and demands.

As to the second issue—the Board instructing its negotiator in private—it likewise follows that this is authorized on the same grounds and reasoning above. The "other side" (teachers' negotiator) is being "coached" and given advices privately and from time to time during the bargaining period; it is only common sense and fair play that "our team" have the same advantage in order to be effective in his efforts. It might be noted that in a case like the present where the negotiator is an *attorney* that certainly he is entitled to consult with the Board on matters regarding preliminary advices.[10] He is also thereby guided toward an effective result. It is not that appellees are "hiding" anything but simply trying to get the best "bargain" available for the public schools and not to be placed at a disadvantage in their efforts. It therefore follows that this is not in violation of the "Sunshine Law" for the Board to instruct and to consult with its labor negotiator in private without it being a violation of § 286.011. . . .

Affirmed.

CARLTON and McCAIN, JJ., and DREW, J. (Retired), concur.

[The concurring opinion of Chief Justice Roberts is omitted.]

ADKINS, Justice (dissenting) :

---

p. 3.—As quoted from The Law and Practice of Teacher Negotiations by Wollett and Chanin, p. 4:2.

This is also the view of the Attorney General of Wisconsin, where the statute provides that no formal action of any kind may be introduced, deliberated upon, or adopted at any closed meeting of the school board. The Attorney General's informal opinion reads as follows:

"I believe it may be broadly stated that preliminary negotiations between a representative of a municipal employer and a representative of its employees are not subject to requirements of Sec. 14.90, Stats., (Anti-Secrecy Law), but that deliberations and adoption of any specific recommendation on the part of the municipality must comply with that statute. School Board and Teacher Negotiations in Wisconsin Public Schools at pp. 11-12, Wisconsin Assn. of School Boards, Winneconne, Wisconsin (1967), as stated in Wollett and Chanin, supra."

[10] The Sacramento Newspaper Guild v. The Sacramento County Board of Supervisors, 263 Cal. App. 2d 41, 69 Cal. Rptr. 480 (1968), cf. Times Publ. Co. v. Williams, 222 So. 2d 470, 475–476 (2d DCA Fla. 1969).

I dissent. The questions involved in this litigation would never have arisen if the Legislature by statute had implemented the provisions of Fla. Const. art. I (Declaration of Rights), § 6, F.S.A., reading:

"The right of employees, by and through a labor organization, to bargain collectively shall not be denied or abridged. Public employees shall not have the right to strike."

In limiting our consideration of this case solely to the powers of the judicial branch of government, we should only determine whether or not Fla. Stat. § 286.011 (government in the sunshine law), F.S.A., is applicable to collective bargaining by public employees.

Thus far the government in the sunshine law has withstood various attacks where a few misguided local boards and agencies have attempted to seek a means by which they could circumvent the law so as to resume secret meetings.

Appellees say that meaningful collective bargaining would be destroyed if full publicity were accorded at each step of the negotiations. It should be recognized that every taxpayer is an interested party in negotiations concerning the salaries to be paid public employees. The members of the school board are mere representatives of the public and any action taken by the school board is the action of the public.

We have previously defined a secret meeting in the following language:

"A secret meeting occurs when public officials meet at a time and place to avoid being seen or heard by the public. When at such meetings officials mentioned in Fla. Stat. § 286.011, F.S.A., transact or agree to transact public business at a future time in a certain manner they violate the government in the sunshine law, regardless of whether the meeting is formal or informal." City of Miami Beach v. Berns, 245 So. 2d 38, 41 (Fla. 1971).

Also in Board of Public Instruction of Broward County v. Doran, 224 So. 2d 693 (Fla. 1969), we held that the statute was intended to cover any gathering dealing with some matter on which foreseeable action would be taken by the Board.

The statute does not make reference to the existence of a quorum, so that a meeting of any agency or authority of the Board may be a public meeting which should be open to the public at all times. The important question is not whether a quorum must be present, but whether the agency or authority of the Board deals with any matter on which foreseeable action may be taken by the Board.

The right of the public to be present, to be heard, and to participate should not be circumvented by having secret meetings of various committees appointed by the Board and vested with authority to make recommendations or suggestions to the Board concerning a matter on which foreseeable action may be taken. It is true that during the early years of our democracy public officials felt that most meetings concerning governmental decisions should be secret, but they soon became aware that an enlightened public is the foremost safeguard for the continued existence of our form of government. It is even more important that local boards, subject to the immediate scrutiny of the local citizen, be required to conduct their meeting in the presence of those who will be directly affected by the decisions of the Board. This is a renovation of the "town hall meeting" where public officials were able to secure the benefit of the thoughts and ideas of those most interested in government—that is, the citizens who pay the taxes.

The government in the sunshine law prevents the Board from functioning secretly under the guise of small committees. If this were done, each member would have an opportunity to commit himself on some matter, on which foreseeable action will be taken, by expressing himself at a secret committee meeting in the absence of the public and without giving the public an opportunity to be heard. The ultimate action of the entire Board in public meetings would merely be an affirmation of the various secret committee meetings held in violation of the law.

There is testimony, and the trial judge held, that meaningful collective bargaining would be destroyed if full publicity were accorded at each step of the negotiations. Therefore, the trial judge held that the statute would be unconstitutional if applied to collective bargaining, as Fla. Const., art. I, § 6, F.S.A., guarantees the right to "bargain collectively." It is also said that the public's representative must be afforded at least an equal position with that enjoyed by those with whom they deal. Such reasoning overlooks the provision in the constitution which prohibits strikes by public employees, thereby removing the only weapon by which labor may insure good faith collective bargaining.

In other words, the constitution contemplates open collective bargaining in good faith without secrecy and without strikes. The standards of performance in bargaining collectively as contemplated in the National Labor Relations Act are discussed in The Law of Labor Relations, by Werne, at page 255.

"While the Act, as amended, defines the duty to bargain collectively, it leaves to the Board and to the courts the determination of what tests shall be applied for the purpose of ascertaining whether employers and unions are performing such duty. The standard of performance is said to be negotiation in good faith to the end that agreement shall be reached with respect to wages, hours and conditions of work, and reduction of the agreement to a signed contract for a fixed reasonable period. Mere gestures in such a direction do not constitute collective bargaining. Nor does the requirement that the employees submit a list of demands, which are either accepted or rejected without explanation, satisfy the requirements.

"The submission of proposals by a union or by an employer, with a 'take-it-or-else' attitude, does not constitute collective bargaining. 'Negotiations with an intent only to delay and postpone a settlement until a strike can be broken' are not collective bargaining.

" 'Interchange of ideas, communication of facts peculiarly within the knowledge of either party, personal persuasion, and the opportunity to modify demands in accordance with the total situation thus revealed at the conference is of the essence of the bargaining process.'

"The nature of the good-faith requirement indicates that whether the standard of performance is met will depend on the facts in each case where the issue is raised. The guide posts for performance and the manifestations of non-performance are considered in connection with refusals to bargain collectively."

The primary requirement is good faith. Certainly, negotiations in public would not detract from good faith bargaining. In fact, it may be said that bad faith emanates from closed doors. There is no case cited which requires that collective bargaining negotiation must be behind closed doors; therefore, for the Court to make this an exception to the government in the sunshine law would be legislation.

It is within the province of the Legislature, as a matter of policy, to determine whether collective bargaining should be an exception to the government in the sunshine law. I express no opinion on such a matter of public policy, but believe that it is not a violation of Fla. Const., art. I, § 6, F.S.A., to require such collective bargaining to take place in public at a public meeting.

In Board of Public Instruction of Broward County v. Doran, *supra*, we held that the statute did not authorize secret meetings on privileged matter. Under this decision the instructions to the negotiator should also be a matter of public concern. Even though this may, on its face, seem to give the negotiator for the teacher an unfair advantage, it will be necessary for him to bargain in good faith with full knowledge that his position cannot be enhanced by the use of the one weapon which ensures true collective bargaining in the classical sense, the strike. This puts each side on an equal footing so that public negotiation may result in benefits to the teachers, the Board, and the public. The Board is without benefit of secrecy and the teachers are without benefit of the threat of strike. . . .

BOYD, J., concurs.

NOTES

1. The Michigan Board in Menominee Board of Education, 1968 MERC Lab. Op. 383, 386, held that a party's insistence on bargaining in public constituted a refusal to negotiate in good faith, reasoning:

> Collective bargaining cannot be effective in the presence of either press or public. Representatives of employer and labor organizations (perhaps because they are human) tend to speak for the public and the news media rather than engage in the collective bargaining procedure. . . .
> We will not impose on the parties the obligation to bargain in a public arena if they are unwilling to do so. Such an obligation would tend to prolong negotiations and damage the procedure of compromise inherent in collective bargaining.

In Mayor Samuel E. Zoll and the City of Salem, MLRC Case No. MUP-309 (1972), the Massachusetts Labor Relations Commission held that a proposal for public view bargaining is not a mandatory subject of bargaining and that, therefore, an employer's insistence on public view bargaining "as a precondition to any agreement is unlawful as a failure to bargain in good faith." The MLRC also held that such insistence unlawfully interfered with the employees' right to bargain through representatives of their own choosing since a natural consequence of such insistence was "that negotiations be conducted in the presence of the rank and file members of the bargaining unit. . . ." *Accord,* Bethlehem Area School Directors, Penn. Lab. Rel. Bd. Case No. PERA-C-2861-C, GERR No. 505, E-1 (1973). On the other hand, the Connecticut State Board of Labor Relations in Town of Stratford, Decision No. 1069 (1972), held "that the publicity to be given to the initial proposals, as well as to any other stages of the negotiations, are mandatory subjects of bargaining." In so ruling, the Board held that a public employer committed an unfair labor practice when it unilaterally promulgated an ordinance which required its chief bargaining representative to "furnish to the Council Clerk of the Town Council and to the Town Clerk, a copy of the initial entire salary and other proposals, and subsequent proposals if increased, submitted for negotiation by said organizations or association, whether oral or written, as soon as practicable, but no later than ten (10) days after receipt of same."

2.　Whether the parties are required to bargain in public is occasionally set forth in the applicable act. The Minnesota Public Employment Labor Relations Act provides that "All negotiations, mediation sessions, and hearings between public employers and public employees or their respective representatives shall be public meetings, except when otherwise provided by the Director [of the Bureau of Mediation Services]." MINN. STAT. ANN. ch. 179, § 179.69 (2) (1973). The Montana Professional Negotiations Act for Teachers provides that "Professional negotiating sessions between employers and teachers, or their representatives, may be open to the public, but meetings of school boards wherein professional negotiating proposals are discussed prior to any professional negotiating sessions shall be closed to the public." MONT. REV. CODES ANN. § 75-6127 (1971).

3.　Is it an unfair labor practice for a public employer or a public employee union to insist upon using a tape recorder or having a stenographer take a verbatim transcript of bargaining sessions? The NLRB has held that such insistence constitutes, in many situations, bad faith bargaining. See, e.g., Architectural Fibre Glass, Div. of Architectural Pottery, 165 N.L.R.B. 238 (1967); Reed & Prince Mfg. Co., 96 N.L.R.B. 850 (1951), enf'd 205 F.2d 131 (1st Cir.), cert. denied, 346 U.S. 887 (1953). The reasons why insistence upon a verbatim transcript of collective bargaining sessions has been viewed as being inconsistent with the duty to bargain collectively were set forth in the following excerpt from the concurring opinion of Members Fanning and Brown in St. Louis Typographical Union No. 8, 149 N.L.R.B. 750, 754-55 (1964):

> Although, by mutual consent, parties have engaged reporters to make verbatim records of collective-bargaining sessions, many authorities and practitioners in the field are of the opinion that the presence of a stenographer at such meetings has an inhibiting effect. The use of a stenographer or a mechanical recorder to create a verbatim transcript does

tend to encourage negotiators to concentrate upon and speak for the purpose of making a record rather than directing their efforts toward a solution of the issues before them. The existence of mutual trust and confidence between the parties is basic to an effective and harmonious collective-bargaining relationship. Yet, as in the instant case, the very suggestion that a verbatim record be made may raise suspicions as to the ultimate use for which it is to be put and, thereby, inject into the relationship an added basis for mistrust and contention. Imposing a stenographer upon a negotiator who, in good faith, believes that the presence of the reporter will only inhibit his ability to bargain effectively can only serve to undermine and seriously impair the collective-bargaining process. Recent studies indicate that both management and unions recognize these inhibiting factors and predominantly tend to avoid the use of a stenographer.

The very nature of the proposal to make a stenographic transcript of all bargaining sessions is such that the matter should be weighed carefully before it is advanced and, if any opposition thereto is expressed, it should be withdrawn. An adamant insistence upon such a demand in the context of present day bargaining is itself, in our opinion, a rejection of the bargaining duty. We would, therefore, hold that requiring a transcript, whether at the option of one of the parties, as proposed by the Employer here, or by means of collective bargaining, as suggested by the majority decision, constitutes an undermining of the collective-bargaining relationship. . . .

The foregoing concurring opinion of Members Fanning and Brown was quoted with approval by the Massachusetts Labor Relations Commission in Mayor Samuel E. Zoll and the City of Salem, MLRC Case No. MUP-309 (1972). *Cf.* Town of New Canaan, Conn. St. Bd. of Labor Rel. Decision No. 865 (1969) (law requiring executive or administrative bodies to report proceedings of meeting not applicable to bargaining sessions).

While making a verbatim transcript of bargaining sessions is frowned upon and may constitute an unfair labor practice, keeping accurate minutes of bargaining sessions is considered essential by most practitioners. As Edward B. Shils and C. Taylor Whittier have observed,

It is very important that the school board negotiating team have a resource person who is so familiar with the problems and the subject matters being discussed that he can keep a running record of questions and answers as well as issues settled. These minutes should be reviewed before each new session. They are important records for the board, the superintendent, and the advisory committee. We do not recommend using a tape recording machine. It is bad for morale on both sides to know that every word is being recorded. There is something harmful about this technique and we believe that it violates the requirement for good faith and good fellowship.

On the other hand, a good fast writer, or a team member blessed with stenographic skills, is most valuable in taking notes that can be used by joint subcommittees charged to draft language and to iron out problems of wording and intent. These notes will be worth their weight in gold when the school board attorney meets with his opposite number to write the final language of the contract: one side or the other may make charges that the language of the final draft is different from understandings reached at the bargaining table. E. SHILS & C.T. WHITTIER, TEACHERS, ADMINISTRATORS, AND COLLECTIVE BARGAINING 400 (1968).

Chapter 5

UNION SECURITY IN PUBLIC EMPLOYMENT

A. Introduction

There are five basic types of union security provisions—closed shop, union shop, maintenance of membership, agency shop, and dues checkoff. The general characteristics of each of these forms of union security are as follows:

1. *Closed Shop.* A closed shop provision requires that an employee as a condition of employment must become a member of the union prior to being employed and must remain a member. The closed shop was lawful under the National Labor Relations Act as originally enacted in 1935, but since 1947 has been prohibited under the Taft-Hartley Amendments. For all intents and purposes the closed shop is illegal in both the public and private sectors.

2. *Union Shop.* A union shop clause requires that an employee as a condition of employment become a member of the union within a stipulated period, usually 30 days, after being hired or after the effective date of the collective bargaining agreement, whichever is later. The NLRA specifically provides that private sector employers and unions may negotiate union shop agreements, except where such agreements are prohibited by state right-to-work laws. Sixty-two per cent of the collective bargaining agreements negotiated in the private sector include union shop clauses. BNA, COLLECTIVE BARGAINING NEGOTIATIONS AND CONTRACTS 87:1. In the public sector Alaska, Kentucky, Vermont, and Washington have legislatively authorized the negotiation of union shop provisions. The Alaska law, ALAS. STAT. ch. 40, § 23.40.110 (b) (1) (Supp. 1972), specifically provides:

> Nothing in this chapter prohibits a public employer from making an agreement with an organization to require as a condition of employment (1) membership in the organization which represents the unit on or after the 30th day following the beginning of employment or on the effective date of the agreement, whichever is later.

The Kentucky fire fighter statute which is only applicable to the City of Louisville and the Vermont municipal act contain virtually identical provisions. KY. REV. STAT. ch. 345, § 345.50 (1) (c) (Supp. 1972) ; VT. STAT. ANN. tit. 21, § 1726 (8) (Supp. 1973).

The Washington statute covering teachers in institutions of higher education provides that following certification the exclusive bargaining representative may request an election to determine whether a majority of the employees in the bargaining unit approve of requiring membership in the certified exclusive bargaining representative as a condition of employment on or after the 30th day following the beginning of employment or the date of such election, whichever is the later. The statute provides that "the failure of an employee to comply with such condition of employment shall constitute cause for dismissal." Like the NLRA, membership for this purpose is "satisfied by the payment of monthly or other periodical dues." There is also a special provision "to safeguard the right of nonassociation of public employees based on bona fide religious tenets or teachings of a church or religious body of which such public employee is a member. . . ." WASH. REV. CODE § 28B.16.100 (1) (1973).

3. *Maintenance of Membership.* A maintenance of membership clause requires that once an employee becomes a member of a union he must continue to be a member as a condition of employment. There is no requirement, however, that an employee initially become a member. Maintenance of membership agreements are permitted under the NLRA, although they are prohibited in those states with right-to-work laws. Only one state—Pennsylvania—specifically permits public employers and unions to negotiate maintenance of membership clauses. PA. STAT. ANN. tit. 43, § 1101.705 (Supp. 1972). Presumably, however, maintenance of membership clauses would also be permissible in states that permit the negotiation of union shop clauses.

4. *Agency Shop.* An agency shop clause requires that an employee as a condition of employment pay an amount equal to the periodic union dues uniformly required as a condition of acquiring or retaining membership. The agency shop is legal under the NLRA, but is prohibited by most state right-to-work laws. The negotiation of agency shop clauses—increasingly referred to as "fair share" agreements by public sector unions— is specifically permitted by law in at least seven states: Alaska, ALAS. STAT. ch. 40, § 23.40.110 (b) (2) (Supp. 1972) ; Michigan, MICH. COMP. LAWS ANN. § 423.210(1)(c), as amended by Act 25, L. 1973; Montana, MONT. REV. CODES ANN. ch. 441, § 5(1)

(c), L. 1973, GERR Ref. File 51:3512; Oregon, ORE. LAWS ch. 536, § 4(1)(c), L. 1973, GERR Ref. File 51:4612; Rhode Island, R.I. GEN. LAWS ANN. tit. 26, ch. 11, § 36-11-2 (1972) ; Vermont, VT. STAT. ANN. tit. 21, § 1726 (8) (Supp. 1973) ; and Wisconsin (municipal employees), WIS. STAT. ANN. § 111.70 (h) (Supp. 1972). In sharp contrast to these statutory provisions which permit the parties to voluntarily agree upon an agency shop clause, the Hawaii public sector law requires an employer, wholly independent of negotiations, to deduct from the pay of all employees in the appropriate unit services fees and remit same to the exclusive representative "upon receiving from an exclusive representative a written statement which specifies an amount of reasonable service fees necessary to defray the costs for its services rendered in negotiating and administering an agreement and computed on a pro rata basis among all employees within its appropriate bargaining unit. . . ." HAWAII REV. STAT. tit. 7, § 89-4 (Supp. 1971). Similarly, the Minnesota law provides that "the employer upon notification by the exclusive representative . . . shall be obligated to check off" from non-members "a fair share fee for services rendered by the exclusive representative." MINN. STAT. ANN. § 179.65 (2) (Supp. 1973). Massachusetts has analogous statutory provisions applicable to the City of Boston and Suffolk County. MASS. ANN. LAWS ch. 335, § 61-2 (Amend. 1969).

5. *Dues Checkoff.* Although not technically considered as such, the dues checkoff is, as a practical matter, a form of union security and will be so considered for the purposes of this chapter. A dues checkoff clause typically provides that upon receipt of a written authorization from an employee the employer will deduct from the employee's pay his periodic union dues and remit same directly to the union. Most of the comprehensive public sector collective bargaining laws specifically permit the checkoff of union dues. In addition, several states that have not enacted public sector bargaining laws have specific statutory provisions that permit the checkoff of union dues.

B. General Policy Considerations

NEW YORK STATE COMMISSION ON THE QUALITY, COST, AND FINANCING OF ELEMENTARY AND SECONDARY EDUCATION, Vol. 3, Appendix 13C, pp. 10-16 (1972)

The Commission has considered whether it ought to recommend to the Legislature that the Taylor Law be amended so as to authorize public employers and employee organizations to negotiate some form of organizational security provision. Since it is unlikely that the Legislature would consider authorizing the union shop because of the serious constitutional questions raised by compulsory membership, our discussion and tentative recommendations will concern only the agency shop.

There have been a number of cogent arguments advanced in support of legislative authorization of the agency shop. Foremost among them is the "free rider" argument: if it is public policy that public employees be granted collective bargaining rights, and that public employers be required to enter into collective agreements with organizations representing these employees, then it follows that those employees benefiting from this new arrangement have some obligation to lend financial support to the organization that wins these benefits. In short, the employee organization, through its authority to participate in the bilateral determination of economic benefits and other quasi policy issues, now serves a public purpose. To require employees to lend financial support to an employee organization is but the counterpart of requiring citizens to pay taxes to support local and state governments.

A second argument often advanced in support of legislative authorization of the agency shop is that those employers granting this provision find generally that their labor relations have become more stabilized. It is usually very difficult for rival organizations to unseat an incumbent organization when all employees in the bargaining unit are already paying dues. This means not only that the employer will be relatively free from the problems posed by frequent changes in bargaining agents, but also that there will be less pressure on the incumbent to outdo the "out" organization by becoming more strident in its pronouncements and more intransigent in its bargaining posture. By the same token, an agency shop allows the employee organization to become somewhat immune from the sometimes unreasonable demands of dissidents within the ranks; such dissidents lack the numerical strength to unseat current leadership, and there is no rival organization to which they can turn.

A third argument in support of legalizing agency shop arrangements is that they provide the employer with a certain amount of sorely needed bargaining leverage, yet at no cost to the taxpayer or to management prerogatives. If school management is determined to bargain hard on this issue—for example, if it refuses to grant the agency shop concession unless the employee organization agrees to remove some undesirable features from the existing contract—it is conceivable that certain gains, particularly in the area of administrative efficiency, will be achieved.

How persuasive are these arguments? To most teacher leaders, and probably to a majority of labor relations experts as well, they are quite persuasive. Yet there are counterarguments, and these too have cogency.

First, an agency shop provision would probably reduce by a significant degree whatever political leverage "satellite" personnel now enjoy within the employee organization. The language of criterion (c) of Section 207 of the Taylor Law, "the unit shall be compatible with the joint responsibilities of the public employer and public employees to serve the public," has generally been construed to mean that it is not in the public interest to fragment or "balkanize" bargaining units. Thus such satellite groups as counselors, nurse teachers, librarians and sometimes department chairmen and assistant principals are deemed to share a community of interest with teachers and are therefore included in the latter's bargaining units. To establish separate bargaining units for each of the above groups would not only invite whipsawing and leapfrogging tactics—to the detriment of both the employer and the public—but also require the employer to spend virtually all his time negotiating with each of the dozen or so bargaining agents representing these various groups.

Consequently, a number of nonteaching school employees are locked into the teacher unit. Relatively few in number, they lack political influence with the teacher organization leadership, which must direct most of its attention to winning benefits for the dominant political majority, the teachers. Thus satellite employees can only hope that when bargaining benefits are distributed the leadership will be generous. If such is not the case, under present circumstances they can threaten to withdraw membership. Thus the employee organization is instructed that even though satellite votes may not have much influence, there are other options open to them.

Under an agency shop arrangement it would not be possible to exercise this kind of leverage. Thus the complaints heard even now from satellite employees about the failure of the teacher organization to represent them fairly, will most assuredly be increased as teacher organizations become more politicized (majoritarian) and budget stringencies more acute.

As for the argument that the agency shop would engender greater stability in employer-employee relations, little can be said in opposition. Certainly the incumbent organization would become relatively immune from raids by rival organizations, just as the leadership of these organizations would enjoy greater insulation from the political machinations of dissident minorities within the ranks. But it can also be said that while stability is a laudable goal in labor relations, so too is freedom of choice. "Unions of their own choosing" was the slogan that accompanied the passage of the Wagner Act, and there is some merit in the argument that industrial democracy is better served if employee organizations are occasionally put to the political test by those whom they represent. This does not mean that the leadership is to be put to the test as there already exists adequate machinery to unseat unresponsive union leaders; it means that the organization itself ought to face the possibility of being voted out of office. Obviously, organizational security tends to reduce the chances of this happening. It is also arguable that a law that obliges an employee organization to win financial support by establishing a record as an effective and responsive bargaining agent, may prove in the long run to be more consistent with the public interest than a statutory provision that in many cases makes a dues collector out of the employer, willing as that employer may be.

The most troublesome feature of the agency shop, however, rests with its enforcement procedures. It was pointed out earlier that the enforcement technique most frequently applied is for the employer to agree to discharge any employee refusing to authorize deductions of the agency fee from his paycheck. What this means, and what it has meant in practice in the state of Michigan, where agency shop provisions are widespread, is that teachers cannot rely on the teacher tenure law for protection.

True, the situation in Michigan is somewhat different from New York State. There the stated grounds for dismissal under the tenure law is for "reasonable and just cause." The Michigan Teacher Tenure Commission and the lower courts have sustained the dismissal of tenured teachers under agency shop provisions, arguing that the failure to render dues to a teacher organization is indeed "reasonable and just cause" for discharge. Under New York State's tenure law the only grounds for dismissal of a tenured teacher are " (a) insubordination, immoral character or conduct unbecoming a teacher; (b) inefficiency, incompetency, physical or mental disability or neglect of duty." It would be difficult, unless one put a strained interpretation on the term "insubordination," to so interpret any of the above grounds for dismissal to cover refusal to render funds to a private organization. Surely the tenure law would have to be amended if the Legislature were to authorize the agency shop, particularly if the statute permitted enforcement procedure that included dismissal of noncomplying tenured teachers.

It is anyone's guess as to how many tenured teachers in the state would on grounds of principle refuse to sign an agency fee authorization card, thereby leaving no option to the employer but to initiate dismissal proceedings. Surely there would be several—probably not enough to cause irreparable damage to public education, but enough to give pause to those who value the rights of individuals at least as much as they value employee bargaining power and organizational security.

The question, then, is how to balance the advantages of some form of organizational security against the obvious disadvantages of forcing upon tenured teachers the option of signing an agency shop fee authorization card or face automatic dismissal. A legislative proposal of the New York State Teachers Association (NYSTA) would provide one answer, empowering employers to deduct agency shop fees without individual authorizations. Thus an employee who chose not to join the organization would have his fee deducted anyway, along with income tax and social security deductions, which are also obligatory.

While this arrangement would resolve the dilemma of forced dismissal of recalcitrant tenured teachers, it would also raise certain constitutional issues, particularly those rights that citizens enjoy under the Fourteenth Amendment. It could at least be argued that the state, acting through one of its agencies, the school boards, would be denying individuals of their property (agency fees) without due process of law.

What the issue comes down to is whether there is sufficient merit in the agency shop provision for the Legislature to authorize it. While such authorization does not require the parties to incorporate the agency shop into the agreement, it is nevertheless implicit that this provision would not be contrary to the public interest as it is rare that legislatures deliberately act *against* the latter. A secondary consideration is whether the Legislature should allow for enforcement procedures including possible dismissal of tenured teachers refusing to authorize the agency fee deduction.

The arguments allowing for some form of organizational security are persuasive, although they become less so in the concept of statewide collective bargaining. While it is not known what the status of membership in local organizations now is, and while it is certainly not known what level of membership is required before an employee organization can represent it effectively, there is evidence that in a number of cases employee organizations need greater protection than now enjoyed if they are to carry out obligations under the law and at the same time be reasonably immune from those pressures that so frequently provoke irresponsible behavior. In one region, for example, NYSTA affiliates represent over 6,000 teachers, yet membership

is slightly more than 3,000. Certainly it is difficult for these employee organizations to carry out their "public purpose" functions under such circumstances.

It does not follow, however, that enforcement by dismissal of
those who refuse to comply with the agency shop agreement—
or even the denial of options, as NYSTA has proposed—is consistent with public policy. What is needed is a mechanism that,
without impeding opportunities to engage volunteer workers and
in general attain more flexible staff arrangements, will also provide contractual protection for struggling organizations. In the
context of local bargaining, we therefore propose legislative authorization that (1) would allow for contractual provisions requiring newly hired personnel to permit some form of fee deduction to support the collective bargaining activity, but that (2)
would render those teachers already on the payroll immune
from the provisions. Thus a new teacher would have the option
of accepting or rejecting a position in New York State education
where the payment of an agency fee was a condition of continuing employment, just as he might refuse employment because
he did not like the pay, hours, or course load involved. However,
this recommendation does not meet the objections raised by
some satellite personnel that an agency shop clause would practically guarantee underrepresentation at the bargaining table.
Conceivably, Section 209-a of the Taylor Law (improper practices) could be strengthened so as to provide a remedy for this
problem. The proposal would seem, however, to provide a
modicum of organizational security without undermining the
spirit of the teacher tenure law.

NOTE

Is there any relationship between the policy, espoused by
many experts, of encouraging the establishment of broad bargaining units in the public sector and the negotiation of union
security agreements? One commentator made the following observation:

> Even if a union succeeds in winning recognition in a large
> unit employees in that unit are generally not required to
> become members of the union. The relative lack of union
> security clauses in the collective bargaining agreements of
> the public service assures that, to a degree unparalleled in
> the private sector, dissident small-unit groups are able to
> maintain their separate identities and to prolong the battle
> for break-off from the larger group's exclusive bargaining
> agent. Rock, *The Appropriate Unit Question in the Public*

Service: The Problem of Proliferation, 67 MICH. L. REV. 1001, 1005 (1969).

GOTBAUM,* COLLECTIVE BARGAINING AND THE UNION LEADER, in PUBLIC WORKERS AND PUBLIC UNIONS 77, 84-85 (S. Zagoria ed. 1972)†

The Less Union Security, the More Militant Leadership

In an open shop situation, the percentage of dues-paying members give you an indication of the labor leader's militancy: the smaller the percentage of membership, the greater the militancy. In a newly organized situation or where organization hovers around the 50 percent area, the union leader knows that he must come up with something new and dramatic or at least look dramatic, in order to increase membership. Where organization approaches the 100 percent level, the union leader can afford the luxury of dealing with issues on their merits.

In one television discussion John DeLury was magnificently stylistic and involved himself in some beautiful rank and file prose. My wife, who watched the program, queried me as to whether this was going to bring the public over to his side. I submitted to her that it would be nice for him to bring the public over to his side, but it was much more important that in an open shop situation the New York City sanitationmen were 99 percent organized. Good public will is of little help to a leader whose union is poorly organized and whose opposition grows troublesome.

In an open shop situation you do not want your contract just ratified: you want it *overwhelmingly* ratified. The opposition does not need a majority, all it needs is to keep the leadership off guard. If you lose a point at the bargaining table it is not considered by the opposition to be a part of normal bargaining. "You sold out" becomes the rallying cry for the opposition. In addition you never know how many members you are going to lose because you did not satisfy their specific desires. So you become an "irresponsible union boss" or a "pirate."

The fight for an agency shop in the public sector is almost ridiculous. Management's insistence on an open shop situation is the most counterproductive imaginable. It is to management's interest that the union be stable and representative of

* Victor Gotbaum is the Executive Director of District Council 37 (New York City) of the American Federation of State, County and Municipal Employees, AFL-CIO.

all the people in its unit. This would give the union leader maneuverability and flexibility. It would make him less demanding, less insecure, and less verbose. The agency shop is eminently fair; yet very few governments allow it. This makes little sense and is another example of public administration immaturity. It perhaps should be regarded in the same light as the public administrator who refuses to accept the role of management.

LARSON,* PUBLIC EMPLOYEES AND THEIR "RIGHT TO WORK"†

It is easy to figure out why union officials put compulsory membership at the top of their "want list" when negotiating with public agencies. There are more than twelve million public employees, including nearly three million Federal employees. If every public employee were under compulsion to pay union dues of $5 a month, the take would amount to $700 million a year—not counting millions in initiation fees!

The stakes are enormous and the union bosses are at work. As Jerry Wurf said, "Our potential is nothing less than fantastic . . . right now six out of every ten new jobs being created are jobs in government." He added that his union would have a million members now instead of just 400,000 if all his contracts called for compulsory unionism!

It is obvious to us that union officials, with the help of some politicians, who receive campaign support from union treasuries, are making fantastic progress in a massive, coast-to-coast, community-by-community program aimed ultimately at locking every public employee into a contract forcing him to pay dues into a union treasury in order to keep his job.

To us the real threat in the compulsory unionization of government workers lies in the fact that it provides a thinly disguised pipeline diverting enforced salary deductions in the form of union dues to provide campaign funds for union-controlled politicians—politicians who as public officials are the government employee's bosses, and who are the very persons who forced him to pay the union in the first place.

The action of Mayor Lindsay is an excellent example of this problem and graphically illustrates why the AFL-CIO recently made an unprecedented decision at the national level to participate fully in campaigns for mayors and other local officials.

---

* Reed Larson is Executive Vice President of the National Right to Work Committee.

† Reprinted by permission of Mr. Reed Larson, The National Right to Work Committee, 1990 M Street, N.W., Washington, D.C., 20036.

In the past this has always been left to the local unions, some of which are effective and some of which are not. Our interpretation of this new emphasis is that it is part of an overall program aimed at obtaining union-controlled public officials at the local level who will—to put it bluntly—roll over and play dead whenever they are confronted by a union organizer representing a handful of militant employees.

The crux of the problem here is the inordinate influence of union political power on public officials charged with the responsibility of setting employee policies. In private industry, the interests of union officials are being served primarily on one side of the bargaining table. But in public employee bargaining we can see what amounts to an agent of union power representing both the employer and the organized employees. The solution, as we see it, is to make compulsory unionism illegal; to take the choice of membership or nonmembership in an employee union out of the hands of the politician and the union professionals, and keep it where it belongs—with the individual employee.

It is the widespread practice of compulsory unionism in private industry that frees union officials from the normal responsibilities of operating a voluntary organization. It is compulsory unionism that releases a major percentage of union resources directly for political action rather than for selling and maintaining membership. According to union spokesmen, retention and expansion of compulsory membership is essential if they are to continue and expand the political activity which they consider necessary and desirable.

Union representative Walter H. Barnes, of the Teamsters Local 636 in New Jersey, let the cat out of the bag last fall after the New Jersey legislature, over the veto of Governor Richard Hughes, passed a Right to Work law covering the state's public employees. Barnes said, "Since we can't get the union shop I have orders from the President of our local to stop trying to organize the Department of Public Works in Englewood because it just isn't worthwhile."

The late President John F. Kennedy clearly recognized the danger involved in the forced unionization of public employees when he insisted that his 1962 Executive Order 10988, authorizing the unionization of Federal employees, also protect the right *not* to join. That order reads: "Employees of the Federal government shall have, and shall be protected in the exercise of the right, freely and without fear of penalty or reprisal, to form, join and assist any employee organization or to refrain from such activity." That part of the Kennedy Executive Order can properly be called the Federal employees' Right to Work law. And as long as it remains in existence compulsory unionism cannot exist for Federal employees.

President Kennedy's Secretary of Labor, Arthur Goldberg, in explaining the order in a speech to members of the American Federation of Government Employees AFL-CIO said,

> I know you will agree with me that the union shop and the closed shop are inappropriate to the Federal government. And because of this, there is a larger responsibility for enlightenment on the part of the government union. In your own organization you have to win acceptance by your own conduct, your own action, your own wisdom, your own responsibility and your own achievements. . . . So you have an opportunity to bring into your organization people who come in because they want to come in and who will participate, therefore, in the full activity of your organization.
> . . . .

As a single-purpose organization the National Right to Work Committee is concerned only with compulsory versus voluntary unionism. We believe the drive for compulsory dues underlies most of the current turmoil in public employee-management relations. And we believe strongly that any meaningful labor legislation—for industrial as well as public employees—must have as its foundation the elimination of compulsory unionism. It is our firm belief that the record shows that voluntarism will go far to provide the checks and balances necessary to keeping union leadership responsive to the individual member.

K. HANSLOWE, THE EMERGING LAW OF LABOR RELATIONS IN PUBLIC EMPLOYMENT 114-15 (1967)†

. . . [A] democratic political structure has limits as to the amount of organized group pressure it can tolerate. At some point the risk arises of a dangerous dilution of governmental authority by its being squeezed to death by conflicting power blocks. If that point is reached, foreign policy is made by defense industry, agricultural policy by farmers, and public personnel policy by employee organizations, and *not* by government representing the wishes of an electorate consisting of individual voters. If that point is reached, an orderly system of individual liberty under lawful rule would seem to be the victim. For surely it is difficult to conceive of a social order without a governmental

---

† Reprinted by permission of the New York State School of Industrial and Labor Relations, Cornell University.

repository of authority, which is authoritative for the very reason that it is representative and democratic.

To illustrate: Problems may arise, if public employee organizations begin to press, as they have already commenced to do, for union security arrangements of one sort or another, making financial support of the employee organization a condition of public employment. On the face of it, this sounds innocent enough, and legal objections of incompatibility with civil service concepts of merit employment are likely to be overridden. If an exclusive bargaining agent is empowered, and is therefore required, to represent all employees in the bargaining unit, it seems fair to require all those benefiting from such representation to contribute to its cost.

But the Supreme Court of the United States has decided, as to the private sector, that the contractual obligation (in the form of the union shop) to contribute to the costs of the representation may not lawfully include, as a condition of employment, coerced support of *political* activities of the organization to which an individual member objects. Support of *collective bargaining activity* is all that may be compelled. Yet, in the public sector, political activity is unavoidably part and parcel of the process of *bargaining with politicians.* Thus there arises the possibility of involuntary contributions to organizational support of politicians who, while ready to improve the working conditions of public employees, on other questions take positions of which such public employees disapprove. Unless careful protections are worked out, enabling individual public employees to "contract out" from compelled support of unwanted political parties, politicians, and public policies, the union shop in public employment has the potential of becoming a neat mutual back-scratching mechanism, whereby public employee representatives and politicians each reinforce the other's interests and domain, with the individual public employee and the individual citizen left to look on, while his employment conditions, and his tax rate, and public policies generally are being decided by entrenched and mutually supportive government officials and collective bargaining representatives over whom the public has diminishing control.

Such dangers are perhaps not immediate. The point needs, however, to be reiterated that there are limits on the amount of stress which a democratic governmental structure can tolerate from organized group pressure. At some point its fibre can be broken, and democratic rule under law be replaced by authoritarian rule by clique.

NOTE

See generally Smith, *The Agency Shop: An Old Issue in a New Environment,* CALIFORNIA PUBLIC EMPLOYEE RELATIONS No. 17 (June 1973) ; Gromfine, *Union Security Clauses in Public Employment,* N.Y.U. 22D ANN. CONF. ON LABOR 285 (1970) ; Comment, *Union Security and the Non-Union Public Employee: Harmony or Conflict?,* 21 CATHOLIC U.L. REV. 615 (1972) ; Comment, *Impact of the Agency Shop on Labor Relations in the Public Sector,* 55 CORNELL L. REV. 547 (1970).

C. Legality of Union Security Provisions in the Absence of Public Sector Collective Bargaining Legislation

PETRUCCI v. HOGAN

New York Supreme Court, Bronx County
5 Misc. 2d 480, 27 N.Y.S.2d 718 (1941)

LOUIS A. VALENTE, J. Plaintiffs are former employees of the Interborough Rapid Transit System, having been connected with its operating and maintenance divisions. While in its employ they joined the Transport Workers Union of Greater New York, of which defendants are now officers. In June, 1940, the City of New York acquired the Interborough and plaintiffs then became city employees and were classified in its civil service. The Transport Workers Union had previously entered into a contract with the Interborough relating to the wages and working conditions of its employees, which contract, on April 3, 1940, was assumed by the Board of Transportation of the City of New York on the date of the consummation of transit unification. Thereafter, and at various times during 1940 and 1941, plaintiffs resigned from membership in the union and severed their association with it. Obviously, the reason for plaintiffs disassociating themselves from the union is that they no longer required its intercession or protection, for as civil service employees they have obtained a security of position and other satisfactory related benefits, which make union membership unnecessary. As a further reason for their resignation, plaintiffs aver that the officers of the union "have been closely associated with the communistic movement in the City of New York" and they do not wish to aid such a cause; and that as a consequence of their withdrawal the defendants and their agents have picketed the homes of the plaintiffs and have distributed leaflets or circulars concerning some of the plaintiffs, charging that after the defendants had secured certain benefits for the plaintiffs they are now undermining the union by lapsing their membership. Plaintiffs also allege that they were subject to other embarrassment and annoyance to themselves and the members of their families, which do not require a detailed recital here. Suffice it to say that they are typical of controversies of this kind.

The facts for the most part are not challenged by the defendants. In fact, they admit the picketing and the distribution of the circulars. Factually there seems to be little at issue. The defendants claim that as a union they have the right to engage in the activities to which the plaintiffs object. Plaintiffs have now applied for a temporary injunction to restrain the defendants, their agents and members from interfering with the plaintiffs in the enjoyment of their civil rights and from picketing their homes and otherwise harassing and annoying them and their families. . . .

The implication is clear from the principal affidavit submitted by the defendants, as well as from the memorandum submitted by their counsel, that the union is of the belief that it may demand the discharge of the plaintiffs who are no longer members of the union and do not wish to be affiliated with it. If the union were possessed of this power, it could establish a "closed shop." In such event employment in the city service would be dependent upon membership in the union, which would be the vital consideration, the provisions of the Constitution of the State of New York and the Civil Service Law to the contrary notwithstanding. Section 6 of article V of the Constitution relating to civil service appointments and promotions, declares: "Appointments and promotions in the civil service of the state, and of all the civil divisions thereof, including cities and villages, shall be made according to merit and fitness to be ascertained, so far as practicable, by examinations, which, so far as practicable, shall be competitive. . . . Laws shall be made to provide for the enforcement of this section." The Civil Service Law was enacted to carry into effect this article of the Constitution, which has as its underlying principle the desire to afford everyone who has the necessary qualifications an equal opportunity of securing appointment. (Matter of Mendelson v. Finegan, 168 Misc. 102, affd. 253 App. Div. 709.) Section 8 of the Civil Service Law provides: "No officer or officers having the power of appointment or employment shall select or appoint any person for appointment, employment, promotion or reinstatement except in accordance with the provisions of this chapter under the rules and regulations prescribed thereunder." Section 6 of the Civil Service Law provides: "The state civil service commission shall. . . . Prescribe . . . suitable rules and regulations for carrying into effect the provisions of this chapter and of section six of article five of the constitution of the state of New York, as herein provided. The rules prescribed by the state and municipal commissions pursuant to the provisions of this chapter shall have the force and effect of law." Subdivision 5 of section 11 of the Civil Service Law substantially grants the same power to the municipal commission of each city, and in subdivision 1 "The mayor or other duly authorized appointing authority of each city in this state shall appoint and employ three suitable persons to prescribe, amend and enforce rules for the classification of the offices, places and employments in the classified service of said city, and for appointments and promotions therein and examinations therefor."

Obviously appointments and promotions in the Civil Service must be determined upon merit and fitness, under suitable regulations adopted by commissions created by the Civil Service Law under the mandate of the Constitution. The right to appointment depends upon merit and fitness, not upon membership in a labor organization. Inasmuch as plaintiffs have acquired civil service status, they may be removed only for causes recognized by law (§ 22, subd. 2) and not for their failure to resume union membership.

Concededly, the purpose of the picketing is to coerce the plaintiffs into retaining or resuming union membership and thus effect the creation or maintenance of a closed shop. The purpose of picketing is the ultimate object thereof, such as to obtain higher wages, or less hours of employment, or the closed shop. (1 Teller on Labor Disputes and Collective Bargaining, § 109.) Of necessity the initial step is union affiliation, which is followed by a demand for the closed shop. The theory of the maintenance of a "closed shop" by a municipality being repugnant to the Constitution, which prescribes standards other than union membership for the selection of Civil Service employees, the observations in Williams v. Quill (277 N.Y. 1) that a labor union may call a strike and picket premises of an employer with the intent of inducing him to employ only union labor, are therefore not decisive of the instant controversy.

It seems to be well settled, and the courts have generally acknowledged, the right of the employee to picket peacefully. In Senn v. Tile Layers Protective Union (301 U.S. 468) the United States Supreme Court held that peaceful picketing did not require statutory sanction but was a right granted by the Constitution, subject, of course, to the right of the State to regulate the methods and means of publicity, as well as the use of the public streets. (Exchange Bakery & Restaurant v. Rifkin, 245 N.Y. 260, *supra.*) So, too, picketing without a strike is no more unlawful than a strike without picketing. The rationale of those cases which permit picketing in the absence of a strike is set forth in that case. The test to be applied is whether the end and the means are lawful. As Judge ANDREWS pointed out in Exchange Bakery & Restaurant v. Rifkin (*supra*, p. 262): "As always, what is done, if legal, must be to effect some lawful result by lawful means." There is nothing inherently illegal in picketing for the purpose of inducing an employer to employ only union labor. (National Protective Assn. of Steam Fitters & Helpers v. Cumming, 170 N.Y. 315.) This, however, would presuppose a situation where the employer is free to contract with such union, regardless of restrictions imposed either by the Constitution or statute. The city is not at liberty to act in derogation of the provisions of the Constitution or the Civil Service Law, and picketing that has for its ultimate object establishment of a "closed shop" wherein only those shall be employed who are members of the union cannot be viewed as legal. . . .

NOTE

Would it be illegal for a public employer to actively seek out and give preference to union members in hiring employees as long as such policy was not included in a collective bargaining agreement or incorporated in an ordinance? In Chapin v. Board of Educ. of the City of Peoria, Docket No. 21255 (Ill. Cir. Ct. 1939), reprinted in RHYNE, LABOR UNIONS AND MUNICIPAL EMPLOYE LAW 157, 158 (1946), the court, in the course of holding that a closed shop clause in an agreement was illegal, stated:

> It may be true that without any contract the board can employ members of the local in question to the exclusion of non-members. It may be within its discretion to do so. The board cannot, however, by contract, foreclose the possibility of a non-member securing employment. The law finds no fault with a school board employing union labor or with the employees belonging to labor unions, but it does not permit the board to bind itself by contract to employ only those who belong to a particular association or organization.

Would such reasoning be valid if the applicable collective bargaining legislation provided, as most of the public sector statutes do, that it is an unfair labor practice for an employer by discrimination in regard to hire or tenure of employment or any term of condition of employment to *encourage* or discourage membership in any labor organization?

FOLTZ v. CITY OF DAYTON

Court of Appeals of Ohio
27 Ohio App. 2d 35, 56 Ohio Op. 2d 213,
272 N.E.2d 169 (1970)

SHERER, Judge.

This appeal is on questions of law from an order of the Common Pleas Court of Montgomery County, 22 Ohio Misc. 27, 254 N.E.2d 395, permanently enjoining the city of Dayton, a charter city, from effectuating a union security agreement entered into by the city with Dayton Public Service Union, local 101, hereinafter referred to as D.P.S.U., and permanently enjoining such union, its officers, representatives, and members from taking any action for the purpose of inducing the city of Dayton to comply with such agreement and from intimidating, coercing or threatening employees of the city of Dayton with disciplinary action for failure to sign an agency shop or union dues authorization.

Defendant city of Dayton and defendant D.P.S.U., entered into an agreement concerning wages, hours, and working conditions of the employees of the city of Dayton who are in the classified civil service. A portion of the agreement provided for an agency shop. The essence of such provision is that all employees of the city of Dayton, within the bargaining unit, not paying dues directly to the union or authorizing the city to check off dues *must pay* a service fee to the union equivalent to the union dues. Failure to do so results in an employee's suspension for a minimum of one day for each month the employee fails to pay such dues or service fee. The discipline provided can include discharge.

The union, on June 16, 1969, forwarded to the city of Dayton a list of 96 city employees, not members of the union who had failed to pay the service fee provided for in the agreement. Plaintiff's exhibit "C" contains this statement:

"These recalcitrant employees now become subject to the penalty provided in the agreement."

Article IV, paragraph 3, of the agreement, provides that:

"Upon written notice from the Union, the City shall discipline an employee covered herein for failure to pay such contract administration charge up to and including discharge, but in no event less than a suspension of one day for each month the employee fails to make such payment."

After the execution of the agreement, the Civil Service Board of the city of Dayton, acting under authority granted to it by section 96 of the charter of the city of Dayton, amended section

2 (O) of rule 18. Rule 18 sets forth a number of grounds for which charges may be brought against an employee for disciplinary action. Section 2 (O) of rule 18 originally provided, as follows:

"Has failed to pay or make reasonable provision for future payment of his just debts due or owing by him, causing thereby annoyance to his superior officer or scandal to the service."

Section 2 (O) was then amended by the Civil Service Board to read as follows:

"Has failed to pay or make reasonable provision for future payment of his just debts due or owing by him or has failed to pay a monthly service charge to a labor organization as may be required by an agreement between the city and such labor organization, causing thereby annoyance to his superior officer or scandal to the service."

The plaintiff, Walter Foltz, appellee herein, brought this action as an individual, as a taxpayer of the city of Dayton, and as a representative of a class of persons similarly situated.

He alleges that he is a taxpayer of the city of Dayton; that he is holding a position in the classified service of the city of Dayton as painter 1; that he is not a member of the union; that he has refused to authorize the city of Dayton to check off union dues or the service charge provided in the contract; that unless restrained, the city and the union will unlawfully discipline and discharge him and others similarly situated; and that he and they will thereby suffer irreparable injuries for which they have no adequate remedy at law.

Plaintiff alleges that civil service employees of the city of Dayton are governed by Chapter 143 of the Ohio Revised Code and other civil service laws and that the agreement aforesaid violates Ohio law.

The judgment entry of the Common Pleas Court recites:

"Accordingly, the Court finds that the Union Security Agreement, Article 14 of the Agreement between the Defendant D.P.S.U., Local 101, and the City of Dayton, dated May 13, 1969, is in conflict with the general law of this State and that it does not accomplish a governmental, public or municipal purpose as distinguished from private, and in consequence thereof is ultra vires and invalid."

The court said that the union security agreement was in conflict with R.C. 9.41 which provides that a municipality may check off the wages of its employees for the payment of dues to a labor union only upon written authorization by the employee.

The Common Pleas Court based its conclusions on the holding of the Supreme Court in Hagerman v. Dayton, 147 Ohio St. 313, 71 N.E.2d 246, wherein the following paragraphs of the syllabus read:

"5. A municipal ordinance which provides for or authorizes a check-off of the wages or salary of civil service appointees is a police regulation and is in conflict with Section 6346-13, General Code [now R.C. 1321.32]. (Sections 3 and 7 of Article XVIII, Ohio Constitution.)

"6. The appointment, tenure, promotion, removal, transfer, lay-off, suspension, reduction, reinstatement or dismissal and working conditions of persons in the classified civil service of the state, the several counties, cities and city school districts thereof, are regulated exclusively by Section 10 of Article XV of the Ohio Constitution and the laws, rules and regulations enacted in pursuance thereof.

"7. There is no authority for the delegation of any powers or functions of either a municipality or its civil service appointees to any organization of any kind."

In that case, the city of Dayton enacted an ordinance authorizing the Director of Finance to make payroll dues deductions as requested by the city employees to be paid to the Dayton Public Service Union. Following the enactment of the ordinance, the Director of Finance of the city of Dayton filed his petition in the Common Pleas Court of Montgomery county asking for a declaratory judgment to determine its legality and validity, and a determination of to what extent, if any, he might lawfully utilize the services of his employees to comply with the provisions of the ordinance.

At page 328, 71 N.E.2d at page 253 the court said:

"There is no municipal purpose served by the check-off of wages of civil service employees. Counsel for appellees argue that a check-off is a convenience to both the municipal appointee and the labor union. We must be realistic and take judicial notice, of what is generally known that the check-off is a means of maintaining membership. Indeed, the record in this case shows that each so-called contract member is required to give a cognovit note for twenty months dues in advance and these proposed check-off payments are to be applied on such notes. The check-off is contrary to the spirit and purpose of the civil service laws of the state."

The court quoted Section 10, Article XV of the Constitution of Ohio, which provides:

"Appointments and promotions in the civil service of the state, the several counties, and cities, shall be made according to merit and fitness, to be ascertained, as far as practicable, by competitive examinations. Laws shall be passed providing for the enforcement of this provision."

The court then said at pages 328, 329, 71 N.E.2d at page 254:

"Under this section of the Constitution and the laws enacted pursuant thereto, labor unions have no function which they may discharge in connection with civil service appointees."

Judge Zimmerman, concurring, quoted from the case of Fitzgerald v. City of Cleveland, 88 Ohio St. 338, 344, 103 N.E. 512, 514, relative to the powers of local self-government and said that the powers of local self-government "are clearly such as involve the exercise of the functions of government."

Judge Zimmerman also quoted from 37 American Jurisprudence 734, Municipal Corporations, Section 120, as follows:

"Generally, a public purpose has for its objective the promotion of the public health, safety, morals, general welfare, security, prosperity, and contentment of all the inhabitants or residents within the municipal corporation, the sovereign powers of which are used to promote such public purpose. The phrase 'municipal purpose' used in the broader sense is generally accepted as meaning public or governmental purpose as distinguished from private."

The city and the union contend that the city's action here in adopting rule 18, 2 (O) is not a "local police regulation" but is a proper exercise of its powers of local self-government conferred upon it by Section 3, Article XVIII of the Ohio Constitution and relies upon the holding of the Supreme Court in the case of State ex rel. Canada v. Phillips, 168 Ohio St. 191, 151 N.E.2d 722, in which the court, at page 196, 151 N.E.2d at page 726, quoted with approval the following language of the court in the earlier case of State ex rel. Lentz v. Edwards, 90 Ohio St. 305, 107 N.E. 768:

"It would not be contended that the civil service of a city is not a matter of municipal concern, nor that the power of regulating that service is not one of the powers of local self-government. . . .

"The manner of regulating the civil service of a city is peculiarly a matter of municipal concern. One of the powers of local self-government is the power of legislating with reference to the local government within the limitations of the constitutional provisions above referred to. [Section 10, Article XV.] As long as the provisions made in the charter of any municipality with reference to its civil service, comply with the requirement of Section 10 of Article XV, and do not conflict with any other provisions of the Constitution, they are valid, and under the cases referred to discontinue the general law on the subject as to that municipality. That provisions adopted by a city might differ from the general laws within the limits defined was not only expected, but the very purpose of the amendment was to permit such differences and make them effective.

". . . [T]he city of Dayton fully complied with the letter and the spirit of Section 10 of Article XV by providing for appointments and promotions in the civil service of the city according to merit and fitness to be ascertained by competitive examinations."

Section 1 of the charter provides in general terms that the city of Dayton:

"may pass such ordinances as may be expedient for maintaining and promoting the peace, good government and welfare of the City and for the performance of the functions thereof."

It is further provided in such section that:

"The city shall have and may exercise, all other powers which, under the constitution and laws of Ohio, it would be competent for this Charter to enumerate."

The charter makes specific provision for civil service in sections 93 to 107, inclusive. In section 96, the charter provides that:

"The Board, subject to the approval of the Commission, shall adopt, amend, and enforce a code of rules and regulations, providing for appointment and employment in all positions in the classified service, based on merit, efficiency, character, and industry, which shall have the force and effect of law; shall make investigations concerning the enforcement and effect of this chapter and of the rules adopted. It shall make an annual report to the Commission."

In *Canada,* the question involved was whether section 151, of the charter of the city of Columbus providing that the appointing authority could appoint any one of the three highest on a civil service eligible list was a local police regulation in conflict with R.C. 143.34, providing for the appointment of the one highest on the civil service eligible list or whether it was a proper exercise of the city's powers of local self government. The court held that the method adopted by a city for making appointments within its civil service is a matter of local self government limited only by the provisions of Section 10, Article XV of the Ohio Constitution, providing for appointments and promotions in the civil service of cities according to merit and fitness to be ascertained by competitive examinations.

In paragraph 8 of the syllabus in *Canada,* the court approved and followed paragraph 2 of the syllabus of Hile v. City of Cleveland, 118 Ohio St. 99, 160 N.E. 621, which held:

"Section 96 of the charter of the city of Cleveland, which provides that one seeking a promotion or appointment in the city civil service shall pass a competitive civil service examination 'unless he shall have served with fidelity for at least two years immediately preceding in a similar position under the city,' does not contravene section 10, art. XV of the Ohio Constitution, but is in full accord therewith, and authorizes promotions and appointments of persons in the civil service of the city without civil service competitive examination, who have previously so served under the city."

A cogent argument is made in the case before us that the action of the city of Dayton adopting section 2 (O) of rule 18 of the civil service rules is a valid exercise of the city's powers of local self government and that it does not conflict with Section 10, Article XV of the Ohio Constitution.

The civil service employees of a city have a right to bargain collectively with the city respecting their wages, hours and conditions of their employment and have a right to designate a union to represent them in such bargaining.

The question here is whether the city's agreement with such a union whereby the city is obligated, upon complaint of the union, to discharge its employees if they fail to pay union dues or to pay a service charge to the union in the amount of such dues is a police regulation in conflict with the provisions of chapter 143 of the Revised Code and R.C. 9.40, or whether it is a valid exercise of its powers of local self government not in conflict with Section 10, Article XV of the Ohio Constitution.

We are unable to distinguish the facts in this case in any significant way from the facts in the *Hagerman* case and we are bound by the Court's conclusion in that case. We conclude, therefore, that the Common Pleas Court did not err in holding that Section 2 (O) of rule 18 of the civil service rules of the city of Dayton is a police regulation in conflict with the general laws of Ohio relating to civil service and is invalid. . . .

We have examined and considered all errors assigned by defendants and find none well taken.

The judgment of the Common Pleas Court will be affirmed. Judgment affirmed.

CRAWFORD, J., concurs in judgment.

With great reluctance, I concur in the judgment, being constrained to do so by Hagerman v. Dayton (1947), 147 Ohio St. 313, 34 O.O. 238, 46 Ohio Law Abst. 141, 71 N.E.2d 246, 170 A.L.R. 199.

Many commentaries cite this case as illustrative of a definitely conservative point of view. Vast changes have occurred and are still occurring in the social, economic and governmental structure which tend to weaken the philosophical basis of that decision. Here the city and the union are alike seeking to give effect to their agreement for an agency shop.

The technical objection to a wage assignment noted in *Hagerman* appears inapplicable. The present plaintiff made no assignment. On the contrary, he resists the deduction. He is apparently content to accept the benefits which the union may accomplish in his behalf, but unwilling to share its costs. Yet, if the union should become an ineffective bargaining agent for the employees, they, including plaintiff, may withdraw its authority by democratic processes.

Whether, in the light of present trends, without a wage assignment, the city may observe the agency shop agreement by requiring all employees to support the bargaining agent, is a question which now deserves careful review.

It is no longer valid to say that these deductions support only a private, personal and selfish purpose. Satisfactory relations between government and its employees is a matter of the utmost public concern, directly conducive to the general welfare.

"Under some circumstances . . . public administrators may deem collective bargaining the most satisfactory method of handling the government's relations with its employees." 21 U. Cinc. L. Rev. 354.

In all the years since *Hagerman,* apparently only once has the Supreme Court expressly mentioned that decision. See State ex rel. Leach v. Price (1959), 168 Ohio St. 499, at 504, 156 N.E.2d 316.

It is earnestly to be hoped that present day conditions may prompt careful review of the problem

[The concurring opinion of Judge Kerns is omitted.]

NOTE

The Missouri Attorney General has ruled that in the absence of authorizing legislation "there is no authority for the State to make check-offs of union dues as such." He also ruled in the same opinion that the State did "not have the authority . . . to accept maintenance of membership or agency clauses which respectively require that union members maintain their membership in the union as a condition of employment and that non-union employees, as a condition of employment pay a union service charge." Mo. Op. Att'y Gen. No. 473, GERR No. 370, B-8 to B-10 (1970) .

D. Legality of Union Security Provisions in States with Public Sector Collective Bargaining Legislation

BAUCH v. CITY OF NEW YORK

New York Court of Appeals
21 N.Y.2d 599, 237 N.E.2d 211, 289 N.Y.S.2d 951
Cert. denied, 393 U.S. 834 (1968)

Fuld, Chief Judge.

This appeal, taken upon constitutional grounds, poses the question—of first impression in this court—whether the City of New York may grant a dues "check-off" privilege to a union representing a majority of the municipal employees in a city-wide bargaining unit and yet deny such privilege to a minority union.[1]

In 1956, the city's Board of Estimate adopted a resolution which granted the check-off privilege to all organizations of city employees whose members authorized the necessary payroll deductions. At that time, the city did not recognize any union as an agent for collective bargaining. Later, the city began to recognize unions as exclusive bargaining agents if they were chosen by a majority of the employees in an appropriate bargaining unit. Even then, however, the Board of Estimate resolution extending the check-off privilege to all unions alike was not changed and the city continued to give effect to its provisions.

---

[1] In labor relations parlance, the "check-off" is the practice whereby an employer deducts the amount of a union member's dues from his pay, usually on the employee's express authorization, and remits it directly to the union.

In April, 1967, the city modified its union recognition policies by means of an executive order of the Mayor. The order provided (1) that appropriate bargaining units for municipal employees were to be established on a city-wide basis or, in some circumstances, on a departmental basis and (2) that the organization chosen by a majority of the employees in each such unit was to be recognized as the exclusive bargaining representative for all employees in the unit.

The Mayor proposes to round out this policy by means of a further executive order which will give the privilege of dues check-off solely to the exclusive bargaining agents and will withdraw it from all other unions. It is the declared opinion of the Mayor and the city's Director of Labor Relations that this plan for a restricted check-off policy, common in private industry, will afford the majority representatives a form of "union security," will increase their prestige and responsibility and will, in consequence, stabilize the collective bargaining process.

Local 832 (International Brotherhood of Teamsters, Chauffeurs, Warehousemen and Helpers of America) and District Council 37 (American Federation of State, County and Municipal Employees, AFL-CIO) are two unions which include persons employed by the city in nonsupervisory clerical titles. District Council 37 has been recognized by the city as the exclusive bargaining representative for such employees; under the proposed plan it will thus have the exclusive benefit of the dues check-off. Local 832, on the other hand, is a minority union and, accordingly, it will be deprived, under the proposed plan, of the check-off privilege it has enjoyed since 1956.[2] Strongly objecting, the latter organization, Local 832, has commenced this article 78 proceeding—through its president and several of its members on behalf of themselves and all others similarly situated —to require the city to continue the check-off of dues to it, and to enjoin the city from granting exclusive check-off privileges to District Council 37 or any other labor organization. The court at Special Term dismissed the petition and the Appellate Division unanimously affirmed the resulting order.

Under the 1963 New York City Charter (§ 8), the Mayor is authorized to "exercise all the powers vested in the city, except as otherwise provided by law." He is the successor to the residual powers originally possessed by the Board of Estimate under a

---

[2] District Council 37 has majority representation status in city-wide units covering over 57,000 employees and in department-wide units covering some 1,300 more. In sharp contrast, Local 832, having an over-all membership in the neighborhood of 1,700 represents only about 1,000 nonsupervisory clerical workers.

similarly worded provision of the 1938 New York City Charter (§ 70) in effect in 1956, when that body adopted the "non-discriminatory" check-off policy. (See, also, New York City Charter [1963], § 1142.) The city—and, thus, the Mayor on its behalf—is empowered to enter into contracts, to regulate the terms of employment and compensation of city employees and to determine the manner of transacting the city's business and affairs (General City Law, Consol. Laws, c. 21, § 20, subds. 1, 17, 19; § 23, subd. 1). The Charter also specifically authorizes the Mayor to supervise city offices and departments, fix salaries, adopt wage plans and prescribe rules governing working conditions (New York City Charter [1963], §§ 123, 124, 813 subd. i). His executive power and discretion thus amply extend to and encompass the proposed action here under review, and no further legislative sanction is required.

Contrary to the petitioners' contention, the Mayor's discretion to decide which employee organization should have check-off privileges is not curtailed by section 93-b of the General Municipal Law Consol. Laws, c. 24. That section provides, in its subdivision 1, that a municipality is "authorized" to deduct dues from its employees' pay.[4] It is unmistakably permissive, not obligatory. It does not control a municipality's selection of the unions, if any, to which it may grant privilege of the check-off; and it certainly does not mandate the continuance of the check-off to minority unions. The only requirements which the section imposes are that, if a municipality does adopt the check-off for any union, (1) it must obtain an employee's written consent before deducting his dues; (2) it must allow the employee to withdraw that consent at any time; and (3) the procedure must be made available only to organizations of civil service employees. These conditions are met in the Mayor's proposed order.

That this State's legislative policy is not antagonistic to the check-off plan embodied in the proposed executive order is manifest also from the terms of the Public Employees' Fair Employment Act (Civil Service Law, Consol. Laws, c. 7, art. 14; L. 1967, ch. 392, known also as the Taylor Act). As the court noted in the course of its opinion at Special Term, that statute—

---

[4] Subdivision 1 of section 93-b reads, in part, as follows: "The fiscal or disbursing officer of every municipal corporation . . . is hereby authorized to deduct from the . . . salary of any employee of such municipal corporation . . . such amount that such employee may specify in writing filed with such . . . officer for the payment of dues in a duly organized association or organization of civil service employees and to transmit the sum so deducted to the said . . . organization. Any such written authorization may be withdrawn by such employee or member at any time by filing written notice of such withdrawal with [such] officer."

which did not take effect until some months after it announced its decision—explicitly gives majority unions of public employees the right to have their members' check-off requests honored, and is silent concerning the right to such check-off on behalf of minority unions (Civil Service Law, § 208). Although our decision in this case will have prospective effect, we need not decide whether the Taylor Act is applicable; it is sufficient to observe that, if the act does apply, it can only reinforce the decision which we reach on the basis of the pre-existing law. In short, the Mayor's proposed policy is plainly consistent with the scheme set forth in the Taylor Act for according recognition, and a degree of union security, to bargaining agents for public employees; to mention but one provision, section 208 makes it mandatory upon a public employer to extend a "right" of membership dues deduction to a union "certified" or "recognized" pursuant to the statute. (See, also, Civil Service Law, §§ 204, 212.) Whatever discretion a public employer may have, under the act, to grant the check-off to a minority union not recognized as a bargaining agent—and that question is not before us—the employer is plainly under no obligation to do so.

Since we find no statutory obstacle in the way of the city's proposed check-off policy, we turn to a consideration of whether that policy would, as Local 832 urges, deprive it of due process or equal protection of the laws. We agree with the courts below that it would not. The requirements of due process are satisfied as long as the challenged measure is reasonably related to the attainment of a permissible objective. (See, e.g., Railway Employes' Dept. v. Hanson, 351 U.S. 225, 233-235, 76 S. Ct. 714, 719, 100 L. Ed. 1112; Virginian Ry. v. System Federation, 300 U.S. 515, 558-559, 57 S. Ct. 592, 605, 81 L. Ed. 789.) Similarly, the standards of equal protection are met if a classification, or a distinction among classes, has some reasonable basis. (See, e.g., Baxstrom v. Herold, 383 U.S. 107, 111, 86 S. Ct. 760, 762, 15 L. Ed. 2d 620; Morey v. Doud, 354 U.S. 457, 464-465, 77 S. Ct. 1344, 1349, 1 L. Ed. 2d 1485; Bucho Holding Co. v. State Rent Comm., 11 N.Y.2d 469, 477, 230 N.Y.S.2d 977, 983, 184 N.E.2d 569, 574.)

In the case before us, the existence of such a reasonable relationship and basis is apparent. The maintenance of stability in the relations between the city and employee organizations, as well as the avoidance of devastating work stoppages, are major responsibilities of the city administration. The Mayor seeks to further these objectives by introducing into city labor relations a practice which has become commonplace in private industry and in the labor policies of other governmental bodies. For example, the

Federal Railway Labor Act specifically empowers the carrier and the exclusive bargaining agent to agree on an exclusive dues check-off (U.S. Code, tit. 45, § 152, subd. *Eleventh,* par. [b]); the practice is authorized for organizations of Federal civil service employees (Code of Fed. Reg., tit. 5, § 550.304, subd. [a], par. [5]; Executive Order 10988, §§ 5, 6, Jan. 17, 1962, 27 Federal Register 551); and it is also followed—according to the record before us—by the New York City Housing Authority and the New York City Transit Authority. The city program is in accord with national labor policy, which has been built on the premise that a majority organization is the most effective vehicle for improving wages, hours and working conditions. (See NLRB v. Allis-Chalmers Mfg. Co., 388 U.S. 175, 180, 87 S. Ct. 2001, 2006, 18 L. Ed. 2d 1123.) Be that as it may, we may not consider the merits or the ultimate wisdom of the policy (see Williamson v. Lee Opt. Co., 348 U.S. 483, 488, 75 S. Ct. 461, 464, 99 L. Ed. 563); it is enough, as already indicated, that a method of implementing union security, so widely utilized and so long tested as the one proposed by the Mayor, may not be said to lack a reasonable basis or to be unrelated to the city's legitimate purposes.

The petitioners also argue that the withdrawal of the dues check-off will weaken their minority union to the point of threatening its very existence. They will thus be deprived, they assert —pointing to such decisions as Bates v. City of Little Rock, 361 U.S. 516, 80 S. Ct. 412, 4 L. Ed. 2d 480, N.A.A.C.P. v. State of Alabama, 357 U.S. 449, 78 S. Ct. 1163, 2 L. Ed. 2d 1488 and Thomas v. Collins, 323 U.S. 516, 65 S. Ct. 315, 89 L. Ed. 430[5]— of their right of freedom of association guaranteed by the First and Fourteenth Amendments of the Federal Constitution and by article I of the State Constitution. Their claim lacks substance. Nothing in the city's labor policy denies members of the petitioners' union the right to meet, to speak, to publish, to proselytize and to collect dues by the means employed by thousands of organizations of all kinds, that do not have the benefit of a dues check-off. Neither the First Amendment nor any other constitutional provision entitles them to the special aid of the city's collection and disbursing facilities.

The order appealed from should be affirmed, with costs.

---

[5] The petitioners' reliance on these decisions is misplaced. The cited cases involved attempts by states to hinder organizations by some affirmative prohibition upon, or intrusion into, their activities. There is not the slightest suggestion that a state or other body must provide services to an organization to help it maintain its competitive position with its rivals.

BURKE, SCILEPPI, BERGAN, KEATING, BREITEL and JASEN, JJ., concur.

Order affirmed.

NOTES

1. *Accord,* Sacramento County Employees Organization, Local 22 v. County of Sacramento, 28 Cal. App. 3d 424, 104 Cal. Rptr. 619, — P.3d — (1972). The Nevada Local Government Employee-Management Relations Board has held that the exclusive bargaining representative has the exclusive right to contract for the checkoff of union dues and that it is not a prohibited practice for an employer to refuse to grant a minority union the right to check off the dues of its members. Operating Engineers Local Union No. 3 v. City of Reno, Item #7 (1972); AFT Local 1800 v. Clark County School Dist., Item #2 (1970).

2. The Wisconsin Supreme Court in Board of School Directors of City of Milwaukee v. WERC, 42 Wis. 2d 637, 168 N.W.2d 92 (1969), held that granting a majority union an exclusive dues checkoff was a prohibited practice. The court approved the WERC's test that " *[t]hose rights or benefits which are granted exclusively to the majority representative,* and thus denied its minority organizations, *must in some rational manner be related to the functions of the majority organization in its representative capacity,* and must not be granted to entrench such organization as the bargaining representative.' " [168 N.W.2d 97] The court, however, rejected the WERC's conclusion that granting an exclusive dues checkoff was permissible, stating:

> The WERC made no attempt to explain how the granting of exclusive checkoff was rationally related to the functioning of the majority organization *in its representative capacity*; nor can we see any relationship whatsoever. The sole and complete purpose of *exclusive* checkoff is self-perpetuation and entrenchment. While a majority representative may negotiate for checkoff, he is negotiating for all the employees, and, if checkoff is granted for any, it must be granted for all. 168 N.W.2d at 98.

FARRIGAN v. HELSBY

New York Supreme Court, Albany County
68 Misc. 2d 952, 327 N.Y.S.2d 909 (1971)
Aff'd 42 App. Div. 2d —, 346 N.Y.S.2d 39 (1973)

JOHN T. CASEY, J. The issue presented by this article 78 proceeding is whether the Public Employment Relations Board (PERB) acted in an arbitrary manner when it held that the

Monroe-Woodbury Board of Education did not commit an unfair labor practice by refusing to negotiate with petitioner concerning an "agency shop" proposal.

During the course of collective negotiations with the Monroe-Woodbury Board of Education, the petitioner, a teacher's association, submitted an item entitled "Support of Exclusive Teacher Representative" for negotiation. According to its terms, in order to retain his employment a teacher had to be either a member of the association (petitioner) or execute an authorization whereby the employer (Board of Education) would deduct an amount equal to the dues paid by a member of the association from such nonmember's salary and pay over that amount to the association. The proposal is commonly called an "agency shop." The board refused to negotiate concerning this item and asked the association to withdraw the proposal from negotiations. The association refused.

Subsequently, petitioner filed an unfair labor practice with PERB alleging that the Board of Education had violated paragraph (d) of subdivision 1 of section 209-a of the Civil Service Law. Specifically, it claimed the Board of Education had failed to bargain in good faith when it refused to negotiate concerning the agency shop. The matter was referred to a hearing officer and the parties agreed upon a stipulated set of facts. Thereafter, the hearing officer rendered a decision and recommended order. PERB agreed with the recommendations of the hearing officer and issued the order that is the subject of this proceeding.

According to PERB, an agency shop proposal could be negotiated by the Board of Education and the petitioner. PERB also concluded, however, that the proposal was illegal and, therefore, was not a mandatory item of negotiations. This being so, PERB continued, the Board of Education could refuse to negotiate concerning the proposal and such action could not be characterized as a failure to negotiate in good faith.

Pursuant to subdivision (a) of section 213 of the Civil Service Law, petitioner commenced this article 78 proceeding to review PERB's determination. The petitioner claims PERB acted arbitrarily because (1) it lacked the power to determine whether the agency shop proposal was legal, or (2) if PERB had such power, its characterization of the agency shop as illegal was arbitrary.

PERB may not, petitioner argues, classify the agency shop as a permissive item of negotiations upon the ground that it is illegal. Instead, according to the petitioner, PERB is limited to determining whether an agency shop is a term or condition of employment within the ambit of subdivision 4 of section 201 of the Civil Service Law; and if PERB finds it falls within sub-division 4 of section 201, the parties must negotiate concerning that item.

An administrative body may not issue unconstitutional orders. (Matter of Sloat v. Board of Examiners, 274 N.Y. 367.) There-fore, if a party to negotiations charged another with committing unfair labor practice by failing to bargain over an obviously unconstitutional term or condition of employment, a directive by PERB to bargain on that item would be erroneous. (Cf., Matter of Sloat v. Board of Examiners, supra.) This being so, it is not difficult to conclude that an order by PERB directing a party to bargain concerning an obviously illegal item would be erroneous.

The agency shop proposal is clearly illegal. Section 202 of the Civil Service Law provides: "Public employees shall have the right to form, join and participate in, or to refrain from form-ing, joining or participating in, any employee organization of their own choosing." Under that section, the public employee is given the right to determine whether he wishes to form, join or participate in the union. The agency shop, which under threat of dismissal requires a teacher to either join or pay dues to the association, contravenes the legislative policy contained therein.[1] (Ritto v. Fink, 58 Misc. 2d 1032.) Furthermore, PERB found, and I agree, that the agency shop would be prohibited under sub-division 2 of section 3012 of the Education Law* and section 93-b of the General Municipal Law.**

---

[1] I am aware of the decision in Smigel v. Southgate Community School District, 180 N.W.2d 215, 63 Labor Cases 52,341 (Mich. App.) wherein an agency shop proposal was not declared invalid. It appears from that decision that the Michigan statutes relating to public employees did not contain an absolute grant of a right to public employees to refrain from forming, joining or participating in an organization. The absence of such legislation distinguishes *Smigel* from the present case.

* Editors' Note: Section 3012 (2) of the Education Law provides that teachers

. . . who have served the probationary period . . . shall hold their re-spective positions during good behavior and efficient and competent service, and shall not be removed except for any of the following causes . . . : (a) insubordination, immoral character or conduct unbecoming a teacher; (b) inefficiency, incompetency, physical or mental dis-ability, or neglect of duty; (c) failure to maintain certification as required by this chapter and by the regulations of the commissioner of education.

** Editors' Note: Section 93-b (1) of the General Municipal Law reads as follows:

The fiscal or disbursing officer of every municipal corporation or other civil division or political subdivision of the State is hereby authorized to deduct from the wage or salary of any employee of such municipal corporation or civil division or political subdivision of the State such amount that such employee may specify in writing filed with such fiscal or disbursing officer for the payment of dues in a duly organized asso-ciation or association of civil service employees and to transmit the sum

In sum, where an item submitted for negotiations is clearly illegal, PERB must recognize such illegality. Furthermore, once having done so, PERB does not act in an arbitrary manner by failing to find that a party has committed an unfair labor practice by refusing to negotiate concerning such an item.

I do not intend this decision to mean that PERB may question and determine the legality of items which are not obvious. That issue was not before me and was not decided.

The petition is dismissed.

NOTES

1. *Accord,* New Jersey Turnpike Employees, Local 194 v. New Jersey Turnpike Authority, 117 N.J. Super. 349, 284 A.2d 566 (1971), *aff'd,* 123 N.J. Super. 461, 303 A.2d 599 (Super. Ct., App. Div. 1973).

2. In Devita v. Scher, 52 Misc. 2d 138, 276 N.Y.S.2d 913 (Sup. Ct. Monroe Cty. 1966), the City of Rochester and the Firefighters had agreed to an agency shop clause in which the city agreed " '. . . to deduct an amount equal to the normal monthly dues paid by members of the Association from the earnings' " of employees in the bargaining unit who were not members of the Association. The court found that the clause in question was invalid, relying on the New York statutory provision which permits a public employer to deduct association dues if the employee files a written authorization and further provides that said written authorization may be withdrawn at any time. Accordingly, the court held that before any dues deduction could be made by the city, an employee had to submit a written authorization, *i.e.,* the city had no authority to make a payroll deduction when no current valid written authorization is on file.

3. Wholly apart from statutory provisions such as those relied on by the court in the principal case, do public employees have a constitutional right to refrain from joining a union? In other words, does it follow that since public employees have a firmly established constitutional right to join or form unions that they also have a constitutional right to refrain from joining or forming unions? If such a constitutional right to refrain from union activities exists, any inconsistent state statutes or state court decisions would necessarily be deemed invalid by virtue of the supremacy clause of the Constitution.

---

so deducted to the said organization or association. Any such written authorization may be withdrawn by such employee or member at any time by filing written notice of such withdrawal with the fiscal or disbursing agent.

TREMBLAY v. BERLIN POLICE UNION
New Hampshire Supreme Court
108 N.H. 416, 237 A.2d 668 (1968)

PER CURIAM.

[Paul Tremblay, the City Marshall, and two police officers filed a petition for declaratory judgment to test the validity of the "union shop" clause, as well as certain other provisions, in the collective bargaining agreement between the City of Berlin and AFSCME, Local 1444. In the agreed statement of facts, the parties stipulated that the two petitioning police officers had initially refused to sign check off authorizations for the deduction of union dues, but had later done so because they were told that their failure to do so would result in their dismissal from the police force.]

The so-called union shop clause (article 3, section 1) is qualified and limited by its terms. The clause in full reads as follows: *"Whenever re-employments are made, or the police department hires new employees,* they shall, within sixty working days become members of the Union Local ♯ 1444 by presenting to the police department a proper authorization, approved by the Union president, for the collection of their dues." (emphasis supplied) There is no requirement in this clause, or any other, for maintenance of membership in good standing. This clause, together with the "check off" clause (article 4, section 1) for union dues, imposes a financial obligation only. The union cannot cause the discharge of an employee, who has resigned from or has been expelled by the union for any reason other than his withdrawal of the check off authorization.

It is argued that this union shop clause of the collective bargaining agreement is invalid as an unlawful delegation of municipal power and is "ultra vires and void." There is no law which prohibits a union shop in this state and RSA 275:1 prohibits any effort to coerce or compel any person into an agreement "not to join or become a member of any labor organization" as a condition of securing or continuing in any employment. The Legislature has declared as a matter of public policy that collective bargaining for municipal employees is a proper public purpose. In making this declaration it has not excluded police departments (as some statutes do) or other public employees in equally essential positions. *Cf.,* Laws 1963, 278:1, now RSA 38-A:18, II (supp), which applies to transit employees. Opinions may differ as to the desirability of collective bargaining for public employees but that discretionary decision has been lodged in the municipalities. One city may determine that union recognition results in efficient operation of its departments; another city may decide that

public employees should have less rights than private citizens.
See Weisenfield, Public Employees—First or Second Class Citizens, 16 Lab. L.J. 685 (1965); Cornell, Collective Bargaining by Public Employees Groups, 107 U. Pa. L. Rev. 43 (1958).

In the present case the police commissioners and the union have, in effect, declared in advance under the collective bargaining agreement that union security is a reasonable requirement for the efficient and orderly administration of the police department. Stutz, Collective Bargaining by City Employees, 15 Lab. L.J. 696 (1964). This is a decision they have the right to make because (1) the Legislature authorized it, (2) ultimate control remains in the municipality and the police commissioners to hire and fire personnel and manage the police department, (3) the overriding provisions of the collective bargaining agreement provide that the powers delegated to the union are subordinate to and must be consistent with the powers of the city and its agents in its control over the administration of the police department. Laws 1963, 275:4, 5. See, Comment, Labor Problems in Public Employment, 61 Nw. U.L. Rev. 105, 133 (1966). . . .

Petition dismissed.

NOTE

In *Tremblay* the court relied in part on the statutory prohibition of coerced nonmembership and the absence of a statutory provision giving public employees a right to refrain from joining a union. Suppose an employer and a union entered into a union shop agreement and there were several employees who were members of a minority union. Would the union shop provision be legal if it had the effect of forcing the employees who were members of the minority union to forego their membership?

SMIGEL v. SOUTHGATE COMMUNITY SCHOOL DISTRICT
Michigan Supreme Court
388 Mich. 531, 202 N.W.2d 305 (1972)

T.M. KAVANAGH, C.J. (*for reversal and remand*). We concur with Justice SWAINSON that the pure legal issues concerning construction of our statutes are not peculiarly within the scope of the expertise of the Michigan Employment Relations Commission and as such were properly brought before the circuit court.

However, we do not agree that the trial court correctly denied the plaintiffs injunctive relief. The determinative issue which must be resolved in this case is:

Does the "agency shop" provision involved in the instant case create the practical equivalent of a "union shop" and, as such, is it prohibited by § 10 of the public employment relations act?

It should be emphasized at the outset that this case involves public employees and is therefore controlled by the so-called public employment relations act. The historical backdrop against which we must view this statute is most significant. The original act had as its stated purposes the prohibition of strikes by certain public employees and the provision for mediation of grievances. It was not until its amendment in 1965 that the statute granted public employees the right to organize and bargain collectively. 1965 PA 379 not only authorized the formation of public employees' unions, but also incorporated the policy of the National Labor Relations Act—that an employer must assume a posture of complete neutrality regarding union membership. He must do nothing to either advance or retard union organizing. Likewise must he refrain from practices which either encourage or discourage membership in labor organizations.

In this respect there is a significant distinction in Michigan's labor law between public and private employees. Though MCLA 423.16; MSA 17.454 (17) is nearly identical to MCLA 423.210; MSA 17.455 (10) in respect to the requirement of employer neutrality, the statute regarding private employment includes one very important provision which is not found in the public employment relations act. MCLA 423.14; MSA 17.454 (15) constitutes an authorization of union security clauses whether in the form of "closed shop," "union shop" or "agency shop."

Prior to the 1965 amendment of the public employment relations act, public employees had no right to organize collectively for bargaining purposes. Defendant union de-emphasizes the significance of this fact in an attempt to show that public employees now have been granted, with the exception of the right to strike, all rights conferred upon private employees.

However, as we have already indicated, the specification of rights for public employment is narrower than for private employment. The Legislature accomplished this result by not including in the public employment relations act the right, specified in MCLA 423.14; MSA 17.454 (15), to enter into agreements containing union security clauses.

Defendant union urges the position that an "agency shop" agreement is not an "all-union" agreement as contemplated by MCLA 423.14; MSA 17.454 (15) and that therefore it need not be specifically authorized by the public employment relations act. While this might be true where an "agency shop" provision accomplishes no more than reimbursement to the union for services rendered to a nonmember, it is certainly not true whenever an "agency shop" agreement has the effect of either encour-

aging or discouraging union membership in violation of MCLA
423.210; MSA 17.455 (10) .

The traditional "agency shop" provision is a well known type of
union security clause. Its terms are often such as to render it
the practical equivalent of a union shop and as such it by definition contravenes the policy and purposes of the public employment relations act.

The United States Supreme Court has on at least two occasions
opined that an "agency shop" provision imposing on employees
the only enforceable membership obligation—payment of initiation fees and regular dues—is the practical equivalent of an all-
union shop. Retail Clerks International Association, Local 1625,
AFL-CIO v. Schermerhorn, 373 U.S. 746; 83 S. Ct. 1461; 10
L. Ed. 2d 678 (1963) ; National Labor Relations Board v. General Motors Corp., 373 U.S. 734; 83 S. Ct. 1453; 10 L. Ed. 2d
670 (1963) .

Significant here is the specific choice of language in article
II, paragraph 2 of the contract. The payroll deduction for nonmembers is "a representation fee *equivalent to the dues and
assessments of the Association* (including the National and
Michigan Education Associations) ." (Emphasis added.) There
is not even the pretense that the sum to be deducted is a pro rata
share of representation expenses, or that it will even be used for
such purpose. In Retail Clerks v. Schermerhorn, supra, the "agency
shop" clause, though specifically earmarking the funds for aiding
the union in meeting collective bargaining expenses, was nevertheless found objectionable under the Florida "right-to-work"
law. The Court reasoned (373 U.S. 746, 752-754) :

> "There is no ironclad restriction imposed upon the use of
> nonmember fees, for the clause merely describes the pay-
> ments as being for 'the purpose of aiding the Union' in
> meeting collective bargaining expenses. The alleged restric-
> tion would not be breached if the service fee was used for
> both collective bargaining and other expenses, for the union
> would be 'aided' in meeting its agency obligations, not only
> by the part spent for bargaining purposes but also by the
> part spent for institutional items, since an equivalent amount
> of other union income would thereby be freed to pay the
> costs of bargaining agency functions.

> "But even if all collections from nonmembers must be
> directly committed to paying bargaining costs, this fact is
> of bookkeeping significance only rather than a matter of
> real substance. It must be remembered that the service fee
> is admittedly the exact equal of membership initiation fees

and monthly dues. . . .[6] Unions 'rather typically' use their membership dues 'to do those things which the members authorize the union to do in their interest and on their behalf.' If the union's total budget is divided between collective bargaining and institutional expenses and if nonmember payments, equal to those of a member, go entirely for collective bargaining costs, the nonmember will pay more of these expenses than his pro rata share. The member will pay less and to that extent a portion of his fees and dues is available to pay institutional expenses. The union's budget is balanced. By paying a larger share of collective bargaining costs the nonmember subsidizes the union's institutional activities. In over-all effect, economically, and we think for the purposes of § 14 (b) , the contract here is the same as the *General Motors* agency shop arrangement. Petitioners' argument if accepted, would lead to the anomalous result of permitting Florida to invalidate the agency shop but forbidding it to ban the present service fee arrangement under which collective bargaining services cost the nonmember more than the member."

Following this reasoning we are compelled to conclude that the "agency shop" provision in the instant contract is repugnant on its face to the provisions of our public employment relations act.

We hold that any such clause as this which makes no effort to relate to nonmembers' economic obligations to actual collective bargaining expenses is clearly prohibited by § 10 of the public employment relations act, as of necessity either encouraging or discouraging membership in a labor organization.

Having so concluded, we hold that the trial court erred in denying plaintiffs injunctive relief. We see no need for an order remanding for proof of *de facto* discrimination in the assessment against nonmembers because there appears upon the face of the contract we have before us *de jure* discrimination of a magnitude sufficient to invalidate the clause.

"[6] 'Rather typically, unions use their members' dues to promote legislation which they regard as desirable and to defeat legislation which they regard as undesirable, to publish newspapers and magazines, to promote free labor institutions in other nations, to finance low cost housing, to aid victims of natural disaster, to support charities, to finance litigation, to provide scholarships, and to do those things which the members authorize the union to do in their interest and on their behalf.'

"We cannot take seriously petitioners' unsupported suggestion at the oral argument that we must assume that the union spends all of its income on collective bargaining expenses. The record is entirely silent on this matter one way or the other and it would be unique indeed if the union expended no funds for noncollective bargaining purposes."

Reversed and remanded to the trial court for the entry of injunctive relief consistent herewith.

ADAMS and T.G. KAVANAGH, JJ., concurred with T.M. KAVA-NAGH, C.J.

WILLIAMS, J. (*concurring in part and dissenting in part*). I concur in part with and dissent in part from the opinions of Chief Justice T.M. KAVANAGH, Justice T.E. BRENNAN and Justice SWAINSON. I concur in reversal and remand.

On the question of court jurisdiction *vis-a-vis* MERC to construe the pertinent statutes, I agree with what the Chief Justice and Justice SWAINSON wrote that the Court has such jurisdiction.

On the question whether PERA § 10 permits an "agency shop," I agree with the Chief Justice and Justice T.E. BRENNAN that it does not. This is because PERA fails to include a savings clause for union security such as § 14 in private employment. National Labor Relations Board v. General Motors Corp., 373 U.S. 734, 738-739; 83 S. Ct. 1453; 10 L. Ed. 2d 670 (1963). See also Retail Clerks International Association, Local 1625, AFL-CIO v. Schermerhorn, 373 U.S. 746, 751; 83 S. Ct. 1461; 10 L. Ed. 2d 678 (1963). Otherwise, an "agency shop" can be compatible with a normal "right-to-work" law. Meade Electric Co. v. Hagberg, 129 Ind. App. 631; 159 N.E.2d 408 (1959).

On the question of the validity of an "agency shop" requirement that non-union members pay the union a sum equivalent to initiation fees, and periodic dues, I agree with Justice SWAINSON that where the "agency shop" is valid such a provision is valid. National Labor Relations Board v. General Motors Corp., supra, 742-744.

T.E. BRENNAN, J. (*for reversal*). The issue here is whether the collective bargaining agreement entered into by the defendant school district would, if enforced, obligate the defendant, a public employer, to violate MCLA 423.210; MSA 17.455 (10).

That section provides:

"Sec. 10. It shall be unlawful for a public employer or an officer or agent of a public employer . . . (c) to discriminate in regard to hire, terms or other conditions of employment in order to encourage or discourage membership in a labor organization; . . . ."

We said in Judges of the 74th Judicial District v. Bay County, 385 Mich. 710 (1971):

"The Bay County Commissioners in this case had entered into an all-union or closed shop agreement with the defendant International Union.

"In the private sector, such all-union agreements are permissible, despite the language of MCLA § 423.16[3] (Stat. Ann. 1968 Rev. § 17.454[17][3]), which makes it unlawful for an employer to discriminate in regard to hire, terms or other conditions of employment in order to encourage or discourage membership in any labor organization.

"All-union agreements are permissible in the private sector because MCLA § 423.14 (Stat. Ann. 1968 Rev. § 17.454 [15]) specifically permits them.

" 'Sec. 14. Nothing in this act shall be construed to interfere with the right of an employer to enter into an all-union agreement with one labor organization if it is the only organization established among his employes and recognized by him, by consent, as the representative of a majority of his employes; nor shall anything in this act be construed to interfere with the right of the employer to make an all-union agreement with more than one labor organization established among his employes if such organizations are recognized by him, by consent, as the representatives of a majority of his employes.'

"In public employment, all-union agreements are not permitted. MCLA § 423.210 (c) (Stat. Ann. 1968 Rev. § 17.455 [10][c]) prohibits discrimination by a public employer to encourage or discourage membership in a labor organization. The language of that subsection is identical to the language of MCLA § 423.16 (3) (Stat. Ann. 1968 Rev. § 17.454[17][3]) .

"But no section parallel to MCLA § 423.14 (Stat. Ann. 1968 Rev. § 17.454[15]) appears in PA 1947, No. 336 (MCLA § 423.201 et seq.; Stat. Ann. 1968 Rev. § 17.455[1] et seq.) ."

It is argued, however, that the Southgate agreement is not a prohibited all-union agreement, but merely a so-called agency shop agreement, by which nonmembers of the exclusive bargaining agent organization are required to pay fees to the union as consideration for services rendered at the bargaining table.

MCLA 423.210 does not address itself merely to all-union or closed shop agreements. In the present context, it prohibits terms or conditions of employment which are designed to encourage membership in a labor organization.

The Southgate agreement makes the payment of dues and assessments of the Southgate, Michigan and National Education Associations, *or the equivalent* of such dues and assessments a condition of employment.

The payment of initiation fees and regular dues are the only obligations enforceable by discharge under § 8[a][3] of the National Labor Relations Act.

It follows that a so-called agency shop contract which imposes the same obligation upon nonmembers, is the practical equivalent of a union shop contract. National Labor Relations Board v. General Motors Corp., 373 U.S. 734; 83 S. Ct. 1453; 10 L. Ed. 2d 670 (1963).

MCLA 423.210 (c) is in effect a "right to work" law, limited to public employment. Other states, construing similar provisions, have held agency shop agreements invalid. Baldwin v. Arizona Flame Restaurant, 82 Ariz. 385; 313 P.2d 759 (1957); Higgins v. Cardinal Mfg. Co., 188 Kan. 11; 360 P.2d 456 (1961); see also, Retail Clerks International Association, Local 1625, AFL-CIO v. Schermerhorn, 373 U.S. 746; 83 S. Ct. 1461; 10 L. Ed. 2d 678 (1963).

The judgment of the trial court should be reversed and the cause remanded.

SWAINSON, J. *(for affirmance in part and reversal in part).* This case involves the validity of the agency shop provision in the public sector under the public employment relations act (hereinafter called PERA) and the teachers' tenure act.

In 1965, the Michigan Legislature amended the PERA and provided for the right of public employees to form or join unions and bargain collectively. Pursuant to § 12 of this act (MCLA 423.212; MSA 17.455[12]), a petition was filed with the Michigan Labor Mediation Board which held a secret ballot election. The Southgate Education Association (hereinafter referred to as SEA) was chosen over the Southgate Federation of Teachers, and was certified as the sole bargaining representative for teachers employed by the Southgate Community School District (hereinafter called the Board).

The Board and the SEA negotiated contracts for the 1966-1967 and 1967-1968 school years. Another petition was filed and a secret ballot election was held in February 1968. The SEA received 96 votes and the Federation 87. The SEA remained certified as the sole bargaining representative and commenced negotiations with the Board, which is a public employer within the meaning of PERA. Agreement on a contract was reached September 4, 1968, for the 1968-1969 and 1969-1970 school years. The agreement was very detailed and was divided into 26 articles concerning wages, working conditions, grievance procedures, *et cetera.* Article 2, § A, of the agreement contained the disputed agency shop provisions. This article provided in part:

"ARTICLE II—MEMBERSHIP, FEES AND PAYROLL DEDUCTIONS

"A. All teachers as a condition of continued employment *shall either:*

"1. Sign and deliver to the Board an assignment authorizing deduction of *membership dues* and assessments of the Association (including the National and Michigan Education Associations) and such authorization shall continue in effect from year to year unless revoked in writing between June 1 and September 1 of a given year. Such sums shall be deducted during the eight (8) consecutive pay periods commencing the 1st pay of October from the salary of all teachers authorizing deductions and remitted within thirty (30) days to the Association. Teachers joining the Association at the beginning of the second semester and signing and delivering to the Board an assignment authorizing deduction of said membership dues, may have dues for that semester deducted from the six (6) consecutive pay periods commencing the 1st pay of February, or

"2. Sign and deliver to the Board an assignment authorizing deduction of a representation fee equivalent to the dues and assessments of the Association (including the National and Michigan Education Associations). Such sums shall be deducted during the eight (8) consecutive pay periods commencing the 1st pay of October from the salary of all teachers authorizing deductions and remitted within thirty (30) days to the Association. Teachers beginning their employment at the beginning of the second semester and signing and delivering to the Board an assignment authorizing deduction of said representation fees may have fees for that semester deducted from the six (6) consecutive pay periods commencing the 1st pay of February. Any teacher who wishes to pay cash for this fee must pay the full amount to the Treasurer of the S.E.A. within thirty (30) days of the commencement of employment.

"In the event the representation fee shall not be paid, the Board upon receiving a signed statement from the Association indicating the teacher has failed to comply with this condition, shall immediately notify said teacher that his services shall be discontinued at the end of the current semester. The Board shall follow the dismissal procedure of the Michigan Tenure Act. The refusal of said teacher to contribute fairly to the costs of negotiation and administration of this and subsequent agreements is recognized as just and reasonable cause for termination of employment. However, if at the end of the semester, the teacher, or teachers, receiving the termination notice shall then be engaged in pursuing any legal remedies contesting the discharge under this provision before the Michigan Tenure Commission, or a court of competent jurisdiction, such teacher's service shall not be terminated until such time as such teacher or teachers have either obtained a final decision as to the validity or legality of such charge, or such teacher or teachers have ceased to pursue the legal remedies available to them by not making a timely appeal of any decision rendered in said manner by the Tenure Commission, or a court of competent jurisdiction.

"This Section is subject to an indemnity agreement executed September 3, 1968 between the parties which is incorporated herein by reference."

The SEA by memorandum dated September 16, 1968, and sent to all nonmembers of the SEA, gave notice of its intention to enforce all the provisions of the collective bargaining agreement negotiated on behalf of all employees in the bargaining unit. On September 26, 1968, plaintiffs, public school teachers employed by the Board but not members of the SEA,[5] filed complaint in Wayne County Circuit Court requesting injunctive relief from the collective bargaining agreement and specifically Article 2, § A, the agency shop provision, and sought damages in the amount of $100,000 against the Board, the SEA, Donald Kouba, its President, and Jack Frucci, Chairman of its negotiating team. The trial court upheld the validity of the agency shop provision and denied the temporary injunctive relief requested. The trial court certified that a controlling question of law was involved, and plaintiffs herein made application to the Court of Appeals for leave to appeal and, also, filed application for leave to appeal to this Court prior to decision of the Court of Appeals. On June 26, 1969, we denied such application.

The Court of Appeals reversed and remanded for a hearing to determine what percentage of the fees provided to be paid to SEA is used for the cost of administering and negotiating the contract. The Court of Appeals held that the agency fee could be neither higher nor lower than this amount without violating §10, subd. (c), of the PERA.[6] The Court of Appeals further

[5] Plaintiff Smigel was an officer of the rival Southgate Federation of Teachers.

[6] Section 10 (c), MCLA 423.210; MSA 17.455 (10), reads:

"It shall be unlawful for a public employer or an officer or agent of a public employer . . . (c) to discriminate in regard to hire, terms or other conditions of employment in order to encourage or discourage membership in a labor organization."

held that on remand the SEA and the Board had the burden of "going forward" with the evidence and the proof on this issue. If such a percentage could be determined, the Court of Appeals held, then the agency shop provision was valid. 24 Mich. App. 179.

The defense moved for clarification of the opinion, for reconsideration, and for a hearing en banc by the Court of Appeals. These motions were denied on August 3, 1970. In view of the overriding importance of this issue to labor relations in the public sector, we granted leave to appeal. 384 Mich. 772.

In addition to the parties to the appeal, the Detroit Federation of Teachers, the American Federation of State, County and Municipal Employees, the Michigan Employment Relations Commission and the Michigan Conference of Teamsters were permitted to file briefs as Amicus Curiae.

Several issues have been raised on this appeal, the threshold one being whether the Michigan Employment Relations Commission has primary and exclusive jurisdiction of this matter, and thus whether the circuit court properly had jurisdiction herein?

Another basic issue presented is whether the agency shop provision between the Southgate Community School District and the Southgate Educational Association is valid under Michigan law and under the United States and Michigan Constitutions? Both parties view this issue as divisible into sub-issues, and each will be dealt with within the framework of this issue.

The question of the jurisdiction of the circuit court to hear this case has been raised on appeal for the first time by defendants and by the Michigan Employment Relations Commission as Amicus Curiae. Both parties urge that the Michigan Employment Relations Commission has primary jurisdiction of this matter and that the circuit court erred in considering same. Plaintiffs correctly point out that defendants did not object to the jurisdiction of the circuit court and even relied on circuit court opinions regarding similar situations in support of their view of the validity of the agency shop provision. However, it is well settled that lack of subject matter jurisdiction cannot be waived. Warner v. Noble, 286 Mich. 654, 659 (1938). A court may and, indeed, has a duty to inquire into its jurisdiction. This has been accepted as law in Michigan since Greenvault v. Farmers & Mechanics' Bank, 2 Doug. (Mich.) 498 (1847). We thus turn to the issue of whether the circuit court properly had jurisdiction in this matter.

Primary Jurisdiction

The Michigan Employment Relations Commission as Amicus Curiae, contends that the circuit court lacked jurisdiction over this matter. It contends that plaintiffs should have first sought relief through the MERC and that the MERC could have provided adequate relief. It further contends that an adequate appeal is provided to the Court of Appeals by the provisions of the PERA.

The deference of courts to administrative agencies and the declining of jurisdiction in favor of these agencies is designed to meet several policy goals. The most important one is the belief that these agencies possess special expertise which are well suited in the first instance to deal with the factual questions involved. The United States Supreme Court accepted this theory in the field of labor relations in Myers v. Bethlehem Shipbuilding Corp., 303 U.S. 41; 58 S. Ct. 459; 82 L. Ed. 2d 638 (1938). The National Labor Relations Board had issued a complaint against Bethlehem charging it with an unfair labor practice. The defendant obtained an injunction in district court against the holding of the hearing before the NLRB. The United States Supreme Court reversed the lower court and held the district court had no jurisdiction to issue an injunction. The Court further held that the NLRB had exclusive jurisdiction in such cases.

Our Court has recognized the doctrine of primary jurisdiction and judicial deference to the expertise of administrative agencies. . . .

There are, however, exceptions to the doctrine of primary jurisdiction as stated above. In Diggs v. State Board of Embalmers and Funeral Directors, 321 Mich. 508 (1948), plaintiff filed an action to set aside revocation of his license after a hearing by the Board. The Board's motion to dismiss was denied, and the Supreme Court affirmed. Plaintiff alleged that the statute under which the hearing was held was unconstitutional. The Court stated (pp. 513-514):

"If plaintiff's position is correct, *in other words, if the entire statute is unconstitutional,* then the provisions with reference to an appeal from an order of defendant board would necessarily fall with the rest of the act. It is scarcely logical to say that plaintiff is bound to press a remedy ostensibly granted by the statute the validity of which he assails.

"This Court has repeatedly held that in cases where an irreparable injury will result from the acts of public officials in attempting to proceed under an invalid law, *the jurisdic-*

tion of equity may be invoked for the purpose of obtaining injunctive relief and a determination as to the constitutionality of the statute that is involved." (Emphasis added.)

This exception, where a plaintiff challenges the unconstitutionality of the statute, was followed in Asta v. Department of Revenue, 338 Mich. 505 (1953). In the recent case of Judges of the 74th Judicial District v. Bay County, 385 Mich. 710 (1971), our Court upheld in part the right of plaintiffs to obtain declaratory relief without the necessity of exhausting their administrative remedies. It appears to us that the present case would fit under this exception to the rules requiring that a party exhaust his administrative remedies prior to seeking judicial relief.

The basic facts are agreed upon by the parties. The questions involved are questions of law which this Court must ultimately decide. Plaintiffs in their complaint contend that the agency shop provision violated both the teachers' tenure act and The Michigan Penal Code (MCLA 750.353 *et seq.;* MSA 28.585 *et seq.*). The special expertise of the Commission is not helpful to the Court in determining these questions of law. Moreover, as Professor Roger Crampton succinctly points out in an article entitled, The Doctrine of Exhaustion of Administrative Remedies in Michigan, 44 Mich. State Bar Journal, No. 7, July 1965, pp. 10-20, one other factor that the courts consider in determining whether to require exhaustion of administrative remedies, is the importance of the question involved. The briefs filed by both parties and the Amicus Curiae briefs filed by the several additional parties, indicate that the validity or invalidity of the agency shop provision will have far-reaching consequences upon collective bargaining in the public sector in Michigan. Professor Crampton asserts that this is an additional factor for the courts to consider in dispensing with the requirement of exhaustion of administrative remedies, and we agree. Thus, we hold that the complaint for injunctive relief was a proper procedure in this case and the circuit court did have jurisdiction of this matter.

Plaintiffs contend that since the PERA does not explicitly permit the agency shop, it, therefore, must forbid it. They cite Benson v. School District No. 1 of Silver Bow County, 136 Mont. 77; 344 P.2d 117 (1959). In that case, plaintiffs, teachers who had refused to join the union, brought a proceeding for mandamus and declaratory judgment. The Supreme Court of Montana ruled in their favor. The School District had approved a master agreement on April 2, 1956, which provided salary increases based on the training and experience of the teachers and, also, required union membership (union shop) by September 4, 1956. The contract further provided that in the event nonunion teachers who had tenure failed to join the union, they should not receive any of the benefits or salary increases that were awarded to other teachers. The difference in salary between union and nonunion teachers the first year was $300. The Court stated (p. 85) :

> "Hence, we come to the question whether the Union Security Clause in the contract is void and illegal as contended by plaintiffs. We hold that it is.
>
> "It is not competent for the school trustees to require union membership as a condition to receiving the increased salary. So far as this case is concerned it is sufficient to say that the Legislature has not given the school board authority to make the discrimination sought to be imposed here."

This case is distinguishable from the present situation because of the blatant discrimination against nonunion teachers. Nonunion teachers were forbidden to receive raises and, hence, there was a clear economic inducement and discrimination in favor of union members. This, of course, would violate § 10 (c) of the PERA. However, no discrimination is made between union and nonunion members in regard to wages or other working conditions in the Southgate contract. Both members and nonmembers receive the same pay scale depending on seniority and education.

In Tremblay v. Berlin Police Union, 108 N.H. 416; 237 A.2d 668 (1968), the Court had before it a declaratory judgment dealing with the validity of certain provisions of the union contract negotiated between a policemen's local union and the Berlin Police Commission. The case was transferred to the Supreme Court on an agreed statement of facts. The contract created a union shop and the Supreme Court upheld the validity of the contract, construing it as an agency shop provision. The Court stated (pp. 422-423) :

> "It is argued that this union shop clause of the collective bargaining agreement is invalid as an unlawful delegation of municipal power and is 'ultra vires and void.' There is no law which prohibits a union shop in this state and RSA 275:1 prohibits any effort to coerce or compel any person into an agreement 'not to join or become a member of any labor organization' as a condition of securing or continuing in any employment. The Legislature has declared as a matter of public policy that collective bargaining for municipal employees is a proper public purpose. . . . Opinions may differ as to the desirability of collective bargaining for public employees but that discretionary decision has been lodged in the municipalities. . . .

"In the present case the police commissioners and the union have, in effect, declared in advance under the collective bargaining agreement that union security is a reasonable requirement for the efficient and orderly administration of the police department. Stutz, Collective Bargaining by City Employees, 15 Lab. L.J. 696 (1964). This is a decision they have the right to make because (1) the Legislature authorized it, (2) ultimate control remains in the municipality and the police commissioners to hire and fire personnel and manage the police department, (3) the overriding provisions of the collective bargaining agreement provide that the powers delegated to the union are subordinate to and must be consistent with the powers of the city and its agents in its control over the administration of the police department. Laws 1963, 275:4, 5. See, Comment, Labor Problems in Public Employment, 61 Nw. U.L. Rev. 105, 133 (1966).

"Our conclusion [is] that this union shop clause, as construed, is valid. . . ."

We agree with the reasoning of the Court in *Tremblay*. The School District and the SEA in negotiating this contract believed that the agency shop provision would promote the goals set out in the PERA. The failure of the Legislature to specifically include a union shop provision does not mean that it cannot be negotiated and agreed upon by the parties. We, therefore, hold that an agency shop provision may be voluntarily agreed upon by the parties and that such an agreement does not violate the provisions of the PERA.

Plaintiffs rely on the report of the Advisory Committee on Public Employee Relations submitted to Governor George Romney, February 15, 1967, and the fact that bills have been introduced in the Legislature to allow agency shops as proof that it is not permitted under current law. The statements of legislators and other citizens provide only some evidence of legislative intent; they are not conclusive on this Court. The question of the validity of the agency shop has been one of uncertainty under Michigan law. The fact that certain legislators attempted to clarify this question by new legislation before a Court decision is not inconsistent with the belief that agency shop is permitted under present law.

Plaintiffs also contend that since the PERA adopts in some sections the wording of the NLRA almost verbatim, it must mean that where the PERA does not follow the NLRA it meant to exclude its terms. However, the legislative history of the two acts are not parallel and, as defendants point out, § 7 of the

NLRA permits workers to join unions or refrain from joining unions, but § 9 of the PERA has no similar proviso for not joining unions. This would mean that under plaintiffs' analysis all workers must join unions. This, of course, is not required by the PERA, but does point up the difficulty in attempting to compare the two pieces of legislation and in assuming that any section of the NLRA left out in the PERA was meant to be excluded.

Finally, plaintiffs contend that the difference in private employment and public employment requires a different result under the PERA than under the NLRA. They contend that the PERA was not adopted to strengthen the collective economic power of public employees. Plaintiffs contend that public employment differs radically from private employment and that public employees should not have the rights of private employees. However, while this theory was the prevailing view in 1947,[11] when the Hutchinson Act was passed, it is not true today. The Legislature, by amendment in 1965, clearly gave public employees many of the rights that employees in the private sector enjoy, including the right to join a labor organization, and the obligation of an employer to bargain with such organization.

Teachers' Tenure Act

Plaintiffs contend that the teachers' tenure act (MCLA 38.71 et seq.; MSA 15.1971 et seq.) precludes the discharge of teachers for failure to pay the agency fee as provided in the Southgate contract. They cite Rehberg v. Ecorse Township School District No. 11, 330 Mich. 541 (1951), where, in discussing the purpose of the tenure act, the Court stated (p. 545):

"The teachers' tenure act has not been construed in Michigan, but the following has been said about such acts elsewhere:

"Its purpose is to maintain an adequate and competent teaching staff, free from political and personal arbitrary interference. Ehret v. Kulpmont Borough School District, 333 Pa. 518 (5 A.2d 188) [1939].

"It promotes good order and the welfare of the State and of the school system by preventing removal of capable and experienced teachers at the personal whims of changing office holders. State, ex rel. Anderson v. Brand, 214 Ind. 347 (5 N.E.2d 531, 913, 110 A.L.R. 778, 781) [1937]. Also, same

---

[11] See Wayne County Civil Service Commission v. Board of Supervisors, 384 Mich. 363, 371-372 (1971), for discussion of the view of the employees' rights under the Hutchinson Act of 1947 (No. 336).

on rehearing, 214 Ind. 347 (7 N.E.2d 777) [1938] 303 U.S. 95 (58 S. Ct. 443, 82 L. Ed. 685, 113 A.L.R. 1482) [1938]; and Lost Creek School Township v. York, 215 Ind. 636 (21 N.E. 2d 58, 127 A.L.R. 1287) [1939].

"In State, ex rel. Wood v. Board of Education of City of St. Louis, 357 Mo. 147 (206 S.W.2d 566, 567 [1947]), it is stated that the purpose of the act is to protect and improve State education by retaining in their positions teachers who are qualified and capable and who have demonstrated their fitness, and to prevent the dismissal of such teachers without just cause. See, also, The Teachers' Contractual Status by I. M. Allen, page 77, Bureau of Publications, Teachers College, Columbia University (1928)."

The teachers' tenure act was first passed in 1937. The act is designed to apply to an innumerable variety of situations that may arise. Article IV, § 1, of the teachers' tenure act, MCLA 38.101; MSA 15.2001, provides in part:

"Discharge or demotion of a teacher on continuing tenure may be made only for reasonable and just cause, and only after such charges, notice, hearing, and determination thereof, as are hereinafter provided."

The words "reasonable and just cause" are not defined, but are to be determined on a case-by-case basis. The legislative policy behind this section is clearly to prevent the firing of qualified teachers because of arbitrary and capricious actions on the part of school boards.

In the instant case the requirement of the agency shop fee is neither arbitrary nor capricious. It was arrived at after mutual bargaining by the Board and the elected representatives of all the teachers. All teachers prior to commencing their employment were notified as to what was required of them. Article 2 of the Southgate contract clearly states what was required of the teachers in regard to the agency fee. Any teacher violating this provision of the contract would be entitled to all the safeguards provided by the tenure act and could not be discharged until after notice and hearing by the tenure board. The requirement of the agency shop provision is not different from a contract which, for example, changed the starting time from 9 o'clock to 8:30. In both cases, the teachers have notice of what is required of them, and a teacher is not being discharged merely because he favors or does not favor a union. Thus, the Southgate agency shop provision does not violate the terms of the teachers' tenure act permitting dismissal for "reasonable and just cause" after such charges, notice, hearing and determination thereof.

The Court of Appeals, in construing the validity of the agency shop fee, held that the amount of the agency fee could only be the nonmembers' proportionate share of the cost of negotiating and administering the contract involved, which might or might not be equivalent to membership dues. The Court of Appeals' opinion cited no authority for the proposition, and we have been unable to find a case so holding. While the Legislature could pass such a law involving a proportionate determination of union dues, it has not done so, and we hold that the provisions of the PERA are not violated when nonmembers are required to pay an equivalent amount as the union dues as an agency shop fee.

In National Labor Relations Board v. General Motors Corp., 373 U.S. 734; 83 S. Ct. 1453; 10 L. Ed. 2d 670 (1963), the United States Supreme Court upheld the validity of an agency shop provision which required nonunion members to pay to the union a sum equivalent to the initiation fee and periodical dues of union members. The Court held that the agency shop provision did not violate the NLRA, § 8 (a) (3), which makes it an unfair labor practice to encourage or discourage membership in a labor organization.

The Court of Appeals held the SEA provision violative of the PERA, § 10 (c), which makes it an unfair labor practice to discriminate in regard to hire, terms, or other conditions of employment in order to encourage or discourage membership in a labor organization. We believe that the PERA does permit the charging of a fee equivalent to the dues of union members for nonunion members. We further believe there are several problems with the rule laid down by the Court of Appeals.

It would be difficult, if not impossible, to determine the exact percentage of union dues which make up the cost of negotiating and administering a contract. For example, if a representative of the NEA or the MEA meets with a negotiating team of the SEA and attempts to assist them in their negotiations with the school board, the SEA and all of the teachers in the Southgate School District may be aided. However, exactly how much is this worth? The local union officers may gain certain bargaining skills by attending NEA or MEA sponsored seminars concerned with collective bargaining. What is the dollar value of such a seminar? What about travel and accommodation expenses for attending the seminar? These types of questions—and others —would have to be answered if the Court of Appeals' test were to be followed. In the absence of a direct statutory directive, we decline to follow that test.

The rule stated by the Court of Appeals would also interfere with the powers of the MERC. The Court of Appeals in holding that any amount over the proportionate share would violate § 10 (c) of the PERA, directed the circuit court to hold a hearing on the matter. However, the Legislature has decreed that the MERC has jurisdiction where charges of unfair labor practices are made.[16] Thus, the decision of the Court of Appeals has directly invaded the function of the MERC and overruled the specific legislative intent to vest the MERC with jurisdiction in matters involving unfair labor practices.

Finally, the Court of Appeals' holding would require a union to disclose a great deal of information on the internal functioning of the union. This may, in many cases, violate the members' constitutional rights of freedom of association and the right to privacy (NAACP v. Alabama, 357 U.S. 449; 78 S. Ct. 1163; 2 L. Ed. 2d 1488 [1958]; Bates v. Little Rock, 361 U.S. 516; 80 S. Ct. 412; 4 L. Ed. 2d 480 [1960]), as well as unduly interfering with the internal functions of a union. Mayo v. Great Lakes Greyhound Lines, 333 Mich. 205 (1952).

Thus, the Court of Appeals erred in remanding for a hearing on the proportionate cost of the representation fee to the cost of negotiating the contract, and we hold that a representation fee equivalent to the amount of union dues is valid and not discriminatory to the nonunion members of the labor organization who receive like benefits as members through the collective bargaining process conducted by the duly designated representative bargaining unit.

The Court of Appeals is reversed insofar as it remanded this matter to the circuit court for determination of the agency fee, and is affirmed in its upholding of the validity of the agency shop provision. No costs, a public question being involved.

NOTES

1. Following the issuance of the Supreme Court's decision in *Smigel*, the Michigan Public Employment Relations Act was amended to specifically authorize the negotiation of an agency shop clause requiring "as a condition of employment that all employees in the bargaining unit pay to the exclusive bargaining representative a service fee equal to the amount of dues uniformly required of members of the exclusive bargaining representa-

---

[16] MCLA 423.216; MSA 17.455 (16), states:

"Violations of the provisions of section 10 shall be deemed to be unfair labor practices remediable by the labor mediation board. . . ."

tive. . . ." MICH. COMP. LAWS ANN. § 423.210 (1) (c) , as amended by Act 25, L. 1973.

2. The Pennsylvania Public Employe Relations Act provides that "membership dues deductions and maintenance of membership are proper subjects of bargaining with the proviso that as to the latter, the payment of dues and assessments while members, may be the only requisite employment condition." PA. STAT. ANN. tit. 43, § 1101.705 (Supp. 1972) . In PLRB v. Freeport Area School Dist., Case No. PERA-C-2777-W (1973) , the Pennsylvania Labor Relations Board held that it was an unfair labor practice for a school board to refuse to enforce an arbitrator's award requiring the termination of a teacher if the teacher failed to maintain her membership in the employee organization as required by the maintenance of membership provision in the parties' collective bargaining agreement. In rejecting the school board's argument that implementation of the arbitrator's award would violate the Public School Code, the PLRB stated:

> The Public School Code was enacted to govern the professional relationship between the school district and the teachers, setting forth generally in Section 1122 valid causes for discharge which largely bear upon the professional duties and responsibilities of the teachers. The Public Employe Relations Act, however, governs only the labor relations between the teachers and the school district, an entirely distinct and different phase of the relationship between the parties than the aforementioned professional relationship. The Public Employe Relations Act does not purport to amend or repeal any of the grounds for dismissal set forth in Section 1122 of the Public School Code. The Public Employe Relations Act, however, provides ground for dismissal which has no relationship to the professional status of teachers in the public schools. Simply stated, each statute embraces a different subject matter and the Public Employe Relations Act is not a substitute for the Public School Code. There is no positive repugnancy between the two enactments since their respective provisions are reconcilable and a consonant construction of each is achieved when viewing the vastly different subject matter of each enactment.

TOWN OF NORTH KINGSTOWN v. NORTH KINGSTOWN TEACHERS ASSOCIATION

Rhode Island Supreme Court
297 A.2d 342 (1972)

JOSLIN, J. This dispute arose under the School Teachers' Arbitration Act [G.L. 1956 (1968 Reenactment) ch. 9.3 of title

28]. A Superior Court justice certified it to this court for hearing and determination on an agreed statement of facts.

It appears that the School Committee of the Town of North Kingstown Teachers Association, bargaining agent for the certified teachers in that town's public school system, met for the purpose of determining what terms and conditions of employment for the school year 1971-72 should be included in a proposed collective bargaining agreement.

When an impasse in negotiations developed, the unresolved issues were submitted to arbitration pursuant to § 28-9.3-9. Included in the submission were association proposals for an agency shop, course reimbursement and longevity pay. Plaintiffs, being dissatisfied with the arbitrators' decision thereon, sought judicial review. Initially they filed a complaint in the Superior Court; they then moved that the case be certified to this court for hearing and determination on an agreed statement of facts. The case arrived here under a consent order which certifies three stated questions for our determination. . . .

We consider the case . . . as if it were properly certified on an agreed statement of facts. In that frame of reference, the issue is whether the arbitrators acted in excess of their jurisdiction with respect to three of the unresolved issues submitted to them.

The first of those issues relates to the arbitrators' authority to order execution of a collective bargaining agreement embodying a provision for what is known in the field of labor relations as an "agency shop." In general, such a provision requires a charge or fee to be paid to a certified labor organization by those employees who, although not members of that organization, are nonetheless part of the collective bargaining unit for which it, as bargaining agent, speaks. In this case, the arbitrators directed the parties "to write" language into their agreement which would give "full effect" to that portion of their award which states:

"... prior to the first payday in October, all teachers as a condition of employment would have to have paid to the Association dues or a sum equal to dues in the united profession. Such an arrangement does not require membership in the Association, it only requires that dues or an amount equal to dues be paid by all teachers in order to hold employment in the North Kingstown School System."

That directive's legality becomes suspect because of possible conflict between it and the right-to-work provision of the School Teachers' Arbitration Act (§ 28-9.3-7) which guarantees public school teachers the freedom ". . . to join *or to decline to join* any association or organization regardless of whether it has been certified as the exclusive representative of certified public school teachers." (emphasis added)

The plaintiffs argue that the two provisions are completely at odds. They rely upon the judgment of the Supreme Court that an agency shop conditions employment "upon the practical equivalent of union 'membership.' "[3] NLRB v. General Motors Corp., 373 U.S. 734, 743, 83 S. Ct. 1453, 1459, 10 L. Ed. 2d 670, 676 (1963). It is unthinkable to them that our Legislature would grant teachers freedom to choose whether or not to affiliate with a labor organization, and simultaneously compel those who opt against joining to pay that organization a "sum equal to [union] dues" in order to obtain or hold employment.

The defendant, on the other hand, sees nothing incongruous between the two. It argues that the legislators who enacted the School Teachers' Arbitration Act in 1966 must certainly have been aware that several states had by then enacted "right-to-work laws"; that while some of those laws were silent on whether nonunion members of a bargaining unit could be compelled to contribute to the union, most were restrictive and specifically prohibited the exaction of union dues or other fees from those nonmembers; and that the failure of our Legislature to pattern our act upon the more restrictive models clearly evidences its intention to allow, rather than to ban, the agency shop as a permissible form of union security arrangement.[4]

This approach finds support in Meade Elec. Co. v. Hagberg, 129 Ind. App. 631, 159 N.E.2d 408 (1959) where it was employed as a rationale for recognizing the legality of an agency shop. It is further aided by the rule of strict construction.[5]

---

[3] In NLRB v. General Motors Corp., 373 U.S. 734, 83 S. Ct. 1453, 10 L. Ed. 2d 670 (1963), the Court held that the National Labor Relations Act does not prohibit inclusion of an agency shop clause in a collective bargaining agreement covering employment in a state having a right-to-work law. In the companion case of Retail Clerks, Local 1625, AFL-CIO v. Schermerhorn, 373 U.S. 746, 83 S. Ct. 1461, 10 L. Ed. 2d 678 (1963), it was held that the question of whether such an arrangement violated Florida law was for the Florida court to decide.

[4] Among the states then having constitutional or statutory right-to-work provisions specifically banning the agency shop were: Alabama, Arkansas, Georgia, Iowa, Louisiana, Mississippi, Nebraska, North Carolina, South Carolina, Tennessee, Utah, Virginia, and Wyoming. A typical provision was Ga. Code Anno. #54-903 (Rev. ed. 1961) which read as follows:

"No individual shall be required as a condition of employment, or of continuance of employment, to pay any fee, assessment, or other sum of money whatsoever, to a labor organization."

[5] In this state we follow the rule that statutes in derogation of the common law should be strictly construed. Hodge v. Osteopathic Gen. Hosp., 107 R.I. 135, 144, 265 A.2d 733, 738-39 (1970); Pucci v. Algiere, 106 R.I. 411, 420-21, 261 A.2d 1, 7 (1970); Atlantic Ref. Co. v. Director of Pub. Works, 104 R.I. 436, 441, 244 A.2d 853, 856 (1968).

Application of that rule in this instance justifies the conclusion that the Legislature, by failing to abrogate, either specifically or by clear implication, the common law right of labor and management to include an agency shop clause in a collective bargaining agreement, is presumed not to have intended a change in that law. Hopfl, *The Agency Shop Question*, 49 Cornell L.Q. 478, 483 (1964).

Decisions elsewhere, however, reject these arguments and, in what apparently is the majority view, hold that a right-to-work law, even though lacking a specific prohibition against taxation of nonunion members, will not tolerate an agency shop. Higgins v. Cardinal Mfg. Co., 188 Kan. 11, 360 P.2d 456 (1961); Baldwin v. Arizona Flame Restaurant, Inc., 82 Ariz. 385, 313 P.2d 759 (1957); Schermerhorn v. Local 1625, Retail Clerks, AFL-CIO, 141 So. 2d 269 (Fla. 1962).

What underlies those decisions is the concept that legislation which ". . . clearly bestows on the workingman a right to join or not join a labor union, as he sees fit, without jeopardizing his job" must of necessity be repugnant to a contract stipulation which ". . . requires the nonunion employee to purchase from the labor union a right . . ." which the right-to-work law has given him. Schermerhorn v. Local 1625, Retail Clerks, AFL-CIO *supra* at 272-73. They rest also on the notion that "the real and rather well-hidden meaning" of a right-to-work law's ban on compulsory unionism includes by necessary implication a prohibition against any forced payment by a worker to a labor organization as the price for obtaining or holding employment. Higgins v. Cardinal Mfg. Co., *supra* at 23, 360 P.2d at 465.

The plaintiffs advance two further arguments in support of the position that it was illegal for the arbitrators to require an agency shop provision to be embodied in this agreement.

The first of those arguments declares that we must assume that the Legislature intended to ban the agency shop, inasmuch as a contrary assumption would subvert the purpose of the tenure laws which in G.L. 1956 (1969 Reenactment) § 16-13-3 make "good and just cause" the only ground for dismissing a tenured teacher.[6] The short answer is that the Legislature which established grounds for dismissal can also provide that noncompliance with an agency shop provision will constitute one of those grounds.

In their other and final argument, plaintiffs, in substance, observe that the School Teachers' Arbitration Act declares this

---

[6] The challenged portion of the award excepts "tenured teachers presently in the system" from the agency shop provision, and we are, therefore, not concerned with problems which might arise had they not been so excluded.

state's public policy as affording public school teachers the rights to organize, to be represented, to negotiate professionally, and to bargain on a collective basis; that in similar declarations the Firefighters' and the Policemen's Arbitration Acts extend to firemen and policemen in § 28-9.1-2 and § 28-9.2-2, respectively, ". . . *all of the rights of labor* other than the right to strike, or engage in any work stoppage or slowdown." (emphasis added) The differences, plaintiffs say, are significant, and they argue that the more restrictive declaration of teachers' rights evidences a legislative intent to invalidate the agency shop as a union security arrangement. That argument, while perhaps ingenious, is nonetheless speculative for the differences on which they rely as a premise in nowise support their conclusion.

We have averted sufficiently to the arguments pro and con to make it apparent that for each which points to a possible legislative intention, there is a satisfactory counter pointing to an opposite intention. This is understandably so because nothing either in the language of the Act, or in the report of the legislative commission[7] preceding its enactment, even hints at an attitudinal approach. Neither is there anything in the objectives which the Act was designed to serve or in the circumstances attendant upon its enactment from which a legislative intention can be ascertained. Instead, there is nothing but obscurity. It is as if there were a complete lack of awareness that there might someday be a proposal to include an agency shop provision in a labor agreement.

As we cannot extract meaning from an intention cloaked in obscurity, we must legislate "between gaps" and fill "the open spaces in the law." Cordozo, The Nature of the Judicial Process 113 (1921). We are guided in that task by "considerations . . . exactly of the same nature as those which ought to dominate legislative action itself, since it is a question in each case, of satisfying, as best may be, justice and social utility by an appropriate rule." Id. at 120. This, Judge Jerome Frank said, is "an activity which, no matter how one may label it, is in part legislative." Guiseppi v. Walling, 144 F.2d 608, 621 (2d Cir. 1944), aff'd sub nom. Gemsco, Inc. v. Walling, 324 U.S. 244, 65 S. Ct. 605, 89 L. Ed. 921 (1945).

In evaluating those considerations which in our judgment would be likely to prompt legislative action, foremost is the argument that a certified labor organization, as sole bargaining agent for all employees in the bargaining unit, is bound by law

---

[7] Report of Commission to Study Mediation and Arbitration as authorized in R.I. Acts and Resolves 1300-02 (1965).

to negotiate for both unions and nonunion members; that the negotiations are costly; that it would be manifestly inequitable to permit those who see fit not to join the union to benefit from its services without at the same time requiring them to bear a fair and just share of the financial burdens; and that no member of a bargaining unit, be he a joiner or a nonjoiner, should expect or be allowed a "free-ride."

Because this argument is persuasive on the general question of the legitimacy of the agency shop does not mean that it is similarly convincing with respect to the validity of a provision calling for nonunion members to pay more than a just portion of the costs of the benefits conferred upon them. To accept such a provision as valid would, in effect, sanction an inverse "free-rider" situation in which the union member, rather than the nonjoiner, would be the "free-rider."

Accordingly, our approval is expressly limited to that kind of agency shop provision which neither requires a nonjoiner to share in expenditures for benefits he is not entitled to receive, nor exacts from him more than a proportionate share of the costs of securing the benefits conferred upon all members of the bargaining unit. An agency shop provision thus limited has been recognized both judicially[8] and at the bargaining table.[9]

The accounting problems which may result from its use, although perhaps burdensome, should not be impossible. Hopfl, 49 Cornell L.Q., *supra* at 480. . . .

The papers in the case, with our decision endorsed thereon, are ordered sent back to the Superior Court for entry of judgment in accordance with said decision.

NOTES

1. Did Chief Justice Kavanagh in his majority opinion in *Smigel* say that agency shop clauses which required that public

---

[8] In Navy v. City of Detroit, Wayne County No. 123-642, 60 CCH Lab. Cas. 66,958 (Mich. Cir., April 23, 1969) the court said:

"It could be that thorough consideration might be given to the specific amount of contribution required under the agency shop provisions so that a non-union member would be making his fair contributions, only to the actual cost of the bargaining and the contract administration and not to the additional costs of other union expenses or activities which bear no relation to the services rendered and in which he plays no part or has no voice." *Id.* at 66,960.

[9] In New Jersey Turnpike Employees, Local 194, AFL-CIO v. New Jersey Turnpike Authority, 117 N.J. Super. 349, 67 CCH Lab. Cas. 68,560 (1971) it is reported at 349-50, 67 CCH Lab. Cas. at 68,561 that the union proposal required ". . . monthly payment by non-members of the union of *their respective fair share of the cost* of collective negotiations, processing of grievances and other activities related to union representation, as a condition of employment." (emphasis added)

employees as a condition of employment pay to the union an amount equal to the pro rata portion of the cost of representing unit employees were illegal under the Michigan law? In terms of actual result, is there any difference between the decision in *Town of North Kingstown* and the majority opinion in *Smigel?*

2. The court in *Town of North Kingstown* cited New Jersey Turnpike Employees, Local 194 v. New Jersey Turnpike Authority, 117 N.J. Super. 349, 284 A.2d 566 (1971), *aff'd*, 83 L.R.R.M. 2350 (N.J. Super. Ct., App. Div. 1973), to demonstrate that agency shop clauses limited to paying an amount equal to the pro rata cost of representing unit employees had been negotiated. The court neglected to note, however, that the New Jersey Superior Court in the case in question held that such a limited agency shop clause was invalid ". . . in view of the legislative declaration of the right of public employees to refrain from union activity, even assisting a union, and in the absence of legislative authorization for an agency shop in public employment."

3. Is it illegal for an employer to attempt to negotiate a limited agency shop agreement that would be applicable to only part of the employees in the bargaining unit? In City of Detroit, 1971 MERC Lab. Op. 1112, the Michigan Employment Relations Commission, in a decision issued before the Michigan Supreme Court's decision in *Smigel,* held that all employees in a bargaining unit must be treated alike with respect to union security provisions. The MERC stated:

> The legislature, by enactment of the proviso in Section 13 of PERA, requires that for collective bargaining purposes all employees in a fire fighters unit except the primary supervisor be treated in the same manner. . . . If all employees in the bargaining unit are required by contract to pay a service fee, there is neither discouragement nor encouragement of union membership. All employees must be treated alike; the differentiation between the fire fighter and other ranks is contrary to this principle.

4. The Massachusetts act covering municipal employees provides that nothing therein "shall diminish the authority and power of the civil service commission." MASS. ANN. LAWS ch. 149, § 178H (Supp. 1972). In Karchmar v. City of Worcester, 84 L.R.R.M. 2410 (Mass. Sup. Jud. Ct. 1973), a municipality argued that by virtue of this provision civil service employees could not be required to pay an agency service fee to a union as a condition of employment. In rejecting this contention, the

Massachusetts Supreme Judicial Court held that the legislature had "the power to prescribe, add to, or otherwise amend the rules of eligibility for appointment, and the conditions of, or grounds for, suspension or removal of all public employment" and that the amendment to the Massachusetts act which permitted the negotiation of clauses in collective bargaining agreements requiring the payment of agency service fees as a condition of employment was such an amendment. The court also rejected arguments that the agency service fee provision, insofar as it applied to civil service employees, violated the due process and equal protection clauses of the Fourteenth Amendment.

Chapter 6

UNION COLLECTIVE ACTION—THE RIGHT TO STRIKE AND PICKET IN THE PUBLIC SECTOR

Like their private sector brethren, labor union adherents in the public sector have established labor organizations which are not mere fraternal societies having polite social functions. Many public sector unions have become militant groups formed for the primary purpose of advancing what are conceived to be the economic interests of their members, and they have not been content to rely exclusively on the art of persuasion through negotiation in wresting concessions from public employers. Even though concerted activity, in the form of the strike and the picket line, has usually been proscribed by law, public sector unions have nevertheless frequently resorted to "economic action" to gain leverage at the bargaining table.

This chapter deals with this troublesome phase of public sector labor relations. In a sense, the construction of the chapter may be unrealistic, because union collective action is treated as a problem separate and distinct from the issue of impasse resolution. It surely is legitimate to contend that the crucial issue is not whether strikes should be prohibited in public sector labor relations, but whether the bargaining process itself and dispute settlement procedures can be made so effective that the need for work stoppages will be obviated. However, given our present state of knowledge, it is unlikely that we can devise a system that would totally supplant the need (or desire) for strikes. In this chapter we present some of the considerations surrounding the difficult strike issue which, combined with the various impasse resolution devices available, may offer some suggestions as to how to achieve stable and harmonious labor relations in the public sector.

A. The Nature of the Problem

Statistics gathered by the Department of Labor Bureau of Labor Statistics illustrate the meteoric rise of the public sector strike from near oblivion in 1958 to large proportions in 1970.

Table 1. Work Stoppages in Government, 1958-70[1]

Year	Total			State Government			Local Government		
	Number		Man-days Idle	Number		Man-days Idle	Number		Man-days Idle
	Stoppages	Workers Involved		Stoppages	Workers Involved		Stoppages	Workers Involved	
1958	15	1,720	7,510	1	30	60	14	1,590	7,460
1959	26	2,240	11,500	4	410	1,650	22	1,830	9,850
1960	36	28,600	58,400	3	970	1,170	33	27,600	57,200
1961	28	6,610	15,300	...	...	...	28	6,610	15,300
1962	28	31,100	79,100	2	1,660	2,260	21	25,300	43,100
1963	29	4,840	15,400	2	280	2,160	27	4,560	13,300
1964	41	22,700	70,800	4	280	3,170	37	22,500	67,700
1965	42	11,900	146,000	...	...	1,280	42	11,900	145,000
1966	142	105,000	455,000	9	3,090	6,010	133	102,000	449,000
1967	181	132,000	1,250,000	12	4,670	16,300	169	127,000	1,230,000
1968	254	201,800	2,545,200	16	9,300	42,800	235	190,900	2,492,800
1969	411	160,000	745,700	37	20,500	152,400	372	139,000	592,200
1970	412	333,500	2,023,200	23	8,800	44,600	386	168,900	1,330,500

[1] Includes stoppages lasting a full day or shift or longer and involving 6 workers or more.

Moreover, the incidence of strike activity in the public sector vis-à-vis the total economy has increased markedly during this same period.

Table 2. Workers Involved as a Percent of Total Employment, 1958-70

Year	All Work Stoppages	Government Work Stoppages		
		Total	State	Local
1958	3.9	0.022	0.002	0.04
1959	3.3	.028	.030	.04
1960	2.4	.340	.060	.60
1961	2.6	.077	—	.14
1962	2.2	.350	.100	.50
1963	1.1	.052	.020	.09
1964	2.7	.240	.020	.40
1965	2.5	.120	—	.20
1966	3.0	.970	.100	1.70
1967	4.3	1.140	.200	1.90
1968	3.8	1.650	.400	2.70
1969	3.5	1.311	.807	2.013
1970	4.7	2.661	.329	2.359

Note: Data on stoppages and workers involved refer to all stoppages beginning in the year; man-days idle refer to all stoppages in effect during year.

However, it is interesting that the number of reported strikes conducted by government employees in 1971 was well below the number in 1970, 327 and 412 respectively. Man-days of idleness decreased substantially to 893,000 in 1971, compared to 2,023,200 in 1970, and the percent of working time lost dropped from 0.06 percent to 0.03 percent.

Many theories have been propounded to explain the cause of strikes in the public sector. Some have attributed it to the increased militancy of public sector unions which, for the first time, possess enough power to use effectively the traditional methods of economic coercion. Others cite a shift in emphasis in public employment from the traditional concerns over job security to the more difficult issues of wages and conditions of employment. Indeed, statistical evidence seems to bear out this theory, as most of the increase in work stoppages in public employment between 1958 and 1970 has been caused by disputes over wages and supplementary benefits rather than other items.

Table 3. Work Stoppages in Government, by Major Issue, 1958-1968.

Year	General Wage Changes and Supplementary Benefits			Union Organization and Security			Job Security		
	Stoppages	No. Involved	Mandays Idle	Stoppages	No. Involved	Mandays Idle	Stoppages	No. Involved	Mandays Idle
1958	8	1,130	4,760	2	340	1,990	.	....	.....
1959	7	950	2,640	9	820	4,580	.	....	.....
1960	19	16,600	40,800	8	6,220	9,610	.	....	.....
1961	22	5,970	13,600	1	20	20	.	....	.....
1962	10	25,500	40,300	5	380	840	2	30	200
1963	15	1,700	8,350	5	2,750	6,060	2	90	170
1964	26	9,620	37,300	8	2,550	7,680	.	....	.....
1965	25	9,830	128,000	12	850	11,500	1	80	80
1966	78	58,200	355,000	36	11,600	45,600	2	170	1,680
1967	128	118,000	1,040,000	29	6,670	99,300	2	730	1,430
1968	146	110,300	759,200	60	33,600	90,100	2	90	200

Year	Administration Matters			Interunion and Intraunion Matters			Other Working Conditions		
	Stoppages	No. Involved	Mandays Idle	Stoppages	No. Involved	Mandays Idle	Stoppages	No. Involved	Mandays Idle
1958	...	.. ...	. ...	.	....	60	5	250	700
1959	...	......	....	2	40	180	8	430	4,060
1960	...	......	....	1	10	10	8	5,770	8,010
1961	...	......	....	1	10	20	4	610	1,640
1962	8	2,380	6,100	3	2,870	31,700	.	....	.....
1963	5	170	340	1	30	120	1	100	400
1964	7	10,600	25,900	.	....	....	.	....	.....
1965	1	10	50	2	980	6,160	.	....	.....
1966	21	33,300	46,500	5	1,760	5,840	.	....	.....
1967	19	2,670	5,630	1	90	360	2	4,030	99,900
1968	33	53,200	1,684,200	5	2,700	4,900	5	1,700	6,200

Whatever the causes for these strikes, it is noteworthy that they have persisted during a period when, for the most part, strikes by public employees have been illegal. Thus, whatever may be said about the causes of public employee strikes, it is apparent that the present methods of dealing with them have not proved adequate to prevent them.

On the basis of these statistics an ostrich-like approach to the problem is not indicated. If, as in the usual view, public sector strikes are inimical to the public interest and should be eliminated or kept to a minimum, action either in terms of eliminating the causes of strikes or in deterring them, or both, is needed. Alternatively, it is arguable that not all public sector strikes seriously damage the public interest and that public policy, therefore, should not reflect an absolute condemnation of strike action, but rather, as in the private sector, should accept strike action except when a strong public interest (such as in health or safety) is involved. In facing the problem of strike action this over-all evaluation must surely be a threshold matter.

NOTES

1. Comprehensive statistical analyses of the problem are to be found in Hall, *Work Stoppages in Government,* 91 MONTHLY LAB. REV. 53 (July 1968); White, *Work Stoppages of Government Employees,* 92 MONTHLY LAB. REV. 29 (Dec. 1969); Young and Brewer, *Strikes by State and Local Government Employees,* 9 IND. REL. 356 (1970); and U.S. BUREAU OF LABOR STATISTICS, WORK STOPPAGES IN GOVERNMENT, 1958-1968, *reprinted in* 71 GERR RF 1011.

2. Some commentators have suggested that strikes in the public sector will be reduced by extending private sector recognition and grievance procedures into the public sector. *See, e.g.,* Clark, *Public Employee Strikes: Some Proposed Solutions,* 23 LAB. L.J. 111 (1972); Zack, *Why Public Employees Strike,* 23 ARB. J. 69, 82-83 (1968). Available statistics lend some credence to these predictions, as they indicate that the incidence of recognition and grievance strikes has been markedly reduced in those states providing for recognition and unfair labor practice regulation. *See* Burton and Krider, *The Role and Consequence of Strikes by Public Employees,* 79 YALE L.J. 418, 439 (1970).

B. Constitutional Considerations

1. Private Sector Precedents

UAW-AFL LOCAL 232 v. WISCONSIN EMPLOYMENT RELATIONS BOARD

United States Supreme Court
336 U.S. 245, 69 S. Ct. 516, 93 L. Ed. 651 (1949)

MR. JUSTICE JACKSON delivered the opinion of the Court . . . .

Briggs & Stratton Corporation operates two manufacturing plants in the State of Wisconsin engaging approximately 2,000 employees. These are represented by the International Union, Automobile Workers of America, A. F. of L., Local No. 232, as collective bargaining agent, it having been duly certified as such by the National Labor Relations Board in proceedings under the National Labor Relations Act. Under such certification, the Union had negotiated collective bargaining agreements, the last of which expired on July 1, 1944. Negotiation of a new one reached a deadlock and bargaining sessions continued for some time without success.

On November 3, 1945, its leaders submitted to the Union membership a plan for a new method of putting pressure upon the employer. The stratagem consisted of calling repeated special meetings of the Union during working hours at any time the Union saw fit, which the employees would leave work to attend. It was an essential part of the plan that this should be without warning to the employer or notice as to when or whether the employees would return. The device was adopted and the first surprise cessation of work was called on November 6, 1945; thereafter, and until March 22, 1946, such action was repeated on twenty-six occasions. The employer was not informed during this period of any specific demands which these tactics were designed to enforce nor what concessions it could make to avoid them.

This procedure was publicly described by the Union leaders as a new technique for bringing pressure upon the employer. It was, and is, candidly admitted that these tactics were intended to and did interfere with production and put strong economic pressure on the employer, who was disabled thereby from making any dependable production plans or delivery commitments. And it was said that "this can't be said for the strike. After the initial surprise of the walkout, the company knows what it has to do and plans accordingly." It was commended as a procedure which would avoid hardships that a strike imposes on employees and was considered "a better weapon than a strike."

The employer did not resort to any private disciplinary measures such as discharge of the employees; instead, it sought a much less drastic remedy by plea to the appropriate public authority under Wisconsin law to investigate and adjudge the Union's conduct under the law of the State. After the prescribed procedures, the Board ordered the Union to cease and desist from " (a) engaging in any concerted efforts to interfere with production by arbitrarily calling union meetings and inducing work stoppages during regularly scheduled working hours; or engaging in any other concerted effort to interfere with production of the complainant except by leaving the premises in an orderly manner for the purpose of going on strike."

Two court proceedings resulted from the Board's order: one by the Board to obtain enforcement and the other by the Union to obtain review. They are here considered, as they were below, together.

The Supreme Court of Wisconsin sustained the Board's order but significantly limited the effect of its otherwise general prohibitions. It held that what the order does, and all that it does, is to forbid individual defendants and members of the Union from engaging in concerted effort to interfere with production by doing the acts instantly involved. . . .

Our only question is, therefore, whether it is beyond the power of the State to prohibit the particular course of conduct described.

The Union contends that the statute as thus applied violates the Thirteenth Amendment in that it imposes a form of compulsory service or involuntary servitude. However, nothing in the statute or the order makes it a crime to abandon work individually (compare Pollock v. Williams, 322 U.S. 4) or collectively. Nor does either undertake to prohibit or restrict any employee from leaving the service of the employer, either for reason or without reason, either with or without notice. The facts afford no foundation for the contention that any action of the State has the purpose or effect of imposing any form of involuntary servitude.

It is further contended that the statute as applied invades rights of free speech and public assemblage guaranteed by the Fourteenth Amendment. We recently considered a similar contention in connection with other state action concerning labor relations. Lincoln Federal Labor Union v. Northwestern Iron & Metal Co., and Whitaker v. North Carolina, 335 U.S. 525, and American Federation of Labor v. American Sash & Door Co., 335 U.S. 538. For reasons there stated, these contentions are without merit.

No serious question is presented by the Commerce Clause of the Constitution standing alone. It never has been thought to prevent the state legislatures from limiting "individual and group rights of aggression and defense" or from substituting "processes of justice for the more primitive method of trial by combat." . . .

But it is claimed that the congressional labor legislation confers upon or recognizes and declares in unions and employees certain rights, privileges or immunities in connection with strikes and concerted activities, and that these are denied by the State's prohibition as laid down in this case. It is elementary that what Congress constitutionally has given, the state may not constitutionally take away. Hill v. Florida, 325 U.S. 538.

The argument is that two provisions, found in §§ 7 and 13 of the National Labor Relations Act, not relevantly changed by the Labor Management Relations Act of 1947, grant to the Union and its members the right to put pressure upon the employer by the recurrent and unannounced stoppage of work. Both Acts provide that "Employees shall have the right to self-organization, to form, join, or assist labor organizations, to bargain collectively through representatives of their own choosing, and to engage in concerted activities, for the purpose of collective bargaining or other mutual aid or protection."[12] Because the acts forbidden by the Wisconsin judgment are concerted activities and had a purpose to assist labor organizations in collective bargaining, it is said to follow that they are federally authorized and thereby immunized from state control. . . .

[The Court found that, since the Union activity was not protected by Section 7 of the NLRA, no exclusion of state authority to regulate the conduct was intended.]

Reliance also is placed upon § 13 of the National Labor Relations Act, which provided, "Nothing in this Act shall be construed so as to interfere with or impede or diminish in any way the right to strike." . . . The 1947 Amendment carries the same provision but that Act includes a definition. Section 501 (2) says that when used in the Act "The term 'strike' includes any strike or other concerted stoppage of work by employees (including a stoppage by reason of the expiration of a collective-bargaining agreement) and any concerted slow-down or other concerted interruption of operations by employees." . . .

This provision, as carried over into the Labor Management Relations Act, does not purport to create, establish or define the right to strike. On its face it is narrower in scope than § 7—the latter would be of little significance if "strike" is a broader term than "concerted activity." Unless we read into § 13 words which Congress omitted and a sense which Congress showed no intention of including, all that this provision does is to declare a rule of interpretation for the Act itself which would prevent any use of what originally was a novel piece of legislation to qualify or impede whatever right to strike exists under other laws. It did not purport to modify the body of law as to the legality of strikes as it then existed. This Court less than a decade earlier had stated that law to be that the state constitutionally could prohibit strikes and make a violation criminal. It had unanimously adopted the language of Mr. Justice Brandeis that "Neither the common law, nor the Fourteenth Amendment, confers the absolute right to strike." Dorchy v. Kansas, 272 U.S. 306, 311. Dissenting views most favorable to labor in other cases had conceded the right of the state legislature to mark the limits of tolerable industrial conflict in the public interest. Duplex Co.

---

[12] § 7 of National Labor Relations Act, 49 Stat. 449, 452. The Labor Management Relations Act of 1947 added a proviso that employees also have the right to refrain from any or all activities mentioned in this section, except to the extent that the right to refrain might conflict with an agreement requiring membership in a union as a condition of employment as authorized by the Act. 61 Stat. 140.

v. Deering, 254 U.S. 443, 488. This Court has adhered to that view. Thornhill v. Alabama, 310 U.S. 88, 103. The right to strike, because of its more serious impact upon the public interest, is more vulnerable to regulation than the right to organize and select representatives for lawful purposes of collective bargaining which this Court has characterized as a "fundamental right" and which, as the Court has pointed out, was recognized as such in its decisions long before it was given protection by the National Labor Relations Act. . . .

That Congress has concurred in the view that neither § 7 nor § 13 confers absolute right to engage in every kind of strike or other concerted activity does not rest upon mere inference; indeed the record indicates that, had the courts not made these interpretations, the Congress would have gone as far or farther in the direction of limiting the right to strike. . . .

If we were to read § 13 as we are urged to do, to make the strike an absolute right and the definition to extend the right to all other variations of the strike, the effect would be to legalize beyond the power of any state or federal authorities to control not only the intermittent stoppages such as we have here but also the slowdown and perhaps the sit-down strike as well. Cf. Allen-Bradley Local v. Wisconsin Employment Relations Board, 315 U.S. 740, 751. And this is not all; the management also would be disabled from any kind of self-help to cope with these coercive tactics of the union except to submit to its undeclared demands. To dismiss or discipline employees for exercising a right given them under the Act or to interfere with them or the union in pursuing it is made an unfair labor practice and if the rights here asserted are rights conferred by the Labor Management Relations Act, it is hard to see how the management can take any steps to resist or combat them without incurring the sanctions of the Act. It is certain that such a result would be inconsistent with the whole purpose disclosed by the Labor Management Relations Act amendments to the National Labor Relations Act. Nor do we think such is the result of any fair interpretation of the text of the Act.

We think that this recurrent or intermittent unannounced stoppage of work to win unstated ends was neither forbidden by federal statute nor was it legalized and approved thereby. Such being the case, the state police power was not superseded by congressional Act over a subject normally within its exclusive power and reachable by federal regulation only because of its effects on that interstate commerce which Congress may regulate. . . .

The judgments are affirmed.

[The dissenting opinions of Douglas, J., with whom Black, and Rutledge, JJ., concurred, and of Murphy, J., with whom Rutledge, J., concurred, are omitted.]

NOTES

1. As the decision illustrates, the right to strike in the private sector is not now and has never been an absolute right. Although most work stoppages are protected by the NLRA, there are numerous instances where strikes are either unprotected or legally forbidden:

(a) Use of violence—*see* NLRB v. Fansteel Metallurgical Corp., 306 U.S. 240, 59 S. Ct. 490, 83 L. Ed. 627 (1939); NLRB v. Thayer Co., 213 F.2d 748 (1st Cir. 1954), *cert. denied,* 348 U.S. 883 (1954).

(b) Unlawful means—*see* NLRB v. Fansteel Metallurgical Corp., 306 U.S. 240, 59 S. Ct. 490, 83 L. Ed. 627 (1939) and Apex Hosiery Co. v. Leader, 310 U.S. 469, 60 S. Ct. 982, 84 L. Ed. 1311 (1940) (sit-down strikes); C.G. Conn Ltd. v. NLRB, 108 F.2d 390 (7th Cir. 1939); Valley City Furniture Co., 110 N.L.R.B. 1589, *enf'd,* 230 F.2d 947 (6th Cir. 1956) (partial strike or slowdown); Allen Bradley Co. v. IBEW Local 3, 325 U.S. 797, 65 S. Ct. 1533, 89 L. Ed. 1939 (1945); United Mine Workers v. Pennington, 381 U.S. 657, 85 S. Ct. 1585, 14 L. Ed. 2d 626 (1965) (combination with business to violate antitrust laws); Carnegie-Illinois Steel Co. v. United Steelworkers, 353 Pa. 420, 45 A.2d 857 (1946) (mass picketing).

(c) Strikes in pursuit of unlawful objectives—*see, e.g.,* NLRB v. IBEW Local 1212, 364 U.S. 573, 81 S. Ct. 330, 5 L. Ed. 2d 302 (1961) ("jurisdictional strike" in violation of Section 8 (b) (4) (D) of the NLRA); Brooks v. NLRB, 348 U.S. 96, 75 S. Ct. 176, 99 L. Ed. 125 (1954) (strike by uncertified union to gain recognition during period when another union has been certified).

2. In the private sector, strikes in violation of a no-strike commitment constitute unprotected activity. *See, e.g.,* NLRB v. Sands Mfg. Co., 306 U.S. 332, 59 S. Ct. 508, 83 L. Ed. 682 (1939). A union breach of a contractual no-strike pledge may be remedied by a damage action under Section 301 of the Labor Management Relations Act. *See* Atkinson v. Sinclair Ref. Co., 370 U.S. 238, 82 S. Ct. 1318, 8 L. Ed. 2d 462 (1962). Furthermore, in the private sector it is now clear that a federal or state court may issue an injunction to halt a strike over a

grievable or arbitrable matter where "a collective bargaining contract contains a mandatory grievance adjustment or arbitration procedure." Boys Markets, Inc. v. Retail Clerks Local 770, 398 U.S. 235, 90 S. Ct. 1583, 26 L. Ed. 2d 199 (1970).

3. Peaceful picketing in furtherance of a labor objective may raise special constitutional questions. In Thornhill v. Alabama, 310 U.S. 88, 60 S. Ct. 296, 84 L. Ed. 460 (1940), the Supreme Court equated peaceful picketing to freedom of speech and, as such, it was protected against abridgement under the First and Fourteenth Amendments, though subject to the same legislative restrictions as other forms of speech. However, the broad pronouncements of *Thornhill* were modified and limited by a later series of cases in which the Court held that picketing, because it involved not only communication of ideas but also elements of patrolling and signaling, was not immune from all state regulation. Since union picketers are not only exercising their right of speech but also are engaging in an exercise of economic power, the Court has held that when such activity is "counter to valid state policy in a domain open to state regulation" it can be restricted, even though it arises in the course of a labor controversy. *See, e.g.,* Teamsters v. Vogt, Inc., 354 U.S. 284, 77 S. Ct. 1166, 1 L. Ed. 2d 1347 (1957); Giboney v. Empire Storage Co., 336 U.S. 490, 69 S. Ct. 684, 93 L. Ed. 834 (1949).

In 1968 the Supreme Court seemingly revitalized the *Thornhill* doctrine in Amalgamated Food Employees v. Logan Valley Plaza, 391 U.S. 308, 88 S. Ct. 1601, 20 L. Ed. 2d 603 (1968), a case involving picketing of an employer within a privately owned shopping center. The employer, Weiss Markets, operated a nonunion supermarket in a large suburban shopping-center complex. Although the market building was posted with a sign prohibiting trespassing or soliciting by anyone other than employees on the adjacent porch and parking lot, nonemployee union members picketed outside the market with signs stating that the Weiss market was nonunion. The areas picketed were all part of the center owned by Logan Valley Plaza, Inc. Picketing was peaceful at all times. Weiss and Logan obtained a state court *ex parte* restraining order, later made final, restraining picketing and trespassing by prohibiting picketing within the shopping center and requiring the union to limit its picketing to areas outside the shopping center. The Supreme Court did not pass on the question of federal preemption. Instead, it evaluated the union's conduct solely in the light of First Amendment protection. Relying on *Thornhill*, the Court premised its ruling on the proposition "that peaceful picketing carried on in a location open generally to the public is, absent other factors involving the purpose or manner of the picketing, protected by the First Amendment." The Court, citing Marsh v. Alabama, 326 U.S. 501, 66 S. Ct. 276, 90 L. Ed. 265 (1946), found the shopping center picketing constitutionally protected, notwithstanding its occurrence on private property, "because the shopping center serves as the community business block 'and is freely accessible and open to the people in the area and those passing through.' "

However, even though the Court found the picketing to be constitutionally protected in *Logan Valley*, it nevertheless ruled that picketing may be "regulated" by state and municipal governments. The Court stated the following pertinent principles:

"We do not hold that respondents, and at their behest the State, are without power to make reasonable regulations governing the exercise of First Amendment rights on their property. Certainly their rights to make such regulations are at the very least co-extensive with the powers possessed by States and municipalities, and recognized in many opinions of this Court, to control the use of public property. Thus where property is not ordinarily open to the public, this Court has held that access to it for the purpose of exercising First Amendment rights may be denied altogether. See Adderley v. Florida, 385 U.S. 39 (1966). Even where municipal or state property is open to the public generally, the exercise of First Amendment rights may be regulated so as to prevent interference with the use to which the property is ordinarily put by the State. Thus we have upheld a statute prohibiting picketing 'in such a manner as to obstruct or unreasonably to interfere with the free ingress or egress to and from any . . . county . . . courthouses.' Cameron v. Johnson, *ante*. . . . Likewise it has been indicated that persons could be constitutionally prohibited from picketing 'in or near' a court 'with the intent of interfering with, obstructing, or impeding the administration of justice.' Cox v. Louisiana, 379 U.S. 559 (1964).

"In addition, the exercise of First Amendment rights may be regulated where such exercise will unduly interfere with the normal use of the public property by other members of the public with an equal right of access to it. Thus it has been held that persons desiring to parade along city streets may be required to secure a permit in order that municipal authorities be able to limit the amount of interference with use of the sidewalks by other members of the public by regulating the time, place, and manner of the parade. Cox v. New Hampshire, 312 U.S. 569 (1941); Poulos v. New Hampshire, 345 U.S. 395 (1953). Compare Kovacs v. Cooper,

336 U.S. 77 (1949) (use of sound trucks making 'loud and raucous noises' on public streets may be prohibited)."

Following the Court's decision in *Logan Valley*, the NLRB decided Solo Cup Co., 172 N.L.R.B. No. 110, 68 L.R.R.M. 1385 (1968), in which it compared union solicitation by nonemployees in a privately owned industrial park to the public aspect of the shopping center in *Logan Valley*, holding the employer's exclusion of nonemployee union organizers from park premises violated § 8 (a) (1). The Board was reversed by the Seventh Circuit, which distinguished *Logan Valley*. "Here, the public was not invited into the District. None of the companies located there held itself out as being open to the public, and the general public had no reason to enter the area." NLRB v. Solo Cup Co., 422 F.2d 1149, 1151 (7th Cir. 1970).

The continuing validity of the *Logan Valley* decision was made questionable by two subsequent Supreme Court decisions. *See* Central Hardware Co. v. NLRB, — U.S. —, 92 S. Ct. 2238, 33 L. Ed. 2d 122 (1972); Lloyd v. Tanner, — U.S. —, 92 S. Ct. 2219, 33 L. Ed. 2d 131 (1972).

4. Given the rationale of the WERB case and the rather extensive limitations on the right to strike in the private sector noted above, can you draft a comprehensive definition of the right to strike as it presently exists in the private sector? It is crucial to understand the precise parameters of this right in order to evaluate the argument that denying public employees the right to strike is a violation of the Fourteenth Amendment's equal protection clause.

2. The Constitutional Issues in the Public Sector

UNITED FEDERATION OF POSTAL CLERKS v. BLOUNT
325 F. Supp. 879 (D.D.C.)
Aff'd, 404 U.S. 802 (1971)

PER CURIAM: This action was brought by the United Federation of Postal Clerks (hereafter sometimes referred to as "Clerks"), an unincorporated public employee labor organization which consists primarily of employees of the Post Office Department, and which is the exclusive bargaining representative of approximately 305,000 members of the clerk craft employed by defendant. Defendant Blount is the Postmaster General of the United States. The Clerks seek declaratory and injunctive relief invalidating portions of 5 U.S.C. § 7311, 18 U.S.C. § 1918, an affidavit required by 5 U.S.C. § 3333 to implement the above statutes, and Executive Order 11491, C.F.R., Chap. II, p. 191. A three-judge court was convened pursuant to 28 U.S.C. § 2282 and § 2284 to consider this issue.

The Statutes Involved

5 U.S.C. § 7311 (3) prohibits an individual from accepting or holding a position in the federal government or in the District of Columbia if he

> " (3)   participates in a strike . . . against the Government of the United States or the government of the District of Columbia. . . ."

Paragraph C of the appointment affidavit required by 5 U.S.C. § 3333, which all federal employees are required to execute under oath, states (POD Form 61) :

> "I am not participating in any strike against the Government of the United States or any agency thereof, and I will not so participate while an employee of the Government of the United States or any agency thereof."

18 U.S.C. § 1918, in making a violation of 5 U.S.C. § 7311 a crime, provides:

> "Whoever violates the provision of section 7311 of title 5 that an individual may not accept or hold a position in the Government of the United States or the government of the District of Columbia if he . . .
>
> " (3)   participates in a strike, or asserts the right to strike, against the Government of the United States or the District of Columbia . . .
>
> "shall be fined not more than $1,000 or imprisoned not more than one year and a day, or both."

Section 2 (e) (2) of Executive Order 11491 exempts from the definition of a labor organization any group which:

> "asserts the right to strike against the Government of the United States or any agency thereof, or to assist or participate in such a strike, or imposes a duty or obligation to conduct, assist or participate in such a strike. . . ."

Section 19 (b) (4) of the same Executive Order makes it an unfair labor practice for a labor organization to:

> "call or engage in a strike, work stoppage, or slowdown; picket an agency in a labor-management dispute; or condone any such activity by failing to take affirmative action to prevent or stop it; . . . ."

Plaintiff's Contentions

Plaintiff contends that the right to strike is a fundamental right protected by the Constitution, and that the absolute prohibition of such activity by 5 U.S.C. § 7311 (3) and the other provisions set out above thus constitutes an infringement of the employees' First Amendment rights of association and free speech and operates to deny them equal protection of the law. Plaintiff also argues that the language to "strike" and "participates in a strike" is vague and overbroad and therefore violative of both the First Amendment and the due process clause of the Fifth Amendment. For the purposes of this opinion, we will direct our attention to the attack on the constitutionality of 5 U.S.C. § 7311 (3), the key provision being challenged. To the extent that the present wording of 18 U.S.C. § 1918 (3) and Executive Order 11491 does not reflect the actions of two statutory courts in Stewart v. Washington, 301 F. Supp. 610 (D.C.D.C. 1969) and N.A.L.C. v. Blount, 305 F. Supp. 546 (D.C.D.C. 1969), said wording, insofar as it inhibits the *assertion* of the right to strike, is overbroad because it attempts to reach activities protected by the First Amendment and is therefore invalid. With this *caveat,* our treatment of the issue raised by plaintiffs with respect to the constitutionality of 5 U.S.C. § 7311 (3) will also apply to 18 U.S.C. § 1918, the penal provision, and to Form 61, the affidavit required by 5 U.S.C. § 3333. For the reasons set forth below, we deny plaintiff's request for declaratory and injunctive relief and grant defendant's motion to dismiss.

I. PUBLIC EMPLOYEES HAVE NO CONSTITUTIONAL RIGHT TO STRIKE.

At common law no employee, whether public or private, had a constitutional right to strike in concert with his fellow workers. Indeed, such collective action on the part of employees was often held to be a conspiracy. When the right of private employees to strike finally received full protection, it was by statute, Section 7 of the National Labor Relations Act, which "took this conspiracy weapon away from the employer in employment relations which affect interstate commerce" and guaranteed to employees in the private sector the right to engage in concerted activities for the purpose of collective bargaining. See discussion in International Union, U.A.W.A., A.F. of L. Local 232 v. Wisconsin Employment Relations Board, 336 U.S. 245, 257-259, 69 S. Ct. 516, 93 L. Ed. 651 (1948). It seems clear that public employees stand on no stronger footing in this regard than private employees and that in the absence of a statute, they too do not possess the right to strike. The Supreme Court has spoken approvingly of such a restriction,

see Amell v. United States, 384 U.S. 158, 161, 86 S. Ct. 1384,
16 L. Ed. 2d 445 (1965), and at least one federal district court
has invoked the provisions of a predecessor statute, 5 U.S.C.
§ 118p-r, to enjoin a strike by government employees. Tennessee
Valley Authority v. Local Union No. 110 of Sheet Metal
Workers, 233 F. Supp. 997 (D.C.W.D. Ky. 1962). Likewise, scores of state cases have held that state employees
do not have a right to engage in concerted work stoppages,
in the absence of legislative authorization. . . . It is fair to
conclude that, irrespective of the reasons given, there is a
unanimity of opinion in the part of courts and legislatures that
government employees do not have the right to strike. See
Moberly, The Strike and Its Alternative in Public Employment,
University of Wisconsin Law Review (1966) pp. 549-550, 554.

Congress has consistently treated public employees as being in
a different category than private employees. The National Labor
Relations Act of 1937 and the Labor Management Relations
Act of 1947, (Taft-Hartley) both defined "employer" as not
including any governmental or political subdivisions, and thereby
indirectly withheld the protections of § 7 from governmental
employees. Congress originally enacted the no-strike provision
separately from other restrictions on employee activity, i.e., such
as those struck down in Stewart v. Washington and N.A.L.C. v.
Blount, supra, by attaching riders to appropriations bills which
prohibited strikes by government employees. See for example the
Third Urgent Deficiency Appropriation Act of 1946, which provided that no part of the appropriation could be used to pay the
salary of anyone who engaged in a strike against the Government.
Section 305 of the Taft-Hartley Act made it unlawful for a federal employee to participate in a strike, providing immediate discharge and forfeiture of civil service status for infractions.
Section 305 was repealed in 1955 by Public Law 330, and reenacted in 5 U.S.C. § 118p-r, the predecessor to the present
statute.

Given the fact that there is no constitutional right to strike, it
is not irrational or arbitrary for the Government to condition
employment on a promise not to withhold labor collectively, and
to prohibit strikes by those in public employment, whether
because of the prerogatives of the sovereign, some sense of higher
obligation associated with public service, to assure the continuing functioning of the Government without interruption, to
protect public health and safety or for other reasons. Although
plaintiff argues that the provisions in question are unconstitutionally broad in covering all Government employees regardless
of the type or importance of the work they do, we hold that it

makes no difference whether the jobs performed by certain public employees are regarded as "essential" or "non-essential," or whether similar jobs are performed by workers in private industry who do have the right to strike protected by statute. Nor is it relevant that some positions in private industry are arguably more affected with a public interest than are some positions in the Government service. While the Fifth Amendment contains no Equal Protection Clause similar to the one found in the Fourteenth Amendment, concepts of Equal Protection do inhere in Fifth Amendment Principles of Due Process. Bolling v. Sharpe, 347 U.S. 497, 74 S. Ct. 693, 98 L. Ed. 884 (1954). The Equal Protection Clause, however, does not forbid all discrimination. Where fundamental rights are not involved, a particular classification does not violate the Equal Protection Clause if it is not "arbitrary" or "irrational," i.e., "if any state of facts reasonably may be conceived to justify it." McGowan v. Maryland, 366 U.S. 420, 426, 81 S. Ct. 1101, 1105, 6 L. Ed. 2d 393 (1961). Compare Kramer v. Union Free School District, 395 U.S. 621, 627-628, 89 S. Ct. 1886, 23 L. Ed. 2d 583 (1969). Since the right to strike cannot be considered a "fundamental" right, it is the test enunciated in *McGowan* which must be employed in this case. Thus, there is latitude for distinctions rooted in reason and practice, especially where the difficulty of drafting a no-strike statute which distinguishes among types and classes of employees is obvious.

Furthermore, it should be pointed out that the fact that public employees may not strike does not interfere with their rights which are fundamental and constitutionally protected. The right to organize collectively and to select representatives for the purposes of engaging in collective bargaining is such a fundamental right. . . . But, as the Supreme Court noted in International Union, etc., Local 232 v. Wisconsin Employment Relations Board, *supra,* "The right to strike, because of its more serious impact upon the public interest, is more vulnerable to regulation than the right to organize and select representatives for lawful purposes of collective bargaining which this Court has characterized as a 'fundamental right' and which, as the Court has pointed out, was recognized as such in its decisions long before it was given protection by the National Labor Relations Act." 336 U.S. at 259, 69 S. Ct. at 524.

Executive Order 11491 recognizes the right of federal employees to join labor organizations for the purpose of dealing with grievances, but that Order clearly and expressly defines strikes, work stoppages and slow-downs as unfair labor practices. As discussed above, that Order is the culmination of a long-standing policy. There certainly is no compelling reason to imply the existence of the right to strike from the right to associate and bargain collectively. In the private sphere, the strike is used to equalize bargaining power, but this has universally been held not to be appropriate when its object and purpose can only be to influence the essentially political decisions of Government in the allocation of its resources. Congress has an obligation to ensure that the machinery of the Federal Government continues to function at all times without interference. Prohibition of strikes by its employees is a reasonable implementation of that obligation.

II. THE PROVISIONS ARE NEITHER UNCONSTITUTIONALLY VAGUE NOR OVERBROAD.

Plaintiff contends that the word "strike" and the phrase "participates in a strike" used in the statute are so vague that "men of common intelligence must necessarily guess at [their] meaning and differ as to [their] application," Connally v. General Construction Co., 269 U.S. 385, 391, 46 S. Ct. 126, 127, 70 L. Ed. 322 (1926), and are therefore violative of the due process clause of the Fifth Amendment. Plaintiff also contends that the provisions are overly broad. While there is no sharp distinction between vagueness and overbreadth, an overly broad statute reaches not only conduct which the Government may properly prohibit but also conduct which is beyond the reach of governmental regulation. A vague statute is merely imprecise in indicating which of several types of conduct which could be restricted has in fact been prohibited.

These concepts of "striking" and "participating in a strike" occupy central positions in our labor statutes and accompanying caselaw, and have been construed and interpreted many times by numerous state and federal courts. "Strike" is defined in § 501 (2) of the Taft-Hartley Act to include "any strike or other concerted stoppage of work by employees . . . and any concerted slowdown or other concerted interruption of operations by employees." On its face this is a straightforward definition. It is difficult to understand how a word used and defined so often could be sufficiently ambiguous as to be constitutionally suspect. "Strike" is a term of such common usage and acceptance that "men of common intelligence" need not guess at its meaning. Connally v. General Construction Co., supra, at 391, 46 S. Ct. at 127.

Plaintiff complains that the precise parameters of "participation" are so unclear that employees may fail to exercise other, protected First Amendment rights for fear of overstepping the line, and that in any event, "participates" is too broad to withstand judicial scrutiny. Plaintiff urges that Congress is required to more specifically define exactly what activities are to be caught up in the net of illegality.

The Government, however, represented at oral argument that it interprets "participate" to mean "striking," the essence of which is an actual refusal in concert with others to provide services to one's employer. We adopt this construction of the phrase, which will exclude the First Amendment problems raised by the plaintiff in that it removes from the strict reach of these statutes and other provisions such conduct as speech, union membership, fund-raising, organization, distribution of literature and informational picketing, even though those activities may take place in concert during a strike by others. We stress that it is only an actual refusal by particular employees to provide services that is forbidden by 5 U.S.C. § 7311 (3) and penalized by 18 U.S.C. § 1918. However, these statutes, as all criminal statutes, must be read in conjunction with 18 U.S.C. §§ 2 (aiding and abetting) and 371 (conspiracy). We express no views as to the extent of their application to cases that might arise thereunder as it is practically impossible to fashion a meaningful declaratory judgment in such a broad area.

This case does not involve a situation where we are concerned with a prior construction by a state supreme court, but rather one in which we are faced with the interpretation to be given a federal statute in the first instance by a federal court. Under such circumstances federal courts have broad latitude, the language of the statute permitting, to construe a statute in such terms as will save it from the infirmities of vagueness and overbreadth. Kent v. Dulles, 357 U.S. 116, 78 S. Ct. 1113, 2 L. Ed. 2d 1204 (1958). This principle of interpretation is equally true of cases which involve rights under the First Amendment. United States v. C.I.O., 335 U.S. 106, 120-122, 68 S. Ct. 1349, 92 L. Ed. 1849 (1948); Chaplinsky v. New Hampshire, 315 U.S. 568, 573-574, 62 S. Ct. 766, 86 L. Ed. 1031 (1942); see also Williams v. District of Columbia, 136 U.S. App. D.C. 56, 419 F.2d 638 (en banc, 1969). Such construction of the word "strike" and the phrase "participates in a strike" achieves the objective of Congress and, in defining the type of conduct which is beyond the reach of the statute, saves it from the risk of vagueness and overbreadth.

Accordingly, we hold that the provisions of the statute, the appointment affidavit and the Executive Order, as construed above, do not violate any constitutional rights of those employees who are members of plaintiff's union. The Government's motion to dismiss the complaint is granted. Order to be presented.

J. SKELLY WRIGHT, Circuit Judge (concurring) :

I concur in Part II of the majority's opinion and in the result. My following comments are addressed to the main issue raised in Part I of the opinion—the validity of the flat ban on federal employees' strikes under the Fifth Amendment of the Constitution. This question is, in my view, a very difficult one, and I cannot concur fully in the majority's handling of it.

It is by no means clear to me that the right to strike is not fundamental. The right to strike seems intimately related to the right to form labor organizations, a right which the majority recognizes as fundamental and which, more importantly, is generally thought to be constitutionally protected under the First Amendment—even for public employees. See Melton v. City of Atlanta, 324 F. Supp. 315 (N.D. Ga. 1971) ; Atkins v. City of Charlotte, 296 F. Supp. 1068 (W.D.N.C. 1969). If the inherent purpose of a labor organization is to bring the workers' interests to bear on management, the right to strike is, historically and practically, an important means of effectuating that purpose. A union that never strikes, or which can make no credible threat to strike, may wither away in ineffectiveness. That fact is not irrelevant to the constitutional calculations. Indeed, in several decisions, the Supreme Court has held that the First Amendment right of association is at least concerned with essential organizational activities which give the particular association life and promote its fundamental purposes. See Williams v. Rhodes, 393 U.S. 23, 89 S. Ct. 5, 21 L. Ed. 2d 24 (1968) ; United Mine Workers, etc. v. Illinois State Bar Assn., 389 U.S. 217, 88 S. Ct. 353, 19 L. Ed. 2d 426 (1967). I do not suggest that the right to strike is co-equal with the right to form labor organizations. Nor do I equate striking with the organizational activities protected in Williams (access to the ballot) or United Mine Workers (group legal representation). But I do believe that the right to strike is, at least, within constitutional concern and should not be discriminatorily abridged without substantial or "compelling" justification.

Hence the real question here, as I see it, is to determine whether there is such justification for denying federal employees a right which is granted to other employees of private business. Plaintiff's arguments that not all federal services are "essential" and that some privately provided services are no less "essential" casts doubt on the validity of the flat ban on federal employees' strikes. In our mixed economic system of governmental and private enterprise, the line separating governmental from private functions may depend more on the accidents of history than on substantial differences in kind.

Nevertheless, I feel that I must concur in the result reached by the majority in Part I of its opinion. As the majority indicates, the asserted right of public employees to strike has often been litigated and, so far as I know, never recognized as a matter of law. The present state of the relevant jurisprudence offers almost no support for the proposition that the government lacks a "compelling" interest in prohibiting such strikes. No doubt, the line between "essential" and "non-essential" functions is very, very difficult to draw. For that reason, it may well be best to accept the demarcations resulting from the development of our political economy. If the right of public employees to strike—with all its political and social ramifications—is to be recognized and protected by the judiciary, it should be done by the Supreme Court which has the power to reject established jurisprudence and the authority to enforce such a sweeping rule.

NOTES

1. Prohibitions against public employee strikes have been challenged on almost every conceivable basis. To date nearly every court ruling on this question has held that these prohibitions do not violate the Constitution. The case law includes:

(a) *First Amendment Challenges:* Abbott v. Myers, 20 Ohio App. 2d 65, 49 Ohio Op. 2d 85, 251 N.E.2d 869 (1969); Board of Educ. Community School Dist. No. 2 v. Redding, 32 Ill. 2d 567, 207 N.E.2d 427 (1965); City of Wauwatosa v. King, 49 Wis. 2d 398, 182 N.W.2d 530 (1971); Jefferson County Teachers Ass'n v. Board of Educ. of Jefferson County, 463 S.W.2d 627 (Ky. 1970), *cert. denied,* 404 U.S. 865 (1971); Board of Educ. of Kankakee School Dist. No. 111 v. Kankakee Fed'n of Teachers Local 886, 46 Ill. 2d 439, 264 N.E.2d 18 (1970), *cert. denied,* 403 U.S. 904 (1971); State v. Heath, 177 N.W.2d 751 (N.D. 1970); Regents of Univ. of Wisconsin v. Teaching Assistants' Ass'n, 74 L.R.R.M. 2049 (Wis. Cir. Ct. 1970); Rogoff v. Anderson, 34 App. Div. 2d 154, 310 N.Y.S.2d 174 (1970); Holland School Dist. v. Holland Educ. Ass'n, 380 Mich. 314, 157 N.W.2d 206 (1968); City of Pawtucket v. Pawtucket Teachers Alliance Local 930, 87 R.I. 364, 141 A.2d 621 (1958).

(b) *Thirteenth Amendment Challenges:* City of Evanston v. Buick, 421 F.2d 595 (7th Cir. 1970); *In re* Block, 50 N.J. 494, 236 A.2d 592 (1967); Pinellas County Classroom Teachers Ass'n Inc. v. Board of Public Instruction of Pinellas County, 214 So. 2d 34 (Fla. 1968); Holland School Dist. v. Holland Educ. Ass'n, *supra.*

(c) *Fourteenth Amendment Challenges:* Abbott v.
Myers, *supra;* City of New York v. DeLury, 23 N.Y.2d 175,
162 Misc. 2d 901, 243 N.E.2d 128, 295 N.Y.S.2d 901 (1968),
appeal dismissed, 394 U.S. 455 (1969) ; Head v. Special
School Dist. No. 1, 288 Minn. 496, 182 N.W.2d 887, *cert.
denied,* 404 U.S. 886 (1970) ; *In re* Block, *supra;* Jefferson
County Teachers Ass'n v. Board of Educ. of Jefferson County,
supra; Holland School Dist. v. Holland Educ. Ass'n, *supra.*

(d) *Bill of Attainder Challenges:* Abbott v. Myers, *supra;*
DiMaggio v. Brown, 19 N.Y.2d 283, 225 N.E.2d 871, 279
N.Y.S.2d 161 (1967) .

2. The relevant case law to date also appears to support the
proposition that strikes by public employees engaged in propriety as well as governmental functions are illegal: Delaware
River & Bay Authority v. International Organization of Masters,
Mates & Pilots, 45 N.J. 138, 211 A.2d 789 (1965) ; Port of
Seattle v. ILWU, 52 Wash. 2d 317, 324 P.2d 1099 (1958) ; City
of Alcoa v. IBEW Local 760, 203 Tenn. 12, 308 S.W.2d 476
(1957) ; City of Los Angeles v. Los Angeles Bldg. Constr. Trades
Council, 94 Cal. App. 2d 36, 210 P.2d 305 (1949) .

3. Violation of an injunction prohibiting public employees
from striking is punishable by contempt and there is no constitutional right to trial by jury in such a contempt proceeding. *See,
e.g.,* City of New York v. DeLury, 23 N.Y.2d 175, 162 Misc. 2d
901, 243 N.E.2d 128, 295 N.Y.S.2d 901 (1968), *appeal dismissed,*
394 U.S. 455 (1969) ; Rankin v. Shanker, 23 N.Y.2d 111, 242
N.E.2d 802, 295 N.Y.S.2d 625 (1968) ; *In re* Block, 50 N.J. 494,
236 A.2d 592 (1967) .

4. Judge Wright in *Blount* claims that "the relevant jurisprudence offers almost no support for the proposition that the
government lacks a 'compelling' interest in prohibiting such
strikes." What reasons cited by the majority in *Blount* seem
most compelling? The court seems to reject out of hand the argument that it is irrational to totally prohibit strikes of municipal
librarians, for example, while allowing strikes of telephone
workers. Why?

C. Theoretical Considerations Relating to the Right to Strike

In dealing with theoretical considerations in this area, it might
be well to question the assumption that strikes are not a fundamental and necessary part of the American collective bargaining
system. Can a labor relations system work in the absence of some
compulsion on both parties? If not, are there alternative devices to

introduce compulsion into the system which are as effective as the strike yet not so disruptive?

WELLINGTON & WINTER, STRUCTURING COLLECTIVE BARGAINING IN PUBLIC EMPLOYMENT, 79 Yale L.J. 805, 822 (1970)†

A. *The Role of the Strike*

We have argued that distortion of the political process is the major, long-run social cost of strikes in public employment. The distortion results from unions obtaining too much power, relative to other interest groups, in decisions affecting the level of taxes and the allocation of tax dollars. This distortion may, therefore, result in a redistribution of income by government, one in which union members are subsidized at the expense of other interest groups. And, where non-monetary issues, such as the decentralization of the governance of schools or the creation of a civilian board to review police conduct, are resolved through bargaining in which the strike or threat thereof is used, the distortion of the political process is no less apparent.

It has been earnestly argued, however, that if public employee unions are successfully denied the strike, they will have too little relative power. To unpack the claims in this argument is crucially important. In the private sector collective bargaining depends upon the strike threat and the occasional strike. It is how deals are made, how collective bargaining works, why employers agree to terms and conditions of employment better than they originally offered. Intuition suggests that what is true of the private sector also is true of the public. Without the strike threat and the strike, the public employer will be intransigent; and this intransigence will, in effect, deprive employees of the very benefits unionization was intended to bring to them. Collective bargaining, the argument goes, will be merely a facade for "collective begging."

Initially, it must be noted that even in the absence of unionism and bargaining the market imposes substantial limitations on the ability of public employers to "take advantage" of their employees. Because they must compete with private employers, and other units of government as well, to hire workers, public employers cannot permit their wages and conditions of employment to be relatively poorer than those offered in the private sector and still get the needed workers. And, as we noted in the *Limits* article,[1] the fact that most public employees work in areas in

---

† Reprinted by permission of The Yale Law Journal Company and Fred B. Rothman & Company.

[1] Wellington & Winter, *The Limits of Collective Bargaining in Public Employment,* 78 YALE L.J. 1107 (1969). [Ed.]

which there are numerous alternative employment opportunities reduces the likelihood that many public employers are monopsonists. Even if they are, moreover, the lack of a profit motive reduces the likelihood that government's monopsony power, if it exists, will be exercised.

Much of the argument about the role of the strike is, in any event, overstated. First, it exaggerates the power of the strike weapon in the private sector. As we argued in the *Limits* article, the power of private sector unions to gain comparative advantages, while real, is inherently limited by what we there called the employment-benefit tradeoff.

Second, the very unionization of public employees creates a powerful interest group, at least in large urban centers, that seems able to compete very well with other groups in the political decision-making process. Indeed, collective bargaining (the strike apart) is a method of channeling and underscoring the demands of public employees that is not systematically available to other groups. Public employee unions frequently serve as lobbying agents wielding political power quite disproportionate to the size of their membership. The failure of the Hartford firefighters, mentioned earlier, to seek formal status as a bargaining agent demonstrates how much punch such organizations can wield. And where a strong local labor council exists, association with it can significantly increase the power of public employee unions. This is some assurance, therefore, that public employees, even if prohibited from striking, will not be at a comparative disadvantage in bargaining with their employers.

Thus, on the merits, when one takes the trouble to unpack its claims, the argument for the strike in public employment is hardly inexorable.

BURTON & KRIDER, THE ROLE AND CONSEQUENCES OF STRIKES BY PUBLIC EMPLOYEES, 79 Yale L.J. 418, 424-32 (1970)†

Wellington and Winter's discussion ["The Limits of Collective Bargaining in Public Employment," 78 Yale L. J. 1107 (1969)] of the cost of substituting collective for individual bargaining in the public sector includes a chain of causation which runs from (1) an allegation that market restraints are weak in the public sector, largely because the services are essential; to (2) an assertion that the public puts pressure on civic officials to arrive at a quick settlement; to (3) a statement that other pressure groups have no weapons comparable to a strike; to (4) a conclusion

---

† Reprinted by permission of The Yale Law Journal Company and Fred B. Rothman & Company.

that the strike thus imposes a high cost since the political process is distorted.

Let us discuss these steps in order:

(1) *Market Restraints:* A key argument in the case for the inappropriateness of public sector strikes is that economic constraints are not present to any meaningful degree in the public sector. This argument is not entirely convincing. First, wages lost due to strikes are as important to public employees as they are to employees in the private sector. Second, the public's concern over increasing tax rates may prevent the decision-making process from being dominated by political instead of economic considerations. The development of multilateral bargaining in the public sector is an example of how the concern over taxes may result in a close substitute for market constraints. In San Francisco, for example, the Chamber of Commerce has participated in negotiations between the city and public employee unions and has had some success in limiting the economic gains of the unions. A third and related economic constraint arises for such services as water, sewage, and, in some instances, sanitation, where explicit prices are charged. Even if representatives of groups other than employees and the employer do not enter the bargaining process, both union and local government are aware of the economic implications of bargaining which leads to higher prices which are clearly visible to the public. A fourth economic constraint on employees exists in those services where subcontracting to the private sector is a realistic alternative. Warren, Michigan, resolved a bargaining impasse with an American Federation of State, County and Municipal Employees (AFSCME) local by subcontracting its entire sanitation service; Santa Monica, California, ended a strike of city employees by threatening to subcontract its sanitation operations. If the subcontracting option is preserved, wages in the public sector need not exceed the rate at which subcontracting becomes a realistic alternative.

An aspect of the lack-of-market-restraints argument is that public services are essential. Even at the analytical level, Wellington and Winter's case for essentiality is not convincing. They argue:

> "The Services performed by a private transit authority are neither less nor more essential to the public than those that would be performed if the transit authority were owned by a municipality. A railroad or a dock strike may be much more damaging to a community than 'job action' by teachers. This is not to say that government services are not essential. They are both because they may seriously injure a city's economy and occasionally the physical welfare of its citizens."

This is a troublesome passage. It ends with the implicit conclusion that all government services are essential. This conclusion is important in Wellington and Winter's analysis because it is a step in their demonstration that strikes are inappropriate in all governmental services. But the beginning of the passage, with its example of "job action" by teachers, suggests that essentiality is not an *inherent* characteristic of government services but depends on the specific service being evaluated. Furthermore the transit authority example suggests that many services are interchangeable between the public and private sectors. The view that various government services are not of equal essentiality and that there is considerable overlap between the kinds of services provided in the public and private sectors is reinforced by our field work and strike data from the Bureau of Labor Statistics. Examples include:

1. Where sanitation services are provided by a municipality, such as Cleveland, sanitationmen are prohibited from striking. Yet, sanitationmen in Philadelphia, Portland, and San Francisco are presumably free to strike since they are employed by private contractors rather than by the cities.

2. There were 25 local government strikes by the Teamsters in 1965-68, most involving truck drivers and all presumably illegal. Yet the Teamsters' strike involving fuel oil truck drivers in New York City last winter was legal even though the interruption of fuel oil service was believed to have caused the death of several people.

(2) *Public Pressure:* The second argument in the Wellington and Winter analysis is that public pressure on city officials forces them to make quick settlements. The validity of this argument depends on whether the service is essential. Using as a criterion whether the service is essential in the short run, we believe a priori that services can be divided into three categories: (1) essential services—police and fire—where strikes immediately endanger public health and safety; (2) intermediate services—sanitation, hospitals, transit, water, and sewage—where strikes of a few days might be tolerated; (3) nonessential services—streets, parks, education, housing, welfare and general administration—where strikes of indefinite duration could be tolerated. These categories are not exact since essentiality depends on the size of the city. Sanitation strikes will be critical in large cities such as New York but will not cause much inconvenience in smaller cities where there are meaningful alternatives to governmental operation of sanitation services.

Statistics on the duration of strikes which occurred in the public sector between 1965 and 1968 provide evidence not only that public services are of unequal essentiality, but also that the a priori categories which we have used have some validity. . . . [S]trikes in the essential services (police and fire) had an average duration of 4.7 days, while both the intermediate and the nonessential services had an average duration of approximately 10.5 days. It is true that the duration of strikes in the intermediate and non-essential services is only half the average duration of strikes in the private sector during these years. However, this comparison is somewhat misleading since all of the public sector strikes were illegal, and many were ended by injunction, while presumably a vast majority of the private sector strikes did not suffer from these constraints. It would appear that with the exception of police and fire protection, public officials are, to some degree, able to accept long strikes. The ability of governments to so choose indicates that political pressures generated by strikes are not so strong as to undesirably distort the entire decision-making process of government. City officials in Kalamazoo, Michigan, were able to accept a forty-eight day strike by sanitationmen and laborers; Sacramento County, California, survived an eighty-seven day strike by welfare workers. A three month strike of hospital work-ers has occurred in Cuyahoga County (Cleveland), Ohio.

(3) *The Strike as a Unique Weapon:* The third objection to the strike is that it provides workers with a weapon unavailable to the employing agency or to other pressure groups. Thus, unions have a superior arsenal. The Taylor Committee Report opposes strikes for this reason, among others, arguing that "there can scarcely be a countervailing lockout." Conceptually, we see no reason why lockouts are less feasible in the public than in the pri-vate sector. Legally, public sector lockouts are now forbidden, but so are strikes; presumably both could be legalized. Actually, pub-lic sector lockouts have occurred. The Social Service Employees Union (SSEU) of New York City sponsored a "work-in" in 1967 during which all of the caseworkers went to their office but refused to work. Instead, union-sponsored lectures were given by representatives of organizations such as CORE, and symposia were held on the problems of welfare workers and clients. The work-in lasted for one week, after which the City locked out the case-workers.

A similar assertion is made by Wellington and Winter, who claim that no pressure group other than unions has a weapon comparable to the strike. But this argument raises a number of questions. Is the distinctive characteristic of an inappropriate method of influencing decisions by public officials that it is economic as opposed to political? If this is so, then presumably the threat of the New York Stock Exchange to move to New

Jersey unless New York City taxes on stock transfers were lowered and similar devices should be outlawed along with the strike.

(4) *Distortion of the Political Process:* The ultimate concern of both the Taylor Committee and Wellington and Winter is that "a strike of government employees . . . introduces an alien force in the legislative process." It is "alien" because, in the words of the Taylor Committee Report:

> "Careful thought about the matter shows conclusively, we believe, that while the right to strike normally performs a useful function in the private enterprise sector (where relative economic power is the final determinant in the making of private agreements), it is not compatible with the orderly functioning of our democratic form of representative government (in which relative political power is the final determinant)."

The essence of this analysis appears to be that certain means used to influence the decision-making process in the public sector —those which are political—are legitimate, while others—those which are economic—are not. For several reasons, we believe that such distinctions among means are tenuous.

First, any scheme which differentiates economic power from political power faces a perplexing definitional task. . . . The former concept would seem to be encompassed by the latter. The degree of overlap is problematical since there can be economic aspects to many forms of persuasion and pressure. It may be possible to provide an operational distinction between economic power and political power, but we do not believe that those who would rely on this distinction have fulfilled their task.

Second, even assuming it is possible to operationally distinguish economic power and political power, a rationale for utilizing the distinction must be provided. Such a rationale would have to distinguish between the categories either on the basis of characteristics inherent in them as a means of action or on the basis of the ends to which the means are directed. Surely an analysis of ends does not provide a meaningful distinction. The objectives of groups using economic pressure are of the same character as those of groups using political pressure—both seek to influence executive and legislative determinations such as the allocation of funds and the tax rate. If it is impossible effectively to distinguish economic from political pressure groups in terms of their ends, and it is desirable to free the political process from the influence of all pressure groups, then effective lobbying and petitioning should be as illegal as strikes.

If the normative distinction between economic and political power is based, not on the ends desired, but on the nature of the means, our skepticism remains undiminished. Are all forms of political pressure legitimate? Then consider the range of political activity observed in the public sector. Is lobbying by public sector unions to be approved? Presumably it is. What then of participation in partisan political activity? On city time? Should we question the use of campaign contributions or kickbacks from public employees to public officials as a means of influencing public sector decisions? These questions suggest that political pressures, as opposed to economic pressures, cannot *as a class* be considered more desirable.

Our antagonism toward a distinction based on means does not rest solely on a condemnation of political pressures which violate statutory provisions. We believe that perfectly legal forms of political pressure have no automatic superiority over economic pressure. In this regard, the evidence from our field work is particularly enlightening. First, we have found that the availability of political power varies among groups of employees within a given city. Most public administrators have respect for groups which can deliver votes at strategic times. Because of their links to private sector unions, craft unions are invariably in a better position to play this political role than a union confined to the public sector, such as AFSCME. In Chicago, Cleveland and San Francisco, the public sector craft unions are closely allied with the building trades council and play a key role in labor relations with the city. Prior to the passage of state collective bargaining laws such unions also played the key role in Detroit and New York City. . . .

Second, the range of issues pursued by unions relying on political power tends to be narrow. The unions which prosper by eschewing economic power and exercising political power are often found in cities, such as Chicago, with a flourishing patronage system. These unions gain much of their political power by cooperating with the political administration. This source of political power would vanish if the unions were assiduously to pursue a goal of providing job security for their members since this goal would undermine the patronage system. In Rochester, for example, a union made no effort to protect one of its members who was fired for political reasons. For the union to have opposed the city administration at that time on an issue of job security would substantially have reduced the union's influence on other issues. In Chicago, where public sector strikes are rare (except for education) but political considerations are not, the unions have made little effort to establish a grievance procedure to protect their members from arbitrary treatment.

Third, a labor relations system built on political power tends to be unstable since some groups of employees, often a substantial number, are invariably left out of the system. They receive no representation either through patronage or through the union. In Memphis, the craft unions had for many years enjoyed a "working relationship" with the city which assured the payment of the rates that prevailed in the private sector and some control over jobs. The sanitation laborers, however, were not part of the system and were able to obtain effective representation only after a violent confrontation with the city in 1968. Having been denied representation through the political process, they had no choice but to accept a subordinate position in the city or to initiate a strike to change the system. Racial barriers were an important factor in the isolation of the Memphis sanitation laborers. Similar distinctions in racial balance among functions and occupations appear in most of the cities we visited.

C. CONCLUSIONS IN REGARD TO STRIKES AND THE POLITICAL PROCESS

Wellington and Winter and the Taylor Committee reject the use of the Strike Model in the public sector. They have endorsed the No-Strike Model in order "to ensure the survival of the 'normal' American political process." Our field work suggests that unions which have actually helped their members either have made the strike threat a viable weapon despite its illegality or have intertwined themselves closely with their nominal employer through patronage-political support arrangements. If this assessment is correct, choice of the No-Strike Model is likely to lead to patterns of decision making which will subvert, if not the "normal" American political process, at least the political process which the Taylor Committee and Wellington and Winter meant to embrace. We would not argue that the misuse of political power will be eliminated by legalizing the strike; on balance, however, we believe that, in regard to most governmental functions, the Strike Model has more virtues than the No-Strike Model.

NOTES

1. The literature on the theoretical aspects of the strike ban is voluminous with the following articles being perhaps the most comprehensive on the point: Anderson, *Strikes and Impasse Resolution in Public Employment,* 67 MICH. L. REV. 943 (1969) ; Bilik, *Toward Public Sector Equality: Extending the*

Strike Privilege, 21 Lab. L.J. 338 (1970) ; Comment, *Collective Bargaining for Public Employees and the Prevention of Strikes in the Public Sector,* 68 Mich. L. Rev. 260 (1969) ; Edwards, *The Developing Labor Relations Law in the Public Sector,* 10 Duquesne L. Rev. 357 (1972) ; Kheel, *Resolving Deadlocks Without Banning Strikes,* 92 Monthly Lab. Rev. 62 (July 1969) and *Strikes and Public Employment,* 67 Mich. L. Rev. 931 (1969) ; Note, *The Strike and Its Alternatives in Public Employment,* 1966 Wis. L. Rev. 549; Smith, *State and Local Advisory Reports on Public Employment Labor Legislation: A Comparative Analysis,* 67 Mich. L. Rev. 891 (1968) ; Taylor, *Public Employment: Strikes or Procedures,* 20 Ind. & Lab. Rel. Rev. 617 (1967) ; Wellington & Winter, The Unions and the Cities (Brookings Institution, 1971) .

2.   Should different treatment be accorded to public employees working in small versus large municipalities? It has been argued that strikes by public employees in smaller towns and cities may be tolerable, especially in non-essential services, but that in a city like New York any strike by public sector employees, because of its political and economic consequences, is too severe to be tolerated; therefore, it is claimed that the strike proscription in the largest cities must of necessity be absolute. Do you agree? Does it make sense to distinguish between large and small communities? Would such a distinction survive constitutional challenge?

3.   A very important (and sometimes neglected) factor in the theoretical considerations is that any calculation of the legitimacy of public sector strikes on the basis of "essentiality" may be likely to have considerable spill-over effects in the private sector. Arvid Anderson, Chairman of the New York City Office of Collective Bargaining, raised this point in Anderson, *Strikes and Impasse Resolution in Public Employment,* 67 Mich. L. Rev. 943, 950-51 (1969) :

> For one thing, the ultimate resolution of public policy toward the strike issue is likely to affect the private as well as the public sector because it is difficult to distinguish between essential public and private services. Resolution of this problem is in turn complicated by the fact that federal law protects the right to strike in private employment, while public employment disputes are a matter for state regulation. The impact of certain critical disputes in the private sector has recently raised the question whether the NLRA machinery is adequate to deal with local emergencies. For example, during the strike against Consolidated Edison

Company in the New York City area, the New York City Corporation Counsel considered whether the emergency procedures of the Taft-Hartley Act could be applied. A strike by fuel oil drivers resulted in the declaration by the Emergency Control Board of the City of New York that the city was in a state of imminent peril. The strike, which occurred during the midst of a flu epidemic, brought severe hardships to apartment dwellers, home owners, and hospital patients. Thus, any test which purports to relate the right to strike to the essentiality of the service involved cannot operate to prohibit strikes in the public sector alone; the private sector also provides countless vital services affecting the health and safety of the public.

See generally Howlett, The Right to Strike in the Public Sector, 53 CHI. B. REC. 108 (1971). Some commentators have noted that the utility of the strike in the private sector is increasingly being questioned. See, e.g., Clark, Public Employee Strikes: Some Proposed Solutions, 23 LAB. L.J. 111 (1972). If public sector employees are given the right to strike, will this result in the extension of a right to the public sector which may be of doubtful value in the private sector?

D. The Definition of Strikes and Other Collective Action Subject to Regulation

UNITED FEDERATION OF POSTAL CLERKS v. BLOUNT, 325 F. Supp. 879, 884 (D.D.C.), aff'd, 404 U.S. 802 (1971). In response to plaintiff's claim that the federal statutory proscriptions against striking and participating in a strike were unconstitutionally vague, the court noted that:

These concepts of "striking" and "participating in a strike" occupy central positions in our labor statutes and accompanying case law, and have been construed and interpreted many times by numerous state and federal courts. "Strike" is defined in § 501 (d) of the Taft-Hartley Act to include "any concerted stoppage of work by employees . . . and any concerted slow-down or other concerted interruption of operations by employees." On its face this is a straightforward definition. It is difficult to understand how a word used and defined so often could be sufficiently ambiguous as to be constitutionally suspect. "Strike is a term of such common usage and acceptance that 'men of common intelligence' need not guess of its meaning." . . . The Government . . . interprets "participate" to mean "striking," the essence of which is an actual refusal in concert with others to provide services to one's employer. We adopt this construction of the phrase. . . .

In re FORESTVILLE TRANSPORTATION ASSOCIATION
4 PERB ¶ 8020 (1971)

Before: I. Markowitz, Hearing Officer, New York State Public Employment Relations Board . . . .

On or about September 25, 1969, the respondent herein entered into an agreement with the Forestville Central School Board of Education. While this agreement is unusually short (1 page), it, in fact, pertains to terms and conditions of employment and was intended by the signatories to be a collective agreement. It was signed by the President of the Board of Education and by Phyllis Swanson who was denominated "President, Bus Drivers' Association." (sic) The agreement ran from July 1, 1969 through June 30, 1970.

During the term of the agreement, the bus drivers became dissatisfied with the maintenance of discipline among the students they were carrying to and from school. As a result of this dissatisfaction, on April 16, 1970, Phyllis Swanson wrote to the Board of Education requesting a meeting with the Board on Monday, April 20th, at 8:30 a.m. The letter was delivered to Dr. Thomas Marshall, supervising principal of the school district. On April 17, Dr. Marshall informed Mrs. Swanson that the Board could not meet at the requested time, but that a meeting could take place on April 22, at 8:00 p.m.

On Monday, April 20, twelve of the district's sixteen bus drivers called in sick. The absence continued through April 24 with the number dropping from 12 to 11 on this date.

On April 21, the school district caused a temporary restraining order to be served on the bus drivers. On the following evening three of the drivers met with three Board members at which time the drivers indicated that a return to work could be effected by the dropping of further injunctive proceedings and the resolution of the disciplinary problems. On April 24, eleven drivers tendered their resignations.

An accord was reached whereby the resignations would not be acted upon and the drivers would return to work Monday morning, April 27, 1970. The return to work accordingly took place.

Unlike most strikes in both the public and private sectors of our economy, the action herein took place not during contract negotiations, but well after the collective agreement has been executed. While such an action is by no means unique, and if proven to be a strike, no less illegal, the defenses of the respondent make this case somewhat extraordinary.

. . . The respondent asserts that it did not "cause, instigate, encourage, conduct, or engage in a strike." Such a denial suggests two questions. First, was the action complained of a strike, and second, what was the connection of the association with the action?

As to the first question, the respondent claims that the incidents occurring between April 20 and April 24 did not constitute a strike, but were in fact absences due to illness. This mass sickness, it is argued, was occasioned by both disciplinary problems and the emotional strain caused by Dr. Marshall's alleged refusal to deal with these problems. The absences are further justified by the respondent by reference to the *Manual of Instructions* of *School Bus Drivers* prepared by the New York State Education Department. This manual states at p. 29 "A school bus driver must never drive a school bus when he is ill, emotionally upset or fatigued." Thus it is argued that since an individual driver suffering from emotional upset has a responsibility to call in sick, 12 drivers acting in this manner cannot be considered to be conducting a strike. It is further contended that only an individual driver is capable of determining his emotional fitness for driving, the implication being that if a driver says he is emotionally upset, there is no way to show that he was not.

Under the Taylor Law, a strike is defined to include a "concerted stoppage of work or slowdown by public employees." (CSL § 201.10) It is well established that a mass sick call may not be used as a subterfuge for an illegal strike within this definition. In the Matter of the City School District of the City of Elmira 3 PERB 8122 (8124) the hearing officer stated:

"Certainly the subterfuge for an illegal strike by resort to the use of mass illness and the like is not a new phenomenon in labor relations. It has been uniformly held that such employee practices are deemed a strike or concerted stoppage of work." (See also the matter of Mahopac Civil Service Employees Association 3 PERB 8130.)

What must now be determined is whether or not the instant sick call constituted a concerted work stoppage or was in actuality the mere coincidence of a large number of employees becoming "emotionally upset" at the same time and for the same duration. In this connection, the testimony has indicated that normal absenteeism due to sickness was no more than two drivers per day. This alone raises serious doubt as to the probability that 12 employees could, independently of each other, get sick or upset at the same time. Additionally, the fact that all employees apparently "recovered" at the same moment increases this doubt.

The testimony of the drivers themselves does little to strengthen their case. By and large those who testified stated that they were upset either because of the summons served upon them or because of specific disciplinary incidents occurring on their respective busses. While it is conceivable that the service of process in conjunction with other difficulties could upset an employee, it is difficult to imagine that all employees would be equally upset and would remain so upset for exactly the same length of time. It is even more difficult to conceive that disciplinary problems were such that employees having them could report for work for several days after the problem occurred, and *then* become so upset that they could not report for work on the very day when a majority of other employees also became emotionally upset.

The sum and substance of respondent's argument is that the Drivers' Manual be interpreted to mean that any time an emotionally upsetting problem occurs in labor relations, drivers (or anyone else dealing with the health or safety of children) be permitted to strike. Thus, not only might a subpoena trigger an emotional upset but a low salary package might as well. This clearly is not the intent of the Taylor Law, nor is it the intent of any instructional or safety manual which the State might issue. The right to strike has been denied the public employee by the legislature and only the legislature may now grant that right. Thus, the Safety Manual notwithstanding, the mass sickness constituted a strike within the definition of the Taylor Law.

We now come to the question of whether or not the respondent caused, instigated, encouraged, condoned or engaged in the strike. To make this determination the Taylor Law sets up two specific guidelines (CSL § 210.3 (e)). The first of these is whether the employee organization called the strike or tried to prevent it. The second is whether the employee organization made or was making good faith efforts to terminate the strike.

As has been indicated, the testimony shows that the employee organization has an unusually informal structure, and is not often looked to for guidance by the employees. This, of course, makes it somewhat difficult to determine what the respondent effectively did or did not do during the time of the strike.

On the other hand, its responsibilities during a strike are somewhat easier to ascertain. Thus, it has been held that even where there is no strike vote and the consensus to strike is obtained informally

"Where the officers and a majority of the membership of an employee organization engaged in a strike, the employee organization is responsible for such strike. 'As long as the union functions as a union, the union is responsible for the mass action of its members. This means when the members go out and act in a concerted fashion and do an illegal act, the union is responsible.' " In the Matter of School Bus Drivers' Association, Elmira City School District 3 PERB 8149 (8152).

Here, as we have indicated, the respondent did, in fact, function as a union, complete with officers and a negotiating team. At least 12 of the 16 drivers employed by the district participated in the strike. Most importantly, the officers of the respondent, as well as the members of its negotiating team did not attempt to prevent the strike, but instead actually participated in it. Lastly, it was only after the strike was a week old that a good faith effort by the respondent was made to terminate it. In short, it is clear that the respondent made no effort at any time between April 20 and April 24 to bring the employees back to work. At best it did nothing; at worst, it caused the strike to continue by the participation of its officers and negotiating team.

. . . The actions of the respondent from April 20 through April 24, 1970 constituted a strike in defiance of the "no-strike" provision of CSL § 210.1.

NOTES

1. In Kiernan v. Bronstein, 83 L.R.R.M. 3095 (N.Y. Sup. Ct. 1973), the Court sustained penalties of fines and probation imposed on policemen who were absent from work on the date when an unlawful strike occurred. The New York Taylor Law provides that "an employee who is absent from work without permission, or who abstains wholly or in part from the full performance of his duties . . . on the date or dates when a strike occurs, shall be presumed to have engaged in such strike. . . ." The Court ruled that this provision did not violate due process because there was "no difficulty in overcoming the presumption and burden of proof by affidavit, ranging from death in the family to donating blood." For other cases which have dealt with the definitional problems related to strikes in the public sector, see Board of Educ., Borough of Union Beach v. New Jersey Educ. Ass'n, 53 N.J. 29, 247 A.2d 867 (1968); Board of Educ. of New York City v. Shanker, 283 N.Y.S.2d 548, 54 Misc. 2d 541, aff'd, 286 N.Y.S.2d 453 (Sup. Ct. App. Div. 1967); Holland School Dist.

v. Holland Educ. Ass'n, 380 Mich. 314, 157 N.W.2d 206 (1968).
In all three cases the strike ban was held to cover the disputed
activities. Even more interesting problems arise in considering
police "strikes" in which the police, rather than walking off the
job, perform their job so strictly as to cause great public annoyance. Should such assiduity be classified as a strike?

2. *See also* Comment, *Collective Bargaining for Public Em-
ployees and the Prevention of Strikes in the Public Sector*, 68
MICH. L. REV. 260, 263-65 (1969); Kheel, *Strikes and Public
Employment*, 67 MICH. L. REV. 931, 935 (1969); Wortman,
Collective Bargaining Tactics in Federal Civil Service, 15 LAB.
L.J. 482 (1964).

BOARD OF EDUCATION OF COMMUNITY UNIT SCHOOL DISTRICT NO. 2 v. REDDING

Supreme Court of Illinois
32 Ill. 2d 567, 207 N.E.2d 427 (1965)

DAILY, Justice.

This action in chancery was brought in the circuit court of
Bond County by plaintiff, the Board of Education of Community Unit School District No. 2 of said county, to enjoin defendants from conducting a strike against the board and from
picketing its schools in support of such strike. The named defendants were a national union, its local counterpart, officials
of the local, and thirteen members of the union who had been
custodial employees of the board. After a hearing, the trial
court denied injunctive relief and dismissed the complaint.
Plaintiff has appealed directly to this court since questions arising under the State and Federal constitutions are involved. More
specifically, it is the contention of plaintiff that the strike and
picketing interfere with the constitutional duty of our General
Assembly to "provide a thorough and efficient system of free
schools," (const. of 1870, art. VIII, sec. 1, S.H.A.,) whereas defendants assert the picketing complained of is a valid exercise
of free speech under the State and Federal constitutions.

Although the legal issues presented are narrow and well defined, we believe a consideration of those issues requires a statement in some detail of the facts surrounding the controversy.
The plaintiff, duly and lawfully organized under the laws of
Illinois, operates seven attendance centers, consisting of three
grade schools, a junior high school and a senior high school in
Greenville, and grade schools in Pocahontas and Sorento. It
has approximately 2500 students enrolled at the seven centers,
and employs 153 teachers and other personnel. Prior to September 2, 1964, its custodial force consisted of 13 employees,

all of whom are defendants in this suit. The latter employees had joined or became affiliated with a local and national "Teamsters, Chauffeurs and Helpers" union and, on August 3, 1964, union officers presented to the plaintiff-board a proposed collective bargaining agreement on behalf of the thirteen employees. Plaintiff refused to sign the agreement for various reasons, the validity or propriety of which form no part of the issues in this proceeding.

On September 2, 1964, a regularly scheduled school day, the thirteen custodial employees did not report for work, but, with the help and financial support of the union, set up picket lines at each of the seven attendance centers. These lines have been maintained at all times pertinent to the case, and it appears that the picketing has been peaceful. In addition, there is no showing in the record that any of the defendants coerced or advised any persons not to cross the picket lines. The pickets carried and paraded with signs, the exact wording of which does not appear in the record; however, as recalled by witnesses, the placards stated in substance that members of "Teamsters Local No. 525" were "on strike" against "Bond County Unit District No. 2."

During the next eight days, except for nonschool days, normal school operations were disrupted as follows: (1) attendance figures were abnormally low, a circumstance which could indirectly affect State aid plaintiff would get on the basis of daily attendance averages; (2) milk and bread deliveries, as well as the deliveries of surplus foods, were not made to the school cafeterias when deliverymen would not cross the picket lines; (3) schools were not cleaned and no personnel were available for such cleaning; (4) the employees of a roofing contractor refused to cross the picket line to complete repairs on a leak in a school roof; (5) the transportation of pupils to schools was affected; and (6) the board closed the schools completely from September 8 through 10.

The complaint for injunctive relief was filed September 8 and, on such date, it appears that local union officials dispatched a telegram to plaintiff stating that the striking employees would "maintain essential sanitary services" upon request, but no such request was made. . . .

Between September 11 and 24 the picketing continued and the schools operated, but with the following deviations from normal: (1) cleaning was done by volunteers and temporary replacements but the cleanliness of the buildings was below standard; (2) no personnel were available to fire furnaces or operate hot water systems; (3) physical education classes had to be curtailed in the junior high school due to lack of hot water; (4) it became necessary to buy a new type water heater for one of the cafeterias in order for dishes to be washed; and (5) principals and other supervisory personnel were forced to perform many duties aside from their regular educational duties. As we interpret the record, union officials advised deliverymen they could cross the picket line if they chose and the delivery of milk and bread was resumed. Some drivers delivering other supplies, however, chose to honor the picket lines, and school personnel used their own cars to go to warehouses for essential supplies. The employees of the roofing contractor continued their refusal to cross the line and, during and after rains, the leak in the roof became worse and plaster fell from the ceiling. Vandalism occurred in one of the schools over a weekend, but there is no showing that it occurred at a time when the regular custodial personnel would have been present.

The trial court refused to enjoin either the strike or the picketing, and its order dismissing the complaint found that plaintiff had failed to show irreparable injury, that the picketing was peaceful and a valid exercise of the constitutional rights of free speech, and that there was no danger of interference with the operations of the schools. . . .

The scope of our review is limited to a consideration of whether such employees may strike against their school board employer, and whether they may picket to support their strike. . . .

[The court went on at length to find that the lower court erred by refusing to enjoin an unlawful strike].

Turning to the matter of picketing, which the trial court also refused to restrain, it is the position of defendants, and was apparently that of the trial court, that the right of working men to communicate their complaints by peaceful picketing is completely inviolable. That is to say, defendants insist that picketing is a form of free speech and when done in a peaceful and truthful manner may not otherwise be regulated or enjoined. However, the premise that peaceful picketing is immune from all regulation and control is a false one. While picketing has an ingredient of communication, the cases make it clear that it cannot be dogmatically equated with constitutionally protected freedom of speech, and that picketing is more than free speech because picket lines are designed to exert, and do exert, influences which produce actions and consequences different from other modes of communication. Indeed, these by-products of picketing which go beyond free speech are self-evident in this case. It is now well established that the latter aspects of picketing may be subject to restrictive regulations. (Bakery & Pastry

Drivers and Helpers Local 802 of Intern. Brotherhood of Teamsters v. Wohl, 315 U.S. 769, 62 S. Ct. 816, 86 L. Ed. 1178,) and while the specific situation must control decision, it is more than clear that a State may, without abridging the right of free speech, restrain picketing where such curtailment is necessary to protect the public interest and property rights and where the picketing is for a purpose unlawful under State laws or policies, whether such policies have been expressed by the judicial organ or the legislature of the State. (Hughes v. Superior Court of State of California, etc., 339 U.S. 460, 70 S. Ct. 718, 94 L. Ed. 985; International Brotherhood of Teamsters Local 695, etc. v. Vogt, Inc., 354 U.S. 284, 77 S. Ct. 1166, 1 L. Ed. 2d 1347; Building Service Employees International Union, Local 262 v. Gazzam, 339 U.S. 532, 70 S. Ct. 784, 94 L. Ed. 1045.)

As stated by the late Mr. Justice Frankfurter in the Hughes case: "It has been amply recognized that picketing, not being the equivalent of speech as a matter of fact, is not its inevitable legal equivalent. Picketing is not beyond the control of a State if the manner in which picketing is conducted or the purpose which it seeks to effectuate gives ground for its disallowance. . . . 'A state is not required to tolerate in all places and all circumstances even peaceful picketing by an individual.'" 339 U.S. at 465-466, 70 S. Ct. at 721, 722, 94 L. Ed. at 992.

The picketing here, though peaceful, was for the purpose of fostering and supporting an unlawful strike against a governmental employer and, being for an unlawful purpose, should have been enjoined for this reason alone. Apart from this, however, the effect of the influences exerted by the picketing was to impede and obstruct a vital and important governmental function—the proper and efficient education of our children—making its curtailment necessary to protect the patently overriding public interest.

Reversed and remanded, with directions.

NOTES

1. Most state courts have followed the view of *Redding* when confronted with the question of the legality of peaceful picketing in the public sector. *See, e.g.*, City of Minot v. Teamsters Local 74, 142 N.W.2d 612 (N.D. 1966); State v. Heath, 117 N.W.2d 751 (N.D. 1970); Trustees of California State Colleges v. Local 1352, San Francisco State College Fed'n of Teachers, 13 Cal. App. 3d 863, 92 Cal. Rptr. 134 (1970). However, peaceful picketing in support of a public sector labor dispute has, on occasion, been allowed even in face of an illegal strike. *Cf.* Peters v. South Chicago Community Hosp., 44 Ill. 2d 22, 253

N.E.2d 375 (1969). Peaceful picketing which was not related to or in furtherance of an illegal strike was permitted in *Regents of Univ. of Wis. v. Teaching Assistants Ass'n*, 74 L.R.R.M. 2049 (Wis. Cir. Ct. 1970).

2. The Illinois Court in *Redding* seemed to rely heavily on the fact that the picketing involved tended to disrupt the orderly functioning of the school. However, picketing which occurs away from the site of the dispute may also be enjoined. *City of Wauwatosa v. King*, 49 Wis. 2d 530, 182 N.W.2d 530 (1971); *Petrucci v. Hogan*, 5 Misc. 2d 480, 27 N.Y.S.2d 718 (Sup. Ct. 1941).

3. In *Board of Educ., Union Free School Dist. No. 3, Town of Brookhaven v. NEA*, 30 N.Y.2d 938 (1972), the New York Court of Appeals reversed the Appellate Division and denied injunctive relief to prevent the teachers' association from distributing statements urging teachers not to work for the school district. The court relied on the fact that the record did not show that the school district operations were so disrupted that the right of freedom of expression could be curtailed by the injunctive relief sought.

E.   The Strike Proscription

1.   At Common Law

ANDERSON FEDERATION OF TEACHERS, LOCAL 519 v. SCHOOL CITY OF ANDERSON, 252 Ind. 558, 251 N.E.2d 15 (1969), *cert. denied*, 399 U.S. 928 (1970). In upholding a trial court restraining order against a teachers' strike and a finding that the union was in contempt of court for violating the restraining order, the Indiana Supreme Court notes that:

> . . . [B]oth the federal and state jurisdictions and men both liberal and conservative in their political philosophies have uniformly recognized that to allow a strike by public employees is not merely a matter of choice of political philosophies, but is a thing which cannot and must not be permitted if the orderly function of our society is to be preserved. This is not a matter for debate in the political arena for it appears fundamental, as stated by Governor Dewey, public strikes would lead to anarchy, and, as stated by President Roosevelt, the public strike "is unthinkable and intolerable" . . . .

The majority opinion cites a long list of state court opinions to support the proposition "that strikes by public employees are or should be prohibited and that injunctions should be granted to halt or prevent them." Chief Justice DeBruler, in a lengthy dissent, argues that "the majority opinion offers absolutely no justification for its holding that every strike by any public employees, including teachers is illegal, and therefore, enjoinable regardless of how peaceful and non-disruptive the strike is. . . ." Chief Justice DeBruler also argued extensively that since Indiana had an anti-injunction statute, the trial court should be reversed because it did not follow the procedures required by that statute and, therefore, it had no jurisdiction to issue a temporary restraining order or injunction without notice or hearing in a matter involving a labor dispute. On this point, the majority had ruled that Indiana's "Little Norris-LaGuardia Act" was not applicable to disputes concerning public employees.

NOTE

Despite the impassioned exhortations of Chief Justice DeBruler, it is well established that at common law public employee strikes are illegal. In addition to the extensive list of cases cited in the majority opinion, see Board of Educ. of Kankakee School Dist. No. 111 v. Kankakee Fed'n of Teachers Local 886, 46 Ill. 2d 439, 264 N.E.2d 18 (1970), *cert. denied*, 403 U.S. 904 (1971); City of Evanston v. Buick, 421 F.2d 595 (7th Cir. 1970); City of San Diego v. AFSCME Local 127, 87 Cal. 258, 8 Cal. App. 3d 308 (1970); Delaware River Bay Authority v. International Organization of Masters, Pilots, and Mates, 45 N.J. 138, 211 A.2d 789 (1965); Kirker v. Moore, 308 F. Supp. 615 (1970), *aff'd,* 436 F.2d 423 (4th Cir.), *cert. denied,* 404 U.S. 824 (1971); State v. Heath, 177 N.W.2d 751 (N.D. 1970); Trustees of California State Colleges v. Local 1352, San Francisco State College Fed'n of Teachers, 13 Cal. App. 3d 863, 92 Cal. Rptr. 134 (1970).

SCHOOL COMMITTEE OF THE TOWN OF WESTERLY v. WESTERLY TEACHERS ASSOCIATION

Supreme Court of Rhode Island
— R.I. —, 82 L.R.R.M. 2623 (1973)

KELLEHER, J. Last September when the public school bells rang to announce the beginning of a new school year, there was one group whose response was something less than unanimous. It was the schoolteachers. In several communities they appeared at the schoolhouse doors not to teach but to picket. A phrase was heard which until recently was usually uttered by those engaged in the private sector of employment. It was "no contract, no work." . . .

September 5, 1972 was teachers' orientation day. A substantial number of the teachers failed to attend the scheduled meetings.

The next day was the first day of school. The students appeared but, once again, the teachers were conspicuous by their absence from the classrooms. At 10 a.m., the committee closed the schools and shortly thereafter a complaint was submitted to a justice of the Superior Court. He then issued an ex parte temporary restraining order which enjoined the strike and ordered the teachers to return to work. On September 7, 1972, the association sought from us certiorari and a stay of the Superior Court's order. We issued the writ but denied the request for a stay. Thereafter, the strike ended and school began in Westerly.

Our issuance of the writ has been motivated by the fact that within recent times, each and every time the public schools of our state have resumed operations after summer vacation, teachers in many of the public school systems have refused to return to their classrooms claiming that they have a right to strike. We have agreed to review the issuance of the Superior Court's restraining order because it is intertwined with an issue of substantial public interest which is capable of repetition yet evading review. . . .

In doing so we are reassessing a position first taken in City of Pawtucket v. Pawtucket Teachers' Alliance, 87 R.I. 364, 141 A.2d 624 (1958), and reaffirmed just about six years ago in Pawtucket School Committee v. Pawtucket Teachers' Alliance, 101 R.I. 243, 221 A.2d 806 (1966). The holding first expressed in 1958 states that striking by public schoolteachers is illegal and subject to being enjoined. We see no reason why this principle should be modified.

There is no constitutionally protected fundamental right to strike. In 1926, Mr. Justice Brandeis wrote that neither the common law nor the Fourteenth Amendment conferred the absolute right to strike. Dorchy v. Kansas, 272 U.S. 306, 47 S. Ct. 86, 71 L. Ed. 248 (1926). It was pointed out in United Federation of Postal Clerks v. Blount, 325 F. Supp. 879 (D.D.C. 1971), aff'd, 404 U.S. 802, 92 S. Ct. 80, 30 L. Ed. 2d 38 (1971), that at common law no employee whether private or public had a constitutional right to strike in concert with fellow workers because such an association was often regarded as an illegal conspiracy which was punishable under the criminal law. The conspiracy weapon was removed and the private employees' right to strike became fully protected with the passage of sec. 7 of the National Labor Relations Act, 49 Stat. 449 (1935). . . . In the years that have ensued since the first Pawtucket schoolteachers' case, there has not been any instance where any court has held that public employees have a constitutional right to strike.

The diffusion of knowledge through the use of the public school system so that the advantages and opportunities afforded by education will be made available to the people is the constitutional responsibility of the state Article XII, sec. 1 of the Rhode Island constitution. This responsibility is carried on at the local level by the school committee as an agent of the state.

The state has a compelling interest that one of its most precious assets—its youth—have the opportunity to drink at the font of knowledge so that they may be nurtured and developed into the responsible citizens of tomorrow. No one has the right to turn off the fountain's spigot and keep it in a closed position. Likewise, the equal protection afforded by the Fourteenth Amendment does not guarantee perfect equality. There is a difference between a private employee and a public employee, such as a teacher who plays such an important part in enabling the state to discharge its constitutional responsibility.

The need of preventing governmental paralysis justifies the "no strike" distinction we have drawn between the public employee and his counterpart who works for the private sector within our labor force.

A thorough compilation of cases covering all facets of a public employee's right to strike can be found in Annot., 37 A.L.R.3d 1147 (1971). A study of this annotation makes it perfectly clear that a judicial or legislative interdiction against strikes by public employees does not constitute involuntary servitude or an unwarranted impingement on one's constitutional rights be they of free speech, assembly, due process or equal protection.

The teachers argue, however, that in the time that has elapsed since the first Pawtucket schoolteachers' case, the United States Supreme Court has treated public employees in such a way as to afford them rights previously denied them. They point to the holdings in Keyishian v. Board of Regents, 385 U.S. 589, 87 S. Ct. 675, 17 L. Ed. 2d 629 (1967) and Garrity v. New Jersey, 385 U.S. 493, 87 S. Ct. 616, 17 L. Ed. 2d 562 (1967).

In *Keyishian*, the Supreme Court described the classroom as the "marketplace of ideas" and invalidated the New York teachers' oath and loyalty law on the basis that their vagueness and ambiguity posed an unconstitutional threat to the teachers' right of free speech. The *Garrity* case dealt with a criminal conviction based upon evidence given by some defendants after they had been told that if they exercised their right against self-incrimination during an investigation of their conduct as policemen, they might be discharged. These cases are of no assistance to the teachers because here there is no effort being made to inhibit the give-and-take that goes on in the classroom between teacher and pupil nor are we concerned with any violation of the Fifth Amendment right.

Having failed in their efforts to persuade us that the right to strike has been elevated to constitutional status, the teachers point to various actions taken by the General Assembly and take the position that they have an implied right to strike. They embark on this effort by first pointing out that the General Assembly in its several enactments according collective bargaining rights to various groups of public employees has specifically stated that they shall not have the right to strike and then stress the absence of any such language as it concerns the teaching profession. The teachers look upon the legislative silence as implicit permission to go on strike. We disagree. . . .

While [the statute] fails to contain an express prohibition against a strike, it certainly does not give the public schoolteachers the right to strike. On such a vital issue, we will not attribute to the General Assembly an intent to depart from the common law unless such an intent is expressly and unmistakably declared. . . . If the Legislature wishes to give the public school pedagogues the right to strike, it must say so in clear and unmistakable language. Accordingly, we find no legislation implicitly granting such a right to the teachers of this state.

The sentiments we have just expressed relative to the implicit right to strike apply equally as well to the teachers' contention that their dispute with the school committee was subject to the anti-injunction provisions of § 28-10-2. In the first Pawtucket schoolteachers' case we rejected this argument. The only additional comment that might be made is that if striking public employees are to be given the advantages of the anti-injunction statute, such action will have to result from legislative action rather than judicial construction.

The teachers' inability to enjoy the benefits of the legislation which severely limits the Superior Court's jurisdiction to enjoin a labor dispute does not mean that every time there is a concerted work stoppage by public employees, it shall be subject to an automatic restraining order. Rule 65 (b) of Super. R. Civ. P. specifically states that no temporary restraining order shall be granted without notice to the adverse party unless it clearly appears from specific facts by affidavit or verified complaint that irreparable harm will result before notice can be served and a hearing held.

We must concede that the mere failure of a public school system to begin its school year on the appointed day cannot be classified as a catastrophic event. We are also aware that there has been no public furor when schools are closed because of inclement weather, or on the day a presidential candidate comes to town, or when the basketball team wins the championship. The law requires that the schools be in session for 180 days a year. General Laws 1956 (1969 Reenactment) § 16-2-2. There is a flexibility in the calendaring of the school year that not only permits the makeup of days which might have been missed for one reason or another but may also negate the necessity of the immediate injunction which could conceivably subject some individuals to the court's plenary power of contempt.

It is true that the issuance of an interlocutory injunction lies within the sound discretion of the trial justice. The temporary restraining order was entered in the case at bar upon the verified complaint of the chairman of the school committee in which it is averred that schools had not opened as scheduled and that irreparable harm would be sustained by the students, parents and citizens of Westerly. We think that in the light of what we have just said such a declaration will no longer justify ex parte relief. . . .

Ex parte relief in instances such as teachers-school committee disputes can make the judiciary an unwitting third party at the bargaining table and potential coercive force in the collective bargaining processes. We embrace the position taken in School District v. Holland Education Ass'n, 380 Mich. 314, 157 N.W.2d 206 (1968), where it was held that the trial court, before giving affirmative relief, should normally conduct a hearing where it would review what has gone on between the disputants and then determine whether injunction should issue and if so, on what terms and for what period of time.

In conclusion, we would emphasize that the solution to the complex problem involving public schools, teachers and collective bargaining rests within the capable hands of the members of our Legislature. They will not want for proposed answers. During its January, 1969 session, the General Assembly created a "Commission to Study the Ways and Means of Avoiding and Resolving Impasses Which Arise During Contract Negotiations Between School Teachers' Organizations and School Committees." The Commission's report was published on March 2, 1970. A majority of the commission recommended compulsory and binding arbitration on all matters. Another commissioner asked for a qualified right to strike while two others declared that "teachers have an ethical, moral and professional right to withhold their services." One commission member took a neutral position by endorsing neither the Majority Report nor any of the Minority Reports. The diverse opinions expressed within the commission are ample proof that the policy to be followed is the one which must be laid out by the members of the Senate and House of Representatives.

The petition for certiorari is granted; the temporary restraining order is quashed pro forma and the papers in the case are returned to the Superior Court.

. . . .

MR. CHIEF JUSTICE ROBERTS, dissenting. . . .

The right to strike was never explicitly granted to any employees, public or private. The labor union and the strike arose out of economic struggle and not by the action of any legislature. Chief Justice Taft recognized the right of employees to strike long before the National Labor Relations Act (NLRA), 29 U.S.C.A. § 141 et seq., was passed. He described the development of the strike as follows:

"Is interference of a labor organization by persuasion and appeal to induce a strike against low wages under such circumstances without lawful excuse and malicious? We think not. Labor unions are recognized by the Clayton Act as legal when instituted for mutual help and lawfully carrying out their legitimate objects. They have long been thus recognized by the courts. They were organized out of the necessities of the situation. A single employee was helpless in dealing with an employer. He was dependent ordinarily on his daily wage for the maintenance of himself and family. If the employer refused to pay him the wages that he thought fair, he was nevertheless unable to leave the employ and to resist arbitrary and unfair treatment. Union was essential to give laborers opportunity to deal on equality with their employer. They united to exert influence upon him and to leave him in a body in order by this inconvenience to induce him to make better terms with them. They were withholding their labor of economic value to make him pay what they thought it was worth. The right to combine for such a lawful purpose has in many years not been denied by any court. The strike became a lawful instrument in a lawful economic struggle or competition between employer and employees as to the share or division between them of the joint product of labor and capital." American Steel Foundries v. Tri-City Central Trades Council, 257 U.S. 184, 208-09, 42 S. Ct. 72, 78, 66 L. Ed. 189, 199-200 (1921).

Nowhere in the NLRA or other labor legislation does Congress expressly grant to employees the right to strike. Rather, in my opinion, this legislation was enacted for the protection of a right already possessed. Such protection was necessary to curb the repressive attitude of many state courts toward labor organizations and their activities. . . .

Having concluded that the right to strike accrues to labor not by legislative grant, but by the irresistible thrust of socio-economic forces, I turn to the question of whether the right to strike is within the protection of the constitutional guarantees. The Supreme Court has long recognized that the right of labor to organize and to bargain collectively is a fundamental right with constitutional protection. NLRB v. Jones & Laughlin Steel Corp., 301 U.S. 1, 33-34, 57 S. Ct. 615, 622-23, 81 L. Ed. 893, 909 (1937). Obviously, the right to strike is essential to the viability of a labor union, and a union which can make no credible threat of strike cannot survive the pressures in the present day industrial world. If the right to strike is fundamental to the existence of a labor union, that right must be subsumed in the right to organize and bargain collectively. Bayonne Textile Corp. v. American Federation of Silk Workers, 116 N.J. Eq. 146, 152-53, 172 A. 551, 554-55 (1934).

I am persuaded that if the right to organize and to bargain collectively is constitutionally protected, then the right to strike, that is, for persons similarly situated to act in concert to promote and protect their economic welfare, must be an integral part of the collective bargaining process.

That being so, it follows that it must be within the protection of the constitutional guarantees of the First Amendment. The collective bargaining process, if it does not include a constitutionally protected right to strike, would be little more than an exercise in sterile ritualism.

I find further support for the proposition of the right of employees to strike in the First and Fifth Amendments to the Constitution of the United States. The First Amendment's protection of freedom of speech and freedom of association have been extended to union organizational activities. Thomas v. Collins, 323 U.S. 516, 532, 65 S. Ct. 315, 323-24, 89 L. Ed. 430, 441 (1945): Hague v. CIO, 307 U.S. 496, 59 S. Ct. 954, 83 L. Ed. 1423 (1939). Moreover, the right to select bargaining representatives has been declared to be a property interest protected by the Clayton Act. Texas & N.O.R.R. v. Brotherhood of Ry. & S.S. Clerks, 281 U.S. 548, 571, 50 S. Ct. 427, 434, 74 L. Ed. 1034, 1046-47 (1930). Such property interest would also be protected by the due process clause of the Fifth Amendment. In view of the fact that the protection of the First and Fifth Amendments is not alien to labor activity, I would conclude that the penumbra of those amendments protects individual workers while acting in concert to further their economic goals. Such activity by necessity includes the right to strike. . . .

I subscribe, then, to the proposition that the right to strike is fundamental and is an integral part of the collective bargaining process. I further hold that the right to strike as an inherent component of the collective bargaining process is constitutionally protected for the benefit of those employed in the public sector as well as those employed in the private sector. I recognize, however, that the state may, by a valid exercise of the police power, proscribe an exercise of the right to strike with respect to those employed in areas of the public service where to permit its exercise would be to make probable an adverse effect on the public health, safety, or welfare.

2. Statutory Proscription: The Question of Appropriate Penalties

The common-law prohibition against public sector strikes has one feature which makes it noteworthy, i.e., its simplicity. In essence the common-law strike proscription has usually been understood to mean that all strikes by all public employees are always illegal. Under this common-law rule, little attention has been paid to issues of enforcement schemes, sanctions, or mitigating circumstances which arguably tend to shift the onus of proving a strike unjustified to a public employer. Rather, at common law, public employers have relied upon the power of the judiciary to enjoin illegal strikes and to enforce civil and criminal contempts against those who fail to obey injunctions.

A large number of states have adopted the common-law strike proscription model in state statutes covering public employees. Perhaps typical of the ratification of the common-law approach is the strike proscription contained in the Connecticut collective bargaining statute: CONN. STAT. ANN. tit. 7, Sec. 7—

Nothing in this act shall constitute a grant of the right to strike to employees of any municipal employer and such strikes are prohibited.

While this approach is superficially appealing, it has one great drawback, namely, it has not worked. The great increase in public sector strikes occurred in a period when a majority of the states relied upon the common-law approach to the problem. Partly for this reason, some states have used somewhat more inventive approaches in dealing with the strike prohibition. Alternatives to the traditional strike proscription which show some ingenuity may be seen in the Pennsylvania, New York and Hawaii state statutes covering public employees which are reprinted in the *Statutory Appendix*.

An interesting study in contrasting theories concerning the problem of enforcement of a statutory ban is found in the statements submitted by the governors' advisory committees in Michigan and New York in 1967 and 1969, respectively.

REPORT TO GOVERNOR ROMNEY BY THE MICHIGAN ADVISORY COMMITTEE ON PUBLIC EMPLOYEE RELATIONS*

. . . The question has been raised whether the basic "no-strike" policy expressed in the present law should be revised so as to recognize the right to strike either generally (i.e., without any specific prohibition) or at least in non-critical situations. On this issue there appear to be (or to be developing) highly polarized positions between public employers and most organizations representing public employees. The former insist that the "no-strike" prohibition represents sound public policy, and that it must be applied uniformly and be supported by adequate sanctions. The organizations, for the most part, disagree, although we find a general consensus among them that police officers and firemen should not strike. "Neutral" opinion is divided, although predominantly, so far as our inquiries indicate, accepting the view that for a variety of reasons the strike is inappropriate in public employment. However, there appears to be wide disagreement on the kinds of sanctions which should or can, with effectiveness, be used.

We think the ultimate disposition of the strike issue is far from clear. Experience in the United States and in other countries over the next several years will clarify the underlying considerations and increase the experience necessary for sound evaluation.

We think, however, that existing Michigan policy with respect to the strike issue—which is reflective of state and federal policy generally—should be continued, at least pending further experience. Consistently therewith, certain changes should be made in the law which, on the one hand, will fairly and appropriately implement that policy, and, on the other hand, will clarify it in the important matter of the distinction between group or concerted action and individual employee action.

The legislature, in enacting the amendments of 1965, continued to make strikes by public employees illegal. Controversy exists as to whether it intended to restrict available sanctions to discipline or discharge action taken by the employer. We think in any event that there should, in addition, be available in appropriate circumstances the remedy of the injunction. We

---

* The members of the Advisory Committee included Gabriel N. Alexander, Edward L. Cushman, Ronald W. Haughton, Charles C. Killingsworth and Russell A. Smith, Chairman.

reject, however, the views, variously expressed, that criminal penalties should be applied; that strikers should automatically forfeit all job rights and be denied the opportunity for re-employment; that injunctions should always be sought and, whenever sought, should always be issued, regardless of circumstances, upon a finding that a strike has occurred or is threatened; that an injunction, once issued, should be supported by a fixed scale of fines for violation of the court's order, which may not be "forgiven"; and that other sanctions, such as loss of representation rights, should be used. In our opinion these provisions could be unduly punitive, or impractical, or damaging to the collective bargaining process.

We think that, where strikes are undertaken *before* the required statutory bargaining and other dispute settlement procedures are fully exhausted (and, in the case of police and firefighters, at any time), injunctive relief should be mandatory when requested. In all other cases, the courts should be authorized to exercise their traditional right to make the injunctive remedy available if warranted in terms of the total equities in the particular case (including, of course, as a primary consideration, the impact of a strike on the public) and should retain their traditional right to adapt sanctions imposed for violation of injunctions to the particular situation.

The court, under this approach, would be expected to inquire into all the circumstances pertinent in the case, including any claim made by the defendants that the employer has failed to meet some statutory obligation. This approach assumes that not all strikes will be enjoined, or at least enjoined forthwith, but by the same token it seems to us to be inconceivable that a strike which involved serious damage to the public interest will not be enjoined. It has been argued that the circuit courts should be removed from responsibility in the area of injunctive relief since they are subject to varying "political" pressures and are too close to the scene of the dispute. To the contrary, we believe the very facts that courts are in the locale of the dispute, bear a direct and immediate responsibility for total law enforcement, and are part of the "political" process in the broadest sense, mean that the responsibility for administering the statutory no-strike policy should rest with them whenever this legal remedy is sought. . . .

NEW YORK GOVERNOR'S COMMITTEE ON PUBLIC EMPLOYEE RELATIONS (1969 Taylor Committee Report)

. . . Our emphasis has been, and continues to be, the development of procedures for the resolution of impasses which will assure equitable treatment for public employees and which will constitute an effective substitute for the strike. Notwithstanding the development of these procedures, there is an evident need for effective deterrents against illegal strikes. In our 1968 Interim Report we stated:

> In face of the safeguards set up in the Taylor Law for the employees, it seems indisputable that the interest of the public as a whole deserves at least the kind of protection reserved in the law as the ultimate method of concluding the most obstinate dispute.
>
> It is safe to say that however carefully the law may undertake to see that public employees are treated fairly and equitably, there will be those who, through impatience or in a desire to achieve more than is fair and equitable, will thoughtlessly advocate and support the use of the strike weapon. Aside from the harm this will inflict on the public and on the labor movement itself, it will promote lawlessness and disrespect for the law and the courts, which can lead to serious consequences. The fact of the matter is that Federal laws prohibiting strikes by public employees have been observed far more scrupulously, and court injunctions against strikes have been given a far higher level of respect and compliance.

It is primarily because we believe that interruption of services will not assure equity for all public employees and the public that we recommended in our 1966 Report that penalties be stipulated. Our hope was that they would serve as additional deterrents to those leaders who believe they are justified in using muscle they uniquely possess, rather than persuasion and orderliness, in advancing the cause of those they represent. The strongest deterrent should, of course, be the realization that justice can be obtained through the techniques set up in the legislation, without use of the public-punishing strike.

a. *Union Deterrents*

1. *Deterrents Related to Contempt Proceedings*

At present, the Taylor Law provides that where an employee organization has violated an order of the Court enjoining an illegal public employees' strike, the Court's discretion to levy fines for such criminal contempt is substantially limited. Section 751 (2) of the Judiciary Law, as amended by the Taylor Law, limits such fine to one week's dues collections of the respondent organization or $10,000, whichever is less, or a minimum fine of $1,000, for each day that the contempt persists.

In our judgment this is an inequitable limitation and does not serve as an effective deterrent. Some large employee organizations are not deterred from asserting the right to strike because the penalties impose no real economic burden upon them. Less affluent unions may find the provision to be an effective deterrent.

We believe that limits now imposed upon the discretion of the Court in the assessment of fines for criminal contempt of its orders are unwise. We would therefore recommend that such limits as to fines for employee organizations be removed.[2]

There seems to be considerable merit, however, in the mandatory and permissive guidelines in the present Taylor Law setting forth the criteria to be applied by the court in the assessment of fines. The provisions in the present law permitting deferral of payment of the fine until the appeal is finally determined and the granting a preference in appellate review of contempt convictions seem to be salutary.

We feel impelled to comment upon the imprisonment of union officials, and others, in consequence of the violation by them of an injunction against an illegal strike. From the standpoint of sound government-employee relations alone we are convinced that the possibility of such imprisonment is not an effective deterrent against engaging in illegal strikes. We have never recommended it. Nor is it a part of the Taylor Law. Indeed, achievement of the objectives of the Taylor Law could very well be enhanced if an imposition of this penalty was not a

---

[2] Our 1968 Interim Report states in part:

We also thought, and recommended, that full discretion in the enforcement of its decrees restraining illegal strikes should be returned to the court. We are of the opinion that the court would be in the best position to determine the appropriate steps to compel compliance with its orders. In the Taylor Law, however, there is a stipulated maximum fine against a defiant labor organization of the lesser of $10,000 per day or one week's dues. To one union this may be very severe; to another it may be brushed off. Indeed, one union advocating the use of the strike publicly announced that it could purchase immunity from violation of the court's injunction for a price of 25 cents per member per day.

We would prefer to leave the appropriate penalties to the court's discretion. Respect for law and the courts should not be sold off at bargain rates. We proposed that there be no limit placed on the criminal contempt fines which the court might impose on a non-complying labor organization in order to assure compliance. We have no special comment to make about the permissible punishment that may be inflicted by the courts on individuals who refuse to comply, for if the shield is taken away from the labor organizations, we believe the likelihood is that there will be less non-compliance. In any event we did not suggest any change in the level of punishment that has been customarily imposed by the courts on individuals found to be in criminal contempt. The penalty of imprisonment for individual criminal contempt did not originate in the Taylor Law nor was it discussed in our 1966 Report.

possibility. On the other hand, whether or not such a penalty is deemed by the courts to be essential for the preservation of the judicial process, upon which all of us depend for the protection of our basic rights, is a question which goes beyond the matter of government-employee relations with which we are here particularly concerned. This is a matter, therefore, for courts to determine.

2. *Deterrents Related to Administrative Proceedings*

The Taylor Law presently limits the authority of the State Board to suspend the right of check-off of an employee organization found to have been responsible for an illegal strike. There is a similar restriction upon the contempt power of the courts, pursuant to Section 751 (2) of the Judiciary Law involving a union in an exempted municipality under Section 212 of the Taylor Law. In each case, the maximum period of suspension is 18 months.

Our belief is that an uncertainty of the extent of this sanction would operate as a more effective deterrent. The limitations which now appear in Section 210 (3) of the Taylor Law and Section 751 (2) of the Judiciary Law restrict the effectiveness of this approach. We believe, therefore, that the deterrent as limited by the Taylor Law is not completely effective.

We recommend, accordingly, that an illegal strike should subject the responsible employee organization to a loss of the right or privilege of check-off. An employee organization having been denied this right should be accorded an opportunity to petition the State Board or the court and the suspension should be lifted only after the organization has proved that it has conformed to the law prohibiting strikes and has affirmed its readiness, willingness, and ability to conform to such law. In the ordinary case the organization could not be accorded the opportunity to prove its bona fides until there had passed without incident at least one full contract term next succeeding the term in which the strike occurred. The suspension of check-off by the State Board or the court, therefore, would be open-ended, subject to resumption upon convincing proof of the organization's record and its readiness to conform to the law.

b. *Individual Deterrents*

Section 210 of the Taylor Law presently provides that a public employee who violates the prohibition against strikes *shall* be subject to certain disciplinary penalties provided by Civil Service Law for misconduct in accordance with procedures established by that law. Notwithstanding the fact that the language is mandatory rather than permissive, it appears that proceedings for individual misconduct under Section 75 of the Civil Service Law have not been undertaken to the extent necessary to serve as an effective deterrent to the participation in an illegal strike. This sanction remains within the control of the public employer. It has often become a negotiable matter in reaching a strike settlement. Where it has not been expressly waived by the public employer as a condition of restoring public services, public employers reportedly have been reluctant to impose these sanctions after a strike. It's easier that way.

In full recognition of these pragmatic considerations, we nonetheless believe that public employers have a responsibility to enforce the law. We believe it would be helpful if the officers or bodies having the power and responsibility to discipline public employees involved in a strike were required to submit to the chief executive officer of the government involved a written report dealing with the carrying out of their responsibilities to enforce disciplinary penalties upon individuals who engage in an illegal strike. Such a report should be submitted within one month after the termination of a strike, should be made public and should provide the following information: (i) the circumstances surrounding the commencement of the strike, (ii) the efforts used to terminate the strike, (iii) the names of those employees whom the officer or body had reason to believe were responsible for causing, instigating or encouraging the strike as well as findings as to their varying degrees of responsibility, and (iv) related to the varying degrees of individual responsibility, the sanctions imposed against such individual employees by such officer or body under the provisions of Section 75 of the Civil Service Law.

NOTES

1. Controversy over the Taylor Act and its predecessor, the Condon-Wadlin Act of 1948, has been high-spirited and, at times, acrimonious. Some of the more temperate and helpful comments include Gould, *The New York Taylor Law: A Preliminary Assessment,* 18 LAB. L.J. 323 (1967); Montana, *Striking Teachers, Welfare, Transit and Sanitation Workers,* 19 LAB. L.J. 273 (1968); Rains, *New York Public Employee Relations Laws,* 20 LAB. L.J. 264 (1969); Waldman, *Damage Actions and Other Remedies in the Public Employee Strike,* in PROCEEDINGS OF THE TWENTIETH NEW YORK UNIVERSITY CONFERENCE ON LABOR 259 (1968); Wolk, *Public Employee Strikes—A Survey of the Condon-Wadlin Acts,* 13 N.Y.L. FORUM 69 (1967); and Raskin, *Politics Up-Ends the Bargaining Table,* in PUBLIC WORK-

ERS AND PUBLIC UNIONS 122 (S. Zagoria ed. 1972), which provides an interesting analysis of the political machinations of New York City during the first five years of the Taylor Act.

2. A survey of some of the more inventive state legislation banning strikes shows a wide variety of sanctions being used. Some of the more stringent state laws include Georgia (GA. CODE ANN. ch. 89-13, §§ 1301-1303, covering state employees providing for five years probation for employees coupled with no pay increase for three years); Nevada (NEV. REV. STAT. ch. 288, §§ 288.-230—.260, covering state and local employees, providing for injunctions, a maximum fine of $50,000 per day against the union, a maximum fine of $1,000 per day against union officials coupled with an indeterminate prison sentence, and dismissal or suspension of the union rank and file); and South Dakota (S.D. COMP. LAWS ch. 3-18, §§ 3-18-9—3-18-14, covering state and local employees, providing for injunctive relief and misdemeanors for inciting or encouraging strikes punishable by a fine up to $50,000 for the union and up to $1,000 or one year in prison for the employees).

3. The penalty provisions of the Taylor Act survived constitutional challenge in Kiernan v. Lindsay, 334 F. Supp. 588 (S.D.N.Y. 1971), aff'd, 96 S. Ct. 1295 (1972); and Lawson v. Board of Educ. of Vestal Central School Dist. No. 1, 315 N.Y.S. 2d 877, 35 App. Div. 2d 878 (1970). See also Pruzan v. Board of Educ. of New York City, 25 Misc. 2d 945, 209 N.Y.S.2d 966 (Sup. Ct. 1960), upholding the constitutionality of the Condon-Wadlin Act's penalty provision.

4. For a construction of what constitutes mitigating circumstances under New York's Taylor Act, see Associated Teachers of Huntington, Inc., 1 PERB ¶399.84 (1968); compare Troy Firemen's Ass'n, 2 PERB ¶3077 (1969), with Island Free Teachers, 2 PERB ¶3068 (1969). See also City of New York v. Social Service Employees' Union, 48 Misc. 2d 820, 266 N.Y.S.2d 277 (1965), aff'd, 25 App. Div. 2d 953, 271 N.Y.S.2d 585 (1966); City of New York v. DeLury, 75 L.R.R.M. 2275 (N.Y. Sup. Ct. 1970).

5. Some statutes provide that reemployment of strikers is forbidden for a certain period following the strike. Should such provisions be subject to waiver at the discretion of the employer? Compare City of Detroit v. Division 26, A.A.S.S.R. & M.C.E., 332 Mich. 237, 51 N.W.2d 228 (1952), with East Bay Municipal Employees Local 390 v. County of Alameda, 83 Cal. 503, 3 Cal. App. 3d 578 (1970) (agreement to reinstate strikers is binding re-

gardless of contention that illegality of the strike served to negate consideration for the promise) and Durkin v. Board of Commissioners, 48 Wis. 2d 112, 180 N.W.2d 1 (1970). Should the answer to this question also govern agreements to pay strikers for time missed while on strike? *See* Head v. Special School Dist. No. 1, 288 Minn. 496, 182 N.W.2d 887 (1970), *cert. denied,* 404 U.S. 886 (1971). Should a city be allowed to make special overtime payments to non-striking supervisory employees for emergency work performed during a strike? *See* Mone v. Pezzano, 77 L.R.R.M. 2605 (N.Y. Sup. Ct. 1971).

6. Should an illegal strike constitute a defense to an employer's alleged violation of its statutory duty to bargain? *See* Saginaw Township Bd. of Educ., 1970 MERC Lab. Op. 127.

F. Enforcement Devices

1. Injunction

HOLLAND SCHOOL DISTRICT v. HOLLAND EDUCATION ASSOCIATION
Michigan Supreme Court
380 Mich. 314, 157 N.W.2d 206 (1968)

O'HARA, Justice:—Leave to appeal was granted in this case to review an order of the Court of Appeals. The order denied a stay of proceedings previously granted and denied the prayer of the appellants to dissolve a temporary injunction. The order remanded the cause to the circuit court for hearing on the merits.

This is a chancery case. The constitutional provision (Const. 1963, art. 6, § 5) abolishes the distinctions between law and equity *proceedings*. It did not abolish the historic difference between law and equity. We note this because it is as a Court of Equity we sit in the case at bar. In this, as in all other cases clearly in equity, we hear appeals *de novo*. The reason for this restatement of principle will appear decisionally later in our opinion.

In 1947, the legislature enacted what is generally referred to as the Hutchinson Act. CL 1948, § 423.201 et seq., as amended by PA 1965, No. 379 (Stat. Ann. 1960 Rev. and Stat. Ann. 1968 Cum. Supp. § 17.455[1] et seq.).

We herewith set forth the title to the act as amended by PA 1965, No. 379:

"An act to prohibit strikes by certain public employees; to provide review from disciplinary action with respect thereto; to provide for the mediation of grievances and the holding of elections; to declare and protect the rights and privileges of public employees; and to prescribe means of enforcement and penalties for the violation of the provisions of this act."

Its first section, as amended by PA 1965, No. 379, defines a strike:

"As used in this act the word 'strike' shall mean the concerted failure to report for duty, the wilful absence from one's position, the stoppage of work, or the abstinence in whole or in part from the full, faithful and proper performance of the duties of employment, for the purpose of inducing, influencing or coercing a change in the conditions, or compensation, or the rights, privileges or obligations of employment."

The second section specifies the employees affected:

"No person holding a position by appointment or employment in the government of the state of Michigan, or in the government of any 1 or more of the political subdivisions thereof, or in the public school service, or in any public or special district, or in the service of any authority, commission, or board, or in any other branch of the public service, hereinafter called a 'public employee,' shall strike."

In the late summer of 1967 the teachers in the School District for the City of Holland, Ottawa and Allegan Counties, acting through their duly certified collective bargaining agency, did not resume their teaching duties on the day set by the board of education. If they were employees within the meaning of the statute they were on strike as that term is defined in the statute.

The school district sought an injunction restraining the teachers from withholding their services. A hearing was held and the trial chancellor issued a temporary injunction. The Court of Appeals denied continuation of a stay order previously granted and the prayer to dissolve the injunction. We likewise denied a stay order and declined to dissolve the injunction but granted leave to appeal. The case is before us in that posture. Regrettably, we have a meager record, the pleadings, transcribed colloquies between court and counsel, and oral argument. To the extent possible, in order that our decision be precedentially meaningful, we will discuss those basic issues which relate to the legal concepts which we consider must govern, and will not limit ourselves to the narrow question of the propriety of the issuance of the temporary injunction. . . .

It is argued that if the act be constitutional, as we have here held, it is inapplicable to appellants for 2 reasons: first, because appellants are not "employees" within the meaning of the act, and second, that as to teachers, injunctive relief may not be granted because an alternative exclusive remedy is to be found in the act.

We consider the first. The principal thrust of this argument is that, because no contracts of employment were in force between appellants and appellee school district at the time the injunction issued, the involved teachers cannot be employees as a matter of law. It is contended that the school code, specifically CLS 1961, § 240.569, as amended by PA 1965, No. 14 (Stat. Ann. 1968 Rev. § 15.3569), mandates such conclusion. Appellants refer to this argument as the "keystone issue." . . .

In finality, we have come to the conclusion that Garden City School District v. Labor Mediation Board, 358 Mich. 258, of necessity must control. In that case the positions of the parties herein were reversed. In Garden City, the school board sought injunctive restraint against the State labor mediation board in its attempted mediation between teachers and the board. The school board challenged that jurisdiction, in part, on the ground that the school code required written contracts, and that the mediation board had no jurisdiction over the terms thereof. This Court said (pp 262, 263):

"Public school teachers are certainly persons 'holding a position by appointment or employment . . . in the public school service.'

"Appellant school board contends, however, that the provisions of the school code of 1955 (CLS 1956, § 340.569 [Stat. Ann. 1959 Rev. § 15.3659]), by providing that teachers shall be hired by written contract, denies jurisdiction to the labor mediation board for mediation as to any terms which might be included in such contracts.

"The written contract provision was first adopted in 1927, and the legislature was certainly familiar with its requirements when it adopted PA 1947, No. 336, which we have quoted. We read these 2 acts together as allowing mediation of salary disputes *in advance* of the determination of the salary provisions of individual teacher contracts." (Emphasis supplied.)

Since this Court concluded that there is jurisdiction to mediate grievances *"in advance* of the determination of salary provisions," it follows that such jurisdiction would necessarily attach in advance of the *executing* of the written contracts themselves, which are required in the case of teachers, by the School Code.

If teachers as we have held *are* subject to the provision of the Hutchinson Act dealing with the mediation of grievances *in advance* of signing written contracts, we can hardly hold with consistency that they *are not* subject to the no-strike provision of the same act for the same reason. We are constrained to hold that appellants were "employees" within the terms of the act.

We next turn to the exclusivity of remedy argument. It is based on § 6 of the act, which provides:

"Notwithstanding the provisions of any other law, any person holding such a position who, by concerted action with others, and without the lawful approval of his superior, wilfully absents himself from his position, or abstains in whole or in part from the full, faithful and proper performance of his duties for the purpose of inducing, influencing or coercing a change in the conditions or compensation, or the rights, privileges or obligations of employment shall be deemed to be on strike but the person, upon request, shall be entitled to a determination as to whether he did violate the provisions of this act. The request shall be filed in writing, with the officer or body having power to remove or discipline such employee, within 10 days after regular compensation of such employee has ceased or other discipline has been imposed. In the event of such request the officer or body shall within 10 days commence a proceeding for the determination of whether the provisions of this act have been violated by the public employee, in accordance with the law and regulations appropriate to a proceeding to remove the public employee. The proceedings shall be undertaken without unnecessary delay. The decision of the proceeding shall be made within 10 days. If the employee involved is held to have violated this law and his employment terminated or other discipline imposed, he shall have the right of review to the circuit court having jurisdiction of the parties, within 30 days from such decision, for determination whether such decision is supported by competent, material and substantial evidence on the whole record."

In this regard we find ourselves in harmony with the holding of the Court of Appeals:

"The claim of the defendants that § 6 of the public employees relations act is the only remedy available to the school board cannot be accepted by this Court. Its provisions for discipline of striking public employees and review procedure for them cannot be interpreted to imply removing the historic power of courts to enjoin strikes by public employees. See 31 ALR 2d 1142 and the cases cited therein."

Additionally, we deem it necessary to observe that the whole section deals with after-the-fact remedies by the employee. The withholding of services and the cessation of compensation for services has had to have taken place before the section can operate. It must be said that appellants' position is eminently, indeed inexorably logical in this regard. The section cannot operate within a situation where injunctive restraint of the withholding of such service has already been granted. We would find ourselves in a complete logical self-contradiction if we were to hold as we have here that courts retain their jurisdiction to issue a restraining order against withholding of services by public employees, and at the same time hold § 6 to be an exclusive remedy. The section seems to us to support the conclusion that the legislature intended that injunctive relief could be granted, but that courts are not required to grant it in every case involving a strike by public employees. To attempt to compel legislatively, a court of equity in every instance of a public employee strike to enjoin it would be to destroy the independence of the judicial branch of government.

Having held that the Hutchinson Act is without constitutional infirmity, that appellants are public employees and as such subject to its no-strike provisions, and that the courts have jurisdiction to restrain prohibited strikes by public employees, but are not required to do so in every case, we turn to the question of whether in the case at bar the chancellor had before him that quantum of proof or uncontradicted allegations of fact which would justify the issuance of an injunction in a labor dispute case.

We here hold it is insufficient merely to show that a concert of prohibited action by public employees has taken place and that *ipso facto* such a showing justifies injunctive relief. We so hold because it is basically contrary to public policy in this State to issue injunctions in labor disputes absent a showing of violence, irreparable injury, or a breach of the peace. For a recent discussion of this question, see Cross Company v. UAW Local No. 155 (AFL-CIO), 371 Mich. 184. . . . We further so hold because such an interpretation of the act would as before noted raise a serious constitutional question. . . .

We recognize that great discretion is allowed the trial chancellor in the granting or withholding of injunctive relief. We do not, in ordinary circumstances, substitute our judgment for his. We hold here, however, that there was a lack of proof which would support the issuance of a temporary injunction.

The order of the Court of Appeals, affirming the circuit court is reversed. Hearing the matter as we do *de novo,* we dissolve the temporary injunction hereinbefore issued, and remand to the circuit court for further proceedings. We suggest that such proceedings inquire into whether, as charged by the defendants, the plaintiff school district has refused to bargain in good faith, whether an injunction should issue at all, and if so, on what terms and for what period in light of the whole record to be adduced. No costs, a public question.

BLACK and ADAMS, JJ., concurred with O'HARA, J.

SOURIS, Justice concurring:—I agree that the temporary injunction should be vacated, but for reasons other than those stated by my Brethren.

It is my judgment that the individual defendants had not become employees of the plaintiff school district when the complaint was filed. None had entered into the contracts of employment with the school district our Legislature saw fit to require "be in writing and signed by a majority of the board in behalf of the district, or by the president and secretary, or by the superintendent of schools when so directed at a meeting of the board." Section 569, school code of 1955, as amended (CLS 1961, § 340.569, as amended by PA 1965, No. 14 [Stat. Ann. 1968 Rev. § 15.3569]). Absent such written contracts of employment, the teachers were not yet employees of the school district subject to the "no-strike" provisions of the Hutchinson Act. The act's definition of "strike" clearly supports my conclusion that the individual defendants, not yet employees of the school district, did not "strike" in violation of the act. Until written contracts of employment were executed, they were under no obligation to report for duty; they could not absent themselves from their positions, for they had none; they could not stop work, for they had not begun yet to work nor had they agreed even to work; and, finally, they could not abstain from performing the duties of employment for any purpose, for they had not assumed yet any such duties. . . .

No employment relationship yet having arisen between the individual defendants and the plaintiff school district when this action was filed, it follows that the injunctive order enjoining defendants from concerted abstention from employment violated the involuntary servitude provisions of the Thirteenth Amendment of the United States Constitution and Article I, section 9 of our state Constitution.

I note my agreement with the latter part of Mr. Justice O'Hara's opinion regarding the judicial inadequacy of the record to support the injunction issued. In other words, even were these defendants employees, I would agree with Justice O'Hara that the chancellor, on the record then before him, should not have granted injunctive relief.

The injunction should be vacated. Defendants should be allowed to tax their costs.

KAVANAGH, C.J., concurred with SOURIS, J.

BRENNAN, Justice (dissenting) :—The tests for granting an injunction *pendente lite* are different than the criterion used in granting permanent injunctive relief. We said in the case of Niedzialek v. Barbers Union, 331 Mich. 296, at page 300, 28 LRRM 2626:

> "Under the record before us, it appears beyond cavil that when trial on the merits is had the issue will be: Should the picketing by defendants be permitted or should it be enjoined? The final result will depend upon the proof produced at the hearing bearing upon the issue of whether the picketing was pertinent to a lawful labor objective. And the issue may also be presented as to whether or not the picketing was peaceful or otherwise. Neither of these issues can be decided until there is a hearing on the merits. It is also clear, at least reasonably certain, that if in the instant case the picketing is continued in the interim until a hearing on the merits plaintiff will suffer irreparable injury. The contrary cannot be persuasively urged; nor can it reasonably be inferred from the record that enjoining picketing in the interim would result in any permanent or irreparable injury to defendants, even if the ultimate determination should be that the picketing was lawful. It is the settled policy of this Court under such circumstances to grant to a litigant who is threatened with irreparable injury temporary injunctive relief and thereby preserve the original status quo."

The function of an injunction *pendente lite* is to prevent irreparable harm which would result from natural delay in reaching a trial on the merits. It may be argued that in this case the status quo was summer vacation and that the temporary injunction permitted a change in the status quo by permitting schools to open at the usual time. But the maintenance of actual status quo is not the only function of an injunction *pendente lite*. The court can consider whether under all the facts and circumstances of the case the issuance of the temporary injunction will maintain the parties in that status which is least likely to do irreparable injury to the party who ultimately prevails.

In this case, the plaintiff school board will be entitled to a permanent injunction unless at the trial on the merits the circuit judge should conclude that by reason of its failure or refusal to do equity to the school teachers, it has forfeited its claim to equitable relief. Such a judgment cannot be made by the circuit judge until he has heard testimony on the extent of the bargaining and on the position taken by both sides at the bargaining table. If at the hearing on the merits it should appear that the school board's treatment of the teachers has been and is equitable and reasonable, a permanent injunction will issue and the teachers will have no basis for complaint concerning the temporary injunction.

If, on the other hand, it should appear at the trial on the merits that the school board has not offered to do equity and has not taken a reasonable position at the bargaining table, then a permanent injunction will be denied and the temporary injunction will be dissolved. Under such circumstances the temporary injunction will merely have delayed the strike until the justice of the teachers' cause and the necessity for their strike will have been vindicated in a court of equity. Such delay is a benefit, not an injury, to the teachers.

The temporary injunction should be affirmed and the case remanded to the circuit court for a full evidentiary hearing on the question of whether a final injunction should issue. It is further directed that the court proceed with dispatch so that a decision on a final injunction can be made before the end of the present school year.

NOTES

1. The *Holland* case stands as the major exception to the general rule that injunctive relief is available to public employers without a showing of irreparable injury or clean hands. *See, e.g.,* Board of Educ. Community Unit School Dist. No. 2 v. Redding, 32 Ill. 2d 567, 207 N.E.2d 427 (1965); Board of Educ., Borough of Union Beach v. New Jersey Educ. Ass'n, 53 N.J. 29, 247 A.2d 867 (1968). However, some courts in other jurisdictions have indicated that temporary injunctions are extraordinary remedies and should be used ". . . only in cases of great emergency and gravity." *See, e.g.,* City of Rockford v. Firefighters Local 413, 98 Ill. App. 2d 36, 240 N.E.2d 705 (1968). *See also* School Comm. of the Town of Westerly v. Westerly Teachers Ass'n, 82 L.R.R.M. 2623 (R.I. Sup. Ct. 1973).

2. In Board of Junior College Dist. No. 508 v. Cook County College Teachers' Union Local 1600, 262 N.E.2d 125 (Ill. App. 1970), the court rejected a joint request made by the employer and the union to dismiss a temporary injunction, stating: "Under no theory can a party that obtains an injunction bind the issuing

court with condonation of contemptuous or illegal acts of those who violate the lower court's order. To give effect to such a theory would usurp the highest function of our courts." *Accord, In re* Buehrer, 236 A.2d 592 (N.J. 1967).

3. Does a court lack jurisdiction to entertain a complaint in equity to enjoin a strike which is threatened but which has not yet occurred? *See* Philadelphia Fed'n of Teachers v. Ross, GERR No. 498, F-1 (Comm. Ct. of Pa. 1973) (Held: jurisdiction proper).

2. The Effect of Anti-Injunction Statutes

As noted in ANDERSON FEDERATION OF TEACHERS LOCAL 519 v. SCHOOL CITY OF ANDERSON, 252 Ind. 558, 251 N.E.2d 15 (1969), *cert. denied*, 399 U.S. 928 (1970), *supra*, the Indiana court ruled that Indiana's "Little Norris-LaGuardia Act," also known as the anti-injunction statute, was not applicable to disputes concerning public employees. The majority opinion correctly observed that "The overwhelming weight of authority in the United States is that government employees may not engage in a strike for any purpose." Chief Justice DeBruler, who dissented on this point, raised some interesting issues with respect to the applicability of the anti-injunction statute to a public sector labor dispute.

NOTES

1. United States v. United Mine Workers, 330 U.S. 258, 67 S. Ct. 677, 91 L. Ed. 884 (1947), which Chief Justice DeBruler seeks to distinguish in his dissent in *Anderson*, has been the most frequently cited decision on this subject. The Supreme Court holding there that the Norris-LaGuardia Act does not apply to public sector labor disputes, has been widely adopted by state courts considering the question. *See, e.g.*, Board of Educ. v. Montgomery County Educ. Ass'n, 67 L.R.R.M. 2745 (Md. Cir. Ct. 1968); City of Minot v. Teamsters Local 74, 142 N.W.2d 612 (N.D. 1966); City of Pawtucket v. Pawtucket Teachers Alliance Local 930, 87 R.I. 364, 141 A.2d 624 (1958); Delaware River and Bay Authority v. International Organization of Masters, Mates & Pilots, 45 N.J. 138, 211 A.2d 789 (1965); Hansen v. Commonwealth, 344 Mass. 214, 181 N.E.2d 843 (1962); *In re* Block, 50 N.J. 494, 236 A.2d 589 (1967); New Jersey Turnpike Authority v. AFSCME Local 1511, 83 N.J. Super. 389, 200 A.2d 134 (1964); Petrucci v. Hogan, 5 Misc. 2d 480, 27 N.Y.S.2d 718, (Sup. Ct. 1941); Port of Seattle v. ILWU, 52 Wash. 2d 317, 324 P.2d 1099 (1958); Rankin v. Shanker, 23 N.Y.2d 111, 242 N.E.2d

802, 295 N.Y.S.2d 625 (1968), *appeal dismissed,* 396 U.S. 120 (1969).

2. In Illinois, the applicability of the state anti-injunction act to public sector labor disputes is somewhat confused. In Peters v. South Chicago Community Hosp., 44 Ill. 2d 22, 253 N.E.2d 375 (1969), the Illinois Supreme Court ruled that employees of a non-profit hospital could not be enjoined from striking (including peaceful picketing) even though this tended to disrupt the normal functioning of the hospital. The ruling was based both on the Illinois anti-injunction statute, which the court felt was applicable, and the fact that no public policy prevented strikes by these employees. However, the opinion cited with approval the decision in Board of Educ. v. Redding, *supra,* and thus left somewhat in doubt the question of public employees in general. But in County of Peoria v. Benedict, 47 Ill. 2d 166, 265 N.E.2d 141, *cert. denied,* 402 U.S. 929 (1970), the Illinois Supreme Court squarely held that the state's anti-injunction act applied to prevent an injunction restraining a strike (and peaceful picketing) by the employees of a county-owned and operated nursing facility. *See also* City of Pana v. Crowe, 299 N.E.2d 770 (1973). In Allen v. Maurer, 6 Ill. App. 3d 633, 286 N.E.2d 135 (1972), the court distinguished *County of Peoria* and held that the anti-injunction act is not applicable to petitions to enjoin teacher strikes since there was a duty under the state constitution "to provide public schools."

3. Contempt Proceedings

SOUTHEASTERN PENNSYLVANIA TRANSPORTATION AUTHORITY v. TRANSPORT WORKERS LOCAL 234

Pennsylvania Court of Common Pleas
66 CCH Lab. Cas. ¶ 52,593 (1971)

JAMIESON, P.J. This is a contempt proceeding initiated under the Public Employee Relations Act (hereinafter PERA), Act of July 23, 1970, P.L. xx, No. 195, 43 P.S. § 1101 et seq.

The Transport Workers Union of Philadelphia, Local No. 234 (UNION), the President of the Union, Dom DiClerico, the Secretary-Treasurer, Joseph Donato, and thirteen members of the Executive Board have been held in contempt following a hearing held on the petition of plaintiff, Southeastern Transportation Authority (SEPTA). Petitions for contempt citations have been served but are as yet unheard against thirty-four other members of the Union.

The foregoing contempt citations were heard and/or served during the period of a transit strike which continued illegally after granting of an injunction. The strike has now ended.

Those defendants against whom contempt verdicts have been entered now argue that they have been denied the procedural rights to which defendants in contempt actions are entitled, and that the contempt verdicts against them must be vacated.

On April 12, 1971, the approximately fifty-two hundred members of the Union, having exhausted the collective bargaining procedures set forth in PERA, commenced a strike which paralyzed the principal commuter lines in Philadelphia. At approximately 5:30 o'clock P.M., on April 14, 1971, on motion of Septa, we granted an injunction, following hearing, having found that the strike created a threat to the health, safety or welfare of the public. Several hours after the preliminary injunction was granted, the Union, acting through its Executive Board, voted to defy the Court order to return to work. This decision was announced at approximately 8:10 o'clock P.M., by the Union officers on city-wide television and radio. It was made quite clear that the Union would refuse to abide by the Court order to return to work.

About one and a half hours later, the Court, at about 9:40 o'clock P.M., held a hearing on the petition of Septa asking that we hold the Union and the Executive Members of the Board in contempt. Based upon the admitted flagrant violation of the Court order, stated by counsel and reiterated by DiClerico and Donato in open court, we imposed a fine of $100,000.00 per day on the Union, said fine to double for each day that violation continued, and $250.00 per day on each member of the Executive Board, said fine to double for each day the violation continued, and sentenced the Union President, Dom DiClerico, and Secretary-Treasurer, Joseph Donato, to stand committed for a period of six months or until they purged themselves of contempt. The following day we remitted the doubling features of the fines and directed the release of DiClerico and Donato, with the order that they direct the Union members to return to work.

Later the same day, April 15, 1971, at approximately 6:30 o'clock P.M., the Executive Board voted to advise the Union membership to return to work. However, the injunction was not obeyed until April 21, 1971. On the evening before the strike terminated, Septa petitioned the Court to hold thirty-four additional members of the Union in contempt.

At the contempt hearings on April 14, 1971, and again on April 15, 1971, (when we released the two Union officers) we indicated that we would consider whatever legal and factual arguments the defendants might subsequently present on the question of the punishment to be imposed.

Defendants now argue, as already noted, that the contempt proceedings were procedurally irregular, contending, primarily, that they were deprived of the procedural rights to which they were entitled in indirect criminal and/or civil contempt proceedings.

The contempt hearing on the evening of April 14, 1971, was obviously summary in nature. Less than two hours after the Union's widely pronounced declaration of defiance, Septa had petitioned for a contempt citation and all interested parties, the Union, the Union officers, DiClerico and Donato, and the members of the Executive Board were present in Court. Defendants made no issue over the facts, freely admitting the heart of Septa's complaint, to wit, that the Executive Board, speaking for the Union, had decided that the Union members would not return to work.

We are now asked to retrace our steps and grant a new hearing at which the factual issue to be resolved, possibly by a jury, will be the same which the Union, DiClerico and Donato have so openly admitted. Because of the particularly wilful, widely publicized violation, we are not strongly motivated to pursue defendants' arguments further. However, because of the complex nature of contempt actions and the necessity to avoid any possible abuse of the Court's use of the awesome power of contempt, we now afford defendants the reflective review to which they are legally entitled.

The gravamen of defendants' complaint, quite in contradistinction to the usual complaint that our overburdened courts have denied litigants the right to speedy trial, is that in this case we moved too quickly. We reluctantly agree.

Septa argues that public employees have only a limited right to strike, it is essential that violations of injunctions prohibiting strikes affecting public health, welfare or safety, be dealt with promptly, the Legislature so intended when it adopted PERA and that hearing on petition, as in the instant case, is procedurally all that defendants are entitled to receive.

We agree with the proposition that illegal strikes by public employees vitally affecting the public should be dealt with promptly. We disagree, however, with Septa's contention that PERA has superseded, specifically or by implication, the usual procedures in criminal and/or civil contempt actions.

Simply stated, there is no provision in PERA establishing a procedure in contempt actions against public employees different from contempt actions against any other category of persons or associations.

Section 1005, PERA, *supra,* provides that: ". . . the public employer shall initiate an action for contempt" where the public employee refuses to comply with the lawful order of Court. There is no indication how the action shall be initiated or what procedure shall be followed. Sections 1006 through 1010 deal comprehensively with the punishment and the factors to be taken into account in determining the amount of fine or imprisonment once there had been a contempt verdict. In the absence of anything more than the mere direction to "initiate an action for contempt," we must obviously look to established common law and statutory procedures in contempt. Statutes are never presumed to make any innovation in the rules and principles of the common law or prior-existing law beyond what is expressly declared in their provisions. In Re Holton's Estate, 399 Pa. 241, 247 (1960).

Septa cites Rankin v. Shanker, 59 LC ¶ 51,970 (1968), to support the proposition that the Legislature intended a simple, summary-type hearing without benefit of jury trial. In *Shanker,* the New York Court of Appeals held that public employees are not entitled to trial by jury in a criminal contempt proceeding brought under the *Taylor Act,* the law upon which PERA is patterned. It is sufficient to say that we find this case distinguishable for the reason that the New York Court of Appeals relied in major part upon prior New York cases (the interpretation of which was vigorously contested by the dissenters) holding that the right of trial by jury in criminal contempt proceedings in labor disputes does not apply to public employees. Pennsylvania is without such precedent. We thus turn to the existing law of contempt to determine whether the procedure followed in the instant case has been correct.

"The Courts have always possessed the inherent power to enforce their orders and decrees by imposing penalties and sanctions for failure to obey or comply therewith." Brocker v. Brocker, 429 Pa. 513, at 519 (1968).

Contempts broadly fall into two categories, civil and criminal. Criminal contempts are further sub-divided into direct and indirect contempts.

"A direct criminal contempt consists of misconduct of a person in the presence of the Court, or so near thereto to interfere with its immediate business and punishment for such contempts may be inflicted summarily." . . .

An indirect criminal contempt, on the other hand, is a violation of an order or decree of court which occurs outside the presence of the court. Marco Industries, Inc. v. United Steel Workers of America, 401 Pa. 284 (1960). Punishment may not be inflicted summarily and the Act of June 23, 1931, P.L. 925, 1, 17 P.S. 2047, provides such procedural safeguards as admission to bail, notice, a reasonable time to make a defense and affords the right of trial by jury. In addition, Section 2 of the foregoing Act limits punishment to a maximum of a $100.00 fine or fifteen days imprisonment or both. 17 P.S. 2048.

Criminal contempts are punitive in their nature and are usually instituted by the Court in the interest of the general public and not of any particular individual or suitor. The purpose in criminal contempt is (1) to vindicate the dignity and authority of the Court and (2) to protect the interest of the general public. Knaus v. Knaus, *supra,* at 376, 377.

Civil contempt is primarily remedial, as distinguished from punitive, in nature. As stated in Knaus v. Knaus, *supra,* at page 377:

". . . where the act of contempt complained of is the refusal to do or refrain from doing some act ordered or prohibited primarily for the benefit of a private party, proceedings to enforce compliance with the decree of the court are civil in nature. The purpose of a civil contempt proceeding is remedial, and judicial sanctions are employed (1) to coerce the defendant into compliance with the Court's order and (2) in some instances to compensate the complainant for losses sustained: United States v. United Mine Workers of America, 330 U.S. 258, 303."

It is significant in relation to the instant case that civil contempt, although primarily for the benefit of a private party, is likewise available to the government or governmental agencies where the purpose of the decree is to compensate for losses sustained. United States v. United Mine Workers of America, *supra.*

A contempt may be both civil and criminal in nature and whether it is one or both depends upon the facts and the objective of the Court's order.

"The dominant purpose and objective of the court's order is the controlling factor in the determination of whether the contempt was civil or criminal. Not only is the dividing line between civil and criminal contempt sometimes shadowy or obscure but the same facts or conduct may constitute or amount to both civil and criminal contempt." Brocker v. Brocker, 429 Pa. 513 (1968), at 519; United States v. United Mine Workers of America, *supra.*

In a civil contempt proceeding, proper procedure calls for rule to show cause why an attachment should not issue, answer and hearing, rule absolute (arrest), hearing on the contempt citation and adjudication of contempt. Commonwealth ex rel. Magaziner v. Magaziner, 434 Pa. 1 (1969).

The dominant purposes in the contempt proceedings before us have quite obviously been two-fold: (1) to vindicate the dignity and authority of the Court and (2) to protect the interest of the general public. At the hearing on April 14th and April 15, we did not indicate to whom the fines should be paid but it is fair to state that it was the Court's intention to direct that the fines be payable to the City and County of Philadelphia. The jail sentence imposed and withdrawn within less than twenty-four hours clearly had both a punitive and coercive purpose—punitive for violation of the Court's decree and coercive in that DiClerico and Donato were originally to be confined for a period not in excess of six months or until they chose to abide by the Court's decree. An incidental purpose of the Court order, of course, was to benefit Septa by causing the employees to return to work. However, it was the protection of the authority of the Court and the riding public in which we were primarily interested. Hence the contempt was primarily criminal in nature.

Based upon the admission by counsel in the presence of the Court that the Executive Board had chosen to defy the injunction, the substantiation of this fact in the testimony of DiClerico and the further testimony of Donato that he could not comply with the Court's order, it might be argued that the Union, DiClerico and particularly Donato were guilty of a direct criminal contempt and need be given no further hearing. We are constrained, however, to reach a different conclusion. Firstly, the parties were present in Court for the reason that they had allegedly committed a contempt, which we now conclude could not be a direct criminal contempt,[8] in caucusing out of the presence of the Court and reaching and announcing the intention to defy the order to return to work. The admissions made by counsel and DiClerico were simply statements that this occurrence had taken place and there was no direct exhibition of defiance by counsel or DiClerico in the presence of the Court. Secondly, although Donato did indicate that he would not attempt to obey the injunction, since the hearing was primarily criminal in nature, we erred in not advising him, or for that matter, the other individual defendant, DiClerico, of their rights against self-incrimination.[9] Thirdly, there is no evidence in the record that defendants waived the procedures to which they were entitled in either indirect

---

[8] "So near thereto" as used in the definition of direct criminal contempt means geographic vicinity of the Court rather than misbehavior having some direct relation to the work of the Court. Nye v. United States, 313 U.S. 33, 61 S. Ct. 810 (1941).

[9] The privilege against self-incrimination is personal and cannot be invoked by unincorporated associations. United States v. White, 64 S. Ct. 1248, 322 U.S. 69 (1944).

criminal contempt or civil contempt actions. Both indirect criminal contempt and civil contempt actions are procedurally so constructed as to permit adequate and timely notice of the alleged violations, an opportunity to defend, and in the case of indirect contempt, the right of jury trial. These are rights established by statute and precedent and, although they might be waived, we believe it inadvisable to presume so, particularly with regard to the right of jury trial, from a silent record, cf. Smith v. Patterson, 409 Pa. 500 (1963). In settling upon this course of action, we are mindful of the requirement that procedural protection in contempt actions must be observed with particular care. As stated in Bloom v. Illinois, 391 U.S. 194, 20 L. Ed. 2d 522, 88 Sup. Ct. 1477, . . . (holding that there is the right of jury trial in the case of serious criminal contempts):

> "We cannot see that the need to further respect for judges and courts is entitled to more consideration than the interest of the individual not to be subjected to serious criminal punishment without the benefit of all the procedural protections worked out carefully over the years and deemed fundamental to our system of justice. Genuine respect, which alone can lend true dignity to our judicial establishment will be engendered not by the fear of unlimited authority but by the firm administration of the law through those institutionalized procedures which have been worked out over the centuries."

The contempt petition for which defendants were brought to Court on April 14, 1971, as aforementioned, charged an indirect criminal contempt for which punishment could not be inflicted summarily. 17 P.S. § 2047. At the heart of the statutory procedure, as already indicated, is a reasonable time to prepare a defense and the right of trial by jury. Although the wide publicity given to the Union determination to violate the decree would seem to establish abundantly that factual issue, this is no justification for denying to defendants their established statutory, if not constitutional, right to have the factual issue presented to a jury for determination, or to waive that right. As incongruous as it may seem on the record before us, we simply cannot justify the contempt verdicts without first affording each defendant the procedural opportunities to which he is entitled.

Nor can we sustain the contempt verdicts on the theory that defendants have been guilty of civil contempt. Firstly, the procedure set forth in Magaziner, *supra*, has not been followed. Assuming that this procedure need not be followed in those instances where the facts also justify a finding of indirect criminal contempt, we note simply that defendants have not had the advantage of indirect criminal contempt procedure either.

Nor can we find any waiver on the part of defendants of their procedural rights in civil contempt. The sanctions which may be imposed in civil proceedings, including confinement, are as substantial as those which may follow upon conviction of a criminal contempt. To suggest, therefore, that the standards for waiver are somehow less in civil than in criminal contempt actions would be a distinction not based on reason.

For the foregoing reasons, we vacate the contempt verdicts and grant each defendant a hearing on the petition for contempt citation originally filed by Septa. Septa may amend the petition and/or file such supplemental petitions as it deems proper to bring to the attention of the Court all instances of alleged violations of the Court order as require punitive or remedial action.

Since the strike has ended, the necessity for remedial relief by way of an order of imprisonment to compel individual members of the Union to comply with the order to return to work is now moot. . . . The injunction entered on April 14, 1971, has not been dissolved. Accordingly, jurisdiction continues in this Court to impose a remedial fine to compensate Septa for losses sustained as a result of the illegal strike.

NOTES

1. The contempt proceeding generally may not be used as a vehicle for contesting the validity of the underlying injunction. *See, e.g.,* County of Peoria v. Benedict, 47 Ill. 2d 166, 265 N.E.2d 141 (1970), *cert. denied,* 402 U.S. 929 (1971); Dade County Classroom Teachers Ass'n v. Rubin, 238 So. 2d 284 (Fla. 1970), *cert. denied,* 400 U.S. 1009 (1971); *In re* Jersey City Educ. Ass'n, 115 N.J. Super. 42, 278 A.2d 206 (Super. Ct. App. Div.), *cert. denied,* 404 U.S. 948 (1971).

2. Perhaps the most frequently litigated issue involving the contempt process is whether the charged party has a right to a jury trial. In this regard, it may be helpful to distinguish between the varieties of contempt along the lines which the court in the *S.E.P.T.A.* case did—namely, civil as opposed to direct and indirect criminal contempts, although the distinctions may be artificial. Nonetheless, it is clear that in the case of a purely civil contempt, the right to trial by jury is not a constitutional mandate and arises, if at all, from statute. Shillitani v. United States, 384 U.S. 364, 86 S. Ct. 1531, 16 L. Ed. 2d 622 (1966). As to criminal contempt, however, the situation is somewhat different. It is clear that in the case of an indirect criminal

contempt, trial by jury is a necessity if the crime is deemed "serious." Bloom v. Illinois, 391 U.S. 194 (1968). The seriousness of the offense is usually determined by the penalty actually imposed (due to the plenary power of the court to administer criminal contempt sanctions), and a jury trial is not required for contempts which do not carry with them at least six months imprisonment. Cheff v. Schnackenberg, 384 U.S. 373, 86 S. Ct. 1523, 16 L. Ed. 2d 629 (1966). In the absence of a statute similar to the one relied on by the court in *S.E.P.T.A.,* most courts have held that a jury trial is not required in a criminal contempt proceeding. *See* Board of Educ. of Newark v. AFT Local 481, 114 N.J. Super. 306, 276 A.2d 175 (App. Div. 1971); *In re* Block, 50 N.J. 494, 236 A.2d 589 (1967); Rankin v. Shanker, 23 N.Y.2d 111, 242 N.E.2d 802, 295 N.Y.S.2d 625 (1968); City of New York v. DeLury, 23 N.Y.2d 175, 162 Misc. 2d 693, 243 N.E.2d 128, 295 N.Y.S.2d 901 (1968), *appeal dismissed,* 394 U.S. 455 (1969); and State v. Heath, 177 N.W.2d 751 (N.D. 1970). It is interesting to note in this context that Sections 11 and 12 of the Norris-LaGuardia Act, 29 U.S.C. §§ 111-112, providing for a jury trial plus change of presiding judge in any indirect contempt proceeding arising from failure to obey an injunction issued by a federal court in a labor dispute, were repealed in 1948.

3. The contempt proceeding, in depending so heavily upon the discretion of the judge, is generally carefully scrutinized to insure against bias of the judge. *See In re* Murchison, 349 U.S. 133, 75 S. Ct. 623, 99 L. Ed. 942 (1955). Accordingly, the Illinois Supreme Court held it error to deny a change of venue (based solely upon allegations of prejudice on the part of the judge) in a criminal contempt proceeding arising from the violation of an injunction restraining an illegal teachers' strike, and reversed the contempt convictions founded thereon. Board of Educ. of Township High School Dist. No. 201 v. Morton Council West Suburban Teachers Local 571, 50 Ill. 2d 258, 278 N.E.2d 769 (Ill. Sup. Ct. 1972).

4. It is generally held that punishments for criminal contempt are permissible only for a wilful violation of an injunction. *In re* Jersey City Educ. Ass'n, 115 N.J. Super. 42, 278 A.2d 206 (App. Div.), *cert. denied,* 404 U.S. 948 (1971). However, knowledge of an injunction may be implied due to news media coverage. *Id.*

5. Penalties imposed for contempt are subject to review on appeal, and it has been held that the imposition of greater sanctions by a reviewing court, without adequate reasons adduced therefor, is reversible error. *See* Dade County Classroom Teachers

v. Rubin, 258 So. 2d 275 (Fla. Dist. Ct. App. 1972), *citing* North Carolina v. Pearce, 395 U.S. 711 (1969).

6. In United States v. Robinson, 449 F.2d 925 (9th Cir. 1971), striking federal air traffic controllers were convicted of criminal contempt for violating the terms of a preliminary injunction forbidding the strike activity. The Ninth Circuit, in an extended opinion, upheld the contempt convictions and rejected the defendants' claim that the preliminary injunction was too vague to be criminally enforced.

SCHOOL COMMITTEE OF NEW BEDFORD v. DLOUHY
Massachusetts Supreme Judicial Court
271 N.E.2d 655 (1971)

QUIRICO, Justice: These are two bills in equity entered in the Superior Court on September 16, 1968, and September 3, 1969, respectively. The plaintiffs in each bill are (a) the school committee of New Bedford (school committee) and (b) the city of New Bedford (city). The defendants in each bill are (a) certain named persons who are made defendants individually and in their representative capacities as officers and members of an unincorporated association (Association) which is the collective bargaining agent for all of the schoolteachers employed by the city, (b) all the members of the Association, and (c) Frederick J. Lambert who is described as the Director of Field Services of the Massachusetts Teachers Association of which the Association in New Bedford is an affiliate.

The plaintiffs seek by each bill to restrain and enjoin the defendants other than Lambert from engaging in a work stoppage or withholding of their services from the city, or engaging in or inducing or encouraging the withholding of services by the teachers of the city's school department. They also seek by each bill to restrain and enjoin the defendant Lambert from inducing or encouraging a work stoppage or withholding of services by these teachers. In each case the court granted such relief in the following stages: by a restraining order, by a preliminary injunction, and by a final decree. The final decree in the 1969 case further held forty-eight defendants, including Lambert, in civil contempt of court and imposed compensatory fines on them, and also held Lambert in criminal contempt of court and imposed a fine on him therefor. The cases are before us on the defendants' appeals from the final decrees in both cases.

1. *Appeal from Final Decree in 1968 Case.* The final decree in the 1968 case permanently enjoined the defendants other than Lambert "from engaging in a work stoppage or withholding of

services . . . or inducing or encouraging the withholding of
services by the teachers of the New Bedford School Department,"
and it permanently enjoined Lambert "from inducing or encouraging a work stoppage or withholding of services by teachers employed by the City of New Bedford." The decree states that "all
parties by counsel in open court" consented to its entry. "The
decree appearing to be made by consent, the appeal cannot be
sustained." Winchester v. Winchester, 121 Mass. 127, 128. See
Evans v. Hamlin, 164 Mass. 239, 240; New York Cent. & Hudson
River R.R. v. T. Stuart & Son Co., 260 Mass. 242, 248; Fishman v.
Alberts, 321 Mass. 280, 281-282. The final decree in the 1968 case,
having been entered by consent of all of the parties, must stand.

2. *Appeal from Final Decree in 1969 Case—Permanent Injunction.* Paragraphs numbered 1 and 2 of the final decree in the
1969 case permanently enjoin the defendants in that case in substantially the same language used in the final decree entered in
the 1968 case discussed above. There is a difference in the names
of the persons, other than Lambert, who are enjoined, but that
difference does not affect our decision. . . . What we have said
above with reference to the final decree in the 1968 case applies
equally to them.

3. *Appeal from Final Decree in 1969 Case—Adjudication of
Civil Contempt.* On September 3, 1969, a judge of the Superior
Court issued a restraining order against the defendants in the
1969 case, using therein the same language which he later incorporated in the first two numbered paragraphs of the final decree
discussed above. On September 4, 1969, the plaintiffs filed a petition alleging that the defendant Lambert and 183 named teachers
who were members of the New Bedford Educators' Association
had violated the restraining order and asked that Lambert and
such teachers be adjudged in contempt for such violation. When
this petition was reached for hearing, counsel for the defendants
stated to the court: "[M]y clients are all now, each and individually, every one of them, prepared and ready to plead guilty to
what they understand is a charge of civil contempt." Thereupon
the judge stated: "[T]he clerk will call the name of each person
who has been cited for contempt. The clerk will inquire after the
name has been called: Do you admit the allegation of contempt, or
do you deny it. If you admit it, then I want each defendant as
their name is called, to say, 'I admit.' If you deny it, then as your
name is called, you say, 'I deny.' " The clerk then called the
names of Lambert and of forty-seven other persons who were
defendants in the petition for contempt. As each name was called,

the person whose name was called replied, "I admit" or "I admit it."

. . . By reason of their admission of guilt of civil contempt, such defendants cannot now require us to decide the many legal and constitutional, but nonjurisdictional, questions which they raised before the trial judge prior to admitting their guilt. . . .

4. *Appeal from Final Decree in 1969 Case: Amounts of Fines Imposed for Civil Contempt.* As a part of the final decree which adjudged certain defendants guilty of civil contempt, the court also imposed a fine of $50,000 on them and the defendant Lambert. As to each of these fines the decree stated that it was "to compensate the . . . [city] for damages as a result of said civil contempt." It also provided that the payment of $50,000 to the city "by one or all of said respondents on the civil contempts shall constitute full compliance with said orders for payment for civil contempts."

After such defendants admitted their guilt of civil contempt and before fixing the amount of the fines therefor, the judge held a hearing to receive evidence on the amount of damages which their contempt had caused to the city. The superintendent of schools testified that despite the work stoppage, many principals, directors, teachers, substitute teachers and cafeteria workers reported for work at schools which had to be closed and those persons had to be paid, that school buses were operated to the schools which had to be closed, that there were charges for utilities serving the schools on the days they had to be closed, and that the days of school thus lost would have to be made up later at which time the same expenditures would be required. He estimated that the total expense to the city for these categories would be about $79,172[4] and that there were some variables and additional items of expense to the city which he could not compute at that time but which he thought would bring the total expense to the city to $100,000. He believed the latter figure to be a "fair figure" and a "conservative figure."

After hearing the evidence and statements by counsel the judge reviewed the background of the controversy and then stated: "It is my judgment that the responsibility for the situation that arose must be shared equally by the . . . [plaintiffs] as well as by

---

[4] In arriving at this figure the superintendent said he was including payments of $60 a day to forty principals for eight days each and he computed this item at $11,200. The correct computation should be $19,200. With this correction, the categories of damages to which he testified included the following: $64,000 paid to teachers, $960 for school buses, $19,200 paid to principals, and $4,992 paid to cafeteria workers. These items alone amount to a total of $89,152 instead of the $79,172 stated by the witness.

the . . . [defendants]. . . . I find on the evidence that the loss
to the . . . [city] is $100,000." He then imposed the fines of
$50,000. The judge's finding that the loss to the city was $100,000
was supported by the testimony of the superintendent of schools
who was the only witness on that subject.

"In cases of civil contempt such as the one before us, a fine
may be assessed for the benefit of a party who has suffered injury because of the contempt. As are damages in tort, the fine
is designed to compensate the injured party for actual losses sustained by reason of the contumacious conduct of the defendant,
i.e., for the pecuniary injury caused by the act of disobedience."
Lyon v. Bloomfield, 355 Mass. 738, 744; Root v. MacDonald,
260 Mass. 344, 361-365. The fine in such a case may also be designed to reimburse the plaintiff for counsel fees and other expenses incurred in enforcing his rights. Grunberg v. Louison, 343
Mass. 729, 736; Parker v. United States, 126 F.2d 370, 379-380
(1st Cir.) . . . .

   5.   *Appeal from Final Decree in 1969 Case: Adjudication that
Lambert is Guilty of Criminal Contempt.* After the judge heard
the evidence from the superintendent of schools on the damages
sustained by the city, and before he announced his decision thereon, he asked counsel for the plaintiffs what the evidence he
"would have presented to the Court in the event of a trial . . .
[would disclose] as to the leader in this strike, the guiding influence." Counsel answered in part that "the officers of the Association and Mr. Lambert would have been shown to have influenced the events of the last few days." The judge asked counsel
for the defendants for some background information on Lambert
and it was given to him. Without further hearing or evidence
the judge then announced his finding that "Lambert was the
director of the conduct of the other defendants and all the members of the New Bedford Educators Association . . . [and] that
his directing provided irresponsible leadership." He also stated:
"I find Frederick J. Lambert guilty of criminal and civil contempt. On the criminal contempt, I impose a . . . fine of $5,000."
This finding and fine were incorporated in the final decree, in
addition to the findings and fines on civil contempt.

The defendant Lambert's admission of guilt was limited to
civil contempt. He was never asked specifically whether he admitted guilt of criminal contempt, and he never specifically admitted such guilt. He was never put to trial on the question of
criminal contempt, and no evidence was presented against him on
that charge. The burden of proving that charge was on the plaintiffs, and it was not incumbent on Lambert to disprove it. This

was not a case of a contempt which had occurred or been committed in the presence of the judge. It was a contempt sometimes referred to or described as an "indirect or constructive" contempt to distinguish it from a "direct" contempt committed in the presence of a judge who may act thereon summarily. Berlandi v. Commonwealth, 314 Mass. 424, 445-446.

"The punishment of . . . [criminal contempt] is solely for the vindication of public authority and the majesty of the law. In general, the proceedings leading up to the punishment should be in accordance with the principles which govern the practice in criminal cases. In a broad sense, the prosecution of such an offender is a criminal case, and the sentence to punishment is a judgment." Hurley v. Commonwealth, 188 Mass. 443, 445. Woodbury v. Commonwealth, 295 Mass. 316, 323. Dolan v. Commonwealth, 304 Mass. 325, 327. In such a prosecution, "the accused should be advised of the charges and have a reasonable opportunity to meet them by way of defense or explanation." Cooke v. United States, 267 U.S. 517, 537; Garabedian v. Commonwealth, 336 Mass. 119, 124-125.

The proceedings which concluded with the finding that Lambert was guilty of criminal contempt and the imposition of a fine of $5,000 on him did not comply with the basic requirements applicable to such cases. That adjudication therefore cannot stand.

In summary, (a) the final decree in the 1968 case is affirmed with costs of appeal to the plaintiffs, and (b) the final decree in the 1969 case is modified by striking therefrom so much of paragraph numbered 3 as holds the defendant Lambert guilty of criminal contempt and by striking therefrom paragraph numbered 4 imposing a fine of $5,000 on him for criminal contempt; as thus modified that final decree is affirmed.

So ordered.

4. Fines, Dismissal, Damages, Taxpayer Suits

NATIONAL EDUCATION ASSOCIATION v. LEE COUNTY BOARD OF PUBLIC INSTRUCTION

Supreme Court of Florida
260 So. 2d 206 (1972)

DEKLE, J. The United States Court of Appeals for the Fifth Circuit in its cause numbered 28195 on appeal from the United States District Court, Middle District of Florida (September 16, 1971), has (in the continuing good relationship which is reflected by such certified questions on State issues) certified to us the following question of law based upon recited facts, pursuant to FLA. STAT. § 25.031 and Rule 4.61 F.A.R.:

Under the facts as stated was the Lee County Board of Public Instruction authorized by Fla. Stat. § 230.22 (5), or any other section of the Florida School Code or implementing regulation, to condition the return of resigned teachers to their status prior to a teacher work stoppage, upon payment by each teacher of $100 to the School Board?

This litigation is an aftermath of a well-publicized period of teacher "strikes" over the State of Florida in February 1968. Included in the turmoil were 400 Lee County (Ft. Myers) school teachers who participated in a state-wide teacher "work stoppage." A temporary restraining order was obtained by the School Board enjoining the teachers from striking but recognizing their right to effect lawful resignations. The teachers thereupon submitted such resignations in writing and after a proper waiting period these were accepted by the Board. Ultimately, the teachers were advised by their state organization to return to the classrooms provided they did not suffer any reprisals or reductions in status. It was after negotiations through citizen mediators that both the teacher group and the School Board voted to accept a proposal whereby all teachers would be permitted to return to their former positions, provided that each pay the School Board $100.

U.S. District Judge Krentzman concluded that the payments were "fines" for leaving their positions and as such violated the due process clause of the 14th Amendment to the U.S. Constitution the (determination of which is of course reserved for any determination by the Court of Appeals). Judge Krentzman also held that such payment would violate state law. It is upon this proposition that the Court of Appeals makes its certification for opinion as a question of law which may be determinative of the cause and "on which there appear to be no clear, controlling precedents in the decisions of the Supreme Court of Florida," as provided in the statute.

Our review of the facts under Florida law leads us to the conclusion that the certified question should be and is answered in the affirmative, i.e., that payment of the $100 was authorized as liquidated damages under Fla. Stat. § 230.22 (5).[1]

This was in reality an agreement between the Board and plaintiffs-teachers to do what was done. The quarrel seems to

---

[1] "(5) PERFORM DUTIES AND EXERCISE RESPONSIBILITY.—The school board may perform those duties and exercise those responsibilities which are assigned to it by law or by regulations of the state board and, in addition thereto, those which it may find to be necessary for the improvement of the district school system in carrying out the purposes and objectives of the school code."

be with labels given to their actions. No good reason appears why there could not be such an agreement, inasmuch as teachers and the Board may within legal limits have agreements on employment with terms as they may fix.

The agreement was generally recognized as an acceptable solution to both sides after extensive negotiations between them in order to arrive at a solution which would end a stalemate then existing. These teachers had submitted written resignations which were accepted effective March 1, 1968; yet they desired after the difficulty at that time had subsided, to return to their former positions in *continuing seniority and standing* rather than as new teachers. The Board did not really object to this, apparently, but was in the position of having to follow the statute[2] and also having sustained alleged damages because of the closing of the schools and the additional expenses due to the resignations of the teachers. The teachers' action created a dilemma: It rendered the teachers ineligible for employment with tenure after the effective date of March 1 under the Florida School Code in that there was no existing legal method by which the departed teachers could be reemployed except as *new* teachers (a condition clearly unacceptable to their state association). This action of the teachers also invoked the School Board's constitutional duty to recover from the teachers any monetary loss occasioned by the teacher walkout. Article XII, Sections 9 and 13, of the Constitution of 1885, then in force, forbade expenditure of school funds for any purpose other than the support and maintenance of public free schools. For the School Board to have forgone collection of damages which it sustained because of the walkout would have been tantamount to subsidizing teacher lobbying and political activity.[5] It seems to us a strange and ironclad system of administration and of law which does not allow a reasonable latitude to "reopen" a gate which has of necessity been closed —yet not locked. The law looks to just results and reasonable conclusions. Such a conclusion was sought by an emergency regulation adopted by the State Board of Education of Florida, providing in part:

---

[2] FLA. STAT. § 231.36 (2), F.S.A., bars from employment for one year any teacher who leaves his position without first being released by the county board, and § 231.36 (3) (a)2, restricts issuance of continuing contracts to teachers performing service which is "continuous except for *leave duly authorized and granted.*" (emphasis ours)

[5] Even aside from the constitutional prohibitions set forth in Art. XII, public funds and public personnel may not be used for the advancement of a partisan political cause. McCarty v. Florida State Road Dept., 211 So. 2d 226 (1st DCA Fla. 1968).

"During a period of emergency as defined in Section 236.0711, Florida Statutes, the state superintendent of public instruction is authorized to waive such rules and regulations as he may consider necessary. . . ."[6]

Pursuant thereto the state superintendent waived the provisions of Section 130-1.76 State of Florida regulations,[7] the effect of which was to permit county boards to grant personal leave *retroactively* so that teachers participating in the walkout could return to their jobs with no loss of tenure.

This was fine as to the walkout. The Lee County teachers, however, had *resigned* and their resignations had been accepted, so that they were no longer employed teachers who could be granted leave, even retroactively. Their situation called for a further solution. One was found in the aforesaid agreement for the teachers return with status and a corresponding compliance with Florida constitutional requirements by payment to cover any damages. This took into consideration both sides of the problem in reaching a fair result which placed the school system in the State of Florida back into operation and at the same time protected the interest of teachers who manifested the same concern. In a sense, the School Board, in the exercise of its broad discretionary powers conferred by law, took about as much "Kentucky windage" in taking the teachers back with tenure as it did in letting them pay for the results of their actions. . . .

Teachers place great emphasis upon the word "fine" which was employed in the agreement. The fact that the language of the agreement used the words "that any such teacher shall forfeit a *fine* of $100" does not in itself control or determine the legal effect of the payment merely because it is labeled a "fine." Just because the cat has her kittens in the oven does not make them biscuits. It is understandable that some teachers would have sensitive feelings on the subject and its effect upon their professional stature. This would warrant in their minds the view that such "fine" was entirely an act of retribution and punishment. This, however, does not make it so, particularly if there is evidence, constitutionally supported, basing the payments upon a reimbursement for additional expenses incurred in a tumultuous upset of the schools and the necessary expenses to reopen. And so it is that the teachers are visited in this connection regarding the use of the term "fine," with the same condemnation employed

---

[6] State Board of Education Regulation 120-0.01 (3) (emergency) 2-20-68.

[7] Providing in part, "Leave shall be officially granted in advance, and no action purporting to grant leave retroactively shall be recognized. . . ."

in their argument that the payment cannot be "liquidated damages" merely by designating it as such.

The real test in each instance is what in fact the payment *is* and whether there were in fact damages as a basis for a consensually imposed amount to be paid. The earlier recriminations and feelings were thereby resolved which are urged as constituting this really a "fine." The teachers are thereby refusing to recognize the very solution which obtained the results they desired. It is essential to a compromise, that earlier positions be mutually merged into the final result.

We consider the agreed payment here as a proper one of liquidated damages which may be shown. On such basis it is not violative of any state statute. It very happily afforded for each side precisely what they wanted. This was simply the vehicle for accomplishing it. The Court should not interfere with such a contract thus accomplished. The result accords with the public interest as well as with the protection of the private rights of the parties upon mutual considerations.

In an era of crisis living which churns up crisis litigation, there seems to us to be no place for needless roadblocks to reasonable solutions, if we are to retain a court or jury of reasonable men. The solution provided was like opening a gate which had been closed by the resignations duly accepted by the Board, following the teachers initial departure from their classrooms "in breach of their school contracts for the year and in violation of Florida law."[11]

To hold that the School Board could not accept payment from the teachers as recompense for financial loss is to force litigation between the parties. Surely the Board, like other parties, has authority to agree upon an amount of money as liquidated damages occasioned by a breach of contract. The teachers obtained their desired tenure for the nominal $100. Mutual consideration which establish legal obligations between two or more parties form the basis of a binding contract.

We hold that the substance of the accord did not violate the public policy or the laws of Florida. Indeed, the common sense solution urged upon the Board by public-spirited citizen mediators—and finally acceded to by the Board upon the representation that the teachers had approved it—may well have been the only avenue which would have served to reopen the schools of Lee County. This was the school Board's primary responsibility which it was required to perform.

---

[11] Dade County Classroom Teachers' Ass'n, Inc. v. Rubin, 217 So. 2d 293 (Fla. 1968); Pinellas County Classroom Teachers Ass'n, Inc. v. Board of Public Instruction of Pinellas County, 214 So. 2d 34 (Fla. 1968).

We accordingly answer the certified question in the affirmative, that the School Board's action was correct and violated no state law of Florida. . . .

The further suggested question of whether an award of damages to teachers would violate Florida law, we answer in the affirmative upon the authority of Board of Public Instruction of Marion County v. Cannon, 92 So. 148 (Fla. 1922), and Haddock v. Board of Public Instruction for Manatee County, 139 So. 147 (Fla. 1932), holding:

> "The Constitution (article 12, § 9) provides that county school funds shall be used 'solely for the support and maintenance of public free schools.' Even if a three-year teacher's contract is contemplated by the law and such contract is illegally breached by the county board of public instruction, whereupon the teacher takes other employment at less salary, such teacher cannot recover against the county school fund the difference between the contract salary and the smaller salary earned in other employments, since that would in effect violate the constitutional command and that such fund shall be used 'solely for the support and maintenance of public free schools.' "

Having thus responded we dispatch with this opinion, and with our profound respects, the entire file in the cause to the Court of Appeals for the Fifth Circuit of these United States.

NOTES

1. Following the decision in the principal case, the Fifth Circuit Court of Appeals had occasion again to consider the matter. *See* National Educ. Ass'n v. Lee County Bd. of Public Instruction, 467 F.2d 447 (5th Cir. 1972), where, in an opinion written by Chief Judge Brown, the court ruled:

> Essentially the teachers' theory is that the forced exaction of a $100 payment from each of them in exchange for their returning to work with their pre-resignation status intact amounted to a fine or penalty for a legislatively undefined wrong, violative of their right to procedural due process because they were afforded no hearing or other opportunity to protest the payments or to contest their legality. . . .
>
> Concededly it is now established to a point beyond all dispute that "public employment, including academic employment, may [not] be conditioned upon the surrender of constitutional rights which could not be abridged by direct governmental action." Keyishian v. Board of Regents, 1967, 385 U.S. 589. . . .

However, none of these cases have any application here unless the teachers were in fact compelled to forego the exercise of a Federal constitutional right in return for re-employment. The critical flaw in their argument is the un-critical (and, on this record, insupportable) assumption that the $100 payments constituted a *deprivation* of property without due process of law within the prohibition of the Fourteenth Amendment. The agreement clearly provided that the teachers would receive a benefit to which concededly they were not otherwise entitled—reemployment with full tenure rights and other accompanying privileges which they had enjoyed before their resignations—in return for a pay-ment of $100. In substance, they were offered an opportunity to surrender one "property right" in order to acquire an-other "property right" that was plainly of greater value to them. Such a mutually advantageous exchange cannot be characterized as a *deprivation* of property, regardless of whether the teachers' payments are pejoratively denominated as "fines" and regardless of whether the subjective inten-tion of the Board members who voted for it was to "punish" alleged past misconduct. . . . [W]e may concede that the teachers here were involuntarily subjected to choosing be-tween paying consideration for an employment benefit of at least equivalent value and foregoing employment altogether. The choice between these options was admittedly coerced. But regardless of whether it was accepted or rejected the Board's offer did not entail a deprivation of property. Ac-cordingly, the payment of the $100 could not have involved the surrender of the right to protection of that property guaranteed by the due process clause of the Fourteenth Amendment.

Obviously the teachers would be in an entirely different position if they were somehow able to establish that they were legally entitled to tenure without payment of $100 and were therefore unilaterally deprived of that money without due process. Instead they are forced to concede that they had effectively resigned their positions and that the Board was not even legally obligated to rehire them at all. In such circumstances their claim fares no better than that of a teacher who, having neither de facto tenure nor an objective expectancy of reemployment, is discharged for un-specified reasons without notice or a hearing.

2. Section 210 of the Taylor Law permits a public employer to determine if an employee has engaged in a strike and, if such a determination is made, to place the employee on probation and

to deduct from his pay twice the daily rate of pay for each day
the employee is on strike. In holding that these provisions do
not constitute a denial of due process, the court in Sanford
v. Rockefeller, 40 App. Div. 2d 82, 337 N.Y.S.2d 688 (1972),
stated:

> Petitioners in these four proceedings are employees of the
> State of New York in permanent positions in the competitive
> class of the Civil Service. On or about May 1, 1972 petition-
> ers and approximately 7,500 other Civil Service employees
> of the State received notices from respondent, Director of
> the Office of Employee Relations, notifying them that they
> had engaged in a strike on April 1 and 2, 1972 in violation
> of subdivision 1 of section 210 of the Civil Service Law.
>
> The notice advised petitioners that the public employer
> must impose penalties of probation for a period of one year,
> during which the employees must serve without tenure, and
> deduction from the employees' salaries of an amount equal
> to twice the daily rate of pay for every day he was in viola-
> tion. (Civil Service Law, § 210, subd. 2, pars. [f] and [g].)
>
> Within 20 days of the date on which the notice was
> mailed, petitioners filed affidavits containing a statement of
> facts to show that they had not engaged in a strike. . . .
>
> The basic issue on this appeal is whether due process
> requires that an employee should be granted a hearing on
> his objections prior to the imposition of the penalties pre-
> scribed by paragraphs (f) and (g) of subdivision 2 of section
> 210 of the Civil Service Law in all cases involving strikes by
> public employees.
>
> There is no provision of either the Federal or State Con-
> stitutions which prevents the State from outlawing strikes by
> public employees. (Rankin v. Shanker, 23 N.Y.2d 111, 69
> LRRM 2746; City of New York v. De Lury, 23 N.Y.2d 175,
> 69 LRRM 2865.) It has also been held that section 210 is
> not unconstitutional because it permits the imposition of
> penalties without a prior hearing. . . .
>
> The contention that the penalty provisions of section 210
> are unconstitutional and that such provisions operate as a
> bill of attainder and deprive public employees of property
> without due process of law, is without merit. The statute
> requires that a written notice of charge be served upon each
> employee who is found to have engaged in a strike, who may
> then object to such determination by filing an affidavit and
> supporting proof. The chief executive officer then determines
> whether to uphold the employee's objection, to dismiss it,
> or grant a hearing to review the facts upon which the objec-

tion is based. Any determination against the employee by either the chief executive officer or the hearing officer is reviewable in an article 78 proceeding. If the initial determination is reversed upon an employee's objection, tenure is restored and payroll deductions refunded. . . .

Special Term, relying mainly on the case of Fuentes v. Shevin (— U.S. —, 32 L. Ed. 2d 556), held that the provisions of section 210 which establish a procedure to object to the determination that the employee engaged in a strike "insofar as it fails to provide for an opportunity for a hearing before the imposition of the statutory penalties is inadequate to satisfy the requirements of due process."

The Fuentes' opinion held that due process was violated by replevin laws of a State insofar as they denied the right of a prior opportunity to be heard before chattels were taken from their possessor, notwithstanding that he could regain possession by posting a security bond, and that he would have an opportunity for a post-seizure hearing and, further, that such laws served no such important governmental or general public interest justifying postponement of the due process right to an opportunity for a hearing until after the seizure of the property.

While we recognize that the penalties provided by section 210, both as to loss of tenure and loss of pay, affect property rights of the employees, we find that the public interest involved justifies the procedure outlined by section 210 which imposes penalties prior to a hearing on the determination by the chief executive officer that the public employee had engaged in a strike.

In GARAVALIA v. CITY OF STILLWATER, 283 Minn. 354, 168 N.W.2d 336 (1969), Garavalia and five other plaintiffs were employees of the defendant City's fire department. Their open dissatisfaction with wages and working conditions led eventually to the appointment, pursuant to the Minnesota Public Employees Labor Relations Act, of an adjustment panel to make findings of fact and recommendations to the city council. The panel's recommendations included changes in working conditions and pay raises for police and firemen to be paid for out of savings elsewhere in the city budget. When the city council appeared to be delaying action on these recommendations, the plaintiffs walked off their jobs, although they informed the fire chief of their willingness to respond to siren calls. The city responded by terminating their employment. After the city refused to rehire the plaintiffs, they brought an action for declaratory judgment to establish their status as employees.

The trial court found that the two plaintiffs who were not veterans of the armed services were discharged for proper cause under sections 179.51 and 179.54 of the Public Employees Labor Relations Act. Section 179.51 prohibits strikes by public employees and section 179.54 provides that one who violates the anti-strike provision is deemed to have abandoned his employment. However, the trial court also found that the four plaintiffs who were service veterans were denied the right to a hearing guaranteed by the Minnesota Veterans Preference Act. The Minnesota Supreme Court reversed the trial court with respect to this latter holding and remanded the case for dismissal. Following is an excerpt of the court's opinion:

The record here presents the issue of whether the requirement of § 197.46, commonly known as the Veterans Preference Act, that an honorably discharged veteran shall not be removed from a position of public employment without a hearing, upon due notice, upon stated charges in writing, applies to a veteran who was engaged in a strike or walkout in violation of § 179.51 and under § 179.54 would otherwise thereby have abandoned and terminated his appointment or employment. We think the court improperly found that the veteran-plaintiffs were discharged, when in fact they abandoned and terminated their own employment by their own acts. Therefore, the requirement of § 197.46 of hearing before *removal* has no application in this situation since that act controls the city's power to terminate the veteran's employment, and in this case the veteran-plaintiffs' employment was terminated by their own act and by operation of law. The trial court found as a fact that "the coordinated action of the plaintiffs constituted a strike or walk out in violation of M.S.A. 179.51 and 179.54." In the face of that finding, the court proceeded as if these statutes stated that such actions were proper grounds for discharge of the employees by the city and as if the city had availed itself of this ground and discharged the veteran-plaintiffs, even though the court in reference to plaintiffs Garavalia and Schrode found that "by their action they abandoned their employment with the City of Stillwater." The same is true of the other plaintiffs. Minn. St. 179.54 clearly provides that "any public employee who violates the provisions of sections 179.51 to 179.58 shall thereby abandon and terminate his appointment or employment. . . ." Under the terms of the statute, no authority to discharge is given the city if a violation occurs. The statute, instead of establishing grounds for discharge of municipal employees by the city, imposes restrictions upon the city's rights to contract with its employees. The contracts of all public employers with their employees are subject to these restrictions. See, City of Detroit v. Division 26 of Amalgamated Assn., 332 Mich. 237, 51 N.W. (2d) 228.

It is thus clear that when any municipal employee violates the provisions of §§ 179.51 to 179.58, his employment with the city is automatically terminated without any action by or on behalf of the city. Furthermore, the city under the terms of § 179.54 has no alternative except to consider such employment terminated, as is further illustrated by § 179.55 which places restrictions upon the right of a public employer to reemploy an employee who has violated §§ 179.51 to 179.58. Thus, the specific intent which plaintiffs may have entertained in this case becomes immaterial since the only material fact is that they violated the statute, which caused the termination of their employment to arise by operation of law due to their own conduct. The requirement of the Veterans Preference Act that there must be a hearing before removal of an employee entitled to the protection of that act has no application in this situation, since that statute controls the city's power to terminate the veteran's employment and, as stated, in this case the veteran-plaintiffs' employment was terminated by operation of law because of their own acts. . . .

CASO v. GOTBAUM
New York Supreme Court
67 Misc. 2d 205, 323 N.Y.S.2d 742 (1971)

HARNETT, J.: Surrounded by walls of precedent, and moated by centuries of channelized thinking, the law can easily suppress newness and find itself critically apart from the social amalgam which is its very reason for existence. And, the risk of analyzing fine points in isolation is the loss of total fairness and justice in the sense it is understood by the society to be served. Such are the dangers in the case at hand.

The dispute here arises as a result of work stoppages affecting sewage treatment and garbage disposal in New York City instigated during June 1971. Nassau County, as well as the County Executive of Nassau County, and the Supervisors of the Towns of North Hempstead and Oyster Bay, in their individual and official capacities, sued the Executive Director of District Council 37, American Federation of State, County and Municipal Employees and the President of Local 237, International Brotherhood of Teamsters in their individual and representative capacities. The public officials (including Nassau County) charged the union leaders with conspiring and causing unlawful acts of work stoppage and coercion at City pollution control plants, pumping stations and yards, which resulted in contaminating the waters of Long Island Sound off the North Shore of the two involved towns. In their main complaint, the public officials ask for a permanent injunction against the union officials repeating their conduct, compensatory damages of $1,000,000 and punitive damages of $5,000,000. While this main action is pending, the public officials, by motion, have asked this court for a preliminary injunction against the union officials, and also to be permitted to examine these officials right away in preparation for an injunction hearing.

The union leaders have so far responded by moving to dismiss the complaint, essentially on the grounds that the complained of conduct is over, that the public officials have no right to be suing them, and that no damage has been demonstrated. . . .

For purposes of those motions then, the union leaders seek to win on the following necessary assumptions:

1. They conspired with others, used intimidation, and with malice, caused raw sewage to be poured into tidal waters;

2. They did this to pressure the New York State Legislature, and to injure those using the waters or living in proximity to them;

3. The waters were polluted and the ecological balances harmed as a result of their deliberate acts;

4. At least the expense of testing and patrolling the waters was occasioned to the County and Towns.

While these may not be the ultimate facts proven at the trial, the union officials claim on their motions to dismiss that they should win as a matter of law even if those are the facts. The Court disagrees.

The union leaders, in a well-reasoned attack, would pick their way through to success on a series of ripostes to arguments thrust forth by the public officials. They essentially argue four legal grounds:

1. The Taylor Law, dealing with strikes by municipal employees;

2. Public Health Law, sec. 1150;

3. Navigation Law, sec. 33; and

4. The Common Law.

Each of these will be dealt with separately.

1. *Taylor Law*

The complaint alleges that the public officials have instituted this action "as taxpayers pursuant to Civil Service Law, sec. 210, subd. 4 and pursuant to the other applicable statutes pertaining hereto." Despite the claim of legal grounds under the Taylor Law (Civil Service Law, sec. 200 *et seq.*), which is reiterated by the public officials in an affidavit submitted in support of this motion, the public officials concede, at page 17 of their reply memorandum, that:

> "they have no standing to sue under the Taylor Act for the simple reason that Nassau County, not being the employer of the striking unions' New York City employees, is not a proper party."

This admission is in accord with the provisions of the Taylor Law which provide a remedy against unlawful strikes of public employees only to the "government involved." Civil Service Law, sec. 211. Moreover, New York City, the involved employer, did sue.

2. *Public Health Law, section 1150*

Public Health Law, section 1150 (1) says:

> "No person, corporation or municipality, shall place or cause to be placed or discharged or cause to be discharged into any of the waters of the State, in quantities injurious to the public health, any sewage, garbage, offal or any decomposable or putrescible matter of any kind or the effluent from any sewage disposal plant . . . or any refuse or waste matter . . . from any sewer or drainage system. . . ."

The statute is enforceable by the Board of Health and the State Commissioner of Health. The public officials assert that those bodies are not intended to be the sole enforcers, but even that argument must fail, for the right to maintain civil actions for violations is expressly limited to cities and villages. Public Health Law, sec. 1157.

3. *Navigation Law, section 33*

In Navigation Law, section 33, the State had decreed that:

> "[n]o person shall drain, deposit or cast any . . . offal, excrement, garbage or other putrid or offensive matter into the navigable waters of the states, except as the same may be authorized by the state department of health. Every person violating the provisions of this section shall upon

conviction by any court of competent jurisdiction be guilty of a misdemeanor. . . ."

The statute vests enforcement rights in the District Attorney of the county where the offense was committed or exists. Clearly, this statute is penal in nature. The public officials argue, however, that it also confers a civil right of action.

The violation of a penal statute may, under certain circumstances, give rise to civil liability. This occurs where the penal statute was enacted for the benefit and protection of a particular class, where the plaintiff in the civil action is a member of the protected class, and where the harm which was done is that which the statute was intended to prevent (see Brody v. Save Way Northern Boulevard, Inc., 37 Misc. 2d 240, revd. 19 A.D. 2d 714, revd. 14 N.Y.2d 576; Murzer v. Braisdell, 183 Misc. 773, aff'd 269 App. Div. 970).

Under the law, the operation of such a rule must be misty. Can one distinguish penal statutes of "particular benefit" from those for the benefit of the public at large? Should such a concept exist? Is the whole approach anything different than seeking to find in the books an existing base for a legal duty, even in a penal statute? If so, is not the true problem of the case the one of duty under the circumstances, and this finally brings us to the crux of the motions to dismiss.

4.　The Common Law

The public officials have argued they have legal rights under the common law, and could win in the main action apart from such statutory specifics as the Labor, Public Health and Navigation Laws. The Court here agrees with the public officials, although without embracing all their reasoning or articulation.

C.　Responsibility for Wilful Wrong to the Environment

1.　A Legal Need

The law obviously cannot provide a civil remedy for every personal conflict in the world. Flamm v. Van Neirop, 56 Misc. 2d 1059. However, there are instances where substantial damage can be done to the public interest which do not fall within the usual categories of causes of action, and yet, redress should be provided for such demonstrated wrong. Battalla v. State, 10 N.Y. 2d 237; Calloway v. Munzer, 57 Misc. 2d 163. As the Court of Appeals has noted:

> "a cause of action arises where that is done which should not be done." Gonzalez v. Industrial Bank (of Cuba), 12 N.Y.2d 33, 38.

See also, Merchants Mutual Ins. Co. v. Jackson Trucking Co., 21 Misc. 2d 1005.

The courts should not dismiss or reject claims merely because the claim is novel or a similar claim has not previously been asserted. Bolivar v. Monnat, 232 App. Div. 33. This rule should be particularly applicable where, as here, a substantial public right is involved.

The communications media daily remind us of the current ecological crisis which threatens the quality of our daily life. Paralleling those problems in importance to the continuation of orderly and healthy society is the need for obedience to lawful mandates. The facts as conceded in this motion present an unusual combination of the two, a blend resulting from the disregard of these union officials for the lawful processes, thereby affecting the health and welfare of people living on or near the water of Long Island Sound, those utilizing those waters for recreation, and marine life. It is an inadequate remedy to enjoin such behavior after it has occurred, for the damage to the environment is then already done. Organizations, whether unions or corporations, public or private, should not be permitted to escape the penalties of the acts which they wilfully perform to the detriment of the public or its physical setting.

Plainly, the legitimate interests of millions of people lie behind the institution of this suit by public officials elected by and representing those people. While courts have traditionally been reluctant to permit municipalities to take action on behalf of their residents in the absence of statutory authority, those cases generally deal with private rights. Marcus v. Village of Mamaroneck, 283 N.Y. 325; Buckley v. Baldwin, 230 App. Div. 245; Wollitzer v. Nat. Title Guaranty Co., 148 Misc. 529, affd. 241 App. Div. 757. Here, the public officials are acting in protection of public rights and public health. See, Nassau County Government Law, section 901; Public Health Law, section 347; People ex rel. Bennett v. Laman, 277 N.Y. 368.

2. *A New Rule of Law*

The Court does not rest this decision on any enunciated interpretation of the Public Health Law or the County Charter. Nor does the Court rest its decision on a policy interpolation from section 33 of the Navigation Law, even though that might be appropriate here. Nor does the Court seek to squeeze a prior case or judicial statement into some conformable pattern to lend authority.

Instead, the court will simply state as its basis a new rule that persons maliciously polluting or contaminating the environment may be enjoined by the chief executive officer of a county or town whose residents are adversely affected by the offensive conduct, or by private citizens reasonably affected. Offensive effect may include economic loss, health hazard, whether immediate or reasonably threatening, recreational or aesthetic impairment, or destruction of wild life. In addition to injunctive sanction, an offending polluter can be answerable in such compensatory damage as may be proven by or on behalf of an injured party, and made to pay punitive damages for deliberate or contemptuous disregard of the environmental rights of others.

a. Standing to Sue

The court cannot be persuaded by the mechanical application of the "standing to sue" to deny the rights of the public officials to bring this action.

Typically, it is stated a party cannot sue unless he is "aggrieved" or has an "interest," usually a financial one. These are historical notions of property law, and have no application to the articulation of public rights. In the growth of consumerism, and emerging public participation in legal processes, the elected executive of a municipality is the major unifying thread of the whole spectrum of his community. Moreover, he controls the extended resources necessary to do legal battle on behalf of the public interest, whether the opposition be giant business, giant labor or giant government. It is necessary that he be able to sue to protect the environment.

b. Wrong and Recompense

Under the facts conceded for the purposes of this motion, New York City sewage plants discharge over 580,000,000 gallons of sewage each day into the Upper East River. The prevailing tides and mixtures carry the receiving waters to Long Island Sound including the tributory bays along the North Shore of Nassau County. The work stoppage here involved resulted in discharge of substantial untreated raw sewage into the river and thence to the Long Island Sound and the North Shore bays. The bacteria count tripled, and in some places increased much more. Algae disturbances resulted. The waters themselves developed a brown scum appearance. The fortuity of absence of normal rainfall permitted the Nassau County bay beaches to remain open, although the beaches on Manhasset Bay were placed on an alert.

The entire area is heavily residential with countless numbers of people involved in diverse residential, recreational and commercial respects.

Further, under the assumed facts, the polluting conduct was deliberate and willful, motivated by a desire to pressure the

State Legislature. There was no cloak of legality for the offensive conduct.

The preliminary injunction issued by the New York County Supreme Court is not a permanent one. Moreover, the record is replete with socially hostile statements supposedly made by the defendants, and disputes as to their context. It is not clear that the union leaders will, in fact, in 1972 get what they want. Accordingly, it is for the trial court to weigh the facts and reach a decision with respect to future jeopardy and a possible permanent injunction. There are at least damages for testing and patrolling the area of conceivable effect. And, finally, the sanction of punitive damage must overhang those who would for their own ends wound the public interest in its environment.

Under all these assumed circumstances, how could a court in this society conclude legal redress is unavailable? Could it turn its back on an admitted wrong, perpetuated on such a large scale, protested by the very elected representatives the system projects? Should it?

The conscience of our community is saturated with environmental awareness, and those deliberately contaminating the environment as an illegal tactic are conspicuously wrongdoers. For the law to ignore this would be to forfeit all credibility. Just as new torts have emerged with new technology, new torts must emerge with changing population pressures and acknowledged social responsibilities.

If the rule of this case is not the law, it should be. And if not now, when?

3. Directions to File Answer

Since the union officials' motions to dismiss are denied, they will be given ten days to file their answers to the complaint, and the matter will thereafter proceed according to law. CPLR 3211 (f).

Short form order signed.

NOTES

1. The decision in the principal case was given further judicial support in Caso v. District Council 37, 71 L.C. ¶ 53,122 (N.Y. Sup. Ct. 1973). In rejecting the purely pecuniary interest test, the court in Caso seems to follow the lead of cases such as Scenic Hudson Preservation Conference v. F.P.C., 354 F.2d 608 (2d Cir. 1965), cert. denied, 384 U.S. 941 (1966). See also Air Transport Ass'n v. Professional Air Traffic Controllers Organization, 313 F. Supp. 181 (E.D.N.Y. 1970). On the liberalization

of standing requirements in general in public actions, see Jaffe, Judicial Control of Administrative Action 459-545 (1965).

2. Even though the standing requirement is treated more liberally in *Caso,* notice that the court finds no right to sue for damages under the Taylor Act, which gives a remedy solely to the employer. For a similar holding in a private damage suit, see Jamur Productions Corp. v. Quill, 51 Misc. 2d 501, 273 N.Y.S. 2d 348 (Sup. Ct. 1966). *See also* Waldman, *Damage Actions and Other Remedies in the Public Employee Strike,* 20th Ann. N.Y.U. Conf. on Labor Law 259 (T. Christensen ed. 1968).

3. Taxpayer suits under statutory provisions prohibiting strikes usually have taken the form of a mandamus action or suits to prevent waste of public treasury moneys. Suits to specifically enforce the penalty provisions of the state no-strike law were upheld in *In re* Weinstein, 61 L.R.R.M. 2323 (N.Y. Sup. Ct. 1966) and Head v. Special School Dist. No. 1, 288 Minn. 496, 182 N.W.2d 887 (1970) (suit brought jointly by Attorney-General and private individuals). *See also* City of Cincinnati v. Cincinnati Dist. Council 51, AFSCME, 72 L.C. ¶ 53,136 (Ohio Sup. Ct. 1973). However, it has been held that where strike penalties are discretionary rather than mandatory, no private remedy is available. Markowski v. Backstrom, 39 Ohio Op. 2d 247, 10 Ohio Misc. 139, 226 N.E.2d 825 (C.P. Lucas County 1967). Similarly, overtime payments to non-strikers is a proper municipal function and may not be enjoined. Mone v. Pezzano, 77 L.R.R.M. 2605 (N.Y. Sup. Ct. 1971). On the question of individual actions for injunctions, see Dade County Classroom Teachers' Ass'n v. Rubin, 238 So. 2d 284 (Fla. 1970), *cert. denied,* 400 U.S. 1009 (1971). *Compare* Durkin v. Board of Police & Fire Comm'rs, 48 Wisc. 2d 112, 180 N.W.2d 1 (1970) (city elector could institute complaint against director of firemen's union which had been on strike, notwithstanding an amnesty agreement between the city and strikers), *with In re* Shanks v. Donovan, 32 App. Div. 2d 1037, 303 N.Y.S.2d 783 (1969), and Shanks v. Procaccino, 70 L.R.R.M. 2741 (Sup. Ct. 1968), *aff'd,* 306 N.Y.S.2d 416 (App. Div. 1969).

4. In Allen v. Maurer, 6 Ill. App. 3d 633, 286 N.E.2d 135 (1972), the court rejected the "public trust" concept in a taxpayer action to enjoin a teachers' union from engaging in a strike against the public school system; the opinion held, in part, that:

> Here, the issue is whether or not taxpayers who have children in the public schools can maintain an action for injunc-

tive relief grounded upon the duty of the State to maintain a free, efficient and high quality system of public education. We are not faced with an alleged misuse of public funds or conveyance of public property. We are concerned with the constitutionally mandated duty of the State to maintain a public school system. Can taxpayer-parents sue to enjoin a teachers strike in order to secure the performance of that constitutional duty under the facts presented by this record? We hold that they cannot.

The Illinois Constitution S.H.A., provides that "a fundamental goal of the People of the State is the educational development of all persons to the limits of their capacities" and that "the State shall provide for an efficient system of high quality public educational institutions and services." Ill. Const., Art. X, Sec. 1. Hence, the State has a constitutional duty to provide and the public has a right to receive an efficient, high quality educational system. This duty is discharged by the State through local boards of education who are primarily responsible for fulfilling this constitutional mandate.

The parties to this appeal have not cited, nor has our research disclosed, any precedent which would confer standing upon individual taxpayer-parents under the situation presented by the facts of this case. We hold that in the circumstances present here, the authority to seek an injunction rests in the State and its official representative, the Board of Education, the members of which are elected by the people to implement the command of the constitution. Any other decision would have the effect of usurping the Board of Education's control of the local educational system.

G.   The Limited Right to Strike in the Public Sector

EDWARDS, THE DEVELOPING LABOR RELATIONS LAW IN THE PUBLIC SECTOR, 10 Duquesne L. Rev. 357, 376-78 (1972)†

The last group of states—those with a legislatively granted limited right to strike—is certainly the most daring of the four. The problem in granting such a limited right to strike, in general, has been to define precisely the tolerable degree of pressure which the government and the public can withstand. Almost invariably, this is done by attempting to draw a line between essential services (wherein a strike is impermissible) and non-essential services where a strike may be tolerated. However, in most laws this line

---

† Reprinted by permission of the Duquesne Law Review.

is very imprecisely delineated—usually by a formula based on some variant of "the public health, safety, or welfare" standard. Such a definition, while admirably flexible, may not be a sufficiently precise formulation to give meaningful guidance.

Another problem with the essential/non-essential calculus is that, in general, it fails to take into account the temporal dimension. A strike, for example, in a highly automated industry, such as the telephone system, may be tolerable for a time. As it endures and the machines begin to break down, it may become intolerable. Other problems of a practical nature—such as who is to make the decision as to essentiality, when this decision is to be made, and whether the strike ban should be mandatory or imposed at the employer's option—are also involved in any partial strike programs.

While the difficulties are legion, there are four states—Hawaii, Pennsylvania, Montana, and Vermont—which have given public employees a limited right to strike. Of the four states, the most limited right is found in Montana, where a nurses law permits strikes, provided that another health care facility within a radius of 150 miles has not simultaneously been shut down. Of more general applicability is the Vermont Act covering municipal employees, which provides that "no public employee may strike or recognize a picket line of a labor organization while performing his official duties, if the strike or recognition of a picket line will endanger the health, safety or welfare of the public." Vermont totally prohibits strikes by "state employees," but it appears to insulate teachers' strikes from injunctive orders in the absence of a showing of a "clear and present danger to a sound program of school education."

Neither of these states have shown the creativity of Hawaii and Pennsylvania in responding to the problem. The Hawaii law, covering all public employees, conditions the right to strike upon:

(1) Good faith compliance with statutory impasse procedures;

(2) Passage of sixty days after findings and recommendations of a fact-finding board are made public; and

(3) The giving of 10 days' notice of desire to strike PERB and employer.

And while all categories of public employees are covered by the act, the Hawaii law also provides:

When the strike occurring, or is about to occur, endangers the public health or safety, the public employer concerned may petition the board to make an investigation. If the board finds that there is imminent a present danger to the health and safety of the public, the board shall set requirements that must be complied with to avoid or remove any such imminent or present danger.

Pennsylvania has adopted a slightly different approach. First, the law prohibits strikes by guards at mental hospitals or prisons or personnel necessary to functioning of the courts. (Police/Fire workers are covered by a separate compulsory arbitration statute.) For all other personnel, strikes are permitted if:

(a) Mediation and fact-finding procedures "have been completely utilized and exhausted"; and

(b) "[U]nless or until such a strike creates a clear and present danger or threat to the health, safety, or welfare of the public."

The basic difference between the Hawaii and Pennsylvania approaches is that when a strike endangers the public health, safety, or welfare, Hawaii's law allows the PERB to make adjustments as it sees fit to eliminate the dangerous aspects of the strike (such as requiring essential employees to work), while Pennsylvania presumably would ban the strike in toto. In the first court decision on record, Pennsylvania's judiciary has indicated the unsoundness of leaving the decision as to the tolerable limits of public employee strikes entirely to the courts. In *SEPTA v. Transport Workers of Philadelphia*,[3] the question of whether a strike of municipal transportation workers was prohibited by the threat to public welfare was answered affirmatively. The court based its holding on some rather tenuous findings that the strike caused increased traffic congestion. The court said that congestion was more than mere inconvenience since it caused a distinct threat to the safety and welfare of those travelling by car as well as pedestrians. It also increased the risk of crime and fire, prevented the aged from obtaining required medical assistance, and markedly interfered with the operation of job training programs, the school system, and the economic welfare in general. Under the rationale of the court in *SEPTA,* few if any public sector strikes will be held to be protected under the new state law. . . .

---

[3] 77 L.R.R.M. 2489 (1971). *But see* Hazelton Area School Dist. v. Education Ass'n, 2 CCH State Lab. Cases ¶ 52,684 (Pa. Comm. Pleas 1971).

ARMSTRONG EDUCATION ASSOCIATION v. ARMSTRONG SCHOOL DISTRICT
Commonwealth Court of Pennsylvania
291 A.2d 120 (1972)

BLATT, Judge: This is an appeal from an Order of the Court of Common Pleas of Armstrong County enjoining the appellant, the Armstrong Education Association ("Association"), from continuing to engage in a strike against the appellee, the Armstrong School District ("District"). The District has approximately 12,000 students, and it employs approximately 550 teachers, for whom the Association is the certified bargaining agent. Since December, 1970, the District and the Association have been engaged in negotiations in an effort to arrive at a collective bargaining agreement for the 1971-1972 school year.

In their negotiations, the parties followed the procedures outlined in the Public Employe Relations Act, Act of July 23, 1970, P.L. —, No. 195, 43 P.S. § 1101.101, et seq. (hereinafter "Act No. 195"), but they reached an impasse. In an effort to resolve this impasse, Association members began a strike against the District on April 27, 1971, and, in response to a complaint in equity filed on behalf of the District, the Court of Common Pleas of Armstrong County enjoined the strike on May 11, 1971, and ordered the teachers back to work. The teachers obeyed this Order and returned to work, finishing out the school year of 1970-1971.

Although negotiations continued, no agreement was reached and the teachers went out on strike again on August 30, 1971, just as the 1971-1972 school year was about to begin. Another complaint in equity was filed on behalf of the District, contending that the strike created "a clear and present danger or threat to the health, safety or welfare of the public," thus bringing the matter within the provisions of Section 1003 of Act No. 195, 43 P.S. § 1101.1003, and making it ripe for injunctive relief. Hearings were held by the Court of Common Pleas on September 1 and September 14, 1971, and the testimony at these hearings was substantially as follows:

The District Superintendent testified that the District was required to supply 180 instructional days prior to June 30, 1972 or be in danger of losing state subsidies, and that, with the school year scheduled to end on June 2, 1972, there might not be enough days remaining before June 30 to make up the time lost because of the strike.

The Assistant Superintendent testified that the strike had caused the cancellation of all extracurricular activities and varsity sports, and that, if permitted to continue, it would interfere with arrangements for "inservice days," which the District considered valuable for the teachers.

The testimony of the District Supervisor of Child Services was to the effect that a continuation of the strike would cause difficulties in obtaining qualified school bus drivers, and would bring about other problems concerning pupil transportation.

The Superintendent of Public Affairs testified that the strike had caused an interruption in his routine office procedures and that the negotiations had consumed so much of his time that a considerable backlog in his work was resulting.

The President of the School Board testified to several instances in which she and other Directors had been harassed by picketing and other disturbances at their homes and by the receipt of numerous unpleasant phone calls. She also testified as to the disorderly atmosphere in which a recent School Board meeting had been conducted, and as to the need for sheriff's deputies to be called in to keep order at the meeting. She at no time stated, however, that the matters complained of had been caused by Association members; in a few instances, she specifically denied that any teachers had been involved.

Following the September 1 hearing, the Court denied the request for an injunction on the ground that it was premature, but, following the September 14 hearing, the Court issued the requested injunction, finding that a clear and present danger or threat to the health, safety or welfare of the public existed. Such a finding was based on the strained atmosphere in the community as evidenced by the harassment of School Board Directors and of the Judge, and on the fact that 12 days of school, which would have to be made up, had already been lost. The teachers were ordered back to work as of September 15, 1971. It is from this injunction that the Association has appealed.

In reviewing the lower court's action in issuing an injunction, our scope of review, as with other types of equity matters, is limited. " '(W)e will look only to see if there were any apparently reasonable grounds for the action of the court below, and we will not further consider the merits of the case or pass upon the reasons for or against such action, unless it is plain that no such grounds existed or that the rules of law relied on are palpably wrong or clearly inapplicable: . . . .' "

It was long the law in almost all jurisdictions that strikes by public employees were illegal, and Pennsylvania was no exception to this rule. The last decade, however, has brought a tremendous increase in the unionization of public employees and a corresponding increase in illegal strikes by these employees, who claim to have found their remedies under the law inadequate. The leaders in this new militancy, perhaps with good reason, have often been school teachers.

In order to deal with the problem of public employee labor relations, the legislature in 1970 enacted Act No. 195.

This Act explicitly recognized the right of public employees to organize and to bargain collectively, and it also established specific procedures for collective bargaining which were intended to lessen the possibility of the development of an impasse. The Act provided, however, that if all the procedures have been complied with, and yet an impasse has developed, the right of the employees to strike must be recognized. The public employer is then given the right to seek equitable relief, including injunctions, in the court of common pleas of the jurisdiction where the strike occurs. Section 1003 of Act No. 195 provides, however, that an injunction may not issue unless ". . . the court finds that the strike creates a clear and present danger or threat to the health, safety or welfare of the public."

The determination of what is a "clear and present" danger under Act No. 195 presents some problems. The phrase has almost invariably been used heretofore in cases involving government interference with First Amendment rights. See, Dennis v. United States, 341 U.S. 494, 71 S. Ct. 857, 95 L. Ed. 1137 (1951); Terminiello v. City of Chicago, 337 U.S. 1, 69 S. Ct. 894, 93 L. Ed. 1131 (1949); Schenk v. United States, 249 U.S. 47, 39 S. Ct. 247, 63 L. Ed. 470 (1919). A definition of the term, however, which seems to be applicable here was stated in Communist Party of the United States v. Subversive Activities Control Board, 223 F.2d 531 (D.C. Cir. 1954), reversed on other grounds, 351 U.S. 115, 76 S. Ct. 663, 100 L. Ed. 1003 (1956), as follows:

> "The 'clear' in that epigram is not limited to a threat indubitably etched in every microscopic detail. It includes that which is not speculative but real, not imagined but actual. The 'present' in the epigram is not restricted to the climactically imminent. It includes that which exists as contrasted with that which does not yet exist and that which has ceased to exist." 223 F.2d at 544.

In this light, the determination of whether or not a strike presents a clear and present danger to the health, safety or welfare of the public must, therefore, require the court to find that the danger or threat is real or actual and that a strong likelihood exists that it will occur. Additionally, it seems to us that the "danger" or "threat" concerned must not be one which is normally incident to a strike by public employees. By enacting Act No. 195 which authorizes such strikes, the legislature may be understood to have indicated its willingness to accept certain inconveniences, for such are inevitable, but it obviously intended to draw the line at those which pose a danger to the public health, safety or welfare.[3]

The reasons indicated by the court for granting the injunction here fall generally into three categories: a) the disruption of routine procedures; b) the harassment of School Board Directors; and c) the danger of losing state subsidies because of the inability of the District to provide the full schedule of 180 instructional days.

The disruption and the harassment were certainly "clear and present," but they did not constitute a "danger" or "threat" as envisaged by Act No. 195. On the other hand, the loss of school subsidies was a "danger," but it was not, at least not yet, "clear and present."

The disruption of routine administrative procedures, the cancellation of extracurricular activities and sports and other such difficulties are most certainly inconvenient for the public, and especially for students and their parents. But these problems are inherent in the very nature of any strike by school teachers. If we were to say that such inconveniences, which necessarily accompany any strike by school teachers from its very inception, are proper grounds for enjoining such a strike, we would in fact be nullifying the right to strike granted to school teachers by the legislature in Act No. 195.

A more serious problem is raised by the community unrest and the harassment of public officials which have apparently occurred in reaction to the strike. The testimony gives no indication as to who has been involved in these incidents, although it was made clear as to some situations that the Association's members were *not* so involved. We deplore such activities and sympathize with the lower court's wish to bring them to an end. Enjoining the

---

[3] "A strike by teachers . . . might be tolerated for an extended period of time before it could be demonstrated that continuation of the strike would constitute a similar threat [of danger to the public]. Teachers are customarily absent from their classrooms during weekends and holidays. Perhaps more significant is the fact that teacher services can be suspended for three months during the summer without any apparent adverse effect on the public welfare. The contrast between employment which normally involves such interruptions in service, and the necessity of continuous service by policemen, dramatizes the reason that the tolerance level for work stoppages differs so markedly.

"Although it has been suggested that a teacher strike might never create an immediate threat to public welfare, a court could conceivably find such a threat where a teacher strike continued for so long that make-up classes would not be feasible before a new school term would begin, or perhaps when the remaining vacation time for make-up classes becomes very short." Note, *Striking a Balance in Bargaining with Public School Teachers,* 56 Iowa L. Rev. 598, 610-611 (1971).

strike, however, was not a proper method of accomplishing this purpose. In this situation it does not seem to be the strike which was the "danger" to the public, but the reaction to it by persons unknown. We cannot find that Section 1003 of Act No. 195 was intended to permit striking employees to be penalized by having their strike enjoined because a number of citizens oppose their stand and choose to show this by disrupting the community. There are other laws available to deal with such disorders.

The danger that the District will lose state subsidies because of a strike would be proper grounds for enjoining the strike if such danger were "clear and present." And, although it is not certain that subsidies will in fact have to be withheld because of the strike, it is a possibility which cannot be ignored. If the strike lasted so long, therefore, that any continuation would make it unlikely that enough days would be available to make up the 180 required, the teachers could be properly enjoined from continuing it. At the time of the last hearing, however, the strike had lasted only 12 days, and the District had 20 days available in June plus 19 holiday dates which could be used to make up time lost. The possibility that the strike would extend longer than the make-up time available did not yet exist. If a strike is to be enjoined on the basis that insufficient make-up time actually will exist, the strike must at the very least have reached the point where its continuation would make it either clearly impossible or extremely difficult for the District to make up enough instructional days to meet the subsidy requirement within the time available. This strike was far from that point when the Court below enjoined it. The fact that students and teachers might have to remain in school later in June than originally planned may be unfortunate, of course, but again it is merely an inconvenience inherent in the right of school teachers to strike, a right now guaranteed them by the law.

We must hold that at the time this injunction was issued, there were no reasonable grounds on which the lower court could find that the strike by the Association was a "clear and present danger or threat to the health, safety or welfare of the public." This is not to say, of course, that public employees may strike with impunity and ignore the public interest, nor that such inconveniences as those noted herein as incidental to a strike might not conceivably accumulate to such an extent, be continued so long or be aggravated by some unexpected development, so that the public health, safety and welfare would in fact then be endangered.

We must hold, however, that the proper purpose of an injunction under Act No. 195 is to avert present danger, not to prevent danger which may never occur at all or which can only occur, if it does occur, at some future time before which the grievances concerned can reasonably be expected to be settled.

For the reasons stated, the order of the lower court is reversed and the injunction is hereby dissolved.

NOTES

1. In Los Angeles Metropolitan Transit Authority v. Brotherhood of Railroad Trainmen, 54 Cal. Rptr. 2d 684, 355 P.2d 905 (1960), the California Supreme Court held that the statute creating the Los Angeles Metropolitan Transit Authority gave employees the right to strike by providing that employees should have the right to bargain collectively and to engage in "other concerted activities for the purpose of collective bargaining or other mutual aid or protection." *See also* Local 266, IBEW v. Salt River Project, Agricultural Improvement & Power Dist., 78 Ariz. 30, 275 P.2d 393 (1954) where the court upheld the right to strike of public employees to enforce a demand for collective bargaining where it was found that employer was engaged in proprietary and not governmental functions.

2. Public employee unions are prohibited from striking by the New York Taylor Act, and may be penalized for violation of the strike proscription; however, Section 210-2 (f) of the statute instructs PERB to "consider all relevant facts and circumstances, including but not limited to: (i) the extent of any wilful defiance . . . (ii) the impact of the strike on the public health, safety, and welfare of the community and (iii) the financial resources of the employee organization; and the board may consider (i) the refusal of the employee organization of the appropriate public employer . . . to submit the [dispute] to mediation and fact-finding . . . and (ii) whether, if so alleged by the employee organization, the appropriate public employer . . . engaged in such acts of extreme provocation as to detract from the responsibility of the employee organization for the strike." *See In re* Massapequa Local 1442, AFT, 4 PERB ¶ 8000 (1970) (giving definition to the statutory defense of "extreme provocation") .

BERNSTEIN, ALTERNATIVES TO THE STRIKE IN PUBLIC LABOR RELATIONS, 85 Harv. L. Rev. 459, 469-475 (1971)†

. . . It is reasonably clear that in public employment, the strike ban does not work; yet in most jurisdictions legalization of the strike is not a real possibility. And, I submit, the strike as it is

---

† Reprinted by permission of The Harvard Law Review Association and Professor Merton C. Bernstein, Ohio State University College of Law.

known in the private sector would not function in the same way in the public sector and does not fit the peculiarities of public collective bargaining—diffuse responsibility and the consequent need for longer periods of time to reach settlements than in the private sector. Compulsory arbitration has serious drawbacks, not the least of which are its unacceptability to large segments of public management and unions and the likely instability of its results.

Therefore I suggest[4] that we explore the possibilities of two other arrangements which have never been considered in the public sector[5] but which, I suggest, fit the needs of *all* the parties more adequately than either present practices or the currently proposed alternatives.

It will help to give a rough sketch of the functioning of these two arrangements before I go into them in detail. In a nonstoppage strike, operations would continue as usual, but both the employees and the employer would pay to a special fund an amount equal to a specified percentage of total cash wages. Thus, while both parties would be under pressure to settle, there would be no disruption of service. In a graduated strike, employees would stop working during portions of their usual workweek and would suffer comparable reductions of wages. Here, there would be pressure not only on employees and employer but also

---

[4] I want to emphasize that the proposed procedures should be part of a comprehensive public labor relations scheme which provides protection of employees against reprisal for collective activity, procedures for ascertaining appropriate bargaining units, elections to determine employee preferences, recognition and mandatory bargaining, sanctions against improper union activity, mediation procedures for bargaining disputes, and factfinding with recommendations in the case of bargaining deadlock. Such procedures are necessary conditions to the proper functioning of the nonstoppage and graduated strikes. Happily, it is also the case that these procedures will work more effectively if the pressure devices I propose are available.

[5] Several proposals for "nonstoppage" or "statutory" (because imposed by statute) strikes were made for the private sector starting in the late 1940's. They were, in chronological order, Marceau & Musgrave, *Strikes in Essential Industries: A Way Out*, 27 HARV. BUS. REV. 287 (1949); Goble, *The Non-Stoppage Strike*, 2 LAB. L.J. 105 (1951); N. CHAMBERLAIN & J. SCHILLING, SOCIAL RESPONSIBILITY AND STRIKES 279-86 (1952); Gregory, *Injunctions, Seizure and Compulsory Arbitration*, 26 TEMP. L.Q. 397, 402 (1953). The major variations are summarized and assessed in McCalmont, *The Semi-Strike*, 15 IND. & LAB. REL. REV. 191 (1962); Marshall & Marshall, *Nonstoppage Strike Proposals—A Critique*, 7 LAB. L.J. 299 (1956).

All of these proposals envisioned that employees continue at work and that the employer lose some income; and most involved a reduction of pay between declaration of the nonstoppage and settlement. All were limited to the private sector. The proposal I make here is the first to suggest application to the public sector and differs in several respects from each of the earlier versions.

The graduated strike is, to the best of my knowledge, original with me.

on the community; however, the decrease in public service would not be as sudden or complete as in the conventional strike. I believe that these two new types of strike substitutes would work best in tandem.

A. *The Nonstoppage Strike*

Under my proposal, a public employee union would be free to declare a nonstoppage strike after all other bargaining procedures failed to produce a settlement. Employees would be obliged to continue to work full time but would forego a portion of their take-home pay. I suggest that, initially, ten percent would suffice. This money would be paid by the public employer directly into a special fund (more fully discussed below). In addition to paying the equivalent of regular wages, the employer would also put into the fund an extra amount equal to what the employees have given up; this latter sum would constitute a loss to the employer. The union would have the option periodically to increase the amount of the foregone wages and employer payment, perhaps by increments of ten percent every two weeks. The public employer would have the option to require the union to switch to a graduated strike. If the employer did this, the employees would continue to lose the same rate of pay, but the employer would forego services rather than pay out additional funds.

I believe that exercise of the option to initiate the nonstoppage strike and increase the percentage can be limited to the union. The union has little other leverage, since the conventional strike would still be prohibited. Also, were the public employer able to initiate a procedure under which employees would work without pay, questions of involuntary servitude might arise. In any event, the employer would still have the strategic bargaining advantage of instituting, after a deadlock in negotiations, certain changes in pay or other terms of employment which have been offered to the union and rejected.

The nonstoppage strike would accommodate the peculiarities of public labor relations. It would attract the attention of and put pressure on both the public officials who deal directly with the union involved and other members of the executive branch whose own budgets might be affected, the local legislature, and state officials. And while a stoppage strike would not precipitate a crisis, its pressure would be steady and increasable. Thus, it may provide the necessary incentive for the various bodies of government to act, while allowing them the time they need to do so effectively. Moreover, it does not disturb consideration of the merits of the dispute with the hysteria and histrionics now typical of illegal strikes.

While nonstoppage strikes would create additional expense for public employers—many of whom are hard pressed as it is— they should also put an end to the present practice of paying the employees at overtime rates when a strike ends to reduce the backlog of work accumulated during the strike. Also, hopefully, the expense should be only temporary, and, as will be explained below, the money will not go to waste. In any event, the price does not seem too high to pay for a substantially improved process of bargaining.

Nonstoppage strikes offer significant advantages to employees, perhaps even more than would legalization of conventional strikes. In the first place, their rate of loss of pay would be lower at any given time than if there were an all-out strike. For employees with mortgage and other installment obligations to meet, this continuity of income is highly desirable. And, to the extent that the nonstoppage strike encourages more responsive bargaining without any stoppages, the total loss of pay may be less. In addition, in a full-scale strike, especially one of long duration, the employer is not liable for fringe benefit payments. Thus, life insurance policies may lapse or require payment by employees at a time when their income is interrupted, and group medical care insurance may have to be kept in force at the higher-cost individual rates. In a nonstoppage strike these benefits should continue.

Second, in actual strikes employees run the risk of losing their jobs. A common sanction in illegal strikes is to fire strikers. In the private strike, too, replacement of economic strikers has long been permitted, and while I have seen no data on public employer activity of this sort, I think it highly probable that permanent, nondiscriminatory replacement of strikers will become a feature of the legal public employee strike. In nonstoppage strikes, of course, jobs would be secure. Moreover, the absence of even temporary replacements would eliminate a traditionally potent source of violence, which everyone has a stake in averting.

Third, long-run employee and union interests are best served by a method that is legal and discomfits the community as little as possible. As union leadership knows from its post-World War II experience, unpopular strikes lead to distasteful legislation. And, by the same token, strikers, even if they feel their conduct justified, often must incur the disapproval of friends, neighbors, and others in the community. A peaceful method of pursuing demands seems clearly preferable.

The public employer would need some means of assuring union and employee compliance with the ground rules. Obviously, working full time for less than full pay might encourage some employees to slow down or "call in sick"—a favored device in strike-ban jurisdictions. Two procedures would minimize violations. First, the unions must see that it is to their advantage to persuade members that it is to *their* advantage to abide by the rules. That is, all must be made aware that the "struck" employer is indeed under strike-like pressure. Second, the statute should provide for an expedited (and I mean quick) unfair labor practice procedure to hear and determine charges of slowdown or improper absence. However, these areas are so sensitive and have such a potential for emotional overreaction that employer discipline of employees should be limited to those cases where impartial hearing officers make a finding that the improper action has taken place.

One serious problem with the nonstoppage strike is finding a suitable use for the special fund to which the public employer and employees have contributed. In order to insure that the loss will actually discipline the parties' conduct in bargaining, the fund would have to be placed effectively beyond their recapture.[6] I recommend that the fund be put at the disposal of a tripartite Public Purposes Committee in which respected community figures outnumber the total number of union and government members. This committee would be charged with the task of applying the money to publicly desirable, preferably short term projects that are not currently in the public budget—creation of scholarships or construction of public recreation facilities, for example. Certainly public employees would get little direct advantage from such a use of the money. Moreover, since these projects would not be currently funded, the committee's action would not discharge any of the government's present obligations; and since such contributions would occur irregularly, the government could not count on being relieved of any future burdens. Consequently, given public officialdom's abhorrence of losing control over money, this use of the funds should also provide an incentive for public employers to bargain.

Finally, I would like to dispel what may perhaps be a lingering doubt about nonstoppage strikes. Although they were initially proposed for use in the private sector more than two decades ago, they have had little acceptance by private parties. There are a number of reasons for this. First, although strikes have been

---

6 It might, however, be worthwhile to experiment with partial recapture as an incentive to rapid settlement. Thus, the amounts lost by the parties in the week in which they reach a settlement might be returned to them.

the subject of some academic disapproval and periodic editorial dismay, they remain an acceptable device in the private sector. There has been, therefore, little real pressure for a substitute. Second, for a nonstoppage strike in the private sector to be as effective as the conventional strike, the contributions of the employer to the fund must be geared to the amount of profits it is spared from losing. Because of the obvious difficulty of calculating this figure, achieving a formula for employer contribution which is satisfactory to both parties could easily be more formidable an obstacle than resolving their basic economic differences. Third, any statutory imposition of a nonstoppage plan would, while solving in a crude way the complexities of computing the formula, raise the claim by employers of deprivation of property without due process and the analogous employee claim of involuntary servitude.

Clearly the first reason does not apply in the public sector, for strikes are not currently acceptable. Nor does the second carry much weight. There is no need in the public sector to base a formula on profits because there are no profits; what should be required by the employees is that there be sufficient pressure on the public employer, and I believe my proposal provides that. The third, too, is inapplicable. Government may of course impose conditions on itself; and since it is constitutional totally to deprive public employees of the right to strike, it should be permissible to provide them with a halfway measure, especially when it is the union which voluntarily initiates its use. In short, no significant barriers to adoption of nonstoppage strikes exist in the public sector.

B. *The Graduated Strike*

A nonstoppage strike may be insufficient to induce responsive bargaining. More direct pressure may be required, and the graduated strike would provide it.

In a graduated strike the union would call work to a halt in stages. During the first week or two of the strike the employees would not work for half a day; during the next period, if the union so chose, they would not work for one full day per week; and so on, until they reached some floor short of total stoppage. Employees' take-home pay would be cut proportionately.

The effect of a graduated strike would be to give the public a taste of reduced service without the shock of immediate and total deprivation. This would start in motion the political machinery I described earlier, but would not overload it. Citizens would make complaints about their inconvenience known to their elected representatives. Local officials, both executive and legislative, would thus be under pressure to *do* something, but would nevertheless be able to consult with each other and with the officials at higher levels of government. They would therefore be able to negotiate with the union in a reasonably coordinated and authoritative manner. Free of resentment and of posturing over illegality, the complicated political process of sorting out preferences between higher costs and fewer services and among competing demands could then work itself out.

To insure that employees really suffer proportionate loss of wages would require, first, that they be unable, after the strike, to reduce backlogs at overtime rates. This could probably be accomplished simply by a limitation on overtime pay for some period following the strike. It does not seem necessary to do more: to the extent the employees ultimately recoup their lost wages, the public will have the lost service restored; and in any case it is unlikely that either side's losses will ever be totally recovered. Second, it would be necessary that the shutdown not exceed the announced level. While enforcement of this requirement would not be easy, it would probably be satisfactory for an impartial body with an expedited hearing procedure to determine the actual extent of the employee stoppage and to mete out appropriate penalties, including reduction of wages. In addition, there would be another strong inducement to proper observance of the ground rules: union and employee recognition that they have an effective, fair, and acceptable weapon to encourage good faith bargaining.

As I stated before, I think that the graduated strike and nonstoppage strike would work best in tandem. Because a nonstoppage strike would cause the public less disruption, we should perhaps require that unions try it for at least four weeks; they would then have the option of instituting a graduated strike. However, since both types of strikes are certain to put pressure on the public employer, I think we should give the employer some limited options. If it feels itself financially hard pressed, it can select the graduated strike, which would result in no additional expense. If it believed that the service performed by the employees was so essential to the public that cessation could not be tolerated—for example, fire and police protection—it should have the opportunity to persuade an impartial, preferably expert, tribunal that the services are in reality so indispensable. If successful, it could limit the union to the ever-more-expensive nonstoppage strike.

V. Conclusion

A blanket ban on strikes by public employees does not work. Illegal strikes are bad for labor relations and even worse for the rule of law. However, conventional strikes, if legalized, would be ill adapted to the complex procedures of public labor relations. Yet the public must accord its employees reasonable procedures that produce responsible bargaining. Under my proposals, bargaining could perform its salutary function, but without the disruption caused by the conventional strike and in ways adapted to the peculiarities of the public's needs and the government's intricate procedures for allocating resources.

Our federal system is complex and often awkward, but it enables us to experiment with various means of regulating public labor-management relations so that neither the public nor public employees are victimized. We should test the nonstoppage strike, the graduated strike, and indeed any other promising arrangement as we grope in this old field mined with so many new problems.

NOTES

1. Under the Canadian Public Service Staff Relations Act, CAN. REV. STAT. c. 72 (1967), covering federal employees, the exclusive bargaining agent is required, at the inception of the bargaining relationship, to decide which of two paths the relationship will follow: (1) Binding arbitration (with no right to strike) or; (2) Conciliation with the right to strike. If the latter alternative is chosen, certain employees whose jobs "consist in whole or in part of duties, the performance of which at any given time or after any specified period of time is or will be necessary in the interest of the safety or security of the public" are forbidden to strike. These employees are chosen, within twenty days of the decision on the conciliation alternative, by the employer, whose decision becomes final if no objection to it is filed. In the event of such an objection, the Public Service Staff Relations Board (PSSRB) established by law, holds a hearing to decide the matter. The PSSRB also provides accurate wage cost data to facilitate the fact finding for negotiation purposes. *See generally* Arthurs, *Collective Bargaining in the Public Service of Canada: Bold Experiment or Act of Folly?*, 67 MICH. L. REV. 971 (1969).

2. The Minnesota Public Employment Relations Act was recently amended to grant strike rights to nonessential employees if an employer refuses to submit to binding arbitration or to adhere to a binding impasse arbitration award. Essential employees are those whose work involves services essential to public health or safety. *See* GERR No. 526, B-11.

3. *See generally Exploring Alternatives to the Strike*, 96 MONTHLY LAB. REV. 33-66 (Sept. 1973).

Chapter 7

SETTLEMENT OF COLLECTIVE BARGAINING IMPASSES

A. Introduction

1. Impasse Disputes

Three kinds of impasse disputes arise in the course of union-management relations whether in the public or private sectors. In customary parlance these are referred to as "representational," "grievance" (or "rights"), and "collective bargaining" (or "interest") disputes, respectively. "Representational" disputes are those arising out of attempts by one or more unions to obtain bargaining rights. These kinds of disputes are the subject matter of Chapter Three. "Grievance" ("rights") disputes are those which arise subsequent to the negotiation of a collective bargaining agreement and ordinarily concern the interpretation or implementation of the agreement. These disputes are customarily handled in accordance with contractually negotiated grievance procedures, which are discussed in Chapter Eight.

"Interest" disputes are disputes arising in the process of an attempt to negotiate the terms of a collective bargaining agreement. This chapter is devoted to a consideration of the various methods or procedures which have been devised in the public sector, or have been advocated for use, to resolve these kinds of disputes. With respect to the problem of the settlement of public sector collective bargaining impasses, the Taylor Report[1] warned:

> The design of dispute settlement procedures must constantly avoid at least two serious pitfalls. The first is that impasse procedures often tend to be overused; they may become too accessible and as a consequence, the responsibility and problem-solving virtues of constructive negotiations are lost. Dispute settlement procedures can become habit-forming, and then negotiations become only a ritual. The second pitfall is that a standardized dispute settlement pro-

---

[1] Governor's Committee on Public Employee Relations, Final Report to Governor Nelson Rockefeller, State of New York, March 31, 1966, p. 33.

cedure is not ideally suited to all parties and to all disputes.
Procedures work best which have been mutually designed,
are mutually administered, and have been mutually shaped to
the particular problem at hand.

2.   A Survey of Impasse Procedures and Their Rationale

D. BOK AND J. DUNLOP, LABOR AND THE AMERICAN COMMUNITY 333-34, 337-38 (1970)†

Once a negotiating relationship has been established, the concern shifts to the resolution of disputes over the terms of employment. The settlement of these disputes calls for the design of procedures to govern collective negotiation and to provide effective
alternatives to conflict. In the first instance, it is probably wise to
ask the parties involved to design their own machinery. Employee
organizations differ widely in their objectives and methods: Governmental units are of varying size and confront diverse budgetary
restraints and procedures. The scope of civil-service regulations
and collective negotiations are far from uniform, and great differences appear in the nature of government operations and the
authority of government negotiators. The influence of employee
organizations and the labor movement in the community also
varies sharply. It stands to reason, therefore, that no one procedure, imposed legislatively, will suit all the situations to which
it would apply.

There are already a variety of procedures available in the public
sector, and inventiveness in this field is at an early stage. The parties may develop some variant of the prevailing-wage approach
and identify the procedures and the comparable sectors to be used
in making these determinations. They may establish various study
committees to operate during the term of the agreement, particularly on difficult prospective issues, with resort to fact finding and
recommendations before a body of their own design and choice.
They may design a system of public hearings with settlement
through normal political processes. As George Meany has observed, "Perhaps the best answer in this field is some system of
voluntary arbitration."

In the absence of procedures agreed to by the parties to resolve
disputes over provisions of an agreement, or in the event that
such machinery fails, the government involved in the dispute has
an obligation to provide a general procedure. There is wide agreement that provision should be made for mediation between the
employee organization and the governmental unit if the parties
fail to resolve the dispute by direct negotiations. But what should

---

† Reprinted by permission of Simon & Schuster, Inc.

happen in the event that the dispute remains unresolved and the parties have reached a serious impasse?

There are three groups of major contending views on impasse procedures: 1) Government employees should be allowed to strike except when the public health or safety is in jeopardy. 2) If the impasse cannot otherwise be settled, no strike of public employees is permissible and the dispute should be resolved by compulsory arbitration binding on both the governmental employer and the employee organization. 3) Recommendations should be made by a fact-finding body, and in the event further mediation around these recommendations does not resolve the dispute, the appropriate legislative body should review the dispute and enact a statute prescribing the terms and conditions of employment. The recommendations of the fact finders should have presumptive validity, but should not be binding on the legislature. . . .

The third alternative impasse procedure is fact finding with final resolution to be made, if necessary, by the legislative body. This procedure provides a role for both expert opinion of neutrals and for legislative judgment on questions beyond the province of the labor-management specialist.

Where it works well, fact finding can be a useful and even a powerful device. It seems to focus public opinion and to economize on the legislators' time, while providing them with the guidance they need. Fact finding is also a flexible procedure; it provides maximum opportunity for mediation, before, during, and after recommendations made privately or publicly. The exposure to hard facts also helps to deflate extreme positions; it allows neutrals to develop and "try on for size" possible accommodations, while permitting the parties to modify a recommendation to their mutual advantage. The uncertainty of the ultimate legislative action may stimulate a settlement, and the parties can preserve the opportunity for reaching such an agreement even after recommendations have been made.

In some instances, of course, the legislative body will unwisely reject the recommendations of a fact-finding board. Thus, critics may argue that the procedure is inherently unfair, since the employer—that is, the government—has the ultimate power to decide, even unfairly, in its own case. But what is the alternative? Some observers will suggest that the union be allowed to strike whenever the government refuses to accept the recommendations of the fact-finding body. But fact finders can make egregious errors, and surely they are not qualified to weigh the added labor costs of a settlement against tax increases and competing public programs and expenditures. Decisions of this kind may be more appropriately resolved by political processes and elected officials than by strikes or labor arbitrators. If so, the union is not without recourse, for it can bring political pressure to bear through its constituents and lobbyists. In this respect, the union occupies a very different position vis-à-vis the government than it would vis-à-vis a private employer with final power to fix the terms of employment. It is true that the union may have very little political influence and some legislative bodies may disregard its pleas for this reason. But similar drawbacks will exist in any system; if strikes were allowed, for example, many public employees would also have too little power to protect their legitimate interests. As a result, considering all the interests at stake, the wisest course may lie in letting the legislative body decide on the recommendations of a neutral panel. If the legislature disregards the recommendations too freely and too unfairly, strikes are likely to occur, regardless of the law, to bring home the interests of the employees. Short of this, the strike seems an inappropriate way to resolve the impasse.

HILDEBRAND, THE RESOLUTION OF IMPASSES, in THE ARBITRATOR, THE NLRB, AND THE COURTS, PROCEEDINGS OF THE TWENTIETH ANNUAL MEETING OF THE NATIONAL ACADEMY OF ARBITRATORS 289-92 (D. Jones ed. 1967)†

[The author first discusses impasse procedures used in the private sector and rejects as unworkable a full assimilation of those procedures to the public sector. After deciding that the public sector provides very special and necessary services, as a monopoly enterprise, which demands continuity of operations, the author continues:]

If these judgments are correct, then the government sector is indeed a special case. Accordingly, the critical task becomes that of designing a set of procedures that will accomplish three major objectives. The first one is to develop as fully as possible a role for collective bargaining as a method for achieving accommodation and mutual consent. The second is to protect the integrity of the bargaining process by insuring the independence of public management so that the process will not become transformed into a type of machine politics, hence political bargaining. Political bargaining is not collective bargaining. Whatever may be its own rationale, it carries real dangers to collective bargaining in the public service, and it cannot be defended by arguments in behalf of collective bargaining as such. If we seek the latter, we must insure the independence of public managements, and we must make it possible for such managements to sign binding agreements.

---

† Reprinted by permission of The Bureau of National Affairs, Inc.

Third, the basic procedure must recognize the need to preserve continuity of operations, but, more than this, it should restrain reliance upon coercion as much as possible, so that bargained settlements can become the rule rather than the exception.

The first objective can be served best by provision for an independent public agency to deal with questions of representation and unfair labor practices. In addition, the enabling statute should provide the parties with incentive to devise their own procedures for resolving impasses, failing which one will be mandated by law.

Treatment of Impasses

The second objective is self-evident, and needs no elaboration. The third refers to the treatment of impasses, about which the rest of my paper will be concerned.

Because the budget-making activities of public bodies are controlled by the calendar, the timing of negotiations becomes critical. They must begin early enough to permit the incorporation of settlements in the budget, and the negotiating period must allow for the possibility of intervention if voluntary agreement cannot be reached. Clearly, too, the whole process must provide sufficient opportunity for legislative consideration, open hearings, and clearance with civil service officials.

Because timing is so important, the procedure should make mediation available whenever serious conflict develops, at the option of either side or of the top public official within the jurisdiction. Obviously, too, this official must be kept continuously informed regarding the progress of negotiations. Furthermore, in my judgment it may well be desirable to provide for preventive mediation at the initiative of the independent agency charged with dealing with representation issues and unfair practices.

But suppose mediation fails. Then what? Here two alternative remedies are possible—compulsory arbitration and fact-finding without compulsory arbitration at its terminus. Recourse to either assumes, of course, that the parties have not built in their own procedure for resolving impasses, a procedure that in turn must be compatible with the fundamental policy laid down by statute.

To my mind, there are two basic weaknesses in the method of compulsory arbitration for dealing with disputes in the public service. One is that the certainty that it can be invoked constitutes an open invitation to extremist strategies. Ask for all you can, because you stand a chance of getting part of it. The insidious consequence is that this will vitiate the very process of collective bargaining. The pressures will then be shifted to what in fact is a juridical mechanism. What begins as collective bargaining ends in something quite different.[2] In the second place, compulsory arbitration amounts to a delegation of the responsibilities of public management and of the lawmakers to outsiders. In my view, this is incompatible with the basic principles of representative government. In fact, it can become a most convenient way to duck hard issues by passing them on to a board that is only temporarily in office and that is not responsible to the electorate. The result is likely to be labor policies that are unsound, because they will be more responsive to power relations than to the equitable accommodation of all interests—those of taxpayers, the citizens who use the service, management, and the whole body of public employees viewed collectively.

The Fact-Finding Approach

The second technique for dealing with impasses is that of fact-finding, following, of course, negotiations and mediation. In my view, and for the reasons just stated, this method should be an open-ended one. That is, if it issues in ultimate failure, compulsory arbitration should not be available at its terminus. I shall submit my reasons for leaving the process open-ended for subsequent consideration.

As I see the matter, fact-finding begins when mediation fails. I favor an all-public tripartite board for this purpose, to increase the likelihood of unanimity. Recourse to such a board should be at the initiative of either party or of the top public official, after the mediation period has run out. Precise time limits are required for hearing the dispute and rendering a report. It also seems to me desirable to provide that the recommendations of the board first should be submitted privately to the parties, coupled with a final mediatory effort by the board itself. If this step proves unsuccessful, the recommendations then should be made public, in hopes of building up public opinion in their behalf. If acceptance still cannot be gained, there may be some merit in having the chief executive assemble a carefully selected private committee to attempt quietly to persuade the intractable side to settle on the basis of these recommendations.

There is much to be said for the fact-finding approach. It is a logical extension of the process of collective bargaining because it continuously keeps open the possibility of voluntary settlement. I know of no other method that would serve this end as well. Moreover, it leaves the ultimate responsibility of the lawmakers intact, and, even more, it can produce a set of guidelines to a fair

---

[2] This danger might be reduced if the arbitration proceeding were made very costly to the parties, and its availability were made uncertain by provision of a choice-of-weapons approach.

resolution of the dispute at their hands. In turn, this latter feature reduces the disabilities of attempting to legislate in a context of crisis, by men mostly lacking in the necessary expertise.

B. AARON, L. BAILER & H. BLOCK, AN EMPLOYEE RELATIONS ORDINANCE FOR LOS ANGELES COUNTY, REPORT AND RECOMMENDATION OF CONSULTANTS' COMMITTEE 31-34 (July 25, 1968)

We have previously adverted to the rising incidence of strikes by public employees. We believe that such strikes are and should be unlawful, but to say so is merely to add a dimension to the problem and does not contribute to its solution. The only meaningful way to deal with strikes in the public sector is to devise settlement procedures which the parties will be willing to substitute for trial by economic combat. We offer no magic formula, no foolproof panacea; but we believe that our recommendations, if adopted, would substantially reduce the need for or the likelihood of strikes by County employees.

We assume that potential strike situations typically have their origin in disputes over proposed new wages, hours, and terms and conditions of employment. Disputes over existing terms and conditions involve rights, as opposed to interests; these disputes are classified as grievances and can be handled in accordance with established grievance procedures. In negotiating over new terms and conditions, however, the County and a certified employee organization may reach an impasse. We recommend that in such a case either party be permitted to invoke the assistance of the Commission [independently staffed, governmentally paid Employer-Employee Commission]. In order to prevent premature involvement of the Commission in the merits of the dispute, we also recommend that either party be permitted to raise the factual issue, to be decided by the Commission, whether an impasse has actually been reached. If that issue were raised and the Commission found that an impasse had not yet been reached, the parties would be obliged to continue their negotiations.

In the case of a genuine impasse, however, the Commission would itself be free to attempt to mediate a settlement of the dispute. Failing in that effort, it would ascertain whether the parties were willing, voluntarily, to submit the dispute to arbitration. If mediation failed and the parties would not mutually agree to arbitrate, the Commission would be empowered under the recommended ordinance to call in one or more neutral outsiders to assist in finding a solution to the dispute. Depending upon the requests of the parties and its own estimate of the situation, the Commission would ask the neutrals to undertake further mediation, or fact-finding with or without recommendations. Failure of any party to cooperate fully with the Commission or its agents at any stage of this procedure would constitute an unfair employee relations practice. The costs, if any, of such proceeding would be borne equally by the parties to the dispute.

Mediation reports would be filed with the Commission and would be kept confidential. Fact-finding reports would be filed with the Commission and transmitted by it to the parties within five calendar days after receipt. Release of the fact-finding report and recommendations, if any, in a given case, would be within the discretion of the Commission.

Release of a fact-finding report would exhaust the legal authority and responsibility of the Commission under the recommended ordinance in a given case. This would not preclude either party, however, from urging the Board of Supervisors to summon the disputants to a hearing to show cause why the recommendations of fact-finders had not been accepted.

KHEEL, STRIKES AND PUBLIC EMPLOYMENT, 67 Mich. L. Rev. 931, 940-41 (1969)†

[After concluding that most compulsory arbitration procedures are unsatisfactory, because of issue framing difficulties and the lack of binding effect on the legislature, Mr. Kheel states:]

The simple lesson is that compulsory arbitration for all disputes and all issues is neither legally sound nor practically feasible. It would be a great mistake to adopt this procedure as the usual method prescribed in advance for all disputes in the expectation that it would signal an end to labor strife in public employment.

I believe, rather, that we should acknowledge the failure of unilateral determination, and turn instead to true collective bargaining, even though this must include the possibility of a strike. We would then clearly understand that we must seek to improve the bargaining process and the skill of the negotiators to prevent strikes. For in the end, the solution to the wide range of labor problems involving the many aspects of a dynamic and complicated human relationship must depend on the human factor. The most elaborate machinery is no better than the people who man it. It cannot function automatically. With skillful and responsible negotiators, no machinery, no outsiders, and no fixed rules are needed to settle disputes. For too long our attention has been directed to the mechanics and penalties rather than to the participants and the process. It is now time to change that, to seek to

† Reprinted by permission of The Michigan Law Review.

prevent strikes by encouraging collective bargaining to the fullest extent possible.

For the few strikes that might jeopardize public health or safety, I would favor legislation authorizing the governor of a state to seek an injunction for a specified period through procedures similar to those for emergency disputes under the Taft-Hartley Act. During the cooling-off period, the parties could continue their search for the basis of accommodation to end the dispute. If these procedures prove unavailing, then the legislature could consider means, but not the specific terms, of settlement, including the possibility of submitting the remaining issues to arbitration within specified bounds. In a particular situation, with issues sharply limited and defined through bargaining, arbitration imposed as a last resort by the legislature can effectively protect the public interest without making a sham of the bargaining process. Our primary reliance would then be placed, as I believe it must if we are to prevent strikes, on joint determination by parties in a true bargaining atmosphere.

I suggest, in short, that there is no workable substitute for collective bargaining—even in government—and that our best chance to prevent strikes against the public interest lies in improving the practice of bargaining. In an environment conducive to real bargaining, strikes will be fewer and shorter than in a system where employees are in effect invited to defy the law in order to make real the promise of joint determination. In a real bargaining environment, the employee representatives, I am convinced, can more effectively meet their dual responsibility to negotiate and to lead. Only if leaders do both can there be constructive labor relationships in place of the chaos resulting when agreements reached in negotiations are rejected by angry rank and file or defied by subterfuge forms of strikes such as working to the rule.

NOTES

1. The preceding excerpts emphasize the need for impasse settlement procedures to provide a substitute for strike action. Is the theory, then, that such procedures will or must involve pressure tactics roughly the equivalent of those which would be generated by a strike or lockout? Alternatively, is the theory that settlement procedures properly designed and skillfully used can or should obviate the need for resort to or availability of the strike or lockout? Given that impasse resolution procedures in the public sector are usually mediation and fact-finding with recommendations, or, in some instances binding arbitration, does the question whether specific procedures are appropriate depend upon which of the suggested underlying theories is sound? Are such

theories relevant to the determination of mediation and fact-finding methodology (*e.g.*, with respect to the role of the mediator, and the question whether fact-finding recommendations are to be made public)? *See* Anderson, *Strikes and Impasse Resolution in Public Employment,* 67 MICH. L. REV. 943, 947-48 (1969) (contending that strikes are not essential to effective dispute settlement given skilled bargainers and sound impasse resolution procedures); R. DOHERTY & W. OBERER, TEACHERS, SCHOOL BOARDS AND COLLECTIVE BARGAINING: A CHANGING OF THE GUARD 96-113 (1967) (favoring binding arbitration to replace the need for strikes); and Taylor, *Using Factfinding and Recommendation in Impasses,* 92 MONTHLY LAB. REV. 63 (July 1969) (suggesting that the strike must be replaced by other equally effective processes for inducing equitable settlements).

2. If regardless of the *de jure* prohibition of strikes, strikes in fact occur to the point that there is really a *de facto* recognition of them as a part of the collective bargaining process, is it not obvious that an evaluation of existing or proposed dispute settlement procedures poses different theoretical and analytical considerations than if it were assumed that strikes are not only illegal, but because illegal will not occur? Does the situation then become roughly comparable to that obtaining in the private sector? If so, is Hildebrand wrong in rejecting the private sector "model?" To put the matter in different terms, is there any justification for structuring dispute settlement procedures as typically now done, mandating mediation and, in addition, fact-finding (or arbitration) for all disputes? For discussions of these questions and alternatives to the no strike ban, see: Garber, *Compulsory Arbitration in the Public Sector: A Proposed Alternative,* 26 ARB. J. 226 (1971) (proposing "final last offer arbitration," but permitting the arbitrator to choose the more reasonable solution offered by the parties on each disputed issue); Bernstein, *Alternatives to the Strike in Public Labor Relations,* 85 HARV. L. REV. 459, 470-75 (1971) (finding strikes inevitable and proposing the use of the graduated strike and the nonstoppage strike, as necessary to give employees sufficient bargaining strength, while not totally disrupting society); Clark, *Public Employee Strikes: Some Proposed Solutions,* 23 LAB. L.J. 111 (1972) (questioning whether any categories of public employees should have the right to strike); Note, *The Strike and Its Alternatives in Public Employment,* 1966 WIS. L. REV. 549, 554-59 (reasons for denying right to strike). For a criticism of even a partial right to strike, see Foegan, *The Partial Strike: A Solution in Public Employment?,* 30 PUB. PER. REV. 83 (1969).

3. Should impasse resolution procedures in the public sector be designed to assure "equitable" settlements irrespective of the relative bargaining strength or weakness of the particular group of employees or the public employer; or, alternatively, should impasse procedures be primarily designed to induce settlements and avoid strikes? The 1966 report by the Michigan Advisory Committee on Public Employee Relations suggested that:

> We think the primary objectives of the law should be to maximize the opportunities for equitable settlement of employee relations disputes in the public sector while rejecting, at this juncture, both resort to the strike and (except in the case of police and firefighters) compulsory third party determination of unresolved new contract issues.

Report to Governor George Romney by the Advisory Committee on Public Employee Relations (1966), *reprinted in* COLLECTIVE BARGAINING IN THE PUBLIC SERVICE 100, 104 (D. Kruger and C. Schmidt eds. 1969).

For two different proposals of procedures which might increase chances of equitable solutions, see Lev, *Strikes by Government Employees: Problems and Solutions,* 57 A.B.A.J. 771 (1971) (suggesting the creation of a Federal Public Employee Mediation Board with mediators designated to issue awards in public sector impasse disputes and, in addition, federal contributions to assist local legislatures to meet monetary terms of awards); and Cole, *Devising Alternatives to the Right to Strike,* 92 MONTHLY LAB. REV. 60 (July 1969) (suggesting a public employment advisory council, which could recommend an appropriate level of increased labor costs to be absorbed by each governmental unit in each fiscal year). *See also Exploring Alternatives to the Strike,* 96 MONTHLY LAB. REV. 33-66 (Sept. 1973).

B. Existing Legislative Approaches

1. Federal Level

EXECUTIVE ORDER 11491[3]

SEC. 15. *Approval of agreements.* An agreement with a labor organization as the exclusive representative of employees in a unit is subject to the approval of the head of the agency or an official designated by him. An agreement shall be approved if it conforms to applicable laws, existing published agency policies and regulations (unless the agency has granted an exception to

---

[3] The full text of the Executive Order is reprinted in the *Statutory Appendix.*

a policy or regulation) and regulations of other appropriate authorities. A local agreement subject to a national or other controlling agreement at a higher level shall be approved under the procedures of the controlling agreement, or, if none, under agency regulations.

SEC. 16. *Negotiation disputes.* The Federal Mediation and Conciliation Service shall provide services and assistance to Federal agencies and labor organizations in the resolution of negotiation disputes. The Service shall determine under what circumstances and in what manner it shall proffer its services.

SEC. 17. *Negotiation impasses.* When voluntary arrangements, including the services of the Federal Mediation and Conciliation Service or other third-party mediation, fail to resolve a negotiation impasse, either party may request the Federal Service Impasses Panel to consider the matter. The Panel, in its discretion and under the regulations it prescribes, may consider the matter and may recommend procedures to the parties for the resolution of the impasse or may settle the impasse by appropriate action. Arbitration or third-party fact finding with recommendations to assist in the resolution of an impasse may be used by the parties only when authorized or directed by the Panel.

NOTES

1. Executive Order 11491 as amended by E.O. 11616 provides that the federal labor-management relations program shall be administered by five bodies: The Federal Labor Relations Council, the Assistant Secretary of Labor for Labor-Management Relations, the Federal Mediation and Conciliation Service (FMCS), the Civil Service Commission, and the Federal Service Impasses Panel (FSIP). The two groups having primary responsibility for assisting contract negotiations are the FMCS and the FSIP. The FSIP consists of seven members appointed by the President for indefinite terms. There are three channels of access to the Panel: Request by the FMCS; request by either or both parties; request by the Executive Secretary of the Panel. To this date the FMCS has never on its own sought the assistance of the FSIP and the Executive Secretary has only infrequently initiated FSIP intervention. Case experience suggests that FSIP will not intervene unless the services of the FMCS have been used.

One of five determinations can be made by the FSIP: that it has no jurisdiction; that negotiations should be resumed; that negotiations should be resumed with more mediation; that other voluntary arrangements such as arbitration should be utilized; or that the Panel should order fact-finding. Of the first thirty-two cases submitted to FSIP, fact-finding was used in five, eleven cases were sent back for more mediation and negotiation, the Panel declined to hear fifteen, and one was referred to other voluntary arrangements. If fact-finding is used, the report is not released; only the recommendations of the fact-finders are made known. After the recommendations are made to the parties, they have thirty days to accept them or otherwise settle. During this period the FMCS may assist the parties. *See* Note, *Federal Service Impasses Panel: Procedural Flexibility and Uncertainty,* 9 HARV. J. LEGIS. 694, 704 (1972).

2. The major criticism of Executive Order 11491 centers on the inability of the procedure to cope with emergency problems and the lack of a clearly defined relationship between the operations of the five organizations. Except for the 30-day limit after fact-finding, no other time restrictions are placed on the parties to reach a settlement. It is contended that making use of the FSIP dependent upon the request of a party and, thereafter a matter of FSIP discretion, reduces the effectiveness of the impasse resolution procedure. On the other hand, many have argued that flexibility and uncertainty should be built into any impasse resolution scheme. In this regard, compare the impasse procedures under Executive Order 11491 with the more rigid formula adopted pursuant to the Postal Reorganization Act, which is reprinted in full in the *Statutory Appendix. See also* Willoughby, *The FMCS and Dispute Mediation in the Federal Government,* 92 MONTHLY LAB. REV. 27 (May 1969); Hampton, *The Framework of E.O. 11491, Labor-Management Relations in the Federal Service,* 17 FED. B. NEWS 70 (1970); and Note, *Federal Service Impasses Panel: Procedural Flexibility and Uncertainty,* 9 HARV. J. LEGIS. 694 (1972).

3. The glaring differences between the rigid procedures of the Postal Reorganization Act and the somewhat undirected flexibility of procedures under Executive Order 11491 may be more attributable to history than to any inherent differences in negotiation problems. The Postal strike of 1970 gave impetus for special legislation which was designed to prohibit further strikes and, presumably, to cure the need for strikes by providing specific procedures for contract settlements. The various steps in the impasse procedures, which include binding arbitration, are mandatory. However, it is not clear that the procedure will cope with a strike, in the event one should occur. What fail-safe mechanisms can be incorporated in a statutory impasse procedure to deal with unlawful strikes? *See* Kennedy, *The Postal Reorganization Act of 1970: Heading Off Future Postal Strikes?,* 59 GEO.

L.J. 305 (1970). *See also* Cohn, *Labor Features of the Postal Reorganization Act,* 22 LAB. L.J. 44 (1971).

2. State and Local Levels

a. A Survey of Legislation

DISPUTE SETTLEMENT IN THE PUBLIC SECTOR: THE STATE-OF-THE-ART, REPORT TO DEPARTMENT OF LABOR, DIVISION OF PUBLIC EMPLOYMENT RELATIONS SERVICES 8-16
(T. Gilroy & A. Sinicropi eds. 1971)

By August of 1971, at least thirty-four states had enacted legislation dealing with interest dispute procedures in public employment. These states were: Alaska, California, Connecticut, Delaware, Florida, Hawaii, Georgia, Idaho, Illinois, Iowa, Kansas, Louisiana, Maine, Maryland, Massachusetts, Michigan, Minnesota, Missouri, Montana, Nebraska, Nevada, New Hampshire, New Jersey, New York, North Dakota, Oklahoma, Oregon, Pennsylvania, Rhode Island, South Dakota, Vermont, Washington, Wisconsin, Wyoming.

Public employee statutes in the above states range in employee coverage from one specific occupational group, such as teachers, to statutes with comprehensive coverage of most public employees in the state. Moreover, a number of states have separate statutes for different types of employees. Oregon has separate laws for state and municipal employees, teachers, and nurses; Wisconsin for state and municipal employees; and Washington for municipal employees, elementary and secondary teachers, public utility district employees and port authority employees.

In addition to variations in coverage, state legislation presents a diversified pattern of impasse procedures such as voluntary systems devised by the parties, mediation, factfinding, arbitration, and "show cause" hearings. Individual statutes often call for one or a combination of the above mentioned procedures. It should be noted that most of the state legislation which includes interest dispute procedures has been passed since 1967. . . .

The following is a summary of the pattern of impasse procedures in state law.

Mediation

At least twenty-five states provided in some way for mediation of negotiation disputes. These states were: Alaska, California, Connecticut, Delaware, Hawaii, Idaho, Kansas, Maine, Maryland, Massachusetts, Michigan, Minnesota, Nebraska, Nevada, New Hampshire, New Jersey, New York, North Dakota, Oregon, Pennsylvania, Rhode Island, South Dakota, Vermont, Washington, Wisconsin.

The provisions for mediation differ among and within states with respect to how the procedure is initiated, who provides the service, the use of one mediator or a panel, the relationship of mediation to other impasse procedures, and provisions for payment of costs.

In most states, mediation can be requested by either party. However, under statutes in at least six states (California, Maine, Maryland, Nevada, North Dakota, and Wisconsin), both parties must request this service. In some states, such as Kansas and New York, the Public Employment Relations Board will intervene either by request or on its own initiative.

The agencies providing mediation services vary among states and in some cases within a state for different groups of employees. Some states, such as New Jersey, provide mediation services through a public employment relations board or commission. Other states use an agency previously established to handle private sector disputes. An example of the latter is the Wisconsin Employment Relations Commission. In some states, more than one agency is involved in mediation. In Connecticut, municipal mediation is handled by the State Board of Mediation and Arbitration while teacher disputes are handled by the Secretary of the State Board of Education. Under the Minnesota teachers statute, the parties may select their own adjustment panel to mediate a dispute. Nebraska law provides that a Court of Industrial Relations may provide panels of mediators for use by the parties. The Vermont teacher law allows the parties to request mediation assistance from the American Arbitration Association.

While most states provide for a single mediator, several states provide for a panel. Frequently, a tripartite panel is utilized in which each party selects one member of the panel, with the partisan members agreeing on a third panel member. The Minnesota state and municipal employees laws are examples of the use of tripartite panels, while Alaska uses a five-member panel.

Twenty-two of the twenty-five states providing for mediation also make available other impasse procedures. Alaska, California, and Maryland are the three states making no specific reference to other procedures, while one of two statutes in North Dakota and one of three statutes in Oregon make no provision for other procedures.

With respect to the costs of mediation, in the private sector the costs are generally borne by the mediation agency. However, in the public sector, there is often an implication or requirement that the parties pay part of the mediation costs.

Factfinding

Unlike the private sector, where factfinding is limited primarily to so-called national emergency disputes, the public sector relies more heavily on this technique in negotiation impasse resolution. At least twenty-three states authorized the use of factfinding. These states were: Connecticut, Delaware, Georgia, Hawaii, Idaho, Kansas, Maine, Massachusetts, Michigan, Minnesota, Montana, Nebraska, Nevada, New Hampshire, New Jersey, New York, North Dakota, Oregon, Pennsylvania, South Dakota, Vermont, Washington, Wisconsin.

The normal procedure is that factfinding may be initiated by either party, a tripartite or neutral panel is utilized, and recommendations for settlement are made by that panel. These recommendations are either made public following the decision, or delayed pending further negotiation based on those recommendations.

As with mediation, there is considerable variation in the relationship of factfinding to other procedures within states. For example, in Montana, factfinding is the only impasse procedure specified in the law.

At least twelve of the twenty-three states authorizing factfinding provided other procedures beyond factfinding. These states were: Connecticut, Hawaii, Kansas, Maine, Michigan, Nebraska, Nevada, New Jersey, New York, Oregon, Pennsylvania, Vermont.

In Connecticut, factfinding is included in the statute covering municipal employees but not in the statute covering teachers. In Delaware the opposite is true. The Pennsylvania public employee statute includes factfinding while the municipal police and fire statute provides for the parties to go directly to binding arbitration.

There are other variations from the general pattern of factfinding mentioned above. New York law requires that the members of factfinding panels all be public representatives rather than using the tripartite system. With regard to costs, the Pennsylvania public employee statute provides that the state pays half of the cost of factfinding and the parties share the other half of the costs. In Michigan, New York and Hawaii, factfinding service is without charge.

In most states, factfinders are not specifically authorized to attempt to mediate the dispute. However, Connecticut, Massachusetts, Minnesota, Oregon, Vermont, and Wisconsin do make specific provisions for factfinders to attempt mediation.

At least two states, Nebraska and Minnesota, detail criteria for use in making factfinding reports. Nebraska requires that rates of pay and conditions of employment which are comparable to those maintained elsewhere for similar work be established. Minnesota provides that factfinders make findings and recommendations taking into consideration (1) tax limitations imposed by law, (2) wages, hours, and conditions of public employees performing comparable duties for other government agencies and in private employment, (3) internal consistency in classes of positions, and (4) any other factors deemed appropriate.

Arbitration

Twenty three states had legislation authorizing voluntary or compulsory arbitration for the resolution of some or all outstanding issues in certain public sector disputes. These states were: Connecticut, Delaware, Florida, Hawaii, Illinois, Iowa, Louisiana, Maine, Massachusetts, Michigan, Minnesota, Missouri, Nebraska, Nevada, New Jersey, New York, Oklahoma, Oregon, Pennsylvania, Rhode Island, South Dakota, Vermont, Wyoming.

Seventeen states provided for voluntary arbitration of certain interest disputes. As to the nature of arbitration decisions in these states, in six states the decisions are advisory, in eight they are binding and in six states the nature of the decision is left to the agreement of the parties. Several states provide for more than one type of arbitration decision under different statutes or in the same law.

Eleven states (Florida, Illinois, Louisiana, Maine, Michigan, Nebraska, Pennsylvania, Rhode Island, South Dakota, Vermont, Wyoming) provided for compulsory arbitration of certain interest disputes. In all of these states except Florida and Illinois binding decisions are authorized. Maine and Rhode Island authorize both types of decision depending on the negotiation issue in question.

Five states (Illinois, Maine, Pennsylvania, Rhode Island and Vermont) provide for both voluntary and compulsory arbitration. These five states demonstrate some of the variety of interest dispute legislation. Illinois provides in its firefighters statute for compulsory arbitration with an advisory decision, and in its transit workers statute for voluntary arbitration with the parties deciding if the decision is binding. Pennsylvania imposes binding arbitration in disputes involving certain state employees, but allows in other disputes, voluntary advisory arbitration. In police or firemen's disputes, either party may invoke binding arbitration. Rhode Island allows either party in municipal employee or teacher impasses to voluntarily request binding arbitration on matters not involving the expenditure of money. In police and fire impasses, compulsory binding arbitration is imposed upon the parties. Maine provides for voluntary binding arbitration of municipal employment disputes under some circumstances and both compulsory advisory and compulsory binding arbitration in others. Vermont provides for voluntary and compulsory arbitration in the same statute, making binding arbitration compulsory as a final step in settlement of firefighters disputes while allowing the parties in other municipal labor disputes to voluntarily go to binding arbitration as a final step.

Interesting variations in other arbitration laws include the Oklahoma statute covering police and firemen which provides for an advisory decision by an arbitrator whose decision becomes binding on both parties if accepted by the municipality, and the Nevada municipal employees statute which allows either party, before factfinding commences, to request that the Governor declare that the factfinder's report will be binding.

In all states which provide for compulsory arbitration, the dispute is referred to an arbitration board rather than an individual arbitrator. Kansas and New York provide for hearings by the legislative body which may take such action as it deems to be in the public interest, including the interest of the involved public employees. In Nebraska, the dispute is resolved by the State Court of Industrial Relations.

Most of the states authorizing arbitration either impose no limit on the issues which may be resolved through this device or are silent on the matter. In Delaware, a limit is specified, while in Louisiana, one is implied. On the other hand, the Maine statute does not appear to limit the scope of arbitration when its use is voluntary, but does provide that determinations shall be advisory when the issues are salaries, pensions and insurance, and binding on other issues when arbitration is utilized. In Rhode Island, which authorizes compulsory arbitration, there is no limit with respect to issues in the case of policemen and firemen, whereas arbitration determinations for municipal employees and teachers are binding except on matters involving the expenditure of money.

In at least six states, specific criteria for arbitration awards have been established. The Vermont firefighters statute allows the arbitration panel wide latitude using as a basis "the relative hardship to the firefighters and the public, conditions in the general area, the relative equities or the peculiarities of the employment." Florida, Maine, Michigan, Nebraska and Rhode Island also outline criteria for arbitration awards. The Michigan statute includes such criteria as the authority of the employer, financial ability of the employer, the interests of the public, consumer prices and comparable wages.

Some statutes, notably those in Michigan and Wyoming, specifically provide for appeal of arbitration awards. Michigan permits appeals if the order is unsupportive by competent material and substantial evidence on the whole record. Wyoming permits appeals to vacate an award for such reasons as corruption, fraud, or partiality, or if the arbitrators exceed their authority. A court may modify or correct an award when there is miscalculation, or mistakes, the arbitrators decided an issue not submitted to them, or the award is imperfect in form. . . .

County and Municipal

While these jurisdictions are in many cases covered by the state legislation previously referred to, in many other instances their labor relations activities take place within the framework of local resolutions or ordinances. In some cases, negotiations take place without any clear legislated guidelines. This is particularly true of larger cities in states without public employment statutes and also in local school districts.

The most comprehensive study of county and municipal labor relations laws to date has been done by the Advisory Commission on Intergovernmental Relations (ACIR), the International City Management Association, National Association of Counties, National League of Cities and the State Personnel Administrator's Association. Their survey of counties and municipalities of over 10,000 population covered "various types of municipal laws—including city charter provisions, ordinances, city council resolutions, personnel rules, and other directives, rather than state laws dealing with public employee organizations and the conduct of negotiations." The distinction between legislative enactment and policy becomes somewhat blurred here.

Two areas of this survey are pertinent to this study. The survey, in part, covered authorizations for arbitration of disputes involving general employees and arbitration for public safety employees. Listing the responses under municipal laws, the survey found nineteen percent of the responding cities with authorized arbitration of disputes with general employees, fourteen percent not authorizing arbitration, and sixty-three percent with no policy. For public safety employees, the survey found eighteen percent with authorized arbitration, fourteen percent not authorizing arbitration, and sixty-four percent with no policy. At the county level, it was found that twenty-one percent of the responding counties authorized arbitration of disputes with general employees, eighteen percent did not authorize it, and fifty-four percent had no policy. For public safety employees, the survey found thirty percent authorizing dispute arbitration, twenty percent not authorizing arbitration, and fifty-six percent with no policy. It is not clear whether these figures on arbitration refer to grievance and/or contract negotiation disputes. They are, however, the only reference to dispute settlement procedures under what are categorized in the tables as "laws." With regard to their county survey, the ACIR cautions against overgeneralizing the results and states that "the findings then point up subtle trends rather than definitive patterns."

Another recent study of interest regarding counties and municipalities has been done in California. This research focuses on resolutions, ordinances, etc., implementing the California state public employee relations act in counties and municipalities. While not required to implement this legislation, this study found that thirty-seven of California's counties and seventeen of the thirty-six cities over 75,000 had done so. With respect to impasse procedures, this study reported that of the seventeen cities with their own rules, thirteen specify interest dispute procedures. Most allow either party to initiate the procedure and usually leave the specific system to mutual determination by the parties. Mediation and factfinding are most often mentioned as part of these dispute resolution systems.

Of the thirty-seven counties with rules, twenty-two list impasse procedures. At the county level, this study found the counties were less specific about impasse procedures than the cities and provided less structure to the process. Overall, the study points up in one state the variety of policies to be found at the county and municipal level.

A number of the larger cities across the country have adopted ordinances which include reference to impasse procedures. The City of Baltimore, for example, provides for the use of mediation and tripartite factfinding with recommendations. Criteria for factfinding decisions are included in the ordinance. The costs of these procedures are shared by the parties. The City of Los Angeles provides that an Employee Relations Board may be used by the parties to resolve negotiation impasses. The Board may appoint mediators or factfinders and the city shares the cost of these procedures with the employee organizations. The City of New York also provides, through its Office of Collective Bargaining, for mediation and factfinding of negotiation disputes with municipal employees.

b. Some Specific Models

WISCONSIN MUNICIPAL EMPLOYMENT LAW—WIS. STAT. ANN.
§ 111.70 (4) (c). *See Statutory Appendix.*

NOTE

There are three statutes covering three separate categories of public employees in Wisconsin: State, municipal, and municipal police and fire fighters. The Wisconsin Employment Relations Commission supervises impasse procedures under all three statutes.

There are two separate statutory impasse procedures for police and fire fighters disputes. One covers police and fire fighters in cities with populations of 5,000 to 500,000 and provides for compulsory arbitration of interest disputes at the request of either party. WIS. STAT. ANN. ch. 247, § 111.77. (The statute specifies "final offer" arbitration, unless the parties jointly elect otherwise.) The other covers only the Milwaukee police force and it, too, provides for compulsory arbitration of interest disputes. However, the statute covering Milwaukee police does not adopt the "final offer" approach. WIS. STAT. ANN. § 111.70 (4) - (jm) 1-13 (Supp. 1972). *See generally* GERR No. 451, B-5 (1972) for a discussion of recent amendments of the Wisconsin State Employment Labor Relations Act, and GERR No. 428, B-6 (1972) for a discussion of the 1972 amendments to the Wisconsin Municipal Employment Law.

• • •

PENNSYLVANIA PUBLIC EMPLOYEE RELATIONS ACT—PA. STAT.
ANN. tit. 43, ch. 19, §§ 1101.801-1101.807, 1101.1002-1101.1003.
See Statutory Appendix.

NOTE

Pennsylvania requires binding arbitration of disputes involving prison and mental hospital guards and court personnel if an impasse is reached. *See Statutory Appendix,* PA. STAT. ANN. § 1101.805 (Supp. 1971). A different statute, PA. STAT. ANN. §§ 217.1-217.10 (Supp. 1971), provides for compulsory arbitration to resolve disputes involving police and fire fighters. All other public employees may strike after statutory dispute resolution procedures have been exhausted, unless or until the strike endangers the public health, safety or welfare.

• • •

NEW YORK PUBLIC EMPLOYEES' FAIR EMPLOYMENT ACT (TAYLOR LAW) —§ 209 of the Taylor Law. *See Statutory Appendix.*

NOTE

Some criticize the New York approach in that it places the task of ultimate dispute resolution in the legislative body after fact-finding. The suggestion is that this will decrease serious bargaining efforts in the expectation that more favorable treatment will come from the legislature. Are there countervailing arguments? Statistics released by the New York PERB covering the years 1967 through 1972 indicate that most disputes in which mediation or fact-finding were used were resolved short of legislative action.

For general discussions of the Taylor Act see Doering, *Impasse Issues in Teacher Disputes Submitted to Fact Finding in New York,* 27 ARB. J. 1 (1972); Sabghii, *The Taylor Act: A Brief Look After Three Years,* 1970 SUPPLEMENT TO REPORT OF TASK FORCE ON STATE AND LOCAL GOVERNMENT LABOR RELATIONS (Chicago: Public Personnel Association 1971); Wollett, *The Taylor Law and the Strike Ban,* in PUBLIC EMPLOYEE ORGANIZATION AND BARGAINING: A REPORT ON THE JOINT CONFERENCE OF THE ASS'N OF LABOR MEDIATION AGENCIES AND THE NATIONAL ASS'N OF STATE LABOR RELATIONS AGENCIES 29-37 (A. Anderson ed. 1968); Drotning & Lipsky, *The Outcome of Impasse Procedures in New York Schools Under the Taylor Law,* 26 ARB. J. 87 (1971); Yaffe & Goldblatt, *Factfinding in Public Employment Disputes in New York State: More Promise Than Illusion,* ILR Paperback No. 10 (1971).

. . .

HAWAII PUBLIC EMPLOYMENT RELATIONS ACT—HAWAII REV. STAT. §§ 89-11 and 89-12. *See Statutory Appendix.*

NOTE

In allowing strike action after resort to the prescribed impasse procedures, Hawaii's statute departs sharply from the norm. Yet it encompasses features of others in providing for mediation fact-finding, and it also includes a detailed procedure for voluntary binding arbitration. Is the right to strike sufficiently restricted to minimize probable resort to strike action? *See* Pendleton, *Collective Bargaining in the Public Sector,* REPORT OF THE INDUSTRIAL RELATIONS CENTER, University of Hawaii (May, 1971).

. . .

NEW YORK CITY COLLECTIVE BARGAINING LAW—§§ 1173-5.0a and 1173-7.0 in ADMINISTRATIVE CODE, ch. 54, Local Law 53-1967, as amended by Local Laws 1 & 2 of 1972. *See Statutory Appendix.*

NOTES

1. New York City evolved its collective bargaining ordinance during the same period when the state level approach under the Taylor Act was being developed. The Office of Collective Bargaining began operations in New York City on January 2, 1968. The OCB was created by the New York City Council and implemented by Mayor John V. Lindsay's Executive Order No. 52 as a result of the 1967 agreement between the City and most of the municipal unions with which it bargained. The agreement was developed under the auspices of the Labor Management Institute of the American Arbitration Association which had begun the task at the request of Mayor Robert F. Wagner in 1965 and completed its work at the request of Mayor Lindsay in 1966. The Chairman of the tripartite panel was Saul Wallen. The other public members were Father Philip A. Carey of the Xavier Institute of Industrial Relations, Professor Vern Countryman of Harvard Law School and Peter Seitz, attorney and arbitrator. *See generally* Raskin, *Politics Up Ends the Bargaining Table,* in PUBLIC WORKERS AND PUBLIC UNIONS 122 (S. Zagoria ed. 1972) ; Anderson, *Strikes and Impasse Resolution in Public Employment,* 67 MICH. L. REV. 943 (1969) ; Gotbaum, *Finality in Collective Bargaining Disputes: The New York Experience,* 21 CATHOLIC U.L. REV. 589 (1972) ; Schilian, *The Taylor Law, The O.C.B. and the Public Employee,* 35 BROOKLYN L. REV. 214 (1969).

2. It was hoped by City officials and union heads alike that the ordinance and OCB structure would prevent strikes. Strikes were not specifically prohibited, but the strike prohibitions and sanctions of the Taylor Act remained applicable. Initially, unions and City officials hailed the ordinance and administrative implementation as a national model, and it continues to have strong support, at least for New York City. But there were some problems, especially in the collective bargaining dispute settlement area. The 1968 sanitation worker strike, followed by police sick-ins and a large backlog of unresolved cases placed the OCB under stress. The New York ordinance was finally amended in 1972 to empower the OCB Board of Collective Bargaining to appoint Impasse Panels to resolve bargaining disputes. An Impasse Panel is authorized to take whatever action it considers necessary to end the dispute, including mediation or final and binding recommendations for settlement. *See* § 1173-7.0c of the New York law. *See also* GERR No. 435, B-10 (1972).

• • •

VANDALIA, OHIO EMPLOYER-EMPLOYEE RELATIONS ORDINANCE No. 72-15, §§ 144.03 (n), (p) & (q), 144.15 (1972) (reported in GERR No. 471, E-1). The impasse resolution procedures of the Vandalia Ordinance provide as follows:

(n) "Fact finding" means identifying the major issues in a particular dispute; reviewing the positions of the parties; investigating and reporting of the facts by one or more impartial factfinders; and making recommendations for settlement.

(p) "Impasse" shall mean the failure of the parties to an existing agreement to achieve agreement thirty (30) days prior to the expiration date thereof, or the failure of the City and an Employee Organization to reach agreement on an initial agreement within ninety (90) days after negotiations have commenced.

(q) "Mediation" shall mean the effort of an impartial third person or persons, functioning as intermediaries, to assist the parties in reaching a voluntary resolution to an impasse through interpretation, suggestion and advice.

144.15 IMPASSE PROCEDURE.

(a) In the event that City management representatives and the certified employee organization are unable to agree on the terms of a "Memorandum of Understanding," by December 1st of each year, then either party may request the assistance of the Board in resolving the impasse.

(b) If the Board determines that an impasse exists, it shall investigate the issues disputed by the parties. It may hold hearings and take testimony. The investigative proceedings shall be private. The Board shall limit its role to the issues referred for impasse settlement. The Board may attempt to mediate a dispute at any time during the investigative proceedings.

(c) If the impasse procedure in subsection (b) is not successful by January 1st of the succeeding year, the City and the Employee Organization shall each appoint a member to a fact-finding committee. The two members so appointed shall mutually agree upon the third member who shall be disinterested in the dispute and representative of the public. If for any reason the public member is not appointed promptly, such member shall be appointed by the Vandalia Municipal Judge. However, if both parties to the controversy agree, the matter may be taken directly to the Council for a decision.

(d) If fact-finding assistance is requested, then any costs incurred shall be shared equally by the City and the employee organization, and such fact-finding shall take place as follows:

(1) After the fact-finding committee has obtained enough information from the parties in the controversy, it shall then, based on the background it has on the issue and any other additional information, present a written statement of facts and their recommendations for resolving the dispute to the parties involved. The committee may submit majority and dissenting findings and recommendations, if appropriate.

During the fact-finding committee's appointment and work, the City and the Employee Organization in the dispute shall be under an obligation to cooperate with the committee and continue to negotiate for the purpose of resolving the dispute.

(e) If the parties involved in the dispute are unable to reach agreement within five (5) days of receipt of the fact-finder's recommendation, the fact-finders shall make its written recommendations public and shall forward their recommendations to the Council. The Council shall conduct a hearing within fifteen (15) days from the date of filing the recommendations to allow City Management representatives or the certified employee organization representatives, an opportunity to present their positions with respect to the fact-finder's recommendations. Upon conclusion of the hearing, the Council shall have the choice of the following three decisions:

(1) The Council may adopt the position of City Management representatives.

(2) The Council may adopt the position of the certified employee organization.

(3) The Council may adopt the position and recommendations of the fact-finders.

(f) The effective date of any agreement reached under the provision of this section shall be the actual date of signing by the employee organization unless otherwise specified.

. . .

DAYTON, OHIO CITY ORDINANCE, § 142-9 (D) - (F) (1972) (reported in GERR No. 452, E-1). The Dayton ordinance, which was adopted in 1972, is another example of a local experiment with impasse procedures designed to resolve interest disputes involving municipal employees. The ordinance provides for fact-finding and then provides:

D. If this dispute remains unresolved for forty-five (45) days following the submission of the Board's findings and recommendations, the findings and recommendations shall be considered by the Commission, and, upon a majority vote, the Commission will render a decision in the dispute at a regular meeting. The Clerk of the Commission shall notify the Employee Organization of the decision in writing.

E. The decision of the Commission shall be final unless within ten (10) days following receipt of such notice by the employee organization either the City Manager or the employee organization files a written protest with the Clerk of the Commission. The matter shall thereupon be resolved by advisory arbitration as set forth in paragraph F of this section: provided however, that upon the agreement of the employee organization and the vote of a majority of the Commission, all or any part of such arbitration may be authorized as final and binding on the parties.

F. The City and the Employee Organization may mutually agree upon an arbitrator, or a joint letter requesting Federal Mediation and Conciliation Service to submit the names of five (5) arbitrators will be signed and mailed by the City and the Employee Organization. Upon receipt of such names, the City and the Employee Organization shall alternately cross off one name until one name remains, that person being selected as the arbitrator. A date for arbitration shall be set as soon as possible in accordance with the wishes of the City and the Employee Organization and the availability of the arbitrator. Both the City and the Employee Organization shall share equally the expenses and fees of the arbitrator and other expenses incident to the arbitration hearing.

C. Mediation and Fact-Finding

1. Underlying Principles and Theories

PICKETS AT CITY HALL, REPORT AND RECOMMENDATIONS OF THE TWENTIETH CENTURY FUND TASK FORCE ON LABOR DISPUTES IN PUBLIC EMPLOYMENT 21-24 (1970)†

Mediation

The function of mediation, as it works for an agreement that the negotiators could not find themselves, is to maintain communication between the parties, who may believe they have said

---

everything they have to say and done everything they are able to do; to inject a neutral presence into what, because of the impasse, has become an adversary situation; to strip away the non-essential matters and frame the core issues in dispute; and to propose suggestions for settlement.

Mediation works best when it is jointly sought by the disagreeing parties. Each is acknowledging that outside help may be useful, a posture that launches the mediation effort under the most favorable auspices. But if one, or both, of the parties refuse to invite mediation, it should be initiated anyway, preferably by the labor agency we recommend be established.

Mediation has no power to compel. It is fruitful only through logic and persuasion. The parties may freely accept or reject a mediator's suggestions if he chooses to make them; they abdicate none of their sovereignty. Mediation has, nevertheless, been the most effective process for the resolution of labor disputes. Only if it is employed to its limit and fails should other processes be invoked.

The quality of the mediator, his experience and skills, may mean the difference between success and failure. The parties must believe that he has no bias against them. He must have a broad knowledge of labor relations, knowing all of the formulas that have been used to settle issues such as the one he confronts, and he must be able to articulate them. He should be inventive in producing new formulas if the situation requires. Above all he must be patient and persevering in his effort to bring the alienated parties into agreement, meanwhile keeping their confidence.

A cadre of professional mediators with experience in the private sector is attached to the Federal Conciliation and Mediation Service, to various state agencies and to some local governments. In some disputes nonprofessionals who seem to have the necessary qualities are enlisted as mediators. In communities which do not have mediation resources, access to an established mediation service should be established, or such a service of their own should be created. It will have a central role in labor relations policy.

But while much private sector mediation expertness is readily transferable to use in public employment disputes, working with government as a party in negotiations and with a union proscribed from striking requires special techniques that must, in many instances, still be acquired. One example of a problem a mediator is likely to face in the public sector is the question of who, on behalf of the employer, can make and effectuate a final decision on disputed issues. Those who represent government in the negotiations may not have such authority. The mediator may have to work to persuade them, then seek and find the true locus of authority—governor, mayor, legislature, council or board—and persuade still further. In any agency, department or subdivision of government, that locus can vary. As the mediator in the private sector must operate with an awareness that the position taken by union representatives in the negotiations is influenced by whether or not they think their membership will ratify any agreement reached, the public sector mediator must be aware that not only is this same factor present but there is also the need for ratification on the employer side at a higher authority level than is often represented in the negotiations.

Fact-Finding

If mediation should fail to achieve agreement in a dispute, there should follow, as a link in a chain, the process of fact-finding. It will be best initiated through appointive action by the independent agency, the establishment of which we have recommended. If such an agency does not exist, it should be initiated by a high level public official who has had no involvement in the dispute.

Fact-finding has been most effective in both the private and public sector where it has been conducted by an individual or by a panel (usually three in number) qualified as impartial, judicious-minded experts in labor relations whose standing and character attest to their competence and lack of bias. Such men start their work with the advantage of being acceptable to the parties in dispute.

The degree of formality in fact-finding proceedings is usually determined by the fact-finders themselves, depending on what manner appears most promising. In any event, full opportunity will be provided for both the disputing parties to make their case. This may include the testimony of witnesses, the submission of documents and statistics, the presentation of briefs, arguments and rebuttals. The fact-finders may want information beyond that presented and may undertake their own research and call witnesses on their own motion. Their first objective is to establish the true facts which, in the normal dispute, are inevitably in controversy.

Once the sifting and winnowing have disclosed the true facts to the panel's satisfaction—as opposed to what the parties may have alleged during negotiations—the fact-finders will frequently essay a mediatory role. They will try to disabuse one or the other or both parties of false notions or assertions and try to get the parties themselves to agree on settlement terms. In many instances the fact-finding process has succeeded at this point in bringing the disputants into agreement and this has completed its work.

Should the dispute still persist after such an effort, it is incumbent upon the panel to exercise its own judgment as to what the settlement terms should be.

A multiplicity of considerations are to be taken into account and weighed as the fact-finders formulate their conclusions. If disputes involve labor costs, as most do, the panel will have heard or studied cost of living figures, rates paid by other employers for comparable work, the historical trend of wage adjustments for the instant employees, non-wage benefit levels and, among much other data, the employer's ability or inability to meet union demands.

Virtually all of the matters that come under fact-finders' scrutiny in a private industry dispute will be within the purview of a panel sitting on a government employee case. But if labor costs are involved, the fact-finders in public employment will most likely have to be concerned with another factor indigenous to public employment: where and how the incidence of increased labor costs will fall. Will it require the imposition of new or higher taxes? Will it have to be paid by curtailing some public service not involved in the case before the panel? Will an upward wage adjustment deprive some other group of public employees who are bound under the same limited budget appropriation of a deserved increase?

Fair-minded and conscientious men, assuming the responsibility of making a judgment on behalf of the whole community, which includes employees, government-as-employer and the public at large, will ponder these implications. For their conclusions to be as fair as humanly possible to all interests concerned, they will have to find some balance between the competing needs and equities.

When it has formulated the terms it will endorse, the panel may decide it will be most effective by not immediately making them public but communicating them privately to the parties. When this technique is followed, a revival of direct negotiations often occurs. The disputants learn the fact-finders' conclusions and have some sense of the public pressure they will be under to accept them when the conclusions of the impartial body that has made a careful study of the issues become widely known.

In this advanced stage of resumed negotiations, focused on the fact-finders' decision, concessions by one or the other or both sides may be offered and agreement may be reached. Or willingly or reluctantly, they may submit to the panel's terms as being the best possible way out of their dispute.

If, however, the time allotted for such further negotiations does not bring results, the fact-finders must make their conclusions public and hope that public opinion will make the unwilling party or parties accept them.

SIMKIN, FACT-FINDING: ITS VALUES AND LIMITATIONS, in ARBITRATION AND THE EXPANDING ROLE OF NEUTRALS, PROCEEDINGS OF THE TWENTY-THIRD ANNUAL MEETING OF THE NATIONAL ACADEMY OF ARBITRATORS 165-72 (G. Somers ed. 1970)†

The principal theme of this paper is that the words—fact-finding—should be substantially eliminated from the labor relations vocabulary or, more accurately, that they should be relegated to more limited usefulness. This has happened already in the private sector. Some day—but not soon—I predict it will also occur in the public sector.

The words fact-finding—conjure up notions of preciseness, of objectivity, of virtue. They even have a godlike quality. Who can disagree with facts? In contrast, the word—mediation—that I do espouse, tends to have an aura of compromise, of slipperiness, of connivance and of furtiveness. Since these are frequent impressions, why prefer the vulgar to the sublime?

There is a problem of semantics. Close examination of the actual functioning of Fact-Finding Boards and of mediators or of Mediation Boards shows that the labels are quite secondary. The abilities and proclivities of the individuals named to those Boards and—more important—the reactions of the parties to the process determine what really happens. Fact-finders do or do not mediate. Some fact-finders who mediate find no facts. Persons appointed as mediators frequently do not mediate in any meaningful way but may announce some real or alleged facts and conclusions.
. . .

Fact-Finding Without Recommendations

The basic notion about this type of fact-finding is that somebody does not know the real facts and that establishment and proclamation of the facts will somehow assist in settlement.

Who is that somebody who is ignorant of the facts? Is it the parties—the general public—or the public opinion makers?

Experienced negotiators will seldom be surprised or influenced very much by the results of such fact-finding.

In a limited number of situations, publications of unpleasant facts may bring pressure on the negotiators by their constitu-

---

† Reprinted by permission of The Bureau of National Affairs, Inc.

encies. Facts that are damaging to a union, published during a long strike, may result in diminished strike morale and more willingness of employees to compromise. Or, publicized facts detrimental to a company position may bring pressure on the company negotiators from the Board of Directors. However, these results are infrequent for a simple reason. Most labor disputes are so complicated that a mere portrayal of facts does not provide a "handle" for action or even suggest clear directional signals towards a likely settlement area.

Publication of facts will be of some minor interest to the general public but will not usually provide an adequate basis for translation into an informed opinion about the total dispute.

The opinion makers (columnists, editorial writers, etc.) may welcome such a report. They will make fewer goofs of factual content and have a new reason for writing something. But the facts will seldom change any preconceived ideas they may have already expressed.

On a few occasions, fact-finders not empowered to make recommendations on the issues have indulged in assessing blame on one of the parties. This device seldom accomplishes anything. It is much more likely to exacerbate the dispute.

In short, fact-finding without recommendations is likely to be an exercise in futility.

These observations may require modification in some current public employee disputes. Bargainers in the public sector sometimes lack some of the sophistication that is more typical in the private sector. Moreover, since the taxpayers are the employers, however far removed from the bargaining table, their appraisal of facts can assume more significance than is the case in a private dispute.

There is a potential and sometimes utilized variety of this general type of fact-finding that is seldom discussed. It is the use of impartial technicians—long in advance of negotiations—to work with the parties to develop pertinent background facts on such issues as pensions and insurance.

Fact-Finding with Recommendations

When fact-finders are given the responsibility to make specific recommendations on the issues in dispute, the process becomes very familiar to an arbitrator. . . . It is arbitration with two major points to distinguish it from grievance arbitration. (1) Recommendations are not final and binding decisions. Either or both parties can reject. (2) The recommendations do not develop out of a contractual framework. They are legislative value judgments. Recommendations are not facts, nor are they based exclusively or even primarily on facts.

Many of you will disagree honestly with the last statement. One concept of this type of fact-finding is that the recommendations flow almost automatically out of the facts. In my considered opinion, this notion has little or no validity. . . .

In arms length fact-finding, where is the fact-finder to find a basis for his value judgments? In the last analysis, all he can do is to exercise his best intellectual powers and search his own soul. He has no adequate opportunity to gauge acceptability by the parties. No hearings can ever meet that need adequately.

This is especially true because the parties have known that recommendations will be forthcoming. During the interval between the appointment of the fact-finder and the issuance of his report, any bargaining that may have occurred is almost certain to stop. All efforts of the parties have been directed to getting the best possible set of recommendations. Nor is it an adequate refuge to conclude—as is sometimes the case—that the exposure of the parties to the fact-finder so frightens them that they will reach agreement to avoid recommendations.

We come now to the receipt of the recommendations. Either or both parties can say: "No." If that is not the situation, it is de facto arbitration and should be so labeled. If a "No" is voiced, the dispute has not been settled. The fact-finder has been rebuffed and usually he has no place to go. If he reacts defensively as he is likely to do, the dispute may be exacerbated. What has been a two-way dispute up to that point may become a three-way controversy. . . .

Where fact-finding has been successful, I would suggest—but cannot prove—that the fact-finder has mediated—deliberately, instructively or surreptitiously. When fact-finding without mediation has succeeded in the public sector, I would suspect that it is a transitory phenomenon. Until recently and even now in some jurisdictions, public employees have been so far behind that fact-finders have a broad target range. I would predict that the range will narrow in the years immediately ahead of us.

What do I mean by mediation? Time does not permit analysis of the remarkably wide spectrum of mediation activity—things that a mediator can do—or not do. At one end, the spectrum begins by a decision not to intervene at all—to provide no third party assistance. At the other end of the band, the mediator can issue public recommendations. A major principle is to maximize bargaining and minimize the role of the mediator—to exercise enough patience to let bargaining work. But the mediator must also be able and willing to "grasp the nettle"—to recognize when patience is not a virtue and to act accordingly. Most mediation decisions are decisions as to strategy and timing —not decisions on the specific issues.

In the hands of a skilled mediator, facts are potent tools. It is seldom that publication of facts is either necessary or desirable. But they can be most useful in hard-hitting deflation of extreme positions. This is accomplished in separate head-to-head conferences or meetings, absent the embarrassment of the other side's presence and certainly not in the press. Public reference to the facts, if required at all, comes after a settlement to help save face.

The mediator has unusual opportunities to explore a wide variety of solutions—to "try them on for size." Thus, he acquires a strong intuitive sense, if not the certainty, of the vital element of acceptability.

Package recommendations are a last resort device, to be utilized only if all else fails and maybe not issued even then. The mediator is never committed to use of that device and he will steadfastly refuse to take such action unless he is convinced or has a strong hunch that it may be productive.

2. Problem Areas—Mediation

W. SIMKIN, MEDIATION AND THE DYNAMICS OF COLLECTIVE BARGAINING 350-51 (1971)†

Separate Mediation Agency?

At the state level, it has been noted that PERB and OCB in New York and PERC in New Jersey have been established separate and apart from the mediation agencies for private disputes. In most other states, public disputes are handled by the same agency that mediates private disputes. In the Federal Government, consideration was given to establishment of a separate federal disputes mediation agency, but Executive Order 11491 reflects a decision to assign this work to the agency that handles private disputes (the FMCS). What are the pros and cons of these two courses of action?

There are major advantages to the single-agency approach. Economy of operation is one that is almost self-evident. Even the largest mediation agencies are small. Administrative costs of two separate agencies would be greater, and a single agency is likely to attract more competent leadership than two smaller ones. Moreover, mediators usually function best when they are sta-

---

† Reprinted by permission of The Bureau of National Affairs, Inc.

tioned near the source of a dispute, and a larger agency can maintain offices in more cities. There is more flexibility of case assignment in each area and to adjacent areas if there is more than one mediator at a regular station.

It might be argued that the differences between public sector and private sector mediation demand specialization and therefore separate agencies. Granted that differences exist, the similarities are even more pronounced. Required mediation skills are essentially the same. It is much easier and quicker to acquaint a skilled mediator with the peculiar features of public disputes than to make a competent mediator out of an individual who happens to have knowledge of the special features of government employment but lacks mediation experience. A larger agency can do a much better job than a small one in training new mediators and in the continuous process of keeping experienced mediators up to date on changes in collective bargaining practices.

It might also be argued that mediators who work in the private sector will seek to transplant unwanted private practices and contract clauses into government agency contracts. Admittedly this is a danger. However, it is equally clear that there are some advantages to cross-fertilization. Moreover, the dangers will not be eliminated by having two separate mediation staffs. The unions (and agency management less frequently) will attempt to inject private sector experience in any case whenever it is to their advantage. The mediator who knows both the advantages and disadvantages of private sector practice is best able to know whether it should be transplanted, modified, or disregarded in a public sector dispute.

On balance, the advantages of a single agency for mediation of public and private disputes are overwhelming—if the agency restricts itself primarily to mediation.

NOTES

1. For a different view, see Zack, *Improving Mediation and Fact Finding in the Public Sector*, 21 LAB. L.J. 264 (1970).

2. Should there be separate mediation agencies to deal with local, state and federal public employee disputes, respectively? The FMCS avoids involvement in local and state public sector bargaining disputes except in instances where no other mediation assistance is available and both parties have requested the aid of FMCS mediators. Such a request is then considered and approved in Washington, D.C. if it is determined that a bargaining impasse has developed after genuine good faith bargaining.

3. In *Collective Bargaining in State and Local Government,* FINAL REPORT OF THE GREAT LAKES ASSEMBLY, East Lansing, Michigan (1973), the following recommendations were made by the seventy-five participants representing public employers, public employee unions, impartials, academicians and government officials:

> Public sector collective bargaining is relatively new. Therefore, the availability and use of skilled mediators provided by a state agency is even more important than in the private sector. Mediation should be available at the request of either party or at the initiation of the administrative agency. In situations in which mediation has not succeeded in resolving disputes, fact-finding procedures should be available, upon the request of either party. Care should be taken to keep fact-finding from becoming a routine procedure and to insure that it is utilized only after *bona fide* collective bargaining assisted by mediation has failed to resolve the dispute. Otherwise, fact-finding could become automatic and impede the collective bargaining process.

4. Some commentators have argued that the availability of fact-finding impairs the effectiveness of mediation and impedes the bargaining process. *See, e.g.,* Zack, *Impasses, Strikes, and Resolutions,* in PUBLIC WORKERS AND PUBLIC UNIONS 101 (S. Zagoria ed. 1972). For other views, see A. Anderson, *The Use of Fact-Finding in Dispute Settlement,* and Saxton, *The Employers View,* in ARBITRATION AND SOCIAL CHANGE, PROCEEDINGS OF THE TWENTY-SECOND ANNUAL MEETING OF THE NATIONAL ACADEMY OF ARBITRATORS 107, 127 (G. Somers ed. 1970).

5. Compare the following statutory methods for instituting fact-finding and their relationship to any prior mediation stage.

9 NEV. REV. STAT. §§ 288.190-288.200:

> 288.190. Negotiation; mediation. The parties shall promptly commence negotiations. During the course of negotiations the parties may mutually agree to utilize the services of a mediator to assist them in resolving their dispute.
>
> 288.200. Submission of dispute to factfinder: Selection, compensation, duties of factfinder; effect of findings, recommendations; criteria for recommendations, awards.
>
> 1. If by March 1, the parties have not reached agreement, either party, at any time up to April 1, may submit the dispute to an impartial factfinder for his findings and recommendations. These findings and recommendations are

not binding on the parties except as provided in subsections 6 and 7.

2. If the parties are unable to agree on an impartial factfinder within 5 days either party may request from the American Arbitration Association a list of seven potential factfinders. The parties shall select their factfinder from this list by alternately striking one name until the name of only one factfinder remains, who will be the factfinder to hear the dispute in question. The employee organization shall strike the first name.

26 ME. REV. STAT. ANN. § 965 (Supp. 1972)

2. *Mediation.* Mediation procedures shall be followed whenever the parties jointly agree to use such services.

3. *Fact-finding.* If the parties, either with or without the services of a mediator, are unable to effect a settlement of their controversy, they may jointly agree either to call upon the Maine Board of Arbitration and Conciliation for factfinding services with recommendations or to pursue some other mutually acceptable fact-finding procedure.

If the parties do not jointly agree to call upon the Maine Board of Arbitration and Conciliation or to pursue some other procedure, either party to the controversy may request the commissioner to assign a fact-finding board. If so requested, the commissioner shall appoint a fact-finding board, ordinarily of 3 members, in accordance with rules and procedures prescribed by the commissioner for making such appointment. The fact-finding board shall be appointed from a list maintained by the commissioner and drawn up after consultation with representatives of state and local government administrators, agencies with industrial relations and personnel functions and representatives of employee organizations and of employers. Any person who has actively participated as the mediator in the immediate proceedings for which fact-finding has been called shall not sit on that fact-finding board.

21 VT. STAT. ANN. § 1707 (Supp. 1972)

Sec. 1707.   Impasse procedure.

(a)   Mediation: If a public employer and its employees are unable to arrive at a satisfactory agreement through collective bargaining after a reasonable period of time, but not less than sixty days, either party may petition the commissioner of labor and industry to appoint a mediator. The commissioner shall thereupon appoint a mediator, who shall communicate with the employer and the employees or their representatives and endeavor by mediation to obtain an amicable settlement.

The mediator shall be a person of high standing in no way actively connected with labor or industry.

(b)   Fact finding, recommendations: If mediation fails after a reasonable period of time, but not less than fifteen days after the appointment of a mediator, either party may by a demand in writing furnished to the other party, personally or by certified mail, require that any and all unresolved issues be submitted to a fact-finding board. . . .

See also Wis. Stat. Ann. § 111.70 (4) (c) (1) and (3a), and 43 Conn. Gen. Stat. Ann. ch. 113 § 7-473 (a) - (b), set forth in full in the *Statutory Appendix.*

3.   Problem Areas—Fact-Finding

a.   Make-up of the Panel

REPORT TO GOVERNOR GEORGE ROMNEY BY THE MICHIGAN ADVISORY COMMITTEE ON PUBLIC EMPLOYEE RELATIONS (1966)

The "fact-finding" function (which should include the making of recommendations) should be carried out through the instrumentality of a Public Employment Relations Panel, the members of which should be appointed by the Governor to serve for terms of two years. There should be twelve members of the Panel, one of whom should be designated as Chairman. The members of the Panel should be persons of recognized stature, competence, and fairness. The Governor should be authorized to enlarge the membership of the Panel, ad hoc, to the extent necessary. The Panel, for its initial two years of operation, should be attached to the executive offices of the Governor. Members of the Panel should serve as needed and be reimbursed for their expenses and compensated on a per diem basis. An Executive Secretary should be provided to assist in coordinating the operations of the Panel.

Upon the certification of the SLMB [State Labor Mediation Board] of an unsettled dispute to the Panel, the Chairman (or, in his absence a Vice-Chairman designated by him) should assign the matter to one or more members of the Panel to carry out the functions of the Panel. . . .

Several reasons support the establishment of the suggested Panel procedure, as distinguished from retaining the fact-finding function in the SLMB or its designees, or providing for the appointment of fact finders on a case by case basis by the Governor.

The designation of a Panel by the Governor would enhance the prestige and increase the effectiveness of the fact finders. Advance designation of the members of the Panel, to serve for a stipulated period of time, would accomplish the desirable objective of reducing involvement and pressures upon the Governor in particular disputes. Moreover, it could reasonably be expected that establishment of the Panel would help assure the availability of competent persons to serve the fact-finding function, build up a body of experience which would be useful in view of the comparatively unique aspects of public employee relations, and tend toward some consistency of approach. . . .

NOTES

1. Are these recommendations sound? What are the various alternative methods of selecting the fact-finder (s)? The Vermont statute provides (Vt. Stat. Ann. § 1707 (b) (Supp. 1972)):

The fact-finding board shall consist of three members. Each party shall appoint one member of the board and the members so appointed shall elect the third member who shall be chairman of the board. If the two members of the board shall fail to select the third member within seven days after their appointment, the commissioner of labor and industry upon notice in writing by either party, shall thereupon appoint the third member unless the parties by agreement in writing approve a different method of selection.

2. Is access to fact-finding without an evaluation of prior negotiation efforts undesirable? The Wisconsin and Connecticut statutes provide for a review of prior negotiations to determine whether a genuine impasse has been reached. If there should be such review, should it be by the fact-finder or by the agency administering the basic collective bargaining law? See McKelvey, *Fact-Finding in Public Employment Disputes: Promise or Illusion?*, 22 Ind. & Lab. Rel. Rev. 528, 535 (1969), suggesting that in those two states fact-finding has not been as addictive as in New York where the statute does not provide for such review. *But see* Yaffe and Goldblatt, *Factfinding in Public Employment in New York State: More Promise Than Illusion,* ILR Paperback No. 10, 25 (1971).

3. Under the New York City OCB procedures the OCB submits a list of seven names from its register of impasse panel members, and each party informs the Director of its preferences, which are respected to the extent there is agreement. The other members are designated by the Director. *See* New York City Col-

lective Bargaining Law, § 1173.7.0 (c) , set forth in *Statutory Appendix.*

b. Functions of the Fact-Finder

DOERING, IMPASSE ISSUES IN TEACHER DISPUTES SUBMITTED TO FACT FINDING IN NEW YORK, 27 Arb. J. 1, 12-16 (March 1972)†

What . . . are the criteria upon which fact finders base their recommendations? There seem to be two major considerations involved, and one or both may be operative in any one situation. The standards of "acceptability" (what the parties will agree to) and of "equity" (the requirements of the fact finder's notions of fairness and good labor relations) appear to be determinative.

The weighting of these criteria will depend to some extent upon the fact finder's view of his own role: whether he sees his primary function as making proposals which will produce a settlement, or as a neutral third party whose major role is to make public the facts of the dispute and try to suggest an "equitable" (not merely "acceptable") resolution of issues. Actually both of these functions are part of the fact finder's role, and they need not necessarily be conflicting. If, however, they are not entirely compatible, the fact finder must choose which criterion to modify in light of the other.

Acceptability

"Acceptability" as an abstract criterion by which to decide the issues in dispute is fairly self evident—"to the lion shall go the lion's share." It means convincing the parties that the recommendations represent the best bargain they could have gotten based upon the power balance between them in free collective bargaining if stoppages were not illegal.

While the concept of "acceptability" is easily defined in the abstract, specific definition of the "acceptable" solution for any set of circumstances is often difficult. The neutral party must get the sense of the situation from the parties themselves and from that try to gauge the area of possible settlement. In addition to correctly judging what the area of settlement is, he must convince the parties that his interpretation is accurate and that the recommendations based upon it represent the best they will be able to get.

Sometimes the problem of persuasion becomes part of the criterion itself. A recalcitrant individual on one of the negotiating teams may have to be taken into consideration in defining the area of settlement, and the criterion of "acceptability" may end

---

† Reprinted by permission of The American Arbitration Association, Inc.

up relating as much to personalities and emotions around the bargaining table as to the facts in the case. The situation is peculiar to public sector bargaining. In a private sector strike situation, the personalities and rhetoric of the negotiators soon give way to a test of economic strength. In public employment, impasse procedures are designed to avoid such tests, and it is more difficult to call a bluff. Personalities and emotions creep into the process and cannot be ignored if settlement is the object. Another factor which may make the neutral person's job more difficult is the fact that in the public sector there are politics on both sides of the table. Management as well as union spokesmen are elected officials.

Although some pressure can be brought to bear through publication of the fact finder's report, research indicated that attempts to arouse public interest have had only minimal effects on the actual settlement of the dispute. Thus the fact finder looking for a settlement is pretty well limited to the facts, both economic and political, and the personalities at the table.

Equity

In addition to his appraisal of acceptability, the fact finder usually arrives at some notion of the "equity" involved before making his recommendations. The term equity here denotes considerations by the neutral party which are not influenced by the power balance between the parties, but by the arguments put forward and such abstract standards of justice as the fact finder may have.

From the presentations made by the parties the fact finder usually obtains several indications as to the equity of their proposals. Perhaps the most useful of these indicators are past practice within the district, and present practice in other neighboring and/or similar districts, with emphasis usually on the latter. Past practice within the district, except where a district has been a leader in a certain field, is usually de-emphasized because it is no longer current. Furthermore, the practices may be in dispute. Comparison with similar and neighboring districts has the advantage of being both an outside standard and a current one.

Through comparisons with neighboring and similar districts the fact finder can ascertain the level of settlements (or at least the relative positions of the parties if bargaining is incomplete) in other districts faced with the same geography, similar tax problems and the same increases in the cost of living. From this the fact finder gains an idea of the "going rate" and also of the competitive recruiting salaries. If neighboring districts are dissimilar in terms of size or tax-base, the fact finder may modify or weight the criterion of comparability accordingly.

In addition to comparability, past practice, and other arguments presented by the parties, the fact finder himself has professional standards from his training and experience in labor relations which may influence his findings. Certain issues may be handled from the point of view of good labor relations rather than on a basis of comparability, past practice, or even acceptability.

The Weighting of the Criteria

Acceptability and equity are most likely to conflict when acceptability is less dependent on economics, and more a matter of personalities or politics. If agreement is to be achieved, such needs and individuals must be accommodated, sometimes at the expense of equity. Where acceptability is measured in economic terms it usually produces contracts similar to those negotiated in comparable districts if only because those districts also had to find acceptable solutions.

In mediation, which precedes fact finding, settlements (if they are achieved) are achieved on the basis of acceptability. If the mediator is successful in convincing the parties of his impression of the "acceptable" solution, there is no need to go on to fact finding. The disputes most likely to be carried further are those in which acceptability depends upon the personalities at the bargaining table, or on political rather than economic factors; in these disputes there is the greatest conflict between acceptability and equity and one party will undoubtedly feel aggrieved. One or both of the parties may opt for fact finding in hopes of finding someone with a different appraisal of acceptability, or someone who will modify what has already been identified as the "acceptable solution" in light of some higher equity. That is, teachers sometimes feel that if a position is morally right and equitable it should prevail even if the power balance in the community would not support such a position. They occasionally go to fact finding in the hope that the fact finder will lend his support to their position.

Fact finding gives the parties a second neutral interpretation of the "acceptable solution" and often an opinion of the equity as well. Having thus identified acceptability and equity as the major criteria, and having suggested that acceptability may be the more important since fact finding is a dispute settlement procedure, it would be interesting to know with what accuracy fact finders judge the area of settlement. If fact finders cannot be reasonably sure of correctly assessing acceptability, it would suggest that they ought not to place inordinate weight on this criterion, or that they should at least give equity the benefit of the doubt in situations where they perceive a conflict between the two criteria.

GOULD, PUBLIC EMPLOYMENT: MEDIATION, FACT-FINDING AND ARBITRATION, 55 Am. Bar Ass'n J. 835, 837-38 (1969)†

Is the fact finder's position . . . that of a judge or arbitrator, who makes a determination predicated upon purely objective criteria? Or is he more akin to the mediator, whose function is to be acceptable to the parties so that he may bring them together on an amicable basis? It is easy to see that the weight given to either of these functions may depend on the statutory timetable or lack of one.

Chairman Robert Howlett of the Michigan Labor Mediation Board has recently expressed his board's hostility toward mediation efforts by fact finders. . . .

In my judgment, the fact-finding process necessarily partakes of both the mediatory and judicial disciplines. While the process is a fluid one about which the drawing of hard and fast lines is still an audacious act, I am convinced that Chairman Howlett's analogy to "in chambers" settlements is a good one. For it seems difficult for the fact finder to introduce himself as a mediator, gain the parties' confidence and trust and then—having failed to bring them together without recommendations—to put on his judicial robes and hear formal testimony on the issues in dispute. The parties are bound to feel confused and betrayed by this role switching, which can result in a "judge's" reliance on information obtained through informal and frank off-the-record mediation sessions.

On the other hand, the skillful fact finder may be able to find a stage of the proceeding when, in his opinion, a settlement is near and when it is therefore propitious to adjourn the hearing for a limited period of time. Sometimes the opportunity is presented through the appearance of misunderstandings by one side of the other's position. An attempt to obtain clarification concerning the differences between the parties may give the fact finder the chance to don his mediator's hat. But, at this "in chambers" stage—as distinguished from the beginning of the hearing—the parties should have acquired some measure of respect for and confidence in the fact finder. If not, his request to adjourn for clarification or for anything else will be met with a refusal or lack of enthusiasm.

However, even when the fact finder is proceeding down the "in chambers" route, the parties are very often inclined to hold

---

† Reprinted by permission of the American Bar Association.

back, anticipating the possible resumption of formal hearings. The fact finder must convince the parties that he will keep the two procedures separate in his own mind. It is an understatement to note that this is not always the easiest feat to carry off.

HOWLETT, COMMENT, in ARBITRATION AND THE EXPANDING ROLE OF NEUTRALS, PROCEEDINGS OF THE TWENTY-THIRD ANNUAL MEETING OF THE NATIONAL ACADEMY OF ARBITRATORS 175, 179-80 (G. Somers ed. 1970)†

We are convinced, however, that if there has been effective mediation, the role of the fact-finder is primarily judicial. If the mediator has performed his role with excellence, a second mediator is generally not helpful. In our 1970 fact-finders' education seminar, two lawyers representing the Michigan Education Association and the Michigan Federation of Teachers, a lawyer representing school districts, and the executive secretary of the Michigan Association of School Boards were in accord that the role of a fact-finder should be judicial and not mediatory. As one lawyer said: "Fact-finding should not be super mediation. If it is used by the fact-finder to club a settlement, the value of the process will be destroyed."

After our initial wandering in the wilderness, we announced that we will not appoint fact-finders until the mediator assigned to the negotiations certifies that mediation has been exhausted and that every effort has been made to narrow the issues to those two or three key items which may make the difference between settlement and failure. Failure may result in a strike. The "strike" is a factor in settlement, as public employees retain the power to strike, even though they do not have that privilege. We do not authorize a fact-finder to return to the dispute after the issuance of his report. We require that our mediators re-enter each case after the fact-finding report if the report is not accepted immediately. Reports have been instrumental in mediated settlements, even though the fact-finder's report was not, per se, accepted.

The debate over whether to combine mediation and fact-finding appears to arise principally from those jurisdictions that do not have an established, competent mediation staff, as we do have in Michigan. I can understand a combination of mediation and fact-finding in those states that use ad hoc mediation and ad hoc fact-finding, with the same person performing both services. In Michigan, ad hoc mediation is seldom needed.

---

† Reprinted by permission of The Bureau of National Affairs, Inc.

Nor have we found that our fact-finders react defensively if employer and union do not accept their recommendations. Perhaps this is because our fact-finders do not return to the bargaining scene, but are succeeded by a mediator. My knowledge of the ability and balance of our fact-finders, however, leads me to conclude that even though these men should engage in post-fact-finding mediation, few of them would react defensively or be unduly concerned at the failure of employer and union to accept their recommendations. Possibly Michigan fact-finders are more thick-skinned than fact-finders in other states, but I doubt it. Contacts with my "opposite numbers" in other states lead me to conclude that they, too, have able fact-finders who perform a significant role in resolving impasses and who are neither prima donnas nor live in a world of fantasy in which they believe that their dictates will, ipso facto, be accepted.

Bill Simkin opines that the fact-finder "has no adequate opportunity to gauge acceptability by the parties." Our experience denies the validity of this criticism *if the fact-finder is competent.* He has greater flexibility than the arbitrator, for he may meet with the parties separately because—in spite of our jaundiced view of mediation by fact-finders—fact-finders do engage in the "search for a solution." A fact-finder, unlike an arbitrator, may discuss the case with each party separately. The arbitrator, who renders a "legal" and binding solution, may not "trim." The fact-finder may, because his primary task is to find *an* equitable —not necessarily *the most* equitable—settlement.

NOTES

1. *See also* A. Anderson, *Strikes and Impasse Resolution,* 67 MICH. L. REV. 943, 964-66 (1969) ; Zack, *Impasses, Strikes and Resolutions,* in PUBLIC WORKERS AND PUBLIC UNIONS 101, 114 (S. Zagoria ed. 1972) .

2. Should parties be required to submit to the fact-finder a jointly agreed upon statement of the issues? Should the fact-finder commence the hearing as if nothing had gone on before or should he regard the last offer of a party as its minimum position?

c. Procedure and Practice

The states are laboratories for experimentation with the fact-finding process. Variations exist as to a variety of incidentals of procedure including (1) who may invoke the process (whether a party or only the public labor relations law administrative agency) , (2) how the tribunal is chosen, (3) who pays for its services, (4) time limitations on its functioning, (5) whether its procedures are to be public or private, (6) how "evidence" is to be presented, (7) which party is required to proceed first at the hearing, (8) what is the "burden of proof," if any, and where does it rest, (9) whether an official record of the "hearing" is to be taken, and, if so, who pays for it, (10) whether the tribunal is restricted to that record as the basis for its conclusions of fact, and (11) whether the tribunal's report and recommendations are to be made public. Differences in approach also exist, as must be apparent at this point, with respect to the question whether there is a "next step" (beyond additional bargaining) after the tribunal issues its report.

4. Appraisal of Experience

DISPUTE SETTLEMENT IN THE PUBLIC SECTOR: THE STATE-OF-THE-ART, REPORT SUBMITTED TO THE U.S. DEP'T OF LABOR, DIVISION OF PUBLIC EMPLOYEE LABOR RELATIONS 59-60 (T. Gilroy & A. Sinicropi eds. 1971)

The effectiveness of factfinding is very difficult to measure. As stated earlier, the process is fluid, often drifting from "mediation" to "arbitration." Also, factfinding usually is saddled with the tougher cases which mediation did not resolve. Moreover, some factfinding is merely reporting without recommendations and factfinding without recommendations is said to be about "as useful as a martini without gin."

Taking note of the misunderstanding and apprehensions concerning factfinding it is not surprising to learn that there has been no accurate manner to standardize the process for review and analysis. McKelvey summarized the assessments made through 1968 and the criteria used to make those appraisals, but she cautioned that such limited findings may only be "illusions." Nevertheless, some data on factfinding have become available and are worthy of note.

The figures most often cited as the percentage of cases going to factfinding that are resolved is ninety percent. It is estimated that sixty to seventy percent of the cases going to factfinding are recorded as having the factfinder's recommendations serve as a basis for settling the dispute. However, at the present time there is no way to determine how close to the recommendations the settlement comes. Stern cites an example of a case considered settled on the basis of a factfinder's recommendations where the actual agreement gave the union only one-third of what the factfinder had recommended.

The use of mediation techniques in factfinding further clouds any accurate assessment of the factfinding process. New York and New Jersey encourage factfinders to mediate and both states report that between twenty-five and thirty percent of all cases going to factfinding are resolved through mediation efforts. Yaffe and Goldblatt report that nearly eighty percent of factfinders in New York engage in mediation. The same study shows that where the factfinder engaged in mediation and where recommendations were subsequently issued, seventy-four percent of such recommendations served as a basis for settlement as against fifty-eight percent of the recommendations for cases where the factfinder did not engage in mediation. Gould points out that the participants themselves prefer the factfinder to act as a mediator and indicates that this most often does occur, even in Michigan where the policy is to separate the roles of the mediator and the factfinder.

Those who support factfinding do so with reservations. Zack states while factfinding works, it offers the risk of "perpetually extending procedures . . . so that good faith bargaining occurs (only) at the last stages, if at all." McKelvey fears that "factfinding may become, as it has under the Railway Labor Act, an addictive habit, the first and not the final step in collective negotiations." Davey and Simkin reluctantly accept it, claiming it to be the least desirable (most undesirable, excluding the strike) method of settling negotiation impasses.

On the positive side, most of the above writers and several others applaud the record of factfinding, particularly as it continues to offer a means in resolving disputes short of the strike and as it educates and assists in the maturation of the parties. However, all of the observations and comments are offered without sufficient evidence. . . .

The concluding note of the Yaffe and Goldblatt study perhaps best describes the status of factfinding: "Accordingly, the New York state experience seems to support the conclusion that factfinding offers more promise than illusion as a mechanism to facilitate the resolution of interest disputes in public sector negotiations."

NOTE

See generally Clark, *Compulsory Arbitration in Public Employment,* 37 PUBLIC EMPLOYEE REL. LIBRARY (1972) ; Stern, *The Wisconsin Public Employee Factfinding Procedure,* 20 IND. & LAB. REL. REV. 3 (Oct. 1966) ; Zack, *Improving Mediation and Fact-Finding in the Public Sector,* 21 LAB. L.J. 264 (1970) ; Zack, *Impasses, Strikes and Resolutions,* in PUBLIC WORKERS AND PUBLIC UNIONS 111 (S. Zagoria ed. 1972) ; A. Anderson, *The Use of Fact-Finding in Dispute Settlement,* in ARBITRATION AND SOCIAL CHANGE, PROCEEDINGS OF THE TWENTY-SECOND ANNUAL

MEETING OF THE N.A.A. 107 (G. Somers ed. 1970) ; McKelvey, *Fact Finding in Public Employment Disputes: Promise or Illusion?*, 22 IND. & LAB. REL. REV. 528 (1969) ; Yaffe & Goldblatt, *Factfinding in Public Employment in New York State: More Promise Than Illusion*, ILR Paperback No. 10 (1971) ; Doering, *Impasse Issues in Teacher Disputes Submitted to Fact Finding in New York*, 27 ARB. J. 1 (March 1972) ; Gould, *Public Employment: Mediation, Fact-Finding and Arbitration*, 55 AM. BAR ASS'N J. 835 (1969) ; Krinsky, *Public Employment Factfinding States*, 17 LAB. L.J. 532 (1966) ; Drotning & Lipsky, *The Outcome of Impasse Procedures in New York Schools Under the Taylor Law*, 26 ARB. J. 87 (1971).

D. The Problem of "Finality"

1. Alternative Procedures Following Mediation and Fact-Finding

The question of "finality" poses the following difficult issue: What mechanisms should be used to resolve interest disputes in the public sector in the event that negotiation, mediation and fact-finding have failed to produce a settlement? In the private sector, if an impasse is reached, the union has two options: (1) Accept the employer's last offer and settle; or (2) strike in an effort to gain leverage at the bargaining table.

Most public employees are legally forbidden to strike; therefore, the weapon of economic coercion is presumably removed as a bargaining stratagem. In the public sector, therefore, the issue arises as to whether there are any legitimate and viable substitutes for the strike weapon which can produce settlements of interest disputes on terms which are reasonable and are not necessarily limited to the public employer's last offer. In an effort to deal with this problem, numerous municipal, state and federal jurisdictions have adopted a variety of legislative schemes in an attempt to obtain finality in the resolution of public sector labor disputes.[4] The most popular among these legislative schemes may be summarized as follows:

(1) *Fact-finding Recommendations Backed by Show Cause Procedures*—This approach addresses the problem of how to make fact-finding with recommendations work well in providing a final solution to bargaining impasses. In a typical situation, only one party will accept the fact-finder's recommendations. The

---

[4] For an excellent general summary of the various legislative schemes, see *Dispute Settlement in The Public Sector: The State-of-the-Art*, Report Submitted to the U.S. Dep't of Labor, Div. of Public Empl. Lab. Rel. 29-46 (T. Gilroy & A. Sinicropi eds. 1971).

other party, for a number of reasons, rejects them in whole or in part. In the event that this occurs, some have suggested that the party rejecting the fact-finder's recommendations should be required in a quasi-judicial proceeding, to justify its failure to adopt the terms of the proposed settlement.[5] A modified version of this approach has been adopted in the Kansas statute, which provides for a show cause hearing before the governing body of the public employer. 6 KAN. STAT. ANN. § 75-4332 (d) (Supp. 1971) .

(2)   *Legislative Determination*—Under this approach, the failure of either party to accept a fact-finder's recommendations, in whole or in part, leads to hearings by the governing legislative body which thereafter decides the terms of the final settlement. This approach is best reflected in Section 209-3 (e) of the New York Taylor Act, which provides:

(e)   in the event that either the public employer or the employee organization does not accept in whole or part the recommendations of the fact-finding board, (i) the chief executive officer of the government involved shall, within ten days after receipt of the findings of fact and recommendations of the fact-finding board, submit to the legislative body of the government involved a copy of the findings of fact and recommendations of the fact-finding board, together with his recommendations for settling the dispute; (ii) the employee organization may submit to such legislative body its recommendations for settling the dispute; (iii) the legislative body or a duly authorized committee thereof shall forthwith conduct a public hearing at which the parties shall be required to explain their positions with respect to the report of the fact-finding board; and (iv) thereafter, the legislative body shall take such action as it deems to be in the public interest, including the interest of the public employees involved.

Under this procedure, it has been held that PERB cannot intercede in an interest dispute to compel a public employer to show cause why a fact-finder's recommendations should not be adopted. City of Albany v. Helsby, 317 N.Y.S.2d 955 (Sup. Ct. 1972) .

(3)   *Executive Declaration of Finality*—Nevada provides that prior to the submission of an interest dispute to fact-finding, either party may request that the governor exercise his emergency

---

[5] *See* Davey, *Dispute Settlement in Public Employment,* in DISPUTE SETTLEMENT IN THE PUBLIC SECTOR 12, 21 (T. Gilroy ed. 1972).

powers and declare that the recommendations shall be binding. Fact-finding then proceeds as usual, observing the criteria set out in the statute. *See* 9 NEV. REV. STAT. § 288.200 (1971). A somewhat different approach is taken under the New York City law, which makes the recommendations of an Impasse Panel final and binding as accepted or modified by the Board of Collective Bargaining. The details of the New York City scheme are set forth in the *Statutory Appendix* in § 1173-7.0c of the New York City Collective Bargaining Law.

(4) *Limited Right to Strike*—Several states, including Hawaii and Pennsylvania, have sought to resolve the finality problem by granting a limited right to strike to certain categories of public employees. The limited right to strike is discussed in Part G of Chapter Six.

(5) *"Advisory" Arbitration*—Several states have made "advisory" arbitration (i.e. non-binding arbitration), an alternative or a sequel to fact-finding. The Maine law provides for both binding and advisory arbitration depending on the issue. Arbitration may be requested by either side, with a tripartite panel made up of one member selected by each side and a neutral third member selected by the other two members or by the American Arbitration Association. The recommendations of the arbitration panel are advisory with respect to salaries, pensions and insurance. *See* ME. REV. STAT. ANN. tit. 26, § 965 (4) (Supp. 1972).

Rhode Island statutes covering municipal employees and teachers also provide for voluntary arbitration, which is only binding with respect to matters not involving the expenditure of money. *See* R.I. GEN. LAWS ANN. §§ 28-9.4-10 to 15 and §§ 28-9.3-9 to 14. However, the Rhode Island laws covering police and firemen make compulsory arbitration mandatory and binding as to all issues. *See* R.I. GEN. LAWS ANN. §§ 28-9.2-7 to 11 and §§ 28-9.1-7 to 11.

The Pennsylvania Law covering prison and hospital guards and court personnel provides that all bargaining impasses "shall be submitted to a panel of arbitrators whose decision shall be final and binding . . . with the proviso that the decisions of the arbitrators which would require legislative enactment to be effective shall be considered advisory only." PA. STAT. ANN. § 1101.85. *See Statutory Appendix*. There is also a separate statutory provision in Pennsylvania requiring compulsory and binding arbitration (at the request of either party) on all issues in interest disputes involving policemen and firemen. PA. STAT. ANN. tit. 43, §§ 217.4-8. It is also noteworthy that the Pennsylvania Public Employee Relations Act provides for "voluntary binding arbitration" of public employee interest disputes which are not otherwise covered by the compulsory arbitration provisions in the Pennsylvania law. *See* PA. STAT. ANN. § 1101.84. Voluntary binding arbitration arises only pursuant to an agreement by the parties and, if it is utilized, "the decisions of the arbitrator which . . . require legislative enactment to be effective shall be considered advisory only."

In Oklahoma, in disputes involving police and firemen, either party may request advisory arbitration; the arbitration award is made binding only if it is accepted by the municipality. *See* OKLA. SESS. LAWS, ch. 14, §§ 7-11.

Some commentators believe that with advisory as contrasted with binding arbitration the parties are more likely to negotiate seriously prior to arbitration. The argument is that one or the other party may believe it has a good chance of receiving more favorable treatment through arbitration than through negotiations, whereas advisory arbitration is less stultifying of the bargaining process since the "award" can be rejected. For good discussions of the use of advisory arbitration in the telegraph and wire service industries, see Bryan, *Avoiding Confrontation by Advisory Arbitration,* and Groner, *Why Advisory Arbitration of New Contracts?* in ARBITRATION AND THE EXPANDING ROLE OF NEUTRALS, PROCEEDINGS OF THE TWENTY-THIRD ANNUAL MEETING, NATIONAL ACADEMY OF ARBITRATORS 55 (G. Somers ed. 1970). Is there any real difference between advisory arbitration and fact-finding with recommendations?

(6) *Voluntary, Binding Arbitration*—At least twelve states (Connecticut, Delaware, Hawaii, Maine, Minnesota, Nevada, New York, New Jersey, Oregon, Pennsylvania, Rhode Island, and Vermont) permit voluntary, binding arbitration in interest disputes involving various categories of public sector employees and employers. The Postal Reorganization Act of 1970, which is set forth in the *Statutory Appendix,* provides for voluntary binding arbitration, but also for compulsory arbitration if a voluntary arrangement is not reached. The Canadian Public Service Staff Relations Act gives unions at the federal level a choice, to be exercised in advance of bargaining, between strike action and submission of disputes to binding arbitration, except that, if the strike route is elected, essential employees may not strike. *See generally* Arthurs, *Collective Bargaining in the Public Service of Canada: Bold Experiment or Act of Folly?,* 67 MICH. L. REV. 971 (1969).

2. Compulsory Binding Arbitration

a. Commentary

H. WELLINGTON & R. WINTER, THE UNIONS AND THE CITIES 178-80 (1971)†

Compulsory and binding arbitration seeks to prevent strikes in two ways, neither of which is completely successful. First, it attempts to enforce a settlement by application of legal sanctions. Ordinarily this will be enough for all but the aberrational case. And the occasional strikes that still occur sometimes may be prevented if the law responds with very harsh penalties. Such penalties, however, often do not have the support of the community and may stir a feeling of revulsion. In those circumstances they are unlikely to be effective and, in any event, workers willing to accept such penalties can still make a strike effective. Legal sanctions, therefore, do not provide total protection.

Compulsory and binding arbitration, however, seeks to prevent strikes in a second way. Because the strike in private employment is viewed by many as a fundamental right located well within the foothills of the Constitution, there is in some places a corresponding sense that laws against strikes in the public sector are unfair. This attitude—which survives in a fierce state of tension with counter attitudes—emboldens public employees to break the law. A procedure that offers public employees a seemingly fair alternative to the strike, however, may change the community's sense of the propriety of the strike and may in the long run influence the attitude of public employees. They may in time reach that desirable state of accepting an award that they find less than totally fair. This is the goal of compulsory arbitration, and is what differentiates it from nonfinality procedures. No moral imperative, above and beyond the preexisting moral imperative of not breaking the no-strike law, is generated by nonfinality procedures such as fact-finding with recommendations. They are advisory only. An aim of arbitration binding on both parties is to generate just such an imperative. Again, however, total success cannot be expected.

The second factor limiting the effectiveness of arbitration is that it deters collective bargaining. The point is simple enough. Either the public employer or the union will reckon that an arbitration award will be more advantageous than a negotiated settlement. That party will then employ tactics to ensure arbitration by bargaining without a sincere desire to reach agreement.

---

† Copyright © 1971 by The Brookings Institution, Washington, D.C. Reprinted by permission.

It is almost impossible wholly to solve this problem; but the route to partial and perhaps satisfactory resolution is to fashion a procedure sufficiently diverse and uncertain as to make a negotiated settlement more attractive to the parties than arbitration.

The composition of an arbitration panel can importantly influence its award. Honest men acting disinterestedly often see things differently. The behaviorists are surely right in thinking that results are influenced by the perspectives of decision makers. Thus, to the extent that the composition of an arbitration panel is unknown beforehand and is outside the control of the parties, some uncertainty will exist. On the other hand, the parties are more likely to have confidence in an award rendered by arbitrators they have chosen. This tension can be eased by allowing each party to select one member of a three-man panel.

G. TAYLOR, IMPASSE PROCEDURES—THE FINALITY QUESTION, GOVERNOR'S CONFERENCE ON PUBLIC EMPLOYMENT RELATIONS 5-6 (New York City, October 15, 1968)

There is considerable wishful thinking that the involvement of the legislative and executive branches of government can be minimized—or even avoided altogether—by having a board of impartial labor relations experts make a final and binding decision to resolve an impasse. While recognizing the apparent simplicity of compulsory arbitration, one should not be unaware of the consequences of the broad delegation of governmental authority which is entailed. An arbitration board would become a powerful arm of government acting without the checks and balances upon which we depend in the fashioning of our laws. Some additional difficult questions have to be faced. Is it sound and wise to consider the claims of one particular group of employees for their share of limited public funds in isolation from the claims of other employees? Or, to do so without regard to the leap-frogging effect upon the total wage bill of a decision made in narrow context? What effect would all this have upon the allocations of limited resources for other sorely needed services to the public? And, if a legislative body cannot or will not do what it takes to carry out an award by the impartial arbitrators, is it intended that a court will compel them to do so? Bringing such questions into the appraisal of compulsory arbitration transforms an apparently easy answer into a very doubtful one.

A. ANDERSON, COMPULSORY ARBITRATION IN PUBLIC SECTOR DISPUTE SETTLEMENT—AN AFFIRMATIVE VIEW, in DISPUTE SETTLEMENT IN THE PUBLIC SECTOR 2-3 (T. Gilroy ed. 1972)†

[I]mpasse panel procedures may prove to be an interim step on the road to a system which features binding arbitration of contract terms in the public sector. In some cases, the parties have taken the additional step of agreeing to be bound by the recommendations of the impasse panel. In other instances, the parties have, in effect, requested the arbitrator to confirm their bargain by taking the responsibility of making an award confirming the agreement of the parties. There has also been an increase in the use of voluntary arbitration of contract terms in the public sector. Such arbitration is authorized by the Taylor Law.

President George Meany of the AFL-CIO, while expressing strong reservations about the use of arbitration in the private sector for resolving bargaining impasses, has suggested the use of binding arbitration in some circumstances in the public sector. The procedure for binding arbitration of contract terms under the new Postal Corporation Act was endorsed by the AFL-CIO. Mr. Meany, in supporting the Postal Corporation Act, stated that any procedure which preserves workers' rights without strikes is acceptable. Labor leaders who endorse the right to strike in public employment have at times qualified such advocacy by supporting binding arbitration of disputes for employees engaged in essential services such as law enforcement and fire fighting. In addition to the new laws and changed attitudes, the number of cases already submitted to arbitration in police and fire disputes in Pennsylvania and Michigan make an examination of compulsory arbitration procedures worthwhile.

The traditional attitudes of labor relations experts toward the binding arbitration process is that it's bad because it won't work and because it will destroy free collective bargaining. Arbitration of contract terms in public employment has been considered to be illegal in some jurisdictions because the process results in the unconstitutional delegation of responsibility to a third party, who is a private person of legislative and executive authority, to fix the terms and conditions of employment and the resulting budget changes and tax rates. Furthermore, it is charged that arbitration will not work because it will not prevent strikes or bring about settlements and will destroy the free collective bargaining process and the willingness of the parties to solve their own disputes. It is argued that compulsory arbitration will result in the piling up

---

† Reprinted by permission of the Center for Labor and Management, College of Business Administration, University of Iowa.

of all kinds of disputes to be submitted for resolution to a third party who neither understands the problems nor has a continuing responsibility for the results of the settlement. . . .

The adoption of compulsory and binding arbitration statutes in such jurisdictions as Michigan, Pennsylvania, Rhode Island, Maine and Wyoming for police and fire disputes is based on the premise that since the right to strike is legally denied and cannot be realistically conferred on employees engaged in vital services, then a substitute bargaining balancer, the right to invoke binding arbitration by a neutral third party, is an effective and equitable substitute as a dispute settlement procedure. Arbitration transfers some of the powers of decision making about contract terms from the economic and political power of the parties involved to neutral arbitrators. Therefore, I don't accept the premise that the right to strike is the *sine qua non* to make the bargaining process work in the public sector. I think arbitration can work and has worked effectively for public employees as a substitute for the strike weapon.

NOTE

For two valuable discussions of compulsory arbitration's application and success in resolving disputes between the protective services and their employers, see Loewenberg, *Compulsory Arbitration for Police and Fire Fighters in Pennsylvania in 1968,* 23 IND. & LAB. REL. REV. 367 (1969) (containing excellent statistical breakdowns by size of cities, location, salary, and the experience of the negotiators or arbitrators) and A. Anderson, *A Survey of Statutes with Compulsory Arbitration Provisions for Fire and Police,* in ARBITRATION OF POLICE AND FIREFIGHTERS DISPUTES, PROCEEDINGS OF A CONFERENCE ON ARBITRATION OF NEW CONTRACT TERMS FOR THE PROTECTIVE SERVICES, AM. ARB. ASS'N, New York (March 9, 1971) (discussing various state approaches, their relative success and providing numerous criticisms and suggestions) .

b. *Legality*

CLARK, COMPULSORY ARBITRATION IN PUBLIC EMPLOYMENT, 37 PERL 16-18 (1972)†

Not surprisingly, the constitutionality of many of the compulsory arbitration statutes that have been enacted in recent years has been challenged. Two principal contentions have been made: First, that compulsory arbitration involves the unconstitutional delegation of legislative authority; and second, that the statutes

---

† Reprinted by permission of the International Personnel Management Association.

do not contain adequate standards to guide the arbitrators. The courts, however, have not found these contentions convincing.

Unconstitutional Delegation of Authority

The Pennsylvania statute providing for compulsory arbitration of police and firemen collective bargaining disputes was challenged on the ground, *inter alia,* that the decision of the arbitration board would determine how public funds would be spent, and that this was a governmental function that could not be delegated without violating the one man, one vote principle. In upholding the constitutionality of the statute, the Pennsylvania Supreme Court in *Harney v. Russo*[6] held that the mere fact that the arbitration panel in the case before us could affect the spending of public funds is clearly not sufficient to make that body "legislative" and thus subject to the one man, one vote principle. Similarly, the Rhode Island Supreme Court in *City of Warwick v. Warwick Regular Firemen's Association*[7] upheld the constitutionality of the Rhode Island Fire Fighters' Arbitration Act. In rejecting the contention that it constituted an unconstitutional delegation of legislative authority, the court stated:

> We are of the opinion that when the legislature, in an exercise of its law-making authority, enacts a statute the purpose of which is to secure to the public some right or benefit, it may delegate to an appropriate agency or officer some residuals of its legislative power in order to permit the selected agent to accomplish the ends contemplated in the original legislation.

Nor did the Rhode Island Supreme Court find merit in the argument that the delegation of legislative authority was defective because it was granted to private individuals. The court observed that each member of the arbitration board "is a public officer and that collectively these officers constitute an administrative or governmental agency." The Wyoming Supreme Court in *State of Wyoming v. Laramie*[8] upheld the constitutionality of the Wyoming Fire Fighters' Compulsory Arbitration Act, noting that the legislature had the authority to make "provision for unresolved matters to be submitted to arbitration or determined in some other manner." In the court's opinion "there could be no collective bargaining if the bargaining necessarily had to end with terms and conditions dictated by the City." . . .

---

6 435 Pa. 183, 189 (1969).

7 256 A.2d 206 (R.I. Sup. Ct. 1969).

8 437 P.2d 295 (Wyo. Sup. Ct. 1968).

Adequacy of Standards

Both the Pennsylvania and Rhode Island statutes were also challenged on the basis that there were not sufficient standards to guide the arbitrators. The Rhode Island Supreme Court in *Warwick* had little difficulty with this contention. The court noted that the Act set out " a number of comprehensive limits on the actions of a board of arbitrators when exercising the power delegated," and these standards were clearly "sufficient to meet the constitutional requirement that the delegated power be confined by reasonable norms or standards." The Rhode Island Supreme Court observed that the standards served a dual purpose, stating:

> . . .They not only operate to direct or limit the action of the recipients of such delegated power, but they are standards pursuant to which on judicial review a court may determine whether the action taken by the recipients of such powers was capricious, arbitrary, or in excess of the delegated authority. In our opinion, this is an important consideration in determining the sufficiency of the standards prescribed in the legislation. In this case it is our opinion that they are sufficient for such purpose.

The Pennsylvania Supreme Court in *Harney* had a more difficult time since the Pennsylvania Act does not set forth specific criteria to be considered by the arbitration panel in rendering decisions. The court, however, was able to get over this hurdle by noting that there was "an obvious legislative policy to protect the public from strikes by policemen and firemen." Accordingly, the court held that the Act passed constitutional muster, observing:

> To require a more explicit statement of legislative policy in a statute calling for labor arbitration would be sheer folly. The great advantage of arbitration is, after all, the ability of the arbitrators to deal with each case on its own merits in order to arrive at a compromise which is fair to both parties. The arbitrators' services are particularly valuable where, as the legislative scheme here requires, the parties have been unable to reach an agreement through collective bargaining. Certainly that is what the Legislature envisioned in its attempt to insure labor peace in this critical public area, and this is adequate. . . .

It should be noted that not all courts would view so cavalierly the failure to prescribe specific standards. For example, the New Jersey Supreme Court struck down a statute providing for compulsory arbitration of public utility disputes because of the act's failure to prescribe sufficient standards.[9]

One of the more ingenious arguments against compulsory arbitration was raised in the *Harney* case. There the public employer asserted that it would be denied due process since it could be held in contempt if it could not implement an award, even though no funds were available. The Pennsylvania Supreme Court, however, noted that there was no evidence in the record to indicate that taxes could not be raised to pay the arbitrator's award. While there was no need to go any further, the court, in dicta, observed that if it did have occasion to hear a case which the tax rates could not

. . . permissibly be raised so as to provide sufficient funds to pay the required benefits to the employees, it will still be open to this Court to rule that the Act . . . impliedly authorizes a Court-approved millage ceiling increase to pay the arbitration award where necessary, or to hold that the municipal budget must be adjusted in other places in order to provide resources for policemen's and firemen's salaries.

c. *A Survey of Legislation: Practice and Procedure; Decisional Standards; Judicial Review and Enforcement of Awards*

McAVOY, BINDING ARBITRATION OF CONTRACT TERMS: A NEW APPROACH TO THE RESOLUTION OF DISPUTES IN THE PUBLIC SECTOR, 72 Colum. L. Rev. 1192-1205 (1972)†

In an effort to avoid the work stoppages that may follow deadlocked negotiations, Michigan and other jurisdictions have instituted binding arbitration of contract terms in the public sector.[10] Though the earliest statutes covering public employees were passed in 1947, the majority of them have been enacted since 1968. As of June, 1972, there were thirty-six such statutes and one mayoral executive order in twenty states and ten cities.[11]

---

[9] Van Riper v. Traffic Tel. Workers Fed'n of New Jersey, 66 A.2d 616, 15 LC ¶ 64769 (1949). Subsequently, the New Jersey Legislature amended the statute to provide specific standards to guide the arbitration panel, and the constitutionality of the statute, as thus amended, was upheld. New Jersey Bell Tel. Co. v. Communication Workers of America, 5 N.J. 354, 75 A.2d 721 (1950).

† Reprinted by permission of Columbia Law Review.

[10] *See* MICH. COMP. LAWS ANN. § 423.231 (Supp. 1972). The Michigan statute covering police and firemen was originally enacted on an experimental basis for only three years. Although it was scheduled to expire on June 30, 1972, the Legislature in 1972 acted affirmatively to extend it an additional three years. MICH. COMP. LAWS ANN. § 423.245 (Supp. 1972), *as amended* by Enrolled House Bill No. 5087 (1972).

[11] Firefighters Arbitration Act of New Albany, Indiana (effec. Feb. 22, 1972) (BNA GOV'T EMPLOYEE RELATIONS REP. No. 447, B-13 (April 10, 1972));

The essential characteristics of binding arbitration are submission of unresolved issues to a panel and a decision by the panel that is final and binding on both parties. The term does not include "one-sided" arbitration, where the award is binding on the employees only if accepted by the employer, who has the option to reject it. The statutes, which may provide for awards

---

ASTORIA, ORE., CODE § 1.211 (1970); DAYTON, OHIO, CODE OF GENERAL ORDINANCES § 142-9 E & F (1972) (BNA GOV'T EMPLOYEE RELATIONS REP. No. 452, E-2 (May 15, 1972)); DEL. CODE ANN. tit. 19, § 1310 (Supp. 1970); DEL. CODE ANN. tit. 2, § 1613 (Supp. 1970); CITY AND COUNTY OF DENVER, COL., Charter §§ C5.80-5 to C5.80-7 (1971); Exec. Order No. 70-229 of the Commissioner of D.C., Part III (4) (effec. June 19, 1970), as implemented by District Personnel Manual ch. 25A, § 12 (c) (BNA GOV'T EMPLOYEE RELATIONS REP. 51:6011, RF-10 (1970)); EUGENE, ORE., CODE § 2.876 (1971) (BNA GOV'T EMPLOYEE RELATIONS REP. No. 423, G-1 (Oct. 18, 1971)); HAWAII REV. STAT. § 89-11 (Supp. 1971); ch. 264, §§ 2 (p), 12 [1971] Kan. Acts 577; LA. STAT. ANN. tit. 23, § 890 (West Supp. 1972); ME. REV. STAT. ANN. tit. 26, § 965, subdiv. 4 (Supp. 1972); MICH. COMP. LAWS ANN. § 423.231 to § 423.240 (Supp. 1972), as amended by Enrolled House Bill No. 5087 (1972); ch. 33, § 12, subdiv. 11 [1971] Minn. Laws 2730: MINN. STAT. ANN. § 179.38 (Supp. 1971); NEB. REV. STAT. ch. 48, art. 8 (1968); NEV. REV. STAT. ch. 288 (1971) (2 CCH LAB. L. REP., STATE LAWS, Nev. ¶ 47,215 (Aug. 6, 1971)); N.H. REV. STAT. ANN. ch. 98-C (Supp. 1971); N.J. STAT. ANN. § 34:13A-3 (d) (Supp. 1972-73); N.J. STAT. ANN. § 34:13A-7 (1965); N.Y.C. ADMIN. CODE ch. 54, § 1173-7.0 (effec. Jan. 12, 1972) (2 CCH LAB. L. REP., STATE LAWS, N.Y. ¶ 47,450.12 (Jan. 28, 1972)), amending N.Y.C. ADMIN. CODE ch. 54, § 1173-7.0 (1971); N.Y. CIV. SER. LAW § 209 (2) (McKinney Supp. 1971-72); ORE. REV. STAT. § 243.751 (2) (1969); PA. STAT. ANN. tit. 43, §§ 1101.804-1101.805 (Purdon Supp. 1972-73); PA. STAT. ANN. tit. 43, § 217 (Purdon Supp. 1972-73); PA. STAT. ANN. tit. 53, § 39951 (Purdon Supp. 1972-73); PA. STAT. ANN. tit. 55, § 563.2 (Purdon 1964); R.I. GEN. LAWS ANN. tit. 28, ch. 9.1 (Supp. 1971), amending R.I. GEN. LAWS ANN. tit. 28, ch. 9.1 (1968); R.I. GEN. LAWS ANN. tit. 28, ch. 9.2 (Supp. 1971), amending R.I. GEN. LAWS ANN. tit. 28, ch. 9.2 (1968); R.I. GEN. LAWS ANN. tit. 28, ch. 9.3 (1968); R.I. GEN. LAWS ANN. tit. 28, ch. 9.4 (1968); S.D. COMPILED LAWS ANN. ch. 9-14A (Supp. 1971); SPRINGFIELD, ORE., CHARTER AMENDMENT (1972); VALLEJO, CAL., CHARTER, art. VIII, § 810 (1971); no. 230, § 5 [1969] VT. PUB. ACTS, 50th Biennial Adj. Sess. 188 (1970), amending VT. STAT. ANN. tit. 21, § 1705 (Supp. 1971); VT. STAT. ANN. tit. 3, § 925 (1972); ch. 247, § 3 [1971] Wis. Laws 432-434; ch. 246, § 1 [1971] Wis. Laws 429-431 (covers Milwaukee police only); WYO. STAT. ANN. tit. 27, ch. 14 (1967).

Binding arbitration of contract terms between the federal government and its employees "may be used by the parties only when authorized or directed by the [Federal Service Impasses] Panel." Exec. Order 11491, as amended § 17, 3 C.F.R. 510 (unamended), 5 U.S.C. § 7301 (Supp. 1972). As of April 17, 1972, arbitration had never been used, although the Executive Secretary of the Federal Service Impasses Panel has indicated that it may become necessary to resort to arbitration in the near future. Telephone interview with David T. Roadley, Executive Secretary of the Federal Service Impasses Panel, April 17, 1972.

Binding arbitration of contract terms between the Postal Service and its employees is required if no agreement is reached within a specified period following the commencement of negotiations. The arbitration board is composed of three arbitrators, one selected by each party and the third selected by the first two arbitrators. The parties, however, may adopt their own arbitration procedure in lieu of the tripartite board. Postal Reorganization Act, 39 U.S.C. § 1207 (1970).

containing both binding and advisory provisions, fall generally into three categories: those that mandate arbitration; those that permit one party to mandate arbitration; and those that allow the parties to agree to arbitration. . . .

I. *Statutory Provisions*

A. *Employees Covered*

The present pattern of coverage of arbitration statutes seems to reflect a degree of uncertainty as to the wisdom or desirability of such measures. The applicability of the few state statutes that mandate arbitration if agreement is not reached within a stated time period is usually limited to firefighters or police.[12] Both the number and scope of the statutes increase as the parties are granted a voice in the implementation of the arbitration procedure. Statutes of eight states that require arbitration when requested by one party cover, in addition to firemen and police,[13] hospital[14] and public transportation[15] workers, Port Authority employees[16] and others.[17] The largest category of statutes, which covers "public employees generally," applies only when both parties agree to the arbitration procedure.[18] Smaller legislative

---

12 *See* R.I. GEN. LAWS ANN. tit. 28, ch. 9.1 (Supp. 1971), *amending* R.I. GEN. LAWS ANN. tit. 28, ch. 9.1 (1968) (firefighters); R.I. GEN. LAWS ANN. tit. 28, ch. 9.2 (Supp. 1971), *amending* R.I. GEN. LAWS ANN. tit. 28, ch. 9.2 (1968) (police); WYO. STAT. ANN. tit. 27, ch. 14 (1967) (firefighters); no. 230, § 5 [1969] VT. PUB. ACTS, 50th Biennial Adj. Sess. 188 (1970) (firefighters); ch. 33, § 12, subdiv. 3, 11 [1971] Minn. Laws 2727, 2730 ("essential employees"); PA. STAT. ANN. tit. 43, § 1101.805 (Purdon Supp. 1972-73) (prison and mental hospital guards; court employees).

13 MICH. COMP. LAWS ANN. § 423.231 (Supp. 1972); PA. STAT. ANN. tit. 43, § 217 (Purdon Supp. 1972-73); S.D. COMPILED LAWS ANN. ch. 9-14A (Supp. 1971); ch. 247, § 3 [1971] Wis. Laws 432-434; ch. 246, § 1 [1971] Wis. Laws 429-431.

14 MINN. STAT. ANN. §§ 179.35, 179.38 (Supp. 1971), *amending* MINN. STAT. ANN. §§ 179.35, 179.38 (1966).

15 LA. STAT. ANN. tit. 23, § 890 (E) (West Supp. 1972); PA. STAT. ANN. tit. 53, § 39951 (Purdon Supp. 1972-73).

16 PA. STAT. ANN. tit. 55, § 563.2 (Purdon 1964).

17 NEB. REV. STAT. §§ 48-801, 48-810 (1968) (employees performing "governmental service in a proprietary capacity"); NEV. REV. STAT. ch. 288 (1971) (2 CCH LAB. L. REP., STATE LAWS, Nev. ¶¶ 47,206 to 47,207 (Aug. 8, 1971)) (public employees not employed by the state, subject to governor's consent).

18 DAYTON, OHIO, CODE OF GENERAL ORDINANCES §§ 142-4, 142-6 (1972) (BNA GOV'T EMPLOYEE RELATIONS REP. No. 452, E-1 & 2 ("May 15, 1972) (municipal employees generally with some exceptions)); DEL. CODE ANN. tit. 19, §§ 1301, 1310 (Supp. 1970) (public employees generally); DEL. CODE ANN. tit. 2, § 1613 (Supp. 1970) (employees of a local transportation authority); Exec. Order No. 170-229 of the Commissioner of D.C., Part III (4) (effec. June 19, 1970), *as implemented* by District Personnel Manual ch. 25A, § 12 (c) (BNA GOV'T EMPLOYEE RELATIONS REP. 51:6011, RF-10 (1970)) (employees of D.C.); HAWAII REV. STAT. §§ 89-2, 89-11 (Supp. 1971) (public employees generally); ch. 264, §§ 2 (a), (f), (p), 12 (a), (e) [1971] Sess. Laws

units display a greater willingness to mandate arbitration, since five of seven municipal ordinances apply to all public employees, with limited exceptions.[19] Generally, arbitration is most likely to be required with respect to employees, such as firemen and police, whose services may be deemed "vital," and more often merely authorized with respect to other types of employees. Pennsylvania, for example, has three types of statutes: mandating arbitration for prison and mental hospital guards and court employees; authorizing arbitration at the request of one party for firemen, police, public transportation and Port Authority employees; and providing for arbitration at the request of both parties for public employees generally.

B. *Timing of Award*

Submission to arbitration deprives the public employer of the power to determine the proportion of its budget it will allocate for employee salaries. As a result, reallocation of previously budgeted funds may be required to satisfy the terms of an award. Many statutes, including the majority of those authorizing arbitration upon agreement of both parties, do not attempt to deal with the problem; however, eleven statutes seek to require

---

of Kan. 575-577 (effec. March 1, 1972) (public employees generally); Los Angeles County Employee Relations Ordinance (BNA Gov'T EMPLOYEE RELATIONS REP. No. 261, F-6 (Sept. 9, 1968)) (public employees generally); N.H. REV. STAT. ANN, § 98-C:4 (Supp. 1971) (state employees); ME. REV. STAT. ANN. tit. 26, §§ 962, 965, subdiv. 4 (Supp. 1972) (municipal employees); ch. 33, subdiv. 12 [1971] Minn. Laws 2730 (public employees generally); N.J. STAT. ANN. § 34:13A-3 (d) (Supp. 1971-72) (public employees generally); N.J. STAT. ANN. § 34:13A-7 (1965); N.Y. CIV. SER. LAW § 209 (2) (McKinney Supp. 1971-72) (public employees generally): NEV. REV. STAT. ch. 288 (1971) (2 CCH LAB. L. REP., STATE LAWS, Nev. ¶¶ 47,207 (Aug. 6, 1971), 47,215 (Jan. 14, 1972)) (public employees generally) ; ORE. REV. STAT. §§ 243.711, 243.751 (2) (1969) (public employees generally): PA. STAT. ANN. tit. 43, §§ 1101.301, 1101.804 (Purdon Supp. 1972-73) (public employees generally); VT. STAT. ANN. tit. 21, § 1705 (Supp. 1971) (municipal employees); VT. STAT. ANN. tit. 3, §§ 902, 925 (1972) (state employees).

19 N.Y.C. ADMIN. CODE ch. 54, §§ 1173-4.0, 1173-7.0, subdiv. c (effec. Jan. 12, 1972) (2 CCH LAB. L. REP., STATE LAWS, N.Y. ¶¶ 47,450.09 and 47,450.12 (Jan. 28, 1972), *amending* N.Y.C. ADMIN. CODE ch. 54, §§ 1173-4.0, 1173-7.0, subdiv. c. (1971)): VALLEJO, CAL., CHARTER, art. VIII, § 810 (1971); EUGENE, ORE., CODE § 2.876 (1971) (BNA GOV'T EMPLOYEE RELATIONS REP. No. 423, G-1 (Oct. 18, 1971)) ; SPRINGFIELD, ORE., CHARTER § XI (Nov. 3, 1970); ASTORIA, ORE., CODE § 1.211 (1969) (public employees generally); CITY AND COUNTY OF DENVER, COL., CHARTER § C5.80 (1971); Firefighters Arbitration Act of New Albany, Indiana (effec. Feb. 22, 1972) (BNA GOV'T EMPLOYEE RELATIONS REP. No. 447, B-13 (April 10, 1972)) (firefighters). (The provisions of the NYC Collective Bargaining Law are not "applicable to the negotiation of any immediate successor agreement to a collective bargaining agreement which expired on or before December 31, 1970." Local Laws, 1972, No. 2, City of New York, § 5 (2 CCH LAB. L. REP., STATE LAWS, N.Y. ¶ 47,450 (Jan. 28, 1972)). As of September, 1972, no binding arbitration had occurred pursuant to these provisions.)

completion of arbitration prior to the last date on which money can be appropriated for the new fiscal year. The manifest purpose of these provisions is to afford the employer the opportunity to tailor its budget requests with a view to the allocations required by all awards effective for the new fiscal year.

Most statutes that look to completion of arbitration prior to a budget appropriation date provide a detailed timetable, specifying dates for the commencement of bargaining, submission to arbitration, selection of arbitrators, holding of hearings, and issuance of the award. Although most statutes mandating arbitration contain such a schedule, only Minnesota's statute expressly requires the issuance of an award before a date related to appropriations.

As an alternative solution, South Dakota and Michigan minimize the disruptive effect of an arbitration award on the employer's budget by providing that the effective date of any determination on wages shall be the beginning of the next fiscal year. Nevada's law requires that in a regular legislative year the arbitration hearing be stayed up to ten days following the adjournment of the legislature *sine die*. Thus the arbitrator can be aware of legislative appropriations before making a determination that must be based on a current ability to pay.

C. Composition of the Panel

Although most statutes authorizing arbitration upon the agreement of both parties permit an ad hoc determination of the size of the panel, the great majority of arbitration laws provide for a tripartite panel composed of one member selected by each party plus a chairman chosen by the two appointees. This type of panel carries the collective bargaining process over into arbitration, since the first two appointees are likely to maintain a partisan stance. In justification of such an approach, it is argued that the labor and employer members will be more familiar with the issues and their sponsors' positions and thus able to help the neutral arbitrator avoid any serious error that might result in an award completely unacceptable to one side. In contrast, statutes in Minnesota and Denver remove collective bargaining procedures from the arbitration process by providing that the parties select the entire tripartite panel from a list of seven names submitted by an independent, neutral board.

D. Dissenting Opinions

Most statutes providing for tripartite panels permit a decision by majority vote, thus creating the possibility of a dissent, either in whole or in part, by one of the arbitrators. Undoubtedly, in jurisdictions that require each party to appoint an arbitrator, the dissenter will most probably be a partisan, rather than the neutral chairman. Present experience is inadequate to indicate what effect such dissents will have on the use of arbitration procedures. A dissenting opinion by the employee-arbitrator may cause the union membership to reject the settlement, while an employer might seek repeal of the arbitration statute following too many dissents by its panel member. Tripartite panels are in fact not mandated in New York City because of apprehension concerning the dissents in other jurisdictions. On the other hand, after a dissent, a party may pursue collective bargaining more aggressively in an attempt to avoid arbitration. Such a result might lead to smoother negotiation of subsequent contracts.

E. Residency Requirement

The majority of statutes have no residency requirement for panel members, although a few impose such a requirement on a judge-appointed chairman of a tripartite panel selected when the two other members, who normally select a chairman, are unable to agree. Only Minnesota's law directs that the names of the arbitrators submitted to the parties contain "whenever possible . . . names of persons from the geographical area in which the public employer is located."

When a city must lay off employees and reduce city services to comply with a binding arbitration award, a likely result is public resentment against an "outside" arbitrator who need not live with the consequences of his award. In 1970, the Mayor of Detroit blamed an award covering policemen for the necessity to reduce city services, to lay off at least 542 city employees, and to increase working hours from 35 to 40 a week. Amidst the ensuing turmoil, the Mayor announced that he was looking for alternative procedures to propose to the state legislature. One of the proposals he considered was to replace the "out-of-town arbitrator" with a permanent umpire who would be familiar with the problems of the city and the unions.

F. Criteria for Award

Most statutes mandating arbitration establish some criteria for the arbitrators to follow in making their award. Vermont's provision, for example, is both concise and general:

The arbitrators may make their determination of disputed issues based upon a consideration of (1) The relative hardship to the firefighters and the public; (2) Conditions in the

general area; (3) The relative equities; or (4) The peculiarities of the employment.

The Rhode Island Policemen's Arbitration Act typifies the use
of longer and more specific criteria:

The factors, among others, to be given weight by the arbitrators in arriving at a decision shall include:

(a)   Comparison of wage rates or hourly conditions of em-
       ployment of the police department in question with pre-
       vailing wage rates or hourly conditions of employment
       of skilled employees of the building trades and industry
       in the local operating area involved.
(b)   Comparison of wage rates or hourly conditions of em-
       ployment of the police department in question with
       wage rates or hourly conditions of employment of police
       departments in cities or towns of comparable size.
(c)   Interest and welfare of the public.
(d)   Comparison of peculiarities of employment in regard to
       other trades or professions, specifically:

    (1)   Hazards of employment
    (2)   Physical qualifications
    (3)   Educational qualifications
    (4)   Mental qualifications
    (5)   Job training and skills.

In contrast to the statutes mandating arbitration, there are no
criteria in seven of the eleven statutes that require arbitration
upon the request of one party, and there are no criteria in most
of the statutes that authorize arbitration upon the consent of
both parties.

Among the statutes with standards, few attempt to deal with
the complex question of the employer's ability to pay, which
may be computed by reference to either revenues presently
available or the community's capacity to tax and its utilization
of its fiscal resources as compared to other communities. As public employers increasingly claim inability to provide higher
compensation and to cover the costs of non-salary demands, arbitrators, in the absence of specific guidelines, will probably tend
to base awards on the jurisdiction's potential ability to increase
its revenues.

Nevada's statute provides the clearest standard concerning an
employer's ability to pay. The arbitrators must first determine
that there is

a current financial ability to grant monetary benefits based
on all existing available revenues as established by the local

government employer, and with due regard for the obligation of the local government employer to provide facilities
and services. . . .

Once that finding has been made, "normal criteria for interest
disputes" may be employed. Such a formulation avoids the possibility of an award that would necessitate increased taxes, employee lay-offs or reduced municipal services.

When a statute does not prescribe rules for decision, arbitrators will presumably apply "general standards." In these circumstances, articulation of the rationale underlying the award
is important to forestall a charge of arbitrariness by a disgruntled
party. Similarly, decisions that demonstrably correspond to prevailing wages, terms, and conditions of employment in comparable jurisdictions will be more readily accepted by the parties.

G. Terms of an Award

All but four jurisdictions permit arbitrators wide latitude in
the selection of settlement terms. Minnesota, Wisconsin, Michigan, and Eugene, Oregon, however, limit awards to either of
the parties' final offers. The Michigan statute provides for a
choice on each economic issue, while the others mandate a selection of a "package" deal. The primary effect of these provisions
is to encourage reasonable bargaining positions at the negotiation
stage, since an unreasonable offer will probably lead to adoption of the other party's position in the arbitration award.

The Michigan approach, termed "last offer" arbitration, is
favored by at least one commentator who would allow the arbitrator to

> make a choice between the final offers of the parties on an
> issue-by-issue basis. In this way, the arbitrator would have
> the prerogative of considering each issue on its merits and of
> accepting the "most reasonable" offer.

It would thus not be necessary to choose between two packages,
each possibly containing some unreasonable demands, and intransigence would never be rewarded.

Despite the seeming superiority of "last offer" arbitration,
Professor Carl Stevens advocates the "one-or-the-other" method
used by Minnesota, Wisconsin and Eugene. If arbitrators are
forced to choose between two "objectionable and arbitrary"
offers, he argues, they can remand the case to the parties requesting more reasonable packages. Remand, however, may exacerbate
rather than ease a tense situation involving two determined
parties. Furthermore, the Michigan statute demonstrates that a
provision for remand can be used in conjunction with "last offer"

arbitration as well. Finally, the public interest requires the elimination of as many irrational items in an award as possible, a goal best achieved under the Michigan approach. . . .

H. *Limitations on an Award*

Although it seems clear that an arbitrator cannot require either party to act illegally or beyond its authority, a few statutes contain provisions explicitly dealing with the possibility of a conflict between an arbitrator's award and existing law. The Vallejo law seeks to avoid any conflict *ab initio* by defining the efficacy of an award by reference to "applicable law." An after-the-fact approach is taken by provisions in Vermont and Minnesota that void portions of an award found to contravene pre-existing statutes. In contrast to these absolute provisions, the New York City ordinance and a Pennsylvania statute adopt a median course. When a term of an award would require enabling legislation, New York City stays its effect "until the appropriate legislative body enacts such [a] law," while Pennsylvania considers the term "advisory only." In such a case the employer's obligation is probably limited to sponsoring and supporting the necessary legislation.

A unique provision of the Pennsylvania statute covering firemen and police attempts to guarantee the binding effect of any award:

> Such determination shall constitute a mandate to the head of the political subdivision which is the employer, or to the appropriate officer of the Commonwealth, if the Commonwealth is the employer, with respect to matters which can be remedied by administrative action, and to the lawmaking body of such political subdivision or of the Commonwealth with respect to matters which require legislative action, to take the action necessary to carry out the determination of the board of arbitration.

Despite the vigor of this language, the Pennsylvania Supreme Court has limited its scope by ruling that in the case of direct conflict, existing laws need not be altered, and the offending terms of the award are therefore void. [City of Washington v. Police Dep't, 436 Pa. 168, 179, 259 A.2d 437, 443 (1969).]

Five statutes limit an arbitration panel's power to affect a jurisdiction's taxing or budgeting operations by rendering advisory terms relating to monetary expenditures. Practical assessment of the significance of these provisions is difficult. A public employer may feel great pressure to accept what is technically a recommendation when it is part of an award containing other binding terms. The pressure will be especially intense if the award fails to distinguish nonbinding from binding provisions and thus raises the expectation of employees that the employer must accept the entire package. In addition arbitrators may well make less costly determinations knowing their decisions are only advisory. Such a result is probably intended by the statutes, which implicitly warn the parties that excessively costly terms may be rejected.

I. *Judicial Review*

The majority of statutes are silent on the question of appeal from an award, and while no reported decisions have considered the issue as to them, the absence of a specific provision usually will not preclude judicial review on grounds such as fraud, lack of impartiality or wrongful assumption of power by the panel. Ten statutes, however, do explicitly provide for a right to appeal to the courts. South Dakota allows the broadest "appeal de novo"; Michigan permits review on the grounds, *inter alia,* that "the order is unsupported by competent, material and substantial evidence on the whole record." Other laws authorize review of questions of law, and, more narrowly, allegations of fraud, misconduct, and wrongful assumption of power. Consistent with the legislative intent that awards covering firemen and police be absolutely binding, a Pennsylvania statute denies any right to appeal from an award. The Pennsylvania Supreme Court, however, has held that this provision allows review to determine if the panel has exceeded its authority.

J. *Expenses*

Since a right to arbitrate at the expense of the other party may lead to obstinacy at the bargaining table, who must compensate the arbitrators is a question of some importance. Most statutes require the parties to share the costs of arbitration. The majority of the laws authorizing arbitration by mutual consent are silent on the question, in keeping with the statutory purpose of permitting, but not requiring, the parties to work out their own arrangements.

NOTE

For more detailed discussions of the "final offer" or "last offer" approach in compulsory arbitration, *see generally* Clark, *Public Employee Strikes: Some Proposed Solutions,* 23 LAB. L.J. 111 (1972) ; Gilroy, *Finality and Final Selection,* in DISPUTE SETTLEMENT IN THE PUBLIC SECTOR 25 (T. Gilroy ed. 1972); Garber, *Compulsory Arbitration in the Public Sector: A Proposed*

Alternative, 26 ARB. J. 226 (1971); Stevens, *The Management of Labor Disputes in the Public Sector,* 51 ORE. L. REV. 191 (1971). For two of the earliest reported cases adopting the "final offer" approach, see City of Indianapolis, 58 L.A. 1302 (1972); City of Eugene, GERR No. 451, B-1 (1972).

d.   Enforcement of Decisional Standards

DETROIT POLICE OFFICERS ASSOCIATION AND CITY OF DETROIT

Compulsory Arbitration Arising Pursuant To
Act No. 312, Michigan Public Acts of 1969 (July 1, 1970)

WILLIAM HABER, Chairman:

[The parties stipulated that nine "economic" issues should be submitted for decision by the Arbitration Panel. These included the matter of base salary for patrolmen and patrolwomen, shift differentials, premium pay for overtime and a cost-of-living escalator. At stake was the resolution of these issues for the City's fiscal year beginning July 1, 1970. With respect to base salaries the City had, in bargaining, proposed a 6% increase, which would have produced a starting salary of $8,480 and a top (5th year) salary of $11,448. The DPOA had proposed $11,712 and $13,315, respectively. The Panel majority awarded a 6% increase in starting salary in the second, third, and fourth years, but an 11.1% increase (to $12,000) for the fifth year and thereafter. The following are certain portions of the majority opinion.]

(a)   *The position of the City,* briefly stated, is that the City's offer is "fair, equitable and reasonable, under all the circumstances;" the patrolman's "package" includes more than his salary; and, when taking into account his fringe benefits, particularly the pension system, the cost of each patrolman is, in effect, $18,490.59 per year; the Panel must compare cities "in the same class," and that the suburban and other Michigan communities whose salary scale was cited by the Union "were not comparable communities;" that the economic impact of a police pay raise in suburban communities is far smaller from what it is in Detroit, and such comparisons in salary levels should not be made; that when compared with other large cities and with the cities in the Michigan group which were cited, "Detroit is a leader and is not behind the times;" that the patrolmen's salary rose 89.1% during a ten-year period in Detroit compared to general City employees whose pay in the same period has increased only 66.8%. Thus, the patrolman has fared quite well even without comparing a superior pension system and other fringe benefits. In addition, some weight must be given to the continuity and stability of employment for police in spite of the "grim economic future of the community."

Quite apart from its view about the equitable character of a 6% wage offer, the City contends that "The Arbitration Panel's jurisdiction is limited by the extent of the legal authority of the municipality;" that the Panel is not "free to render any decision it pleases;" that it is restricted not only by the Compulsory Arbitration Act, but by the Michigan Constitution, the Home Rule Act, the Michigan Taxation and Assessment Statutes, the Municipal Finance Act, the applicable Charter and Ordinance provisions, and the general body of law of this State; that the Panel is bound to take into account "the lawful authority of the employer," among other factors.

The City has a duty to produce a balanced budget; it is not given a free hand to raise money to pay its bills; the City is not in a good financial condition.

In view of all this, the jurisdiction of this Panel is limited, and "any award of the Panel which requires additional expenditures must be contingent on the City securing additional revenues other than as reflected in the existing budget." The Panel has only the power to determine the amount and extent of a wage rate or other conditions of employment: it cannot determine priorities since only elected officials can do that.

Finally, the City's fiscal picture is dismal; the non-recurring revenues in the current year will not be available in 1971-72; there will be an anticipated deficit on June 30, 1970, and a much larger one on June 30, 1972. In addition, there will be a "revenue gap" of impressive proportions in the 1971-72 budget. Moreover, Detroit's population has been decreasing, the tax base is declining, the personal property assessments are diminishing; the City cannot justify any more borrowing.

(b)   *The position of the Union.* The Union urges the Panel not to be unduly influenced by the City's argument on the issue of ability-to-pay. It emphasizes that during negotiations the City had indicated that it was not going to rely on a claim of inability to pay. It quotes the Mayor that he was prepared to seek a pay package that was fair to all, and will not require excuses related to inability to pay. It cites the testimony of the City Controller to the effect that it is not fair to attempt to meet budget crises by failing to make a decent, reasonable, and equitable wage offer. In other words, states the Union, the official view of the City Administration is that the police should not have to subsidize the general taxpayer by working at a salary that is less than fair and equitable. It cites one of its witnesses to the effect that it is illogical to lean heavily on the ability-to-pay position; that no one would seriously suggest such an argument to private contractors or propose to pay them less or to seek discounts on items purchased on the ground of the local government not being able to pay the established price.

The Union's brief makes reference to the City's budget, and observes that its financial difficulties are due to its own decisions concerning priorities; that it has not made any serious effort to reduce existing positions; that it is spending funds for activities far less essential than police work; that the City's expenditures can be reduced; that the pension liabilities could be funded during a longer period than thirteen years; that the City is overstating its plea of poverty and fiscal helplessness; that the City is crying "wolf" before the wolf is on the scene.

In its plea for higher salaries, the Union calls attention to its testimony and in its brief to the hazards of the police officer's work, to the "potential dangers," "the daily tensions;" it introduces a "chilling picture" of statistics concerning the number of officers assaulted on duty, injured while making arrests, injured by gunshot and knives—a total of 431 in the calendar year of 1968; there were an additional 1,000 various types of accidents while in a scout car, motorcycle or otherwise. The 1969 story is somewhat similar, with 404 such assaults in addition to four officers killed. A former Commissioner testified that one out of each nine policemen could be expected to be injured in the line of duty each year.

The Union emphasizes particularly the comparison of salaries between policemen in Detroit with communities in the Detroit Metropolitan area. Detroit, it contends, is not competing with New York, Philadelphia or San Francisco: it is competing with Livonia, St. Clair Shores and Westland. It calls attention to the higher crime rate in Detroit and in the thirteen largest cities in the country. It cites Philadelphia, with a much larger population and a crime rate of 1,819 per 100,000 people, compared to Detroit ratio of 6,879. It refers to Milwaukee, with a rate of 2,517 per 100,000 people—about one-third of the Detroit rate. It urges that such rates indicate radically different working conditions, and that it is really not appropriate to compare police salaries in these cities with those in Detroit in view of the significant difference in the crime situation—that is to say, working conditions. Detroit police officers, the Union pleads, should be paid more than those in these communities which have been used for comparison. Moreover, it urges that the Panel should take into consideration the general level of pay of the Detroit area, which is higher than in most of the comparable communities; it should consider whether collective bargaining prevails; whether there are traditional patterns of pay which would make mere wage comparisons inadequate. While the Union makes comparisons between police salaries and the earnings of other employees such as skilled tradesmen, it states that there are no employee groups comparable with policemen in respect to the nature of their duties and the responsibilities involved. It maintains that the 6% pay offer made by the City would leave Detroit patrolmen behind other communities in the Detroit Metropolitan area if account is taken of payments in those communities for such items as gun allowance, shift premium and uniform allowance.

In brief, in the Union's view, when compared to improvements in basic salary in several other Michigan communities and in other cities throughout the country, and when considered in relationship to the risks which accompany the policeman's work and the need to provide an adequate incentive to attract, to hold and to reward, its proposal for salaries is not unreasonable.

Moreover, according to the Union, its request for beginning wage and the annual steps over a four-year period is also designed to remunerate policemen for what is in effect "off-duty" services which are required of every policeman. While not universal throughout the country, Detroit patrolmen are required to carry their weapons when off duty, when shopping, and even when attending social affairs. It is unfair, according to the Union, to require such services without special compensation.

Similarly, patrolmen are required to "line up" for roll call 15 minutes before their eight hour day begins and to report to headquarters for 10 minutes at the conclusion of the shift. The officer should be entitled to compensation for this period. When the request for gun pay is coupled with remuneration for these required appearances and services, the Union considers it reasonable to propose a scale which begins at $11,715 and advances in the 5th year to $13,315. . . .

The Arbitration Panel carefully examined the entire transcript consisting of nearly 1,500 pages and the exhibits particularly relevant to the wage and salary issue. It has taken into account those exhibits which compare Detroit's present and proposed wages with those prevailing in other large urban centers throughout the country, taking due note of the observations that not all of these cities are necessarily comparable. In Washington, D.C., for example, the wages are, in the final analysis set or largely influenced by Congressional authority; in another large city salaries are set by the state legislature; in several other cities the collective bargaining procedure does not prevail; and in some the wage and salary levels for 1970-71 have not yet been determined and the prevailing levels were not an adequate guide to the Panel in considering the scale for 1970-71. Moreover, when the general level of employee compensation in both public and private employment in a community is considerably below national levels because of historic or other influence, to use such areas as a standard of comparison of the wages of policemen in Detroit is not appropriate. . . .

Similarly, comparing Detroit's wage scale proposed by the City with other Michigan communities, while not entirely irrelevant, is not especially helpful to the Arbitration Panel. These communities are relatively smaller; the size of the police force is nominal; the impact of any salary change is not overwhelming, the crime rates and general tensions associated with police work are of an entirely different order of magnitude than those prevailing in the City of Detroit. . . .

The Union contends that Detroit should really be compared with suburban communities and other Michigan cities. It refers to these in its brief as the only "true comparisons" because "Detroit is actively competing with these cities." It observes that the City is constantly losing trained and experienced officers to suburban departments and cities. Both in the transcript and its brief it calls the Panel's attention to testimony of personnel turnover, to the number of patrolmen who have gone to suburban areas "in the last few years." The turnover rate, however, in the Panel's view, is definitely not alarming. In fact, it is rather modest.

There are many advantages for a patrolman in smaller suburban communities. The pressures and tensions are undoubtedly less demanding. The Union also emphasizes favorable salary differences and implies that this is the reason why some 48 patrolmen left for the smaller communities in recent years. That some have left cannot be questioned, and that others will continue to do so is to be expected. Many factors account for this. Differences in the maximum salary may be an important factor. The evidence cited in the Exhibits is clearly not conclusive. The base salary at the maximum effective July 1, 1970, is higher in all six instances cited than that presently prevailing in Detroit, but below that of Detroit as proposed in this award. The higher totals of remuneration referred to in the Union's brief for all but two of these communities includes other elements than the base salary.

Salaries in private employment in Detroit are not, in the Panel's view, a useful guide in judging the adequacy or equity of salaries paid to police in Detroit. Many of these occupations have a long tradition of collective bargaining. Others have had for many years wage changes related to productivity or escalation factors based upon the Consumers Price Index. Moreover, many trades and skills in private employment do not have the continuity or stability of employment which characterizes City employment in general and police work in particular. Nor are the salary scales of most other city employees a helpful guide to the Panel. These employees are not subjected to the strains and tensions which are often (although not always) associated with police work. . . .

The Panel did not make an exhaustive inquiry into the problem of hazards, tension and strains associated with police work. It was told that these hazards, according to casualty insurance criteria, are not any greater than for a large number of other occupations such as carpenters or other building trades, and, in fact, a considerable number of other employment classifications on the City's payroll. The Chairman of the Panel is not too impressed with these comparisons. A carpenter may be injured or may, in fact, lose his life because of an occupational accident. A police officer, on the other hand, who is disabled or perhaps killed is often exposed not primarily because of an accident, but because of the inherent risk, especially in high crime areas. . . .

[T]he Panel has concluded that the City's proposal for a flat 6% increase for all patrolmen is inadequate if account is taken of change in the cost of living as well as the need to provide a more adequate remuneration for the risks of police work and the need to attract the best possible candidates, hopefully with higher educational achievements, beyond high school. The proposal of the City for a 6% increase is accepted, and becomes part of this award only for police officers with four years or less. For fifth year patrolmen the award calls for an increase which takes into account not only the changes in the purchasing power of the patrolman's dollar but also provides a substantial increase in prevailing salary for officers in their fifth year and all with higher than five years seniority. . . .

The logic of this Finding and Award is that the salary should remain modest for the starting patrolman and during his first four years in service. Having completed four years, it is reasonable to assume that the patrolman is now an experienced officer; that he has resisted the temptation to leave and seek employment in another community or in another vocation. He should be adequately rewarded with a salary that represents some improvement over the cost of living change that is associated with some status and dignity and will insure the commitment and devotion which the City has a right to expect from its police officers. . . .

The 5th year patrolman with an increase of $1,200 above his present salary of $10,800 is provided a salary boost of 11.1% above last year's salary. This is considerably above the cost of living increase. It may be thought of as including what used to be referred to as an "improvement factor." In other words, this is a merit increase which hopefully will lead to genuine "improvement" and an increase in the policeman's "productivity" by such measures of productivity as may be developed. . . .

This salary of $12,000 for the 5th year will make the Detroit police officer one of the best paid police officers in the United States. Even so, however, the difference between Detroit and several other cities with which it might be compared is not of substantial magnitude. . . .

It is clear to the Panel that comparable large cities are beginning to approach for officers with 5 years experience salary levels which are in excess of $11,000 or $11,500. It is a defensible concept that if that is the national direction, a salary of $12,000 for experienced officers with at least four years seniority is appropriate for a city like Detroit. This salary, at the maximum over four years, should make it possible for the City to consider revising its requirements for minimum qualifications for patrolmen. It should be in a position to attract to the police force men (and women) especially qualified; it should seek out candidates with educational qualifications beyond the high school diploma and possessing those personal and intelligence factors which are likely to ensure success in the delicate task of police work in a modern urban community. The higher salary provides a large opportunity and it would be unfortunate if it were not exploited.

On the basis of the data submitted to the Panel, the maximum salary of $12,000 beginning with the 5th year, would apply to 2,421 of Detroit's police officers represented by the Detroit Police Officers Association. The Panel is aware of the fact that while the Award directly covers the members of the DPOA, the number affected is substantially larger since the Award would undoubtedly be applied to supervision. Approximately 1,397 officers, almost all DPOA members, have been on the police force for less than 5 years and would not receive the maximum amount until after they have completed their 4th year.

The basic salary award (6% for the first four years and $1,200 for officers with more than 4 years of service) when applied to the DPOA membership subject to this arbitration, is estimated to cost about $1,340,000 above the City's 6% offer. The Panel is aware that this estimate will be increased by the fact that the

City may have to apply increases to other police officers not covered by this arbitration.

2.   The Ability-to-Pay Issue

The Panel has not taken lightly the legislative requirement that in making its award it take into consideration "the interest and welfare of the public and the financial ability of the unit of government to meet these costs." It recognizes that the Act lists "ability-to-pay" as one of many factors to be considered by the Panel. A responsible decision which did not take this into account would be indefensible, even if the law did not require the Panel to consider it. This is true in any employment relationship, and particularly so when the employer is a unit of government which has definite constitutional and charter limitations concerning the imposition of additional taxes. A private employer may under certain circumstances, depending upon the competitive situation in the market and the demand for his product, raise prices and thus transfer all or part of the extra costs of a change in the rate of pay to his employees, to the consumers of its product. A unit of government does not have that freedom unless its legislative body authorizes additional taxes, and that it has authority to levy such additional taxes. Again, a private employer may be quite ruthless in cutting costs and in reallocating his limited funds in order to meet the requirements of a new wage agreement or award.

A unit of government, while it has some degree of freedom in reallocation of its limited funds, is much more restricted. It is simple to say that much less should be spent for recreation. To do so may merely compound the problems of delinquency and crime and complicate even further the tasks of the police department. Similarly, it is easy to suggest that less money should be spent for parks, equipment, capital improvements, the public library, new employees—all matters cited in the Union's brief. The City has much less freedom in these matters than is assumed by the questions asked, and not analyzed, in that brief. In any event, it is not the role of this Arbitration Panel to pass upon these matters. It has no authority nor responsibility. Only the elected representatives of the people in the City Hall or Lansing can pass upon the degree to which one type of expenditure should have a higher priority than another. Consequently, the Panel is not in any position to give weight to the Union's view as to what expenditure could be cut back or what services are less essential than others.

Similarly, the Panel has read with special care the testimony of the Auditor General, the Assistant Auditor General, the City

Controller and the brief of the Corporation Counsel. This testimony and the City's brief are largely concerned with the ability-to-pay issue. The brief of the Corporation Counsel, in effect, argues that the Panel is without authority to provide any increase in salaries above its offer, and by implication it cannot make any changes in the other conditions covered by the nine stipulations submitted to the Panel, if cost consequences result.

The record indicates there will be an anticipated deficit of at least $20 million on June 30, 1970; that unless certain legislative enactments occur in Lansing there may be a deficit as large as $43.5 million on June 30, 1971. Certain income available in 1970-71 will not be available in the following year; the property tax limit has been reached. The search for additional revenues has been unproductive. Moreover, an anticipated revenue gap in the 1971-72 budget of $80 million is likely to develop (TR pp. 389-390-441, the testimony of the individuals referred to above and the Corporation Counsel's brief, page 21). Accordingly, in the City's view, either directly stated or by implication, the Panel has no authority in effect to deal with the issues submitted to it since any resolution might cost money. And the City has no money!

The Chairman of the Panel, and hopefully his colleagues on the Arbitration Board, has no choice but to dismiss this argument. Act 312, Section 1, states that since it is the public policy of this state to prohibit strikes by public police, the maintenance of morale of police employees and efficient operations of such departments make it necessary "to afford an alternative, expeditious, effective and binding procedure for the resolution of disputes." To that end, provision is made for compulsory arbitration. The Panel cannot comprehend why the City chose to proceed and to agree to binding arbitration (Joint Exhibit 1, III c) if, in its view, the Panel had no authority to make a finding with regard to the issues before it, unless its finding completely agreed with the City's offer.

The Panel fully recognizes that its action must be responsible; that its award must take into consideration the City's ability to pay. The legislature, however, did not indicate that this was the sole factor to be considered. This was one of the factors, although a critically important one. In fact, the very sentence referring to this factor links the "financial ability of the unit of government" with "the interest and welfare of the public." The Panel has done that. Having taken into account the equities involved in the proposals by the DPOA, it cannot conclude that it is impotent and has no authority to make any award because it costs money.

If that logic were to be persuasive and controlling, the City itself might be guilty of violating the brief which its Corporation Counsel submitted to the Panel. It proposed a basic salary increase of 6% effective July 1, 1970. The financial picture of the City outlined in its brief and inferred in the voluminous testimony and many of the 77 exhibits which were submitted, suggest that even its proposed increase might be barred by its own logic, if that were to be given a strict construction. All of the obstacles against adopting a deficit budget cited in the City's brief may very well apply even to the budget which contains the City's 6% increase.

The Panel has concluded that such logic would defeat the intent of Act 312, the interests of the police officers, and compound rather than simplify the problem of the City in its fight against crime and in the maintenance of law and order. Failure to provide proper public support for police officers in dealing with their sense of grievance concerning salaries and related matters could in fact further aggravate the City's fiscal capacity.

Having declined to accept as conclusive the thrust of the City's brief dealt with in 25 of its 29 pages, the Panel wishes to make it clear that it is not unaware of the serious fiscal problems faced by the City of Detroit. On paper, the budget for 1970-71 appears balanced. This balance, however, is achieved by anticipating income of more than $20 million, largely dependent upon favorable action by the Legislature on a series of items not all of which are likely to materialize. Consequently, the budget for 1970-71 may in effect contain a deficit.

These facts are not subject to serious dispute. This is, however, not an entirely new experience for the City of Detroit. The record contains some evidence to the fact that such deficits have occurred heretofore. The Chairman assumes that the issue is related to the size of the deficit and the degree to which the City officials have room to maneuver. Such deficits or serious cash shortages have faced the City time and again and challenged the ingenuity of city officials in grappling with them. They are entitled to public congratulation for their resourcefulness in overcoming one fiscal obstacle after another.

The Panel is also aware of the fact that the property tax rate is already up to the maximum allowed by law. No relief is possible from that source. It can not express a judgment with regard to services which ought to have a subordinate priority. This is not its function and it would be presumptuous for it to even express an opinion as to what services are less important to the life of the City than the protection against crime, the enforcement of City ordinances and the provisions of countless essential services made available by the Police Department. The Panel recognizes the near primacy of that service in a modern urban community deeply troubled by its concern for personal security, the maintenance of order and the protection of property.

It is not the Panel's task to spell out in detail or even in general terms how the City ought to go about dealing with its complex problems. The record submitted to it indicates that its population has been declining (from 1,850,000 to 1,500,000 in a period of 20 years). Much construction which has been taking place has been of a tax exempt nature. Reference has been made to the fact that some businesses have left the City either due to the population trend, the City income tax or other factors.

These overwhelming problems are generally recognized. As with the issue of priorities, it would also be presumptuous for the Panel to suggest how the City should resolve these difficulties. Mayor Roman Gribbs in his remarks to Union representatives of City employees in March of this year was quoted in the record to the effect that the City desires to provide a fair pay package, "one that will not require excuses in the way of inability to pay." The Panel does not think that the 6% increase represents such a package for experienced officers with five or more years of service.

Mr. Robert Roselle, Controller of the City, observed in his appearance before the Panel that it would not be fair to meet budget crises through not paying employees. To be sure, in his view, the City's offer was equitable. This the Panel has not accepted except for the beginning officers with less than 5 years of service. The Controller asserted that the City has an obligation "to try to find the money." If that is not possible, he observed that the City would have to examine the nature of its municipal services in order to minimize the deficit.

Other witnesses before the Panel observed that ability-to-pay is a criterion employed only with respect to salaries and wages of City employees. It could not be used with a private contractor by suggesting to him that he reduce his employees' wages when he has a contract with the City, nor would it make sense for the City to plead poverty in order to pay less than the market price for supplies which it purchases.

The [recommendations of the] Fact Finding Panel of 1968 . . . observed that the ability-to-pay criterion rigidly applied would result in a "highly irrational pattern of employee compensation." The idea of this criterion has never been widely accepted and has been used only to postpone rather than to deny wage adjustments.

DETROIT POLICE OFFICERS ASSOCIATION AND CITY OF DETROIT

Findings And Recommendations On Unresolved
"Economic" And Other Issues (February 27, 1968)

[In 1968, prior to the enactment of Michigan's compulsory arbitration statute, the DPOA and the City of Detroit submitted unresolved "economic" and other bargaining issues to a "Detroit Police Dispute Panel." The agreement for submission resulted from the mediation efforts of a "Detroit Citizens Committee," headed by Bishop Richard Emrich, which constituted in the wake of serious bargaining difficulties, which in turn, had led to "blue flu" and other interruptions in police operations and retaliatory suspensions. The Mayor and the DPOA agreed "to do all in their power to put the panel's recommendations into effect as promptly as possible." The Dispute Panel consisted of three "neutrals," Professors Ronald W. Haughton of Wayne State University, Charles C. Killingsworth of Michigan State University, and Russell A. Smith, Chairman, of the University of Michigan. Base salaries at the time were $7,424 (starting) and $8,335 (5th year). The DPOA demanded a starting salary of $7,500 and a 5th year salary of $10,000, as well as additional fringe and other economic benefits. The parties' stipulation of issues included the following:

No. 1: Considering all the circumstances, should the City raise the pay of patrolmen and policewomen to a maximum of $10,000 per annum for the fiscal year July 1, 1967 to July 1, 1968, or any lesser sum above the present base maximum of $8,335.00. If a lesser sum, how much of a rise should be granted?

No. 2: If a raise is recommended pursuant to Issue No. 1 above, does the City of Detroit have the funds available from which the recommended raise may be legally paid?

No. 3: If the answer to Issue No. 2 is in the negative, how can the funds to pay the raises recommended in Issue 1 legally be obtained or provided?

No. 4: If the answers to the preceding issues are that no raises be granted or that no funds to grant raises are available or can be legally obtained for the fiscal year 1967-68, what is recommended with respect to the amounts of pay raises and the methods of financing them for future fiscal years?

The Panel unanimously determined that the base for the fifth year salary should be $10,000. Following are certain excerpts from the Panel's Opinion]:

The Question of Ability to Pay

As already noted, the City's principal emphasis in discussing the wage question is on ability to pay. We believe that, for analytical purposes, the City's arguments can be considered to have five aspects, as follows:

1) Now that the 1967-68 budget has been closed, the City is forbidden by law to grant any wage increases or other economic benefits that would require an increase in any item in the closed budget; the only exception would be in an emergency created by a natural disaster or some comparable unforeseen event.

2) Even prior to the closing of the budget, it was clear that legal limitations on the City's taxing powers and the magnitude and urgency of other needs made it impossible to finance any wage increases for any City employees in the 1967-68 budget.

3) The cost of granting a police salary increase would be far larger than the amounts paid to the policemen, because as a matter of equity any economic concession to the police would have to be matched by similar concessions to all other City employees; this is especially true since other City employees accepted the "no-increase" decision for 1967-68 while the police engaged in an illegal "strike," for which they should not be rewarded.

4) Legal restrictions aside, as a practical matter the only way to get money for a substantial police salary increase within the framework of the 1967-68 budget would be to institute massive layoffs of other City employees, and that would mean disastrous curtailment of essential services.

5) It is anticipated that the City's operations during the current fiscal year will result in an enormous deficit, now estimated at about $20,000,000, and essential expenditures in the 1968-69 fiscal year are estimated to exceed presently available revenues by as much as $39,000,000. In these circumstances, as a matter of sound fiscal policy the City should not commit itself to any salary increases unless major new sources of revenue are made available by action of the State Legislature.

Because of the importance and complexity of the purely legal questions raised by the City, we have chosen to deal with those questions in a separate Memorandum Concerning Legal Questions, which is attached to and hereby made a part of this Opinion. The conclusion reached in the Memorandum is that the City has failed to establish that there are purely legal barriers to the granting of a salary increase to police officers in the current or next fiscal years. Therefore, it is appropriate to discuss other aspects of the ability-to-pay issue.

The formulation of the 1967-68 Budget. We recognize, and we believe that all informed persons recognize, that the City of Detroit was confronted by serious financial difficulties when it was formulating the 1967-68 budget. We also recognize that it would have been quite difficult to finance a large, across-the-board increase for all City employees. Nevertheless, it is clear from the record before us that the City had the legal authority to raise substantially more money from property taxes than it elected to raise, and that this added revenue would have been adequate to finance a significant salary increase at least for police officers. In other words, the City's alleged inability to pay increased police salaries is in some measure a self-imposed inability.

The basic limitation on the City's power to tax property is that the levy may not legally exceed 2 percent of State Equalized Valuation (with certain exemptions). In 1967-68, the net property tax levied subject to the limitation was $82,907,396. Two percent of equalized valuation, however, was $96,153,958. Thus, there was a margin of $13,245,562 available. If the City had elected to do so, it could have increased the property tax rate enough to yield some part or all of this amount for general revenue purposes, including the financing of salary increases. Instead, the City chose to absorb virtually all of that margin, as permitted by law, by the authorization of faith and credit budget bonds. The amount of such bonds authorized in any given fiscal year must be counted against the 2 percent limitation in that year, even though amounts appropriated for debt service are not counted against that limitation. The budget bonds were for a variety of capital improvements—for example, Art Institute building additions, park improvements and land acquisitions, street openings and widenings, street lighting improvements, street railway equipment and buildings, and so on.

We do not question the desirability of any of these capital improvements. Neither do we question the statement of the City Budget Director that, ideally, the capital improvement program should be much larger for a city the size of Detroit. We note, however, that many of the improvements were deferrable, and that most of the money was spent on outside contracts rather than for City payroll employees; i.e., deferral of most of the projects would not have resulted in layoffs for regular City employees. We note further that the City plans to reduce sharply the total amount of capital improvements to be financed by budget bonds in the coming fiscal year.

The important point is that limitations on the City's taxing powers did not make it literally impossible to obtain the revenue to finance a salary increase for police officers in the 1967-68 budget. If the City had chosen to cut back its capital improvement program, it would have had the legal authority to increase its revenues from property taxes.

We note that, in the 1967-68 fiscal year, the General City property tax rate was held at the same level that it had been for two preceding fiscal years, which is $23.972 per thousand assessed valuation. We are aware of the unpopularity of increases in taxes, especially property taxes. Nevertheless, the City cannot now successfully plead that it lacked ability to pay any salary increases in formulating the 1967-68 budget, when it had unused taxing powers.

We recognize, of course, that the City cannot now reconsider the basic decisions that were made in the formulation of the current budget. Certainly it cannot now retroactively increase the property tax rate. But our discussion of this matter is not mere idle second-guessing of decisions that cannot be changed. We believe that the analysis has a bearing on the questions of equity and fiscal policy that the City also asks us to consider.

Equitable Considerations. We do not accept the proposition that any economic concession to the policemen represented by DPOA would have to be accompanied by comparable concessions to all other City employees. The City has not cited any provision of law or custom that compels such uniformity of treatment of all City employees. Indeed, the evidence shows the opposite. In the 1966-67 fiscal year, policemen and firemen were given a much larger increase than the general increase for all City employees; building tradesmen have been given substantial increases when other City employees got none; and in the current fiscal year—a "no-increase" year—registered nurses in City hospitals were given a substantial increase in earnings through increases in shift premiums, for the stated purpose of relieving an acute staff shortage. In any event, under present circumstances we believe that it would be a disastrous policy to compel policemen to advance only in lockstep with all other City employees.

We must emphasize that we are dealing here with the argument that *all* City employees must be given uniform treatment. We recognize that, in Detroit, firemen have long had "parity" with policemen. We pass no judgment and offer no recommendations or opinion on the desirability of continuing this relationship. This matter is not included within the scope of this proceeding. Neither are we passing judgment on the merits of any economic demands that may be presented by other groups of City employees. These matters are also outside the scope of this proceeding, and any judgment we might express would be uninformed, because obviously we have not been provided with any of the evidence that would be essential for an informed judgment. Drawing upon general knowledge, however, we can say that—with one possible exception—there is no major group of municipal employees other than policemen concerning whom there is such a broad national consensus on the need for immediate and substantial wage increases. The possible exception is teachers; and as is well-known, Detroit teachers recently received increases totalling $1,700 over two years.

We also reject the contention that a wage increase which is otherwise justified—indeed, urgently necessary—should be denied because of an alleged illegal strike by policemen last June. Before the issues involved in the "blue flu" episode had been fully litigated, the City agreed to "hold in abeyance" all legal proceedings, and it reinstated all suspended patrolmen and ultimately paid them for lost time. DPOA likewise agreed to hold in abeyance its charges against the City of illegal refusal to bargain. As DPOA correctly points out, if we were to give weight to one set of charges, we would be compelled in fairness to give weight to the other set as well. Whatever the outcome might have been if both sets of charges had been pursued to a final, authoritative adjudication, it seems clear that the charges have been rendered moot by the subsequent conduct of both parties. Hence, neither set of charges should be deemed relevant to the questions which the parties have asked us to answer.

The Sources of Funds Within the 1967-68 Budget. The accompanying Memorandum points out some legally available sources of funds for police salary increases within the 1967-68 budget. On the basis of these findings and the others already set forth at length, we have concluded that the DPOA request for a $10,000 maximum base pay for patrolmen should be granted, and we shall so recommend. The effective date, related adjustments in the patrolman salary schedule, and estimated costs will be discussed in detail below.

We do not believe that it is either feasible or desirable for us to specify to the last penny precisely from which sources the necessary funds to pay the increased salaries should come. It is likely that some hard choices will be required, and they should be made by the Common Council, the Mayor, and his principal subordinates. We will not go beyond an indication of what seems to us a reasonable order of priorities.

(A)   Because of the persistent undermanning of the police force, there should be some funds available within the existing salary appropriation. Some part of the unused salary funds have been designated for the payment of overtime by Common Council action; remaining funds should be used for the payment of the higher salaries recommended.

(B)   Revenue from traffic fines has been running about one-third below normal for many months as a consequence of an alleged ticket-writing "slowdown" by the police officers. To the extent that this is the case we presume that the slowdown will cease immediately, thus resulting in a substantial increase in the current income to the City from this source. In addition, we urge the appropriate City officials to consider immediate action to raise the general level of traffic fines, either by agreement with the judges or by Common Council action to specify higher minimum fines for various offenses. It seems particularly appropriate that traffic law violators should bear a significant part of the increased cost of maintaining an adequate police force in the City of Detroit.

(C)   The City should immediately institute a "savings program" with the specific goal of saving a minimum of 5 percent of all unexpended balances in appropriations, wherever possible. Such a program was instituted in Detroit during the 1957-58 fiscal year, and it resulted in an apparent saving of about $2.8 million. That program was undertaken in December, but even a program undertaken now should realize significant savings. A stringent standard of necessity should be applied; all but the most urgent equipment purchases, for example, should be deferred. DPOA has pointed to a number of individual items in the current budget that would not be included in a true "austerity" budget. While some of these budget items now represent expenditures already made, it seems reasonable to presume that there are still others on which significant savings could be effected during the remainder of this fiscal year.

(D)   There is at least one significant item of unexpected revenue which the City will receive during the current fiscal year and which was not included in the budget. This is the City's share of the State income tax revenues. The Budget Director estimates this revenue at about $960,000. He insists that it "must" be applied to the reduction of the anticipated deficit in the current budget, but we do not find any legal requirement for that disposition; apparently this is viewed as a matter of desirable fiscal policy. Under the exigent circumstances of this case, we believe that the financing of an immediate salary increase for patrolmen should be given priority over reduction of the anticipated deficit.

(E) All of the foregoing should be more than sufficient to permit the transfer of funds to the Police Department in amounts adequate to meet the direct and immediate cost of the recommended salary increase in the current fiscal year. However, if the funds thus made available prove to be insufficient, or if the City decides that it must give simultaneous increases to closely-related groups—for example, to police officers above the rank of patrolman—and cannot find the necessary funds, then we believe that consideration must be given to ways and means of financing the required expenditures on a deficit basis. According to the testimony, the Sanitation Division of the Department of Public Works is expected to have a payroll deficit of approximately $1,000,000 (Tr. 1082-83). We were not told what formalities, if any, must be undertaken to authorize such a deficit; but as a final resort, if all other efforts fail—which we regard as an unlikely prospect—then consideration must be given to the incurrence of a payroll deficit in the Police Department.

The 1968-69 and Later Fiscal Years. Although it might be gathered from the wording of Issue No. 4 that we should undertake to specify in detail how recommended increases in police salaries should be financed in 1968-69 and ensuing fiscal years, the City recognized in the course of our hearings that, as a practical matter, it is impossible to provide us with sufficiently detailed information about prospective revenues and expenditures to permit detailed recommendations of this kind. Subsequent to the hearings, we have been provided with the interim report of a Task Force studying the problem which states that essential expenditures in the 1968-69 fiscal year in the City of Detroit are likely to exceed presently available revenues by as much as $39,000,000. Obviously, we are not in a position to provide a detailed blueprint for the solution of this unquestionably serious fiscal problem, and we are even less in a position to guarantee that the State Legislature will grant the City the added taxing authority that it obviously needs. Nevertheless, we can offer some general comments that are pertinent to the general subject.

We may take it as clearly established that, as matters now stand, Detroit lacks the "ability to pay" higher wages to any substantial group of City employees in the next and ensuing fiscal years without enlarging its prospective deficits. In the long run, how much weight should be given the "ability to pay" factor in wage determination for municipal employees? Judge Leonard provided us with an answer from his own extensive background and thinking, as follows:

> Generally speaking, favorable consideration for pay increases for municipal employees is often rejected by the city on the grounds that it is unable to pay. This is rather an illogical position to assume. A city would not suggest to a private contractor that they reduce the pay to employees performing work under the contract because the city is not in a position to pay the higher rate, nor would the city suggest that discounts be provided for commodities to be purchased by the city on the ground that they could not meet a fairly-established price. Neither should the temporary financial condition of the city be a controlling factor, as there are means of leveling off obligations, or providing for additional revenue. In the last analysis, the city should be a fair and model employer. This, of course, does not suggest that city employees be paid substantially more than outside employees performing the same general type of service, as this would be an unjustified gratuity that the taxpayer should not be expected to provide.

This answer touches on points that we consider worthy of further emphasis. If the "ability to pay" criterion is to be fair to all parties, it must work *both* ways. If employee wages are to be held *below* a fair market level when the municipality is short of money, then those wages should be raised *above* the market level when the City is in a surplus condition. Obviously, such a policy would not be viable; wide fluctuations in employee earnings from year to year would be unsatisfactory to everyone concerned, and a highly irrational pattern of employee compensation could develop. Because of considerations like these, the ability-to-pay approach has never gained wide acceptance in industry generally. In the few instances in which it has been given significant weight, this factor has usually been relied upon to justify some postponement of wage adjustments called for by the labor market but not to deny them permanently. As we read the record now before us, the wages of the Detroit police force have been lagging below the levels called for by the labor market for a number of years. The comparison with wage levels in the Michigan State Police, set forth at some length above, illustrates the point. This lag has tended to grow larger, not smaller, during the past decade. The lag has now contributed to the development of a manpower crisis in the Detroit Police Department. In these circumstances, continued reliance on inability to pay the salary levels that are clearly justified is not only unfair to the men and women directly affected; it is also a clear and present danger to the welfare of the community. The first order of business must be the adjustment in police salaries that is now urgently required. The second order of business must be to make those budgetary adjustments that are necessary, including the seeking of new revenue sources.

Nothing that we have said here should be interpreted as a denial that the City of Detroit urgently needs new taxing authority which can be granted only by the State Legislature. Judged by any normal standards, the current (1967-68) budget is a very "tight" one; and it should be clear that the various sources of "savings" that we have suggested herein are feasible only as emergency, short-term measures. Detroit is in serious financial trouble, and we join others who have urged that the State Legislature take steps to raise the authorized level of the municipal income tax, to restore the authority to levy local excise taxes, and to revise the 2 percent restriction on property tax levies.

We are aware that acceptance of our recommendations regarding patrolmen will add to the pressures which the City already faces to increase wage and salary levels of other groups of City employees in the coming fiscal year if not immediately. We note that, according to news reports (Daily Express, January 16, 1968), the City Controller has already advised Common Council that pay raises for all City employees will be included in the proposed 1968-69 budget, because of increases already granted in private industry and in other governmental units. It is impossible at this point to say to what extent, if at all, the recommended patrolman increase might compel the City to grant its other employees increases which are larger than those already planned in response to pressures existing before the announcement of our recommendations.

There will probably be some such effect, and to the extent that there is, this will add to the City's financial problems. In all probability, as noted above, the City will not be able to solve these problems without finding new sources of revenue or sharply curtailing many kinds of City services and programs. But we do not think the City of Detroit, any more than other public employers, can expect its employees to subsidize the public service for any extended period by working at salaries substantially below the levels which, in terms of applicable criteria, are proper. If the citizenry are unwilling to pay a fair price for employment services, they will, in our judgment, have to be willing to live with reduced services.

CITY OF DETROIT AND DETROIT FIRE FIGHTERS ASSOCIATION

Compulsory Arbitration Arising Pursuant To
Act No. 312, Michigan Public Acts of 1969 (1970)

HARRY H. PLATT, Chairman:

[Following the compulsory arbitration involving the Detroit policemen, an unresolved dispute between the Detroit Fire Fighters Association and the City proceeded to arbitration, principally on "economic" issues. In the matter of base salaries which, for many years, had been the same as for police, the Association's demand, as modified downward subsequent to the police arbitration decision, was for parity with the police. By a unanimous award the Panel granted this demand. Following are excerpts from the Panel's Opinion.] . . .

The central issue in this dispute concerns the amount of salary increase Detroit fire fighters should receive in the fiscal year July 1, 1970 to June 30, 1971. While in its original formulation of the wage demand the Association requested $13,062.00 annual salary for the fire fighters based on the wages paid by the City to its skilled trades employees plus 10 cents per hour hazard pay, it did not press this request in final argument. Instead, it makes two claims: (1) based on the applicable criteria—cost of living, comparison factors, wage trends, other wage influencing factors and criteria which are customarily taken into account in collective bargaining and by arbitrators—an annual base (top) salary for fire fighters of at least $13,000.00 would be fair and reasonable; (2) in the alternative, a top salary of $12,000.00 a year should be awarded in order to maintain the established historical parity relationship between police and fire pay.

Discussion

A basic condition for the success of any system of compulsory arbitration in public employment, which necessarily entails delegation of authority to a Board of Arbitration to make decisions which traditionally had been entrusted to elected officials would seem to require a specific legislative prescription of standards to govern decision. Act 312 of the Michigan Public Acts of 1969 does this. Section 8 of the Act provides that the Board's determination "shall be just and reasonable and based upon the factors prescribed in Sections 9 and 10." . . .

Read together, the above sections leave no doubt that the legislative intent was not to limit the Board of Arbitration but to allow it the broadest scope in considering what factors it deems "applicable" in reaching its decision. In this case, the Board's function is to determine a fair, rational, and objective economic solution based on economic facts. More specifically, it is our task to fix an annual base salary for the City's fire fighters which will be just and reasonable.

There is of course no magic formula for determining salary levels. Certainly, there is no single standard that can be relied upon to give a conclusive answer. And persons with equal intelligence and integrity might well differ as to the applicability of any one factor or number of factors or as to the weight to be given to any of them. Clearly, under the Michigan Act, there is an area of discretion left to the Board of Arbitration in deciding which criteria are most appropriate or controlling. Suffice it to say that in this case we have deemed applicable the following factors to which we gave varying degrees of weight: (1) the public interest and welfare and financial ability of the City to meet the costs of a pay increase; (2) comparison of the salaries, hours, and conditions of employment of the Detroit fire fighter classes with those of fire fighters in comparable communities; (3) cost of living changes; (4) total compensation of Detroit fire fighters, including basic salary, fringe benefits, continuity and stability of employment, and all other benefits; (5) changes in any of the foregoing circumstances during the pendency of the arbitration proceedings; and (6) factors normally taken into consideration by parties in collective bargaining, mediators, fact-finders, and arbitrators. It goes without saying, that it is the total combination of factors considered which produces a wage decision, not any one alone.

Cost of Living

It is well to note at the outset that the Board finds the City's offer of a flat 6% pay increase to all fire fighters for the fiscal year 1970-71 regardless of their years of service, less than adequate. We are convinced by the evidence that the determining factor in making this offer was the City's estimate of its then financial condition and that, with the possible exception of cost of living changes, no other wage determining criteria received serious consideration. Even so, while the change in cost of living was acknowledged to be 6.8%, the raise offered was 6%. Furthermore, it was the same percentage increase as other general City employees were offered, without taking into account past wage relationships between those employee groups or differences in their duties, responsibilities, skill requirements, job hazards, hours, and other working conditions. Plainly, the City's financial ability to meet the costs of a higher pay increase than 6% cannot be the sole criterion of the adequacy of its offer.

The Public Welfare and Interest and Ability to Pay

Section 9 (c) of Act 312 of Michigan Public Acts of 1969 provides that one of the factors to be considered by the Board of Arbitration, if deemed applicable, concerns the public interest and welfare as well as the City's financial ability to meet the costs of a pay increase. There therefore remains the question whether in consideration of those criteria some modification of the award which would otherwise be made is required in order to lessen the cost impact of the Association's pay demand.

The phrase "interest and welfare of the public" is not defined in the statute. Nor is it a phrase that has a commonly understood, fixed meaning. However, in the context in which it is used, it undoubtedly refers to an important social value, the general welfare, which calls for protection of the citizenry in matters affecting public safety and security, which includes the right to a reasonable steady flow of essential services upon which the public safety and security depend.

The City strongly urges us to take into account its precarious financial condition and to find that it lacks the "ability to pay" any salary increase in excess of 6%. Indeed, we do find that the City's financial adversity will unquestionably require it to continue to operate on a deficit financing basis. Yet we are mindful that an efficient fire department which pays fair compensation and provides adequate benefits to its employees is essential to the public welfare. Unquestionably, fire fighting services, like other essential public safety services, are becoming more expensive. So are the personal and family needs of the fire fighters. If, as we believe it to be the case, the general public and the taxpayers wish to continue to have a modern, efficient fire fighting service in the City of Detroit they must be willing to bear the increased cost.

We are fully aware that many employers cite unsatisfactory circumstances when supporting a claim of inability to meet employee demands. We are equally mindful that virtually all of these employers somehow find some source of necessary funds after the demands are met.

In the case at hand we are also aware, as the Association has pointed out, that year-end deficits and revenue gaps have been a "normal" way of life in Detroit for many years. We also understand that the increase in the real estate tax rate, the enactment of the excise tax on utilities, and the Urban Assistance Grant, all of which occurred after the original salary offer was made, have alleviated the fiscal problems somewhat. We do not, in other words, accept the stated inability of the City to meet fire fighter demands as a reason in and of itself for rejecting those demands. Nor would the provisions of the Act permit us to do so.

But we do not believe the City's financial condition can be ignored or that it is a wholly irrelevant consideration in determining pay levels which are above the level of substandard or minimum pay. Indeed, we must, as a practical matter and in prudence and good conscience, try to balance the needs of fire fighters for a pay increase and the City's ability and the taxpayers' willingness to meet the cost.

Apart from the financial data that has been presented, what adds great credence to the City's claim of inability to pay the amount of increase requested by the Association and to give that factor considerable weight is the testimony of City witnesses regarding several steps which have already been taken by the City Administration in the direction of cutting operation costs. These steps prove that the City does unquestionably believe that the existing fiscal situation is indeed desperate. They must be viewed as previews of further actions of comparable severity if costs of operation do increase.

For example, City witnesses testified that the current financial condition has prevented the filling of many budget positions, including those in essential service areas. Subsequent published figures update this testimony and disclose that there were in mid-November some 2,365 unfilled positions on the City's tax supported payroll. This figure, we believe, is directly translatable into discontinued and reduced municipal services to the citizens of Detroit.

Even more indicative of the validity of the City's claim is the information which it has presented relative to layoffs. There is evidence that some 539 City employees have been laid off from their jobs in recent months solely for budgetary reasons and that the City has not as yet been able to recall most of them or to place them in other positions.

Perhaps most important, evidence was offered that the layoff of some 329 City employees was announced on July 2, 1970, in an effort to reduce costs and that an additional 214 employees were similarly dropped from the payroll following an announcement on July 30. Moreover, it was indicated that these layoffs were made despite the fact that some 1,700 budgeted positions have not been filled as of July 1, that the City had increased the work week to 40 hours in many departments from the long standing 37½-hour work week, and that various City programs and activities had been curtailed or discontinued in the further effort to cope with the serious financial situation.

The implication of this testimony was that the cost of meeting fire fighter demands was translatable in terms of additional layoffs and reductions in municipal services. City witnesses held no hope that additional impositions on the budget could be borne without this type of response. It is these substantial reductions in services and the layoff of employees which convinces this Board that the City's ability to meet the costs of the fire fighters demands is indeed limited. We know of no other community in which the effort to cut costs has been nearly so drastic. Having taken these steps, the City's leadership has demonstrated to our satisfaction that it does consider its fiscal condition to be most precarious and that it does not see the possibility of acquiring additional funds as a solution to its dilemmas.

As a Board, we must therefore face the likelihood that increased costs ensuing from our decision, quite apart from the merits of the fire fighters' demands, would probably produce still further impacts on the City's ability to carry out its obligations to the people of Detroit.

Accordingly, we have strived to temper our decision in keeping with our perception of the City's fiscal facts of life. Our conclusion is that while the financial condition in which the City finds itself does not warrant a denial of a fair and equitable pay increase for fire fighters in the current fiscal year, a postponement of the effective date of part of our pay award, which will lessen the cost impact of a full application of the parity principle, is appropriate. Our pay award is therefore as follows:

Pay parity between the police and fire service has been an established City policy for more than 63 years and, no sufficient showing having been made to justify a disruption of that parity relationship, it shall be continued. Accordingly, effective July 1, 1970 and January 1, 1971, the salary schedule for fireman classes shall be:

	Effective July 1, 1970	Effective January 1, 1971
Fire Fighters, start (first year)	$ 8,480	. . . . . .
Second year	9,222	. . . . . .
Third year	9,964	. . . . . .
Fourth year	10,706	. . . . . .
Fifth year and more	11,448	$12,000

The above represents a 6% pay increase for all fire fighters effective July 1, 1970 and a further increase of 5.1% of present base salary, effective January 1, 1971, for firemen in their fifth year or more of service. Other departmental ranks and classifications enumerated in the parties' submission agreement shall receive corresponding increases, *i.e.*, 6% effective July 1, 1970 and a further increase of 5.1% of present base salary effective January 1, 1971. The practical effect of this award is to continue the historical parity relationship between police and fire pay on and after January 1, 1971. Postponement of the effective date of the second step increases will of course result in a large money saving for the City in this current year.

NOTES

1. In the 1971-72 compulsory arbitration involving the Detroit Fire-Fighters Association and the City of Detroit, the Panel Chairman, Charles C. Killingsworth, stated (p. 12) :

> If the legislature had intended that a showing that the governmental unit was having serious financial difficulties should preclude considerations of any other factors, the language to express such an intent could easily have been written into Act 312. No such language appears in the Act, of course.

The decision of the Panel also compared the City of Detroit with other cities and concluded (p. 13) :

> . . . [T]he experienced practitioner can evolve from a number of such comparisons—some of which will obviously be more persuasive than others—what this writer conceptualizes as a *zone of reasonableness*. This zone has a lower limit, below which most informed and reasonable persons would agree it would be unreasonable to go in the particular case; and it has an upper limit which most informed and reasonable persons would agree it would be unreasonable to exceed. Within this zone of reasonableness, the ability-to-pay factor may properly exert an influence.

2. In the 1971-72 compulsory arbitration involving the City of Detroit and the Detroit Police Officers Association, the Panel was also confronted with an assertion that the City was "sinking into a financial quagmire." In evaluating the evidence regarding the City's ability to pay, Panel Chairman Gabriel N. Alexander observed (pp. 11-12) :

> The evidence establishes that the City has been unable to extricate itself from a steadily increasing year to year deficit for several years, and that it is powerless to do any-

thing by way of increasing revenues without additional legislation from other governments, state or federal. I am convinced to a depressing certainty that the City cannot survive as an independent unit of government as that concept
was understood, say, a decade ago.

DPOA argues, and I agree, that the "financial ability" criterion set forth in Section 9 (c) is not controlling. If it were,
I might well conclude that there should be no salary increases, or even (considering what has happened on some
occasions in private employment) that salaries should be
reduced. But this is beside the point. The city acknowledges
that some increase is appropriate. The statute commands us
to take into account other criteria, in addition to financial
ability, and what I have asserted as the ruling is a reflection
of the amalgam of all the considerations pro and con which
bear upon the ultimate point in issue. As DPOA points out,
Detroit cannot buy coal for its generating plants or salt for
its streets for less than the "going rate" because it is impoverished. Why then should it be able to "buy" the labor of
its policemen for less than the "going rate" because it is
impoverished? Of course the answer lies in the statute which
defines the "going rate" (in statutory words "just and
reasonable") as that rate which shall be fixed by the Panel
after taking into account, among other things, the "financial ability of the unit of government to meet those costs."

3.   For some excellent discussions of the problem of ability to
pay, *see generally* Zack, *Ability to Pay in Public Sector Bargain-
ing,* in PROCEEDINGS OF NEW YORK UNIVERSITY TWENTY-THIRD
ANNUAL CONFERENCE ON LABOR (Christenson ed. 1970) ; Ross,
The Arbitration of Public Employee Wage Disputes, 23 IND. &
LAB. REL. REV. 3 (1969) ; Block, *Criteria in Public Sector Inter-
est Disputes,* in ARBITRATION AND THE PUBLIC INTEREST, PRO-
CEEDINGS OF THE TWENTY-FOURTH ANNUAL MEETING OF THE
NATIONAL ACADEMY OF ARBITRATORS 171 (G. Somers ed. 1971).

4.   On the question of the competence of arbitrators to deal
with issues arising pursuant to a government employer's claim of
"inability to pay," see Smith, *Comment,* in ARBITRATION AND THE
PUBLIC INTEREST, PROCEEDINGS OF THE TWENTY-FOURTH ANNUAL
MEETING OF THE NATIONAL ACADEMY OF ARBITRATORS 180, 184-87
(G. Somers ed. 1971). Professor Smith argues that "inability to
pay" is not a difficult issue in a case where the employer is "utterly
without financial resources to fund *any* increase in labor costs";
however, he makes the following additional observations with
respect to the problem:

[T]hese simplistic remarks dodge a whole series of problems for the neutral ranging from the factual to the basic questions of principle. I suggest that among the very serious questions are several that are not within the realm of expertise of labor dispute arbitrators on the basis solely of their private sector experience. The initial question is in a sense factual only. It is: What is the public body's actual fiscal position in terms of its ability to absorb *any* increased operating costs? Any sound analysis of this matter often requires an exhaustive and knowledgeable inquiry into budget allocations, revenue sources, transferability of appropriations, borrowing capability, and the like. The second question is whether, if the public body's ability to absorb increased operating costs is limited (which is probably the typical situation), the neutral should attempt to determine the gross amount of increased labor costs, if any, which the public body can finance. This in itself may turn out to be a fairly complicated problem. But, assuming this gross amount can be determined, the next and crucial question is whether the neutral should assume that this fund is all that can be provided, by way of increases, for any and all groups of employees—given the repercussionary effects of an increase awarded to the group before him—or should act on the basis that this fund can be enlarged by the public body by reductions in force or rearrangements of priorities. Obviously related is the question whether the neutral should attempt to determine the impact his award will have in terms of affecting the economic demands of other groups of employees and their ultimate settlement. Bear in mind, of course, that it is assumed that these other groups of employees, and their bargaining representatives, if any, are not parties to his proceeding or represented in it.

Now I submit that inquiries of these kinds pose problems which are so serious and difficult as to make the criterion ability to pay or, more realistically, alleged inability to pay, one which, if deemed to be relevant or required by law to be taken into consideration, is likely to be taken less seriously than others, such as comparison data. One of Howard Block's observations is that he "is inclined to agree with those who insist that when a neutral rules out inability to pay as a valid defense, he should also assume some responsibility for finding the funds to implement his award," although he also adds, apparently as a proviso, "if the parties have authorized him to do so." I interpret this remark as implying that Howard not only regards ability to pay as a proper criterion for consideration, where advanced by a party, but further as stating that the neutral does, indeed, have the full responsibility, somehow, of dealing with the series of problems which, I have suggested, then must be addressed. But I doubt very much that he can or should attempt any assignment of that magnitude except perhaps in a situation where all parties concerned, including other unions, have deliberately vested in him what would be tantamount to the full authority of the public body with respect to its budget, allocations, and priorities.

What, then, is the likely result where ability to pay is accepted by the neutral, or by law forced upon him, as a factor to be taken into account? Only a searching analysis of arbitral decisions would provide anything like an accurate answer. I have knowledge of some, however, including several in which I have participated. My impression is that a number of arbitrators, absent any statutory compulsion to take fiscal matters into account, tend to regard them as substantially irrelevant. But my impression, further, is that where, as under the Michigan police and firefighter compulsory arbitration law, this is one of the several factors specified for consideration as applicable, there has been a more or less valiant effort to analyze the public body's fiscal position, and, upon finding a very tight situation, to make an award on economic issues which would be somewhat less, or stated as being somewhat less, than otherwise would have been considered justified, but yet not to let the fiscal factor predominate.

INTERNATIONAL ASSOCIATION OF FIRE FIGHTERS, LOCAL 1285, LAS VEGAS, NEVADA AND CITY OF LAS VEGAS (1972)

HOWARD S. BLOCK, Fact-Finder:

[The parties came to impasse in negotiations over a number of "economic" issues, including wages. NEV. REV. STAT. § 288.200-7 empowers the Governor to make the anticipated findings and recommendations of the factfinder binding at the request of either party. The Fire Fighters invoked this provision and, after a hearing, Governor O'Callaghan ordered that the factfinder's recommendations be final and binding as to six issues, including wages. Subsequent to the hearing, the parties jointly selected Howard S. Block to serve as Factfinder (from a list submitted by the American Arbitration Association). The decision was as follows with respect to "binding monetary issues":] . . .

1. Binding Monetary Issues

(a) *Salary Grade Adjustments*—The parties are ordered to negotiate the issue of Salary Grade Adjustments for the classifications of Alarm Operator and Hydrant Repairman. The Factfinder reserves jurisdiction to determine this issue if the parties are unable to resolve it within thirty days from the date of this Report.

(b) As to all other monetary issues, the Factfinder rules that the City does not have the financial ability to pay the additional wages and benefits proposed by the Fire Fighters. . . .

For the current (1972-73) fiscal year, the City offered an across-the-board wage increase of 5% to all employees which, when added to the reclassification study increase, amounts to a total wage advance averaging 6.6% for Fire Fighters. This does not include instep and longevity increases already built into the salary schedule, and a number of minor fringe benefit items, which together add 4.39% to the average income of City employees. According to the Fire Fighters, this 4.39% figure is significantly less in the Fire Department.

The City's 1972-73 wage proposal was accepted by the City Employees Association. It was rejected by the Police Protective Association and the resulting impasse was submitted to Factfinder Joseph F. Gentile who submitted a comprehensive report on May 5, 1972 (City Exhibit 1) which concluded that the City did not have the financial ability to grant additional monetary benefits. Chronologically, that brings us down to the instant case to which we now turn.

Preliminary Determination Pursuant to NRS 288.200-8(a)

For a Factfinder, the crux of the Nevada Statute is found in NRS 288.200-8 (a) which delineates the criteria he must apply in arriving at his decision. Because of its importance in this proceeding, that statutory language is set forth below:

"8. Any factfinder, whether acting in a recommendatory or binding capacity, shall base his recommendations or award on the following criteria:

"(a) *A preliminary determination shall be made as to the financial ability* of the local government employer based on all existing available revenues as established by the local government employer, and with due regard for the obligation of the local government employer to provide facilities and services guaranteeing the health, welfare and safety of the people residing within the political subdivision.

"(b) Once the factfinder has determined in accordance

with paragraph (a) that there is a current financial ability to grant monetary benefits, he shall use normal criteria for interest disputes regarding the terms and provisions to be included in an agreement in assessing the reasonableness of the position of each party as to each issue in dispute.

"The factfinder's report shall contain the facts upon which he based his recommendations or award." [Emphasis added.]

It is clear from the foregoing provision that the Legislature has established a two-step procedure, with the first step being a preliminary determination of financial ability. What is not at all clear is the test to be applied in making this "preliminary determination," and the parties are in sharp disagreement on this point. Thus, the "preliminary determination" question poses two issues for the Factfinder: (1) the meaning that can reasonably be ascribed to this statutory requirement and (2) how that meaning should be applied to the instant case.

The City's position on the first issue was summarized by Counsel as follows:

". . . if the Board of City Commissioners with reference to the budget have made the allocations reasonably, that the Factfinder cannot tamper with them. In essence, turning the coin around, it is the City's position that the Factfinder has to be able to say that as a matter of law the Commission's allocations were unreasonable."

In other words, the City maintains that its budgetary allocations are conclusive upon all parties unless it can be determined that some of its allocations are unreasonable. The Factfinder cannot accept this interpretation for the following two principal reasons: (1) it is readily apparent to the most casual observer that, over at least the past several years, financial constraints upon local government in Nevada, and elsewhere across the United States, make it impossible to satisfy all of the requirements that would fall within the broad classification of a "reasonable allocation." Therefore, if a Union's right to negotiate matters within the scope of representation were limited to funds "unreasonably allocated," it would make the negotiating process a meaningless ritual; and (2) if the Legislature intended the budgetary allocations of local government to be conclusive, it could have easily said so. There is simply no justification for "reading-in" such an interpretation which, in practical effect, would restore employer-employee relations to where they were before the Dodge Act was passed.

In the Factfinder's opinion, if the criteria imposed by NRS 288.200-8 (a) are to be reconciled, in any meaningful way, with the duty to negotiate over wages, hours and conditions of employment as prescribed by NRS 288.150, then, once the City has determined the sums that are necessary ". . . to provide facilities and service guaranteeing the health, welfare and safety of the people residing within [the City limits] . . ." [NRS 288.200-8 (a)], it must then establish priorities in its allocation of remaining funds as between all claimants—*e.g.* capital expenditures, employee requests, taxpayer proposals, and all of the other competing claims upon the limited funds available. The ranking of these priorities may be reviewed by a Factfinder as to its reasonableness. Indeed, this is ordinarily the principal function of the interest dispute factfinder in the public sector where, as here, there are insufficient funds to meet all legitimate demands. Were the Factfinder barred from reviewing the order of priorities, as the City has argued, then this entire factfinding procedure would serve little, if any, purpose. The Factfinder rules, therefore, that a review of City established priorities is proper under the statutory language.

We turn now to the principal and remaining question bearing on the "preliminary determination" issue—whether the City's priorities should be revised in order to meet the Union's demands. Or, stating the question in statutory terms, whether the City has the financial ability to pay such demands. The parties focused their attention on this key issue because the answer to it determines, in large measure, the extent to which the Union's demands can be satisfied, if at all.

Both the Fire Fighters and the City offered an analysis of budget expenditures and revenues through expert testimony. In addition, each submitted comprehensive exhibits into evidence which compared the City's salaries and benefits with Fire Fighters in other public jurisdictions of Nevada, California and elsewhere in the United States. All of these data were then summarized and ably argued by Counsel for each side in his closing argument. The exigencies of time make it impractical for the Factfinder to review all of the arguments advanced or even most of them. However, on the basis of a careful scrutiny of the entire record of this proceeding, the Factfinder concludes that he would not be justified in altering the priorities established by the Board of City Commissioners. He has reached this conclusion for the following principal reasons:

    1. The Fire Fighters salary schedule compares favorably with those of other Nevada jurisdictions. On the basis of the record before him, the Factfinder cannot agree with the Union's argument that the proper comparison is with the salary schedule of the City of Los Angeles. In support of

this contention, the Union relied upon the following two principal arguments: (a) this was the recommendation of Factfinder Johns in his 1971 Report and (b) the Los Angeles rates were the guideline for voter approval, in 1968, of the $144 increase for Fire Fighters.

As to the first point, it must be noted that Professor Johns' recommendation was not adopted by the Board of City Commissioners; furthermore, this Factfinder would hesitate to adopt the conclusions of a prior Factfinder without examining the evidence upon which his conclusions were based—evidence which is not before him. With regard to the second argument advanced by the Union, it does appear from Fire Fighters Exhibit 41 that the 1968 $144 increase was based upon a comparison with Los Angeles rates, although that explanation did not appear on the ballot (City Exhibit 51). Whatever may have been the motivation in basing the 1968 increase on Los Angeles rates, the record since then negates any intent to use Los Angeles as a guideline. For this Factfinder to conclude that the Los Angeles and Las Vegas Fire Fighter salary schedules should be linked together permanently, it would take far more persuasive evidence than is present in this record.

2. The 6.6% increase offered by the City (5% general increase and 1.6% reclassification) approximates the change in the cost of living since the last general increase and, in addition, is comparable to the increases granted other public employees in Clark County.

3. The Fire Fighters cannot be viewed in isolation from other City employees. While the relationship of their salaries and benefits to other employees in the City cannot be decisive, it is, nevertheless, a factor entitled to considerable weight. The evidence reveals that Policemen (450 unit employees) and Fire Fighters (250 unit employees), and to a lesser extent members of the City Employees Association (700 unit employees) have been granted similar increases in prior years. For this Factfinder to depart from the established past practice in granting such general increases, it would require clear and convincing proof—a level of proof that cannot be discerned in the record of this proceeding.

4. An analysis of the fund allocations in the 1972-73 budget, taken together with the respectable relationship between income and expenditures in prior years, is convincing to the Factfinder that current budget projections are realistic. Any significant revision or reduction in the expendi-

tures as allocated by the City in the current budget could seriously impair its ability to furnish essential facilities and services.

The finding on this crucial point of ability to pay disposes of all monetary issues save one—Salary Grade Adjustments. For the reasons set forth below in the discussion of this item, the Factfinder has remanded it back to the parties for negotiation. The sum required to meet the Union's demand on this issue is not significant, and is well within the City's ability to pay. Following consideration of Salary Grade Adjustments, the Factfinder will then take up the nonmonetary issues, namely, Benefits, Duration, Savings Clause, Civil Service Rules, and Sick Leave.

NOTE

Did Fact-Finder Block assume more responsibility than the statute really authorized? Does the interpretation by Block result in a usurpation of legislative authority? Did Block avoid this legal question by refusing to alter the City's priorities? Is this statutory analysis, if valid, impetus for Las Vegas public employees to try to negotiate as one group?

3.   The Canadian "Arbitrate or Strike" Legislation

ARTHURS, COLLECTIVE BARGAINING IN THE PUBLIC SERVICE ACT OF CANADA: BOLD EXPERIMENT OR ACT OF FOLLY?, 67 Mich. L. Rev. 971, 987-93 (1969)†

[The Canadian Public Service Staff Relations Act, CAN. REV. STAT. c. 72 (1967), covering federal employees] requires both the employing agency and the bargaining agent, upon timely notice, "to bargain collectively in good faith and make every reasonable effort to conclude a collective agreement." As a reflection of the statute's general adherence to private sector principles, this admonition is hardly surprising. It is the procedure for impasse resolution which represents the most novel (and, some say, the most radical) feature of the statute. Following certification, the bargaining agent for each certified union is required to choose between two procedures "for resolution of any dispute to which it may be a party": arbitration or a process of conciliation. Since arbitral awards are "binding on the employer and the bargaining agent . . . and on the employees," choice of the arbitration option forecloses the possibility of a strike. However, no comparable binding effect accompanies the report of a conciliation board, and there are no prohibitions elsewhere in the statute which

---

† Reprinted by permission of the Michigan Law Review.

would preclude a post-conciliation strike. By inference, then, strikes are permitted following exhaustion of the conciliation process.

The failure to announce affirmatively the existence of a right to strike is hardly surprising. In the first place, no Canadian court has ever clearly held that strikes by public servants are per se illegal; thus there was no need for Parliament to reverse an existing legal norm. Second, while it is true that Canadian labor relations statutes have seldom contained an express reference to the right to strike, the courts have recognized that such legislation impliedly incorporates the common-law right to strike.

The Act does not, however, entirely abandon the public interest in the continued operation of government to the whim of negotiators. If a union has elected to resolve its collective bargaining impasses by a process of conciliation—and, impliedly, by a strike—rather than by arbitration, the Act forbids certain "designated employees" within the bargaining unit from striking because their duties "consist in whole or in part of duties the performance of which at any particular time or after any specified period of time is or will be necessary in the interest of the safety or security of the public." But it should be noted that the definition of "designated employees" is very circumscribed. The Act denies the right to strike only to those persons whose absence from work would imperil interests which are absolutely vital; employees whose absence would merely imperil the "public interest," "convenience," or "welfare" are still permitted to strike.

The procedure for identifying "designated employees" is designed to avoid controversy over this issue during the course of a strike when the pressures of conflict would make resolution of the matter especially difficult. Within twenty days after either party has served a notice to bargain, the employing agency must establish a list of essential employees. If the union does not object to the employer's list, all of the persons so identified are taken to be "designated." However, in the event that the bargaining agent files an objection, the Board must hold a hearing to determine whether the listed employees are really essential to the "safety and security of the public."

In practice, the various government employers have exercised great self-restraint in designating critical employees. Of approximately 33,000 employees in bargaining units governed by the strike option, the government has "designated" only eighty-six. In each case, the union has accepted the employer's unilateral judgment. Thus, the Board has not had occasion to determine authoritatively the meaning of the statutory phrase "safety and security of the public." Nevertheless, some clue to the meaning of this standard may be gleaned from the *Air Traffic Controllers* case, where the only "designated" employees were those controllers thought necessary to provide emergency assistance to overflying and noncommercial aircraft at various airports throughout the country. Obviously, such a small number of "designated" controllers would be inadequate to service regular domestic commercial air traffic, which would necessarily be suspended for the duration of a strike within this particular bargaining unit.

The Act does not expressly provide for the designation of additional employees during a strike if the employing agency or the Board initially misjudged the number or type of employees necessary to protect the public interest. The PSSRB would undoubtedly mobilize its full statutory resources to cope with such a crisis, including its power to "review, rescind, amend, alter or vary any decision or order made by it." It might well be argued that the employer and the Board should have anticipated all contingencies in making the original choice of designated employees, but this argument might have the unfortunate effect of prompting the employer to exaggerate at the outset the number of designated employees on the basis of remote contingencies.

A second series of problems concerns the relationship between striking employees and designated employees in the same bargaining unit. If a government employer determines that a skeleton staff is necessary during a strike in order to provide services essential to the "safety and security of the public," how is such a staff to be selected from among the employees in a bargaining unit? What happens if some of the designated employees resign or become ill? Must the same individuals continue to work throughout the strike, or can the strikers serve in rotation? What of the risks of sabotage, deliberate slow-downs, or "work-to-rule" campaigns by designated employees? And what of the wages paid to designated employees: if the remuneration for continuing on the job exceeds strike pay, should the designated employees be required to turn the surplus over to the union strike fund? Although these as yet unanswered questions are potentially troublesome, the statutory procedure for designating employees in advance of an actual strike situation is fundamentally sound. The fact that the parties are not locked in conflict makes it more likely that they will agree upon the list of designated employees. If there is disagreement, the Board can undertake the difficult adjudicative problems of defining and identifying employees in essential services without the extra pressure of a strike situation. Finally, if a large proportion of employees in a bargaining unit must be designated as essential, thus impairing the union's ability to strike, that fact is made obvious so that the union can opt for arbitration at an early stage in the proceedings. . . .

[T]he institutional arrangements provided by the statute undoubtedly contribute to the amicable settlement of disputes. Perhaps most important in this regard is the provision of a factual framework for enlightened bargaining. The Pay Research Bureau, established in 1957, has obtained the cooperation and confidence of the government and the employee associations both in gathering and in disseminating data useful in the bargaining process. By largely removing factual issues from the realm of controversy, the Bureau enables negotiators to focus attention on the admittedly difficult task of choosing the criteria by which those facts are to be evaluated. Second, if the parties fail to resolve their differences in direct negotiation, the dispute does not pass directly to arbitration. Instead, the Act provides for the intervention of a conciliator on the request of either party. Only if the conciliator fails to bring the parties together does the focus shift from bargaining to binding third-party determination.

If and when it is necessary to resort to arbitration, the Act contains elaborate provisions to ensure that the issue will be clearly and narrowly defined for the arbitrator. The Arbitration Tribunal, moreover, is not simply left to speculate upon the principles by which public employment working conditions are to be fixed. The Act provides the Arbitration Tribunal—and presumably negotiators seeking to avoid arbitration—with specific criteria for determining wages and working conditions. While these standards are admittedly broad, they at least constitute an attempt by Parliament to discharge its legislative obligations by stating that public employees are to enjoy employment conditions comparable to those in the private sector. Coupled with the data generated by the Pay Research Bureau and submitted to the scrutiny of an Arbitration Tribunal staffed by highly competent men, these legislative guidelines are likely to produce a decision which the disputants will respect. Certainly, neither party need fear that arbitration involves risks of irresponsible or ill-informed third-party determinations. Indeed, the very rationality of the arbitration process may encourage the parties to simulate it in private negotiations, and thus avoid arbitration altogether.

In the case of bargaining units which opted for the right to strike, the experience to date is somewhat less than conclusive. While the air traffic controllers were able to negotiate an agreement without recourse to a strike, 25,000 postal workers who apparently felt obliged to employ the ultimate sanction called a postal strike which lasted for nineteen days—from July 18 to August 8, 1968. This was hardly a surprising development. In

1965 the postal workers had resorted to a seventeen-day walkout; on several other occasions, national and local union groups had threatened strike action. A number of factors contributed to the militancy of these groups: deep-seated grievances against poor working conditions; departmental management which was under-staffed and ill-prepared for collective bargaining; a new union leadership cognizant of the fact that their predecessors had been purged as "moderates"; and overtones of French Canadian na-tionalism in the Montreal local union. Circumstances beyond the immediate control of the parties added several ingredients to this witches' brew: a federal election occurred in the midst of bar-gaining; a new Postmaster-General took office; critics called for an overhaul of postal services and mail rates; and the government attempted to restrain inflation by encouraging a policy of wage restraint throughout the economy.

Bargaining began at a slow, almost fatalistic pace. While the parties made some progress on minor items, and although a board of conciliation succeeded in resolving other issues, the govern-ment made no response to the union's unrealistically high wage demand until the very eve of the strike. Predictably, this last-minute move proved "too little, too late," and the first legal strike of Canadian federal workers began. Much more unpredictable was the comparatively mild reaction of the Canadian public. To some extent, the press was sympathetic to the grievances of the employees and critical of the government's failure to make an earlier wage offer; thus, it initially adopted a fairly neutral atti-tude. Having learned the lessons of the previous mail strike in 1965, many businesses had made arrangements to continue serving customers and collecting accounts for the duration of the strike. Welfare agencies and similar organizations also provided emer-gency services to their clientele through alternate devices. While there was some inconvenience and extra expense, the strike did not appear to cause a major communications crisis.

As the strike progressed, however, the patience of the public began to wear thin, and pressure mounted for legislation to end the walkout. The government's position was awkward indeed. It was reluctant to withdraw the right to strike on the very first occasion upon which it had been exercised, and it was equally hesitant to undertake the task of suppressing the almost certain defiance which a back-to-work order would bring. On the other hand, the government could hardly afford to capitulate to union demands. The postal workers were seeking wage increases beyond those which had been accepted by unions subject to arbitration; moreover, it was doubtful that the militant union members would even accept any recommendation made by its negotiating team.

Thus, while the government was under increasing pressure to end the strike, it could not afford to reach a settlement with the postal workers which would destroy the faith of other unions in the efficacy of the arbitration option. Finally, such factors as veiled threats of special antistrike legislation, increasing public hostility toward the strike, and financial pressure on the individual union members (who received no strike pay) helped to move the union toward settlement. After further concessions by the employer and the vigorous and imaginative efforts of a special mediator, the parties reached an agreement. By a narrow margin, the union membership ratified the agreement, and the postal strike was over.

The postal strike, then, can be seen either as vindicating the predictions of doom by detractors of the new statute or as proving the good sense of its draftsmen. Critics would contend that the Act proferred the right to strike to "irresponsible" unionists who used it at the first opportunity to the considerable inconvenience, if not the lasting detriment, of the country. Conversely, proponents of the Act might argue that a postal strike was inevitable, that the statute merely circumvented awkward problems of law enforcement, and that the community's actual loss was negligible. Moreover, they would contend that public inconvenience was a small price to pay for the preservation of free collective bargaining and that the ultimate resolution of the conflict within the range of settlements among bargaining units subject to arbitration augurs well for the future of the system.

CRISPO, DISPUTE SETTLEMENT IN THE CANADIAN PUBLIC SERVICE, in PROCEEDINGS OF THE INTERNATIONAL SYMPOSIUM ON PUBLIC EMPLOYMENT LABOR RELATIONS 89, 92-95 (1971)†

Even though Canada's federal experiment with public service dispute settlement has, on balance, thus far proven successful, this does not mean that in any significant way it strengthens the case for compulsory arbitration. This is because Canada's federal model falls considerably short of the latter. In essence it is really arbitration at the exclusive option of the employee bargaining agents, who can individually reverse their positions before their next set of negotiations if they are not satisfied with an award growing out of their latest impasse with the government. From the point of view of the employee body, the likelihood is that arbitration at its discretion should ensure that the arbitration tribunals are not just normative in their judgment, but are at

---

† Reprinted by permission of the Institute for Labor and Industrial Relations, University of Michigan.

least accommodative to some extent. Assuming the bargaining agents' veto power over the continuation of the arbitral process does give rise to such a shift in emphasis, it should work to the advantage of the employees.

The point is that little that is happening in public service dispute settlement at the federal level in Canada can be construed to negate the traditional arguments marshalled against compulsory arbitration. Although time will not permit even a quick review of these arguments here, one of them does require renewed emphasis in this age of rank-and-file union membership militancy. It is not just that compulsory arbitration poses manning and criteria problems, or that it tends to undermine the collective bargaining process. Equally important is the disturbing effect it can have on union leaders. Harried as they are by more intense and unmanageable internal trade-off problems, it is little wonder that labour leaders sometimes privately crave the imposition of arbitration. Then they could blame the arbitrator for unpopular but unavoidable decisions, which might otherwise seriously undermine their internal political positions. It is in this troubling sense that compulsory arbitration could lead to increasingly irresponsible union leadership.

Like so many other problems to which compulsory arbitration can give rise, this is less likely to happen under Canada's new federal public service model, because union officials cannot just blame the arbitration process or the arbitrators. They can avoid both by convincing their members to opt next time round for strike action. To repeat, then, praiseworthy as the new federal model in Canada may be, it does not bolster the weak case to be made for compulsory arbitration, which, in the author's view, should be employed only on an ad hoc basis, as a last resort, when all else fails and the public health, welfare and safety are jeopardized.

What Canada's approach to bargaining in the federal civil service does suggest is that more effort should be made to improve the acceptability of forms of arbitration short of the compulsory variety. Much could no doubt be done to make voluntary, optional, and other types of arbitration more viable, and even attractive.

Other Considerations

Before concluding, there are one or two other aspects of Canada's federal approach that merit attention. Mentioned earlier were the potentially damaging effects which the government's abortive wage guidelines had on the new civil service bargaining system. Just as the promulgation of these guidelines led the government to try to hold the line at six percent with its employees so too, did it stimulate their bargaining agents to make that amount their minimum objective. In several cases, at least in the parties' public pronouncements, other criteria were almost forgotten as the parties battled around this symbolic figure. More impasses were inevitably reached than would otherwise have been the case, with a corresponding increase in both arbitrations and strikes. If nothing else, however, the new federal bargaining system probably spared Canadian civil servants the degree of discriminatory treatment under a general guidelines program that has been their counterparts' fate in other jurisdictions.

One feature of the new system that has not received much attention is the vulnerability of the government to a kind of whipsaw. It stands to reason that arbitration awards under this new optional system cannot diverge significantly from the fruits of bargaining where a strike is the alternative, or the arbitration route will be discredited. As the Chairman of the Public Service Staff Relations Board pointed out in a speech last year:

"Unless there is a reasonable relationship between the benefits gained under both schemes (arbitration and strike), there is a danger that, in the not-too-distant future, bargaining agents that have opted for arbitration may alter their specification of a dispute resolution process."

Strategically, this tends to put the government in a vulnerable position, since groups with strike leverage may use it to extract high settlements which weaker groups will then try to emulate through arbitration. According to one observer:

"This provides a bargaining agent with a very powerful weapon in collective bargaining. Groups which are unwilling or unable to engage in effective strike action can compel the government to submit disputes to compulsory arbitration. Other groups which may find the strike an effective weapon can in fact engage in work stoppages."

If this potential for whipsawing begins to show up as a serious problem, the solution might lie in providing the government with the alternative of declining a group option to go to arbitration, in which event the affected employees would be permitted to strike over their unmet demands. It is at least worth contemplating the effect of such a double option, although some would no doubt dismiss the suggestion out of hand as a mischievous and irresponsible one.

NOTES

1. A danger inherent to any arbitration procedure, is that one party will refuse to accept the award. Such was the case with the Montreal police, who refused to accept what they considered an inadequate award and struck. *See* Arthurs, *The Arbitral Process,* in PROCEEDINGS OF THE INTERNATIONAL SYMPOSIUM ON PUBLIC EMPLOYMENT LABOR RELATIONS 134, 137-38 (1971) (discussing the policemen's strike and the effect any increased settlement would have on future adherence to arbitration awards). Arthurs suggests that by providing compulsory arbitration as an alternative the parties may have little incentive to reach agreement voluntarily. He notes, however, that as yet this has not happened. In A. Anderson, *Compulsory Arbitration in Public Sector Dispute Settlement—An Affirmative View,* in DISPUTE SETTLEMENT IN THE PUBLIC SECTOR 1, 5-6 (T. Gilroy ed. 1972), it is reported that 75 percent of the agreements reached pursuant to the Canadian Public Service Staff Relations Act by the parties without recourse to any third-party assistance and that 17 percent were settled with the assistance of a conciliator.

2. The Minnesota Public Employment Relations Act was amended in 1973 to grant strike rights to nonessential employees if an employer refuses to submit to binding arbitration or to adhere to a binding impasse arbitration award. Essential employees are those whose work involves services essential to public health or safety. *See* GERR No. 526, B-11.

Chapter 8

ENFORCEMENT OF THE COLLECTIVE BARGAINING AGREEMENT

A. Private Sector Concepts Concerning the Legal Status of the Collective Agreement

The Legal Status of the Collective Agreement[1]

Early court decisions advanced at least three separate theories, along with variants, to explain the legal nature and effect of the collective agreement.

1. The labor agreement establishes local customs or usages, which are then incorporated into the individual employee's contract of hire. This seems to have been the orthodox view of the American courts, at least prior to the era of the labor relations acts.[2] Under the original form of this theory, the collective agreement itself was not regarded as a contract. It had legal effect only as its terms were absorbed into individual employment contracts. Somewhat similar is the traditional English concept that collective agreements are merely "gentlemen's agreements" or moral obligations not enforceable by the courts. Some American scholars also have voiced an occasional plea that court litigation over collective agreements should be rejected as detrimental to the parties' continuing relationship.[3] Nevertheless, judicial enforcement at the behest of either employers or unions became generally accepted in this country well before the passage of the LMRA in 1947, and was confirmed by that act. To account for the recognition eventually granted to both the union and individuals as possessors of enforceable rights under labor agreements, a refinement of the custom and usage theory posits the existence of two bilateral contracts. One contract consists "partly of promises running to the benefit of the union as an organization . . . and partly of provisions relating to wages, hours and job security

---

[1] From R. Smith, L. Merrifield, and T. St. Antoine, Labor Relations Law: Cases and Materials (4th ed., 1968).

[2] See Rice, *Collective Labor Agreements in American Law,* 44 Harv. L. Rev. 572, 582 (1931).

[3] See Shulman, *Reason, Contract, and Law in Labor Relations,* 68 Harv. L. Rev. 999 (1955).

which the employer promises to incorporate in a second bilateral contract—the contract of hire between the employer and the individual employees."[4]

2.   The collective agreement is a contract that is negotiated by the union as the agent for the employees, who become the principals on the agreement. This so-called agency theory was adopted by a few courts which could not rationalize the enforceability of an instrument executed by an unincorporated association lacking juristic personality. Suits between individual employees and employers were maintainable, however, on the theory the union had merely served as the employees' agent in negotiations.

3.   The collective agreement is a third party beneficiary contract, with the employer and union the mutual promisors and promisees, and with the employees the beneficiaries. Despite arguable shortcomings (is the employer to be left without recourse against the employee beneficiary, who has made no promises?), the third party beneficiary theory became rather widely accepted as the best explanation of the collective agreement in terms of traditional common-law concepts.[5]

Today, collective-bargaining agreements in industries affecting commerce are enforced as a matter of federal law under § 301 of the LMRA. This means that the Supreme Court's views on the nature of the labor contract are now of primary concern. Two characteristics of the Court's thinking stand out. First, the Court is eclectic in its approach to common-law doctrines; it refuses to confine itself to any single theory, but draws upon whatever elements may be helpful in a variety of theories. Second, the Court has increasingly emphasized what may be described as the "constitutional" or "governmental" quality of the labor agreement. Thus, the collective agreement has been described as "not an ordinary contract" but rather a "generalized code" for "a system of industrial self-government."[6] In analogizing the plant or industrial community to a political society, it might be said the collective agreement serves as a sort of basic legislation or constitution, and the grievance and arbitration procedure for the reso-

---

[4] Cox, *The Legal Nature of Collective Bargaining Agreements,* 57 MICH. L. REV. 1, 20 (1958); *see* Association of Westinghouse Salaried Employees v. Westinghouse Elec. Corp., 210 F.2d 623 (3rd Cir. 1954), *aff'd,* 348 U.S. 437 (1955).

[5] *See* C. GREGORY, LABOR AND THE LAW 447 (2d rev. ed. 1961).

[6] *See* John Wiley & Sons, Inc. v. Livingston, 376 U.S. 543, 550 (1964); United Steelworkers v. Warrior & Gulf Nav. Co., 363 U.S. 574, 578-80 (1960); Aeronautical Ind. Dist., Lodge 72 v. Campbell, 337 U.S. 521, 528 (1949).

lution of day-to-day disputes arising under the agreement constitutes a sort of judicial system.[7]

The Supreme Court's eclectic approach to the nature of the
labor contract is reflected in the following well-known comments
by Mr. Justice Jackson in J.I. Case Co. v. NLRB, 321 U.S. 332,
334-35 (1944):

> Contract in labor law is a term the implications of which
> must be determined from the connection in which it appears.
> Collective bargaining between employer and the representa-
> tives of a unit, usually a union, results in an accord as to
> terms which will govern hiring and work and pay in that
> unit. The result is not, however, a contract of employment
> except in rare cases; no one has a job by reason of it and no
> obligation to any individual ordinarily comes into existence
> from it alone. The negotiations between union and manage-
> ment result in what often has been called a trade agreement,
> rather than in a contract of employment. Without pushing
> the analogy too far, the agreement may be likened to the
> tariffs established by a carrier, to standard provisions pre-
> scribed by supervising authorities for insurance policies, or
> to utility schedules of rates and rules for service, which do
> not of themselves establish any relationships but which do
> govern the terms of the shipper or insurer or customer rela-
> tionship whenever and with whomever it may be established.
> Indeed, in some European countries, contrary to American
> practice, the terms of a collectively negotiated trade agree-
> ment are submitted to a government department and, if
> approved, become a governmental regulation ruling employ-
> ment in the unit.
>
> After the collective trade agreement is made, the individ-
> uals who shall benefit by it are identified by individual
> hirings. The employer, except as restricted by the collective
> agreement itself and except that he must engage in no unfair
> labor practice or discrimination, is free to select those he
> will employ or discharge. But the terms of the employment
> already have been traded out. There is little left to individual
> agreement except the act of hiring. This hiring may be by
> writing or by word of mouth or may be implied from con-
> duct. In the sense of contracts of hiring, individual contracts
> between the employer and employee are not forbidden,

[7] For elaboration, see Chamberlain, *Collective Bargaining and the Concept of Contract*, 48 COLUM. L. REV. 829 (1948); Cox, *The Legal Nature of
Collective Bargaining Agreements*, 57 MICH. L. REV. 1, 25-36 (1958).

but indeed are necessitated by the collective bargaining procedure.

But, however engaged, an employee becomes entitled by virtue of the Labor Relations Act somewhat as a third party beneficiary to all benefits of the collective trade agreement, even if on his own he would yield to less favorable terms. The individual hiring contract is subsidiary to the terms of the trade agreement and may not waive any of its benefits, any more than a shipper can contract away the benefit of filed tariffs, the insurer the benefit of standard provisions, or the utility customer the benefit of legally established rates.

NOTE

Much has been written on the legal nature of the collective agreement, with most commentators noting its unique characteristics and the difficulties and dangers of adopting traditional doctrines developed in other fields of contract law. *See* Burstein, *Enforcement of Collective Agreements by the Courts,* in N.Y.U. Sixth Annual Conference on Labor 31 (1953) ; Chamberlain, *Collective Bargaining and the Concept of Contract,* 48 Colum. L. Rev. 829 (1948); Cox, *Rights Under a Labor Agreement,* 69 Harv. L. Rev. 601 (1956) ; Cox, *The Legal Nature of Collective Bargaining Agreements,* 57 Mich. L. Rev. 1 (1958) ; Gregory, *The Law of the Collective Agreement,* 57 Mich. L. Rev. 635 (1959) ; Gregory, *The Collective Bargaining Agreement: Its Nature and Scope,* 1949 Wash. U.L.Q. 3; Rice, *Collective Labor Agreements in American Law,* 44 Harv. L. Rev. 572 (1931) ; Shulman, *Reason, Contract, and Law in Labor Relations,* 68 Harv. L. Rev. 999 (1955) ; Warns, *The Nature of the Collective Bargaining Agreement,* 3 U. Miami L.Q. 235 (1949) ; Witmer, *Collective Labor Agreements in the Courts,* 48 Yale L.J. 195 (1938) .

B.   The Enforcement of the Collective Agreement Through the Grievance Procedure and Arbitration

PICKETS AT CITY HALL: REPORT AND RECOMMENDATIONS OF THE TWENTIETH CENTURY FUND TASK FORCE ON LABOR DISPUTES IN PUBLIC EMPLOYMENT 17-18 (1970)†

In any agreement negotiated, the public employer and the union should be strongly encouraged to provide a system for the presentation and disposition of grievances as they may be alleged

---

by employees. One of the most positive values to be found in a union-employer relationship is that it establishes a formal process through which complaints that might otherwise be unknown and unattended by management are brought into the light.

No matter how detailed the agreement between union and management may be, it cannot take into account all of the problems that will arise during its term. Nor can it anticipate what differences there may be over interpreting provisions in the agreement and their application. Hence the grievance procedure is a safety valve. Rather than let a difference that arises while the agreement is in force develop into a deadlock which might disrupt the work place or lead to a strike, formal grievance machinery should be established. As it functions, the individual employee has assurance that he will not suffer from management arbitrariness while the union has assurance that it will be heard and management has assurance that employee claims will not be supported by coercive pressures.

The lack of formal grievance machinery has led to public employee disputes, as employees have no alternative method of pressing a claim against unfair treatment, real or imagined. Established grievance procedures, leading ultimately to arbitration, have proved essential in achieving peaceful resolution of disputes in the private sector. Such procedures are equally essential for public employment.

Giving an outsider (the arbitrator) power to render a binding decision on a grievance involving internal organizational or operational matters may appear to be a momentous step for the responsible administrator of a government agency. His protection is that despite any ruling by an arbitrator, he cannot be required to do something beyond his legal authority or contrary to law. Against this hazard he will be protected by the courts. If his interpretation or application of the terms of an agreement seem wrong to his employees, with no opportunity to appeal they cannot escape a frustration that can seriously damage employee relations.

Unless specifically proscribed by law from agreeing to binding arbitration—and where such laws exist they should be repealed—a government agency should accept the arbitration of grievance matters in its own protection against unresolved and potentially explosive disputes. In jurisdictions where binding arbitration remains impermissible, the arbitrator's award should be taken as advisory and, if necessary, referred for implementation to the body or official with authority to order it.

1. The Grievance Procedure

One of the most significant accomplishments of labor law in the private sector has been the development of a system of industrial jurisprudence, a system whereby the parties themselves establish the machinery for the resolution of day-to-day disputes over the interpretation and application of the collective bargaining agreement. Almost all of these disputes are settled by means of this machinery; few disputes get as far even as the last step in the process, which is usually some form of arbitration.

> The essence of a grievance procedure is to provide a means by which an employee, without jeopardizing his job, can express a complaint about his work or working conditions and obtain a fair hearing through progressively higher levels of management. Under collective bargaining, four important and related features have been added to this concept. First, the collective bargaining contract, while it drastically limits the area of legitimate complaints by establishing the basic conditions of employment and rules for day-to-day administration deemed to be fair by mutual agreement, at the same time may create a source of grievances and disagreements through ambiguities of language and omissions, as do changing circumstances and violations. Second, the union is recognized and accepted as the spokesman for the aggrieved worker, and an inability to agree on a resolution of the issue becomes a dispute between union and management. Third, because an unresolved grievance becomes a union-management dispute, a way ultimately must be found to reach settlements short of a strike or lockout or substitutes for such actions. Final and binding arbitration is the principal means to this end. Fourth, the process of adjusting grievances and grievance disputes is itself defined in the agreement, and, along with other aspects of collective bargaining, tends to become increasingly formal.[8]

Private sector grievance procedures typically consist of a series of steps, with the employee-grievant and the management seeking to resolve the dispute at successively higher levels. The employee normally takes his grievance first to his foreman or to his union steward. If the union steward is consulted first, he will present the grievance on behalf of the employee to the foreman. Normally, the employee is entitled to union representation at each step. If no resolution is achieved, the matter may be taken to a higher company official, often the foreman's immediate su-

---

[8] U.S. BUREAU OF LABOR STATISTICS BULL. NO. 1425-1, MAJOR COLLECTIVE BARGAINING AGREEMENTS: GRIEVANCE PROCEDURES 1 (1964).

perior; this is the second step. If no solution is found here, the matter may then go to a still higher company official or to a hearing before a union shop committee and certain company officials who have been designated to meet regularly with this committee. If the grievance is denied at this level, but the union continues to deem it meritorious, it may go to a conference of regional union officials and high company officers. Failure to settle the grievance at this step may result in a union demand that the matter be arbitrated. The number of steps in the procedure will of course vary from contract to contract, and the nature of the proceedings at each step may differ, but the pattern is fairly well established in the private sector.

Public sector grievance procedures in the past have generally not followed the private sector pattern. There are two major reasons for this.[9] First, the sovereignty doctrine led many public employers to conclude that they were powerless to negotiate any kind of procedure which would result in the sharing of decision-making authority or its transfer to any third party. Second, a negotiated grievance procedure was thought to be superfluous; often, a grievance procedure already existed in the form of a civil service appeals system.

There are major differences, however, between civil service appeals procedures in the public sector and a private sector model grievance procedure.[10] A civil service procedure is normally established unilaterally by the public employer or through the legislative process, though employee organizations are generally consulted. In contrast, a negotiated grievance procedure is by definition established bilaterally through collective bargaining; it exists by virtue of the effort and approval of both parties. Processing a grievance is usually an individual matter in a civil service procedure, though the individual is generally allowed union representation at some stage of the proceedings; in a negotiated procedure, however, it is a union matter, the union taking up the cudgel for the employee and determining how far and how fast to process the grievance dispute. A civil service procedure is an "appeals" procedure; the employee is seen as appealing to higher authority from the decision of a public official. A negotiated grievance procedure, however, is less an appeal than a continuation of the collective bargaining process, a method by which the rights and responsibilities of the parties

9 Ullman & Begin, *The Structure and Scope of Appeals Procedures for Public Employees,* 23 IND. & LAB. REL. REV. 323 (1970).

10 Amundson, *Negotiated Grievance Procedures in California Public Employment: Controversy and Confusion,* 6 CAL. PUB. EMPL. REL. 2 (August 1970).

are continually clarified in the developing "common law of the shop."

Further distinctions between civil service appeal procedures and grievance procedures are detailed in Massey, *Employee Grievance Procedures,* in Developments in Public Employee Relations 64-65 (1965):

> [A] civil service commission is not like an arbitrator. An arbitrator, hopefully at least, is a disinterested party. On the other hand, when a commission is hearing an appeal, it is passing on the application by an operating agency of regulations issued by the commission pursuant to law. It is enforcing its own regulations.
>
> Also, a civil service commission is not an integral part of management, as is the personnel department of a private business. While many commissions have taken a positive role in personnel administration and have become to a degree an arm of management, they are not in a position to be an integral part of management. They have a legal existence independent of management. Moreover, historically, they were established as the protector of job applicants and employees against political favoritism by management, and they are now regarded by employees as the protector of a number of employee rights. Incidentally, some unions of government employees seem to consider it an advantage to apply more-or-less continuous pressure on the commissions. Of course, some other organizations with a considerable population of government employees as members—veterans' organizations, for example—do the same. Thus, civil service commissioners are likely to have a dual loyalty—to management, on the one hand, and to employees, on the other. This arrangement has endured for many years and may have its advantages. It is, however, a different arrangement than is found in private business.

Conceptually, there is also a great difference in the subject matter covered by the two types of procedures. A grievance procedure, as a matter of contract, may cover such subjects as wages, fringe benefits, working conditions, and other matters not normally covered by civil service appeals procedures. The scope of a civil service appeals procedure, on the other hand, depends on the applicable statute or city ordinance; typically, civil service laws deal almost exclusively with the manner of appointment, promotions, discharges and changes of status of employees. Civil service regulations in these areas have historically been considered non-negotiable.

As a practical matter, however, there is often a considerable overlap of grievance and appeals procedures. Indeed, employees sometimes may have a choice of procedures, or the procedure may be mandated by the type of incident that has occurred. An "adverse action," for example—an official reprimand, suspension or discharge—may require an appeal to the civil service commission or supervisory political body rather than a grievance within the management structure.

In the last few years there has been increasing reliance on the private sector model in the formulation of public sector grievance procedures.[11] In part, this is due to the trend away from viewing the doctrine of sovereignty as a complete bar to the adoption and enforcement of public sector collective bargaining agreements containing grievance procedures, even those which culminate in binding arbitration.[12] In part, too, it is due to the recognition that negotiated grievance procedures are capable of coexisting with or supplanting civil service appeals procedures.

Whatever the motivating factors, one recent study shows negotiated grievance procedures to be on the increase.[13] In the federal service, it was found that about 38 percent of the employees were covered by collective bargaining agreements, approximately half of which contained negotiated procedures. Among state and local government employees, 21 percent were covered by collective agreements; 90 percent of these agreements contained negotiated procedures.

In the private sector, 32 percent of employees are under collective agreements,[14] almost all of which have negotiated grievance procedures and 94 percent of which culminate in binding arbitration.[15] Fifty-three percent of state and local government contracts also provide for binding arbitration;[16] binding arbitration is yet rare in federal labor agreements, though 40 per-

---

[11] Begin, *The Private Grievance Model in the Public Sector*, 10 IND. REL. 21 (1971).

[12] *See, e.g.*, Tremblay v. Berlin Police Union, 108 N.H. 416, 237 A.2d 668, 68 L.R.R.M. 2070 (1968); Board of Educ. of Union Free School Dist. No. 3 v. Associated Teachers of Huntington, 30 N.Y.2d 122, 331 N.Y.S. 2d 17 (1972). *Also see* Note, *Legality and Propriety of Agreements to Arbitrate Major and Minor Disputes in Public Employment*, 54 CORNELL L. REV. 129 (1968).

[13] Ullman & Begin, *The Structure and Scope of Appeals Procedures for Public Employees*, 23 IND. & LAB. REL. REV. 323 (1970).

[14] *Id.* at 327.

[15] U.S. BUREAU OF LABOR STATISTICS, BULL. No. 1425-6, MAJOR COLLECTIVE BARGAINING AGREEMENTS: ARBITRATION PROCEDURES 5 (1966).

[16] Ullman & Begin, note 13 *supra* at 329.

cent of them do provide for advisory arbitration.[17] The National Postal Agreement of 1971 does provide for binding arbitration, but the U.S. Postal Service Corporation is not a typical federal agency; by virtue of the passage of the Postal Reorganization Act,[18] it is now under the jurisdiction of the National Labor Relations Board.

REPORT OF THE COMMITTEE ON THE LAW OF FEDERAL GOVERNMENT EMPLOYEE RELATIONS, SECTION OF LABOR RELATIONS LAW, AMERICAN BAR ASSOCIATION 1972 COMMITTEE REPORTS 144-46 (1972)†

The Federal Labor Relations Council, charged with the responsibility of overseeing the Federal service labor relations program, is not only charged with a decision-making role, . . . but is responsible for recommending to the President changes in the program.

In accordance with this responsibility, the Council conducted public hearings in October 1970 to review the program. After a substantial delay, the Council made recommendations to the President in June 1971. . . .

The Council's recommendation [in the area of grievances and arbitration] were accepted by the President, who issued Executive Order 11616 on August 26, 1971, amending Executive Order 11491. The . . . major changes are as follows:

The Council was concerned with the right of employees to select a representative other than the exclusive representative to process grievances arising under the negotiated grievance procedure. It felt that permitting employees to select a rival union to process employee grievances which were related to the negotiated agreement was undesirable. Accordingly, the Order was amended to provide that only a representative approved by the exclusive bargaining agent which negotiated the agreement could represent employees in processing grievances under the agreement.

Employees or groups of employees were, however, given the right to present their own grievances without the intervention of the exclusive representative. The rights of the exclusive representative to administer the agreement were protected by a proviso

---

[17] *Id.* A major reason for the restricted use of binding arbitration in the federal service has been that § 8 (b) of Executive Order 10988 provided for advisory arbitration only. In 1969, Executive Order 11491 eliminated this restriction, opening the door for the first time to negotiated grievance procedures containing binding arbitration provisions.

[18] 39 U.S.C.A. § 101 *et seq.* (Supp. 1972).

† Reprinted by permission of the American Bar Association.

that if the employee presents his own grievance the exclusive union representative shall be given an opportunity to be present at the adjustment and the adjustment of the grievance shall not be inconsistent with the terms of the agreement.

The Council found that the existing mix of employee "grievances" and union "disputes" involving agency regulations, application of laws, or agency policy, all considered under a negotiated grievance procedure, created a situation under which employees were faced with complicated choices in seeking relief. In order to correct this problem, the Order was amended to confine the negotiated grievance procedure to grievances, whether employee or union instigated, concerning the interpretation or application of the terms of the agreement and not other matters.

The Council noted that a grievance procedure limited to the interpretation or application of the agreement would not only simplify grievance processing, but "in addition, an incentive will be created for unions to negotiate substantive agreements within the full scope of negotiations authorized by the Order." The extent to which this goal has been achieved is unknown at this time. Whether unions are seeking or will seek more substantive agreements and thereby broaden the scope of the agreement in order to provide wider latitude to process grievances remains to be seen.

The Council's recommendations, which were adopted by the President, further clarified the situation by permitting all other grievances, i.e., those not involving the interpretation or application of the terms of the agreement, to be processed through any other avenue available to the employees. In the case of grievances not cognizable under the agreement, the employees could select any representative they desired to represent them. The prior practice of excluding matters covered by statutory appeals procedures was retained.

In order to enhance further the role of the exclusive representative, the amendments eliminated the requirement that the employee agree to arbitration. Furthermore, the employer was also given the right to invoke arbitration.

Finding the need for a procedure to resolve questions as to what is grievable or arbitrable, the Council recommended that such disagreements be resolved by the Assistant Secretary of Labor. In the private sector, those issues are customarily disposed of by arbitration or in the courts. The Council stated that the machinery created by the amendments to handle these disagreements "is appropriate in order to insure consistent application

of the recommended revisions with respect to negotiated grievance procedures." It should be noted that the courts have indicated that they do not have jurisdiction over matters arising
under the Executive Order or agreements which result from the
Executive Order. Bronx-Manhattan Postal Union v. Gronouski,
350 F.2d 451.

Subsequent to the amendments of Executive Order 11491, the
Federal Labor Relations Council, on March 22, 1972, issued an
Information Bulletin to clarify certain provisions of the amended
order as they related to the grievance procedure.

Inasmuch as the Council found that a substantial number of
agreements executed under the Order did not contain any type
of grievance procedure, it resolved this problem by mandating
that all negotiated agreements entered into, renewed or extended,
after the effective date of the amendments, November 24, 1971,
must contain a grievance procedure. The grievance procedure
could contain binding arbitration and the sharing of the cost
of arbitration was made negotiable.

NOTES

1. Though a method for handling grievances is a nearly
universal feature of collective bargaining agreements in both
the public and private sectors, not all contracts define "grievance" in the same way. Some contracts, in fact, detail the procedure without defining the term at all. The language outlining
the scope of the grievance procedure may be very broad, or it
may detail the matters which are subject to the procedure in
very specific terms. Other provisions generally exclude certain
subjects from the grievance procedure as matters of management
prerogative.

2. The scope of the grievance procedure should not be confused with the scope of arbitration. The two are often not co-
extensive. Some disputes may be grievable even though they
concern matters which the parties have not agreed to submit
to arbitration. In most cases, however, at least in the private
sector, the scope of the grievance procedure and the scope of
arbitration coincide.[19]

2. Negotiating the Grievance Procedure

In the private sector, the most important element in negotiating a grievance procedure is the intent of the parties as to
what should and what should not be a grievable dispute. In the

---

[19] U.S. BUREAU OF LABOR STATISTICS BULL. NO. 1425-6, MAJOR COLLECTIVE
BARGAINING AGREEMENTS: ARBITRATION PROCEDURES 6, 8 (1966).

public sector, other factors are also important. Principal among those other factors is the intent of the legislature. Did the state legislature or city council, in enacting a public employee bargaining law, intend that the area in question be subject to the grievance procedure, or did they intend that it be left to the unbridled discretion of the public employer? Also relevant is the effect of past or existing civil service systems. In addition to the procedures they establish, civil service appeals procedures also create customs and attitudes as to the proper way to do things. How are the procedures and their attendant customs to be accommodated?

In negotiating a grievance procedure, the following questions are likely to be of concern to the parties:

1. Is the procedure to culminate in final and binding arbitration?

2. How extensively is the employee organization to be involved in the procedure? Are stewards or other union representatives to be present from the initial stages of the grievance? Will the individual employee or the organization have the final say as to whether the grievance is processed through the succeeding stages of the procedure, settled, or dropped? Unions typically want control of the procedure to insure uniformity in its operation and to facilitate the development of informal channels of communication, customs, practices and settlement mechanisms. On the other hand, the individual in civil service systems has always been responsible for processing his own appeals, with union advice but not control; the practice is not easily supplanted.

3. What are the time limits to be for filing and processing grievances? Should time limits begin to run from the time of a grievable occurrence or from the time the employee realizes he has a grievance?

4. Should the union have the right to file general "policy" grievances or should it be restricted to filing specific grievances on behalf of designated employee grievants?

5. What should be considered a grievable dispute? What type of complaints is the grievance procedure designed to handle? Generally, employee organizations seek to broaden the scope of the procedure to include as many specific subjects as possible and to open the door to new grievable matters by adding "past practices" and other open-ended clauses. Management, just as in the private sector, seeks to reserve as much as possible to its own discretion by the insertion of a broad "management rights" clause. Of course, the scope is often circumscribed by the legis-

lature. Other problems not often encountered in the private sector also arise, as the following case indicates.

TREPEDINO v. DUMPSON
New York Court of Appeals
24 N.Y.2d 705, 249 N.E.2d 751, 301 N.Y.S.2d 967 (1969)

Fuld, Chief Judge.

In July of 1963, the petitioners, who were employed as social investigators, with tenure, by the Department of Welfare of the City of New York (hereafter referred to as the Department), addressed a letter, as representatives of a labor union, to the Director of the Bureau of Family Services of the United States Department of Health, Education and Welfare in Washington, D.C. Consisting of two pages, it combined criticism of existing procedures[1] and a request for information which (it was asserted) the petitioners had been unable to obtain from their superiors. The letter was not made public, and no copies were distributed. A month later, the City Commissioner of Welfare suspended the petitioners from their jobs and filed charges of misconduct against them; more specifically, they were accused (1) of making a number of false or misleading statements in the letter and (2) of exceeding the scope of their privileges as representatives of a minority labor organization. The Commissioner found them guilty and suspended them without pay for a period of 67 days. That determination was confirmed by the Appellate Division in this article 78 proceeding, and the appeal is before us, as of right, on constitutional grounds.

The Supreme Court, in Pickering v. Board of Educ. of Township High School Dist. 205, Will County, Illinois, 391 U.S. 563, 88 S. Ct. 1731, 20 L. Ed. 2d 811, held that those engaged in public employment may not "constitutionally be compelled to relinquish the First Amendment rights they would otherwise enjoy as citizens to comment on matters of public interest in connection with the operation of the [agency] in which they work" (p. 568, 88 S. Ct., p. 1734), and that—in the light of New York Times Co. v. Sullivan, 376 U.S. 254, 84 S. Ct. 710, 11 L. Ed. 2d 686—they may not be disciplined in the absence of proof that they made the statements in question "with knowledge of their falsity or with reckless disregard of their truth or falsity." (See, also, Puentes v. Board of Educ. of Union Free School District No. 21, 392 U.S. 653, 88 S. Ct. 2271, 20 L. Ed. 2d 1341.) After

---

[1] It was stated, for instance, that social service workers were required to handle a physically unmanageable case load and that the State had failed to reduce such case load to comply with what the petitioners believed was the prescribed standard to qualify for Federal contribution.

the *Pickering* case was handed down, respondent Commissioner, departing from his initial position, frankly acknowledged that his determination could not stand. In short, he concedes that the petitioners' suspension "may not be" "based upon the falsity of [their] statements" and suggests that "the order appealed from should be reversed and [his] determination . . . annulled." This, we note, is precisely the result arrived at in Matter of Puentes v. Board of Educ., 24 N.Y.2d 996, 302 N.Y.S.2d 824, 250 N.E.2d 232, also decided today.

However, the respondent urges, the matter should be remanded to him so that he may consider whether the communication written by the petitioners violated the "grievance procedures" mandated by the Department.

There can be no doubt that it is highly disruptive and not conducive to maintaining the morale of an officer or the efficiency of its workers if employees were to be permitted to go outside their organization initially to register complaints concerning its operations. If, therefore, a designated grievance procedure has been prescribed, it is desirable, nay necessary, that the employees pursue and exhaust such procedure. It was for that reason that the Supreme Court in *Pickering* left the door open to "narrowly drawn grievance procedures" which would require employees "to submit complaints about the operation [of their departments] to their superiors for action thereon prior to bringing the complaints before the public" (391 U.S., at p. 573, 88 S. Ct., at p. 1737, n.4).

The communication to the Director of the Federal Bureau in Washington was ill-considered, apparently written by the petitioners out of pique because they believed they were being saddled with an unduly heavy and burdensome case load. However, be that as it may, the record in the present case demonstrates that the subject matter of the letter, critical though it may have been of the Welfare Department's operations, could not be appropriately raised or dealt with through its grievance machinery. The procedure established by the Commissioner in his Executive Order No. 389 simply establishes machinery in the Department for dealing with the *individual* problems of employees. The plan of this so-called "grievance procedure" is not unlike those found in private collective bargaining agreements which are neither designed nor intended to deal with such broad issues as those raised in the petitioners' letter to the Federal Bureau in Washington.[2] The matters which the petitioners

---

[2] In view of this conclusion, we need not reach the difficult question whether that Executive Order (No. 389) constitutes the sort of carefully or "narrowly drawn grievance procedure" which, the Supreme Court indicated

mentioned in the letter were not personal to them but concerned the entire Department, involving as it did general policies and practices in carrying out the Department's functions. As bearing on this, it is of some significance that the Commissioner himself did not consider the procedure provided for in his Executive Order applicable as a method for resolving the matter. This is evidenced by the fact that the petitioners were not accused of a failure to exhaust specific "grievance procedures."[3]

It is not amiss to point out that—regardless of the possible impact a communication such as that before us may have in another case—there was neither claim nor showing here that the petitioners interfered with New York City's welfare program or neglected their duties as employees or that the letter created discipline problems or disharmony among the petitioners' fellow employees.

Under all the circumstances, to paraphrase what we said in the *Puentes* case, 24 N.Y.2d, at p. 999, 302 N.Y.S.2d, at p. 826, 250 N.E.2d, at p. 233, the single letter, which formed the predicate for the charges, "was permitted . . . to be elevated into an issue" out of all proportion "to the occasion." As already indicated, it furnishes insufficient basis for disciplinary action.

The order appealed from should be reversed, without costs, and the determination of the Commissioner of Welfare annulled.

NOTES

1. Issues similar to those in the principal case were raised in Board of Educ., Union Free School Dist. No. 27 v. West Hempstead Chapter, New York State Teachers' Ass'n, 63 Misc. 2d 335, 311 N.Y.S.2d 708 (Sup. Ct. 1970). That case involved telegrams sent by the teachers' association to certain school officials demanding their resignations. The school board's application to enjoin the teachers' association from making such public statements and for a judgment requiring the use of the grievance procedure was denied. The court held that neither the board nor the association could present grievances, since this right was reserved to individuals under the contract. The court also noted that the action "encompasses broad issues not within the grievance procedure. . . ." 311 N.Y.S.2d at 710.

---

in the *Pickering* case, 391 U.S., at p. 572, 88 S. Ct., at p. 1737, 20 L. Ed. 2d 811, n.4, employees may be required to follow before "bringing the complaints before the public."

[3] The specifications charged that the petitioners' "acts of misconduct . . . even if committed by [them] in [their] capacity as representatives or spokesmen of a minority labor organization, were outside the scope of the privileges accorded to minority labor organizations by the Mayor's Executive Order No. 49 or the Commissioner's Executive Order No. 389". . . .

2. In Dade County Classroom Teachers' Ass'n, Inc. v. Ryan, 225 So. 2d 903 (Fla. 1969), the Florida Supreme Court held that a public employee union could not act as the sole collective bargaining representative for all employees in a unit. Though the Court did not challenge the authority of the school board to enter into a collective bargaining agreement with the teachers' association, it held that the grievance procedure did not apply to nonconsenting teachers.

3. For an early in-depth study of public employee grievance procedures, see Berger, *Grievance Process in the Philadelphia Public Service*, 13 IND. & LAB. REL. REV. 568 (1960). Later studies may be found in Ullman and Begin, *The Structure and Scope of Appeals Procedures for Public Employees*, 23 IND. & LAB. REL. REV. 323 (1970) and Begin, *The Private Grievance Model in the Public Sector*, 10 IND. REL. 21 (1971). For a survey of the scope and content of grievance procedures in New York State, see NEW YORK STATE PUBLIC EMPLOYMENT RELATIONS BOARD, REPORT ON GRIEVANCE PROCEDURES IN COUNTY CONTRACTS WITH PUBLIC EMPLOYEE ORGANIZATIONS, NEW YORK STATE (1971).

With respect to grievance procedures in the public sector, see generally: Amundson, *Negotiated Grievance Procedures in California Employment: Controversy and Confusion*, 6 CAL. PUB. EMP. REL. 1 (1970); U.S. BUREAU OF LABOR STATISTICS, BULL. NO. 1661, NEGOTIATION IMPASSE, GRIEVANCE, AND ARBITRATION IN FEDERAL AGREEMENTS (1970); Koretz, *Labor Relations Law*, 22 SYRACUSE L. REV. 133, 136-139 (1971); HANDLING EMPLOYEE GRIEVANCES (R. Helms ed. PERL No. 2, 1968); E. SHILS & C.T. WHITTIER, TEACHERS, ADMINISTRATORS AND COLLECTIVE BARGAINING (1968); Wolf, *Grievance Procedures for School Employees*, in EMPLOYER-EMPLOYEE RELATIONS IN THE PUBLIC SCHOOLS 133 (R. Doherty ed. 1967); Pragan, *Grievance Procedures in the Federal Service*, 89 MONTHLY LAB. REV. 609 (1966); Segal, *Grievance Procedures for Public Employees*, 9 LAB. L.J. 921 (1958).

3. Grievance Arbitration

Almost universally in the private sector and increasingly in the public sector,[20] negotiated grievance procedures are capped by an arbitration provision. Grievance arbitration involves the adjudication of disputes which the parties have been unable to settle among themselves by a neutral third-party or panel. The

---

[20] Howlett, *Arbitration in the Public Sector*, PROCEEDINGS OF THE SOUTHWESTERN LEGAL FOUNDATION 15TH ANNUAL INSTITUTE ON LABOR LAW 262 (1969).

neutral may be a single arbitrator or a multi-member (either tripartite or all-neutral) panel; an arbitrator or panel may be *ad hoc* (temporary, invited by the parties to hear one or a series of cases) or permanent (as an umpire who is hired to hear all disputes between the parties). The arbitrator's decision may be final and binding on the parties or advisory only.

In the private sector, grievance arbitration performs a number of very important functions.[21] First, it provides a relatively speedy and inexpensive means of settling disputes. Secondly, it gives the employee the security of knowing that the ultimate recourse for the resolution of any grievance he may have lies with a neutral and not with his employer. Thirdly, it helps conserve judicial resources by providing a means to settle most disputes without court action. Fourthly, and most importantly, it serves national labor policy as a mechanism for the maintenance of industrial peace, providing an alternative to the strike in the resolution of day-to-day disputes.

Arbitration of grievances is a method of industrial self-regulation, a private rather than a governmental proceeding. Yet, private sector arbitration enjoys the sanction and support of law. Section 203 (d) of the Labor Management Relations Act of 1947[22] states: "Final adjustment by a method agreed upon by the parties is hereby declared to be the desirable method for settlement of grievance disputes arising over the application or interpretation of an existing collective-bargaining agreement. . . ." In the 1957 case of *Textile Workers Union v. Lincoln Mills*,[23] the Supreme Court held that arbitration agreements were specifically enforceable in the federal courts under § 301 (a) of the LMRA;[24] and in the 1960 *Steelworkers' Trilogy*[25] cases, the Court determined that arbitration agreements and awards should be reviewable by the courts only according to a very narrowly prescribed standard, thus discouraging both refusals to arbitrate and appeals from arbitration awards.

The reasons for enforcing arbitration agreements and awards in the private sector apply in the public sector as well. Some objection has been voiced against the legality of grievance arbi-

---

[21] *See generally* R. SMITH, L. MERRIFIELD & D. ROTHSCHILD, COLLECTIVE BARGAINING AND LABOR ARBITRATION (1970).

[22] 29 U.S.C. § 173 (d).

[23] 353 U.S. 448 (1957).

[24] 29 U.S.C. § 185 (a).

[25] United Steelworkers v. American Mfg. Co., 363 U.S. 564, 80 S. Ct. 1343, 4 L. Ed. 2d 1403 (1960); United Steelworkers v. Warrior & Gulf Nav. Co., 363 U.S. 574, 80 S. Ct. 1347, 4 L. Ed. 2d 1409 (1960); United Steelworkers v. Enterprise Wheel Car Corp., 363 U.S. 593, 80 S. Ct. 1358, 4 L. Ed. 2d 1424 (1960).

tration on the grounds that it is a derogation of the right of legislatures to determine public policy.[26] However, this judicially created principle, that an agreement to arbitrate constitutes an unlawful delegation of power, is beginning to lose some of its force and the courts seem increasingly inclined to follow the enforcement rules developed in *Lincoln Mills* and *Steelworkers' Trilogy* in dealing with public sector grievance arbitration.

There are two quite different types of labor arbitration: grievance arbitration, or "arbitration of rights," and impasse arbitration or "arbitration of interests." In dealing with public sector labor relations, it is particularly important to be aware of the differences between the two. In the private sector, impasse arbitration is seldom used; references to "arbitration" almost always mean grievance arbitration. But in the public sector, where strikes by public employees are usually illegal, impasse arbitration is important and occasionally mandated by statute. Grievance arbitration involves the determination of rights under an *existing* contract by an arbitrator acting in a judicial capacity. Impasse arbitration, on the other hand, is utilized when the parties are unable to agree to the provisions of a labor contract at the bargaining table; it is a substitute for the economic weaponry of strikes and lockouts in the determination of what the contract rights of the parties *shall be*. The impasse arbitrator is a combination policy-maker, administrator, and chancellor at equity; in contrast to the grievance arbitrator, he is a formulator, rather than a follower of the parties' contract.

ROCKLAND PROFESSIONAL FIRE FIGHTERS ASSOCIATION v. CITY OF ROCKLAND

Supreme Judicial Court of Maine
261 A.2d 418 (1970)

WEATHERBEE, Justice.

In 1957 our Legislature enacted "An Act Relating to Arbitration Pursuant to Collective Bargaining Contracts." This legislation as amended is now 26 M.R.S.A. § 951, et seq. Section 951 reads:

"A written provision in any collective bargaining contract to settle by arbitration a controversy thereafter arising out of such contract or out of the refusal to perform the whole or any part thereof, or an agreement in writing to submit to arbitration an existing controversy arising out of such a contract, or such refusal, herein designated in this

---

[26] *See, e.g.,* Fellows v. LaTronica, 151 Colo. 300, 377 P.2d 547 (1962).

subchapter as 'a written submission agreement,' shall be valid, irrevocable and enforceable, save upon such grounds, independent of the provisions for arbitration, as exist at law or in equity for the revocation of any contract."

Section 954 provides for the appointment of arbitrators by the Court in the event that the collective bargaining contract fails to establish a method for their appointment or if the method so provided is ignored by one party. Section 956 details methods for obtaining testimony of witnesses at the arbitration hearing, and for the fees of witnesses. Section 957 provides for the enforcement by the Superior Court of the award of arbitration upon application of a party that judgment shall be entered for the party. Section 958 enumerates grounds which would justify vacating an award.

In 1965 the Legislature enacted a statute which is referred to as the Fire Fighters Arbitration Law which is now 26 M.R.S.A. § 980, et seq. In doing so the Legislature declared it to be the public policy of the State that this particular class of municipal employees in their position of high responsibility should be given the right to organize and bargain collectively with the municipalities in arriving at a contract of employment.

Section 981 reads:

"The protection of the public health, safety and welfare demands that the permanent uniformed members of any paid fire department in any municipality not be accorded the right to strike or engage in any work stoppage or slowdown. This necessary prohibition does not, however, require the denial to such municipal employees of other recognized rights of labor such as the right to organize, to be represented by a labor organization of their choice, and the right to bargain collectively concerning wages, rates of pay and other terms and conditions of employment."

Following the broad statement of policy of section 981 the Fire Fighters Arbitration Law proceeds to empower the fire fighters to compel the municipality to meet with the fire fighters' bargaining agent to bargain collectively in the formation of a written contract of employment. Section 986 provides that if the parties cannot reach a contract the unresolved issues shall be submitted to arbitration at the option of the association. Section 987 sets out the method of selecting the arbitrators. Section 988 describes the rules under which hearings shall be conducted and specifies that a less-than-unanimous decision of the arbitrators shall not be binding on either party.

Section 991 includes the words

"Any collective bargaining agreement negotiated under this chapter shall specifically provide that the fire fighters who are subject to its terms shall have no right to engage in any work stoppage, slowdown or strike, the consideration for such provision being the right to a resolution of disputed questions." . . .

Under the authority of the Fire Fighters Arbitration Law the firemen of Rockland organized and entered into a contract of employment for the calendar year of 1967. . . .

[The contract established a grievance procedure] consisting of four steps, the third of which provided for a hearing before an Appeal Grievance Board. . . .

The contract then provided that:

"Arbitration shall be in accordance with Title 26, Sect. 987 of the Maine Revised Statutes Annotated."

. . . [H]owever, section 987 only sets up machinery for the organization and operation of an arbitration board for the purpose of resolving disputes concerning the negotiation of a labor contract and makes no provision for arbitration of disputes arising later under the contract.

On April 27, 1967 Walter R. Dyer, a Rockland fireman, was suspended for six days allegedly for insubordinate conduct. Dyer and the Plaintiff exhausted the grievance processes provided in the contract and the matter went on to arbitration. The parties followed the provisions of section 987 in selecting the members of the arbitration board but on June 12, before the Board could hear the matter, Dyer was discharged for a similar reason.

Plaintiff and Defendant then combined the two grievances and submitted to the arbitration board the single issue of whether the discharge of Dyer was for sufficient cause. After hearing, a majority of the board returned an award which read:

"1.   There was not sufficient cause for the discharge of Walter R. Dyer on June 12, 1967.

2.   If Dyer resigns from office in Local 1584 of the International Association of Firefighters, the City of Rockland shall offer him reinstatement to his former position without back pay."

Dyer did resign from office in the union but the city refused to reinstate him. Plaintiff then brought an application for judgment upon the arbitration award in the Superior Court in Knox County. Defendant moved to dismiss the application for judgment on the grounds that:

1)   The award was not unanimous and therefore was in-
      valid.
2)   The board abused its discretion and exceeded the pow-
      ers given it in going beyond the single question sub-
      mitted to them.
3)   The city has the right to discharge any employee when,
      in his best judgment, the City Manager considers that
      the city's interest requires it.

The matter was heard before a Justice of the Superior Court
who granted Defendant's motion to dismiss the application for
judgment on the award. The ruling of the Justice was based
on his conclusion that

". . . [T]he Legislature intended that whatever benefits
it was conferring upon the Fire Fighters, the right to organize, bargain collectively, arbitrate and all other rights
being granted, were to to be viewed entirely in the light of
the language of the Fire Fighters Arbitration Law. . . ."

As the Fire Fighters Arbitration Law provided only for arbitration of disputes surrounding the *making* of a contract, the Justice held the Fire Fighters had been given no right to arbitration
of disputes arising *subsequent* to the contract and therefore had
no right to enforcement of an award. . . .

We find that the Fire Fighters Arbitration Law, in spite of
the scope suggested by its title, provides for arbitration only
as to the negotiation of a labor contract. The parties here did
negotiate a contract as the Fire Fighters Arbitration Law empowered them to do. The contract bound the parties to submit
unresolved grievances to arbitration at the option of the union.
The legislature intended the Fire Fighters to have all the rights
of labor organizations except those specifically withheld and in
section 951, years earlier, the Legislature had given all labor
organizations the right to provide in their contracts for arbitration of grievances arising out of such contracts. The fire fighters'
authority to agree with the city to submit their unresolved grievances to arbitration is found in section 951. The provision in
Plaintiff and Defendant's contract that arbitration of their labor
grievances should be in accordance with section 987 appears to
us to be best explained by the fact that the 1957 general statute
authorizing arbitration makes no provision for the method in
which the arbitrators shall be chosen (except that if the contract fails to provide a method or if a party refuses to proceed
under the method agreed upon, resort may be had to the Court
for appointment of the arbitrator.) It leaves the parties to state
in their contracts the method they prefer for selecting arbitrators.

We view the reference to section 987 as the parties' agreement that the arbitrators should be chosen by the method provided in section 987. . . .

Applying the *in pari materia* rule of construction and reading in connection with the Fire Fighters Arbitration Law the 1957 general arbitration statute having the same general purpose, it appears clear that the grant to the fire fighters of "all of the rights of labor other than the right to strike, or engage in any work stoppage or slowdown" found in section 981 included the right to submit grievances to binding arbitration. We hold that the Plaintiff was entitled to submit to arbitration grievances arising under the labor contract and was not limited to the specific issue of formation of a contract.

The Justice in the Superior Court did not reach the issues concerning the validity of the award itself. . . . They remain to be determined in the Superior Court. . . .

NOTES

1. It has frequently been held that state statutes pertaining to employer-employee relations "must be construed to apply only to private industry, at least until such time as the legislature shows a definite intent to include political subdivisions." Wichita Public Schools Employees Union, Local 513 v. Smith, 194 Kan. 2, 397 P.2d 357 (1964). *See also* Miami Water Works Local 654 v. City of Miami, 157 Fla. 445, 26 So. 2d 194 (1946). The 1957 grievance arbitration statute in the principal case was not made specifically applicable to the public sector. How, then, did the Supreme Court of Maine determine that this statute was applicable to the collective bargaining agreement between the city and the firemen's union? Did the Court rule in effect that the Fire Fighters Arbitration Law was itself sufficient to compel the enforcement of the arbitration award?

2. *In pari materia* means, generally, "on the same subject." Statutes *in pari materia,* according to the rules of statutory construction, are intended by the legislature to be part of a single legislative scheme and are intended to be construed together. Do you think that the Maine legislature intended that the 1957 arbitration law and the Fire Fighters Arbitration Act were to be construed together? Are they part of a "single legislative scheme" or were they enacted to serve altogether different functions?

3. The principal case was cited as authority and a nearly identical result was reached in Providence Teachers Union Local 958 v. School Committee of Providence, 108 R.I. 444, 276

A.2d 762 (1971). Look again at the language of section 981 of the Maine Fire Fighters Arbitration Law, reprinted in the principal case. The court in *Providence Teachers* found that the presence of similar language in the Rhode Island law demonstrated that the state legislature intended public sector unions to have the same rights as other labor organizations, except for those rights specifically withheld. Does the right to bargain collectively necessarily imply the right to enter into contracts providing for the binding arbitration of grievances?

4. On the subject of grievance arbitration generally, see R. SMITH, L. MERRIFIELD & D. ROTHSCHILD, COLLECTIVE BARGAINING AND LABOR ARBITRATION (1971); R. FLEMING, THE LABOR ARBITRATION PROCESS (1965); F. ELKOURI & E. ELKOURI, HOW ARBITRATION WORKS (1960). On grievance arbitration in the public sector, see Rock, *The Role of the Neutral in Grievance Arbitration in Public Employment,* in COLLECTIVE BARGAINING IN GOVERNMENT 141 (J. Loewenberg and M. Moskow, eds. 1972); U.S. BUREAU OF LABOR STATISTICS, BULL. NO. 1661, NEGOTIATION IMPASSE, GRIEVANCE, AND ARBITRATION IN FEDERAL AGREEMENTS (1970); Note, *Legality and Propriety of Agreements to Arbitrate Major and Minor Disputes in Public Employment,* 54 CORNELL L. REV. 129 (1968); Krislov, *Prospects for the Use of Advisory Grievance Arbitration in Federal Service,* 18 IND. & LAB. REL. REV. 420 (1965); Krislov & Schmulowitz, *Grievance Arbitration in State and Local Government Units,* 18 AM. ARB. J. 171 (1963); Killingsworth, *Grievance Adjudication in Public Employment,* 13 AM. ARB. J. 3 (1958); ARBITRATION CASES IN PUBLIC EMPLOYMENT (E. Tracy ed. 1969).

4. Grievance and Arbitration at the Federal Level: The Role of the Comptroller General

KAGEL, GRIEVANCE ARBITRATION IN THE FEDERAL SERVICE: HOW FINAL AND BINDING?, 51 Ore. L. Rev. 134, 146-49 (1971)†

As head of the General Accounting Office, the Comptroller General is charged with assuring that public funds are disbursed in accordance with law. By express statute, his office is independent of the executive branch.[27] He is empowered to issue decisions on legal questions asked by agency disbursing officers as well as to audit their accounts. A finding by advance decision that expenditures are lawful is binding on the heads of execu-

---

† Reprinted by permission. Copyright © 1971 by The University of Oregon.
[27] 31 U.S.C. § 41 (1970).

tive departments and agencies[28] as well as on the Government Accounting Office.[29]

The Comptroller General's advance decisions may be sought whenever a disbursing officer or agency head[30] believes that an advance opinion will shield him from later liability for illegally disbursing government funds, and since such advance permission can be obtained, his decision will presumably be sought before nonroutine government expenditures are made. . . . In 1845 in *United States v. Ames*,[31] the court held that a government officer has no power to bind the United States to an arbitration clause unless authorized by statute. The Comptroller General has consistently rendered decisions which follow *Ames*.[32] . . . The Comptroller General's view of arbitration has adversely affected federal service labor arbitrations. One advisory arbitration decision[33] held that a schedule change by an agency violated its collective bargaining agreement. The decision recommended that employees be compensated for any losses incurred as a result of the violation. The agency then sought a determination by the Comptroller General with respect to whether it could comply with the advisory decision. Although the schedule change was a violation of the bargaining agreement, the Comptroller General, relying in part on Executive Order 10,988, § 12 (b) which spells out broad management rights that cannot be bargained away by an agency, held that the agency acted within its right to "maintain the efficiency of government operations." He reasoned that since schedule changes were authorized by regulation, the bargaining agreement therefore authorized changes and the agency acted in accordance with its rights. "[I]t does not appear that the . . . work week . . . established in accordance with . . . regulations . . . would be subject to arbitration."[34] The award, therefore, could not be paid by the agency. . . . Under Executive Orders 10,988 and 11,491, there

---

[28] 31 U.S.C. § 44 (1970).

[29] 31 U.S.C. § 74 (1970). *See generally* Comment, *The Control Powers of the Comptroller General,* 56 COLO. L. REV. 1199 (1956).

[30] 31 U.S.C. § 74 (1970).

[31] 24 Fed. Cas. 784, No. 14, 411 (C.C. Mass. 1845).

[32] *See generally,* Katzman, *Arbitration in Government Contracts: The Ghost at the Banquet,* 24 ARB. J. 133 (1969); Mosk, *Arbitration in Government,* in ARBITRATION AND PUBLIC POLICY 168 (Proceedings of the Fourteenth Annual Meeting, Nat'l Acad. of Arbitrators, BNA ed. 1961).

[33] Dec. Comptroller Gen. E-163422, Apr. 8, 1971, Current Gov't Emp. Rel. Rep. No. 401, at E-1 (May 17, 1971). This is not an isolated case. *See also* Current Gov't Emp. Rel. Rep. No. 408, at A-10 (July 5, 1971) citing from Dec. Comp. Gen. E-172671 (June 14, 1971), holding to the same effect.

[34] Dec. Comptroller Gen. B-163422 (Apr. 8, 1971).

have been and will be arbitration cases recommending or ordering back pay or other economic relief to employees because of
agency agreement violations. Unlike Executive Order 10,988,
however, the situation concerning nonadvisory arbitration under
Executive Order 11,491 could be interpreted differently by the
Comptroller General. Under § 13 (b) of Executive Order 11,491,
as amended, agencies can file exceptions to the award with the
Federal Labor Relations Council. That section was designed to
police arbitration decisions and especially to determine whether
decisions comply with applicable law and regulations. Section
13 (b) will, to some extent, provide the same review as the
Comptroller General's and should therefore "police" the legality
of the award for the Comptroller General. Deference by him to
the Federal Labor Relations Council's decision would then be in
order.

Other considerations, however, militate against a conclusion
that this approach will be adopted. Apparently, an agency or
federal officer cannot be precluded by the terms of an Executive
Order from appealing to the Comptroller General for his decision
with respect to whether payment of any funds required by an
arbitration award is proper. In addition, appeal may not be taken
to the Council because of failure to comply with requisite time
limits. In the cases cited, the Comptroller General, in addition to
interpreting the Executive Order, has directly involved himself
in the determination of the merits of those cases.

Accordingly, the choice of seeking a Comptroller General's
decision gives agencies a second avenue of appeal, one that is
possibly more responsive to the agency's view than the arbitrator's
decision or the limited appeal to the Federal Labor Relations
Council. An appeal to the Comptroller General, in view of the
attitude shown to date with respect to arbitration, is apparently
a dependable method to overturn virtually all arbitration decisions where monetary relief is granted. The dilemma for the
agency is that even if it wanted to comply with such an arbitration decision in good faith, the disbursing agency could find
himself in a position where his disbursement would later be disallowed if no advance opinion was sought.

In all future cases in which an agency seeks a determination from the Comptroller General whether to abide by an arbitration award, it is conceivable that payment of otherwise valid
awards will be disallowed. The Comptroller General could use
§ 12 (b) of Executive Order 11,491 to preclude arbitration for
most fact situations. Section 12 (b) is broad in scope and could
be used to justify any decision the Comptroller General wishes
to make.

The Comptroller General's decisions thus pose a difficult obstacle if arbitration is to be an effective process in federal labor relations.

NOTES

1. Section 12 (b) of Executive Order 11491, as amended by Executive Order 11616, reads as follows:

Management officials of the agency retain the right, in accordance with applicable laws and regulations—

(1)   to direct employees of the agency;

(2)   to hire, promote, transfer, assign and retain employees within the agency, and to suspend, demote, discharge, or take other disciplinary action against employees;

(3)   to relieve employees from duties because of lack of work or for other legitimate reasons;

(4)   to maintain the efficiency of the Government operations entrusted to them;

(5)   to determine the methods, means, and personnel by which such operations are to be conducted; and

(6)   to take whatever actions may be necessary to carry out the mission of the agency in situations of emergency. . . .

Section 13 (b) of the amended Executive Order 11491 provides that either party to a collective bargaining agreement authorized by that Order may file an exception to an arbitrator's award with the Federal Labor Relations Council. One of the principal functions of the Council is to review arbitration awards; it is possible, therefore, as suggested by Kagel, that the Comptroller General may adopt a policy of deference to the decision of the Council. Nothing in the law requires this, however.

2. In Dec. Comptroller Gen. B-175867, GERR No. 460, A-9 (1972), the Comptroller General ruled that there was no authority in federal personnel law which would allow the payment of overtime pay to a Hill Air Force Base employee, who was denied the opportunity to put in eight hours of overtime work in violation of the labor agreement between the Utah base and a union local, despite a favorable ruling on the grievance which the employee later filed.

The applicable clause in the agreement between Hill AFB and American Federation of Government Employees Local 1592, while stating that the administration of overtime is solely a function of management, also provided that "first consideration" for overtime shall be given employees currently assigned to the job in question, and that "second consideration" shall go to those qualified to do the job in the area or function in which overtime work is required. The grievant claimed that the contract had been violated when another man, who was entitled only to "second consideration," worked the overtime instead of the grievant, who had "first consideration" rights. Following a hearing, the Secretary of the Air Force agreed that the contract had indeed been violated, and proposed the payment of the eight hours' overtime as a remedy. Before doing so, however, the agency sought clearance from the Comptroller General. In denying the claim for back pay, the Comptroller General ruled that, "although there appears to have been a violation of . . . the union-management agreement . . . it is our opinion that there is no authority for the payment of overtime compensation in the instant case since no actual work has been performed by the employee."

C. Judicial Enforcement of the Collective Bargaining Agreement

1. The Authority of Government Employers to Execute Collective Bargaining Agreements

BOARD OF EDUCATION OF UNION FREE SCHOOL DISTRICT NO. 3 OF THE TOWN OF HUNTINGTON v. ASSOCIATED TEACHERS OF HUNTINGTON, INC.*

Court of Appeals of New York
30 N.Y.2d 122, 282 N.E.2d 109, 331 N.Y.S.2d 17 (1972)

FULD, Chief Judge.

We are called upon to decide (1) whether a school board has the authority to enter into a collective bargaining agreement granting economic benefits to schoolteachers, absent specific statutory authorization to do so and (2) whether such a board lacks the power to enter into a collective bargaining agreement containing a clause which provides for the arbitration of disputes concerning disciplinary action taken against tenure teachers. . . .

Each of the provisions under attack relates to a term or condition of employment and, accordingly, the Board was, in light of the Taylor Law, required to negotiate—unless its contentions, to which we turn, compel a different conclusion.

Although the Board raises specific objections that are peculiar to each of the challenged items, its basic premise is the same— that, absent a statutory provision *expressly* authorizing a school board to provide for a particular term or condition of employment, it is legally prohibited from doing so. Proceeding from that premise, the Board would have us hold that school boards possess only those powers granted by a single provision, section 1709,

---

* The full text of this opinion appears in Chapter Four.

of the Education Law. Quite apart from the fact that that section contains a broad grant of powers[5] the Board's premise is fallacious. Under the Taylor Law, the obligation to bargain as to all terms and conditions of employment is a broad and unqualified one, and there is no reason why the mandatory provision of that act should be limited, in any way, except in cases where some other applicable statutory provision explicitly and definitively prohibits the public employer from making an agreement as to a particular term or condition of employment.

Were it otherwise, a school board would have a hard time bargaining effectively with its teachers concerning terms of employment, since it would frequently be difficult, if not impossible, to find an express grant of power with respect to any particular subject. To adhere to the restrictive view advanced by the Board "would," the Appellate Division recently wrote in Matter of Teachers Assn. (Bd. of Educ.) (34 A.D.2d, *supra,* at p. 356, 312 N.Y.S.2d 252, 257), "virtually destroy the bargaining powers which public policy has installed in the field of public employment and throttle the ability of a Board of Education to meet the changing needs of employer-employee relations within its district."

Public employers must, therefore, be presumed to possess the broad powers needed to negotiate with employees as to all terms and conditions of employment. The presumption may, of course, be rebutted by showing statutory provisions which expressly prohibit collective bargaining as to a particular term or condition but, "[i]n the absence of an express legislative restriction against bargaining for that term of an employment contract between a public employer and its employees, the authority to provide for such [term] resides in the [school board] under the broad powers and duties delegated by the statutes." (Matter of Teachers Assn. [Bd. of Educ.], 34 A.D.2d 351, 355, 312 N.Y.S.2d 252, 256, *supra;* see, also, Rayburn v. Board of Educ., 71 LRRM 2177, 2178 [Mich. Cir. Ct.].) It is hardly necessary to say that, if the Board asserts a lack of power to agree to any particular term or condition of employment, it has the burden of demonstrating the existence of a specific statutory provision which circumscribes the exercise of such power. It has failed to meet this burden in the present case. . . .

It is of more than passing significance that the Taylor Law explicitly vests employee organizations with the right to repre-

---

[5] Subdivision 33 of section 1709 recites that the Board shall have "all the powers reasonably necessary to exercise powers granted expressly or by implication and to discharge duties imposed expressly or by implication by this chapter or other statutes."

sent public employees not only in connection with negotiations as to the terms and conditions of employment but also as to *"the administration of grievances arising thereunder"* (Civil Service Law, § 203; italics supplied). Indeed, it is the declared policy of this State to encourage "public employers and . . . employee organizations to agree upon procedures for resolving disputes" (§ 200, subd. [c]). And arbitration is, of course, part and parcel of the administration of grievances. . . . There is, therefore, no reason to infer that the Legislature intended that the provisions of the Tenure Law should, by implication, deprive employee organizations of a right to represent employees in the administration of disciplinary grievances.[7]

Nor can we agree that a board of education is better qualified than an arbitrator to decide whether a teacher in its employ should be dismissed for incompetency or misconduct. It may not be gainsaid that arbitrators, selected because of their impartiality and their intimate knowledge of school board matters are fully qualified to decide issues such as those under consideration. . . .

We would but add that there is no basis for the fear expressed that to permit the grievance to go to arbitration will enable the employee to appeal—pursuant to section 3020-a, subdivision 5, of the Education Law—to the arbitrator *after* he has lost before the commissioner or the court or, conversely, to the Commissioner of Education or the Supreme Court *after* he has submitted to arbitration and lost before the arbitrator.[8] Once the controversy is heard and a decision arrived at *either* by the arbitrator *or* by the commissioner *or* by the judge, that is the end of the matter. As already indicated, the collective bargaining agreement does no more than give the employee a possible third means of reviewing a Board determination.

The order appealed from should be modified, without costs, by reversing so much thereof as holds illegal the provision permitting arbitration with respect to the disciplining of tenure teachers and, except as so modified, affirmed.

[The opinion of Judge Breitel, dissenting in part, is omitted.]

NOTES

1. Generally, the authority to bargain collectively is given to the public employer by state statute or city ordinance. But this

---

[7] Likewise unfounded is the Board's claim that the limited definition of the term "grievance" found in the General Municipal Law (§ 682, subd. 4) is to be incorporated into the Taylor Law and restrict the meaning of that term as there used.

[8] We assume, of course, that the arbitration proceeding is fair and regular and free from any procedural infirmities that might invalidate the award. (Cf., e.g., Spielberg Manufacturing Company, 112 N.L.R.B. 1080).

authority may not be sufficient to validate the collective bargaining agreement. Before the court can decide whether it will enforce the agreement, a number of preliminary questions must be answered: (a) Does the statute apply to the parties to the agreement? Some statutes are made applicable only to certain specific groups of public employees, as, for example, firemen, policemen, or teachers. (b) Are there any explicit constitutional or statutory provisions which would prevent the parties from making agreements in certain subject matter areas? (c) Are there any constitutional or statutory provisions which would by implication prevent the parties from reaching agreements in certain areas?

2. The absence of conflicting state law or policy was found to be an important factor in the decision of the New Hampshire Supreme Court in upholding the validity of a contested union security provision in Tremblay v. Berlin Police Union, 108 N.H. 416, 237 A.2d 668, 68 L.R.R.M. 2070 (1968). There the Court said:

> It is argued that this union shop clause of the collective bargaining agreement is invalid as an unlawful delegation of municipal power and is "ultra vires and void." There is no law which prohibits a union shop in this state. . . . The Legislature has declared as a matter of public policy that collective bargaining for municipal employees is a proper public purpose. In making this declaration it has not excluded police departments (as some statutes do) or other public employees in equally essential positions. . . . Opinions may differ as to the desirability of collective bargaining for public employees but that discretionary decision has been lodged in the municipalities.

3. Not all state statutes are construed so liberally as was the Taylor Law in *Huntington*. The California Winton Act, for example, a "meet and confer" type statute covering elementary and secondary school teachers, has been interpreted rather narrowly by California courts. The decision of the Orange County Superior Court in Placentia Unified Educ. Ass'n v. Board of Educ., Placentia Unified School Dist., 77 L.R.R.M. 3137 (Cal. Super. Ct. 1971), is indicative:

> [T]he public policy of the State, as expressed by legislation and judicial decision, is to circumscribe narrowly the powers of school districts, in the interests of state-wide uniformity. In particular, the Legislature has attempted by the Winton Act (EDUCATION CODE, Secs. 13080-13088) to formulate *sui generis* a regulation of the role of public

employees and their employee organizations in the decision-
making process. In light of its terms and legislative history
and of the scope, nature and legislative history of other legislation (particularly the Meyers-Milias-Brown Act, Gov. CODE,
Secs. 3500-3511), dealing with employer-employee relations
in the private and public sectors, the Court concludes that
the Winton Act does not authorize a school board, in the
course of procedures therein outlined, to enter into legally
enforceable contracts with employee organizations, whether
relating to binding grievance arbitration or otherwise.

This decision paralleled the result reached by the Los Angeles
County Superior Court in Hayes v. Association of Classroom
Teachers, 76 L.R.R.M. 2140 (Cal. Super. Ct. 1970).

In the above California cases the courts determined that a fairly
comprehensive legislative scheme for the resolution of disputes
excluded the possibility of binding grievance arbitration as a
competitive alternative. Other legislative approaches lead to similarly restrictive interpretations. In Zderick v. Silver Bow County,
154 Mont. 118, 460 P.2d 749 (1969), the Montana Supreme
Court disallowed a claim by an employee against the county for
accumulated sick leave. The Court based its decision on the fact
that the state legislature had made piecemeal grants of authority
to political subdivisions in a number of fringe benefit areas but
had not acted with respect to accumulated sick leave.

4.   The idea that the legislature is *delegating power* to the government employer to enter into enforceable contracts with public
employee unions is a constant feature of cases dealing with the
enforcement of collective bargaining agreements in the public sector. Even if the power is not held to be inherently nondelegable,
there are still two principal questions the court must answer:
(1) Did the legislature intend to delegate the power to contract?
(2) If the legislature did so intend, did it provide adequate
standards for the exercise of the power? It is important to distinguish a power which cannot be delegated from an ineffective
delegation of power. For a case involving ineffective delegation,
see Ohio Civil Service Employees Ass'n v. Division 11, Ohio
Dep't of Highways, 79 L.R.R.M. 2559 (Ohio Ct. App. 1971).

5.   The opinion of Chief Judge Fuld in the *Huntington
Teachers* case held that the validity of a contract provision turned
on whether it constituted a term or condition of employment.
However, although an employer may be required to negotiate
with respect to a particular provision, the resulting agreement
on that provision may not be enforceable against the public
employer until the legislature has given final approval. This is

particularly true where fiscal matters are concerned, since the general rule is that the parties to an agreement cannot bind a legislative body to make an appropriation of public funds in order to pay for agreed upon increases in wages or fringe benefits. *But see* Wheatley v. City of Covington, 79 L.R.R.M. 2614 (Ky. Cir. Ct. 1972). In New York, the Taylor Act, N.Y. CIVIL SERVICE LAW § 204-(1)(a), requires that the following clause be included in contracts of public employment:

> It is agreed . . . that any provision of this agreement requiring legislative action to permit its implementation by amendment of law or by providing the additional funds therefor, shall not become effective until the appropriate legislative body has given approval.

The Connecticut Municipal Employee Relations Act, CONN. GEN. STAT. ANN. tit. 7, §§ 7-467 to 7-475 (Supp. 1972), likewise reserves final judgment for the legislature at the same time that it alleviates the problem of conflict with existing legislation:

> Any agreement reached by the negotiators shall be reduced to writing. . . . [A] request for funds necessary to implement such written agreement and for approval of any provisions of the agreement which are in conflict with any charter, special act, ordinance, rule or regulation adopted by the municipal employer or its agents, such as a personnel board or civil service commission, or any general statute directly regulating the hours of work of policemen or firemen . . . shall be submitted by the bargaining representative of the municipality within fourteen days . . . to the legislative body which may approve or reject such request as a whole by a majority vote . . . ; but, if rejected, the matter shall be returned to the parties for further bargaining. [*Id.* at § 7-474 (b)]

However, the Connecticut statute provides further that:

> Notwithstanding any provision of any general statute, charter, special act or ordinance to the contrary, the budget-appropriating authority of any municipal employer shall appropriate whatever funds are required to comply with a collective bargaining agreement, provided the request . . . [for funds] has been approved by the legislative body. . . . [*Id.* at § 7-474 (c)]

In Massachusetts, as in other states, the public employer is obligated to request the legislature to appropriate the funds necessary to give effect to the contract. MASS. STAT. ANN. ch. 149, § 1781 (Supp. 1971). Is there any way to guarantee that the government employer will present the strongest possible case for the appropriation to the legislature?

2.   What Constitutes an Enforceable Contract?

PATROLMEN'S BENEVOLENT ASSOCIATION v. CITY OF NEW YORK
Court of Appeals of New York
27 N.Y.2d 410, 267 N.E.2d 259, 318 N.Y.S.2d 477 (1971)

BERGAN, Judge.

The action is to enforce a purported collective bargaining agreement between the Patrolmen's Benevolent Association and the City of New York for the period October 1, 1968 to December 31, 1970. The complaint alleges the agreement was made January 28, 1969 between the association and the city and that among its provisions was the establishment of a ratio of 3 to 3.5 between patrolmen's and sergeants' salaries to be maintained during the term of contract; that sergeants' salaries were increased by the city December 18, 1969 and that accordingly patrolmen are entitled to an increase conformably to the ratio.

The action is described in the moving affidavit for summary judgment by plaintiff Edward J. Kiernan, president of the association, as "a simple action for the breach of the salary provisions of a collective bargaining agreement." Plaintiffs have had summary judgment at Special Term, which has been affirmed by a divided court at the Appellate Division.

The issue on appeal as it reaches this court is whether the existence of a purported integrated agreement is left so uncertain in the record as to require a trial; or whether it appears so clearly that plaintiffs are entitled to summary judgment on the papers without trial.

There is a threshold difficulty as to summary judgment in the form the plaintiffs have chosen to plead the contract terms and to formulate their motion for judgment. A party seeking judgment on the basis of a writing must show the writing he relies on is the writing agreed to. But the text of agreement pleaded in the complaint and recited in the moving Kiernan affidavit is the text of a descriptive circular sent by the association to its members February 3, 1969 to be voted on.

The text of this circular is not shown to have been accepted by the city; and the initialed agreement relied on by plaintiffs in this court as showing there had been a written contract was expressed in a different text. In an action based, as this one is, on a specific writing, summary judgment ought not be granted on showing a different writing, even though the two texts have similarity, without appropriate amendment of pleading and proof to conform the basis for relief claimed to the actual writing relied upon.

There is a more fundamental obstacle to summary judgment here. Not any of the papers or writings in the record, signed or unsigned, show a complete collective bargaining agreement between the association and the city embracing all the terms and conditions which had been canvassed by negotiators.

There is a writing initialed on January 29 by a representative of the association and of the city which shows an accord on some terms, including the ratio with sergeants' salaries, but both in what it says and what it covers it is not a complete or independent collective bargaining agreement. This is the specific instrument which plaintiffs in this court say is an independently enforceable agreement on which they are entitled to summary judgment.

The affidavit of Herbert L. Haber, Director of Labor Relations of the city, who handled the negotiations with the association and who initialed the January 29 accord, filed in opposition to plaintiffs' motion for summary judgment, states not only that there was "no written collective bargaining agreement" between the association and the city as of May 7, 1970, but that for the preceding year "the parties [including the association and city] have been attempting to set forth the terms of the entire agreement in a formal written collective bargaining contract."

He swore further that in the fall of 1969 the association had submitted "a proposed draft of a written contract." On the motion for summary judgment these statements must be accepted as true and they require a trial on the issue whether it was the intention of the parties to integrate their preliminary understandings and accords reached in the course of negotiation into a formal and final writing covering the full contractual relation.

The issue, then, is whether it was the intention of the parties that the accord as to part of the subjects of negotiation should become an independent agreement; or whether it was intended, as the Haber affidavit indicates, there should be further and ultimate formalization in writing. The Restatement notes that "An agreement is integrated" when the parties adopt a writing or writings "as the final and complete expression of the agreement" (Restatement, Contracts, § 228). The draft of Restatement, Second (§ 235, subd. [3]) broadens this somewhat but is in the same sense. On the showing made on this record the question whether there has been integration here is a question of fact.

The decisional law in New York is consistent with this. In Scheck v. Francis, 26 N.Y.2d 466, 311 N.Y.S.2d 841, Chief Judge Fuld wrote for the court that "if the parties to an agreement do not intend it to be binding upon them until it is reduced to writing and signed by both of them, they are not bound and may not be held liable until it has been written out and signed.". . .

Corbin regards this kind of situation as typically presenting a question of fact, i.e., where the parties have "the understanding during this process [settling some details] that the agreement is to be embodied in a formal written document." (1 Corbin, Contracts, pp. 97, 98.)

If there are conditions which are regarded as important still left for adjustment it may be held that there has been no enforceable agreement. In Arliss v. Herbert Brenon Film Corp., 230 N.Y. 390, 130 N.E. 587, Judge Hogan, writing for the court, was of opinion that the evidence disclosed an intention that a contract should not be deemed to have been made "until such conditions should be mutually agreed upon and embodied in a written contract.". . .

In support of the Haber affidavit stating that it was the intention of the parties to formalize their understanding in a complete contract is the text of the written accord of January 29 itself. Its fragmentary internal structure strongly suggests other things were necessary to full integration of the agreement of the parties.

This instrument describes itself as a "Modification of 'Proposed Collective Bargaining Agreement'" between the association and the city. The proposed agreement to which this refers is the text of a draft distributed to the association members November 21, 1968. This proposed agreement had been previously rejected by the members of the association.

It seems obvious that this modification of a proposed agreement is not itself a complete agreement and the change in details all hang on some final formalization. Some of them, e.g., that referring to the time of work of the 5% night shift, is unintelligible without being filled in by some other interpretive writing.

The court inquired of the city on the argument about its custom followed in executing complete collective bargaining agreements, formalizing all terms. There has been filed with the court the texts of some 28 complete collective bargaining agreements executed between 1966 and 1969.

The city on January 4, 1971, in lieu of a sur-rebuttal brief, filed with the court the constitution and by-laws of plaintiff association which require that collective bargaining agreements with the city shall be reduced to writing. Plaintiffs reply under the same date that this is what was done here; but, of course, the question remains whether it was intended by the parties in this negotiation that there should be a further rounded agreement.

Plaintiffs argue also in support of summary judgment that the city had recognized "the agreement" by paying the salaries which had been fixed in the accord of January 29, 1969. The city did pay those salaries retroactively to October 1, 1968 under the authority of an order made by the Mayor March 28, 1969, but it expressly provided that positions covered by it "shall not be eligible for any further salary or fringe benefit increases prior to January 1, 1971," the end of the contract period.

This would seem to negate a contemporaneous intention by the city to have the tie-in with sergeants' salaries effect an increase before the end of the contract period and would bear on one of the issues to be tried out in the action.

The evident fact seems to be that this was a piecemeal negotiation and settlement in writing of contract terms. That, however, does not make the terms binding if there were any condition to their being binding dependent upon a more formal writing or upon agreement on other material terms. Whether there were such conditions is shown by the papers to be a sharply controverted issue, and, hence, one not determinable on summary judgment.

Nor does the issue of fact dissolve into one determinable as a matter of law because there was part performance of the written piecemeal agreement. That would occur, despite the conditions if they existed, if the parties were satisfied that any future agreement must and would contain the elements performed, namely, the salary increase.

The important and only issue in this case is whether the piecemeal agreement, and such agreement there certainly was, for a ratio between sergeants and patrolmen, was conditional, either on a full collective agreement signifying total agreement of all issues in dispute, or on a formal written collective agreement signifying not only full agreement on all terms but documentation removing risks of dispute as to terms. That issue is, on the present record of affidavits, and concededly incomplete and unapproved drafts and counter-drafts, an issue of fact.

The counterclaim of the city was properly dismissed.

The order should be modified by reversing so much thereof as grants summary judgment to plaintiffs on the complaint and otherwise affirmed, without costs.

FULD, Chief Judge (dissenting).

Contrary to intimations in the city's argument, no one could seriously urge a court to announce an inflexible rule that a collective bargaining agreement must be embodied in a formal written document and that neither party is bound by its terms until each has signed and executed it. Having in mind the manner in which collective bargaining has been carried on between public employers and their employees, such a principle would be completely unworkable. In any event, though, absent such an inexorable rule, we see no escape from the conclusion, reached by the courts below, that no issue of fact exists as to the city's acquiescence in the terms of the parity provision—which is the heart of this controversy—or as to the intent of the parties that there be a binding collective bargaining agreement even though not reduced to a formal written contract. Accordingly, we would affirm the order granting summary judgment to the plaintiffs for the reasons set forth in the memorandum decision of the Appellate Division and the opinion of the court at Special Term.

BREITEL, JASEN and GIBSON, JJ., concur with BERGAN, J.

FULD, C.J., dissents and votes to affirm in a separate opinion in which BURKE and SCILEPPI, JJ., concur.

Ordered accordingly.

NOTES

1. The progression of the *Patrolmen's Benevolent Ass'n* case through the New York State court system provides an interesting study of the difficulties encountered by an employer who fails to coordinate commitments to various groups of employees. The heart of the problem was the City's very real fear that if a contract were found to exist between the PBA and the city, it would set in motion an unending cycle of wage demands. The City had entered into three wage ratio commitments: a 3.0-3.5 PBA-police sergeants' wage ratio agreement, a 3.0-3.8 firemen's-fire officers' wage ratio agreement, and an agreement to maintain wage parity between police sergeants and fire lieutenants. If the PBA agreement were honored, one or the other of the other two ratios would always be out of balance. One raise would always trigger a demand for another. Before the New York County Supreme Court, the city argued that the contract was void because of impossibility of performance. Patrolmen's Benevolent Ass'n v. City of New York, 75 L.R.R.M. 2293 (N.Y. Sup. Ct. 1970). The court found no merit to this argument, holding that the city had voluntarily entered into the contracts; the difficulty was of the city's own making and therefore the impossibility of performance doctrine did not apply. The Appellate Division affirmed the Supreme Court's summary judgment finding that a valid contract existed, concluding:

> A realistic appraisal of the habits of the parties in dealing with each other must lead persuasively to the recognition that there is a contract between the parties as binding as though engrossed and bearing a dozen seals. Patrolmen's Benevolent

Ass'n v. City of New York, 35 App. Div. 2d 697, 314 N.Y.S.2d 762, 763 (1970).

Following the Court of Appeals remand, the Supreme Court again held, this time after trial, that the PBA and the City had reached a mutually enforceable agreement. Patrolmen's Benevolent Ass'n v. City of New York, 76 L.R.R.M. 3087 (N.Y. Sup. Ct. 1971).

2. In State *ex rel.* Bain v. Clallam County Bd. of County Comm'rs, 77 Wash. 2d 542, 463 P.2d 617 (1970), mandamus was sought to require the county commissioners to adopt and perform an oral collective bargaining agreement calling for a pay increase for employees of the City of Port Angeles. The Washington Supreme Court found the agreement to be too vague and uncertain to be susceptible to a decree of specific enforcement. The court also held that the state collective bargaining statute requires agreements to be in writing, suggesting the following policy reason for its decision:

> Obviously, the legislature in authorizing and in empowering county commissioners to enter into *written* agreements did so to avoid the very thing that happened here: conducting county business privately—as in the Elks' Club—from which the public could be excluded, possibly binding the county and its treasury to contractual obligations established only by parol evidence, and leaving the county dependent on the memory and recollection of the negotiators. 463 P.2d 621.

Where a collective bargaining contract is found to be clear and unambiguous in its terms, however, specific performance has been held to be a proper remedy. Cheyenne Firefighters Local 279 v. Jacobson, 75 L.R.R.M. 2563 (Wyo. Dist. Ct. 1970).

3. **Prior Exhaustion of Contractual and Administrative Remedies**

MORTON v. SUPERIOR COURT, FRESNO COUNTY

California Court of Appeals
9 Cal. App. 3d 977, 88 Cal. Rptr. 533 (1970)

GARGANO, Justice: The City of Fresno and its Chief of Police, H.R. Morton, have applied for a writ of prohibition to prevent further proceedings in the lawsuit now pending in the Superior Court of Fresno County, in which real parties in interest, hereafter referred to as real parties, seek a writ of mandate and declaratory relief. Petitioners contend that the superior court lacks jurisdiction because real parties did not exhaust their administrative remedy before filing the action. Petitioners allege that real parties are city employees with a labor grievance, and that they by-passed the grievance procedure adopted by the city manager to resolve such grievances. . . .

It is undisputed that the action which petitioners seek to enjoin is primarily concerned with a labor dispute between real parties and the City of Fresno; real parties are police officers employed by the city, and they brought the action on behalf of themselves and all members of the Fresno Police Relief Association to secure a judicial declaration that the time consumed by policemen in putting on and taking off their uniforms and during lunch periods is compensable overtime. It is also undisputed that real parties intentionally by-passed the city's grievance procedure. Real parties contend that their controversy with the city does not come within the scope of that procedure and that in any event, the exhaustion doctrine does not apply to this case. Because it is settled that the exhaustion of an administrative remedy, where one is available, is a condition precedent to obtaining judicial relief, and that "a court violating the rule acts in excess of jurisdiction" . . . we shall consider petitioners' application for a writ of prohibition on the merits. . . . If there was any question about the applicability of the grievance procedure, it was incumbent upon real parties to present the question to the city manager so that he could decide the issue in the first instance. It lies within the power of the administrative agency (in this case the city manager) to determine, in the first instance and before judicial relief may be obtained, whether a given controversy falls within its granted jurisdiction. . . .

Real parties apparently believe that because an employee is not required to file a written grievance, he may resort to the judicial process without first submitting to the grievance procedure. The basic purpose for the exhaustion doctrine is to lighten the burden of overworked courts in cases where administrative remedies are available and are as likely as the judicial remedy to provide the wanted relief. It is the rule that if an administrative remedy is available, it must be exhausted even though the administrative remedy is couched in permissive language. . . .

Understandably, a city employee is not required to file a grievance if he does not wish to do so, but he must first pursue this administrative remedy before resorting to the judicial process.

The city's grievance procedure is somewhat cumbersome, and in some cases partially regressive; for example, real parties' request for overtime credit was refused by the chief of police, and under the grievance procedure they were required to back-track and file a grievance with their immediate supervisor who is a subordinate to the chief. Nevertheless, the procedure provides for a thorough review of an employee's grievance by a representative committee, and then for an appeal to the city manager who must make a decision. Had the present controversy been presented to the city manager, and had he decided that real parties were entitled to overtime credit under the city charter or municipal ordinance for time consumed in putting on and taking off their uniforms and during lunch periods, he could have enforced this interpretation of the law by ordering the chief of police to approve the overtime. . . .

We turn to real parties' contention that they were not required to exhaust their administrative remedy in this case, first because their lawsuit is a class action, and second, because the action is primarily concerned with questions of law.

We do not believe that a city employee may dispense with the city's grievance procedure merely because his grievance affects more than one employee or member of a class. If we were to permit a city employee, on important policy questions which vitally affect the city, to by-pass the very office charged with the duty of managing the city's affairs solely because his grievance affects more than one employee, we would foist upon the judicial branch the arduous task of solving governmental policy questions without giving the responsible governmental branch the opportunity to solve its own problems at the administrative level.

We conclude that because real parties have failed to demonstrate that the city grievance procedure was inadequate to protect the members of the class they allegedly represent, they cannot prevail on this point. If real parties had filed a grievance, and if the city manager had ruled in their favor, the ruling would have applied to all police officers similarly affected. By the same token, if the city manager's decision had been adverse to real parties, it would have had the finality necessary to enable them to bring a class action. . . .

There is authority for the rule that the exhaustion doctrine is inapplicable when constitutional or jurisdictional issues or questions of law are raised. However, the decisions are by no means uniform, and this view is not followed in California. In United States v. Superior Court, 19 Cal. 2d 189, the California Supreme Court held that the exhaustion doctrine not only applies to orders which are erroneous but also to those assailed as nullities because illegally adopted. In Security First Nat. Bank v. County of Los Angeles, 35 Cal. 2d 319, 217 P.2d 946, our Supreme Court held that resort to the administrative remedy was required even though the statute sought to be applied and enforced by the administrative agency was challenged upon constitutional grounds.

It stands to reason that the exhaustion doctrine is applicable in a case such as this, which not only raises mixed questions of law and fact but also involves fundamental policy questions which should be resolved on the local level if at all possible.

The writ is granted.

Stone, P.J., concurred.

NOTES

1.   Steele v. Haley, 335 F. Supp. 659 (D. Mass. 1971), *aff'd,* 451 F.2d 1105 (1st Cir. 1971), involved a suit by a public school teacher arising under 42 U.S.C. §§ 1983 and 1985. Plaintiff claimed that he had been denied his constitutional right to due process when the school committee terminated his appointment as acting head of the Physical Education Department without sufficient notice or hearing. The court declined to consider the constitutional issues because the matter had already been submitted to arbitration. The court noted, in this regard, that:

> Where by contract the parties have established a machinery for handling and arbitrating grievances, they have in effect set up their private system of administrative remedies. If a plaintiff succeeds in the private administrative process, it will be unnecessary to have a federal judicial hearing. If he fails, he is not estopped from presenting to the judiciary a constitutional claim.

The *Steele v. Haley* decision and related matters are discussed in detail in the section dealing with "Exhaustion of Remedies as a Prerequisite to Suit by an Individual Employee," *infra.*

2.   It is generally accepted that judicial enforcement of a collective bargaining agreement will be foreclosed to parties who have established a binding arbitration procedure to deal with contract grievance disputes. *See, e.g.,* Central School District v. Litz, 60 Misc. 2d 1009, 1010-11, 304 N.Y.S.2d 372 (1969), *aff'd,* 34 App. Div. 2d 1092, 314 N.Y.S.2d 176 (1970), where it was held that:

> Once a valid agreement has been entered into providing for arbitration, any controversy arising between the parties to the contract which is within the compass of those provisions must go to arbitration.

However, judicial enforcement of a collective bargaining agreement may lie, notwithstanding the presence of an arbitration procedure where (1) there is fraud or duress; (2) the subject matter of the alleged contract breach is excluded from arbitration or (3) there has been a breach of the duty of fair representation.

See, e.g., Board of Education, Central School District No. 1 v. Grand Island Teachers Ass'n, 67 Misc. 2d 859, 324 N.Y.S.2d 717 (Sup. Ct. 1970), *aff'd,* 38 App. Div. 2d 669, 326 N.Y.S.2d 1023 (1971), *appeal denied,* 30 N.Y.2d 481 (1972); Nassau Chapter, Civil Service Employees Ass'n v. Board of Educ., School Dist. No. 3, Town of Hempstead, 63 Misc. 2d 49, 310 N.Y.S.2d 381 (Sup. Ct. 1970); Kaufman v. Goldberg, 64 Misc. 2d 524, 315 N.Y.S.2d 35 (Sup. Ct. 1970).

D.   Enforcement of Voluntary Arbitration Agreements

1.   The Private Sector Precedents: Lincoln Mills and the "Trilogy"

H. WELLINGTON, LABOR AND THE LEGAL PROCESS 97-100 (1968)†

When Congress enacted the Taft-Hartley Act, it was not centrally concerned with the question of judicial enforcement of the collective agreement. Congressional tolerance for strikes and other types of labor disputes, however, was low, and the strike during contract time was one of the many sorts of union activity that came in for censure. Some thought was given to making any such strike an unfair labor practice; but this was not done. Procedures were erected limiting the union's freedom to strike, and the strike in breach of the collective agreement was itself "left to the usual processes of law"—whatever they might be. The procedural difficulties involved in suing a union because it was an unincorporated association, however, did engage the attention of Congress, and unions were made suable as entities. The legislative process in the end produced a seemingly innocuous section providing in part that: "Suits for violation of contracts between an employer and a labor organization representing employees in an industry affecting commerce . . . may be brought in any district court of the United States having jurisdiction of the parties, without respect to the amount in controversy or without regard to the citizenship of the parties." But this section—301 of the Labor Management Relations Act—has proved to be far reaching in its impact. Indeed, the reach given to it by the Supreme Court of the United States is well beyond any that Congress could have foreseen. The law of the collective agreement has been turned around. Today it is one of the most rapidly developing segments of American jurisprudence.

Textile Workers v. Lincoln Mills[35] is the case that began this quiet revolution. It was decided by the Supreme Court in 1957,

---

† Reprinted by permission of The Yale University Press.
[35] 353 U.S. 448 (1957).

and it grew out of the effort of a union to compel an employer to submit grievances to arbitration. The union brought suit in a federal district court under section 301. It asserted that the employer had promised in the collective agreement to arbitrate grievances which arose during contract time; that he had broken this promise, and that, therefore, the court should order specific performance of the promise to arbitrate. The employer in turn raised some interesting defenses going to the question of whether the court had the power to grant equitable relief in these circumstances.

The first of these defenses relied on the Norris-LaGuardia Act's prohibition against federal courts issuing injunctions in labor disputes. But while an order compelling specific performance is quite properly thought of as a mandatory injunction, it is not the type of injunction which is a central concern of the Norris-LaGuardia Act, and the Supreme Court ultimately had little difficulty in concluding that the anti-injunction statute did not apply in a suit for specific performance of an arbitration promise.[36]

Much less easily resolved, however, was another of the employer's contentions. At common law in most states the promise to arbitrate was not enforceable by an order of specific performance.[37] This was so whether the promise was contained in a commercial contract or in a collective agreement. Theoretically one might recover damages for breach of this promise, but practically one could never show damages. This state rule was also the federal rule.[38] Some states,[39] and the federal government,[40] had legislation which, for some types of contracts at least, changed the common law rule. But the law of the relevant state apparently could not help the union in *Lincoln Mills,* and there was serious doubt whether the United States Arbitration Act applied to arbitration promises in collective bargaining agreements.[41]

Moreover, it was unclear which body of law governed a suit brought under section 301. The statute appeared to be no more than a grant of jurisdiction to the federal courts. It said nothing

---

[36] 353 U.S. at 457-59. . . .

[37] *See, e.g.,* Rowe v. Williams, 97 Mass. 163 (1867). *Cf.* Cogswell v. Cogswell, 70 Wash. 178, 126 P. 431 (1912).

[38] *See* Red Cross Line v. Atlantic Fruit Co., 264 U.S. 109, 120-22 (1924).

[39] The statutes are collected in 4 BNA LABOR RELATIONS REPORTER.

[40] 9 U.S.C. §§ 1-14 (1964).

[41] *Compare* United Furniture Workers v. Colonial Hardwood Flooring Co., 168 F.2d 33 (4th Cir. 1948), *with* Mercury Oil Refining Co. v. Oil Workers Int'l Union, 187 F.2d 980 (10th Cir. 1951) *and* Tenney Engineering Inc. v. United Elec. Workers, 207 F.2d 450 (3rd Cir. 1953).

about the substantive rights of the parties. The early law—
what there was of it—on the subject of rights under the collective agreement was, as noted, of state, not federal, origin. Nor was
it clear whether the law governing the availability of the equitable remedy of specific performance was the law of the forum
or the law which created the cause of action.

All of these problems were serious. They had split the lower
courts for ten years; they had worried the commentators and
disturbed the private orders. All of these serious problems were
solved by the Supreme Court in the *Lincoln Mills* case by judicial
fiat. No serious attempt was made by that Court to bridge with
reasoned elaboration the gap between question and conclusion.
The majority opinion is simply an *ipse dixit*.

The Court held that section 301 was a charter to the courts to
develop a federal "common law" of the collective bargaining
agreement, and that section 301 itself empowered the courts to
grant specific performance of the promise to arbitrate.

R. SMITH & D. JONES, THE SUPREME COURT AND LABOR DISPUTE ARBITRATION: THE EMERGING FEDERAL LAW, 63 Mich. L. Rev. 751, 755-60 (1965)†

The so-called "Trilogy" of 1960 consisted of three cases in
which, in each instance, the union involved was the United Steelworkers of America. The cases have been stated, dissected, and
critically examined to the point that we now have a wealth of
literature concerning them. A brief review of the issues presented
and the decisions is, nevertheless, desirable as part of our background recital.

In *Warrior & Gulf*,[42] the grievances brought by the Union protested the contracting out of certain maintenance work clearly
encompassed by the bargaining unit. There was a layoff situation
at the time the grievances were filed which, in part, was due to
the contracting out of such work. The labor agreement was silent
on the subject of contracting out; however, it undoubtedly contained recognition, wage, and seniority provisions. The agreement
also contained a no-strike provision. Excluded from the arbitration
process were matters that were "strictly a function of management," but otherwise the arbitration clause was unusually broad.
It stated:

> "Should differences arise between the Company and the
> Union or its members . . . as to the meaning and applica-
> tion of the provisions of this Agreement, or should any local

---

† Reprinted by permission of The Michigan Law Review.
42 United Steelworkers v. Warrior & Gulf Nav. Co., 363 U.S. 574 (1960).

trouble of any kind arise, there shall be no suspension of
work on account of such differences, but an earnest effort
shall be made to settle such differences in the following
manner [referring to the grievance and arbitration pro-
cedure]."

In a suit by the Union under section 301 to compel arbitration,
the district court granted the Company's motion to dismiss, holding that the agreement did not confide in an arbitrator the right
to review the defendant's business judgment in contracting out
work and that contracting out was strictly a function of management within the meaning of the exclusionary language of the
arbitration clause. The court of appeals affirmed, but the Supreme
Court reversed and the Company was forced to arbitrate.

In *American Manufacturing*,[43] the question was whether the
Company was required to submit to arbitration a grievance based
on its refusal to reinstate an employee who had suffered an industrial injury. In a consent decree settlement of a workmen's compensation claim, the employee had been awarded a lump-sum
payment plus costs on the basis that he had incurred a permanent
partial disability of twenty-five per cent. His subsequent demand
for reinstatement was predicated on a statement by his physician
(who had supported the earlier claim of permanent partial disability) that the employee "is now able to return to his former
duties without danger to himself or to others." Contractually, the
demand was based on a provision in the seniority article of the
labor agreement which recognized "the principle of seniority as a
factor in the selection of employees for promotion, transfer, layoff,
re-employment, and filling of vacancies, where ability and efficiency are equal." The arbitration clause was standard in that it
permitted arbitration of "any disputes, misunderstandings, differences or grievances arising between the parties as to the meaning,
interpretation and application of the provisions of this agreement." The district court and court of appeals refused to require
the Company to arbitrate, although they disagreed on the basis of
decision. The district court used an estoppel theory; the court of
appeals held that estoppel did not go to the question of arbitrability, but it examined the cited seniority provisions and concluded that the grievance was "a frivolous, patently baseless
one" and hence not within the arbitration clause. Again, the
Supreme Court reversed and ordered arbitration.

In *Enterprise*,[44] the grievance sought the reinstatement of

---

43 United Steelworkers v. American Mfg. Co., 363 U.S. 564 (1960).

44 United Steelworkers v. Enterprise Wheel & Car Corp., 363 U.S. 593
(1960).

certain employees who had been discharged because they had left their jobs in protest against the discharge of a fellow employee. The Company refused to arbitrate the grievance, but was ordered to do so by a federal district court. The arbitrator's decision reduced the penalty of discharge to a ten-day disciplinary layoff and ordered the grievants reinstated with back pay adjusted for the ten-day penalty. The decision was handed down five days after the labor agreement had expired, and the Company refused to comply with the award on the ground, *inter alia,* that the arbitrator lacked the authority either to order back pay for any period subsequent to the expiration date of the labor agreement or to order reinstatement. The district court directed the Company to comply with the award, but the court of appeals reversed on the ground urged by the Company. The Supreme Court, however, once more upheld the authority of the arbitrator.

Seven Justices concurred in these decisions. Mr. Justice Whittaker dissented, and Mr. Justice Black did not participate. The principal opinion for the majority was written by Mr. Justice Douglas. Mr. Justice Frankfurter did not join in this opinion, but concurred in the results in each case. Justices Brennan and Harlan, while joining the Douglas opinion in each case, also added "a word" in *Warrior & Gulf* and *American Manufacturing.*

The decisions have been viewed as indicating a strong federal policy favoring the arbitration process as a means of resolving disputes concerning the interpretation or application of collective bargaining agreements and as restricting the role of the courts in this area. This interpretation, we think, is correct, although it derives its principal support from the content of the opinions, especially the opinion by Mr. Justice Douglas, rather than from the specific dispositions of the issues presented. . . .

Considering at this point only the 1960 decisions, the following propositions seem to have been declared as a matter of federal substantive law with respect to labor agreements subject to enforcement under section 301 of the Labor Management Relations Act of 1947:

(1) The existence of a valid agreement to arbitrate, and the arbitrability of a specific grievance sought to be arbitrated under such an agreement, are questions for the courts ultimately to decide (if such an issue is presented for judicial determination) unless the parties have expressly given an arbitrator the authority to make a binding determination of such matters.

(2) A court should hold a grievance non-arbitrable under a valid agreement to use arbitration as the terminal point in the grievance procedure only if the parties have clearly

indicated their intention to exclude the subject matter of the grievance from the arbitration process, either by expressly so stating in the arbitration clause or by otherwise clearly and unambiguously indicating such intention.

(3) Evidence of intention to exclude a claim from the arbitration process should not be found in a determination that the labor agreement could not properly be interpreted in such manner as to sustain the grievance on its merits, for this is a task assigned by the parties to the arbitrator, not the courts.

(4) An award should not be set aside as beyond the authority conferred upon the arbitration, either because of claimed error in interpretation of the agreement or because of alleged lack of authority to provide a particular remedy, where the arbitral decision was or, if silent, might have been the result of the arbitrator's interpretation of the agreement; if, however, it was based not on the contract but on an obligation found to have been imposed by law, the award should be set aside unless the parties have expressly authorized the arbitrator to dispose of this as well as any contract issue.[45]

---

[45] See also Report of Special Warrior & Gulf Committee, in 1963 PROCEEDINGS OF THE ABA SECTION OF LABOR RELATIONS LAW 196-97, in which the following six general propositions with respect to arbitration under collective bargaining agreements were said to have been established by the Trilogy: "(1) Arbitration is a matter of contract, not of law; parties are required to arbitrate only if, and to the extent that, they have agreed to do so. (2) The question of arbitrability under a collective bargaining agreement is a question for the courts, not for the arbitrator, unless the parties specifically provide otherwise in their agreement. (3) Since arbitration under a collective bargaining agreement is an alternative to strike, rather than to litigation, as in commercial arbitration, the traditional judicial reluctance toward compelling parties to arbitrate is not applicable to labor arbitration. (4) When the parties have provided for arbitration of all disputes as to the application or interpretation of a collective bargaining agreement, the courts should order arbitration of any grievance which claims that management has violated the provisions of the agreement, irrespective of the courts' views as to the merits of the claim. (5) When the parties have coupled with a provision for arbitration of all disputes a clause specifically excepting certain matters from arbitration, the courts should order arbitration of a claim that the employer has violated the agreement unless it may be said with positive assurance that the subject matter falls within the exception clause. (6) An arbitral award should be enforced (absent fraud or similar vitiating circumstance) unless it is clear that the arbitrator has based that award upon matters outside the contract he is charged with interpreting and applying."

2.   Compelling Arbitration

A.F.S.C.M.E., LOCAL 1226, RHINELANDER CITY EMPLOYEES
v. CITY OF RHINELANDER

Supreme Court of Wisconsin
35 Wis. 2d 209, 151 N.W.2d 30 (1967)

HANLEY, Justice.

On December 10, 1964, the plaintiff, Frances Bischoff, was discharged from her job as an administrative assistant in the water department of the city by order of the city mayor. At that time Mrs. Bischoff was a member of the union. The local union was the exclusive bargaining agent for city employees in several city departments, including the water department. The city and the union had a written collective bargaining agreement which in Article X provided [for a grievance procedure concluding in binding arbitration]. . . .

Mrs. Bischoff felt that by her discharge her rights and privileges under the collective bargaining agreement had been violated, and submitted the problem to the union grievance committee. The union determined that a grievance existed and processed Mrs. Bischoff's grievance through the first four steps of the Article X proceeding without solution satisfactory to both sides. Thereupon the union chose its member of the arbitration panel as provided in Article X of the collective bargaining agreement. The city refused to choose its member of the arbitration board and refused to follow the procedures set out in the agreement for choosing the third member chairman of the arbitration board.

Mrs. Bischoff and the union commenced this action for specific performance of the arbitration clause of the agreement for Mrs. Bischoff's grievance on her discharge. The city demurred upon the ground that the plaintiffs' complaint failed to state facts sufficient to constitute a cause of action. The trial court sustained the demurrer, basically upon the ground that the city had no statutory authority to enter into a binding arbitration agreement, and that therefore no cause of action will lie to specifically enforce such an agreement. From the judgment sustaining the demurrer, the plaintiffs appeal. . . .

The following issues are presented on this appeal:

1.   Is the arbitration clause contained in the collective bargaining agreement binding on the city?

2.   If the clause is binding, is it specifically enforceable in the courts?

3.   Is the question of whether Mrs. Bischoff was discharged for just cause an arbitrable issue under the agreement?

1. *Binding effect of the agreement to arbitration.*

At the conclusion of the agreement, prior to the signatures of the officials of the city and the union, is the following provision:

"This Agreement shall be binding upon both the Employer and the Union."

The initial question is whether that part of the "agreement," Article X, which provides an arbitration procedure as a final step in the processing of grievances is binding upon the city.

We think it is binding. By sec. 111.70 (4) (i), Stats., the legislature has decreed that written collective bargaining agreements between municipal employers and labor organizations "shall be binding" if they contain express language to that effect. Here we have such an agreement which contains such express language. Thus the contract comes exactly within the provision of the statute and is binding.

2. *Specific enforceability of the agreement to arbitrate grievances.*

In the leading case on the point of enforceability, Local 1111 of United Electrical, Radio, & Machine Workers of America v. Allen-Bradley Co. (1951), 259 Wis. 609, 49 N.W.2d 720, this court held that a collective bargaining contract containing provisions for the arbitration of grievances was legal and in full force in Wisconsin, but that without some statutory basis the courts have no power to order an employer to perform its agreement to arbitrate. The basis of the court's opinion was that courts may specifically enforce agreements to arbitrate differences arising under an existing contract only under sec. 298.01, Stats. Since sec. 298.01 specifically does not apply to contracts between employers and employees, except as provided in sec. 111.10, Stats., the court reasoned that the union was not entitled to a judgment requiring the employer to arbitrate.

It should be noted that in Local 1111 etc., v. Allen-Bradley, supra, the court was divided. Mr. Justice CURRIE, joined by Mr. Justice BROADFOOT, dissented on the grounds that Wisconsin courts are not so impotent as to be unable to enforce valid and lawful agreements and that the declaratory judgment statute under which the action was brought authorized the court to grant supplementary relief when necessary and proper.

Mr. Justice CURRIE in his dissenting opinion, at page 618, 49 N.W.2d at page 725, stated:

"I cannot subscribe to the theory that the common law is an inflexible instrument which does not permit growth and adjustment to meet the social needs of the times. This court in the past has repudiated this very theory. Mr. Justice Nelson in his opinion in Schwanke v. Garlt, 219 Wis. 367, 371, 263 N.W. 176, 178, declared:

" 'While we are at all times bound to uphold the Constitution of this state and to give due effect to its paramount provisions, we may not ignore the fact "that the common law is susceptible of growth and adaptation to new circumstances and situations, and that the courts have power to declare and effectuate what is the present rule in respect of a given subject without regard to the old rule. . . . The common law is not immutable, but flexible, and upon its own principles adapts itself to varying conditions." Dimick v. Schiedt, 293 U.S. 474, 55 S. Ct. 296, 301, 79 L. Ed. 603. To the same effect is Funk v. United States, 290 U.S. 371, 54 S. Ct. 212, 78 L. Ed. 369.' "

We believe the rule that the enforcement of an arbitration provision in a collective bargaining agreement is not enforceable at common law should be repudiated.

The very purpose of grievance arbitration is to prevent individual problems from blossoming into labor disputes which cause strikes and lockouts and which require collective bargaining to restore peace and tranquility.

We now adopt the view expressed by Mr. Justice CURRIE in his dissent in *Local 1111,* supra, and conclude that it is illogical to hold in this case that the arbitration provisions are valid but the court is powerless to enforce them by compelling the city to arbitrate Mrs. Bischoff's grievance, especially in the light of the legislative enactment in sec. 111.70 (4) (i), Stats., that ". . . Such agreements shall be binding. . . ."

The city and the trial court in its decision contend that the legislative history of sec. 111.70 (4), Stats., demonstrates that the legislature rejected the use of grievance arbitration as a means of settling disagreements which arise under collective bargaining agreements with municipal employees. Actually, if the legislative history demonstrates anything, it is that the legislature rejected the idea of extending the jurisdiction to the Wisconsin Employment Relations Board to handle or enforce arbitration agreements in municipal employment relations. . . .

3. Arbitrability of the discharge.

The city contends that even if Article X of the collective bargaining agreement is binding upon the city, Mrs. Bischoff's discharge is not a grievance subject to arbitration under the terms of that article. The trial court did not consider this question, but the parties have argued it and it is a question of law which the court will consider in order to avoid additional appeals.

According to Article X of the agreement, the following matters are subject to the grievance procedure:

". . . differences [which may] arise between the Employer and the Union as to the meaning and application of the provisions of this agreement or as to any question relating to wages, hours, and conditions of employment. . . ."

Article IV of the agreement provides the following with respect to probationary employees:

"Section 1. New employees without prior service shall be employed on a six (6) months probationary basis, and during said period may be discharged for cause without recourse through the Union."

Mrs. Bischoff was apparently a permanent employee who claims that this section of the agreement, at least by implication, protects her from discharge without cause, and that she was discharged without cause. It would thus seem that Mrs. Bischoff's grievance, processed by the union, can fairly be said to be a difference "as to the meaning and application of the provisions" of the agreement, if not a "question relating to wages, hours, and conditions of employment." Moreover, Mrs. Bischoff felt that her rights and privileges under the agreement were violated by her discharge. The question of her discharge would thus seem to be arbitrable under sec. 2 of Article X, which in part provides:

"Should an employee feel that his rights and privileges under this Agreement have been violated he shall first submit the problem to the Union Grievance Committee. If it is determined after investigation by the Union that a grievance does exist it shall be processed in the manner described below: . . . ."

4. Arbitration is not an unlawful infringement on the legislative power of the city.

The city has contended that to require the city to submit to binding arbitration is an unlawful infringement upon the legislative power of the city council and a violation of its home rule powers. Yet in all of its arguments the city is talking about arbitration in the collective bargaining context—arbitration to set the terms of a collective bargaining agreement. Such is not this case, which involves arbitration to resolve a grievance arising under an existing agreement to which the city is a party. The legislature has passed statutes doubtless of statewide concern, which provide that the city's agreement to arbitrate grievances is binding on the city.

We conclude that the arbitration clause contained in the collective bargaining agreement is binding upon the city and is specifically enforceable in the courts and that Mrs. Bischoff's discharge is an arbitrable issue under the agreement.

Judgment reversed and cause remanded for further proceedings in conformity with the opinion.

BOARD OF EDUCATION, CENTRAL SCHOOL DISTRICT NO. 1 OF THE TOWN OF GRAND ISLAND v. GRAND ISLAND TEACHERS' ASSOCIATION

New York Supreme Court
67 Misc. 2d 859, 324 N.Y.S.2d 717 (Sup. Ct. 1970)
Aff'd mem., 38 App. Div. 2d 669, 326 N.Y.S.2d 1023 (1971)
Appeal denied, 30 N.Y.2d 481 (1972)

WALTER J. MAHONEY, J. There is now before this court an application by the petitioner herein, pursuant to CPLR 7503 (subd. [c]) to stay arbitration of an alleged dispute between petitioner and respondents herein.

From the pleadings presented it would appear that the petitioner, Board of Education, Central School District No. 1 of the Town of Grand Island, Erie County, New York (hereinafter referred to as the "Board"), is a public employer, and, that the respondent, Grand Island Teachers' Association (hereinafter referred to as the "Association"), is a public employee organization and the duly recognized employee representative of the teachers of the Grand Island Central School District. By an agreement entitled Agreement Relating To Terms and Conditions of Employment (hereinafter referred to as "Agreement"), entered into by and between the Board and the Association, effective for the period July 1, 1969 through June 30, 1970, a detailed four-level grievance procedure was prescribed under article XX thereof. The fourth and last stage of said procedure provides for arbitration of unresolved grievances.

Pertinent to this proceeding, said Agreement, under article IX, entitled "Teacher Evaluation," and article X entitled "The Probationary Teacher," contains various provisions including certain procedural specifications relative to the subject matter of the respective articles. . . .

It would further appear from the pleadings submitted that pursuant to section 3013 of the Education Law, six probationary teachers of Board's school district and members of the Association were notified in writing by the Board on April 8 and 13, 1970 that their employment would terminate at the end of the 1969-70 school year. Thereafter, on or about May 6, 1970, in accordance with "Stage 1" of the grievance procedure article of the Agreement, the respondent, Richard S. Meredith, as chairman of the Grievance Committee of the Association, filed a grievance report charging the chief school officer and the Board with violations of provisions contained in articles IX and X of the Agreement, specifying that: "The Grand Island Board of Education has failed to direct their Administrative Staff to follow and comply with the provisions of Articles IX and X. The dismissal by the Board of Education of those probationary teachers on April 8 and 13, 1970 without benefit of their rights granted under Articles IX and X of the agreement between the Board and the Association."

It is significant to the proceeding now before this court that the particularization of the relief sought on said grievance report is specified as follows: "That the Grand Island Board of Education direct its Administrative Staff to comply with all the provisions of Articles IX and X in respect to probationary teachers."

. . .

Petitioner's contentions in support of relief herein sought would appear to be: (a) that the notice or complaint of the Association fails to identify the alleged grievance; (b) that the alleged grievance sought to be arbitrated by the Association is excluded by the terms of the Agreement; and (c) that the demanded arbitration would result in the fractionalizing of remedies, contrary to law.

Whether, under the facts here presented, there be merit to any or all of said petitioner's contentions, it must preliminarily be acknowledged that the subject matter jurisdiction of the court in a proceeding of this nature is statutorily restricted by CPLR 7501 and CPLR 7503 (subd. [b]). As was held in Central School Dist. v. Litz (60 Misc. 2d 1009, 1010-1011, affd. 34 A.D.2d 1092):

> "CPLR 7503 provides for a stay of arbitration if there was not a valid agreement, the agreement has not been complied with or the claim is barred by statutory limitations.
>
> "Once a valid agreement has been entered into providing for arbitration, any controversy arising between the parties to the contract which is within the compass of those provisions must go to arbitration. (*Matter of Exercycle Corp.* [*Maratta*], 9 N.Y.2d 329.) The only exceptions to which a court will enjoin arbitration are: 1. where there is fraud or duress, 2. where there is no bona fide dispute between the parties, 3. where the performance which is the subject for the demand for arbitration is prohibited, or 4. where a condition precedent to arbitration under the contract has not been fulfilled. If the issue involved is solely one of construction or interpretation, it is for the arbitrators to decide the meaning

of the contract. (*Matter of Exercycle Corp.* [*Maratta*], *supra.*)" . . .

Neither fraud nor duress is either alleged or inferentially present under the facts here presented.

The existence of a bona fide dispute between the parties concerning compliance by the Board with various provisions contained in articles IX and X of the Agreement is patently clear.

Nor, in proper perspective, can it be said that the performance, which is the subject of the demand for arbitration, i.e., compliance with provisions contained in afore-mentioned articles of the Agreement, is prohibited. Petitioner's contention that section 3013 of the Education Law, vesting absolute discretion in the Board with respect to the termination of employment of probationary teachers, combined with the provision contained in article III, paragraph 2 of the Agreement, constitutes an effective exclusion from the arbitration provision of the Agreement, is not in the present posture of the proceedings now before this court. . . . Without expressing any opinions upon the merits of the dispute (CPLR 7501), the Association as a party to the notice and demand for arbitration may well have a viable interest in the Board's compliance with its contractual obligations concerning the subject matter in dispute.

Lastly, the contended inadequacy and deficiency in identifying and specifying the alleged grievance in the notices served by the Association is not sustained by the facts presented and cannot warrant this court's intervention on the basis that a condition precedent to arbitration under the Agreement has not been fulfilled.

By reason of the foregoing, the petitioner's application to stay arbitration must be denied, and petitioner is directed to proceed to arbitration of the dispute concerning compliance or noncompliance by the petitioner with those specified provisions contained in articles IX and X of the Agreement, in the manner so provided under article XX thereof.

BOARD OF EDUCATION OF THE TOWNSHIP OF ROCKAWAY v. ROCKAWAY TOWNSHIP EDUCATION ASSOCIATION

New Jersey Superior Court
81 L.R.R.M. 2462 (1972)

STAMLER, Judge:—Plaintiff is The Board of Education of the Township of Rockaway in Morris County. Defendants are Rockaway Township Education Association (hereinafter RTEA) and Joseph Youngman, a teacher in the employ of the Board. The Board asks that defendants be enjoined from proceeding before

the American Arbitration Association on the question of interference with the "academic freedom" of the teacher in violation
of a contract between the Board and RTEA. . . .

On June 23, 1971, the Board and RTEA entered into a contract which provided for the terms and conditions of employment of teachers in the Rockaway Township School District. In
February 1972, Youngman, a teacher of Humanities, was directed
by the Superintendent of the school district not to conduct in
his 7th grade class a previously announced "debate" on the
subject of abortion. The 7th grade class is composed of eleven
and twelve year old children. . . .

Defendants contend that the preclusion decision of the Superintendent and its affirmance by the Board was a denial of
"academic freedom" to defendants and a violation of Article
XXVII, Paragraph C of the collective bargaining contract between the parties.

Paragraph C reads as follows:

> "The Board and the Association agree that academic free-
> dom is essential to the fulfillment of the purposes of the
> Rockaway Township School District. Free discussion of con-
> troversial issues is the heart of the democratic process.
> Through the study of such issues, political, economic or
> social, youth develops those abilities needed for functional
> citizenship in our democracy. *Whenever appropriate for
> the maturation level of the group,* controversial issues may
> be studied in an unprejudiced and dispassionate manner.
> It shall be the duty of the teacher to foster the study of an
> issue and not to teach a particular viewpoint in regard to
> it." (Emphasis supplied.)

Defendants demanded of the Board that the issue of the alleged
violation of Article XXVII, Par. C as well as the issue of academic
freedom of a member of the teaching staff be processed as a
"grievance" before the American Arbitration Association as provided in the contract. Notice of its intention to proceed before
the Arbitration Association was given to the Board. The Board
filed its complaint seeking an injunction, asserting that the appropriate forum is a proceeding before the Commissioner of Education. . . .

Article III, Paragraph A (1) of the contract defines "grievance" as:

> "The term 'grievance' means a complaint by an employee
> of the Association that, as to him, there has been a personal
> loss or injury because of an administrative decision affecting

said employee, or an unjust application, interpretation or violation of a policy, or agreement. The term 'grievance' and the procedure relative thereto shall not apply to a complaint of a non-tenure teacher which arises by reason of his not being re-employed after only two years on probation."

It is clear that both the Board and RTEA agreed that "academic freedom" is essential to the fulfillment of the purposes of the School District. The heart of the problem is the fourth sentence in the quoted section of Article XXVII (C) :

"Whenever appropriate for the maturation level of the group, controversial issues may be studied in an unprejudiced and dispassionate manner." . . .

To determine "maturation level" requires expertise in education. One proposition upon which the authors of the articles cited above agree: a trial court is not so qualified.

This then places the obligation on either the teacher or the Board or both. When disagreement arises, shall it be settled before a panel selected from the American Arbitration Association or before the Commissioner of Education with review by the State Board of Education and thereafter the Appellate Courts?

The New Jersey Employer-Employee Relations Act, P.L. 1968, Ch. 303, requires a public employer, including a board of education, to negotiate with the majority representative of an appropriate unit of its employees concerning the terms and conditions of employment. Specifically to be negotiated is a grievance procedure. N.J.S.A. 34:13A-53. In N.J.S.A. 34:13A-10 the following appears:

"Nothing in this act shall be construed to annul or modify, or to preclude the renewal or continuation of any agreement heretofore entered into between any public employer and any employee organization, *nor shall any provision hereof annul or modify any statute or statutes of the state.*" (Emphasis added.)

It cannot be argued, therefore, that Title 18 "Education" insofar as it is concerned with relationship between Boards, teachers *and* pupils has been superseded. Even were this language eliminated from Chapter 303, our Supreme Court has held that the general rule of statutory construction, in the absence of clear legislative direction to the contrary, requires a determination that a later statute will not be deemed to repeal or modify an earlier one, but all existing statutes pertaining to the same subject matter "are to be construed together as a unitary and harmonious whole, in order that each may be fully effective." Clifton

v. Passaic County Board of Taxation, 28 N.J. 411, 421 (1958).
Thus, the provisions of both Title 18A and Chapter 303 must
be read together so that both are harmonized and each is given
its appropriate role.

The selection of courses to be presented to students and the
subjects to be presented or discussed cannot be a "term or condition of employment." Defendants argue "there can be no doubt
that the methods of selecting courses and even more clearly,
the procedures and methods by which these courses are to be
presented, may be negotiated at least in broad terms." This proposition is untenable.

The Board is responsible for the production of a "thorough
and efficient" school system (N.J. Constitution, Art. 8 Sec. 4 P.1)
and particularly the statutory obligation to provide "courses of
study suited to the ages and attainments of all pupils." N.J.S.
18A:33-1. The Board has a continuing obligation placed upon it
by the Legislature to adopt and alter courses of study. . . .

In Porcelli v. Titus, 108 N.J. Super. 301, 2 FEP Cases 344
(App. Div. 1970), cert. denied 55 N.J. 310 (1970), the following appears at p. 312, 2 FEP Cases at 348:

> " 'The public schools were not created, nor are they sup-
> ported for the benefit of the teachers therein, . . . but for
> the benefit of the pupils, and the resulting benefit to their
> parents and the community at large.' "

The courts have recognized that public employees cannot
make contracts with public agencies that are contrary to the
dictates of the Legislature. Lullo v. International Association of
Fire Fighters, 55 N.J. 409, 73 LRRM 2680 (1970). Nor can
public agencies such as a board of education "abdicate or bargain away their continuing legislative or executive obligations or
discretion." Lullo, supra, 440, 73 LRRM at 2693.

It is concluded therefore that if the contract is read to delegate to a teacher or to a teacher's union the subject of courses of
study, the contract in that respect is *ultra vires* and unenforceable.
It must follow therefore that the American Arbitration Association cannot be the subdelegee of the Board and of the teachers.
Additionally, it is to be noted that the American Arbitration Association may be well qualified to "arbitrate" compensation,
hours of work, sick leave, fringe-benefits and the like, but they
and their panels possess no expertise in arbitrating the maturation level of a 7th grade student in the elementary schools of
Rockaway Township.

However, defendants who were dissatisfied with the action
of the Superintendent and the Board are not without a remedy.

N.J.S. 18A:6-9 provides that the Commissioner of Education "shall have jurisdiction to hear and determine, without cost to the parties, all controversies and disputes arising under the school laws. . . ." On subsequent appeal, our appellate courts will have the benefit of the special experience of the administrative agencies operating in the vital area of education, especially of the young. . . .

BOARD OF EDUCATION OF CENTRAL SCHOOL DISTRICT NO. 1, TOWN OF CLARKSTOWN v. CRACOVIA

New York Supreme Court, Appellate Division
36 App. Div. 2d 851, 321 N.Y.S.2d 496 (1971)

In a proceeding to stay arbitration which had been demanded by respondent Clarkstown Teachers' Association, petitioner appeals from an order of the Supreme Court, Rockland County, entered August 20, 1970, which denied the application, granted respondents' cross motion to compel arbitration, directed petitioner to proceed to arbitration and enjoined petitioner from commencing or prosecuting any action with respect to the dispute ordered to be arbitrated.

Order affirmed, with $10 costs and disbursements.

In September, 1969 petitioner entered into a collective bargaining agreement with respondent Clarkstown Teachers' Association effective July 1, 1969 to June 30, 1970. Paragraph (a) of Article XVI of the agreement contained a provision relative to class size which read as follows:

"Maximum Class Sizes—Facilities permitting, for the maximum teacher effectiveness and pupil involvement class sizes will be no larger than (25) twenty-five on the elementary and (27) twenty-seven on the secondary levels."

The agreement also included an extensive grievance procedure in Article XXIII, which contained four separate stages. The fourth and final stage was the arbitration stage which in part stated:

"The decision of the arbitrator shall be final and binding only with respect to grievances concerning the interpretation or application of the specific terms of this Agreement; provided that binding arbitration shall not be had for any grievance concerning provisions of this contract that involve the Board's discretion or right to set policy. In grievances other than those covered in the above sentence, while the decision shall be advisory, each side will have a moral obligation to seriously consider the recommendation."

On January 20, 1970, the Teachers' Association duly served a notice of intention to arbitrate an alleged grievance relating to "Maximum Class Sizes" which remained unresolved after completion of the first three stages of the grievance procedure.

In its petition in this stay proceeding petitioner contended that the provisions of the agreement excerpted above bound it to so-called "advisory arbitration" and not "binding arbitration." Its position is that article 75 of the CPLR does not empower a court to direct parties to arbitrate a dispute which results in an award which can only be advisory in nature. The Teachers' Association cross-moved to compel arbitration.

In our opinion, it is no longer necessary, as it was under section 1448 of the Civil Practice Act, that a contractual dispute be of a justiciable nature before arbitration will be ordered. Such limitation has been expressly removed by the Legislature in its enactment of CPLR 7501 which reads:

"A written agreement to submit any controversy . . . is enforceable without regard to the justiciable character of the controversy."

We can see no compelling reason why article 75 of the CPLR should not be applicable to "advisory arbitration" if that is what the parties intended. Arbitration is a creature of contract and its scope can be very broad or very narrow, depending on the provisions of the contract. At bar, the parties have agreed to submit their disputes to arbitration although additionally agreeing to limit the impact of the arbitrator's award to that of merely an advisory nature in some instances.

We do not now decide whether the posed grievances are subject to an arbitration decision which is binding.

NOTES

1. If the courts can enforce an agreement to arbitrate, even though the subject matter of the dispute is not justiciable, as in the *Cracovia* case, can the courts enforce the resulting award? *See* Johnson v. Village of Plymouth, 288 Minn. 300, 180 N.W.2d 184 (1970) ; Schwartz v. North Salem Bd. of Educ., 65 Misc. 2d 472, 318 N.Y.S.2d 774 (Sup. Ct. 1971) .

2. Should the courts compel arbitration even if the grievance sought to be arbitrated is of doubtful merit? In the private sector, in cases arising under Section 301 of the Labor-Management Relations Act, the Supreme Court has ruled that:

The collective agreement calls for the submission of grievances in the categories which it describes, irrespective of whether a court may deem them to be meritorious. . . . The function of the court is very limited when the parties have agreed to submit all questions of contract interpretation to the arbitrator. It is confined to ascertaining whether the party seeking arbitration is making a claim which on its face is governed by the contract. Whether the moving party is right or wrong is a question of contract interpretation for the arbitrator. In these circumstances the moving party should not be deprived of the arbitrator's judgment, when it was his judgment and all that it connotes that was bargained for.

United Steelworkers v. American Mfg. Co., 363 U.S. 564, 567-68; 80 S. Ct. 1343, 4 L. Ed. 2d 1403 (1960). Should this rule be applied in the public sector, or should the courts take a more active role in weighing the merits of a dispute before compelling arbitration? *See In re* Board of Educ., Union Free School Dist. No. 7 v. Deer Park Teachers' Ass'n, Inc., 66 Misc. 2d 794, 322 N.Y.S.2d 110 (Sup. Ct. 1971). Is there any merit to the argument that disputes involving public employees should be settled in a public forum rather than a "private" proceeding? What if the dispute involves back pay or other economic issues?

3. *See generally* Note, *Legality and Propriety of Agreements to Arbitrate Major and Minor Disputes in Public Employment*, 54 CORNELL L. REV. 129 (1968); Killingsworth, *Grievance Adjudication in Public Employment*, 13 ARB. J. 3 (1958); Howlett, *Arbitration in the Public Sector*, PROCEEDINGS OF THE SOUTHWESTERN LEGAL FOUNDATION 15TH ANNUAL INSTITUTE ON LABOR LAW 231 (1969).

3. Deciding Questions of Arbitrability

BOARD OF EDUCATION OF SCHOOL DISTRICT OF THE CITY OF ROCKFORD v. ROCKFORD EDUCATION ASSOCIATION

Appellate Court of Illinois, Second District
4 Ill. App. 2d 29, 280 N.E.2d 286 (1972)

ABRAHAMSON, Justice.

The Rockford Education Association, Inc. and Howard L. Getts, defendants below, prosecute this appeal from a declaratory judgment entered February 12, 1971 in favor of the Board of Education in and for the School District of the City of Rockford, No. 205, Winnebago County.

In May, 1969, the Board of Education, the governing body of the school district, created an administrative position described as Director of Personnel and Recruitment and distributed an

"Announcement of Vacancy" to members of the instructional staff. The announcement included a résumé of the duties of the position and invited applications from interested parties. Howard Getts, employed as a guidance counsellor by the district, applied for the job along with several other members of the staff. Getts was recommended by the superintendent of schools for the position but the Board, on October 13, 1969, rejected his application together with those of the other applicants and declined to fill the position. It remains unfilled to this day.

The Rockford Education Association, Inc. is a not-for-profit corporation organized to represent the school teachers and members of the instructional staff in the negotiation of collective bargaining agreements with the Board. The Association and Board had entered into a collective bargaining agreement, designated as the "Professional Agreement," effective for the period from July 1, 1969 to June 30, 1970. Getts was a member of the Association and, as a certified member of the instructional staff, was employed under the provisions of the Professional Agreement.

On October 27, 1969, Getts filed a grievance alleging, among other things, a violation of the Agreement by the Board in that it had improperly failed to promote him to the position of Director of Personnel and Recruitment. Getts' grievance was processed through various preliminary steps to the superintendent of schools who stated that he was unable to pass on it. Thereafter, on November 26, the Association and Getts filed a demand for arbitration with the American Arbitration Association. The Board answered that demand, in the nature of a special appearance, and maintained that the matter of selection or employment of employees was not intended to be included in the Professional Agreement and could not, in any event, be delegated by the Board and, therefore, it was not an arbitrable issue. The matter was considered by an arbitrator on that sole question and, after briefs had been submitted and arguments made, he concluded, on February 16, 1970, that the grievance was arbitrable and set it for a hearing on the merits on April 10.

On April 2, the Board brought its complaint to stay the arbitration pursuant to Section 102 (b) of the Uniform Arbitration Act (Ill. Rev. Stat. 1969, ch. 10, sec. 102 (b)) and for declaratory judgment pursuant to Section 57.1 of the Civil Practice Act (Ill. Rev. Stat. 1969, ch. 110, sec. 57.1) to declare that the Professional Agreement was void to the extent that it related to arbitration of selection or promotion of employees. The Association and Getts filed motions to dismiss and for summary judgment. The trial court considered the matter on the pleadings, briefs and oral argument and then denied the motions of the defendant, set aside the award of the arbitrator that the matter was arbitrable and declared that the Agreement was "to the extent it relates to arbitration of matters of selection or promotion of employees . . . void and without force of law. . . ."

The grievance filed by Getts contained the specific allegation that the Board violated Article XXXIII of the Professional Agreement. Article XI, Section A, defines a grievance as a "claim by the Association or a staff member that there has been a violation, misinterpretation or misapplication of any of the provisions of the Agreement." Article XI, Section E, provides that if the superintendent is unable to satisfactorily resolve the grievance, it would be submitted to binding arbitration under the rules of the American Arbitration Association.

Article XXXIII provides that all promotional positions would be filled according to certain procedures and "on the basis of qualification for the vacant post. . . ." A promotional position is described as a position among others, on the "administrative-supervisory level." The arbitrator concluded that on the basis of the language of the Agreement, the complaint of Getts was a "grievance" and, as such, subject to binding arbitration.

It has been held that a board of education does not require legislative authority to enter into a collective bargaining agreement and that such an agreement is not against public policy. Chicago Div. Ill. Ed. Ass'n. v. Board of Ed., 76 Ill. App. 2d 456, 472, 222 N.E.2d 243. However, a board may not, through a collective bargaining agreement or otherwise, delegate to another party those matters of discretion that are vested in the board by statute. The School Code provides that the board has the duty "To appoint all teachers and fix the amount of their salaries. . . ." Ill. Rev. Stat. 1969, Ch. 122, sec. 10-20 and 10-20.7. The cases have held that these are among the powers and duties of a board that cannot be delegated or limited by contract. . . .

The appellants contend, as did the arbitrator, that the Board actually exercised, rather than delegated, its responsibilities in regard to the employment of a Director. They argue that the Board created the position, defined the duties to be performed, and fixed the salary. Thereafter, an applicant for the position was to be appointed within the guidelines properly established by the Board and there was no further discretionary function to be exercised. We do not agree.

Article I of the Professional Agreement recognized the undisputable statutory limitations on the Board in providing "There is reserved exclusively to the Board all responsibilities, powers, right and authority expressly or inherently vested in it by laws and constitutions of Illinois and the United States, excepting where expressly and in specific terms limited by the provisions of this agreement." This Article in itself contains an anomaly since clearly the Board could not, in any event, agree to limit those powers granted exclusively to it by the School Act. However, there is nothing in the Agreement that could be construed as an express or specific limitation on the discretion of the Board to employ or not to employ anyone as Director of Personnel and Recruitment. Although, a promotional procedure is established in Article XXXIII, the appointment is to be based on "qualification." The ultimate determination of "qualification" was not, nor could it be, delegated by the Board to any outside agency including the American Arbitration Association.

We therefore conclude that the judgment of the trial court was correct and should be affirmed.

Affirmed.

NOTES

1. Courts seem to be much more willing to declare a dispute non-arbitrable in the public sector than in the private sector. In large part, this has probably resulted because public employers are seen to retain broader discretion and "management rights" to control the employment circumstance than are their private sector counterparts. Additionally, collective agreements in the public sector are likely to exclude, in specific terms, more subjects from arbitration, and statutes and public policy considerations often reserve other areas for decision by management alone. While no general rule delineates non-arbitrable subjects in the public sector, since the language of the contract or of the applicable state legislation may be a crucial factor, the following case summaries may give some hint of the trend of judicial opinion (especially in New York) in this area.

Arbitrable disputes: The determination of whether teachers complied with a contractual provision relating to the time for filing a grievance was for the arbitrator, not the court. Central School Dist. No. 1 v. Harrison Ass'n of Teachers, 79 L.R.R.M. 3085 (N.Y. Sup. Ct. 1972).

The "procedure" used by a school board in terminating the employment of a non-tenure teacher is arbitrable even if the *grounds* for termination cannot be challenged by arbitration. *In re* Associated Teachers of Huntington v. Board of Educ., Union Free School Dist. No. 3, 60 Misc. 2d 443, 303 N.Y.S.2d 469 (Sup. Ct. 1969).

It is for the arbitrator to determine the arbitrability of the question of whether the school district kept its promise to use best efforts to maintain the pupil-teacher ratio. Central School Dist. No. 1 v. Litz, 60 Misc. 2d 1009, 304 N.Y.S.2d 372 (1969), *aff'd*, 34 App. Div. 2d 1092, 314 N.Y.S.2d 176 (Sup. Ct. App. Div. 1970).

See also Pittsburgh City Fire Fighters Local 1 v. Barr, 408 Pa. 325, 184 A.2d 588 (1962) (formula for fixing future wage increases *was* an arbitrable grievance); Board of Educ., Middle Country Central School Dist. No. 1 v. Middle Country Teachers' Ass'n, 78 L.R.R.M. 2092 (N.Y. Sup. Ct. 1971) (board of education was not entitled to stay of arbitration of union grievance concerning staffing of classrooms, there being no clear and unquestionable exclusion of the matter from arbitration).

Non-arbitrable disputes: Because of a financial crisis, the New York legislature passed a special law in 1971 prohibiting the granting of sabbatical leaves to public employees. In Central School Dist. No. 2 v. Ramapo Central School Dist. No. 2 Teachers Ass'n, 67 Misc. 2d 317, 324 N.Y.S.2d 260 (Sup. Ct. 1971), the questions before the Rockland County Supreme Court were whether certain teachers had enforceable contractual rights to sabbatical leave before the new law took effect and whether the court or the arbitrator should decide this issue. The court granted the petition to stay arbitration, concluding:

> The Court fully subscribes to the line of cases which encourage the arbitration of disputes arising under collective bargaining agreements. However, where a major public policy is involved, as expressed in section 82, the Court is of the opinion that the public interest requires that issues of law and of fact as to the application of such legislation should be resolved by a Court rather than an arbitrator. 324 N.Y.S.2d at 263.

A dispute over the fixing of salary and insurance levels under a reopening provision in a contract was not an arbitrable grievance, since the contract required arbitration only with respect to disputes concerning the meaning, application, or interpretation of the agreement. This dispute involved *new* provisions to be included in the contract and not the *existing* terms of the agreement. North Bellmore Teachers' Ass'n v. Board of Educ., Union Free School Dist. No. 4, 68 Misc. 2d 238, 326 N.Y.S.2d 571 (Sup. Ct. 1971).

Withdrawal of recognition of a union is not an arbitrable subject. De Sensi v. Osborne, 62 L.R.R.M. 2186 (Pa. C.P., Wash. County 1966).

A dispute involving the dismissal of a school nurse during the term of her probationary status was held not arbitrable, since it was a "personal" but not a contract grievance. Lehman v. Dobbs Ferry Bd. of Educ., Union Free School Dist. No. 3, 66 Misc. 2d 996, 323 N.Y.S.2d 283 (1971), aff'd, 38 App. Div. 2d 849 (1972).

Tenure questions are not subject to arbitration. Board of Educ., Central School Dist. No. 1 v. Lakeland Fed'n of Teachers, Local 1760, 79 L.R.R.M. 2618 (N.Y. Sup. Ct. 1971); Legislative Conference of City University of New York v. Board of Higher Educ. of the City of New York, 38 App. Div. 2d 478, 330 N.Y.S.2d 688 (1972), appeal denied, 30 N.Y.2d 481 (1972).

The method used to select a new assistant fire chief could not be the basis for an arbitrable grievance. Ringler v. Yarnell, 4 Pa. Cmwlth 540, 287 A.2d 893 (Pa. Cmwlth Ct. 1972).

An unconstitutional contract provision is not arbitrable. Central School Dist. No. 4 of Brookhaven v. Bellport Teachers Ass'n, 74 L.R.R.M. 2221 (N.Y. Sup. Ct. 1970).

A dispute arising over a set of regulations promulgated by a Hartford, Conn. school board which prescribed emergency duties for teachers was held to be non-arbitrable by a Connecticut Superior Court, even though the regulations allegedly deprived the teachers of the one free period per day given to them by the collective bargaining agreement. The court held that the school board was not free to bargain away its power to act in an emergency. Board of Educ. of City of Hartford v. Hartford Fed'n of Teachers, 75 L.R.R.M. 2397 (Conn. Super. Ct. 1970).

2. In the federal service, the question of arbitrability is covered by Section 13 (d) in the amended Executive Order 11491, which provides that:

[Q]uestions that cannot be resolved by the parties as to whether or not a grievance is on a matter subject to the grievance procedure in an existing agreement, or is subject to arbitration under that agreement, may be referred to the Assistant Secretary [of Labor] for decision.

Thus, if the parties are unable to agree either on the arbitrability of the dispute or on whether to submit the dispute to the arbitrator for his determination with respect to arbitrability, the parties may submit the dispute to the Assistant Secretary of Labor for a determination.

3. In the private sector, issues concerning "procedural arbitrability" are generally held to be matters to be decided by the arbitrator, not the court. In John Wiley & Sons, Inc. v. Livings-

ton, 376 U.S. 543, 544, 84 S. Ct. 909, 11 L. Ed. 2d 898 (1964),
it was held that:

> Once it is determined . . . that the parties are obligated to
> submit the subject matter of a dispute to arbitration, "pro-
> cedural" questions which grow out of the dispute and bear
> on its final disposition should be left to the arbitrator. Even
> under a contrary rule, a court could deny arbitration only
> if it could confidently be said not only that a claim was
> strictly "procedural," and therefore within the purview of
> the court, but also that it should operate to bar arbitration
> altogether, and not merely limit or qualify an arbitral award.
> In view of the policies favoring arbitration and the parties'
> adoption of arbitration as a preferred means of settling dis-
> putes, such cases are likely to be rare indeed. In all other
> cases, those in which arbitration goes forward, the arbitrator
> would ordinarily remain free to reconsider the ground
> covered by the Court insofar as it bore on the merits of the
> dispute, using the flexible approaches familiar to arbitration.
> Reservation of "procedural" issues for the courts would thus
> not only create the difficult task of separating related issues,
> but would also produce frequent duplication of effort.

In essence, the basis of the decision in *Wiley* on this issue was
that the "procedural disagreements," to use the Court's term,
were aspects of the merits of the dispute and that such matters
should usually be decided by arbitrators, not courts. The rule of
Wiley has seemingly found favor in the public sector, too. *See,
e.g.*, City of Auburn v. Nash, 34 App. Div. 2d 345, 312 N.Y.S.
2d 700 (1970) (dispute with respect to city employee's compliance with provision of collective bargaining agreement relating
to time for requesting arbitration of grievance was held to be
determinable by the arbitrator and not by the court).

4. Judicial Review of Arbitration Awards

TOWN OF BABYLON v. LOCAL 237 OF INTERNATIONAL BROTHERHOOD OF TEAMSTERS

New York Supreme Court, Special Term, Part I
Suffolk County
79 L.R.R.M. 2892 (1971)

THOM, Justice:—Application by Petitioners, Town of Babylon and Robert A. Hanington, Superintendent of Highways of
the Town of Babylon, (hereinafter referred to as the "Town")
to vacate the arbitration award of the Respondent-Arbitrator, Lou
V. Tempera, Commissioner of Labor of Suffolk County (hereinafter referred to as the "Arbitrator"). Respondent, Local 237

of the International Brotherhood of Teamsters (hereinafter referred to as "Local 237") cross-moves to dismiss the petition on the grounds that it fails to state a cause of action.

Certain employees of the Petitioners filed grievances under the grievance procedures formulated by the Town and Local 237. A hearing was scheduled before the Arbitrator on April 14, 1971, at which time the Town moved to dismiss the proceeding on the grounds that the grievances were not filed within the time provided by the written agreement between the parties. Testimony was taken and exhibits received in evidence upon this issue by the Arbitrator and on May 12, 1971 the arbitrator made an award to the effect that the dispute between the parties was timely filed and was arbitrable, and the motion to dismiss was denied. The Town now seeks to vacate that award on the grounds that in view of the written agreements between the parties as to the grievance procedure, the award of the arbitrator constituted a "perverse misconstruction" of the agreement, having no rational basis in fact or law, and, therefore, should be vacated.

In the Matter of Wilkins, 169 N.Y. 494, 496, 497, 62 N.E. 575, 576, the Court of Appeals stated: "Where the merits of a controversy are referred to an arbitrator selected by the parties, his determination, either as to the law or the facts is conclusive; and a court will not open an award unless perverse misconstruction or positive misconduct upon the part of the arbitrator is plainly established. . . . The award of an arbitrator cannot be set aside for mere errors of judgment either as to the law or the facts. If he keeps within his jurisdiction, and is not guilty of fraud, corruption, or other misconduct affecting his award, it is unassailable, operates as a final and conclusive judgment. . . ." CPLR, Section 7511 (b) sets forth the grounds upon which an award of an arbitrator may be vacated or modified by a court. The doctrine of "perverse misconstruction," since matter of Wilkens, has been discussed but has been generally found to be inapplicable by the courts. (S. & W. Fine Foods, Inc. v. Office Employees International Union, 8 A.D.2d 130, 32 LA 660, affd. 7 N.Y.2d 1018, 35 LA 649; Matter of Camps Corp. (Pacific Mills), 275 A.D. 634: District Marine Engineers Beneficial Association v. Isbrandtsen Co., 36 Misc.2d 408). In the case of S. & W. Fine Foods, Inc. (supra) the Court interpreted the language in the Matter of Wilkins as follows: "The words 'perverse misconstruction' bracketed in the disjunctive with the words 'positive misconduct,' must be taken to refer to misbehavior of the arbitrator in the way of evident partiality, corruption, exceeding powers and the like. . . . If so, the perverse misconstruction must be

more than an egregious error of law before it satisfies the statute;
it must be one which is so divorced from rationality that it can
be accounted for only by one of the kinds of misconduct recited in the statute. In that event, the vacatur is granted not for
error of law or misconstruction of documents but for misconduct
under one or more of the permitted categories, which misconduct has been established. Nothing like that was established in
this case. It is notable that no case since Matter of Wilkins has
found it necessary or desirable to use 'perverse misconstruction'
as a ground for vacatur of arbitration awards (citations)."

After reading the minutes of the hearing before the Arbitrator, and the papers and proofs submitted upon this application, the Court is of the opinion that the Petitioners have failed
to establish any of the grounds as set forth above for vacating the
award of the arbitrator, and, accordingly, the petition is dismissed.

Since the Court has ruled on the merits of petitioners' application, Respondents' cross-motion is denied as moot.

NOTES

1. In the private sector, the Supreme Court has made it clear
that "the courts . . . have no business weighing the merits of the
grievance, considering whether there is equity in a particular
claim, or determining whether there is particular language in
the written instrument which will support the claim." United
Steelworkers of America v. American Mfg. Co., 363 U.S. 564,
80 S. Ct. 1343, 4 L. Ed. 2d 1403 (1960). "[T]he judicial inquiry
. . . must be strictly confined to the question of whether the [par-
ties] did agree to arbitrate the grievance or did agree to give
the arbitrator power to make the award he made." United
Steelworkers of America v. Warrior & Gulf Navigation Co., 363
U.S. 574, 80 S. Ct. 1347, 4 L. Ed. 2d 1409 (1960). An arbitrator's
"award is legitimate only so long as it draws its essence from
the collective bargaining agreement"; however, "a mere ambiguity in the opinion accompanying an award, which permits
the inference that the arbitrator may have exceeded his authority, is not a reason for refusing to enforce the award." United
Steelworkers of America v. Enterprise Wheel & Car Co., 363 U.S.
593, 80 S. Ct. 1358, 4 L. Ed. 2d 1424 (1960).

2. There are few cases dealing with judicial review of grievance arbitration awards in the public sector. To date, in those
few cases where the issue has arisen, the courts have shown an
inclination to apply the same standards as are utilized in reviewing private sector awards. In Board of Higher Educ. of the City

of New York v. United Fed'n of College Teachers, Local 1460, 4 PERB 8230 (N.Y. Sup. Ct. 1971), the court denied a motion to vacate an arbitrator's award, concluding:

It does not appear that the arbitrator was either arbitrary or capricious. The arbitrator determined the issues before him and did not give any provisions of the agreement a completely irrational construction nor can it fairly be said that he made a new contract for the parties by his award.

There is, however, some reason to believe that the courts will be somewhat more active in reviewing the merits of arbitration awards in the public sector granting economic benefits. In the private sector there is usually no question of the power of the arbitrator to order back pay or other "make whole" remedies in appropriate cases; nor is there any question of the authority of the employer to comply with the award. In the public sector, however, public policy considerations may raise special problems with respect to the enforcement of the "make whole" remedies. Antonopoulou v. Beame, 67 Misc. 2d 851, 325 N.Y.S.2d 12 (1971), aff'd, 332 N.Y.S.2d 464, 80 L.R.R.M. 2652 (Sup. Ct., App. Div. 1972), reversed, 32 N.Y.2d 126, 296 N.E.2d 247 (1973) serves as an example of this, even though the case involved the settlement of a grievance at a step short of arbitration. In Antonopoulou, a lecturer at Queen's College was refused in her request that she be allowed to return to work prior to the end of her scheduled maternity leave. At the second step of the grievance procedure, the Chancellor of the University directed that Mrs. Antonopoulou be reinstated with back pay. The City Comptroller rejected the back pay award, contending that since it covered a period during which no services were performed, it constituted a gift of public funds, thus violating the state constitution. In a proceeding to annul the Comptroller's decision, the New York Supreme Court stated that although grievance settlements are "clearly entitled to the same dignity and effect as arbitration awards" the corollary proposition was also true that "[i]f the arbitrator exceeds his power or if the award or grievance settlement contravenes public policy, it cannot be enforced." The lower court found the awarding of back pay for a period during which no services were performed to be in contravention of public policy and thus refused to enforce the grievance settlement. The Appellate Division, in affirming the decision, agreed with the position of the Comptroller. However, the New York Court of Appeals reversed and ruled that:

"In the instant case, the collective bargaining agreement, contemplating as it does a continuing process of grievance resolution through the prescribed grievance procedures, created an enforceable contractual right on the subsequent settlement. Absent a showing . . . that the grievance did not relate to the terms or conditions of employment, the settlement is as binding as any other arbitration award. Consequently, there was a legal obligation on the part of the municipality to comply with the settlement decision, and payment thereunder cannot be considered a 'gift'."

3. Some of the opinions cited elsewhere in this chapter indicate that the courts will likely be more active in reviewing the "merits" of arbitration awards in the public sector in cases involving (1) constitutional questions; (2) conflicting statutory regulations; (3) important questions of "public policy"; (4) tenure questions in public education; and (5) public fiscal and budgetary matters. *See, e.g.,* Associated Teachers of Huntington, Inc. v. Board of Educ. of Union Free School Dist. No. 3, Town of Huntington, GERR No. 487, B-4 (N.Y. Sup. Ct., App. Div. 1973).

4. By definition, voluntary arbitration requires the consent of both parties. In the public sector, much more than in the private, there are the constant problems of determining who may consent to arbitration on behalf of the employer and how this consent is to be manifested. The public sector official with apparent authority to bind the employer to arbitrate an issue may not have actual authority; unless those with actual authority have consented to arbitration, which often must be in a quite formal manner, the resulting award may be unenforceable. *See* Sheahan v. School Comm. of Worcester, 270 N.E.2d 912 (Mass. 1971).

5. Cases involving "interest arbitration" may provide clues to the standards the courts will use in reviewing grievance arbitration awards in the public sector. In some states, judicial standards for review of interest arbitration awards are legislatively mandated (*e.g.,* N.J. STAT. ANN. § 34:13B-23 (1965); FLA. STAT. ANN. § 453.10 (Supp. 1972); BURNS' IND. STAT. ANN. § 40-2412 (1965); 43 PA. STAT. ANN. § 213.13 (1964). The Supreme Court of Pennsylvania, in City of Washington and Police Dep't of City of Washington, 436 Pa. 168, 259 A.2d 437 (1969), ruled that even though no judicial appeal was permissible under a state law providing for interest arbitration, an appeal would nevertheless lie to challenge an arbitration award on any of the following grounds: (1) a question of arbitral jurisdiction; (2) an issue over the regularity of the arbitration proceedings; (3) a

question as to whether the arbitrator exceeded his power; and (4) constitutional questions.

The case of Mount St. Mary's Hospital v. Catherwood, 26 N.Y. 2d 493, 260 N.E.2d 508, 311 N.Y.S.2d 863 (1970), raised the interesting question of whether a different standard should be used in evaluating interest arbitration awards than that applied with respect to grievance awards. Judge Breitel of the New York Court of Appeals, for the majority, suggested that while the substantial evidence rule was sufficient for evaluating grievance awards, compulsory interest arbitration awards must not be arbitrary or capricious and "must be justified by the public interest." Chief Judge Fuld disagreed, stating in his concurring opinion that the legislative standard for the review of arbitration awards (N.Y. CIV. PRAC. LAW AND RULES § 7511 (McKinney Supp. 1971)) was the same for both interest and grievance arbitration, compulsory or consensual. "The Legislature did not intend . . . to permit the harassing and time-consuming delays which would inevitably result from the introduction of judicial proceedings to review arbitration awards." 311 N.Y.S.2d at 884.

6.   For a good discussion of the problem of review of arbitration awards in the federal service, see Kagel, *Grievance Arbitration in the Federal Service: How Final and Binding?*, 51 ORE. L. REV. 134 (1971).

E.   Individual Rights Under the Collective Bargaining Agreement

1.   Introduction

H. WELLINGTON & R. WINTER, THE UNIONS AND THE CITIES 162-64 (1971)†

The interest of the individual employee is generally well served in the grievance procedure by his representative, the union. Typically, it is the union that brings the grievance and pursues it through the several steps spelled out in the contract, and, if necessary, on to arbitration. But, as we have learned from experience in the private sector, it would be a terrible mistake to assume that congruity of interests between union and individual always exists. Divergence is possible because of a reasonable disagreement as to what the contract provides, because the interests of the individual and those of a majority of employees do not coincide, because the individual is a political rival of the union president, because he is black and a majority of the union is white, because he is disliked, against union policy, unwilling to do what he is told to do, and so forth. And divergence of interests may occur at any stage of the grievance procedure. The union may decline to process a grievance at all, take it through some steps and drop it, or refuse to go to arbitration.

While potential conflict between individual and union exists at the precontract negotiation stage as well, it is most troublesome during contract administration. This may be because at that stage the employee is viewed as having rights that grow out of an existing agreement, rather than amorphous and hard-to-define interests in a yet to be achieved contractual settlement.

Be that as it may, the private sector has developed a bewilderingly complicated and relatively unsatisfactory body of law to deal with the problem. The law is complicated largely because of the complexities in the underlying problem. On the one hand, if collective bargaining is to be an orderly, efficient process that brings stability to labor relations, it is desirable to place the employer in a position where he is able to work out binding settlements with the union, and the union alone. On the other hand, the individual needs protection from the union that fails adequately to represent his interests.

One approach to the problem is to give the individual employee a cause of action against the union if it fails to represent him fairly; but to give him no redress against the employer. Indeed, the duty of fair representation exists in the private sector under federal law. It has, however, been much hedged about. The other approach is to give the employee a direct and individual right in the collective agreement, recognize the fact that this right may undercut efficiency and stability, but recognize also that the effect of this can be grossly overestimated and that institutions have ways of adapting themselves. Federal law recognizes individual rights in the contract. It also hedges them about.

Whatever one's position as to what the law should be in the private sector, it seems clear that in municipal collective bargaining the individual should have access, as an individual, to the grievance procedure, arbitration, and the courts. Without collective bargaining, there is no comparable right in private employment. In public employment such a right generally does obtain and is administered by civil service commissions. While it has been argued that these commissions have no legitimate role in the resolution of grievances where collective bargaining is established, the protection afforded the individual under civil service should not be lost with their demise. Such protection may be retained by giving the employee generous individual rights in the collective agreement.

Of course, the union's interests must be protected. It should be able to argue for its interpretation of the contract at each level of the grievance procedure, in arbitration, and before the court. Nor, where its antagonistic position is reasonable, should it have to bear the costs of the individual's case. But these are minor and easily resolved difficulties when compared to some of the . . . problems that must be faced when techniques of contract administration are transplanted from the private to the public sector.

2. Exhaustion of Remedies as a Prerequisite to Suit by an Individual Employee

STEELE v. HALEY
U.S. District Court, District of Massachusetts
335 F. Supp. 659 (1971)

WYZANSKI, Chief Judge:—Invoking 42 U.S.C. §§ 1983 and 1985, plaintiff, a public school teacher, brings this action against present and former members of a public school committee on a complaint that they denied him, and conspired to deny him, his constitutional right to due process of law under the Fourteenth Amendment by terminating his appointments to perform, at extra compensation, extra duties as acting head of the Physical Education Department, Director of Athletics, and Football Coach at Westford Academy, a public school, without giving him what he regarded as a sufficiently detailed notice of the grounds and without affording him a public and adversary hearing.

The parties have stipulated the facts, and each side has moved for summary judgment. . . .

[After the school committee had voted to relieve plaintiff of his athletic duties, the matter was appealed to arbitration under the collective bargaining agreement between the Westford Teachers Association and the Westford School Committee.] . . . Contending that plaintiff was not entitled to the protection of the contract in respect to his athletic appointments, the Committee, by an equity action in the Middlesex Superior Court of the Commonwealth of Massachusetts, sought "to restrain arbitration." But on May 27, 1970 that court ordered the parties to submit the grievance to arbitration. After hearings, the arbitrator, having canvassed all the issues in a comprehensive opinion, on October 5, 1970 made the following award:

"In refusing to supply Mr. Steele or the Association with the information needed for a defense against the Committee's charges, and by its further refusal to hear his defense and give it consideration in reviewing its termination action, the Westford School Committee violated the Grievance Procedure, Article 5 of its Agreement, when it terminated the appointment of Chesley A. Steele as Athletic Director, Acting Head of the Physical Education Department and Varsity Football Coach, on or about January 15, 1970.

"The School Committee is directed to reinstate Mr. Steele to all three positions forthwith, and reimburse him for any salary loss occasioned by its improper action."

It stipulated that "Subsequent to the rendering of the Arbitrator's award, the then members of the Westford School Committee filed a petition in the Middlesex Superior Court under G.L. (Ter. Ed.) Chapter 150C, Sections 11 and 12, praying that the award be vacated or modified. This petition is still under consideration by the Superior Court. . . ."

June 25, 1970, that is, between the time the state court directed that the parties should proceed with the arbitration sought by plaintiff and the date when the arbitrator made his award, plaintiff filed in this court the present complaint alleging causes of action under 42 U.S.C. §§ 1983 and 1985. He claims that the defendants deprived him of his constitutional rights because they terminated his athletic appointments without giving him "the opportunity to present evidence, confront or cross-examine his accusers, hear the evidence presented against him," or "be informed of the specific charges against him," and because the Committee's action was "taken without prior promulgation of a regulation or order defining what kinds of conduct would be deemed grounds for terminating the Plaintiff's employment in the capacities as acting head of the Department of Physical Education, Athletic Director and Football Coach." The complaint also alleges that the Committee members entered into a conspiracy to deprive plaintiff of his athletic positions without the benefit of constitutional rights.

The threshold question in the case at bar is what is the effect upon plaintiff's causes of action under 42 U.S.C. §§ 1983 and 1985 of the arbitration award proceedings pending in the state court.

The least effect of the state court proceedings is to make it incumbent upon this court to abstain from a decision of the merits of any constitutional issue with respect to the termination of plaintiff's athletic appointments. Since the claims pending in the state court, if sustained, will obviate the necessity of determining whether plaintiff is entitled to be restored to his appointments and to receive damages, this court might find that it was relieved of the necessity of determining the Fourteenth Amendment or other constitutional questions. Askew v. Hargrave, 401 U.S. 476 (1971).

But there is a more fundamental obstacle to this court entertaining the present complaint. Plaintiff has not exhausted the arbitral remedies which are available to him, and which, unlike the situation in U.S. Bulk Carriers v. Arguelies, 400 U.S. 351 (1971), he has elected to pursue. Where by contract the parties have established a machinery for handling and arbitrating grievances, they have in effect set up their private system of administrative remedies. If a plaintiff succeeds in the private administrative process, it will be unnecessary to have a federal judicial hearing. If he fails, he is not estopped from presenting to the judiciary a constitutional claim. It is difficult to see any sound reason for not requiring a § 1983 plaintiff to exhaust his contractual administrative remedies as he is required to exhaust his statutory administrative remedies. . . .

In both situations there is always a possibility that "official abuse can be corrected without resort to lengthy and costly trial" [Note Exhaustion of State Remedies under the Civil Rights Act, 68 Colum. L. Rev. 1201, 1206 (1968) quoted in Eisen v. Eastman, 421 F.2d 560 (1969), 567-568 note 11].

Complaint dismissed.

STEELE v. HALEY
U.S. Court of Appeals, First Circuit
451 F.2d 1105 (1971)

COFFIN, Circuit Judge: Plaintiff Chesley A. Steele brought this action under 42 U.S.C. § 1983 and § 1985, with jurisdiction based on 28 U.S.C. § 1343, to challenge as violative of procedural due process the action of the Westford, Massachusetts School Committee in dismissing him from the non-tenured positions of football coach, athletic director, and head of the department of physical education at Westford Academy, a public high school. He now appeals the district court's dismissal for failure to exhaust arbitral remedies. . . .

We do not reach the merits of either Steele's constitutional claim or the defendants' assertion that, having initiated arbitration, Steele must await the completion of state court challenges to the arbitrator's award before bringing suit under § 1983. For the reasons discussed below, we conclude that this is a proper case for abstention.

Steele's federal claim is in a curious posture. Having prevailed thus far under the collective bargaining agreement, he would nevertheless have the federal courts grant substantially the same relief on constitutional grounds to protect him against the possibility that the arbitrator's award may be vacated by the state court. His fear derives from the opinion of the Massachusetts

Supreme Judicial Court in DeCanio v. School Committee of Boston, 1970 Mass. Adv. Sh. 1223, 260 N.E.2d 676, appeal dismissed, 401 U.S. 929 (1971). But that case holds merely that a hearing before discharge of a probationary teacher is not mandated by Massachusetts statute, the Massachusetts Constitution, or the United States Constitution. In contrast, the arbitrator's award in the present case was based upon his construction of the collective bargaining agreement. . . . While it is surely an open question, we think that there is a substantial possibility that the arbitrator's award will be upheld.

While we thus abstain from deciding Steele's federal claim under the Fourteenth Amendment, we direct the district court to retain jurisdiction. As the Supreme Court indicated in Zwickler v. Koota, 389 U.S. 241, 244 n. 4 (1967), "It is better practice, in a case raising a federal constitutional or statutory claim, to retain jurisdiction, rather than to dismiss. . . ."

Remanded with directions to retain jurisdiction.

NOTES

1. *Steele v. Haley* deals with the problem of failure to exhaust arbitral remedies as a prerequisite to a federal action under 42 U.S.C. §§ 1983 and 1985; however, the principle of exhaustion of contract remedies has generally been applied in situations where individual employees seek judicial enforcement of a collective agreement without ever seeking redress of their claims pursuant to the contractually established grievance procedure. Thus, in the private sector, the Supreme Court has ruled that an individual employee cannot sue an employer directly for an alleged breach of contract without first processing his claim through the contractual grievance procedure. Republic Steel Corp. v. Maddox, 379 U.S. 650, 85 S. Ct. 614, 13 L. Ed. 2d 580 (1965).

On the duty of exhaustion in the public sector, see Coffee v. Board of Educ. of the City of New York, 65 Misc. 2d 931, 319 N.Y.S.2d 249 (Sup. Ct. 1971); Clampitt v. Board of Educ., Warren Consolidated Schools, 68 L.R.R.M. 2996 (Mich. Cir. Ct. 1968).

The Supreme Court has also held that, in the private sector, an individual suit for breach of contract will be heard if the union has breached its duty of fair representation by a wrongful refusal to process an individual claim under a contract grievance or arbitration procedure. Vaca v. Sipes, 386 U.S. 171, 87 S. Ct. 903, 17 L. Ed. 2d 842 (1967).

Defenses against a failure to exhaust also include repudiation of the collective bargaining agreement by the employer or evidence showing that the pursuit of grievance remedies would almost inevitably prove futile. *Cf.,* Glover v. St. Louis-San Francisco Ry., 393 U.S. 324, 89 S. Ct. 548, 21 L. Ed. 2d 519 (1969) ; Ricciotti v. Warwick School Committee, 319 F. Supp. 1006 (D.R.I. 1970) ; *In re* Tischler v. Board of Educ., Monroe-Woodbury Central School Dist. No. 1, 37 App. Div. 2d 261, 323 N.Y.S.2d 508 (1971). The concept of futility may also involve questions with respect to the *adequacy* of the remedy itself. *See, e.g.,* Ricciotti v. Warwick School Committee, *supra.*

2.   In reaching its decision in *Steele v. Haley,* the District Court cites Eisen v. Eastman, 421 F.2d 560 (2d Cir. 1969), *cert. denied,* 400 U.S. 841 (1970). That case held that state administrative remedies must be exhausted before a suit can be brought in federal court under the Civil Rights Act of 1871, at least where the case is heard by a single district court judge. This appears to be a minority view. Where the case is heard by a three-judge panel it is clear that exhaustion is not required:

> Decisions of this Court . . . establish that a plaintiff in an action brought under the Civil Rights Act, 42 U.S.C. § 1983, 28 U.S.C. § 1343, is not required to exhaust administrative remedies where the constitutional challenge is sufficiently substantial, as here to require the convening of a three-judge court. King v. Smith, 392 U.S. 309 at 312, n.4.

While Eisen v. Eastman, *supra,* has been supported by at least one district court, Holland v. Beto, 309 F. Supp. 784 (S.D. Tex. 1970) ; Schwartz v. Galveston Independent School Dist., 309 F. Supp. 1034 (S.D. Tex. 1970) ; Burnett v. Short, 311 F. Supp. 586 (S.D. Tex. 1970), other courts have held that exhaustion is not required even in single-judge § 1983 cases. *See, e.g.,* Whitner v. Davis, 410 F.2d 24 (9th Cir. 1969) ; Reichenberg v. Nelson, 310 F. Supp. 248 (D. Neb. 1970) ; James v. Ogilvie, 310 F. Supp. 661 (N.D. Ill. 1970). Unequivocal language of Supreme Court opinions both before and after *Eisen* appears to support the view of this latter group of courts. *See* McNeese v. Board of Educ., Community Unit School Dist. No. 187, 373 U.S. 668, 83 S. Ct. 1433, 10 L. Ed. 2d 622 (1963) ; Monroe v. Pape, 365 U.S. 167, 81 S. Ct. 473, 5 L. Ed. 2d 492 (1961) ; Damico v. California, 389 U.S. 416, 88 S. Ct. 526, 19 L. Ed. 2d 647 (1967) ; King v. Smith, 392 U.S. 309, 88 S. Ct. 2128, 20 L. Ed. 2d 1118 (1968) ; Wilwording v. Swenson, 404 U.S. 249, 92 S. Ct. 407, 30 L. Ed. 2d 418 (1971).

The Court stated in McNeese v. Board of Educ., Community Unit School Dist. 187, 373 U.S. 668, 83 S. Ct. 1433, 10 L. Ed. 2d 622 (1963), that one of the purposes of the Civil Rights Act of 1871 was "to provide a remedy in the federal courts supplementary to any remedy any state might have" and, therefore, "relief under the Civil Rights Act may not be defeated because relief was not just sought under state law which provided [an administrative] remedy."

If a plaintiff is not required to exhaust state *administrative* remedies in § 1983 cases, should he be required to exhaust *contract* remedies? Would it have made a difference in *Steele v. Haley* if the remedial process under the contract had been at an earlier stage when the court suit was filed? Suppose Steele had filed a § 1983 suit immediately, before the controversy had gone to arbitration. Should the court have entered an order compelling arbitration? Suppose the arbitration award had been unfavorable to Steele. Should he then have had the opportunity to "retry" the case before a federal judge? In James v. Board of Educ. of Central Dist. No. 1 of Addison, 461 F.2d 566 (2d Cir. 1972), the Second Circuit made it clear that a Civil Rights plaintiff would not be barred from pursuing a suit under § 1983 by an adverse determination in a state administrative proceeding.

3. The Fifth Circuit, in Beale v. Blount, 461 F.2d 1133 (1972), ruled that federal government employees are required to exhaust administrative remedies before bringing suit under § 1981 of the Civil Rights Act. The decision in *Beale* is set forth in Chapter Nine.

3. The Union's Duty of Fair Representation

KAUFMAN v. GOLDBERG

New York Supreme Court, Special Term, Kings County
64 Misc. 2d 524, 315 N.Y.S.2d 35 (1970)

LIEBOWITZ, Justice.

[Petitioner Kaufman, an employee of the New York City Department of Social Services, complained that he had been punitively transferred and demoted from Resource Consultant to Caseworker, with a loss of seniority. In accordance with procedures established in a collective bargaining agreement between the City and the Social Service Employees Union, Local 371, the petitioner filed a grievance alleging violation of the agreement on the part of the Department of Social Services. The grievance was denied at Steps I, II, and III of the grievance procedure. Kaufman claimed he then requested that the union take the grievance to Step IV by demanding arbitration, but that the request was refused because of Kaufman's non-membership in the union. The petitioner then brought this action against the Commissioner of the Department of Social Services, the Director of the Office of Labor Relations, and the City Civil Service

Commission, seeking an order to vacate the determinations which denied the grievance at each step of the procedure and to direct the Civil Service Commission to reinstate his seniority and restore his title of Resource Consultant. After determining that the petitioner had failed to establish any contractual violation on the part of the Department of Social Services, the court went on to discuss whether Kaufman had in fact demanded arbitration and whether the union had wrongfully refused to proceed to arbitration on his behalf.]

If petitioner had established that his "transfer" was in violation of the contract, there would remain the issue as to whether petitioner could resort to direct action in face of the Step IV provision for arbitration which, pursuant to the contract, could be prosecuted only by the Union, and whether there was truth in his statement that his request for arbitration was rejected by the Union because of his non-membership.

The law is well established that by union membership an employee indicates he "has entrusted his rights to his union representative" and ordinarily has no individual right to demand or control the arbitration procedures (Parker v. Borock, 5 N.Y.2d 156, 182 N.Y.S.2d 577, 156 N.E.2d 297; Matter of Soto [Goldman], 7 N.Y.2d 397, 198 N.Y.S.2d 282, 165 N.E.2d 855; Chupka v. Lorenz-Schneider, 12 N.Y.2d 1, 233 N.E.2d 929, 186 N.E.2d 191). There is however, a line of cases in other jurisdictions which imposes on a union the duty of fair representation to its members and that the violation of that duty permits the employee to proceed directly against the employer. The authorities are exhaustively researched and discussed in Jenkins v. Schluderberg-T, etc., Co., 217 Md. 556, 144 A.2d 88 (see 45 Corn. L.Q. 25). In *Jenkins*, the court held that where the union acted in an arbitrary and discriminatory manner in failing to proceed on behalf of the employee against the employer, the employee may proceed directly. The court quoted (at pp. 564-565, 144 A.2d at p. 93) from the article by Professor Cox in 69 Harvard Law Review 601, 652:

> " 'While the rule which bars an individual employee from bringing an action on the contract when the union is unwilling to take the case to arbitration is sound if the union has made an adjustment or is satisfied that the grievance lacks merit, nevertheless it would work injustice in situations where the union is unwilling to press the claim because of indifference or reluctance to suffer the expense. Both factors come into play under open-shop contracts when a grievance having no precedent value is filed by a non-member, whose failure to pay dues means that he contrib-

utes nothing to the cost of acting as his representative. One solution would be to open arbitration proceedings to individual grievants. Another alternative is to allow the employees to bring suit against the employer and union as codefendants upon analogy to the bill in equity which the beneficiary of a trust may maintain against the trustee who fails to press a claim against a third person. The suit would fail on the merits if it appeared that the collective bargaining representative had dropped the grievance for *lack of merit or had negotiated a reasonable adjustment.'* "

The court also quoted (p. 565, 144 P.2d p. 93) from Professor Cox's article, "Individual Enforcement of Collective Bargaining Agreements," (8 Lab. L.J. 850, 858), which is most pertinent to a situation where the employee is a non-member of the union, as follows:

" 'In my opinion the presumption should be against individual enforcement of a collective bargaining agreement *unless the union has unfairly refused* to act. . . . The bargaining representative would be guilty of a breach of duty if it refused to press a justifiable grievance either because of laziness, prejudice or *unwillingness to expend* money *on behalf of employees who were not members of the union.* Individual enforcement would then become appropriate. . . .' (Emphasis added.) "

The broad authority of the union as exclusive bargaining agent, even where it springs from statute, in the negotiation and administration of a collective bargaining agreement, is accompanied by the responsibility of fair representation (Humphrey v. Moore, 375 U.S. 335, 342, 84 S. Ct. 363, 11 L. Ed. 2d 370; Vaca v. Sipes, 386 U.S. 171, 177, 87 S. Ct. 903, 17 L. Ed. 2d 842). In *Vaca,* the court, in firm dictum, stated (pp. 184-186, 87 S. Ct. p. 914):

"However, if the wrongfully discharged employee himself resorts to the courts before the grievance procedures have been fully exhausted, the employer may well defend on the ground that the exclusive remedies provided by such a contract have not been exhausted. Since the employee's claim is based upon breach of the collective bargaining agreement, he is bound by terms of that agreement which govern the manner in which contractual rights may be enforced. For this reason, it is settled that the employee must at least attempt to exhaust exclusive grievance and arbitration procedures established by the bargaining agreement. Republic

Steel Corp. v. Maddox, 379 U.S. 650, 85 S. Ct. 614, 13 L. Ed. 2d 580. However, because these contractual remedies have been devised and are often controlled by the union and the employer, they may well prove unsatisfactory or unworkable for the individual grievant. The problem then is to determine under what circumstances the individual employee may obtain judicial review of his breach-of-contract claim despite his failure to secure relief through the contractual remedial procedures.

. . . .

"We think that another situation when the employee may seek judicial enforcement of his contractual rights arises if, as is true here, the union has sole power under the contract to invoke the higher stages of the grievance procedure, *and* if, as is alleged here, the employee-plaintiff has been prevented from exhausting his contractual remedies by the union's *wrongful* refusal to process the grievance. It is true that the employer in such a situation may have done nothing to prevent exhaustion of the exclusive contractual remedies to which he agreed in the collective bargaining agreement. But the employer has committed a wrongful discharge in breach of that agreement, a breach which could be remedied through the grievance process to the employee-plaintiff's benefit were it not for the union's breach of its statutory duty of fair representation to the employee. To leave the employee remediless in such circumstances would, in our opinion, be a great injustice. We cannot believe that Congress, in conferring upon employers and unions the power to establish exclusive grievance procedures, intended to confer upon unions such unlimited discretion to deprive injured employees of all remedies for breach of contract. Nor do we think that Congress intended to shield employers from the natural consequences of their breaches of bargaining agreements by wrongful union conduct in the enforcement of such agreements. Cf. Richardson v. Texas & N.O.R. Co., 242 F.2d 230, 235-236 (C.A. 5th Cir.) .

For these reasons, we think the wrongfully discharged employee may bring an action against his employer in the face of a defense based upon the failure to exhaust contractual remedies, provided the employee can prove that the union as bargaining agent breached its duty of fair representation in its handling of the employee's grievance. . . ."

(See, also, Thomas P. Lewis, "Fair Representation in Grievance Administration: Vaca v. Sipes" in the Supreme Court Review

[1967], p. 81; see, also, dictum in Belinski v. Delco Appliance Corporation, 23 A.D.2d 805, 258 N.Y.S.2d 61, lv. to app. den. 16 N.Y.2d 482, 261 N.Y.S.2d 1026, 209 N.E.2d 563, citing Humphrey v. Moore, 375 U.S. 335, 84 S. Ct. 363, 11 L. Ed. 2d 370).

The authority of the Social Service Employees Union in the case at bar arises from statute (N.Y.C. Collective Bargaining Law, Administrative Code, Chap. 54; Local Law 53-1967; and implemented by the Mayor's Executive Order No. 52). The Union by its contract undertook to represent *all* Caseworkers as their "sole and exclusive" agent (Art. I). As such it was under a duty to entertain and consider petitioner's alleged grievance on the merits so as to determine whether to prosecute it to arbitration if, in fact, a demand had been made upon it for such relief. The court determines, however, that the Union did not violate this duty since it finds as a fact that petitioner at no time made a request of the Union to demand arbitration of his alleged grievances. Under the circumstances, it may not be said that petitioner has fully exhausted his contractual grievance procedures, since, as expressed in Vaca v. Sipes (*supra,* citing Republic Steel Corp. v. Maddox, 379 U.S. 650, 85 S. Ct. 614, 13 L. Ed. 2d 580), the employee must at least *attempt* to exhaust exclusive grievance and arbitration procedures established by the bargaining agent as a condition precedent to proceeding against the employer. (See, also, Bilinski v. Delco Appliance Division, General Motors Corporation, 23 A.D.2d 805, 258 N.Y.S.2d 61, lv. to app. den. 16 N.Y.2d 482, 261 N.Y.S.2d 1026, 209 N.E.2d 563, *supra,* but cf. Pattenge v. Wagner Iron Works, 275 Wis. 495, 82 N.W.2d 172).

Assuming, therefore, that the petitioner was transferred in violation of the collective bargaining agreement (which the court found earlier not to be the case), it is, nonetheless, clear that the petitioner would not be entitled to relief, even under the theory of "Jenkins," "Vaca" and allied cases, because petitioner failed to first exhaust his contractual remedies.

Accordingly, judgment is directed dismissing the petition on the merits.

McGRAIL v. DETROIT FEDERATION OF TEACHERS

Michigan Circuit Court, Wayne County
82 L.R.R.M. 2623 (1973)

DINGEMAN, Judge: This controversy arises out of a contract agreement between the defendants, Detroit Board of Education (DBE) and the Detroit Federation of Teachers (DFT) for the school years '67-'69. The plaintiff William J. McGrail institutes this suit as a class action representing himself individually, and the class of Emergency Substitutes (ES) class 1, and Emergency

Substitutes in a Regular Position (ESPR) class 3. Plaintiff alleges that these two classes were "sold down the river" by the DFT and DBE because they did not receive a pay raise as all the other teachers employed by the DBE in the 67-68 period, although they did receive an increase for the period of 68-69. The complaint itself alleges that there was hostile discrimination on the part of the union (DFT) in dealing with the above classes and that this amounted to a breach of the duty to fairly represent all employees. The DBE is brought into this suit on a conspiracy theory because they participated in the negotiations and agreed to the resulting contract which resulted in the denial of the pay raise. Both defendants move for summary and/or accelerated judgment under the court rules, alleging: 1. Plaintiffs have failed to state a cause of action; 2. There is no genuine issue of material fact; 3. Plaintiff lacks capacity to sue due to the lack of proper class action being presented; 4. Plaintiff has failed to follow grievance procedure.

Plaintiff has alleged that the union has breached its duty to fairly represent the classes (1 & 3) above. He also has alleged that the DBE conspired with the union in this denial of a raise. These allegations are sufficient with respect to notice pleading but as to the DBE there have been no real facts to substantiate the allegation of conspiracy. There have been many facts (submitted by affidavit, depositions, etc.) which plaintiff argues substantiate his allegation, but taken altogether they do not support a conspiracy theory, nor do they even give rise to a reasonable inference of conspiracy. Almost the same is true with respect to the cause of action against the DFT. Plaintiff alleges that simply because they did not get a pay increase for the 67-68 school term, the union breached its duty to fairly represent them. No sufficient facts are alleged to substantiate this breach.

The case law dealing with this type cause of action seems to support the position that plaintiff has not alleged sufficient facts to sustain his action. The law basically says that the union should have broad discretion in negotiating contracts, weighing advantages and disadvantages of different proposals, and that to allow every dissatified person to challenge the validity of certain contracts without showing a strong indication of a breach of the duty to fairly represent, would create havoc in the field of labor law. The case of Ford Motor Company v. Huffman, 345 U.S. 330, 97 L. Ed. 1048, 73 S. Ct. 681 (1953) is indicative of these propositions. In that case the plaintiffs were employees of Ford Motor Company who were receiving seniority credit for post employment service. The new union contract allowed seniority credit for pre-employment service. The plaintiffs argued that because of this, their status was considerably lowered. The court acknowledged the fact that this was not beneficial to plaintiffs and that it did lessen their status. In laying out the law on the fair representation duty the court says:

> "That the authority of bargaining representatives, however, is not absolute is recognized in Steele v. Louisville & N.R. Co., 323 U.S. 192, 198, 199, 89 L. Ed. 173, 180, 181, 65 S. Ct. 226, 15 LRRM 708. . . . There statutory obligation to represent all members of an appropriate unit requires them to make an honest effort to serve the interest of all of those members, without hostility to any. (Citations omitted)
>
> *"Any authority to negotiate derives its principal strength from a delegation to the negotiators of a discretion to make such concessions and accept such advantages as, in the light of all relevant considerations, they believe will best serve the interests of the parties represented. A major responsibility of negotiators is to weigh the relative advantages and disadvantages of differing proposals."* (Emphasis added)

The court later continues, saying:

> "The mere existence of such differences does not make them invalid. The complete satisfaction of all who are represented is hardly to be expected. A wide range of reasonableness must be allowed a statutory bargaining representative in serving the unit it represents subject always to complete good faith and honesty of purpose in the exercise of its discretion.
>
> *"Compromises on a temporary basis, with a view to long range advantages are natural incidents of negotiation. Differences in wages, hours and conditions of employment reflect countless variables."* (Emphasis added)

The court here says that the union must be allowed a rather broad range of reasonableness subject to complete good faith and honesty of purpose, because they must serve the interest of all employees. They have the power to accept and reject proposals and to evaluate the advantages and disadvantages of these proposals in light of all relevant consideration. The court acknowledges the fact that all members will never be satisfied and differences will always exist. See also Cortez v. Ford Motor Company, 349 Mich. 108 (1957).

It is clear from the above cases that absent a showing of bad faith, arbitrary or discriminatory action, or fraud, the union has complete discretion to negotiate contracts in the interest of the members as a whole. The Michigan Court of Appeals in Field v.

Local 652, UAW AFL-CIO, 6 Mich. App. 140 (1967) discusses the judiciary's reluctance to get more involved in labor relations, saying:

> "To allow individual employees to overrule and supersede their union would work havoc in the union themselves and seriously disturb the field of labor relations. In order for a court to take such serious steps, a disappointed employee carries a strong burden of proof that the union acted in bad faith, fraudulently and arbitrarily. Pleadings must go beyond conclusions and state facts sufficient to raise the presumption that there has been unfair representation."

In the present case before the court the plaintiff has simply alleged a breach of a duty to fair representation and bases this solely on the fact that the classes he represents did not receive a raise during a certain period covered under a contract. This in itself does not constitute arbitrary or discriminatory action, bad faith or fraud. At most, the facts plaintiff shows amount to a temporary compromise for the benefit of all, which the union is entitled to make.

The motions for summary judgment are granted.

Appropriate orders may be submitted or noticed for presentment within ten days.

NOTES

1. In Lowe v. Hotel & Restaurant Employees Union, Local 705, 389 Mich. 123 (1973), the Michigan Supreme Court upheld a jury verdict in favor of an employee against his union representatives for a breach of the duty of fair representation. The employee had been discharged from his job and the union refused to process his grievance to arbitration under the collective bargaining agreement. In rejecting defendants' argument that the suit should have been dismissed because the employee failed to exhaust his internal union remedies, the Michigan court set forth the following general principles with respect to duty of fair representation:

> In the case before us, plaintiff's complaint alleges a duty of representation and a breach of that duty. It does not allege the conclusion that the defendant union's action was arbitrary and the product of bad faith, but it does allege facts from which such conclusions could be drawn.

The trial judge instructed the jury in these words:

> "In other words, it is a question of pure reasonableness in the assessment of the action of the Union. Did they do

what any prudent outfit would do in the circumstances that faced them? Did they make an honest effort to find out who was right and who was wrong, and did they let the blame fall right where it should; or did they take an arbitrary position, and not do what they should have done on behalf of this man?"

Defendants did not object to the charge. Under the charge as given, the jury was properly advised that the plaintiff should recover only if they found the union's refusal to take plaintiff's grievance to arbitration was arbitrary and not a fair, reasonable and honest judgment on their part.

If that standard is less exacting than has appeared in other cases, it reflects a belief that a union owes a greater duty to its members than merely to refrain from persecuting them.

Every man's employment is of utmost importance to him. It occupies his time, his talents, and his thoughts. It controls his economic destiny. It is the means by which he feeds his family and provides for their security. It bears upon his personal well-being, his mental and physical health.

In days gone by, a man's occupation literally gave him his name. Even today, continuous and secure employment contributes to a sense of identity for most people.

It is no solace to a man fired from his job that his union acted without spite, animosity, ill will, and hostility toward him. If he has been wrongfully discharged by his employer, in violation of his contract of employment, a collective bargaining agreement made for his benefit and protection, it is unthinkable that he should be denied relief—denied justice—by the courts.

But it is argued that precedential authority places the worker in a cross fire between two rules of law.

He cannot bring an action against his employer because the grievance procedure established by the collective bargaining agreement must be exhausted as a condition precedent to such action. Leadon v. Detroit Lumber Co., 340 Mich. 74 (1954); Cortez v. Ford Motor Co., 349 Mich. 108 (1957); and Spencer v. Wall Wire Products Co., 357 Mich. 296 (1959). And he cannot exhaust his contract remedy because the final stages of the grievance machinery can only be activated by the union. . . .

This, of course, is the precise dilemma propounded so eloquently by Mr. Justice Black in his ringing dissent in *Vaca v. Sipes:*

"Today the Court holds that an employee with a meritorious claim has no absolute right to have it either litigated or arbitrated."

Indeed, the rule in *Vaca,* as observed by Mr. Justice Black, gives the employee either two remedies or none. Absent union bad faith, he can recover against neither the union nor the company. Given union bad faith, he has an action against both. . . .

In this case . . . there is no basis to conclude that the trial court thought, or led the jury to believe, that the question of whether or not Lowe had been wrongfully discharged was dispositive of the issue of the union's liability.
. . .

In summary, we hold that the testimony adduced at the trial of this cause and the evidence presented to the jury, taken in the light most favorable to the plaintiff, was sufficient for the jury to have concluded that the plaintiff was wrongfully discharged by his employer and that the defendant union violated its obligation toward him to afford him fair representation by making no effort whatsoever to settle his grievance, by ignoring his grievance, by processing it in a perfunctory manner, and that the plaintiff was not required, either as a matter of fact or law, to make a formal appeal to the international president or the international executive board as a condition precedent to this action against the employer and the union.

2.   In Bodensack v. AFSCME, Local 587, 81 L.R.R.M. 2639 (Wis. Cir. Ct. 1972), it was held that the Wisconsin Employment Relations Commission has exclusive jurisdiction of claims that a union has breached its duty of fair representation.

3.   In the private sector, allegations of a breach of the duty of fair representation may appear in two different contexts: as a defense to the charge of failure to exhaust contract remedies in a breach of contract suit against the employer, Vaca v. Sipes, 386 U.S. 171, 87 S. Ct. 903, 17 L. Ed. 2d 842 (1967), or as the basis for a direct action against the union itself, Syres v. Oil Workers Local 23, 223 F.2d 739 (5th Cir.), *rev'd per curiam,* 350 U.S. 892 (1955). *Also see generally,* Steele v. Louisville & Nashville R.R., 323 U.S. 192, 65 S. Ct. 226, 89 L. Ed. 173 (1944); Brotherhood of Ry. Trainmen v. Howard, 343 U.S. 768, 72 S. Ct. 1022, 96 L. Ed. 1283 (1952); Ford Motor Co. v. Huffman, 345 U.S. 330, 73 S. Ct. 681, 97 L. Ed. 1048 (1953); Conley v. Gibson, 355 U.S. 41, 78 S. Ct. 99, 2 L. Ed. 2d 80 (1957); Humphrey v. Moore, 375 U.S. 335, 84 S. Ct. 363, 11 L. Ed. 2d 370 (1964).

The burden of proving a breach of the duty of fair representation is not one which is easily carried. "A breach of the statutory duty of fair representation occurs only when a union's conduct toward a member of the collective bargaining unit is arbitrary, discriminatory, or in bad faith." Vaca v. Sipes, *supra,* 386 U.S. at 189-90.

Consider the duty of fair representation in light of the principle of majority rule. Should the burden of proof in a breach of fair representation case be so stringent? Evaluate the following arguments:

For a lighter burden of proof: By establishing itself as exclusive representative (where this is permitted by law in the public sector) a union acquires great power to affect the wages and working conditions of the employees in the unit. The union's responsibility to members of the collective bargaining unit should be commensurate with its power. A lighter burden of proof would enable the courts to better protect the interests of members of minority racial and ethnic groups, minority-union and non-union members of this unit, and others who might be subject to union discrimination. In addition, the unions themselves would be helped; they would be forced to remain constantly aware of their obligation to represent *all* the employees in the unit.

For the continuation of a heavy burden of proof: Private dispute settlement in employment relationships can operate efficiently only if union officials remain relatively free to compromise grievance claims and even to refuse to press unmeritorious grievances. If burden of proof standards were lowered, union officials would feel more pressure to avoid charges of unfair representation by taking each claim to the final stage of the grievance procedure. Early settlement would be discouraged; frivolous claims would be encouraged. In addition, judges would be more inclined to evaluate the merits of arbitration cases, thus hampering the efficacy of the arbitration process. The individual employee has other ways of vindicating his rights through the courts (as by Title VII or § 1983 suits) which do not involve harm to private dispute settlement mechanisms. There is no reason, therefore, to change the rule that a union is presumed to be acting in the best interest of the employees in the unit and will not be found guilty of unfair representation in the absence of clear proof of willful misconduct.

4. Most collective bargaining agreements specify that the right to invoke the grievance procedure, including arbitration, is a union prerogative. *Cf.* Black-Clawson Co. v. IAM Lodge 355, 313 F.2d 179 (2d Cir. 1962). Should an employee have the

right to have his grievance arbitrated, even if the union does not concur?

5. Should an arbitration award be vacated on the basis of charges by the affected employee that the union failed to properly represent him at the hearing? *See* De Losa v. Transport Workers Union, 73 L.R.R.M. 2620 (N.Y. Sup. Ct. 1970).

6. On the duty of fair representation generally, see Cox, *The Duty of Fair Representation,* 2 VILL. L. REV. 151 (1957); Gregory, *Fiduciary Standards and the Bargaining and Grievance Process,* 8 LAB. L.J. 843 (1957); Wellington, *Union Democracy and Fair Representation: Federal Responsibility in a Federal System,* 67 YALE L.J. 1327 (1958); Aaron, *Some Aspects of the Union's Duty of Fair Representation,* 22 OHIO ST. L.J. 39 (1961); Aaron, *The Union's Duty of Fair Representation Under the Railway Labor and National Labor Relations Act,* 34 J. AIR L. & COM. 167 (1968); Sherman, *Union's Duty of Fair Representation and the Civil Rights Act of 1964,* 49 MINN. L. REV. 771 (1965); Gould, *Labor Arbitration of Grievances Involving Racial Discrimination,* 118 PA. L. REV. 40 (1969); Lewis, *Fair Representation in Grievance Administration: Vaca v. Sipes,* 1967 SUP. CT. REV. 81; Note, *The Employee's Remedy for a Union's Breach of the Duty of Fair Representation: Vaca v. Sipes,* 14 U.C.L.A. L. REV. 1351 (1967); Note, *Union Discretion and the Abridgement of Employee Rights,* 51 ORE. L. REV. 248 (1971).

F. Legally Imposed Financial Limitations on Public Employers

NORTON TEACHERS ASSOCIATION v. TOWN OF NORTON
Massachusetts Supreme Judicial Court
— Mass. —, 279 N.E.2d 659 (1972)

REARDON, Justice: This is a bill brought under G.L. c. 231A, in which the Norton Teachers Association and the Norton School Committee seek a determination of the validity of certain provisions of a collective bargaining contract entitling teachers to a salary increase in 1969. The plaintiffs seek also an order requiring the town of Norton and Edward S. Smith, Jr., its treasurer, to make payments in accordance with the provisions of the agreement. The defendants appeal from a final decree ordering them to pay the sums due under the agreement for 1969.

The trial judge made certain findings, rulings, and an order, which he adopted as a report of material facts. We summarize those facts, together with others we find for ourselves.

On September 3, 1968, the plaintiffs entered into a collective bargaining agreement pursuant to G.L. c. 149, §§ 178G-178N. The agreement, which covered the period between September 2, 1968, and August 31, 1970, provided for a higher salary schedule than one previously in effect.[1] The contract contained provisions for renegotiation on compensation. The 1968 appropriation of the school committee was insufficient to cover the increased salaries for the period September 2, 1968, to December 31, 1968. For that period the teachers were thus paid at a rate lower than that called for by the September 3 agreement.

On March 4, 1969, the annual town meeting voted down the following item in the warrant requested by the school committee: "To see if the Town will vote to raise sufficient money for teachers' salary and interest from September 1, 1968, to December 31, 1968, or take any action relative thereto." At that same meeting $1,287,462 was appropriated for the schools for 1969. It was a blanket appropriation and not detailed item by item.

On March 26, 1969, the collective bargaining agreement was amended for the second time. The amendment revised the salary schedule in the following way: (a) salaries for the period September 3-December 31, 1968, were reduced to correspond with the amounts actually paid; (b) salaries for January 1, 1969-March 9, 1969, were left at the levels originally provided for by the September 3, 1968, agreement; (c) salaries for March 10, 1969, to June 30, 1969, were higher than provided for in the September 3, 1968, agreement. The preamble to the amendment suggests the purpose of placing the teachers and other professional employees covered by the agreement in the financial position which would have been theirs had the school committee been able to meet its salary obligations under the original agreement from September 2 to December 31, 1968, or had the town voted in favor of the warrant item requested by the committee. The total appropriation for the 1969 school budget was sufficient to cover the higher salaries provided for in the amendment. The trial judge found that "the School Committee at all times was acting in good faith in an effort to meet its obligations under said contract of September 3, 1968 . . . and without any intent or purpose to evade the provisions of G.L. c. 44, § 31."

We face another in a long line of cases where the powers and duties of the school committee under G.L. c. 71 are challenged as being in conflict with certain provisions of the Municipal Finance Act, G.L. c. 44. See Casey v. Everett, 330 Mass. 220, 222, and cases cited.

---

[1] On December 9, 1968, the contract was first amended to provide for an even higher salary schedule effective September 2, 1969. This amendment is not in issue.

The defendants base their argument on two sections of G.L. c. 44. Section 31, as amended by St. 1955, c. 259, provides, in pertinent part, the "[n]o department financed by municipal revenue . . . shall incur a liability in excess of the appropriation made for the use of such department. . . ." (It is uncontested that the 1968 school appropriation was insufficient to pay the salaries of the professional employees as agreed upon by the school committee and the teachers association for the period September 2, 1968, to December 31, 1968.)

Section 64, inserted by St. 1941, c. 179, provides: "Any town having unpaid bills of previous years which may be legally unenforceable due to the insufficiency of an appropriation in the year in which such bills were incurred, may, at an annual meeting by a four-fifths vote, or at a special meeting by a nine-tenths vote, of the voters present and voting at a meeting duly called, appropriate money to pay such bills. . . ." As noted above, the annual town meeting on March 4, 1969, rejected the school committee's request under this section to pay the teachers' salary increase for the period September 1, 1968 to December 31, 1968.

The defendants argue that the school committee, in the face of the town's rejection of its request, should not be allowed to achieve the same result indirectly by an increase in the 1969 salary level sufficient to compensate teachers for what they lost in 1968. It is further argued that the school committee in 1968 was prohibited from entering into a contract increasing salaries in excess of the amount appropriated because of G.L. c. 44, § 31. Picking up the increase in the form of a higher 1969 salary schedule, according to the defendants, constitutes a mere gratuity and an invalid action. The defendants further argue that this was, in substance, the payment of a bill for salaries incurred in a prior year without compliance with G.L. c. 44, § 64.

We held in Callahan v. Woburn, 306 Mass. 265, that the school committee could bind the city by contracts of employment with teachers in excess of appropriations available at the time the contracts were made. Before us is a case distinguishable from the Callahan case since in this instance there was no discrepancy between the amount appropriated by the town for the schools for 1968 and the amount requested by the school committee. Yet as indicated in the preamble to the March 26 amendment, the higher salaries were provided for by this amendment in recognition that the teachers were required to accept lower salaries in the latter part of 1968 than they contracted for.

It does not follow necessarily that the increases for 1969 were gifts of what could not have legally been paid to the teachers in 1968. It is significant that only those teachers who actually worked in 1969 received the increase. This situation is to be contrasted with Whittaker v. Salem, 216 Mass. 483, 485. There a school committee's grant to a principal of a year's leave of absence at one half his regular salary was held invalid as a "pure gratuity." This was held notwithstanding that the principal in question had overworked during the previous year and endangered his health. On the other hand, in Averell v. Newburyport, 241 Mass. 333, 335, we said in upholding the school committee provision for paid sick leave, "Although the rule increasing the possible length of absence without loss of pay was adopted after the salaries for the year had been fixed by vote of the committee, that is not decisive against the plaintiff. *In principle it stands on the same footing as an increase of salary during the period of a contract. It was not a mere gratuity. It may have been regarded as an additional incentive to superior work*" (emphasis supplied). See Attorney Gen. v. Woburn, 317 Mass. 465, 467; Fitchburg Teachers Assn. v. School Comm. of Fitchburg, — Mass. —, —, 77 LRRM 3132. We think the statement in the Averell case is sound.

We are further supported in our determination by the unwavering line of cases enforcing, when possible, "the supremacy of the school committee's authority in matters pertaining to the management of the public schools." Casey v. Everett, 330 Mass. 220, 222, and cases cited. In particular, we have often held that the school committee has complete power to fix the compensation of teachers. See Leonard v. School Comm. of Springfield, 241 Mass. 325, 329-330; Watt v. Chelmsford, 323 Mass. 697, 700; Lynch v. Fall River, 336 Mass. 558, 559; Collins v. Boston, 338 Mass. 704, 707. The only question is the sufficiency of funds available to the school committee. Fitchburg Teachers Assn. v. School Comm. of Fitchburg, — Mass. —, —, 77 LRRM 3132. Here it was uncontested that the total appropriation for the 1969 school budget was sufficient to cover the increases due under the amendment.

The problem of Callahan v. Woburn, 306 Mass. 265, came here in part because the contracts with the teachers did not run from year to year concurrently with the town's successive fiscal years. We held in the Callahan case, at page 268, that such contracts were nonetheless proper.

Furthermore, it cannot be denied that if the original agreement of September 3, 1968, had contained those salary schedules as finally provided for by the March 26, 1969, amendment (i.e., with the increases not coming into effect until 1969), there would be no question as to its validity. The impact on the town would have been the same. All circumstances considered, the agreement

with the March 26 amendment is valid and enforceable. There
was no error.

Decree affirmed.

NOTES

1. In Providence Teachers' Union Local 958 v. School Committee of Providence, 108 R.I. 444, 276 A.2d 762 (1971), a dispute concerning retirement benefit provisions in an executed
collective bargaining agreement was submitted to arbitration.
One of the grounds urged by the School Committee as a defense
to an award directing payment of the questioned benefits was
the unavailability of appropriated funds. The court rejected the
defense and held that the money due under the award was a
debt of the city. *See also* Town of Scituate v. Scituate Teachers
Ass'n, 82 L.R.R.M. 2005, *appeal dismissed*, 296 A.2d 466, 82
L.R.R.M. 2007 (R.I. Sup. Ct. 1972).

2. In Newark Teachers Ass'n v. Board of Educ. of Newark,
57 N.J. 100, 270 A.2d 14 (1970), defendant Board of Education
adopted a salary schedule calling for increases in the pay of
teachers. The teachers' association was informed, however, that
the schedule would not go into effect until the City appropriated
the funds necessary to implement it. Had it been applicable to the
current (1969-70) school year, the resolution would have provided for salary increases in excess of the budget. In an action
to compel the school board to pay the salary increases effective
immediately, the New Jersey Supreme Court affirmed a lower
court judgment that state law did not require a school board's
resolution to be given immediate effect.

See also Association of New Jersey State College Faculties v.
Board of Higher Educ., 75 L.R.R.M. 2613 (N.J. Super. Ct. 1970).

3. The Maine Supreme Court issued a preliminary injunction
preventing the School Committee of Kittery from rolling back
teacher pay increases negotiated by the Kittery Teachers Association. Justice Wernick found that the School Committee violated the state's Municipal Employees Relations Law in attempting to eliminate the salary increases after the Town Council
eliminated $55,000 off the school budget with a recommendation
that $20,000 of the reduction come from the teacher salary item.
On the School Committee's claim that it was merely following
the Town Council's mandate in rolling back the salary increase,
Justice Wernick ruled that the Council was "without authority
to restrict to a specific purpose or use" part of the total funds
allocated to the Committee. *See* GERR No. 418, B-12 (1971).
A similar decision was reached in Board of Educ. of the City

of Buffalo and Buffalo Teachers Federation, Inc., 4 PERB ¶ 4-3090 (1971).

4. In District Council 33, AFSCME v. Philadelphia, 81 L.R.R.M. 2539 (Pa. C.P., Phila. County 1971), the court directed the City of Philadelphia to appropriate funds necessary to continue payments of disability benefits to firemen and teachers. The court ruled in effect that the exhaustion of funds in a municipal budget did not relieve the city of its obligations under a collective bargaining agreement. In reaching this result, the court cited Harney v. Russo, 435 Pa. 183, 255 A.2d 560 (1969), where the Pennsylvania Supreme Court upheld the constitutionality of the compulsory arbitration act for policemen and firemen to settle bargaining impasses; the court in *Harney* stated, in part, that:

> . . . [I]f we do hear a case in which tax millage, as a matter of record, cannot permissibly be raised so as to provide sufficient funds to pay the required benefits to the employees, it will still be open to this Court to rule that the Act of June 24, 1968 impliedly authorizes a court-approved millage ceiling increase to pay the arbitration award where necessary, or to hold that the municipal budget must be adjusted in other places in order to provide resources for policemen's or firemen's salaries.

See also City of Washington and Police Dep't of City of Washington, 436 Pa. 168, 259 A.2d 437 (1969).

G. Breach of Contract as an Unfair Labor Practice

1. Contract Disputes Before a State Agency

BOARD OF EDUCATION, UNION FREE SCHOOL DISTRICT NO. 3, TOWN OF HEMPSTEAD, NASSAU COUNTY AND EAST MEADOW TEACHERS ASSOCIATION

New York Public Employment Relations Board
4 PERB ¶ 4-3018 (1971)

The East Meadow Teachers Association (EMTA) filed an improper practice charge against the Board of Education, Union Free School District No. 3, Town of Hempstead, Nassau County (respondent).

The charge alleged a violation of § 209-a.1 (d) [1] of the Public Employees' Fair Employment Act (Act) in that the respondent unilaterally changed the terms and conditions relating to sab-

---

[1] "to refuse to negotiate in good faith with the duly recognized or certified representatives of its public employees."

batical leaves by requiring all applicants for such leaves to agree to return to the employment of respondent for a period of two years following the termination of the sabbatical leave.

EMTA and respondent entered into a written agreement in July, 1969 setting forth the terms and conditions of employment for teaching personnel. The agreement became effective on September 1, 1969, and terminated on August 31, 1970.

The agreement provided in ¶ 5.1:

"Sabbatical Leave—The existing practices, policies and procedures respecting sabbatical leaves to teaching personnel are confirmed and shall remain in effect except that (a) a teacher eligible for sabbatical may select a half-year sabbatical at full pay for full-time study or its equivalent upon approval of the Superintendent of Schools, either in the United States or abroad and (b) in selecting among applicants for sabbatical leave, length of service in the District shall be one of the prime considerations."

In April, 1970 the respondent changed its policy relating to sabbatical leave to require, as a condition to the granting thereof, an agreement to work for respondent for a two-year period following the leave. It is conceded that in effecting this change respondent did not negotiate with EMTA.

The hearing officer concluded that procedures and policies relating to sabbatical leave are a mandatory subject of collective negotiations and that there is an obligation on the part of the respondent to negotiate with EMTA "prior to implementing a change in its sabbatical leave policy."

The hearing officer, after giving consideration to several affirmative defenses asserted by respondent and finding them lacking in merit, thereupon found that respondent violated § 209-a.1 (d) of the Act.

Respondent has excepted to the decision and recommended order of the hearing officer.

The arguments in defense of the position of respondent may be summarized as (1) Sabbatical Leave is not a term or condition of employment under the Act; (2) The conduct of respondent alleged as the basis of the charge herein would constitute a breach of the agreement between the parties and, therefore, the grievance procedure set forth in the contract is the sole remedy available to EMTA; (3) The question has become moot in that in the subsequent agreement between the parties there is a contractual provision covering sabbatical leave, the point at issue. . . .

First, we agree with the hearing officer that the issue of sabbatical leave is a term and condition of employment and thus is a proper subject of collective negotiations. The provisions of § 1709, subdivision 16 of the Education Law does not negate this conclusion.

Therefore, either party has the duty to negotiate concerning this subject if requested by the other. This duty to negotiate, of course, does not compel one party to agree to the proposal of the other. Rather, this duty requires each party to negotiate in good faith on all mandatory subjects of negotiations.

As to respondent's second contention that the respondent's conduct herein should be relegated to the grievance procedure agreed upon by the parties in their negotiated agreement, the hearing officer reasoned that the "claim here does not relate to the interpretation of any clause of the collective agreement." The hearing officer concluded that, "this dispute is not one of contract interpretation but of statutory obligation" and, therefore, EMTA could properly invoke the improper practice section of the Act, rather than the grievance procedures in the negotiated agreement.

This issue raised by respondent is one of first impression before this Board and raises some basic questions. The first question is: Does this Board have general jurisdiction to police and enforce negotiated agreements between public employers and employee organizations within this state?

We conclude that it does not. The legislature of this state has not dealt explicitly with this problem, as have the legislatures of Wisconsin,[2] or Hawaii,[3] in making the breach of a collective bargaining agreement an unfair labor practice. While the legislature of this state has stated that, in the administration of improper practices, decisions in the private sector shall not be binding or controlling precedent[4] nevertheless such statutory mandate does not by its terms preclude this Board from considering the vast reservoir of experience in the private sector.

In decisions construing the National Labor Relations Act, it appears to be well-settled that the National Labor Relations Board does not have general jurisdiction over alleged violations of collective bargaining agreements.[5] In reaching this conclusion, the Supreme Court relied upon the legislative history of the enactment of the Taft-Hartley Act[6] and concluded that Congress

---

[2] State Employment Labor Relations Act, § 111.84 (1) (e).

[3] State of Hawaii, Act 171, L. 1970, § 13 (a) (8).

[4] CSL § 209-a. 8.

[5] NLRB v. C & C Plywood Corp., 385 U.S. 421; NLRB v. M & M Oldsmobile Inc., 377 F.2d 712.

[6] NLRB v. C & C Plywood Corp., supra, footnote 5.

"deliberately chose to leave the enforcement of collective agreements to the usual processes of law."[7]

There is no such legislative history as to the Act herein. Nevertheless, we find the conclusion reached by the Supreme Court in the private sector to be a salutary approach, particularly since the legislature of this state did not provide that a breach of a negotiated agreement would constitute an improper practice. However, this is not dispositive of the issue raised by respondent, for all that has been concluded so far is that a breach of contract is not *per se* an improper labor practice.

A second question arises whether conduct which constitutes a breach of contract may also constitute an improper practice. This question requires an affirmative answer in the light of facts of this case.

Respondent herein agreed, in the negotiated agreement, to maintain existing policies, practices and procedures relating to sabbatical leave. Respondent unilaterally changed such practices, policies and procedures without negotiating such change with the representative of its employees. This constitutes a violation of § 209-a.1 (d) of the Act in that it violates respondent's obligation "to negotiate in good faith" with such representative.

The fact that respondent, in effecting such change, contends that it acted in the public interest, does not cure the violation herein. The Act mandates that a public employer negotiate terms and conditions of employment with the certified or recognized representative of its employees. This obviously precludes the unilateral imposition of terms and conditions of employment.

We do not reach the question here of whether, in such circumstances, this Board should defer to the grievance and arbitration procedures in an agreement because the subject contract does not provide for binding arbitration.

The third defense, to wit, the allegation that the question has become moot, is not a defense at all; rather, its relevance in this case is only to the nature of the remedial order to be issued by this Board. . . .

2.   Deference to Arbitration

NEW YORK CITY TRANSIT AUTHORITY AND TRANSPORT WORKERS OF AMERICA LOCAL 100

New York Public Employment Relations Board
4 PERB ¶ 4504 (1971)

J. AXELROD, Hearing Officer—On April 13, 1970, pursuant to Part 204 of the Rules of Procedure (herein referred to as the

---

[7] Charles Dowd Box Co. v. Courtney, 368 U.S. 518.

Rules) of the New York State Public Employment Relations Board (herein referred to as the Board), Harry Bordansky (herein referred to as the charging party) filed a charge[2] against the New York City Transit Authority (herein referred to as respondent Transit Authority) and the Transport Workers Union of America, AFL-CIO and Local 100, Transport Workers Union of America, AFL-CIO (herein referred to as respondent TWU), alleging that they had violated § 209-a.1 (a) [3] and § 209-a.2 (a) [4] respectively, of the Public Employees' Fair Act (herein referred to as the Act) by discriminating against the charging party in the assignment of overtime work because of his non-union status. The charging party also alleged that a grievance on this issue which he had filed under the contractual grievance procedure established by the respondents was then stalled at Step 4 because of respondent Transit Authority's failure to file a timely determination.

Thereafter, each respondent filed an answer denying the material allegations of the charge and also raising certain affirmative defenses, including, on the part of respondent Transit Authority, the charging party's alleged failure to exhaust his administrative remedies.

At a pre-hearing conference conducted by me on May 11, 1970, the parties agreed by stipulation to adjourn a hearing on the charge, *sine die,* "pending the charging party's exhaustion of his remedies under the contractual grievance procedure" which included binding arbitration. On August 4, the designated impartial arbitrator, Theodore Kheel, issued an award dismissing the grievance as without merit.

A formal hearing was then held before me on October 13. At the hearing, respondent Transit Authority sought dismissal of the charge without a hearing on the merits, on the ground that the issues raised in the charge had already been resolved by the arbitral award to which PERB should defer in furtherance of the recognized public policy of encouraging voluntary dispute settlement procedures. Respondent Transit Authority pointed out, in support of its contention, that the U.S. Supreme Court

[2] Mr. Bordansky filed the charge on behalf of himself and several other employees.

[3] This section makes it an improper practice for an employer "deliberately . . . to interfere with, restrain or coerce public employees in the exercise of their rights guaranteed in section two hundred two for the purpose of depriving them of such rights. . . ."

[4] This section makes it an improper practice for an employee organization "deliberately . . . to interfere with, restrain or coerce public employees in the exercise of the rights granted in section two hundred two, or to cause, or attempt to cause, a public employer to do so. . . ."

had long recognized the efficacy of arbitration as a stabilizing force in labor relations and had approved the National Labor Relations Board's policy[5] of accepting an arbitral determination as dispositive of an unfair labor practice case where the same issue was being litigated, the proceedings were fair and regular, and the award did not conflict with the precepts or provisions of the National Labor Relations Act.[6] Following litigation of the circumstances of the arbitral award in the instant case, I granted the respondent Transit Authority's motion to dismiss the charge, and said I would explain my ruling in a decision.

Facts

Respondent TWU has for many years been the recognized negotiating representative of, *inter alia,* hourly paid operating and maintenance employees of the respondent Transit Authority, including the charging party. At all times pertinent herein, the charging party was not a member of respondent TWU.

Article VIII of the collective agreement between respondents establishes a five-step grievance procedure and then provides for arbitration before a designated impartial arbitrator, whose determination ". . . shall be final and binding on both parties." Any individual employee may invoke the grievance machinery on his own behalf.[7]

In mid March, 1970, the charging party filed a grievance at Step 2 of the contractual grievance procedure alleging that he had been discriminatorily by-passed in the assignment of overtime on March 16 because of his non-union status.[8] Unsatisfied with the determination at Step 2, the charging party processed the grievance to Step 3, and then Step 4. When the Step 4 determination was not forthcoming following the expiration of the contractual deadline, the charging party filed the instant charge on April 13.

As of May 11, the date of the pre-hearing conference in the instant case, the grievance had been processed through a Step 5 hearing and, as noted above, the parties agreed to adjourn further proceedings herein until the contractual grievance arbitration machinery had been exhausted.

Thereafter, following the issuance of a Step 5 determination

---

[5] See, e.g., Spielberg Manufacturing Co., 112 NLRB 1080 (1955).

[6] Carey v. Westinghouse Electric Corp., 375 U.S. 261, 55 LRRM 2042 (1964).

[7] Under certain circumstances TWU, although not representing a grieving employee, must be notified of and be allowed to participate in each step of the procedure.

[8] The subject of overtime assignment is covered in a written schedule of working conditions and is clearly grievable.

dismissing his grievance, the charging party submitted the matter to arbitration. . . .

At the arbitration, in accordance with a long standing custom of the parties, the arbitrator took notes in lieu of a formal transcript.[9] The charging party admittedly was afforded unlimited opportunity to present all information and documents he wished in support of his grievance. Respondent Transit Authority also presented evidence but respondent TWU, although represented, did not present independent evidence.

The arbitrator, Mr. Kheel, in his decision and award, framed the grievance as follows:

> "Harry Bordansky, a Bus Maintainer B, who is not a member of the Union, claims that the Authority discriminated against non-Union men in his shop in the assignment of overtime during the pick year ending in May 1970. Mr. Bordansky alleges that the average of overtime hours awarded to non-Union men was less than average for Union men and there were specific occasions when the Authority exhibited distinct favoritism to Union men over non-Union men in the assignment of overtime."

The arbitrator evaluated the overtime assignments on one such "specific" occasion, March 16, and found no evidence to support Mr. Bordansky's claim. . . .

Discussion

Preliminarily, it will be useful to isolate the precise matter at issue in this proceeding. The Board's authority to hear and determine an improper practice charge in the face of an outstanding arbitral determination resolving the same point alleged in the charge *is not* at issue. The Legislature has entrusted the Board, under § 205.5 (d) of the Act, with the task of "establishing procedures for the prevention of improper employer and employee organization practices as provided in section two hundred nine-a of this article" except for cases involving parties under the jurisdiction of the New York City Office of Collective Bargaining. The commission of improper employer and employee organization practices threatens the established public policy of maintaining "harmonious and cooperative relationships between government and its employees." Such practices thus are public wrongs with ramifications for the public interest far beyond their effects on

---

[9] Mr. Kheel, the designated impartial arbitrator, was out of the country on the assigned day for the arbitration hearing. The parties agreed to have Mr. Messina, an associate of Mr. Kheel, sit as the arbitrator, with the understanding that Mr. Kheel would render the decision based upon Mr. Messina's notes.

the parties immediately concerned. Clearly, then, the Legislature could not have intended that the determination in a private forum of a matter alleged to be an improper practice would oust the Board of its statutory jurisdiction over the matter. But, while the Board may consider the matter *de novo* under such circumstances, it is not bound to do so if it is satisfied that the public interest will be otherwise served. This brings me to the only question which *is* at issue in this proceeding, namely, the effect the Board should give to an existing arbitral award resolving the same matters raised by an improper practice charge.

Consideration of the role of arbitration in labor relations is a necessary predicate to any discussion of the issue at bar. The United States Supreme Court has for many years held that national labor policy in the private sector accords arbitration a position of primacy as a medium for settling labor disputes and preserving industrial stability. . . .

The importance to public sector labor relations of voluntary dispute settlement procedures, including arbitration, was recognized in the 1966 "Report of the Governor's Committee on Public Employee Relations" (Taylor Committee), a document widely regarded as the most complete source of legislative history of the ensuing Taylor Act. . . .

The Legislature took to heart the Committee's advice to encourage private dispute settlement procedures. Section 200 of the Act, entitled "Statement of Policy," declares:

". . . it is the public policy of the State and the purpose of this Act to promote harmonious and cooperative relationships between government and its employees and to protect the public by assuring, at all times, the orderly and uninterrupted operations and functions of government. These policies are best effectuated by . . . (c) encouraging . . . public employers and . . . employee organizations to agree upon procedures for resolving disputes. . . ."

It follows that every effort must be made to insure the integrity of those private arrangements which the parties have devised for conclusively resolving disputes. Where an alleged improper practice has been litigated in a forum designated by the parties for the final and binding resolution of disputes, this objective can best be accomplished if the resulting private determination is given conclusive effect in the improper practice proceeding. However, to satisfy the public interest, which is always at stake in an improper practice proceeding but rarely involved in a private proceeding, the Board should defer to the arbitration award only under the following circumstances:

1. the same issue raised in the improper practice charge
    was aired and determined in the arbitration proceeding;
2. the arbitration proceeding was conducted with fairness
    and regularity of procedure;
3. the resulting award is final and binding on the parties;
    and
4. the award does not contravene the Act or offend public
    policy.

By deferring to an award meeting these standards, the Board
will be able to implement its statutory mandate to redress improper practices while carrying out the statutory objective of
encouraging private dispute settlement procedures.

I now turn to an application of these policy considerations to
the case at bar. At the hearing in the instant case, the charging
party contended that the award should be disregarded because
no stenographic record was kept during the arbitration hearing,
and the award did not answer every question raised by the charging party during the arbitration. Contrary to the charging party's
assertion, neither of these facts impugns the fairness or the regularity of the arbitration proceeding nor the integrity of the
award. As to the former point, it is an accepted custom in many
arbitration proceedings to dispense with a formal transcript and
to have the matter decided upon the exhibits and the arbitrator's
notes. Regarding the issue about the completeness of the award,
the arbitrator conclusively disposed of the grievance for clearly
stated reasons. There is no requirement that an arbitral (or for
that matter, a judicial) determination provide specific answers
to each argument made during the course of a proceeding and any
such expectation would be manifestly unreasonable.

As previously noted, the charging party invoked the contractual grievance machinery, even prior to filing the instant charge.
The issue submitted to arbitration was identical to that raised
in the charge. At the arbitration proceeding, the charging party
had every opportunity to air his grievance and present evidence.
The arbitrator, after evaluating the competing contentions in his
binding award dismissed the grievance as unsubstantiated by the
evidence. Finally, the award does not offend the policies of the
Act. Accordingly, I find that the four criteria set forth *supra* have
been satisfied and this Board therefore should decline to exercise
jurisdiction.

In view of the above findings of fact and conclusions of law, I
therefore recommend that the charge be dismissed in its entirety.

[The decision of the Hearing Officer was adopted and affirmed
by the New York Public Employment Relations Board in New
New York City Transit Authority, 4 PERB ¶ 4-3031 (1971).]

BOARD OF EDUCATION OF THE CITY OF BUFFALO AND BUFFALO TEACHERS FEDERATION, INC.

New York Public Employment Relations Board
4 PERB ¶ 4-3090 (1971)

The Buffalo Teachers Federation, Inc. (Federation) filed an improper practice charge against the Board of Education of the City of Buffalo (employer) on August 5, 1971. The charge alleges a violation of Section 209-a.1 (a) and (d) of the Public Employees' Fair Employment Act (Act) [1] in that the employer unilaterally decided not to implement certain provisions concerning terms and conditions of employment contained in a current contract between the employer and the Federation.

Facts

Employer and Federation entered into a contract in March, 1970 covering the academic years, 1970-71 and 1971-72.

In January, 1971 the employer submitted its budget to the Mayor of the City of Buffalo, as the employer is fiscally dependent upon the City of Buffalo.

The budget, as submitted, was in the amount of $89,311,837. This budget was approximately $19,000,000 in excess of the previous year's budget.

The Mayor submitted the budget for the employer's operations to the City Council in April, 1971. However, the Mayor reduced the amount in the employer's budget to about $71,200,-000. The City Council took no action on the budget so, pursuant to the City Charter, the budget as proposed by the Mayor became the official budget of the employer as of June 1, 1971.

The employer was told in May that it was not going to receive all the funds it had requested and, thus, was considering areas in its proposed budget where cuts could be effected. The employer met with representatives of the Federation on two occasions—one in the latter part of May and the second in the middle of June. The employer spoke about possible areas where the budget might be reduced and wanted "reaction" from the Federation. The Federation advised the employer that they would not renegotiate the existing contract and that the Federation would insist upon full implementation of the terms and conditions as set forth in the contract.

---

[1] These sections make it an improper practice for an employer deliberately " (a) to interfere with, restrain or coerce public employees in the exercise of their rights guaranteed in section two hundred two for the purpose of depriving them of such rights; . . . (d) to refuse to negotiate in good faith with the duly recognized or certified representatives of its public employees." Clearly, the main thrust of the charging party's case is a violation of (d) and only derivatively of (a).

The employer was required to adopt its operating budget by July 1st, based on the sum allocated by the City. The operating budget as adopted by the employer on July 1, 1971 did not provide funds to implement contractual obligations in four areas: (1) hiring of specialty teachers; (2) hiring of additional teachers; (3) hiring of teachers' aides; (4) preparation periods for teachers.[2]

The employer met with Federation representatives on July 6th to discuss the adopted budget, but the teachers declined to negotiate any change in the agreement.

Thereafter, this improper practice charge was filed on August 5, 1971.

The employer's Superintendent of Schools did testify that the lump-sum appropriation of $71,000,000 allotted by the City would have been sufficient to meet its contractual obligations, as well as all other mandated programs.[3] However, the employer contended that this would have necessitated a curtailment of other programs and activities which, though not mandated, were beneficial to the students.

The hearing officer found that, "The employer violated § 209-a.1 (d) of the Act when it deliberately decided not to comply with four of the terms of the existing contract."

The employer filed exceptions to the hearing officer's decision and stated in its brief in support of such exceptions that the sole issue raised in the exceptions was whether the Board "should take jurisdiction of this particular matter. . . ."

The employer asserts, in support of its exceptions that (a) arbitration of any alleged violation of the contract was available to the charging party; (b) the charge was prematurely brought in that none of the alleged violations had occurred when the charge was filed; and (c) since the filing of the charge, the employer has complied with its contractual obligations.

Discussion

(a)   Availability of Arbitration

The subject contract between the parties provides for arbitration of unresolved grievances relating to "claims of violation . . . of this contract." The employer contends that this Board should defer to arbitration and decline jurisdiction herein.

---

[2] Under the contract, the teachers were to receive an 8% salary increase. The budget as adopted on July 1st did not provide for this increase, but on July 23, 1971 the City gave to the employer an additional $3.1 million, which funded the increase.

[3] The employer did, in its adopted operating budget, fulfill a contractual obligation of salary increases for its clerical employees.

In a previous decision, we concluded that a contract violation is not *per se* an improper practice. It is only where the violation of contract is also a violation of a right under the Act that the matter is within the jurisdiction of this Board.[4] However, that decision did not reach the question which is raised herein, namely, whether this Board should defer to arbitration where an improper practice charge is filed alleging a violation of Section 209-a.1 (d) and the facts underlying the charge would be subject to the grievance arbitration procedures of the contract.

The legislature of this State granted to this Board the power and function "to establish procedures for the prevention of improper . . . practices" and provided further that "the board shall exercise exclusive non-delegable jurisdiction of the powers granted to it" in this regard.[5] However, the same legislature also declared it to be the public policy of this State "to promote harmonious and cooperative relationships between government and its employees," and that this policy can be, in part, effectuated by "encouraging . . . public employees and . . . employee organizations to agree upon procedures for resolving disputes." Thus, it would seem that some accommodation is required between these two legislative mandates.

The experience of the National Labor Relations Board (NLRB) in this regard, while not controlling, is worthy of some consideration.[8] We would first point out that the NLRB observes a distinction between two situations—one where there has been an arbitral award and the other where arbitration has not been initiated.[9] It is the latter situation which confronts us here, so we will limit our observations to that situation.

In a very recent case, the NLRB decided that, where the dispute is essentially a dispute over the terms and meaning of the contract between the parties, the dispute should be resolved pursuant to the as yet not invoked grievance arbitration procedures of the contract.[10] For a long time previously the NLRB has deferred to contractual arbitration procedures which had already been invoked[11] and the Supreme Court of the United States

---

[4] Board of Education, Union Free School District No. 3, Town of Hempstead, Nassau County, 4 PERB ¶ 4-3018, 3659.

[5]   CSL § 205.5 (d).

[8] Section 10 (a) of LMRA provides that the National Labor Relations Board "is empowered to prevent any person from engaging in any unfair labor practice. . . . This power shall not be affected by any other means of adjustment or prevention that has been or may be established by agreement, law, or otherwise. . . ." 29 USC 160 (a).

[9] Collyer Insulated Wire, 192 NLRB No. 150; 77 LRRM 1931.

[10] Ibidem.

[11] Crown Zellerbach, 95 NLRB 753; 28 LRRM 1357.

has indicated its approval of the NLRB's deference to agreed procedures for resolution of disputes.[12] Nevertheless, it cannot be said that the NLRB will always defer to the grievance arbitration procedure where a charge is made of a unilateral change in terms and conditions allegedly in violation of contract. A *sine qua non* for such deference would appear to be that the unilateral action taken is based upon a substantial claim of contractual privilege.[13]

In the case before us, it cannot be said that the subject unilateral changes were based upon a substantial claim of contractual privilege; rather, the record seems clear that the unilateral changes herein complained of were made without any color of right under the contract. This is not a situation where the employer's actions were based upon a good-faith interpretation of a contractual provision. Rather, we are faced with a situation where an employer, though it had available funds to fulfill its contractual obligations, decided to violate the contract in order to use the funds for other purposes which, in its judgment, would be more beneficial.

We conclude that this is not a situation where this Board should withhold its jurisdiction and defer to the grievance arbitration procedure.

(b) *Employer's Duty to Negotiate*

In reaching this conclusion, we are aware of the fundamental distinctions between labor relations in the public sector and those in the private sector. A public employer has a grave and, at times, an awesome responsibility in providing such essential services as police and fire protection and medical care services that its constituents rightfully not only expect, but demand— services that could properly be said to be one of the reasons for the very existence of a government. On the other hand, public employees in this State are not permitted to strike regardless of the provocation. Because of this strike prohibition, it would seem clear that the scope of a public employer's obligation to negotiate with the representative of its employees transcends the obligation of a private employer.

The duties and obligations of a public employer to its constituents and its statutory obligations to its employees must be balanced. Admittedly, there may be occasions where the former must be given greater weight than the latter. We do not find, however, that the situation here is such an occasion. The em-

---

[12] Carey v. Westinghouse Electric Corporation, 375 U.S. 261, 271.

[13] Jos. Schlitz Brewery Company, 175 NLRB No. 23, 70 LRRM 1472, Collyer Insulated Wire, supra.

ployer here did not act to undermine the Federation; rather, it reacted to the financial squeeze imposed upon it by another entity—the City of Buffalo. Further, the record would appear to support the conclusion that it acted in a manner that it deemed to be the proper discharge of its obligation to its constituency. Nevertheless, it did act unilaterally in abrogating certain provisions of the contract between it and the Federation. The Federation is the negotiating representative for the public employees herein and, as such, the employer is mandated to negotiate with it on terms and conditions of employment. Such unilateral action in the abrogation of contract terms by an employer is clearly a violation of this obligation to negotiate. The financial squeeze imposed upon the employer here does not exculpate it, for the employer did have sufficient funds to meet its mandated programs and to fulfill its contractual obligations with the Federation. However, as pointed out by the hearing officer, "It elected to pick and choose its own priorities and elected to fund 'non-mandated' programs . . . and to pick and choose which 'non-mandated' articles of the Federation's contract it would comply with. The Act does not permit such freedom of action on the part of a public employer who is required to negotiate with an employee organization." We agree with the hearing officer and with his conclusion that the employer violated its obligation to negotiate in good faith.

(c)   Prematurity of the Charge

We overrule the employer's exception that the charge was prematurely brought. This point was fully considered by the hearing officer and rejected by him. We endorse the reasoning of the hearing officer.

(d)   Mootness of the Charge

We overrule this exception of the employer. Although it is true that, subsequent to the hearing officer's recommendation, the employer has complied with its contractual obligations, this subsequent compliance does not cure the statutory violation by the employer. It merely goes to the nature of the remedy to be afforded to the Federation.

Conclusion

As no such case as this had ever arisen in the past, the employer was not fully cognizant of its statutory duty to its employees during the time when it was under fiscal pressures. Because of this, and because it has complied with its contractual obligations to its employees since the issuance of the charge herein, no remedial order is necessary.

H. Taxpayer Suits as an Enforcement Mechanism

In private sector collective bargaining, members of the public are remote third parties to the process, involved to the extent that they are consumers and stockholders, yet not really participants. In the public sector, members of the public are afforded many more opportunities to participate at key points in the bargaining process—at school board and city council meetings, in the legislature where legislative approval of collective bargaining agreements is required, and even in millage elections where the fate of negotiated increases in employee benefits may be decided. In part, public participation in public sector bargaining is attributable to the close relationship between the bargaining and political processes; public participation is invited as a matter of democratic privilege. In part, too, participation is enhanced by the essential nature of many public employee services. Yet another factor is the popular perception of a much more direct financial link between the citizen as taxpayer and the wages of public servants than is the case between the citizen as stockholder or consumer and the wages of the private sector employee.

Most states now permit taxpayer suits challenging the constitutionality of legislation or charging administrative agencies with abuse of discretion, provided that the taxpayer can show a sufficient financial stake in the outcome. *See* Jaffe, *Standing to Secure Judicial Review: Public Actions,* 74 HARV. L. REV. 1265, 1276-81 (1961) ; Comment, *Taxpayers' Suits: A Survey and Summary,* 69 YALE L.J. 895 (1960). In some states the taxpayer is regarded as a private attorney general seeking to vindicate the public interest. *See* the concurring opinion of Justice Douglas in Flast v. Cohen, 392 U.S. 83, 108, notes 2-5 (1968). This concept is applicable to the collective bargaining process in the public sector in those cases in which the interests of the public employer and the public unions seem to be arrayed against the interests of the taxpayer. This is especially true where a taxpayer suit may be the only means of invoking the provisions of a punitive law, as the following cases illustrate.

LEGMAN v. SCHOOL DISTRICT OF CITY OF SCRANTON
Pennsylvania Supreme Court, Eastern District
432 Pa. 342, 247 A.2d 566 (1968)

ROBERTS, Justice:—Appellee instituted this action in equity to enjoin the school district from paying increased salaries to certain teachers in the Scranton school system who allegedly went on strike in December 1967. The gravamen of his complaint is that such action by the school board (which has already progressed to the point of approving this raise in the 1968 budget) would violate the Strike by Public Employees Act, Act of June 30, 1947, P.L. 1883, § 1 et seq., 43 P.S. § 215.1 et seq. This statute provides that whenever a "public employee" goes "on strike" such employee may return to his previous employment only on the condition that his compensation remain the same as before the walkout for a period of three years. Appellants (a group which now includes as intervening parties the two teachers' unions) filed preliminary objections to the complaint. It is from the dismissal of these objections that appellants lodge this appeal.

Their first contention is that equity has no jurisdiction to hear this case. The argument is based on the proposition that the Strike by Public Employees Act contains the exclusive means for determining whether a violation of the act has occurred. The section relied upon provides:

> "Notwithstanding the provisions of any other law, any person holding such a position who, without the lawful approval of his superior, fails to report for duty or otherwise absents himself from his position or abstains, in whole or in part, from the full, faithful and proper performance of his position shall be deemed on strike: Provided, That such person, upon request, shall be entitled to establish that he did not violate the provisions of this act. Such request must be filed in writing within ten days after regular compensation of such employee has ceased. In the case of a public employee who is entitled by law to a hearing upon dismissal or removal, such written request shall be filed with the officer or body having power to remove such employee, and such officer or body shall within ten days conduct a hearing to determine whether the provisions of this act have been violated by such public employee in the manner provided by law, appropriate to a proceeding to dismiss or remove such public employee."

We agree that this part of the statute clearly provides the *sole* procedure by which it may be determined whether a school employee violated the act. But this conclusion is not dispositive of the issue before this Court. Here we have a taxpayer of the school district complaining that the school board is about to make illegal payments. He seeks to guarantee by restraining the school board that no such payments are made. Thus it is a controversy between the taxpayer and the school board. This type of litigation clearly does not come within the language of section 5 of the Strike by Public Employees Act which directs: "That such person, [public employee allegedly on strike] upon request, shall be entitled to establish that he did not violate the provisions of the act." The section five procedure only comes into play *once* the school board has determined that one or more of its employees has been "on strike" and decides that such striking employee or employees are not entitled to increased compensation because of the penalty provision of section 4 of the act.

What the taxpayer in the instant action seeks is to restrain illegal payments by the school board; if successful in obtaining the injunction, the school board will be required to make the initial determination whether or not any of its employees were on strike. Once it decides which, if any, of the teachers were on strike and refuses to pay the increased compensation to those employees because of the section 4 penalty, *then* section 5 becomes operative. This latter section will provide a procedure by which teachers who have been adjudged "on strike" and who wish to appeal such determination may have their grievances adjudicated.

But section 5 may never come into play if the school board decided that it would be appropriate to disregard the penalties imposed by section 4. Thus some procedure is required to compel the school board to give effect to the act. Certainly the Strike by Public Employees Act provides no such procedure, let alone the exclusive procedure as alleged by appellants. However, for this purpose an action in equity is perfectly suitable. Equity can mold a decree which precludes the school district from ignoring the act. In fact, equity can be said to supply the *only* adequate and complete remedy available to appellee in this case. See Schrader v. Heath, 408 Pa. 79, 182 A.2d 696 (1962). Moreover, when the sustaining of preliminary objections will result in a denial of claim, or a dismissal of suit, preliminary objections should be sustained only in cases which are clear and free from doubt. Conrad v. Pittsburg, 421 Pa. 492, 218 A.2d 906 (1966); Baker v. Brennan, 419 Pa. 222, 213 A.2d 362 (1965); Schrader v. Heath, supra. . . .

The order of the court below dismissing the preliminary objections is affirmed. Each party to pay own costs.

COHEN, Justice (dissenting) :—I cannot agree with the majority because plaintiff-appellee has failed to state a cause of action. The only allegation of impropriety on the part of the school board is that in its budget the board provided for salary increases. Such allegation should not elicit the courts' intrusion into the local affairs of a school board as a "super board" or as a policeman. Members of the school board know that any illegal act will expose them to surcharge. We cannot restrain anticipated illegalities or improprieties on the mere allegation that a budget provides the funds for such anticipated improprieties. I would reverse the lower court and dismiss the complaint.

DURKIN v. BOARD OF POLICE AND FIRE COMMISSIONERS FOR THE CITY OF MADISON

Wisconsin Supreme Court
48 Wis. 112, 180 N.W.2d 1 (1970)

The Board of Police and Fire Commissioners for the City of Madison, Wisconsin, appellant, entered an order determining that Edward D. Durkin, respondent, had violated sec. 111.70 (4) (1), Stats., SLL 60:244, and certain rules of the fire department of the city of Madison, and thereupon suspended the respondent from the fire department. Respondent petitioned the circuit court for Dane County for review. The trial court entered judgment reversing the order of the Board and the Board has appealed from the judgment of the circuit court.

This action was commenced before the Board of Police and Fire Commissioners for the City of Madison, Wisconsin, upon a complaint of an elector of the city of Madison against Edward D. Durkin, a captain of the fire department for the city of Madison and president of the City Fire Fighters Union Local No. 311.

On March 27, 28 and 29, 1969, there occurred a strike by the firemen for the city of Madison. During this period negotiations were conducted between the city of Madison (City) and the Fire Fighters Union Local No. 311 (Union), which resulted in the signing of an agreement by the City and the Union and an end to the strike. The agreement included a clause whereby the Union and members of the fire department were granted amnesty for their activity in connection with the strike.

Following the settlement, an investigation of the strike was conducted by the appellant, but no charges were filed against any member of the fire department. Thereafter, on June 27, 1969, an elector of the city of Madison, filed a complaint with the appellant charging respondent with having counseled, abetted and led a strike by the Union, and with having participated in that strike by absenting himself from duty during his assigned hours. The complaint alleged that respondent was guilty of violating sec. 111.70 (4) (1), Stats., which prohibits strikes by municipal employees, and of "contumacious conduct endangering the public safety." A hearing on the complaint pursuant to sec. 62.13 (5), was requested.

A hearing on the complaint was conducted by appellant, and on August 24, 1969, an order was entered finding that respondent had participated in the strike and was guilty of violating sec. 111.70 (4) (1) , Stats., "contumacious conduct endangering the public safety," and of violating Rules 34, 89 and 100 of the Rules of the Fire Department of Madison, Wisconsin. Respondent was suspended from the fire department for a period of one hundred eighty days.

On petition of the respondent, the order was reviewed by the circuit court for Dane County. The court entered judgment reversing appellant's order on a finding that the order was affected by an error of law in that appellant did not consider itself bound by the terms of an amnesty clause in the collective bargaining agreement signed by the City and the Union. The circuit court held that the amnesty clause prevented appellant from suspending respondent and, therefore, ordered the respondent reinstated, with back pay. . . .

The collective bargaining agreement between the City and the Union included a clause by which the City agreed to dismiss all legal proceedings commenced by it and pending against the Union and its members, to waive all other causes of action arising out of the negotiations or the strike, and to refrain from directly or indirectly commencing an action that would in any way discipline any employee for participation in the strike.

The narrow issue presented by this case is whether the amnesty clause above referred to and contained in the collective bargaining agreement abrogates the statutory right of an elector to file a complaint with the appellant contained in sec. 62.13 (5) (b) , Stats. We are of the opinion that it does not.

The first paragraph of the agreement specifically refers to proceedings commenced by the City and to causes of action by the City. The filing of a complaint by an elector with the Board constitutes neither.

The second paragraph of the agreement recites, "Consistent with appropriate Wisconsin statutes, it is the express policy of the City that *it* will not directly or indirectly commence an action that will in any way discipline. . . ." (Emphasis added.)

It is the contention of the appellant that the processing of the elector's complaint by the appellant constitutes the City indirectly commencing an action to discipline the respondent. However, the elector has a statutory right to file charges and if the city council could somehow foreclose the right of the Board to process charges filed by the elector, it follows that the lawful right of an elector to file charges as provided in sec. 62.13 (5) (b) , Stats., would be rendered meaningless. The Board is required to process charges filed with it by an elector in accordance with the statutes of the State of Wisconsin and such rules and regulations as it may adopt which are not inconsistent therewith. The ultimate disposition by the Board of the charges so filed by an elector will be considered later in this opinion.

We find no authority which is particularly helpful on this issue and have considered all authorities advanced by both parties. Among other authorities, our attention has been directed to Muskego-Norway C.S.J. S.D. No. 9 v. W.E.R.B. (1967), 35 Wis. 2d 540, 151 N.W.2d 617, and Joint School Dist. No. 8 v. W.E.R.B. (1967), 37 Wis. 2d 483, 155 N.W.2d 78. Respondent advances an argument on the same principle as that adopted in Joint School Dist. No. 8 v. W.E.R.B., supra, that since sec. 111.70, Stats., was enacted subsequent to sec. 62.13 (5), the latter must yield to sec. 111.70 (4) (i), SLL 60:244, and thus a city may agree to a provision granting amnesty when entering into a binding, collective bargaining agreement pursuant to sec. 111.70 (4) (i) even though it would defeat the lawful right of an elector to file charges. The argument, however, assumes that sec. 111.70 (4) (i), does authorize a municipality to agree to an amnesty clause in a collective bargaining agreement which would abrogate the right of an elector to file charges. We find no authority to support such a position. . . .

We conclude that the case must be remanded to the Board for further proceedings for the reason that the respondent was not afforded due process.

Respondent had notice of and an opportunity to defend against charges that he was guilty of violating sec. 111.70 (4) (1), Stats., and of "contumacious conduct endangering the public safety." The charges filed by the elector against the respondent did not allege that he had violated any rules of the fire department. It appears the respondent had no notice of these alleged rule violations until it was pronounced by the Board that he had so violated the three rules in its written decision filed after the hearing. Due process of law requires that an individual have notice of and an opportunity to defend against charges proffered against him. In General Electric Co. v. Wisconsin E. R. Board (1958), 3 Wis. 2d 227, 241, 88 N.W.2d 691, 700, 42 LRRM 2187, 2192, this court held:

> "The principle of fair play is an important factor in a consideration of due process of law. Parties in a legal proceeding have a right to be apprised of the issues involved, and to be heard on such issues. A finding or order made in a proceeding in which there has not been a 'full hearing' is a denial of due process and is void. . . ."

No court of review has the means of determining whether the Board would have imposed the same penalty had it found the respondent in violation of only two of the violations charged in the complaint.

On this appeal, the respondent contends that based upon the evidence before it, the order of the Board was arbitrary and discriminatory and also unreasonable. However, this issue was not passed upon by the circuit court; and also in view of our remand to the Board for further proceedings because of the lack of due process, it is not properly raised in this court. Nevertheless, we would observe that the Board does have the authority to dismiss the complaint after it has been processed if, in its judgment it should determine such was a proper disposition of the charges filed by the elector. Also, should the Board decide further proceedings are necessary, on the basis of the record now before us, various factors should be taken into consideration by the Board in its ultimate decision. Among these are: (1) The amnesty clause in the agreement which unequivocally sets forth the position of the city council in its relation with the Union and its members; (2) the decision of the Board, as such, and its individual members, not to file charges against any fireman; and (3) the fact that the Board had knowledge of the fact that over 270 firemen participated in the strike and that no charges were filed against anyone except the respondent.

We reach our conclusions as to the disposition of this case upon different grounds than those considered by the circuit court. However, the effect of our decision is that the judgment of the circuit court which reverses the order of the Board of Police and Fire Commissioners is affirmed. That part of the judgment ordering the Madison fire department to forthwith reinstate the respondent, and that he be paid as though he had been in continuous service, is reversed, and the cause is remanded to the Board of Police and Fire Commissioners for further proceedings consistent with this opinion.

By the Court—Affirmed in part; reversed in part.

NOTES

1. The final result of the *Legman* case was a victory for the teachers and the school board. In Legman v. School Dist. of City of Scranton, 438 Pa. 157, 263 A.2d 370 (1970), the Pennsylvania Supreme Court held that, regardless of the legality of the initial action under the Pennsylvania Public Employees Anti-Strike Act of 1947, the school board's action in raising the salaries of teachers who had participated in the strike was ratified by the legislature by the passage of an amendment to the 1968

School Code, 43 PA. STAT. ANN. §§ 215.1 to 215.5. In 1970 the Public Employees Anti-Strike Act was repealed in large part by the Public Employee Relations Act, 43 PA. STAT. ANN. § 1101.101 *et seq.*, § 1101.2201 (Supp. 1972).

2. An important consideration raised in both the *Legman* and *Durkin* cases is the question of whether a statute designed to punish striking public employees is self-executing. If the statute is not self-executing, and the public employer chooses not to invoke the provisions of the statute, does a later invocation of the statute by a taxpayer violate the striking employee's right to due process? *Compare* the principal cases *with* Goldberg v. City of Cincinnati, 26 Ohio St. 228, 271 N.E.2d 284 (1971).

3. Is a taxpayer required to accept a public employer's findings of fact with respect to a violation of the law? In Head v. Special School Dist. No. 1, 80 L.R.R.M. 2459 (Minn. Dist. Ct. 1971), the court held that taxpayers seeking to enjoin a board of education from making illegal payments to striking teachers were entitled to an order requiring the teachers to give depositions as to their conduct during the strike. The taxpayers were entitled to determine for themselves whether the board acted arbitrarily in deciding that the teachers, who did not work during the period of the strike, were nonetheless not themselves on strike. *See also* Head v. Special School Dist. No. 1, 288 Minn. 496, 182 N.W.2d 887 (1970), where taxpayers were allowed to join with State Attorney General to challenge and upset a strike settlement agreement between school board and teachers' association.

4. Other courts are less willing to allow taxpayer intervention in the employer-employee relationship. In Wilson v. Evans, 70 L.R.R.M. 2094 (N.Y. Sup. Ct. 1968), an action was brought by parents and taxpayers seeking an injunction to prevent a school custodian from interfering with academic instruction by failing to provide custodial services. The court held that it was without jurisdiction to intervene in a purely administrative matter between a civil service employee and his employer. If the actions of the custodian are deemed to be a strike, the court said, school officials have the power to deal with them under the applicable state law.

Chapter 9

THE POLITICAL AND CIVIL RIGHTS OF PUBLIC EMPLOYEES

No study of labor relations law in the public sector would be complete without some analysis of the political and civil rights of public employees. The line that divides the "public" and the "private" employment sectors is frequently obscure. Nevertheless, partly because of certain overriding constitutional principles, the history of regulation of employment relations in the public sector in the United States has posed many special problems which have not been seen in the private sector. As Robert M. O'Neil so aptly noted in his book, *The Price of Dependency: Civil Liberties In The Welfare State,* 61-62 (1970):

> Much of what government can do *for* its own work force, it can also require private employers to do for their workers. The harder question remains, and will be the crux of this chapter: What can government do *to* its employees—what conditions and restrictions can it impose upon them—which it could not do to employees of private firms?

On the one hand, history has demonstrated that public employees in the United States may be made subject to rigid conditions of employment. The most familiar general restrictions on public employment relate to political activities and associations. However, several other types of employment restrictions have also proven to be controversial in the public service; among these have included loyalty oaths, bans on partisan political activities, reprisals for criticizing government officials or policies, and employment disabilities created by criminal records, personal appearance, sexual activity, private associations and deviant conduct.

On the other hand, although it is clear that the public employee may be burdened by special job conditions and restrictions, it is likewise clear that, as a public servant, the government worker cannot be saddled with unconstitutional conditions or restrictions of employment. Public workers, therefore, enjoy certain constitutional protections, privileges and rights which provide a framework for the regulation of employment relations in the government service. For example, constitutional issues concerning the freedom of association and expression, the privilege against self incrimination, due process as a protection against dismissal, and protections against race, sex, national origin and religious discrimination, have an important and direct bearing on employment relations law in the public sector.

Since these constitutional issues and related statutory applications are matters transcending labor relations law and collective bargaining in the public sector, they cannot be ignored. With this in mind, the following materials are presented to help the student of labor relations law in the public sector to comprehend some of the important legal principles, both constitutional and statutory, which affect the political and civil rights of public employees.

McAULIFFE v. MAYOR OF NEW BEDFORD, 155 Mass. 216, 29 N.E. 517 (1892) . In a decision written by Justice Oliver Wendell Holmes, the Massachusetts court upheld a city rule which prohibited policemen from joining labor unions. In reaching this conclusion, the court rendered its now famous dictum that:

> The petitioner may have a constitutional right to talk politics, but he has no constitutional right to be a policeman. There are few employments for hire in which the servant does not agree to suspend his constitutional right of free speech, as well as of idleness, by the implied terms of his contract. The servant cannot complain, as he takes the employment on the terms which are offered him.

O'NEIL, THE PRIVATE LIVES OF PUBLIC EMPLOYEES, 51 Ore. L. Rev. 70, 82-83 (1971)†

The public employee's legal status is vastly better today than at the time when Justice Holmes remarked that Officer McAuliffe might "have a constitutional right to talk politics, but . . . no right to be a policeman."[1] If it is true that the Supreme Court has never squarely relieved the government worker of Holmes' dilemma, one who enters the public service may still (save in California[2] and Oregon[3]) be compelled to steer clear of partisan politics.[4] But that is one of the few lacunae remaining from a time when public employment and other government benefits

---

† Reprinted by permission. Copyright © by The University of Oregon.

[1] McAuliffe v. New Bedford, 155 Mass. 216, 220, 29 N.E. 517 (1892).

[2] Bagley v. Washington Township Hosp. Dist., 65 Cal. 2d 499, 421 P.2d 409, 55 Cal. Rptr. 401 (1966); Fort v. Civil Serv. Comm'n, 61 Cal. 2d 331, 392 P.2d 385, 38 Cal. Rptr. 625 (1964).

[3] Minielly v. State, 242 Ore. 490, 411 P.2d 69 (1966).

[4] United Public Workers v. Mitchell, 330 U.S. 75 (1947). Despite a constant barrage from scholars and critics and growing pressures for reform

were classed as "privileges which could be conditioned, denied, or terminated as agency heads or legislators saw fit."

All that has changed. The principal catalyst for reform has been the recent development of the doctrine of unconstitutional conditions, applied with particular force to government employment.[5] Courts have consistently repudiated the notion that because government was under no legal obligation to offer employment to any person, it might therefore withhold such employment on arbitrary or discriminatory grounds or encumber public service with onerous and instrusive conditions. In a host of recent decisions, the Supreme Court has cautioned that "public employment . . . may [not] be conditioned upon the surrender of constitutional rights which could not be abridged by direct government action."[6]

A.   Restrictions and Privileges of Public Employment

1.   Loyalty Oaths

GARNER V. BOARD OF PUBLIC WORKS OF LOS ANGELES, 341 U.S. 716, 71 S. Ct. 909, 95 L. Ed. 1317 (1951). Held valid a municipal ordinance which required municipal employees, as a condition of employment, to sign an affidavit disclosing whether they were or ever had been a member of the Communist Party and to take an oath declaring that for five years prior to the effective date of the ordinance they did not advocate the overthrow of government by force or belong to any organization that advocated such doctrine. In upholding both the oath and affidavit portions of the ordinance, the Court ruled that it was not invalid as a bill of attainder and held further that "we are unable to conclude that punishment is imposed by a general regulation which merely provides standards of qualification and eligibility for employment." 341 U.S. at 722.

---

within the civil service, the Hatch Act survives. *See, e.g.,* Esman, *The Hatch Act: A Reappraisal,* 60 YALE L.J. 986 (1951); Nelson, *Public Employees and the Right to Engage in Political Activity,* 9 VAND. L. REV. 27 (1955); Rose, *A Critical Look at the Hatch Act,* 75 HARV. L. REV. 510 (1962); Note, *The Public Employee and Political Activity,* 3 SUFFOLK L. REV. 380 (1969).

[5] *See* especially the works of the two most thoughtful commentators on this development, Linde, *Justice Douglas on Liberty in the Welfare State: Constitutional Rights in the Public Sector,* 40 WASH. L. REV. 10 (1965); and Van Alstyne, *The Constitutional Rights of Public Employees: A Comment on the Inappropriate Uses of an Old Analogy,* 16 U.C.L.A.L. Rev. 751 (1969). For more specialized comments on a particular application of the doctrine, see O'Neil, *Public Employment, Antiwar Protest and Preinduction Review,* 17 U.C.L.A.L. REV. 1028 (1970).

[6] Keyishian v. Board of Regents, 385 U.S. 589, 605-06, 87 S. Ct. 675, 17 L. Ed. 2d 629 (1967).

BAGGETT V. BULLITT, 377 U.S. 360, 84 S. Ct. 1316, 12 L. Ed. 2d 377 (1960). Held unconstitutional two loyalty oaths required by the State of Washington: a "positive loyalty oath" imposed on teachers, making them subscribe that they "will by precept and example promote respect for the flag and [federal and state] institutions, reverence for law and order and undivided allegiance to the [federal] government;" and a "negative disclaimer" imposed on all state employees, requiring them to disclaim being a "subversive person" or members of a "subversive organization." "Subversive person" was defined pursuant to state law to mean "any person who commits, attempts to commit, or aids in the commission, or advocates, abets, advises or teaches by any means any person to commit, attempt to commit, or aids in the commission of any act intended to overthrow, destroy or alter [or 'to assist' in same] the constitutional form of . . . government . . . or with knowledge that the organization is [subversive] . . . becomes or remains a member of a subversive organization. . . ." "Subversive organization" was defined in similar terms under the state law and the Communist Party was declared subversive. The Court held, per Justice White writing for the majority, that "Persons required to swear they understand this oath may quite reasonably conclude that any person who aids the Communist Party or teaches or advises known members of the Party is a subversive person because such teaching or advice may now or at some future date aid the activities of the Party. Teaching and advising are clearly acts, and one cannot confidently assert that his counsel, aid, influence or support which adds to the resources, rights and knowledge of the Communist Party or its members does not aid the Party in its activities, activities which the statute tells us are all in furtherance of the stated purpose of overthrowing the Government by revolution, force, or violence."

The Court also indicated that the Washington statute was unconstitutionally vague.

> "A person is subversive not only if he himself commits the specified acts but if he abets or advises another in aiding a third person to commit an act which will assist yet a fourth person in the overthrow or alteration of constitutional government. The Washington Supreme Court has said that knowledge is to be read into every provision and we accept this construction. . . . But what is it that the Washington professor must 'know'? Must he know that his aid or teaching will be used by another and that the person aided has the requisite guilty intent or is it sufficient that he knows that his aid or teaching would or might be useful to others in the commission of acts intended to overthrow the Gov-

ernment? Is it subversive activity, for example, to attend and participate in international conventions of mathematicians and exchange views with scholars from Communist countries? . . .

"The Washington oath goes beyond overthrow or alteration by force or violence. It extends to alteration by 'revolution' which, unless wholly redundant and its ordinary meaning distorted, includes any rapid or fundamental change. Would, therefore, any organization or any person supporting, advocating or teaching peaceful but far-reaching constitutional amendments be engaged in subvervise activity?"

Finally, the Court ruled that the "positive loyalty oath" offended "due process because of vagueness." On this last point, the Court noted that: "The range of activities which are or might be deemed inconsistent with the required promise is very wide indeed. . . . The uncertain meanings of the oaths require the oath-taker—teachers and public servants—to 'steer far wider of the unlawful zone' . . . than if the boundaries of the forbidden areas were clearly marked. Those with a conscientious regard for what they solemnly swear or affirm, sensitive to the perils posed by the oath's indefinite language, avoid the risk of loss of employment, and perhaps profession, only by restricting their conduct to that which is unquestionably safe. Free speech may not be so inhibited."

ELFBRANDT v. RUSSELL, 384 U.S. 11, 86 S. Ct. 1238, 16 L. Ed. 2d 321 (1966). The Court invalidated an Arizona law which required an oath from state employees. The oath was the conventional one whereby the employee swore or affirmed that he would support the United States Constitution and the constitution and laws of the State of Arizona. However, the state legislature had put a gloss on the oath by subjecting to a prosecution for perjury and for discharge from public office anyone who took the oath and who "knowingly and willfully becomes or remains a member of the Communist Party of the United States . . ." or any other organization having for one of its purposes the overthrow of the government of Arizona. Petitioner, a public school teacher and a member of the Quaker faith, claimed that good conscience prevented her from taking the oath because she did not know what the oath meant and she had been unable to get a hearing at which the scope and definition of the oath could be determined. Petitioner thus brought a suit for declaratory relief. The Court held that the oath, as it had been construed by the state legislature, violated petitioner's right to freedom of association. The Court noted in particular that

the oath was overly broad because it applied to mere membership in the Communist Party, or to any subversive organization,
without requiring "the specific intent" to further the illegal
aims of the organization. Consequently, the oath was read to be
founded on the impermissible doctrine of "guilt by association."
The Court cited *Baggett* and held that a statute touching rights
protected by the First Amendment must be narrowly drawn, to
define and punish specific conduct as constituting a clear and
present danger to a substantial interest of the state. Mr. Justice
White, along with Justices Clark, Harlan and Stewart, dissented.
The dissenting opinion cited earlier Court opinions which had
indicated that a state is permitted to require its public employees, as a condition of employment, to abstain from knowing membership in organizations advocating the violent overthrow of government and that the state is constitutionally free
to inquire into such associations and to discharge those public
employees who decline to affirm or deny them.

NOTE

For an excellent analysis of the evolution of the law in this
area, see Israel, *Elfbrandt v. Russell—The Demise of the Oath?*,
1966 SUP. CT. REV. 193. *See also* Leahy, *Loyalty and the First
Amendment—A Concept Emerges*, 43 N.D.L. REV. 53 (1966);
Comment, 77 YALE L. J. 739 (1968).

KEYISHIAN v. BOARD OF REGENTS
Supreme Court of the United States
385 U.S. 589, 87 S. Ct. 675, 17 L. Ed. 2d 629 (1967)

MR. JUSTICE BRENNAN delivered the opinion of the Court.

Appellants were members of the faculty of the privately owned
and operated University of Buffalo, and became state employees
when the University was merged in 1962 into the State University of New York, an institution of higher education owned
and operated by the State of New York. As faculty members
of the State University their continued employment was conditioned upon their compliance with a New York plan, formulated partly in statutes and partly in administrative regulations,
which the State utilizes to prevent the appointment or retention
of "subversive" persons in state employment. . . .

[Each of the appellants] refused to sign, as regulations then
in effect required, a certificate that he was not a Communist,
and that if he had ever been a Communist, he had communicated that fact to the President of the State University of New
York. Each was notified that his failure to sign the certificate
would require his dismissal. . . .

Appellants brought this action for declaratory and injunctive relief, alleging that the state program violated the Federal Con stitution in various respects. . . .

We considered some aspects of the constitutionality of the New York plan 15 years ago in Adler v. Board of Education, 342 U.S. 485. That litigation arose after New York passed the Feinberg Law which added § 3022 to the Education Law. The Feinberg Law was enacted to implement and enforce two earlier statutes. The first was a 1917 law, now § 3021 of the Education Law, under which "the utterance of any treasonable or seditious word or words or the doing of any treasonable or seditious act" is a ground for dismissal from the public school system. The second was a 1939 law which was § 12-a of the Civil Service Law when *Adler* was decided and, as amended, is now § 105 of that law. This law disqualifies from the civil service and from employment in the educational system any person who advocates the overthrow of government by force, violence, or any unlawful means, or publishes material advocating such overthrow or organizes or joins any society or group of persons advocating such doctrine.

The Feinberg Law charged the State Board of Regents with the duty of promulgating rules and regulations providing procedures for the disqualification or removal of persons in the public school system who violate the 1917 law or who are ineligible for appointment to or retention in the public school system under the 1939 law. . . .

The Board of Regents thereupon promulgated rules and regulations containing procedures to be followed by appointing authorities to discover persons ineligible for appointment or retention under the 1939 law, or because of violation of the 1917 law. The Board also announced its intention to list "subversive" organizations after requisite notice and hearing, and provided that membership in a listed organization after the date of its listing should be regarded as constituting prima facie evidence of disqualification, and that membership prior to listing should be presumptive evidence that membership has continued, in the absence of a showing that such membership was terminated in good faith. Under the regulations, an appointing official is forbidden to make an appointment until after he has first inquired of an applicant's former employers and other persons to ascertain whether the applicant is disqualified or ineligible for appointment. In addition, an annual inquiry must be made to determine whether an appointed employee has ceased to be qualified for retention, and a report of findings must be filed.

Adler was a declaratory judgment suit in which the Court held, in effect, that there was no constitutional infirmity in former § 12-a or in the Feinberg Law on their faces and that they were capable of constitutional application. But the contention urged in this case that both § 3021 and § 105 are unconstitutionally vague was not heard or decided. . . .

Moreover, to the extent that *Adler* sustained the provision of the Feinberg Law constituting membership in an organization advocating forceful overthrow of government a ground for disqualification, pertinent constitutional doctrines have since rejected the premises upon which that conclusion rested. *Adler* is therefore not dispositive of the constitutional issues we must decide in this case. . . .

Section 3021 requires removal for "treasonable or seditious" utterances or acts. The 1958 amendment to § 105 of the Civil Service Law, now subdivision 3 of that section, added such utterances or acts as a ground for removal under that law also. The same wording is used in both statutes—that "the utterance of any treasonable or seditious word or words or the doing of any treasonable or seditious act or acts" shall be ground for removal. But there is a vital difference between the two laws. Section 3021 does not define the terms "treasonable or seditious" as used in that section; in contrast, subdivision 3 of § 105 of the Civil Service Law provides that the terms "treasonable word or act" shall mean "treason" as defined in the Penal Law and the terms "seditious word or act" shall mean "criminal anarchy" as defined in the Penal Law.

Our experience under the Sedition Act of 1798, 1 Stat. 596, taught us that dangers fatal to First Amendment freedoms inhere in the word "seditious." See New York Times Co. v. Sullivan, 376 U.S. 254, 273-276. And the word "treasonable," if left undefined, is no less dangerously uncertain. Thus it becomes important whether, despite the omission of a similar reference to the Penal Law in § 3021, the words as used in that section are to be read as meaning only what they mean in subdivision 3 of § 105. Or are they to be read more broadly and to constitute utterances or acts "seditious" and "treasonable" which would not be so regarded for the purposes of § 105?

Even assuming that "treasonable" and "seditious" in § 3021 and § 105, subd. 3, have the same meaning, the uncertainty is hardly removed. The definition of "treasonable" in the Penal Law presents no particular problem. The difficulty centers upon the meaning of "seditious." Subdivision 3 equates the term "seditious" with "criminal anarchy" as defined in the Penal Law. Is the reference only to Penal Law § 160, defining criminal anarchy as "the doctrine that organized government should be overthrown by force or violence, or by assassination of the executive head or of any of the executive officials of government, or by any unlawful means"? But that section ends with the sentence "The advocacy of such doctrine either by word of mouth or writing is a felony." Does that sentence draw into § 105, Penal Law § 161, proscribing "advocacy of criminal anarchy"? If so, the possible scope of "seditious" utterances or acts has virtually no limit. For under Penal Law § 161, one commits the felony of advocating criminal anarchy if he ". . . publicly displays any book . . . containing or advocating, advising or teaching the doctrine that organized government should be overthrown by force, violence or any unlawful means." Does the teacher who carries a copy of the Communist Manifesto on a public street thereby advocate criminal anarchy? It is no answer to say that the statute would not be applied in such a case. We cannot gainsay the potential effect of this obscure wording on "those with a conscientious and scrupulous regard for such undertakings." Baggett v. Bullitt, 377 U.S. 360, 374. . . . The crucial consideration is that no teacher can know just where the line is drawn between "seditious" and nonseditious utterances and acts.

Other provisions of § 105 also have the same defect of vagueness. Subdivision 1 (a) of § 105 bars employment of any person who "by word of mouth or writing wilfully and deliberately advocates, advises or teaches the doctrine" of forceful overthrow of government. This provision is plainly susceptible of sweeping and improper application. It may well prohibit the employment of one who merely advocates the doctrine in the abstract without any attempt to indoctrinate others, or incite others to action in furtherance of unlawful aims. See Herndon v. Lowry, 301 U.S. 242; Yates v. United States, 354 U.S. 298; Noto v. United States, 367 U.S. 290; Scales v. United States, 367 U.S. 203. And in prohibiting "advising" the "doctrine" of unlawful overthrow does the statute prohibit mere "advising" of the existence of the doctrine, or advising another to support the doctrine? Since "advocacy" of the doctrine of forceful overthrow is separately prohibited, need the person "teaching" or "advising" this doctrine himself "advocate" it? Does the teacher who informs his class about the precepts of Marxism or the Declaration of Independence violate this prohibition?

Similar uncertainty arises as to the application of subdivision 1 (b) of § 105. That subsection requires the disqualification of an employee involved with the distribution of written material "containing or advocating, advising or teaching the doctrine" of forceful overthrow, and who himself "advocates, advises, teaches, or embraces the duty, necessity or propriety of adopting the doctrine contained therein." Here again, mere advocacy of abstract doctrine is apparently included. . . .

Like the language of § 105, subd. 1 (a), this language may reasonably be construed to cover mere expression of belief. For example, does the university librarian who recommends the reading of such materials thereby "advocate . . . the . . . propriety of adopting the doctrine contained therein"?

We do not have the benefit of a judicial gloss by the New York courts enlightening us as to the scope of this complicated plan. In light of the intricate administrative machinery for its enforcement, this is not surprising. The very intricacy of the plan and the uncertainty as to the scope of its proscriptions make it a highly efficient *in terrorem* mechanism. It would be a bold teacher who would not stay as far as possible from utterances or acts which might jeopardize his living by enmeshing him in this intricate machinery. . . .

The result must be to stifle "that free play of the spirit which all teachers ought especially to cultivate and practice. . . ." That probability is enhanced by the provisions requiring an annual review of every teacher to determine whether any utterance or act of his, inside the classroom or out, came within the sanctions of the laws. . . .

There can be no doubt of the legitimacy of New York's interest in protecting its education system from subversion. But "even though the governmental purpose be legitimate and substantial, that purpose cannot be pursued by means that broadly stifle fundamental personal liberties when the end can be more narrowly achieved." Shelton v. Tucker, 364 U.S. 479, 488. . . .

Our Nation is deeply committed to safeguarding academic freedom, which is of transcendent value to all of us and not merely to the teachers concerned. That freedom is therefore a special concern of the First Amendment, which does not tolerate laws that cast a pall of orthodoxy over the classroom. . . .

We emphasize once again that "[p]recision of regulation must be the touchstone in an area so closely touching our most precious freedoms," N.A.A.C.P. v. Button, 371 U.S. 415, 438; "[f]or standards of permissible statutory vagueness are strict in the area of free expression. . . . Because First Amendment freedoms need breathing space to survive, government may regulate in the area only with narrow specificity." *Id.*, at 432-433. New York's complicated and intricate scheme plainly violates that standard. When one must guess what conduct or utterance may lose him his position, one necessarily will "steer far wider of the unlawful zone. . . ." Speiser v. Randall, 357 U.S. 513, 526.

For "[t]he threat of sanctions may deter . . . almost as potently as the actual application of sanctions." . . .

The regulatory maze created by New York is wholly lacking in "terms susceptible of objective measurement." . . . Vagueness of wording is aggravated by prolixity and profusion of statutes, regulations, and administrative machinery, and by manifold cross-references to interrelated enactments and rules.

We therefore hold that § 3021 of the Education Law and sub-divisions 1 (a), 1 (b) and 3 of § 105 of the Civil Service Law as implemented by the machinery created pursuant to § 3022 of the Education Law are unconstitutional.

Appellants have also challenged the constitutionality of the discrete provisions of subdivision 1 (c) of § 105 and subdivision 2 of the Feinberg Law, which make Communist Party member-ship, as such, prima facie evidence of disqualification. . . . Subdivision 2 of the Feinberg Law was, however, before the Court in *Adler* and its constitutionality was sustained. But con-stitutional doctrine which has emerged since that decision has rejected its major premise. That premise was that public em-ployment, including academic employment, may be conditioned upon the surrender of constitutional rights which could not be abridged by direct government action. Teachers, the Court said in *Adler*, "may work for the school system upon the reasonable terms laid down by the proper authorities of New York. If they do not choose to work on such terms, they are at liberty to retain their beliefs and associations and go elsewhere." . . .

However . . . "the theory that public employment which may be denied altogether may be subjected to any conditions, regard-less of how unreasonable, has been uniformly rejected." Keyishian v. Board of Regents, 345 F.2d 236, 239. . . .

We proceed then to the question of the validity of the provi-sions of subdivision 1 (c) of § 105 and subdivision 2 of § 3022, barring employment to members of listed organizations. Here again constitutional doctrine has developed since *Adler*. Mere knowing membership without a specific intent to further the unlawful aims of an organization is not a constitutionally ade-quate basis for exclusion from such positions as those held by appellants. . . .

Elfbrandt and *Aptheker* state the governing standard: legisla-tion which sanctions membership unaccompanied by specific in-tent to further the unlawful goals of the organization or which is not active membership violates constitutional limitations.

Measured against this standard, both Civil Service Law § 105, subd. 1 (c), and Education Law § 3022, subd. 2, sweep over-broadly into association which may not be proscribed. The presumption of disqualification arising from proof of mere membership may be rebutted, but only by (a) a denial of membership, (b) a denial that the organization advocates the overthrow of government by force, or (c) a denial that the teacher has knowledge of such advocacy. . . .

Thus proof of nonactive membership or a showing of the absence of intent to further unlawful aims will not rebut the presumption and defeat dismissal. This is emphasized in official administrative interpretations. . . .

The Feinberg Certificate was even more explicit: "Anyone who is a *member* of the Communist Party or of any organization that advocates the violent overthrow of the Government of the United States or of the State of New York or any political subdivision thereof cannot be employed by the State University." . . .

Thus § 105, subd. 1 (c), and § 3022, subd. 2, suffer from impermissible "overbreadth." . . . They seek to bar employment both for association which legitimately may be proscribed and for association which may not be proscribed consistently with First Amendment rights. . . .

We therefore hold that Civil Service Law § 105, subd. 1 (c), and Education Law § 3022, subd. 2, are invalid insofar as they proscribe mere knowing membership. . . .

MR. JUSTICE CLARK, with whom MR. JUSTICE HARLAN, MR. JUSTICE STEWART and MR. JUSTICE WHITE join, dissenting. . . .

It is clear that the Feinberg Law, in which this Court found "no constitutional infirmity" in 1952, has been given its death blow today. Just as the majority here finds that there "can be no doubt of the legitimacy of New York's interest in protecting its education system from subversion" there can also be no doubt that "the be-all and end-all" of New York's effort is here. And, regardless of its correctness, neither New York nor the several States that have followed the teaching of Adler v. Board of Education, 342 U.S. 485, for some 15 years, can ever put the pieces together again. No court has ever reached out so far to destroy so much with so little. . . .

[I]n 1952, in Adler v. Board of Education, *supra,* this Court passed upon the identical statute condemned here. It, too, was a declaratory judgment action—as in this case. However, there the issues were not so abstractly framed. Our late Brother Minton wrote for the Court:

"A teacher works in a sensitive area in a schoolroom. There he shapes the attitude of young minds towards the society in which they live. In this, the state has a vital concern.

It must preserve the integrity of the schools. That the school authorities have the right and the duty to screen the officials, teachers, and employees as to their fitness to maintain the integrity of the schools as a part of ordered society, cannot be doubted." At 493.

And again in 1958 the problem was before us in Beilan v. Board of Education, *supra*. There our late Brother Burton wrote for the Court:

"By engaging in teaching in the public schools, petitioner did not give up his right to freedom of belief, speech or association. He did, however, undertake obligations of frankness, candor and cooperation in answering inquiries made of him by his employing Board examining into his fitness to serve it as a public school teacher." 357 U.S., at 405.

And on the same day in Lerner v. Casey, 357 U.S. 468, our Brother HARLAN again upheld the severance of a public employee for his refusal to answer questions concerning his loyalty. And also on the same day my Brother BRENNAN himself cited *Garner* with approval in Speiser v. Randall, 357 U.S. 513 (1958).

Since that time the *Adler* line of cases has been cited again and again with approval: Shelton v. Tucker, 364 U.S. 479 (1960), in which both *Adler* and *Beilan* were quoted with approval, and *Garner* and *Lerner* were cited in a like manner; likewise in Cramp v. Board of Public Instruction, 368 U.S. 278 (1961), *Adler* was quoted twice with approval; and, in a related field where the employee was discharged for refusal to answer questions as to his loyalty after being ordered to do so, Nelson v. Los Angeles County, 362 U.S. 1 (1960), the Court cited with approval all of the cases which today it says have been rejected, *i.e.*, *Garner, Adler, Beilan* and *Lerner*. Later Konigsberg v. State Bar, 366 U.S. 36 (1961), likewise cited with approval both *Beilan* and *Garner*. And in our decision in *In re* Anastaplo, 366 U.S. 82 (1961), *Garner, Beilan* and *Lerner* were all referred to. Finally, only three Terms ago my Brother WHITE relied upon *Cramp,* which in turn cited *Adler* with approval twice. See Baggett v. Bullitt, 377 U.S. 360 (1964).

In view of this long list of decisions covering over 15 years of this Court's history, in which no opinion of this Court even questioned the validity of the *Adler* line of cases, it is strange to me that the Court now finds that the "constitutional doctrine which has emerged since . . . has rejected [*Adler's*] major premise." With due respect, as I read them, our cases have done no such thing. . . .

But even if *Adler* did not decide these questions I would be obliged to answer them in the same way. The only portion of the Feinberg Law which the majority says was not covered there and is applicable to appellants is § 105, subd. 1 (a), 1 (b) and 1 (c). These have to do with teachers who advocate, advise, or teach the doctrine of overthrow of our Government by force and violence, either orally or in writing. This was the identical conduct that was condemned in Dennis v. United States, [341 U.S. 494 (1951)]. There the Court found the exact verbiage not to be unconstitutionally vague, and that finding was of course not affected by the decision of this Court in Yates v. United States, 354 U.S. 298. . . .

The majority says that the Feinberg Law is bad because it has an "overbroad sweep." I regret to say—and I do so with deference—that the majority has by its broadside swept away one of our most precious rights, namely, the right of self-preservation. Our public educational system is the genius of our democracy. The minds of our youth are developed there and the character of that development will determine the future of our land. Indeed, our very existence depends upon it. The issue here is a very narrow one. It is not freedom of speech, freedom of thought, freedom of press, freedom of assembly, or of association, even in the Communist Party. It is simply this: May the State provide that one who, after a hearing with full judicial review, is found to have wilfully and deliberately advocated, advised, or taught that our Government should be overthrown by force or violence or other unlawful means; or to have wilfully and deliberately printed, published, etc., any book or paper that so advocated *and to have personally* advocated such doctrine himself; or to have wilfully and deliberately become a member of an organization that advocates such doctrine, is prima facie disqualified from teaching in its university? My answer, in keeping with all of our cases up until today, is "Yes"!

I dissent.

CONNELL v. HIGGINBOTHAM

Supreme Court of the United States
403 U.S. 207, 91 S. Ct. 1772, 29 L. Ed. 2d 418 (1971)

PER CURIAM.

This is an appeal from an action . . . challenging the constitutionality of . . . various loyalty oaths upon which appellant's employment as a school teacher was conditioned.

The three-judge U.S. District Court declared three of the

five clauses contained in the oaths to be unconstitutional,* and enjoined the State from conditioning employment on the taking of an oath including the language declared unconstitutional. The appeal is from that portion of the District Court decision, 305 F. Supp. 445, which upheld the remaining two clauses in the oath: I do hereby solemnly swear or affirm (1) "that I will support the Constitution of the United States and of the State of Florida"; and (2) "that I do not believe in the overthrow of the Government of the United States or of the State of Florida by force or violence." . . . Appellant was dismissed from her teaching position on March 18, 1969, for refusing to sign the loyalty oath required of all Florida public employees, Fla. Stat. § 876.05.

The first section of the oath upheld by the District Court, requiring all applicants to pledge to support the Constitution of the United States and of the State of Florida, demands no more of Florida public employees than is required of all state and federal officers. U.S. Const., Art. VI, cl. 3. The validity of this section of the oath would appear settled. . . . The second portion of the oath, approved by the District Court, falls within the ambit of decisions of this Court proscribing summary dismissal from public employment without hearing or inquiry required by due process. Slochower v. Board of Education, 350 U.S. 551, 76 S. Ct. 637, 100 L. Ed. 692 (1956) . . . .

Mr. Justice MARSHALL, with whom Mr. Justice DOUGLAS and Mr. Justice BRENNAN join, concurring in the result.

I agree that Florida may require state employees to affirm that they "will support the Constitution of the United States and of the State of Florida." Such a forward-looking, promissory oath of constitutional support does not in my view offend the First Amendment's command that the grant or denial of governmental benefits cannot be made to turn on the political viewpoints or affiliations of a would-be beneficiary. I also agree that Florida may not base its employment decisions, as to state teachers or any other hiring category, on an applicant's willingness *vel non* to affirm "that I do not believe in the overthrow of the Government of the United States or of the State of Florida by force or violence."

---

* The clauses declared unconstitutional by the court below required the employee to swear: (a) "that I am not a member of the Communist Party"; (b) "that I have not and will not lend my aid, support, advice, counsel or influence to the Communist Party"; and (c) "that I am not a member of any organization or party which believes in or teaches, directly or indirectly, the overthrow of the Government of the United States or of Florida by force or violence."

However, in striking down the latter oath, the Court has left the clear implication that its objection runs, not against Florida's determination to exclude those who "believe in the overthrow," but only against the State's decision to regard unwillingness to take the oath as conclusive, irrebuttable proof of the proscribed belief. Due process may rightly be invoked to condemn Florida's mechanistic approach to the question of proof. But in my view it simply does not matter what kind of evidence a State can muster to show that a job applicant "believe[s] in the overthrow." For state action injurious to an individual cannot be justified on account of the nature of the individual's beliefs, whether he "believe[s] in the overthrow" or has any other sort of belief. "If there is any fixed star in our constitutional constellation, it is that no official, high or petty, can prescribe what shall be orthodox in politics, nationalism, religion, or other matters of opinion. . . ." West Virginia State Board of Education v. Barnette, 319 U.S. 624, 642, 63 S. Ct. 1178, 1187, 87 L. Ed. 1628 (1943).

I would strike down Florida's "overthrow" oath plainly and simply on the ground that belief as such cannot be the predicate of governmental action.

COLE v. RICHARDSON
Supreme Court of the United States
405 U.S. 676, 92 S. Ct. 1332, 31 L. Ed. 2d 593 (1972)

MR. CHIEF JUSTICE BURGER delivered the opinion of the Court.

In this appeal we review the decision of the three-judge District Court holding a Massachusetts loyalty oath unconstitutional, 300 F. Supp. 1321. . . .

[Appellee], Mrs. Richardson, was asked to subscribe to the oath required of all public employees in Massachusetts. The oath is as follows:

"I do solemnly swear (or affirm) that I will uphold and defend the Constitution of the United States of America and the Constitution of the Commonwealth of Massachusetts and that I will oppose the overthrow of the government of the United States of America or of this Commonwealth by force, violence or by any illegal or unconstitutional method."
. . .

[Appellee was advised that she could not continue as an employee of the Boston State Hospital unless she subscribed to the oath. When she refused to comply, her employment was terminated.] . . .

A three-judge District Court held the oath statute unconstitutional and enjoined the appellant from applying the statute to prohibit Mrs. Richardson from working for Boston State Hospital. The District Court found the attack on the "uphold and defend" clause, the first part of the oath, foreclosed by Knight v. Board of Regents, 269 F. Supp. 339 (S.D.N.Y. 1967), affirmed, 390 U.S. 36, 88 S. Ct. 816, 19 L. Ed. 2d 812 (1968). But it found that the "oppose and overthrow" clause was "fatally vague and unspecific," and therefore a violation of First Amendment rights. The court granted the requested injunction but denied the claim for damages. . . .

We conclude that the Massachusetts oath is constitutionally permissible. . . .

A review of the oath cases in this Court will put the instant oath into context. We have made clear that neither federal nor state governments may condition employment on taking oaths which impinge rights guaranteed by the First and Fourteenth Amendments respectively, as for example those relating to political beliefs. . . . Nor may employment be conditioned on an oath that one has not engaged, or will not engage, in protected speech activities such as the following: criticizing institutions of government; discussing political doctrine that approves the overthrow of certain forms of government; and supporting candidates for political office. Keyishian v. Board of Regents, 385 U.S. 589, 87 S. Ct. 675, 17 L. Ed. 2d 629 (1967); Baggett v. Bullitt, 377 U.S. 360, 84 S. Ct. 1316, 12 L. Ed. 2d 377 (1964); Cramp v. Board of Public Instruction, 368 U.S. 278, 82 S. Ct. 275, 7 L. Ed. 2d 285 (1961). Employment may not be conditioned on an oath denying past, or abjuring future, associational activities within constitutional protection; such protected activities include membership in organizations having illegal purposes unless one knows of the purpose and shares a specific intent to promote the illegal purpose. Whitehill v. Elkins, 389 U.S. 54, 88 S. Ct. 184, 19 L. Ed. 2d 228 (1967); Keyishian v. Board of Regents, *supra;* Elfbrandt v. Russell, 384 U.S. 11, 86 S. Ct. 1238, 16 L. Ed. 2d 321 (1966); Wieman v. Updegraff, 344 U.S. 183, 73 S. Ct. 215, 97 L. Ed. 216 (1952). . . . And, finally, an oath may not be so vague that " 'men of common intelligence must necessarily guess at its meaning and differ as to its application, [because such an oath] violates the first essential of due process of law.' " Cramp v. Board of Public Instruction, 368 U.S., at 287, 82 S. Ct. at 280. . . .

An underlying, seldom articulated concern running throughout these cases is that the oaths under consideration often required individuals to reach back into their pasts to recall minor, sometimes innocent, activities. They put the government into "the censorial business of investigating, scrutinizing, interpreting, and then penalizing or approving the political viewpoint" and past activities of individuals. Law Students Civil Rights Research Council v. Wadmond, 401 U.S., at 192, 91 S. Ct. at 740 (Marshall, J., concurring).

Several cases recently decided by the Court stand out among our oath cases because they have upheld the constitutionality of oaths, addressed to the future, promising constitutional support in broad terms. These cases have begun with a recognition that the Constitution itself prescribes comparable oaths in two articles. Article II, §1, cl. 7, provides that the President shall swear that he will "faithfully execute the office . . . and will to the best of my ability preserve, protect and defend the Constitution of the United States." Article VI, cl. 3, provides that all state and federal officers shall be bound by an oath "to support this Constitution." . . .

Bond v. Floyd, 385 U.S. 116, 87 S. Ct. 339, 17 L. Ed. 2d 235 (1966), involved Georgia's statutory requirement that state legislators swear to "support the Constitution of this State and of the United States," a paraphrase of the constitutionally required oath. The Court there implicitly concluded that the First Amendment did not undercut the validity of the constitutional oath provisions. Although in theory the First Amendment might have invalidated those provisions, approval of the amendment by the same individuals who had included the oaths in the Constitution suggested strongly that they were consistent. The Court's recognition of this consistency did not involve a departure from its many decisions striking down oaths which infringed First and Fourteenth Amendment rights. The Court read the Georgia oath as calling simply for an acknowledgment of a willingness to abide by "constitutional processes of government." 385 U.S., at 135, 87 S. Ct. 339, 349, 17 L. Ed. 2d 235. . . .

Although disagreeing on other points, in *Wadmond, supra,* all members of the Court agreed on this point. Mr. Justice Marshall noted there, while dissenting as to other points,

"The oath of constitutional support requires an individual assuming public responsibilities to affirm . . . that he will endeavor to perform his public duties lawfully." 401 U.S., at 192, 91 S. Ct. at 740.

The Court has further made clear that an oath need not parrot the exact language of the constitutional oaths to be constitutionally proper. Thus in Ohlson v. Phillips, 397 U.S. 317, 90 S. Ct. 1124, 25 L. Ed. 2d 337 (1970), we sustained the constitutionality of a state requirement that teachers swear to "uphold" the Constitution. . . . The District Court in the instant case properly recognized that the first clause of the Massachusetts oath, in which the individual swears to "uphold and defend" the constitutions of the United States and the Commonwealth, is indistinguishable from the oaths this Court has recently approved. Yet the District Court applied a highly literalistic approach to the second clause to strike it down. We view the second clause of the oath as essentially the same as the first.

The second clause of the oath contains a promise to "oppose the overthrow of the government of the United States of America or of this Commonwealth by force, violence or by any illegal or unconstitutional method." The District Court sought to give a dictionary meaning to this language and found "oppose" to raise the specter of vague, undefinable responsibilities actively to combat a potential overthrow of the government. That reading of the oath understandably troubled the court because of what it saw as vagueness in terms of what threats would constitute sufficient danger of overthrow to require the oath-giver to actively oppose overthrow, and exactly what actions he would have to take in that respect. . . . We have rejected such rigidly literal notions and recognized that the purpose leading legislatures to enact such oaths, just as the purpose leading the Framers of our Constitution to include the two explicit constitutional oaths, was not to create specific responsibilities but to assure that those in positions of public trust were willing to commit themselves to live by the constitutional processes of our system as Mr. Justice Marshall suggested in *Wadmond*, 401 U.S., at 192, 91 S. Ct. 720. Here the second clause does not require specific action in some hypothetical or actual situation. Plainly "force, violence or . . . any illegal or unconstitutional method" modifies "overthrow" and does not commit the oath taker to meet force with force. Just as the connotatively active word "support" has been interpreted to mean simply a commitment to abide by our constitutional system, the second clause of this oath is merely oriented to the negative implication of this notion; it is a commitment not to use illegal and constitutionally unprotected force to change the constitutional system. The second clause does not expand the obligation of the first; it simply makes clear the application of the first clause to a particular issue. Such repetition, whether for emphasis or cadence, seems to be wont with authors of oaths. That the second clause may be redundant is no ground to strike it down; we are not charged with correcting grammar but with enforcing a constitution.

The purpose of the oath is clear on its face. We cannot presume that the Massachusetts legislature intended by its use of such general terms as "uphold," "defend," and "oppose" to impose obligations of specific, positive action on oath takers. Any such construction would raise serious questions whether the oath was so vague as to amount to a denial of due process. . . . Nor is the oath as interpreted void for vagueness. . . . It is punishable only by a prosecution for perjury and, since perjury is a knowing and willful falsehood, the constitutional vice of punishment without fair warning cannot occur here. Nor here is there any problem of the punishment inflicted by mere prosecution. See Cramp v. Board of Public Instruction, 368 U.S., at 284, 82 S. Ct. at 279, 7 L. Ed. 2d 285. There has been no prosecution under this statute since its 1948 enactment, and there is no indication that prosecutions have been planned or begun. The oath "triggered no serious possibility of prosecution" by the Commonwealth. Were we confronted with a record of actual prosecutions or harassment through threatened prosecutions, we might be faced with a different question. . . .

Appellee mounts an additional attack on the Massachusetts oath program in that it does not provide for a hearing prior to the determination not to hire the individual based on the refusal to subscribe to the oath. All of the cases in this Court which require a hearing before discharge for failure to take an oath involved impermissible oaths. In Slochower v. Board of Education, 350 U.S. 551, 76 S. Ct. 637, 100 L. Ed. 692 (1956) (not an oath case), the State sought to dismiss a professor for claiming the Fifth Amendment privilege in a United States Senate committee hearing; the Court held the State's action invalid because the exercise of the privilege was a constitutional right from which the State could not draw any rational inference of disloyalty. Appellee relies on Nostrand v. Little, 362 U.S. 474, 80 S. Ct. 840, 4 L. Ed. 2d 892 (1960), and Connell v. Higginbotham, 403 U.S. 207, 91 S. Ct. 1772, 29 L. Ed. 2d 418 (1971), but in those cases the Court held only that the mere refusal to take the particular oath was not a constitutionally permissible basis for termination. In the circumstances of those cases only by holding a hearing, showing evidence of disloyalty, and allowing the employee an opportunity to respond might the State develop a permissible basis for concluding that the employee was to be discharged.

Since there is no constitutionally protected right to overthrow a government by force, violence, or illegal or unconstitutional means, no constitutional right is infringed by an oath to abide by the constitutional system in the future. Therefore there is no requirement that one who refuses to take the Massachusetts oath be granted a hearing for the determination of some other fact before being discharged.

The judgment of the District Court is reversed and the case is remanded for further proceedings consistent with this opinion.

Mr. Justice DOUGLAS, dissenting.

The part of the oath that says "I will oppose the overthrow of the government of the United States of America or of this Commonwealth by force, violence or by any illegal or unconstitutional method" is plainly unconstitutional by our decisions. See Board of Education v. Barnette, 319 U.S. 624, 634, 63 S. Ct. 1178, 87 L. Ed. 1628.

Advocacy of basic fundamental changes in Government, which might popularly be described as "overthrow," is within the protection of the First Amendment even when it is restrictively construed. . . . The same idea was put in somewhat different words in Noto v. United States, 367 U.S. 290, 297-298, 81 S. Ct. 1517, 1521, 6 L. Ed. 2d 836 that "abstract teaching" of overthrow is protected activity as contrasted to "preparing a group for violent action and steeling it to such action." . . . And see Yates v. United States, 354 U.S. 298, 318, 77 S. Ct. 1064, 1076, 1 L. Ed. 2d 1356.

The present oath makes such advocacy a possible offense under a restrictive reading of the First Amendment.

The views expressed by Mr. Justice Black and me give the First Amendment a more expansive reading. We have condemned loyalty oaths as "manifestation[s] of a national network of laws aimed at coercing and controlling the minds of men. Test oaths are notorious tools of tyranny. When used to shackle the mind they are, or at least should be, unspeakably odious to a free people." Wieman v. Updegraff, 344 U.S. 183, 193, 73 S. Ct. 215, 220, 97 L. Ed. 216 (1952) (Black, J., concurring) . . . .

The line between the permissible control by a State and the impermissible control is "the line between ideas and overt acts." . . . "The First Amendment . . . leaves the way wide open for people to favor, discuss, advocate, or incite causes and doctrines however obnoxious and antagonistic such views may be to the rest of us." . . . This oath, however, requires that appellee "oppose" that which she has an indisputable right to advocate. Yet the majority concludes that the promise of "opposition"—exacted as a condition of public employment—is a mere redundancy which does not impair appellee's freedom of expression[3] . . .

---

[3] . . . If the oath is void for vagueness or overbreadth, it is because the common meaning of its words is so imprecise or so far-reaching as to place a "chilling effect" upon constitutionally protected expression. This vice—readily apparent in the present oath—is emphasized rather than avoided by the majority's opinion. The tortured route which the majority takes to give

Mr. Justice MARSHALL, with whom Mr. Justice BRENNAN joins, dissenting. . . .

It is the second half of the oath to which I object. I find the language "I will oppose the overthrow of the government of the United States of America or of this Commonwealth by force, violence or any illegal or unconstitutional method" to be impermissibly vague and overbroad. . . .

The most striking problem with the oath is that it is not clear whether the last prepositional phrase modifies the verb "oppose" or the noun "overthrow." Thus, an affiant cannot be certain whether he is swearing that he will "oppose" governmental overthrow by utilizing every means at his disposal, including those specifically prohibited by the laws or constitutions he has sworn to support, or whether he has merely accepted the responsibility of opposing illegal or unconstitutional overthrows. The first reading would almost surely be unconstitutional since it is well established that a State cannot compel a citizen to waive the rights guaranteed him by the Constitution in order to obtain employment. . . . This reading would also make the second half of the oath inconsistent with the first half. It is far from clear to me which reading the Massachusetts Legislature intended. A reasonable man could certainly read the oath either way, and the State has not offered to make a binding clarification of its purport.

Even assuming that the second reading were unconditionally adopted by the State and communicated to prospective employees, the vice of vagueness is still not cured, for the affiant is left with little guidance as to the responsibilities he has assumed in taking the oath. In what form, for example, must he manifest his opposition to an overthrow? At oral argument in the District Court, the State's attorney asserted that citizens have three standards of obligation to their government to oppose overthrows:

> "The ordinary citizen who has taken no oath has an obligation to act *in extremis;* a person who has taken the first part of the present oath would have a somewhat larger obligation, and one who has taken the second part has one still larger." 300 F. Supp. 1321, at 1322.

I agree with the conclusion of the District Court that "[t]he very fact that such varied standards . . . can be suggested is enough to condemn the language as hopelessly vague." *Id.,* at 1323. . . .

---

this oath a supposedly constitutional interpretation merely emphasizes the unconstitutional effect those words would have were they to be given their natural meaning.

The Court's prior decisions represent a judgment that simple affirmative oaths of support are less suspect and less evil than negative oaths requiring a disaffirmance of political ties, group affiliations, or beliefs. Compare Connell v. Higginbotham, 403 U.S. 207, 91 S. Ct. 1772, 29 L. Ed. 2d 418 (1971); . . . with Whitehill v. Elkins, *supra;* Baggett v. Bullitt, *supra;* Cramp v. Board of Public Instruction, 368 U.S. 278, 82 S. Ct. 275, 7 L. Ed. 2d 285 (1961); Speiser v. Randall, 357 U.S. 513 (1958). . . .

Yet, I think that it is plain that affirmative oaths of loyalty, no less than negative ones, have odious connotations and that they present dangers. See Asper, The Long and Unhappy History of Loyalty Testing in Maryland, 13 Am. J. Leg. Hist. 97, 104 (1969); Askin, Loyalty Oaths in Retrospect; Freedom and Reality, 1968 Wis. L. Rev. 498, 502; Note, Loyalty Oaths, 77 Yale L.J. 739, 763 (1968). We have tolerated support oaths as applied to all government employees only because we view these affirmations as an expression of "minimal loyalty to the Government." . . . That they are minimal intrusions into the freedom of government officials and employees to think, speak, and act makes them constitutional; it does not mean that greater intrusions will be tolerated. On the contrary, each time this Court has been faced with an attempt by government to make the traditional support oath more comprehensive or demanding, it has struck the oath down. See, *e.g.,* Connell v. Higginbotham, *supra;* Baggett v. Bullitt, *supra;* cf. Bond v. Floyd, 385 U.S. 116, 87 S. Ct. 339, 17 L. Ed. 2d 235 (1966).

When faced with an "imminent clear and present danger," governments may be able to compel citizens to do things which would ordinarily be beyond their authority to mandate. But, such emergency governmental power is a far cry from compelling every state employee in advance of any such danger to promise in any and all circumstances to conform speech and conduct to opposing an "overthrow" of the government. The Constitution severely circumscribes the power of government to force its citizens to perform symbolic gestures of loyalty. . . .

NOTES

1. Does the majority opinion in *Cole* reflect a somewhat strained effort to save the challenged oath from constitutional infirmity? Is the rationale in *Cole* consistent with the approach taken in United States v. Robel, 389 U.S. 258, 88 S. Ct. 419, 19 L. Ed. 2d 508 (1967)? In *Robel*, section 5 (a) (1) (D) of the Subversive Activities Control Act of 1950—which imposed criminal sanctions on any member of a Communist action group who en-

gaged in employment in a defense facility—was declared to be unconstitutional for want of clarity and precision. In *Robel,* the Court refused to save the challenged statute from constitutional infirmity by limiting its application to active members of Communist action organizations who had the specific intent of furthering the unlawful goals of the organizations.

2. For some useful comments on the general subject of loyalty oaths and related topics, see Bruff, *Unconstitutional Conditions upon Public Employment: New Departures in the Protection of First Amendment Rights,* 21 HASTINGS L.J. 129 (1969); Leahy, *The Public Employee and the First Amendment—Must He Sacrifice His Civil Rights To Be a Civil Servant,* 4 CALIF. W.L. REV. 1 (1968); Van Alstyne, *The Constitutional Rights of Public Employees: A Comment on the Inappropriate Use of an Old Analogy,* 16 U.C.L.A.L. REV. 751 (1969); Israel, *Elfbrandt v. Russell—The Demise of the Oath?,* 1966 SUP. CT. REV. 193; Van Alstyne, *The Demise of the Right—Privilege Distinction in Constitutional Law,* 81 HARV. L. REV. 1439 (1968).

2. Privilege Against Self Incrimination and the Duty of Disclosure

GARRITY v. NEW JERSEY

Supreme Court of the United States
385 U.S. 493, 87 S. Ct. 616, 17 L. Ed. 2d 562 (1967)

MR. JUSTICE DOUGLAS delivered the opinion of the Court.

Appellants were police officers in certain New Jersey boroughs. The Supreme Court of New Jersey ordered [an investigation of] alleged fixing of traffic tickets.

Before being questioned, each appellant was warned (1) that anything he said might be used against him in any state criminal proceeding; (2) that he had the privilege to refuse to answer if the disclosure would tend to incriminate him; but (3) that if he refused to answer he would be subject to removal from office.

Appellants answered the questions. No immunity was granted. . . . Over their objections, some of the answers given were used in subsequent prosecutions for conspiracy to obstruct the administration of the traffic laws. Appellants were convicted and their convictions were sustained over their protests that their statements were coerced, by reason of the fact that, if they refused to answer, they could lose their positions with the police department. . . .

We postponed the question of jurisdiction to a hearing on the merits. 383 U.S. 941. The statute whose validity was sought to be "drawn in question," 28 U.S.C. § 1257 (2), was the forfeiture statute.[3] But the New Jersey Supreme Court refused to reach that question (44 N.J., at 223, 207 A.2d, at 697), deeming the voluntariness of the statements as the only issue presented. *Id.,* at 220-222, 207 A.2d, at 695-696. The statute is therefore too tangentially involved to satisfy 28 U.S.C. § 1257 (2), for the only bearing it had was whether, valid or not, the fear of being discharged under it for refusal to answer on the one hand and the fear of self-incrimination on the other was "a choice between the rock and the whirlpool" which made the statements products of coercion in violation of the Fourteenth Amendment. We therefore dismiss the appeal, treat the papers as a petition for certiorari (28 U.S.C. § 2103), grant the petition and proceed to the merits.

We agree with the New Jersey Supreme Court that the forfeiture-of-office statute is relevant here only for the bearing it has on the voluntary character of the statements used to convict petitioners in their criminal prosecutions. . . .

The choice given petitioners was either to forfeit their jobs or to incriminate themselves. The option to lose their means of livelihood or to pay the penalty of self-incrimination is the antithesis of free choice to speak out or to remain silent. That practice, like interrogation practices we reviewed in Miranda v. Arizona, 384 U.S. 436, 464-465, is "likely to exert such pressure upon an individual as to disable him from making a free and rational choice." We think the statements were infected by the coercion inherent in this scheme of questioning and cannot be sustained as voluntary under our prior decisions. . . .

In these cases . . . though petitioners succumbed to compulsion, they preserved their objections, raising them at the earliest possible point. . . . The cases are therefore quite different from the

---

[3] "Any person holding or who has held any elective or appointive public office, position or employment (whether state, county or municipal), who refuses to testify upon matters relating to the office, position or employment in any criminal proceeding wherein he is a defendant or is called as a witness on behalf of the prosecution, upon the ground that his answer may tend to incriminate him or compel him to be a witness against himself or refuses to waive immunity when called by a grand jury to testify thereon or who willfully refuses or fails to appear before any court, commission or body of this state which has the right to inquire under oath upon matters relating to the office, position or employment of such person or who, having been sworn, refuses to testify or to answer any material question upon the ground that his answer may tend to incriminate him or compel him to be a witness against himself, shall, if holding elective or public office, position or employment, be removed therefrom or shall thereby forfeit his office, position or employment and any vested or future right of tenure or pension granted to him by any law of this state provided the inquiry relates to a matter which occurred or arose within the preceding five years. Any person so forfeiting his office, position or employment shall not thereafter be eligible for election or appointment to any public office, position or employment in this state." N.J. Rev. Stat. § 2A:81-17.1 (Supp. 1965).

situation where one who is anxious to make a clean breast of the whole affair volunteers the information.

Mr. Justice Holmes in McAuliffe v. New Bedford, 155 Mass. 216, 29 N.E. 517, stated a dictum on which New Jersey heavily relies:

"The petitioner may have a constitutional right to talk politics, but he has no constitutional right to be a policeman. There are few employments for hire in which the servant does not agree to suspend his constitutional right of free speech, as well as of idleness, by the implied terms of his contract. The servant cannot complain, as he takes the employment on the terms which are offered him. On the same principle, the city may impose any reasonable condition upon holding offices within its control." *Id.*, at 220, 29 N.E., at 517-518.

The question in this case, however, is not cognizable in those terms. Our question is whether a State, contrary to the requirement of the Fourteenth Amendment, can use the threat of discharge to secure incriminatory evidence against an employee.

We held in Slochower v. Board of Education, 350 U.S. 551, that a public school teacher could not be discharged merely because he had invoked the Fifth Amendment privilege against self-incrimination when questioned by a congressional committee:

"The privilege against self-incrimination would be reduced to a hollow mockery if its exercise could be taken as equivalent either to a confession of guilt or a conclusive presumption of perjury. . . . The privilege serves to protect the innocent who otherwise might be ensnared by ambiguous circumstances." *Id.*, at 557-558.

We conclude that policemen, like teachers and lawyers, are not relegated to a watered-down version of constitutional rights. . . .

Reversed.

Mr. Justice Harlan, whom Mr. Justice Clark and Mr. Justice Stewart join, dissenting. . . .

The majority is apparently engaged in the delicate task of riding two unruly horses at once: it is presumably arguing simultaneously that the statements were involuntary as a matter of fact, in the same fashion that the statements in Chambers v. Florida, 309 U.S. 227, and Haynes v. Washington, 373 U.S. 503, were thought to be involuntary, and that the statements were inadmissible as a matter of law, on the premise that they were products of an impermissible condition imposed on the constitutional privilege. These are very different contentions and require separate replies, but in my opinion both contentions are plainly mistaken, for reasons that follow. . . .

As interrogation commenced, each of the petitioners was sworn, carefully informed that he need not give any information, reminded that any information given might be used in a subsequent criminal prosecution, and warned that as a police officer he was subject to a proceeding to discharge him if he failed to provide information relevant to his public responsibilities. . . .

All of the petitioners testified at trial, and gave evidence essentially consistent with the statements taken from them. . . .

The issue remaining is whether the statements were inadmissible because they were "involuntary as a matter of law," in that they were given after a warning that New Jersey policemen may be discharged for failure to provide information pertinent to their public responsibilities. What is really involved on this score, however, is not in truth a question of "voluntariness" at all, but rather whether the condition imposed by the State on the exercise of the privilege against self-incrimination, namely dismissal from office, in this instance serves in itself to render the statements inadmissible. Absent evidence of involuntariness in fact, the admissibility of these statements thus hinges on the validity of the consequence which the State acknowledged might have resulted if the statements had not been given. If the consequence is constitutionally permissible, there can surely be no objection if the State cautions the witness that it may follow if he remains silent. If both the consequence and the warning are constitutionally permissible, a witness is obliged, in order to prevent the use of his statements against him in a criminal prosecution, to prove under the standards established since Brown v. Mississippi, 297 U.S. 278, that as a matter of fact the statements were involuntarily made. The central issues here are therefore identical to those presented in *Spevack v. Klein:* whether consequences may properly be permitted to result to a claimant after his invocation of the constitutional privilege, and if so, whether the consequence in question is permissible. For reasons which I have stated in *Spevack v. Klein,* in my view nothing in the logic or purposes of the privilege demands that all consequences which may result from a witness' silence be forbidden merely because that silence is privileged. The validity of a consequence depends both upon the hazards, if any, it presents to the integrity of the privilege and upon the urgency of the public interests it is designed to protect.

It can hardly be denied that New Jersey is permitted by the Constitution to establish reasonable qualifications and standards of conduct for its public employees. Nor can it be said that it is arbitrary or unreasonable for New Jersey to insist that its employees furnish the appropriate authorities with information pertinent to their employment. Cf. Beilan v. Board of Education, 357 U.S. 399; Slochower v. Board of Education, 350 U.S. 551. Finally, it is surely plain that New Jersey may in particular require its employees to assist in the prevention and detection of unlawful activities by officers of the state government. The urgency of these requirements is the more obvious here, where the conduct in question is that of officials directly entrusted with the administration of justice. . . .

NOTES

1. In Spevack v. Klein, 385 U.S. 511, 87 S. Ct. 625, 17 L. Ed. 2d 574 (1967), the companion case to *Garrity*, the Court held an attorney's refusal to testify at a judicial investigation of his alleged professional misconduct and refusal to produce certain financial records on the ground that to do so might tend to incriminate him, an impermissible basis for his disbarment. After reaffirming the idea that the Fifth Amendment's privilege against self-incrimination was made applicable to the states by the Fourteenth Amendment, the Court stated that "[t]he threat of disbarment and the loss of professional standing, professional reputation, and of livelihood are powerful forms of compulsion to make a lawyer relinquish the privilege" and furthermore that "the imposition of any sanction which makes assertion of the Fifth Amendment privilege 'costly' " was, in this context, the imposition of a penalty. The Court pointed out that the Self-Incrimination Clause "extends its protection to lawyers as to other individuals and that it should not be watered down by imposing the dishonor of disbarment and the deprivation of a livelihood as a price for asserting it," and also that "[l]ike the school teacher in *Slochower* . . . and the policeman in *Garrity* . . . lawyers also enjoy first-class citizenship."

Justice Harlan argued, in dissent, that "so long as state authorities do not derive any imputation of guilt from a claim of the privilege, they may in the cause of a bona fide assessment of an employee's fitness for public employment require that the employee disclose information reasonably related to his fitness, and may order his discharge if he declines." According to the dissenters, "petitioner was not denied his privilege against self-incrimination, nor was he penalized for its use; he was denied his authority to practice law . . . by reason of his failure to satisfy valid obligations imposed by the State as a condition of that authority." In a separate dissenting opinion Mr. Justice White stated that the Court's holding would "seem justifiable only on the ground that it is an essential measure to protect against self-incrimination—to prevent what may well be a successful attempt to elicit incriminating admissions" but that since *Garrity* "excludes such statements . . . from a criminal proceeding . . . [there is] little legal or practical basis . . . for preventing the discharge of a public employee or the disbarment of a lawyer who refuses to talk about the performance of his public duty." In a separate concurring opinion, Justice Fortas suggested that "a public employee who is asked questions specifically, directly, and narrowly relating to the performance of his official duties" could be terminated for declining to answer. But Justice Fortas expressed the view that "a lawyer is not an employee of the State. He does not have the responsibility of an employee to account to the State for his actions. . . . The special responsibilities that he assumes as licensee of the State and officer of the court do not carry with them a diminution, however limited, of his Fifth Amendment rights."

2. The companion cases Gardner v. Broderick, 392 U.S. 273, 88 S. Ct. 1913, 20 L. Ed. 2d 1082 (1968) and Uniformed Sanitation Men Ass'n, Inc. v. Commissioner of Sanitation of the City of New York, 392 U.S. 280 (1968) involved the validity of the terminations of public employees who refused to waive immunity from prosecution or testify at grand jury hearings concerning alleged bribery and corruption. The Court, in striking down the employee dismissals as unconstitutional, stressed the fact that in neither case were the dismissals based on the employees' refusal to answer pertinent questions about their official duties, but instead were for their refusal to waive their constitutionally protected privilege against self-incrimination. The Court, per Justice Fortas, concluded that "if New York had demanded that petitioners answer questions specifically, directly and narrowly relating to the performance of their official duties in pain of dismissal from public employment without requiring relinquishment of the benefits of the constitutional privilege, and if they had refused to do so, this case would be entirely different," but that in the instant case they had instead been presented with a choice between waiving their constitutional rights or losing their jobs. All of the employees had been terminated in accordance with a New York City Charter provision which required the discharge of public servants who invoked the privilege against self-incrimination during authorized investigations of public employees' conduct

or who refused to waive immunity against prosecution prompted by their testimony.

3. The earlier decision of Slochower v. Board of Higher Educ. of New York City, 350 U.S. 551, 76 S. Ct. 637, 100 L. Ed. 692 (1956) held invalid the summary dismissal of a teacher pursuant to a section of the Charter of the City of New York which provided for dismissal of any city employee who invoked the privilege against self-incrimination and thereby refused to answer questions of a legislative committee. The Appellant, a teacher in a college maintained by the city, had been summarily discharged from his position when he refused to answer certain questions asked by a Senate Sub-Committee regarding his alleged membership in the Communist Party some eleven years prior to the hearing. He had stated, however, that he was not currently a member of the Communist Party and would answer all questions relating to the eleven-year period subsequent to his alleged membership. In upholding appellant's dismissal the State's highest court construed the charter section as providing that "the assertion of the privilege against self-incrimination is equivalent to a resignation" thereby attempting to avert conflict with the state law which allowed for discharge of a person in appellant's position "only for cause, and after notice, hearing, and appeal." The Supreme Court, in overturning the dismissal, stated that "[t]he privilege against self-incrimination would be reduced to a hollow mockery if its exercise could be taken as equivalent either to a confession of guilt or a presumption of perjury." Since no inference of guilt was permissible from appellant's assertion of privilege the Court held the dismissal arbitrary, and therefore a denial of Fourteenth Amendment due process of law.

3. Freedom of Association

SHELTON v. TUCKER
Supreme Court of the United States
364 U.S. 479, 81 S. Ct. 247, 5 L. Ed. 2d 231 (1960)

MR. JUSTICE STEWART delivered the opinion of the Court.

An Arkansas statute compels every teacher, as a condition of employment in a state-supported school or college, to file annually an affidavit listing without limitation every organization to which he has belonged or regularly contributed within the preceding five years. At issue in these two cases is the validity of that statute under the Fourteenth Amendment to the Constitution. . . .

The provisions of the Act are summarized in the opinion of the District Court as follows:

"Act 10 provides in substance that no person shall be employed or elected to employment as a superintendent, principal or teacher in any public school in Arkansas, or as an instructor, professor or teacher in any public institution of higher learning in that State until such person shall have submitted to the appropriate hiring authority an affidavit listing all organizations to which he at the time belongs and to which he has belonged during the past five years, and also listing all organizations to which he at the time is paying regular dues or is making regular contributions, or to which within the past five years he has paid such dues or made such contributions. The Act further provides, among other things, that any contract entered into with any person who has not filed the prescribed affidavit shall be void; that no public moneys shall be paid to such person as compensation for his services; and that any such funds so paid may be recovered back either from the person receiving such funds or from the board of trustees or other governing body making the payment. The filing of a false affidavit is denounced as perjury, punishable by a fine of not less than five hundred nor more than one thousand dollars, and, in addition, the person filing the false affidavit is to lose his teaching license." 174 F. Supp. 353-354." . . .

The plaintiffs in the Federal District Court (appellants here) were B.T. Shelton, a teacher employed in the Little Rock Public School System, suing for himself and others similarly situated, together with the Arkansas Teachers Association and its Executive Secretary, suing for the benefit of members of the Association. Shelton had been employed in the Little Rock Special School District for twenty-five years. In the spring of 1959 he was notified that, before he could be employed for the 1959-1960 school year, he must file the affidavit required by Act 10, listing all his organizational connections over the previous five years. He declined to file the affidavit, and his contract for the ensuing school year was not renewed. At the trial the evidence showed that he was not a member of the Communist Party or of any organization advocating the overthrow of the Government by force, and that he was a member of the National Association for the Advancement of Colored People. The court upheld Act 10, finding the information it required was "relevant," and relying on several decisions of this Court, particularly Garner v. Board of Public Works of Los Angeles, 341 U.S. 716; Adler v. Board of Education, 342 U.S. 485; Beilan v. Board of Education, 357 U.S. 399; and Lerner v. Casey, 357 U.S. 468.

The plaintiffs in the state court proceedings (petitioners here) were Max Carr, an associate professor at the University of Arkansas, and Ernest T. Gephardt, a teacher at Central High School in Little Rock, each suing for himself and others similarly situated. Each refused to execute and file the affidavit required by Act 10. . . .

Both were advised that their failure to comply with the requirements of Act 10 would make impossible their re-employment as teachers for the following school year. The Supreme Court of Arkansas upheld the constitutionality of Act 10, on its face and as applied to the petitioners. 231 Ark. 641, 331 S.W.2d 701.

I.

It is urged here, as it was unsuccessfully urged throughout the proceedings in both the federal and state courts, that Act 10 deprives teachers in Arkansas of their rights to personal, associational, and academic liberty, protected by the Due Process Clause of the Fourteenth Amendment from invasion by state action. In considering this contention, we deal with two basic postulates.

First. There can be no doubt of the right of a State to investigate the competence and fitness of those whom it hires to teach in its schools, as this Court before now has had occasion to recognize. . . .

This controversy is thus not of a pattern with such cases as N.A.A.C.P. v. Alabama, 357 U.S. 449, and Bates v. Little Rock, 361 U.S. 516. In those cases the Court held that there was no substantially relevant correlation between the governmental interest asserted and the State's effort to compel disclosure of the membership lists involved. Here, by contrast, there can be no question of the relevance of a State's inquiry into the fitness and competence of its teachers.

Second. It is not disputed that to compel a teacher to disclose his every associational tie is to impair that teacher's right of free association, a right closely allied to freedom of speech and a right which, like free speech, lies at the foundation of a free society. DeJonge v. Oregon, 299 U.S. 353, 364; Bates v. Little Rock, *supra,* at 522-523. Such interference with personal freedom is conspicuously accented when the teacher serves at the absolute will of those to whom the disclosure must be made—those who any year can terminate the teacher's employment without bringing charges, without notice, without a hearing, without affording an opportunity to explain.

The statute does not provide that the information it requires be kept confidential. Each school board is left free to deal with the information as it wishes. The record contains evidence to indicate that fear of public disclosure is neither theoretical nor groundless. Even if there were no disclosure to the general public, the pressure upon a teacher to avoid any ties which might displease those who control his professional destiny would be constant and heavy. Public exposure, bringing with it the possibility of public pressures upon school boards to discharge teachers who belong to unpopular or minority organizations, would simply operate to widen and aggravate the impairment of constitutional liberty. . . .

II.

The question to be decided here is not whether the State of Arkansas can ask certain of its teachers about all their organizational relationships. It is not whether the State can ask all of its teachers about certain of their associational ties. It is not whether teachers can be asked how many organizations they belong to, or how much time they spend in organizational activity. The question is whether the State can ask every one of its teachers to disclose every single organization with which he has been associated over a five-year period. The scope of the inquiry required by Act 10 is completely unlimited. The statute requires a teacher to reveal the church to which he belongs, or to which he has given financial support. It requires him to disclose his political party, and every political organization to which he may have contributed over a five-year period. It requires him to list, without number, every conceivable kind of associational tie—social, professional, political, avocational, or religious. Many such relationships could have no possible bearing upon the teacher's occupational competence or fitness.

In a series of decisions this Court has held that, even though the governmental purpose be legitimate and substantial, that purpose cannot be pursued by means that broadly stifle fundamental personal liberties when the end can be more narrowly achieved. The breadth of legislative abridgment must be viewed in the light of less drastic means for achieving the same basic purpose. . . .

The unlimited and indiscriminate sweep of the statute now before us brings it within the ban of our prior cases. The statute's comprehensive interference with associational freedom goes far beyond what might be justified in the exercise of the State's legitimate inquiry into the fitness and competency of its teachers. The judgments in both cases must be reversed.

It is so ordered.

Mr. Justice Frankfurter, dissenting.

As one who has strong views against crude intrusions by the state into the atmosphere of creative freedom in which alone the spirit and mind of a teacher can fruitfully function, I may find displeasure with the Arkansas legislation now under review. But in maintaining the distinction between private views and constitutional restrictions, I am constrained to find that it does not exceed the permissible range of state action limited by the Fourteenth Amendment. By way of emphasis I therefore add a few words to the dissent of MR. JUSTICE HARLAN, in which I concur.
. . .

Where state assertions of authority are attacked as impermissibly restrictive upon thought, expression, or association, the existence *vel non* of other possible less restrictive means of achieving the object which the State seeks is, of course, a constitutionally relevant consideration. This is not because some novel, particular rule of law obtains in cases of this kind. Whenever the reasonableness and fairness of a measure are at issue—as they are in every case in which this Court must apply the standards of reason and fairness, with the appropriate scope to be given those concepts, in enforcing the Due Process Clause of the Fourteenth Amendment as a limitation upon state action—the availability or unavailability of alternative methods of proceeding is germane. Thus, a State may not prohibit the distribution of literature on its cities' streets as a means of preventing littering, when the same end might be achieved with only slightly greater inconvenience by applying the sanctions of the penal law not to the pamphleteer who distributes the paper but to the recipient who crumples it and throws it away. Hague v. C.I.O., 307 U.S. 496; Schneider v. State, 308 U.S. 147; Jamison v. Texas, 318 U.S. 413. . . . But the consideration of feasible alternative modes of regulation in these cases did not imply that the Court might substitute its own choice among alternatives for that of a state legislature, or that the States were to be restricted to the "narrowest" workable means of accomplishing an end. . . .

In the present case the Court strikes down an Arkansas statute requiring that teachers disclose to school officials all of their organizational relationships, on the ground that "Many such relationships could have no possible bearing upon the teacher's occupational competence or fitness." Granted that a given teacher's membership in the First Street Congregation is, standing alone, of little relevance to what may rightly be expected of a teacher, is that membership equally irrelevant when it is discovered that the teacher is in fact a member of the First Street Congregation *and* the Second Street Congregation *and* the Third Street Congregation *and* the 4-H Club *and* the 3-H Club *and* half a dozen other groups? Presumably, a teacher may have so many divers associations, so many divers commitments, that they consume his time and energy and interest at the expense of his work or even of his professional dedication. Unlike wholly individual interests, organizational connections—because they involve obligations undertaken with relation to other persons—may become inescapably demanding and distracting. Surely, a school board is entitled to inquire whether any of its teachers has placed himself, or is placing himself, in a condition where his work may suffer. . . .

If I dissent from the Court's disposition in these cases, it is not that I put a low value on academic freedom. See Wieman v. Updegraff, 344 U.S. 183, 194 (concurring opinion); Sweezy v. New Hampshire, 354 U.S. 234, 255 (concurring opinion). It is because that very freedom, in its most creative reaches, is dependent in no small part upon the careful and discriminating selection of teachers. This process of selection is an intricate affair, a matter of fine judgment, and if it is to be informed, it must be based upon a comprehensive range of information. I am unable to say, on the face of this statute, that Arkansas could not reasonably find that the information which the statute requires—and which may not be otherwise acquired than by asking the question which it asks—is germane to that selection. Nor, on this record, can I attribute to the State a purpose to employ the enactment as a device for the accomplishment of what is constitutionally forbidden. Of course, if the information gathered by the required affidavits is used to further a scheme of terminating the employment of teachers solely because of their membership in unpopular organizations, that use will run afoul of the Fourteenth Amendment. It will be time enough, if such use is made, to hold the application of the statute unconstitutional. . . .

I am authorized to say that MR. JUSTICE CLARK, MR. JUSTICE HARLAN and MR. JUSTICE WHITTAKER agree with this opinion.

MR. JUSTICE HARLAN, whom MR. JUSTICE FRANKFURTER, MR. JUSTICE CLARK and MR. JUSTICE WHITTAKER join, dissenting. . . .

The legal framework in which the issue must be judged is clear. The rights of free speech and association embodied in the "liberty" assured against state action by the Fourteenth Amendment (see DeJonge v. Oregon, 299 U.S. 353, 364; Gitlow v. New York, 268 U.S. 652, 672, dissenting opinion of Holmes, J.) are not absolute. Near v. Minnestota, 283 U.S. 697, 708; Whitney v. California, 274 U.S. 357, 373 (concurring opinion of Brandeis, J.). Where official action is claimed to invade these rights, the controlling inquiry is whether such action is justifiable on the basis of a superior governmental interest to which such individual rights must yield. When the action complained of pertains to the realm of investigation, our inquiry has a double aspect: first, whether the investigation relates to a legitimate governmental purpose; second, whether, judged in the light of that purpose, the questioned action has substantial relevance thereto. See Barenblatt v. United States, 360 U.S. 109; Uphaus v. Wyman, 360 U.S. 72.

In the two cases at hand, I think both factors are satisfied. It is surely indisputable that a State has the right to choose its teachers on the basis of fitness. And I think it equally clear, as the Court appears to recognize, that information about a teacher's associations may be useful to school authorities in determining the moral, professional, and social qualifications of the teacher, as well as in determining the type of service for which he will be best suited in the educational system. . . .

Despite these considerations this statute is stricken down because, in the Court's view, it is too broad, because it asks more than may be necessary to effectuate the State's legitimate interest. Such a statute, it is said, cannot justify the inhibition on freedom of association which so blanket an inquiry may entail. Cf. N.A.A.C.P. v. Alabama, *supra;* Bates v. Little Rock, *supra.*

I am unable to subscribe to this view because I believe it impossible to determine *a priori* the place where the line should be drawn between what would be permissible inquiry and overbroad inquiry in a situation like this. Certainly the Court does not point that place out. There can be little doubt that much of the associational information called for by the statute will be of little or no use whatever to the school authorities, but I do not understand how those authorities can be expected to fix in advance the terms of their enquiry so that it will yield only relevant information. . . .

NOTES

1. Is Justice Frankfurter's dissenting opinion persuasive? Is it not possible for a school board to judge a teacher's performance without knowing of his outside associations?

2. How should the Arkansas statute have been drafted so as to avoid constitutional infirmity? In a situation like the one posed in the *Shelton* case, is it possible to determine where the line should be drawn between what would be permissible inquiry and overbroad inquiry?

4. Freedom of Expression

PICKERING v. BOARD OF EDUCATION
Supreme Court of the United States
391 U.S. 563, 88 S. Ct. 1731, 20 L. Ed. 2d 811 (1968)

Mr. Justice Marshall delivered the opinion of the Court.

Appellant Marvin L. Pickering, a teacher in Township High School District 205, Will County, Illinois, was dismissed from his position by the appellee Board of Education for sending a letter to a local newspaper in connection with a recently proposed tax increase that was critical of the way in which the Board and the district superintendent of schools had handled past proposals to raise new revenue for the schools. Appellant's dismissal resulted from a determination by the Board, after a full hearing, that the publication of the letter was "detrimental to the efficient operation and administration of the schools of the district" and hence, under the relevant Illinois statute, Ill. Rev. Stat., c. 122, § 10-22.4 (1963), that "interests of the school require[d] [his dismissal]." . . . At the hearing the Board charged that numerous statements in the letter were false and that the publication of the statements unjustifiably impunged the "motives, honesty, integrity, truthfulness, responsibility and competence" of both the Board and the school administration. The Board also charged that the false statements damaged the professional reputations of its members and of the school administrators, would be disruptive of faculty discipline, and would tend to foment "controversy, conflict and dissension" among teachers, administrators, the Board of Education, and the residents of the district. . . .

The Illinois courts reviewed the proceedings solely to determine whether the Board's findings were supported by substantial evidence and whether, on the facts as found, the Board could reasonably conclude that appellant's publication of the letter was "detrimental to the best interests of the schools." Pickering's claim that his letter was protected by the First Amendment was rejected on the ground that his acceptance of a teaching position in the public schools obliged him to refrain from making statements about the operation of the schools "which in the absence of such position he would have an undoubted right to engage in." . . .

To the extent that the Illinois Supreme Court's opinion may be read to suggest that teachers may constitutionally be compelled to relinquish the First Amendment rights they would otherwise enjoy as citizens to comment on matters of public interest in connection with the operation of the public schools in which they work, it proceeds on a premise that has been unequiv-

ocally rejected in numerous prior decisions of this Court. . . .
At the same time it cannot be gainsaid that the State has interests
as an employer in regulating the speech of its employees that
differ significantly from those it possesses in connection with regulation of the speech of the citizenry in general. The problem in
any case is to arrive at a balance between the interests of the
teacher, as a citizen, in commenting upon matters of public concern and the interest of the State, as an employer, in promoting
the efficiency of the public services it performs through its
employees. . . .

Because of the enormous variety of fact situations in which
critical statements by teachers and other public employees may
be thought by their superiors, against whom the statements are
directed, to furnish grounds for dismissal, we do not deem it
either appropriate or feasible to attempt to lay down a general
standard against which all such statements may be judged. However, in the course of evaluating the conflicting claims of First
Amendment protection and the need for orderly school administration in the context of this case, we shall indicate some of the
general lines along which an analysis of the controlling interests
should run.

An examination of the statements in appellant's letter objected
to by the Board reveals that they, like the letter as a whole, consist essentially of criticism of the Board's allocation of school funds
between educational and athletic programs, and of both the
Board's and the superintendent's methods of informing, or preventing the informing of, the district's taxpayers of the real reasons why additional tax revenues were being sought for the
schools. The statements are in no way directed towards any person with whom appellant would normally be in contact in the
course of his daily work as a teacher. Thus no question of maintaining either discipline by immediate superiors or harmony
among coworkers is presented here. Appellant's employment
relationships with the Board and, to a somewhat lesser extent,
with the superintendent are not the kind of close working relationships for which it can persuasively be claimed that personal
loyalty and confidence are necessary to their proper functioning.
Accordingly, to the extent that the Board's position here can be
taken to suggest that even comments on matters of public concern
that are substantially correct . . . may furnish grounds for dismissal if they are sufficiently critical in tone, we unequivocally
reject it.

We next consider the statements in appellant's letter which we
agree to be false. The Board's original charges included allegations that the publication of the letter damaged the professional

reputations of the Board and the superintendent and would foment controversy and conflict among the Board, teachers, administrators, and the residents of the district. However, no evidence to support these allegations was introduced at the hearing. So far as the record reveals, Pickering's letter was greeted by everyone but its main target, the Board, with massive apathy and total disbelief. The Board must, therefore, have decided, perhaps by analogy with the law of libel, that the statements were *per se* harmful to the operation of the schools.

However, the only way in which the Board could conclude, absent any evidence of the actual effect of the letter, that the statements contained therein were *per se* detrimental to the interest of the schools was to equate the Board members' own interests with that of the schools. Certainly an accusation that too much money is being spent on athletics by the administrators of the school system . . . cannot reasonably be regarded as *per se* detrimental to the district's schools. Such an accusation reflects rather a difference of opinion between Pickering and the Board as to the preferable manner of operating the school system, a difference of opinion that clearly concerns an issue of general public interest. . . .

More importantly, the question whether a school system requires additional funds is a matter of legitimate public concern on which the judgment of the school administration, including the School Board, cannot, in a society that leaves such questions to popular vote, be taken as conclusive. On such a question free and open debate is vital to informed decision-making by the electorate. Teachers are, as a class, the members of a community most likely to have informed and definite opinions as to how funds allotted to the operation of the schools should be spent. Accordingly, it is essential that they be able to speak out freely on such questions without fear of retaliatory dismissal.

In addition, the amounts expended on athletics which Pickering reported erroneously were matters of public record on which his position as a teacher in the district did not qualify him to speak with any greater authority than any other taxpayer. The Board could easily have rebutted appellant's errors by publishing the accurate figures itself, either via a letter to the same newspaper or otherwise. We are thus not presented with a situation in which a teacher has carelessly made false statements about matters so closely related to the day-to-day operations of the schools that any harmful impact on the public would be difficult to counter because of the teacher's presumed greater access to the real facts. Accordingly, we have no occasion to consider at this time whether under such circumstances a school board could reasonably require that a teacher make substantial efforts to verify the accuracy of his charges before publishing them.[4]

What we do have before us is a case in which a teacher has made erroneous public statements upon issues then currently the subject of public attention, which are critical of his ultimate employer but which are neither shown nor can be presumed to have in any way either impeded the teacher's proper performance of his daily duties in the classroom[5] or to have interfered with the regular operation of the schools generally. In these circumstances we conclude that the interest of the school administration in limiting teachers' opportunities to contribute to public debate is not significantly greater than its interest in limiting a similar contribution by any member of the general public.

The public interest in having free and unhindered debate on matters of public importance—the core value of the Free Speech Clause of the First Amendment—is so great that it has been held that a State cannot authorize the recovery of damages by a public official for defamatory statements directed at him except when such statements are shown to have been made either with knowledge of their falsity or with reckless disregard for their truth or falsity. New York Times Co. v. Sullivan, 376 U.S. 254 (1964) ; St. Amant v. Thompson, 390 U.S. 727 (1968). Compare Linn v. United Plant Guard Workers, 383 U.S. 53 (1966). The same test has been applied to suits for invasion of privacy based on false statements where a "matter of public interest" is involved. Time, Inc. v. Hill, 385 U.S. 374 (1967). It is therefore perfectly clear that, were appellant a member of the general public, the State's power to afford the appellee Board of Education or its members any legal right to sue him for writing the letter at issue here would be limited by the requirement that the letter be judged by the standard laid down in *New York Times.*

This Court has also indicated, in more general terms, that statements by public officials on matters of public concern must be accorded First Amendment protection despite the fact that the statements are directed at their nominal superiors. Garrison v. Louisiana, 379 U.S. 64 (1964) ; Wood v. Georgia, 370 U.S.

---

[4] There is likewise no occasion furnished by this case for consideration of the extent to which teachers can be required by narrowly drawn grievance procedures to submit complaints about the operation of the schools to their superiors for action thereon prior to bringing the complaints before the public.

[5] We also note that this case does not present a situation in which a teacher's public statements are so without foundation as to call into question his fitness to perform his duties in the classroom. In such a case, of course, the statements would merely be evidence of the teacher's general competence, or lack thereof, and not an independent basis for dismissal.

375 (1962). In *Garrison,* the *New York Times* test was specifically applied to a case involving a criminal defamation conviction stemming from statements made by a district attorney about the judges before whom he regularly appeared.

While criminal sanctions and damage awards have a somewhat different impact on the exercise of the right to freedom of speech from dismissal from employment, it is apparent that the threat of dismissal from public employment is nonetheless a potent means of inhibiting speech. We have already noted our disinclination to make an across-the-board equation of dismissal from public employment for remarks critical of superiors with awarding damages in a libel suit by a public official for similar criticism. However, in a case such as the present one, in which the fact of employment is only tangentially and insubstantially involved in the subject matter of the public communication made by a teacher, we conclude that it is necessary to regard the teacher as the member of the general public he seeks to be.

In sum, we hold that, in a case such as this, absent proof of false statements knowingly or recklessly made by him, a teacher's exercise of his right to speak on issues of public importance may not furnish the basis for his dismissal from public employment. Since no such showing has been made in this case regarding appellant's letter . . . his dismissal for writing it cannot be upheld and the judgment of the Illinois Supreme Court must, accordingly, be reversed and the case remanded for further proceedings not inconsistent with this opinion.

It is so ordered.

Mr. Justice White, concurring in part and dissenting in part. . . .

The core of today's decision is the holding that Pickering's discharge must be tested by the standard of New York Times Co. v. Sullivan, 376 U.S. 254 (1964). To this extent I am in agreement. . . .

The Court devotes several pages to re-examining the facts in order to reject the determination below that Pickering's statements harmed the school system, *ante,* at 570-573, when the question of harm is clearly irrelevant given the Court's determination that Pickering's statements were neither knowingly nor recklessly false and its ruling that in such circumstances a teacher may not be fired even if the statements are injurious.

. . . Deliberate or reckless falsehoods serve no First Amendment ends and deserve no protection under that Amendment. The Court unequivocally recognized this in *Garrison,* where after reargument the Court said that "the knowingly false statement and the false statement made with reckless disregard of the truth, do not enjoy constitutional protection." 379 U.S., at 75. The Court today neither explains nor justifies its withdrawal from the firm stand taken in *Garrison*. As I see it, a teacher may be fired without violation of the First Amendment for knowingly or recklessly making false statements regardless of their harmful impact on the schools. As the Court holds, however, in the absence of special circumstances he may not be fired if his statements were true or only negligently false, even if there is some harm to the school system. I therefore see no basis or necessity for the Court's foray into fact-finding with respect to whether the record supports a finding as to injury. If Pickering's false statements were either knowingly or recklessly made, injury to the school system becomes irrelevant, and the First Amendment would not prevent his discharge. For the State to be constitutionally precluded from terminating his employment, reliance on some other constitutional provision would be required. . . .

NOTES

1. In Watts v. Seward, 454 P.2d 732 (Alas.), *cert. denied*, 397 U.S. 921 (1969), it was held that teachers could properly be dismissed for circulating an open letter and making other statements (some of which were found to be false) criticizing the school superintendent who had a close relationship with teachers and students. The court distinguished *Pickering* by finding that the conduct was detrimental to discipline and harmony within the school system, that the teachers' criticism did not relate to the expenditure of school funds, but rather, to day-to-day operations of the school, and that available grievance procedures had not been followed.

2. A California appellate court in Norton v. City of Santa Anna, 15 Cal. App. 3d 419, 93 Cal. Rptr. 37 (1971), used the so-called "*Bagley* formula" to weigh the interests of the governmental agency against the constitutional interests of a policeman, who had been discharged for bringing a lawsuit against the police chief. In sustaining the dismissal, the court ruled that:

> When such a conflict does arise, the governmental agency seeking to impose restrictions on the exercise of an employee's constitutional rights must demonstrate that: (1) the governmental restraint rationally relates to the enhancement of the public service; (2) the benefits that the public gains by the restraint outweigh the resulting impairment of the constitutional right; and (3) no alternatives less subversive to the constitutional right are available. (Bagley v.

Washington Township Hosp. Dist., 65 Cal. 2d 499, 501-502, 55 Cal. Rptr. 401, 421 P.2d 409.) In other words, a public employee may speak freely so long as he does not impair the administration of the public service in which he is engaged. (Belshaw v. City of Berkeley, 246 Cal. App. 2d 493, 497, 54 Cal. Rptr. 727.) Similarly, a public employee may engage in political activity providing it does not affect the administrative functioning or public integrity of the governmental agency. 93 Cal. Rptr. at 41.

Is the "*Bagley* formula" significantly different from the tests set forth in *Pickering?*

3. The Courts have applied the *Pickering* tests and requirements in various areas and circumstances of public employment. In Tinker v. Des Moines Community School Dist., 393 U.S. 503, 509, 89 S. Ct. 733, 21 L. Ed. 2d 731 (1969), the Court held that the problem presented by public school children wearing black armbands (during school hours, on school property and in violation of a school regulation) as a symbolic act to publicize their objections to the hostilities in Vietnam, did not involve aggressive, disruptive action or even group demonstration. Rather, the conduct was viewed as involving direct, primary First Amendment rights akin to "pure speech." The Court stated:

> In order for the State . . . to justify prohibition of a particular expression of opinion, it must be able to show that its action was caused by something more than a mere desire to avoid the discomfort and unpleasantness that always accompany an unpopular viewpoint. Certainly where there is no finding and no showing that engaging in the forbidden conduct would "materially and substantially interfere with the requirements of appropriate discipline in the operation of the school" the prohibition cannot be sustained.

In Swaaley v. United States, 376 F.2d 857 (Ct. Cl. 1967), Swaaley, a naval shipyard worker, wrote the Secretary of the Navy a petition for redress of grievances which included charges that some of his superior officials were guilty of favoritism in the matter of promotions. He was discharged. The Court held that the defamatory statements were not shown to have been wilfully false or made with reckless disregard for truth or falsity and that Swaaley's discharge was improper. A similar ruling was made by the same Court in Burkett v. United States, 402 F.2d 1002 (Ct. Cl. 1968). *See also* Murray v. Vaughn, 300 F. Supp. 688, 703-05 (D.R.I. 1969), which involved a Peace Corps volunteer, and Puentes v. Board of Educ. of Union Free School Dist. No. 21, 24

N.Y.2d 996, 250 N.E.2d 232, 302 N.Y.S.2d 824 (Ct. App. 1969), in which a teacher (a union official) wrote letters to teachers and administrators within the school district criticizing the failure of the school administration to renew the employment of a probationary teacher and was suspended without pay. The Court of Appeals of New York cited *Pickering* and said:

> There is no suggestion in the record that petitioner's indiscretions led to any deleterious effects within the school system and it is unlikely that they should have. Indiscreet bombast in an argumentative letter, to the limited extent present here, is insufficient to sanction disciplinary action. . . .
>
> Concededly, petitioner's direct teaching and in-class performance were correct and not affected by the writing or sending of the letter. 250 N.E.2d at 233.

See also the prior case of Trepedino v. Dumpson, 24 N.Y.2d 705, 249 N.E.2d 751 (1969) (involving social workers). For other applications of the *Pickering* principle, see Muller v. Conlisk, 429 F.2d 901 (7th Cir. 1970) ; McGee v. Richmond Unified School Dist., 306 F. Supp. 1052 (N.D. Cal. 1969) ; Meehan v. Macy, 425 F.2d 469 (D.C. Cir. 1968), *aff'd after rehearing en banc,* 425 F.2d 472 (D.C. Cir. 1969).

JAMES v. BOARD OF EDUCATION
United States Court of Appeals, Second Circuit
461 F.2d 566 (1972)

IRVING R. KAUFMAN, Circuit Judge:

[T]he issue in this case is whether, in assuming the role of judge and disciplinarian, a Board of Education may forbid a teacher to express a political opinion, however benign or noncoercive the manner of expression. We are asked to decide whether a Board of Education, without transgressing the first amendment, may discharge an 11th grade English teacher who did no more than wear a black armband in class in symbolic protest against the Vietnam War, although it is agreed that the armband did not disrupt classroom activities, and as far as we know did not have any influence on any students and did not engender protest from any student, teacher or parent. We hold that the Board may not take such action. . . .

James appealed his dismissal to the New York State Commissioner of Education, Ewald B. Nyquist, asserting that his dismissal infringed upon his first amendment rights and deprived him of due process of law. The "hearing" before the Commissioner, as we were informed at the argument of this appeal, was no more than an informal roundtable discussion between the Commissioner, the parties and their attorneys. No transcript of the proceedings was made. On September 23, 1970, Commissioner Nyquist filed his decision. Although he recognized that a board of education does not have unfettered discretion to dismiss a probationary teacher, he concluded that James had violated "sound educational principles" and that his actions "were not constitutionally protected." In addition, he reaffirmed the Board of Education's absolute right to dismiss a probationary teacher without affording the teacher a hearing or explaining the basis of the discharge.

Thereupon, James instituted this action in the Western District of New York. . . . Judge Burke denied James's motion for summary judgment and granted the defendants' motion for a judgment, summarily dismissing the complaint on the merits, seemingly on two grounds: first, that the issues raised by the complaint were *res judicata,* and second, that none of James's federally protected rights was violated. . . .

At the outset we are presented with the contention that the claims asserted below are *res judicata.* We consider this to be wholly without merit. Appellees argue that James, at his own choosing, was given the full opportunity to litigate his claims before the Commissioner of Education, a "judicial officer" of the State, and therefore that James should be bound by the Commissioner's decision. Judge Burke buttressed their position with a pointed reference to James's failure to appeal the Commissioner's decision to the New York courts.

It is no longer open to dispute that a plaintiff with a claim for relief under the Civil Rights Act, 42 U.S.C. § 1983, is not required to exhaust state judicial remedies. It is still the law in this Circuit, however, that a Civil Rights plaintiff must exhaust state administrative remedies. It hardly can be suggested that a plaintiff having followed the course laid out by *Eisen,* was to be barred henceforth from pressing his claim to final judicial review or to be deprived of his opportunity to litigate his constitutional claims in the judicial forum of his choice. To adopt the full implication of appellees' argument would be to effect a judicial repeal of 42 U.S.C. § 1983 and strike down the Supreme Court's decision in Monroe v. Pape, *supra.* James would be placed in the paradoxical position of being barred from the federal courts if he had not exhausted administrative remedies and barred if he had.

We come now to the crucial issue we must decide—did the Board of Education infringe James's first amendment right to freedom of speech?

Any meaningful discussion of a teacher's first amendment right to wear a black armband in a classroom as a symbolic protest against this nation's involvement in the Vietnam War must begin with a close examination of the case which dealt with this question as it applied to a student. Tinker v. Des Moines Independent Community School District [393 U.S. 503 (1969)]. Mary Beth Tinker, a junior high school student, her older brother and his friend, both high school students, were suspended from school for wearing black armbands in school to publicize their opposition to the war in Vietnam. Noting that neither students nor teachers "shed their constitutional rights to freedom of speech or expression at the schoolhouse gate," 393 U.S. at 506, 89 S. Ct. at 736, the Supreme Court held that a school cannot bar or penalize students' exercise of primary first amendment rights akin to "pure speech" without "a showing that the students' activities would materially and substantially disrupt the work and discipline of the school." *Id.* at 513, 89 S. Ct. at 740.

With respect to both teacher and student, the responsibility of school authorities to maintain order and discipline in the schools remains the same. The ultimate goal of school officials is to insure that the discipline necessary to the proper functioning of the school is maintained among both teachers and students. Any limitation on the exercise of constitutional rights can be justified only by a conclusion, based upon reasonable inferences flowing from concrete facts and not abstractions, that the interests of discipline or sound education are materially and substantially jeopardized, whether the danger stems initially from the conduct of students or teachers. Although it is not unreasonable to assume that the views of a teacher occupying a position of authority may carry more influence with a student than would those of students *inter sese,* that assumption merely weighs upon the inferences which may be drawn. It does not relieve the school of the necessity to show a reasonable basis for its regulatory policies. . . .

"The problem in any case is to arrive at a balance between the interests of the teacher, as a citizen, in commenting upon matters of public concern and the interest of the State, as an employer, in promoting the efficiency of the public services it performs through its employees." Pickering v. Board of Education, 391 U.S. 563, 568, 88 S. Ct. 1731, 1734, 20 L. Ed. 2d 811 (1968).

It is to be noted that in this case, the Board of Education has made no showing whatsoever at any stage of the proceedings that Charles James, by wearing a black armband, threatened to disrupt classroom activities or created any disruption in the school. . . .

Appellees urge us not to conclude that schools must wait until disruption is on the doorstep before they may take protective action. We do not suggest this course, but if anything is clear from the tortuous development of the first amendment right, freedom of expression demands breathing room. To preserve the "marketplace of ideas" so essential to our system of democracy, we must be willing to assume the risk of argument and lawful disagreement. . . . This is entirely different, however, from saying that the school must await open rebellion, violence or extensive disruption before it acts. . . .

That does not end our inquiry, however. The interest of the state in promoting the efficient operation of its schools extends beyond merely securing an orderly classroom. . . . Accordingly, courts consistently have affirmed that curriculum controls belong to the political process and local school authorities. "Courts do not and cannot intervene in the resolution of conflicts which arise in the daily operation of school systems and which do not directly and sharply implicate constitutional values." Epperson v. Arkansas, 393 U.S. 97, 104, 89 S. Ct. 266, 270, 21 L. Ed. 2d 228 (1968).[16]

Appellees argue that this broad power extends to controlling a teacher's speech in public schools, that "assumptions of the 'free marketplace of ideas' on which freedom of speech rests do not apply to school-aged children, especially in the classroom where the word of the teacher may carry great authority." Note, Developments in the Law-Academic Freedom, 81 Harv. L. Rev. at 1053. Certainly there must be some restraints because the students are a "captive" group. But to state the proposition without qualification is to uncover its fallacy. More than a decade of Supreme Court precedent leaves no doubt that we cannot countenance school authorities arbitrarily censoring a teacher's speech merely because they do not agree with the teacher's political philosophies or leanings. This is particularly so when that speech does not interfere in any way with the teacher's obligations to teach, is not coercive and does not arbitrarily inculcate doctrinaire views in the minds of the students. . . .

Although sound discussions of ideas are the beams and buttresses of the first amendment, teachers cannot be allowed to patrol the precincts of radical thought with the unrelenting goal of indoctrination, a goal compatible with totalitarianism and not democracy. When a teacher is only content if he persuades his students that his values and only his values ought to be their values, then it is not unreasonable to expect the state to protect impressionable children from such dogmatism. But, just as clearly,

[16] Even in this area there are constitutional limitations. In *Epperson*, for example, the Court held that a state could not prevent a high school biology teacher from teaching students about Darwin's theory of evolution because the regulation would be an establishment of religion in violation of the first amendment. Nor can a state prevent the teaching of modern foreign languages under the guise of promoting "civic development." Meyer v. Nebraska, 262 U.S. 390, 43 S. Ct. 625, 67 L. Ed. 1042 (1923).

those charged with overseeing the day-to-day interchange between teacher and student must exercise that degree of restraint necessary to protect first amendment rights. The question we must ask in every first amendment case is whether the regulatory policy is drawn as narrowly as possible to achieve the social interests that justify it, or whether it exceeds permissible bounds by unduly restricting protected speech to an extent "greater than is essential to the furtherance of" those interests. . . .

Several factors present here compel the conclusion that the Board of Education arbitrarily and unjustifiably discharged James for wearing the black armband. Clearly, there was no attempt by James to proselytize his students. It does not appear from the record that any student believed the armband to be anything more than a benign symbolic expression of the teacher's personal views. Moreover, we cannot ignore the fact that James was teaching 11th grade (high school) English. His students were approximately 16 or 17 years of age, thus more mature than those junior high school students in *Tinker*. . . .

Finally, James was first removed from class while he was teaching poetry. There is no suggestion whatsoever that his armband interfered with his teaching functions, or, for that matter, that his teaching ever had been deficient in any respect.

We emphasize that we do not question the broad discretion of local school authorities in setting classroom standards, nor do we question their expertise in evaluating the effects of classroom conduct in light of the special characteristics of the school environment. The federal courts, however, cannot allow unfettered discretion to violate fundamental constitutional rights. . . .

It is characteristic of resolutions of first amendment cases, where the price of freedom of expression is so high and the horizons of conflict between countervailing interests seemingly infinite, that they do not yield simplistic formulas or handy scales for weighing competing values. "The best one can hope for is to discern lines of analysis and advance formulations sufficient to bridge past decisions with new facts. One must be satisfied with such present solutions and cannot expect a clear view of the terrain beyond the periphery of the immediate case." Eisner v. Stamford Board of Education, 440 F.2d 803, 804 n.1 (2d Cir. 1971).

It is appropriate, however, lest our decision today (which is based on the total absence of any facts justifying the Board of Education's actions) be misunderstood, that we disclaim any intent to condone partisan political activities in the public schools which reasonably may be expected to interfere with the educational process.

Accordingly, we conclude that the district court erred. The judgment of the district court is reversed and the case remanded for proceedings not inconsistent with this opinion.

NOTES

1. Should *Pickering* have been distinguished in the *James* decision because the first amendment rights in *Pickering* were exercised outside of the classroom? *See* Goldwasser v. Brown, 417 F.2d 1169 (D.C. Cir.), *cert. denied*, 397 U.S. 922 (1969) (*Pickering* test applies to teacher's classroom speech at Air Force language school).

2. In Hanover v. Northrup, 325 F. Supp. 170 (D. Conn. 1970), it was held that it was a violation of first amendment rights to dismiss a junior high school teacher who refused to lead her class in the Salute to the Flag because she believed the phrase "with liberty and justice for all" was an untrue statement. Does the decision in *Hanover* comport with the principles outlined in *James?*

3. *See generally* Kaufman, I., *The Medium, the Message and the First Amendment*, 45 N.Y.U.L. REV. 761 (1970).

5. Regulation of the Private Lives of Public Employees

McCONNELL v. ANDERSON

United States Court of Appeals, Eighth Circuit
451 F.2d 193 (1971)
Cert. denied, 405 U.S. 1046 (1972)

STEPHENSON, Circuit Judge.

This case has its origin in a July 9, 1970 resolution of the University of Minnesota Board of Regents not to approve the application of James Michael McConnell to head, at the rank of Instructor, the cataloging division of the University's St. Paul campus library on the ground that his "personal conduct, as represented in the public and University news media, is not consistent with the best interest of the University." McConnell's complaint alleged that he was offered the division head appointment in April 1970; that he accepted the offer in May 1970, but that the offer was withdrawn, pursuant to the foregoing resolution, after he and another male publicly applied for a marriage license at the Hennepin County, Minnesota Clerk's office. . . . In addition to the allegations above, his complaint asserted that he was a homosexual and that the Board's resolution not to approve his employment application was premised on the fact of his homosexuality and upon his desire, as exemplified by the marriage license incident, specifically to publicly profess his "earnest" belief that homosexuals are entitled to privileges equal to those afforded heterosexuals. . . .

Federal jurisdiction was claimed, *inter alia,* under 42 U.S.C.A. § 1983 and 28 U.S.C.A. § 1343 (3). Judge Neville, after conducting an oral hearing at which evidence was taken, entered judgment for McConnell and enjoined the Board from refusing to employ him "solely because, and on the grounds that he is a homosexual." . . .

Judge Neville stayed the judgment and suspended the injunction pending disposition of this appeal. We must reverse. . . .

McConnell apparently is well-educated and otherwise able, possessing both an academic degree and a master's degree; that he formerly was employed as Acquisitions Librarian at Park College in Missouri; that he is a member of the organization known as FREE (Fight Repression of Erotic Expression); that on May 18, 1970, McConnell and a friend referred to in the record as "Jack Baker" encountered Dr. Hopp and informed him of their intention to obtain a license to marry; that during this conversation Dr. Hopp expressed concern that such an occurrence might well jeopardize favorable consideration of McConnell's employment application; that about three hours later on the same day, McConnell and Jack Baker appeared at the Hennepin County Clerk's office and made formal application for the license; that this event received the attention of the local news and television media; that the Board's Faculty, Staff and Student Affairs Committee, on June 24, 1970, convened to initially consider the matter of McConnell's proposed appointment and voted that it be not approved; that McConnell promptly was so advised and given notice that he could request a hearing at the Committee's next scheduled meeting on July 9; that McConnell requested a hearing; that he and his counsel appeared at the meeting and were furnished copies of the resolution in its proposed form; that McConnell and his counsel took advantage of this opportunity to present information they deemed supportive of his application, and that at the conclusion of the presentation on McConnell's behalf, the Committee adopted the resolution. It perhaps is well at this point to note that McConnell makes no claim that the Board denied him procedural due process.

The Board's primary demand for reversal is based upon a most fundamental contention. It is the Board's claim that Judge Neville, in issuing the injunction, exceeded his proper function and authority by superimposing his own situational judgment upon legitimate Board action supported by substantial and material factual data. . . .

We focus our initial attention upon our standard of review of the Board's action. The Minnesota Supreme Court has had no less than five occasions to determine and review the proper role and function of the Board of Regents in the management, control and administration of the University of Minnesota. From these decisions we think it can be said generally that, insofar as Minnesota's highest court is concerned, the Board is vested with plenary and exclusive authority to govern, control and oversee the administration of the University and that the role of Minnesota courts in reviewing Board action is limited to determining whether the Board has kept within the scope of its constitutional powers. . . .

[T]he discretion of the Board necessarily is broad and subject only to such judicial review as normally is available to litigants allegedly aggrieved by administrative action generally. We think the attitude and approach to the Board's role by Minnesota's court is sound and instructive and we adopt it as our own.

Without question, then, the Board is on relevant and sound ground in asserting that the decision embodied in its resolution cannot be overturned in the absence of a clear and affirmative showing that it was premised upon arbitrary or capricious conduct. That a court is, in reviewing a determination of an administrative body, limited to deciding whether the administrative action was arbitrary, unreasonable or capricious long has been settled. . . .

It is McConnell's position that the Board's decision not to approve his employment application reflects "a clear example of the unreasoning prejudice and revulsion some people feel when confronted by a homosexual." That being so, he argues that the Board's action was arbitrary and capricious and thus violative of his constitutional rights. We do not agree.

It is our conclusion that the Board possessed ample specific factual information on the basis of which it reasonably could conclude that the appointment would not be consistent with the best interests of the University. . . .

[I]t is at once apparent that this is not a case involving mere homosexual propensities on the part of a prospective employee. Neither is it a case in which an applicant is excluded from employment because of a desire clandestinely to pursue homosexual conduct. It is, instead, a case in which something more than remunerative employment is sought; a case in which the applicant seeks employment on his own terms; a case in which the prospective employee demands, as shown both by the allegations of the complaint and by the marriage license incident as well, the right to pursue an activist role in *implementing* his unconventional ideas concerning the societal status to be accorded homosexuals and, thereby, to foist tacit approval of this socially repugnant concept upon his employer, who is, in this instance, an institution of higher learning.[7] We know of no constitutional fiat or binding principle of decisional law which requires an employer to accede to such extravagant demands. We are therefore unable fairly to categorize the Board's action here as arbitrary, unreasonable or capricious. . . .

Reversed, with directions to dissolve the injunction and to dismiss the action on the merits.

NORTON v. MACY
United States Court of Appeals, District of Columbia Circuit
417 F.2d 1161 (1969)

BAZELON, Chief Judge:

Appellant, a former GS-14 budget analyst in the National Aeronautics and Space Administration (NASA), seeks review of his discharge for "immoral conduct" and for possessing personality traits which render him "unsuitable for further Government employment." As a veterans preference eligible, he could be dismissed only for "such cause as will promote the efficiency of the service." Since the record before us does not suggest any reasonable connection between the evidence against him and the efficiency of the service, we conclude that he was unlawfully discharged.

Appellant's dismissal grew out of his arrest for a traffic violation. In the early morning of October 22, 1963, he was driving his car in the vicinity of Lafayette Square. He pulled over to the curb, picked up one Madison Monroe Procter, drove him once around the Square, and dropped him off at the starting point. The two men then drove off in separate cars. Two Morals Squad officers, having observed this sequence of events, gave chase, traveling at speeds of up to 45 miles per hour. In the parking lot of appellant's Southwest Washington apartment building, Procter

---

[7] Compare Pickering v. Board of Education, 391 U.S. 563, 568-575, 88 S. Ct. 1731, 20 L. Ed. 2d 811 (1968). In the District Court McConnell apparently argued that he has the right to apply for a marriage license and that such is "symbolic speech" within the protection of the Free Speech and Due Process clauses of the First and Fourteenth Amendments. See McConnell v. Anderson, p. 815 of 316 F. Supp. He relies largely on Tinker v. Des Moines Ind. School Dist., 393 U.S. 503, 89 S. Ct. 733, 21 L. Ed. 2d 731 (1969), a case from this circuit. Although this contention is not pressed here, we feel constrained to observe that we do not believe that *Tinker*, when read in light of its distinctive facts, can afford McConnell any comfort in this regard.

told the police that appellant had felt his leg during their brief circuit of Lafayette Square and had then invited him to appellant's apartment for a drink. The officers arrested both men and took them "to the Morals Office to issue a traffic violation notice."

Pending issuance of the traffic summons, the police interrogated appellant and Procter for two hours concerning their activities that evening and their sexual histories. Meanwhile, pursuant to an arrangement, the head of the Morals Squad telephoned NASA Security Chief Fugler, who arrived on the scene at 3:00 a.m. in time to hear the last of the interrogation. . . . Throughout, appellant steadfastly denied that he had made a homosexual advance to Procter. . . .

[However, during a later] interrogation, appellant allegedly conceded that he had engaged in mutual masturbation with other males in high school and college, that he sometimes experienced homosexual desires while drinking, that on rare occasions he had undergone a temporary blackout after drinking, and that on two such occasions he suspected he might have engaged in some sort of homosexual activity. . . .

NASA concluded that appellant did in fact make a homosexual advance on October 22, and that this act amounted to "immoral, indecent, and disgraceful conduct." It also determined that . . . appellant possesses "traits of character and personality which render [him] . . . unsuitable for further Government employment." A Civil Service Appeals Examiner and the Board of Appeals and Review upheld these conclusions. In appellant's action for reinstatement, the District Court granted appellee's motion for summary judgment.

Congress has provided that protected civil servants shall not be dismissed except "for such cause as will promote the efficiency of the service." The Civil Service Commission's regulations provide that an appointee may be removed, *inter alia*, for "infamous . . . , immoral, or notoriously disgraceful conduct" and for "any . . . other disqualification which makes the individual unfit for the service." We think—and appellant does not strenuously deny— that the evidence was sufficient to sustain the charge that, consciously or not, he made a homosexual advance to Procter. Accordingly, the question presented is whether such an advance, or appellant's personality traits as disclosed by the record, are "such cause" for removal as the statute requires.

The Fifth Circuit Court of Appeals recently refused to consider a substantive attack on a dismissal for private homosexual conduct, apparently believing that it had no authority to review on the merits a Civil Service determination of unfitness.[5] The courts have, it is true, consistently recognized that the Commission enjoys a wide discretion in determining what reasons may justify removal of a federal employee; but it is also clear that this discretion is not unlimited. The Government's obligation to accord due process sets at least minimal substantive limits on its prerogative to dismiss its employees: it forbids all dismissals which are arbitrary and capricious. These constitutional limits may be greater where, as here, the dismissal imposes a "badge of infamy," disqualifying the victim from any further Federal employment, damaging his prospects for private employ, and fixing upon him the stigma of an official defamation of character. The Due Process Clause may also cut deeper into the Government's discretion where a dismissal involves an intrusion upon that ill-defined area of privacy which is increasingly if indistinctly recognized as a foundation of several specific constitutional protections. Whatever their precise scope, these due process limitations apply even to those whose employment status is unprotected by statute. And statutes such as the Veterans' Preference Act were plainly designed to confer some additional job security not enjoyed by unprotected federal employees. . . .

Accordingly, this court has previously examined the merits of a dismissal involving a statutorily protected employee charged with off-duty homosexual conduct. In other cases, we have recognized that, besides complying with statutory procedural requirements, the employer agency must demonstrate some "rational basis" for its conclusion that a discharge "will promote the efficiency of the service." . . .

Preliminarily, we must reject appellee's contention that once the label "immoral" is plausibly attached to an employee's off-duty conduct, our inquiry into the presence of adequate rational cause for removal is at an end. A pronouncement of "immorality" tends to discourage careful analysis because it unavoidably connotes a violation of divine, Olympian, or otherwise universal

---

[5] Anonymous v. Macy, 398 F.2d 317 (5 Cir. 1968). The Court said only: Counsel for appellant . . . argue at great length, and with considerable ability, that homosexual acts constitute private acts upon the part of such employees, that they do not affect the efficiency of the service, and should not be the basis of discharge. That contention is not accepted by this Court. See Hargett v. Summerfield, 100 U.S. App. D.C. 85, 243 F.2d 29 (1957).

398 F.2d at 318. Although Hargett v. Summerfield eschews any absolute bar to judicial review of a discharge on the merits, it contains language which approaches such a bar. Thus, it is not altogether clear whether the Fifth Circuit thought it had no authority to consider the arguments presented or whether it thought only that the particular matters raised fell within the area of agency discretion.

standards of rectitude. However, the Civil Service Commission has neither the expertise nor the requisite anointment to make or enforce absolute moral judgments, and we do not understand that it purports to do so. Its jurisdiction is at least confined to the things which are Caesar's, and its avowed standard of "immorality" is no more than "the prevailing mores of our society." ...

We are not prepared to say that the Commission could not reasonably find appellant's homosexual advance to be "immoral," "indecent," or "notoriously disgraceful" under dominant conventional norms. But the notion that it could be an appropriate function of the federal bureaucracy to enforce the majority's conventional codes of conduct in the private lives of its employees is at war with elementary concepts of liberty, privacy, and diversity. And whatever we may think of the Government's qualifications to act *in loco parentis* in this way, the statute precludes it from discharging protected employees except for a reason related to the efficiency of the service. Accordingly, a finding that an employee has done something immoral or indecent could support a dismissal without further inquiry only if all immoral or indecent acts of an employee have some ascertainable deleterious effect on the efficiency of the service. The NASA official who fired him, Mr. Garbarini, testified that appellant was a "competent employee" doing "very good" work. ...

Appellant's duties apparently did not bring him into contact with the public, and his fellow employees were unaware of his "immorality." Nonetheless, Garbarini's advisers told him that dismissal for any homosexual conduct was a *"custom* within the agency," and he decided to follow the custom because continued employment of appellant might "turn out to be embarrassing to the agency" in that "if an incident like this occurred again, it could become a public scandal on the agency."

Thus, appellee is now obliged to rely solely on this possibility of embarrassment to the agency to justify appellant's dismissal. The assertion of such a nebulous "cause" poses perplexing problems for a review proceeding which must accord broad discretion to the Commission. We do not doubt that NASA blushes whenever one of its own is caught *in flagrante delictu;* but if the possibility of such transitory institutional discomfiture must be uncritically accepted as a cause for discharge which will "promote the efficiency of the service," we might as well abandon all pretense that the statute provides any substantive security for its supposed beneficiaries. A claim of possible embarrassment might, of course, be a vague way of referring to some specific potential interference with an agency's performance; but it might also be a smokescreen hiding personal antipathies or moral judgments which are excluded by statute as grounds for dismissal. A reviewing court must at least be able to discern some reasonably foreseeable, specific connection between an employee's potentially embarrassing conduct and the efficiency of the service. Once the connection is established, then it is for the agency and the Commission to decide whether it outweighs the loss to the service of a particular competent employee.

In the instant case appellee has shown us no such specific connection. Indeed, on the record appellant is at most an extremely infrequent offender, who neither openly flaunts nor carelessly displays his unorthodox sexual conduct in public. Thus, even the potential for the embarrassment the agency fears is minimal. We think the unparticularized and unsubstantiated conclusion that such possible embarrassment threatens the quality of the agency's performance is an arbitrary ground for dismissal.
. . .

Lest there be any doubt, we emphasize that we do not hold that homosexual conduct may never be cause for dismissal of a protected federal employee. Nor do we even conclude that potential embarrassment from an employee's private conduct may in no circumstances affect the efficiency of the service. What we do say is that, if the statute is to have any force, an agency cannot support a dismissal as promoting the efficiency of the service merely by turning its head and crying "shame."

Since we conclude that appellant's discharge cannot be sustained on the grounds relied on by the Commission, the judgment of the District Court must be

Reversed.

TAMM, Circuit Judge (dissenting) : . . .

This court plainly held in the case of Hargett v. Summerfield, 100 U.S. App. D.C. 85, 88, 243 F.2d 29, 32 (1957), that "employee removal and discipline are almost entirely matters of executive agency discretion," and "that, so long as there [is] substantial compliance with applicable procedures . . . the administrative determination [is] not reviewable as to the wisdom or good judgment of the department . . . exercising [its] discretion." (Citations omitted.) I have felt constrained to follow this view time and again, see, e.g., dissenting opinion in Meehan v. Macy, U.S. App. D.C. (No. 20.812, decided May 12, 1969) (en banc), although in so doing I remain a vox clamantis in deserto.
. . . Homosexuals, sadly enough, do not leave their emotions at Lafayette Square and regardless of their spiritual destinies they still present targets for public reproach and private extortion. I

believe this record supports the finding that this individual presents more than a potential risk in this regard and that his termination will serve the efficiency of the service. Despite the billows of puffery that continue to float out of recent opinions on this subject, I believe that the theory that homosexual conduct is not in any way related to the efficiency and effectiveness of governmental business is not an evil theory—just a very unrealistic one.

NOTES

1. In Morrison v. State Bd. of Educ., 1 Cal. 3d 214, 82 Cal. Rptr. 175, 461 P.2d 375 (1969), the California Supreme Court held that a school teacher could not be dismissed for a single homosexual act. The court noted, in dictum, that a broad prohibition against "immoral acts" would raise serious constitutional questions. In this regard, the court observed that "school officials concerned with enforcing such broad prohibitions might be inclined to probe into the private life of each and every teacher, no matter how exemplary his classroom conduct. Such prying might all too readily lead school officials to search for 'telltale signs' of immorality in violation of the teacher's constitutional rights."

2. The court in *Morrison* suggests that an individual cannot be removed from the teaching profession in the absence of a showing that his retention in the public service poses a significant danger of harm to either students, school employees, or others who might be affected by his actions as a teacher. Other courts have subscribed to this view in cases involving hair style, private correspondence, and heterosexual relations. *See, e.g.,* Mindel v. United States Civil Serv. Comm'n, 312 F. Supp. 485 (N.D. Cal. 1970); Forstner v. City and County of San Francisco, 243 Cal. App. 2d 625, 52 Cal. Rptr. 621 (1966); Jarvella v. Willoughby-Eastlake City School Dist. Bd. of Educ., 12 Ohio Misc. 288, 41 Ohio Op. 2d 423, 233 N.E.2d 143 (C.P. Lake County 1967). *Compare* the holding in *Morrison with* Board of Trustees v. Stubblefield, 16 Cal. App. 3d 820, 94 Cal. Rptr. 318 (1971) (extra-marital involvement with student).

3. In contrast to the decision in *Norton v. Macy*, the court in *McConnell* appears wholly insensitive to homosexuality, describing it as a "socially repugnant concept." However, is it clear that the D.C. Circuit would have decided *McConnell* differently than the 8th Circuit if it had heard and decided the case? The D.C. Circuit in *Norton* suggests that, pursuant to the Veterans' Preference Act, the government employer must show "some rea-

sonably foreseeable, specific connection between an employee's potentially embarrassing conduct and the efficiency of the service." What is the standard of review expressed in *McConnell* and where does the burden of proof lie?

4. In O'Neil, *The Private Lives of Public Employees,* 51 ORE. L. REV. 70, 105-106 (1971), the author suggests that the courts must evaluate the following factors in weighing the substantiality of governmental interests against infringement of personal freedoms in cases involving the regulation of the private lives of public employees: What is the effect, if any, upon the individual's job performance? What is the effect, if any, upon the efficiency of the agency? What is the effect, if any, on the image of and public confidence in the agency? O'Neil concludes that "judgments about governmental interests cannot be made in the abstract . . . [and that] the following factors . . . have been deemed pertinent by courts in passing upon recent public employment dismissals: (a) How sensitive is the position held or sought? . . . (b) Have other members of the agency or institution been involved? . . . (c) Was the behavior recent and is it recurrent? . . . (d) What is the probability of repetition? . . . (e) How does the transgression relate to the employee's entire record? . . . What is the status of the behavior outside the public service? . . . How clear and specific is the standard of conduct? . . . What less onerous alternatives are available to the agency? . . . What procedures are provided within the agency?"

CARTER v. UNITED STATES
United States Court of Appeals, District of Columbia Circuit
407 F.2d 1238 (1968)

LEVENTHAL, Circuit Judge:

Appellant Carter brought an action asserting that his discharge from Government service deprived him of statutory and constitutional rights. He appeals to this court on the ground that the District Court erred when it granted judgment in favor of the Government without a trial.

The facts shown on the record before us are these. Carter was hired by the Federal Bureau of Investigation (FBI) in 1960 as a clerk in its identification division. His employment with the Bureau was interrupted by his enlistment in the Air Force. After completing his military service in 1965 he was reinstated at his old job. In August 1965, the FBI received an anonymous letter complaining that Carter was "sleeping with young girls and carrying on." When questioned about the matter by his supervisor, Carter admitted that a female friend had twice stayed overnight at his apartment. He admitted that they slept together, although not nude, in the same bed, but insisted that they did not have sexual relations. He told his supervisor that the lady had been visiting Washington from out of town for a period of three days, that they had been going together for several years, and that he was seriously considering marriage. On one occasion she had visited at his home in Kentucky and stayed with his brother and sister-in-law. . . .

Carter was dismissed by the FBI for "conduct unbecoming an employee of this Bureau." . . . Carter sued for reinstatement and back pay, and served interrogatories. Without answering, the Government pressed a motion for summary judgment, which the District Court granted, holding that appellant was not entitled to a trial.

We affirm the District Court's ruling that Carter had no statutory rights to employment under the Civil Service laws or the Veterans Preference Act. However we cannot agree with the District Court's conclusion that Carter was not entitled to a trial to determine whether the discharge violated Section 9 (c) of the Universal Military Training and Service Act, 50 U.S.C. App. § 459 (c) (1964). We do not rule on appellant's claim of unconstitutional arbitrariness.[4]

Because of the exemption of the FBI from the civil service laws, the Bureau is generally free to discharge its employees for any reasons it chooses, subject only to constitutional limitations. Obviously, however, that discretion is subject to any specific limitations that Congress has chosen to impose. This much is conceded by appellee. Thus, like any other employer, the FBI is subject to the provisions of § 9 (c) of the Universal Military Training and Service Act by which Congress granted special rights and protections to the returning veteran: the right to reinstatement in the civilian job he held prior to military service; the right to be free in the first year after resumption of civilian life from discharge for other than "cause."

The law giving a returning veteran a right to be free of discharge except for "cause" puts on the employer the burden of coming forward with a cause sufficient to justify the discharge. . . .

The FBI asserts that it had "cause" to dismiss Carter. Essentially the contention is that any FBI employee would be fired for this conduct, and the application of a general FBI personnel

---

[4] It seems plain to us that no discharge could be for "cause" within the meaning of § 9 (c) if it were so arbitrary and unreasonable as to violate due process. We therefore need not reach constitutional questions in this case.

policy which does not discriminate against veterans must be upheld unless so arbitrary as to violate due process.

A private employer may have the right, in the absence of
statute or contract to the contrary, to fire an employee for personal reasons, unrelated to job function, that appeal to the employer, the color of hair, a dislike of men who smoke, or have a
tattoo, etc. That does not mean that the employer can fire a
returning veteran for the same reason as constituting "cause."
. . .

The "cause" provision was inserted by Congress to provide the
reemployed veteran with a protection of reasonableness similar to
that enjoyed by a union member protected by provisions in a
collective bargaining agreement limiting discharge to cause. The
ultimate criterion, whether the employer acted reasonably, is the
one generally applied where an employment contract is terminated by an employer because of employee misconduct, and that
standard is appropriate under this Federal statute. Kemp v. John
Chattillon & Sons, 169 F.2d 203 (3rd Cir. 1948). We think a discharge may be upheld as one for "cause" only if it meets two
criteria of reasonableness: one, that it is reasonable to discharge
employees because of certain conduct, and the other, that the
employee had fair notice, express or fairly implied, that such
conduct would be ground for discharge. . . .

The District Judge granted summary judgment on the ground
that regardless of whether Carter's action was moral or immoral,
he had been indiscreet in carrying on his relationship. The
Government's brief also treats the nexus of the case as including: "that appellant's sexual misadventures had become sufficiently public knowledge to cause an anonymous complaint to the
FBI" (p. 15).

That theory is not maintainable on the present record so as to
support summary judgment without a trial. The only conduct
before us on this record was limited to two occasions, and in
Carter's own apartment. There is no suggestion here that Carter
was notoriously promiscuous, consorted with prostitutes or anything of that sort. Certainly Carter's admitted conduct cannot
be equated with that generally "loose" conduct likely to become
a matter of public notoriety. The only basis for inferences as to
the extent to which Carter's conduct was known outside the
circle of his roommates—also employed by the FBI—is an
anonymous letter. The letter does not indicate how the writer
came to know of Carter's acts. . . .

The FBI may well have made an informed appraisal, or investigation, that permitted it to ascertain that Carter so conducted
himself as to turn a private relationship ino a public affront. But

that is a question of fact and Carter is entitled to a trial of that fact.

We turn to the issue whether "cause" for discharge was established as a matter of law by Carter's admitted overnight "necking" and "petting" with his young lady in his apartment on two occasions. . . .

Appellant's counsel point out that Carter did nothing more than the "bundling" condoned in Puritan New England. As for more modern precedent, the law is clear that an unmarried man does not have an "immoral" character for purposes of exclusion from citizenship even if he goes beyond necking and engages in heterosexual relations. Judge Learned Hand pointed out, "we have answered in the negative the question whether an unmarried man must live completely celibate, or forfeit his claim to a 'good moral character.' " Schmidt v. United States, 177 F.2d 450, 452 (2d Cir. 1949).

The Government's motion put before the court, as an exhibit, the Handbook for FBI Employees, distributed to all FBI employees. We consider whether that Handbook shows that Carter was put on notice that his admitted conduct was prohibited. The Handbook is a description of the FBI and its work, as well as a "guide" to "help you refrain from doing anything which would in any way detract from the Bureau's reputation or embarrass it in any manner." The sole relevant passage is one stating—"personal misbehavior of Bureau employees reflecting unfavorably upon them or the Bureau, and neglect of duty cannot be tolerated."

The Government invokes the standard of the lady from Dubuque and argues that as the FBI relies on the cooperation of the citizenry it is reasonable to compel moral standards for all employees—clerks as well as agents—that would satisfy that most upright lady. Pretermitting the issue whether the standard of the lady from Dubuque would have been reasonable if announced, there is a threshold problem, whether the employees have adequate notice of such a standard. The FBI employees are expressly told in the Handbook that legal gambling is permitted, as is off-duty use of intoxicants, yet these sit poorly with many upright citizens. We do not think a court can deny an employee a trial of the issue on the ground that this Handbook clearly puts FBI employees on notice that they must meet not only the general standards of their own community, but also the special standards of the lady from Dubuque. . . .

The question is whether the limitation on private life now asserted to apply to all FBI employees is something the average FBI clerical employee should and does know as contemplated by "ordinarily expected standards of personal conduct." We cannot say that the answer is so clear that Carter is not even entitled to a trial....

The order of the District Court is vacated and the case remanded for further proceedings.

So ordered.

DANAHER, Circuit Judge (dissenting) : ....

This court on many occasions has recognized the principle that the power to remove inferior Government employees is an incident of the power to appoint them, following the statement in Myers v. United States, 272 U.S. 52, 161, 47 S. Ct. 21, 71 L. Ed. 160 (1925). Put another way the interest of a Government employee in retaining his job can be summarily denied. "It has become a settled principle that government employment, in the absence of legislation, can be revoked at the will of the appointing officer." Cafeteria and Restaurant Workers etc. v. McElroy, 367 U.S. 886, 896, 81 S. Ct. 1743, 1749, 6 L. Ed. 2d 1230 (1961) ; Vitarelli v. Seaton, 359 U.S. 535, 539, 79 S. Ct. 968, 3 L. Ed. 2d 1012 (1959). No matter who has stated the law, no one has said it better than Mr. Justice Reed speaking for the Court of Claims in Batchelor v. United States, 169 Ct. Cl. 180, 183, cert. denied, 382 U.S. 870, 86 S. Ct. 147, 15 L. Ed. 2d 109 (1965), where we read:

> "The Supreme Court in Keim v. United States, 177 U.S. 290 (1900), considered the question of whether or not the courts may supervise the acts of an executive department head in discharging an employee. The Court's decision in that case clearly placed the removal of executive department employees within the ambit of executive discretion, and ruled that until Congress, by 'special and direct legislation makes provisions to the contrary,' the courts cannot review the soundness or propriety of the exercise of the department head's discretion. This case stands as a solid milestone in a long line of unbroken authorities holding that where there are no established procedures or statutes to be followed, removal of an employee is solely within the discretion of agency officials and accordingly may be effected without giving reason. See Cafeteria Workers v. McElroy, 367 U.S. 886, 896-97 (1961) and cases cited therein." ...

It has been suggested that the Handbook for FBI Employees is not sufficiently specific in pointing out that the Bureau cannot tolerate personal misbehavior of its employees "reflecting unfavorably upon them or the Bureau." It is true that the Handbook does not say that an FBI employee may not use profane and obscene language in denouncing his superiors in the presence of others. A fingerprint clerk is not enjoined against mocking or vilifying a police officer who brings in a "lifted" fingerprint for classification in furtherance of cooperation with the Bureau. Myriad examples of unspecified misbehavior will suggest themselves. Something is lacking, it is argued, in that the Handbook did not particularize with respect to any such illustration, or by way of denouncing the very conduct under discussion here, admitted by Carter who "told exactly what happened." If an employee of the Bureau did not know that he was expected to comply satisfactorily with "ordinarily accepted standards of personal conduct," I would suppose he did not belong in the Bureau in the first place. Were I required to do so, I would rule that the Director had ample cause for dismissing Carter. . . .

BRUNS v. POMERLEAU
319 F. Supp. 58 (D. Md. 1970)

NORTHROP, Chief Judge.

The plaintiff, a practicing nudist, has brought his complaint against the defendants pursuant to Title 42, U.S.C.A. Section 1983—"Civil Rights Act"—on the ground that the defendants wrongfully refused to accept the plaintiff's application for employment as a probationary patrolman and that such refusal was tantamount to a violation of the plaintiff's civil rights, as guaranteed by the First, Fifth and Fourteenth Amendments of the United States Constitution. . . .

The criteria established by the [City of Baltimore] Commissioner of Police and by the Civil Service Commission is designed to allow the Commissioner to employ certain procedures, such as investigation, personal contacts, etc., after the threshold written examination is administered by the Civil Service Commission. The policy of the police department is to accept as a probationary patrolman any applicant who passed the written examination given by the Civil Service Commission and who passed the personal interview. The test to qualify for this position of probationary patrolman is thus not limited solely to the successful completion of the written examination, but rather to the passing of all requirements established by both authorities. . . .

It is conceded that plaintiff stood first of the sixty applicants for the two hundred positions of probationary patrolman, both in the written and in the preliminary interview examinations, and that no derogatory information was turned up by the indepth investigation. It is stipulated by both parties that there was no reason for his exclusion, other than the fact that he was a nudist. . . .

Commissioner Pomerleau testified before this court that he had made that policy decision and, for his reasons, stated that: (1) Nudism is not generally accepted as a way of life by the general public and (2) Because of this, a nudist might possibly subject police officers in general and the Department in particular to public criticism; (3) A nudist would possibly be harassed by fellow members of the Department making his position intolerable; (4) He possibly could not perform his duties where his views might differ in vice control work, such as with lewd shows, indecent exposure, etc., because of a nudist's belief that nudism is not improper, providing the motive behind exposure is not of a pornographic nature; (5) The feeling that a nudist could have a psychological impediment which would inhibit his proper performance under certain circumstances; and (6) He further felt that being a nudist might have an adverse effect upon his testimony in any given instance, especially before a jury during a court proceeding.

He testified that a policeman has an extremely sensitive job, and that there has been difficulty recently in recruiting individuals because of the nature of the work and the considerable magnitude of recent problems in law enforcement. He therefore decided that he could not afford to experiment with an individual who did not conform to what might be considered normal socially acceptable activities. . . .

There is no question but that now there is a different test of one's constitutional right to public employment than that announced by Justice Holmes in McAuliffe v. Mayor, etc., of City of New Bedford, 155 Mass. 216, 29 N.E. 517 (1892), when he said (speaking for the Massachusetts Supreme Judicial Court), (o)ne "may have a constitutional right to talk politics, but he has no constitutional right to be a policeman." Id. at 220, 29 N.E. at 517. The efficacy of this statement has been eroded by subsequent court decisions in which the "right-privilege" distinction has been narrowed to forbid a state the power to compel the surrender of constitutional rights as a condition of public employment. . . .

The Supreme Court has left little doubt that the right of association is specifically encompassed and protected by the First Amendment. . . . The First and Fourteenth Amendments protect this right to associate with any person of one's choosing for the purpose of advocating and promoting legitimate, albeit controversial, political, social or economic views. . . .

By limiting the power of the states to interfere with freedom of speech and freedom of association, the Fourteenth Amendment protects all persons, no matter what their views or means of expression. It is too late in the day to doubt that his freedom of association extends only to political or conventional associations and not to the social or the unorthodox. A nudist has the benefit of this constitutional right to associate with other nudists when his actions are in conformity with valid state statutes. This is a right of constitutional stature that a state may not condition by the exaction of a price. . . . In order to justify a state's infringement, the state has the burden of showing a compelling or sufficiently important governmental interest to justify the intrusion upon the constitutional right. . . .

It is the failure of defendant Pomerleau, as Commissioner of the Baltimore City Police Department, to establish a sufficiently compelling governmental interest in excluding the plaintiff from becoming a probationary patrolman, solely because of his being a practicing nudist, that we find an unconstitutional infringement upon plaintiff's rights. . . .

Neither the plaintiff nor the defendants have introduced any evidence relative to the general public attitude toward nudism. It is conceded that there are a number of camps located across the United States where interested families and persons may go, in an unobtrusive manner, to practice recreational activities in the nude. There is no indication that the plaintiff would attempt to procure other adherents to his views in the police department making such solicitation disruptive of departmental operations. While the testimony reveals a policeman is, in effect, on duty twenty-four hours a day, seven days a week, and must at all times have his weapon on his person, it is a matter of common knowledge that in participating in other recreational activities, when not nude, the weapon is not always so available. . . .

The defendant's contention that plaintiff and the department would possibly be subjected to public criticism is not, standing alone, a valid reason for infringing upon one's constitutional right. The Constitution protects the unorthodox views as well as the orthodox. . . .

This court has uniformly held that nudism *per se* is not immoral or obscene. United States v. 25,000 Magazines, Entitled "Revue," 254 F. Supp. 1014 (D. Md.), aff'd *sub nom.*, United States v. Central Magazine Sales (Ltd.), 381 F.2d 821 (4th Cir. 1966); United States v. 1,000 Copies of Magazine Entitled "Solis," 254 F. Supp. 595 (D. Md. 1966). There is hardly an art museum or gallery to which one can go where completely nude statues and pictures are not on constant and prominent exhibition. Many popular books and magazines, far too numerous to list, frequently publish human nudity without offending the law. Nudism may be unappealing and unattractive to some people. It may be repulsive and vulgar to others. But that does not limit its right to constitutional protection. Whether or not it appeals to or repels an individual's sensitivities is irrelevant when a court is bound to apply First Amendment rights which do not incorporate such subjective standards.

Plaintiff's activities at Pine Tree Associates in no way intrudes upon the public's sensibilities. He is a member of a group whose activities are neither illegal nor immoral and which are carried on unobtrusively. . . .

It cannot be denied that the behavioral pattern of a policeman off duty as well as on is of paramount interest to the Department. His associations are limited by his law enforcement employment. But it can only be limited to such associations or off duty activities that affect his morals and integrity or are inimical to the Department. What he does in his private life, as with other public employees, should not be his employer's concern unless it can be shown to affect in some degree his efficiency in the performance of his duties. There is nothing in the record before us to show that plaintiff's association would be inimical to his work or the Department. To deny his application consideration solely because of the defendant's bare allegations, without more, is to engage in speculation and presumptions. Constitutional freedoms cannot be limited on such hollow arguments. . . .

It is therefore the opinion of this court that defendant Pomerleau has failed to show by clear and convincing evidence such a paramount governmental interest as would justify an intrusion upon plaintiff's First Amendment right, and his policy of total exclusion of all nudists is arbitrary and capricious. . . .

MURRAY v. JAMISON
333 F. Supp. 1379 (W.D.N.C. 1971)

McMILLAN, D. J.: The plaintiff was discharged from employment as a switchboard operator or dispatcher by the Building Inspection Department of the City of Charlotte immediately after his supervisors discovered that he was the Grand Dragon of the Ku Klux Klan of North Carolina. Under the circumstances this discharge was unlawful under the First and Fourteenth Amendments to the United States Constitution, and the defendants will be directed to take appropriate remedial action. . . .

The Ku Klux Klan is known and shown by this record to be a segregationist "white supremacy" organization. Its bloody history is well known. Its oath of allegiance requires secrecy; its history is totally repugnant to all who favor constitutional government or who believe that all persons are entitled to due process and to equal protection of laws.

Klansmen, like Negroes, are people. They are entitled to associate together and to speak their minds. They are not by virtue of Klan membership disqualified from holding public employment any more than is a Presbyterian or a Black Panther or a member of the United Daughters of the Confederacy or of the Daughters of the American Revolution or the American Legion or the NAACP.

If membership in the Klan does prevent adequate performance of public duty it may be cause for discharge or discipline. The objectives of employment are usually fairly well defined, and they do not ordinarily include using the employer's time or the position of the job to further private pursuits. However, in the absence of a showing that Klansmanship has produced or is genuinely likely to produce a lower quality of performance of the employee's duties, the constitutional rights of free speech and free association and the interests of society in the encouragement of free thought and debate prevent public authorities from discharging public employees merely because of views and associations not approved of by the temporary bearer of the supervisory duty. Constitution of the United States, First and Fourteenth Amendments; Wieman v. Updegraff, 344 U.S. 183 (1952) ; Battle v. Mulholland, 439 F.2d 321 (5th Cir., 1971) .

Plaintiff was wrongfully discharged.

NOTES

1. The *Bruns* and *Murray* decisions were founded on principles of freedom of speech and association gleaned from the First and Fourteenth Amendments. However, several courts have found restrictions on public employees' appearance and private activity to be arbitrary and discriminatory and thus violative of the equal protection clause. *See, e.g.,* Ramsey v. Hopkins, 320 F. Supp. 477 (N.D. Ala. 1970) , remanded for assessment of back wages, 447 F.2d 128 (5th Cir. 1971) (school regulation against teacher's wearing a mustache) ; Braxton v. Board of Public Instruction, 303 F. Supp. 958 (M.D. Fla. 1969) (school regulation against teachers' wearing beards) . What is the standard of review employed by these courts in judging the challenged state action? Does the standard comport with the narrow test stated in McConnell v. Anderson, *supra?*

2. To what extent should the "right of privacy" protect public employees against arbitrary employment regulations? *Cf.* Griswold v. Connecticut, 381 U.S. 479 (1965) (invalidating Connecticut's ban against giving information about contraception or using birth control devices) ; Stanley v. Georgia, 394 U.S. 557 (1969) (holding that the private and personal use and viewing of obscene materials may not be made a crime).

3. Some courts have also utilized substantive due process to overturn public employer rules regulating the private life styles of public employees. *See, e.g.,* Finot v. Pasadena City Bd. of Educ., 250 Cal. App. 2d 189, 58 Cal. Rptr. 520 (1967) (teacher's wearing of a beard was personal liberty protected by due process clause). An interesting historical reference on this point is Justice McReynolds' opinion in Meyer v. Nebraska, 262 U.S. 390, 399 (1923) (holding invalid a state law which forbade the teaching of any modern language, other than English, to any child below the ninth grade in any private, parochial or public school).

B. Procedural Due Process as a Protection Against Dismissal from Public Employment

BOARD OF REGENTS v. ROTH

Supreme Court of the United States
408 U.S. 564, 92 S. Ct. 2701, 33 L. Ed. 2d 548 (1972)

Mr. Justice Stewart delivered the opinion of the Court.

In 1968 the respondent, David Roth was hired for his first teaching job as assistant professor of political science at Wisconsin State University-Oshkosh. He was hired for a fixed term of one academic year. The notice of his faculty appointment specified that his employment would begin on September 1, 1968, and would end on June 30, 1969. The respondent completed that term. But he was informed that he would not be rehired for the next academic year.

The respondent had no tenure rights to continued employment. Under Wisconsin statutory law a state university teacher can acquire tenure as a "permanent" employee only after four years of year-to-year employment. Having acquired tenure, a teacher is entitled to continued employment "during efficiency and good behavior." A relatively new teacher without tenure, however, is under Wisconsin law entitled to nothing beyond his one-year appointment. There are no statutory or administrative standards defining eligibility for re-employment. State law thus clearly leaves the decision whether to rehire a nontenured teacher for another year to the unfettered discretion of University officials. . . . Rules promulgated by the Board of Regents provide that a nontenured teacher "dismissed" before the end of the year may have some opportunity for review of the "dismissal." But the Rules provide no real protection for a nontenured teacher who simply is not re-employed for the next year. He must be informed by February first "concerning retention or non-retention for the ensuing year." But "no reason for non-retention need be given. No review or appeal is provided in such case."

In conformance with these Rules, the President of Wisconsin State University-Oshkosh informed the respondent before February 1, 1969, that he would not be rehired for the 1969-1970 academic year. He gave the respondent no reason for the decision and no opportunity to challenge it at any sort of hearing.

The respondent then brought this action in a federal district court alleging that the decision not to rehire him for the next year infringed his Fourteenth Amendment rights. He attacked the decision both in substance and procedure. First, he alleged that the true reason for the decision was to punish him for certain statements critical of the University administration, and that it therefore violated his right to freedom of speech.[5] Second, he alleged that the failure of University officials to give him notice of any reason for nonretention and an opportunity for a hearing violated his right to procedural due process of law.

The District Court granted summary judgment for the respondent on the procedural issue, ordering the University officials to provide him with reasons and a hearing. 310 F. Supp. 972. The Court of Appeals, with one judge dissenting, affirmed this partial summary judgment. 446 F.2d 806. We granted certiorari. 404 U.S. 909, 92 S. Ct. 227, 30 L. Ed. 2d 181. The only question presented to us at this stage in the case is whether the respondent had a constitutional right to a statement of reasons and a hearing on the University's decision not to rehire him for another year.[6] We hold that he did not.

---

[5] While the respondent alleged that he was not rehired because of his exercise of free speech, the petitioners insisted that the non-retention decision was based on other, constitutionally valid grounds. The District Court came to no conclusion whatever regarding the true reason for the University President's decision. . . .

[6] The courts that have had to decide whether a nontenured public employee has a right to a statement of reasons or a hearing upon nonrenewal of his contract have come to varying conclusions. Some have held that neither procedural safeguard is required. *E.g.,* Orr v. Trinter, 444 F.2d 128 (CA6); Jones v. Hopper, 410 F.2d 1323 (CA10); Freeman v. Gould Special School District, 405 F.2d 1153 (CA8). At least one court has held that there is a right to a statement of reasons but not a hearing. Drown v. Portsmouth School District, 435 F.2d 1182 (CA1). And another has held that both re-

The requirements of procedural due process apply only to the deprivation of interests encompassed within the Fourteenth Amendment's protection of liberty and property. When protected interests are implicated the right to some kind of prior hearing is paramount.[7] But the range of interests protected by procedural due process is not infinite. . . .

Undeniably, the respondent's re-employment prospects were of major concern to him—concern that we surely cannot say was insignificant. And a weighing process has long been a part of any determination of the *form* of hearing required in particular situations by procedural due process. But, to determine whether due process requirements apply in the first place, we must look not to the "weight" but to the *nature* of the interest at stake. See Morrissey v. Brewer, 405 U.S. —, —, 92 S. Ct. 2593, 32 L. Ed. 2d —. We must look to see if the interest is within the Fourteenth Amendment's protection of liberty and property.

"Liberty" and "property" are broad and majestic terms. They are among the "[g]reat [constitutional] concepts . . . purposely left to gather meaning from experience. . . . [T]hey relate to the whole domain of social and economic fact, and the statesmen who founded this Nation knew too well that only a stagnant society remains unchanged." National Mutual Ins. Co. v. Tidewater Transfer Co., 337 U.S. 582, 646, 69 S. Ct. 1173, 1195, 93 L. Ed. 1556 (Frankfurter, J., dissenting). For that reason the Court has fully and finally rejected the wooden distinction between "rights" and "privileges" that once seemed to govern the applicability of procedural due process rights.[9] The Court has also made clear that the property interests protected by procedural due process extend well beyond actual ownership of real estate, chattels, or money.[10] By the same token, the Court has required

---

quirements depend on whether the employee has an "expectancy" of continued employment. Ferguson v. Thomas, 430 F.2d 852, 856 (CA5).

[7] Before a person is deprived of a protected interest, he must be afforded opportunity for some kind of a hearing, "except for extraordinary situations where some valid governmental interest is at stake that justifies postponing the hearing until after the event." . . .

[9] In a leading case decided many years ago, the Court of Appeals for the District of Columbia Circuit held that public employment in general was a "privilege," not a "right," and that procedural due process guarantees therefore were inapplicable. Bailey v. Richardson, 86 U.S. App. D.C. 248, 182 F.2d 46, aff'd by an equally divided Court, 341 U.S. 918, 71 S. Ct. 669, 95 L. Ed. 1352. The basis of this holding has been thoroughly undermined in the ensuing years. For, as Mr. Justice Blackmun wrote for the Court only last year, "this Court now has rejected the concept that constitutional rights turn upon whether a governmental benefit is characterized as a 'right' or as a 'privilege.'" Graham v. Richardson, 403 U.S. 365, 374, 91 S. Ct. 1848, 1853, 29 L. Ed. 2d 534.

[10] See, *e.g.*, Connell v. Higginbotham, 403 U.S. 207, 208, 91 S. Ct. 1772, 1773, 29 L. Ed. 2d 418; Bell v. Burson, 402 U.S. 535, 91 S. Ct. 1586, 29

due process protection for deprivations of liberty beyond the sort of formal constraints imposed by the criminal process.

Yet, while the Court has eschewed rigid or formalistic limitations on the protection of procedural due process, it has at the same time observed certain boundaries. For the words "liberty" and "property" in the Due Process Clause of the Fourteenth Amendment must be given some meaning. . . .

The State, in declining to rehire the respondent, did not make any charge against him that might seriously damage his standing and associations in his community. It did not base the nonrenewal of his contract on a charge, for example, that he had been guilty of dishonesty, or immorality. Had it done so, this would be a different case. For "[w]here a person's good name, reputation, honor, or integrity is at stake because of what the government is doing to him, notice and an opportunity to be heard are essential." . .

In such a case, due process would accord an opportunity to refute the charge before University officials. In the present case, however, there is no suggestion whatever that the respondent's interest in his "good name, reputation, honor or integrity" is at stake.

Similarly, there is no suggestion that the State, in declining to re-employ the respondent, imposed on him a stigma or other disability that foreclosed his freedom to take advantage of other employment opportunities. The State, for example, did not involve any regulations to bar the respondent from all other public employment in State universities. Had it done so, this, again, would be a different case. . . .

To be sure, the respondent has alleged that the nonrenewal of his contract was based on his exercise of his right to freedom of speech. But this allegation is not now before us. The District Court stated proceedings on this issue, and the respondent has yet to prove that the decision not to rehire him was, in fact, based on his free speech activities.[14]

L. Ed. 2d 90; Goldberg v. Kelly, 397 U.S. 254, 90 S. Ct. 1011, 25 L. Ed. 2d 287.

[14] See n. 5, *infra.* The Court of Appeals, nonetheless, argued that opportunity for a hearing and a statement of reasons were required here "as a *prophylactic* against non-retention decisions improperly motivated by exercise of protected rights." 446 F.2d, at 810 (emphasis supplied). While the Court of Appeals recognized the lack of a finding that the respondent's nonretention was based on exercise of the right of free speech, it felt that the respondent's interest in liberty was sufficiently implicated here because the decision not to rehire him was made "with a background of controversy and unwelcome expressions of opinion." *Ibid.*

When a State would directly impinge upon interests in free speech or free press, this Court has on occasion held that opportunity for a fair adversary

Hence, on the record before us, all that clearly appears is that the respondent was not rehired for one year at one University. It stretches the concept too far to suggest that a person is deprived of "liberty" when he simply is not rehired in one job but remains as free as before to seek another. Cafeteria Workers v. McElroy, 367 U.S. at 895-896, 81 S. Ct. at 1748-1749, 6 L. Ed. 2d 1230.

The Fourteenth Amendment's procedural protection of property is a safeguard of the security of interests that a person has already acquired in specific benefits. These interests—property interests—may take many forms.

Thus the Court has held that a person receiving welfare benefits under statutory and administrative standards defining eligibility for them has an interest in continued receipt of those benefits that is safeguarded by procedural due process. Goldberg v. Kelly, 397 U.S. 254, 90 S. Ct. 1011, 25 L. Ed. 2d 287. Similarly, in the area of public employment, the Court has held that a public college professor dismissed from an office held under tenure provisions, Slochower v. Board of Education, 350 U.S. 551, 76 S. Ct. 637, 100 L. Ed. 692, and college professors and staff members dismissed during the terms of their contracts, Wieman v. Updegraff, 344 U.S. 183, 73 S. Ct. 215, 97 L. Ed. 216, have interests in continued employment that are safeguarded by due process. Only last year, the Court held that this principle "proscribing summary dismissal from public employment without hearing or inquiry required by due process" also applied to a teacher recently hired without tenure or a formal contract, but nonetheless with a clearly implied promise of continued employment. Connell v. Higginbotham, 403 U.S. 207, 208, 91 S. Ct. 1772, 1773, 29 L. Ed. 2d 418.

Certain attributes of "property" interests protected by procedural due process emerge from these decisions. To have a property interest in a benefit, a person clearly must have more than an abstract need or desire for it. He must have more than a unilateral expectation of it. He must, instead, have a legitimate claim of entitlement to it. It is a purpose of the ancient institution of property to protect those claims upon which people rely in their daily lives, reliance that must not be arbitrarily undermined. It is a purpose of the constitutional right to a hearing to provide an opportunity for a person to vindicate those claims.

---

hearing must precede the action, whether or not the speech or press interest is clearly protected under substantive First Amendment standards. . . .

In the respondent's case, however, the State has not directly impinged upon interests in free speech or free press in any way comparable to a seizure of books or an injunction against meetings. Whatever may be a teacher's rights of free speech, the interest in holding a teaching job at a state university, *simpliciter,* is not itself a free speech interest.

Property interests, of course, are not created by the Constitution. Rather they are created and their dimensions are defined by existing rules or understandings that stem from an independent source such as state law—rules or understandings that secure certain benefits and that support claims of entitlement to those benefits. Thus the welfare recipients in Goldberg v. Kelly, *supra,* had a claim of entitlement to welfare payments that was grounded in the statute defining eligibility for them. The recipients had not yet shown that they were, in fact, within the statutory terms of eligibility. But we held that they had a right to a hearing at which they might attempt to do so.

Just as the welfare recipients' "property" interest in welfare payments was created and defined by statutory terms, so the respondent's "property" interest in employment at the Wisconsin State University-Oshkosh was created and defined by the terms of his appointment. Those terms secured his interest in employment up to June 30, 1969. But the important fact in this case is that they specifically provided that the respondent's employment was to terminate on June 30. They did not provide for contract renewal absent "sufficient cause." Indeed, they made no provision for renewal whatsoever.

Thus the terms of the respondent's appointment secured absolutely no interest in re-employment for the next year. They supported absolutely no possible claim of entitlement to re-employment. Nor, significantly, was there any state statute or University rule or policy that secured his interest in re-employment or that created any legitimate claim to it.[16] In these circumstances, the respondent surely had an abstract concern in being rehired, but he did not have a *property* interest sufficient to require the University authorities to give him a hearing when they declined to renew his contract of employment. . . .

We must conclude that the summary judgment for the respondent should not have been granted, since the respondent has not shown that he was deprived of liberty or property protected by the Fourteenth Amendment. The judgment of the Court of Appeals, accordingly, is reversed and the case is remanded for further proceedings consistent with this opinion. It is so ordered. Reversed and remanded.

---

[16] To be sure, the respondent does suggest that most teachers hired on a year-to-year basis by the Wisconsin State University-Oshkosh are, in fact, rehired. But the District Court has not found that there is anything approaching a "common law" of re-employment, see Perry v. Sindermann, 405 U.S. — at —, 92 S. Ct. 2694, at —, 32 L. Ed. 2d —, so strong as to require University officials to give the respondent a statement of reasons and a hearing on their decision not to rehire him.

Mr. Justice Douglas, dissenting. . . .

Though Roth was rated by the faculty as an excellent teacher, he had publicly criticized the administration for suspending an entire group of 94 Black students without determining individual guilt. He also criticized the university's regime as being authoritarian and autocratic. He used his classroom to discuss what was being done about the Black episode; and one day, instead of meeting his class, he went to the meeting of the Board of Regents. . . .

Professor Will Herberg of Drew University in writing of "academic freedom" recently said:

". . . it is sometimes conceived as a basic constitutional right guaranteed and protected under the First Amendment.

"But, of course, this is not the case. Whereas a man's right to speak out on this or that may be guaranteed and protected, he can have no imaginable human or constitutional right to remain a member of a university faculty. Clearly, the right to academic freedom is an acquired one, yet an acquired right of such value to society that in the minds of many it has verged upon the constitutional." Washington Evening Star, Jan. 23, 1972.

There may not be a constitutional right to continued employment if private schools and colleges are involved. But Prof. Herberg's view is not correct when public schools move against faculty members. For the First Amendment, applicable to the States by reason of the Fourteenth Amendment, protects the individual against state action when it comes to freedom of speech and of press and the related freedoms guaranteed by the First Amendment; and the Fourteenth protects "liberty" and "property" as stated by the Court in *Sindermann*.

No more direct assault on academic freedom can be imagined than for the school authorities to be allowed to discharge a teacher because of his or her philosophical, political, or ideological beliefs. . . .

When a violation of First Amendment rights is alleged, the reasons for dismissal or for nonrenewal of an employment contract must be examined to see if the reasons given are only a cloak for activity or attitudes protected by the Constitution. A statutory analogy is present under the National Labor Relations Act, 29 U.S.C. § 151 et seq. While discharges of employees for "cause" are permissible (Fibreboard Paper Products Corp. v. National Labor Relations Board, 379 U.S. 203, 217, 85 S. Ct. 398, 406, 13 L. Ed. 2d 233), discharges because of an employee's union activities is banned by § 8 (a) (3), 29 U.S.C. § 158 (c) (3). So the search is to ascertain whether the stated ground was the real one or only a pretext. See J.P. Stevens & Co. v. National Labor Relations Board, 380 F.2d 292, 300 (2nd Cir.) . . . .

There is sometimes a conflict between a claim for First Amendment protection and the need for orderly administration of the school system, as we noted in Pickering v. Board of Education, 391 U.S. 563, 569, 88 S. Ct. 1731, 1735, 20 L. Ed. 2d 811. That is one reason why summary judgments in this class of cases are seldom appropriate. Another reason is that careful factfinding is often necessary to know whether the given reason for nonrenewal of a teacher's contract is the real reason or a feigned one. . . . In Wieman v. Updegraff, 344 U.S. 183, 73 S. Ct. 215, 97 L. Ed. 216, we held that an applicant could not be denied the opportunity for public employment because he had exercised his First Amendment rights. And in Speiser v. Randall, 357 U.S. 513, 78 S. Ct. 1332, 2 L. Ed. 2d 1460, we held that a denial of a tax exemption unless one gave up his First Amendment rights was an abridgement of Fourteenth Amendment rights.

As we held in Speiser v. Randall, *supra,* when a State proposes to deny a privilege to one who it alleges has engaged in unprotected speech, Due Process requires that the State bear the burden of proving that the speech was not protected. "The 'protection of the individual against arbitrary action' . . . [is] the very essence of due process." Slochower v. Board of Higher Education, 350 U.S. 551, 559, 76 S. Ct. 637, 641, 100 L. Ed. 692 (1956), but where the State is allowed to act secretly behind closed doors and without any notice to those who are affected by its actions, there is no check against the possibility of such "arbitrary action." . . .

Mr. Justice MARSHALL, dissenting. . . .

I would go further than the Court does in defining the terms "liberty" and "property."

The prior decisions of this Court, discussed at length in the opinion of the Court, establish a principle that is as obvious as it is compelling—*i.e.,* federal and state governments and governmental agencies are restrained by the Constitution from acting arbitrarily with respect to employment opportunities that they either offer or control. Hence, it is now firmly established that whether or not a private employer is free to act capriciously or unreasonably with respect to employment practices, at least absent statutory or contractual controls, a government employer is different. The government may only act fairly and reasonably.

This Court has long maintained that "the right to work for a living in the common occupations of the community is of the very essence of the personal freedom and opportunity that it was the purpose of the [Fourteenth] Amendment to secure." Truax v. Raich, 239 U.S. 33, 41, 36 S. Ct. 7, 10, 60 L. Ed. 131 (1915) (Hughes, J.) . See also Meyer v. Nebraska, 262 U.S. 390, 399, 43 S. Ct. 625, 626, 67 L. Ed. 1042 (1923) . . . .

In my view, every citizen who applies for a government job is entitled to it unless the government can establish some reason for denying the employment. This is the "property" right that I believe is protected by the Fourteenth Amendment and that cannot be denied "without due process of law." And it is also liberty—liberty to work—which is the "very essence of the personal freedom and opportunity" secured by the Fourteenth Amendment.

This Court has often had occasion to note that the denial of public employment is a serious blow to any citizen. See, e.g., Joint Anti-Fascist Refugee Committee v. McGrath, 341 U.S. 123, 185, 71 S. Ct. 624, 655, 95 L. Ed. 817 (1951) (Jackson, J., concurring) ; United States v. Lovett, 328 U.S. 303, 316-317, 66 S. Ct. 1073, 1079, 90 L. Ed. 1252 (1946) . Thus, when an application for public employment is denied or the contract of a government employee is not renewed, the government must say why, for it is only when the reasons underlying government action are known that citizens feel secure and protected against arbitrary government action.

Employment is one of the greatest, if not the greatest, benefits that governments offer in modern-day life. When something as valuable as the opportunity to work is at stake, the government may not reward some citizens and not others without demonstrating that its actions are fair and equitable. And it is procedural due process that is our fundamental guarantee of fairness, our protection against arbitrary, capricious, and unreasonable government action.

We have often noted that procedural due process means many different things in the numerous contexts in which it applies. See, e.g., Goldberg v. Kelly, 397 U.S. 254, 262, 90 S. Ct. 1011, 1017, 25 L. Ed. 2d 287 (1970) ; Bell v. Burson, 402 U.S. 535, 91 S. Ct. 1586, 29 L. Ed. 2d 90 (1971) . Prior decisions have held that an applicant for admission to practice as an attorney before the United States Board of Tax Appeals may not be rejected without a statement of reasons and a chance for a hearing on disputed issues of fact;[4] that a tenured teacher could not be summarily dismissed without notice of the reasons and a hearing;[5]

---

[4] Goldsmith v. United States Board of Tax Appeals, 270 U.S. 117, 46 S. Ct. 215, 70 L. Ed. 494 (1926).

[5] Slochower v. Board of Higher Education, 350 U.S. 551, 76 S. Ct. 637, 100 L. Ed. 692 (1956).

that an applicant for admission to a state bar could not be denied the opportunity to practice law without notice of the reasons for the rejection of his application and a hearing;[6] and even that a substitute teacher who had been employed only two months could not be dismissed merely because she refused to take a loyalty oath without an inquiry into the specific facts of her case and a hearing on those in dispute.[7] I would follow these cases and hold that respondent was denied due process when his contract was not renewed and he was not informed of the reasons and given an opportunity to respond.

It may be argued that to provide procedural due process to all public employees or prospective employees would place an intolerable burden on the machinery of government. Cf. Goldberg v. Kelly, *supra*. The short answer to that argument is that it is not burdensome to give reasons when reasons exist. Whenever an application for employment is denied, an employee is discharged, or a decision not to rehire an employee is made, there should be some reason for the decision. It can scarcely be argued that government would be crippled by a requirement that the reason be communicated to the person most directly affected by the government's action.

Where there are numerous applicants for jobs, it is likely that few will choose to demand reasons for not being hired. But, if the demand for reasons is exceptionally great, summary procedures can be devised that would provide fair and adequate information to all persons. As long as the government has a good reason for its actions it need not fear disclosure. It is only where the government acts improperly that procedural due process is truly burdensome. And that is precisely when it is most necessary. . . .

Moreover, proper procedures will surely eliminate some of the arbitrariness that results not from malice, but from innocent error. . . . When the government knows it may have to justify its decisions with sound reasons, its conduct is likely to be more cautious, careful, and correct. . . .

Mr. Chief Justice BURGER, concurring.

I concur in the Court's judgments and opinions in *Perry* and *Roth,* but there is one central point in both decisions that I would like to underscore since it may have been obscured in the comprehensive discussion of the cases. That point is that the

---

[6] Willner v. Committee on Character, 373 U.S. 96, 83 S. Ct. 1175, 10 L. Ed. 2d 224 (1963).

[7] Connell v. Higginbotham, 403 U.S. 207, 91 S. Ct. 1772, 29 L. Ed. 2d 418 (1972).

relationship between a state institution and one of its teachers is essentially a matter of state concern and state law. The Court holds today only that a state-employed teacher who has a right to re-employment under state law, arising from either an express or implied contract, has, in turn, a right guaranteed by the Fourteenth Amendment to some form of prior administrative or academic hearing on the cause for nonrenewal of his contract. Thus whether a particular teacher in a particular context has any right to such administrative hearing hinges on a question of state law. . . .

NOTES

1. In an earlier case, Cafeteria and Restaurant Workers Union, Local 473 v. McElroy, 367 U.S. 886, 896, 81 S. Ct. 1743, 6 L. Ed. 2d 1230 (1961), the Court held that a cafeteria employee on a naval base was not entitled to a hearing and statement of the reasons why she was denied security clearance by the Security Officer and consequently dismissed from the job which she had held for six years. After stating that the claimed breach of due process required an inquiry into the "nature of the government function involved as well as of the private interest . . . affected by governmental action," the Court then characterized the private interest involved as merely "the opportunity to work at one isolated and specific military installation" whereas the governmental function was characterized as that of managing "the internal operation of an important federal military establishment." The Court also pointed out that in its "proprietary military capacity, the Federal Government . . . has traditionally exercised unfettered control" and, further, that the Supreme Court itself had "consistently recognized that an interest closely analogous to . . . [that of petitioner], the interest of a government employee in retaining his job, can be summarily denied." To what extent has the holding in *McElroy* been diminished by the Court's decision in *Roth*?

2. In Taylor v. New York City Transit Authority, 433 F.2d 665 (2d Cir. 1970), plaintiff claimed that his dismissal by the New York City Transit Authority violated his rights under the due process clause of the Fourteenth Amendment. The court held that although the circumstances described by plaintiff raised serious due process questions normally cognizable by the federal courts, defendant was entitled to a summary judgment due to plaintiff's failure to raise the issues which comprised the crux of his federal cause of action when he had presented his case to the state Civil Service Commission, even though both he and his

lawyer had full knowledge of the facts and circumstances at that time. The court stated that the plaintiff had failed to meet the reasonable requirement prescribed by the state that, having chosen to appeal to the Commission, he accord that body an adequate opportunity to pass on the claim. *See also* Eisen v. Eastman, 421 F.2d 560 (2d Cir.), *cert. denied,* 400 U.S. 841 (1969). *Cf.* Paton v. Poirier, 286 A.2d 243 (R.I. Sup. Ct. 1972).

3. *See generally* Note, *Non-Tenure Teachers: Procedural Rights upon Dismissal,* 3 Loy.-Chi. L.J. 114 (1972); Van Alstyne, *The Constitutional Rights of Teachers and Professors,* 1970 Duke L.J. 841; Van Alstyne, *Demise of the Right-Privilege Distinction in Constitutional Law,* 81 Harv. L. Rev. 1439 (1968); Frakt, *Non-Tenure Teachers and the Constitution,* 18 U. Kan. L. Rev. 27 (1969); O'Neil, The Price of Dependency: Civil Liberties in the Welfare State 115-95 (1970); Note, *Developments in the Law of Academic Freedom,* 81 Harv. L. Rev. 1045 (1968); Leahy, *From McAuliffe to McLaughlin: A Revolution in the Constitutional Rights of Public Employees,* 57 Ill. B.J. 910 (1969); Rosenbloom, *The Constitution and the Civil Service: Some Recent Developments, Judicial and Political,* 18 U. Kan. L. Rev. 839 (1970).

PERRY v. SINDERMANN
Supreme Court of the United States
408 U.S. 593, 92 S. Ct. 2694, 33 L. Ed. 2d 570 (1972)

Mr. Justice Stewart delivered the opinion of the Court.

From 1959 to 1969 the respondent, Robert Sindermann, was a teacher in the state college system of the State of Texas. After teaching for two years at the University of Texas and for four years at San Antonio Junior College, he became a professor of Government and Social Science at Odessa Junior College in 1965. He was employed at the college for four successive years, under a series of one-year contracts. He was successful enough to be appointed, for a time, the cochairman of his department.

During the 1968-1969 academic year, however, controversy arose between the respondent and the college administration. The respondent was elected president of the Texas Junior College Teachers Association. In this capacity, he left his teaching duties on several occasions to testify before committees of the Texas Legislature, and he became involved in public disagreements with the policies of the college's Board of Regents. In particular, he aligned himself with a group advocating the elevation of the college to four-year status—a change opposed by the

Regents. And, on one occasion, a newspaper advertisement appeared over his name that was highly critical of the Regents.

Finally, in May 1969, the respondent's one-year employment contract terminated and the Board of Regents voted not to offer him a new contract for the next academic year. The Regents issued a press release setting forth allegations of the respondent's insubordination.[1] But they provided him no official statement of the reasons for the nonrenewal of his contract. And they allowed him no opportunity for a hearing to challenge the basis of the nonrenewal. . . .

The Court of Appeals reversed the judgment of the District Court. Sindermann v. Perry, 430 F.2d 939. First, it held that, despite the respondent's lack of tenure, the nonrenewal of his contract would violate the Fourteenth Amendment if it in fact was based on his protected free speech. Since the actual reason for the Regents' decision was " in total dispute" in the pleadings, the court remanded the case for a full hearing on this contested issue of fact. *Id.* at 942-943. Second, the Court of Appeals held that, despite the respondent's lack of tenure, the failure to allow him an opportunity for a hearing would violate the constitutional guarantee of procedural due process if the respondent could show that he had an "expectancy" of re-employment. It, therefore, ordered that this issue of fact also be aired upon remand. . . .

The first question presented is whether the respondent's lack of a contractual or tenure right to re-employment, taken alone, defeats his claim that the nonrenewal of his contract violated the First and Fourteenth Amendments. We hold that it does not.

For at least a quarter century, this Court has made clear that even though a person has no "right" to a valuable governmental benefit and even though the government may deny him the benefit for any number of reasons, there are some reasons upon which the government may not act. It may not deny a benefit to a person on a basis that infringes his constitutionally protected interests—especially, his interest in freedom of speech. For if the government could deny a benefit to a person because of his constitutionally protected speech or associations, his exercise of those freedoms would in effect be penalized and inhibited. This would allow the government to "produce a result which [it] could not command directly." Speiser v. Randall, 357 U.S. 513, 526, 78 S. Ct. 1332, 1342, 2 L. Ed. 2d 1460. Such interference with constitutional rights is impermissible. . . . We have applied the principle regardless of the public employee's contractual or other

---

[1] The press release stated, for example, that the respondent had defied his superiors by attending legislative committee meetings when college officials had specifically refused to permit him to leave his classes for that purpose.

claim to a job. Compare Pickering v. Board of Education, *supra*, with Shelton v. Tucker, *supra*.

Thus the respondent's lack of a contractual or tenure "right" to re-employment for the 1969-1970 academic year is immaterial to his free speech claim. Indeed, twice before, this Court has specifically held that the nonrenewal of a nontenured public school teacher's one-year contract may not be predicated on his exercise of First and Fourteenth Amendment rights. Shelton v. Tucker, *supra*; Keyishian v. Board of Regents, *supra*. We reaffirm those holdings here.

In this case, of course, the respondent has yet to show that the decision not to renew his contract was, in fact, made in retaliation for his exercise of the constitutional right of free speech. The District Court foreclosed any opportunity to make this showing when it granted summary judgment. Hence, we cannot now hold that the Board of Regents' action was invalid.

But we agree with the Court of Appeals that there is a genuine dispute as to "whether the college refused to renew the teaching contract on an impermissible basis—as a reprisal for the exercise of constitutionally protected rights." 430 F.2d, at 943. The respondent has alleged that his nonretention was based on his testimony before legislative committees and his other public statements critical of the Regents' policies. And he has alleged that this public criticism was within the First and Fourteenth Amendment's protection of freedom of speech. Plainly, these allegations present a *bona fide* constitutional claim. For this Court has held that a teacher's public criticism of his superiors on matters of public concern may be constitutionally protected and may, therefore, be an impermissible basis for termination of his employment. Pickering v. Board of Education, *supra*.

For this reason we hold that the grant of summary judgment against the respondent, without full exploration of this issue, was improper.

The respondent's lack of formal contractual or tenure security in continued employment at Odessa Junior College, though irrelevant to his free speech claim, is highly relevant to his procedural due process claim. But it may not be entirely dispositive.

We have held today in Board of Regents v. Roth, *supra*, that the Constitution does not require opportunity for a hearing before the nonrenewal of a nontenured teacher's contract, unless he can show that the decision not to rehire him somehow deprived him of an interest in "liberty" or that he had a "property" interest in continued employment, despite the lack of tenure or a formal contract. In *Roth* the teacher had not made a showing on either point to justify summary judgment in his favor.

Similarly, the respondent here has yet to show that he has been deprived of an interest that could invoke procedural due process protection. As in *Roth,* the mere showing that he was not rehired in one particular job, without more, did not amount to a showing of a loss of liberty.[5] Nor did it amount to a showing of a loss of property.

But the respondent's allegations—which we must construe most favorably to the respondent at this stage of the litigation—do raise a genuine issue as to his interest in continued employment at Odessa Junior College. He alleged that this interest, though not secured by a formal contractual tenure provision, was secured by a no less binding understanding fostered by the college administration. In particular, the respondent alleged that the college had a *de facto* tenure program, and that he had tenure under that program. He claimed that he and others legitimately relied upon an unusual provision that had been in the college's official Faculty Guide for many years:

> "*Teacher Tenure:* Odessa College has no tenure system. The Administration of the College wishes the faculty member to feel that he has a permanent tenure as long as his teaching services are satisfactory and as long as he displays a cooperative attitude toward his co-workers and his superiors, and as long as he is happy in his work."

Moreover, the respondent claimed legitimate reliance upon guidelines promulgated by the Coordinating Board of the Texas College and University System that provided that a person, like himself, who had been employed as a teacher in the state college and university system for seven years or more has some form of job tenure. Thus the respondent offered to prove that a teacher, with his long period of service, at this particular State College had no less a "property" interest in continued employment than a formally tenured teacher at other colleges, and had no less a procedural due process right to a statement of reasons and a hearing before college officials upon their decision not to retain him.

We have made clear in *Roth* . . . that "property" interests subject to procedural due process protection are not limited by a few rigid, technical forms. Rather, "property" denotes a broad range of interests that are secured by "existing rules or understandings." . . . A person's interest in a benefit is a "property"

---

[5] The Court of Appeals suggested that the respondent might have a due process right to some kind of hearing simply if he *asserts* to college officials that their decision was based on his constitutionally protected conduct. 430 F.2d at 944. We have rejected this approach in Board of Regents v. Roth, *supra,* 408 U.S. at — n.14, 92 S. Ct., at 2708 n.14.

interest for due process purposes if there are such rules or mutually explicit understandings that support his claim of entitlement to the benefit and that he may invoke at a hearing.

A written contract with an explicit tenure provision clearly is evidence of a formal understanding that supports a teacher's claim of entitlement to continued employment unless sufficient "cause" is shown. Yet absence of such an explicit contractual provision may not always foreclose the possibility that a teacher has a "property" interest in re-employment. For example, the law of contracts in most, if not all, jurisdictions long has employed a process by which agreements, though not formalized in writing, may be "implied." 3 Corbin on Contracts, §§ 561-672A. Explicit contractual provisions may be supplemented by other agreements implied from "the promisor's words and conduct in the light of the surrounding circumstances." *Id.*, at § 562. And, "[t]he meaning of [the promisor's] words and acts is found by relating them to the usage of the past." *Ibid.*

A teacher, like the respondent, who has held his position for a number of years, might be able to show from the circumstances of this service—and from other relevant facts—that he has a legitimate claim of entitlement to job tenure. Just as this Court has found there to be a "common law of a particular industry or of a particular plant" that may supplement a collective-bargaining agreement, United Steelworkers v. Warrior & Gulf Nav. Co., 363 U.S. 574, 579, 80 S. Ct. 1347, 1351, 4 L. Ed. 2d 1409, so there may be an unwritten "common law" in a particular university that certain employees shall have the equivalent of tenure. This is particularly likely in a college or university, like Odessa Junior College, that has no explicit tenure system even for senior members of its faculty, but that nonetheless may have created such a system in practice. See Byse & Joughin, Tenure in American Higher Education 17-28.

In this case, the respondent has alleged the existence of rules and understandings, promulgated and fostered by state officials, that may justify his legitimate claim of entitlement to continued employment absent "sufficient cause." We disagree with the Court of Appeals insofar as it held that a mere subjective "expectancy" is protected by procedural due process, but we agree that the respondent must be given an opportunity to prove the legitimacy of his claim of such entitlement in light of "the policies and practices of the institution." 430 F.2d, at 943. Proof of such a property interest would not, of course, entitle him to reinstatement. But such proof would obligate college officials to grant a hearing at his request, where he could be informed of the grounds for his nonretention and challenge their sufficiency.

Therefore, while we do not wholly agree with the opinion of the Court of Appeals, its judgment remanding this case to the District Court is affirmed.

Affirmed.

Mr. Justice MARSHALL, dissenting in part. . . .

For the reasons stated in my dissenting opinion in . . . *Roth,* I would modify the judgment of the Court of Appeals to direct the District Court to enter summary judgment for respondent entitling him to a statement of reasons why his contract was not renewed and a hearing on the disputed issues of fact.

NOTE

In Kennedy v. Sanchez, 349 F. Supp. 863, GERR No. 477, F-1 (N.D. Ill. 1972), a non-probationary federal employee in the competitive service was discharged from his position as field representative with the Chicago branch of the Office of Economic Opportunity for making public statements critical of his superiors. In an action before a three-judge court, plaintiff sought declaratory and injunctive relief on the grounds that the discharge procedure and standards followed by OEO denied him due process of law and infringed on his right to freedom of speech. The court found merit in plaintiff's claims and ordered his reinstatement with back pay; in reaching this conclusion, the court clearly rejected the notion that government employment may be revoked summarily at the will of the appointing officer. The court ruled that since the plaintiff was a non-probationary employee in the competitive service, who could be removed or suspended without pay "only for such cause as will promote the efficiency of the service" [5 U.S.C. § 7501 (a)], he had a sufficient "property" interest in continued employment to come within the protection of the due process guarantees. The court noted in particular that plaintiff had a right to a "full evidentiary hearing prior to termination, with the right to be heard by an impartial hearing officer; the right to present witnesses; and the right to a written decision indicating the reasons for discharge or suspension and the evidence relied upon." The court also held that the statutory reference to "such cause as will promote the efficiency of the service" [in 5 U.S.C. § 7501 (a)] was not "sufficiently specific to justify the removal or suspension without pay of employees for making public statements critical of their superiors." This portion of the statute was held to be unconstitutional due to vagueness and overbreadth insofar as it purported to regulate the speech of competitive service employees working for the federal government.

But see Shelton v. EEOC, GERR No. 498, A-7 (W.D. Wash. 1973), involving a constitutional challenge to 5 U.S.C. § 7501 by a former Director of an EEOC district office who had been terminated for cause. In rejecting the plaintiff's suit, the court ruled that procedural due process did not always and inflexibly require a full-scale adversary hearing prior to every termination of a tenured federal employee. The court observed that plaintiff had been accorded due process of law when he was allowed to review the material relied upon to support his discharge and to present either an oral or written reply. *Kennedy v. Sanchez* was distinguished on the ground that it dealt primarily with First Amendment rights of free speech.

C.   Regulation of Partisan Political Activities of Public Employees

1.   The Hatch Act

COMMENT, THE HATCH ACT—A CONSTITUTIONAL RESTRAINT OF FREEDOM?, 33 Albany L. Rev. 345-47 (1969)†

The Hatch Act was the product of two Congressional enactments[7] and was intended to prevent what Congress deemed to be "pernicious political activities"[8] among certain federal,[9] state and local[10] employees. In the opinion of one author, the purpose of the act was to insure the political neutrality of federal and state bureaucracies because "political neutrality among career civil servants is a necessary corollary to efficient and responsible administration."[11] It has been claimed that the Hatch Act, by eliminating partisan political activity among federal employees, combats four evils: the act prevents the bureaucracy from becoming a united political power bloc; it prevents the party in power from using government workers to promote the continued dominance of the party; it prevents competition between the party and the department head for the employee's loyalty; and it prevents employee demoralization which results from promotions and rewards based on politics rather than merit.[12]

With regard to political activity, the act prohibits specified employees of the federal executive department from either affecting

---

† Reprinted by permission of the Albany Law Review.

[7] Act of Aug. 2, 1939, ch. 410, 53 Stat. 1147; Act of July 19, 1940, ch. 640, 54 Stat. 767.

[8] *Id.*

[9] 5 U.S.C. §§ 7321-7327 (Supp. III, 1968).

[10] 5 U.S.C. §§ 1501-1508 (Supp. III, 1968).

[11] Esman, *The Hatch Act—A Reappraisal*, 60 YALE L.J. 986, 995 (1951).

[12] *Id.* at 994-95.

the result of an election or from actively participating in political management or political campaigns.[13] Generally, every employee in the executive branch of the federal government falls within the prohibition of the act. However, there are several notable exceptions. The prohibition against political management and political campaigns does not apply to any person employed as the head or assistant head of an executive department, or paid from the appropriations of the President's office, or appointed as a member of the executive department, by the President with the advice and consent of the Senate.[14] Likewise, not all political activities are prohibited. Section 7326 exempts nonpartisan political activities from the scope of the act.[15] Penalties for violations of the act range from thirty days suspension without pay to removal from office.[16]

With respect to state and local government employees, the act

---

[13] 5 U.S.C. § 7324 provides: " (a) An employee in an Executive agency or an individual employed by the government of the District of Columbia may not—

(1) use his official authority or influence for the purpose of interfering with or affecting the result of an election; or

(2) take an active part in political management or in political campaigns."

This language was adopted from Executive Order No. 642 (June 3, 1907). This order became a rule of the Civil Service Commission until 1939 when it was adopted as § 9 (a), 53 Stat. 1147. See also 5 C.F.R. § 4.1 (1968).

[14] 5 U.S.C. § 7324 (d) (Supp. III, 1968): "Subsection (a) (2) of this section does not apply to—

(1) an employee paid from the appropriation for the office of the President;

(2) the head or the assistant head of an Executive department or military department;

(3) an employee appointed by the President, by and with the advice and consent of the Senate, who determines policies to be pursued by the United States in its relations with foreign powers or in the nationwide administration of Federal laws; . . . ."

[15] 5 U.S.C. § 7326 (Supp. III, 1968) provides: "Section 7324 (a) (2) of this title does not prohibit political activity in connection with—

(1) an election and the preceding campaign if none of the candidates is to be nominated or elected at that election as representing a party any of whose candidates for presidential elector received votes in the last preceding election at which presidential electors were selected; or

(2) a question which is not specifically identified with a National or State political party or political party of a territory or possession of the United States.

For the purpose of this section, questions relating to constitutional amendments, referendums, approval of municipal ordinances, and others of a similar character, are deemed not specifically identified with a National or State political party or political party of a territory or possession of the United States."

[16] 5 U.S.C. § 7325 (Supp. III, 1968). The appropriate Civil Service Commission Regulations may be found in 5 C.F.R. §§ 733.101-733.808 (1968).

seeks to regulate the political conduct of only those employees who work for state or local agencies and whose activities are "financed in whole or in part by loans or grants made by the United States or Federal agency."[17] Thus, for example, most employees of a state department of social welfare come within the act since this department probably receives federal funds under the categorical assistance programs of the Social Security Act.[18] One important exception to the act's restrictions involves those individuals "employed by an educational or research institution, establishment, agency or system which is supported in whole or in part by a State or political subdivision thereof."[19] Similar to the provisions for federal employees, various non-partisan activities of state and local government employees are exempt.[20] Employees who violate the act are liable for removal from office.[21] Additionally, should the state or local government either fail to remove the offending employee or reappoint the employee to another state agency, the Civil Service Commission may direct the appropriate federal agency to withhold from the state agency

---

[17] 5 U.S.C. § 1502 (Supp. III, 1968) provides: " (a) A State or local officer or employee may not—
  (1) use his official authority or influence for the purpose of interfering with or affecting the result of an election or a nomination for office;
  (2) . . .
  (3) take an active part in political management or in political campaigns."
5 U.S.C. § 1501 (4) (Supp. III, 1968) defines a state or local officer or employee as "an individual employed by a State or local agency whose principal employment is in connection with an activity which is financed in whole or in part by loans or grants made by the United States or Federal Agency. . . ."

[18] E.g., Title IV (Aid to Dependent Children) 42 U.S.C. §§ 601-09 (1964); Title XIX (Medical Assistance) 42 U.S.C. §§ 1396-96d (Supp. I, 1965); Title I (Aid to the Aged) 42 U.S.C. §§ 301-06 (1964). The same applies to employees of state labor departments which receive grants under Title III (Unemployment Compensation) of the Social Security Act. 42 U.S.C. §§ 501-03 (1964).

[19] 5 U.S.C. § 1501 (4) (B) (Supp. III, 1968). In addition, § 1502 (c) (1) specifically exempts the governor and lieutenant governor from the provisions of 1502 (a) (3).

[20] 5 U.S.C. § 1503 (Supp. III, 1968) provides: "Section 1502 (a) (3) of this title does not prohibit political activity in connection with—
  (1) an election and the preceding campaign if none of the candidates is to be nominated or elected at that election as representing a party any of whose candidates for presidential elector received votes in the last preceding election at which presidential electors were selected; or
  (2) a question which is not specifically identified with a National or State political party.
For the purpose of this section, questions relating to constitutional amendments, referendums, approval of municipal ordinances, and others of a similar character, are deemed not specifically identified with a National or State political party."

[21] 5 U.S.C. § 1505 (2) (Supp. III, 1968).

a sum equal to two years' salary of the employee charged with the violation.[22]

UNITED PUBLIC WORKERS OF AMERICA v. MITCHELL
Supreme Court of the United States
330 U.S. 75, 67 S. Ct. 556, 91 L. Ed. 754 (1947)

MR. JUSTICE REED delivered the opinion of the Court.

The Hatch Act, enacted in 1940, declares unlawful certain specified political activities of federal employees. Section 9 forbids officers and employees in the executive branch of the Federal Government, with exceptions, from taking "any active part in political management or in political campaigns." Section 15 declares that the activities theretofore determined by the United States Civil Service Commission to be prohibited to employees in the classified civil service of the United States by the Civil Service Rules shall be deemed to be prohibited to federal employees covered by the Hatch Act. These sections of the Act cover all federal officers and employees whether in the classified civil service or not and a penalty of dismissal from employment is imposed for violation. There is no designation of a single governmental agency for its enforcement. . . .

The present appellants sought an injunction before a statutory three-judge district court of the District of Columbia against appellees, members of the United States Civil Service Commission, to prohibit them from enforcing against appellants the provisions of the second sentence of § 9 (a) of the Hatch Act . . . [which] reads, "No officer or employee in the executive branch of the Federal Government . . . shall take any active part in political management or in political campaigns." . . .

None of the appellants, except George P. Poole, has violated the provisions of the Hatch Act. They wish to act contrary to its provisions and those of § 1 of the Civil Service Rules and desire a declaration of the legally permissible limits of regulation. Defendants moved to dismiss the complaint for lack of a justiciable case or controversy. The District Court determined that each of these individual appellants had an interest in their claimed privilege of engaging in political activities, sufficient to give

---

[22] 5 U.S.C. § 1506 (Supp. III, 1968). For a more thorough analysis of the provisions of the Hatch Act, see, Clark, *Federal Regulation of Campaign Activities,* 6 FED. B.J. 5 (1944); Friedman and Klinger, *The Hatch Act: Regulation by Administrative Action of Political Activities of Governmental Employees,* 7 FED. B.J. 5 (1945); Howard, *Federal Restrictions upon Political Activity of Government Employees,* 35 AM. POL. SCI. REV. 470 (1941). For a comprehensive list of those activities which are barred by the Hatch Act see Friedman and Klinger, *supra,* at 9-13.

them a right to maintain this suit. United Federal Workers of America (C.I.O.) v. Mitchell, 56 F. Supp. 621, 624. The District Court further determined that the questioned provision of the Hatch Act was valid and that the complaint therefore failed to state a cause of action. It accordingly dismissed the complaint and granted summary judgment to defendants. . . .

At the threshold of consideration, we are called upon to decide whether the complaint states a controversy cognizable in this Court. . . .

As is well known, the federal courts established pursuant to Article III of the Constitution do not render advisory opinions. For adjudication of constitutional issues, "concrete legal issues, presented in actual cases, not abstractions," are requisite. This is as true of declaratory judgments as any other field. These appellants seem clearly to seek advisory opinions upon broad claims of rights protected by the First, Fifth, Ninth and Tenth Amendments to the Constitution. As these appellants are classified employees, they have a right superior to the generality of citizens, compare Fairchild v. Hughes, 258 U.S. 126, but the facts of their personal interest in their civil rights, of the general threat of possible interference with those rights by the Civil Service Commission under its rules, if specified things are done by appellants, does not make a justiciable case or controversy. Appellants want to engage in "political management and political campaigns," to persuade others to follow appellants' views by discussion, speeches, articles and other acts reasonably designed to secure the selection of appellants' political choices. Such generality of objection is really an attack on the political expediency of the Hatch Act, not the presentation of legal issues. It is beyond the competence of courts to render such a decision.

The power of courts, and ultimately of this Court, to pass upon the constitutionality of acts of Congress arises only when the interests of litigants require the use of this judicial authority for their protection against actual interference. A hypothetical threat is not enough. We can only speculate as to the kinds of political activity the appellants desire to engage in or as to the contents of their proposed public statements or the circumstances of their publication. It would not accord with judicial responsibility to adjudge, in a matter involving constitutionality, between the freedom of the individual and the requirements of public order except when definite rights appear upon the one side and definite prejudicial interferences upon the other. . . . We should not take judicial cognizance of the situation presented on the part of the appellants considered in this subdivision of the opinion. These reasons lead us to conclude that the determination of the trial court, that the individual appellants, other than Poole, could maintain this action, was erroneous.

The appellant Poole does present by the complaint and affidavit matters appropriate for judicial determination.[23] The affidavits filed by appellees confirm that Poole has been charged by the Commission with political activity and a proposed order for his removal from his position adopted subject to his right under Commission procedure to reply to the charges and to present further evidence in refutation.[24] We proceed to consider the controversy over constitutional power at issue between Poole and the Commission as defined by the charge and preliminary finding upon one side and the admissions of Poole's affidavit upon the other. Our determination is limited to those facts. This proceeding so limited meets the requirements of defined rights and a

---

[23] "I have for a long time been interested in political activities. Both before and since my employment in the United States Mint, I have taken an active part in political campaigns and political management. In the 28th Ward, 7th Division in the City of Philadelphia I am and have been a Ward Executive Committeeman. In that position I have on many occasions taken an active part in political management and political campaigns. I have visited the residents of my Ward and solicited them to support my party and its candidates; I have acted as a watcher at the polls; I have contributed money to help pay its expenses; I have circulated campaign literature, placed banners and posters in public places, distributed leaflets, assisted in organizing political rallies and assemblies, and have done any and all acts which were asked of me in my capacity as a Ward Executive Committeeman. I have engaged in these activities both before and after my employment in the United States Mint. I intend to continue to engage in these activities on my own time as a private citizen, openly, freely, and without concealment.

"However, I have been served with a proposed order of the United States Civil Service Commission, dated January 12, 1944, which advises me that because of the political activities mentioned above, and for no other reason, 'it is, . . ., the opinion of this Commission that George P. Poole, an employee of the United States Mint at Philadelphia, Pennsylvania, has been guilty of political activity in violation of Section 1, Civil Service Rule I' and that unless I can refute the charges that I have engaged in political activity, I will be dismissed from my position as a Roller in the United States Mint at Philadelphia, Pennsylvania."

[24] The tentative charge and finding reads:

I.

"It is charged: That . . .

"The said George P. Poole held the political party office of Democratic Ward Executive Committeeman in the City of Philadelphia, Pennsylvania.

"The said George P. Poole was politically active by aiding and assisting the Democratic Party in the capacity of worker at the polls on general election day, November 5, 1940, and assisted in the distribution of funds in paying party workers for their services on general election day, November 5, 1940."

III.

"The above described activity constitutes taking an active part in political management and in a political campaign in contravention of Section 1, Civil Service Rule I, and the regulations adopted by the Commissioners thereunder."

definite threat to interfere with a possessor of the menaced rights by a penalty for an act done in violation of the claimed restraint. . . .

This brings us to consider the narrow but important point involved in Poole's situation. Poole's stated offense is taking an "active part in political management or in political campaigns." He was a ward executive committeeman of a political party and was politically active on election day as a worker at the polls and a paymaster for the services of other party workers. The issue for decision and the only one we decide is whether such a breach of the Hatch Act and Rule 1 of the Commission can, without violating the Constitution, be made the basis for disciplinary action.

When the issue is thus narrowed, the interference with free expression is seen in better proportion as compared with the requirements of orderly management of administrative personnel. Only while the employee is politically active . . . must he withhold expression of opinion on public subjects. We assume that Mr. Poole would be expected to comment publicly as committeeman on political matters, so that indirectly there is an attenuated interference. We accept appellants' contention that the nature of political rights reserved to the people by the Ninth and Tenth Amendments are involved. The right claimed as inviolate may be stated as the right of a citizen to act as a party official or worker to further his own political views. Thus we have a measure of interference by the Hatch Act and the Rules with what otherwise would be the freedom of the civil servant under the First, Ninth and Tenth Amendments. And, if we look upon due process as a guarantee of freedom in those fields, there is a corresponding impairment of that right under the Fifth Amendment. Appellants' objections under the Amendments are basically the same.

We do not find persuasion in appellants' argument that such activities during free time are not subject to regulation even though admittedly political activities cannot be indulged in during working hours. The influence of political activity by government employees, if evil in its effects on the service, the employees or people dealing with them, is hardly less so because that activity takes place after hours. Of course, the question of the need for this regulation is for other branches of government rather than the courts. Our duty in this case ends if the Hatch Act provision under examination is constitutional.

Of course, it is accepted constitutional doctrine that these fundamental human rights are not absolutes. The requirements of residence and age must be met. The essential rights of the First Amendment in some instances are subject to the elemental need for order without which the guarantees of civil rights to others would be a mockery. The powers granted by the Constitution to the Federal Government are subtracted from the totality of sovereignty originally in the states and the people. Therefore, when objection is made that the exercise of a federal power infringes upon rights reserved by the Ninth and Tenth Amendments, the inquiry must be directed toward the granted power under which the action of the Union was taken. If granted power is found, necessarily the objection of invasion of those rights, reserved by the Ninth and Tenth Amendments, must fail. Again this Court must balance the extent of the guarantees of freedom against a congressional enactment to protect a democratic society against the supposed evil of political partisanship by classified employees of government. . . .

[T]he practice of excluding classified employees from party offices and personal political activity at the polls has been in effect for several decades. Some incidents similar to those that are under examination here have been before this Court and the prohibition against certain types of political activity by office-holders has been upheld. The leading case was decided in 1882. Ex parte Curtis, 106 U.S. 371. There a subordinate United States employee was indicted for violation of an act that forbade employees who were not appointed by the President and confirmed by the Senate from giving or receiving money for political purposes from or to other employees of the government on penalty of discharge and criminal punishment. Curtis urged that the statute was unconstitutional. This Court upheld the right of Congress to punish the infraction of this law. The decisive principle was the power of Congress, within reasonable limits, to regulate, so far as it might deem necessary, the political conduct of its employees. A list of prohibitions against acts by public officials that are permitted to other citizens was given. This Court said, p. 373:

> "The evident purpose of Congress in all this class of enactments has been to promote efficiency and integrity in the discharge of official duties, and to maintain proper discipline in the public service. Clearly such a purpose is within the just scope of legislative power, and it is not easy to see why the act now under consideration does not come fairly within the legitimate means to such an end."

The right to contribute money through fellow employees to advance the contributor's political theories was held not to be protected by any constitutional provision. It was held subject to regulation. . . . The conclusion of the Court, that there was no constitutional bar to regulation of such financial contributions of public servants as distinguished from the exercise of political privileges such as the ballot, has found acceptance in the subsequent practice of Congress and the growth of the principle of required political neutrality for classified public servants as a sound element for efficiency. The conviction that an actively partisan governmental personnel threatens good administration has deepened since *Ex parte Curtis*. Congress recognizes danger to the service in that political rather than official effort may earn advancement and to the public in that governmental favor may be channeled through political connections.

In United States v. Wurzbach, 280 U.S. 396, the doctrine of legislative power over actions of governmental officials was held valid when extended to members of Congress. The members of Congress were prohibited from receiving contributions for "any political purpose whatever" from any other federal employees. Private citizens were not affected. The argument of unconstitutionality because of interference with the political rights of a citizen by that time was dismissed in a sentence. Compare United States v. Thayer, 209 U.S. 39.

The provisions of § 9 of the Hatch Act and the Civil Service Rule 1 are not dissimilar in purpose from the statutes against political contributions of money. The prohibitions now under discussion are directed at political contributions of energy by government employees. These contributions, too, have a long background of disapproval. Congress and the President are responsible for an efficient public service. If, in their judgment, efficiency may be best obtained by prohibiting active participation by classified employees in politics as party officers or workers, we see no constitutional objection. . . . To declare that the present supposed evils of political activity are beyond the power of Congress to redress would leave the nation impotent to deal with what many sincere men believe is a material threat to the democratic system. Congress is not politically naive or regardless of public welfare or that of the employees. It leaves untouched full participation by employees in political decisions at the ballot box and forbids only the partisan activity of federal personnel deemed offensive to efficiency. With that limitation only, employees may make their contributions to public affairs or protect their own interests, as before the passage of the Act.

The argument that political neutrality is not indispensable to a merit system for federal employees may be accepted. But because it is not indispensable does not mean that it is not desirable or permissible. Modern American politics involves organized political parties. Many classifications of government employees have been accustomed to work in politics—national, state and local—as a matter of principle or to assure their tenure. Congress may reasonably desire to limit party activity of federal employees so as to avoid a tendency toward a one-party system. It may have considered that parties would be more truly devoted to the public welfare if public servants were not overactive politically. . . .

It is only partisan political activity that is interdicted. It is active participation in political management and political campaigns. Expressions, public or private, on public affairs, personalities and matters of public interest, not an objective of party action, are unrestricted by law so long as the government employee does not direct his activities toward party success.

It is urged, however, that Congress has gone further than necessary in prohibiting political activity to all types of classified employees. It is pointed out by appellants "that the impartiality of many of these is a matter of complete indifference to the effective performance" of their duties. Mr. Poole would appear to be a good illustration for appellants' argument. The complaint states that he is a roller in the mint. We take it this is a job calling for the qualities of a skilled mechanic and that it does not involve contact with the public. Nevertheless, if in free time he is engaged in political activity, Congress may have concluded that the activity may promote or retard his advancement or preferment with his superiors. Congress may have thought that government employees are handy elements for leaders in political policy to use in building a political machine. For regulation of employees it is not necessary that the act regulated be anything more than an act reasonably deemed by Congress to interfere with the efficiency of the public service. There are hundreds of thousands of United States employees with positions no more influential upon policy determination than that of Mr. Poole. Evidently what Congress feared was the cumulative effect on employee morale of political activity by all employees who could be induced to participate actively. It does not seem to us an unconstitutional basis for legislation. . . .

We have said that Congress may regulate the political conduct of government employees "within reasonable limits," even though the regulation trenches to some extent upon unfettered political action. The determination of the extent to which political activities of governmental employees shall be regulated lies primarily with Congress. Courts will interfere only when such regulation passes beyond the generally existing conception of governmental power. That conception develops from practice, history, and changing educational, social and economic conditions. The regulation of such activities as Poole carried on has the approval of long practice by the Commission, court decisions upon similar problems and a large body of informed public opinion. Congress and the administrative agencies have authority over the discipline and efficiency of the public service. When actions of civil servants in the judgment of Congress menace the integrity and the competency of the service, legislation to forestall such danger and adequate to maintain its usefulness is required. The Hatch Act is the answer of Congress to this need. We cannot say with such a background that these restrictions are unconstitutional. . . .

The judgment of the District Court is accordingly

Affirmed.

[The dissenting opinions of JUSTICE DOUGLAS and JUSTICE BLACK, concurred in by JUSTICE RUTLEDGE, and the concurring opinion of JUSTICE FRANKFURTER, are omitted.]

NOTES

1. In Oklahoma v. United States Civil Serv. Comm'n, 330 U.S. 127 (1947), decided the same day as *Mitchell*, the Supreme Court upheld the constitutionality of those provisions of the Hatch Act which limited the right of certain state employees to participate in partisan politics. Oklahoma brought suit to review a determination of the Civil Service Commission that a member of the state's highway commission had, by acting as chairman of the Democratic State Central Committee, violated the Hatch Act. The Commission directed the state to remove this member.

The state contended that the Hatch Act was unconstitutional because it regulated the internal affairs of a state and intruded upon state sovereignty in violation of the Tenth Amendment. While concluding that the federal government could not directly regulate the political activities of state or local employees, the Court held that the federal government could do so indirectly by fixing the terms and conditions upon which federal moneys would be allotted to the states. The Court held that the Tenth Amendment did not deprive the federal government of its power to use any necessary and proper means in the exercise of a granted power to attain a permissible goal. The Court defined the permissible goal as "better public service" which was to be attained by "requiring those who administered funds for national needs to abstain from active political partisanship." 330 U.S. at 143.

2. The holding in *Mitchell* has been soundly criticized over the years. For example, in Hobbs v. Thompson, 448 F.2d 456, 457 (5th Cir. 1971), the court considered the constitutionality

of a city ordinance which provided that no employee of the fire department

> . . . "shall take an active part in any primary or election, and all [such] employees are hereby prohibited from contributing any money to any candidate, soliciting votes or prominently identifying themselves in a political race with or against any candidate for office."

The court rejected the argument that the constitutionality of the ordinance should be determined by the *Mitchell* "rational basis" balancing test. Instead, the court ruled that the treatment in *Mitchell* of First Amendment rights was inconsistent with other First Amendment cases decided in the same time period as well as those decided subsequently and that the "privilege theory" of public employment, seemingly adopted by the Court in *Mitchell*, was no longer tenable. The court applied traditional overbreadth principles to the ordinance and held it to be "fatally overbroad and vague" because it "failed to focus narrowly upon a substantial state interest which might justify some proscription of the political activity of . . . firemen." 448 F.2d at 475.

3. For a good discussion of many of the court decisions since *Mitchell* dealing with state and federal legislation, see Shartis, *The Federal Hatch Act and Related State Court Trends—A Time for a Change?*, 1970 THE BUSINESS LAWYER 1381. *See also* Esman, *The Hatch Act—A Reappraisal*, 60 YALE L.J. 986 (1951); Heady, *The Hatch Act Decisions*, 41 AM. POL. SCI. REV. 687 (1947); Mosher, *Government Employees Under the Hatch Act*, 22 N.Y.U.L.Q. REV. 233 (1947); Note, *Political Sterilization of Government Employees*, 47 COLUM. L. REV. 295 (1947); Note, *Restrictions on the Civil Rights of Federal Employees*, 47 COLUM. L. REV. 1161 (1947); Note, *Constitutional Limitations on Political Discrimination in Public Employment*, 60 HARV. L. REV. 779 (1947); Bruff, *Unconstitutional Conditions upon Public Employment: New Departures in the Protection of First Amendment Rights*, 21 HASTINGS L.J. 129 (1969); Comment, *The Hatch Act—A Constitutional Restraint of Freedom?*, 33 ALBANY L. REV. 345 (1969); Note, *The Public Employee and Political Activity*, 3 SUFFOLK L. REV. 380 (1969); Buckley, *Political Rights of Government Employees*, 19 CLEV. ST. L. REV. 568 (1970); Leahy, *The Public Employee and the First Amendment—Must He Sacrifice His Civil Rights To Be a Civil Servant?*, 4 CALIF. W.L. REV. 1 (1968); Note, *The First Amendment and Public Employees—An Emerging Constitutional Right To Be a Policeman?*, 37 GEO. WASH. L. REV. 409 (1968); Van Alstyne, *The Constitutional Rights of Public Employees: A Comment on the In-*

appropriate Use of an Old Analogy, 16 U.C.L.A.L. REV. 751 (1969).

4. A federal government Commission on Political Activity of Government Personnel concluded that the existing political restrictions imposed on public servants are far in excess of what appears to be needed. *See* Jones, Charles O., *Reevaluating the Hatch Act: A Report on the Commission on Political Activity of Government Personnel,* 29 PUBLIC ADMIN. REV. 249 (1969). The Commission indicated that there should become clear relationship between the dangers feared and the corrective measures used to regulate political activities. For cases which have tended to adopt this view, see Fort v. Civil Serv. Comm'n, 61 Cal. 2d 331, 38 Cal. Rptr. 625, 392 P.2d 385 (1964); Bagley v. Washington Township Hosp. Dist., 65 Cal. 2d 449, 55 Cal. Rptr. 401, 421 P.2d 409 (1966); Minielly v. State, 242 Ore. 490, 411 P.2d 69 (1966); De Stefano v. Wilson, 96 N.J. Super. 592, 233 A.2d 682 (1967); Gray v. City of Toledo, 323 F. Supp. 1281 (N.D. Ohio 1971) (upholding a state statute restricting policeman's right to engage in political activity, but indicating that only partisan political action which directly and adversely affected the employee's ability to perform his job efficiently, could be constitutionally prohibited).

See also Huerta v. Flood, 103 Ariz. 608, 447 P.2d 866 (1968) and City of Miami v. Sterbenz, 203 So. 2d 4 (Fla. 1967) (both holding unconstitutional laws against solicitation for political contributions as too indefinite as to the acts which were illegal). *But see* State *ex rel.* Baldwin v. Strain, 152 Neb. 763, 42 N.W. 2d 796 (1950); Lecci v. Looney, 33 App. Div. 2d 916, 307 N.Y. S.2d 594, 595 (1970) (citing *Mitchell* and *McAuliffe,* the court held that the law prohibiting a policeman from being "a delegate or representative to, or tak[ing] active part in any movement for the nomination or election of candidates for political office or public office" is constitutional); Lecci v. Cahn, 37 App. Div. 2d 779, 325 N.Y.S.2d 400, *cert. denied,* 405 U.S. 1073 (1971) (holding constitutional a state law making contributions to or collections on behalf of political clubs by policemen, a misdemeanor); Fishkin v. United States Civil Serv. Comm'n, 309 F. Supp. 40 (N.D. Cal. 1969), *appeal dismissed,* 396 U.S. 278, *reh. den.,* 397 U.S. 958 (1970).

5. *Standing:* The courts have generally rejected the holding in *Mitchell* that a party must be charged with a violation of the act challenged in order to have standing. Most courts have held, as in Hobbs v. Thompson, *supra* note 2, that where the act challenged may have adverse affects on the parties challenging it,

the parties have standing. In N.A.A.C.P. v. Button, 371 U.S. 415, 83 S. Ct. 328, 9 L. Ed. 2d 405 (1963), the Court stated, in this regard, that:

> the instant decree may be invalid if it prohibits privileged exercises of First Amendment rights whether or not the record discloses that the petitioner has engaged in privileged conduct. For in appraising a statute's inhibitory effect upon such rights, this Court has not hesitated to take into account possible applications of the statute in other factual contexts besides that at bar. Thornhill v. Alabama, 310 U.S. 88, 97-98, 60 S. Ct. 736, 741-742, 84 L. Ed. 1093; Winters v. New York, supra, 333 U.S. at 518-520, 68 S. Ct. at 671-672. Cf. Staub v. City of Baxley, 355 U.S. 313, 78 S. Ct. 277, 2 L. Ed. 2d 302. [371 U.S. at 432.]

UNITED STATES CIVIL SERVICE COMMISSION v. NATIONAL ASSOCIATION OF LETTER CARRIERS
Supreme Court of the United States
— U.S. —, 93 S. Ct. 2880, 37 L. Ed. 2d 796 (1973)

MR. JUSTICE WHITE delivered the opinion of the Court.

On December 11, 1972, we noted probable jurisdiction of this appeal, 409 U.S. 1058, based on a jurisdictional statement presenting the single question whether the prohibition in § 9 (a) of the Hatch Act, now codified in 5 U.S.C. § 7324 (a) (2), against federal employees taking "an active part in political management or in political campaigns," is unconstitutional on its face. Section 7324 (a) provides:

> "An employee in an Executive agency or an individual employed by the government of the District of Columbia may not—
>
> "(1) use his official authority or influence for the purpose of interfering with or affecting the result of an election; or
>
> "(2) take an active part in political management or in political campaigns.
>
> "For the purpose of this subsection, the phrase 'an active part in political management or in political campaigns' means those acts of political management or political campaigning which were prohibited on the part of employees in the competitive service before July 19, 1940, by determinations of the Civil Service Commission under the rules prescribed by the President."

A divided three-judge court sitting in the District of Columbia had held the section unconstitutional. 346 F. Supp. 578 (1972). We reverse the judgment of the District Court.

I

The case began when the National Association of Letter Carriers, six individual federal employees and certain local Democratic and Republican political committees filed a complaint, asserting on behalf of themselves and all federal employees that 5 U.S.C. § 7324 (a) (2) was unconstitutional on its face and seeking an injunction against its enforcement.

Each of the plaintiffs alleged that the Civil Service Commission was enforcing, or threatening to enforce, the Hatch Act's prohibition against active participation in political management or political campaigns with respect to certain defined activity in which that plaintiff desired to engage. The Union, for example, stated among other things that its members desired to campaign for candidates for public office. The Democratic and Republican Committees complained of not being able to get federal employees to run for state and local offices. Plaintiff Hummel stated that he was aware of the provision of the Hatch Act and that the activities he desired to engage in would violate that Act as, for example, his participating as a delegate in a party convention or holding office in a political club.

A three-judge court was convened, and the case was tried on both stipulated evidence and oral testimony. The District Court then ruled that § 7324 (a) (2) was unconstitutional on its face and enjoined its enforcement. The court recognized the "well-established governmental interest in restricting political activities by federal employees which [had been] asserted long before enactment of the Hatch Act," 346 F. Supp., at 579, as well as the fact that the "appropriateness of this governmental objective was recognized by the Supreme Court of the United States when it endorsed the objective of the Hatch Act. United Public Workers v. Mitchell, 330 U.S. 75 . . . (1947) . . . ." Id., at 580. The District Court ruled, however, that Mitchell left open the constitutionality of the statutory definition of "political activity," ibid., and proceeded to hold that definition to be both vague and overbroad, and therefore unconstitutional and unenforceable against the plaintiffs in any respect. The District Court also added, id., at 585, that even if the Supreme Court in Mitchell could be said to have upheld the definitional section in its entirety, later decisions had so eroded the holding that it could no longer be considered binding on the District Court.

II

As the District Court recognized, the constitutionality of the Hatch Act's ban on taking an active part in political management or political campaigns has been here before.

This very prohibition was attacked in the *Mitchell* case by a labor union and various federal employees as being violative of the First, Ninth, and Tenth Amendments and as contrary to the Fifth Amendment as being vague and indefinite, arbitrarily discriminatory, and a deprivation of liberty. . . . As to the plaintiff Poole, [in *Mitchell*] the court noted that "he was a ward executive committeeman of a political party and was politically active on election day as a worker at the polls and a paymaster for the services of other party workers." 330 U.S., at 94. Plainly, the Court thought, these activities fell within the prohibition of § 9 of the Hatch Act against taking an active part in political management or political campaigning; and "[t]hey [were] also covered by the prior determinations of the [Civil Service] Commission," *id.*, at 103 (footnote omitted), as incorporated by § 15 of the Hatch Act[4] the Court relying on a Civil Service Commission publication, Political Activity and Political Assessments, Form 1236, September 1939, for the latter conclusion. *Id.*, at 103, n. 38. Poole's complaint thus presented a case or controversy for decision, the question being solely whether the Hatch Act "without violating the Constitution, [could make this conduct] the basis for disciplinary action." 330 U.S. at 94. The court held that it could. . . .

We unhesitatingly reaffirm the *Mitchell* holding that Congress had, and has, the power to prevent Mr. Poole and others like him from holding a party office, working at the polls and acting as party paymaster for other party workers. An Act of Congress going no farther would in our view unquestionably be valid. So would it be if, in plain and understandable language, the statute forbade activities such as organizing a political party or club; actively participating in fund-raising activities for a partisan candidate or political party; becoming a partisan candidate for, or campaigning for, an elective public office; actively managing the campaign of a partisan candidate for public office; initiating or circulating a partisan nominating petition or soliciting votes for a partisan candidate for public office; or serving as a delegate,

---

[4] Section 15 of the Hatch Act, now codified in 5 U.S.C. § 7324 (a) (2), see n. 1, *supra*, defined the prohibition against taking "an active part in political management or in political campaigns" as proscribing those activities that the Civil Service Commission had determined up to the time of the passage of the Hatch Act were prohibited for classified civil service employees. The role and scope of § 15 are discussed in the text, *infra*.

alternate or proxy to a political party convention. Our judgment is that neither the First Amendment nor any other provision of the Constitution invalidates a law barring this kind of partisan political conduct by federal employees.

A

Such decision on our part would no more than confirm the judgment of history, a judgment made by this country over the last century that it is in the best interest of the country, indeed essential, that federal service should depend upon meritorious performance rather than political service, and that the political influence of federal employees on others and on the electoral process should be limited. . . .

The original Civil Service rules were promulgated on May 7, 1883, by President Arthur. Civil Service Rule I repeated the language of the Act that no one in the executive service should use his official authority or influence to coerce any other person or to interfere with an election, but went no further in restricting the political activities of federal employees. 8 Richardson, Messages and Papers of the Presidents 161 (1899). Problems with political activity continued to arise. Twenty-fourth Annual Report of the Civil Service Commission, 7-9 (1908), and one form of remedial action was taken in 1907 when in accordance with Executive Order 642 issued by President Theodore Roosevelt, 1 Report of Commission on Political Activity, *supra,* at 9, § 1 of Rule I was amended to read as follows:

"No person in the Executive civil service shall use his official authority or influence for the purpose of interfering with an election or affecting the results thereof. *Persons who, by the provisions of these rules are in the competitive classified service, while retaining the right to vote as they please and to express privately their opinions on all political subjects, shall take no active part in political management or in political campaigns.*" Twenty-fourth Annual Report of the Civil Service Commission, *supra,* at 104 (emphasis added).

It was under this rule that the Commission thereafter exercised the authority it had to investigate, adjudicate, and recommend sanctions for federal employees thought to have violated the rule. See Howard, Federal Restrictions on the Political Activity of Government Employees, 35 Am. Pol. Sci. Rev. 470, 475 (1941). In the course of these adjudications, the Commission identified and developed a body of law with respect to the conduct of federal employees that was forbidden by the prohibition against taking an active part in political management or political campaigning. Adjudications under Civil Service Rule I spelled out the scope and meaning of the rule in the mode of the common law, 86 Cong. Rec. 2341-2342; and the rules fashioned in this manner were from time to time stated and restated by the Commission for the guidance of the federal establishment. Civil Service Form 1236 of September 1939, for example, purported to publish and restate the law of "Political Activity and Political Assessments" for federal office holders and employees.

Civil Service Rule I covered only the classified service. The experience of the intervening years, particularly that of the 1936 and 1938 political campaigns, convinced a majority in Congress that the prohibition against taking an active part in political management and political campaigns should be extended to the entire federal service. 84 Cong. Rec. 4304, 9595, 9604, and 9610. A bill introduced for this purpose, S. 1871, "to prevent pernicious political activities," easily passed the Senate, 84 Cong. Rec. 4191-4192; but both the constitutionality and the advisability of purporting to restrict the political activities of employees were heatedly debated in the House. *Id.,* at 9594-9639. The bill was enacted, however, 53 Stat. 1147. This was the so-called Hatch Act, named after the Senator who was its chief proponent. . . .

Section 9 (a) , which provided the prohibition against political activity now found in 5 U.S.C. § 7324 (a) (2) , with which we are concerned in this case, essentially restated Civil Service Rule I, with an important exception. *Id.,* at 1148. It made it

> "unlawful for any person employed in the executive branch of the Federal Government, or any agency or department thereof, to use his official authority or influence for the purpose of interfering with an election or affecting the result thereof. No officer or employee of the executive branch of the Federal Government, or any agency or department thereof, shall take any part in political management or in political campaigns. All such persons shall retain the right to vote as they may choose and to express their opinions on all political subjects." . . .

Section 9 differed from Civil Service Rule I in important respects. It applied to all persons employed by the Federal Government, with limited exceptions; it made dismissal from office mandatory upon an adjudication of a violation; and, whereas Civil Service Rule I had stated that persons retained the right to express their private opinions on all political subjects, the statute omitted the word "private" and simply privileged all employees "to express their opinions on all political subjects."

On the day prior to signing the bill, President Roosevelt sent a message to Congress stating his conviction that the bill was constitutional and recommending that Congress at its next session consider extending the Act to state and local government employees. 84 Cong. Rec. 10745-10747 and 10875. This, Congress quickly proceeded to do. The Act of July 19, 1940, c. 640, 54 Stat. 767, in § 12 (a), *ibid.*, amended the Hatch Act by extending its provisions to officers and employees of state and local agencies "whose principal employment is in connection with any activity which is financed in whole or in part by loans or grants made by the United States. . . ." The Civil Service Commission was empowered under § 12 (b), *id.*, at 768, to investigate and adjudicate violations of the Act by state and local employees. Also relevant for present purposes, § 9 (a) of the Hatch Act was amended so that all persons covered by the Act were free to "express their opinions on all political subjects *and candidates.*" *Id.*, at 767 (emphasis added). Moreover, § 15, *id.*, at 771, defined § 9 (a) 's prohibition against taking an active part in political management or in political campaigns as proscribing "the same activities on the part of such persons as the United States Civil Service Commission has heretofore determined are at the time this section takes effect prohibited on the part of employees in the classified Civil Service of the United States by the provisions of the civil service rules prohibiting such employees from taking any active part in political management or in political campaigns.". . .

In 1966, Congress determined to review the restrictions of the Hatch Act on the partisan political activities of public employees. For this purpose, the Commission on Political Activity of Government Personnel was created. 80 Stat. 868. The Commission reported in 1968, recommending some liberalization of the political activity restrictions on federal employees, but not abandoning the fundamental decision that partisan political activities by government employees must be limited in major respects. 1 Report of Commission on Political Activity of Government Personnel, *supra*. Since that time, various bills have been introduced in Congress, some following the Commission's recommendations and some proposing much more substantial revisions of the Hatch Act. In 1972, hearings were held on some proposed legislation; but no new legislation has resulted.

This account of the efforts by the Federal Government to limit partisan political activities by those covered by the Hatch Act should not obscure the equally relevant fact that all 50

States have restricted the political activities of their own employees.

B

Until now, the judgment of Congress, the Executive and the country appears to have been that partisan political activities by federal employees must be limited if the Government is to operate effectively and fairly, elections are to play their proper part in representative government and employees themselves are to be sufficiently free from improper influences. *E.g.,* 84 Cong. Rec. 9598, 9603; 86 Cong. Rec. 2360, 2621, 2864, 9376. The restrictions so far imposed on federal employees are not aimed at particular parties, groups or points of view, but apply equally to all partisan activities of the type described. They discriminate against no racial, ethnic or religious minorities. Nor do they seek to control political opinions or beliefs, or to interfere with or influence anyone's vote at the polls.

But as the Court held in Pickering v. Board of Education, 391 U.S. 563, 568 (1968), the government has an interest in regulating the conduct and "the speech of its employees that differ[s] significantly from those it possesses in connection with regulation of the speech of the citizenry in general. The problem in any case is to arrive at a balance between the interest of the [employee], as a citizen, in commenting upon matters of public concern and the interest of the [government], as an employer, in promoting the efficiency of the public services it performs through its employees." Although Congress is free to strike a different balance than it has, if it so chooses, we think the balance it has so far struck is sustainable by the obviously important interests sought to be served by the limitations on partisan political activities now contained in the Hatch Act. . . .

III

But however constitutional the proscription of identifiable partisan conduct in understandable language may be, the District Court's judgment was that § 7324 (a) (2) was both unconstitutionally vague and fatally overbroad. . . .

Section 7324 (a) (2) provides that an employee in an executive agency must not take "an active part in political management or in political campaigns" and goes on to say that this prohibition refers to "those acts of political management or political campaigning which were prohibited on the part of employees in the competitive service before July 19, 1940, by determinations of the Civil Service Commission under the rules prescribed by the President." Section 7324 (b) privileges an employee to vote as he chooses and to express his opinion on political subjects and candidates, and § 7324 (c) and (d), as well as § 7326, also limit the applicability of the section.[15] The principal issue with respect to this statutory scheme is what Congress intended when it purported to define "an active part in political management or in political campaigns," as meaning the prior interpretations by the Civil Service Commission under Civil Service Rule I which contained the identical prohibition.

Earlier in this opinion it was noted that this definition was contained in § 15 of the 1940 Act. As recommended by the Senate Committee, S. Rep. No. 1236, 76th Cong., 3d Sess., 2, 4, § 15 conferred broad rule-making authority on the Civil Service Commission to spell out the meaning of "an active part in political management and political campaigns." There were, in any event, strong objections to extending the Hatch Act to those state employees working in federally financed programs, e.g., 86 Cong. Rec. 2486, 2793-2794, 2801-2802, and to § 15, in particular, as being an unwise and invalid delegation of legislative power to the Commission. E.g., id., at 2352, 2426-2427, 2579, 2794, 2875. The matter was vigorously debated; and ultimately Senator Hatch, the principal proponent and manager of the bill, offered a substitute for § 15, id., at 2928 and 2937, limiting the reach of the prohibition to those same activities that the Commission "has heretofore determined are at the time of the passage of this Act prohibited on the part of employees" in the classified service by the similar provision in Civil Service Rule I. The matter was further debated, and the amendment carried. Id., at 2958-2959.

The District Court and appellees construe § 15, now part of § 7324 (a) (2), as incorporating each of the several thousand adjudications of the Civil Service Commission under Civil Service Rule I, many of which are said to be undiscoverable, inconsistent, or incapable of yielding any meaningful rules to govern present or future conduct. In any event, the District Court held the prohibition against taking an active part in political management and political campaigns to be itself an insufficient guide

---

[15] 5 U.S.C. § 7324 provides:

" (a) An employee in an Executive agency or an individual employed by the government of the District of Columbia may not—

" (1) use his official authority or influence for the purpose of interfering with or affecting the result of an election; or

" (2) take an active part in political management or in political campaigns. "For the purpose of this subsection, the phrase 'an active part in political management or in political campaigns' means those acts of political management or political campaigning which were prohibited on the part of employees in the competitive service before July 19, 1940, by determinations of the Civil Service Commission under the rules prescribed by the President."

to employee behavior and thought the definitional addendum of § 15 only added additional confusion by referring the concerned employees to an impenetrable jungle of Commission proceedings, orders, and rulings. 346 F. Supp. 582-583, 585.

We take quite a different view of the statute. As we see it, our task is not to destroy the Act if we can, but to construe it, if consistent with the will of Congress, so as to comport with constitutional limitations. With this in mind and having examined with some care the proceedings surrounding the passage of the 1940 Act and adoption of the substitute for § 15, we think it appears plainly enough that Congress intended to deprive the Civil Service Commission of rule-making power in the sense of exercising a subordinate legislative role in fashioning a more expansive definition of the kind of conduct that would violate the prohibition against taking an active part in political management or political campaigns. But it is equally plain, we think, that Congress accepted the fact that the Commission had been performing its investigative and adjudicative role under Civil Service Rule I since 1907 and that the Commission had, on a case-by-case basis, fleshed out the meaning of Rule I and so developed a body of law with respect to what partisan conduct by federal employees was forbidden by the rule. 86 Cong. Rec. 2342, 2353. It is also apparent, in our view, that the rules that had evolved over the years from repeated adjudications were subject to sufficiently clear and summary statement for the guidance of the classified service. Many times during the debate on the floor of the Senate, Senator Hatch and others referred to a summary list of such prohibitions, e.g., id., at 2929, 2937-2938, 2942-2943, 2949, 2952-2953, the Senator's ultimate reference being to Civil Service Form No. 1236 of September 1939, the pertinent portion of which he placed in the Record, id., at 2938-2940,[18] and which was the Commission's then current effort to restate the

---

[18] See Appendix, *infra*. Senator Hatch did not have Form 1236 with him on the floor during debate on § 15 and provided the pertinent portion from the Form for insertion into the Congressional Record after debate had been completed on the section. 86 Cong. Rec. 2938, 2940. However, the Senator had provided the Senate with a card listing 18 rules which were described as the Civil Service Commission's construction of Civil Service Rule I, *id.*, at 2937-2938, 2943. The card, prepared by Senator Hatch with assistance from the Commission, was a summary of pertinent portions of Form 1236, *id.*, at 2937-2938, and was inserted into the Congressional Record, *id.*, at 2943. It provided:

"The pertinent language in section 9 is practically a duplication of the civil-service rule prohibiting activity of employees under the classified civil service.

"The section provides in substance, among other things, that no such officer or employee shall take any active part in political management or in political campaigns.

prevailing prohibitions of Civil Service Rule I, as spelled out in its adjudications to that date. It was this administrative restatement of Civil Service Rule I law, modified to the extent necessary to reflect the provisions of the 1939 and 1940 Acts themselves, that, in our view, Congress intended to serve as its definition of the general proscription against partisan activities. It was within the limits of these rules that the Civil Service Commission was to proceed to perform its role under the statute.

Not only did Congress expect the Commission to continue its accustomed role with respect to federal employees, but also in

---

"The same language of the civil-service rule has been construed as follows:

"1. Rule prohibits participation not only in national politics but also in State, county, and municipal politics.

"2. Temporary employees, substitutes, and persons on furlough or leave of absence with or without pay are subject to the regulation.

"3. Whatever an official or employee may not do directly he may not do indirectly or through another.

"4. Candidacy for or service as delegate, alternate, or proxy in any political convention is prohibited.

"5. Service for or on any political committee is prohibited.

"6. Organizing or conducting political rallies or meetings or taking any part therein except as a spectator is prohibited.

"7. Employees may express their opinions on all subjects, but they may not make political speeches.

"8. Employees may vote as they please, but they must not solicit votes; mark ballots for others; help to get out votes; act as checkers, marker, or challenger for any party or engage in other activity at the polls except the casting of his own ballot.

"9. An employee may not serve as election official unless his failure or refusal so to do would be a violation of State laws.

"10. It is political activity for an employee to publish or be connected editorially, managerially, or financially with any political newspaper. An employee may not write for publication or publish any letter or article signed or unsigned in favor of or against any political party, candidate, or faction.

"11. Betting or wagering upon the results of a primary or general election is political activity.

"12. Organization or leadership of political parades is prohibited but marching in such parades is not prohibited.

"13. Among other forms of political activity which are prohibited are distribution of campaign literature, assuming political leadership, and becoming prominently identified with political movements, parties, or factions or with the success or failure of supporting any candidate for public office.

"14. Candidacy for nomination or for the election to any National, State, county, or municipal office is within the prohibition.

"15. Attending conventions as spectators is permitted.

"16. An employee may attend a mass convention or caucus and cast his vote, but he may not pass this point.

"17. Membership in a political club is permitted, but employees may not be officers of the club nor act as such.

"18. Voluntary contributions to campaign committees and organizations are permitted. An employee may not solicit, collect, or receive contributions. Contributions by persons receiving remuneration from funds appropriated for relief purposes are not permitted."

§ 12 (b) of the 1940 Act Congress expressly assigned the Commission the enforcement task with respect to state employees now covered by the Act. The Commission was to issue notice, hold hearings, adjudicate and enforce. This process, inevitably and predictably, would entail further development of the law within the bounds of, and necessarily no more severe than, the 1940 rules and would be productive of a more refined definition of what conduct would or would not violate the statutory prohibition of taking an active part in political management and political campaigns.

It is thus not surprising that there were later editions of Form 1236, or that in 1970 the Commission again purported to restate the law of forbidden political activity and, informed by years of intervening adjudications, again sought to define those acts which are forbidden and those which are permitted by the Hatch Act. These regulations, 5 CFR Part 733, are wholly legitimate descendants of the 1940 restatement adopted by Congress and were arrived at by a process that Congress necessarily anticipated would occur down through the years. We accept them as the current and, in most respects, the long-standing interpretations of the statute by the agency charged with its interpretation and enforcement. It is to these regulations purporting to construe § 7234 as actually applied in practice, as well as to the statute itself, with its various exclusions, that we address ourselves in rejecting the claim that the Act is unconstitutionally vague and overbroad.

Whatever might be the difficulty with a provision against "taking active part in political management or in political campaigns," the Act specifically provides that the employee retains the right to vote as he chooses and to express his opinion on political subjects and candidates. The Act exempts research and educational activities supported by the District of Columbia or by religious, philanthropic or cultural organizations, 5 U.S.C. § 7324 (c); and § 7326 exempts nonpartisan political activity: questions, that is, that are not identified with national or state political parties are not covered by the Act, including issues with respect to constitutional amendments, referendums, approval of municipal ordinances and the like. Moreover, the plain import of the 1940 amendment to the Hatch Act is that the proscription against taking an active part in the proscribed activities is not open-ended but is limited to those rules and proscriptions that had been developed under Civil Service Rule I up to the date of the passage of the 1940 Act. Those rules, as refined by further adjudications within the outer limits of the 1940 rules, were restated by the Commission in 1970 in the form of regulations specifying the conduct that would be prohibited or permitted by § 7324 and its companion sections.

We have set out these regulations in the margin.[21] We see nothing impermissibly vague in 5 CFR § 733.122, which specifies

---

[21] The pertinent regulations, appearing in 5 CFR Part 733, provide:

"PERMISSIBLE ACTIVITIES

"§ 733.111 Permissible activities.

"(a) All employees are free to engage in political activity to the widest extent consistent with the restrictions imposed by law and this subject. Each employee retains the right to—

"(1) Register and vote in any election;

"(2) Express his opinion as an individual privately and publicly on political subjects and candidates;

"(3) Display a political picture, sticker, badge, or button;

"(4) Participate in the nonpartisan activities of a civic, community, social, labor, or professional organization, or of a similar organization;

"(5) Be a member of a political party or other political organization and participate in its activities to the extent consistent with law;

"(6) Attend a political convention, rally, fund-raising function; or other political gathering;

"(7) Sign a political petition as an individual;

"(8) Make a financial contribution to a political party or organization;

"(9) Take an active part, as an independent candidate, or in support of an independent candidate, in a partisan election covered by § 733.124;

"(10) Take an active part, as a candidate or in support of a candidate, in a nonpartisan election;

"(11) Be politically active in connection with a question which is not specifically identified with a political party, such as a constitutional amendment, referendum, approval of a municipal ordinance or any other question or issue of a similar character;

"(12) Serve as an election judge or clerk, or in a similar position to perform nonpartisan duties as prescribed by State or local law; and

"(13) Otherwise participate fully in public affairs, except as prohibited by law, in a manner which does not materially compromise his efficiency or integrity as an employee or the neutrality, efficiency, or integrity of his agency.

"(b) Paragraph (a) of this section does not authorize an employee to engage in political activity in violation of law, while on duty, or while in a uniform that identifies him as an employee. The head of an agency may prohibit or limit the participation of an employee or class of employees of his agency in an activity permitted by paragraph (a) of this section, if participation in the activity would interfere with the efficient performance of official duties, or create a conflict or apparent conflict of interests.

"PROHIBITED ACTIVITIES

"§ 733.121 Use of official authority; prohibition.

"An employee may not use his official authority or influence for the purpose of interfering with or affecting the result of an election.

"§ 733.122 Political management and political campaigning; prohibitions.

"(a) An employee may not take an active part in political management or in a political campaign, except as permitted by this subpart.

"(b) Activities prohibited by paragraph (a) of this section include but are not limited to—

"(1) Serving as an officer of a political party, a member of a National, State, or local committee of a political party, an officer or member of a committee of a partisan political club, or being a candidate for any of these positions;

in separate paragraphs the various activities deemed to be prohibited by § 7324 (a) (2). There might be quibbles about the meaning of taking an "active part in managing" or about "actively participating in fund-raising" or about the meaning of becoming a "partisan" candidate for office; but there are limitations in the English language with respect to being both specific and manageably brief, and it seems to us that although the prohibitions may not satisfy those intent on finding fault at any cost, they are set out in terms that the ordinary person exercising ordinary common sense can sufficiently understand and comply with, without sacrifice to the public interest. . . .

The Act permits the individual employee to "express his opinion on political subjects and candidates," 5 U.S.C. § 7324 (b) ; and the corresponding regulation, 5 CFR § 733.111 (a) (2), privileges the employee to "[e]xpress his opinion as an individual privately and publicly on political subjects and candidates." The section of the regulations which purports to state the partisan acts that are proscribed, *id.,* § 733.122, forbids in subparagraph (a) (10) the endorsement of "a partisan candidate for public office or political party office in a political advertisement, a broadcast, campaign literature or similar material," and in subparagraph (a) (12), prohibits "[a]ddressing a convention, caucus, rally or similar gathering of a political party in support of or in opposition to a partisan candidate for public office or political

---

" (2) Organizing or reorganizing a political party organization or political club;

" (3) Directly or indirectly soliciting, receiving, collecting, handling, disbursing, or accounting for assessments, contributions, or other funds for a partisan political purpose;

" (4) Organizing, selling tickets to, promoting, or actively participating in a fund-raising activity of a partisan candidate, political party, or political club;

" (5) Taking an active part in managing the political campaign of a partisan candidate for public office or political party office;

" (6) Becoming a partisan candidate for, or campaigning for, an elective public office;

" (7) Soliciting votes in support of or in opposition to a partisan candidate for public office or political party office;

" (8) Acting as recorder, watcher, challenger, or similar officer at the polls on behalf of a political party or partisan candidate;

" (9) Driving voters to the polls on behalf of a political party or partisan candidate;

" (10) Endorsing or opposing a partisan candidate for public office or political party office in a political advertisement, a broadcast, campaign literature, or similar material;

" (11) Serving as a delegate, alternate, or proxy to a political party convention;

" (12) Addressing a convention, caucus, rally, or similar gathering of a political party in support of or in opposition to a partisan candidate for public office or political party office; and

" (13) Initiating or circulating a partisan nominating petition."

party office." Arguably, there are problems in meshing § 733.111 (a) (2) with §§ 733.122 (a) (10) and (12), but we think the latter prohibitions sufficiently clearly carve out the prohibited political conduct from the expressive activity permitted by the prior section to survive any attack on the grounds of vagueness or in the name of any of those policies that doctrine may be deemed to further.

It is also important in this respect that the Commission has established a procedure by which an employee in doubt about the validity of a proposed course of conduct may seek and obtain advice from the Commission and thereby remove any doubt there may be as to the meaning of the law, at least insofar as the Commission itself is concerned.

Neither do we discern anything fatally overbroad about the statute when it is considered in connection with the Commission's construction of its terms represented by the 1970 regulations we now have before us. The major difficulties in this respect again relate to the prohibition in § 733.122 (a) (10) and (12) on endorsements in advertisements, broadcasts, and literature and on speaking at political party meetings in support of partisan candidates for public or party office. But these restrictions are clearly stated, they are political acts normally performed only in the context of partisan campaigns by one taking an active role in them, and they are sustainable for the same reasons that the other acts of political campaigning are constitutionally proscribable. They do not, therefore, render the remainder of the statute vulnerable by reason of overbreadth.

Even if the provisions forbidding partisan campaign endorsements and speech making were to be considered in some respects unconstitutionally overbroad, we would not invalidate the entire statute as the District Court did. The remainder of the statute, as we have said, covers a whole range of easily identifiable and constitutionally proscribable partisan conduct on the part of federal employees, and the extent to which pure expression is impermissibly threatened, if at all, by § 733.122 (a) (10) and (12), does not in our view make the statute substantially overbroad and so invalid on its face.

For the foregoing reasons, the judgment of the District Court is reversed.

NOTE

In Broadrick v. Oklahoma, — U.S. —, 93 S. Ct. 2908, 37 L. Ed. 2d 830, 41 L.W. 5111 (1973), decided the same day as the principal case, the Supreme Court upheld the constitutionality of the Oklahoma state merit system act. The state statute prohibited any state classified employee from being "an officer or member" of a "partisan political club" or a candidate for "any paid public office." The law also forbade the solicitation of contributions "for any political organization, candidacy or other political purpose" and the taking part "in the management or affairs of any political party or in any political campaign." Appellants argued that the statute was unconstitutionally vague and that its prohibitions were too broad in their sweep, failing to distinguish between conduct that may be proscribed and conduct that must be permitted. In rejecting these arguments, the Court ruled that:

> where conduct and not merely speech is involved, we believe that the overbreadth of a statute must not only be real, but substantial as well, judged in relation to the statute's plainly legitimate sweep. It is our view that § 818 is not substantially overbroad and that whatever overbreadth may exist should be cured through case-by-case analysis of the fact situations to which its sanctions, assertedly, may not be applied.
>
> Unlike ordinary breach of the peace statutes or other broad regulatory acts, § 818 is directed, by its terms, at political expression which if engaged in by private persons would plainly be protected by the First and Fourteenth Amendments. But at the same time, § 818 is not a censorial statute, directed at particular groups or view points. Cf. Keyishian v. Board of Regents, *supra*. The statute, rather, seeks to regulate political activity in an even-handed and neutral manner. . . .
>
> Under the decision in *Letter Carriers*, there is no question that § 818 is valid at least insofar as it forbids classified employees from: soliciting contributions for partisan candidates, political parties, or other partisan political purposes; becoming members of national, state, or local committees of political parties, or officers or committee members in partisan political clubs, or candidates to any paid public office; taking part in the management or affairs of any political party's partisan political campaign; serving as delegates or alternates to caucuses or conventions of political parties; addressing or taking an active part in partisan political rallies or meetings; soliciting votes or assisting voters at the polls or helping in a partisan effort to get voters at the polls; participating in the distribution of partisan campaign literature; initiating or circulating partisan nominating petitions; or riding in caravans for any political party or partisan political candidate.

These proscriptions are taken directly from the contested paragraphs of § 818, the Rules of the State Personnel Board and its interpretive circular, and the authoritative opinions of the State Attorney General. . . .

Appellants further point to the Board's interpretive rules purporting to restrict such allegedly protected activities as the wearing of political buttons or the use of bumper stickers. It may be that such restrictions are impermissible and that the § 818 may be susceptible of some other improper applications. But as presently construed, we do not believe that § 818 must be discarded *in toto* because some persons' arguably protected conduct may or may not be caught or chilled by the statute. Section 818 is not substantially overbroad and is not, therefore, unconstitutional on its face.

2.   Political Activity by Unions Representing Employees in the Public Sector

H. WELLINGTON AND R. WINTER, THE UNIONS AND THE CITIES 24-25, 28-31 (1971)†

Although the market does not discipline the union in the public sector to the extent that it does in the private, the municipal employment paradigm, nevertheless, would seem to be consistent with what Robert A. Dahl has called the " 'normal' American political process," which is "one in which there is a high probability that an active and legitimate group in the population can make itself heard effectively at some crucial stage in the process of decision," for the union may be seen as little more than an "active and legitimate group in the population." With elections in the background to perform, as Mr. Dahl notes, "the critical role . . . in maximizing political equality and popular sovereignty," all seems well, at least theoretically, with collective bargaining and public employment.

But there is trouble even in the house of theory if collective bargaining in the public sector means what it does in the private. The trouble is that if unions are able to withhold labor—to strike—as well as to employ the usual methods of political pressure, they may possess a disproportionate share of effective power in the process of decision. Collective bargaining would then be so effective a pressure as to skew the results of the " 'normal' American political process."

One should straightway make plain that the strike issue is not simply the importance of public services as contrasted with

---

† Copyright © 1971 by The Brookings Institution, Washington, D.C. Reprinted by permission.

services or products produced in the private sector. This is only part of the issue, and in the past the partial truth has beclouded analysis. The services performed by a private transit authority are neither less nor more important to the public than those that would be performed if the transit authority were owned by a municipality. A railroad or a dock strike may be more damaging to a community than "job action" by police. This is not to say that governmental services are not important. They are, both because the demand for them is inelastic and because their disruption may seriously injure a city's economy and occasionally impair the physical welfare of its citizens. Nevertheless, the importance of governmental services is only a necessary part of, rather than a complete answer to, the question: Why be more concerned about strikes in public employment than in private?

The answer to the question is simply that, because strikes in public employment disrupt important services, a large part of a mayor's political constituency will, in many cases, press for a quick end to the strike with little concern for the cost of settlement. This is particularly so where the cost of settlement is borne by a different and larger political constituency, the citizens of the state or nation. Since interest groups other than public employees, with conflicting claims on municipal government, do not, as a general proposition, have anything approaching the effectiveness of the strike—or at least cannot maintain that relative degree of power over the long run—they may be put at a significant competitive disadvantage in the political process. . . .

The strike and its threat, moreover, exacerbate the problems associated with the scope of bargaining in public employment. This seems clear if one attends in slightly more detail to techniques of municipal decision making.

Few students of our cities would object to Herbert Kaufman's observation that:

> Decisions of the municipal government emanate from no single source, but from many centers; conflicts and clashes are referred to no single authority, but are settled at many levels and at many points in the system: no single group can guarantee the success of any proposal it supports, the defeat of every idea it objects to. Not even the central governmental organs of the city—the Mayor, the Board of Estimate, the Council—individually or in combination, even approach mastery in this sense.
>
> Each separate decision center consists of a cluster of interested contestants, with a "core group" in the middle, invested by the rules with the formal authority to legitimize

decisions (that is to promulgate them in binding form) and a constellation of related "satellite groups" seeking to influence the authoritative issuances of the core group.

Nor would many disagree with Nelson W. Polsby when, in discussing community decision making that is concerned with an alternative to a "current state of affairs," he argues that the alternative "must be politically palatable and relatively easy to accomplish; otherwise great amounts of influence have to be brought to bear with great skill and efficiency in order to secure its adoption."

It seems probable that such potential subjects of bargaining as school decentralization and a civilian police review board are, where they do not exist, alternatives to the "current state of affairs," which are not "politically palatable and relatively easy to accomplish." If a teachers' union or a police union were to bargain with the municipal employer over these questions, and were able to use the strike to insist that the proposals not be adopted, how much "skill and efficiency" on the part of the proposals' advocates would be necessary to effect a change? And, to put the shoe on the other foot, if a teachers' union were to insist through collective bargaining (with the strike or its threat) upon major changes in school curriculum, would not that union have to be considerably less skillful and efficient in the normal political process than other advocates of community change? The point is that with respect to some subjects, collective bargaining may be too powerful a lever on municipal decision making, too effective a technique for changing or preventing the change of one small but important part of the "current state of affairs."

Unfortunately, in this area the problem is not merely the strike threat and the strike. In a system where impasse procedures involving third parties are established in order to reduce work stoppages—and this is common in those states that have passed public employment bargaining statutes—third party intervention must be partly responsive to union demands. If the scope of bargaining is open-ended, the neutral part, to be effective, will have to work out accommodations that inevitably advance some of the union's claims some of the time. And the neutral, with his eyes fixed on achieving a settlement, can hardly be concerned with balancing all the items on the community agenda or reflecting the interests of all relevant groups. . . .

Collective bargaining by public employees and the political process cannot be separated. The costs of such bargaining, therefore, cannot be fully measured without taking into account the

impact on the allocation of political power in the typical municipality. If one assumes, as here, that municipal political processes
should be structured to ensure "a high probability that an active
and legitimate group in the population can make itself heard
effectively at some crucial stage in the process of decision," then
the issue is how powerful unions will be in the typical municipal
political process if a full transplant of collective bargaining is
carried out.

The conclusion is that such a transplant would, in many cases,
institutionalize the power of public employee unions in a way that
would leave competing groups in the political process at a permanent and substantial disadvantage. . . .

A teachers' strike may not endanger public health or welfare.
It may, however, seriously inconvenience parents and other citizens who, as voters, have the power to punish one of the parties—
and always the same party, the political leadership—to the dispute.
How can anyone any longer doubt the vulnerability of a municipal employer to this sort of pressure? Was it simply a matter of
indifference to Mayor Lindsay in September 1969 whether another
teachers' strike occurred on the eve of a municipal election? Did
the size and the speed of the settlement with the United Federation of Teachers (UFT) suggest nothing about one first-rate politician's estimate of his vulnerability? And are the chickens now
coming home to roost because of extravagant concessions on pensions for employees of New York City the result only of mistaken
actuarial calculations? Or do they reflect the irrelevance of long-
run considerations to politicians vulnerable to the strike and compelled to think in terms of short-run political impact?

RASKIN, POLITICS UP-ENDS THE BARGAINING TABLE, in PUBLIC WORKERS AND PUBLIC UNIONS 122, 142-43 (S. Zagoria ed. 1972)†

It is in this area of the scope of bargaining that bitter battles lie
ahead for New York City's ultra-political labor movement. Every
union contract is a limit on management's freedom, and nowhere
is that tug-of-war more difficult to resolve than in governmental
service. Everything a teachers' union does affects the quality of
education, and in New York the cross-over from straight bread-
and-butter concerns to the nature of the educational system is
profound. The United Federation of Teachers was not only dominant in the legislative hassle over school decentralization but it

---

† A.H. Raskin, *Politics Up-Ends the Bargaining Table,* in PUBLIC WORKERS
AND PUBLIC UNIONS (Sam Zagoria ed.). Copyright © 1972 by The American
Assembly, Columbia University. Reprinted by permission of Prentice-Hall,
Inc.

incorporated into its contracts a provision for double-manned "More Effective Schools" as the chief vehicle for educational reform. The extent to which such incursions into policy determination would be prohibited by the proposed curbs in Albany has already prompted the UFT to fuse its strength with that of other teacher groups all over the state to mount a militant counteroffensive next year.

Realistically, no legal walls are going to keep civil service unions from moving increasingly into the policy field. Private industry learned many years ago that unions are ingenious enough to find a hundred expedients for punching holes in "management's rights" clauses. Manpower is so much a bedrock of all municipal services that public unions will find ways to tie considerations of job security or working conditions into every policy issue they want to have a voice in.

NOTE

Wellington and Winter argue that if traditional collective bargaining is transplanted in the public sector, "such a transplant would, in many cases, institutionalize the power of public employee unions in a way that would leave competing groups in the political process at a permanent and substantial disadvantage." Assuming that this view is correct, can the dangers and problems posed be effectively protected against by strict enforcement of the Hatch Act or comparable legislation? Does the Hatch Act purport to deal with the kind of problems posed by Wellington and Winter? *See generally* Love and Sulzner, *Political Implications of Public Employee Bargaining,* 11 IND. REL. 18 (Feb. 1972).

3. The Right To Petition

Section 7102 of the statute governing employee relations in the federal service provides that:

> The right of employees individually or collectively, to petition Congress, or a Member of Congress, or to furnish information to either House of Congress, or to a Committee or Member thereof, may not be interfered with or denied. [5 U.S.C. § 7102 (Supp. IV 1969)]

This section, which first appeared as part of the Lloyd-LaFollette Act of 1912 (37 Stat. 555), was specifically directed at the "gag rule" initiated by President Theodore Roosevelt in 1902. As first instituted, the "gag rule" absolutely prohibited employees of the executive department from petitioning Congress to remedy job grievances. (Exec. Order No. 163, Jan. 31, 1902, *reprinted in*

48 Cong. Rec. 5223 (1912).) Later, in 1909, President Taft issued a similar executive order. The Taft "gag rule" (Exec. Order 1142, Nov. 26, 1909, *reprinted in* 48 Cong. Rec. 4513 (1912)), broadly prohibited employee petitions seeking "congressional action of any kind," however, it did allow employees to present petitions with the "consent and knowledge" of their department heads.

The "gag rule" was severely criticized, especially by postal employees who comprised the largest block of civil servants affected by the rule and against whom the rule was strictly enforced. As a consequence, Congress passed section 6 of the 1912 Act, which read as follows:

> The right of persons employed in the civil service of the United States, either individually or collectively, to petition Congress, or any Member thereof, or to furnish information to either House of Congress, or to any Committee or member thereof, shall not be denied or interfered with.

This section subsequently appeared as 5 U.S.C. § 652 (d) [62 Stat. 356 (1948)], which is the forerunner of the current provision in 5 U.S.C. § 7102. An excellent review of the legislative history of the act may be found in Comment, *Dismissals of Public Employees for Petitioning Congress: Administrative Discipline and 5 U.S.C. Section 652 (d)*, 74 YALE L.J. 1156, 1161 (1965), where it is reported that:

> The dominant theme in the House and Senate debates seems to have been that the act was designed to insure that unjust treatment of government employees would promptly and effectively be brought to the attention of Congress. Many Congressmen felt that redress of job grievances could not be satisfactorily obtained by employee appeals to superiors; the gag rule "instead of promoting discipline and efficiency, produces the worst kind of tyranny" by department heads. . . .
>
> It is apparent, then, that section 652 (d) was intended to encompass job grievance petitions. It also seems clear that Congress meant to prevent the *act* of petitioning from being used as grounds for discipline or dismissal. . . . [citations omitted]

See also Note, *The Right of Government Employees to Furnish Information to Congress: Statutory and Congressional Aspects*, 57 VA. L. REV. 885, 893-95 (1971),† which gives the following

---

† Reprinted by permission of the Virginia Law Review and Fred B. Rothman & Company.

summary of the leading judicial opinions construing Section 7102:

> The judicial history of section 7102 is confined to seven cases,[23] of which only two have examined the scope of the protection afforded petitions submitted to Congress. In *Steck v. Connally*,[24] Judge Holtzoff of the District Court for the District of Columbia ordered the reinstatement of a federal employee who had been dismissed on charges that he had circulated among his fellow employees a petition which he forwarded to a member of Congress. The Court explained that section 7102 guaranteed to all civil servants the right to furnish information to Congress "free from *any restriction* or interference on the part of their superior officers." It further found that a department head could not censor the contents of the petition or dismiss the petitioner even if the statements in the petition were untrue. In response to the argument that administrative efficiency, discipline, and morale required that the statute be narrowly construed, the court noted: "[t]o be sure an activity of this kind can adversely affect the morale of a Government department. It can be vexatious and annoying at times if the employee acts unreasonably, but the statute contains no limitation."
>
> Despite this broad holding, in *Turner v. Kennedy*,[25] the District Court for the District of Columbia rendered summary judgment against an FBI agent who asked the court to overturn a Civil Service Commission's finding that letters he wrote to several members of Congress were false, irresponsible, and unjustified, and therefore demonstrated his unsuitability for continued employment in the FBI. The court did not discuss the scope of protection guaranteed by section 7102, and seemingly assumed that it did not protect the

---

23 Of the five cases that did not examine the legislative history of section 7102 to determine its scope, four involved statements made either to both Congress and the public, or solely to the public: Meehan v. Macy, 392 F.2d 822 (D.C. Cir.), *modified*, 425 F.2d 469 (1968), *vacated*, 425 F.2d 472 (1969) (en banc, per curiam); Levine v. Farley, 107 F.2d 186 (D.C. Cir. 1939), *cert. denied*, 308 U.S. 622 (1940); Eustace v. Day, 198 F. Supp. 233 (D.D.C. 1961); Ruderer v. United States, 412 F.2d 1285 (Ct. Cl. 1969), *cert. denied*, 398 U.S. 914 (1970). In each of these cases, the court held that the right to petition Congress under section 7102 did not encompass the right to direct statements at the public to induce others to write to their Congressmen. In Swaaley v. United States, 376 F.2d 857 (Ct. Cl. 1967), the court cited section 7102 as analogous protection of the right of government employees to petition their department head.

24 199 F. Supp. 104 (D.D.C. 1961).

25 Civil No. 3160-62 (D.D.C., Oct. 5, 1962), *aff'd*, 332 F.2d 304 (D.C. Cir.), *cert. denied*, 379 U.S. 901 (1964).

plaintiff's activities. In a four-line per curiam decision—
which alluded neither to the statutory history nor to *Steck
v. Connally*—the Court of Appeals affirmed.[26]

Circuit Judge Fahy dissented, relying on the broad language of section 7102 and citing *Steck* with approval. After
examining the legislative history, he concluded that the
tenor of the debate indicated Congressional intent "that
full First Amendment rights were to be extended to a Civil
Service employee by Section [7102]." Nevertheless, Judge
Fahy went on to reason that "perhaps his right is conditioned
to a degree by the circumstance that he is in government
service." He therefore proposed to limit the protection of section 7102 in the same way that the Supreme Court, in *New
York Times Co. v. Sullivan*,[27] had limited the right of freedom of the press. Adapting the *New York Times* rules to the
Turner case, Fahy would have excluded from the protection
of section 7102 all statements "made with actual malice,
that is, with knowledge that they were false or with reckless
disregard of whether [they were] false or not."[28] In a footnote
he cautioned that he did not reach such questions as whether
"the contents of a petition furnishing classified information
or confidential information of a nature that is in the public
interest not to disclose is privileged."

The significance of *Turner v. Kennedy* lies not so much
in its holding as in the suggestion, implicit in the District
Court's opinion and in the per curiam and dissenting opinions of the Court of Appeals, that section 7102 is susceptible
of limitation despite its sweeping language and its legislative
history. In the future courts confronted with the issue of
the statute's scope of protection are faced with two alternatives. On the one hand, they may leave to the executive
branch the decision whether the information in question is
of "a nature that is in the public interest not to [be] disclosed" or constitutes activity that "causes the agency immediate and substantial harm."[29] There is considerable prece-

---

[26] 332 F.2d 304 (D.C. Cir. 1964).

[27] 376 U.S. 255 (1964).

[28] 332 F.2d at 307. Consequently, Judge Fahy would have remanded the
case to the Civil Service Commission for a determination of whether the
statements met the test he formulated. *Id.*

[29] The Civil Service Commission used the latter standard in *Turner*. In
Meehan v. Macy, 392 F.2d 822, 830 (D.C. Cir. 1968), the Court of Appeals
for the District of Columbia stated its standard of review:

[I]n general the courts defer to the agency as the appropriate judge
of what is an appropriate cause for discharge as needed to promote

dent for this course. As early as 1840, the Supreme Court asserted that "interference of the courts with the performance of the ordinary duties of the executive departments of the government, would be productive of nothing but mischief."[30] The consequences of this abdication are twofold. First, the fate of the federal employee who furnished information to Congress would be placed in the hands of his department head or other superior officers—the precise situation Congress sought to change. Second, as the ultimate arbiter, the executive branch could effectively foreclose to Congress an important source of its information.

On the other hand, courts that seek to safeguard the civil servant's right to petition may adopt a strict standard in reviewing executive action. They would then face the difficult task of striking a balance among conflicting interests. In determining whether a civil servant has the right to furnish information to Congress, the courts would have to decide what information must not be disclosed in the public interest, and under what circumstances the agency's interest in discipline, morale, and efficiency overrides the right of the federal employee to consult his representatives. Clearly, these questions could be resolved more effectively if the legislative and executive branches could agree upon a precise statute that would balance their conflicting interests.

SWAALEY V. UNITED STATES, 376 F.2d 857, 862 (Ct. Cl. 1967), gives definition to the "right of petition" enjoyed by government employees under the First Amendment:

We think the freedom of the press to criticize and it may be, defame, public officials has no better support than the freedom of petition here involved. We agree with Judge Fahy's suggestion that the doctrine of New York Times Co. v. Sullivan, supra, applies to federal employee's petitions. See Turner v. Kennedy, 118 U.S. App. D.C. 104, 332 F.2d 304, 307 (1964), cert. denied 379 U.S. 901, 85 S. Ct. 189, 13 L. Ed. 2d 175 (dissenting opinion).

. . . These suggestions, it is true, relate to petitions to Congress. But, it would seem that whatever rights a civil

---

efficiency of the service, provided its decision is not arbitrary or capricious.

See also De Fino v. McNamara, 287 F.2d 339 (D.C. Cir.), cert. denied, 366 U.S. 976 (1961) (agency is not required to consider the employee's entire performance record in applying its standard); Taylor v. Macy, 252 F. Supp. 1021 (S.D. Cal. 1966) (dismissal based on criminal convictions that had been expunged).

[30] Decatur v. Paulding, 39 U.S. (14 Pet.) 497, 516 (1840).

service employee has under the First Amendment include petitions to the head of his own department as well as those to Congress. Mr. Justice Story, in his Commentaries on the Constitution, Vol. II, Section 1895, at 645, note b (5th ed. 1891), said of the right to petition:

"The statements made in petitions addressed to the proper authority, in a matter within its jurisdiction, are so far privileged that the petitioner is not liable, either civilly or criminally, for making them, though they prove to be untrue and injurious, unless he has made them maliciously."

This statement was also quoted with approval in Turner v. Kennedy, supra, 332 F.2d at 307 (dissenting opinion). In Bridges v. State of California, 314 U.S. 252, 277, 62 S. Ct. 190, 86 L. Ed. 192 (1941), a telegram to the Secretary of Labor was held to be a First Amendment petition. . . .

Therefore, we hold that a petition by a federal employee to one above him in the executive hierarchy is covered by the First Amendment and if it includes defamation of any Federal official, protection is lost only under the circumstances in which a newspaper article would lose such protection if it defamed such official. "Criticism of . . . official conduct does not lose its constitutional protection merely because it is effective criticism and hence diminishes . . . official reputations. If neither factual error nor defamatory content suffices to remove the constitutional shield from criticism of official conduct, the combination of the two elements is no less inadequate." New York Times Co. v. Sullivan, supra, 376 U.S. at 273, 84 S. Ct. at 722.

NOTES

1. Can it be argued that the *New York Times* doctrine should have full application to government employees who criticize superiors "through channels," as in *Swaaley, supra,* but that some lesser standard should apply in cases involving appeals to the public? *Compare* Los Angeles Teachers Union, Local 1021 v. Los Angeles City Bd. of Educ., 71 Cal. 2d 551, 78 Cal. Rptr. 723, 455 P.2d 827 (1969) and Hudson v. Gray, 285 Ala. 546, 234 So. 2d 564 (1970), *with* the holding in Meehan v. Macy, 425 F.2d 469 (D.C. Cir. 1968), *aff'd after rehearing en banc,* 425 F.2d 472 (D.C. Cir. 1969).

2. In T. EMERSON, THE SYSTEM OF FREEDOM OF EXPRESSION 590 (1970), the author argues that:

Restriction on the political conduct of government employees does not abridge their freedom of expression to the extent that it is indispensably required as part of the employment relation; that is to say, is essential to the government's power to carry out its functions through engaging the services of its citizens. Controls are permissible at the point where the expression can be shown to relate to job performance, either by way of indicating the employee's competence, interfering with his capacity to carry out orders, or impairing his relationship with the rest of the organization. Hence regulations concerned with the making of deliberately false statements that may reflect on competence, carrying on political activities during working hours, campaigning against or running for office against an immediate superior, would be justified. So also would controls aimed at eliminating a direct conflict of interest between an employee's political activity and his government position. In addition, needless to say, prohibition of political activities that are no expression at all, such as using official authority for partisan political coercion of subordinates, or refusal to comply with the merit system in promotion, would raise no First Amendment problems.

4. Political Lobbying

Political lobbying is, to some extent, subsumed under the more general heading of the right to petition. Lobbying by public employees is frequently a supplement to or replacement for traditional collective bargaining. Many of the statutes and executive orders regulating collective bargaining in the public sector have narrowly limited the scope of bargaining; for example, section 11 (b) of Executive Order 11491 (see *Statutory Appendix*), specifically excludes from bargaining:

> [M]atters with respect to the mission of the agency; its budget; its organization; the number of employees; and the number, types, and grades of positions of employees assigned to an organizational unit, work project, or tour of duty; the technology of performing its work; or its internal security practices.

Thus, unions representing employees in the federal service are frequently forced to make direct appeals to Congress to achieve bargaining goals.

Even when a public agency or department is authorized to negotiate and agree to certain substantive items, there may remain the requirement of legislative approval of some parts of the agreement. The New York Taylor Law, for example, includes the following requirement:

Any written agreement between a public employer and an employee organization determining the terms and conditions of employment of public employees shall contain the following notice in type not smaller than the largest type used elsewhere in such agreement.

"It is agreed by and between the parties that any provision of this agreement requiring legislative action to permit its implementation by amendment of law or by providing the additional funds therefor, shall not become effective until the appropriate legislative body has given approval." [NEW YORK CIVIL SERVICE LAW § 204-a (McKinney Supp. 1971)]

The Wisconsin State Employment Labor Relations Act, requires that agreements involving state employees must be sent to a joint legislative committee for approval once they have been approved by the union representative. A public hearing must then be held. If the committee approves the agreement, it introduces bills in both legislative houses to implement those portions of the agreement, such as wage adjustments, which require legislative approval. If the committee rejects the agreement, or if it approves but the legislature rejects the resultant bills, the agreement is sent back to the parties for further negotiation. WIS. STAT. ANN. §§ 111.80-111.97 (Wis. Leg. Serv. Supp. 1972).

Given these types of legislative enactments, it would appear that unions in the public sector must necessarily become involved in the "political process" in order to achieve legislative ratification of negotiated benefits.

For a series of articles discussing the lobbying problem, see Moskow, Loewenberg and Koziara, *Lobbying* 216, Nilan, *Union Lobbying at the Federal Level* 221, McLennan and Moskow, *Multilateral Bargaining in the Public Sector* 227, and Belasco, *Municipal Bargaining and Political Power* 235, in COLLECTIVE BARGAINING IN GOVERNMENT (Loewenberg & Moskow eds. 1972).

NOTES

1. The need to gain legislative approval for negotiated agreements, suggests that the legislators should remain neutral arbiters. However, in New York, the Taylor Law does not prohibit a legislator from also acting as a negotiator, even if he is later to decide whether agreement should be approved. *See* County of Broome and Deputy Sheriff's Benevolent Ass'n of Broome County, 3 PERB ¶ 3103 (1970), where the Board, after concluding that it was statutorily permissible for legislators to act as negotiators, stated that,

While we do conclude that the participation of the legislators herein does not constitute a violation of the duty to negotiate in good faith, we repeat the warning set forth in the *Vestal* decision that pragmatically it is most difficult for legislators to participate actively in the negotiations and then step back and act objectively as arbiters, the role which was envisioned for the legislature by the Taylor Law.

2. Can an argument be made that, because of the unique nature of collective bargaining in the public sector, all political activity which is not directly disruptive of departmental efficiency to a harmful degree should be permitted? Many of these problems may be partially alleviated by compulsory binding arbitration or mediation, which may reduce the need for political action by unions in the public sector.

D. Fair Employment Practices

1. Constitutional Proscription Against Discrimination

JOHNSON v. BRANCH

United States Court of Appeals, Fourth Circuit
364 F.2d 177 (1969)

J. SPENCER BELL, Circuit Judge:

This is an appeal from a judgment of the district court dismissing with prejudice the plaintiff's complaint seeking reversal of the action of her school committee which refused to renew her contract of employment as a teacher. She contends that the committee acted either in an arbitrary and capricious manner or acted to penalize her for exercising her constitutional rights. Jurisdiction is based upon Title 28 U.S.C. § 1343 (3), Title 42 U.S.C. §§ 1971, 1981, 1983 and 1985, and the First, Fifth, Thirteenth, Fourteenth and Fifteenth Amendments to the Constitution of the United States.

The record discloses, the defendants concede, and the court found that the plaintiff, a Negro, was a well qualified, conscientious, and competent teacher . . . for a period of nearly twelve years preceding the incidents involved here. In addition to her teaching duties she had done a great deal of "extracurricular" work for the school and for student activities which indicated her devotion to her professional task. During the year 1962-1963 the Principal graded her in all fields as excellent and above average, the two highest possible ratings used in the system of grading teachers by the Halifax school system. Her superintendent, a defendant, testified that she had been an above average teacher and was doing very satisfactory work.

Beginning in the month of April 1963, the town of Enfield became a focal point of civil rights activity which included a voter registration drive, the candidacy of a number of Negroes for public offices, a major federal voting suit, an attempt to use the public library by Negro high school students, and the picketing of places of public accommodation. . . .

The plaintiff was a participant in one of the demonstrations and in the voter registration and voting activity. Both her husband and her father were candidates for public office. Her uncle brought suit in the federal district court in an effort to secure the Negroes an adequate opportunity to register.

The civil rights movement in Enfield became increasingly active and controversial during the summer and fall of 1963 and continued into the winter of 1964. It had not terminated at the time that teaching contracts came up for renewal at the April 23, 1964, meeting of the District School Committee. In March, Mrs. Johnson received from her Principal, L.M. Williams, a letter dated March 10, 1964, listing seven infractions of the school rules which he asked her to correct. The plaintiff offered expert evidence to show, and the district court in its comments appeared to agree, that these infractions individually and collectively were not in themselves justification for failure to re-employ the plaintiff. None of them involved the quality of her classroom work. Instead they covered such matters as being 15 minutes late to supervise an evening athletic contest; arriving at the school building a few minutes after the prescribed sign-in time but before any class was due to commence; failure to furnish a written explanation for not attending a P.T.A. meeting; failure to stand in the door of her classroom to supervise pupils as the classes changed, and failure to see that the cabinets in her home room were clean and free of fire hazard. To all of these, the plaintiff offered explanations, and early in April the plaintiff received a letter dated March 31, 1964, in which the Principal informed her that he had seen improvement "in the areas mentioned" in the letter of March 10th. The letter continued "I am recommending you for re-election for a teacher for the 1964-1965 school term on condition that you continue to show improvement. . . ." Prior to the meeting of the District School Board in April, Principal Williams did in fact sign the plaintiff's contract, thus complying with the state's legal requirement that he recommend her before the Committee could act on her contract. The record discloses that the former pleasant relationship between Mrs. Johnson and the Principal, Williams, became strained over the period of her civil rights activities. The plaintiff contends that Williams was opposed to such activity on the part of school teachers and exhibited his hostility by criticizing her. She concedes that she took offense at his actions. However, she insisted that at no time were their relations such that they interfered with her official duties, and Williams also conceded that he could not specify a single infringement of the rules after the warning of March 10th. In any event, his testimony confirmed his statement of March 31st that she had improved and that he had recommended extending her contract for another year.

The District Committee met on April 23, 1964, to consider renewal of teacher contracts. . . .

All the members of the school committee knew of the civil rights activity in general and of the participation of Mr. Johnson, the plaintiff's husband, therein, though they denied specific knowledge of the plaintiff's part or of her relationship as wife to the Mr. Johnson who was running for the State Senate from that district. At this meeting all the committee members (except the Chairman, Coppage, who had received copies) first became aware of the two letters to Mrs. Johnson. In their testimony before the court they all declared that their decision was based solely on the letters. Superintendent Overman testified that at the meeting Williams renewed his favorable recommendation of March 31st. None of the members was able to testify to any inquiry into further details made at the meeting. . . . [Also present at the meeting] . . . was a member of the County School Board who had previously told Mrs. Johnson's husband that a teacher would be fired for voting activity. The members voted 2 to 1 against renewing Mrs. Johnson's contract. There was no discussion of her conduct. The two members who voted against renewal conceded frankly that they were opposed to integration of the schools. On June 2nd, the Principal told Mrs. Johnson that her contract had not been renewed because of insubordination to him. The district court, after reviewing the record, found that ". . . there was good cause for not re-employing the plaintiff under the circumstances as established by the evidence" because of the "plaintiff's inability to perform those extracurricular duties required of her promptly and in a cooperative manner. . . ." We hold that the court committed clear error in this finding, but before discussing the facts we turn to the law of the case.

The law of North Carolina is clear on the procedure for hiring teachers. All contracts are for one year only, renewable at the discretion of the school authorities. A contract must be signed by the Principal as an indication of his recommendation and then transmitted to the District School Committee, whose business it is either to approve or disapprove in their discretion. (N.C.G.S.

§ 115-72). There is no vested right to public employment. No one questions the fact that the plaintiff had neither a contract nor a constitutional right to have her contract renewed, but these questions are not involved in this case. It is the plaintiff's contention that her contract was not renewed for reasons which were either capricious and arbitrary or in order to retaliate against her for exercising her constitutional right to protest racial discrimination. . . .

[I]n Franklin v. County School Board of Giles County, 360 F.2d 325 (4 Cir. 1966), this court ordered that Negro teachers whose contracts were not renewed because of their race be reinstated. There the Board contended that they had, in the act of failure to renew the contracts, compared the qualifications of the teachers with others in the system and found them inferior, but the record disclosed no objective evidence of such inferiority in the face of equal certification and experience. However wide the discretion of School Boards, it cannot be exercised so as to arbitrarily deprive persons of their constitutional rights. . . .

While there is some ambiguity in the court's findings and conclusions, we think it a fair summary to say that the court found that the plaintiff's civil rights activities consumed so much of her time and interest that they interfered with her "extracurricular" activities at the school; created some dissension between her and the Principal, and caused the Board's refusal to renew her contract. This independent finding of the court is irrelevant because it is not the reason advanced by the Board members for refusing to execute her contract. The statute gives discretion to the school board in deciding whether or not to continue the employment of a teacher. Discretion means the exercise of judgment, not bias or capriciousness. Thus it must be based upon fact and supported by reasoned analysis. In testing the decision of the school board the district court must consider only the facts and logic relied upon by the board itself. It is "a simple but fundamental rule of administrative law . . . that a reviewing court, in dealing with a determination or judgment which an administrative agency alone is authorized to make, must judge the propriety of such action solely by the grounds invoked by the agency. If those grounds are inadequate or improper, the court is powerless to affirm the administrative action by substituting what it considers to be a more adequate or proper basis. To do so would propel the court into the domain which Congress has set aside for the administrative agency." S.E.C. v. Chenery Corp., 332 U.S. 194, 196, 67 S. Ct. 1575, 1577, 91 L. Ed. 1995 (1947). Similarly the district court may not usurp the discretionary power of the school board but must judge the constitutionality of its action on the basis of the facts which were before the Board and on its logic. The testimony of all the members of the Board was that they did not know of the plaintiff's civil rights activities, or at least the extent thereof, and that their action was based solely upon the letters of March 10th and March 31st. We accept the defendant's statements that they were not aware of the extent of the plaintiff's personal participation in this activity because the district court credited them. Thus the record offers no objectively substantiated facts known to the Board with regard to the plaintiff's civil rights activity which would justify the Board's action as found by the court. . . .

That the plaintiff had her disagreements with her Principal is obvious from the record. In such periods of great emotional stress there is no more reason to expect the Negro community to be unanimous than to expect the white to be so. But that these disagreements had been satisfactorily settled by March 31st in such a manner as not to interfere with her school work was shown both by the Principal's letter of that date and by his testimony. He testified that the plaintiff had improved in her attitude toward him and that she had not violated any of the rules since the warning of March 10th. Furthermore, the members of the Board testified that they had not further questioned the Principal and that they acted solely on the strength of the letters and their personal opinions that the Principal did not want the plaintiff's contract renewed. Thus there is no support in the record for the court's finding that the extent of the plaintiff's activities interfered with her school work or that the Principal and the plaintiff had not reached a satisfactory understanding of their differences. We take it to be self-evident that the objections held either by the Board or the Principal to the plaintiff's exercise of her personal and associational liberty to express her feelings about segregation would not justify refusal to renew her contract so long as these activities did not interfere with her performance of her school work. We feel that the infractions enumerated in the March 10th letter were neither individually nor collectively such as to justify failure to renew the contract of a teacher with the plaintiff's record of twelve years. The district court did not seek to rely on these infractions to support the dismissal. These being the only basis for the school board's decision, we find that the action of the school board was arbitrary and capricious.

We, with the district court, accept the defendants' statements that they did not know of the extent of the plaintiff's activities for civil rights but they knew of her attitude towards the civil rights movement. She made no secret of it. The Principal forced her to cancel an invitation to a local civil rights leader to talk to the students in her lecture course, even though he was not to talk about civil rights (she acceded to this order). Mr. Copeland, the member who moved not to renew her contract, was a member of the Town Council which rejected an equal accommodations ordinance strenuously backed by both Mrs. Johnson and her husband several weeks before the April meeting. Three days before the meeting, Mr. Coppage pointed out the plaintiff's husband to his fellow board member Thorne at the polling place.

In this factual context we think the court committed error in separately weighing the facts with respect to the plaintiff's two contentions: first, that the Board either acted arbitrarily or capriciously, or second, that it acted to penalize her for her civil rights activity. In weighing the reason offered by the Board to support its contention that it did not act arbitrarily, we cannot ignore the highly charged emotional background of a small eastern North Carolina community in the throes of a civil rights campaign where more than 51% of the population was Negro and where the two members of the Board who voted against the plaintiff confessed to knowledge of her husband's activity and their opposition to school desegregation. To accept such an analysis we would have to pretend not to know as judges what we know as men. It is apparent on this record that absent the racial question, the issue would not have arisen. The only reasonable inference which may be drawn from the failure to renew Mrs. Johnson's contract in the face of her splendid record of twelve years on such trivial charges was the Board members' objections to her racial activity. We cannot weigh the separate contentions in airtight compartments.

For these reasons the order of the district court is reversed and the case remanded with instructions to enter an order directing the Board to renew her contract for the next school year (1966-1967) and to determine her damages.

Reversed and remanded.

[The dissenting opinion of ALBERT V. BRYAN, Circuit Judge, is omitted.]

NOTES

1. Many of the cases of alleged discrimination in public education have arisen pursuant to court ordered shifts from segregated to unitary school systems in the South. In 1969, the Supreme Court rendered two important decisions in this area. In one, Alexander v. Holmes County Bd. of Educ., 396 U.S. 19, 90 S. Ct. 29, 24 L. Ed. 2d 19 (1969), the Court ruled that the aging order of Brown v. Board of Educ., 347 U.S. 483 (1954), was to take effect "immediately" and that school districts could no longer

operate dual school systems based on race or color. In the second case, United States v. Montgomery County Bd. of Educ., 395 U.S. 225, 89 S. Ct. 1670, 23 L. Ed. 2d 263 (1969), the Court ruled that the legal requirement of desegregation included an obligation to integrate public school faculties. The Court in *Montgomery County* ordered the school board to move toward a goal whereby in each school the ratio of white to Negro faculty members was substantially the same throughout the school system.

2. Another important decision in this area is Singleton v. Jackson Municipal Separate School Dist., 419 F.2d 121, *cert. denied*, 396 U.S. 1032 (5th Cir. 1970). The *Singleton* decision set forth standards to be followed in the event of personnel reductions which occur as a result of the transition to unitary school systems. In essence the court ordered that if, during the process of desegregation, staff reductions, resulting in dismissal or demotion of professional personnel, become necessary, the school district must proceed to select the staff members to be displaced on the basis of previously developed "non-racial objective criteria." The criteria must be made available for public inspection and must be retained by the school district. Additionally, the school district must also "record and preserve the evaluation of staff members under the criteria" and make the evaluation available to the displaced employee upon his request. The court in *Singleton* also made the significant ruling that, in the event of staff displacements—

"no staff vacancy may be filled through recruitment of a person of a race, color, or national origin different from that of the individual dismissed or demoted, until each displaced staff member who is qualified has had an opportunity to fill the vacancy and has failed to accept an offer to do so." 419 F.2d at 1218.

For more recent decisions following the mandate of *Singleton*, see Lee v. Macon County Bd. of Educ., 455 F.2d 978 (5th Cir. 1971) and Lee v. Macon County Bd. of Educ., 456 F.2d 1371 (5th Cir. 1972).

3. Minority teachers may properly be displaced pursuant to a transition from a segregated to a unitary school system, *see, e.g.,* Thomas v. Board of Educ. of the Plum Bayou Tucker School Dist., 457 F.2d 1268 (8th Cir. 1972), however, as the cases clearly recognize, unless objective standards are required, not only would the displaced minority staff remain displaced but, in all probability, the overwhelming numbers of minority applicants

for new employment would remain unhired. The applicable judicial precedents also make it clear that job criteria must bear some provable relationship to the position in question when the use of the criteria results in unfavorable differentials along racial lines. The problems encountered in this area are graphically illustrated by two 1971 Mississippi cases in which the school district imposed the requirement that both incumbent teachers and prospective applicants attain certain scores on the National Teachers Examinations (NTE) and the Graduate Record Examinations (GRE) in order to retain or obtain employment. Baker v. Columbus Municipal Separate School Dist., 329 F. Supp. 706 (N.D. Miss. 1971); Armstead v. Starkville Municipal Separate School Dist., 325 F. Supp. 560 (N.D. Miss. 1971). In both situations the local boards were aware of the fact that a disproportionate number of Blacks, as compared with whites, had failed to achieve these scores and therefore the pool of eligible teachers would be virtually all white. The court in both cases ruled that the use of these criteria as conditions of employment was illegal because (1) the tests had a disproportionately adverse impact on Black versus white job candidates and (2) the tests were never clearly shown to measure or predict a person's ability to be a good teacher. The courts also found that the GRE and NTE were not designed to facilitate the selection or identification of effective teachers. Rather, it was found that the purpose of the GRE was to assist in the identification of candidates for graduate study; and the purpose of the NTE was to measure the academic achievement of seniors in teacher education programs. There was no evidence of positive correlation between scores on either examination and effective teaching skills and ability.

2. Title VII of The Civil Rights Act

(a) Introduction

G. COOPER & H. RABB, EQUAL EMPLOYMENT LAW AND LITIGATION 33-35 (1972)†

Title VII of the Civil Rights Act of 1964, 42 U.S.C. Sec. 2000e *et seq.*, was enacted by Congress as a comprehensive prohibition on private acts of employment discrimination. As amended by the Equal Employment Opportunity Act of 1972, Title VII also now covers virtually all state and local government employees and previously-exempt employees of educational institutions. The

---

† Published in *Materials for a Clinical Law Course*, Employment Rights Project, Columbia Law School, pursuant to a grant from the Equal Employment Opportunity Commission and the New York City Commission for Human Rights.

law authorizes the Equal Employment Opportunity Commission (EEOC) to process, investigate and conciliate employment discrimination complaints and, if necessary, to bring suits against respondents in federal court. Between 1972 and 1974, the Attorney General also has authority to bring "pattern and practice" employment suits concurrently with EEOC. After 1974, EEOC assumes exclusive government authority for enforcement of the law. Title VII also creates a cause of action enforceable in federal court by aggrieved persons or classes of persons. The law provides for injunctive and affirmative relief as well as back pay, and the granting of attorneys' fees to a prevailing party.

Title VII forbids discrimination by an employer of fifteen or more persons engaged in an industry affecting commerce, including employment agencies and labor unions. The most notable employers exempt from coverage are the federal government and private clubs.

Although federal employees are not brought within the jurisdiction of the EEOC, Sec. 717 (d) of the new Title VII obliges the federal government to undertake an affirmative program of equal employment opportunity for all employees and applicants. Under this section the Civil Service Commission is given authority to investigate complaints of discrimination in hiring and to execute appropriate remedies. An individual employee or applicant who is dissatisfied with the government's disposition of his complaint has the same right as an employee in the private sector to bring a court action.

For those persons substantively covered by Title VII, the dictates are broad in that Title VII forbids all discriminatory employment practices based upon race, color, religion, sex or national origin. There are, however, exceptions. The law permits classification or employment referral on the basis of religion, sex or national origin (but not race) in certain very narrow instances where religion, sex or national origin are *bona fide* occupational qualifications. Section 703 (h) of Title VII states that it is not an unlawful employment practice for an employer to act upon the results of "any professionally developed ability test" provided that such test is not designed or used to discriminate, nor is it an unlawful employment practice for an employer to apply different conditions of employment or rates of pay pursuant to a *bona fide* seniority or merit system. . . . Finally, Sec. 703 (j) states that preferential treatment shall not be required merely because of the existence of a statistical imbalance within a group of employees. Despite these exceptions, the substantive coverage of Title VII is still quite broad.

NOTE

The full text of Title VII is included in the *Statutory Appendix*. The 1972 Amendments to the Act reflected several important refinements in the areas of coverage for state and local government employees, including:

(a)   *Extension of the Act to include state and local governments—see* §§ 701 (a) , 701 (b) , and 701 (h) .

(b)   *Extension of the Act to include private and public educational institutions—see* § 702.

(c)   *Suits by the Attorney General against governmental agencies—see* § 706 (f) (1) .

(d)   *Creation of the Equal Employment Coordinating Council—see* § 715.

(e)   *Provisions covering non-discrimination in Federal government employment—see* §§ 717 (a) , 717 (b) , 717 (e) .

(f)   *Provision covering government contractors—see* § 718.

(b)   Judicial Enforcement of Title VII

LOCAL 189, UNITED PAPERMAKERS AND PAPERWORKERS
v. UNITED STATES

United States Court of Appeals, Fifth Circuit
416 F.2d 980 (1969)
Cert. denied, 397 U.S. 919 (1970)

WISDOM, Circuit Judge:

Title VII of the Civil Rights Act of 1964 prohibits discrimination in all aspects of employment. In this case we deal with one of the most perplexing issues troubling the courts under Title VII: how to reconcile equal employment opportunity *today* with seniority expectations based on *yesterday's* built-in racial discrimination. May an employer continue to award formerly "white jobs" on the basis of seniority attained in other formerly white jobs, or must the employer consider the employee's experience in formerly "Negro jobs" as an equivalent measure of seniority? We affirm the decision of the district court. We hold that Crown Zellerbach's job seniority system in effect at its Bogalusa Paper Mill prior to February 1, 1968, was unlawful because by carrying forward the effects of former discriminatory practices the system results in present and future discrimination. When a Negro applicant has the qualifications to handle a particular job, the Act requires that Negro seniority be equated with white seniority. . . .

The parties stipulated most of the basic facts. Crown Zellerbach (Crown) runs a paper mill at Bogalusa, Louisiana. The Company employs about 950 white workers and 250 Negro workers.

Jobs there have always been organized hierarchically within "lines of progression." The jobs within each line for the most part are related functionally so that experience in one job serves as training for the next.

Until May 1964, the Company segregated the lines of progression by race, reserving some lines to white employees and others to Negroes. Local 189 of the United Papermakers and Paperworkers, the white local, had jurisdiction over the more desirable lines; Local 189-A, the Negro local, had jurisdiction over the left-overs. With very few exceptions, the lowliest white jobs paid more and carried greater responsibility than the most exalted Negro jobs. Promotion within each line was determined by "job seniority"; when a vacancy occurred, the workers in the slot below it could bid for the job, and the one who had worked the longest *in the job slot below* had priority.

The Company put new employees on "extra boards." These boards were labor pools used to fill temporary vacancies within the lines of progression. The senior men had first call on vacancies in the entry jobs at the bottom of the various lines. When lay-offs occurred, those at the bottom of the line were bumped back to the extra board. They had first claim, however, on any vacancies in their old jobs under "rights of recall." Crown segregated its extra boards, like its lines of progression, by race, one for Negroes and one for whites.

The Company merged the extra boards in May 1964. Whoever, regardless of race, had the longest term on the board now gained priority to bid on entry jobs in the white lines. Merger opened up the lines to Negro entrants, and helped the relatively recent Negro employees on the board. It did not help more senior Negroes already in the lines of progression. Moreover, the rights of recall gave any white who had served in a white line preference over others on the board in bidding on his old job. That fact slowed the advance of even newer Negro employees. A "transfer provision" added in 1965 enabled Negroes already in black lines of progression to bid on the bottom jobs in white lines on the basis of their "mill seniority," or time worked at the mill. This change meant that they did not have to become junior men on the extra board in order to bid on the starting job in previously white lines. It also meant that they did not have to surrender certain benefits accruing to mill seniority when they made the transfer.

Title VII went into effect with regard to Crown on July 2, 1965. . . .

In January 1966 the unions and the Company amended the collective bargaining agreement so as to merge the progression lines within each department on the basis of existing pay rates. Except for one job in the plant, merger by pay rates merely meant tacking the Negro lines to the bottom of white lines. Whites on the extra boards who had rights of recall to jobs formerly entry jobs retained those rights to the same jobs, even though the positions were now in the middle of the merged lines. More importantly, Crown continued to award promotions according to job seniority: the man with the most years in the job slot below the vacancy had first call. Time worked in the mill counted for nothing as such. As a necessary result, Negroes had no seniority in bidding for formerly white jobs except as against each other and new white employees. They could not have such seniority, since the Company had not allowed them into the white progression lines. Crown gave no recognition to years spent in the Negro lines, and continued to make years spent in formerly white jobs the determinative factor in awarding all former white jobs except those previously at the entry level. The system conditioned job advancement upon a qualification that the Company itself had limited racially, *regardless of whether the qualification*—seniority in previously white jobs—*was necessary to do the work*. The legality of that arrangement is the main issue here. . . .

No one can quarrel with the broad proposition that Title VII operates only prospectively. By specific provision, the Act did not become effective at all until one year after the date of enactment. The central operative provision, § 703 (a) , declares that "it *shall* be an unlawful employment practice" for an employer to discriminate. (Emphasis added.) Section 701 (b) and (e) provide that for staggered effective dates: The Act applied on July 2, 1965, only to employers of 100 employees or more, extending to employers of 75, 50, and 25 at successive yearly intervals. The dispute is whether a seniority system based on pre-Act work credit constitutes present discrimination.

Although the effect of Title VII provoked considerable debate in Congress, the legislative history of the title is singularly uninstructive on seniority rights. Opponents of the Act warned that Title VII would destroy hard-earned seniority rights; proponents responded that it would not affect accrued seniority. In Quarles v. Philip Morris, Inc., E.D. Va. 1968, 279 F. Supp. 505, after a careful review of the legislative history, Judge John D. Butzner, Jr. concluded:

"Several facts are evident from the legislative history. First, it contains no express statement about departmental seniority. Nearly all of the references are clearly to employment seniority. None of the excerpts upon which the company and the union rely suggests that as a result of past discrimination a Negro is to have employment opportunities inferior to those of a white person who has less employment seniority. Second, the legislative history indicates that a discriminatory seniority system established before the act cannot be held lawful under the act. The history leads the court to conclude that Congress did not intend to require 'reverse discrimination'; that is, the Act does not require that Negroes be preferred over white employees who possess employment seniority. It is also apparent that Congress did not intend to freeze an entire generation of Negro employees into discriminatory patterns that existed before the act."

Perhaps the strongest argument for the *Quarles* construction of the Act is § 703 (h) :

"Section 703 (h) expressly states the seniority system must be *bona fide*. The purpose of the act is to eliminate racial discrimination in covered employment. Obviously one characteristic of a *bona fide* seniority system must be lack of discrimination. Nothing in § 703 (h) , or in its legislative history suggests that a racially discriminatory seniority system established before the act is a *bona fide* seniority system under the act." Quarles v. Philip Morris, Incorporated, E.D. Va. 1968, 279 F. Supp. 505, 517.

We agree with this view . . . .

The defendants assert, paradoxically, that even though the system conditions future employment opportunities upon a previously determined racial status the system is itself racially neutral and not in violation of Title VII. The translation of racial status to job-seniority status cannot obscure the hard, cold fact that Negroes at Crown's mill will lose promotions which, *but for* their race, they would surely have won. Every time a Negro worker hired under the old segregated system bids against a white worker in his job slot, the old racial classification reasserts itself, and the Negro suffers anew for his employer's previous bias. It is not decisive therefore that a seniority system may appear to be neutral on its face if the inevitable effect of tying the system to the *past* is to cut into the employees *present* right not to be discriminated against on the ground of race. The crux of the problem is how far the employer must go to undo the effects of past discrimination. A complete purge of the "but-for" effects of previous bias would require that Negroes displace white incumbents who hold jobs that, but for discrimination, the Negroes' greater mill seniority would entitle them to hold. Under this *"freedom now"* theory, allowing junior whites to continue in their jobs constitutes an act of discrimination.

Crown and Local 189 advance a *"status quo"* theory: the employer may satisfy the requirements of the Act merely by ending explicit racial discrimination. Under that theory, whatever unfortunate effects there might be in future bidding by Negroes luckless enough to have been hired before desegregation would be considered merely as an incident of now extinguished discrimination.

A *"rightful place"* theory stands between a complete purge of "but-for" effects maintenance of the status quo. The Act should be construed to prohibit the *future awarding* of vacant jobs on the basis of a seniority system that "locks in" prior racial classification. White incumbent workers should not be bumped out of their *present* positions by Negroes with greater plant seniority; plant seniority should be asserted only with respect to new job openings. This solution accords with the purpose and history of the legislation.

Not all "but-for" consequences of pre-Act racial classification warrant relief under Title VII. For example, unquestionably Negroes, as a class, educated at all-Negro schools in certain communities have been denied skills available to their white contemporaries. That fact would not, however, prevent employers from requiring that applicants for secretarial positions know how to type, even though this requirement might prevent Negroes from becoming secretaries.

This Court recently struck down a nepotism membership requirement of a "white" union which shortly before had ceased overt discrimination. Local 53 of the International Association of Heat and Frost Insulators and Asbestos Workers v. Vogler, 5 Cir. 1969, 407 F.2d 1047. Under the nepotism rule, only the sons of members or close relatives living with members could become "improvers," and only "improvers" could be accepted into the union. Relationship to a member as a prerequisite to admission had the necessary effect of locking non-whites out of the union. The union argued that the desire to provide family security was a rational non-racial basis for the rule and that since the nepotism requirement excluded all persons unrelated to members, regardless of their race, it could not, therefore, be called a racial classification. This court held that the rule served no purpose related to ability to perform the work in the asbestos trade and that it violated Title VII. . . .

The controlling difference between the hypothetical typing requirement and the nepotism rule rejected in *Vogler* is *business necessity*. When an employer or union has discriminated in the past and when its present policies renew or exaggerate discriminatory effects, those policies must yield, unless there is an overriding legitimate, nonracial business purpose. Secretaries must be able to type. There is no way around that necessity. A nepotism rule, on the other hand, while not unrelated to the training of craftsmen, is not essential to that end. To be sure, skilled workers may gain substantial benefits from having grown up in the home of a member of the trade. It is clear, nonetheless, that the benefits secured by nepotism must give way because of its effective continuation and renewal of racial exclusion. That much was decided in *Vogler*.

The decisive question then is whether the job seniority standard, as it is now functioning at the Bogalusa plant, is so necessary to Crown Zellerbach's operations as to justify locking Negroes, hired before 1966, into permanent inferiority in their terms and conditions of employment. The record supports the district court's holding that job seniority is not essential to the safe and efficient operation of Crown's mill. The defendants' chief expert witness, Dr. Northrup, made it clear that he considered mill seniority "disastrous" only to the extent that it allowed *all* men in a slot to bid on the basis of their time at the mill. He stated that mill seniority in that sense would create labor unrest because its main effect would be to allow whites to "jump" other whites and Negroes to "jump" other Negroes. He also expressed fears about allowing anyone to bid on any vacancy in a line of progression, without requiring that he first advance job-by-job through the various levels below it. That problem might be solved, he stated, by imposing a residency requirement for training purposes. Dr. Northrup explicity stated that job seniority does *not* provide the only safe or efficient system for governing promotions. He suggested, in fact, an alternative "job credit" system that would give certain fractional seniority credit to victims of discrimination for the years in which they had been excluded from the white progression lines.

The court took account of Dr. Northrup's apprehensions in fashioning its decree. In place of job security [seniority?] the court ordered the institution of a mill seniority system carefully tailored to assure that no employee would have a right to a job that he could not perform properly. The court's decision put the emphasis where it belongs: absent a showing that the worker has the ability to handle a particular job, the entry job is the proper beginning for any worker. Under the court's decree, employees still must move up through the various lines of progression job-by-job. As a further restraint, if a certain minimum time is needed in one job to train an employee for the next, a residency requirement may be imposed that will slow the rise of Negro employees. Under the system that is in effect at the mill now, and that is unaffected by the decree, that residency period is six months. To meet the problem of labor unrest that might result from "jumping" unrelated to racial issues, the court specifically limited its decree to instances in which Negroes hired before 1966 were among the bidders. Finally, and most importantly, both the court's decree and the existing collective bargaining agreement give Crown Zellerbach the right to deny promotions to employees who lack the ability or qualification to do the job properly.

All these precautions, we think, bear out the plaintiffs' assertion that there are satisfactory alternatives to job seniority at the Bogalusa mill. They lead us to conclude that the imposition of a system that perpetuates and renews the effects of racial discrimination in the guise of job seniority is not necessary or justified at Bogalusa. Job seniority, embodying as it does, the racially determined effects of a biased past, constitutes a form of present racial discrimination. . . .

The defendants maintain that Congress specifically exempts seniority systems such as Crown's from the operation of Title VII. In support of their assertion the defendants cite that portion of § 703 (h) which allows an employer to "apply different standards of compensation, or different terms, conditions, or privileges of employment *pursuant to a bona fide seniority* or merit system . . . provided that such differences are not the result of an intention to discriminate because of race, color, religion, sex, or national origin."

No doubt, Congress, to prevent "reverse discrimination" meant to protect certain seniority rights that could not have existed but for previous racial discrimination. For example a Negro who had been rejected by an employer on racial grounds before passage of the Act could not, after being hired, claim to outrank whites who had been hired before him but after his original rejection, even though the Negro might have had senior status but for the past discrimination. As the court pointed out in *Quarles,* the treatment of "job" or "department seniority" raises problems different from those discussed in the Senate debates: "a department seniority system that has its genesis in racial discrimination is not a bona fide seniority system." 279 F. Supp. at 517.

It is one thing for legislation to require the creation of *fictional* seniority for newly hired Negroes, and quite another thing for it to require that time *actually worked* in Negro jobs be given equal status with time worked in white jobs. To begin with, requiring employers to correct their pre-Act discrimination by creating fictional seniority for new Negro employees would not necessarily aid the actual victims of the previous discrimination. There would be no guaranty that the new employees had actually suffered exclusion at the hands of the employer in the past, or, if they had, there would be no way of knowing whether, after being hired, they would have continued to work for the same employer. In other words, creating fictional employment time for newly-hired Negroes would comprise preferential rather than remedial treatment. The clear thrust of the Senate debate is directed against such preferential treatment on the basis of race. That sentiment was codified in an important portion of Title VII, § 703 (j) . . . .

We find unpersuasive the argument that, whatever its operational effects, job seniority is immune under the statute because not imposed with the *intent* to discriminate. Section 703 (h), quoted earlier, excludes from the strictures of Title VII different working terms dictated by "bona fide" seniority systems "provided that such differences are *not the result of an intention to discriminate because of race. . . .*" Here, however, if Crown did not intend to punish Negroes as such by reinstituting job seniority, the differences between the job status of Negroes hired before 1966 and whites hired at the same time would have to be called the "result" of Crown's earlier, intentional discrimination. . . .

Section 706 (g) limits injunctive (as opposed to declaratory) relief to cases in which the employer or union has "*intentionally engaged in*" an unlawful employment practice. Again, the statute, read literally, requires only that the defendant meant to do what he did, that is, his employment practice was not accidental. The relevant legislative history . . . bears out the language of the statute on that point.

Section 707 (a) allows the Attorney General to enforce the Act only where there is a "pattern or practice of resistance to the full enjoyment of any of the rights secured by this subchapter" and where the pattern or practice "is *intended* to deny the full exercise of the rights herein described." Defendants contend that no such condition existed here. . . .

Here . . . the conduct engaged in had racially-determined effects. The requisite intent may be inferred from the fact that the defendants persisted in the conduct after its racial implications had become known to them. Section 707 (a) demands no more. . . .

Our main conclusions may be summarized as follows: (1) Crown's job seniority system carries forward the discriminatory effects integral to the company's former employment practices. (2) The safe and efficient operation of the Bogalusa mill does not depend upon maintenance of the job seniority system. (3) To the extent that Crown and the white union insisted upon carrying forward exclusion of a racially-determined class, *without business necessity,* they committed, with the requisite intent, in the statutory sense, an unfair employment practice as defined by Title VII. . . .

GRIGGS v. DUKE POWER CO.
Supreme Court of the United States
401 U.S. 424, 91 S. Ct. 849, 28 L. Ed. 2d 158 (1971)

MR. CHIEF JUSTICE BURGER delivered the opinion of the Court.

We granted the writ in this case to resolve the question whether an employer is prohibited by the Civil Rights Act of 1964, Title VII, from requiring a high school education or passing of a standardized general intelligence test as a condition of employment in or transfer to jobs when (a) neither standard is shown to be significantly related to successful job performance, (b) both requirements operate to disqualify Negroes at a substantially higher rate than white applicants, and (c) the jobs in question formerly had been filled only by white employees as part of a longstanding practice of giving preference to whites.

Congress provided, in Title VII of the Civil Rights Act of 1964, for class actions for enforcement of provisions of the Act and this proceeding was brought by a group of incumbent Negro employees against Duke Power Company. All the petitioners are employed at the Company's Dan River Steam Station, a power generating facility located at Draper, North Carolina. At the time this action was instituted, the Company had 95 employees at the Dan River Station, 14 of whom were Negroes; 13 of these are petitioners here.

The District Court found that prior to July 2, 1965, the effective date of the Civil Rights Act of 1964, the Company openly discriminated on the basis of race in the hiring and assigning of employees at its Dan River plant. The plant was organized into five operating departments: (1) Labor, (2) Coal Handling, (3) Operations, (4) Maintenance, and (5) Laboratory and Test. Negroes were employed only in the Labor Department where the highest paying jobs paid less than the lowest paying jobs in the other four "operating" departments in which only whites were employed. Promotions were normally made within each department on the basis of job seniority. Transferees into a department usually began in the lowest position.

In 1955 the Company instituted a policy of requiring a high school education for initial assignment to any department except

Labor, and for transfer from the Coal Handling to any "inside" department (Operations, Maintenance, or Laboratory). When the Company abandoned its policy of restricting Negroes to the Labor Department in 1965, completion of high school also was made a prerequisite to transfer from Labor to any other department. From the time the high school requirement was instituted to the time of trial, however, white employees hired before the time of the high school education requirement continued to perform satisfactorily and achieve promotions in the "operating" departments. Findings on this score are not challenged.

The Company added a further requirement for new employees on July 2, 1965, the date on which Title VII became effective. To qualify for placement in any but the Labor Department it became necessary to register satisfactory scores on two professionally prepared aptitude tests, as well as to have a high school education. Completion of high school alone continued to render employees eligible for transfer to the four desirable departments from which Negroes had been excluded if the incumbent had been employed prior to the time of the new requirement. In September 1965 the Company began to permit incumbent employees who lacked a high school education to qualify for transfer from Labor or Coal Handling to an "inside" job by passing two tests—the Wonderlic Personnel Test, which purports to measure general intelligence, and the Bennett Mechanical Aptitude Test. Neither was directed or intended to measure the ability to learn to perform a particular job or category of jobs. The requisite scores used for both initial hiring and transfer approximated the national median for high school graduates.

The District Court had found that while the Company previously followed a policy of overt racial discrimination in a period prior to the Act, such conduct had ceased. The District Court also concluded that Title VII was intended to be prospective only and, consequently, the impact of prior inequities was beyond the reach of corrective action authorized by the Act.

The Court of Appeals was confronted with a question of first impression, as are we, concerning the meaning of Title VII. After careful analysis a majority of that court concluded that a subjective test of the employer's intent should govern, particularly in a close case, and that in this case there was no showing of a discriminatory purpose in the adoption of the diploma and test requirements. On this basis, the Court of Appeals concluded there was no violation of the Act.

The Court of Appeals reversed the District Court in part, rejecting the holding that residual discrimination arising from prior employment practices was insulated from remedial action. The Court of Appeals noted, however, that the District Court was correct in its conclusion that there was no finding of a racial purpose of invidious intent in the adoption of the high school diploma requirement or general intelligence test and that these standards had been applied fairly to whites and Negroes alike. It held that, in the absence of a discriminatory purpose, use of such requirements was permitted by the Act. In so doing, the Court of Appeals rejected the claim that because these two requirements operated to render ineligible a markedly disproportionate number of Negroes, they were unlawful under Title VII unless shown to be job-related. We granted the writ on these claims. . . .

The objective of Congress in the enactment of Title VII is plain from the language of the statute. It was to achieve equality of employment opportunities and remove barriers that have operated in the past to favor an identifiable group of white employees over other employees. Under the Act, practices, procedures, or tests neutral on their face, and even neutral in terms of intent, cannot be maintained if they operate to "freeze" the status quo of prior discriminatory employment practices.

The Court of Appeals' opinion, and the partial dissent, agreed that, on the record in the present case, "whites fare far better on the Company's alternative requirements" than Negroes.[6] This consequence would appear to be directly traceable to race. Basic intelligence must have the means of articulation to manifest itself fairly in a testing process. Because they are Negroes, petitioners have long received inferior education in segregated schools and this Court expressly recognized these differences in Gaston County v. United States, 395 U.S. 285 (1969). There, because of the inferior education received by Negroes in North Carolina, this court barred the institution of a literacy test for voter registration on the ground that the test would abridge the right to vote indirectly on account of race. Congress did not intend by Title VII, however, to guarantee a job to every person regardless of qualifications. In short, the Act does not command that any

---

[6] In North Carolina, 1960 census statistics show that, while 34% of white males had completed high school, only 12% of Negro males had done so. U.S. Bureau of the Census, U.S. Census of Population: 1960, Vol. 1, Part 35, Table 47.

Similarly, with respect to standardized tests, the EEOC in one case found that use of a battery of tests, including the Wonderlic and Bennett tests used by the Company in the instant case, resulted in 58% of whites passing the tests, as compared with only 6% of the blacks. Decision of EEOC, CCH Empl. Prac. Guide, ¶ 17,304.53 (Dec. 2, 1966). See also Decision of EEOC 70-552, CCH Empl. Prac. Guide, ¶ 6139 (Feb. 19, 1970).

person be hired simply because he was formerly the subject of discrimination, or because he is a member of a minority group. Discriminatory preference for any group, minority or majority, is precisely and only what Congress has proscribed. What is required by Congress is the removal of artificial, arbitrary, and unnecessary barriers to employment when the barriers operate invidiously to discriminate on the basis of racial or other impermissible classification.

Congress has now provided that tests or criteria for employment or promotion may not provide equality of opportunity only in the sense of the fabled offer of milk to the stork and the fox. On the contrary, Congress has now required that the posture and condition of the job seeker be taken into account. It has —to resort again to the fable—provided that the vessel in which the milk is proffered be one all seekers can use. The Act proscribes not only overt discrimination but also practices that are fair in form, but discriminatory in operation. The touchstone is business necessity. If an employment practice which operates to exclude Negroes cannot be shown to be related to job performance, the practice is prohibited.

On the record before us, neither the high school completion requirement nor the general intelligence test is shown to bear a demonstrable relationship to successful performance of the jobs for which it was used. Both were adopted, as the Court of Appeals noted, without meaningful study of their relationship to job-performance ability. Rather, a vice president of the Company testified, the requirements were instituted on the Company's judgment that they generally would improve the overall quality of the work force.

The evidence, however, shows that employees who have not completed high school or taken the tests have continued to perform satisfactorily and make progress in departments for which the high school and test criteria are now used. The promotion record of present employees who would not be able to meet the new criteria thus suggests the possibility that the requirements may not be needed even for the limited purpose of preserving the avowed policy of advancement within the Company. In the context of this case, it is unnecessary to reach the question whether testing requirements that take into account capability for the next succeeding position or related future promotion might be utilized upon a showing that such long range requirements fulfill a genuine business need. In the present case the Company has made no such showing.

The Court of Appeals held that the Company had adopted the diploma and test requirements without any "intention to discriminate against Negro employees." We do not suggest that either the District Court or the Court of Appeals erred in examining the employer's intent; but good intent or absence of discriminatory intent does not redeem employment procedures or testing mechanisms that operate as "built-in headwinds" for minority groups and are unrelated to measuring job capability.

The Company's lack of discriminatory intent is suggested by special efforts to help the undereducated employees through Company financing of two-thirds the cost of tuition for high school training. But Congress directed the thrust of the Act to the *consequences* of employment practices, not simply the motivation. More than that, Congress has placed on the employer the burden of showing that any given requirement must have a manifest relationship to the employment in question.

The facts of this case demonstrate the inadequacy of broad and general testing devices as well as the infirmity of using diplomas or degrees as fixed measures of capability. History is filled with examples of men and women who rendered highly effective performance without the conventional badges of accomplishment in terms of certificates, diplomas, or degrees. Diplomas and tests are useful servants, but Congress had mandated the common-sense proposition that they are not to become masters of reality.

The Company contends that its general intelligence tests are specifically permitted by § 703 (h) of the Act. That section authorizes the use of "any professionally developed ability test" that is not "designed, intended, *or used* to discriminate because of race. . . ." (Emphasis added.)

The Equal Employment Opportunity Commission, having enforcement responsibility, has issued guidelines interpreting § 703 (h) to permit only the use of job-related tests. The administrative interpretation of the Act by the enforcing agency is entitled to great deference. See, *e.g.,* United States v. City of Chicago, — U.S. — (No. 386, O.T. 1970) ; Udall v. Tallman, 380 U.S. 1 (1965) ; Power Reactor Co. v. Electricians, 367 U.S. 396 (1961) . Since the Act and its legislative history support the Commission's construction, this affords good reason to treat the Guidelines as expressing the will of Congress.

Section 703 (h) was not contained in the House version of the Civil Rights Act but was added in the Senate during extended debate. For a period, debate revolved around claims that the bill as proposed would prohibit all testing and force employers to hire unqualified persons simply because they were part of a group formerly subject to job discrimination. Proponents of Title VII sought throughout the debate to assure the critics that the

Act would have no effect on job-related tests. Senators Case of New Jersey and Clark of Pennsylvania, comanagers of the bill on the Senate floor, issued a memorandum explaining that the proposed Title VII "expressly protects the employer's right to insist that any prospective applicant, Negro or white, *must meet the applicable job qualifications.* Indeed, the very purpose of Title VII is to promote hiring on the basis of job qualifications, rather than on the basis of race or color." (Emphasis added.) 110 Cong. Rec. 7247. Despite these assurances, Senator Tower of Texas introduced an amendment authorizing "professionally developed ability tests." Proponents of Title VII opposed the amendment because, as written, it would permit an employer to give any test, "whether it was a good test or not, so long as it was professionally designed. Discrimination could actually exist under the guise of compliance with the statute." Remarks of Senator Case, 110 Cong. Rec. 13504.

The amendment was defeated and two days later Senator Tower offered a substitute amendment which was adopted verbatim and is now the testing provision of § 703 (h). Speaking for the supporters of Title VII, Senator Humphrey, who had vigorously opposed the first amendment, endorsed the substitute amendment, stating: "Senators on both sides of the aisle who were deeply interested in Title VII have examined the text of this amendment and have found it to be in accord with the intent and purpose of that title." 110 Cong. Rec. 13724. The amendment was then adopted. From the sum of the legislative history relevant in this case, the conclusion is inescapable that the EEOC's construction of § 703 (h) to require that employment tests be job-related comports with congressional intent.

Nothing in the Act precludes the use of testing or measuring procedures; obviously they are useful. What Congress has forbidden is giving these devices and mechanisms controlling force unless they are demonstrably a reasonable measure of job performance. Congress has not commanded that the less qualified be preferred over the better qualified simply because of minority origins. Far from disparaging job qualifications as such, Congress has made such qualifications the controlling factor, so that race, religion, nationality, and sex become irrelevant. What Congress has commanded is that any tests used must measure the person for the job and not the person in the abstract.

The judgment of the Court of Appeals is, as to that portion of the judgment appealed from, reversed.

MR. JUSTICE BRENNAN took no part in the consideration or decision of this case.

McDONNELL DOUGLAS CORP. v. GREEN

Supreme Court of the United States
— U.S. —, 93 S. Ct. 1817, — L. Ed. 2d — (1973)

MR. JUSTICE POWELL delivered the opinion of the Court.

The case before us raises significant questions as to the proper order and nature of proof in actions under Title VII of the Civil Rights Act of 1964.

Petitioner, McDonnell Douglas Corporation, is an aerospace and aircraft manufacturer headquartered in St. Louis, Missouri, where it employs over 30,000 people. Respondent, a black citizen of St. Louis, worked for petitioner as a mechanic and laboratory technician from 1956 until August 28, 1964 when he was laid off in the course of a general reduction in petitioner's work force.

Respondent, a long-time activist in the civil rights movement, protested vigorously that his discharge and the general hiring practices of petitioner were racially motivated. As part of this protest, respondent and other members of the Congress on Racial Equality illegally stalled their cars on the main roads leading to petitioner's plant for the purpose of blocking access to it at the time of the morning shift change. . . .

On July 2, 1965, a "lock-in" took place wherein a chain and padlock were placed on the front door of a building to prevent the occupants, certain of petitioner's employees, from leaving. Though respondent apparently knew beforehand of the "lock-in," the full extent of his involvement remains uncertain.

Some three weeks following the "lock-in," on July 25, 1965, petitioner publicly advertised for qualified mechanics, respondent's trade, and respondent promptly applied for re-employment. Petitioner turned down respondent, basing its rejection on respondent's participation in the "stall-in" and "lock-in." Shortly thereafter, respondent filed a formal complaint with the Equal Employment Opportunity Commission, claiming that petitioner had refused to rehire him because of his race and persistent involvement in the civil rights movement, in violation of §§ 703 (a) (1) and 704 (a) of the Civil Rights Act of 1964. 42 U.S.C. §§ 2000e-2 (a) (1) and 2000e-3 (a). The former section generally prohibits racial discrimination in any employment decision while the latter forbids discrimination against applicants or employees for attempting to protest or correct allegedly discriminatory conditions of employment.

The Commission made no finding on respondent's allegation of racial bias under § 703 (a) (1), but it did not find reasonable cause to believe petitioner had violated § 704 (a) by refusing to rehire respondent because of his civil rights activity. After the Commission unsuccessfully attempted to conciliate the dispute, it advised respondent in March 1968, of his right to institute a civil action in federal court within 30 days.

On April 15, 1968, respondent brought the present action, claiming initially a violation of § 704 (a) and, in an amended complaint, a violation of § 703 (a) (1) as well. The District Court dismissed the latter claim of racial discrimination in petitioner's hiring procedures on the ground that the Commission had failed to make a determination of reasonable cause to believe that a violation of that section had been committed. The District Court also found that petitioner's refusal to rehire respondent was based solely on his participation in the illegal demonstrations and not on his legitimate civil rights activities. The court concluded that nothing in Title VII or § 704 protected "such activity as employed by the plaintiff in the 'stall-in' and 'lock-in' demonstrations." . . .

On appeal, the Eighth Circuit affirmed that unlawful protests were not protected activities under § 704 (a) , but reversed the dismissal of respondent's § 703 (a) (1) claim relating to racially discriminatory hiring practices, holding that a prior Commission determination of reasonable cause was not a jurisdictional prerequisite to raising a claim under that section in federal court. The court ordered the case remanded for trial of respondent's claim under § 703 (a) (1) .

In remanding, the Court of Appeals attempted to set forth standards to govern the consideration of respondent's claim. The majority noted that respondent had established a prima facie case of racial discrimination; that petitioner's refusal to rehire respondent rested on "subjective" criteria which carried little weight in rebutting charges of discrimination; that though respondent's participation in the unlawful demonstrations might indicate a lack of a responsible attitude toward performing work for that employer, respondent should be given the opportunity to demonstrate that petitioner's reasons for refusing to rehire him were merely pretextual. In order to clarify the standards governing the disposition of an action challenging employment discrimination, we granted certiorari. . . .

I. We agree with the Court of Appeals that absence of a Commission finding of reasonable cause cannot bar suit under an appropriate section of Title VII and that the District Judge erred in dismissing respondent's claim of racial discrimination under § 703(a)(1). Respondent satisfied the jurisdictional prerequisites to a federal action (i) by filing timely charges of employment discrimination with the Commission and (ii) by receiving and acting upon the Commission's statutory notice of the right to sue. 42 U.S.C. §§ 2000e-5 (a) and 2000e-5 (e) . The Act does not restrict a complainant's right to sue to those charges as to which the Commission has made findings of reasonable cause, and we will not engraft on the statute a requirement which may inhibit the review of claims of employment discrimination in the federal courts. The Commission itself does not consider the absence of a "reasonable cause" determination as providing employer immunity from similar charges in a federal court, 29 CFR § 1601.30, and the courts of appeal have held that, in view of the large volume of complaints before the Commission and the nonadversary character of many of its proceedings, "court actions under Title VII are *de novo* proceedings and . . . a Commission's 'no reasonable cause' finding does not bar a lawsuit in the case." Robinson v. Lorillard Corp., 444 F.2d 791, 800 (4th Cir.); Beverly v. Lone Star Lead Construction Corp., 437 F.2d 1136 (5th Cir.); Flowers v. Local 6, Laborers International Union of North America, 431 F.2d 205 (7th Cir.); Fekete v. U. S. Steel Corp., 424 F.2d 331 (3d Cir.).

Petitioner argues, as it did below, that respondent sustained no prejudice from the trial court's erroneous ruling because in fact the issue of racial discrimination in the refusal to re-employ "was tried thoroughly" in a trial lasting four days with "at least 80%" of the questions relating to the issue of "race." Petitioner therefore requests that the judgment below be vacated and the cause remanded with instructions that the judgment of the District Court be affirmed. We cannot agree that the dismissal of respondent's § 703(a)(1) claim was harmless error. It is not clear that the District Court's findings as to respondent's § 704(a) contentions involved the identical issues raised by his claim under § 703(a)(1). The former section relates solely to discrimination against an applicant or employee on account of his participation in legitimate civil rights activities or protests, while the latter section deals with the broader and centrally important question under the Act of whether, for any reason, a racially discriminatory employment decision has been made. Moreover, respondent should have been accorded the right to prepare his case and plan the strategy of trial with the knowledge that the § 703(a)(1) cause of action was properly before the District Court. Accordingly, we remand the case for trial of respondent's claim of racial discrimination consistent with the views set forth below.

II. The critical issue before us concerns the order and allocation of proof in a private, single-plaintiff action challenging employment discrimination. The language of Title VII makes plain the purpose of Congress to assure equality of employment opportunities and to eliminate those discriminatory practices and devices which have fostered racially stratified job environments to the disadvantage of minority citizens. Griggs v. Duke Power Co., 401 U.S. 424, 429 (1971) . . . .

There are societal as well as personal interests on both sides of this equation. The broad, overriding interest, shared by employer, employee, and consumer, is efficient and trustworthy workmanship assured through fair and racially neutral employment and personnel decisions. In the implementation of such decisions, it is abundantly clear that Title VII tolerates no racial discrimination, subtle or otherwise.

In this case respondent, the complainant below, charges that he was denied employment "because of his involvement in civil rights activities" and "because of his race and color." Petitioner denied discrimination of any kind, asserting that its failure to re-employ respondent was based upon and justified by his participation in the unlawful conduct against it. Thus, the issue at the trial on remand is framed by those opposing factual contentions. The two opinions of the Court of Appeals and the several opinions of the three judges of the court attempted, with a notable lack of harmony, to state the applicable rules as to burden of proof and how this shifts upon the making of a prima facie case. We now address this problem.

The complainant in a Title VII trial must carry the initial burden under the statute of establishing a prima facie case of racial discrimination. This may be done by showing (i) that he belongs to a racial minority; (ii) that he applied and was qualified for a job for which the employer was seeking applicants; (iii) that, despite his qualifications, he was rejected; and (iv) that, after his rejection, the position remained open and the employer continued to seek applicants from persons of complainant's qualifications. In the instant case, we agree with the Court of Appeals that respondent proved a prima facie case. . . . Petitioner sought mechanics, respondent's trade, and continued to do so after respondent's rejection. Petitioner, moreover, does not dispute respondent's qualifications and acknowledges that his past work performance in petitioner's employ was "satisfactory."

The burden then must shift to the employer to articulate some legitimate, nondiscriminatory reason for respondent's rejection. We need not attempt in the instant case to detail every matter which fairly could be recognized as a reasonable basis for a refusal to hire. Here petitioner has assigned respondent's participation in unlawful conduct against it as the cause for his rejection. We think that this suffices to discharge petitioner's burden of proof at this stage and to meet respondent's prima facie case of discrimination.

The Court of Appeals intimated, however, that petitioner's stated reason for refusing to rehire respondent was a "subjective" rather than objective criterion which "carries little weight in rebutting charges of discrimination." . . . This was among the statements which caused the dissenting judge to read the opinion as taking "the position that such unlawful acts as Green committed against McDonnell would not legally entitle McDonnell to refuse to rehire him, even though no racial motivation was involved. . . ." Regardless of whether this was the intended import of the opinion, we think the court below seriously underestimated the rebuttal weight to which petitioner's reasons were entitled. Respondent admittedly had taken part in a carefully planned "stall-in," designed to tie up access and egress to petitioner's plant at a peak traffic hour. Nothing in Title VII compels an employer to absolve and rehire one who has engaged in such deliberate, unlawful activity against it. In upholding, under the National Labor Relations Act, the discharge of employees who had seized and forcibly retained an employer's factory buildings in an illegal sit-down strike, the Court noted pertinently:

> "We are unable to conclude that Congress intended to compel employers to retain persons in their employ regardless of their unlawful conduct—to invest those who go on strike with an immunity from discharge for acts of trespass or violence against the employer's property. . . . Apart from the question of the constitutional validity of an enactment of that sort, it is enough to say that such a legislative intention should be found in some definite and unmistakable expression." NLRB v. Fansteel Corp., 306 U.S. 240, 255 (1939).

Petitioner's reason for rejection thus suffices to meet the prima facie case, but the inquiry must not end here. While Title VII does not, without more, compel rehiring of respondent, neither does it permit petitioner to use respondent's conduct as a pretext for the sort of discrimination prohibited by § 703(a)(1). On remand, respondent must, as the Court of Appeals recognized, be afforded a fair opportunity to show that petitioner's stated reason for respondent's rejection was in fact pretextual. Especially relevant to such a showing would be evidence that white employees involved in acts against petitioner of comparable seriousness to the "stall-in" were nevertheless retained or rehired. Petitioner may justifiably refuse to rehire one who was engaged in unlawful, disruptive acts against it, but only if this criterion is applied alike to members of all races.

Other evidence that may be relevant to any showing of pretextuality includes facts as to the petitioner's treatment of respondent during his prior term of employment, petitioner's reaction, if any, to respondent's legitimate civil rights activities, and petitioner's general policy and practice with respect to minority employment. On the latter point, statistics as to petitioner's employment policy and practice may be helpful to a determination of whether petitioner's refusal to rehire respondent in this case conformed to a general pattern of discrimination against blacks. Jones v. Lee Way Motor Freight, Inc., 421 F.2d 245 (10th Cir. 1970); Blumrosen, Strangers in Paradise: Griggs v. Duke Power Co., and the Concept of Employment Discrimination, 71 Mich. L. Rev. 59, 91-94 (1972). In short, on the retrial respondent must be given a full and fair opportunity to demonstrate by competent evidence that the presumptively valid reasons for his rejection were in fact a coverup for a racially discriminatory decision.

The court below appeared to rely upon *Griggs v. Duke Power Co., supra,* in which the Court stated: "If an employment practice which operates to exclude Negroes cannot be shown to be related to job performance, the practice is prohibited." *Id.* at 431. But *Griggs* differs from the instant case in important respects. It dealt with standardized testing devices which, however neutral on their face, operated to exclude many blacks who were capable of performing effectively in the desired positions. *Griggs* was rightly concerned that childhood deficiencies in the education and background of minority citizens, resulting from forces beyond their control, not be allowed to work a cumulative and invidious burden on such citizens for the remainder of their lives. *Id.* at 430. Respondent, however, appears in different clothing. He had engaged in a seriously disruptive act against the very one from whom he now seeks employment. And petitioner does not seek his exclusion on the basis of a testing device which overstates what is necessary for competent performance, or through some sweeping disqualification of all those with any past record of unlawful behavior, however remote, insubstantial or unrelated to applicant's personal qualifications as an employee. Petitioner assertedly rejected respondent for unlawful conduct against it and, in the absence of proof of pretextual or discriminatory application of such a reason, this cannot be thought the kind of "artificial, arbitrary, and unnecessary barrier to employment" which the Court found to be the intention of Congress to remove. *Griggs,* p. 431.

III. In sum, respondent should have been allowed to amend his complaint to include a claim under § 703(a)(1). If the evidence on retrial is substantially in accord with that before us in this case, we think that respondent carried his burden of establishing a prima facie case of racial discrimination and that petitioner successfully rebutted that case. But this does not end the matter. On retrial respondent must be afforded a fair opportunity to demonstrate that petitioner's assigned reason for refusing to re-employ was pretextual or discriminatory in its application. If the District Judge so finds, he must order a prompt and appropriate remedy. In the absence of such a finding, petitioner's refusal to rehire must stand.

The cause is hereby remanded to the District Court for reconsideration in accordance with this opinion.

NOTES

1. In Gregory v. Litton Systems, Inc., 472 F.2d 631, 5 FEP Cas. 267 (9th Cir. 1972), it was held that an employer's use of arrest records as an employment criterion may be unlawful under Title VII if the use of such records is not shown to be job related and the employment practice has an adverse discriminatory impact on racial minorities. In a similar ruling, in Johnson v. Pike Corp. of America, 332 F. Supp. 490, 495 (C.D. Cal. 1971), the court, in considering the legality of a dismissal of a Black employee who had an excessive number of wage garnishments, stated:

> Where the discrimination shown results, not from disparate treatment, but from the foreseeable effect of a policy neutral on its face, Griggs indicates that under some circumstances the policy may be justified by a showing of "business necessity." Such a showing is an affirmative defense on which the defendant has the burden of proof. In the present case, defendant corporation has argued that Rule 6 is justified on a number of grounds. Specifically, the defendant has argued that the dismissal policy is justified because of the expense and time attendant to responding to attachments and garnishments by various sections of the company's management and clerical staffs, because of the annoyance and time involved in answering letters and telephone calls from its employees' creditors, and, finally, because garnishments result in a loss of efficiency on behalf of the employee whose wages have been garnisheed.

The exact boundaries and contours of the phrase "business necessity" are still uncertain. The court, in Local 189, United Papermakers and Paperworkers v. United States, supra, stated that the policy or practice must be "essential to the safe and efficient operation" of the business. 416 F.2d

at 989. In *Griggs,* the Court stated that a permissible practice must be one which can be shown to be "related to job
performance" or "measuring job capability."

If the defendant's justifications of Rule 6 are examined
in light of the Supreme Court's definition of business necessity, they are not sufficient. The sole permissible reason for
discriminating against actual or prospective employees involves the individual's capability to perform the job effectively. This approach leaves no room for arguments regarding inconvenience, annoyance or even expense to the
employer. While the argument that wage garnishment results
in a loss of efficiency by the employee is entitled to consideration, the court cannot correlate wage garnishment with
work efficiency. Certainly the argument that an employee
whose wages are being partially withheld for the benefit of
his creditors will apply himself less enthusiastically to his
work is at its best only speculative. If he is an unproductive worker, he may be terminated because he is unproductive, but not for a supposedly causal relationship which has
the effect of being racially discriminatory.

It might be argued that *Griggs* should not be followed
since the question whether business necessity includes expense and inconvenience to the employer was not presented
to the Supreme Court. While there may be in many situations a clear distinction between business necessity relating
to job capability and business necessity relating to the employer's expense and inconvenience, it is submitted that the
Court in *Griggs* intended the definition therein outlined to
be exclusive. The Court liberally construed Title VII in
order to implement the congressional directive that members of minority groups be insured equal opportunity in employment. All attempts to depart from this mandate must be
carefully scrutinized. The Court has stated that the only
permissible reason for tolerating discrimination is "business
necessity" which is "related to job performance." The ability
of the individual effectively and efficiently to carry out his
assigned duties is, therefore, the only justification recognized
by the law.

2. *See generally* Fraser, *Racially Neutral Criteria and Discrimination Under Title VII: "Built-In Headwinds" or Permissible Practices?,* 6 MICH. JOURNAL OF LAW REFORM 97 (1972);
Cooper and Sobol, *Seniority and Testing Under Fair Employment Laws: A General Approach to Objective Criteria of Hiring
and Promotion,* 82 HARV. L. REV. 1598 (1969); Note, *Legal
Implications of the Use of Standardized Ability Tests in Em-*

ployment and Education, 68 COLUM. L. REV. 691 (1968); Comment: *Civil Rights—Employee Testing*, 7 WAKE FOREST L. REV. 425 (1971); Case Notes: *Civil Rights—Educational and Testing Requirements—Employment Tests Not to be Given Controlling Force Unless They are Demonstrably a Reasonable Measure of Job Performance*, 40 FORDHAM L. REV. 350 (1971); Recent Decisions: *Title VII of the Civil Rights Act of 1964—Educational and Testing Requirements Invalid Unless Job-Related—Griggs v. Duke Power Company, 401 U.S. 424 (1971)*, 10 DUQUESNE L. REV. 270 (1971).

3. On September 29, 1969, the Labor Department put into effect its revised "Philadelphia Plan," under which federal contractors in the Philadelphia area would have to make good faith efforts to meet specific percentage "goals" for minority group employment in six construction trades. In Contractors Ass'n of Eastern Pennsylvania v. Shultz, 442 F.2d 159 (3d Cir. 1971), *cert. denied*, 404 U.S. 854 (1971), the plan was upheld against constitutional attack on due process and equal protection grounds, and was found to be neither violative of Title VII of the Civil Rights Act nor inconsistent with the NLRA. The court viewed the program as an appropriate requirement of "affirmative action" to eliminate racial discrimination in employment, as called for by Executive Order 11246, and a proper exercise of Presidential authority.

See also Southern Illinois Builders Ass'n v. Ogilvie, 471 F.2d 680, 5 FEP Cas. 229 (7th Cir. 1972).

PHILLIPS v. MARTIN MARIETTA CORP.
Supreme Court of the United States
400 U.S. 542, 91 S. Ct. 496, 27 L. Ed. 2d 613 (1971)

PER CURIAM.

Petitioner Mrs. Ida Phillips commenced an action in the United States District Court for the Middle District of Florida under Title VII of the Civil Rights Act of 1964 alleging that she had been denied employment because of her sex. The District Court granted a summary judgment for Martin Marietta (Martin) on the basis of the following showing: (1) in 1966 Martin informed Mrs. Phillips that it was not accepting job applications from women with pre-school age children; (2) as of the time of the motion for summary judgment, Martin employed men with pre-school age children; (3) at the time Mrs. Phillips applied, 70-75% of the applicants for the position she sought were women; 75-80% of those hired for the position, assembly trainee, were women, hence no question of bias against women as such was presented.

The Court of Appeals for the Fifth Circuit affirmed, 411 F.2d 1 (CA5 1969), and denied a rehearing *en banc*. 416 F.2d 1257 (CA5 1969). We granted certiorari. 397 U.S. 960 (1970).

Section 703 (a) of the Civil Rights Act of 1964 requires that persons of like qualifications be given employment opportunities irrespective of their sex. The Court of Appeals therefore erred in reading this section as permitting one hiring policy for women and another for men—each having pre-school age children. The existence of such conflicting family obligations, if demonstrably more relevant to job performance for a woman than for a man, could arguably be a basis for distinction under § 703 (e) of the Act. But that is a matter of evidence tending to show that the condition in question "is a bona fide occupational qualification reasonably necessary to the normal operation of that particular business or enterprise." The record [before] us, however, is not adequate for resolution of these important issues. See Kennedy v. Silas Mason Co., 334 U.S. 249, 256-257 (1948). Summary judgment was therefore improper and we remand for fuller development of the record and for further consideration.

Vacated and remanded.

MR. JUSTICE MARSHALL, concurring.

While I agree that this case must be remanded for a full development of the facts, I can not agree with the Court's indication that a "bona fide occupational qualification reasonably necessary to the normal operation of" Martin Marietta's business could be established by a showing that some women, even the vast majority, with preschool age children have family responsibilities that interfere with job performance and that men do not usually have such responsibilities. Certainly, an employer can require that all of his employees, both men and women, meet minimum performance standards, and he can try to insure compliance by requiring parents, both mothers and fathers, to provide for the care of their children so that job performance is not interfered with.

But the Court suggests that it would not require such uniform standards. I fear that in this case, where the issue is not squarely before us, the Court has fallen into the trap of assuming that the Act permits ancient canards about the proper role of women to be a basis for discrimination. Congress, however, sought just the opposite result.

By adding the prohibition against job discrimination based on sex to the 1964 Civil Rights Act Congress intended to prevent employers from refusing "to hire an individual based on stereotyped characterizations of the sexes." Equal Employment Opportunity Commission, "Guidelines on Discrimination Because of Sex," 29 CFR § 1604.1 (a) (ii). See Bowe v. Colgate-Palmolive Co., 416 F.2d 711 (CA7 1969); Weeks v. Southern Bell Tel. & Tel. Co., 408 F.2d 228 (CA5 1969). Even characterizations of the proper domestic roles of the sexes were not to serve as predicates for restricting employment opportunity. The exception for "bona fide occupational qualifications" was not intended to swallow the rule.

That exception has been construed by the Equal Employment Opportunity Commission, whose regulations are entitled to "great deference," Udall v. Tallman, 380 U.S. 1, 16 (1965), to be applicable only to job situations that require specific physical characteristics necessarily possessed by only one sex. Thus the exception would apply where necessary "for the purposes of authenticity or genuineness" in the employment of actors or actresses, fashion models, and the like. If the exception is to be limited as Congress intended, the Commission has given it the only possible construction.

When performance characteristics of an individual are involved, even when parental roles are concerned, employment opportunity may be limited only by employment criteria that are neutral as to the sex of the applicant.

NOTES

1. In Diaz v. Pan American World Airways, 442 F.2d 385 (5th Cir. 1971), cert. denied, 404 U.S. 950 (1971), a court held that female sex is not a "bona fide occupational qualification" for the job of flight cabin attendant. The preference of airline passengers for female attendants is not determinative. The test is "business necessity," not "business convenience." Discrimination based on sex is permissible only where the essence of the business operation would be undermined by not having members of one sex exclusively in a particular position. Airlines may still consider the ability of individuals to perform nonmechanical functions, but they may not exclude all males merely because most males might not perform adequately.

Both federal and state courts have consistently struck down as discriminatory under Title VII various state "protective" statutes, which limit the hours women may work or the weights they may lift, or which prohibit them from certain occupations, such as bartending. See, e.g., Rosenfeld v. Southern Pacific Co., 444 F.2d 1219 (9th Cir. 1971); Manning v. General Motors Corp., 3 FEP Cas. 968 (N.D. Ohio 1971); Sail'er Inn, Inc. v. Kirby, 95 Cal. Rptr. 329, 485 P.2d 529 (1971).

2. In Cohen v. Chesterfield County School Bd., 474 F.2d 395 (4th Cir. 1973), the court, sitting *en banc,* reversed the district court and held that a school board regulation which required a teacher to take a leave of absence from her duties at the end of her fifth month of pregnancy was not violative of the Equal Protection Clause. The Court concluded that "pregnancy and motherhood do have a great impact on the lives of women, and, if that impact is reasonably noticed by a governmental regulation, it is not to be condemned as an invidious classification." A strong opinion in dissent was written by Judge Winters. The decision in *Cohen* followed an earlier decision rendered by the Fifth Circuit in Schattman v. Texas Employment Comm'n, 459 F.2d 32 (5th Cir. 1972), *cert. denied,* — U.S. —, 5 FEP Cas. 299 (1973). *But see* LaFleur v. Cleveland Bd. of Educ., 465 F.2d 1184 (6th Cir. 1972); Green v. Waterford Bd. of Educ., 473 F.2d 629, 5 FEP Cas. 443 (2d Cir. 1973) (holding unconstitutional school board rules requiring women employees to take maternity leaves several months in advance of anticipated childbirth). Is the constitutional test of "discrimination," as defined by the courts in *Schattman* and *Cohen,* inconsistent with the test of discrimination enunciated by the courts in decisions arising under Title VII? In Pittsburgh Press Co. v. Pittsburgh Comm'n on Human Relations, — U.S. —, 5 FEP Cas. 1141 (1973), the Court held that a city ordinance forbidding newspapers to carry sex-designated advertising columns for nonexempt job opportunities did not violate a newspaper's First Amendment rights.

3. Section 1604.10 of the 1972 EEOC Guidelines states that an employment policy which automatically excludes women from jobs because of pregnancy will be considered to be a prima facie case of discrimination under Title VII. 29 C.F.R. § 1604.10 (1972). This Guideline is consistent with a 1969 decision rendered by a federal district court in the matter of Cheatwood v. Southern Central Bell Telephone & Telegraph Co., 303 F. Supp. 754 (M.D. Ala., N.D. 1969). The court in that case ruled in effect that all women cannot be excluded from a particular heavy job assignment merely because some of them may become pregnant. The EEOC Guidelines also indicate that employment policies having to do with maternity leaves and health insurance benefits must "be applied to disability due to pregnancy or childbirth on the same terms and conditions as they are applied to other *temporary* disabilities." In this regard, Section 1604.10 (c) of the Guidelines further states:

Where the termination of an employee who is temporarily disabled is caused by an employment policy under which insufficient or no leave is available, such a termination violates the Act if it has disparate impact on employees of one sex and is not justified by business necessity.

4.   In Bartmess v. Drewrys, 444 F.2d 1186 (7th Cir.), *cert. denied,* 404 U.S. 939 (1971), the Seventh Circuit ruled that a retirement plan, adopted pursuant to a collective bargaining agreement which provided that female employees were to retire at age 62 and male employees were to retire at age 65, violated Title VII since it provided for different treatment of men and women. In Danner v. Phillips Petroleum Co., 447 F.2d 159 (5th Cir. 1971), a woman who had worked for 10 years for the company was bumped out of her job and replaced by male employees. The company responded to her claim of sex discrimination by citing a "neutral" company policy of giving seniority and bumping rights only to certain job classifications, such as "roustabouts" or "roughnecks." Since Mrs. Danner was neither a "roustabout" nor a "roughneck," the company argued that she had no right to retain her job. The evidence disclosed, however, that while the system appeared neutral, it was discriminatory in effect because no female employee held a job as either a roustabout or roughneck. The court found further that Mrs. Danner performed substantially the same work as the seniority-protected males and, therefore, she was improperly excluded from the seniority system. This ruling was handed down notwithstanding the special protection for seniority systems in Section 703 (h) which provides that "bona fide" seniority systems will not be considered to violate the Act.

5.   A New York court has declared unlawful a professional baseball league's restriction against the hiring of women umpires. The New York court noted that the bona fide occupational qualification exception must be given a narrow construction and must be affirmatively proved by the party claiming it. The court further concluded that the employer had failed to show a factual basis for the asserted belief that women were not qualified for the job of a professional baseball umpire, notwithstanding the evidence that the job would require some physical strain, travel, and loss of weight, and the possibility of some physical injury. New York State Division of Human Rights v. New York-Pennsylvania Professional Baseball League, 29 N.Y.2d 921, 279 N.E.2d 856, 329 N.Y.S.2d 99 (1972).

6.   *See generally* J. Wilcox, *The Sex Discrimination Provisions of Title VII: A Maturing Controversy,* 3 PAC. L.J. 37 (1972). For other cases and discussions, see *Symposium: Women's Rights,* 23 HASTINGS L.J. 1 (1971); *Symposium on the Legal*

Rights of Women, 17 N.Y.L. FORUM 335 (1971); *Symposium—*
Women and the Law, 5 VALPARAISO L. REV. 203 (1971); E.
Landau and K. Dunahoo, *Sex Discrimination in Employment:*
A Survey of State and Federal Remedies, 20 DRAKE L. REV.
417 (1971); Comment, *Sex Discrimination in Higher Educa-*
tion: Constitutional Equality for Women?, 10 J. FAMILY L. 327
(1971); *Developments in the Law: Employment Discrimination*
and Title VII of the Civil Rights Act of 1964, 84 HARV. L. REV.
1109, 1166-94 (1971); Edwards, *Sex Discrimination in Employ-*
ment: Some Unresolved Issues, 24 Lab. L.J. 411 (1973).

(c) Deferral to Arbitration
RIOS v. REYNOLDS METAL CO.
United States Court of Appeals, Fifth Circuit
467 F.2d 54 (1972)

BELL, Circuit Judge:—Title VII of the Civil Rights Act of
1964 makes it unlawful for an employer to discriminate against
an employee on the basis of race, color, religion, sex, or national
origin. 42 USCA, § 2000e. The Act provides a procedure whereby an aggrieved employee may obtain relief from injuries caused
by discriminatory employment practices. This procedure cul-
minates in a civil action by the employee where other measures
fail. The question presented on this appeal is whether this judicial remedy is available to an employee who first submits his
claim to arbitration under an anti-discrimination clause in a
collective bargaining agreement between his employer and his
union and receives an adverse arbitral determination of the
issues he ultimately presents to the court under Title VII.

We touched on this question in a peripheral manner in a
prior decision of this court. Hutchings v. United States Industries, Inc., 5 Cir., 1970, 428 F.2d 303, 2 FEP Cases 725. There
we held that the doctrines of election of remedies and res judicata
did not bar a subsequent suit under Title VII where the rights
and remedies at issue in an arbitration proceeding differed from
the rights and remedies at issue under Title VII. We left for
the future ". . . the question whether a procedure similar to that
adopted by the Labor Board in deferring to arbitration awards
when certain standards are met might properly be adopted in
Title VII cases." Id. at 314 n.10. The more important fact in
Hutchings was that the collective bargaining agreement and
arbitral process did not expressly include the employer obligation under Title VII. There we said:

"In view of the dissimilarities between the contract
grievance-arbitration process and the judicial process under

Title VII, it would be fallacious to assume that an employee utilizing the grievance-arbitration machinery under the contract and also seeking a Title VII remedy in court is attempting to enforce a single right in two forums. We do not mean to imply that employer obligations having their origin in Title VII are not to be incorporated into the arbitral process. When possible they should be. See generally Gould, Labor Arbitration of Grievances Involving Racial Discrimination, 118 U. Pa. L. Rev. 40 (1969). But the arbitrator's determination under the contract has no effect upon the court's *power* to adjudicate a violation of Title VII rights."

Here the employer obligation in issue under Title VII is expressly included in the arbitral process under the collective bargaining agreement. We also have a prejudgment determination by an arbitrator of an issue which is the same issue as that which the employee subsequently presented to the district court.

In the case at bar the district court held that the arbitrator's determination of this issue barred the civil action under Title VII. For reasons to be stated, we reverse and remand for further proceedings.

I. Appellant Rios was employed at a plant operated by Reynolds Metals Company, appellee. Rios applied for a position as mechanic pipefitter, a position then vacant. After passing a written examination, he assumed the new post on a trial basis. About one month later he was demoted to his former position.

Pursuant to the provisions of the collective bargaining agreement between Reynolds and the Aluminum Workers International Union, Rios filed a grievance in which he claimed that he had not been given a reasonable trial period at his new assignment. Arbitration ensued. At the arbitration hearing, in response to questions raised by his union representative, Rios maintained that one reason for his demotion was that Reynolds had discriminated against him because he was a Mexican-American. The arbitrator rejected this contention and determined that Rios had been given fair treatment during the trial period. The arbitrator concluded that Rios was demoted because he was unable to perform the new job satisfactorily.

Rios initiated this action in the district court before the arbitration hearing was held. The arbitrator's decision followed and thereafter, in light of the decision of the arbitrator, Reynolds moved for summary judgment. Reynolds contended that Rios, having submitted to arbitration, was bound by the arbitrator's determination. The district court accepted this contention.

II. The settlement of labor disputes by arbitration is a favored national labor policy. See, e.g., Boys Markets, Inc. v. Retail Clerks Union, Local 770, 1970, 398 U.S. 235. . . .

For this reason, in developing principles that will govern the availability of judicial relief under Title VII, we must carefully assess the impact of judicial action upon the favored arbitral remedy.

The viability of arbitration depends on the willingness of courts to enforce the arbitrator's award without reopening issues resolved by him. Thus, in such cases, courts customarily defer to the arbitrator's determination. They restrict their inquiry to the single question whether, under the terms of the collective bargaining agreement, the arbitrator had power to decide the issues he decided. If he had such power, his decision is binding. See, e.g., United Steelworkers v. Enterprise Wheel & Car Corp., 363 U.S. at 596.

The question here is whether a similar approach should be followed when, in the first instance, the issues decided by the arbitrator are cognizable in the federal court by virtue of Title VII, which manifests a strong national policy against discriminatory employment practices. We conclude that the traditional approach to the arbitration process is not warranted in this context.

The remedy afforded by Title VII is supplemental. It exists apart from analogous remedies provided by contract or by federal or state law. Indeed, aggrieved employees may seek relief under Title VII without first invoking or exhausting available alternative legal or contractual remedies. See Caldwell v. National Brewing Company, 5 Cir., 1971, 443 F.2d 1044, 3 FEP Cases 600; King v. Georgia Power, 295 F. Supp. 943, 1 FEP Cases 357, 69 L.R.R.M. 2094 (N.D. Ga. 1968). In addition, we have said that even where an employee does pursue an alternative remedy in cases involving Title VII rights, the federal court is to be "the final arbiter." Hutchings, supra, 428 F.2d at 313.

It does not follow, however, that the policies of Title VII require that an employee who has submitted his claim to binding arbitration must always be given an opportunity to relitigate his claim in court. In some instances such a requirement would not comport with elementary notions of equity, for it would give the employee, but not the employer, a second chance to have the same issue resolved. More importantly, such a requirement would tend to frustrate the national policy favoring arbitration. An employer would have little incentive to agree to arbitrate under a system where only the employee, in the event of an adverse arbitral determination, would have an opportunity to relitigate the matter in court.

This, of course, assumes that the national policy favoring arbitration of labor disputes should include grievances concerning rights which are guaranteed by Title VII. As we have noted, the teaching of *Hutchings* is that they may be included in the grievance-arbitration process. But, as *Hutchings* holds, the determination in the arbitration process has no effect upon the power of the federal court to adjudicate a violation of rights under Title VII. The question thus becomes whether the courts may accommodate the national arbitration process policy to Title VII proceedings without thwarting the congressional intent in Title VII to eliminate discriminatory practices in employment. We conclude that the policy which favors arbitration and the remedial policy of Title VII may be accommodated by a procedure which was alluded to in *Hutchings* but saved for decision on another day. It is that a district court may, under limited circumstances, defer to a prior arbitration award.

The apparent analogy is to the deferral procedure followed by the National Labor Relations Board in the exercise of its discretionary powers under the National Labor Relations Act. See Lodge No. 12, etc. v. Cameron Iron Works, Inc., 5 Cir., 1958, 257 F.2d 467, 473; Spielberg Manufacturing Co., 112 N.L.R.B. 1080 (1955).

As we recognized in Lodge No. 12, etc. v. Cameron Iron Works, supra, a prior arbitration award does not divest the NLRB of its statutory jurisdiction to effectuate the policies of the National Labor Relations Act. But we recognized as well that a given controversy may be cognizable both as an arbitrable grievance under a collective bargaining agreement, and as a labor dispute under the National Labor Relations Act. Where such a coincidence of issues exists, it is within the discretionary power of the NLRB to defer to findings made by the arbitrator.

In exercising this power, the NLRB has recognized the limits of its discretion and has developed minimum standards on which to structure the decision to defer vel non. In Spielberg Manufacturing Co., 112 N.L.R.B. at 1082, 36 L.R.R.M. 1152, the Board stated that where "the proceedings appear to have been fair and regular, all parties have agreed to be bound, and the decision of the arbitration panel is not clearly repugnant to the purposes and policies of the Act," it is proper for the Board to defer to a prior arbitration award involving the same issues. This practice has been approved by the courts and reaffirmed by the NLRB as being consistent with national labor policy. See, e.g., Carey v.

Westinghouse Corp., 1964, 375 U.S. 261, 270, n.7, 55 L.R.R.M. 2042; Lodge No. 12, etc. v. Cameron Iron Works, supra.

We hold that the federal district court in the exercise of its power as the final arbiter under Title VII may follow a like procedure of deferral under the following limitations. First, there may be no deference to the decision of the arbitrator unless the contractual right coincides with rights under Title VII. Second, it must be plain that the arbitrator's decision is in no way violative of the private rights guaranteed by Title VII, nor of the public policy which inheres in Title VII. In addition, before deferring, the district court must be satisfied that (1) the factual issues before it are identical to those decided by the arbitrator; (2) the arbitrator had power under the collective agreement to decide the ultimate issue of discrimination; (3) the evidence presented at the arbitral hearing dealt adequately with all factual issues; (4) the arbitrator actually decided the factual issues presented to the court; (5) the arbitration proceeding was fair and regular and free of procedural infirmities. The burden of proof in establishing these conditions of limitation will be upon the respondent as distinguished from the claimant.

In essence, this procedure will amount to a review of the arbitration proceeding in cases involving Title VII rights. It is not as broad as the procedure followed in general grievance-arbitration cases where the court looks only to the question whether under the terms of the collective bargaining agreement the arbitrator had power to decide the issues he decided. United Steelworkers, supra, 363 U.S. at 596. Neither is it as broad as the policy of deferral under res judicata principles which we have applied in cases where facts previously determined by the Labor Board are presented in collateral proceedings in the federal courts. Nix v. International Ass'n of Machinists and Aerospace Workers, 5 Cir., 1971, 452 F.2d 794, 78 L.R.R.M. 2922; H. L. Robertson and Associates, Inc. v. Local No. 519, 5 Cir., 1970, 429 F.2d 520, 74 L.R.R.M. 2872; Brotherhood of Painters, Decorators and Paperhangers v. Edgewood Contracting Co., 5 Cir., 1969, 416 F.2d 1081, 72 L.R.R.M. 2524.

REVERSED and REMANDED for further proceedings not inconsistent herewith.

NOTES

1. In Newman v. Avco Corp., 451 F.2d 743 (6th Cir. 1971), a Black employee was allowed to maintain an action against his employer and union for an allegedly discriminatory discharge despite a prior adverse arbitration decision. The court pointed out that the employee had no choice under the contract but to

submit his grievance to arbitration, that he was challenging the fairness of the arbitration proceeding, and that there was a grave doubt whether the arbitrator had the power under the contract to rule on the racial discrimination charge. The decision in *Newman* appears to modify the Sixth Circuit opinion in Dewey v. Reynolds Metal Co., 429 F.2d 324 (1970), *aff'd by equally divided Court*, 402 U.S. 689 (1971).

2. *See generally* Edwards and Kaplan, *Religious Discrimination and the Role of Arbitration Under Title VII*, 69 MICH. L. REV. 599 (1971); Meltzer, *Labor Arbitration and Overlapping and Conflicting Remedies for Employment Discrimination*, 39 U. CHI. L. REV. 30 (1971).

3. The Civil Rights Acts of 1866 and 1871

WATERS v. WISCONSIN STEEL WORKS OF INTERNATIONAL HARVESTER CO.

United States Court of Appeals, Seventh Circuit
427 F.2d 476
Cert. denied, 400 U.S. 911 (1970)

SWYGERT, Chief Judge:

This appeal raises important questions concerning the availability and scope of various federal remedies for combating racial discrimination in employment. Plaintiffs, William Waters and Donald Samuels, brought a class action seeking damages and injunctive relief against the Wisconsin Steel Works of International Harvester Company and Local 21, United Order of American Bricklayers and Stone Masons. They alleged that Harvester, with the assistance of Local 21, maintained a discriminatory hiring policy designed to exclude Negroes, including the plaintiffs, from employment as bricklayers at Wisconsin Steel Works. Plaintiffs claimed that these allegations of racial discrimination stated a cause of action under four separate statutes: section 1 of the Civil Rights Act of 1866, 42 U.S.C. § 1981; Title VII of the 1964 Civil Rights Act, 42 U.S.C. §§ 2000e to e-15; section 301(a) of the Labor-Management Relations Act, 29 U.S.C. § 185(a); and the National Labor Relations Act, 29 U.S.C. §§ 151 to 167. On the motion of defendants the district court dismissed plaintiff's complaint. The plaintiffs appeal from the order of dismissal. We reverse and remand for trial. . . .

The complaint alleges that prior to June 1964 Harvester, with the acquiescence of Local 21, maintained a discriminatory hiring policy which excluded Negroes from employment as bricklayers. During June 1964 five Negroes, including William Waters, were hired as bricklayers. Waters, a member of Local 21, worked in that capacity from June 13, 1964 until he was laid off on September 11, 1964. Nine other bricklayers including all of the Negroes hired in June were discharged at that time.

Under the collective bargaining agreement workers achieve seniority only after ninety consecutive days on the job. Thus all of the Negro bricklayers hired in June 1964 worked as probationary employees and did not acquire seniority and the accompanying right to preferential reinstatement when bricklayer jobs were again available. Plaintiffs allege that this seniority system, agreed to by Local 21, is part of a systematic attempt to exclude Negroes from employment as bricklayers. . . .

I. The Existence of a Right to Sue Under Section 1981.

In Jones v. Alfred H. Mayer Co., 392 U.S. 409, 88 S. Ct. 2186 (1968), the Supreme Court was asked to determine the scope and constitutionality of 42 U.S.C. § 1982. In its original form section 1982 was part of section 1 of the Civil Rights Act of 1866.[5] The Court held that section 1 and its derivative, section 1982, prohibit "*all* racial discrimination, private as well as public, in the sale or rental of property. . . ." *Jones, supra,* at 413, 88 S. Ct., at 2189. The constitutionality of section 1982 was upheld on the basis of Congress' power to enact legislation to enforce the thirteenth amendment.[6]

Plaintiffs argue by analogy to the *Jones* case that 42 U.S.C. § 1981[7] is also derived from section 1 of the Civil Rights Act of

---

[5] Section 1 of the Civil Rights Act of 1866 provided:

Be it enacted by the Senate and House of Representatives of the United States of America in Congress assembled, That all persons born in the United States and not subject to any foreign power, . . . are hereby declared to be citizens of the United States; and such citizens, of every race and color, without regard to any previous condition of slavery or involuntary servitude . . . shall have the same right, in every State and Territory in the United States, to make and enforce contracts, to sue, be parties, and give evidence, to inherit, purchase, lease, sell, hold, and convey real and personal property, and to full and equal benefit of all laws and proceedings for the security of person and property, as is enjoyed by white citizens, and shall be subject to like punishment, pains, and penalties, and to none other, any law, statute, ordinance, regulation, or custom, to the contrary notwithstanding.

[6] The thirteenth amendment provides:

Section 1:

Neither slavery nor involuntary servitude, except as a punishment for a crime whereof the party shall have been duly convicted, shall exist within the United States, or any place subject to their jurisdiction.

Section 2:

Congress shall have power to enforce this article by appropriate legislation.

[7] 42 U.S.C. § 1981 provides:

All persons within the jurisdiction of the United States shall have the same right in every State and Territory to make and enforce contracts,

1866; that it is a valid exercise of congressional power under the thirteenth amendment; and that it is intended to prohibit private racial discrimination in employment by companies and unions. We agree.

There can be little doubt that section 1981, as well as section 1982, is derived directly from section 1 of the 1866 Civil Rights Act. In this judgment we rest primarily on the views expressed by the Supreme Court in the *Jones* case. In footnote 78, the Court said that "the right to contract for employment, [is] a right secured by 42 U.S.C. § 1981 (. . . derived from § 1 of the Civil Rights Act of 1866 . . .)." *Jones, supra,* at 442, 88 S. Ct., at 2204. This statement is buttressed by further mention of the derivation of section 1981 in footnote 28, *Jones, supra,* at 422, 88 S. Ct. 2186.

The Supreme Court's view of the genesis of section 1981 is also supported by our own analysis. In 1870 Congress reenacted section 1 of the 1866 Act as section 18 of the 1870 Civil Rights Act. As part of the 1870 Act Congress also adopted section 16 which is similar, although somewhat broader, than section 1 of the 1866 Act. For purposes of determining the derivation of section 1981 we believe the enactment of section 16 of the 1870 Act is superfluous since section 18 is sufficiently broad to include the provisions of section 1981. This conclusion is supported by the failure of defendants to present legislative history to demonstrate that Congress intended to narrow the scope of the right "to make and enforce contracts" provision of section 1 of the 1866 Act by the enactment of section 16. In fact, a contrary intent is more likely since Congress by enacting section 16 undoubtedly was attempting to insure that the right to make and enforce contracts without regard to race was supported by the fourteenth as well as the thirteenth amendment.[8]

From the discussion in the *Jones* case, it is also evident that section 1981, as part of section 1 of the 1866 Act, was a valid exercise of Congress' power to enact legislation under the thirteenth amendment. We rest particularly upon the Supreme Court's analysis of Hodges v. United States, 203 U.S. 1, 27 S. Ct. 6, 51 L. Ed. 65 (1906). In *Hodges* a group of white workers were prosecuted under section 1981 for terrorist activities conducted against Negro employees of a saw mill. The Supreme Court reversed the defendants' conviction, holding that section 1981

---

to sue, be parties, give evidence, and to the full and equal benefit of all laws and proceedings for the security of persons and property as is enjoyed by white citizens, and shall be subject to like punishments, pains, penalties, taxes, licenses, and exactions of every kind, and to no other.

[8] The fourteenth amendment was not adopted until 1868.

was not designed to prohibit private acts of discrimination. The Court in *Jones* examined the decision in *Hodges* and ruled:

> The conclusion of the majority in *Hodges* rested upon a concept of congressional power under the Thirteenth Amendment irreconcilable with the position taken by every member of this Court in the Civil Rights Cases and incompatible with the history and purpose of the Amendment itself. Insofar as *Hodges* is inconsistent with our holding today, it is hereby overruled. *Jones, supra,* at 442-443, 88 S. Ct. at 2205 n.78.[9]

Every indicia of congressional intent points to the conclusion that section 1981 was designed to prohibit private job discrimination. The words of the statute, which are almost identical in relevant respects to section 1982, must be construed to extend beyond insuring the bare legal capacity of Negroes to enter into contracts. Thus Congress provided that: "All persons . . . shall have the same right . . . to make and enforce contracts . . . as is enjoyed by white citizens." We are not persuaded that the failure of Congress to expressly mention employment contracts makes section 1981 distinguishable from section 1982. This conclusion is supported by the legislative history of the 1866 Act which demonstrates Congress' intent that section 1 apply to employment contracts. As the Supreme Court noted in *Jones:*

> The congressional debates are replete with references to private injustices against Negroes—references to white employers who refused to pay their Negro workers, white planters who agreed among themselves not to hire freed slaves without the permission of their former masters. *Jones, supra,* at 427, 88 S. Ct., at 2197.

As an example of Congress' concern are the words of Representative Windom delivered on the floor of the House:

> Its object is to secure to a poor, weak class of laborers the right to make contracts for their labor, the power to enforce the payment of their wages, and the means of holding and enjoying the proceeds of their toil. Cong. Globe, 39th Cong., 1st Sess. 1159 (1866) .

This explanation of the purpose of section 1 of the 1866 Act demonstrates that Congress contemplated a prohibition of racial discrimination in employment which would extend beyond state action.

---

[9] *See generally* A. Larson, New Law of Race Relations, 1969 Wis. L. Rev. 470.

Racial discrimination in employment by unions as well as by employers is barred by section 1981. The relationship between an employee and a union is essentially one of contract. Accordingly, in the performance of its functions as agent for the employees a union cannot discriminate against some of its members on the basis of race. . . .

NOTES

1. Judge Swygert's holding should apply equally to the public employment sector. *See* Arrington v. Massachusetts Bay Transp. Auth., 306 F. Supp. 1355 (D. Mass. 1969).

See generally Note, *Racial Discrimination in Employment Under the Civil Rights Act of 1866,* 36 U. CHI. L. REV. 615 (1969); Note, *A "New" Weapon to Combat Racial Discrimination in Employment: The Civil Rights Act of 1866,* 29 MD. L. REV. 158 (1969); Comment, *The Resurrection of the Civil Rights Act of 1866: Its Effect upon Modern Legislation and Current Litigation,* 23 BAYLOR L. REV. 277 (1971); E. Larson, *The Development of Section 1981 as a Remedy for Racial Discrimination in Private Employment,* 7 HARV. CIV. RIGHTS—CIV. LIB. L. REV. 56 (1972); Note, *The "New" Thirteenth Amendment: A Preliminary Analysis,* 82 HARV. L. REV. 1294 (1969).

2. Section 1983 of 42 U.S.C. is far more inclusive than § 1981, as it is not limited to racial discrimination, but proscribes any deprivation of constitutional rights under color of state authority. In Hanover Township Fed'n of Teachers v. Hanover Community School Corp., 318 F. Supp. 757, 761 (N.D. Ind. 1970), *aff'd,* 457 F.2d 456 (7th Cir. 1972), a suit brought by nine teachers under § 1983, claiming discrimination against them for exercising First Amendment rights to join and participate in a union, the court stated:

> The issue here is not whether the plaintiffs have a constitutional right to be teachers or to receive payment for extracurricular activities. The question is whether the termination of the plaintiffs' contracts for teaching and extracurricular activities deprived the plaintiffs of the freedom of association guaranteed them by the Constitution. It is the opinion of the Court that the actions of the defendants were motivated by a desire to retaliate against members of the union, and that, in terminating the contracts of the plaintiffs, the defendants deprived them of their constitutional rights in violation of 42 U.S.C.A. § 1983 and 18 U.S.C.A. § 1343.

3. Section 1981 has been extended in the private sector to allow damage recoveries for racial discrimination; *see* Sanders v. Dobbs Houses, Inc., 431 F.2d 1097 (5th Cir.), *cert. denied,* 401 U.S. 948 (1970) and Lazard v. Boeing Co., 322 F. Supp. 343 (E.D. La. 1971). However, it appears that neither damages nor equitable relief is available against a municipality under 42 U.S.C. § 1983. In Monroe v. Pape, 365 U.S. 167 (1961), the Supreme Court held that a municipality is not a "person" within the meaning of the statute for purposes of an action for money damages under § 1983. The lower federal courts were subsequently split on the issue as to whether cities were proper defendants under § 1983 where equitable relief was sought. *See, e.g.,* League of Academic Women v. Regents of the Univ. of California, 343 F. Supp. 636 (N.D. Cal. 1972) and the cases cited therein. However, the matter was finally resolved in City of Kenosha, Wisconsin v. Bruno, 93 S. Ct. 2222, 2226 (1973), where it was held:

> We find nothing in the legislative history discussed in *Monroe,* or in the language actually used by Congress, to suggest that the generic word "person" in § 1983 was intended to have a bifurcated application to municipal corporations depending on the nature of the relief sought against them. Since, as the Court held in *Monroe,* "Congress did not undertake to bring municipal corporations within the ambit of" § 1983, 365 U.S., at 187, 81 S. Ct. at 484, they are outside of its ambit for purposes of equitable relief as well as for damages. The District Court was therefore wrong in concluding that it had jurisdiction of appellees' complaints under § 1343.

For an excellent discussion of the problem, see Comment, *Suing Public Entities Under the Federal Civil Rights Act: Monroe v. Pape Reconsidered,* 43 U. COLO. L. REV. 105 (1971). *See generally* Note, *A Municipal Corporation May be Sued Under the Civil Rights Act for Equitable Relief,* 70 COLUM. L. REV. 1467 (1970); Comment, *Injunctive Relief Against Municipalities Under Section 1983,* 119 U. PA. L. REV. 389 (1970).

CHANCE v. BOARD OF EXAMINERS
United States Court of Appeals, Second Circuit
458 F.2d 1167 (1972)

FEINBERG, Circuit Judge: . . . .

The named plaintiffs, who are respectively black and Puerto Rican, sued the Board of Examiners under federal civil rights laws, 42 U.S.C. §§ 1981, 1983. Plaintiffs claimed that competitive examinations given by the Board to those seeking permanent appointment to supervisory positions in the City's schools discriminated against blacks and Puerto Ricans and violated the Equal Protection Clause of the fourteenth amendment. Judge Mansfield, after making extensive findings of fact, found sufficient merit in plaintiffs' case to preliminarily enjoin the Board from using the examinations. . . .

I. The appeal comes to us in an unusual posture. Since plaintiffs attacked the method used to fill supervisory positions in the school system of the City of New York, one would surmise that their primary opposition would come from those in charge of that system, the Board of Education of the City of New York and its Chancellor, Harvey B. Scribner, both named as defendants in this action. However, although the Board of Education appeared below, it did not actively oppose the motion for preliminary injunction and has not appealed from the district court's order. The Chancellor has done even less. . . . The Board of Examiners, however, vigorously opposed plaintiffs' motion in the trial court and has appealed. . . .

To obtain a permanent supervisory job in the New York City school system an applicant must not only meet State requirements but also obtain a City license. This dual qualification is in effect in New York State only in Buffalo and New York City; elsewhere in the State, certification by State authorities alone is enough. Moreover, only the New York City School District maintains a Board of Examiners. The Board of Examiners was established by the State legislature near the turn of the century as an independent body to conduct examinations to be used in selecting New York City school system professional personnel. The Board of Education and the Chancellor prescribe the minimum education and experience requirements for supervisors, but the Board of Examiners prepares and administers the examinations. The examination process itself may take as long as two years to complete. If a candidate successfully completes the examination, his name is placed on a list of those eligible for the particular supervisory post; he may then be selected by an appropriate school governing authority to fill an open position for which he is certified. If he is not appointed within four years after being placed on the list, his name is dropped and will not be re-listed until he again passes the examination.

For many hopefuls, the stumbling block to a permanent supervisory position has been the examination prepared by defendant Board of Examiners. That is true for plaintiffs Chance and Mercado, who have necessary State certificates and who meet the educational and experience requirements established by the City

Board of Education. Chance has been employed in the New York City public school system for 15 years. Mercado for 12. They are now serving as acting principals of elementary schools in New York City, selected for those positions by their local community school boards. Unless they pass the Board's examination, however, they are foreclosed from being appointed permanent principals. They brought this suit to challenge that obstacle as racially discriminatory and, therefore, unconstitutional. . . .

After receiving extensive statistical evidence, Judge Mansfield found that:

> [T]he examinations prepared and administered by the Board of Examiners for the licensing of supervisory personnel, such as Principals and Assistant Principals, have the *de facto* effect of discriminating significantly and substantially against Black and Puerto Rican applicants.

330 F. Supp. at 223. The judge further found:

> Such a discriminatory impact is constitutionally suspect and places the burden on the Board to show that the examinations can be justified as necessary to obtain Principals, Assistant Principals and supervisors possessing the skills and qualifications required for successful performance of the duties of these positions. The Board has failed to meet this burden. . . .

II.   Arguing that the injunction now in effect should be reversed, defendant Board of Examiners raises a number of issues on appeal, some primarily factual, others questions of law. In the former category, the Board claims that the statistics before the trial judge had little probative value and were used by him improperly and that the judge's finding that the Board's supervisory examinations were not job-related was clearly erroneous. In opposing plaintiffs' motion for injunctive relief in the district court, the Board itself had argued that:

> If statistics have any relevancy in determining the claim of discrimination, the only meaningful statistic would be a comparison of the pass-fail ratio of [whites with those of] black and Puerto Rican applicants.

As already indicated, the court thereafter ordered the parties to develop a Survey to determine comparative pass rates of different ethnic groups in recent years. The Survey took several months to complete and covered 50 supervisory examinations given during the last seven years, involving approximately 6,000 applicants.
. . .

The district judge read the Survey to show that white candidates passed the various supervisory examinations, considered together, "at almost 1½ times the rate of Black and Puerto Rican candidates." 330 F. Supp. at 210. The court, however, found even more significant the fact that:

> [W]hite candidates passed the examination for Assistant Principal of Junior High School at almost double the rate of Black and Puerto Rican candidates, and passed the examinations for Assistant Principal of Day Elementary School at a rate one-third greater than Black and Puerto Rican candidates.

Id. The statistics for the latter two examinations were thought particularly significant "because they were taken by far more candidates than those taking any other examinations conducted in at least the last seven years," and "because the assistant principalship has traditionally been the route to and prerequisite for the most important supervisory position, Principal." Id. The judge reasoned that these examinations for assistant principal screened minority applicants out of a chance to become full principals, thus in effect magnifying the overall statistical differences between white and non-white pass-fail rates. 330 F. Supp. at 210-11. The court also relied on other statistics, which showed that cities not using New York's system of examinations had a startlingly higher percentage of blacks and Puerto Ricans in supervisory positions. . . .

III. The parties agree that the case did not end with the district court's finding that the examinations prepared and administered by the Board significantly and substantially discriminated against black and Puerto Rican applicants. The district court pointed out that "the existence of such discrimination standing alone, would not necessarily entitle plaintiffs to relief." 330 F. Supp. at 214. The further question was whether the examinations could be "validated as relevant to the requirements of the positions for which they are given, i.e., whether they are 'job related.'" Id. On that issue the court first held that the Board had the burden of making a "strong showing" that the tests were in fact job related; it then concluded that the burden was not met. The correctness of these rulings as well as the constitutional issues surrounding them are discussed in the following section of this opinion. For the moment, however, we confine our attention to the court's factual finding that the examinations had not been validated.

The district court pointed out that two generally accepted methods are used to determine whether a particular examination is job-related or reasonably constructed to measure what it purports to measure. One is "content validation," which requires the examiners to demonstrate that they have formulated examination questions and procedures based on an analysis of the job's requirements, usually determined through empirical studies conducted by experts. An examination has content validity, then, if it elicits "from the candidate information that is relevant to the job for which it is given." 330 F. Supp. at 216. The other method of evaluating job-relatedness is "predictive validation," which requires a showing that there is a correlation between a candidate's performance on the test and his actual performance on the job. Part of the controversy in the trial court was over which of these was the better method for evaluating the Board's examinations. Plaintiffs stressed "predictive validation" as the more relevant test, while defendant argued that "content validation" was the more useful criterion. The district court did not resolve the dispute since it concluded that the Board had failed to establish that examinations were "valid as to content, much less to predictiveness." 330 F. Supp. at 219.

In reaching its finding the court had to choose between conflicting expert testimony covering the issue of job-relatedness. Defendant Board submitted affidavits of several respected leaders in the field of educational testing, who stated that on the information supplied them the Board was apparently following testing methods that reasonably assured content valid examinations. The Board also introduced several research reports written by its staff members as showing its efforts to insure job-relatedness. Against this evidence plaintiffs offered the affidavits of various experts who found the Board's examinations lacking in validity, whether content or predictive. In making his finding the trial judge obviously relied heavily on the expert evidence offered by plaintiffs. The judge noted that the "fatal weakness in the Board's system" lies in its failure to actually implement the "techniques and procedures adopted in principle and approved by independent experts." Id. He further found that the Board's research reports were either irrelevant to developing valid examinations or were grossly inadequate for that purpose. Finally, the court stated that its conclusion based on the expert testimony was "confirmed" by its own study of some of the examinations. The trial judge seems to have felt that, at least from a layman's perspective, the examinations placed more emphasis on measuring a candidate's ability to memorize than on his ability to perform as a supervisor. It should be pointed out, however, that the district court's finding of invalidity was limited to the written part of the examinations. The judge made "no finding as to the content

validity of the oral examinations, standing alone." 330 F. Supp.
at 222. The court also held that the evidence was insufficient to
support a finding that the Board had failed to administer the
examinations objectively. . . .

IV.   We come, then, to the question whether the district court
applied the proper constitutional standards in reaching its conclusions that (1) plaintiffs made out a *prima facie* case of racial
discrimination, and (2) the Board, in turn, failed to meet its
burden of demonstrating that the examinations are justified
notwithstanding their discriminatory effect.

Concededly, this case does not involve intentionally discriminatory legislation, cf. Loving v. Virginia, 388 U.S. 1 (1967), or
even a neutral legislative scheme applied in an intentionally
discriminatory manner, see Yick Wo v. Hopkins, 118 U.S. 356
(1886). Nonetheless, we do not believe that the protection afforded racial minorities by the fourteenth amendment is
exhausted by those two possibilities. As already indicated, the district court found that the Board's examinations have a significant and substantial discriminatory impact on black and Puerto
Rican applicants. That harsh racial impact, even if unintended,
amounts to an invidious *de facto* classification that cannot be ignored or answered with a shrug. At the very least, the Constitution requires that state action spawning such a classification "be
justified by legitimate state considerations." Abate v. Mundt,
403 U.S. 182, 185 (1971). . . .

The Board argues, however, that the statistical differences
found by the district court are insufficient to meet the constitutional test of invidiousness and do not amount to a *prima facie*
case of *de facto* discrimination. In particular, the Board notes
that even according to the district court's analysis, on an overall
basis white candidates passed at only one and one-half times the
rate of black and Puerto Rican candidates. Such a difference, it
is argued, is at most mere underrepresentation and hardly amounts
to the gross unexplained disparity that is required for a *prima
facie* case. See, e.g., Swain v. Alabama, 380 U.S. 202 (1965). But
as we previously indicated, the district court did not merely rely
on the difference in overall pass rates. Of "greater significance"
were the pass rates with respect to the assistant principal examinations and the magnifying effect that results from requiring
candidates to pass the examinations seriatim. Moreover, an additional factor considered was the small percentage in New York
City of minority principals and assistant principals in comparison
with other large metropolitan school systems that do not have
comparable examination requirements. We believe that on this
and other evidence in the record the district court could prop-

erly conclude that plaintiffs had demonstrated a disparity of sufficient magnitude to amount to a *prima facie* case of invidious
de facto discrimination.

We further believe that once such a *prima facie* case was made,
it was appropriate for the district court to shift to the Board a
heavy burden of justifying its contested examinations by at least
demonstrating that they were job-related. First, since the Board
is specifically charged with the responsibility of designing those
examinations, it certainly is in the better position to demonstrate
their validity. Cf. Cooper and Sobol, Seniority and Testing
Under Fair Employment Laws: A General Approach to Objective
Criteria of Hiring and Promotion, 82 Harv. L. Rev. 1598, 1665
(1969). Second, once discrimination has been found it would be
anomalous at best if a public employer could stand back and
require racial minorities to prove that its employment tests were
inadequate at a time when this nation is demanding that private
employers in the same situation come forward and affirmatively
demonstrate the validity of such tests. See Title VII of the Civil
Rights Act of 1964, 42 U.S.C. § 2000e; Griggs v. Duke Power Co.,
401 U.S. 424, 432 (1971). The anomaly would only be emphasized by the recent passage of the Equal Employment Opportunity
Act of 1972, which broadened Title VII to include state and city
public employers.

The Board maintains, however, that the district court applied
an improper standard in determining whether the examinations
had been justified notwithstanding their discriminatory impact.
According to the Board, the district court "clearly erred" in applying the compelling interest standard rather than the rational
relationship test customarily applied in equal protection cases.

Although state action invidiously discriminating on the basis
of race has long called for the "most rigid scrutiny," Korematsu
v. United States, 323 U.S. 214, 216 (1944), the Supreme Court has
yet to apply that stringent test to a case such as this, in which the
allegedly unconstitutional action unintentionally resulted in discriminatory effects. See Dandridge v. Williams, 397 U.S. 471, 485
n.17 (1970); cf. Whitcomb v. Chavis, supra, 403 U.S. at 149-60.
Manifestly, the question whether that test should be applied to
de facto discriminatory classifications is a difficult one and is not
to be resolved by facile reference to cases involving intentional
racial classifications. We think, however, that the district court's
decision may be upheld under the "more lenient equal protection standard" and so find it unnecessary to reach this most difficult question.

To be sure, the district court stated that the *de facto* classification found was "constitutionally suspect" and that the Board was

required to make a "strong showing" that its examinations can
be "justified as necessary." 330 F. Supp. at 223, 216. Such language usually connotes application of the "compelling interest"
test. But the court's actual analysis indicates that it never
reached the point where application of that test would bring
a different result from application of the rational relationship test.
It is true that the court placed a heavy burden of proof on the
Board—properly so, as we have already indicated. But the proposition to be proved was only that the Board's examinations were
job-related. As to that, the court concluded that the Board's procedures for insuring the basic content validity of its tests were
inadequately implemented and that as a result the tests themselves
did not measure what they purported to measure. In short, the
present examinations were not found to be job-related and thus
are "wholly irrelevant to the achievement of a valid state objective." Turner v. Fouche, supra, 396 U.S. at 362; see Reed v. Reed,
404 U.S. 71, 75-76 (1971). The court did not reach the issue
whether—or even suggest that—if the written examinations were
job-related the Board would still be required to demonstrate that
no less discriminatory means of obtaining its supervisory personnel were available. See Loving v. Virginia, supra, 388 U.S. at
11; McLaughlin v. Florida, 379 U.S. 184, 196 (1964); cf. United
States v. Bethlehem Steel Corp., 446 F.2d 652, 662 (2d Cir. 1971).
Had the court done that, the bite of the "compelling interest"
test would apply. Instead the court apparently thought that appropriate examinations could be prepared, but that the Board had
not yet done so. The Board, then, failed to meet its burden even
under the rational relationship standard, which would be the
least justification that the Constitution requires.

V. The last issue before us is whether the district judge
abused his discretion in issuing a preliminary injunction against
the use of Board examinations and lists of eligibles based upon
the results of those tests and in requiring the Board to allow appointment of "acting" supervisors. . . .

We understand the fears of those individuals and groups that
have filed strong and even passionate briefs, urging us to reverse.
We share their concern for the public school system; its strength
is crucial in our society. But emotion has led some of the *amici*
astray in describing the decision of the court below. The judge
did not approve of a quota system for the appointment of supervisory personnel; he specifically rejected the idea. Nor did he
permanently do away with the merit system and substitute nepotism and patronage. The judge did not outlaw other written
examinations or indicate that none could be created to test more
fairly the qualities necessary for a supervisory job. It may well be

that new testing procedures will be devised by the parties themselves and be approved by the district court. Certainly, the case
should not linger on in its present unfinished state. All that the
court below did was to enjoin, on an interim basis, examinations
that it justifiably found to have a discriminatory effect and to be
ill-suited for their purpose and to allow the Board of Education of
New York City and its Chancellor to fill vacancies on an acting
basis with candidates meeting criteria satisfactory to them. That
order was not improper and we affirm it.

PORCELLI v. TITUS

United States Court of Appeals, Third Circuit
431 F.2d 1254 (1970)
Cert. denied, 402 U.S. 944 (1971)

PER CURIAM: The plaintiffs herein, Victor Porcelli et al., ten
white teachers employed by the Newark Board of Education,
brought suit under the Civil Rights Act alleging that as of May
28, 1968, the defendant, Superintendent of Schools in the City of
Newark, Franklyn Titus, acting under color of law for the
Newark School System, subjected the plaintiffs to deprivation of
their rights, privileges or immunities secured to them by the
Constitution of the United States of America. This allegedly was
accomplished by the abolition of a promotional list which had
been in existence since 1953, which provided for oral and written examinations for anyone wishing to aspire to be principals
or vice-principals in the System and which, it was contended by
so doing, racially discriminated against whites whose names appeared on the promotional list for appointment. At the time of
the abolition or suspension of the said promotional list, the first
fifteen thereon had been appointed, but Porcelli, Bigley and
Shapiro, plaintiffs herein, though eligible, had not yet been
appointed.

The school population in the City of Newark in October, 1961,
was 67,134, of which the Negro population was 55.1%. In September, 1968, the total school population was 75,876, with a
Negro student population of 72.5%, reflecting an increase in
seven years of 8,742 students and a percentage increase of Negro
students of 17.4%. During the school year 1967-1968, there were
249 administrative and supervisory positions (superintendents,
principals and vice-principals, senior and junior high school principals, etc.), of which 27, or 10% were held by Negroes. On
August 22, 1968, only one Negro each for principal and vice-
principal was eligible on the promotional list and of the 72 principals in the system none were Negro and 67 vice-principals, 64
were white and 3 Negro.

On February 1, 1967, School Board of the City of Newark entered into a contract with the Teachers Association.[2]

Under date of May 28, 1968, defendant Board of Education passed a resolution suspending and abolishing the making of appointments from this list and instead the defendant, Franklyn Titus, Superintendent of the School System in Newark, presented certain recommendations for the appointments of principals, vice-principals, senior and junior high school principals, which the Board adopted, representing a total of 35 white appointments and 20 Negro appointments. The appointments were designated as temporary appointments and the Board was to later review the appointments recommended, the criteria to be used by the Board having not as yet been finalized. In his recommendation to the Board the Superintendent candidly admitted that color was one of the criteria which he utilized, contending that the pattern by which principals, vice-principals and others were appointed reflected an era in 1953, when the promotional list was adopted, and as of 1968, conditions had so changed in the Newark School System that the promotional list had become outmoded by virtue of the changing population, community-wise and in the school system, which had occurred since its adoption.

This action was begun by a motion for summary judgment on the pleading, but the lower court denied it and ordered a full evidentiary hearing at which both sides were heard at great length. Superintendent Titus, one of the defendants, stated as one of his reasons for the abolition of the promotional list the fact that the Newark Public School System, especially in reading, was well below the national norm which obtained throughout the country; that there was such a great imbalance in the principal and vice-principal positions that, in his professional judgment, he

---

[2] Under the terms of the contract, it was required:

"A. The positions of principal, vice principal, head teacher, department chairman and counselor shall be filled in order of numerical ranking from the appropriate list, which ranking shall be determined by written and oral examination. Appointments to the position of teacher to assist principal (formerly called Administrative Assistant) shall be made annually on a temporary basis if the Superintendent determines that such a position is necessary or desirable, and all appointments to such position shall be made in order of numerical ranking from the appropriate vice-principal's list if such a list exists.

"B. Such examinations shall be given at regularly scheduled intervals and shall be adequately publicized in every school at least sixty (60) days in advance.

"C. All openings for the positions of supervisor, assistant supervisor and director and all positions hereafter created in new categories not existing shall be adequately publicized in every school at least sixty (60) days before the appointment is made and the qualifications for the positions shall be clearly set forth."

felt that by adding a Negro who was qualified to these important positions, thus making the faculty more integrated, would the more readily lend itself to an upgrading of the Public School System in Newark. Although, as has been indicated, color was frankly admitted by all the witnesses for the appellees as being one of the factors in the selection of the principals and vice-principals, and one Simeon Moss, who was the assistant superintendent for elementary education who made the recommendations to the Superintendent for the appointments, stated that color was a prime factor, it was not the only factor, as the procuring of qualified individuals was the real objective.[4] Plaintiffs' position was that this use of color in the selection of principals and vice-principals and the device used to achieve that selection by abolition or suspension of the promotional list was a violation of their Constitutional rights under the Fourteenth Amendment.

With this contention we do not agree. State action based partly on considerations of color, when color is not used per se, and in furtherance of a proper governmental objective, is not necessarily a violation of the Fourteenth Amendment. Proper integration of faculties is as important as proper integration of schools themselves, as set forth in Brown v. Board of Education, 349 U.S. 295 (1955), the thrust of which extends to the selection of faculties. In Kemp v. Beasley, 389 F.2d 178 (1968), the court held, at 189, where race was a consideration in the selection of teachers and faculties, "We reaffirm the principle that faculty selection must remain for the board and sensitive expertise of the School Board and its officials." And, at page 190, "The question thus becomes, when is there such faculty distribution as to provide equal opportunities to all students and to all teachers—whether

---

[4] The findings of fact in the district court opinion, 302 F. Supp. at 732-733, 2 FEP Cases 57, include the following:

"A fair evaluation of the record supports the conclusion that the promotional lists were suspended and the examination system abolished, not simply to appoint Negroes to promotional positions, but to obtain for these positions qualified persons, white or black, whose qualifications were based on an awareness of, and sensitivity to, the problems of educating the Newark school population. . . .

. . . .

"The Court is satisfied that in abolishing the examination procedure, there was no intention on the part of the Board to discriminate against white persons or exclude them from consideration for promotional positions. No inference of any such intention can be gleaned from the record. The testimony of several of the witnesses . . . shows that, despite a desire to provide an avenue for the appointment of more Negro administrators, the ultimate objective of the Board was to promote those persons most qualified to suit the needs of the Newark school system. There is nothing in the record to indicate that the Board was attempting to appoint Negroes in numbers proportionate to the school population."

white or Negro? Students in each school should have the same quality of instruction as in any other school. Every predominantly Negro school should have, wherever possible, substantially as integrated a faculty as the predominantly white school."

Again, in Springfield School Committee v. Barksdale, 348 F.2d 261, 266 (1965), the court stated: "It has been suggested that classification by race is unlawful regardless of the worthiness of the objective. We do not agree. The defendants' proposed action does not concern race insofar as race correlates with proven deprivation of educational opportunity." Further, in United States v. Jefferson County Board of Education, 372 F.2d 836, 895 (1966), it was stated, "As to faculty, we have found that school authorities have an affirmative duty to break up the historical pattern of segregated faculties, the hall-mark of the dual system."

It would therefore seem that the Boards of Education have a very definite affirmative duty to integrate school faculties and to permit a great imbalance in faculties—as obtained on August 22, 1968, when a new plan was proposed to the School Board in Newark for the increasing of qualified Negro administrators— would be in negation of the Fourteenth Amendment to the Constitution and the line of cases which have followed Brown v. Board of Education, supra.

We concur in the carefully considered opinion of Chief Judge Augelli, dated August 14, 1969, wherein he made findings of fact and conclusions of law pursuant to Federal Rule of Civil Procedure 52a (Porcelli v. Titus, 302 F. Supp. 726, 2 FEP Cases 52 (District of New Jersey 1969)). He also entered a final order dismissing the complaint with prejudice on September 17, 1969.

The judgment of the lower court will be affirmed.

CARTER v. GALLAGHER

United States Court of Appeals, Eighth Circuit
452 F.2d 315, 327 (1971)
Cert. denied, 406 U.S. 950 (1972)

On Petition For Rehearing En Banc.

GIBSON, Circuit Judge.

A panel of this court . . . sustained the order and opinion of the Honorable Earl R. Larson, District Court of Minnesota, finding that the employment practices and procedures for determining qualifications of applicants for positions on the Minneapolis Fire Department were racially discriminatory in violation of the Equal Protection Clause of the Fourteenth Amendment and the Civil Rights Act of 1870, 42 U.S.C. § 1981, and approved a number of corrective practices ordered so as to eliminate all racially discriminatory practices; but disapproved that part of

Judge Larson's order providing for absolute minority preference in the employment of the next 20 persons to be hired by the department. The case was brought as a class action and relief was extended to minority groups as a class.

The panel opinion, while sustaining most of Judge Larson's findings and orders granting affirmative relief, did not approve of the absolute preference in Fire Department employment to 20 minority persons who met the qualifications for the positions under the revised qualification standards established by the decree and held that the absolute preference order infringed upon the constitutional rights of white applicants whose qualifications are established to be equal or superior to the minority applicants. . . .

A petition for rehearing en banc by the appellees was granted but limited solely to the issue of the appropriate remedy. . . .

The fact of past racially discriminatory practices and procedures in employment by the Fire Department is accepted and clearly evidenced by the fact that of the 535 men in the Fire Department none are from minority groups.[2] We are thus here concerned only with the appropriateness of the remedy ordered by the District Court. The absolute preference of 20 minority persons who qualify has gone further than any of the reported appellate court cases in granting preference to overcome the effects of past discriminatory practices and does appear to violate the constitutional right of Equal Protection of the Law to white persons who are superiorly qualified.

The panel opinion has recognized the illegality of the past practices, has ordered those practices abandoned, and the affirmative establishment of nondiscriminatory practices and procedures. There is, as the panel pointed out, no claim or showing made that the plaintiffs were identifiable members of the class who had made prior applications for employment and were denied employment solely because of race. This latter situation could be remedied immediately by ordering the employment of such persons. However, in dealing with the abstraction of employment as a class, we are confronted with the proposition that in giving an absolute preference to a minority as a class over those of the white race who are either superiorly or equally qualified would constitute a violation of the Equal Protection Clause of the Fourteenth Amendment to the Constitution.

The defendants-appellants point out the mandatory requirements of the Minneapolis City and the Minnesota Veterans' Preference Act (Minnesota Statute § 197.45). These requirements

---

[2] The total minority population of the Minneapolis area was 6.44 percent in 1970; black population 4.37 percent.

however must give way to the Supremacy Clause of Article 6 of the United States Constitution.

Mr. Justice Black, in speaking for a unanimous court (although Mr. Justice Harlan concurred on the basis of the Fifteenth Amendment rather than on the Fourteenth) in Louisiana v. United States, 380 U.S. 145, 85 S. Ct. 817, 13 L. Ed. 2d 709 (1964), approved the suspension of Louisiana voting laws that had been administered discriminatorily against Negroes and held it was the affirmative duty of the district court to eliminate the discriminatory effects of past practices, stating, "We bear in mind that the court has not merely the power but the duty to render a decree which so far as possible eliminate the discriminatory effects of the past as well as bar like discrimination in the future." 380 U.S. at 154, 85 S. Ct. at 822. It is apparent that remedies to overcome the effects of past discrimination may suspend valid state laws. United States v. Mississippi, 339 F.2d 679 (5th Cir. 1964); United States v. Duke, 332 F.2d 759 (5th Cir. 1963).

Admittedly the District Court has wide power sitting as a court of equity to fashion relief enforcing the congressional mandate of the Civil Rights Act and the constitutional guarantees of the Equal Protection of the Law; and clearly, courts of equity have the power to eradicate the effects of past discriminations. Parham v. Southwestern Bell Telephone Co., 433 F.2d 421 (8th Cir. 1971). We are not here concerned with the anti-preference treatment section 703 (j) of Title VII of the Civil Rights Act of 1964, 42 U.S.C. § 2000e-2(j)[3] as this class action is predicated under § 1981 of the old Civil Rights Act and the provisions of the Fourteenth Amendment. However, even the anti-preference treatment section of the new Civil Rights Act of 1964 does not limit the power of a court to order affirmative relief to correct the effects of past unlawful practices. United States v. IBEW, Local No. 38, 428 F.2d 144 (6th Cir.), cert. denied, 400 U.S. 943, 91 S. Ct. 245, 27 L. Ed. 2d 248 (1970).

---

[3] 42 U.S.C. § 2000e-2 (j) provides as follows:

"Nothing contained in this subchapter shall be interpreted to require any employer, employment agency, labor organization, or joint labor-management committee subject to this subchapter to grant preferential treatment to any individual or to any group because of the race, color, religion, sex, or national origin of such individual or group on account of an imbalance which may exist with respect to the total number or percentage of persons of any race, color, religion, sex, or national origin employed by any employer, referred or classified for employment by any employment agency or labor organization, admitted to membership or classified by any labor organization, or admitted to, or employed in, any apprenticeship or other training program, in comparison with the total number or percentage of persons of such race, color, religion, sex, or national origin in any community, State, section, or other area, or in the available work force in any community, State, section, or other area."

Although this case is not predicated upon Title VII of the Civil Rights Act of 1964 and most of the cases that have dealt with the issue of remedying past discriminatory practices along with prohibiting present discriminatory practices are under that Act, the remedies invoked in those cases offer some practical guidelines in dealing with this issue.

As the panel opinion points out most of these cases deal with discriminations to a specified individual who has been presently discriminated against on account of race, and the remedy is there easily applied as the individual who has been discriminated against can be presently ordered employed without running into the constitutional questions involved in granting preference to any one class over another. However, in United States v. Ironworkers Local 86, 443 F.2d 544 (9th Cir. 1971), cert. denied, 404 U.S. 984, 92 S. Ct. 447, 30 L. Ed. 2d 367 (1971) the Ninth Circuit approved the district court decree ordering building construction unions to offer immediate job referrals to previous racial discriminatees and also approved a prospective order requiring the unions to recruit sufficient blacks to comprise a 30 percent membership in their apprenticeship programs. This was ordered in Seattle which had a black population of approximately 7 percent. See, United States v. Local No. 86, Int. Ass'n of Bridge S., D. and R. Ironworkers et al., 315 F. Supp. 1202 (W.D. Wash. 1970).

In Local 53 of Int. Ass'n of Asbestos Workers v. Vogler, 407 F.2d 1047 (5th Cir. 1969), the trial court ordered the immediate admission into the union of three Negroes who were racially discriminated against in their application for membership and voided a local membership rule that in effect made the union a self-perpetuating nepotistic group, specifically ordering the union to develop objective criteria for membership and prospectively ordering the alternating of white and Negro referrals.

In United States v. Central Motor Lines, Inc., 325 F. Supp. 478 (W.D.N.C. 1970), the trial court issued a preliminary injunction requiring the motor carrier to hire six Negro drivers "promptly," (apparently within two weeks from the date of the order), and that any future drivers hired were to be in an alternating ratio of one black to one white.

Cases arising from Executive Order #11246, prohibiting all contractors and subcontractors on federally financed projects from discriminating in their employment practices, have also upheld plans which establish percentage goals for the employment of minority workers. See Contractors Association of Eastern Pa. v. Secretary of Labor, 442 F.2d 159 (3d Cir. 1971) (upholding the "Philadelphia Plan" requiring minority employment goals in the construction trades ranging from 19 percent-26 percent); Joyce

v. McCrane, 320 F. Supp. 1284 (D.N.J. 1970) (requiring contractors to employ 30 percent-37 percent minority journeymen).

It is also appropriate to note that precedent from our own Circuit establishes that the presence of identified persons who have been discriminated against is not a necessary prerequisite to ordering affirmative relief in order to eliminate the present effects of past discrimination. In United States v. Sheet Metal Workers Local 36, 416 F.2d 123 (8th Cir. 1969), we required substantial changes in union referral systems. In connection with this holding, Judge Heaney noted:

"We recognize that each of the cases cited in n.15 to support our position can be distinguished on the ground that in each case, a number of known members of a minority group had been discriminated against after the passage of the Civil Rights Act. Here, we do not have such evidence, but we do not believe that it is necessary. The record does show that qualified Negro tradesmen have been and continue to be residents of the area. It further shows that they were acutely aware of the Locals' policies toward minority groups. It is also clear that they knew that even if they were permitted to use the referral system and become members of the union, they would have to work for at least a year before they could move into a priority group which would assure them reasonably full employment. In the light of this knowledge, it is unreasonable to expect that any Negro tradesman working for a Negro contractor or a nonconstruction white employer would seek to use the referral systems or to join either Local." Id. at 132.

It may also be pointed out that in actions under Title VII of the Civil Rights Act, 42 U.S.C. § 2000e et seq., Congress has specifically granted authority to the trial courts to "order such affirmative action as may be appropriate, which may include . . . hiring of employees. . . ." 42 U.S.C. § 2000e—5 (g) (emphasis added).

None of the remedies ordered or approved in the above cases involved an absolute preference for qualified minority persons for the first vacancies appearing in an employer's business, in contrast to the remedy ordered in the instant case. The absolute preference ordered by the trial court would operate as a present infringement on those non-minority group persons who are equally or superiorly qualified for the fire fighter's positions; and we hesitate to advocate implementation of one constitutional guarantee by the outright denial of another. Yet we acknowledge the legitimacy of erasing the effects of past racially discriminatory practices. Louisiana v. United States, *supra*. To accommodate these conflicting considerations, we think some reasonable ratio for hiring minority persons who can qualify under the revised qualification standards is in order for a limited period of time, or until there is a fair approximation of minority representation consistent with the population mix in the area. Such a procedure does not constitute a "quota" system because as soon as the trial court's order is fully implemented, all hirings will be on a racially nondiscriminatory basis, and it could well be that many more minority persons or less, as compared to the population at large, over a long period of time would apply and qualify for the positions. However, as a method of presently eliminating the effects of past racial discriminatory practices and in making meaningful in the immediate future the constitutional guarantees against racial discrimination, more than a token representation should be afforded. For these reasons we believe the trial court is possessed of the authority to order the hiring of 20 qualified minority persons, but this should be done without denying the constitutional rights of others by granting an absolute preference.

Ideas and views on ratios and procedures may vary widely but this issue should be resolved as soon as possible. In considering the equities of the decree and the difficulties that may be encountered in procuring qualified applicants from any of the racial groups, we feel that it would be in order for the district court to mandate that one out of every three persons hired by the Fire Department would be a minority individual who qualifies until at least 20 minority persons have been so hired.

Fashioning a remedy in these cases is of course a practical question which may differ substantially from case to case, depending on the circumstances. In reaching our conclusion in the instant case, we have been guided to some extent by the following considerations:

(1)   It has now been established by the Supreme Court that the use of mathematical ratios as "a starting point in the process of shaping a remedy" is not unconstitutional and is "within the equitable remedial discretion of the District Court." Swann v. Charlotte-Mecklenburg Board of Education, 402 U.S. 1, 25, 91 S. Ct. 1267, 1280, 28 L. Ed. 2d 554 (1971).

(2)   Given the past discriminatory hiring policies of the Minneapolis Fire Department, which were well known in the minority community, it is not unreasonable to assume that minority persons will still be reluctant to apply for employment, absent some positive assurance that if qualified they will in fact be hired on a more than token basis.

(3) As the panel opinion noted, testing procedures required to qualify applicants are undergoing revision and validation at the present time. As the tests are currently utilized, applicants must attain a qualifying score in order to be certified at all. They are then ranked in order of eligibility according to their test scores (disregarding for present purposes the veteran's preference). Because of the absence of validation studies on the record before us, it is speculative to assume that the qualifying test, in addition to separating those applicants who are qualified from those who are not, also ranks qualified applicants with precision, statistical validity, and predictive significance. See generally, Cooper & Sobol, Seniority and Testing under Fair Employment Laws: A General Approach to Objective Criteria of Hiring and Promotion, 82 Harv. L. Rev. 1598, 1637-1669 (1969). Thus, a hiring remedy based on an alternating ratio such as we here suggest will by no means necessarily result in hiring less qualified minority persons in preference to more qualified white persons.

(4) While some of the remedial orders relied on by the plaintiffs and the Government ordered one to one ratios, they appear to be in areas and occupations with a more substantial minority population than the Minneapolis area. Thus we conclude that a one to two ratio would be appropriate here, until 20 qualified minority persons have been hired.

The panel opinion is adopted as the opinion of the court en banc with the exception of that part relating to the absolute preference.

The District Court properly retained jurisdiction pending full implementation of its decree and the remedy. Cause is remanded for further proceedings consistent with this opinion. . . .

[The concurring opinion of MATTHES, Chief Judge, is omitted.]

VAN OOSTERHOUT, Senior Circuit Judge (dissenting).

For reasons stated in Division V of the panel opinion in this case, reported at 452 F.2d 324, I dissent from the en banc mandatory determination that one out of three persons hired by the Fire Department shall be a minority person until at least twenty minority persons are hired. Such provision in my opinion is vulnerable to the same constitutional infirmity as Judge Larson's absolute preference provision. This court's minority preference provision will not discriminate against as many white applicants as Judge Larson's decree but it will still give some minority persons preference in employment over white applicants whose qualifications are determined to be superior under fairly imposed standards and tests.

Employment preferences based on race are prohibited by the Fourteenth Amendment. This case is distinguishable from Swann v. Charlotte-Mecklenburg Board of Education relied upon by the majority in that whites have no right to insist upon segregated schools, while white as well as Black applicants cannot be denied employment on the basis of race.

I agree that a court of equity has broad power to frame an appropriate decree but such power does not extend to establishing provisions which deprive persons of constitutionally guaranteed rights.

Present and future applicants for firemen positions are in no way responsible for past discrimination. Plaintiffs have not shown that any plaintiff now seeking employment has personally suffered as a result of past discrimination by being denied employment over a less qualified white person. Past general racial discrimination against Blacks under the circumstances of this case does not justify unconstitutional present racial discrimination against white applicants. The court should of course go as far as is constitutionally permissible to eliminate racial discrimination in employment of firemen. Substantial steps in that direction have been taken by other provisions of Judge Larson's decree and the panel opinion.

MEHAFFY, Circuit Judge, joins in this dissent.

NOTES

1. In NAACP v. Allen, 340 F. Supp. 703 (M.D. Ala. 1972), the court upon finding a clear pattern of discrimination against Blacks in the hiring of state troopers, ordered the State to hire one Black trooper for each white hired, until 25% of the state trooper force was Black. But see Anderson v. San Francisco School Dist., — F. Supp. —, 5 FEP Cas. 362 (N.D. Cal. 1972), where the court held that an affirmative action program, which set forth specific percentage quotas for the employment of minority group members as school administrators, violated the Fourteenth Amendment of the United States Constitution, 42 U.S.C. § 1983 and Title VI of the Civil Rights Act of 1964. The court stated:

Preferential treatment under the guise of "affirmative action" is the imposition of one form of racial discrimination in place of another.

However, the court qualified this statement, acknowledging that racial preferences had been sanctioned by other courts to correct past discrimination and in the instant case there had been no demonstration of past discrimination.

2. In *Carter,* even though the case arose under § 1981, the court relied on judicial opinions rendered pursuant to Title VII to support its remedy of quota hiring; does the reference to Title VII tend to narrow the possible scope of remedies under § 1981? What is the meaning of the anti-preference language in § 703 (j) of Title VII?

3. Is a judicial remedy which suggests "goals" for minority hiring as effective as the remedy provided in *Carter? Cf.* Castro v. Beecher, 459 F.2d 725 (1st Cir. 1972), where the district court merely ordered that a non-discriminatory job test be developed to replace a discriminatory test which had been used to select policemen, but the court of appeals reversed in part and required the establishment of a "priority pool" for the hiring of minority applicants who passed the new test.

4. Should the decision in *Porcelli* be read to mean that it is a denial of equal protection for a public employer not to utilize a racial quota to overcome racial disparities in public employment? Should a public employer be required to establish compensatory training programs to remedy disparities of preparation among various classes of job applicants? These questions were answered in the negative in *Castro, supra,* where the First Circuit stated that:

> Such a result would be to translate what is a discretionary power of courts in giving relief into a mandatory standing obligation for employers. . . . A public employer may constitutionally take its applicants as it finds them.

5. In the cases involving quota or preferential hiring, the courts are often faced with the argument of "reverse discrimination" as seen in *Carter* and *Porcelli.* How should the courts deal with this problem? Can it be argued that any remedy which gives a preference to minority job applicants is violative of equal protection? The courts have tended to avoid this constitutional question by limiting preferential hiring orders. Usually, before an order for preferential hiring is issued, there must be a finding of a history of discrimination against a protected group or statistical evidence showing a pattern of gross discrimination; members of the preferred class are required to satisfy job related employment tests; the order is almost always temporary; the order is sometimes conditioned to take account of the availability of the preferred group in the geographic areas nearby the place of employment; and there is usually a finding that other available affirmative relief would be inadequate to overcome the present effects of the existing discrimination. *See, e.g.,* Castro v. Beecher,

supra; Commonwealth v. O'Neill, 5 FEP Cas. 713 (3rd Cir. 1973); Commonwealth v. Sebastian, 5 FEP Cas. 499 (W.D. Pa. 1972); Shield Club v. City of Cleveland, 5 FEP 566 (N.D. Ohio 1973); Bridgeport Guardians, Inc. v. Commission, 5 FEP 570 (D. Conn. 1973).

4. The Problem of Conflict of Forums

YOUNG v. INTERNATIONAL TELEPHONE & TELEGRAPH CO.
United States Court of Appeals, Third Circuit
438 F.2d 757 (1971)

GIBBONS, Circuit Judge:—Plaintiff appeals from the order of the district court which dismissed his complaint for want of subject matter jurisdiction. The complaint seeks damages and injunctive relief with respect to alleged racial discrimination in employment. . . .

Plaintiff is a black citizen of the United States, a resident of Philadelphia, and a sheet metal journeyman. Defendant International Telephone & Telegraph Co., Nesbitt Division (Nesbitt) operates a plant in Philadelphia where it employs sheet metal workers. Defendant Local #19, Sheet Metal Workers International Association (Local #19) is an unincorporated trade union of sheet metal workers, having union contracts with employers of sheet metal workers in the Philadelphia area. Defendant Kern is the Vice-President of Local #19. Prior to 1965 there were no minority group members of Local #19 due to a policy of racial exclusion implemented by conspiracy between Local #19 and certain employers including Nesbitt, whereby employers kept minority workers in unskilled job classifications. In 1965 plaintiff was admitted to membership in Local #19 as a result of an order by the Philadelphia Human Relations Commission requiring Nesbitt to reinstate plaintiff in a job category which required his admission to Local #19. Since his admission to Local #19 both it and Nesbitt have harassed plaintiff maliciously and wantonly, in retaliation for his enforcing his right of admission to the union, and pursuant to its general practice of discriminating against black employees. Plaintiff filed three complaints with the Philadelphia Human Relations Commission in an unsuccessful effort to end harassment by Nesbitt, but was eventually forced to seek other employment.

In 1969 Local #19 was composed of 1,688 journeymen, of whom only 17 were from minority groups. At the same time, at least 375 minority group workers were qualified to perform the same work as present members of Local #19 but were denied admission to the Union.

Defendant Hershman Sheet Metal Works, Inc. (Hershman) is an employer of Sheet Metal Workers at its plant in Philadelphia. On July 17, 1970 Hershman offered plaintiff employment and on July 20 he resigned from Nesbitt. When plaintiff went to Local #19 to notify it of his new job Kern informed him that Local #19's rules required that he be placed on the Out-of-Work List, in spite of the fact that Local #19's usual procedure with respect to white members is to grant immediate transfer when a new job has been secured by an individual member. On July 20 Local #19 notified Hershman that plaintiff could not work there, and as a result Hershman cancelled plaintiff's job.

Plaintiff on his own behalf seeks damages from Nesbitt, Hershman and Local #19 for lost wages since July 20, 1970, and temporary and permanent injunctions restraining Hershman from breaching his employment contract and Local #19 from interfering with that contract. Claiming to act on behalf of all black sheet metal journeymen who are present and potential members of Local #19, pursuant to Rule 23 (a) and (b) (2), Fed. R. Civ. P., he seeks temporary and permanent injunctions against Nesbitt, Hershman, and Local #19, restraining each from discriminating against blacks with respect to job opportunities and working conditions.

The complaint does not allege that plaintiff has pursued any remedies under Title VII of the Civil Rights Act of 1964, 42 U.S.C. § 2000e-5. Jurisdiction is asserted under 42 U.S.C. § 1981 and § 1985, and under 28 U.S.C. § 1343 (1) and (4). The district court dismissed (1) because § 1981 is not applicable to discrimination in private employment, and (2) because plaintiff's failure to have invoked the administrative processes of Title VII of the 1964 Civil Rights Act is fatal to his cause. We reverse.

I.   The Effect of 42 U.S.C. § 1981

Defendants contend that § 1981 does not give plaintiff a right of action for their acts of discrimination relating to his employment. That statute provides:

> All persons within the jurisdiction of the United States shall
> have the same right . . . to make and enforce contracts . . .
> as is enjoyed by white citizens. . . .

[The court first rejected the defendants' claim that § 1981 was not applicable to "private acts of discrimination in employment." On this score, the court cited Jones v. Alfred H. Mayer Co., 392 U.S. 409, 88 S. Ct. 2186, 20 L. Ed. 2d 1189 (1968), and followed the opinions rendered by the Seventh and Fifth Circuits in Waters v. Wisconsin Steel Works of Int'l Harvester

Co., 427 F.2d 476, *cert. denied,* 400 U.S. 911 (1970) and Sanders v. Dobbs Houses, Inc., 431 F.2d 1097 (5th Cir. 1970)]. . . .

Defendants also contend that assuming the applicability of § 1981 to certain private acts of discrimination, a fair reading of the statute precludes the construction that it was intended to apply to the employment situation. We cannot agree. In the context of the reconstruction it would be hard to imagine to what contract right the Congress was more likely to have been referring. Certainly the recently emancipated slaves had little or nothing other than their personal services about which to contract. If such contracts were not included, what was? Certainly the situation of former slaves with respect to their labor was a matter of grave concern in the Congress when the 1866 Act was passed. We therefore reject the strained reading of § 1981 suggested by defendants.

Since this appeal arises on the pleadings, it presents no precise issue as to the relief which would be available assuming that § 1981 prohibits private discrimination in employment. Sullivan v. Little Hunting Park, supra, indicates that 28 U.S.C. § 1343 (4) creates federal jurisdiction to award damages or equitable relief, and that on the authority of 42 U.S.C. § 1988 a district court may draw from federal or state sources an appropriate federal rule of damages. 396 U.S. at 238-40. Thus, unless another statute has repealed § 1981 by necessary implication, the district court had jurisdiction to grant all the relief which plaintiff requested.

II.   The Effect of 42 U.S.C. § 2000e et seq. on § 1981

Defendants contend that Title VII of the Civil Rights Act of 1964 did by necessary implication deprive the district court of jurisdiction. There could have been no intentional repealer, since in 1964 the Congress had no knowledge that private discrimination was prohibited by either § 1981 or § 1982. Jones v. Alfred H. Mayer Co., supra, was not decided until 1968. In that case the Supreme Court referred to the rules of statutory construction of Posadas v. National City Bank, 296 U.S. 497, 503 (1936):

> There are two well-settled categories of repeals by implication— (1) where provisions in the two acts are in irreconcilable conflict, the latter act to the extent of the conflict constitutes an implied repeal of the earlier one; and (2) if the latter act covers the whole subject of the earlier one and is clearly intended as a substitute, it will operate similarly as a repeal of the earlier act. But, in either case, the intention of the legislature to repeal must be clear and mani-

fest; otherwise, at least as a general thing, the latter act is to be construed as a continuation of, and not a substitute for, the first act and will continue to speak, so far as the two acts are the same, from the time of the first enactment.

Applying these rules of statutory construction, we hold that Title VII of the 1964 Act does not deprive the district courts of jurisdiction over actions brought under § 1981 to remedy private discrimination in employment. . . .

[W]ith respect to employers covered, Title VII coverage is narrower than § 1981. It is broader in coverage of classes of victims of discriminatory acts. And since § 1981 covers other contract rights besides that of employment as well as rights other than the right to contract, Title VII clearly does not cover the whole subject of the earlier act. We are not dealing with a statute intended as a substitute. The remaining question is whether in any respects the two statutes are in irreconcilable conflict. . . .

Defendants contend that the provisions for deferral to state agencies for sixty days and for EEOC conciliation efforts for thirty days are in irreconcilable conflict with § 1981 and that exhaustion of these steps in the administrative process should be considered as jurisdictional prerequisites to a district court suit charging discrimination in private employment. They argue for a pre-emption of the field by the Title VII administrative remedies, to the exclusion of the federal courts, at least until after the administrative remedies have run their course.

Imposing the duty on the EEOC to defer to state or local agencies for sixty days certainly is no evidence of a congressional intention to deprive other appropriate forums of their jurisdiction. At most it indicates an intention to take advantage of existing state agencies having expertise and experience, and thereby to shield the new federal agency from an overburdening caseload. That this must have been the intention is evidenced by the fact that deferral to state or local agencies is only temporary. If results have not been accomplished in sixty days the EEOC must begin its investigation. . . .

The statutory duty of the EEOC to attempt conciliation presents a more complex issue. Here an intention to substitute conciliation and persuasion for friction and contention in the delicate field of labor-management relations is evident. At the same time no reference is made in the statute or in such legislative history as is available to any limitation on the jurisdiction of other agencies. Yet the Congress was aware that the courts and the National Labor Relations Board deal with racial discrimination by unions and employers. . . .

[There is nothing] in the language of the statute indicating an intention to deprive the district courts of any pre-existing jurisdiction, known or unknown.

In Waters v. Wisconsin Steel Works of Internat'l Harvester Co., supra, the Seventh Circuit considered the same argument made by the defendants with respect to the necessary effect of the EEOC duty to conciliate and said:

Because of the strong emphasis which Congress placed up-on conciliation, we do not think that aggrieved persons should be allowed to by-pass the Commission without good reason. We hold therefore, that an aggrieved person may sue directly under section 1981 if he pleads a reasonable excuse for his failure to exhaust EEOC remedies. 427 F.2d at 487, 2 FEP Cases 582.

In that case the plaintiff alleged facts which the court found to be a sufficient justification for failure to proceed before the Commission. Defendants would have us accept the Waters case as holding that either exhaustion of EEOC administrative procedures or some justification for non-exhaustion is a jurisdictional prerequisite for an employment discrimination suit. It is not at all clear that the Seventh Circuit intended its Waters opinion to go that far. But in any event such a holding would not be warranted by any language in Title VII and we decline to so hold. As will be developed hereinafter, due regard to the conciliation jurisdiction of the EEOC can be afforded by the district courts short of the erection of a jurisdictional bar.

Defendants contend that there is an irreconcilable conflict between § 1981 and Title VII because of the difference in applicable statutes of limitations. There is no federal statute of limitations applicable to § 1981, and the federal courts would look to the most nearly analogous state statute of limitations. See Henig v. Odorioso, 385 F.2d 491 (3d Cir. 1967), cert. denied, 390 U.S. 1016 (1968). A charge generally must be filed with the Commission, within ninety days after the alleged unlawful practice occurred. This protective limitation on the business of a new federal agency gives no indication of any congressional intention to limit access to the courts. When the Commission notifies the charging party of its inability to achieve conciliation that party may, within thirty days of such notice, commence a civil action in the district court. 42 U.S.C. § 2000e-5 (e). There is a distinctly separate Title VII purpose for this thirty day statute of limitations, not applicable to § 1981. Title VII provides:

Upon application by the complainant and in such circumstances as the court may deem just, the court may appoint an attorney for the complainant and may authorize the commencement of the action without the payment of fees, costs, or security. Upon timely application, the court may, in its discretion, permit the Attorney General to intervene in such civil action if he certifies that the case is of general public importance. 42 U.S.C. § 2000e-5 (e).

In a Title VII action there is also a provision for the award of reasonable attorney's fees to the prevailing party. 42 U.S.C. § 2000e-5 (k). Moreover, as we pointed out hereinabove, many acts of discrimination other than those coming under § 1981 are prohibited by Title VII. Limiting access to the court under Title VII, therefore, involves governmental and judicial interests distinctly different and greater than are involved under § 1981. The different governmental interests include the broader coverage of Title VII and the possibility of participation in the lawsuit by the Attorney General. The different judicial interests include the possibility of waiver of fees and costs, imposition of counsel fees, and appointment of counsel. The difference in applicable statutes of limitations is in these circumstances no argument for implied repeal or even for the application of the Title VII statute of limitations to § 1981 actions. In Sanders v. Dobbs Houses, Inc., supra, the Fifth Circuit had before it a § 1981 suit commenced forty-six days after the EEOC had notified plaintiff of its inability to achieve conciliation. It held that the action could proceed. It rejected the contention that there was irreconcilable conflict and hence pre-emption by the later statute. We agree.

We conclude that nothing in Title VII of the Civil Rights Act of 1964 imposes any jurisdictional barrier to a suit brought under § 1981 charging discrimination in private employment.

III.   Implementing the Conciliation Policy of Title VII

We do not suggest by this holding that in the course of a suit under § 1981 the conciliation features of Title VII should be entirely disregarded. Even in a suit arising under Title VII the district courts are told:

Upon request, the court may, in its discretion, stay further proceedings for not more than sixty days pending the termination of State or local proceedings described in subsection (b) of this section or the efforts of the commission to obtain voluntary compliance. 42 U.S.C. § 2000e-5 (e).

Most § 1981 cases, and in particular most class actions under § 1981, will seek equitable relief. Obviously the availability of conciliation by the EEOC is a factor to be considered in the exercise of discretion in granting such relief. This is particularly the case with preliminary injunctions. There is ample scope, within the traditional bounds of discretion in the application of equitable remedies, for the district courts to develop on a case by case basis an accommodation between their jurisdiction under § 1981 and the conciliation efforts of the Commission. There may be cases, indeed, where conciliation will be more successful because carried out while a preliminary injunction has preserved, for an aggrieved employee, the status quo.

In this connection we call to the district court's attention the Commission's power, under 42 U.S.C. § 2000e-4 (f) :

> (4)   upon request of (i) any employer, whose employees or some of them, or (ii) any labor organization, whose members or some of them, refuse or threaten to refuse to co-operate in effectuating the provisions of this subchapter, to assist in such effectuation by conciliation or such other remedial action as is provided by this chapter.

This power apparently may be exercised by the EEOC at any time, even during the pendency of a lawsuit brought pursuant to § 1981. The district courts may well find it appropriate to suggest to defendants in certain cases such resort to the healing remedies of conference, conciliation, and persuasion.

Title VII is in our view "a continuation of and not a substitute for" § 1981. Cf. Posadas v. National City Bank, supra, 296 U.S. at 503. By fashioning equitable relief with due regard to the availability of conciliation and by encouraging in appropriate cases a resort to the EEOC during the pendency of § 1981 cases the courts will carry out the policies of both statutes. The order dismissing the complaint for lack of subject matter jurisdiction will be reversed, and the case remanded to the district court for further proceedings consistent with this opinion.

NOTE

There is some legislative history surrounding the 1972 amendments to Title VII which indicates that the opinion in *Young* will probably prevail over the contrary holding by the Seventh Circuit in *Waters v. Wisconsin Steel*, cited in the principal case:

> In establishing the applicability of Title VII to State and local employees, the . . . individual's right to file a civil action in his own behalf, pursuant to the Civil Rights Act of 1870 and 1871, 42 U.S.C. §§ 1981 and 1983, is in no way affected. During the floor debate surrounding the passage of Title VII of the Civil Rights Act of 1964, it was made clear that the Act was not intended to preempt existing rights under the National Labor Relations Act or the Railway

Labor Act. Title VII was envisioned as an independent statutory authority meant to provide an aggrieved individual with an additional remedy to redress employment discrimination. Two recent court decisions, Young v. International Telephone and Telegraph Co., 438 F.2d 757 (3rd Cir. 1971) and Sanders v. Dobbs Houses, 431 F.2d 1097 (5th Cir. 1970), have affirmed this Committee's belief that the remedies available to the individual under Title VII are co-extensive with the individual's right to sue under the provisions of the Civil Rights Act of 1866, 42 U.S.C. § 1981, and that the two procedures augment each other and are not mutually exclusive. The bill, therefore, by extending jurisdiction to State and local government employees does not affect existing rights that such individuals have already been granted by previous legislation. House Committee Report No. 92-238, June 2, 1971, at 18.

BEALE v. BLOUNT
United States Court of Appeals, Fifth Circuit
461 F.2d 1133 (1972)

SIMPSON, Circuit Judge:

Charging that his November 6, 1970 discharge from his position as a substitute letter carrier at the Buena Vista Station branch of the Miami, Florida, Post Office occurred solely because he was black, Howard Beale, Jr., brought suit in the district court for injunctive relief, monetary damages[2] and reinstatement with back pay. Named as defendants were Winston Blount, the Postmaster-General of the United States; T.J. Coleman, the Regional Director of the Post Office Department; and E.M. Dunlap, the postmaster for Miami, Florida. Citing Waters v. Wisconsin Steel Works of International Harvester Company, 7 Cir. 1970, 427 F.2d 476, and Beverly v. Lone Star Lead Construction Corporation, 5 Cir. 1971, 437 F.2d 1136, the court below dismissed the complaint on the ground that available administrative remedies had not been exhausted. On this appeal Beale contends that the doctrine requiring exhaustion of available administrative remedies is inapplicable to a suit alleg-

---

[2] The claim for monetary damages was dropped by Beale during the pendency of the suit below. The damages claim may have been abandoned prematurely in view of the October 15, 1971 decision of the United States Court of Claims in Chambers v. United States, 1971, 451 F.2d 1045, holding that Order 11478, 34 F.R. 12985 (1969) and Title 5, U.S.C., Section 7151, conferred jurisdiction on the Court of Claims under the Tucker Act Title 28, U.S.C., Section 1346 (a) (2), to entertain a suit for back pay by an *applicant* for federal employment who allegedly was denied employment solely for racial reasons.

ing the termination of federal employment solely for racial reasons. For reasons which differ somewhat from the one given by the district court, we affirm the order of dismissal.

I. The Facts

Beale filed his complaint in the district court while postal authorities[3] were administratively reviewing the appropriateness of his termination. In order to put the facts in perspective, we outline separately the chronologies of the administrative and judicial proceedings.

A. The Administrative Proceeding

On November 11, 1968, Beale was hired as a substitute letter carrier at the Buena Vista Station. Beale argued with his immediate supervisor, Braz, on June 22, 1970, over Beale's alleged failure to pay proper attention to his work inside the station. Four days later, on June 26, 1970, Beale and Braz once again exchanged angry words and Beale was alleged to have picked up a stool and made a menacing gesture toward Braz. . . .

On October 23, 1970, defendant Coleman advised Beale in writing that the charge of misconduct had been sustained and that he would be terminated from the postal service as of November 6, 1970. The scheduled termination was automatically postponed by Beale's appeal to F.J. Nunlist, the Assistant Postmaster-General for Operations, and request for a formal hearing. A hearing was held at Miami, Florida, on December 10, 1970, before Hearing Officer Lindler. At the hearing Beale was represented by Tony Montanez, an official of the postal employees union to which he belonged. On December 23, 1970, the hearing officer submitted his report of the December 10 proceeding. The report related that at the hearing Beale had limited his evidence to matters in extenuation, with primary emphasis upon his claim that Braz had provoked him on June 26, 1970.

By letter to Beale dated March 16, 1971, Assistant Postmaster-General Nunlist noted that Beale's representative at the hearing of December 10, 1970, had made several references to alleged racial motivations behind the decision to terminate Beale. Nunlist's letter expressly invited Beale to file a formal claim of racial discrimination with the postal authorities. On March 25, 1971,

---

[3] On August 12, 1970, Public Law 91-375, 84 Stat. 720, the Postal Re-Organization Act of 1970 was approved. This act abolished the Post Office Department and created in its stead the United States Postal Service, "an independent establishment of the executive branch of the Government of the United States." The United States Postal Service officially came into existence on July 1, 1971, at which time it assumed all the functions previously performed by the Post Office Department.

Beale's suit-counsel advised Nunlist in writing that Beale did not "wish to file any administrative charges of racial discrimination since a lawsuit is pending in federal court involving this claim of racial discrimination."

On April 8, 1971, Nunlist advised Beale that he had decided to sustain the decision to terminate him from the postal service. The termination was effective as of April 23, 1971. The Board of Appeals and Review, on August 25, 1971, sustained the decision of the Assistant Postmaster-General to terminate Beale's employment. That Board was the final administrative review authority within the postal establishment.

B. *The Judicial Proceeding*

Beale's complaint was filed in the district court on January 12, 1971. It alleged that Beale was "a member of a class composed of black citizens in or about the Miami area who have been discriminated against by the defendants with respect to employment solely on account of race or color." It continued that the defendants "have pursued and continue to pursue a pattern or practice and custom or usage of racial discrimination which has deprived and tended to deprive the plaintiffs and members of their class of the same right to make and enforce contracts, and the same right to enjoy property as it is enjoyed by white persons." According to the complaint, the defendants had implemented their racially discriminatory policies in numerous ways, among them being: (1) by "subjecting black employees to harsher discipline than white employees"; and (2) by "failing and refusing to take such affirmative steps as may be necessary to correct the effects of their past racially discriminatory practices." Alleging district court jurisdiction pursuant to Title 42, U.S.C., Sections 1981-1988, Title 28, U.S.C., Section 1343, and Title 28, U.S.C., Section 1331, the complaint sought injunctive relief against the named defendants and their subordinates prohibiting continuance of racially discriminatory practices against the class represented by Beale, seeking damages in excess of $10,000.00 to the members of that class, and reinstating Beale with back pay. . . .

On April 8, 1971, the defendants moved to dismiss the complaint for lack of subject-matter jurisdiction and failure to state a claim upon which relief could be granted or, in the alternative, for summary judgment. The defendants' motion was granted, with prejudice, on April 28, 1971. Beale filed his notice of appeal April 30, 1971. On September 3, 1971, he advised this Court that the Board of Appeals and Review had on August 25 sustained the decision to terminate his employment.

II. The Claim for Injunctive Relief

Although the district court did deal in terms with the complaint's request for injunctive relief against the defendants' allegedly racially discriminatory practices, we are of the opinion that such relief is barred by the doctrine of sovereign immunity. This holding is compelled under our decision in Blaze v. Moon, 5 Cir. 1971, 440 F.2d 1348. . . .

Conceding the undetermined possibility that various branches of the former United States Post Office did indeed practice racial discrimination with respect to department employees, the district court was without power to consider such a request for relief in the absence of a specific grant of jurisdiction from Congress to afford antidiscrimination injunctive relief.[6]

III. The Claim for Reinstatement

Traditionally, the procedural avenue to reinstatement for an ex-employee of the federal government claiming to be the victim of improper discharge has been a petition for mandatory injunction or writ of mandamus directed to the head of the agency concerned commanding the re-employment of the petitioner. Schwartz and Jacoby, Litigation with the Federal Government (1970), Chapter XVI. The exhaustion of available administrative remedies was a prerequisite to maintenance of such a mandamus action. Bolger v. Marshall, 1951, 90 U.S. App. D.C. 30, 193 F.2d 37. See, also, Chandler v. Judicial Council of Tenth Circuit of United States, 1970, 398 U.S. 74, 90 S. Ct. 1648, 26 L. Ed. 2d 100. The remedy of mandamus directed against an agency has been regarded as an exception to the doctrine that suits may not be maintained against the United States without its consent. Clackamas County, Oregon v. McKay, 1954, 94 U.S. App. D.C. 108, 219 F.2d 479, vacated as moot 1955, 349 U.S. 909, 75 S. Ct. 599, 99 L. Ed. 1244. In 1962, Congress broadened the availability of the mandamus remedy by investing the district courts generally with jurisdiction to issue the writ which eliminated the previous requirement that reinstatement suits be maintained only in the United States District Court for the

---

[6] Section 401 (1), Title 39, United States Code, empowers the United States Postal Service "to sue and be sued in its official name." The United States Supreme Court has held that a "sue and be sued clause" constitutes a waiver of sovereign immunity. Keifer & Keifer v. Reconstruction Finance Corporation, 1939, 306 U.S. 381, 59 S. Ct. 516, 83 L. Ed. 784; Federal Housing Administration v. Burr, 1940, 309 U.S. 242, 60 S. Ct. 488, 84 L. Ed. 724. Because Beale was terminated from his employment before the United States Postal Service officially came into existence and because when Beale filed his suit in the district court his employer was the United States Post Office Department, we deem it unnecessary to consider the impact of Title 39, U.S.C., Section 401 (1) upon Beale's claim for injunctive relief.

District of Columbia. Public Law 87-748, 76 Stat. 744 (October 5, 1962), codified as Title 28, U.S.C., Section 1361. The legislative history of that act clearly reflects that Congress did not intend to modify the requirement of exhaustion of available administrative remedies in mandamus suits. 1962 U.S. Code Congressional and Administrative News, pp. 2784, 2787.

For purposes of this appeal the complaint's request for Beale's reinstatement with back pay will be considered as an action in the nature of a petition for writ of mandamus. This bypasses the obstacle of the doctrine of sovereign immunity, so that we get directly to the issue of exhaustion of available administrative remedies. The issue of exhaustion, as we find it here, raises two separate questions:

(a) Does the allegation of racial discrimination on the part of a federal agency excuse a discharged employee from the requirement that he exhaust available administrative remedies before bringing suit to compel his reinstatement?

(b) Assuming that exhaustion of available administrative remedies is required where racial discrimination is alleged to have been the motivation behind the decision to terminate employment, has Beale satisfied that requirement in this case?

IV. The Requirement of Exhaustion of Available Administrative Remedies with Respect to Federal Employment

In support of the contention that he is not required to exhaust available administrative remedies before bringing suit in a federal court charging a federal agency with racial discrimination in employment, Beale advances two theories: It is first asserted that the district court's jurisdiction is not limited to that established by Title 28, U.S.C., Section 1361 (mandamus), but extends to the jurisdiction provided by Title 28, U.S.C., Sections 1331 and 1343.[7] The second contention is that the decisions of

---

[7] Title 28, U.S.C., § 1331:

" (a) The district courts shall have original jurisdiction of all civil actions wherein the matter in controversy exceeds the sum or value of $10,000, exclusive of interest and costs, and arises under the Constitution, laws, or treaties of the United States."

Title 28, U.S.C., § 1343:

"The district courts shall have original jurisdiction of any civil action authorized by law to be commenced by any person: . . . (3) [t]o redress the deprivation, under color of any State law, statute, ordinance, regulation, custom or usage, of any right, privilege or immunity secured by the Constitution of the United States or by any Act of Congress providing for equal rights of citizens or of all persons within the jurisdiction of the United States; (4) [t]o recover damages or to secure equitable or other relief under any Act of Congress providing for the protection of civil rights, including the right to vote."

the United States Supreme Court in Monroe v. Pape, 1961, 365 U.S. 167, 81 S. Ct. 473, 5 L. Ed. 2d 492; McNeese v. Board of Education, 1963, 373 U.S. 668, 83 S. Ct. 1433, 10 L. Ed. 2d 622; and Damico v. California, 1967, 389 U.S. 416, 88 S. Ct. 526, 19 L. Ed. 2d 647, dealing with the requirement of exhaustion of *state* administrative remedies in actions brought pursuant to Title 42, U.S.C., Section 1983 have application here.

We find neither theory to be meritorious. Our reasons are simple and uninvolved.

Sections 1331 and 1343, Title 28, United States Code, may not be construed to constitute waivers of the federal government's defense of sovereign immunity. Cotter Corporation v. Seaborg, 10 Cir. 1966, 370 F.2d 686, 692. Beale's complaint thus alleges no proper jurisdictional basis for seeking reinstatement.

The Supreme Court's decisions regarding the supplementary nature of relief under Title 42, U.S.C., Section 1983, are inapplicable to this case, in which Beale alleges a deprivation of rights protected by Title 42, U.S.C., Section 1981. The Section 1983 cases on which Beale heavily relies dealt with the relationships between the several states and the federal government in the field of deprivations of federally protected rights under the color of state law. The Supreme Court found no rational basis for requiring a claimant to exhaust state administrative remedies before being permitted to institute an action in federal court to redress the deprivation of a federal right. But Beale's situation is totally dissimilar from that of a plaintiff in a Section 1983 action. Beale was formerly an employee of a department of the government of the United States. The federal government is on record by Act of Congress as opposed to discrimination on the basis of race in its own employment practices. Title 5, U.S.C., Section 7151.[10] Pursuant to Section 7151, the President has directed the heads of all federal agencies to put into effect positive programs designed to eliminate racial discrimination in federal employment and to resolve complaints of unequal treatment on the basis of race within the governmental establishment. Executive Order 11246 (1965), as amended by Executive Order 11478 (1969).

Beale does not assert that resort to the administrative processes of the postal service designed to deal with complaints of racial discrimination would be a meaningless ritual. He claims simply

---

[10] Title 5, U.S.C., § 7151:

"It is the policy of the United States to insure equal employment opportunities for employees without discrimination because of race, color, religion, sex, or national origin. The President shall use his existing authority to carry out this policy."

that he did not need to present his claim of racial discrimination to the postal authorities before bringing suit in district court. We adhere to the time-tested requirement that available administrative remedies be exhausted prior to the institution of a mandamus action. The federal bureaucracy's efforts to police its own practices with respect to discrimination in employment on the basis of race should not be undermined. This would be the predictable effect of sanctioning resort to the federal courts before completion of the administrative review process. We hold that the teachings of *Monroe, McNeese* and *Damico* and similar decisions have no application to this case.[11]

V. The Exhaustion of Available Administrative Remedies in This Case

Beale claims that a white employee of the Miami, Florida, Post Office would not have been fired for engaging in the conduct with which he was charged, the use of foul language towards and an assault upon a superior. It is asserted that the punishment for a similar offense by a white employee would at most have been three days' suspension. Throughout the administrative review of the decision to take disciplinary action against Beale for his behavior on June 26, 1970, he and his counsel persistently refused to present the issue of racial discrimination to the postal authorities. When he was invited by the Assistant Postmaster-General to make such a claim, Beale declined to do so on the basis that the issue was then pending before a federal court. Beale's sole defense to the charges in the administrative proceedings apparently was his assertion that Braz provoked his actions.

Under these circumstances we reject Beale's alternative claim that available administrative remedies are now exhausted by the adverse decision of the Board of Appeals and Review during the progress of this appeal. We think rather that the doctrine of exhaustion of available administrative remedies requires a federal court plaintiff to establish that all claims which could have been entertained by the administrative agency involved were in fact presented to that agency for resolution. See, Unemployment Compensation Commission of Territory of Alaska v. Aragan, 1946, 329 U.S. 143, 155, 67 S. Ct. 245, 251, 91 L. Ed. 136. See

---

[11] Our ruling in this regard should not be construed as implying that a plaintiff in a § 1983 action would be required to exhaust the available state administrative remedies before bringing his federal lawsuit in the event the State is able to establish the efficacy of those remedies. The Supreme Court's decisions in *Monroe, McNeese* and *Damico* make it clear that such exhaustion is not required of a § 1983 plaintiff no matter what state administrative avenues for relief are open to him.

also, Picard v. Connor, 1971, 404 U.S. 270, 92 S. Ct. 509, 30 L. Ed. 2d 438, requiring in a state prisoner's federal habeas corpus action that full opportunity for state court review of federal constitutional claims must be sought before relief is available in a federal district court.

Beale deliberately refused to permit the postal authorities to consider his claim that he had received the excessive punishment of dismissal solely because of his race. Instead, he withheld that claim in order to raise it in the first instance in a federal court. Such a strategy, it appears to us, is calculated to disrupt the operation of the postal service's internal program aimed at the elimination of racial discrimination in employment. We are constrained to hold that Beale's refusal to raise the racial discrimination issue during the course of the administrative review of the decision to terminate his postal employment is tantamount to a deliberate bypass of available administrative remedies. Exhaustion of those remedies has not taken place.

VI. Conclusion

We recapitulate. Beale's claim for injunctive relief is barred by the doctrine of sovereign immunity; he is required to exhaust his available administrative remedies before seeking reinstatement in federal court, even where the alleged basis for the separation from federal employment is racial discrimination; and Beale, by refusing to raise the issue of racial discrimination in the course of the administrative review of the decision to terminate him, did not exhaust his available administrative remedies. The district court properly refused to entertain Beale's suit. Its judgment is

Affirmed.

NOTE

It is no longer open to dispute that a plaintiff with a claim for relief under the Civil Rights Act, 42 U.S.C. § 1983, is not required to exhaust state *judicial* remedies. *See, e.g.,* Monroe v. Pape, 365 U.S. 167, 81 S. Ct. 473, 5 L. Ed. 2d 492 (1961); Rodriguez v. McGinnis, 456 F.2d 79 (2d Cir. 1972). However, the Second Circuit has held that a civil rights plaintiff must still exhaust state *administrative* remedies before proceeding in federal court on a § 1983 suit. *See* Eisen v. Eastman, 421 F.2d 560 (2d Cir. 1969), *cert. denied,* 400 U.S. 841 (1970). But in James v. Board of Educ., 461 F.2d 566 (2d Cir. 1972), the Second Circuit made it clear that a civil rights plaintiff would not be barred from pursuing a suit under § 1983 by an adverse determination in a state administrative proceeding.

HADNOTT v. LAIRD
United States Court of Appeals, District of Columbia Circuit
463 F.2d 304 (1972)

WILKEY, Circuit Judge:—Plaintiffs appeal from an order of the District Court dismissing an action for injunctive and declaratory relief against the Secretary of Defense and the Administrator of the General Services Administration. Plaintiffs brought the action on their own behalf and "on behalf of all black employees, applicants for employment, and prospective applicants for employment at the southern facilities" of eleven paper product companies having supply contracts with Defense and GSA, alleging that the rights of plaintiffs (and the class they represent) had been violated under the due process clause of the Fifth Amendment by the failure of the Government to enforce the companies' contractual agreements for nondiscrimination. The action sought an injunction against the two government officials, preventing the award of any future contracts and requiring the termination of the existing one, until all alleged racially discriminatory employment practices should be eliminated. The District Court dismissed the action on two grounds, sovereign immunity and the failure of the plaintiffs to exhaust their administrative remedies. Without reaching the first, we affirm on the latter ground.

I. The facts are stated fully in the published opinion of the able trial Judge. Executive Order 11246, last in the series of Presidential orders directed at eliminating discrimination, requires that every government contract include specific provisions binding the contractor not to discriminate against any employee or applicant because of race, color, creed, or national origin, and to take affirmative action to insure that nondiscrimination is a reality. The penalties for violating these contractual obligations include contract cancellation, termination, or suspension, and ineligibility for future government contracts.

The overall enforcement of these nondiscriminatory contract obligations is entrusted not to the specific contracting agencies themselves (although they have primary responsibility for obtaining compliance), but to the Secretary of Labor. Aside from the contracts with his own Department, he has no special interest in any particular contract or contractor, but independently has the specific duty to see that the nondiscriminatory provisions are enforced with all government contractors. To carry out his responsibility the Secretary has created the Office of Federal Contract Compliance and promulgated detailed regulations, which among other things establish a complete procedure under which any employee or applicant for employment may complain of discriminatory practices by a government contractor.[2] Following a complaint the regulations require prompt investigation to determine if there has been a violation of the equal opportunity clause. In accord with the usual common sense principle of avoiding litigation where possible, if investigation indicates a violation, the preferred solution is for the offending contractor to take immediate corrective steps. If the contractor disputes the existence of violations, he is given a hearing, at which time the complainants or witnesses offered by them may be heard.[3] If after hearing a violation is determined, the penalties authorized by the Executive Order may be imposed.[4]

At the time of oral argument, out of the eleven companies involved here, with three the Government had reached new affirm-

---

[2] 41 C.F.R. § 60-1.21–.23.

[3] 41 C.F.R. § 60-1.26 (b) (1) (2) reads as follows:

(b) *Formal hearings*— (1) General *procedure.* The Director or the agency head, with the approval of the Director, may convene formal hearings pursuant to Subpart B of this part. Such hearings shall be conducted in accordance with procedures prescribed by the Director or the agency head. Reasonable notice of a hearing shall be sent by registered mail, return requested, to the last known address of the prime contractor or subcontractor complained against. Such notice shall contain the time and place of hearings, a statement of the provisions of the order and regulations pursuant to which the hearing is to be held, and a concise statement of the matters pursuant to which the action furnishing the basis of the hearing has been taken or is proposed to be taken. Copies of such notice shall be held before a hearing officer designated by the Director or an agency head. Each party shall have the right to counsel, a fair opportunity to present evidence and argument and to cross-examine. Wherever a formal hearing is based in whole or in part on matters subject to the collective bargaining agreement and compliance may necessitate a revision of such agreement, any labor organization which is a signatory to the agreement shall have the right to participate as a party. Any other person or organization shall be permitted to participate upon a showing that such person or organization has an interest in the proceedings and may contribute materially to the proper disposition thereof. The hearing officer shall make his proposed findings and conclusions upon the basis of the record before him.

(2) *Cancellation, termination, and debarment.* No order for cancellation or termination of existing contracts or subcontracts or for debarment from further contracts or subcontracts pursuant to section 209 of the order shall be made without affording the prime contractor or subcontractor an opportunity for a hearing. . . .

41 C.F.R. § 60-2.2 (c) (1) reads as follows:

(1) If the contractor fails to show good cause for his failure or fails to remedy that failure by developing and implementing an acceptable affirmative action program within 30 days, the compliance agency, upon the approval of the Director, shall issue a notice of proposed cancellation or termination of existing contracts or subcontracts and debarment from future contracts and subcontracts pursuant to § 60-1.26 (b), giving the contractor 10 days to request a hearing. If a request for hearing has not been received within 10 days from such notice, such contractor will be declared ineligible for future contracts and current contracts will be terminated for default.

[4] 41 C.F.R., § 60-1.24, 60-1.26, 60-1.127.

ative action agreements correcting violations found by the investigation, compliance reviews had been conducted and were being analyzed to determine the existence of violation in four instances, and the remaining four companies were scheduled for compliance reviews in the near future.[5]

II.   Although administrative action under Executive Order 11246 has been and is taking place, yet nowhere in the record is it asserted that any specific one of the plaintiffs has filed a complaint against one of the named companies and invoked the procedure provided by Executive Order 11246 and the implementing regulations. There is thus no showing by plaintiffs that they have asserted before and been denied rights by the OFCC. Instead, plaintiffs argue, first, that it would be fruitless for them to do so and, second, that because they are asserting constitutional rights they cannot be required to do so before resorting to the federal court.

A.   As to the usefulness of plaintiffs resorting to the administrative procedure set up to achieve precisely the results which plaintiffs desire in this case, i.e., either strict compliance with equal employment opportunity requirements or the debarment of the offending companies from government contracts, we are of the opinion that plaintiffs will never know the result until they try.[7] Plaintiffs have a variety of excuses as to why pursuing the

---

[5] While the Senate Committee on Labor and Public Welfare stated, in its recommendations for the bill to improve the Equal Employment Opportunity Commission which the Senate passed on 2 October 1970, as noted by the plaintiffs.

. . . [T]he committee also believes that an adequate job of providing equal employment opportunity has not, and is not, being provided through the Federal procurement function. There has been far too much non-public discussion and negotiation and far too few understandable results. In many instances the [Labor] Department's claim that something major happened, when measured against the demonstration that something actually happened, is grossly lacking in the clarity that the public and minorities can understand. In short, OFCC is still suffering from a paucity of credible achievements. . . . (S. Rep. No. 91-1137, Equal Employment Opportunities Act (1970), 20), the committee nonetheless "decided not to recommend such changes in the existing legislative structure at the present time" (Id.), thus leaving the federal contract compliance function with the OFCC rather than "overburdening" the Equal Employment Opportunity Commission with it. See also Hearings on S. 2453 Before the Subcommittee on Labor of the Senate Committee on Labor and Public Welfare, 91st Cong., 1st Sess. 37, 38, 92-98, 100, 114, 168-69, 194.

[7] Our dissenting colleague accepts the position of plaintiffs that the administrative remedies available do not provide "any realistic possibility for the relief plaintiffs seek," adding that under these administrative procedures "the government participates in the form of judge or mediator, but a declaration of governmental duties and responsibilities is not contemplated by such procedures." First, considering that Congress labored long and hard to create just these procedures, we are reluctant to hold that all this was in vain be-

prescribed administrative route instead of leaping into court with a constitutional claim would be a waste of their time.

1. Principally plaintiffs claim that in the instances where the investigation has been made and completed, and corrective action taken pursuant to a new, specific affirmative action agreement, the companies are still in violation. If this is true, there is nothing to preclude the plaintiffs from filing another complaint making such factual assertions as they think can be established, and calling for a hearing on such complaint in which the plaintiffs and witnesses offered by them may be allowed to participate.

2. Plaintiffs further assert that neither Executive Order 11246 nor the regulations provide an absolute right to the complainants or witnesses offered by them to participate in such hearings, but the regulations do provide that if there is a hearing the individual complainant may participate in the administrative hearing, if he can show he has an interest in the proceeding and may contribute materially to the proper disposition thereof. Rosado v. Wyman, 397 U.S. 397 (1970), should not discourage plaintiffs. As the trial court pointed out:

> There the Department of Health, Education and Welfare had "no procedures whereby welfare recipients may trigger and participate in the Department's review of state welfare programs." (397 U.S., at 406.) Such is not the case here.

3. Plaintiffs further assert that in some (but not all) of the instances where revised contractual obligations have been put into effect following the compliance investigation triggered by the show-cause order, the new contracts have been refused to the plaintiffs on the grounds that these agreements are confidential. Whether this is true or not, we would assume that if a complaint were filed by the plaintiffs in regard to any one of these companies in this situation, the contract provisions would be a matter of relevant evidence at the hearing.

In the present posture of this case the plaintiffs came into the United States District Court without any administrative record whatsoever, for the apparent reason that plaintiffs had never pursued a complaint, if they had filed any in the first instance,

---

cause these remedies do not provide "any realistic possibility for the relief plaintiffs seek" in precisely those situations for which they were designed. At least we would not so hold on the showing made by plaintiffs here. Secondly, in the absence of final administrative action on plaintiffs' applications here, how can anyone be certain that a judicial declaration of governmental duties and responsibilities is required at all? In the interest of avoiding unnecessary, or duplicitous governmental action, particularly in light of the crowded dockets confronting the judiciary at present, it would appear most sensible for the court to await final administrative action here before proceeding, if the need to do so still remains.

under the administrative procedures provided under Executive Order 11246 and the regulations pursuant thereto.[11] Administrative action should be pursued in cases like this one in view of the comprehensive administrative remedies available to the plaintiffs. Finality would be obtained by plaintiffs themselves presenting and pursuing complaints with the OFCC at whatever stage of the compliance agreement process.[12] We cannot say with exactitude what will occur if the plaintiffs go to the Office of Federal Contract Compliance and file a complaint in each of the eleven instances which they cited to the District Court and now cite to this court. But we are assured that one of several things will happen: (1) the Office of Federal Contract Compliance may actually reject the complaint on the ground that the matter has already been investigated, compliance assured, and the matter closed; (2) the OFCC may accept the complaint, reopen the investigation, but deny plaintiffs any role in such investigation by offering testimony or otherwise; or (3) the OFCC may reopen the investigation, conduct an open hearing, in which plaintiffs are allowed to participate. In either eventuality, the plaintiffs will have definite administrative action to which to point when they then come into the United States District Court for review under the provisions of the Administrative Procedure Act.[13]

---

[11] We are unable to appreciate plaintiffs' argument that pursuing their administrative remedy somehow involves much more labor on their part. Under complaint filed with the Office of Federal Contract Compliance all plaintiffs need establish is that the accused company is in violation. Under the action brought in the District Court the plaintiffs by their own theory must establish (1) the accused company is in violation, and (2) the appropriate government officials have not taken required action. In the OFCC proceeding there is provision for appointed counsel for each complainant (41 C.F.R. § 60-1.26 (b)) in addition to the reasonably expected action of the enforcement officials.

Similarly, under a Title VII court action directed against the companies, discussed under III infra, comparative advantages would accrue to plaintiffs.

[12] The plaintiffs' grievances might arise at any one of three stages: (1) Before any OFCC consideration or action with respect to plaintiffs' complaint; (2) During OFCC consideration or action; or (3) After OFCC consideration and action, in the form either of a finding of no discriminatory practices or acceptance by a company or companies of a compliance agreement, which plaintiffs find is insufficient or not being enforced. In any of these cases, complainants should at first attempt to make full use of the administrative remedies explicitly designed to provide the kind of relief which they seek here—elimination of discriminatory practices on the part of the companies. *Having once fully but unsuccessfully pursued the available administrative remedies, plaintiffs would have exhausted them and they would pose no bar to judicial consideration of the plaintiffs' complaints.*

[13] Plaintiffs beg a further inadequacy, that they are not assured that the Administrative Procedure Act would give them judicial review of administrative action taken pursuant to regulations promulgated under an Execu-

B. Turning now to plaintiffs' second argument against the applicability of the exhaustion doctrine here, the plaintiffs contend that whether their resort to administrative remedies would be useless or useful, they are not relegated to administrative remedies, but can seek redress originally in the federal courts for alleged violation of their constitutional rights by government officials. However, the Supreme Court cases cited by plaintiffs and the dissent here in support of this theory do not involve federal officials but do involve state or other non-federal officers, and furthermore were brought against such officials under the Civil Rights Act.[14]

Aside from the fact that plaintiffs' theory is not supported in the cases cited, there are several affirmative reasons why plaintiffs should not be allowed to bring the action originally against these federal officials on this constitutional ground.

First, if the existence of Executive Order 11246 and the implementing regulations providing administrative enforcement of a nondiscrimination policy with government contractors is completely meaningless, it follows—and plaintiffs on oral argument candidly so agreed—that whenever a government contractor is allegedly violating any other federal statute then an original action in a federal court to compel the government department to cease doing business with the private company would lie as a means of enforcement of the statute (or constitutional provision) being violated. To read the due process clause as containing the remedy of government contract cancellation, available to be invoked by an aggrieved private party is a bit unprecedented.

---

tive Order, in contrast to statute. This bugaboo would seem to have been exercised by Service v. Dulles, 354 U.S. 363 (1957).

While the plaintiffs assert that there have been only three instances in the entire history of the OFCC program in which formal hearings were instituted for the purpose of debarring a government contractor (In Matter of Timken Roller Bearing Co., OFCC Docket No. 100-68; In Matter of Allen-Bradley Co., OFCC Docket No. 101-68; and In Matter of Bethlehem Steel Co., OFCC Docket No. 102-68), and that no contract has ever been cancelled, such hearings and subsequent debarment are not, of course, the only manner in which final administrative action may be obtained before judicial consideration is appropriate. . . .

[14] McNeese v. Board of Education, 373 U.S. 668 (1963); Monroe v. Pape, 365 U.S. 167 (1961); Damico v. California, 389 U.S. 416 (1967). See also 317 F. Supp. 379, 385 (1970). The dissent, in addition to the above-cited Supreme Court cases, cites Chisley v. Richland Parish School Board, 448 F.2d 1251, 3 FEP Cases 1113 (5th Cir. 1971), and Hobbs v. Thompson, 448 F.2d 456 (5th Cir. 1971), for the proposition that "the requirement of exhaustion is rapidly disappearing from that area of our jurisprudence dealing with the vindication of constitutional rights." This overlooks the fact, however, that the two Fifth Circuit cases he cites, as well as the three Supreme Court cases referred to above, are concerned with the question of the necessity for exhausting *state* judicial or administrative remedies prior to seeking relief in the federal courts. . . .

Unprecedented, and likewise fraught with the possibility of complete disruption of the usual procedures for statutory enforcement.

And unnecessary. Executive Order 11246, plus supporting comprehensive regulations, was tailored to afford a specific remedy for any violation of the due process clause by racial discrimination committed by government contractors. There is no need to construe the due process clause as containing any particular remedy and being virtually self-executing. The remedy provided by Executive Order 11246 is precisely what the plaintiffs seek here, and directed against the type violators, government contractors, by whose actions plaintiffs may be really aggrieved.

Finally, in view of plaintiffs' constitutional claims advanced in the instant case and the availability of alternate judicial and administrative remedies, it would be particularly inappropriate for this court to involve itself with such constitutional claims at this point. Involvement might well be unnecessary, if the plaintiffs pursued the range of alternatives available to them described above and immediately hereafter. . . .

III. Our conclusion that plaintiffs should not be permitted to initiate an original court action, demanding the remedy of government contract termination with all companies found racially discriminating in employment practices, with the remedy derived directly from the due process clause, is reinforced by the existence of still another remedy to vindicate their rights unresorted to by plaintiffs. Recognizing that Title VII of the Civil Rights Act of 1964 is not an exclusive remedy and that the action is brought directly against the offending company rather than against government officials as plaintiffs have done here, still, if plaintiffs are interested in securing equal employment opportunities with private companies instead of litigating with government officials, this is precisely the purpose for which Title VII was designed.

Indeed, two of the named plaintiffs have filed complaints with the Equal Employment Opportunity Commission, but, as the District Court noted, they have not taken the next steps requisite to instituting civil actions against the companies. Whereas these two or any of the named plaintiffs, or any other employee or applicant, could file charges with the EEOC, and in the court if voluntary compliance were not secured by the Commission, they have not done so. Such Title VII suits may be class actions under Rule 23, F.R. Civ. P. If the charges are proved, all the class plaintiffs can obtain complete relief from the asserted discriminatory employment practices. In so doing, plaintiffs could have the assistance of court-appointed counsel and bring the action without paying the usual fees.[20]

The manifest disinterest of plaintiffs in pursuing the effective remedies provided by Congress and the Executive can be explained only by their desire to create a hitherto unfound construction and implicit remedy in the Fifth Amendment due process clause, i.e., private party class actions to compel government officials to terminate contracts with private companies having racially discriminatory practices without the benefit of any enabling statute or administrative procedure. To do so would be unwise, unprecedented, and in complete disregard of the carefully thought out remedies provided by both Congress and the Executive to vindicate plaintiffs' rights. The dismissal by the District Court is

Affirmed.

JOHNSON, Chief District Judge, dissenting:—I respectfully dissent. . . .

There is no doubt that plaintiffs' ultimate goal is the end of what they allege are the racially discriminatory hiring and employment practices of the companies mentioned in this action. This case is a direct attempt to achieve that end. Here plaintiffs seek a declaration of the government's duty affirmatively to secure nondiscriminatory policies among governmental contractors who are being economically sustained by government contracts and public funds.

In my judgment the majority has misstated plaintiffs' case by characterizing it as seeking "either strict compliance with equal employment opportunity requirements or the disbarment of the offending companies from government contracts." Rather, the fundamental thrust of plaintiffs' action seeks a judicial declaration outlining the extent to which government officials who contract with companies that engage in racially discriminatory hiring and promotion practices must undertake to end racial discrimination by these companies. To put it more succinctly, plaintiffs are saying that these government officials have failed to fulfill their constitutional duty to contract with only nondiscriminatory companies and have thereby subsidized and continue to subsidize with federal funds widespread, blatant and continuing racial discrimination. Plaintiffs are seeking a judicial declaration of basic constitutional rights.

---

[20] 42 U.S.C. §§ 2000 (e)-5 (e) (k). We do not hold that plaintiffs must allege and prove that they themselves have been discriminated against. It is sufficient if they allege and prove discrimination against any members of the class they purport to represent.

Neither administrative remedies under Executive Order 11246 nor those available under Title VII provide any realistic possibility for the relief plaintiffs seek. Those avenues are for the resolution of employee-employer conflict. Certainly under either procedure the government participates in the form of judge or mediator, but a declaration of governmental duties and responsibilities is not contemplated by such procedures. It may be that administrative remedies are available to government officials to force offending companies to cease such invidious practices. This fact, however, does not mean that the victims of such practices cannot litigate their rights in the federal judicial system.

Even assuming that the majority is correct that plaintiffs could theoretically gain relief through these administrative procedures, there is a strong countervailing consideration which suggests that such relegation in this case is neither required nor appropriate. It is that the requirement of exhaustion is rapidly disappearing from that area of our jurisprudence dealing with the vindication of constitutional rights. . . .

I get the impression that the majority may be saying that federal officials are less obligated than their state counterparts to obey the Constitution; certainly, they are no more immune for their violations. See Bolling v. Sharpe, 347 U.S. 497, 500 (1954). While substantially different from a factual standpoint, the basic legal issue involved in United States of America by John N. Mitchell, Attorney General vs. John S. Frazer, as Director, Alabama Personnel Department, 317 F. Supp. 1079, 2 FEP Cases 847 (M.D. Ala. 1970), regarding the duty of government officials to protect the rights of citizens against infringement by organizations being subsidized with federal funds, is substantially the same. In United States v. Frazer, the Court determined that the United States was subsidizing various programs that were being administered by the defendant State of Alabama officials. After making a finding of discrimination on the basis of race in hiring and promotional practices on the part of State officials, the Court observed, among other things, that:

> . . . Failure on the part of any of these Government officials to take legal action in the event that racial discrimination does exist would constitute dereliction of official duty.
>
> . . . Here, the United States is seeking to enforce the terms and conditions which Congress expressly imposed upon the expenditure of federal funds. To put it another way, the United States is merely attempting to enforce the express terms and conditions which the State of Alabama agreed to meet in receiving federal funds. . . .

In the case now before this Court, the only difference is that here the plaintiffs are the ones being discriminated against by the organizations receiving federal funds through various contracts with the United States government being administered by the defendants.

As for the fact that this case is brought under the Fifth Amendment, rather than 42 U.S.C. § 1983, the majority has simply stated a distinction without a difference. Since § 1983 applies only to state action, it is unavailable for challenges to federal officers. More fundamentally, the proper consideration for whether exhaustion is necessary is the similarity of the rights sought to be protected and the reasoning which justifies dispensing with administrative remedies, not the identity of the jurisdictional provision. The crucial factor is that in this case, as in the prior cases, the plaintiffs are seeking protection of or a declaration concerning basic constitutional rights allegedly infringed upon by government officials. There is no sound reason for concluding that an administrative agency is better equipped or more competent than the federal judiciary to determine the merits of plaintiffs' claims.

The majority has also failed to respond adequately to plaintiffs' contention that the administrative remedies are ineffective and unavailing. For example, it is clear from a reading of the regulations that under either the Executive Order or Title VII, the plaintiffs could file complaints against the offending companies. This would not, however, guarantee plaintiffs the right to participate in the agency proceedings, although they may be permitted to do so. They have no control whatever over the investigation or prosecution of the action. They must file the complaint and then hope for the best. I find this case sufficiently similar to Rosado v. Wyman, 397 U.S. 397 (1970), to render exhaustion inappropriate. . . .

In sum, it seems to me to be highly ironic that this Court is relegating a claim of constitutional violation by federal officials to other federal administrators despite the fact that the administrators have already exhibited their disinterest in safeguarding plaintiffs' rights. It may be that the Fifth Amendment does not require the cancellation of contracts made by government officials with discriminating companies. Plaintiffs, however, have been denied an opportunity to present their evidence since the case went out in the district court without a hearing. I would remand the case for a hearing of the merits.

NOTE

In Farmer v. Philadelphia Elec. Co., 329 F.2d 3 (3rd Cir. 1964), the court details the history of Executive Orders proscribing employment discrimination by federal government contractors. The *Farmer* decision concludes by observing that:

> Defendant does not contend that the requiring of non-discrimination provisions in government contracts is beyond the power of Congress. See Youngstown Sheet & Tube Co. v. Sawyer, 343 U.S. 579, 588, 72 S. Ct. 863, 96 L. Ed. 1153 (1952). Nor does it maintain that the executive orders and regulations were issued without statutory authority. . . .

> [W]e have no doubt that the applicable executive orders and regulations have the force of law. See Lichter v. United States, 334 U.S. 742, 785, 68 S. Ct. 1294, 92 L. Ed. 1694 (1948) ; United States v. Excel Packing Co., 210 F.2d 596 (C.A.10 1954), cert. denied, 348 U.S. 817, 75 S. Ct. 28, 99 L. Ed. 664. However, the matter does not end here for we still must determine whether a violation of the nondiscrimination provisions by a party, a private corporation, to the contract gives the plaintiff a right to bring a civil action in the Federal courts for damages sustained as a result of that violation. No statute in terms confers a private remedy. Plainly the executive orders do not expressly provide for one. Nor do they, in our opinion, do so by implication. The history of the executive orders on the subject from 1951 to the present all point to the conclusion that the enforcement of the nondiscrimination provisions in Government contracts has been entrusted to one or more of the Governmental agencies with the assistance of a committee appointed by the President. . . .

> The history of the orders, the rules and regulations made pursuant to them, and the actual practice in the enforcement of the nondiscrimination provisions are all strong persuasive evidence, it seems to us, that court action as a remedy was to be used only as a last resort, and that the threat of a private civil action to deter contractors from failing to comply with the provisions was not contemplated by the orders. . . .

> We know of no announced overriding federal common law permitting a right of action by an employee against his employer for the latter's failure to comply with the nondiscrimination provision in a government contract. 329 F.2d at 8-10.

See also Farkas v. Texas Instrument, Inc., 375 F.2d 629 (5th Cir.) , *cert. denied,* 389 U.S. 977 (1967) .

Index

References are to page numbers.